Psychology: A Journey

General Psychology 2301

Customized for Dr. Thomas Taulbee | 5th Edition

Coon and Mitterer

CENGAGE
Learning·

Australia • Brazil • Japan • Korea • Mexico • Singapore • Spain • United Kingdom • United States

Psychology: A Journey: General Psychology 2301, 5th Edition

Senior Manager, Student Engagement:

Linda deStefano

Janey Moeller

Manager, Student Engagement:

Julie Dierig

Marketing Manager:

Rachael Kloos

Manager, Production Editorial:

Kim Fry

Manager, Intellectual Property Project Manager:

Brian Methe

Senior Manager, Production and Manufacturing:

Donna M. Brown

Manager, Production:

Terri Daley

Psychology: A Journey, 5th Edition
Dennis Coon | John O. Mitterer

For product information and technology assistance, contact us at
Cengage Learning Customer & Sales Support, 1-800-354-9706
For permission to use material from this text or product,
submit all requests online at **cengage.com/permissions**
Further permissions questions can be emailed to
permissionrequest@cengage.com

This book contains select works from existing Cengage Learning resources and was produced by Cengage Learning Custom Solutions for collegiate use. As such, those adopting and/or contributing to this work are responsible for editorial content accuracy, continuity and completeness.

Compilation © 2014 Cengage Learning

ISBN-13: 978-1-305-02664-3

ISBN-10: 1-305-02664-0

WCN: 01-100-101

Cengage Learning

5191 Natorp Boulevard
Mason, Ohio 45040
USA

Cengage Learning is a leading provider of customized learning solutions with office locations around the globe, including Singapore, the United Kingdom, Australia, Mexico, Brazil, and Japan. Locate your local office at: **international.cengage.com/region.**

Cengage Learning products are represented in Canada by Nelson Education, Ltd. For your lifelong learning solutions, visit **www.cengage.com/custom.** Visit our corporate website at **www.cengage.com.**

Printed in Mexico

To our students: We thank you and wish you all the best with your studies. You are the reason we write about psychology. As an old rock-and-roll band once sang, "If there's no audience, there just ain't no show."

About the Authors

Dr. Coon is the author of *Psychology: Modules for Active Learning* and *Introduction to Psychology: Gateways to Mind and Behavior*, as well as *Psychology: A Journey*. Together, these texts have been used by more than 2 million students. Dr. Coon frequently serves as a reviewer and consultant to publishers, and he edited the best-selling trade book *Choices*. He also helped design modules for PsychNow!, Wadsworth's interactive CD-ROM.

In his leisure hours, Dr. Coon enjoys hiking, photography, painting, woodworking, and music. He also designs, builds, and plays classical and steel string acoustic guitars. He has published articles on guitar design and occasionally offers lectures on this topic, in addition to his more frequent presentations on psychology.

John Mitterer was awarded his Ph.D. in cognitive psychology from McMaster University. Currently, Dr. Mitterer is a faculty member at Brock University, where he has taught more than 25,000 introductory psychology students. He is the recipient of the 2003 Brock University Distinguished Teaching Award, a 2003 Ontario Confederation of University Faculty Associations (OCUFA) Teaching Award, a 2004 National 3M Teaching Fellowship, the 2005 Canadian Psychological Association Award for Distinguished Contributions to Education and Training in Psychology, and the 2010 Brock University Don Ursino Award for Excellence in the Teaching of Large Classes. He also held a three-year Brock Chancellor's Chair for Teaching Excellence from 2006 to 2009.

His first love is in applying cognitive principles to the improvement of undergraduate education. In support of his introductory psychology course, he has been involved in the creation of textbooks and ancillary materials such as CD-ROMs and websites for both students and instructors. Dr. Mitterer has published and lectured on undergraduate instruction throughout Canada and the United States.

In his spare time, Dr. Mitterer strives to become a better golfer and to attain his life goal of seeing all the bird species in the world. To this end he recently traveled to Papua New Guinea, Uganda, the Galapagos, and China.

© Hank Morgan/Rainbow

© Hank Morgan/Rainbow

Brief Contents

Contents

2 Brain and Behavior 59

3 Human Development 95

 **4** Sensation and Perception **139**

 **5** States of Consciousness **189**

6 Conditioning and Learning **233**

 **7** Memory **273**

12 Psychological Disorders **485**

13 Therapies **527**

To the Student—The Journey Begins

Greetings from your authors! We look forward to being your guides as you explore the exciting field of psychology and our ever-evolving understanding of human behavior. In a very real sense, we wrote this book about you, for you, and to you. We sincerely hope you will find, as we do, that what you learn is at once familiar, exotic, surprising, and challenging.

Reading Psychology: A Journey

In Psychology: A Journey, we have done all that we could imagine to make it enjoyable for you to read this book. We trust you will find your first journey through psychology to be quite interesting and useful to you in your everyday life. Each chapter will take you into a different realm of psychology such as personality, abnormal behavior, memory, consciousness, and human development. Each realm is complex and fascinating in its own right, with many pathways, landmarks, and interesting detours to discover. Like any journey of discovery, your exploration of psychology will help you to better understand yourself, others, and the world around you. It's definitely a trip worth taking.

Studying Psychology: A Journey

No one likes to start a new adventure by reading a manual. We just want to step off the airplane and begin our vacation, get right into that new computer game, or just start using our new camera or smart phone. You might be similarly tempted to just start reading this textbook. Please be patient. Successfully learning psychology depends on how you study this book as well as how you read it.

Psychology is about each of us. It asks us to adopt a reflective attitude as we inquire, "How can we step outside ourselves to look objectively at how we live, think, feel, and act?" Psychologists believe the answer is through careful thought, observation, and inquiry. As simple as that may seem, thoughtful reflection takes practice to develop. It is the guiding light for all that follows.

Psychology: A Journey, then, is your passport to an adventure in active learning, not just passive reading. To help you get off to a good start, we strongly encourage you to read our short "manual," Introduction: The Psychology of Studying which precedes Chapter 1. This introduction describes a variety of study skills, including the effective SQ4R method, that you can use to get the most out of this text, your psychology course, and your other courses as well. It also tells how you can explore psychology through digital media such as the Internet, electronic databases, and interactive CDs.

To the Instructor—An Invitation to Teach Psychology

Thank you for choosing Psychology: A Journey for your students and for your course. Marcel Proust wrote, "The real voyage of discovery consists not in seeing new landscapes but in having new eyes." It is in this spirit that we have written this book to promote not just an interest in human behavior but an appreciation for the perspective of the psychologist as well.

Preface

To the Student—The Journey Begins

Greetings from your authors! We look forward to being your guides as you explore the exciting field of psychology and our ever-evolving understanding of human behavior. In a very real sense, we wrote this book about you, for you, and to you. We sincerely hope you will find, as we do, that what you learn is at once familiar, exotic, surprising, and challenging.

Reading *Psychology: A Journey*

In *Psychology: A Journey*, we have done all that we could imagine to make it enjoyable for you to read this book. We trust you will find your first journey through psychology to be quite interesting and useful to you in your everyday life. Each chapter will take you into a different realm of psychology, such as personality, abnormal behavior, memory, consciousness, and human development. Each realm is complex and fascinating in its own right, with many pathways, landmarks, and interesting detours to discover. Like any journey of discovery, your exploration of psychology will help you to better understand yourself, others, and the world around you. It's definitely a trip worth taking.

Studying *Psychology: A Journey*

No one likes to start a new adventure by reading a manual. We just want to step off the airplane and begin our vacation, get right into that new computer game, or just start using our new camera or smart phone. You might be similarly tempted to just start reading this textbook. Please be patient. Successfully learning psychology depends on how you study this book as well as how you read it.

Psychology is about each of us. It asks us to adopt a reflective attitude as we inquire, "How can we step outside ourselves to look objectively at how we live, think, feel, and act?" Psychologists believe the answer is through careful thought, observation, and inquiry. As simple as that may seem, thoughtful reflection takes practice to develop. It is the guiding light for all that follows.

Psychology: A Journey, then, is your passport to an adventure in active learning, not just passive reading. To help you get off to a good start, we strongly encourage you to read our short "manual," *Introduction: The Psychology of Studying*, which precedes Chapter 1. This introduction describes a variety of study skills, including the *reflective SQ4R* method, that you can use to get the most out of this text, your psychology course, and your other courses as well. It also tells how you can explore psychology through digital media such as the Internet, electronic databases, and interactive CDs.

To the Instructor—An Invitation to Teach Psychology

Thank you for choosing *Psychology: A Journey* for your students and for your course. Marcel Proust wrote, "The real voyage of discovery consists not in seeing new landscapes but in having new eyes." It is in this spirit that we have written this book to promote not just an interest in human behavior but an appreciation for the perspective of the psychologist as well.

As we point out to your students in the *Introduction: The Psychology of Studying,* which precedes Chapter 1, there is a big difference between experiencing and reflecting on experience (Norman, 1994). For John Dewey (1910), reflective thinking is the "active, persistent and careful consideration of any belief or supposed form of knowledge in the light of the grounds that support it, and the further conclusion to which it tends." The psychologist's perspective, of course, involves reflecting on human behavior in a variety of ways. When it comes to studying psychology, reflective cognition requires actively thinking *about* what you have just read, which results in deeper understanding and memory. (Please consider taking a look at our *Introduction,* as it explains to your students in some detail how to become a more reflective student and outlines how they can get the most out of this book. By the way, we encourage you, if at all possible, to assign your students to read it as well.)

Throughout this text, we have tried to select only the very "best" material from the many topics that could be presented. Nevertheless, *Psychology: A Journey* covers not only the heart of psychology but also many topics at the cutting edge of current knowledge, including a focus on the practical applications of psychology, the growing importance of neuroscience, and the richness of human diversity. New information, anecdotes, perspectives, and narratives appear throughout the 5th edition. The result is a concise text that is readable, manageable, informative, and motivating. At the same time, we have structured this book to help students consolidate the skills to learn efficiently and to become better critical thinkers. Without such skills, students cannot easily go, as Jerome Bruner (1973) put it, "beyond the information given."

The Teaching Challenge

Wouldn't it be nice if all of our students came to our courses highly motivated to explore psychology and well prepared to cope with the learning challenges we create for them? As the authors of this textbook, we have together accumulated some 60 years of classroom experience, teaching tens of thousands of college and university students. Although we have found most students to be generally well intentioned, our modern world certainly does immerse them in their work, careers, families, intimate relationships, popular culture, and life in general. As we compete for ever more limited student attention, we must do more than just lecture in psychology. We must also motivate our students to read and learn, as well as to educate them about how to learn effectively (Matthew & Sternberg, 2009; Paternoster & Pogarsky, 2009).

We have explicitly designed and written the 5th edition of *Psychology: A Journey* to foster deeper student engagement with the field of psychology, better memory for what has been read and studied, and a deeper understanding of how to become more reflective learners and thinkers. To help you and your students reach these goals, we have organized our design philosophy around three core principles:

1: Readability and Narrative Emphasis

Many introductory psychology students are reluctant readers. Selecting a textbook is half the battle in teaching a successful course. A good text does much of the work of imparting information to your students. This frees class time for your discussion, extra topics, or media presentations. It also leaves students asking for more. When a book overwhelms students or cools their interest, teaching and learning suffer. If students won't read the textbook, they can't very well be reflective about what they have read.

That's why we've worked hard to make this a clear, readable, and engaging text. *Psychology: A Journey* is designed to give students a clear grasp of major concepts without burying them in details. At the same time, it offers a broad overview that reflects psychology's rich heritage of ideas. We think students will find this book informative and intellectually stimulating.

Because we want students to read this book with genuine interest and enthusiasm, not merely as an obligation, we have made a special effort to weave narrative threads through every chapter. Everyone loves a good story, and the story of psychology is among the most compelling to be told. Throughout *Psychology: A Journey,* we have used intriguing anecdotes and examples to propel reading and sustain interest.

Practical Applications

To make psychology even more inviting to students, we have emphasized the many ways that psychology relates to practical problems in daily life. For example, a major feature of this book is the *Psychology in Action* sections found at the end of each chapter. These high-interest discussions bridge the gap between theory and practical applications. We believe it is fair for students to ask, "Does this mean anything to me? Can I use it? Why should I learn it if I can't?" The *Psychology in Action* sections show students how to solve practical problems and manage their own behavior. This allows them to see the benefits of adopting new ideas, and it breathes life into psychology's concepts.

2: Integrated Support for Active Learning

Studying, rather than reading, a textbook requires the active cognitive engagement that psychologist Donald Norman (1993) calls *reflective.* In his recent book, *Thinking, Fast and Slow,* Daniel Kahneman describes it as *System 2* thinking (Kahneman, 2011), Being reflective when you read a textbook involves asking yourself if you understand what you are reading, how it might relate to things you already know, what new questions your reading might trigger, and so on. The resulting elaboration of the just-read new information is, perhaps, the best way to foster understanding and form lasting memories (Anderson, 2010a; Gadzella, 1995; Goldstein, 2011).

It is in this spirit that we have redesigned this edition of *Psychology: A Journey* to encourage students to become more reflective, active learners. To achieve this important pedagogical goal, the traditional SQ4R method has been updated to *reflective SQ4R,* an active-learning format, to make studying psychology an even more rewarding experience. As students explore concepts, they are encouraged to think critically about ideas and relate them to their own experiences. Notice how the steps of the reflective SQ4R method—*survey, question, read, recite, reflect,* and *review*—are incorporated into the chapter design:

Survey

Features at the beginning of each chapter help students build cognitive maps of upcoming topics, thus serving as advance organizers (Ausubel, 1978). A photograph and short *Journey into Psychology* preview arouses interest, gives an overview of the chapter, and focuses attention on the task at hand. A *Journey Theme* and a list of more detailed *Journey Questions* are then given to guide reading. These questions are now also numbered, making it easier for students and instructors to relate the *Journey Questions* to a matched set of learning objectives that appear throughout the materials that accompany this textbook.

The answers to *Journey Questions* open intellectual pathways and summarize psychology's "big ideas." Ultimately, those answers provide a good summary of what students have learned. With these chapter-opening features, we invite students to read with a purpose and actively process information.

Question

How can questioning be built in to a textbook? Each major chapter section begins with one or more *Journey Questions.* As students read a chapter, they can try to discover the answers to these questions. They can then compare their answers with the ones listed in the chapter summary.

Further, throughout each chapter, italicized *Dialogue Questions*, like the one on the previous page, also serve as advance organizers. That is, *Dialogue Questions* prompt students to look for important ideas as they read, thus promoting active learning. They also establish a dialogue in which the questions and reactions of students are anticipated. This clarifies difficult points in a lively give-and-take between questions and responses.

Read

We've made every effort to make this a clear, readable text. To further aid comprehension, we've used a full array of traditional learning aids. These include boldface terms (with phonetic pronunciations), bulleted summaries, a robust illustration program, summary tables, a name index, and an integrated subject index and glossary. As an additional aid, figure and table references in the text are printed in different colored text. These "placeholders" make it easier for students to return to the section they were reading after they have paused to view a table or figure.

We have made the glossary function in this edition even more powerful. The *Main Glossary*, at the end of the book, has been integrated with the *Subject Index*, making it easier to link important definitions to where they are discussed in the text. As before, all glossary items are bolded and defined in-text when a term is first encountered. This aids reading comprehension because students get clear definitions when and where they need them—in the general text itself. In addition, the parallel *Running Glossary* defines key terms in the margins of the relevant pages, making it easy for students to find, study, and review important terms.

Recite

Throughout each chapter, strategically placed built-in *Study Breaks* give students a chance to test their recall and further develop their understanding of preceding topics. Each *Study Break* includes a *Recite* section, a short, noncomprehensive quiz to help students actively process information and assess their progress. *Recite* questions, which are not as difficult as in-class tests, are meant to offer a sample of what students could be asked about various topics. Students who miss any items are encouraged to backtrack and clarify their understanding before reading more. In other words, completing *Recite* questions serves as a form of recitation to enhance learning. The same is true for longer chapter-ending *Test Your Knowledge* quizzes.

Reflect

Since simple recitation is usually not enough to foster deeper understanding, in each chapter we invite students to engage in two distinct types of reflection, self-reflection and critical thinking:

- **Self-Reflection:** Self-reflection (or self-reference) makes new information more meaningful by relating it to what is already known (Klein & Kihlstrom, 1986). We provide many opportunities for self-reflection throughout *Psychology: A Journey*. The text is written with many contemporary references, examples, and stories to make it easier for students to relate what they are reading to their own life experience. As we mentioned previously, each chapter ends with a *Psychology in Action* section that invites students to relate psychology to practical problems in their own daily lives.

  Discovering Psychology boxes in many chapters are "try-it" demonstrations that enable students to observe interesting facets of their own behavior or do self-assessment exercises. In this way, students are given yet another way to link new information to concrete experiences. Finally, to help students further elaborate their new understanding, each *Study Break* includes a series of *Self-Reflect* questions that encourage students to connect new concepts with personal experiences and prior knowledge.

- **Critical Thinking:** Being reflective about psychology involves more than self-reflectively asking "What does this have to do with me and what I already know?" It also involves reflecting more deeply about the field. Our book also invites students to think critically about psychology.

The active, questioning nature of the reflective SQ4R method is, in itself, an inducement to critical thinking. In addition, every *Study Break* also includes *Think Critically* questions. These stimulating questions challenge students to think critically and analytically about psychology. Each is followed by a brief answer with which students can compare their own thoughts. Many of these answers are based on research and are informative in their own right. Many of the *Dialogue Questions* that introduce topics in the text also act as models of critical thinking.

Further, Chapter 1 contains a discussion of critical thinking skills and a rational appraisal of pseudopsychologies. In addition, the discussion of research methods in Chapter 1 is actually a short course on how to think clearly about behavior. It is augmented by suggestions about how to critically evaluate claims in the popular media. Chapter 8, which covers cognition, language, creativity, and intelligence, includes many topics related to critical thinking.

Throughout the text, many boxed highlights promote critical thinking about specific topics that students should approach with healthy skepticism. The *Critical Thinking* boxes model a reflective approach to the theoretical and empirical foundations of critical thinking in psychology. In addition, *Human Diversity* boxes encourage reflection on the variability of the human experience, *Clinical File* boxes encourage reflection on the clinical applications of psychology, and *Brainwaves* boxes foster deeper insight into the brain structures and processes that underlie psychological phenomena. Taken together, these features will help students think more reflectively about your course and the field of psychology, while also gaining thinking skills of lasting value.

Review

As we noted previously, all important terms appear in a *Running Glossary* throughout the book, which aids review. We have also integrated the *Main Glossary* with the *Subject Index*. When reviewing, students can easily link definitions of concepts with the appropriate section of text where those concepts are introduced and discussed.

As also noted, a *Psychology in Action* section shows students how psychological concepts relate to practical problems, including problems in their own lives. The information found in *Psychology in Action* helps reinforce learning by illustrating psychology's practicality.

To help students further consolidate their learning, each *Chapter in Review* includes a *Summary*, which restates all of the major ideas presented earlier in the chapter, organized around the same *Journey Questions* found at the beginning of the chapter. In this way we bring the reflective SQ4R process full circle and reinforce the learning objectives for the chapter.

3: Integrative Themes: *The Whole Person*

No one linear chapter organization can fully capture the interconnectedness of our field. We have, of course, included the usual "for more information see Chapter XX" cross-references. But to better convey this richness, we also explore the natural complexity of psychology by weaving several more detailed themes throughout the chapters of this edition of *Psychology: A Journey*.

One theme is that of *positive psychology*. Over the last decade or so, increasing interest in positive psychology has begun to complement the focus of the previous 100 years on the negative side of human behavior. What do we know, for instance, about love, happiness, creativity, well-being, self-confidence, and achievement? Throughout this book, we have attempted to answer such questions for students, often in periodic, short integrative sections entitled *The Whole Person*. Our hope is that students who read this book will gain an appreciation for the potential we all have for optimal functioning. Also, of course, we hope that they will leave introductory psychology with emotional and intellectual tools they can use to enhance their lives.

Starting in Chapter 1, we also explore the idea that human behavior is better understood when examined from three complementary perspectives, the biological, the psychological, and the sociocultural, again often in *The Whole Person* summaries. You may choose to explicitly present these perspectives to your students. Alternatively, you might leave these for your students to explore and unconsciously absorb.

The Biological Perspective: The Growing Importance of Neuroscience

Our students, partly because of the popular media, are increasingly aware that the brain and the nervous system play a role in shaping human behavior. While our chapter on *Brain and Behavior* deals with the usual topics, such as methods of studying the brain, neural functioning, synaptic transmission, the structure of the nervous system and brain, and the endocrine system, we deliberately include a discussion of the biological perspective in many of the other chapters comprising this book. One way we do this is to incorporate a *Brainwaves* box into some of those chapters. Table P.1 gives a chapter-by-chapter list of topics that are discussed from the biological perspective.

The Psychological Perspective: The Centrality of Self-Knowledge

There are many ways we have threaded the psychological perspective throughout this book. It is, of course, central to psychology. In this edition of *Psychology: A Journey*, we have chosen to place a special thematic emphasis on the self. In doing so, we respond to Timothy Wilson's (2009) criticism that introductory psychology courses do not spend enough time exploring the issue of self-knowledge, despite the fact that students are terribly interested in learning more about themselves. Besides, as you may have already noted, our focus on active, reflective learning is also designed to improve our students' self-awareness. Throughout the book we follow the development of the self from the beginnings of self-recognition in infancy to the development of wisdom in old age. Table P.1 gives a chapter-by-chapter list of the relevant discussions.

The Sociocultural Perspective: Human Diversity, Culture, and Gender

Of course, no introductory psychology textbook would be complete without a discussion of human diversity and the multicultural, multifaceted nature of contemporary society. In *Psychology: A Journey*, students will find numerous discussions of human diversity, including differences in race, ethnicity, culture, gender, abilities, sexual orientation, and age. Too often, such differences needlessly divide people into opposing groups. Our aim throughout this text is to discourage stereotyping, prejudice, discrimination, and intolerance. We've tried to make this book gender neutral and sensitive to diversity issues. All pronouns and examples involving females and males are equally divided by gender. In artwork, photographs, and examples, we have tried to portray the rich diversity of humanity. In addition, a boxed feature, *Human Diversity*, appears throughout the book, providing students with examples of how to be more reflective about human diversity.

In short, many topics and examples in this book encourage students to appreciate social, physical, and cultural differences and to accept them as a natural part of being human. Table P.1 also gives a chapter-by-chapter list of discussions of issues of human diversity, culture, and gender.

Table P.1 Coverage of Neuroscience, Self-Knowledge, Human Diversity, Culture, and Gender Across Chapters in *Psychology: A Journey*, 5th Edition

CHAPTER	NEUROSCIENCE IN PSYCHOLOGY: A JOURNEY	SELF-KNOWLEDGE IN PSYCHOLOGY: A JOURNEY	HUMAN DIVERSITY AND CULTURE IN PSYCHOLOGY: A JOURNEY	GENDER IN PSYCHOLOGY: A JOURNEY
Chapter 1: Thinking Critically About Psychology and Research Methods	Neuroscience and biopsychology, evolutionary psychology, the biological perspective, EEG and dreaming, links between brain and behavior, phrenology, Phineas Gage and case studies	Importance of self-knowledge, ethical research, psychological perspective, self-actualization, testing common sense, critical thinking, personal freedom, scientific thinking, introspection, behaviorism, humanism, eclecticism	Cultural psychology, human diversity, appreciating social and cultural differences, the impact of culture, cultural relativity, a broader view of diversity, human diversity and representative samples	The psychology of gender, gender differences in research, women in psychology, gender and social norms
Chapter 2: Brain and Behavior	Neural function, synaptic transmission, neurotransmitters, parts of the nervous system and brain, localization of function, methods of studying the brain, endocrine system, handedness	Brain and self, localization of function, including self, self-directed neuroplasticity, locked-in syndrome, truth and lies, split-brain and consciousness, intelligence, frontal lobes, strokes and self, hemispheres and self, mirror neurons, thinking styles, emotions	Biological treatments for people with spinal injuries, hypopituitary dwarfism, acromegaly, handedness and laterality, brain interfaces for people with total paralysis, diagnosis of neurological conditions, cultural experiences shape the brain, handedness and culture	Specialization of men's and women's brains, sex differences in lateralization, hormonal differences, sex and steroids
Chapter 3: Human Development	Biological factors in heredity and development, readiness, maturation, prenatal biological influences, sensitive periods, enriched environments and the brain, temperament, biological predisposition to language, cognitive stages and brain maturation, puberty, physical changes in old age	Temperament, newborn sensitivity, imitation, attachment, terrible twos, egocentrism, theory of mind, self-awareness, turn-taking in language development, self-recognition, search for identity, moral development, role confusion, self-acceptance, personal growth, subjective well-being, self-esteem, reactions to impending death	Culture and evolution, ethnic differences in child-rearing, relationship between culture and babbling, parentese in different cultures, sociocultural influences on cognitive development, scaffolding, zone of proximal development, adolescent status and culture, diversity and the adolescent search for identity, ethnicity and personal identity, culture and moral reasoning, ageism and myths about the elderly	Prenatal development, maternal and paternal parenting styles, emotional attachment patterns, gender and puberty, male and female midlife transitions
Chapter 4: Sensation and Perception	Sensory filtering, transduction, sensory localization in the brain, electrical stimulation of sensory experiences in the brain and sensory nerves, physiology of various sense receptors and sensory pathways, sensory gating, neuromatrix theory, perceptual construction and learning	Perceptual experiences, psychophysics, reality testing, perceptual awareness, perceptual learning, perceptual habits and top-down processing	The "other race" effect in facial recognition, culture and the recognition of pictorial depth cues, culture and the Müller-Lyer illusion, cross-racial perceptions (eyewitness accuracy), cultural differences in perception	Sex differences in color deficiency
Chapter 5: States of Consciousness	EEG, stages of sleep, REM and dreaming, biological theories of sleep and dreaming, effects of "sleeping pills," narcolepsy, EEG and hypnosis, brain scans and meditation, how psychoactive drugs affect the brain and neurotransmitters, drug addiction	Consciousness, self-awareness and heightened self-awareness, self-control under hypnosis, autosuggestion, self-control, mindfulness, analyzing dreams, lucid dreaming	States of consciousness and culture, culture and interpretations of dreams and hypnopompic imagery, the cultural context of drug use	REM sleep and dreaming in men and women, caffeine and pregnancy, effects of Ecstasy and alcohol on sexual performance

Chapter				
Chapter 6: Conditioning and Learning	Eyeblink conditioning and diagnosis of autism and minimal consciousness, conditioned emotional reactions and the amygdala, primary reinforcement and intracranial self-stimulation	Awareness of cognitive learning versus unconscious nature of associative learning, self-managed behavior	Spanking and culture	Effects of television on children's perceptions of sex roles, effects of television on children's level of aggression
Chapter 7: Memory	Penfield, brain stimulation, and memory; cerebellum amnesia and types of memory; brain trauma and procedural memory; brain trauma and amnesia; consolidation; long-term potentiation; role of hippocampus in declarative memories; limbic system and flashbulb memories; cortex and long-term memory	Episodic memory, elaborative encoding, experience of partial retrieval, self-reference and memory, mnemonics	Aging and memory, cultural influences on memory, eyewitnesses and cross-racial recognition, labeling and the ability to remember people from other social groups	Recovered memories versus false memories
Chapter 8: Cognition, Language, Creativity, and Intelligence	Synesthesia, imagery and the brain, kinesthetic imagery, sign language and the brain, organic causes of mental disability, heredity and intelligence	Synesthesia, imagery, kinesthetic images, cognitive effects of bilingualism, linguistic relativity, insight, intuition, creativity, giftedness, self-respect and intellectual disability, multiple intelligences, wisdom	Linguistic misunderstandings between cultures; the pros and cons of bilingualism; linguistic relativity; cultural differences in the use of phonemes; the deaf community and gestural languages; cultural barriers to problem solving; age and IQ; the developmentally disabled; race, culture, ethnicity, and intelligence; cultural differences in intelligence (as taught to children); culture-fair intelligence testing	Stereotypes and cognition; sex differences in IQ; men, women, and the definition of intelligence
Chapter 9: Motivation and Emotion	Needs as internal deficiencies; biological motives; homeostasis; circadian rhythms; role of melatonin; biological factors in hunger; hypothalamus and thirst; types of thirst; estrus; sex hormones; sexual orientation; prenatal biological basing effect; physiological changes and emotion; physiological arousal; moods, emotion, and the limbic system, including the amygdala; role of the autonomic nervous system and arousal; parasympathetic rebound; polygraphy; brain scans and lying	Intrinsic motivation and creativity, meta-needs, self-actualization, emotional expression and health, higher emotional intelligence	Cultural values and food preferences; culture, ethnicity, and dieting; pain avoidance and cultural conditioning; sexual scripts; casual sex in America; the influence of culture on emotional expressions; cultural differences in the occurrence of emotion; cultural differences in facial expressions; cultural learning and body language	Eating disorders and gender, how hormones affect sex drive, gender differences in sexual response, sexual activity, sexual orientation, role of hormones in sex drive, gender differences in emotion, alexithymia
Chapter 10: Personality	Behavioral genetics and personality, Big 5 traits and neurotransmitters, limbic system and the unconscious	Long-term consistency of self, self-concept, self-esteem, self-confidence, Freudian ego, free choice, self-actualization, positive personality traits, self-image, congruence (between self-image and ideal self), possible selves, self-efficacy, self-reinforcement, androgyny and self-expression	Character and culture, self-esteem and culture, common traits and culture, culture and gender roles	Social learning of male and female traits, Oedipus versus Electra complexes, gender roles, gender-role stereotypes, culture and gender roles, gender-role socialization, androgyny

Continued

Table P.1 Coverage of Neuroscience, Self-Knowledge, Human Diversity, Culture, and Gender Across Chapters in *Psychology: A Journey*, 5th Edition—cont'd

CHAPTER	NEUROSCIENCE IN *PSYCHOLOGY: A JOURNEY*	SELF-KNOWLEDGE IN *PSYCHOLOGY: A JOURNEY*	HUMAN DIVERSITY AND CULTURE IN *PSYCHOLOGY: A JOURNEY*	GENDER IN *PSYCHOLOGY: A JOURNEY*
Chapter 11: Health, Stress, and Coping	Stress reaction, general adaptation syndrome, psychoneuroimmunology, psychosomatic disorders, biofeedback	Self-screening for illnesses, self-control, wellness, cognitive appraisal, coping, hardiness, optimism, happiness, stress management, humor, sexual self-awareness, sexually responsible behavior, sexuality and self-esteem	Culture shock and acculturative stress, scapegoating of ethnic group members, frustration and minority groups, AIDS and sexual orientation, AIDS worldwide	Rates of HIV/AIDS infection and death, sex differences in seeking social support
Chapter 12: Psychological Disorders	Biological risk factors, organic psychosis, Alzheimer's disease, hereditary and biological causes of schizophrenia, the schizophrenic brain, biology and depression, the psychopathic brain, diathesis-stress model	Self-destructive behaviors, nonconformity, subjective discomfort, loss of self, self-criticism, self-defeating thinking patterns	How culture affects judgments of psychopathology, culture-bound syndromes from around the world, ethnic group differences in psychopathology	How gender affects judgments of psychopathology, gender differences in rates of anxiety disorders, sex differences in rates of clinical depression, gender differences in suicide (attempt and completion)
Chapter 13: Therapies	Drug therapies, ECT, brain stimulation therapy, psychosurgery, future of medical therapies, transcranial magnetic stimulation	Insight, personal growth and psychotherapy, human potential, choosing to become, courage, overcoming irrational beliefs, the fully functioning person, behavioral self-management	Cultural issues in counseling and psychotherapy, culturally aware therapists	
Chapter 14: Social Behavior	"Brainwashing", homogamy, evolution, and mate selection; aggression, biology, and the brain	Social comparison, self-disclosure, self-assertion, solitude	Culture, social roles, in-groups versus out-groups, social status, attitudes, male-female differences in mate preferences, racial prejudice and discrimination, ethnocentrism, social stereotypes, cultural differences in hostility and aggression, symbolic prejudice, rejection and demonization of out-groups, experiments in creating and reducing prejudice, multiculturalism, breaking the prejudice habit, cultural awareness	Stereotype threat and gender, influence of physical attractiveness, male-female differences in mate preferences, evolutionary perspectives on male and female mate selection, critique of evolutionary perspective, levels of testosterone and aggression

Psychology: A Journey—What's New in the Fifth Edition?

Thanks to psychology's vitality and suggestions from professors, this text is updated in many ways. The fifth edition of *Psychology: A Journey* features an improved pedagogy as well as some of the most recent and interesting information in psychology, along with fully updated references and statistics. The following annotations highlight some of the new topics and features that appear in this edition.

Introduction: The Psychology of Studying

- The updated Introduction, which we invite you to have your students read, offers information on how to read effectively, study more efficiently, take good notes, prepare for tests, perform well on various types of tests, create study schedules, and avoid procrastination.
- The SQ4R framework is now referred to as "reflective SQ4R." Our intent is to more clearly combine the comprehension-boosting power of critical thinking approaches with the memory-boosting power of the traditional SQ4R method.
- *Study Breaks* have been more clearly labeled so that students can more easily see the connection with the reflective SQ4R method. Specifically, after the *Recite* section, the *Reflect* section now includes *Think Critically* questions and *Self-Reflect* questions. This combination makes it clearer that relating new information to personal experiences and thinking critically about new information are both forms of self-reflective cognition.

Chapter 1: Thinking Critically About Psychology and Research Methods

- The chapter title has been changed to better reflect our deliberate focus on critical thinking skills.
- We created a new chapter-opening photo and vignette.
- Material on commonsense knowledge has been clarified, with new examples and a new figure.
- Information on research specialties has been integrated into an expanded table and discussion in the section entitled *Psychologists—Guaranteed Not to Shrink*.
- Material on animal research is now found in *Psychologists—Guaranteed Not to Shrink*, including a new photo and caption on orca conservation.
- The section on critical thinking has been revised, beginning with a new definition of critical thinking in psychology. The principle of falsifiability has been added as a fifth principle.
- The coverage of astrology has been reorganized around two major objections to astrology: lack of theory and lack of evidence.
- The concept *fallacy of positive instances* has been replaced with the more widely used *confirmation bias*.
- The section on the scientific method is now organized around a new, more recent research example.

Chapter 2: Brain and Behavior

- A dramatic new chapter-opening photo and vignette highlight chronic traumatic brain injury.
- Experience has shown us that students find it easier to grasp the overall organization of the nervous system before tackling the details of neuronal and synaptic functioning. We have revised our order of coverage accordingly.
- Expanded coverage of neurotransmitters includes a new table. The main neurotransmitters from the table are revisited throughout the remainder of the book.

- The spinal reflex arc is now treated as a simple neural network.
- Material on neuroplasticity and neurogenesis is now collected in a new, unified section, *Neuroplasticity and Neurogenesis*.
- We have updated the discussion about the size of the human brain, stressing the role of corticalization.
- A new feature, *Mirror, Mirror in the Brain*, explores mirror neurons and the provocative "broken mirrors" hypothesis of autism spectrum disorders.
- Another new feature, *Trapped!*, extends our previous coverage of hindbrain damage.
- The hormone oxytocin is now discussed.

Chapter 3: Human Development

- This chapter has been reorganized to offer more extended coverage of adult development relative to coverage of child development.
- Material on infant and early child development has been reorganized and streamlined.
- Harry Harlow's "cloth mother" studies are now covered in the section *Social Development in Infancy*.
- The section *Cognitive Development in Children* has been streamlined and now includes a new feature, *Theory of Mind: I'm a Me!… and You're a You!*
- The section on middle adulthood has been expanded to include coverage of health, family, and career issues.
- We have added coverage of material on death and dying.
- A new *Psychology in Action* section now discusses well-being and happiness.

Chapter 4: Sensation and Perception

- A new chapter-opening photo and vignette highlight the possibility of perceptual *mis*construction.
- The opening section on sensory processes has been reorganized and rewritten and now deals with early, sensory selectiveness (selection, adaptation, analysis, coding).
- Psychophysics and absolute and relative thresholds are now introduced in the opening section.
- Rhodopsin and iodopsin are now clearly identified as rod and cone photosensitive pigments.
- The number of human smell receptors encoded by genes (1000) is now distinguished from the number actually expressed (400).
- Information on gate control and neuromatrix theories of pain is now included in the section on somesthetic senses, along with other material on pain.
- Material on selective attention has been expanded and placed after the section on perception and is no longer grouped with information on sensory gating and sensory adaptation to emphasize that selective attention is a "late" (i.e., brain-based) mechanism, not an "early" (i.e., sense-based) one.
- The material on the Müller-Lyer illusion is now covered in a later section on perceptual learning and perceptual habits.

Chapter 5: States of Consciousness

- The opening vignette and first section have been rewritten to better reflect the notion of levels of consciousness as well as altered states of consciousness.
- The definition of consciousness has been updated to more clearly reflect the current consensus that normal consciousness is of the external world and the internal world.
- Repair/restorative theories of sleep are now discussed.
- The health risks of sleep apnea are now better stressed.
- A section on narcolepsy has been added.

- Sensory deprivation ("floating" or restricted environmental stimulation therapy) is now treated as a type of meditation, and is treated as a boxed feature.
- Drug abuse statistics have been updated throughout the chapter.
- A note about the benefits of legal psychoactive drug use is now included.
- We now cover amphetamine use as "study drugs."
- A new section on narcotics has been added.
- The harm reduction approach to managing substance abuse is now discussed.
- The *Psychology in Action* section has been revised. Ernest Hartmann's contemporary theory of dreaming is now discussed.

Chapter 6: Conditioning and Learning

- The use of the term *reinforcer* has been limited to the usual sense in operant conditioning and is no longer used to refer to classical conditioning.
- A new feature, *In the Blink of an Eye*, discusses the clinical uses of eye blink conditioning.
- John Watson and Little Albert are now mentioned in the discussion of conditioned emotional responses.
- More current examples of the applications of reinforcement and tokens are now given, including a new figure.
- The material on superstitious conditioning has been upgraded to a feature box, *Are We Less Superstitious Than Pigeons?*, and has been elaborated.
- Punishment is now referred to, more traditionally, as positive punishment and negative punishment (or response cost).
- The section on feedback has been expanded to include knowledge of results.
- The section on modeling in the media has been entirely revised, reflecting a growing awareness that violent media may not be as harmful as previously thought.

Chapter 7: Memory

- The opening section on stages of memory has been rewritten to make it easier to understand the Atkinson-Schiffrin model.
- The term *constructive processing* has been replaced by the term *elaborative processing* throughout the chapter and text to refer to the flexibility of long-term memory.
- The new glossary terms, *false memory* and *source confusion*, allow us to better describe a major downside of elaborative memory processing. In addition, *elaborative encoding* has been subsumed under the term *elaborative processing*.
- A new section, *From Encoding to Retrieval in Long-Term Memory*, clarifies the relationship between what is done at encoding and what might be retrieved.
- The section on photographic memory and eidetic imagery has been rewritten for greater clarity.

Chapter 8: Cognition, Language, Creativity, and Intelligence

- Because cognition and language are components of intelligence, they are now covered first, as reflected in the new chapter title.
- A distinction between experiential and reflective processing is introduced in the first section and woven throughout the chapter and elsewhere in the book.
- A new feature, *What's North of My Fork?*, introduces the linguistic relativity hypothesis.
- The section on experts versus novices now includes reference to experiential processing in experts.
- The section "*Hot*" Cognition now includes a new feature on decision stress, "*Extra Hot, Decaf, Double-Shot….*"

- Material on causes of intellectual disability has been expanded.
- Material on artificial intelligence has been relocated to a later section on issues with the definition of intelligence and has been tightened up.

Chapter 9: Motivation and Emotion

- Material on pain has been relocated to the opening section as an example of an episodic, as opposed to the more typical homeostatic, drive.
- The motives of hunger and thirst are combined in a new section.
- Material on the sex drive has been integrated in a new section, *Sex—Mapping the Erogenous Zones*.
- Material on the need for achievement has been reworked and oriented around a new feature, *True Grit*.
- The opening section on emotions, *Inside an Emotion—Caught in That Feeling?*, has been rewritten. The phrase *primary emotions* has been replaced by the more current phrase *basic emotion* and more fully defined. Basic emotions are now linked more clearly to subcortical limbic structures and experiential processing.
- The discussion of lie detection now includes a discussion of the guilty knowledge test.
- Material on alexithymia now appears in the section *Gender and Emotion*.
- The effects of Botox are now discussed in the context of the facial feedback hypothesis.

Chapter 10: Personality

- Freudian slips are now identified as such and a cartoon has been added.
- Humanist theory is now treated before behavioral theory.
- The notion of biological predispositions is clarified. Trait theory and psychoanalytic theory are contrasted with learning theory and humanist approaches in their stress on personality consistencies as being due to genetic dispositions or situational determinants.
- A new section on positive personality traits has been added to the section *Humanistic Theory—Peak Experiences and Personal Growth*.
- The section *Traits and Situations* has been relabeled *Nature and Nurture* to better link up with use of these terms elsewhere in the book.
- The *Psychology in Action* section on shyness has been reorganized and rewritten for greater clarity.

Chapter 11: Health, Stress, and Coping

- Health statistics have been updated throughout the chapter.
- The opening section has been rewritten to immediately introduce the biopsychosocial model and contrast it with the medical model.
- The definition of health psychology has been broadened to include cognitive and behavioral factors.
- The concept of subjective well-being is now discussed in the section *The Whole Human: Subjective Well-Being*.
- Treatment of burnout in college has been expanded.
- A new feature on relative poverty, *So You Think You're Poor*, has been added.
- The treatment of depression has been restructured and now ends with a discussion of the college blues.
- A new section, *The Whole Human: Hardiness, Optimism, and Happiness*, has been added.
- The *Psychology in Action* section now includes a scorable *Undergraduate Stress Questionnaire*.

Chapter 12: Psychological Disorders

- A previous feature on Munchausen by proxy syndrome is now the chapter-opening vignette.
- The opening sections on mental illness in general have been streamlined.
- Material on psychology and the law has been expanded and now includes a discussion of the insanity defense.
- To eliminate confusion, the phrases *organic mental disorder* and *organic psychoses* are no longer stressed as they are not actual DSM-IV or DSM-5 categories.
- A new section on comorbidity has been added, including a distinction between primary and secondary problems.
- Material on the upcoming DSM-5 is now discussed in an expanded section.
- Possible DSM-5 changes in diagnostic categories and labels are identified throughout the chapter.
- Material on psychiatric labeling and stigmatization is now covered before discussions of specific diagnoses.
- Schizophrenia and dissociative identity disorder are more clearly distinguished.
- A section on undifferentiated schizophrenia has been added.

Chapter 13: Therapies

- The chapter now begins with a brief history of therapy, starting with demonology and ending with psychoanalysis.
- Humanistic and cognitive therapies are now covered in successive sections and treated as two contrasting types of "talk" therapies.
- A new section on cognitive behavior therapy has been added.
- The two successive sections on behavior therapies are now more clearly identified as based on classical and operant conditioning principles, respectively.
- The section on medical therapies has been updated. Pharmaceutical action is now linked to major neurotransmitter systems.
- Deep brain stimulation is now identified as such.
- A section labeled *The Future of Therapy—Back to the Future* examines the future of therapy. It includes a new section on *transcranial magnetic stimulation* and positions both group therapies and Internet therapy as the future of psychotherapy.
- The section on therapy at a distance has been updated.

Chapter 14: Social Behavior

- A new chapter-opening vignette and photo have been created.
- Although overall chapter coverage has not shifted dramatically, the chapter organization has.
- The opening section is now on groups.
- A new cluster of social comparison, attribution, and attitudes, collected as examples of social cognition, follows.
- The social influence topics are now covered following coverage of social cognition.
- A new cluster of prosocial behavior topics now includes affiliation, attraction, and helping behavior.
- A new cluster of antisocial behavior includes aggression, prejudice, and intergroup conflict, including a new section on bullying.
- Solitude is distinguished from loneliness.
- Zimbardo's famous prison experiment is now discussed.
- The material on aggression and media violence has been updated.
- The authoritarian personality is more fully described.

Appendix 1: Behavioral Statistics

- A new opening vignette follows a student grappling with statistics. The vignette is woven throughout the appendix. The result is a more engaging approach to traditionally dry material. A new cartoon is intended to reinforce the new tone of the appendix.

Appendix 2: Life After School

- This new appendix briefly invites students to think about life after school.
- The opening section, *It's Off to Work We Go—Hi Ho, Hi Ho*, is aimed primarily at students not pursuing a career in psychology. It urges students to take a *skills orientation* toward what they have learned from psychology.
- Skills students learn are grouped into five categories: study skills, research skills, critical thinking skills, cultural awareness skills, and personal skills.
- The next section, *Careers in Psychology—Are You Reading My Mind?*, is aimed primarily at students looking for a psychology career. The rich variety of the field of psychology is surveyed.
- The final section briefly surveys six other applied fields of psychology: I/O (industrial/organizational) psychology, environmental psychology, educational psychology, psychology and the law, sports psychology, and human factors psychology.

A Complete Course—Teaching and Learning Supplements

The fifth edition of *Psychology: A Journey* is supported by a rich array of learning and teaching supplements, ranging from a traditional study guide and instructor's manual to electronic resources such as a test bank and access to a variety of web-based materials. These supplements are designed to make teaching and learning more effective. Many are available free to professors or students. Others can be packaged with this text at a discount.

Student Support Materials

Introductory students must learn a multitude of abstract concepts, which can make a first course in psychology difficult. The materials listed here will greatly improve students' chances for success.

Further Readings to Accompany Journey: An Introduction

Each selection in this booklet explores a given topic such as "How do concerns about self presentation affect behavior?" and then comes to a set of practical conclusions about the issue. Issues range from the effect of culture on counseling and psychotherapy, the role of touching in personal relationships, how biology influences learning, and more (ISBN: 0-495-01691-8).

Careers in Psychology: Opportunities in a Changing World, 4e

This informative booklet, written by Tara L. Kuther, is a Wadsworth exclusive. The pamphlet describes the field of psychology, as well as how to prepare for a career in psychology. Career options and resources are also discussed. *Careers in Psychology* can be packaged with this text at no additional cost to students (ISBN 1-133-04967-2).

Sniffy™ the Virtual Rat, Lite Version 3.0

There's no better way to master the basic principles of learning than working with a real laboratory rat. However, this is usually impractical in introductory psychology courses. *Sniffy the Virtual Rat* offers a fun, interactive alternative to working with lab animals. This innovative and entertaining software teaches students about operant and classical conditioning by allowing them to condition a virtual rat. Users begin by training Sniffy to press a bar to obtain food. Then they progress to studying the effects of reinforcement schedules and simple classical conditioning. In addition, special "Mind Windows" enable students to visualize how Sniffy's experiences in the Skinner box produce learning. The Sniffy CD-ROM includes a Lab Manual that shows students how to set up various operant and classical conditioning experiments. *Sniffy™ the Virtual Rat, Lite Version 3.0* may be packaged with this text for a discount (ISBN: 1-111-72617-5)

Online Resources

The Internet is providing new ways to exchange information and enhance education. In psychology, Wadsworth is at the forefront in making use of this exciting technology.

CourseMate

Cengage Learning's Psychology CourseMate brings course concepts to life with interactive learning, study, and exam preparation tools that support the printed textbook. Access an integrated eBook, learning tools including glossaries, flashcards, quizzes, videos, Virtual Psychology Labs, and more in your Psychology CourseMate. Go to CengageBrain.com to register or purchase access.

WebTutor

WebTUTOR™

Jump-start your course with customizable, rich, text-specific content within your Course Management System. Whether you want to Web-enable your class or put an entire course online, WebTutor™ delivers. WebTutor offers a wide array of resources including access to the eBook, glossaries, flashcards, quizzes, videos, Virtual Psychology Labs, and more.

Aplia

aplia™

Aplia helps students understand Psychology as a science through fresh and compelling content, brief engagement activities that illustrate key concepts, and thought-provoking questions.

- Engagement activities pique student interest and motivate students to learn about a concept. Short experiments, videos, and surveys provide a range of experiential learning opportunities.
- Questions about real-world situations hone students' critical thinking skills.
- Auto-assigned, auto-graded assignments hold students accountable for the material before they come to class, increasing their effort and preparation.
- Immediate, detailed explanations for every answer enhance student comprehension.
- Gradebook Analytics allow instructors to monitor and address performance on a student-by-student and topic-by-topic basis.

Essential Teaching Resources

As every professor knows, teaching an introductory psychology course is a tremendous amount of work. The supplements listed here should not only make life easier for you, they should also make it possible for you to concentrate on the more creative and rewarding facets of teaching.

Instructor's Resource Manual

The *Instructor's Manual*, by Kelly Bouas Henry, Missouri Western State University, and John Mitterer, Brock University, contains resources designed to streamline and maximize the effectiveness of your course preparation. This IRM is a treasure trove of resources; each chapter includes learning objectives, discussion questions, lecture enhancements, role-playing scenarios, "one-minute motivators," broadening-our-cultural-horizons exercises, journal questions, suggestions for further reading, media suggestions, web links, and handouts. (ISBN: 1-285-19262-1).

Test Bank

The *Test Bank* was prepared by Jeannette Murphey of Meridian Community College. It includes more than 4,500 multiple-choice questions organized by chapter and by learning objectives. All items, which are classified as factual, conceptual, or applied, include correct answers and page references from the text. All questions new to this edition are identified by an asterisk (ISBN: 1-285-19260-5).

WebTutor™

WebTUTOR™

Jumpstart your course with customizable, rich, text-specific content within your Course Management System. Whether you want to Web-enable your class or put an entire course online, WebTutor™ delivers. WebTutor offers a wide array of resources including access to the eBook, glossaries, flashcards, quizzes, videos, and more.

PowerLecture with ExamView for *Psychology: A Journey* 5e

This one-stop digital library and presentation tool includes preassembled Microsoft® PowerPoint® lecture slides. In addition to the full Instructor's Resource Manual and Test Bank, the PowerLecture also includes ExamView® testing software with all the test items from the printed Test Bank in electronic format, enabling you to create customized tests in print or online. With PowerLecture, you'll find all of your video and media resources in one place, including an image library with graphics from the book itself (ISBN: 1-285-09137-X).

Supplementary Books

No text can cover all of the topics that might be included in an introductory psychology course. If you would like to enrich your course, or make it more challenging, the Wadsworth titles listed here may be of interest.

Challenging Your Preconceptions: Thinking Critically about Psychology, Second Edition

This paperbound book (ISBN: 0-534-26739-4), written by Randolph Smith, helps students strengthen their critical-thinking skills. Psychological issues such as hypnosis and repressed memory, statistical seduction, the validity of pop psychology, and other topics arc used to illustrate the principles of critical thinking.

Writing Papers in Psychology, 9e

The ninth edition of *Writing Papers in Psychology,* 9e (ISBN: 1-111-72613-2), by Ralph L. Rosnow and Mimi Rosnow, is a valuable "how to" manual for writing term papers and research reports. This new edition has been updated to reflect the latest APA guidelines. The book covers each task with examples, hints, and two complete writing samples. Citation ethics, how to locate information, and new research technologies are also covered.

Cross-Cultural Perspectives in Psychology

How well do the concepts of psychology apply to various cultures? What can we learn about human behavior from cultures different from our own? These questions lie behind a collection of original articles written by William F. Price and Rich Crapo. The fourth edition of *Cross-Cultural Perspectives in Psychology* (ISBN: 0-534-54653-6) contains articles on North American ethnic groups as well as cultures from around the world.

Summary

We sincerely hope that both teachers and students will consider this book and its supporting materials a refreshing change from the ordinary. Creating it has been quite an adventure. In the pages that follow, we believe students will find an attractive blend of the theoretical and the practical, plus many of the most exciting ideas in psychology. Most of all, we hope that students using this book will discover that reading a college textbook can be entertaining and enjoyable.

Acknowledgments

Psychology is a cooperative effort requiring the talents and energies of a large community of scholars, teachers, researchers, and students. Like most endeavors in psychology, this book reflects the efforts of many people. We deeply appreciate the contributions of all those who have supported this text's evolution, including the following psychologists:

Linda Amos, Altamaha Technical College
Edward Fernandes, Barton College
Danielle D. Gagne, Alfred University
Ann Higgs, Marist College
Angela Lipsitz, Northern Kentucky University
Daniel McConnell, University of Central Florida
Jack Palmer, University of Louisiana at Monroe
Sandy Phipps, Hazard Community & Technical College
James Previte, Victor Valley College
Tommy Turner, Snead State Community College
Dawn Wright, Meridian Community College

We especially wish to thank the following professors, whose sage advice helped improve the fourth and third editions of *Psychology: A Journey*:

Fourth Edition:
Jean Brown, Cambrian College
Anice Bullock, Tomball College
Lisa Clark, Clark Atlanta University
Eric Comstock, Heald College, Concord
David Das, Elgin Community College
Michael Gardner, California State University, Northridge
Dorothy Gomez, Bunker Hill Community College
Frank Hager, Allegany College of Maryland
John Haworth, Florida Community College at Jacksonville
John S. Klein, Castleton State College
Patricia Lanzon, Henry Ford Community College
Denis Laplante, Lambton College
Laura Madson, New Mexico State University
Errol Magidson, Richard J. Daley College

Horace Marchant, Westfield State College
Richard Mascolo, El Camino Community College
Shawn Mikulay, Elgin Community College
Pike Nelson, Chicago State University
Alysia Ritter, Murray State University
Moises Salinas, Central Connecticut State University
Matthew Westra, Longview Community College

Third Edition:
Dana Albright, Clovis Community College
Saundra Ciccarelli, Gulf Coast Community College
Ellen Cotter, Georgia Southwestern State University
Keith Davis, University of South Carolina
Mary Ellen Dello Stritto, Ball State University
Mylo Egipciaco, Los Angeles Pierce College
Richard Epro, Nassau County Community College
Sabra Jacobs, Prestonsburg Community College
Thuy Karafa, Ferris State University
Jimi Leopold, Tarleton State University
Feleccia Moore-Davis, Houston Community College
Todd Nelson, California State University, Stanislaus
Randall Osborne, Southwest Texas State University
Sandra Phipps, Hazard Community College
Robert Wellman, Fitchburg State College
Matthew Zagumny, Tennessee Tech University

Producing *Psychology: A Journey* and its supplements was a formidable task. We are especially indebted to each of the following individuals for supporting this book:

Sean Wakely
Michelle Julet

We also wish to thank the individuals at Cengage who so generously shared their knowledge and talents over the past year. These are the people who made it happen:

Vernon Boes
Jessica Egbert
Jennifer Risden
Jeremy Judson
Jessica Alderman
Mary Noel
Pat Waldo

We would especially like to express our deepest gratitude to our Editor-in-Chief, Linda Schreiber-Ganster, who has actively supported our efforts, and our Publisher Jon-David Hague for helping us define a new vision for *Journey* and make this book the best it can possibly be. Their guidance will make life easier for professors and students who use this book. We also owe a debt to Jeremy Judson, whose able assistance and wonderful friendship has been utterly invaluable. Nicolas Albert and Shannon LeMay-Finn pushed us along our schedules with aplomb and much thoughtful feedback. Kate Mannix, Kelly Henry, Jeannette Murphey, Janell Gibson, Roman Barnes, Vernon Boes, Jessica Alderman, and Jessica Egbert have all made important contributions.

At home, Barbara Kushmier and Kayleigh Hagerman helped with several aspects of the preparation of this book. Last of all, we would like to thank our wives, Sevren and Heather, for making the journey worthwhile.

Journey Theme *Scientific observation is the most powerful way to critically answer questions about behavior.*

© Pete Saloutos/Corbis

Thinking Critically About Psychology and Research Methods

Journey into Psychology: Death Valley

Wendy has a big dream. Before she gets too old, she wants to run a marathon in every state in the United States and every province in Canada. And not just any 26.2 miles, mind you. She calls them "extreme marathons," solo runs through the most forbidding terrain possible. She has already completed four of them. Here she is on her California extreme marathon, right in the middle of Death Valley (her friends don't call her "Windy" for nothing).

What could Wendy possibly be thinking, you might wonder. But then, you might equally wonder why people get married, join the army, go skydiving, grow roses, become suicide bombers, go to college, or live out their lives in monasteries. You might even wonder, at least sometimes, why *you* do the things you do. In other words, the odds are you are curious about human behavior (just like your authors, we should point out). That may even be a part of the reason you are taking a course in psychology and reading this book.

Psychology is an ever-changing vista of people and ideas that can help you better understand yourself and others. Although we might envy those who get to visit Death Valley, perform on Broadway, explore the ocean's depths, or walk on the moon, the ultimate frontier lies much closer to home. Every life is a marathon, and every day is its own little journey. Think of this book as a "road map" of human behavior. We hope that it illuminates, in some small way, your own journey.

Journey Questions

1.1 What is psychology and what are its goals?

1.2 What is critical thinking?

1.3 How does psychology differ from false explanations of behavior?

1.4 How is the scientific method applied in psychological research?

1.5 How did the field of psychology emerge?

1.6 What are the contemporary perspectives in psychology?

1.7 What are the major specialties in psychology?

1.8 How is an experiment performed?

1.9 What is a double-blind experiment?

1.10 What nonexperimental research methods do psychologists use?

1.11 How good is psychological information found in the popular media?

Psychology—Behave!

JOURNEY QUESTION 1.1 *What is psychology and what are its goals?*

Those of us wondering about Wendy's extreme marathons are not the first humans ever to be curious about human behavior. Even the word *psychology* is thousands of years old, coming from the ancient Greek roots *psyche*, meaning "mind," and *logos*, meaning "knowledge or study." However, have you ever actually seen or touched a "mind"? Because the mind can't be studied directly, **psychology** is now defined as the scientific study of overt behavior and mental processes (covert behavior).

To what does "behavior" refer in the definition of psychology? Any directly observable action or response—eating, hanging out, sleeping, talking, or sneezing—is an *overt behavior*. So are studying, gambling, watching television, tying your shoes, giving someone a gift, learning Spanish, reading this book, and, yes, running extreme marathons. But psychologists haven't left out the "mind"; they also study *covert behaviors*. These are private mental events, such as thinking, dreaming, remembering, and other mental processes (Jackson, 2011).

Today, psychology is both a *science* and a *profession*. As scientists, some psychologists do research to discover new knowledge. Others apply psychology to solve problems in fields such as mental health, business, education, sports, law, medicine, and the design of machines (Davey, 2011). Still others are teachers who share their knowledge with students. Later we will return to the profession of psychology. For now, let's focus on how psychologists create knowledge. Whether they work in a lab, a clinic, or a classroom, all psychologists rely on critical thinking and especially information gained from scientific research.

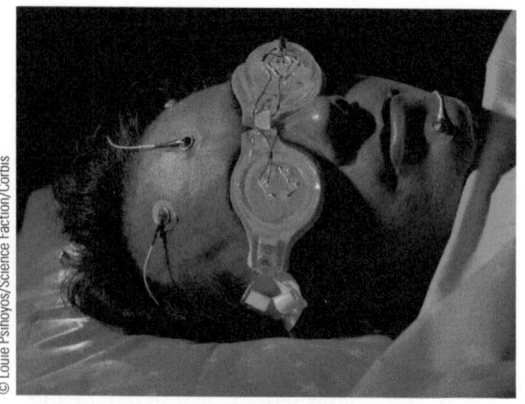

Psychologists are highly trained professionals who have specialized skills in counseling and therapy, measurement and testing, research and experimentation, statistics, diagnosis, treatment, and many other areas. Here psychologist Steven LaBerge wears goggles designed to alert him that he is dreaming, in order to increase his chances of having a lucid dream (Holzinger, LaBerge, & Levitan, 2006). (See Chapter 5 for more details.)

Psychology The scientific study of overt behavior and mental processes (covert behavior).

Scientific observation An empirical investigation structured to answer questions about the world in a systematic and intersubjective (observations can be reliably confirmed by multiple observers) fashion.

Seeking Knowledge in Psychology

Isn't psychology really just a matter of using your common sense? Many people regard themselves as expert "people watchers" and form their own "commonsense" theories of behavior. However, you may be surprised to learn how often self-appointed authorities and long-held commonsense beliefs about human behavior are wrong. For example, have you ever heard that some people are left-brained and some are right-brained? Or that subliminal advertising really works? Or that men and women communicate very differently? It turns out that these widely held beliefs, and many others, are wrong (Lilienfeld et al., 2010).

But how could common sense be wrong so often? We'll spend quite a bit of time in this chapter exploring why this might be so. One problem is that much of what passes for common sense is vague and inconsistent. For example, it is frequently said that you should "strike while the iron is hot." With this in mind, you make a snap decision to buy a cheap cell phone because the offer is time-limited. Later, when you complain to a friend about getting locked into an expensive data plan, she scolds you that everybody knows "haste makes waste."

Further, commonsense statements like these work best after the fact. If your cell phone had worked out, the iron would have, indeed, been "hot." After your purchase turned out to be a bust, it took no insight at all for your friend to point it out.

Another problem with common sense is that it often depends on limited personal observation. For example, have you ever had someone tell you he heard that people in New York City (or Mexico, or Canada, or Paris, or wherever) are rude? But this might mean no more than that someone had a bad encounter on one visit. It may well say nothing about those people in general.

Unlike such casual observation, psychologists rely on **scientific observation**. Although both are based on gathering *empirical evidence* (information gained from direct observation), unlike everyday personal experiences, scientific observation is *systematic*, or carefully planned. Scientific observations are also *intersubjective*, which means that more than one observer can confirm them.

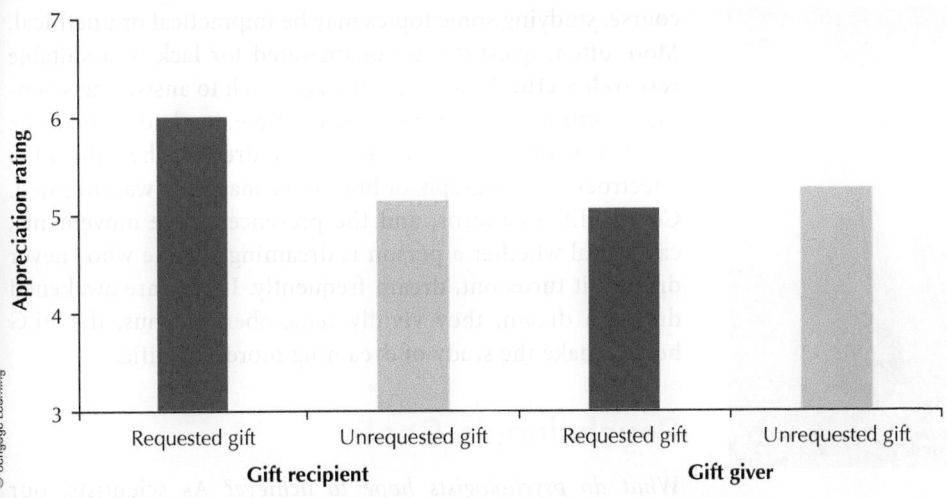

Figure 1.1 Results of an empirical study. The graph shows that the recipients of gifts appreciate gifts they have requested more than gifts chosen by the gift giver. If anything, gift givers were slightly more likely to believe that recipients would prefer to receive an unrequested gift (although the difference was not statistically significant.) (Data adapted from Gino & Flynn, 2011.)

Basically, the scientific approach says, "Let's take a more objective look" (Stanovich, 2010). Psychologists study behavior directly by systematically collecting data (observed facts) so they can draw valid conclusions. Would you say it's true, for instance, that "The clothes make the man"? Or do you believe that "you can't judge a book by its cover"? Why argue about it? As psychologists, we would simply get some people who are well dressed and some who are not and, through scientific observation, find out who makes out better in a variety of situations!

Here's an example of gathering empirical evidence: Have you ever wondered if, when it comes to giving gifts, it really is "the thought that counts"? Francesca Gino and Francis Flynn (2011) decided to find out. They asked gift recipients to rate how much they would appreciate getting a gift they requested as opposed to one chosen by the gift giver. It turns out people would be more appreciative of a gift they requested. In contrast, gift givers thought recipients would be just as appreciative of an unre-quested gift (see **Figure 1.1**).

Isn't the outcome of this study fairly predictable? Not if you started out believing otherwise. Sometimes the results of studies match our personal observations or commonsense beliefs and sometimes they come as a surprise. In this instance, you may have guessed the outcome. Your suspicions were confirmed by scientific observation. However, it could easily have turned out differently.

I like getting money for a gift; does that make a difference? Gino and Flynn (2011) checked that out as well. They found that gift recipients preferred getting money even more than getting a gift they requested even though gift givers thought exactly the opposite. Apparently, we struggle more with the idea of "thoughtful" gifts when we are the givers than when we are the recipients.

Psychological Research

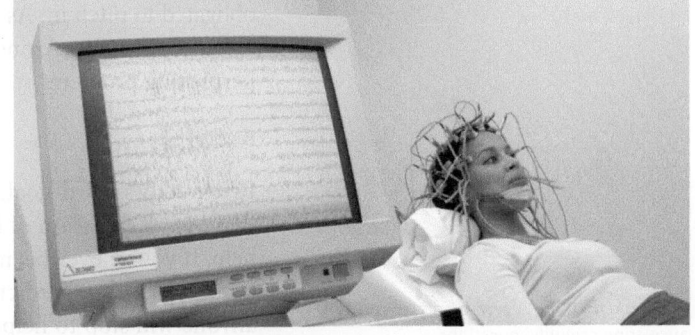

The scientific study of dreaming was made possible by use of the EEG, a device that records the tiny electrical signals generated by the brain as a person sleeps. The EEG converts these electrical signals into a written record of brain activity. Certain shifts in brain activity, coupled with the presence of rapid eye movements, are strongly related to dreaming. (See Chapter 5 for more information.)

Many fields, such as history, law, art, and business, are also interested in human behavior. How is psychology different? Psychology's great strength is that it uses scientific observation to systematically answer questions about all sorts of behaviors (Stanovich, 2010). Of

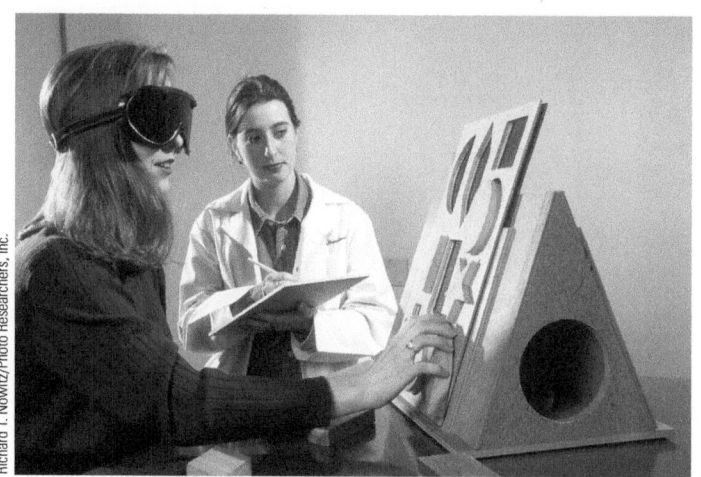

Some psychologists specialize in administering, scoring, and interpreting psychological tests, such as tests of intelligence, creativity, personality, or aptitude. This specialty, which is called psychometrics, is an example of using psychology to predict future behavior.

course, studying some topics may be impractical or unethical. More often, questions go unanswered for lack of a suitable **research method**—a systematic approach to answering scientific questions. In the past, for example, we had to take the word of people who say they never dream. Then the EEG (electroencephalograph, or brainwave machine) was invented. Certain EEG patterns, and the presence of eye movements, can reveal whether a person is dreaming. People who "never dream," it turns out, dream frequently. If they are awakened during a dream, they vividly remember it. Thus, the EEG helped make the study of dreaming more scientific.

Psychology's Goals

What do psychologists hope to achieve? As scientists, our ultimate goal is to benefit humanity (O'Neill, 2005). More specifically, the goals of psychology are to *describe, understand, predict,* and *control* behavior. What do psychology's goals mean in practice? Let's see.

Description

Answering psychological questions often begins with a careful description of behavior. **Description**, or naming and classifying, is typically based on making a detailed record of scientific observations.

But a description doesn't explain anything, does it? Right. Useful knowledge begins with accurate description, but descriptions fail to answer the important "why" questions. *Why* do more women attempt suicide, and *why* do more men complete it? *Why* are people more aggressive when they are uncomfortable? *Why* are bystanders often unwilling to help in an emergency? (And, most importantly, *why* did Wendy start running extreme marathons?)

Understanding

We have met psychology's second goal when we can explain an event. That is, **understanding** usually means we can state the causes of a behavior. For example, research on "bystander apathy" reveals that people often fail to help when *other* possible helpers are nearby. Why? Because a "diffusion of responsibility" occurs. Basically, no one person feels personally obligated to pitch in. As a result, the more potential helpers there are, the less likely it is that anyone will help (Aronson, Wilson, & Akert, 2010; Darley, 2000). Now we can explain a perplexing problem.

Prediction

Psychology's third goal, **prediction**, is the ability to forecast behavior accurately. Notice that our explanation of bystander apathy makes a prediction about the chances of getting help. If you've ever been stranded on a busy freeway with car trouble, you'll recognize the accuracy of this prediction: Having many potential helpers nearby is no guarantee that anyone will stop to help.

Control

Description, explanation, and prediction seem reasonable, but is control a valid goal? Control may seem like a threat to personal freedom. However, to a psychologist, **control** simply refers to the ability to alter the conditions that affect behavior. If a clinical psychologist helps a person overcome a terrible fear of snakes, control is involved. If you suggest changes in a classroom that help students learn better, you have exerted control. Control is also involved in designing cars to keep drivers from making fatal errors. Clearly, psychological control must be used wisely and humanely.

Research method A systematic approach to answering scientific questions.

Description In scientific research, the process of naming and classifying.

Understanding In psychology, understanding is achieved when the causes of a behavior can be stated.

Prediction An ability to accurately forecast behavior.

Control Altering conditions that influence behavior.

In summary, psychology's goals are a natural outgrowth of our desire to understand behavior. Basically, they boil down to asking the following questions:

What is the nature of this behavior? (description)

Why does it occur? (understanding and explanation)

Can we forecast when it will occur? (prediction)

What conditions affect it? (control)

---

 study break The Science of Psychology

RECITE

Check your memory by answering these questions. If you miss any, skim over the preceding material before continuing, to make sure you understand what you just read.

1. Psychology is the _____ study of _____ and _____ processes.
2. Commonsense beliefs are often
   a. vague
   b. inconsistent
   c. based on limited observations
   d. all of the above
3. The best psychological information is typically based on
   a. casual observation
   b. opinions of experts and authorities
   c. anthropomorphic measurements
   d. scientific observation
4. Which of the following questions relates most directly to the goal of *understanding* behavior?
   a. Do the scores of men and women differ on tests of thinking abilities?
   b. Why does a blow to the head cause memory loss?
   c. Will productivity in a business office increase if room temperature is raised or lowered?
   d. What percentage of college students suffer from test anxiety?

REFLECT

THINK CRITICALLY

5. Can you think of some "commonsense" statements that contradict each other?
6. All sciences are interested in controlling the phenomena they study. True or false?

SELF-REFLECT

At first, many students think that psychology is primarily about abnormal behavior and psychotherapy. Did you? How would you describe the field now?

ANSWERS

1. scientific, (overt) behavior, (covert) mental 2. d 3. d 4. b 5. There are many examples. Here are a few more: "The grass is always greener on the other side" versus "There's no place like home"; "Too many cooks spoil the broth" versus "Two heads are better than one." 6. False. Astronomy and archaeology are examples of sciences that do not share psychology's fourth goal. Think about it for a moment: No one can *control* the stars or the past.

Critical Thinking—Take It with a Grain of Salt

JOURNEY QUESTION 1.2 *What is critical thinking?*

How does critical thinking play a role in psychology? Most of us would be skeptical when offered a "genuine" Rolex watch or expensive designer sunglasses for just a few dollars on eBay. And most of us easily accept our ignorance of subatomic physics. But because we deal with human behavior every day, we tend to think that we already know what is true in psychology. All too often, we are tempted to "buy" commonsense beliefs, urban legends, and even outrageous claims about the powers of "healing" crystals, "miraculous" herbal remedies, astrology, psychics describing people's personalities and predicting their future, and so forth.

For this and many more reasons, learning to think critically is one of the lasting benefits of a college education. **Critical thinking** in psychology is a type of reflection (you DID read the *Psychology of Studying*, on pages 2–4, right?) that involves asking whether a particular belief can be supported by scientific theory and observation (Yanchar, Slife, & Warne, 2008). Critical thinkers are willing to challenge conventional wisdom by asking hard questions (Jackson & Newberry, 2012).

Critical thinking (in psychology) A type of reflection involving the support of beliefs through scientific explanation and observation.

For example, when it comes to achieving our goals, is it better to focus on how far we still have to go before we reach a goal or should we focus on what we have already accomplished? Critical thinkers might immediately ask: "Is there any theory to support stressing either a goal focus or an accomplishment focus? Is there any empirical evidence either way? What could we do to find out for ourselves?" (Be on the lookout later in this chapter for some evidence concerning this question.)

Critical Thinking Principles

The heart of critical thinking is a willingness to actively *reflect* on ideas. Critical thinkers evaluate ideas by probing for weaknesses in their reasoning and analyzing the evidence supporting their beliefs. They question assumptions and look for alternate conclusions. True knowledge, they recognize, comes from constantly revising our understanding of the world.

Critical thinking relies on the following basic principles (Elder, 2006; Jackson & Newberry, 2012; Kida, 2006):

1. *Few "truths" transcend the need for logical analysis and empirical testing.* Whereas religious beliefs and personal values may be held as matters of faith, most other ideas can and should be evaluated by applying the rules of logic, evidence, and the scientific method.
2. *Critical thinkers often wonder what it would take to show that a "truth" is false.* Critical thinkers actively seek to *falsify* beliefs, including their own. They are willing to admit when they are wrong. As Susan Blackmore (2000, p. 55) said when her studies caused her to abandon some long-held beliefs, "Admitting you are wrong is always hard—even though it's a skill that every psychologist has to learn." At the same time, critical thinkers can be more confident in beliefs that have survived their attempts at falsification.
3. *Authority or claimed expertise does not automatically make an idea true or false.* Just because a teacher, guru, celebrity, or authority is convinced or sincere doesn't mean you should automatically believe or disbelieve that person. Naïvely accepting (or denying) the word of an "expert" is unscientific and self-demeaning without asking, "Is this a well-supported explanation, or is there a better one? What evidence convinced her or him?"
4. *Judging the quality of evidence is crucial.* Imagine you are a juror in a courtroom, judging claims made by two battling lawyers. To decide correctly, you can't just weigh the *amount* of evidence. You must also critically evaluate the *quality* of the evidence. Then you can give greater weight to the most credible facts.
5. *Critical thinking requires an open mind.* Be prepared to consider daring departures and go wherever the evidence leads. However, don't become so "open-minded" that you are simply gullible. Astronomer Carl Sagan once noted, "It seems to me that what is called for is an exquisite balance between two conflicting needs: the most skeptical scrutiny of all hypotheses that are served up to us and at the same time a great openness to new ideas" (Kida, 2006, p. 51).

To put these principles into action, here are some questions to ask as you evaluate new information (Browne & Keeley, 2010; Jackson & Newberry, 2012):

1. What claims are being made? What are their implications?
2. Are the claims understandable? Do they make logical sense? Is there another possible explanation? Is it a simpler explanation?
3. What tests (if any) of these claims have been made? What was the nature and quality of the tests? Can they be repeated? Who did the tests? How reliable and trustworthy were the investigators? Do they have conflicts of interest? Do their findings appear to be objective? Has any other independent researcher duplicated the findings?
4. How good is the evidence? (In general, scientific observations provide the highest quality evidence.)
5. Finally, how much credibility can the claim be given? High, medium, low, provisional?

A course in psychology naturally enriches thinking skills. In this book, all upcoming chapters include *Think Critically* questions based on the ones you have seen here. Take the time to tackle these questions. The effort will sharpen your thinking abilities and make learning livelier. For an immediate thinking challenge, let's take a critical look at several nonscientific systems that claim to explain behavior.

Pseudopsychologies—Palms, Planets, and Personality

JOURNEY QUESTION 1.3 *How does psychology differ from false explanations of behavior?*

A **pseudopsychology** (SUE-doe-psychology) is any unfounded system that resembles psychology. Many pseudopsychologies give the appearance of being scientific but are actually false. (*Pseudo* means "false.") Pseudopsychologies are types of **superstitions**, unfounded beliefs held without evidence or in the face of falsifying evidence.

Unlike "real" psychology, pseudopsychologies change little over time because followers seek evidence that appears to confirm their beliefs and avoid evidence that falsifies them. Critical thinkers, scientists, and psychologists, in contrast, are skeptical of their own theories (Schick & Vaughn, 2011). They actively look for contradictions as a way to advance knowledge.

Can you give some examples of false psychologies? One pseudopsychology, known as *phrenology*, was popularized in the nineteenth century by Franz Gall, a German anatomy teacher. Phrenology claimed that the shape of the skull reveals personality traits. Psychological research has long since shown that bumps on the head have nothing to do with talents or abilities. In fact, the phrenologists were so far off that they listed the part of the brain that controls hearing as a center for "combativeness"! *Palmistry* is a similarly falsified system that claims lines on the hand reveal personality traits and predict the future. Despite the overwhelming evidence against phrenology and palmistry, these pseudopsychologies are still practiced today. Palmists, in particular, can still be found separating the gullible from their money in many cities.

At first glance, a pseudopsychology called *graphology* might seem more reasonable. Some graphologists claim that personality traits are revealed by handwriting. Based on such claims, some companies even use graphologists to select job candidates. This is troubling because graphologists score close to zero on tests of accuracy in rating personality (Dazzi & Pedrabissi, 2009; Furnham, Chamorro-Premuzic, & Callahan, 2003). In fact, graphologists do no better than untrained college students in rating personality and job performance (Neter & Ben-Shakhar, 1989). Even a graphological society recommends that handwriting analysis should not be used to select people for jobs (Simner & Goffin, 2003). (By the way, graphology's failure at revealing personality should be separated from its value for detecting forgeries.)

Graphology might seem harmless enough until you imagine being denied a job because a graphologist didn't like your handwriting. This false system has been used to determine who is hired, given bank credit, or selected for juries. In these and similar situations, pseudopsychologies do, in fact, harm people.

If pseudopsychologies have no scientific basis, how do they survive and why are they popular? There are several reasons, all of which can be illustrated by a critique of astrology.

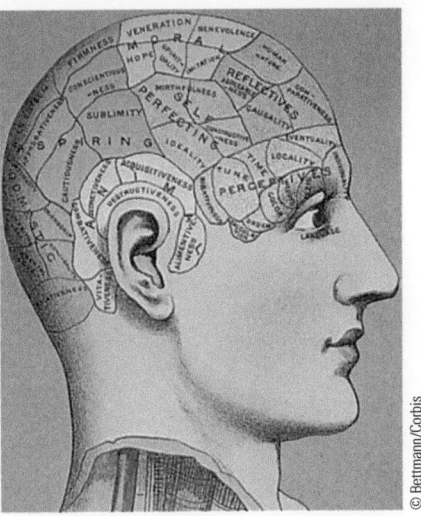

Phrenology was an attempt to assess personality characteristics by examining various areas of the skull. Phrenologists used charts such as the one shown here as guides. Like other pseudopsychologists, phrenologists made no attempt to empirically verify their concepts.

Would you hire this man? Here's a sample of your author's handwriting. What do you think it reveals? Your interpretations are likely to be as accurate (or inaccurate) as those of a graphologist.

Problems in the Stars

Arguably the most popular pseudopsychology, astrology holds that the positions of the stars and planets at the time of one's birth determine personality traits and affect behavior. Like other pseudopsychologies, astrology has repeatedly been shown to have no scientific validity, either theoretically or empirically (Kelly, 1999; Rogers & Soule, 2009):

Pseudopsychology Any false and unscientific system of beliefs and practices that is offered as an explanation of behavior.

Superstition Unfounded belief held without evidence or in spite of falsifying evidence.

1. **The theory of astrology is unconvincing.** Astrology is based on a zodiac map invented several thousand years ago in an ancient civilization called Babylon. Unlike scientific theories, which are regularly falsified and rejected or revised accordingly, the basic underpinnings of astrology have remained relatively unchanged. To date, no astrologer has offered a convincing explanation of *how* the positions of the planets at a person's birth could affect his or her future. Astrologers have also failed to explain *why* the moment of birth should be more important than, say, the moment of conception. (Perhaps it is because it is relatively easy to figure out the moment of birth and much trickier to determine the moment of conception.) Besides, the zodiac has shifted in the sky by one full constellation since astrology was first set up. (In other words, if astrology calls you a Scorpio you are really a Libra, and so forth.) However, most astrologers simply ignore this shift (Martens & Trachet, 1998).

2. **The evidence against astrology** is **convincing.** One study of more than 3,000 predictions by famous astrologers found that only a small percentage were fulfilled. These "successful" predictions tended to be vague ("There will be a tragedy somewhere in the east in the spring") or easily guessed from current events (Culver & Ianna, 1988). Similarly, if astrologers are asked to match people with their horoscopes, they do no better than would be expected by chance. In one famous test, astrologers could not even use horoscopes to distinguish murderers from law-abiding people (Gauquelin, 1970). In fact, there is no connection between people's astrological signs and their intelligence or personality traits (Hartmann, Reuter, & Nyborg, 2006). There is also no connection between the "compatibility" of couples' astrological signs and their marriage and divorce rates or between astrological signs and leadership, physical characteristics, or career choices (Martens & Trachet, 1998).

In short, astrology doesn't work.

Then why does astrology often seem to work? Even the daily horoscopes printed in newspapers can seem uncannily accurate. For many people this apparent accuracy can only mean that astrology is valid. Unfortunately such *uncritical acceptance* overlooks a much simpler psychological explanation (see, for example, Rogers & Soule, 2009). The following discussion explains why.

Uncritical Acceptance

Perceptions of the accuracy of horoscopes are typically based on **uncritical acceptance**—the tendency to believe claims because they seem true or because it would be nice if they were true. Horoscopes are generally made up of mostly flattering traits. Naturally, when your personality is described in *desirable* terms, it is hard to deny that the description has the "ring of truth." How much acceptance would astrology receive if a birth sign read like this:

> **Virgo:** You are the logical type and hate disorder. Your nitpicking is unbearable to your friends. You are cold, unemotional, and usually fall asleep while making love. Virgos make good doorstops.

Confirmation Bias

Even when an astrological description contains a mixture of good and bad traits, it may seem accurate. To find out why, read the following personality description.

> **Your Personality Profile**
> You have many personality strengths, with some weaknesses to which you can usually adjust. You tend to be accepting of yourself. You are comfortable with some structure in your life but do enjoy diverse experiences from time to time. Although on the inside you might be a bit unsure of yourself, you appear under control to others. You are sexually well-adjusted, although you do have some questions. Your life goals are more or less realistic. Occasionally you question your decisions and actions because you're unsure that they are correct. You want to be liked and admired by other people. You are not using your potential to its full extent. You like to think for yourself and don't always take other people's word without thinking it through. You are not

Uncritical acceptance The tendency to believe claims because they seem true or because it would be nice if they were true.

generally willing to disclose to others because it might lead to problems. You are a natural introvert, cautious, and careful around others, although there are times when you can be an extrovert who is the "life of the party."

Does this describe your personality? A psychologist read a similar summary individually to college students who had taken a personality test. Only a few students felt that the description was inaccurate. Another classic study found that people rated the "personality profile" as more accurate than their actual horoscopes (French et al., 1991).

Reread the description and you will see that it contains both sides of several personality dimensions ("You are a natural introvert . . . although there are times when you can be an extrovert . . ."). Its apparent accuracy is an illusion based on **confirmation bias**, in which we remember or notice things that confirm our expectations and forget the rest (Lilienfeld, Ammirati, & Landfield, 2009). The pseudopsychologies thrive on this effect. For example, you can always find "Aquarius characteristics" in an Aquarius. If you looked, however, you could also find "Gemini characteristics," "Scorpio characteristics," or whatever. Perhaps this explains why, in an ironic twist, 94 percent of those sent the full 10-page horoscope of a famous mass murderer accepted it as their own (Gauquelin, 1970).

Confirmation bias is also relied on by various "psychic mediums" who claim that they can communicate with the deceased friends and relatives of audience members. An analysis shows that the number of "hits" (correct statements) made by these people tends to be very low. Nevertheless, many viewers are impressed because of our natural tendency to remember apparent hits and ignore misses. Of course, particularly embarrassing misses are often edited out before such shows appear on television (Nickell, 2001).

The Barnum Effect

Pseudopsychologies also take advantage of the **Barnum effect**, which is a tendency to consider personal descriptions accurate if they are stated in general terms (Kida, 2006). P. T. Barnum, the famed circus showman, had a formula for success: "Always have a little something for everybody." Like the all-purpose personality profile, palm readings, fortunes, horoscopes, and other products of pseudopsychology are stated in such general terms that they can hardly miss. There is

Non Sequitur

always "a little something for everybody." To observe the Barnum effect, read *all 12* of the daily horoscopes found in newspapers for several days. You will find that predictions for other signs fit events as well as those for your own sign do. Try giving a friend the wrong horoscope sometime. Your friend may still be quite impressed with the "accuracy" of the horoscope.

Astrology's popularity shows that many people have difficulty separating valid psychology from systems that seem valid but are not. The goal of this discussion, then, has been to make you a more critical observer of human behavior and to clarify what is, and what is not, psychology. Here is what the "stars" say about your future:

> Emphasis now on education and personal improvement. A learning experience of lasting value awaits you. Take care of scholastic responsibilities before engaging in recreation. The word *psychology* figures prominently in your future.

Remember, pseudopsychologies may seem like no more than a nuisance, but they can do harm. For instance, people seeking treatment for psychological disorders may become the victims of self-appointed "experts" who offer ineffective, pseudoscientific "therapies" (Kida, 2006; Lilienfeld, Ruscio, & Lynn, 2008). Valid psychological principles are based on scientific theory and evidence, not fads, opinions, or wishful thinking.

Confirmation bias The tendency to remember or notice information that fits one's expectations, while forgetting discrepancies.

Barnum effect The tendency to consider a personal description accurate if it is stated in very general terms.

Scientific Research—How to Think Like a Psychologist

JOURNEY QUESTION 1.4 *How is the scientific method applied in psychological research?*

Thinking critically about psychology begins with the careful recording of facts and events, the heart of all sciences. To be *scientific*, our observations must be *systematic*, so that they reveal something reliable about behavior (Stanovich, 2010). To use an earlier example, if you are interested in whether gift recipients prefer gifts they requested or gifts that givers chose for them, you will learn little by making haphazard observations of gift-giving at family birthday parties. To be of value, your observations must be planned and systematic.

The Scientific Method

The **scientific method** is a form of critical thinking based on careful collection of evidence, accurate description and measurement, precise definition, controlled observation, and repeatable results (Jackson, 2011; Yanchar, Slife, & Warne, 2008). In its ideal form, the scientific method has six elements:

1. Making observations
2. Defining a problem
3. Proposing a hypothesis
4. Gathering evidence/testing the hypothesis
5. Building a theory
6. Publishing results

Let's take a closer look at some elements of the scientific method. Earlier we ran across the question of whether goals are more attainable if people maintain a goal focus (stressing how much remains to be done to achieve the goal) or an achievement focus (stressing how much has already been achieved). All the basic elements of the scientific method are found in this example, from Florida State University psychologist Kyle Conlon and his colleagues (2011).

Making Observations

The researchers reviewed previously published studies, noting that both goal-focused and achievement-focused approaches are popular. If the goal is weight loss, for example, one goal-focused approach is to "count down" the pounds (only 10 pounds to go!) while one achievement-focused approach is to celebrate milestones (congratulations on losing the first 10 pounds!).

Defining a Problem

The researchers also noted that maintaining a goal focus seems to inspire more goal-oriented behaviors. Thus, they defined their main problem as, "Will people lose more weight if they maintain a goal focus or if they maintain an achievement focus?"

Proposing a Hypothesis

What exactly is a "hypothesis"? A **hypothesis** (hi-POTH-eh-sis) is a tentative statement about, or explanation of, an event or relationship. In common terms, a hypothesis is a *testable* hunch or educated guess about behavior. For example, you might hypothesize "Frustration encourages aggression." How could you test this hypothesis? First you would have to decide how you are going to frustrate people. (This part might be fun.) Then you will need to find a way to measure whether they become more aggressive. (Not so much fun if

Applying the scientific method to the study of behavior requires careful observation. Here, a psychologist videotapes a session in which a child's thinking abilities are being tested.

Scientific method A form of critical thinking based on careful measurement and controlled observation.

Hypothesis A statement of the predicted outcome of an experiment or an educated guess about the relationship between variables.

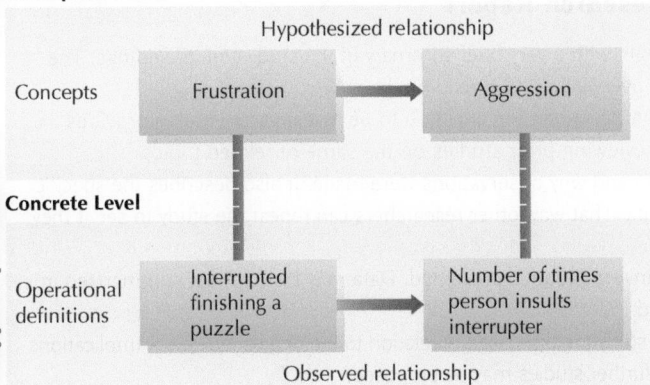

Conceptual Level

Hypothesized relationship

Concepts → Frustration → Aggression

Concrete Level

Operational definitions → Interrupted finishing a puzzle → Number of times person insults interrupter

Observed relationship

Figure 1.2 Operational definitions are used to link concepts with concrete observations. Do you think the examples given are reasonable operational definitions of frustration and aggression? Operational definitions vary in how well they represent concepts. For this reason, many different experiments may be necessary to draw clear conclusions about hypothesized relationships in psychology.

you plan to be nearby.) Your observations would then provide evidence to confirm or disconfirm your hypothesis.

Because we cannot see or touch frustration, we must define it operationally. An **operational definition** states the exact procedures used to represent a concept. Operational definitions allow unobservable ideas, such as covert behaviors, to be tested in real-world terms (see **Figure 1.2**). For example, since you can't measure frustration directly, you might define frustration as "interrupting an adult before he or she can finish a puzzle and win a free movie pass." And aggression might be defined as "the number of times a frustrated individual insults the person who prevented work on the puzzle." In other words, covert behaviors are operationally defined in terms of overt behavior so they can be observed and studied scientifically.

Gathering Evidence/Testing the Hypothesis

Now let's return to the question of whether weight loss is easier when you maintain a goal focus. To gather data, the researchers assigned participants to one of three weight loss groups, goal-focused, achievement-focused, and no-focus control. Each group met for 12 weekly meetings and had access to a special website. As predicted, goal-focused individuals lost more weight than did either achievement-focused or control individuals. They also reported being more committed to reaching their goal weights.

Theory Building

What about theory building? In research, a **theory** is a system of ideas designed to interrelate concepts and facts in a way that summarizes existing data and predicts future observations. Good theories summarize observations, explain them, and guide further research (**Figure 1.3**). Without theories of forgetting, personality, stress, mental illness, and the like, psychologists would drown in a sea of disconnected facts (Stanovich, 2010).

Conlon and his colleagues interpreted their results as consistent with theories of motivation that stress the importance of being aware of how much work still remains to be done to achieve a goal. The results were also portrayed as extending these theories into the field of health psychology and as being relevant to the design of health intervention programs.

Publishing Results

Because scientific information must always be *publicly available*, the results of psychological studies are usually published in professional journals (see **Table 1.1**). That way, other researchers can read about the results and make their own observations if they doubt the study's findings (Jackson, 2011). If others are able to *replicate* (repeat) the results of a study, those results become more credible.

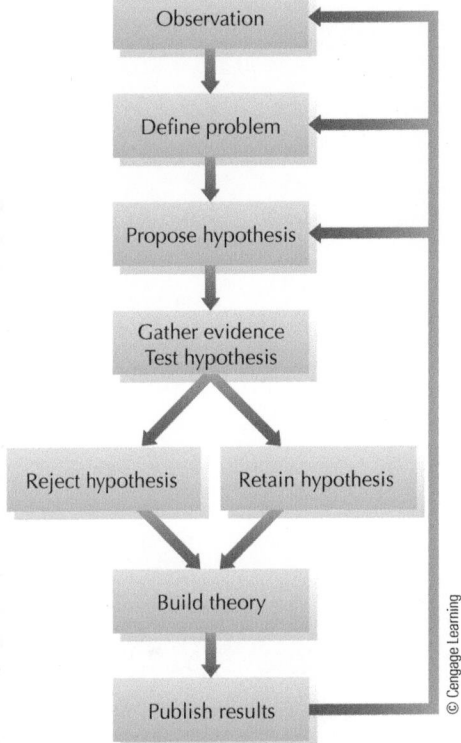

Observation → Define problem → Propose hypothesis → Gather evidence Test hypothesis → Reject hypothesis / Retain hypothesis → Build theory → Publish results

Figure 1.3 Psychologists use the logic of science to answer questions about behavior. Specific hypotheses can be tested in a variety of ways, including naturalistic observation, correlational studies, controlled experiments, clinical studies, and the survey method. Psychologists revise their theories to reflect the evidence they gather. New or revised theories then lead to new observations, problems, and hypotheses.

Operational definition Defining a scientific concept by stating the specific actions or procedures used to measure it. For example, "hunger" might be defined as "the number of hours of food deprivation."

Theory A system of ideas designed to interrelate concepts and facts in a way that summarizes existing data and predicts future observations.

Table 1.1 Outline of a Research Report

- **Abstract** Research reports begin with a very brief summary of the study and its findings. The abstract allows you to get an overview without reading the entire article.
- **Introduction** The introduction describes the question to be investigated. It also provides background information by reviewing prior studies on the same or related topics.
- **Method** This section tells how and why observations were made. It also describes the specific procedures used to gather data. That way, other researchers can repeat the study to see if they get the same results.
- **Results** The outcome of the investigation is presented. Data may be graphed, summarized in tables, or statistically analyzed.
- **Discussion** The results of the study are discussed in relation to the original question. Implications of the study are explored and further studies may be proposed.

© Cengage Learning

In a scholarly article published in the *Journal of Experimental Social Psychology,* Conlon and his colleagues (2011) describe the question they investigated, the methods they used, and the results of their study comparing goal-focused and achievement-focused dieters.

Research Ethics

Aren't there also rules about how scientists have to treat the people they study? You are absolutely right. Psychology experiments sometimes raise *ethical* questions. Stanley Milgram's obedience studies are a classic example (see Chapter 14). Participants were ordered to give what they thought were painful electric shocks to another person (although no shocks were actually given) (Milgram, 1963). Believing that they had hurt someone, many people left the experiment shaken and upset. A few suffered guilt and distress for some time afterward. Such experiments raise serious ethical questions. Did the information gained justify the emotional costs? Was deception really necessary? As a reply to such questions, American Psychological Association guidelines state that "Psychologists must carry out investigations with respect for the people who participate and with concern for their dignity and welfare" (see **Table 1.2**).

Similar guidelines apply to animals, where investigators are expected to "ensure the welfare of animals and treat them humanely" (American Psychological Association, 2010). To assure this, most college and university psychology departments have ethics committees that oversee research. Nevertheless, no easy answers exist for the ethical questions raised by psychology, and debate about specific experiments is likely to continue.

Table 1.2 Basic Ethical Guidelines for Psychological Researchers

Do no harm.

Accurately describe risks to potential participants.

Ensure that participation is voluntary.

Minimize any discomfort to participants.

Maintain confidentiality.

Do not unnecessarily invade privacy.

Use deception only when absolutely necessary.

Remove any misconceptions caused by deception (debrief).

Provide results and interpretations to participants.

Treat participants with dignity and respect.

© Cengage Learning

RECITE

1. Most of psychology can rightfully be called common sense because psychologists prefer informal observation to systematic observation. T or F?
2. *Confirmation bias* refers to graphology's accepted value for the detection of forgeries. T or F?
3. Personality descriptions provided by pseudopsychologies are stated in general terms, which provide "a little something for everybody." This fact is the basis of the

   a. palmist's fallacy   b. uncritical acceptance pattern
   c. confirmation bias   d. Barnum effect

4. A psychologist does a study to see whether exercising increases sense of well-being. In the study, he will be testing an

   a. experimental hypothesis   b. operational definition
   c. empirical definition   d. anthropomorphic theory

5. _____ behaviors are operationally defined in terms of _____ behavior

   a. Overt, covert   b. Observable, overt
   c. Covert, overt   d. Covert, abstract

REFLECT

THINK CRITICALLY

6. Try constructing a few "Barnum statements," personality statements that are so general that virtually everyone will think they apply to themselves. Can you string them together to make a "Barnum profile"? Can you adapt the same statements to construct a "Barnum horoscope"?

SELF-REFLECT

It is nearly impossible to get through a day without encountering people who believe in pseudopsychologies or who make unscientific or unfounded statements. How stringently do you evaluate your own beliefs and the claims made by others?

How might you scientifically test the old saw that you can't teach an old dog new tricks? Follow the steps of the scientific method to propose a testable hypothesis and decide how you would gather evidence. (Well, OK, you don't have to publish your results.)

ANSWERS

1. F 2. F 3. d 4. a 5. c 6. The term "Barnum statement" comes from Levy (2003; but see also Rogers & Soule, 2009), who offers the following examples: You are afraid of being hurt. You are trying to find a balance between autonomy and closeness. You don't like being overly dependent. You just want to be understood.

A Brief History of Psychology—Psychology's Family Album

JOURNEY QUESTION 1.5 *How did the field of psychology emerge?*

As we noted previously, people have been informally observing human behavior and philosophizing about it for thousands of years. In contrast, psychology's history as a science dates back little more than 130 years to Leipzig, Germany. There, in 1879, Wilhelm Wundt (VILL-helm Voont), the "father of psychology," set up a laboratory to study conscious experience.

What happens, Wundt wondered, when we experience sensations, images, and feelings? To find out, he systematically observed and measured stimuli of various kinds (lights, sounds, weights). A **stimulus** is any physical energy that affects a person and evokes a response (stimulus: singular; stimuli [STIM-you-lie]: plural). Wundt then used **introspection**, or "looking inward," to probe his reactions to various stimuli. (Stop reading, close your eyes, carefully examine your covert thoughts, feelings, and sensations, and you will be introspecting.)

Over the years, Wundt studied vision, hearing, taste, touch, memory, time perception, and many other topics. By insisting on systematic observation and measurement, he asked some interesting questions and got psychology off to a good start (Schultz & Schultz, 2012).

Structuralism

Wundt's ideas were carried to the United States by Edward Titchener (TICH-in-er). Titchener called Wundt's ideas **structuralism** and tried to analyze the structure of mental life into basic "elements" or "building blocks."

How could he do that? You can't analyze experience like a chemical compound, can you? Perhaps not, but the structuralists tried "mental chemistry," mostly by using introspection.

Hulton Archive/Getty Images

Wilhelm Wundt, 1832–1920. Wundt is credited with making psychology an independent science, separate from philosophy. Wundt's original training was in medicine, but he became deeply interested in psychology. In his laboratory, Wundt investigated how sensations, images, and feelings combine to make up personal experience.

Stimulus Any physical energy sensed by an organism.

Introspection To look within; to examine one's own thoughts, feelings, or sensations.

Structuralism The school of thought concerned with analyzing sensations and personal experience into basic elements.

William James, 1842–1910. William James was the son of philosopher Henry James, Sr., and the brother of novelist Henry James. During his long academic career, James taught anatomy, physiology, psychology, and philosophy at Harvard University. James believed strongly that ideas should be judged in terms of their practical consequences for human conduct.

John B. Watson, 1878–1958. Watson's intense interest in observable behavior began with his doctoral studies in biology and neurology. Watson became a psychology professor at Johns Hopkins University in 1908 and advanced his theory of behaviorism. He remained at Johns Hopkins until 1920 when he left for a career in the advertising industry!

Functionalism The school of psychology concerned with how behavior and mental abilities help people adapt to their environments.

Natural selection Darwin's theory that evolution favors those plants and animals best suited to their living conditions.

Behaviorism The school of psychology that emphasizes the study of overt, observable behavior.

Response Any muscular action, glandular activity, or other identifiable aspect of behavior.

For instance, an observer might hold an apple and decide that she had experienced the elements "hue" (color), "roundness," and "weight." Another example of a question that might have interested a structuralist is "What basic tastes mix together to create complex flavors as different as broccoli, lime, bacon, and strawberry cheesecake?"

Introspection proved to be a poor way to answer most questions (Benjafield, 2010). Why? Because no matter how systematic the observations, the structuralists frequently *disagreed*. And when they did, there was no way to settle intersubjective differences. Think about it. If you and a friend both introspect on your perceptions of an apple and end up listing different basic elements, who would be right? Despite such limitations, "looking inward" is still used as one source of insight in studies of hypnosis, meditation, problem solving, moods, and many other topics.

Functionalism

American scholar William James broadened psychology to include animal behavior, religious experience, abnormal behavior, and other interesting topics. James's brilliant first book, *Principles of Psychology* (1890), helped establish the field as a separate discipline (Hergenhahn, 2009).

The term **functionalism** comes from James's interest in how the mind functions to help us adapt to the environment. James regarded consciousness as an ever-changing stream or flow of images and sensations—not a set of lifeless building blocks, as the structuralists claimed.

The functionalists admired Charles Darwin, who deduced that creatures evolve in ways that favor survival. According to Darwin's principle of **natural selection**, physical features that help plants and animals adapt to their environments are retained in evolution. Similarly, the functionalists wanted to find out how the mind, perception, habits, and emotions help us adapt and survive.

Behaviorism

Functionalism and structuralism were soon challenged by **behaviorism**, the study of observable behavior. Behaviorist John B. Watson objected strongly to the study of the "mind" or "conscious experience." He believed that introspection is unscientific precisely because there is no way to settle disagreements between observers. Watson realized that he could study the overt behavior of animals even though he couldn't ask them questions or know what they were thinking (Benjafield, 2010). He simply observed the relationship between *stimuli* (events in the environment) and an animal's **responses** (any muscular action, glandular activity, or other identifiable aspect of behavior). These observations were objective because they did not involve introspecting on subjective experience. Why not, he asked, apply the same objectivity to study human behavior?

Watson soon adopted Russian physiologist Ivan Pavlov's (ee-VAHN PAV-lahv's) concept of *conditioning* to explain most behavior. (A *conditioned response* is a learned reaction to a particular stimulus.) Watson claimed, "Give me a dozen healthy infants, well-formed, and my own special world to bring them up in and I'll guarantee to take any one at random and train him to become any type of specialist I might select—doctor, lawyer, artist, merchant-chief, and yes, beggarman and thief" (Watson, 1913/1994).

Would most psychologists agree with Watson's claim? No. The behaviorists believed that all responses are *determined* by stimuli. Today, this is regarded as an overstatement. Just the same, behaviorism helped make psychology a natural science, rather than a branch of philosophy (Schultz & Schultz, 2012).

Radical Behaviorism

The best-known behaviorist, B. F. Skinner (1904–1990), believed that our actions are controlled by rewards and punishments. To study learning, Skinner created his famous conditioning chamber, or "Skinner box." With it, he could present stimuli to animals and record their responses. Many of Skinner's ideas about learning grew out of work with rats and pigeons. Nevertheless, he believed that the same laws of behavior apply to humans. As a "radical behaviorist," Skinner also believed that covert mental events, such as thinking, are not needed to explain behavior (Schultz & Schultz, 2012).

Behaviorists deserve credit for much of what we know about learning, conditioning, and the proper use of reward and punishment. Skinner was convinced that a "designed culture" based on positive reinforcement could encourage desirable behavior. (Skinner opposed the use of punishment because it doesn't teach correct responses.) Too often, he believed, punishment and misguided rewards lead to destructive actions that create problems such as overpopulation, pollution, and war.

Gestalt Psychology

Imagine that you just played "Happy Birthday" on a low-pitched tuba. Next, you play it on a high-pitched flute. The flute duplicates none of the tuba's sounds. Yet we notice something interesting: The melody is still recognizable—as long as the *relationship* between notes remains the same.

Now, what would happen if you played the notes of "Happy Birthday" in the correct order, but at a rate of one per hour? What would we have? Nothing! The separate notes would no longer be a melody. Perceptually, the melody is more than the individual notes that define it.

It was observations like these that launched the Gestalt school of thought. German psychologist Max Wertheimer (VERT-hi-mer) was the first to advance the Gestalt viewpoint. It is inaccurate, he said, to analyze psychological events into pieces, or "elements," as the structuralists did. Accordingly, **Gestalt psychologists** studied thinking, learning, and perception as whole units, not by analyzing experiences into parts. Their slogan was, "The whole is greater than the sum of its parts" (see Figure 1.4). In fact, the German word *Gestalt* means "form, pattern, or whole."

Like a melody, many experiences cannot be broken into smaller units, as the structuralists proposed. For this reason, studies of perception and personality have been especially influenced by the Gestalt viewpoint.

Psychoanalytic Psychology

As American psychology grew more scientific, an Austrian doctor named Sigmund Freud was developing radically different ideas that opened new horizons in art, literature, and history, as well as psychology (Chessick, 2010; Jacobs, 2003). Freud believed that mental life is like an iceberg: Only a small part is exposed to view. He called the area of the mind that lies outside of personal awareness the **unconscious**. According to Freud, our behavior is

B. F. Skinner, 1904–1990. Skinner studied simple behaviors under carefully controlled conditions. The "Skinner box" you see here has been widely used to study learning in simplified animal experiments. In addition to advancing psychology, Skinner hoped that his radical brand of behaviorism would improve human life.

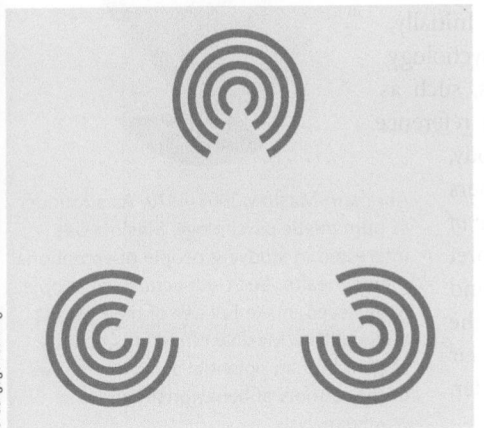

Figure 1.4 The design you see here is entirely made up of broken circles. However, as the Gestalt psychologists discovered, our perceptions have a powerful tendency to form meaningful patterns. Because of this tendency, you will probably see a triangle in this design, even though it is only an illusion. Your whole perceptual experience exceeds the sum of its parts.

Gestalt psychology A school of psychology emphasizing the study of thinking, learning, and perception in whole units, not by analysis into parts.

Unconscious Contents of the mind that are beyond awareness, especially impulses and desires not directly known to a person.

Max Wertheimer, 1880–1941. Wertheimer first proposed the Gestalt viewpoint to help explain perceptual illusions. He later promoted Gestalt psychology as a way to understand not only perception, problem solving, thinking, and social behavior, but also art, logic, philosophy, and politics.

Sigmund Freud, 1856–1939. For more than 50 years, Freud probed the unconscious mind. In doing so, he altered modern views of human nature. His early experimentation with a "talking cure" for hysteria is regarded as the beginning of psychoanalysis. Through psychoanalysis, Freud added psychological treatment methods to psychiatry.

Psychoanalysis A Freudian approach to psychotherapy emphasizing the exploration of unconscious conflicts.

Psychodynamic theory Any theory of behavior that emphasizes internal conflicts, motives, and unconscious forces.

Humanism An approach to psychology that focuses on human experience, problems, potentials, and ideals.

Determinism The idea that all behavior has prior causes that would completely explain one's choices and actions if all such causes were known.

Free will The idea that human beings are capable of freely making choices or decisions.

deeply influenced by unconscious thoughts, impulses, and desires—especially those concerning sex and aggression.

Freud theorized that many unconscious thoughts are *repressed*, or held out of awareness, because they are threatening. But sometimes, he said, they are revealed by dreams, emotions, or slips of the tongue. ("Freudian slips" are often humorous, as when a student who is late for class says, "I'm sorry I couldn't get here any later.")

Like the behaviorists, Freud believed that all thoughts, emotions, and actions are *determined*. In other words, nothing is an accident: If we probe deeply enough we will find the causes of every thought or action. Unlike the behaviorists, he believed that unconscious processes (not external stimuli) were responsible.

Freud was also among the first to appreciate that childhood affects adult personality ("The child is father to the man"). Most of all, perhaps, Freud is known for creating **psychoanalysis**, the first fully developed psychotherapy, or "talking cure." Freudian psychotherapy explores unconscious conflicts and emotional problems (see Chapter 13).

It wasn't very long before some of Freud's students modified Freud's ideas. Known as *neo-Freudians* (*neo* means "new" or "recent"), they accept much of Freud's theory but revise parts of it. Many, for instance, place less emphasis on sex and aggression and more on social motives and relationships. Some well-known neo-Freudians are Alfred Adler, Anna Freud (Freud's daughter), Karen Horney (HORN-eye), Carl Jung (yoong), Otto Rank (rahnk), and Erik Erikson. Today, Freud's ideas have been altered so much that few strictly psychoanalytic psychologists are left. However, his legacy is still evident in various **psychodynamic theories**, which continue to emphasize internal motives, conflicts, and unconscious forces (Moran, 2010).

Humanistic Psychology

Humanism is a view that focuses on subjective human experience. Humanistic psychologists are interested in human potentials, ideals, and problems.

How is the humanistic approach different from others? Carl Rogers, Abraham Maslow, and other humanists rejected the Freudian idea that we are ruled by unconscious forces. They were also uncomfortable with the behaviorist emphasis on conditioning. Both views have a strong undercurrent of **determinism**—the idea that behavior is determined by forces beyond our control. In contrast, the humanists stressed **free will**, our ability to make voluntary choices. Of course, past experiences do affect us. Nevertheless, humanists believe that people can freely *choose* to live more creative, meaningful, and satisfying lives.

Humanists are interested in psychological needs for love, self-esteem, belonging, self-expression, creativity, and spirituality. Such needs, they believe, are as important as our biological urges for food and water. For example, newborn infants deprived of human love may die just as surely as they would if deprived of food.

How scientific is the humanistic approach? Initially, humanists were less interested in treating psychology as a science. They stressed subjective factors, such as one's self-image, self-evaluation, and frame of reference. (*Self-image* is your perception of your own body, personality, and capabilities. *Self-evaluation* refers to appraising yourself as good or bad. A *frame of reference* is a mental perspective used to interpret events.) Today, humanists still seek to understand how we perceive ourselves and experience the world. However, most now do research to test their ideas, just as other psychologists do (Schneider, Bugental, & Pierson, 2001).

Abraham Maslow, 1908–1970. As a founder of humanistic psychology, Maslow was interested in studying people of exceptional mental health. Such self-actualized people, he believed, make full use of their talents and abilities. Maslow offered his positive view of human potential as an alternative to the schools of behaviorism and psychoanalysis.

Table 1.3 The Early Development of Psychology

PERSPECTIVE	DATE	NOTABLE EVENTS
Experimental psychology	1875	• First psychology course offered by William James
	1878	• First American Ph.D. in psychology awarded
	1879	• Wilhelm Wundt opens first psychology laboratory in Germany
	1883	• First American psychology lab founded at Johns Hopkins University
	1886	• First American psychology textbook written by John Dewey
Structuralism	1898	• Edward Titchener advances psychology based on introspection
Functionalism	1890	• William James publishes *Principles of Psychology*
	1892	• American Psychological Association founded
Psychodynamic psychology	1895	• Sigmund Freud publishes first studies
	1900	• Freud publishes *The Interpretation of Dreams*
Behaviorism	1906	• Ivan Pavlov reports his research on conditioned reflexes
	1913	• John Watson presents behaviorist view
Gestalt psychology	1912	• Max Wertheimer and others advance Gestalt viewpoint
Humanistic psychology	1942	• Carl Rogers publishes *Counseling and Psychotherapy*
	1943	• Abraham Maslow publishes "A Theory of Human Motivation"

© Cengage Learning

Maslow's concept of self-actualization is a key feature of humanism. **Self-actualization** refers to developing one's potential fully and becoming the best person possible. According to humanists, everyone has this potential. Humanists seek ways to help it emerge.

Table 1.3 presents a summary of psychology's early development.

The Role of Diversity in Psychology's Early Days

Were all the early psychologists Caucasian men? Although women and ethnic minorities were long underrepresented among psychologists, there *were* pioneers (Minton, 2000). In 1894, Margaret Washburn became the first woman to be awarded a Ph.D. in psychology. By 1906 in America, about 1 psychologist in 10 was a woman. In 1920, Francis Cecil Sumner became

Self-actualization The ongoing process of fully developing one's personal potential.

Margaret Washburn, 1871–1939. In 1908, Washburn published an influential textbook on animal behavior, titled *The Animal Mind*.

Francis Cecil Sumner, 1895–1954. Sumner served as chair of the Psychology Department at Howard University and wrote articles critical of the underrepresentation of African Americans in American colleges and universities.

Inez Beverly Prosser, ca. 1895–1934. Prosser was one of the early leaders in the debate about how to best educate African-American children.

the first African-American man to earn a doctoral degree in psychology. Inez Beverly Prosser, the first African-American female psychologist, was awarded her Ph.D. in 1933.

The predominance of early Caucasian male psychologists is worrisome because it inadvertently introduced a narrowness into psychological theory and research. Biases concerning the race, ethnicity, age, and sexual orientation of researchers and participants in psychological research have definitely limited our understanding (Carroll, 2013; Guthrie, 2004). Far too many conclusions have been created by and/or based on small groups of people who do not represent the rich tapestry of humanity.

Since 2000, however, more than 70 percent of all undergraduate and graduate degrees in psychology have been awarded to women. Similarly, 25 percent of all undergraduate degrees and 16 percent of doctorates in psychology were awarded to persons of color (American Psychological Association, 2003a). Increasingly, psychology is coming to better reflect human diversity (Hyde, 2013).

Psychology Today—Three Complementary Perspectives on Behavior

JOURNEY QUESTION 1.6 *What are the contemporary perspectives in psychology?*

At one time, loyalty to each school of thought in psychology was fierce, and clashes were common. Now, some early systems, such as structuralism, have disappeared entirely, whereas new ones have gained prominence. Also, viewpoints such as functionalism and Gestalt psychology have blended into newer, broader perspectives. The three broad views that shape modern psychology are the *biological, psychological,* and *sociocultural* perspectives (**Table 1.4**).

The Biological Perspective

The **biological perspective** seeks to explain our behavior in terms of biological principles such as brain processes, evolution, and genetics. By using new techniques, *biopsychologists* are producing exciting insights about how the brain relates to thinking, feelings, perception, abnormal behavior, and other topics. Biopsychologists and others who study the brain and nervous system, such as biologists and biochemists, together form the broader field of **neuroscience**. **Evolutionary psychologists** look at how human evolution and genetics might explain our current behavior.

The Psychological Perspective

The **psychological perspective** views behavior as the result of psychological processes within each person. This view continues to emphasize scientific observation, just as the early behaviorists did. However, the psychological perspective now includes *cognitive psychology*, which seeks to explain how mental processes, such as thoughts and feelings, influence our behavior (Goldstein, 2011). Cognitive psychology has gained prominence in recent years as researchers have devised ways to objectively study covert behaviors, such as thinking, memory, language, perception, problem solving, consciousness, and creativity. With a renewed interest in thinking, it can be said that psychology has finally "regained consciousness" (Robins, Gosling, & Craik, 1998).

Freudian psychoanalysis continues to evolve into the broader *psychodynamic view*. Although many of Freud's ideas have been challenged or refuted, psychodynamic psychologists continue to trace our behavior to unconscious mental activity. They also seek to develop therapies to help people lead happier, fuller lives. The same is true of humanistic psychologists, although they stress subjective, conscious experience and the positive side of human nature, rather than unconscious processes.

Biological perspective The attempt to explain behavior in terms of underlying biological principles.

Neuroscience The broader field of biopsychologists and others who study the brain and nervous system, such as biologists and biochemists.

Evolutionary psychology The study of how human evolution and genetics might explain our current behavior.

Psychological perspective The traditional view that behavior is shaped by psychological processes occurring at the level of the individual.

Table 1.4 Contemporary Ways to Look at Behavior

BIOLOGICAL PERSPECTIVE

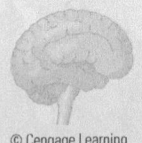
© Cengage Learning

Biopsychological View

Key Idea: *Human and animal behavior is the result of internal physical, chemical, and biological processes.*

Seeks to explain behavior through activity of the brain and nervous system, physiology, genetics, the endocrine system, and biochemistry; neutral, reductionistic, mechanistic view of human nature.

© Cengage Learning

Evolutionary View

Key Idea: *Human and animal behavior is the result of the process of evolution.*

Seeks to explain behavior through evolutionary principles based on natural selection; neutral, reductionistic, mechanistic view of human nature.

PSYCHOLOGICAL PERSPECTIVE

© Cengage Learning

Behavioristic View

Key Idea: *Behavior is shaped and controlled by one's environment.*

Emphasizes the study of observable behavior and the effects of learning; stresses the influence of external rewards and punishments; neutral, scientific, somewhat mechanistic view of human nature.

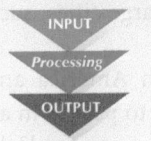
© Cengage Learning

Cognitive View

Key Idea: *Much human behavior can be understood in terms of the mental processing of information.*

Concerned with thinking, knowing, perception, understanding, memory, decision making, and judgment; explains behavior in terms of information processing; neutral, somewhat computer-like view of human nature.

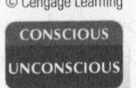
© Cengage Learning

Psychodynamic View

Key Idea: *Behavior is directed by forces within one's personality that are often hidden or unconscious.*

Emphasizes internal impulses, desires, and conflicts—especially those that are unconscious; views behavior as the result of clashing forces within personality; somewhat negative, pessimistic view of human nature.

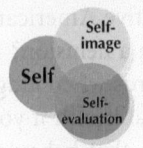
© Cengage Learning

Humanistic View

Key Idea: *Behavior is guided by one's self-image, by subjective perceptions of the world, and by needs for personal growth.*

Focuses on subjective, conscious experience, human problems, potentials, and ideals; emphasizes self-image and self-actualization to explain behavior; positive, philosophical view of human nature.

SOCIOCULTURAL PERSPECTIVE

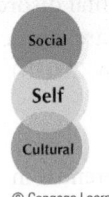
© Cengage Learning   © Cengage Learning

Sociocultural View

Key Idea: *Behavior is influenced by one's social and cultural context.*

Emphasizes that behavior is related to the social and cultural environment within which a person is born, grows up, and lives from day to day; neutral, interactionist view of human nature.

Positive Psychology

Psychologists have always paid attention to the negative side of human behavior. This is easy to understand because of the pressing need to solve human problems. However, more and more psychologists, some of them inspired by the humanists, have begun to ask "What do we know about love, happiness, creativity, well-being, self-confidence, and achievement?" Together, such topics make up **positive psychology**, the study of human strengths, virtues, and optimal behavior (Hefferon & Bonniwell, 2011; Seligman & Csikszentmihalyi, 2000). Many topics from positive psychology can be found in this book. Ideally, they will help make your own life more positive and fulfilling (Snyder, Lopez, & Pedrotti, 2011).

Positive psychology The study of human strengths, virtues, and effective functioning.

As illustrated by this photo from the inauguration of President Barack Obama in 2009, America is becoming more diverse. To fully understand human behavior, personal differences based on age, race, culture, ethnicity, gender, and sexual orientation must be taken into account.

The Sociocultural Perspective

As you can see, it is helpful to view human behavior from more than one perspective. This is also true in another sense. The **sociocultural perspective** stresses the impact that social and cultural contexts have on our behavior. Cultural diversity is becoming the norm. Over 100 million Americans are now African American, Hispanic, Asian American, Native American, or Pacific Islander (Humes, Jones, & Ramirez, 2010). In some large cities, such as Detroit and Baltimore, "minority" groups are already the majority.

In the past, psychology was based mostly on the cultures of North America and Europe. Now, we must ask, do the principles of Western psychology apply to people in all cultures? Are some psychological concepts invalid in other cultures? Are any universal? As psychologists have probed such questions, one thing has become clear: Most of what we think, feel, and do is influenced, in one way or another, by the social and cultural worlds in which we live (Henrich, Heine, Norenzayan, 2010).

Cultural Relativity

Imagine that you are a clinical psychologist. Your client, Linda, who is a Native American, tells you that spirits live in the trees near her home. Is Linda suffering from a delusion? Is she abnormal? Cases like Linda's teach us to be wary of using narrow standards when judging others or comparing groups. Obviously, you will misjudge Linda's mental health if you fail to take her cultural beliefs into account. **Cultural relativity**—the idea that behavior must be judged relative to the values of the culture in which it occurs—can greatly affect our understanding of "other people" including the diagnosis and treatment of mental disorders (Lum, 2011). To be effective, psychologists must be sensitive to people who are ethnically and culturally different from themselves (American Psychological Association, 2003b).

A Broader View of Diversity

In addition to cultural differences, the behavior of people is influenced by differences in age, ethnicity, gender, religion, disability, and sexual orientation, which all affect the **social norms** that guide behavior. Social norms are rules that define acceptable and expected behavior for members of various groups. Too often, the unstated standard for judging what is "average," "normal," or "correct" has been the behavior of middle-aged, white, heterosexual, middle-class Western males (Henrich, Heine, & Norenzayan, 2010). An appreciation of the fuller spectrum of human diversity can enrich your life, as well as your understanding of psychology (Helgeson, 2009).

The Whole Human

Today, many psychologists realize that a single perspective is unlikely to fully explain complex human behavior. As a result, they are *eclectic* (ek-LEK-tik) and draw insights from a variety of perspectives. As we will see throughout this book, insights from one perspective often complement insights from the others as we seek to better understand the whole human. In a moment, we will further explore what psychologists do. First, here are some questions to enhance your learning.

Sociocultural perspective The focus on the importance of social and cultural contexts in influencing the behavior of individuals.

Cultural relativity The idea that behavior must be judged relative to the values of the culture in which it occurs.

Social norms Rules that define acceptable and expected behavior for members of a group.

RECITE

Match:

1. _____ Wundt
2. _____ Structuralism
3. _____ Functionalism
4. _____ Behaviorism
5. _____ Gestalt
6. _____ Psychodynamic
7. _____ Humanistic
8. _____ Cognitive
9. _____ Biopsychology

A. Against analysis; studied whole experiences

B. Relates behavior to the brain, physiology, and genetics

C. Emphasizes self-actualization and personal growth

D. Interested in unconscious causes of behavior

E. Interested in how the mind aids survival

F. Studied stimuli and responses, conditioning

G. Concerned with thinking, language, problem solving

H. Used introspection and careful measurement

I. "Mental chemistry" and introspection

10. A psychotherapist is working with a person from an ethnic group other than her own. She should be aware of how cultural relativity and _____ affect behavior.

   a. the anthropomorphic error
   b. operational definitions
   c. biased sampling
   d. social norms

REFLECT

THINK CRITICALLY

11. Modern sciences like psychology are built on intersubjective observations, those that can be verified by two or more independent observers. Did structuralism meet this standard? Why or why not?

SELF-REFLECT

Which school of thought most closely matches your own view of behavior? Do you think any of the early schools offers a complete explanation of why we behave as we do? What about the three broad contemporary perspectives? Can you explain why so many psychologists are eclectic?

ANSWERS

1. H 2. I 3. E 4. F 5. A 6. D 7. C 8. G 9. B 10. d 11. No, it did not. The downfall of structuralism was that each observer examined the contents of his or her own mind—which is something that no other person can observe.

Psychologists—Guaranteed Not to Shrink

JOURNEY QUESTION 1.7 *What are the major specialties in psychology?*

Do all psychologists do therapy and treat abnormal behavior? Less than 60 percent are clinical and counseling psychologists. Regardless, all **psychologists** are highly trained in the methods, knowledge, and theories of psychology. They usually have earned a master's degree or a doctorate, typically requiring several years of postgraduate training. Twenty-nine percent are employed full-time at colleges or universities, where they teach and do research, consulting, or therapy. The remainder give psychological tests, do research in other settings, or serve as consultants to business, industry, government, or the military (see **Figure 1.5**).

At present, the American Psychological Association (APA) consists of more than 50 divisions, each reflecting special skills or areas of interest. No matter where they are employed or what their area of specialization, many psychologists do research. Some do *basic research*, in which they seek knowledge for its own sake. For example, a psychologist might study memory simply to understand how it works. Others do *applied research* to solve immediate practical problems, such as finding ways to improve athletic performance (Davey, 2011). Some do both types of research. Some of the major specialties are listed in Table 1.5.

Have you ever wondered what it takes to become a psychologist? See "Is a Career in Psychology Right for You?"

Animals and Psychology

Research involving animals was mentioned in some of the preceding examples in Table 1.5. Why is that? You may be surprised to learn that psychologists are interested in the behavior of *any* living creature—from flatworms to humans. Indeed, some comparative psychologists spend their entire careers studying rats, cats, dogs, parrots, or chimpanzees.

Although only a small percentage of psychological studies involve animals, they include many different types of research (Ord et al., 2005). Some psychologists use **animal models** to discover principles that apply to humans. For instance, animal studies have helped us

© Rob Niebrugge/Alamy

Killer whales living along the Pacific Coast near the border between the United States and Canada are listed as endangered. Studies of their social behavior are enhancing efforts to conserve these magnificent creatures (Parsons et al., 2009).

Psychologist A person highly trained in the methods, factual knowledge, and theories of psychology.

Animal model In research, an animal whose behavior is used to derive principles that may apply to human behavior.

Discovering Psychology

Is a Career in Psychology Right for You?

As you read this book we encourage you to frequently reflect on new ideas by relating them to your own life in order to better understand and remember them. "Discovering Psychology" boxes like this one are designed to help you be more reflective about how psychology relates to your own life. Answer the following questions to explore whether you would enjoy becoming a psychologist:

1. I have a strong interest in human behavior. True or False?

2. I am good at recognizing patterns, evaluating evidence, and drawing conclusions. True or False?

3. I am emotionally stable. True or False?

4. I have good communication skills. True or False?

5. I find theories and ideas challenging and stimulating. True or False?

6. My friends regard me as especially sensitive to the feelings of others. True or False?

7. I enjoy planning and carrying out complex projects and activities. True or False?

8. Programs and popular books about psychology interest me. True or False?

9. I enjoy working with other people. True or False?

10. Clear thinking, objectivity, and keen observation appeal to me. True or False?

If you answered "True" to most of these questions, a career in psychology might be a good choice. And remember that many psychology majors also succeed in occupations such as management, public affairs, social services, business, sales, and education (Kuther & Morgan, 2010). To learn more, check out Appendix 2, *Life after School*.

(a) Specialties in Psychology

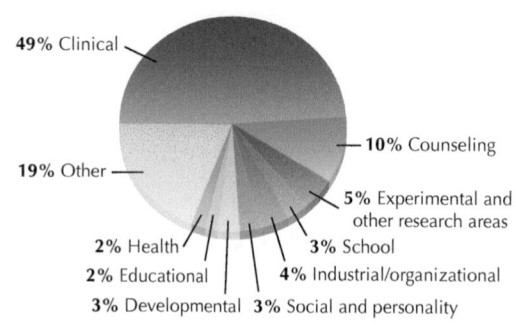

Figure 1.5 (a) Specialties in psychology (APA Center for Workforce Studies, 2010). Percentages are approximate. (b) Where psychologists work (Cheal et al., 2009). (c) This chart shows the main activities psychologists do at work. Any particular psychologist might do several of these activities during a work week. As you can see, most psychologists specialize in applied areas and work in applied settings (Cheal et al., 2009).

(b) Where Psychologists Work

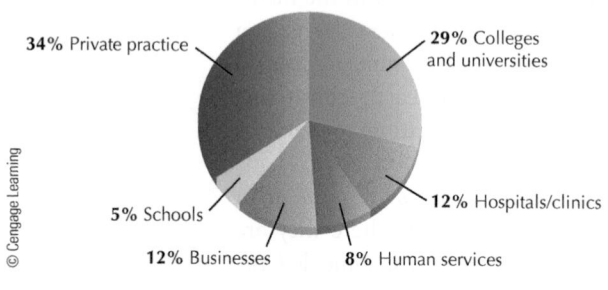

(c) What Psychologists Do (Primary Activity)

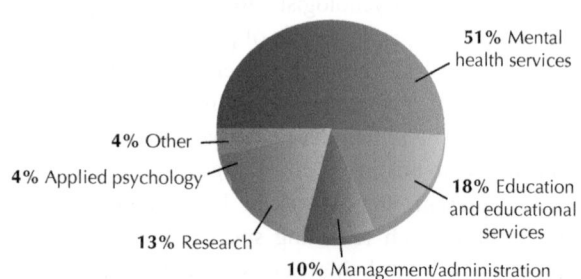

© Cengage Learning

understand stress, learning, obesity, aging, sleep, and many other topics. Psychology can also benefit animals. Behavioral studies can help us better care for domestic animals and those in zoos, as well as conserve endangered species in the wild.

Helping People

Although most psychologists help people in one way or another, those interested in emotional problems usually specialize in clinical or counseling psychology (see **Table 1.5**). **Clinical psychologists** treat psychological problems or do research on therapies and mental disorders. In contrast, **counseling psychologists** tend to treat milder problems, such as troubles at work or school. However, such differences are fading, and many counseling psychologists now work full time as therapists.

To become a clinical psychologist, it is best to have a doctorate (Ph.D., Psy.D., or Ed.D.). Most clinical psychologists have a Ph.D. degree and follow a scientist-as-practitioner model.

Clinical psychologist A psychologist who specializes in the treatment of psychological and behavioral disturbances or who does research on such disturbances.

Counseling psychologist A psychologist who specializes in the treatment of milder emotional and behavioral disturbances.

That is, they are trained to do either research or therapy. Many do both. Other clinicians earn the Psy.D. (Doctor of Psychology) degree, which emphasizes therapy skills rather than research (Peterson, 2001).

Does a psychologist have to have a license to offer therapy? At one time it was possible in many states for anyone to "hang out a shingle" as a "psychologist." Now psychologists must not only meet rigorous educational requirements, they must meet stringent legal requirements as well. To work as a clinical or counseling psychologist, you must have a license issued by a state examining board. However, the law does not prevent you from calling yourself anything else you choose—therapist, rebirther, primal feeling facilitator, cosmic aura balancer, or life skills coach—or from selling your "services" to anyone willing to pay. Beware of people with self-proclaimed titles. Even if their intentions are honorable, they may have little training. A licensed psychologist who chooses to use a particular type of therapy is not the same as someone "trained" solely in that technique.

Psychologists are often inaccurately portrayed in the media as incompetent therapists. Some films have featured psychologists who are more disturbed than their patients (such as Jack Nicholson's character in *Anger Management*) or psychologists who are bumbling buffoons (such as Billy Crystal's character in *Analyze This*). In the Internet series *Web Therapy*, *Friends* star Lisa Kudrow plays a hapless therapist who thinks real therapy can happen over the web in three minutes. Such characters may be dramatic and entertaining, but they seriously distort public perceptions of responsible and hardworking psychologists (Schultz, 2004).

Real clinical and counseling psychologists follow an ethical code that stresses (1) high levels of competence, integrity, and responsibility; (2) respect for people's rights to privacy, dignity, confidentiality, and personal freedom; and, above all, (3) protection of the client's welfare (American Psychological Association, 2010; Barnett et al., 2007). Psychologists are also expected to use their knowledge to contribute to society. Many do volunteer work in the communities in which they live.

Other Mental Health Professionals

Clinical psychologists are not the only people who work in the field of mental health. Often they coordinate their efforts with other specially trained professionals. What are the differences among psychologists, psychiatrists, psychoanalysts, counselors, and other mental health professionals? Each has a specific blend of training and skills.

Psychologists are all shrinks, right? Nope. "Shrinks" (a slang term derived from "head shrinkers") are **psychiatrists**, medical doctors who treat mental disorders, often by doing psychotherapy. Psychiatrists can also prescribe drugs, which is something psychologists usually cannot do. However, this is changing. Psychologists in New Mexico and Louisiana can now legally prescribe drugs. It will be interesting to see whether other states grant similar privileges (McGrath & Moore, 2010).

To be a psychoanalyst, you must have a moustache and goatee, spectacles, a German accent, and a well-padded couch—or so the media stereotype goes. Actually, to become a **psychoanalyst**, you must have an M.D. or Ph.D. degree plus further training in Freudian psychoanalysis. In other words, either a physician or a psychologist may become an analyst by learning a specific type of psychotherapy.

In many states, counselors also do mental health work. A **counselor** is an adviser who helps solve problems with marriage, career, school, work, or the like. To be a licensed counselor (such as a marriage and family counselor, a child counselor, or a school counselor) typically requires a master's degree plus 1 or 2 years of full-time supervised counseling experience. Counselors learn practical helping skills and do not treat serious mental disorders.

Psychiatric social workers play an important role in many mental health programs where they apply social science principles to help patients in clinics and hospitals. Most hold an M.S.W. (Master of Social Work) degree. Often, they assist psychologists and psychiatrists as part of a team. Their typical duties include evaluating patients and families, conducting group therapy, or visiting a patient's home, school, or job to alleviate problems.

In a moment we'll take a closer look at how research is done. Before that, here's a chance to do a little research on how much you've learned.

Psychiatrist A medical doctor with additional training in the diagnosis and treatment of mental and emotional disorders.

Psychoanalyst A mental health professional (usually a medical doctor) trained to practice psychoanalysis.

Counselor A mental health professional who specializes in helping people with problems not involving serious mental disorder; for example, marriage counselors, career counselors, or school counselors.

Psychiatric social worker A mental health professional trained to apply social science principles to help patients in clinics and hospitals.

Table 1.5 Kinds of Psychologists and What They Do

SPECIALTY		TYPICAL ACTIVITIES	SAMPLE RESEARCH TOPIC
Biopsychology	B*	Does research on the brain, nervous system, and other physical origins of behavior	"I've been doing some exciting research on how the brain controls hunger."
Clinical	A	Does psychotherapy; investigates clinical problems; develops methods of treatment	"I'm curious about the relationship between early childhood trauma and the victims' adult relationships so that I can be help adults be more successful in their marriages."
Cognitive	B	Studies human thinking and information processing abilities	"I want to know how reasoning, problem solving, memory, and other mental processes relate to computer game playing."
Community	A	Promotes community-wide mental health through research, prevention, education, and consultation	"How can we prevent the spread of sexually transmitted diseases more effectively? That's what I want to better understand."
Comparative	B	Studies and compares the behavior of different species, especially animals	"Personally, I'm fascinated by the communication abilities of porpoises."
Consumer	A	Researches packaging, advertising, marketing methods, and characteristics of consumers	"My job is to improve the marketing of products that are environment friendly."
Counseling	A	Does psychotherapy and personal counseling; researches emotional disturbances and counseling methods	"I am focused on better understanding why people become hoarders and how to help them stop."
Cultural	B	Studies the ways in which culture, subculture, and ethnic group membership affect behavior	"I am interested in how culture affects human eating behavior, especially the foods we eat and whether we eat with a spoon, chopsticks, or our fingers."
Developmental	A, B	Conducts research on infant, child, adolescent, and adult development; does clinical work with disturbed children; acts as consultant to parents and schools	"I'm focusing on transitions from the teenage years to early adulthood."
Educational	A	Investigates classroom dynamics, teaching styles, and learning; develops educational tests, evaluates educational programs	"My passion is to figure out how to help people with different learning styles be effective learners."
Engineering	A	Does applied research on the design of machinery, computers, airlines, automobiles, and so on, for business, industry, and the military	"I'm studying how people use movement–based computer interfaces, like Kinect."
Environmental	A, B	Studies the effects of urban noise, crowding, attitudes toward the environment, and human use of space; acts as a consultant on environmental issues	"I am concerned about global warming and want to understand what impact rising temperatures have on human culture."
Evolutionary	B	Studies how behavior is guided by patterns that evolved during the long history of humankind	"I am studying some interesting trends in male and female mating choices."
Forensic	A	Studies problems of crime and crime prevention, rehabilitation programs, prisons, courtroom dynamics; selects candidates for police work	"I am interested in improving the reliability of eyewitness testimony during trials."
Gender	B	Does research on differences between males and females, the acquisition of gender identity, and the role of gender throughout life	"I want to understand how young boys and girls are influenced by gender stereotypes."
Health	A, B	Studies the relationship between behavior and health; uses psychological principles to promote health and prevent illness	"How to better help people overcome drug addictions is my field of study."
Industrial-organizational	A	Selects job applicants; does skills analysis; evaluates on-the-job training; improves work environments and human relations in organizations and work settings	"Which plays a greater role in successful management styles, intelligence or emotion? That is my question."
Learning	B	Studies how and why learning occurs; develops theories of learning	"Right now I'm investigating how patterns of reinforcement affect learning. I am especially interested in superstitious conditioning."
Medical	A	Applies psychology to manage medical problems, such as the emotional impact of illness, self-screening for cancer, compliance in taking medicine	"I want to know how to help people take better charge of their own health."
Personality	B	Studies personality traits and dynamics; develops theories of personality and tests for assessing personality traits	"I am especially interested in the personality profiles of people willing to take extreme risks."
School	A	Does psychological testing, referrals, emotional and vocational counseling of students; detects and treats learning disabilities; improves classroom learning	"My focus is finding out how to keep students in school instead of having them drop out."
Sensation and perception	B	Studies the sense organs and the process of perception; investigates the mechanisms of sensation; develops theories about how perception occurs	"I am using a perceptual theory to study how we are able to recognize faces in a crowd."
Social	B	Investigates human social behavior, including attitudes, conformity, persuasion, prejudice, friendship, aggression, helping, and so forth	"My own interest is interpersonal attraction. I place two strangers in a room and analyze how strongly they are attracted to each other."

*Research in this area is typically applied (A), basic (B), or both (A, B). © Cengage Learning

RECITE

Match the following research areas with the topics they cover.

_____ 1. Developmental psychology
_____ 2. Learning
_____ 3. Personality
_____ 4. Sensation and perception
_____ 5. Biopsychology
_____ 6. Social psychology
_____ 7. Forensic psychology

A. Attitudes, groups, leadership
B. Behavior as related to the legal system
C. Brain and nervous system
D. Child psychology
E. Individual differences, motivation
F. Processing sensory information
G. Conditioning, memory

8. A psychologist who specializes in treating human emotional difficulties is called a _____ psychologist.
9. Who among the following would most likely be involved in the detection of learning disabilities?
   a. a consumer psychologist   *b.* a forensic psychologist
   c. an experimental psychologist   *d.* a school psychologist

REFLECT

THINK CRITICALLY

10. If many psychologists work in applied settings, why is basic research still of great importance?

SELF-REFLECT

Which specialty in psychology is most interesting to you? What is it about that specialty that most attracts you?

ANSWERS

1. D 2. G 3. E 4. F 5. C 6. A 7. B 8. clinical or counseling 9. d 10. Because practitioners benefit from basic psychological research in the same way that physicians benefit from basic research in biology. Discoveries in basic science form the knowledge base that leads to useful applications.

The Psychology Experiment—Where Cause Meets Effect

JOURNEY QUESTION 1.8 *How is an experiment performed?*

To get beyond description and fully understand behavior, psychologists must be able to explain *why* we act the way we do. To discover the *causes* of behavior, we must usually conduct an **experiment**. An experiment is a formal trial undertaken to confirm or disconfirm a hypothesis about the causes of behavior (although causes are sometimes revealed by naturalistic observation or correlations). Experiments allow psychologists to carefully control conditions and bring cause-and-effect relationships into sharp focus. Hence, they are generally accepted as the most powerful scientific research tool. To perform an experiment you would do the following:

1. Directly vary a condition you think might affect behavior.
2. Create two or more groups of subjects. These groups should be alike in all ways *except* the condition you are varying.
3. Record whether varying the condition has any effect on behavior.

Suppose you want to find out if using cell phones while driving a car affects the likelihood of having an accident. First, you would form two groups of people. Then you could give the members of one group a test of driving ability while they are using a cell phone. The second group would take the same test without using a cell phone. By comparing average driving ability scores for the two groups, you could tell if cell phone use affects driving ability.

As you can see, the simplest psychological experiment is based on two groups of **experimental subjects**—animals or people whose behavior is investigated. Human subjects are also called **participants**. One group is called the *experimental group*; the other becomes the *control group*. The experimental group and the control group are treated exactly alike except for the condition (or *variable*) you intentionally vary.

Variables and Groups

What are the different kinds of variables? A **variable** is any condition that can change and that might affect the outcome of the experiment. Identifying causes and effects in an experiment involves three types of variables:

1. **Independent variables** are conditions altered or varied by the experimenter, who sets their size, amount, or value. Independent variables are suspected *causes* for differences in behavior.

Experiment A formal trial undertaken to confirm or disconfirm a hypothesis about cause and effect.

Experimental subjects Humans (also referred to as **participants**) or animals whose behavior is investigated in an experiment.

Variable Any condition that changes or can be made to change; a measure, event, or state that may vary.

Independent variable In an experiment, the condition being investigated as a possible cause of some change in behavior. The values that this variable takes are chosen by the experimenter.

2. **Dependent variables** measure the results of the experiment. That is, they reveal the *effects* that independent variables have on *behavior*. Such effects are often revealed by measures of performance, such as test scores.

3. **Extraneous variables** are conditions that a researcher wishes to prevent from affecting the outcome of the experiment.

We can apply these terms to our cell phone/driving experiment in this way:

1. Cell phone use is the independent variable—we want to know if cell phone use affects driving ability.

2. Driving ability (defined by scores achieved on a test of driving ability) is the dependent variable—we want to know if the ability to drive well depends on whether a person is using a cell phone.

3. All other variables that could affect driving ability are extraneous. Examples of extraneous variables are the number of hours slept the night before the test, driving experience, and familiarity with the car used in the experiment.

By the way, psychologist Davis Strayer and his colleagues have confirmed that almost all drivers talking on cell phones drive no better than people who are legally drunk, and that texters are even worse (Drews et al., 2009; Strayer, Drews, & Crouch, 2006; Watson & Strayer, 2010).

As you can see, an **experimental group** consists of participants exposed to the independent variable (cell phone use in the preceding example). Members of the **control group** are exposed to all other variables except the independent variable (driving ability in the preceding example).

Let's examine another simple experiment. Suppose you notice that you seem to study better while listening to your iPod. This suggests the hypothesis that listening to music improves learning. We could test this idea by forming an experimental group that studies with music. A control group would study without music. Then we could compare their scores on a test.

Is a control group really needed? Can't people just study while listening to their iPods to see if they do better? Better than what? The control group provides a *point of reference* for comparison with the scores in the experimental group. Without a control group it would be impossible to tell whether music had any effect on learning. If the average test score of the experimental group is higher than the average of the control group, we can conclude that music improves learning. If there is no difference, it's obvious that the independent variable had no effect on learning.

In this experiment, the amount learned (indicated by scores on the test) is the *dependent variable*. We are asking, Does the independent variable *affect* the dependent variable? (Does listening to music affect or influence learning?)

Experimental Control

How do we know that the people in one group aren't more intelligent than those in the other group? It's true that personal differences might affect the experiment. However, they can be controlled by randomly assigning people to groups. **Random assignment** means that a participant has an equal chance of being in either the experimental group or the control group. Randomization evenly balances personal differences in the two groups. In our musical experiment, this could be done by simply flipping a coin for each participant: Heads, and the participant is in the experimental group; tails, it's the control group. This would result in few average differences in the number of people in each group who are women or men, geniuses or dunces, hungry, hungover, tall, music lovers, or whatever.

Other *extraneous*, or outside, variables—such as the amount of study time, the temperature in the room, the time of day, the amount of light, and so forth—must also be prevented from affecting the outcome of an experiment. But how? Usually this is done by making all conditions (except the independent variable) *exactly* alike for both groups. When all conditions are the same for both groups—*except* the presence or absence of music—then any difference in the amount learned *must* be caused by the music (**Figure 1.6**).

Dependent variable In an experiment, the condition (usually a behavior) that is affected by the independent variable.

Extraneous variables Conditions or factors excluded from influencing the outcome of an experiment.

Experimental group In a controlled experiment, the group of subjects exposed to the independent variable or experimental condition.

Control group In a controlled experiment, the group of subjects exposed to all experimental conditions or variables *except* the independent variable.

Random assignment The use of chance (for example, flipping a coin) to assign subjects to experimental and control groups.

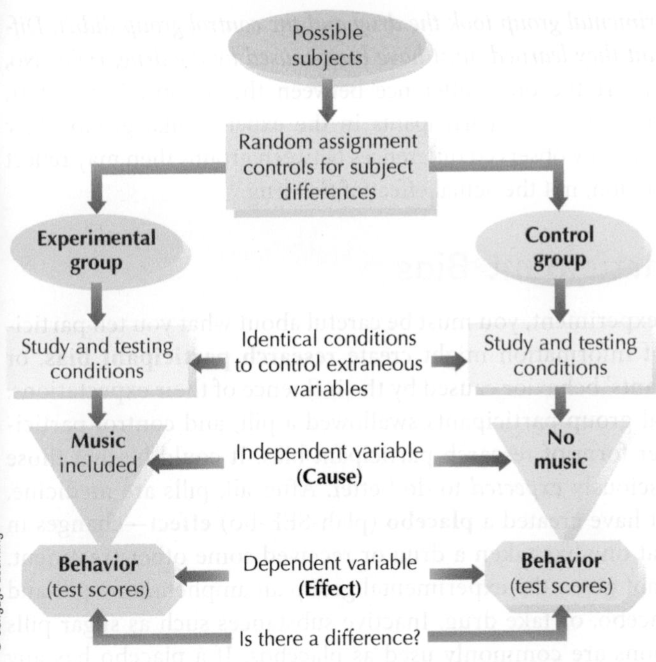

Possible subjects
Random assignment controls for subject differences
Experimental group
Control group
Study and testing conditions
Identical conditions to control extraneous variables
Study and testing conditions
Music included
Independent variable (Cause)
No music
Behavior (test scores)
Dependent variable (Effect)
Behavior (test scores)
Is there a difference?

Figure 1.6 Elements of a simple psychological experiment to assess the effects of music during study on test scores.

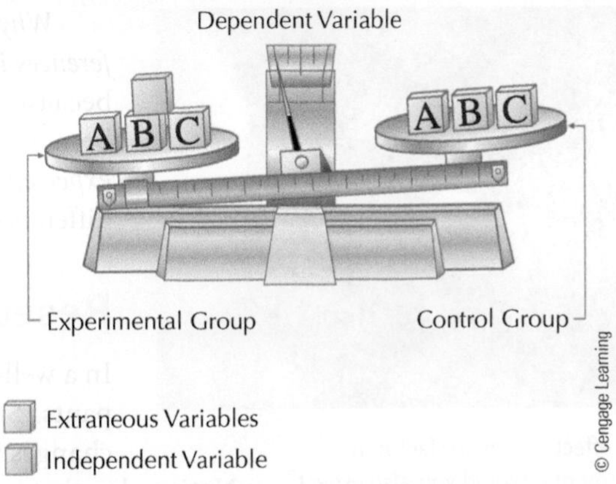

Dependent Variable
A B C
A B C
Experimental Group
Control Group
Extraneous Variables
Independent Variable
© Cengage Learning

Figure 1.7 Experimental control is achieved by balancing extraneous variables for the experimental group and the control group. For example, the average age (A), education (B), and intelligence (C) of group members could be made the same for both groups. Then we could apply the independent variable to the experimental group. If their behavior (the dependent variable) changes (in comparison with the control group), the change must be caused by the independent variable.

Cause and Effect

Now let's summarize. In an experiment two or more groups of subjects are treated differently with respect to the independent variable. In all other ways they are treated the same. That is, extraneous variables are equated for all groups. The effect of the independent variable (or variables) on some behavior (the dependent variable) is then measured. In a carefully controlled experiment, the independent variable is the only possible *cause* for any *effect* noted in the dependent variable. This allows clear cause-and-effect connections to be identified (Figure 1.7).

Evaluating Results

How can we tell if the independent variable really made a difference? This problem is handled statistically (See Appendix 1). Reports in psychology journals almost always include the statement, "Results were **statistically significant**." What this means is that the obtained results would occur very rarely by chance alone. To be statistically significant, a difference must be large enough that it would occur by chance in less than 5 experiments out of 100. Of course, findings also become more convincing when they can be *replicated* (repeated) by other researchers.

Double Blind—On Placebos and Self-Fulfilling Prophecies

JOURNEY QUESTION 1.9 *What is a double-blind experiment?*

Suppose a researcher hypothesizes that the drug amphetamine (a stimulant) improves learning. She explains her hypothesis to her participants and gives experimental group participants an amphetamine pill before they begin studying. Control group members get nothing. Later, she assesses how much each participant learned. Does this experiment seem valid? Actually, it is seriously flawed for several reasons.

Statistically significant Experimental results that would rarely occur by chance alone.

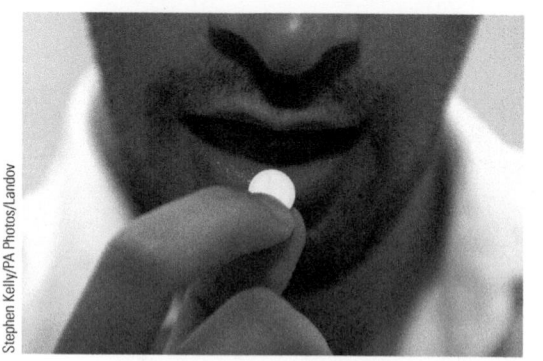

Stephen Kelly/PA Photos/Landov

The placebo effect is a major factor in medical treatments. Would you also expect the placebo effect to occur in psychotherapy? It does, which complicates studies on the effectiveness of new psychotherapies, but likely also enhances the effectiveness of psychotherapy (Justman, 2011).

Why? The experimental group took the drug and the control group didn't. Differences in the amount they learned must have been caused by the drug, right? No, because the drug wasn't the only difference between the groups. For a start, because of what they were told, participants in the experimental group likely *expected* to learn more. Any observed differences between groups then may reflect differences in expectation, not the actual effect of the drug.

Research Participant Bias

In a well-designed experiment, you must be careful about what you tell participants. Small bits of information might create **research participant bias**, or changes in participants' behavior caused by the influence of their expectations. Notice also that experimental group participants swallowed a pill, and control participants did not. This is another form of research participant bias. It could be that those who swallowed a pill unconsciously *expected* to do better. After all, pills are medicine, aren't they? This alone might have created a **placebo** (plah-SEE-bo) **effect**—changes in behavior caused by belief that one has taken a drug or received some other treatment. Suppose the researcher had not given the experimental group an amphetamine pill and instead had given them a placebo, or fake drug. Inactive substances such as sugar pills and saline (saltwater) injections are commonly used as placebos. If a placebo has any effect, it must be based on suggestion, rather than chemistry (McBurney & White, 2010).

Placebo effects can be quite powerful, usually accounting for at least one third of the apparent effectiveness of the "official" treatment. For instance, a saline injection is 70 percent as effective as morphine in reducing pain. That's why doctors sometimes prescribe placebos—especially for complaints that seem to have no physical basis. Placebos have been shown to affect pain, anxiety, depression, alertness, tension, sexual arousal, cravings for alcohol, and many other processes (Justman, 2011; Wampold et al., 2005). (See Chapter 11 for more information on placebos.)

How could an inert substance have any effect? Placebos alter our expectations, both conscious and unconscious, about our own emotional and physical reactions. Because we associate taking medicine with feeling better, we expect placebos to make us feel better, too (Benedetti, 2009). After a person takes a placebo, there is a reduction in brain activity linked with pain, so the effect is not imaginary (Wager et al., 2004).

Controlling Research Participant Bias

How can you avoid research participant bias? To control for research participant bias, we could use a **single-blind experiment**. In this case, participants do not know whether they are in the experimental or the control group or whether they are receiving a real drug or a placebo. All participants are given the same instructions and everyone gets a pill or injection. People in the experimental group get a real drug, and those in the control group get a placebo. Because participants are *blind* as to the hypothesis under investigation and whether they received the drug, their expectations (conscious *and* unconscious) are the same. Any difference in their behavior must be caused by the drug. However, even this arrangement is not enough, because researchers themselves sometimes affect experiments by influencing participants. Let's see how this occurs.

Researcher Bias

How could a researcher influence participants? As we saw above, when the experimenter explained her hypothesis to the participants, she likely biased the results of the study. But even if a researcher uses a single-blind procedure to avoid deliberately biasing participants, **researcher bias**—changes in behavior caused by the unintended influence of a researcher—remains a problem. In essence, experimenters run the risk of finding what they expect to find. This occurs because humans are very sensitive to hints about what is expected of them (Rosenthal, 1994).

Research participant bias Changes in the behavior of research participants caused by the unintended influence of their own expectations.

Placebo effect Changes in behavior due to participants' expectations that a drug (or other treatment) will have some effect.

Single-blind experiment An arrangement in which participants remain unaware of whether they are in the experimental group or the control group.

Researcher bias Changes in participants' behavior caused by the unintended influence of a researcher's actions.

Researcher bias even applies outside the laboratory. Psychologist Robert Rosenthal (1973) reports an example of how expectations influence people: At the U.S. Air Force Academy Preparatory School, 100 airmen were randomly assigned to five different math classes. Their teachers did not know about this random placement. Instead, each teacher was told that his or her students had unusually high or low ability. Students in the classes labeled "high ability" improved much more in math scores than those in "low ability" classes. Yet, initially, all of the classes had students of equal ability.

Although the teachers were not conscious of any bias, apparently they subtly communicated their expectations to students. Most likely, they did this through tone of voice, body language, and by giving encouragement or criticism. Their "hints," in turn, created a self-fulfilling prophecy that affected the students. A **self-fulfilling prophecy** is a prediction that prompts people to act in ways that make the prediction come true. For instance, many teachers underestimate the abilities of ethnic minority children, which hurts the students' chances for success (Weinstein, Gregory, & Strambler, 2004). In short, people sometimes become what we prophesy for them. It is wise to remember that others tend to live *up* or *down* to our expectations for them (Jussim & Harber, 2005).

The Double-Blind Experiment

Because of research participant bias and researcher bias, it is common to keep both participants and researchers "blind." In a **double-blind experiment** neither participants nor researchers know who is in the experimental group or the control group, including who received a drug and who took a placebo. This not only controls for research participant bias, it also keeps researchers from unconsciously influencing participants.

How can the researchers be "blind"; it's their experiment, isn't it? The researchers who designed the experiment, including preparing the pills or injections, typically hire research assistants to collect data from the participants. Even the research assistants are blinded in that they do not know which pill or injection is drug or placebo or whether any particular participant is in the experimental or control group.

Self-fulfilling prophecy A prediction that prompts people to act in ways that make the prediction come true.

Double-blind experiment An arrangement in which both participants and experimenters are unaware of whether participants are in the experimental group or the control group, including who might have been administered a drug or a placebo.

✋ study break The Psychology Experiment

RECITE

1. To understand cause and effect, a simple psychological experiment is based on creating two groups: the _____ group and the _____ group.
2. There are three types of variables to consider in an experiment: _____ variables (which are manipulated by the experimenter); _____ variables (which measure the outcome of the experiment); and _____ variables (factors to be excluded in a particular experiment).
3. A researcher performs an experiment to learn whether room temperature affects the amount of aggression displayed by college students under crowded conditions in a simulated prison environment. In this experiment, the independent variable is which of the following?

   a. room temperature   b. the amount of aggression
   c. crowding   d. the simulated prison environment

4. A procedure used to control both research participant bias and researcher bias in drug experiments is the

   a. correlation method   b. controlled experiment
   c. double-blind experiment   d. random assignment of participants

REFLECT

THINK CRITICALLY

5. There is a loophole in the statement "I've been taking vitamin C tablets, and I haven't had a cold all year. Vitamin C is great!" What is the loophole?

SELF-REFLECT

We all conduct little experiments to detect cause-and-effect connections. If you enjoy music, for example, you might try listening with different types of headphones. The question then becomes, "Does the use of ear buds vs. sound-cancelling headphones (the independent variable) affect the enjoyment of music (the dependent variable)?" Can you think of an informal experiment you've run in the last month? What were the variables? What was the outcome?

ANSWERS

1. experimental, control 2. independent, dependent, extraneous 3. a 4. c 5. The statement implies that vitamin C prevented colds. However, not getting a cold could just be a coincidence. A controlled experiment with a group given vitamin C and a control group not taking vitamin C would be needed to learn whether vitamin C actually has any effect on susceptibility to colds.

Nonexperimental Research Methods—Different Strokes

JOURNEY QUESTION 1.10 *What nonexperimental research methods do psychologists use?*

Determining cause-and-effect relationships between variables lies at the heart of discovering not just *what* we do, but *why* we do it. For this reason, psychologists place a special emphasis on controlled experimentation, or the **experimental method**. However, because it is not always possible to conduct experiments, psychologists gather evidence and test hypotheses in many other ways (Jackson, 2011). They observe behavior as it unfolds in natural settings (*naturalistic observation*); they make measurements to discover relationships between events (*correlational method*); they study psychological problems and therapies in clinical settings (*clinical method*); and they use questionnaires to poll large groups of people (*survey method*). Let's see how each of these is used to advance psychological knowledge.

Naturalistic Observation

Psychologists sometimes rely on **naturalistic observation**, the observation of behavior in a *natural setting* (the typical environment in which a person or animal lives). For example, in 1960, Jane Goodall first observed a wild chimpanzee in Tanzania use a grass stem as a tool to remove termites from a termite mound (Van Lawick-Goodall, 1971). Notice that naturalistic observation provides only *descriptions* of behavior. In order to *explain* observations, we may need information from other research methods. Just the same, Goodall's discovery showed that humans are not the only tool-making animals (Rutz et al., 2010).

Chimpanzees in zoos use objects as tools. Doesn't that demonstrate the same thing? Not necessarily. Naturalistic observation allows us to study behavior that hasn't been tampered with or altered by outside influences. Only by observing chimps in their natural environment can we tell whether they use tools without human interference.

Limitations

Doesn't the presence of human observers affect the animals' behavior? Yes. The observer effect is a major problem. The **observer effect** refers to changes in a subject's behavior caused by an awareness of being observed. Naturalists must be very careful to keep their distance and avoid "making friends" with the animals they are watching. Likewise, if you are interested in why automobile drivers have traffic accidents, you can't simply get in people's cars and start taking notes. As a stranger, your presence would most likely change the drivers' behaviors.

When possible, the observer effect can be minimized by concealing the observer. Another solution is to use hidden recorders. One naturalistic study of traffic accidents was done with video cameras installed in 100 cars (Dingus et al., 2006). It turns out that most accidents are caused by failing to look at the traffic in front of the car (eyes forward!). Hidden stationary video cameras have also provided valuable observations of many animal species. As recording devices have become miniaturized, it has even become possible to attach "critter cams" directly to many species, allowing observations to be made across their natural ranges (Figure 1.8). For example, zoologist Christian Rutz and his colleagues outfitted shy New Caledonian crows with "crow cams" to better understand their use of tools to forage for food (Rutz et al., 2007, 2010). Not only can these clever crows use twigs to reach food, they can use a shorter twig to get a longer twig to get food (Wimpenny et al., 2009). Apparently, humans and other primates are not the only tool-using species.

Observer bias is a related problem in which observers see what they expect to see or record only selected details (Jackson, 2011). For instance, teachers in one classic study were told to watch normal elementary school children who had been labeled (for the study) as "learning disabled," "mentally retarded," "emotionally disturbed," or "normal." Sadly, teachers gave the children very different ratings, depending on the labels used (Foster

Figure 1.8 New Caledonian crows wearing tiny "crow cams" barely half the weight of a silver dollar have been recorded using twigs to forage for food (Rutz et al., 2007).

© Jolyon Troscianko 2006

Experimental method Investigating causes of behavior through controlled experimentation.

Naturalistic observation Observing behavior as it unfolds in natural settings.

Observer effect Changes in an organism's behavior brought about by an awareness of being observed.

Observer bias The tendency of an observer to distort observations or perceptions to match his or her expectations.

& Ysseldyke, 1976). In some situations, observer bias can have serious consequences (Spano, 2005). For example, a police officer expecting criminal behavior might shoot a person who is reaching for his wallet because he appears to be reaching for a gun.

A special mistake to avoid when observing animals is the **anthropomorphic** (AN-thro-po-MORE-fik) **error**. This is the error of attributing human thoughts, feelings, or motives to animals—especially as a way of explaining their behavior (Waytz, Epley, & Cacioppo, 2010). The temptation to assume that an animal is "angry," "jealous," "bored," or "guilty" can be strong. If you have pets at home, you probably already know how difficult it is to avoid anthropomorphizing but it can lead to false conclusions. For example, if your dog growls at your date, you might assume the dog doesn't like your companion. But it's possible that your date is merely wearing a cologne or perfume that irritates the dog's nose.

Psychologists doing naturalistic studies make a special effort to minimize bias by keeping an *observational record*, or detailed summary of data and observations. As suggested by the study of traffic accidents and the use of "critter cams," video recording often provides the most objective record of all. Despite its problems, naturalistic observation can supply a wealth of information and raise many interesting questions. In most scientific research it is an excellent starting point.

Correlational Studies

Let's say a psychologist notes an association between the IQs of parents and their children, or between beauty and social popularity, or between anxiety and test performance. In each case, two observations or events are **correlated**, or linked together in an orderly way. In a **correlational study**, two factors are measured. Then a statistical technique is used to find their degree of correlation. (See the Statistics Appendix near the end of this book for more information.) For example, John Simister and Cary Cooper (2005) decided to find out if there is a correlation between crime and the weather. They obtained data on temperatures and criminal activity in Los Angeles over a 4-year period. When they graphed air temperature and the frequency of aggravated assaults, a clear relationship emerged. Assaults and temperatures rise and fall more or less in parallel (so there may be something to the phrase "hot under the collar"). Knowing the temperature in Los Angeles now allows us to predict the number of aggravated assaults.

Correlation Coefficients

How is the degree of correlation expressed? The strength and direction of a relationship can be expressed as a **coefficient of correlation**. This can be calculated as a number falling somewhere between $+1.00$ and -1.00 (see the Statistics Appendix). Drawing graphs of relationships can also help clarify their nature (see **Figure 1.9**). If the number is zero or close to zero, the association between two measures is weak or nonexistent (see Figure 1.9c). For example, the correlation between shoe size and intelligence is zero. (Sorry, size 12 readers.) If the correlation is $+1.00$, a perfect positive relationship exists (see Figure 1.9e); if it is -1.00, a perfect negative relationship has been discovered (see Figure 1.9a).

Correlations in psychology are rarely perfect. But the closer the coefficient is to $+1.00$ or -1.00, the stronger the relationship. For example, identical twins tend to have almost identical IQs. In contrast, the IQs of parents and their children are only generally similar. The correlation between the IQs of parents and children is .35; between identical twins it's .86.

What do the terms "positive" and "negative" correlation mean? In a *positive correlation*, higher scores in one measure are matched by higher scores in the other. For example, there is a moderate positive correlation between high school grades and college grades; students who do well in high school tend to do well in college (and the reverse) (see Figure 1.9d) In a *negative correlation*, higher scores on one measure are associated with lower scores on the other. We might observe, for instance, a moderate negative correlation between the number of hours that students play computer games and their grades. That is, more play is associated with lower grades (Figure 1.9b). (This is the well-known computer-game-zombie effect.)

Anthropomorphic error The error of attributing human thoughts, feelings, or motives to animals, especially as a way of explaining their behavior.

Correlation The existence of a consistent, systematic relationship between two events, measures, or variables.

Correlational study A nonexperimental study designed to measure the degree of relationship (if any) between two or more events, measures, or variables.

Coefficient of correlation A statistical index ranging from -1.00 to $+1.00$ that indicates the direction and degree of correlation.

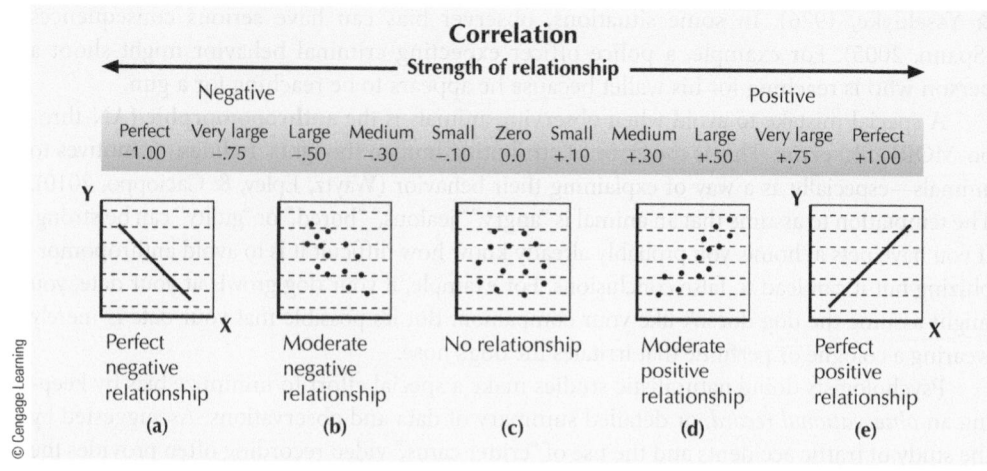

Figure 1.9 The correlation coefficient tells how strongly two measures are related. These graphs show a range of relationships between two measures, X and Y. If a correlation is negative (a), increases in one measure are associated with decreases in the other. (As Y gets larger, X gets smaller.) In a positive correlation (e), increases in one measure are associated with increases in the other. (As Y gets larger, X gets larger.) The center-left graph (b, "moderate negative relationship") might result from comparing time spent playing computer games (Y) with grades (X): More time spent playing computer games is associated with lower grades. The center graph (c, "no relationship") would result from plotting a person's shoe size (Y) and his or her IQ (X). The center-right graph (d, "moderate positive relationship") could be a plot of grades in high school (Y) and grades in college (X) for a group of students: Higher grades in high school are associated with higher grades in college.

Wouldn't that show that playing computer games too much causes lower grades? It might seem so, but as we saw previously, the best way to be confident that a cause-and-effect relationship exists is to perform a controlled experiment.

Correlation and Causation

Correlational studies help us discover relationships and make predictions. However, correlation *does not* demonstrate **causation** (a cause-effect relationship) (Jackson & Newberry, 2012). It could be, for instance, that students who aren't interested in their classes have more time for computer games. If so, then their lack of study and lower grades would be the result of disinterest, and not excessive game playing (which would be another result of disinterest in classes). Just because one thing *appears* to be directly related to another does not mean that a cause-and-effect connection exists.

Here is another example of mistaking correlation for causation: What if a psychologist discovers a correlation between parents who smoke cigarettes and juvenile delinquency in their children? Does this show that parental smoking *causes* juvenile delinquency? Perhaps, but maybe juvenile delinquents drive their parents to take up smoking. Better yet, maybe both parental smoking and juvenile delinquency are related to some third factor, such as socioeconomic status. Poorer parents are more likely to be smokers and poorer juveniles are more likely to become delinquents. To reiterate, just because one thing *appears* to cause another does not *confirm* that it does. The best way to be confident that a cause-and-effect relationship exists is to perform a controlled experiment.

The Clinical Method

It may be impractical, unethical, or impossible to use the experimental method to study rare events, such as unusual mental disorders, childhood "geniuses," or "rampage" school shootings (Harding, Fox, & Mehta, 2002). In such instances, a **case study**—an in-depth focus on a single participant—may be the best source of information. Clinical psychologists rely

Causation The act of causing some effect.

Case study An in-depth focus on all aspects of a single person.

heavily on case studies, especially as a way to investigate mental disorders, such as depression or psychosis. Also, case studies of psychotherapy have provided many useful ideas about how to treat emotional problems (Wedding & Corsini, 2011).

Case studies may sometimes be thought of as *natural clinical tests* (accidents or other natural events that provide psychological data). Gunshot wounds, brain tumors, accidental poisonings, and similar disasters have provided much information about the human brain. One remarkable case from the history of psychology was reported by Dr. J. M. Harlow (1868). Phineas Gage, a young foreman on a work crew, was impaled by a 13-pound steel rod in the front of his brain because of a dynamite explosion (Figure 1.10). Amazingly, he survived the accident. Within 2 months Gage could walk, talk, and move normally, but the injury forever changed his personality. Instead of the honest and dependable worker he had been before, Gage became a surly, foul-mouthed liar. Dr. Harlow carefully recorded all details of what was perhaps the first in-depth case study of an accidental frontal lobotomy (the destruction of front brain matter).

When a Los Angeles carpenter named Michael Melnick suffered a similar injury, he recovered completely, with no lasting ill effects. Melnick's very different reaction to a similar injury shows why psychologists prefer controlled experiments and often use lab animals for studies of the brain. Case studies lack formal control groups. This, of course, limits the conclusions that can be drawn from clinical observations.

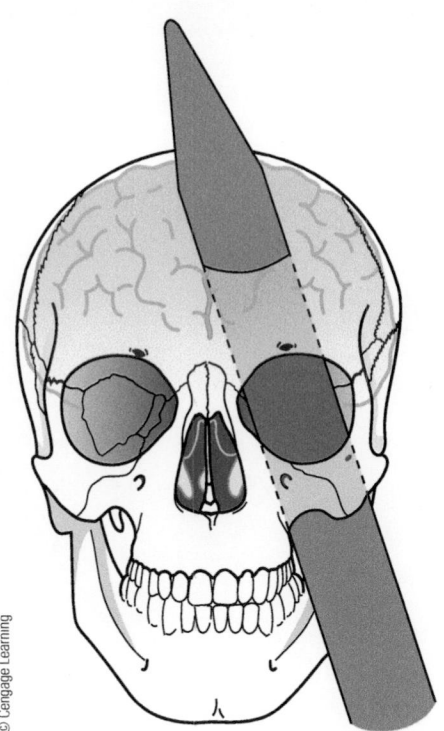

© Cengage Learning

Figure 1.10 Some of the earliest information on the effects of damage to frontal areas of the brain came from a case study of the accidental injury of Phineas Gage.

Survey Method

Sometimes psychologists would like to ask everyone in the world a few well-chosen questions: "What form of discipline did your parents use when you were a child?" "What is the most dishonest thing you've done?" "Why do you think you run extreme marathons?" Honest answers to such questions can reveal much about people's behavior. But, because it is impossible to question everyone, doing a survey is often more practical.

In **surveys**, public polling techniques are often used to answer psychological questions (Babbie, 2013; Thrift, 2010). Typically, people in a representative sample are asked a series of carefully worded questions. A **representative sample** is a small group that accurately reflects a larger population. A good sample must include the same proportion of men, women, young, old, professionals, blue-collar workers, Republicans, Democrats, whites, African Americans, Native Americans, Latinos, Asians, and so on as found in the population as a whole.

A **population** is an entire group of animals or people belonging to a particular category (for example, all college students or all single women). Ultimately, we are interested in entire populations. But by selecting a smaller sample, we can draw conclusions about the larger group without polling each and every person. Representative samples are often obtained by *randomly* selecting who will be included (Figure 1.11). (Notice that this is similar to randomly assigning participants to groups in an experiment.)

How accurate is the survey method? Modern surveys like the Gallup and Harris polls are quite accurate. The Gallup poll has erred in its election predictions by only 1.5 percent since 1954. However, if a survey is based on a biased sample, it may paint a false picture. A *biased sample* does not accurately reflect the population from which it was drawn. Surveys done by magazines, websites, and online information services can be quite biased. Surveys on gun control laws done by *O: The Oprah Magazine* and *Guns and Ammo* magazine would probably produce very different results—neither of which would represent the general population. That's why psychologists using the survey method go to great lengths to ensure that their samples are representative. Fortunately, people can often be polled by telephone or the Internet, which makes it easier to obtain large samples. Even if one person out of three refuses to answer survey questions, the results are still likely to be valid (Hutchinson, 2004)

Internet Surveys

Recently, psychologists have started doing surveys and experiments on the Internet. Web-based research can also be a cost-effective way to reach very large groups of people, especially people who are not easy to survey any other way (Smyth et al., 2010). Internet studies

Survey In psychology, a public polling technique used to answer psychological questions.

Representative sample A small, randomly selected part of a larger population that accurately reflects characteristics of the whole population.

Population An entire group of animals or people belonging to a particular category (for example, all college students or all married women).

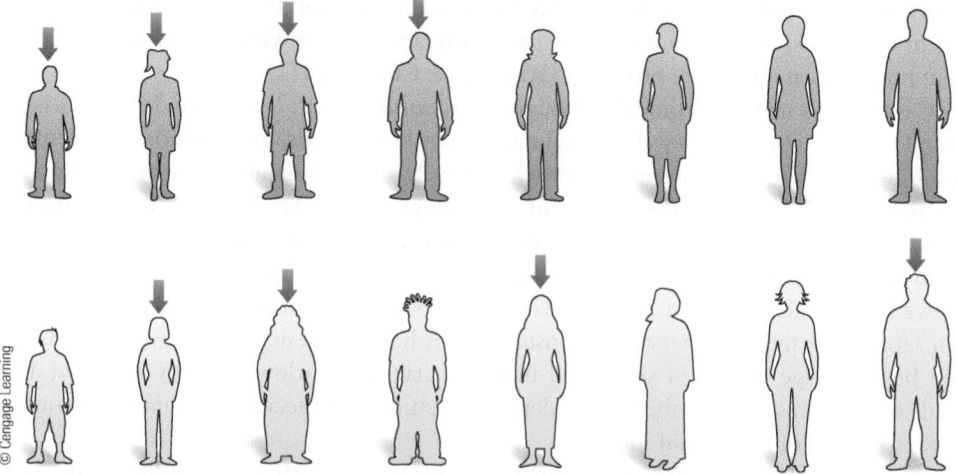

Figure 1.11 If you were conducting a survey in which a person's height might be an important variable, the upper, nonrandom sample would be very unrepresentative. The lower random sample, selected using a table of random numbers, better represents the group as a whole.

have provided interesting information about topics such as anger, decision-making, racial prejudice, what disgusts people, religion, sexual attitudes, and much more. Biased samples can limit web-based research (because it isn't easy to control who actually answers your online questionnaire), but psychologists are getting better at gathering valid information with it (Lewis, Watson, & White, 2009).

Social Desirability

Even well-designed surveys may be limited by another problem. If a psychologist were to ask you detailed questions about your sexual history and current sexual behavior, how accurate would your replies be? Would you exaggerate? Would you be embarrassed? Replies to survey questions are not always accurate or truthful. Many people show a distinct *courtesy bias* (a tendency to give "polite" or socially desirable answers). For example, answers to questions concerning sex, drinking or drug use, income, and church attendance tend to be less than truthful. Likewise, the week after an election, more people will say they voted than actually did (Babbie, 2011).

Summary

Despite their limitations, surveys frequently produce valuable information. For instance, one survey explored the vulnerability of U.S. retail malls to terrorism with the goal of improving our capacity to prevent and respond to an attack (Rigakos et al., 2009). To sum up, the survey method can be a powerful research tool. Like other methods, it has limitations, but new techniques and strategies are providing valuable information about our behavior.

Is so much emphasis on science really necessary in psychology? In a word, yes. As we have seen, science is a powerful way of asking questions about the world and getting trustworthy answers. (Table 1.6 summarizes many of the important ideas we have covered.)

A Look Ahead

To help you get the most out of psychology, each chapter of this text includes a "Psychology in Action" section like the one that follows. There you will find ideas you can actually use, now or in the future. To complete the topics we have been discussing, let's take a critical look at information reported in the popular press. You should find this an interesting way to conclude our opening tour of psychology and its methods.

Table 1.6 Comparison of Psychological Research Methods

	ADVANTAGES	DISADVANTAGES
Experimental Method	Clear cause-and-effect relationships can be identified; powerful controlled observations can be staged; no need to wait for natural event	May be somewhat artificial; some natural behavior not easily studied in laboratory (field experiments may avoid these objections)
Naturalistic Observation	Behavior is observed in a natural setting; much information is obtained, and hypotheses and questions for additional research can be formed	Little or no control is possible; observed behavior may be altered by the presence of the observer; observations may be biased; causes cannot be conclusively identified
Correlational Method	Demonstrates the existence of relationships; allows prediction; can be used in lab, clinic, or natural setting	Little or no control is possible; relationships may be coincidental; cause-and-effect relationships cannot be confirmed
Clinical Method	Takes advantage of "natural clinical trials" and allows investigation of rare or unusual problems or events	Little or no control is possible; does not provide a control group for comparison; subjective interpretation is often necessary; a single case may be misleading or unrepresentative
Survey Method	Allows information about large numbers of people to be gathered; can address questions not answered by other approaches	Obtaining a representative sample is critical and can be difficult to do; answers may be inaccurate; people may not do what they say or say what they do

© Cengage Learning

 study break Nonexperimental Research Methods

RECITE

1. Two major problems in naturalistic observation are the effects of the observer and observer bias. T or F?
2. The _____ error involves attributing human feelings and motives to animals.
3. Correlation typically does not demonstrate causation. T or F?
4. Case studies can often be thought of as natural tests and are frequently used by clinical psychologists. T or F?
5. For the survey method to be valid, a representative sample of people must be polled. T or F?
6. A problem with the survey method is that answers to questions may not always be _____ or _____.

REFLECT

THINK CRITICALLY

7. A psychologist conducting a survey at a shopping mall (The Gallery of Wretched Excess) flips a coin before stopping passersby. If the coin shows heads, he interviews the person; if it shows tails, he skips that person. Has the psychologist obtained a random sample?

SELF-REFLECT

Google "critter cam" and find one you can watch. What species are you watching? What behaviors might you observe and record?

See if you can identify at least one positive correlation and one negative correlation that involves human behavior.

Have you ever known someone who suffered a brain injury or disease? How did his or her behavior change? Was the change clear-cut enough to serve as a natural clinical test?

ANSWERS

1. T 2. anthropomorphic 3. T 4. T 5. T 6. accurate, truthful 7. The psychologist's coin flips *might* produce a reasonably good sample of people *at the mall*. The real problem is that people who go to the mall may be mostly from one part of town, from upper income groups, or from some other nonrepresentative group. The psychologist's sample is likely to be seriously flawed.

Psychology in Action

Psychology in the Media—Are You Fluent in Klingon?

JOURNEY QUESTION 1.11 *How good is psychological information found in the popular media?*

Psychology is a popular topic in contemporary media. Unfortunately, much of what you will encounter is based on entertainment value rather than critical thinking or science. Here are some suggestions for separating high-quality information from misleading fiction:

Suggestion 1: Be skeptical. Have you ever played the game called "telephone" or "pass it down"? One person whispers a sentence to someone else who, in turn, whispers it on down the line. Usually, when the person at the end of the line repeats the message, it has been humorously distorted. Similarly, modern media—especially the Internet—function as a giant "echo chamber" awash with rumors, hoaxes, half-truths, and urban legends like the one about giant alligators living in New York sewers (Hughes, 2008).

One of our all-time favorites was a story about the health department in Oregon seeking a Klingon interpreter for mental health patients who only spoke in the fictional language used on the *Star Trek* television series. This tale started when a newspaper reported that Klingon was on a list of languages that some psychiatric patients claimed they could speak. The article specifically noted that "in reality, no patient has yet tried to communicate in Klingon." Nevertheless, as the story echoed around the web, the idea that Oregon was looking for someone fluent in Klingon had become a "fact" (O'Neill, 2003).

Reports in the popular media tend to be made uncritically and with a definite bias toward reporting "astonishing" findings and telling interesting stories. Remember, saying, "That's incredible" means, "That's not believable"—which is often true.

Suggestion 2: Consider the source of information. It should come as no surprise that information used to sell a product often reflects a desire for profit rather than the objective truth. Here is a typical advertising claim: "Government tests prove that no sleep medicine is stronger or more effective than Coma." A statement like this usually means that there was *no difference* between Coma and the other products tested. No other sleep aid was stronger or more effective. But none was weaker either.

Remember that psychological services may be merchandised as well. Keep the source in mind when reading the claims of makers of home biofeedback machines, sleep-learning devices, subliminal CDs, and the like. Be wary of expensive courses that promise instant mental health and happiness, increased efficiency, memory, extrasensory perception (ESP) or psychic ability, control of the unconscious mind, an end to smoking, and so on. Usually they are promoted with a few testimonials and many unsupported claims (Lilienfeld, Ruscio, & Lynn, 2008).

Psychic claims should be viewed with special caution. Google magician James Randi's Million Dollar Challenge. Randi has long offered $1,000,000 to anyone demonstrating such abilities under controlled conditions. Did you know that no one has even passed the preliminary tests yet?

Stage mentalists make a living by deceiving the public. Understandably, they are highly interested in promoting belief in their nonexistent powers. The same is true of the so-called psychic advisers promoted in television commercials. These charlatans make use of the Barnum effect (the tendency to consider personal descriptions accurate if they are stated in general terms) to create an illusion that they know private information about the people who call them (Nickell, 2001).

Suggestion 3: Beware of oversimplifications, especially those motivated by monetary gain.   Courses or programs that offer a "new personality in three sessions," "six steps to love and fulfillment in marriage," or some newly discovered "secret for unlocking the powers of the mind and the universe" should be immediately suspect.

An excellent example of oversimplification is provided by websites devoted to a video that promises to reveal "the secret to unlimited joy, health, money, relationships, love, youth: everything you have ever wanted." According to these sites, all you need to do is put your desires out to the universe and the universe must respond by granting your wishes. And all it will cost you is the price of ordering the video. (It's no secret that the promoters are the real winners in this game.)

Suggestion 4: Remember, "for example" is no proof.   After reading this chapter you should be sensitive to the danger of selecting single examples. If you read, "Law student passes state bar exam using sleep-learning device," don't rush out to buy one. Systematic research showed long ago that these devices are of little or no value (Druckman & Bjork, 1994). A corollary to this suggestion is to ask: Are the reported observations important or widely applicable? Similarly, in 2002, baseball pitcher Randy Johnson began wearing a particular metal-impregnated twisted rope necklace designed to "stabilize the electricity flow through the body." By the 2010 World Series, hundreds of players were superstitiously wearing one, all without any scientific explanation of, or evidence for, their efficacy (Carroll, 2011).

Examples, anecdotes, single cases, and testimonials are all potentially deceptive. According to numerous testimonials, believers in the power of the "secret" described above have been showered with money, success, and happiness immediately after viewing the video. Someone is bound to win the lottery by sheer luck. Unfortunately, such *individual cases* (or even several) tell us nothing about what is true *in general* (Stanovich, 2010). How many people *didn't* win the lottery after buying the video? How many people bought the "magic necklace" to no avail? Similarly, studies of large groups of people show that smoking increases the likelihood of lung cancer. It is less relevant if you know a lifelong heavy smoker who is 95 years old. The general finding is the one to remember.

Suggestion 5: Ask yourself if there was a control group.   The key importance of a control group in any experiment is frequently overlooked by the unsophisticated—an error to which you are no longer susceptible. The popular media are full of reports of "experiments" performed without control groups: "Talking to Plants Speeds Growth"; "Special Diet Controls Hyperactivity in Children"; "Graduates of Firewalking Seminar Risk Their Soles."

Consider the last example for a moment. Expensive commercial courses have long been promoted to teach people to walk barefoot on hot coals. (Why anyone would want to do this is itself an interesting question.) Firewalkers supposedly protect their feet with a technique called "neurolinguistic programming." Many people have paid good money to learn the technique, and most do manage a quick walk on the coals. But is the technique necessary? And is anything remarkable happening? We need a comparison group.

Fortunately, physicist Bernard Leikind has provided one. Leikind showed with volunteers that anyone (with reasonably callused feet) can walk over a bed of coals without being burned. The reason is that the coals, which are light, fluffy carbon, transmit little heat when touched. The principle involved is similar to briefly putting your hand in a hot oven. If you touch a pan, you will be burned because metal transfers heat efficiently. But if your hand stays in the heated air you'll be fine because air transmits little heat (Kida, 2006; Mitchell, 1987). Mystery solved.

Suggestion 6: Look for errors in distinguishing between correlation and causation.   As you now know, it is dangerous to presume that one thing *caused* another just because they

Firewalking is based on simple physics, not on any form of supernatural psychological control. The temperature of the coals may be as high as 1,200° F. However, coals are like the air in a hot oven: They are very inefficient at transferring heat during brief contact.

are correlated. In spite of this, you will see many claims based on questionable correlations. Here's an example of mistaking correlation for causation: Jeanne Dixon, a well-known astrologer, once answered a group of prominent scientists—who had declared that there is no scientific foundation for astrology—by saying, "They would do well to check the records at their local police stations, where they will learn that the rate of violent crime rises and falls with lunar cycles." Dixon, of course, believes that the moon affects human behavior.

If it is true that violent crime is more frequent at certain times of the month, doesn't that prove her point? Far from it. Increased crime could be due to darker nights, the fact that we expect others to act crazier during a full moon, or any number of similar factors. Besides, direct studies of the alleged "lunar effect" have shown that it doesn't occur (Dowling, 2005). Moonstruck criminals, influenced by "a bad moon rising," are a fiction (Iosif & Ballon, 2005).

Suggestion 7: Be sure to distinguish between observation and inference.   If you see a person *crying*, is it correct to assume that she or he is *sad*? Although it seems reasonable to make this assumption, it could easily be wrong. We can observe objectively that the person is crying, but to *infer* sadness may be in error. It could be that the individual has just peeled 5 pounds of onions. Or maybe he or she just won a million-dollar lottery, or is trying contact lenses for the first time.

Psychologists, politicians, physicians, scientists, and other experts often go far beyond the available facts in their claims. This does not mean that their inferences, opinions, and interpretations have no value; the opinion of an expert on the causes of mental illness, criminal behavior, learning problems, or whatever can be revealing. But be careful to distinguish between fact and opinion.

Summary.   We are all bombarded daily with such a mass of new information that it is difficult to absorb it. The available knowledge in an area like psychology, biology, or medicine is so vast that no single person can completely know and comprehend it. With this situation in mind, it becomes increasingly important that you become a critical, selective, and informed consumer of information (Lilienfeld et al., 2010).

 study break Psychology in the Media

RECITE

1. Popular media reports usually stress objective accuracy. T or F?
2. Stage mentalists and psychics often use deception in their "acts." T or F?
3. Blaming the lunar cycle for variations in the rate of violent crime is an example of mistaking correlation for causation. T or F?
4. If a psychology student uses a sleep-learning device to pass a midterm exam, it proves that the device works. T or F?

REFLECT

THINK CRITICALLY

5. Mystics have shown that fresh eggs can be balanced on their large ends during the vernal equinox when the sun is directly over the equator, day and night are equal in length, and the world is in perfect balance. What is wrong with their observation?

SELF-REFLECT

How actively do you evaluate and question claims made by an authority or found in the media? Could you be a more critical consumer of information? *Should* you be a more critical consumer of information?

ANSWERS

1. F 2. T 3. T 4. F 5. Eggs can actually be balanced any time you like. The lack of a control group gives the illusion that something amazing is happening, but the equinox has nothing to do with egg balancing (Halpern, 2003).

Chapter in Review

Summary

1.1 What is psychology and what are its goals?

- 1.1.1 Psychology is the science of (overt) behavior and (covert) mental processes.
- 1.1.2 Psychologists are professionals who create and apply psychological knowledge.
- 1.1.3 Psychologists engage in critical thinking as they systematically gather and analyze empirical evidence to answer questions about behavior.
- 1.1.4 Psychologists gather scientific data in order to describe, understand, predict, and control behavior.

1.2 What is critical thinking?

- 1.2.1 Critical thinking is central to the scientific method, to psychology, and to the everyday understanding of behavior.
- 1.2.2 Critical thinking in psychology is a type of open-minded reflection involving the support of beliefs with scientific explanation and observation.
- 1.2.3 The validity of beliefs can be judged through logical analysis, evaluating evidence *for* and *against* the claim, and evaluating the *quality* of the evidence.
- 1.2.4 Critical thinkers seek to falsify claims by making up their own minds rather than automatically taking the word of "experts."

1.3 How does psychology differ from false explanations of behavior?

- 1.3.1 Pseudopsychologies are unfounded systems that are frequently confused with valid psychology.
- 1.3.2 Unlike psychology, pseudopsychologies change little over time because followers seek evidence that appears to confirm their beliefs and avoid evidence that contradicts their beliefs.
- 1.3.3 Belief in pseudopsychologies is based in part on uncritical acceptance, confirmation bias, and the Barnum effect.

1.4 How is the scientific method applied in psychological research?

- 1.4.1 In the scientific method, systematic observation is used to test hypotheses about behavior and mental events. A powerful way to observe the natural world and draw valid conclusions, scientific research provides the highest quality information about behavior and mental events.
- 1.4.2 Psychological research begins by defining problems and proposing hypotheses. Concepts must be defined operationally before they can be studied empirically.
- 1.4.3 Next, researchers gather evidence to test hypotheses. The results of scientific studies are made public so that others can evaluate them, learn from them, and use them to suggest new hypotheses, which lead to further research.
- 1.4.4 Psychological research must be done ethically to protect the rights, dignity, and welfare of participants.

1.5 How did the field of psychology emerge?

- 1.5.1 The field of psychology emerged 130 years ago when researchers began to directly study and observe psychological events.
- 1.5.2 The first psychological laboratory was established in Germany in 1879 by Wilhelm Wundt, who studied conscious experience.
- 1.5.3 The first school of thought in psychology was structuralism, a kind of "mental chemistry" based on introspection.
- 1.5.4 Structuralism was followed by functionalism, behaviorism, and Gestalt psychology.
- 1.5.5 Psychodynamic approaches, such as Freud's psychoanalytic theory, emphasize the unconscious origins of behavior.
- 1.5.6 Humanistic psychology accentuates subjective experience, human potentials, and personal growth.
- 1.5.7 Because most of the early psychologists were Caucasian men, bias was inadvertently introduced into psychological research. Today, more women and minorities are becoming psychologists and being studied as research participants.

1.6 What are the contemporary perspectives in psychology?

- 1.6.1 Three complementary streams of thought in modern psychology are the biological perspective, including biopsychology and evolutionary psychology; the psychological perspective, including behaviorism, cognitive psychology, the psychodynamic approach, and humanism; and the sociocultural perspective.
- 1.6.2 Psychologists have recently begun to formally study positive aspects of human behavior, or positive psychology.
- 1.6.3 Most of what we think, feel, and do is influenced by the social and cultural worlds in which we live.
- 1.6.4 Today, there is an eclectic blending of many viewpoints within psychology.

1.7 What are the major specialties in psychology?

- 1.7.1 There are dozens of specialties in psychology, including biopsychology, clinical, cognitive, community, comparative, consumer, counseling, cultural, developmental, educational, engineering, environmental, evolutionary, forensic, gender, health, industrial-organizational, learning, medical, personality, school, sensation and perception, and social psychology.
- 1.7.2 Psychological research may be basic or applied.
- 1.7.3 Psychologists may be directly interested in animal behavior, or they may study animals as models of human behavior.
- 1.7.4 Although psychologists, psychiatrists, psychoanalysts, counselors, and psychiatric social workers all work in the field of mental health, their training and methods differ considerably.

1.8 How is an experiment performed?

- 1.8.1 Experiments involve two or more groups of subjects that differ only with regard to the independent variable. Effects on the dependent variable are then measured. All other conditions (extraneous variables) are held constant.

- 1.8.2 Because the independent variable is the only difference between the experimental group and the control group, it is the only possible cause of a change in the dependent variable

- 1.8.3 The design of experiments allows cause-and-effect connections to be clearly identified.

1.9 What is a double-blind experiment?

- 1.9.1 Research participant bias is a problem in some studies; the placebo effect is a source of research participant bias in experiments involving drugs.

- 1.9.2 A related problem is researcher bias. Researcher expectations can create a self-fulfilling prophecy, in which a participant changes in the direction of the expectation.

- 1.9.3 In a double-blind experiment, neither the research participants nor the researchers collecting data know who was in the experimental group or the control group, allowing valid conclusions to be drawn.

1.10 What nonexperimental research methods do psychologists use?

- 1.10.1 Psychologists also rely on naturalistic observation, the correlational method, case studies, and the survey method.

- 1.10.2 Unlike controlled experiments, nonexperimental methods usually cannot demonstrate cause-and-effect relationships.

- 1.10.3 Naturalistic observation is a starting place in many investigations. Two problems with naturalistic observation are the effects of the observer on the observed and observer bias.

- 1.10.4 In the correlational method, relationships between two traits, responses, or events are measured and a correlation coefficient is computed to gauge the strength of the relationship. Relationships in psychology may be positive or negative. Correlations allow prediction but do not demonstrate cause-and-effect.

- 1.10.5 Case studies provide insights into human behavior that can't be gained by other methods.

- 1.10.6 In the survey method, people in a representative sample are asked a series of carefully worded questions. Obtaining a representative sample of people is crucial when the survey method is used to study large populations.

1.11 How good is psychological information found in the popular media?

- 1.11.1 Information in the mass media varies greatly in quality and accuracy and should be approached with skepticism and caution.

- 1.11.2 It is essential to critically evaluate information from popular sources (or from any source, for that matter) in order to separate facts from fallacies.

- 1.11.3 Problems in media reports are often related to biased or unreliable sources of information, uncontrolled observation, misleading correlations, false inferences, oversimplification, use of single examples, and unrepeatable results.

Interactive Learning

Log in to CengageBrain to access the resources your instructor requires. For this book, you can access:

CourseMate Go to CengageBrain.com to access Psychology CourseMate, where you will find an interactive eBook, glossaries, flashcards, quizzes, videos, Virtual Psychology Labs, and more.

aplia

Aplia If your professor has assigned Aplia:

1. Sign in to your account.
2. Complete the corresponding exercises as required by your professor.
3. When finished, click "Grade It Now" to see which areas you have mastered, which areas need more work, and detailed explanations of every answer.

Test Your Knowledge

Psychology and Research Methods

1. Psychology is the study of _____ behaviors and _____ mental processes.
   - a. subjective, objective
   - b. covert, overt
   - c. psyche, logos
   - d. overt, covert

2. Scientific observation is
   - a. intersubjective
   - b. empirical evidence
   - c. systematically obtained
   - d. all of the above

3. Who among the following is most interested in the effects of stress on the immune system?
   - a. learning theorist
   - b. personality theorist
   - c. comparative psychologist
   - d. health psychologist

4. Research that can explain why people remember better if they relate new information to familiar ideas meets which of psychology's goals?
   - a. describe
   - b. understand
   - c. predict
   - d. control

5. The Barnum effect depends on providing
   - a. specific descriptions
   - b. intersubjectivity
   - c. correlations
   - d. a little something for everybody

6. Belief in astrology is based on the confirmation bias, which is a failure to
   - a. collect relevant correlations
   - b. make use of introspection
   - c. distinguish between observation and inference
   - d. engage in critical thinking

7. A psychologist does a study to see if having control over difficult tasks reduces stress. In the study he will be testing an
   - a. experimental hypothesis
   - b. operational definition
   - c. empirical definition
   - d. anthropomorphic theory

8. After you identify an interesting problem or question about behavior, you will need to establish _____ of important variables before you begin to make controlled observations.
   - a. correlations
   - b. operational definitions
   - c. double-blind controls
   - d. a theory

9. The outcome of a psychology experiment is revealed by measuring changes in behavior. Such measures are the _____ variable of the experiment.
   - a. independent
   - b. correlational
   - c. dependent
   - d. extraneous

10. Double-blind experiments are designed to control for the
    - a. placebo effect
    - b. anthropomorphic fallacy
    - c. unintended influence of operational definitions
    - d. courtesy bias

11. Introspection was especially important to which school of thought in psychology?
    - a. structuralism
    - b. functionalism
    - c. behaviorism
    - d. Gestalt

12. Which two schools of thought have largely disappeared from contemporary psychology?
    - a. behaviorism, Gestalt
    - b. humanism, cognitive behaviorism
    - c. functionalism, structuralism
    - d. structuralism, humanism

13. Who among the following was a historic woman psychologist?
    - a. Sumner
    - b. Wundt
    - c. Washburn
    - d. Watson

14. Who among the following is LEAST likely to treat serious behavioral and emotional disturbances?
    - a. psychologist
    - b. counselor
    - c. psychiatrist
    - d. psychoanalyst

15. To be effective, psychologists must be sensitive to people's
    - a. ethnicity
    - b. culture
    - c. social norms
    - d. all of the above

16. Observer bias and the observer effect are problems in using
    - a. naturalistic observation
    - b. the correlational method
    - c. the experimental method
    - d. naturalistic experiments

17. Because correlation does not demonstrate causation, psychologists often use _____ to answer questions about behavior.
    - a. experimentation
    - b. naturalistic observation
    - c. the survey method
    - d. the clinical method

18. Case studies can often be thought of as
    - a. experiments
    - b. natural clinical tests
    - c. positive correlations
    - d. control groups

19. Obtaining a representative sample is especially important in psychological research involving
    - a. the placebo effect
    - b. hypothesis testing
    - c. the experimenter effect
    - d. the survey method

20. An article in a magazine claims that "Special Learning Software Fosters Deep Learning in Children." This claim is meaningless unless
    - a. the author is an authority on learning
    - b. the software has been tested empirically
    - c. the software is a bestseller
    - d. the author knows of a specific child who benefited from the software

Answers 1. d 2. d 3. d 4. b 5. d 6. d 7. a 8. b 9. c 10. a 11. a 12. c 13. c 14. b 15. d 16. a 17. a 18. b 19. d 20. b

Journey Theme *Brain activity is the source of human consciousness, intelligence, and behavior.*

Brain and Behavior

Journey into Psychology: Punch-Drunk

He died of a self-inflicted gunshot wound to the stomach in February 2011. Not to his head, mind you, because he wanted to leave his brain to science. A two-time Super Bowl winner, Dave Duerson blamed his post-football troubles, including memory loss, trouble spelling words, depression, and moodiness, on the repeated concussions he suffered while on the playing field. Sure enough, an autopsy revealed the same signs of chronic traumatic brain injury that have been found in dozens of other retired NFL players, as well as in athletes from many other violent sports, such as hockey and boxing. The boxers even have a name for it: *punch-drunk*.

We don't normally notice the central role the brain plays in all that makes us human. But a stroke or other brain injury can change that in a flash. (A stroke occurs when an artery carrying blood in the brain bleeds or becomes blocked, causing some brain tissue to die.) Almost instantly, victims realize that something is wrong. You would, too, if you suddenly found that you couldn't move, feel parts of your body, see, or speak. However, some brain injuries are not so obvious. Many involve less dramatic, but equally disabling, changes in personality, thinking, judgment, or emotions. Some, like Dave Duerson's, can take years to become apparent.

Your 3-pound brain is wrinkled like a walnut, the size of a grapefruit, and the texture of tofu. The next time you are in a market that sells beef brains, stop and have a look. What you will see is similar to your own brain, only smaller. How could such a squishy little blob of tissue allow us to become neuroscientists? To make music of exquisite beauty? To seek a cure for cancer? To fall in love? Or to read a book like this one?

Each of the 100 billion neurons—or nerve cells—in your brain is linked to thousands of others. The resulting network of 100 trillion connections allows you to process immense amounts of information. Undeniably, the human brain is the most amazing of all computers. Let's visit this fascinating realm.

Journey Questions

2.1 What are the major divisions of the nervous system?

2.2 How do neurons operate and communicate?

2.3 How are different parts of the brain identified and what do they do?

2.4 How do the left and right hemispheres differ and what are the different functions of the lobes of the cerebral cortex?

2.5 What are the major parts of the subcortex?

2.6 Does the glandular system affect behavior?

2.7 In what ways do right- and left-handed individuals differ?

The Nervous System—Wired for Action

JOURNEY QUESTION 2.1 *What are the major divisions of the nervous system?*

Mike and Molly are out in the park, playing Frisbee. Although this may appear simple, a blaze of activity lights up many of the billions of **neurons** (NOOR-ons)—individual nerve cells—making up their nervous systems. In order to catch Mike's latest toss, a huge amount of information must be collected by Molly's eyes (where's that Frisbee going?), muscles (are my hands in place to catch it?), and other senses (what's that sound behind me?), and sent to the brain to be interpreted. Messages must then be sent back to direct countless muscle fibers (move my body and hands to catch that Frisbee while avoiding that couple chatting on the lawn behind me). And this must happen over and over again, in "real time," for as long as they keep playing. Before we dive into the details, let's get an overview of the "wiring diagram" that makes their game of catch possible (Freberg, 2010).

As you can see in **Figure 2.1**, the **central nervous system (CNS)** consists of the brain and spinal cord. The brain carries out most of the "computing" in the nervous system and communicates with the rest of the body through the large bundle of nerves called the spinal cord. The **peripheral nervous system (PNS)** is the intricate network of nerves that carries information between the CNS and the rest of the body. Thirty-one pairs of *spinal nerves*

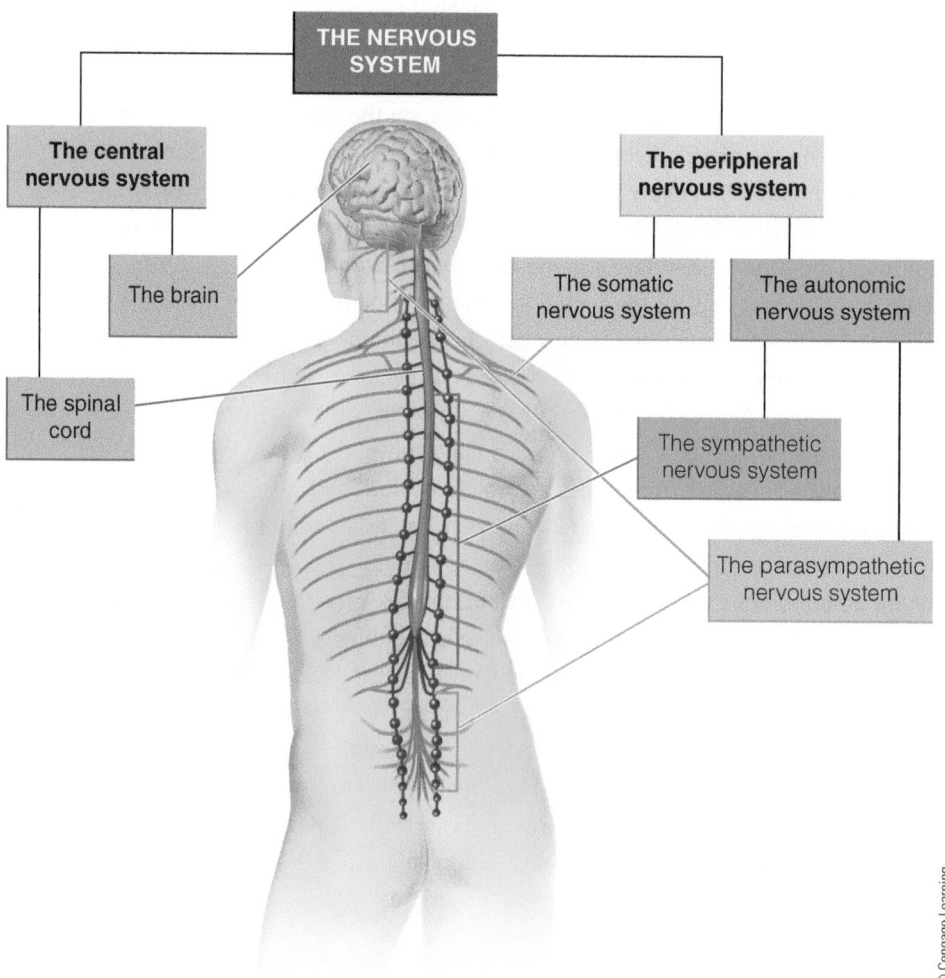

Neuron An individual nerve cell.

Central nervous system (CNS) The brain and spinal cord.

Peripheral nervous system (PNS) All parts of the nervous system outside the brain and spinal cord.

Figure 2.1 The nervous system can be divided into the central nervous system, made up of the brain and spinal cord, and the peripheral nervous system, composed of the nerves connecting the body to the central nervous system. (From Freberg, L.A. *Discovering Biological Psychology*, 2e. Copyright © 2009 Wadsworth, a part of Cengage Learning.)

carry sensory and motor messages to and from the spinal cord. In addition, 12 pairs of *cranial nerves* leave the brain directly without passing through the spinal cord. Together, these nerves keep your entire body in communication with your brain.

Are nerves the same as neurons? No. Neurons are tiny. You would need a microscope to see one. **Nerves** are large bundles of many neuron fibers (called *axons*). You can easily see nerves without magnification.

The Peripheral Nervous System

The peripheral nervous system can be divided into two major parts. The **somatic nervous system (SNS)** carries messages to and from the sense organs and skeletal muscles. In general, it controls voluntary behavior, such as when Mike does his little victory dance whenever he actually catches the Frisbee. In contrast, the **autonomic nervous system (ANS)** serves the internal organs and glands. The word *autonomic* means "self-governing." Activities governed by the autonomic nervous system are mostly "vegetative" or automatic, such as heart rate, digestion, and perspiration. Thus, messages carried by the somatic system can make your hand move, but they cannot cause your eyes to dilate. Likewise, messages carried by the ANS can stimulate digestion, but they cannot help you carry out a voluntary action, such as writing a letter. If Mike feels a flash of anger when he misses a catch, or a surge of love for Molly when she smiles, a brief burst of activity will spread through his autonomic nervous system.

The SNS and ANS work together to coordinate the body's internal reactions to events in the world outside. For example, if a snarling dog lunges at Molly, her SNS will control her leg muscles so that she can run. At the same time, her ANS will raise her blood pressure, quicken her heartbeat, and so forth. The ANS can be divided into the *sympathetic* and *parasympathetic* branches.

How do the branches of the autonomic system differ? Both the sympathetic and the parasympathetic branches are related to emotional responses, such as crying, sweating, heart rate, and other involuntary behavior (**Figure 2.2**). However, the **sympathetic branch** is an "emergency" system. It prepares the body for "fight or flight" during times of danger or high emotion. In essence, it arouses the body for action. In contrast, the **parasympathetic branch** quiets the body and returns it to a lower level of arousal. It is most active soon after an emotional event. The parasympathetic branch also helps keep vital processes such as heart rate, breathing, and digestion at moderate levels. Of course, both branches of the ANS are always active. At any given moment, their combined activity determines if your body is more or less relaxed or aroused.

How do neurons actually process information throughout the brain and the rest of the nervous system? Let's find out.

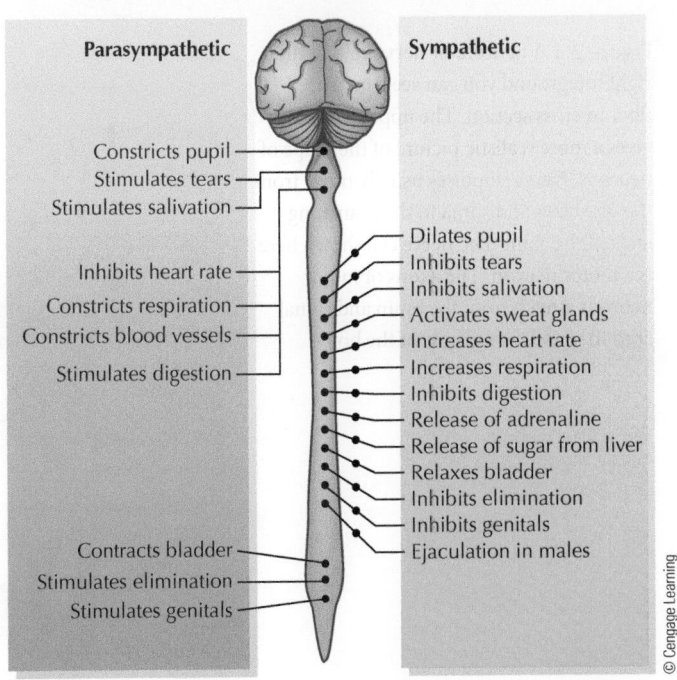

Figure 2.2 Sympathetic and parasympathetic branches of the autonomic nervous system. Both branches control involuntary actions. The sympathetic system generally activates the body. The parasympathetic system generally quiets it. The sympathetic branch relays its messages through clusters of nerve cells outside the spinal cord.

Neurons—Building a "Biocomputer"

JOURNEY QUESTION 2.2 *How do neurons operate and communicate?*

Although these little cells may seem far removed from daily life, everything you think, feel, and do begins with the 100 billion or so neurons in your brain and nervous system (Banich & Compton, 2011). Sustained by at least ten times as many *glial cells* (cells that support neurons in a variety of ways), neurons carry input from the senses to the brain, where they also process that input. Neurons also carry output from the brain in order to activate muscles and glands.

Nerve A bundle of neuron axons.

Somatic nervous system (SNS) The system of nerves linking the spinal cord with the body and sense organs.

Autonomic nervous system (ANS) The system of nerves carrying information to and from the internal organs and glands.

Sympathetic branch The branch of the ANS that arouses the body.

Parasympathetic branch The branch of the ANS that quiets the body.

Figure 2.3 A neuron, or nerve cell. In the right foreground you can see a nerve cell fiber in cross section. The upper left photo gives a more realistic picture of the shape of neurons. Nerve impulses usually travel from the dendrites and soma to the branching ends of the axon. The nerve cell shown here is a motor neuron. The axons of motor neurons stretch from the brain and spinal cord to muscles or glands of the body.

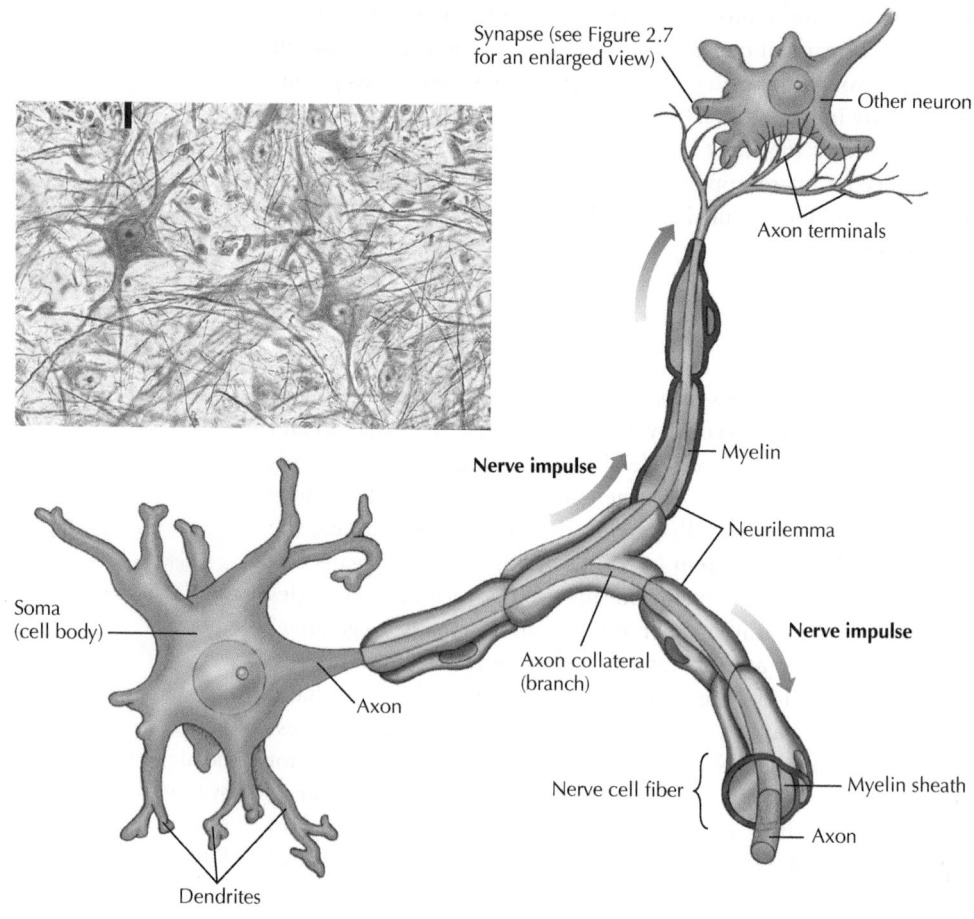

Yet, a single neuron is not very smart—it takes many just to make you blink. Literally billions of neurons may be involved when a singer like Taylor Swift belts out a tune. Your brainpower arises because individual neurons link to one another in spidery webs. Each neuron receives messages from many others and sends its own message on to many others. When neurons form vast networks, they produce intelligence and consciousness (Toates, 2011).

Parts of a Neuron

What does a neuron look like? What are its main parts? No two neurons are exactly alike, but most have four basic parts (Figure 2.3). The **dendrites** (DEN-drytes), which look like tree roots, are neuron fibers that receive messages from other neurons. The **soma** (SOH-mah, or cell body) does the same. In addition, the soma sends messages of its own (via nerve impulses) down a thin fiber called the **axon** (AK-sahn).

Some axons are only 0.1 millimeter long. (That's about the width of a pencil line.) Others stretch up to a meter through the nervous system. (From the base of your spine to your big toe, for instance.) Like miniature cables, axons carry messages through the brain and nervous system. Large bundles of axons comprise most of the spinal cord and the nerves of the peripheral nervous system. Altogether, your brain contains about 3 million miles of axons (Breedlove, Watson, & Rosenzweig, 2010). Axons "branch out" into smaller fibers ending in bulb-shaped **axon terminals**. By forming connections with the dendrites and somas of other neurons, axon terminals allow information to pass from neuron to neuron.

Now let's summarize with a metaphor. Imagine that you are standing in a long line of people who are holding hands. A person on the far left end of the line wants to silently

Dendrites Neuron fibers that receive incoming messages.

Soma The main body of a neuron or other cell.

Axon Fiber that carries information away from the cell body of a neuron.

Axon terminals Bulb-shaped structures at the ends of axons that form synapses with the dendrites and somas of other neurons.

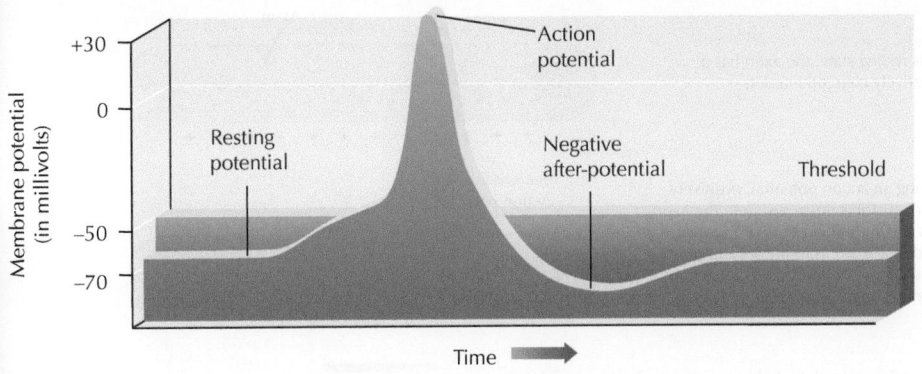

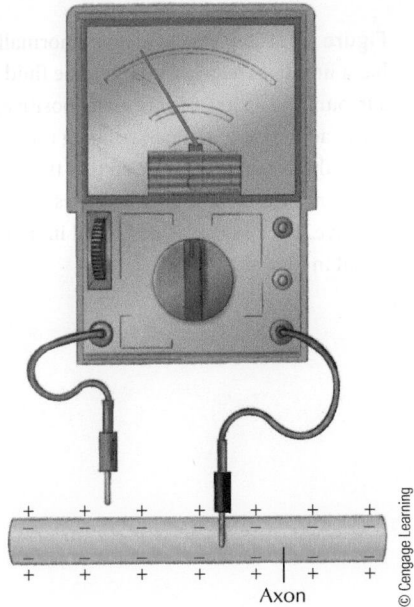

Figure 2.4 Electrical probes placed inside and outside an axon measure its activity. (The scale is exaggerated here. Such measurements require ultra-small electrodes, as described in this chapter.) The inside of an axon at rest is about −60 to −70 millivolts, compared with the outside. Electrochemical changes in a neuron generate an action potential. When sodium ions (Na⁺) that have a positive charge rush into the cell, its interior briefly becomes positive. This is the action potential. After the action potential, positive potassium ions (K⁺) flow out of the axon and restore its negative charge. (See Figure 2.5 for further explanation.)

send a message to the person on the right end. She does this by pressing the hand of the person to her right, who presses the hand of the person to his right, and so on. The message arrives at your left hand (your dendrites). You decide whether to pass it on. (You are the soma.) The message goes out through your right arm (the axon). With your right hand (the axon terminals), you squeeze the hand of the person to your right, and the message moves on.

The Nerve Impulse

Electrically charged molecules called *ions* (EYE-ons) are found inside each neuron. Other ions lie outside the neuron. Some ions have a positive electrical charge, whereas others have a negative charge. When a neuron is inactive (or resting), more of these "plus" charges exist outside the neuron and more "minus" charges exist inside. As a result, the inside of each resting neuron in your brain has an electrical charge of about −60 to −70 millivolts at the axon. (A millivolt is one thousandth of a volt.) This charge allows each neuron in your brain to act like a tiny biological battery.

The electrical charge of an inactive neuron is called its **resting potential**. But neurons seldom get much rest: Messages arriving from other neurons raise and lower the resting potential. If the electrical charge rises to about −50 millivolts, the neuron will reach its *threshold*, or trigger point for firing (see Figure 2.4). It's as if the neuron says, "Ah-ha! It's time to send a message to my neighbors." When a neuron reaches its threshold, an **action potential**, or nerve impulse, sweeps down the axon at up to 200 miles per hour (Figure 2.5). That may seem fast, but it still takes at least a split second to react. That's one reason why hitting a 100-mile-per-hour professional baseball pitch is so difficult.

What happens during an action potential? The axon membrane is pierced by tiny tunnels or holes called *ion channels*. Normally, these tiny openings are blocked by molecules that act like gates or doors. During an action potential, the gates pop open. This allows sodium ions (Na⁺) to rush into the axon (Toates, 2011). The channels first open near the soma. Then, gate after gate opens down the length of the axon as the action potential zips along (Figure 2.6).

Each action potential is an *all-or-nothing event* (the nerve impulse occurs completely or not at all). You might find it helpful to picture the axon as a row of dominoes set on end. Tipping over the dominoes is an all-or-nothing act. Once the first domino drops, a wave of falling blocks will zip rapidly to the end of the line. Similarly, when a nerve impulse is triggered near the soma, a wave of activity (the action potential) travels down the length of the

Resting potential The electrical charge of a neuron at rest.

Action potential The nerve impulse.

Figure 2.5 The inside of an axon normally has a negative electrical charge. The fluid surrounding an axon is normally positive. As an action potential passes along the axon, these charges reverse so that the interior of the axon briefly becomes positive. This process is described in more detail in Figure 2.6.

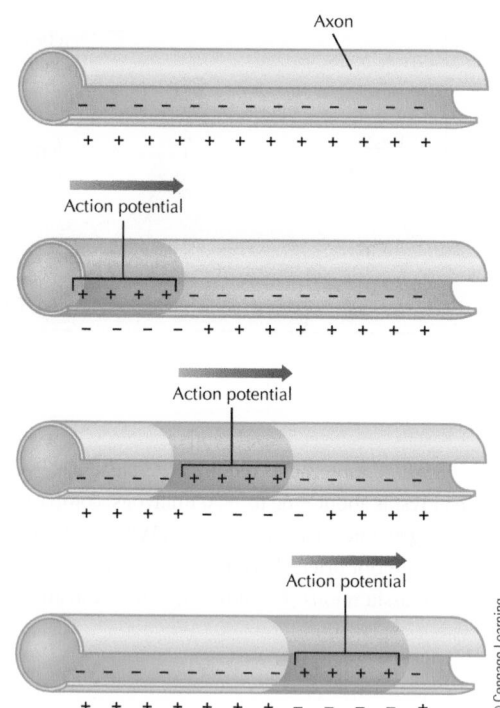

1. In its resting state, the axon has a negatively charged interior.

2. During an action potential, positively charged atoms (ions) rush into the axon. This briefly changes the electrical charge inside the axon from negative to positive. Simultaneously, the charge outside the axon becomes negative.

3. The action potential advances as positive and negative charges reverse in a moving zone of electrical activity that sweeps down the axon.

4. After an action potential passes, positive ions rapidly flow out of the axon to quickly restore its negative charge. An outward flow of additional positive ions returns the axon to its resting state.

axon. This is what happens in long chains of neurons as a dancer's brain tells her feet what to do next, beat after beat.

After each nerve impulse, the cell briefly dips below its resting level and becomes less willing or ready to fire. This **negative after-potential** occurs because potassium ions (K^+) flow out of the neuron while the membrane gates are open (Figure 2.6). After a nerve impulse, ions flow both into and out of the axon, recharging it for more action. In our model, it takes an instant for the row of dominoes to be set up again. Soon, however, the axon is ready for another wave of activity.

Saltatory Conduction

The axons of some neurons (such as the one pictured in Figure 2.3) are coated with a fatty layer called *myelin* (MY-eh-lin). Small gaps in the myelin help nerve impulses move faster. Instead of passing down the entire length of the axon, the action potential leaps from gap to

Negative after-potential A drop in electrical charge below the resting potential.

Figure 2.6 The interior of an axon. The right end of the top axon is at rest. Thus, it has a negative charge inside. An action potential begins when ion channels open and sodium ions (Na^+) rush into the axon. In this drawing, the action potential would travel from left to right along the axon. In the lower axon, the action potential has moved to the right. After it passes, potassium ions (K^+) flow out of the axon. This quickly renews the negative charge inside the axon, so that it can fire again. Sodium ions that enter the axon during an action potential are pumped out more slowly. Removing them restores the original resting potential.

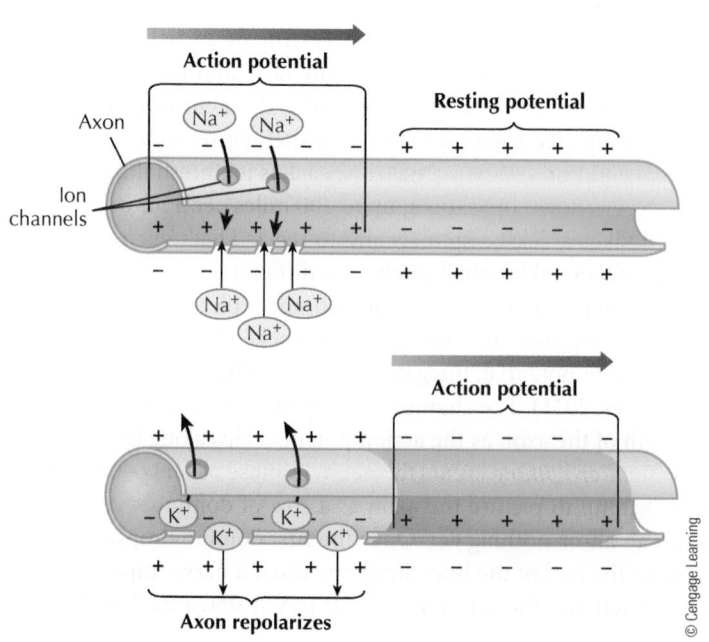

gap, a process called **saltatory conduction**. (The Latin word *saltare* means to jump or leap.) Without the added speed of saltatory action potentials, it would probably be impossible to brake in time to avoid many automobile accidents (or to hit that fastball). When the myelin layer is damaged, a person may suffer from numbness, weakness, or paralysis. That, in fact, is what happens in multiple sclerosis, a disease that occurs when the immune system attacks and destroys the myelin in a person's body (Khan, Tselis, & Lisak, 2010).

Synapses and Neurotransmitters

How does information move from one neuron to another? The nerve impulse is primarily electrical. That's why electrically stimulating the brain affects behavior. To prove the point, researcher José Delgado once entered a bullring with a cape and a radio transmitter. The bull charged. Delgado retreated. At the last instant the speeding bull stopped short. Why? Because Delgado had placed radio activated electrodes (metal wires) deep within the bull's brain. These, in turn, stimulated "control centers" that brought the bull to a halt (Horgan, 2005).

In contrast to nerve impulses, communication between neurons is chemical. The microscopic space between two neurons, over which messages pass, is called a **synapse** (SIN-aps) (Figure 2.7). When an action potential reaches the tips of the axon terminals, **neurotransmitters** (NOOR-oh-TRANS-mit-ers) are released into the synaptic gap. Neurotransmitters are chemicals that alter activity in neurons.

Let's return to our metaphor of people standing in a line. To be more accurate, you and the others shouldn't be holding hands. Instead, each person should have a squirt gun in his or her right hand. To pass along a message, you would squirt the left hand of the person to your right. When that person notices this "message," he or she would squirt the left hand of the person to the right, and so on.

When chemical molecules cross over a synapse, they attach to special receiving areas on the next neuron (see Figure 2.7). These tiny *receptor sites* on the cell membrane are sensitive to neurotransmitters. The sites are found in large numbers on neuron bodies and dendrites. Muscles and glands have receptor sites, too.

Do neurotransmitters always trigger an action potential in the next neuron? No, but they do change the likelihood of an action potential in the next neuron. Some neurotransmitters *excite* the next neuron (move it closer to firing). Others *inhibit* it (make firing less likely).

More than 100 neurotransmitter chemicals are found in the brain. Some examples are acetylcholine, dopamine, GABA, glutamate, norepinephrine, and serotonin (**Table 2.1**).

Why are there so many neurotransmitters? Some neurotransmitters are used by specific "pathways" that interlink regions of the brain. It is as if different pathways speak different languages. Perhaps this helps prevent confusing "crosstalk" or intermixing of messages. For example, the brain has a reward or "pleasure" system that mainly "speaks" dopamine (although other neurotransmitters are also found in the system) (Opland, Leinninger, & Myers, 2010; Salamone, 2007).

Slight variations in neurotransmitter function may be related to temperament differences in infancy and personality differences in adulthood (Ashton, 2007). Outright disturbances of any neurotransmitter can have serious consequences. For example, too much dopamine may cause schizophrenia (Kendler & Schaffner, 2011), whereas too little serotonin may underlie depression (Merens et al., 2008).

Many drugs mimic, duplicate, or block neurotransmitters. For example, the chemical structure of cocaine is similar to that of dopamine. In the short run, cocaine can trigger an

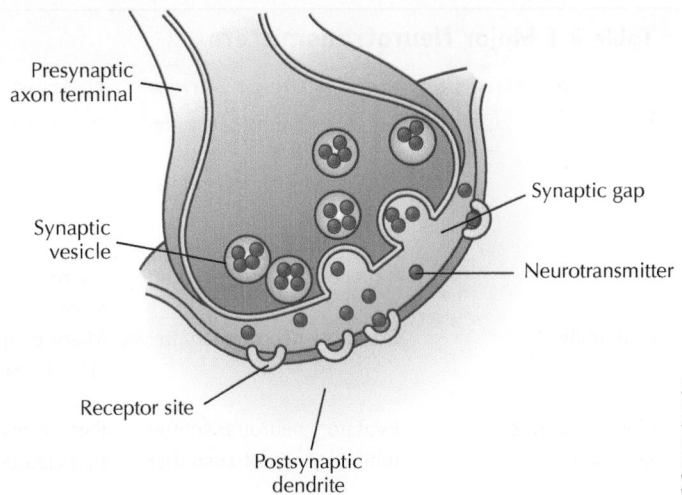

Figure 2.7 A highly magnified view of a synapse. Neurotransmitters are stored in tiny sacs called synaptic vesicles (VES-ih-kels). When a nerve impulse reaches the end of an axon, the vesicles move to the surface and release neurotransmitters. These molecules cross the synaptic gap to affect the next neuron. The size of the gap is exaggerated here; it is actually only about one millionth of an inch. Some transmitter molecules excite the next neuron and some inhibit its activity.

Saltatory conduction The process by which nerve impulses conducted down the axons of neurons coated with myelin jump from gap to gap in the myelin layer.

Synapse The microscopic space between two neurons, over which messages pass.

Neurotransmitter Any chemical released by a neuron that alters activity in other neurons.

Table 2.1 Major Neurotransmitters

NEUROTRANSMITTER	MAIN MODE OF ACTION	FUNCTION IN THE BRAIN	EFFECTS OF IMBALANCE
Acetylcholine	Excitatory neurotransmitter	Participates in movement, autonomic function, learning and memory.	Deficiency may play a role in Alzheimer's disease.
Dopamine	Excitatory neurotransmitter	Participates in motivation, reward, planning of behavior.	Deficiency may lead to Parkinson's disease, reduced feelings of pleasure; excess may lead to schizophrenia.
GABA	Inhibitory neurotransmitter	Major inhibitory effect in the central nervous system; participates in moods.	Deficiency may lead to anxiety.
Glutamate	Excitatory neurotransmitter	Major excitatory effect in the central nervous system; participates in learning and memory.	Excess may lead to neuron death and autism; deficiency may lead to tiredness.
Norepinephrine	Excitatory neurotransmitter	Participates in arousal and vigilance, and mood.	Excess may lead to anxiety.
Serotonin	Inhibitory neurotransmitter	Participates in mood, appetite, and sleep.	Deficiency may lead to depression and/or anxiety.

Adapted from Freberg, 2010; Kalat, 2013.

© Cengage Learning

increase in dopamine in the reward system, resulting in a drug "high" (Briand et al., 2008). In the long run, the overuse of recreational drugs like cocaine overstimulates the reward system and disturbs dopamine function, resulting in drug addiction (Volkow et al., 2007).

As another example, the drug curare (cue-RAH-ree) causes paralysis. Acetylcholine (ah-SEET-ul-KOH-leen) normally activates muscles. By attaching to receptor sites on muscles, curare blocks acetylcholine, preventing the activation of muscle cells. As a result, a person or animal given curare cannot move—a fact known to South American Indians of the Amazon River Basin, who use curare as an arrow poison for hunting. Without acetylcholine, a baseball pitcher couldn't even move, much less throw a fastball.

Neural Regulators

More subtle brain activities are affected by chemicals called **neuropeptides** (NOOR-oh-PEP-tides). Neuropeptides do not carry messages directly. Instead, they *regulate* the activity of other neurons. By doing so, they affect memory, pain, emotion, pleasure, moods, hunger, sexual behavior, and other basic processes. For example, when you touch something hot, you jerk your hand away. The messages for this action are carried by neurotransmitters. At the same time, pain may cause the brain to release neuropeptides called *enkephalins* (en-KEF-ah-lins). These opiate-like neural regulators relieve pain and stress. Related neuropeptide chemicals called *endorphins* (en-DORF-ins) are released by the pituitary gland. Together, these chemicals reduce the pain so that it is not too disabling (Drolet et al., 2001).

We can now explain the painkilling effect of placebos (fake pills or injections); they raise endorphin levels (Price, Finniss, & Benedetti, 2008; Stewart-Williams, 2004). A release of endorphins also seems to underlie "runner's high," masochism, acupuncture, and the euphoria sometimes associated with childbirth, painful initiation rites, and even sport parachuting (Janssen & Arntz, 2001). In each case, pain and stress cause the release of endorphins. In turn, these induce feelings of pleasure or euphoria similar to being "high" on morphine. People who say they are "addicted" to running may be closer to the truth than they realize. Ultimately, neural regulators may help explain depression, schizophrenia, drug addiction, and other puzzling topics.

Neural Networks

Let's put together what we now know about the nerve impulse and synaptic transmission to see how **neural networks**, interlinked collections of neurons, process information in our nervous systems (Zimmer, 2010). The simplest network, a **reflex arc**, occurs when a stimulus provokes an automatic response. Such reflexes arise within the spinal cord, without any help from the brain (Figure 2.8). Imagine that Molly steps on a thorn. (Yes, they're still

Neuropeptides Brain chemicals, such as enkephalins and endorphins, that regulate the activity of neurons.

Neural networks Interlinked collections of neurons that process information in the brain.

Reflex arc The simplest behavior, in which a stimulus provokes an automatic response.

playing Frisbee.) Pain is detected in her foot by a *sensory neuron*—a neuron that carries messages from the senses toward the CNS. Instantly, the sensory neuron fires off a message to Molly's spinal cord.

Inside the spinal cord, the sensory neuron synapses with a *connector neuron* (a neuron that links two others). The connector neuron activates a *motor neuron* (a neuron that carries commands from the CNS to muscles and glands). The muscle fibers are made up of *effector cells* (cells capable of producing a response). The muscle cells contract and cause Molly's foot to withdraw. Note that no brain activity is required for a reflex arc to occur. Molly's body will react automatically to protect itself.

In reality, even a simple reflex usually triggers more complex activity. For example, muscles of Molly's other leg must contract to support her as she shifts her weight. Even this can be done by the spinal cord, but it involves a bigger network of cells and several spinal nerves. Also, the spinal cord normally informs the brain of its actions. As her foot pulls away from the thorn, Molly will feel the pain and think, "Ouch, what was that?"

Perhaps you have realized how adaptive it is to have a spinal cord capable of responding on its own. Such automatic responses leave the brains of our Frisbee stars free to deal with more important information—such as the location of trees, lampposts, and chatting picnickers—as they take turns making grandstand catches.

Neural networks in the brain perform much more complex calculations. Figure 2.9 shows a small neural network involved in making a decision. Five neurons synapse with a single neuron that, in turn, connects with three more neurons. At the point in time depicted in the diagram, the single neuron is receiving one stronger and two weaker excitatory messages (+) as well as two inhibitory ones (−). Does it fire an impulse? It depends: If enough "exciting" messages arrive close in time, the neuron will reach its threshold and fire—but only if it doesn't get too many "inhibiting" messages that push it *away* from its trigger point. In this way, messages are *combined* before a neuron "decides" to fire its all-or-nothing action potential.

Let's try another metaphor. You are out shopping with five friends and find a pair of jeans you want to buy. Three of them think you should buy the jeans; your best friend is especially positive (+); and two think you shouldn't (−). Because, on balance, their input is positive, you go ahead and buy the jeans. Maybe you even tell some other friends they should buy those jeans as well. Similarly, any single neuron in a neural network "listens" to the neurons that synapse with it and combines that input into an output. At any instant, a single neuron may weigh hundreds or thousands of inputs to produce an outgoing message. After the neuron recovers from the resulting action potential, it again combines the inputs, which may have changed in the meantime, into another output, and another, and another.

In this way, each neuron in your brain functions as a tiny computer. Compared with the average laptop computer, a neuron is terribly simple and slow. But multiply these events by billions of neurons and trillions of synapses, all operating at the same time, and you have an amazing computer—one that could easily fit inside a shoebox.

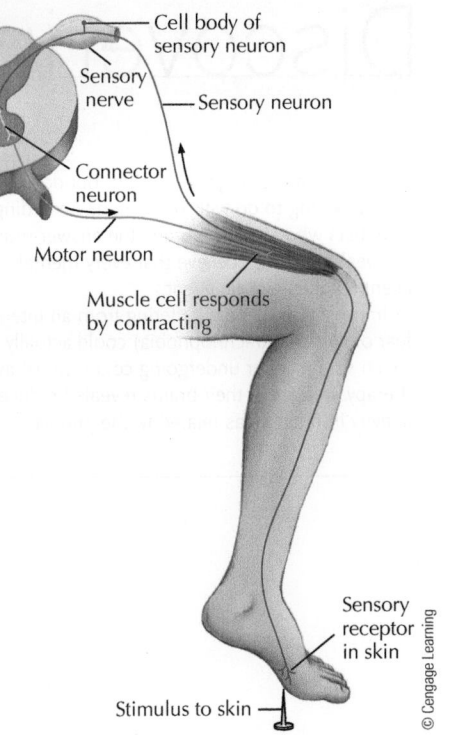

Figure 2.8 A sensory-motor arc, or reflex, is set in motion by a stimulus to the skin (or other part of the body). The nerve impulse travels to the spinal cord and then back out to a muscle, which contracts. Such reflexes provide "automatic" protective devices for the body.

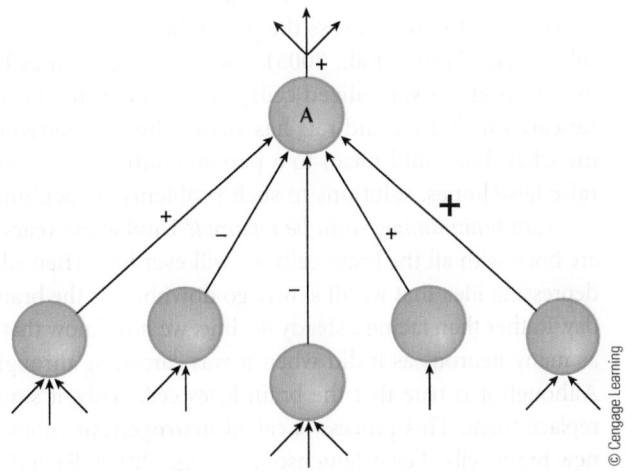

Figure 2.9 A small neural network. Neuron A receives inputs from two weaker and one stronger excitatory connections (+) and two inhibitory connections (−) and combines the inputs into a "decision" to launch an action potential, which may help trigger further synaptic transmissions in other neurons.

Discovering Psychology

You Can Change Your Mind, But Can You Change Your Brain?

You can always change your mind. But does that have anything to do with your brain? According to scientists who study the brain, the answer must be "yes" since they believe that every mental event involves a brain event.

In one study, people suffering from an intense fear of spiders (arachnophobia) could actually touch spiders after undergoing cognitive behavior therapy. Images of their brains revealed reduced activity in brain areas related to the phobia

(Paquette et al., 2003). Not only did they change their minds about spiders, they literally changed their brains.

Another study focused on taxi drivers in London, England, who must learn the names and locations of tens of thousands of streets in order to earn their licenses. Not only do experienced cabbies have superior memory for street information, the parts of their brains responsible for processing this learning are also enlarged

(Woollett & Maguire, 2011). Again, a learning experience changed their brains.

Just think: Every time you learn something, you are reshaping your living brain (Begley, 2006). There is even a fancy phrase to describe what you are doing: *self-directed neuroplasticity*. So as you study this psychology textbook, you are changing your mind—and your brain—about psychology.

Neuroplasticity and Neurogenesis

The term **neuroplasticity** refers to the capacity of our brains to change in response to experience. Synaptic connections may grow stronger and new ones may form. (Figure 2.6 shows one particularly strong synapse—the large +.) In general, the repeated activation of synapses between two neurons strengthens the connection between them. This is known as *Hebb's rule* (Hebb, 1949). Inactive synaptic connections may weaken and even die. Consequently, every new experience you have is reflected in changes to your brain. For example, rats raised in a complex environment have more synapses and longer dendrites in their brains than rats raised in a simpler environment (Kolb, Gibb, & Gorny, 2003). Or consider Nico and Brooke, teenagers who had a large portion of their brains removed as infants. Today they are functioning well; over the years their brains have compensated for their losses (Immordino-Yang, 2008; Kolb et al., 2011).

Are adult human brains also neuroplastic? Although adult brains are less neuroplastic, they can still be changed with patience and persistence. See "You Can Change Your Mind, But Can You Change Your Brain?"

The nervous system is "plastic" for another reason. It has long been known that nerves in the peripheral nervous system can regrow if they are damaged. The axons of most neurons in nerves outside the brain and spinal cord are covered by a thin layer of cells called the *neurilemma* (NOOR-rih-LEM-ah). (Return to Figure 2.3.) The neurilemma forms a "tunnel" that damaged fibers can follow as they repair themselves. Because of this, patients can expect to regain some control over severed limbs once they have been reattached.

In contrast, a serious injury to spinal cord was long thought to be permanent. However, scientists are starting to make progress repairing damaged neurons in the spinal cord (Rossignol & Frigon, 2011). For instance, they have partially repaired cut spinal cords in rats by establishing "cellular bridges" to close the gap. Strategies include coaxing severed nerve fibers to grow across the gap (Cheng, Cao, & Olson, 1996), grafting nerve fibers to fill the gap (Féron et al., 2005), and injecting stem cells (immature cells that can mature into a variety of specialized cells, such as neurons) into the gap (Watson & Yeung, 2011). Research with mice and rats has already been followed up with some human trials. Imagine what that could mean to a person confined to a wheelchair. Although it is unwise to raise false hopes, solutions to such problems are beginning to emerge.

Can brain damage also be repaired? Until a few years ago, it was widely believed that we are born with all the brain cells we will ever have (Ben Abdallah et al., 2010). This led to the depressing idea that we all slowly go downhill, as the brain loses thousands of neurons every day. Rather than facing a steady decline, we now know that a healthy 75-year-old brain has just as many neurons as it did when it was careening through life in the body of a 25-year-old. Although it is true that the brain loses cells daily, it simultaneously grows new neurons to replace them. This process is called **neurogenesis** (noor-oh-JEN-uh-sis), the production of new brain cells (Lee, Clemenson, & Gage, 2011). Each day, thousands of new cells originate

Neuroplasticity The capacity of the brain to change in response to experience.

Neurogenesis The production of new brain cells.

deep within the brain, move to the surface, and link up with other neurons to become part of the brain's circuitry. This was stunning news to brain scientists, who must now figure out what the new cells do. Most likely they are involved in learning, memory, and our ability to adapt to changing circumstances (Canales, 2010).

The discovery of neurogenesis in adult brains is leading to new treatments for some types of brain damage (Ekonomou et al., 2011; Lagace, 2011). Imagine that a patient named Bobby has suffered a stroke, damaging some of the neurons responsible for controlling his left arm. What could be done to help Bobby recover from the resulting partial paralysis? One approach, called *constraint-induced movement therapy*, involves restraining Bobby's good right arm, forcing his impaired left arm to be more active. By using his left arm, Bobby could increase neurogenesis in the damaged part of his brain (Taub, 2004). In another approach, drugs that speed up neurogenesis could be injected into the damaged area of Bobby's brain (Zhang, Zhang, & Chopp, 2005). Such techniques are beginning to offer new hope for people suffering from a variety of other disabilities, such as blindness and Parkinson's disease (Brinton & Wang, 2006; Burke et al., 2007).

We will shortly probe more deeply into the brain. Before we do, it might be wise to explore some of the research tools biopsychologists use. Let's consider some of the basics.

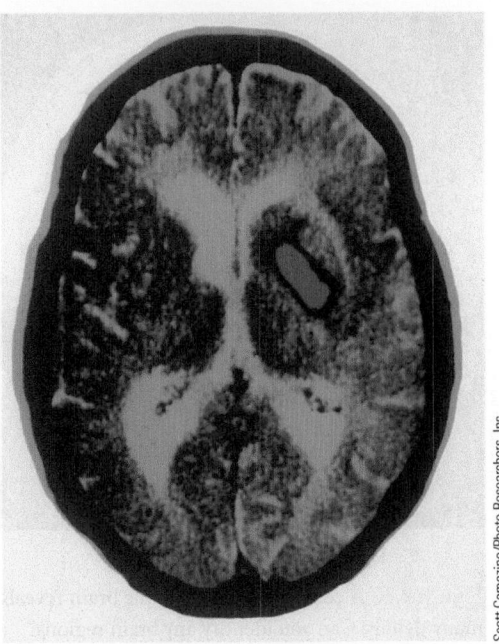

This brain in this photo was damaged by a stroke (shown in red). The location of the stroke will determine what mental or behavioral functions are disrupted.

Scott Camazine/Photo Researchers, Inc.

Research Methods—Charting the Brain's Inner Realms

JOURNEY QUESTION 2.3 *How are different parts of the brain identified and what do they do?*

Biopsychology is the study of how biological processes, especially those occurring in the nervous system, relate to behavior. In their research, many biopsychologists try to learn which parts of the brain control particular mental or behavioral functions, such as being able to recognize faces or move your hands. That is, they try to learn where functions are localized (located) in the brain. Many techniques have been developed to help identify brain structures and the functions they control.

Mapping Brain Structure

Anatomists have learned much about brain structure by dissecting (cutting apart) autopsied human and animal brains and examining them under a microscope. Dissection reveals that the brain is made up of many anatomically distinct areas or "parts." Less intrusive newer methods, such as the CT scan and the MRI scan, can be used to map brain structures in living brains.

CT Scan

Computerized scanning equipment has revolutionized the study of brain structures and made it easier to identify brain diseases and injuries. At best, conventional X-rays produce only shadowy images of the brain. **Computed tomographic (CT) scanning** is a specialized type of X-ray that does a much better job of making the brain visible. In a CT scan, X-rays taken from a number of different angles are collected by a computer and formed into an image of the brain. A CT scan can reveal brain structure as well as the location of strokes, injuries, tumors, and other brain disorders.

MRI Scan

Magnetic resonance imaging (MRI) uses a very strong magnetic field, rather than X-rays, to produce an image of the body's interior. During an MRI scan, the body is placed inside a magnetic field. Processing by a computer then creates a three-dimensional model of the brain or body. Any two-dimensional plane, or slice, of the body can be selected and displayed as an image

Computed tomographic scan (CT scan) A computer-enhanced X-ray image of the brain or body.

Magnetic resonance imaging (MRI) An imaging technique that results in a three-dimensional image of the brain or body, based on its response to a magnetic field.

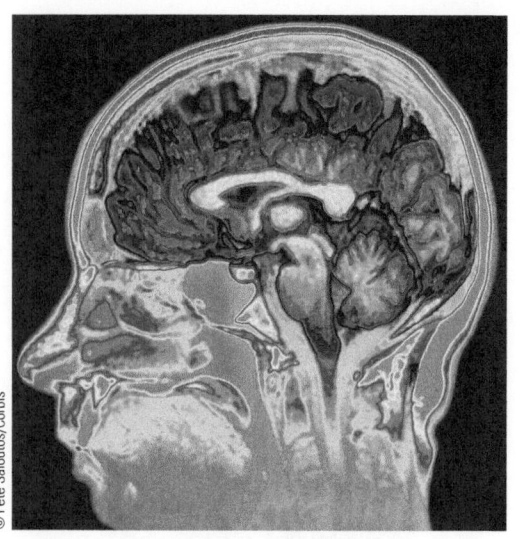

Figure 2.10 A colored MRI scan of the brain reveals many details. Can you identify any brain regions?

on a computer screen. MRI scans produce more detailed images than are possible with CT scans, allowing us to peer into the living brain almost as if it were transparent (Figure 2.10).

Exploring Brain Function

Although it is valuable to be able to examine images of different brain structures, such as those made possible by CT scans and MRIs, it is another matter entirely to visualize what role those structures play in normal brain function.

What parts of the brain allow us to think, feel, perceive, or act? To answer questions like this, we must **localize function** by linking psychological or behavioral capacities with particular brain structures. In many instances, this has been done through **clinical case studies**. Such studies examine changes in personality, behavior, or sensory capacity caused by brain diseases or injuries. If damage to a particular part of the brain consistently leads to a particular loss of function, then we say the function is localized in that structure. Presumably, that part of the brain controls the same function in all of us.

Although major brain injuries are easy enough to spot, psychologists also look for more subtle signs that the brain is not working properly. **Neurological soft signs**, as they are called, include clumsiness, an awkward gait, poor hand-eye coordination, and other problems with perception or fine muscle control (Morgan & Ricker, 2008). These telltale signs are "soft" in the sense that they aren't direct tests of the brain, like a CT scan or MRI scan. Long-term brain damage, like that suffered by Dave Duerson, is usually first diagnosed with soft signs. Likewise, soft signs help psychologists diagnose problems ranging from childhood learning disorders to full-blown psychosis (Schoenberg & Scott, 2008).

Instead of relying on clinical studies, researchers have learned much from **electrical stimulation of the brain (ESB)** (Figure 2.11). For example, the surface of the brain can be "turned on" by stimulating it with a mild electrical current delivered through a thin insulated wire called an **electrode**. When this is done during brain surgery, the patient can describe what effect the stimulation had. (The brain has no pain receptors, so surgery can be done while a patient is awake. Only local painkillers are used for the scalp and skull. Any volunteers?) Even structures below the surface of the brain can be activated by lowering a stimulating electrode, insulated except at the tip, into a target area inside the brain. ESB can call forth behavior with astonishing power. Instantly, it can bring about aggression, alertness, escape, eating, drinking, sleeping, movement, euphoria, memories, speech, tears, and more.

Could ESB be used to control a person against his or her will? It might seem that ESB could be used to control a person like a robot. But the details of emotions and behaviors elicited by ESB are modified by personality and circumstances. Sci-fi movies to the contrary, it would be impossible for a ruthless dictator to enslave people by "radio controlling" their brains.

An alternative approach is **ablation** (ab-LAY-shun), or surgical removal of parts of the brain (see Figure 2.11). When ablation causes changes in behavior or sensory capacity, we

Localization of function The research strategy of linking specific structures in the brain with specific psychological or behavioral functions.

Clinical case study A detailed investigation of a single person, especially one suffering from some injury or disease.

Neurological soft signs Subtle behavioral signs of nervous system dysfunction, including clumsiness, an awkward gait, poor hand-eye coordination, and other perceptual and motor problems.

Electrical stimulation of the brain (ESB) Direct electrical stimulation and activation of brain tissue.

Electrode Any device (such as a wire, needle, or metal plate) used to electrically stimulate or destroy nerve tissue or to record its activity.

Ablation Surgical removal of tissue.

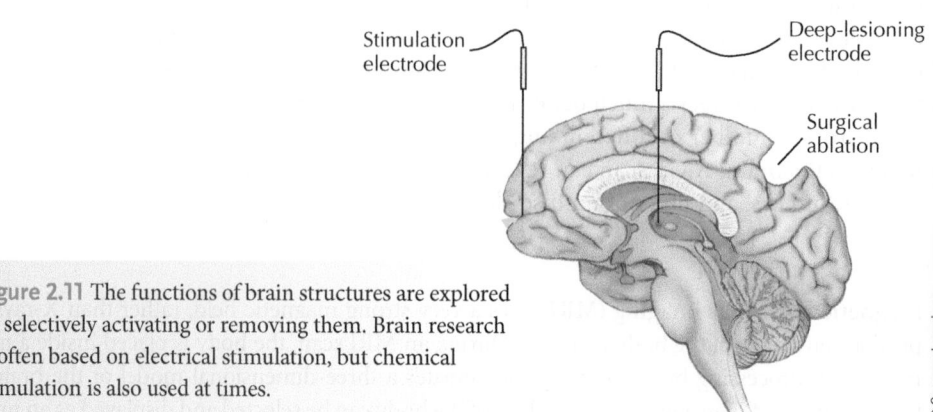

Figure 2.11 The functions of brain structures are explored by selectively activating or removing them. Brain research is often based on electrical stimulation, but chemical stimulation is also used at times.

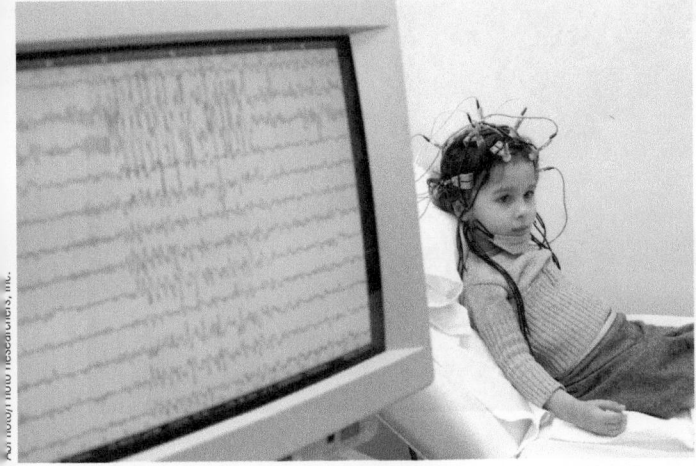
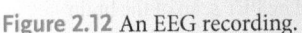

Figure 2.12 An EEG recording.

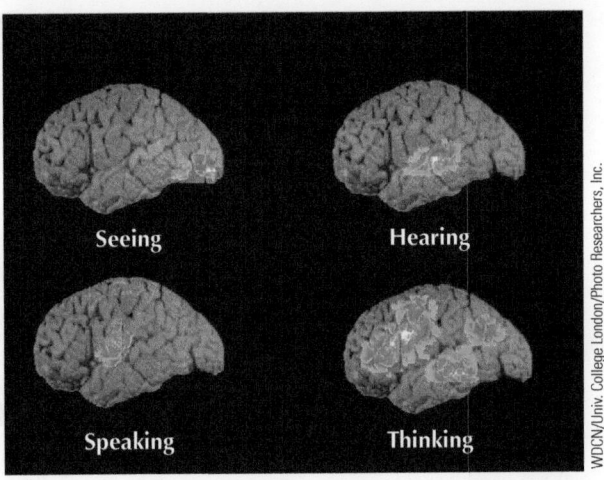

Seeing

Hearing

Speaking

Thinking

Figure 2.13 Colored PET scans reveal different patterns of brain activation when we engage in different tasks.

also gain insight into the purpose of the missing "part." By using a technique called **deep lesioning** (LEE-zhun-ing), structures below the surface of the brain can also be removed. In this case, an electrode is lowered into a target area inside the brain and a strong electric current is used to destroy a small amount of brain tissue (see Figure 2.11). Again, changes in behavior give clues about the function of the affected area.

To find out what individual neurons are doing, we need to do a microelectrode recording. A *microelectrode* is an extremely thin glass tube filled with a salty fluid. The tip of a microelectrode is small enough to detect the electrical activity of a *single* neuron. Watching the action potentials of just one neuron provides a fascinating glimpse into the true origins of behavior. (The action potential shown in Figure 2.4 was recorded with a microelectrode.)

Are any less invasive techniques available for studying brain function? Whereas CT scans and MRIs cannot tell us what different parts of the brain *do*, several other techniques allow us to observe the activity of parts of the brain without doing any damage at all. These include the EEG, PET scan, and fMRI. Such techniques allow biopsychologists to localize areas in the brain responsible for thoughts, feelings, and actions.

EEG

Electroencephalography (ee-LEK-tro-in-SEF-ah-LOG-ruh-fee) measures the waves of electrical activity produced near the surface of the brain. Small disk-shaped metal plates are placed on a person's scalp. Electrical impulses from the brain are detected by these electrodes and sent to an **electroencephalograph (EEG)**. The EEG amplifies these very weak signals (brain waves) and records them on a moving sheet of paper or a computer screen (Figure 2.12). Various brain-wave patterns can identify the presence of tumors, epilepsy, and other diseases. The EEG also reveals changes in brain activity during sleep, daydreaming, hypnosis, and other mental states.

PET Scan

A newer technology, called **positron emission tomography (PET)**, provides much more detailed images of activity both *near* the surface and *below* the surface of the brain. A PET scan detects positrons (subatomic particles) emitted by weakly radioactive glucose (sugar) as it is consumed by the brain. Because the brain runs on glucose, a PET scan shows which areas are using more energy. Higher energy use corresponds with higher activity. Thus, by placing positron detectors around the head and sending data to a computer, it is possible to create a moving, color picture of changes in brain activity. As you can see in Figure 2.13, PET scans reveal that very specific brain areas are active when you see, hear, speak, or think.

Deep lesioning Removal of tissue within the brain by use of an electrode.

Electroencephalograph (EEG) A device that detects, amplifies, and records electrical activity in the brain.

Positron emission tomography (PET) An imaging technique that results in a computer-generated image of brain activity, based on glucose consumption in the brain.

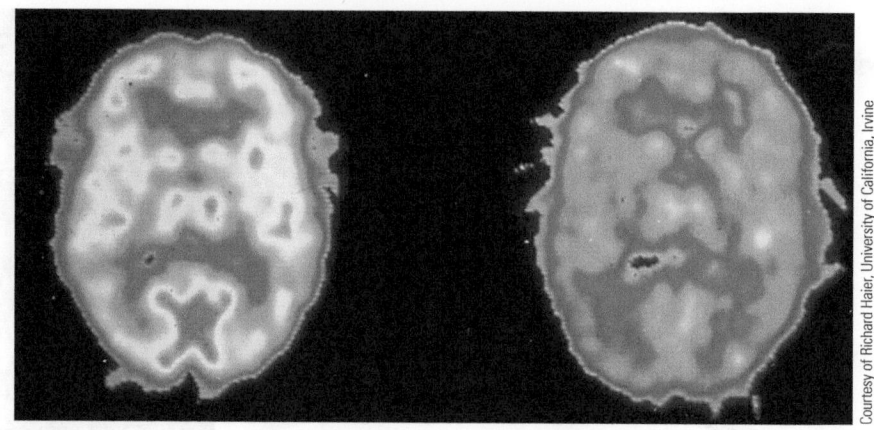

Figure 2.14 In the images you see here, red, orange, and yellow indicate high consumption of glucose; green, blue, and pink show areas of low glucose use. The PET scan of the brain on the left shows that a man who solved 11 out of 36 reasoning problems burned more glucose than the man on the right, who solved 33.

More active brains are good, right? Although we might assume that hardworking brains are smart brains, the reverse appears to be true (Neubauer & Fink, 2009). Using PET scans, psychologist Richard Haier and his colleagues first found that the brains of people who perform well on a difficult reasoning test consume less energy than those of poor performers (Haier et al., 1988) (Figure 2.14). Haier believes this shows that intelligence is related to brain efficiency: Less efficient brains work harder and still accomplish less (Haier, White, & Alkire, 2003). We've all had days like that!

Is it true that most people use only 10 percent of their brain capacity? This is one of the lasting myths about the brain. Brain scans show that all parts of the brain are active during waking hours. Obviously, some people make better use of their innate brainpower than others do. Nevertheless, there are no great hidden or untapped reserves of mental capacity in a normally functioning brain.

fMRI

A **functional MRI (fMRI)** uses MRI technology to make brain activity visible. Like PET scans, fMRIs also provide images of activity throughout the brain. For example, if we scanned you while you are reading this textbook, areas of your brain involved in understanding what you read would be highlighted in an fMRI image. (In contrast, if we used MRI, rather than fMRI, we would get a beautiful image of your brain structure without any clues as to which parts of your brain were more or less active.)

Psychiatrist Daniel Langleben and his colleagues (2005; Hakun et al., 2009) have even used fMRI images to tell whether a person is lying. As Figure 2.15 shows, the front of the brain is more active when a person is lying, rather than telling the truth. This may occur because it takes extra effort to lie, and the resulting extra brain activity is detected with fMRI. Eventually, fMRI may help us distinguish between lies, false statements made with the intention to deceive, and *confabulations*, which are false claims believed to be true (Hirstein, 2005; Langleben, Dattilio, & Gutheil, 2006).

As they learn more about the human brain, researchers are creating digital three-dimensional brain maps. These "atlases" show brain structures and even their accompanying psychological functions. They promise to be valuable guides for medical treatment, as well as for exploring the brain (Jagaroo, 2009; Jellinger, 2009). Clearly, it is just a matter of time until even brighter beacons are flashed into the shadowy inner world of thought.

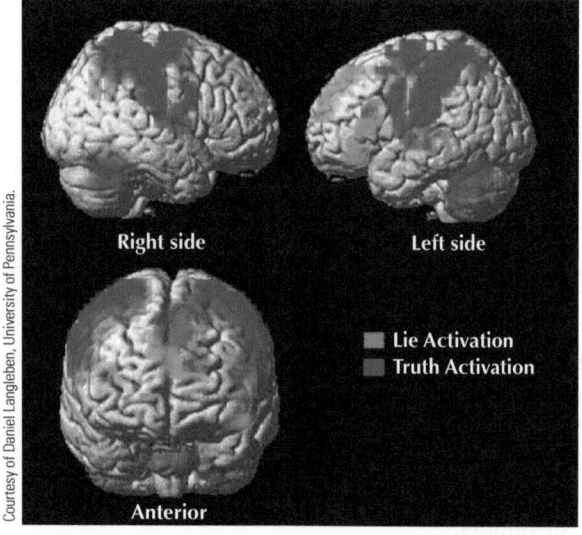

Figure 2.15 Participants were asked to tell the truth or to lie while fMRI images of their brains were taken. When compared with telling the truth *(shown in blue)*, areas toward the front of the brain were active during lying *(shown in red)*. (Adapted from Langleben et al., HUMAN BRAIN MAPPING Copyright © 2005 Daniel Langleben. Reprinted by permission of John Wiley & Sons, Inc.)

Functional MRI (fMRI) MRI technique that records brain activity.

RECITE

1. The somatic and autonomic systems are part of the _____ nervous system.
2. The _____ and _____ are receiving areas where information from other neurons is accepted.
3. Nerve impulses are carried down the _____ to the _____ _____.
4. The _____ potential becomes a(n) _____ potential when a neuron passes the threshold for firing.
5. Sodium and potassium ions flow through ion channels in the synapse to trigger a nerve impulse in the receiving neuron. T or F?
6. Which of the following research techniques has the most in common with clinical studies of the effects of brain injuries?

   a. EEG recording
   b. deep lesioning
   c. microelectrode recording
   d. PET scan

7. CT scans cannot determine which part of your brain plays a role in speech because CT scans

   a. use X-rays
   b. reveal brain structure, not brain activity
   c. reveal brain activity, not brain structure
   d. use magnetic fields

REFLECT

THINK CRITICALLY

8. What effect would you expect a drug to have if it blocked passage of neurotransmitters across the synapse?

SELF-REFLECT

You suspect that a certain part of the brain is related to risk-taking. How could you use clinical studies, ablation, deep lesioning, and ESB to study the structure? You are interested in finding out how single neurons in the optic nerve respond when the eye is exposed to light. What technique will you use? You want to know which areas of the brain's surface are most active when a person sees a face. What methods will you use?

ANSWERS

1. peripheral 2. dendrites, soma 3. axon, axon terminals 4. resting, action 5. F 6. b 7. b 8. Such a drug could have wide-ranging effects. If the drug blocked excitatory synapses, it would depress brain activity. If it blocked inhibitory messages, it would act as a powerful stimulant.

The Cerebral Cortex—My, What a Wrinkled Brain You Have!

JOURNEY QUESTION 2.4 *How do the left and right hemispheres differ and what are the different functions of the lobes of the cerebral cortex?*

In many ways we are pretty unimpressive creatures. Animals surpass humans in almost every category of strength, speed, and sensory sensitivity. However, we do excel in intelligence.

Does that mean humans have the largest brains? No, that honor goes to whales, whose brains tip the scales at around 19 pounds. At 3 pounds, the human brain seems puny—until we compare brain weight to body weight. We then find that a sperm whale's brain is 1/10,000 of its weight. The ratio for humans is 1/60. And yet the ratio for tree shrews (very small squirrel-like insect-eating mammals) is about 1/30. So our human brains are not noteworthy in terms of either absolute or relative weight (Coolidge & Wynn, 2009).

So having a larger brain doesn't necessarily make a person smarter? That's right. Although a small positive correlation exists between intelligence and brain size, overall size alone does not determine human intelligence (Johnson et al., 2008; Witelson, Beresh, & Kigar, 2006). In fact, many parts of your brain are surprisingly similar to corresponding brain areas in other animals, such as lizards. It is your larger **cerebral** (seh-REE-brel or ser-EH-brel) **cortex** that sets you apart.

The cerebral cortex, which looks a little like a giant, wrinkled walnut, consists of the two large hemispheres that cover the upper part of the brain. The two hemispheres are divided into smaller areas known as lobes. Parts of various lobes are responsible for the ability to see, hear, move, think, and speak. Thus, a map of cortex is in some ways like a map of human behavior, as we shall see.

The cerebral cortex covers most of the brain with a mantle of *gray matter* (spongy tissue made up mostly of cell bodies). Although the cortex is only 3 millimeters thick (one tenth of an inch), it contains 70 percent of the neurons in the central nervous system. It is largely responsible for our ability to use language, make tools, acquire complex skills, and live in complex social groups (Coolidge & Wynn, 2009). In humans, the cortex is twisted and folded,

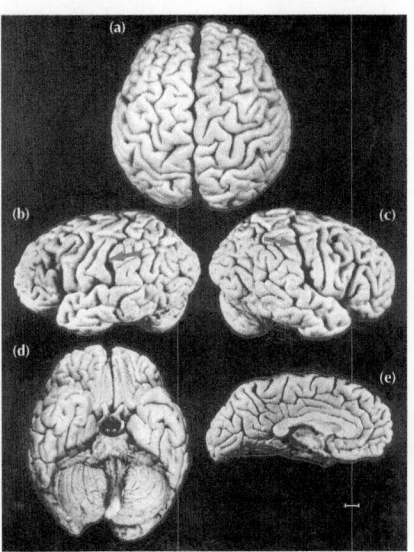

Photographs of views of Einstein's brain: from the top *(a)*, left *(b)*, right *(c)*, bottom *(d)* and middle section *(e)*. Overall brain size was within normal limits. However, the parts of the brain necessary for spatial reasoning in the parietal lobe (see arrows in b and c) had a unique anatomy and were larger than in control brains. (Adapted from Witelson, Kigar, & Harvey, Lancet, 1999, and reprinted with permission of S. F. Witelson.)

© Dr. Sandra F. Witelson

Cerebral cortex The outer layer of the brain.

Figure 2.16 A more wrinkled cortex has greater cognitive capacity. Extensive corticalization is the key to human intelligence.

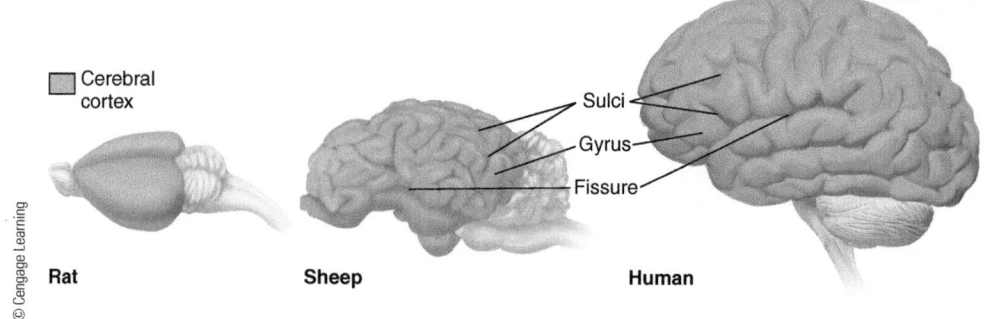

Rat   Sheep   Human

Cerebral cortex

Sulci
Gyrus
Fissure

© Cengage Learning

and it is the largest brain structure. In lower animals, it is smooth and small (Figure 2.16). The fact that humans are more intelligent than other animals is related to this **corticalization** (KORE-tih-kal-ih-ZAY-shun), or increase in the size and wrinkling of the cortex. Without the cortex, we humans wouldn't be much smarter than toads.

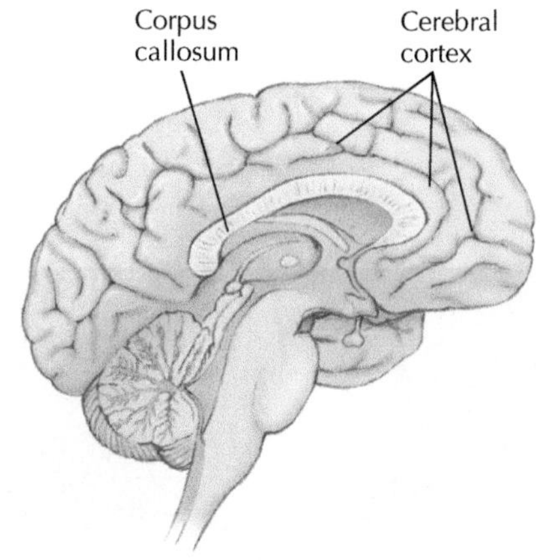

Cerebral Hemispheres

The cortex is composed of two sides, or *cerebral hemispheres* (half-globes), connected by a thick band of axon fibers called the *corpus callosum* (KORE-pus kah-LOH-sum) (Figure 2.17). The left side of the brain mainly controls the right side of the body. Likewise, the right brain mainly controls left body areas. Bobby's stroke damaged his right hemisphere, causing some loss of movement in his left arm.

Damage to one hemisphere may also cause a curious problem called *spatial neglect* (Silveri, Ciccarelli, & Cappa, 2011). A patient with right hemisphere damage may pay no attention to the left side of visual space (Figure 2.18). Often, the patient will not eat food on the left side of a plate. Some even refuse to acknowledge a paralyzed left arm as their own (Hirstein, 2005). If you point to the "alien" arm, the patient is likely to say, "Oh, that's not my arm. It must belong to someone else."

Hemispheric Specialization

In 1981, Roger Sperry (1914–1994) won a Nobel Prize for his remarkable discovery that the right and left brain hemispheres perform differently on tests of language, perception, music, and other capabilities (Corballis, 2010b).

Corpus callosum   Cerebral cortex

© Cengage Learning

Figure 2.17

Model   Patient's copy

Figure 2.18 Spatial neglect. A patient with right-hemisphere damage was asked to copy three model drawings. Notice the obvious neglect of the left side in his drawings. Similar instances of neglect occur in many patients with right-hemisphere damage. (From Left Brain, Right Brain, 5th ed., by Sally P. Springer & Georg Deutsch. © 1981, 1985, 1989, 1993, 1998 by Sally P. Springer and Georg Deutsch. Used with permission of W. H. Freeman and Company.)

Corticalization An increase in the relative size of the cerebral cortex.

"Split Brains"

How is it possible to test only one side of the brain? One way is to work with people who've had a **"split-brain" operation**. In this rare type of surgery, the corpus callosum is cut to control severe epilepsy. The result is essentially a person with two brains in one body (Colvin & Gazzaniga, 2007). After the surgery, it is possible to send information to one hemisphere or the other (Figure 2.19). However, after the right and left brain are separated, each hemisphere will have its own separate perceptions, concepts, and impulses to act.

How does a split-brain person act after the operation? Having two "brains" in one body can create some interesting dilemmas. One split-brain patient, Karen, has to endure an out-of-control left hand. As Karen put it, "I'd light a cigarette, balance it on an ashtray, and then my left hand would reach forward and stub it out. It would take things out of my handbag and I wouldn't realise so I would walk away. I lost a lot of things before I realised what was going on" (Mosley, 2011). However, such conflicts are actually rare. That's because both halves of the brain normally have about the same experience at the same time. Also, if a conflict arises, one hemisphere usually overrides the other.

Split-brain effects are easiest to see in specialized testing. For example, we could flash a dollar sign to the right brain and a question mark to the left brain of a patient named Tom. (Figure 2.19 shows how this is possible.) Next, Tom is asked to draw what he saw, using his left hand, out of sight. Tom's left hand draws a dollar sign. If Tom is then asked to point with his right hand to a picture of what his hidden left hand drew, he will point to a question mark (Sperry, 1968).

In short, for the split-brain person, one hemisphere may not know what is happening in the other. This has to be the ultimate case of the "right hand not knowing what the left hand is doing"! Figure 2.20 provides another example of split-brain testing.

Right Brain/Left Brain

Earlier it was stated that the hemispheres differ in abilities. In what ways are they different? The brain divides its work in interesting ways. Roughly 95 percent of us use our left brain for language (speaking, writing, and understanding). In addition, the left hemisphere is superior at math, judging time and rhythm, and coordinating the

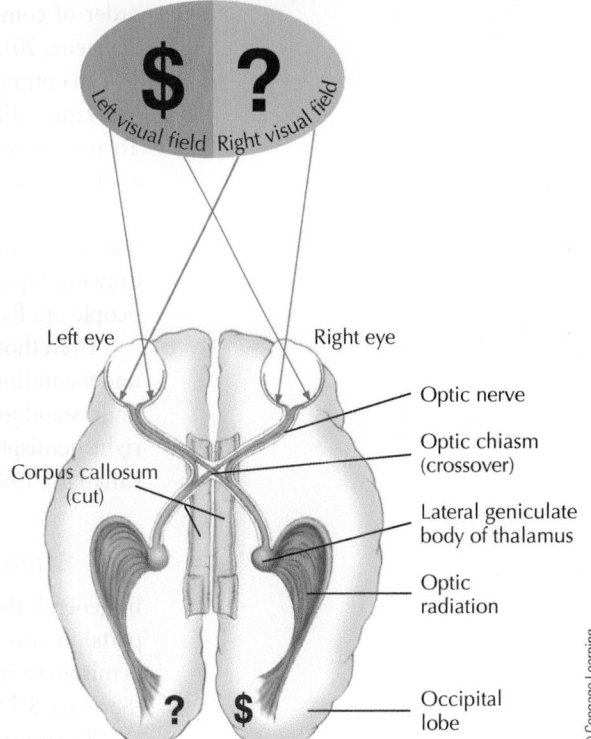

Figure 2.19 Basic nerve pathways of vision. Notice that the left portion of each eye connects only to the left half of the brain; likewise, the right portion of each eye connects to the right brain. When the corpus callosum is cut, a "split brain" results. Then visual information can be sent to just one hemisphere by flashing it in the right or left visual field as the person stares straight ahead.

"Split-brain" operation Cutting the corpus callosum.

Left Brain
- Language
- Speech
- Writing
- Calculation
- Time sense
- Rhythm
- Ordering of complex movements

Right Brain
- Nonverbal
- Perceptual skills
- Visualization
- Recognition of patterns, faces, melodies
- Recognition and expression of emotion
- Spatial skills
- Simple language comprehension

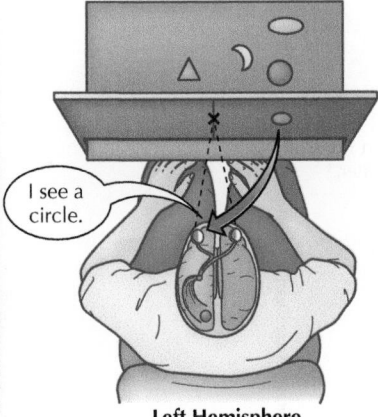

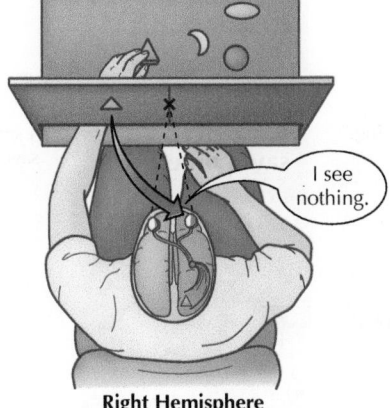

Left Hemisphere

Right Hemisphere

Figure 2.20 A circle is flashed to the left brain of a split-brain patient and he is asked what he saw. He easily replies, "A circle." He can also pick out the circle by merely touching shapes with his right hand, out of sight behind a screen. However, his left hand can't identify the circle. If a triangle is flashed to the patient's right brain, he can't say what he saw (speech is controlled by the left hemisphere). He also can't identify the triangle by touch with the right hand. Now, however, the left hand has no difficulty picking out the triangle. In other tests, the hemispheres reveal distinct skills, as listed above the drawing.

order of complex movements, such as those needed for speech (Kell et al., 2011; Pinel & Dehaene, 2010).

In contrast, the right hemisphere can produce only the simplest language and numbers. Working with the right brain is like talking to a child who can say only a dozen words or so. To answer questions, the right hemisphere must use nonverbal responses, such as pointing at objects (see Figure 2.20).

Although it is poor at producing language, the right brain is especially good at perceptual skills, such as recognizing patterns, faces, and melodies; putting together a puzzle; or drawing a picture. It also helps you express emotions and detect the emotions that other people are feeling (Borod et al., 2002; Castro-Schilo & Kee, 2010).

Even though the right hemisphere is nearly "speechless," it is superior at some aspects of understanding language. If the right side of the brain is damaged, people lose their ability to understand jokes, irony, sarcasm, implications, and other nuances of language. Basically, the right hemisphere helps us see the overall context in which something is said (Beeman & Chiarello, 1998; Dyukova et al., 2010).

One Brain, Two Styles

In general, the left hemisphere is involved mainly with *analysis* (breaking information into parts). It also processes information *sequentially* (in order, one item after the next). The right hemisphere appears to process information *holistically* (all at once) and *simultaneously* (Springer & Deutsch, 1998).

To summarize further, you could say that the right hemisphere is better at assembling pieces of the world into a coherent picture; it sees overall patterns and general connections. The left brain focuses on small details (Figure 2.21). The right brain sees the wide-angle view; the left zooms in on specifics. The focus of the left brain is local, the right is global (Hübner & Volberg, 2005).

Are there left-brained and right-brained people? Numerous books and websites have been devoted to how to use the left brain or the right brain to manage, teach, draw, ride horses, learn, and even make love. But this is a drastic oversimplification since people normally use both sides of their brain at all times. It's true that some tasks may make *more* use of one hemisphere or the other. But in most "real world" activities, the hemispheres share the work. Each does the parts it does best and shares information with the other side.

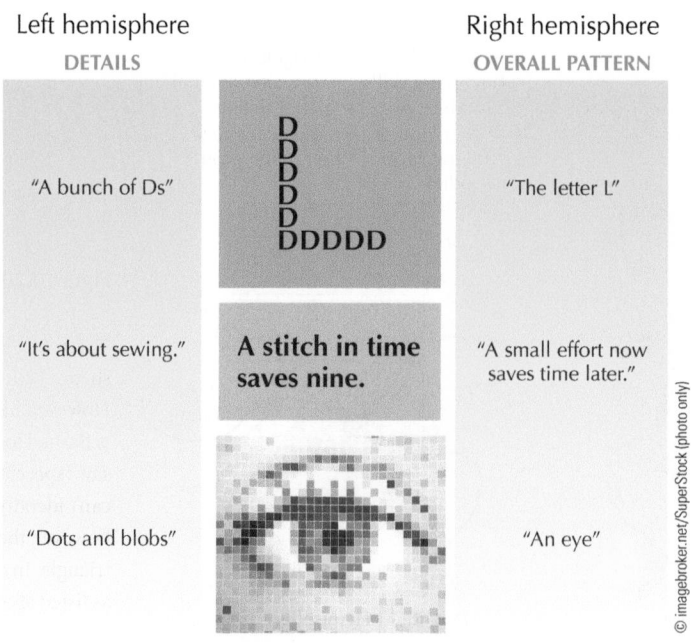

Figure 2.21 The left and right brain have different information processing styles. The right brain gets the big pattern; the left focuses on small details. © Cengage Learning

A smart brain is one that grasps both the details and the overall picture at the same time. For instance, during a concert, a guitarist will use her left brain to judge time and rhythm and coordinate the order of her hand movements. At the same time, she will use her right brain to recognize and organize melodies.

Lobes of the Cerebral Cortex

Each of the two hemispheres of the cerebral cortex can be divided into several smaller *lobes*. Some of the lobes of the cerebral cortex are defined by larger fissures on the surface of the cortex. Others are regarded as separate areas because their functions are quite different (Figure 2.22).

The Frontal Lobes

The **frontal lobes** are associated with higher mental abilities and play a role in your sense of self. This area is also responsible for the control of movement. Specifically, an arch of tissue at the rear of the frontal lobes, called the **primary motor area** (or **primary motor cortex**), directs the body's muscles. If this area is stimulated with an electrical current, various parts of the body will twitch or move. The drawing wrapped around the motor cortex in Figure 2.23 is out of proportion because it reflects the *dexterity* of body areas, not their size. The hands, for example, get more area than the feet (Figure 2.23). If you've ever wondered why your hands are more skilled or agile than your feet, it's partly because more motor cortex is devoted to the hands. Incidentally, due to neuroplasticity, learning and experience can alter these "motor maps." For instance, violin, viola, and cello players have larger "hand maps" in the cortex (Hashimoto et al., 2004).

Motor cortex is one brain area that contains **mirror neurons**. These are neurons that become active when we perform an action *and* when we merely observe someone else carrying out the same action. (For more information about mirror neurons, see "Mirror, Mirror in the Brain.")

The rest of the frontal lobes are often referred to as *frontal association areas*. Only a small portion of the cerebral cortex (the primary areas) directly controls the body or receives information from the senses. All the surrounding areas, which are called **association areas** (or **association cortex**), combine and process information. For example, if you see a rose, association areas will help you connect your primary sensory impressions with memories, so that you can recognize the rose and name it. Some association areas also contribute to higher mental abilities, such as language. For example, a person with damage to association areas in the left hemisphere may suffer **aphasia** (ah-FAZE-yah), an impaired ability to use language.

One type of aphasia is related to **Broca's** (BRO-cahs) **area**, a "speech center" that is part of the left frontal association area (for 5 percent of all people, the area is part of the right frontal association area). Damage to Broca's area causes *motor* (or *expressive*) *aphasia*, a great difficulty in speaking or writing (Grodzinsky & Santi, 2008). Generally, the person knows what she or he wants to say but can't seem to fluently utter the words (Burns & Fahy, 2010). Typically, a patient's

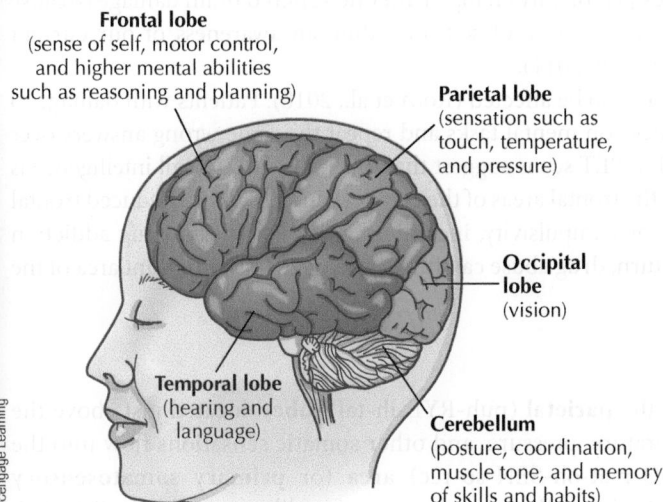

Frontal lobe
(sense of self, motor control, and higher mental abilities such as reasoning and planning)

Parietal lobe
(sensation such as touch, temperature, and pressure)

Occipital lobe
(vision)

Temporal lobe
(hearing and language)

Cerebellum
(posture, coordination, muscle tone, and memory of skills and habits)

Figure 2.22

Frontal lobes Areas of the cortex associated with movement, the sense of self, and higher mental functions.

Primary motor area (primary motor cortex) A brain area associated with control of movement.

Mirror neuron A neuron that becomes active when a motor action is carried out *and* when another organism is observed carrying out the same action.

Association areas (association cortex) All areas of the cerebral cortex that are not primarily sensory or motor in function.

Aphasia A speech disturbance resulting from brain damage.

Broca's area A language area related to grammar and pronunciation.

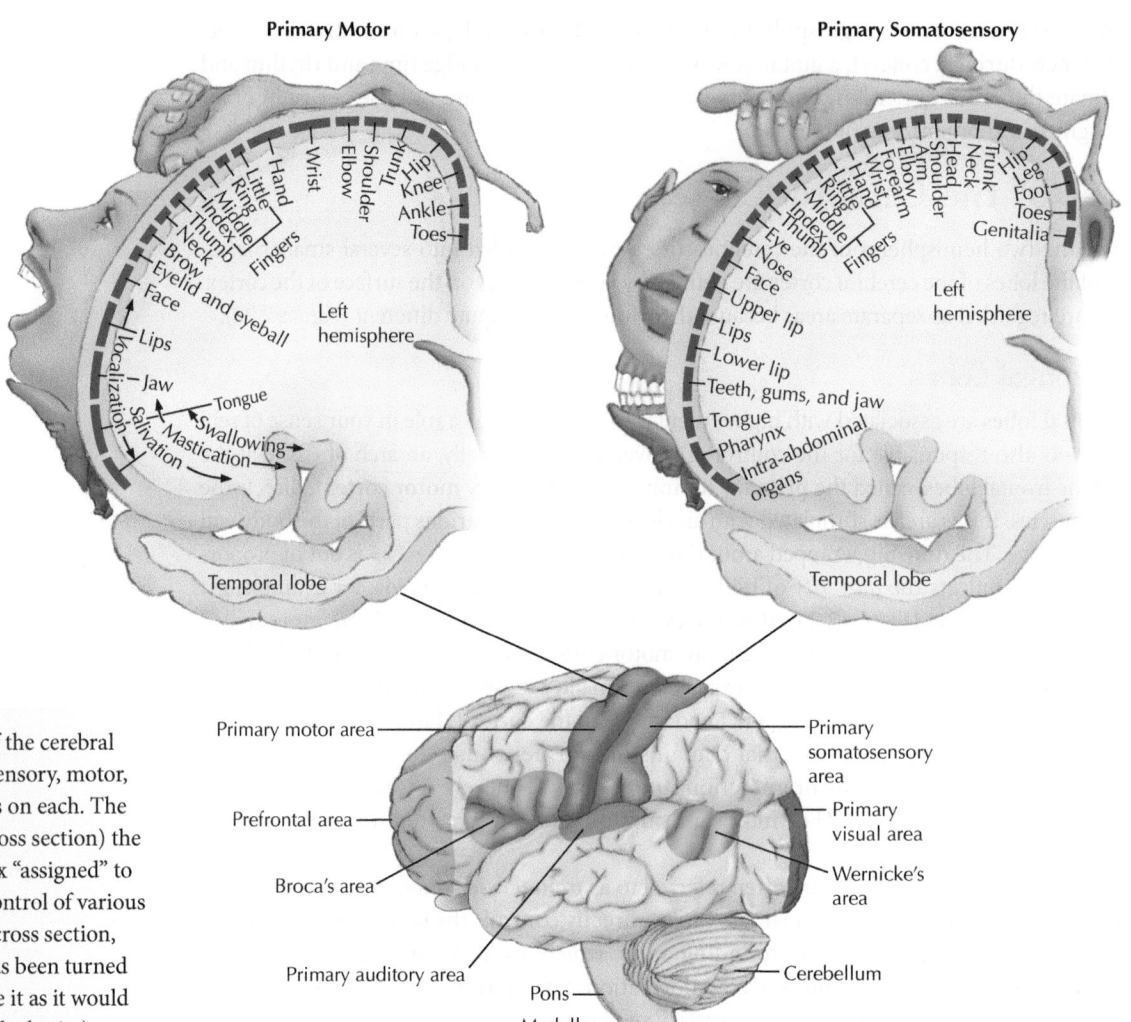

Primary Motor

Primary Somatosensory

Left hemisphere

Left hemisphere

Temporal lobe

Temporal lobe

Primary motor area
Prefrontal area
Broca's area
Primary auditory area
Pons
Medulla
Spinal cord
Primary somatosensory area
Primary visual area
Wernicke's area
Cerebellum

Figure 2.23 The lobes of the cerebral cortex and the primary sensory, motor, visual, and auditory areas on each. The top diagrams show (in cross section) the relative amounts of cortex "assigned" to the sensory and motor control of various parts of the body. (Each cross section, or "slice," of the cortex has been turned 90 degrees so that you see it as it would appear from the back of the brain.)

grammar and pronunciation are poor and speech is slow and labored. For example, the person may say "bife" for bike, "seep" for sleep, or "zokaid" for zodiac.

The very front of the frontal association region is known as the **prefrontal area** (or **prefrontal cortex**). This part of the brain is related to more complex behaviors (Banich & Compton, 2011). If the frontal lobes are damaged, a patient's personality and emotional life may change dramatically. Remember Phineas Gage, the railroad foreman described in Chapter 1? It's likely that Gage's personality changed after he suffered brain damage because the prefrontal cortex generates our sense of self, including an awareness of our current emotional state (Jenkins & Mitchell, 2011).

Reasoning or planning may also be affected (Roca et al., 2010). Patients with damage to the frontal lobes often get "stuck" on mental tasks and repeat the same wrong answers over and over (Stuss & Knight, 2002). PET scans suggest that much of what we call intelligence is related to increased activity in the frontal areas of the cortex (Duncan, 2005). Reduced frontal lobe function also leads to greater impulsivity, including increased risk for drug addiction (Crews & Boettiger, 2009). In turn, drug abuse can further damage this important area of the brain (Perry et al., 2011).

The Parietal Lobes

Bodily sensations register in the **parietal** (puh-RYE-ih-tal) **lobes**, located just above the occipital lobes. Touch, temperature, pressure, and other somatic sensations flow into the **primary somatosensory** (SO-mat-oh-SEN-so-ree) **area** (or **primary somatosensory cortex**) of the parietal lobes. Again we find that the map of bodily sensations is distorted.

Clinical File

Mirror, Mirror in the Brain

Italian researchers had just recorded an increase in the activity of a single neuron in the motor cortex of a monkey as it reached for food. A few seconds later, one of the researchers happened to reach for a snack of his own. The same neuron obligingly responded as if the monkey had reached for the food itself. Unexpectedly, a neuron involved in controlling a particular motor movement was also activated when the monkey merely observed that same motor movement in someone else. Just like that, the Italians discovered *mirror neurons* (Rizzolatti, Fogassi, & Gallese, 2006). Because they *mirror* actions performed by others, such neurons may explain how we can intuitively understand other people's behavior. They may also underlie our ability to learn new skills by imitation (Pineda, 2009; Rizzolatti & Craighero, 2004).

The discovery of mirror neurons has triggered a flood of interest. Recently, researchers have confirmed that mirror neurons are found in various areas of the brain and appear to exist in the human brain as well (Molenberghs, Cunnington, & Mattingley, 2012). In addition, neuroscientists speculate that newborn humans (and monkeys) are able to imitate others because networks of mirror neurons are activated when an infant watches someone perform an action. Then,

the same mirror network can be used to perform that action (Lepage & Théret, 2007). Similarly, human empathy (the ability to identify with another person's experiences and feelings) may arise from activation of mirror neurons (Baird, Scheffer, & Wilson, 2011).

Mirror neurons may even partially explain *autism spectrum disorders*. In early childhood, children with autism begin to suffer from an impaired ability to interact and communicate with other people. Restricted and repetitive behavior, such as head banging, is also common. According to the "broken mirrors" hypothesis, autism may arise in infants whose mirror neuron system has been damaged by genetic defects or environmental risk factors (Ramachandran & Oberman, 2006). This explanation is attractive because autism's primary features of impaired communication and social interaction appear to be related to the role that mirror neurons play in reflecting the actions and words of others.

To date, these are just hypotheses that await empirical confirmation. More importantly, such possibilities are only just now leading to proposals for new therapies for autism (Wan et al., 2010). Nevertheless, the possibilities are exciting.

Attila Kisbenedek/AFP/Getty Images

A chimpanzee imitates researcher Jane Goodall.

In the case of somatosensory cortex, the drawing in Figure 2.23 reflects the *sensitivity* of body areas, not their size. For example, the lips are large in the drawing because of their great sensitivity, whereas the back and trunk, which are less sensitive, are much smaller. Notice that the hands are also large in the map of body sensitivity—which is obviously an aid to musicians, typists, watchmakers, massage therapists, lovers, and brain surgeons.

The Temporal Lobes

The **temporal lobes** are located on each side of the brain. Auditory information projects directly to the **primary auditory area**, making it the main site where hearing first registers. If we did a PET scan of your brain while you listened to your favorite song, your primary auditory area would be the first to light up, followed by association areas in your temporal lobes. Likewise, if we could electrically stimulate the primary auditory area of your temporal lobe, you would "hear" a series of sound sensations.

A left temporal lobe association area called **Wernicke's** (VER-nick-ees) **area** also functions as a language site (see Figure 2.23; again, for 5 percent of all people, the area is on the right temporal lobe). If it is damaged, the result is a *receptive* (or *fluent*) *aphasia*. Although the person can hear speech, he or she has difficulty understanding the meaning of words. Thus, when shown a picture of a chair, someone with Broca's aphasia might say "tssair." In contrast, a Wernicke's patient might *fluently*, but incorrectly, identify the photo as "truck" (Tanner, 2007).

The Occipital Lobes

At the back of the brain, we find the **occipital** (awk-SIP-ih-tal) **lobes,** the area of cortex concerned with vision. Patients with tumors (cell growths that interfere with brain activity) in the **primary visual area**, the part of the cortex to first receive input from the eyes, experience blind spots in their vision.

Temporal lobes Areas of the cortex that include the sites in which hearing registers in the brain.

Primary auditory area Part of the temporal lobe in which auditory information is first registered.

Wernicke's area A temporal lobe brain area related to language comprehension.

Occipital lobes Portion of the cerebral cortex in which vision registers in the brain.

Primary visual area The part of the occipital lobe that first receives input from the eyes.

Human Diversity

Are men's and women's brains specialized in different ways? In a word, yes (Cahill, 2006). Many physical differences between male and female brains have been found, although their effects remain to be better understood. One generalization that may stand the test of time is that men's and women's brains may well be specialized in different ways to arrive at the same capabilities (Piefke et al., 2005; Zaidi, 2010).

For example, in one classic series of studies, researchers observed brain activity as people did language tasks. Both men and women showed increased activity in Broca's area, on the left side of the brain, exactly as expected. Surprisingly, however, the left *and* the right brain were activated in more than half the women tested (Shaywitz & Gore, 1995; **Figure 2.24**). Despite this difference, the two sexes performed equally well on a task that involved sounding out words (Shaywitz et al., 1995).

Another study, this time focused on intelligence, also found that women are more likely than men to use both sides of their brains (Tang et al., 2010). In a different study, brain images of men and women with similar IQ scores revealed major differences in brain areas involved in intelligence (Haier et al., 2004). In general, the men had more gray matter (neuron cell bodies), whereas the women had more white matter (axons coated in myelin). Further, the women had more gray and white matter concentrated in their frontal lobes than the men did. The men's gray matter was split between their frontal and parietal lobes, whereas their white matter was mostly in the temporal lobes.

Using both sides of the brain for language and other forms of intelligence may be a big advantage. For example, when Broca's area is damaged, some women can use the right side of their brains to compensate for the loss, which allows them to resume speaking (Sommer, 2010). A man with similar damage might be permanently impaired. Thus, when a man says, "I have half a mind to tell you what I think," he may be stating a curious truth. Regardless, it seems that nature has given the brains of men and women different routes to the same abilities.

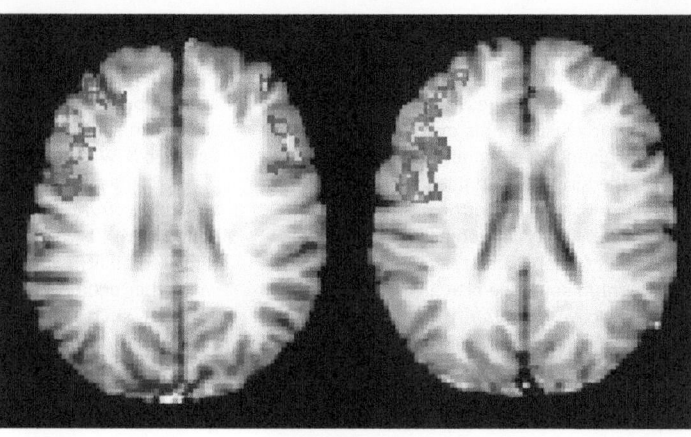

Figure 2.24 Language tasks activate both sides of the brain in many women but only the left side in men.

Do the primary visual areas of the cortex correspond directly to what is seen? Images are mapped onto the cortex, but the map is greatly stretched and distorted (Toates, 2011). That's why it's important to avoid thinking of the visual area as a little television screen in the brain. Visual information creates complex patterns of activity in neurons; it does *not* make a television-like image.

One of the most fascinating results of brain injury is **visual agnosia** (ag-KNOW-zyah), an inability to identify seen objects. Visual agnosia is often caused by damage to the association areas on the occipital lobes (Farah, 2004). This condition is sometimes referred to as "mindblindness." For example, if we show Alice, an agnosia patient, a candle, she can see it and can describe it as "a long narrow object that tapers at the top." Alice can even draw the candle accurately, but she cannot name it. However, if she is allowed to feel the candle, she will name it immediately. In short, Alice can still see color, size, and shape. She just can't form the associations necessary to perceive the meanings of objects.

Are agnosias limited to objects? No. A fascinating form of "mindblindness" is **facial agnosia**, an inability to perceive familiar faces (Farah, 2006; Sacks, 2010). One patient with facial agnosia couldn't recognize her husband or mother when they visited her in the hospital, and she was unable to identify pictures of her children. However, as soon as visitors spoke she knew them immediately by their voices.

Areas devoted to recognizing faces lie in association areas on the underside of the occipital lobes. These areas appear to have no other function. Why would part of the brain be set aside solely for identifying faces? From an evolutionary standpoint it is not really so surprising. After all, we are social animals, for whom facial recognition is very important. This specialization is just one example of what a marvelous organ of consciousness we possess.

How much do individual brains differ? Could we find different specializations from brain to brain? Perhaps. "His and Her Brains?" explains why.

Visual agnosia An inability to identify seen objects.

Facial agnosia An inability to perceive familiar faces.

In summary, the bulk of our daily experience and all of our understanding of the world can be traced to the different areas of the cortex. The human brain is among the most advanced and sophisticated of the brain-bearing species on earth. This, of course, is no guarantee that our marvelous "biocomputer" will be put to full use. Still, we must stand in awe of the potential it represents.

 study break Hemispheres and Lobes of the Cerebral Cortex

RECITE

See if you can match the following.

1. _____ Corpus callosum
2. _____ Occipital lobes
3. _____ Parietal lobes
4. _____ Temporal lobes
5. _____ Frontal lobes
6. _____ Association cortex
7. _____ Aphasias
8. _____ Corticalization
9. _____ Left hemisphere
10. _____ Right hemisphere
11. _____ "Split brain"
12. _____ Agnosia

A. Visual area
B. Language, speech, writing
C. Motor cortex and abstract thinking
D. Spatial skills, visualization, pattern recognition
E. Speech disturbances
F. Causes sleep
G. Increased ratio of cortex in brain
H. Bodily sensations
I. Treatment for severe epilepsy
J. Inability to identify seen objects
K. Fibers connecting the cerebral hemispheres
L. Cortex that is not sensory or motor in function
M. Hearing

REFLECT

THINK CRITICALLY

13. If your brain were removed, replaced by another, and moved to a new body, which would you consider to be yourself, your old body with the new brain, or your new body with the old brain?

SELF-REFLECT

Learning the functions of the brain lobes is like learning areas on a map. Try drawing a map of the cortex. Can you label all the different "countries" (lobes)? Can you name their functions? Where is the primary motor area? The primary somatosensory area? Broca's area? Keep redrawing the map until it becomes more detailed and you can do it easily.

ANSWERS

1. K 2. A 3. H 4. M 5. C 6. L 7. E 8. G 9. B 10. D 11. I 12. J 13. Although there is no "correct" answer to this question, your personality, knowledge, personal memories, and self-concept all derive from brain activity—which makes a strong case for your old brain in a new body being more nearly the "real you."

The Subcortex—At the Core of the (Brain) Matter

JOURNEY QUESTION 2.5 *What are the major parts of the subcortex?*

You could lose large portions of your cerebral cortex and still survive. Not so with the **subcortex**, the brain structures immediately below the cerebral cortex. Serious damage to the subcortex, or lower brain, can be fatal. Hunger, thirst, sleep, attention, sex, breathing, and many other vital functions are controlled by parts of the subcortex. Let's get a quick overview of these brain areas, which can be divided into the brainstem (or hindbrain), the midbrain, and the forebrain. (The forebrain also includes the cerebral cortex, which we discussed separately because of its size and importance.) For our purposes, the midbrain can be viewed as a link between the forebrain and the brainstem. Therefore, let's focus on the rest of the subcortex (**Figure 2.25**).

The Hindbrain

Why are the lower brain areas so important? As the spinal cord joins the brain, it widens into the brainstem. The **brainstem** consists mainly of the medulla (meh-DUL-ah) and the cerebellum (ser-ah-BEL-uhm). The **medulla** contains centers important for the reflex control of vital life functions, including heart rate, breathing, swallowing, and the like. Various drugs, diseases, and injuries can disrupt the medulla and end or endanger your life. You can also be left locked-in (see "Trapped!").

The **pons**, which looks like a small bump on the brainstem, acts as a bridge between the medulla and other brain areas. In addition to connecting with many other locations, including the cerebellum, the pons influences sleep and arousal.

Subcortex All brain structures below the cerebral cortex.

Brainstem The lowest portions of the brain, including the cerebellum, medulla, pons, and reticular formation.

Medulla The structure that connects the brain with the spinal cord and controls vital life functions.

Pons An area on the brainstem that acts as a bridge between the medulla and other structures.

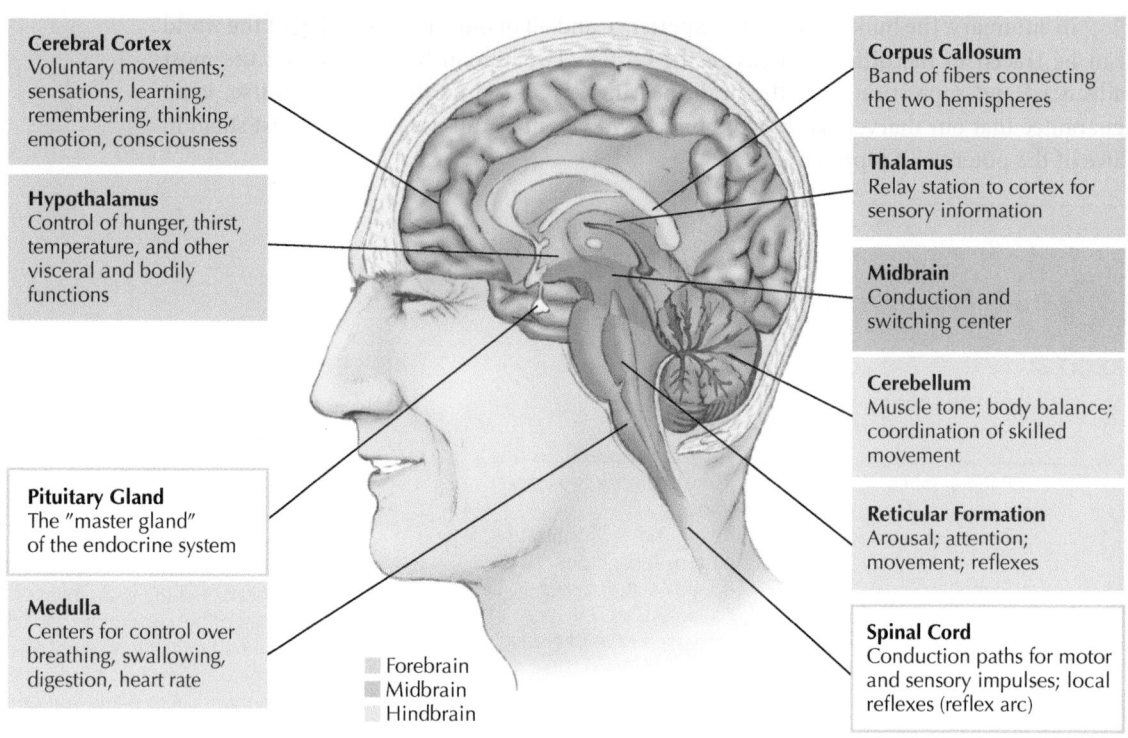

Cerebral Cortex
Voluntary movements; sensations, learning, remembering, thinking, emotion, consciousness

Hypothalamus
Control of hunger, thirst, temperature, and other visceral and bodily functions

Pituitary Gland
The "master gland" of the endocrine system

Medulla
Centers for control over breathing, swallowing, digestion, heart rate

Corpus Callosum
Band of fibers connecting the two hemispheres

Thalamus
Relay station to cortex for sensory information

Midbrain
Conduction and switching center

Cerebellum
Muscle tone; body balance; coordination of skilled movement

Reticular Formation
Arousal; attention; movement; reflexes

Spinal Cord
Conduction paths for motor and sensory impulses; local reflexes (reflex arc)

Forebrain
Midbrain
Hindbrain

Figure 2.25 This simplified drawing shows the main structures of the human brain and describes some of their most important features. (You can use the color code in the foreground to identify which areas are part of the forebrain, midbrain, and hindbrain.)

The cerebellum, which looks like a miniature cerebral cortex, lies at the base of the brain. Although there is growing evidence of a role in cognition and emotion (Schmahmann, 2010), the **cerebellum** primarily regulates posture, muscle tone, and muscular coordination. The cerebellum also stores memories related to skills and habits (Christian & Thompson, 2005). Again we see that experience shapes the brain: Musicians, who practice special motor skills throughout their lives, have larger than average cerebellums (Hutchinson et al., 2003).

What happens if the cerebellum is injured? Without the cerebellum, tasks like walking, running, or playing catch become impossible. The first symptoms of a crippling disease called *spinocerebellar degeneration* are tremor, dizziness, and muscular weakness. Eventually, victims have difficulty merely standing, walking, or feeding themselves.

Reticular Formation

A network of fibers and cell bodies called the **reticular** (reh-TICK-you-ler) **formation (RF)** lies inside the medulla and brainstem. As messages flow into the brain, the RF gives priority to some while turning others aside (Kalat, 2013). By doing so, the RF influences *attention*. The RF doesn't fully mature until adolescence, which may be why children have such short attention spans. The RF also modifies outgoing commands to the body. In this way the RF affects muscle tone, posture, and movements of the eyes, face, head, body, and limbs. At the same time, the RF controls reflexes involved in breathing, sneezing, coughing, and vomiting.

The RF also keeps us vigilant, alert, and awake. Incoming messages from the sense organs branch into a part of the RF called the **reticular activating system (RAS)**. The RAS bombards the cortex with stimulation, keeping it active and alert. For instance, let's say a sleepy driver rounds a bend and sees a deer standing in the road. The driver snaps to attention and applies the brakes. She can thank her RAS for arousing the rest of her brain and averting an accident. If you're getting sleepy while reading this chapter, try pinching your ear—a little pain will cause the RAS to momentarily arouse your cortex.

Cerebellum A brain structure that controls posture, muscle tone, and coordination.

Reticular formation (RF) A network within the medulla and brainstem; associated with attention, alertness, and some reflexes.

Reticular activating system (RAS) A part of the reticular formation that activates the cerebral cortex.

At the age of 33, Kate Adamson had a stroke that caused catastrophic damage to her brainstem. This event left her with *locked-in syndrome:* Just before the stroke she was fine, and the next moment she was totally paralyzed, trapped in her own body and barely able to breathe (Cruse et al., 2011). Unable to move a muscle, but still fully awake and aware, she was unable to communicate her simplest thoughts and feelings to others.

Kate thought she was going to die. Her doctors, who thought she was *brain dead*, did not administer painkillers as they inserted breathing and feeding tubes down her throat. However, in time Kate discovered that she could communicate by blinking her eyes. After a recovery that was miraculous by any measure, she went on to appear before the U.S. Congress and even wrote about her experiences (Adamson, 2004).

Not everyone is so lucky. Just think what might have befallen Kate had she not even been able to blink her eyes (Schnakers et al., 2009). In one chilling study, coma researcher Steven Laureys and his colleagues used fMRI to reexamine 54 patients previously diagnosed as being in a *persistent vegetative state* (brain dead). Patients were repeatedly asked to imagine swinging a tennis racquet or walking down a familiar street. Five of the patients showed clearly different brain activity to the two tasks despite being unable to communicate with doctors in any other way (Laureys & Boly, 2007).

What if they could "will" a computer to speak for them? Right on! These results suggest that not all totally locked-in patients are brain dead and hold out the hope that we may eventually be able to develop brain-computer interfaces to help free them from their bodily prisons (Karim et al., 2006; Monti et al., 2010; Shih & Krusienski, 2012).

The Forebrain

Like buried treasure, two of the most important parts of your body lie deep within your brain. The thalamus (THAL-uh-mus) and an area just below it called the hypothalamus (HI-po-THAL-uh-mus) are key parts of the forebrain (see Figure 2.25).

How could these be any more important than other areas already described? The **thalamus** acts as a final "switching station" for sensory messages on their way to the cortex. Vision, hearing, taste, and touch all pass through this small, football-shaped structure. Thus, injury to even small areas of the thalamus can cause deafness, blindness, or loss of any other sense, except smell.

The human hypothalamus is about the size of a small grape. Small as it may be, the **hypothalamus** is a kind of master control center for emotion and many basic motives (Toates, 2011). The hypothalamus affects behaviors as diverse as sex, rage, temperature control, hormone release, eating and drinking, sleep, waking, and emotion. The hypothalamus is basically a "crossroads" that connects many areas of the brain. It is also the final pathway for many kinds of behavior. That is, the hypothalamus is the last place where many behaviors are organized or "decided on" before messages leave the brain, causing the body to react.

The Limbic System

As a group, the hypothalamus, parts of the thalamus, the amygdala, the hippocampus, and other structures make up the limbic system (Figure 2.26). The **limbic system** has a major role in producing emotion and motivated behavior. Rage, fear, sexual response, and intense arousal can be localized to various points in the limbic system. Laughter, a delightful part of human social life, also has its origins in the limbic system (Cardoso, 2000).

During evolution, the limbic system was the earliest layer of the forebrain to develop. In lower animals, the limbic system helps organize basic survival responses: feeding, fleeing, fighting, and reproduction. In humans, a clear link to emotion remains. The **amygdala** (ah-MIG-dah-luh), in particular, is strongly related to fear (Amano et al., 2011).

The amygdala provides a primitive "quick pathway" to the cortex. Like lower animals, we can be startled and, as such, are able to react to dangerous stimuli before we fully know what is going on (Fellous & LeDoux, 2005). In situations in which true danger exists, such as in military combat, the amygdala's rapid response may aid survival. However, disorders of the brain's fear system can be very disruptive. An example is the war veteran who involuntarily dives into the bushes when he hears a car backfire. The role of the amygdala in emotion may also explain why people who suffer from phobias and disabling anxiety often feel afraid without knowing why (Lamprecht et al., 2009; Schlund & Cataldo, 2010).

Thalamus A brain structure that relays sensory information to the cerebral cortex.

Hypothalamus A small area of the brain that regulates emotional behaviors and motives.

Limbic system A system in the forebrain that is closely linked with emotional response.

Amygdala A part of the limbic system associated with fear responses.

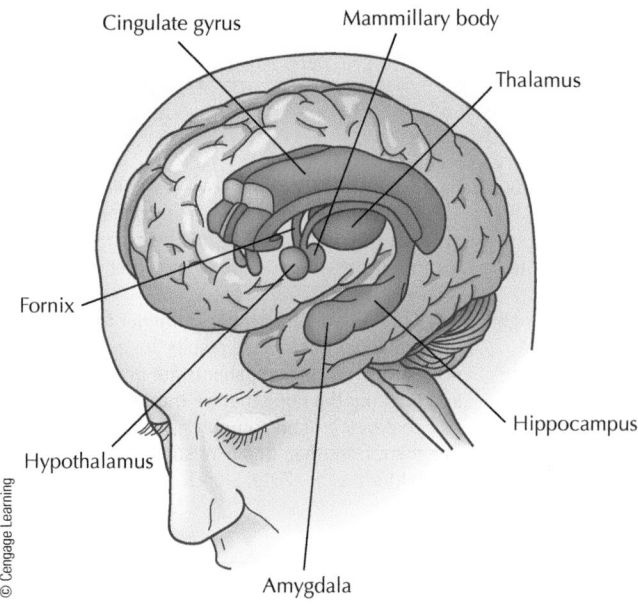

Cingulate gyrus

Mammillary body

Thalamus

Fornix

Hippocampus

Hypothalamus

Amygdala

© Cengage Learning

Figure 2.26 Parts of the limbic system. Although only one side is shown here, the hippocampus and the amygdala extend out into the temporal lobes at each side of the brain. The limbic system is a sort of "primitive core" of the brain strongly associated with emotion.

Some parts of the limbic system have taken on additional, higher-level functions. A part called the **hippocampus** (HIP-oh-CAMP-us) is important for forming lasting memories (Jurd, 2011). The hippocampus lies inside the temporal lobes, which is why stimulating the temporal lobes can produce memory-like or dream-like experiences. The hippocampus also helps us navigate through space. The right side of your hippocampus will become more active, for instance, if you mentally plan a drive across town (Aradillas, Libon, & Schwartzman, 2011).

Psychologists have discovered that animals will learn to press a lever to deliver a dose of electrical stimulation to the limbic system. The animals act like the stimulation is satisfying or pleasurable. Indeed, several areas of the limbic system act as reward, or "pleasure," pathways. Many are found in the hypothalamus, where they overlap with areas that control thirst, sex, and hunger. As we mentioned previously, commonly abused drugs, such as cocaine, amphetamine, heroin, nicotine, marijuana, and alcohol, activate many of the same pleasure pathways. This appears to be part of the reason these drugs are so rewarding (Niehaus, Cruz-Bermúdez, & Kauer, 2009).

You might also be interested to know that music you would describe as "thrilling" activates pleasure systems in your brain. This may explain some of the appeal of music that can send shivers down your spine (Salimpoor et al., 2011). (It may also explain why people will pay so much for concert tickets!)

Punishment, or "aversive," areas have also been found in the limbic system. When these locations are activated, animals show discomfort and will work hard to turn off the stimulation. Because much of our behavior is based on seeking pleasure and avoiding pain, these discoveries continue to fascinate psychologists.

The Whole Person

We have seen that the human brain is an impressive assembly of billions of sensitive cells and nerve fibers. The brain controls vital bodily functions, keeps track of the external world, issues commands to the muscles and glands, responds to current needs, regulates its own behavior, and even creates the "mind" and the magic of consciousness—*all* at the same time.

Two final notes of caution are now in order. First, for the sake of simplicity, we have assigned functions to each "part" of the brain as if it were a computer. This is only a half-truth. In reality, the brain is a vast information-processing system. Incoming information scatters all over the brain and converges again as it goes out through the spinal cord to muscles and glands. The overall system is much, much more complicated than our discussion of separate "parts" implies. Second, we have stressed how the brain underlies all human experience. Again, this is only a half-truth. Human experience also shapes the brain's circuits (Kolb & Whishaw, 2011). For example, as we have seen, practicing cultural knowledge, such as cab driving, mathematics, or music, will not only improve performance, it will also result in a changed brain (Merlin, 2008).

The Endocrine System—My Hormones Made Me Do It

JOURNEY QUESTION 2.6 *Does the glandular system affect behavior?*

Our behavior is not solely a product of the nervous system. The endocrine (EN-duh-krin) glands form an equally important parallel communication system in the body. The **endocrine system** is made up of glands that secrete chemicals directly into the bloodstream or

Hippocampus A part of the limbic system associated with storing memories.

Endocrine system Glands whose secretions pass directly into the bloodstream or lymph system.

lymph system (Figure 2.27). These chemicals, called **hormones**, are carried throughout the body, where they affect both internal activities and visible behavior. Hormones are related to neurotransmitters. Like other transmitter chemicals, hormones activate cells in the body. To respond, the cells must have receptor sites for the hormone. Hormones affect puberty, personality, dwarfism, jet lag, and much more.

How do hormones affect behavior? Although we are seldom directly aware of them, hormones affect us in many ways (Toates, 2011). Here is a brief sample: Hormone output from the adrenal glands rises during stressful situations; androgens ("male" hormones) are related to the sex drive in both males and females; hormones secreted during times of high emotion intensify memory formation; at least some of the emotional turmoil of adolescence is due to elevated hormone levels; different hormones prevail when you are angry rather than fearful. Pregnancy and motherhood cause the release of hormones that lead to the dramatic changes involved in maternal behavior (Beans, 2009). Even disturbing personality patterns may be linked to hormonal irregularities (Evardone, Alexander, & Morey, 2007). Because these are just samples, let's consider some additional effects hormones have on the body and behavior.

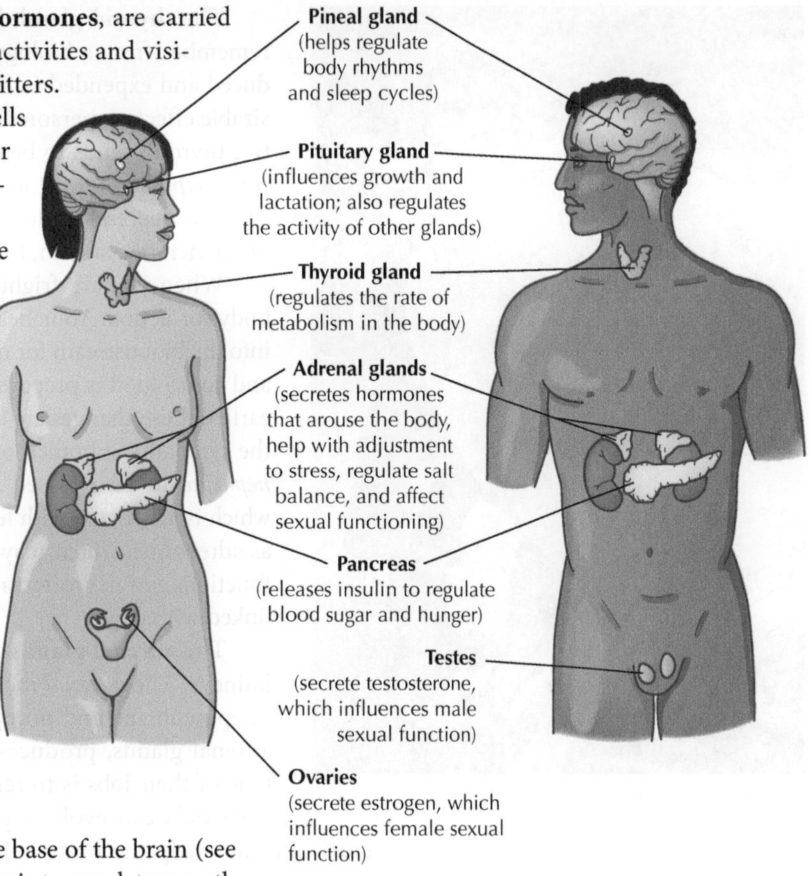

The **pituitary** is a pea-sized globe hanging from the base of the brain (see Figure 2.25). One of the pituitary's more important roles is to regulate growth (Beans, 2009). During childhood, the pituitary secretes a hormone that speeds body development. If too little **growth hormone** is released, a person may remain far smaller than average. If this condition is not treated, a child may be 6 to 12 inches shorter than age-mates. As adults, some will have *hypopituitary* (HI-po-pih-TU-ih-ter-ee) *dwarfism.* Such individuals are perfectly proportioned, but tiny. Regular injections of growth hormone can raise a hypopituitary child's height by several inches, usually to the short side of average.

Too much growth hormone produces *gigantism* (excessive bodily growth). Secretion of too much growth hormone late in the growth period causes *acromegaly* (AK-row-MEG-uh-lee), a condition in which the arms, hands, feet, and facial bones become enlarged. Acromegaly produces prominent facial features, which some people have used as a basis for careers as character actors, wrestlers, and the like.

Oxytocin, another important hormone released by the pituitary, plays a broad role in regulating many behaviors generally involved in happiness (Viero et al., 2010). These include pregnancy, parenthood, sexual activity, social bonding, trust, and even reducing stress reactions (Gordon et al., 2010; Kingsley & Lambert, 2006; Mikolajczak et al., 2010).

The pituitary is often called the "master gland" because it influences other endocrine glands (especially the thyroid, adrenal glands, and ovaries or testes). These glands in turn regulate such body processes as metabolism, responses to stress, and reproduction. But the master has a master: The pituitary is directed by the hypothalamus, which lies directly above it. In this way, the hypothalamus can affect glands throughout the body. This, then, is the major link between the brain and hormones (Kalat, 2013).

The **pineal** (pin-EE-ul) **gland** was once considered a useless remnant of evolution. In certain fishes, frogs, and lizards, the gland is associated with a well-developed light-sensitive organ, or so-called third eye. In humans, the function of the pineal gland is just now coming to light (so to speak). The pineal gland releases a hormone called **melatonin** (mel-ah-TONE-in) in response to daily variations in light. Melatonin levels in the bloodstream rise at dusk, peak around midnight, and fall again as morning approaches. As far as the brain is concerned, it's bedtime when melatonin levels rise (Norman, 2009).

Pineal gland (helps regulate body rhythms and sleep cycles)

Pituitary gland (influences growth and lactation; also regulates the activity of other glands)

Thyroid gland (regulates the rate of metabolism in the body)

Adrenal glands (secretes hormones that arouse the body, help with adjustment to stress, regulate salt balance, and affect sexual functioning)

Pancreas (releases insulin to regulate blood sugar and hunger)

Testes (secrete testosterone, which influences male sexual function)

Ovaries (secrete estrogen, which influences female sexual function)

© Cengage Learning

Figure 2.27 The endocrine system.

Hormone A glandular secretion that affects bodily functions or behavior.

Pituitary gland The "master gland" whose hormones influence other endocrine glands.

Growth hormone A hormone, secreted by the pituitary gland, that promotes body growth.

Oxytocin A hormone, released by the pituitary gland, that plays a broad role in regulating pregnancy, parenthood, sexual activity, social bonding, trust, and even reducing stress reaction.

Pineal gland Gland in the brain that helps regulate body rhythms and sleep cycles.

Melatonin Hormone released by the pineal gland in response to daily cycles of light and dark.

Not all little people have underactive pituitary glands. Peter Dinklage, who has won Emmy and Golden Globe awards for his brilliant role as the scheming Tyrion Lannister in the television series *Game of Thrones*, was born with *achondroplasia*. The most common cause of dwarfism, achondroplasia is a genetic disorder of bone development resulting in disproportionately short limbs.

Thyroid gland Endocrine gland that helps regulate the rate of metabolism.

Epinephrine An adrenal hormone that tends to arouse the body; epinephrine is associated with fear. (Also known as adrenaline.)

Norepinephrine Both a brain neurotransmitter and an adrenal hormone that tends to arouse the body; norepinephrine is associated with anger. (Also known as noradrenaline.)

Adrenal glands Endocrine glands that arouse the body, regulate salt balance, adjust the body to stress, and affect sexual functioning.

The **thyroid gland**, located in the neck, regulates metabolism. As you may remember from a biology course, *metabolism* is the rate at which energy is produced and expended in the body. By altering metabolism, the thyroid can have a sizable effect on personality. A person suffering from *hyperthyroidism* (an overactive thyroid) tends to be thin, tense, excitable, and nervous. An underactive thyroid *(hypothyroidism)* in an adult can cause inactivity, sleepiness, slowness, obesity, and depression (Joffe, 2006). In infancy, hypothyroidism limits development of the nervous system, leading to severe intellectual disability.

When you are frightened or angry, some important reactions prepare your body for action: Your heart rate and blood pressure rise; stored sugar is released into the bloodstream for quick energy; your muscles tense and receive more blood; and your blood is prepared to clot more quickly in case of injury. As we discussed earlier, these changes are controlled by the autonomic nervous system. Specifically, the sympathetic branch of the ANS causes the hormones *epinephrine* and *norepinephrine* to be released by the adrenal glands. **Epinephrine** (ep-eh-NEF-rin), which is associated with fear, tends to arouse the body. (Epinephrine is also known as adrenaline, which may be more familiar to you.) **Norepinephrine** (which also functions as a neurotransmitter in the brain) also tends to arouse the body, but it is linked with anger.

The **adrenal glands** are located just under the back of the rib cage, atop the kidneys. The *adrenal medulla*, or inner core of the adrenal glands, is the source of epinephrine and norepinephrine. The *adrenal cortex*, or outer "bark" of the adrenal glands, produces a set of hormones called *corticoids* (KOR-tih-coids). One of their jobs is to regulate salt balance in the body. A deficiency of certain corticoids can evoke a powerful craving for the taste of salt in humans. The corticoids also help the body adjust to stress, and they are a secondary source of sex hormones.

An oversecretion of the adrenal sex hormones can cause *virilism* (exaggerated male characteristics). For instance, a woman may grow a beard or a man's voice may become so low it is difficult to understand. Oversecretion early in life can cause *premature puberty* (full sexual development during childhood). One of the most remarkable cases on record is that of a 5-year-old Peruvian girl who gave birth to a son (Strange, 1965).

Since we are on the topic of sex hormones, there is a related issue worth mentioning. One of the principal androgens, or "male" hormones, is testosterone, which is supplied in small amounts by the adrenal glands. (The testes are the main source of testosterone in males.) Perhaps you have heard about the use of anabolic steroids by athletes who want to "bulk up" or promote muscle growth. Most of these drugs are synthetic versions of testosterone.

Although there is some disagreement about whether steroids actually improve athletic performance, it is widely accepted that they may cause serious side effects (Sjöqvist, Garle, & Rane, 2008). Problems include voice deepening or baldness in women and shrinkage of the testicles, sexual impotence, or breast enlargement in men (Millman & Ross, 2003). Dangerous increases in hostility and aggression ("roid rage") have also been linked with steroid use (Lumia & McGinnis, 2010). Increased risk of heart attack and stroke, liver damage, and stunted growth are also common when steroids are used by younger adolescents. Understandably, almost all major sports organizations ban the use of anabolic steroids.

In this brief discussion of the endocrine system, we have considered only a few of the more important glands. Nevertheless, this should give you an appreciation of how completely behavior and personality are tied to the ebb and flow of hormones in the body.

A Look Ahead

In the upcoming *Psychology in Action* section, we will return to the brain to see how hand preference relates to brain organization. You'll also find out if being right- or left-handed affects your chances of living to a ripe old age.

RECITE

1. Three major divisions of the brain are the brainstem or
   _____, the _____, and the
   _____.

2. Reflex centers for heartbeat and respiration are found in the
   a. cerebellum   *b.* thalamus   *c.* medulla   *d.* RF

3. A portion of the reticular formation, known as the RAS, serves as
   an _____ system in the brain.
   a. activating   *b.* adrenal
   c. adjustment   *d.* aversive

4. The _____ is a final relay, or "switching station," for
   sensory information on its way to the cortex.

5. "Reward" and "punishment" areas are found throughout the
   _____ system, which is also related to emotion.

6. Undersecretion from the thyroid can cause both _____ and
   _____.
   a. dwarfism   *b.* gigantism
   c. obesity   *d.* intellectual disability

7. The body's ability to resist stress is related to the action of the
   adrenal _____.

REFLECT

THINK CRITICALLY

8. Subcortical structures in humans are quite similar to corresponding
   lower brain areas in animals. Why would knowing this allow you to
   predict, in general terms, what functions are controlled by the
   subcortex?

SELF-REFLECT

What are the major subcortical structures and what functions do they
control?
Why is it especially important to understand the *limbic system* and the
role it plays in your emotional life?

ANSWERS

1. hindbrain, midbrain, forebrain 2. c 3. a 4. thalamus 5. limbic 6. c, d (in infancy) 7. cortex 8. Because the subcortex must be related to basic functions common to all higher animals: motives, emotions, sleep, attention, and vegetative functions, such as heartbeat, breathing, and temperature regulation. The subcortex also routes and processes incoming information from the senses and outgoing commands to the muscles.

Psychology in Action

Handedness—Are You Sinister or Dexterous?

JOURNEY QUESTION 2.7 *In what ways do right- and left-handed individuals differ?*

Throughout history, left-handedness has been frowned upon. "Lefties" have often been characterized as clumsy, awkward, unlucky, or insincere. The Latin word for left is actually *sinister*! In contrast, right-handedness is the paragon of virtue. The Latin word for right is *dexter,* and "righties" are more likely to be referred to as dexterous, coordinated, skillful, and just. But is there any basis in fact for these attitudes?

What causes **handedness** (a preference for the right or left hand)? Why are there more right-handed than left-handed people? How do left-handed and right-handed people differ? Does being left-handed create any problems—or benefits? The answers to these questions lead us back to the brain, where handedness begins. Let's see what research has revealed about handedness, the brain, and you.

Assessing Handedness

Write your name on a sheet of paper, first using your right hand and then your left. You were probably much more comfortable writing with your dominant hand. This is interesting because there's no real difference in the strength or dexterity of the hands themselves. The agility of your dominant hand is an outward expression of superior motor control on one side of the brain. If you are right-handed, there is literally more area on the left side of your brain devoted to controlling your right hand. If you are left-handed, the reverse applies.

The preceding exercise implies that you are either entirely right- or left-handed. But handedness is a matter of degree. To better assess your handedness, complete a few questions adapted from the Waterloo Handedness Questionnaire (Brown et al., 2006) by putting a check mark in the Right, Left, or Either column for each question. The more "Rights" you check, the more right-handed you are.

Handedness A preference for the right or left hand in most activities.

Are You Right- or Left-Handed?

	Right	Left	Either
1. With which hand would you hold a paintbrush to paint a wall?	_____	_____	_____
2. Which hand would you use to pick up a book?	_____	_____	_____
3. With which hand would you use a spoon to eat soup?	_____	_____	_____
4. Which hand would you use to flip pancakes?	_____	_____	_____
5. Which hand would you use to pick up a piece of paper?	_____	_____	_____
6. Which hand would you use to draw a picture?	_____	_____	_____
7. Which hand would you use to insert and turn a key in a lock?	_____	_____	_____
8. Which hand would you use to throw a ball?	_____	_____	_____

About 90 percent of all humans are right-handed; 10 percent are left-handed. Most people (about 75 percent) are strongly right- or left-handed (McManus et al., 2010). The rest show some inconsistency in hand preference. Which are you?

Is there such a thing as being left-footed? Excellent question. Do you have "two left feet"? *Sidedness* is often measured by assessing hand, foot, eye, *and* ear preference (Greenwood et al., 2006). We also generally prefer breathing through one nostril over the other and even have a preference for which direction we lean our head when kissing (van der Kamp & Cañal-Bruland, 2011). (Do you kiss "right"?) Nevertheless, handedness remains the single most important behavioral indicator of sidedness.

If a person is strongly left-handed, does that mean the right hemisphere is dominant? Not necessarily. It's true that the right hemisphere controls the left hand, but a left-handed person's language-producing, **dominant hemisphere** may still be on the left side of the brain.

Brain Dominance

About 95 percent of right-handers process speech in the left hemisphere and are left-brain dominant. A good 70 percent of left-handers produce speech from the left hemisphere, just as right-handed people do. About 19 percent of all lefties and 3 percent of righties use their right brain for language. Some left-handers (approximately 12 percent) use both sides of the brain for language processing. All told, more than 90 percent of the population uses the left brain for language (Coren, 1992; Szaflarski et al., 2011).

Is there any way for a person to tell which of his or her hemispheres is dominant? One clue is the way you write. Right-handed individuals who write with a straight hand, and lefties who write with a hooked hand, are more likely left-brain dominant for language. Left-handed people who write with their hand below the line, and righties who use a hooked position, are more likely right-brain dominant. Another hint is provided by hand gestures. If you gesture mostly with your right hand as you talk, you probably process language in your left hemisphere, and vice versa. Be aware, however, that writing position and gesture are not foolproof. The only sure ways to check brain dominance is to do tests that involve assessing one cerebral hemisphere at a time (Jones, Mahmoud, & Phillips, 2011; Kirveskari, Salmelin, & Hari, 2006).

Causes of Handedness

Is handedness inherited from parents? Yes, at least partly (Corballis, 2010a). Clear hand preferences are apparent even before birth, as can be seen in a fetal ultrasound image (**Figure 2.28**). According to British psychologist Peter Hepper, prenatal handedness

Dominant hemisphere A term usually applied to the side of a person's brain that produces language.

preferences persist for at least 10 years after birth (Hepper, Wells, & Lynch, 2005). This suggests that handedness cannot be dictated. Parents should not try to force a left-handed child to use his or her right hand. To do so may create speech or reading problems (Klöppel et al., 2010).

Studies of identical twins show that hand preferences are not directly inherited like eye color or skin color, however (Ooki, 2005; Reiss et al., 1999). Yet, two left-handed parents are more likely to have a left-handed child than two right-handed parents are (McKeever, 2000). The best evidence to date shows that left-handedness is more common in males and is influenced by a single gene on the X (female) chromosome (Papadatou-Pastou et al., 2008).

On the other hand, environmental factors such as learning, birth traumas, and social pressure to use the right hand can also affect which hand you end up favoring (Bailey & McKeever, 2004; Domellöf, Johansson, & Rönnqvist, 2011). In the past, many left-handed children were forced to use their right hand for writing, eating, and other skills. This is especially true in collectivist cultures like India and Japan, where left-handedness is viewed as especially negative. Not surprisingly, the proportion of left-handers in these societies is only about half that found in individualist cultures such as the United States and Canada (Ida & Mandal, 2003).

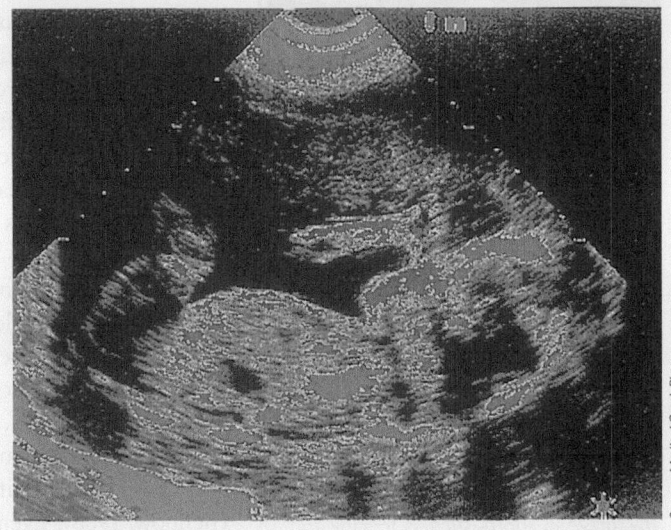

Figure 2.28 In this ultrasound image, a 4-month-old fetus sucks her right thumb. Research by British psychologist Peter Hepper suggests that she will continue to prefer her right hand long after she is born and that she will be right-handed as an adult.

Advantage Right

Are there any drawbacks to being left-handed? A small minority of lefties owe their hand preference to birth traumas (such as prematurity, low birth weight, and breech birth). These individuals have higher rates of allergies, learning disorders, and other problems (Betancur et al., 1990). Similarly, people with inconsistent handedness (as opposed to consistent left-handers) may be at risk for more immune-related diseases (Bryden, Bruyn, & Fletcher, 2005). (Inconsistent handedness means doing some things better with one hand and other things better with the other.)

Is it true that right-handed people live longer than left-handed people? It is true that there is a shortage of very old lefties. One possible explanation lies in the widespread finding that left-handers are more accident-prone (Dutta & Mandal, 2005). However, the supposed clumsiness of lefties may well be a result of living in a right-handed world. One study showed that left-handed locomotive engineers have higher accident rates and suggested that the cause was due to the design of locomotive controls (Bhushan & Khan, 2006). If it can be gripped, turned, or pulled, it's probably designed for the right hand. Even toilet handles are on the right side. On the other hand, the shortage of very old lefties may just reflect the fact that, in the past, more left-handed children were forced to become right-handed. That makes it look like many lefties don't survive to old age. In reality, they do, but many of them are masquerading as righties (Martin & Freitas, 2002)!

Advantage Left

Are there any advantages to being left-handed? Actually, there are some clear advantages to being left-handed (Faurie et al., 2008). Throughout history, a notable number of artists have been lefties, from Leonardo da Vinci and Michelangelo to Pablo Picasso and M. C. Escher. Conceivably, because the right hemisphere is superior at imagery and visual abilities, there is some advantage to using the left hand for drawing or painting (Wilkinson et al., 2009). At the least, lefties are definitely better at visualizing three-dimensional objects. This may be why there are more left-handed architects, artists, and chess players than would be expected (Coren, 1992). Similarly, being right-handed does not guarantee sports superiority. Left-handers have done well in a

Christopher Lee/Getty Images for Ricoh

Left-handers, such as 2011 French Open tennis champion Rafael Nadal, have an advantage in sports such as fencing and tennis. Most likely, their movements are less familiar to opponents, who usually face right-handers.

Lateralization Differences between the two sides of the body; especially, differences in the abilities of the brain hemispheres.

variety of professional sports including boxing, fencing, handball, and tennis (Coren, 1992; Dane & Erzurumluoglu, 2003; Holtzen, 2000).

Lateralization refers to specialization in the abilities of the brain hemispheres. One striking feature of lefties is that they are generally less lateralized than the right-handed. In fact, even the physical size and shape of their cerebral hemispheres are more alike. If you are a lefty, you can take pride in the fact that your brain is less lopsided than most! In general, left-handers are more symmetrical on almost everything, including eye dominance, fingerprints—even foot size (Bourne, 2008; Polemikos & Papaeliou, 2000).

In some situations, less lateralization may be a real advantage. For instance, individuals who are moderately left-handed or are ambidextrous (can do things equally well with both hands) seem to have better than average pitch memory, which is a basic musical skill. Correspondingly, more musicians are ambidextrous than would normally be expected (Springer & Deutsch, 1998).

Math abilities may also benefit from fuller use of the right hemisphere. Students who are extremely gifted in math are much more likely to be left-handed or ambidextrous (Benbow, 1986). Even when ordinary arithmetic skills are concerned, lefties seem to excel (Annett, 2002; Annett & Manning, 1990).

The clearest advantage of being left-handed shows up when there is a brain injury. Because of their milder lateralization, left-handed individuals typically experience less language loss after damage to either brain hemisphere, and they recover more easily (Geschwind, 1979). Maybe having "two left feet" isn't so bad after all.

study break Handedness and Brain Lateralization

RECITE

1. About 95 percent of left-handed people process language on the left side of the brain, the same as right-handed people do. T or F?
2. Left-handed individuals who write with their hand below the writing line are likely to be right-brain dominant. T or F?
3. People basically learn to be right- or left-handed. T or F?
4. In general, left-handed individuals show less lateralization in the brain and throughout the body. T or F?

REFLECT

THINK CRITICALLY

5. News reports that left-handed people tend to die younger have been flawed in an important way: The average age of people in the left-handed group was younger than that of participants in the right-handed group. Why would this make a difference in the conclusions drawn?

SELF-REFLECT

Think for a moment about what you "knew" about handedness and left-handed people before you read this section. Which of your beliefs were correct? How has your knowledge about handedness changed?

ANSWERS

1. F 2. T 3. F 4. T 5. Because we can't tell if handedness or average age accounts for the difference in death rates. For example, if we start with a group of 20- to 30-year-old people, in which some die, the average age of death has to be between 20 and 30. If we start with a group of 30- to 40-year-old people, in which some die, the average age of death has to be between 30 and 40. Thus, the left-handed group might have an earlier average age at death simply because members of the group were younger to start with.

Chapter in Review

Summary

2.1 What are the major divisions of the nervous system?

- 2.1.1 The nervous system can be divided into the central nervous system (CNS) and the peripheral nervous system (PNS). The CNS is made up of the brain, which carries out most of the "computing" in the nervous system, and the spinal cord, which connects the brain to the PNS.

- 2.1.2 The PNS, includes the somatic nervous system (SNS), which carries sensory information to the brain and motor commands to the body, and the autonomic nervous system (ANS), which controls "vegetative" and automatic bodily processes. The ANS has a sympathetic branch and a parasympathetic branch.

2.2 How do neurons operate and communicate?

- 2.2.1 The dendrite and soma of a neuron combine neural input and send it down the axon to the axon terminals for output across the synapse to other neurons.

- 2.2.2 The firing of an action potential (nerve impulse) is basically an electrical event.

- 2.2.3 Communication between neurons is chemical: Neurotransmitters cross the synapse, attach to receptor sites, and excite or inhibit the receiving cell.

- 2.2.4 Chemicals called neuropeptides regulate activity in the brain.

- 2.2.5 All behavior can be traced to networks of neurons. The spinal cord can process simple reflex arcs.

- 2.2.6 The brain's circuitry is not static. The brain can "rewire "itself and even grow new nerve cells in response to changing environmental conditions.

- 2.2.7 Neurons and nerves in the peripheral nervous system can often regenerate. At present, damage in the central nervous system is usually permanent, although scientists are working on ways to repair damaged neural tissue.

2.3 How are different parts of the brain identified and what do they do?

- 2.3.1 Biopsychologists study how processes in the body, brain, and nervous system relate to behavior.

- 2.3.2 A major brain research strategy involves the localization of function to link specific structures in the brain with specific psychological or behavioral functions.

- 2.3.3 Brain structure is investigated though dissection and less intrusive CT scans and MRI scans.

- 2.3.4 Brain function is investigated through clinical case studies, electrical stimulation, ablation, deep lesioning, electrical recording, and microelectrode recording, as well as less intrusive EEG recording, PET scans, and fMRI scans.

2.4 How do the left and right hemispheres differ and what are the different functions of the lobes of the cerebral cortex?

- 2.4.1 The human brain is marked not by overall size but by advanced corticalization, or enlargement of the cerebral cortex.

- 2.4.2 "Split brains" can be created by cutting the corpus callosum. The split-brain individual shows a remarkable degree of independence between the right and left hemispheres.

- 2.4.3 The left hemisphere is good at analysis and it processes small details sequentially. It contains speech or language "centers" in most people. It also specializes in writing, calculating, judging time and rhythm, and ordering complex movements.

- 2.4.4 The right hemisphere detects overall patterns; it processes information simultaneously and holistically. It is largely nonverbal and excels at spatial and perceptual skills, visualization, and recognition of patterns, faces, and melodies.

- 2.4.5 The frontal lobes contain the primary motor area (which includes many mirror neurons) and many association areas, which combine and process information. Damage to one association area—Broca's area—results in motor aphasia, a difficulty speaking or writing. The prefrontal cortex is related to abstract thought and one's sense of self.

- 2.4.6 The parietal lobes contain the primary sensory area, which processes bodily sensations.

- 2.4.7 The temporal lobes contain the primary auditory area and are responsible for hearing and language. Damage to Wernicke's area results in fluent aphasia, a difficulty understanding meanings of words.

- 2.4.8 The occipital lobes contain the primary visual area is responsible for vision.

- 2.4.9 Men's and women's brains are specialized in different ways.

2.5 What are the major parts of the subcortex?

- 2.5.1 The brain can be subdivided into the forebrain, midbrain, and hindbrain. The subcortex includes hindbrain and midbrain brain structures as well as the lower parts of the forebrain, below the cortex.

- 2.5.2 The medulla contains centers essential for reflex control of heart rate, breathing, and other "vegetative" functions. The pons links the medulla with other brain areas.

- 2.5.3 The cerebellum maintains coordination, posture, and muscle tone.

- 2.5.4 The reticular formation directs sensory and motor messages, and part of it, known as the RAS, acts as an activating system for the cerebral cortex.

- 2.5.5 The thalamus carries sensory information to the cortex.

- 2.5.6 The hypothalamus exerts powerful control over eating, drinking, sleep cycles, body temperature, and other basic motives and behaviors.

2.5.7 The limbic system is strongly related to emotion. It also contains distinct reward and punishment areas and an area known as the hippocampus that is important for forming memories.

2.6 Does the glandular system affect behavior?

- 2.6.1 Endocrine glands serve as a chemical communication system within the body. The ebb and flow of hormones from the endocrine glands entering the bloodstream affect behavior, moods, and personality.
- 2.6.2 Many of the endocrine glands are influenced by the pituitary (the "master gland"), which is in turn influenced by the hypothalamus. Thus, the brain controls the body through both the faster nervous system and the slower endocrine system.

2.7 In what ways do right- and left-handed individuals differ?

- 2.7.1 The vast majority of people are right-handed and therefore left-brain dominant for motor skills. More than 90 percent of right-handed persons and about 70 percent of the left-handed also produce speech from the left hemisphere.
- 2.7.2 Brain dominance and brain activity determine if you are right-handed, left-handed, or ambidextrous.
- 2.7.3 Most people are strongly right-handed. A minority are strongly left-handed. A few have moderate or mixed hand preferences or they are ambidextrous. Thus, handedness is not a simple either/or trait.
- 2.7.4 Left-handed people tend to be less strongly lateralized than right-handed people (their brain hemispheres are not as specialized).

Interactive Learning

Log in to CengageBrain to access the resources your instructor requires. For this book, you can access:

CourseMate Go to CengageBrain.com to access Psychology CourseMate, where you will find an interactive eBook, glossaries, flashcards, quizzes, videos, Virtual Psychology Labs, and more.

Aplia If your professor has assigned Aplia:

1. Sign in to your account.
2. Complete the corresponding exercises as required by your professor.
3. When finished, click "Grade It Now" to see which areas you have mastered, which areas need more work, and detailed explanations of every answer.

Test Your Knowledge

Brain and Behavior

1. Nerves are made up of bundles of
   a. dendrites   b. neurotransmitters
   c. synapses   d. axons

2. The somatic nervous system is part of the
   a. PNS   b. ANS
   c. sympathetic branch d. axon terminal

3. Quieting the body and returning it to a lower level of arousal after an emotional event is a specialty of the
   a. parasympathetic system   b. peripheral nervous system
   c. spinal nerves   d. effector cells

4. The point at which information is passed from one neuron to another links the
   a. neurilemma and myelin   b. soma and ion channels
   c. axon terminals and   d. enkephalin and myelin
      dendrites

5. Muscles are activated by a transmitter substance called
   a. neuropeptide   b. acetylcholine
   c. enkephalin   d. endorphin

6. The activity of neurons is regulated by _____, which affect memory, pain, moods, hunger, and other processes.
   a. neuropeptides   b. neurilemmas
   c. resting potentials d. dendrites

7. The brain grows new neurons to replace those that are lost. This process is known as
   a. neurogenesis   b. neurileminal regeneration
   c. autonomic regeneration   d. neuropeptosis

8. To record the electrical activity of a single neuron, you would need to use
   a. an EEG   b. ESB
   c. a microelectrode   d. surface ablation

9. Which research technique provides an image of ongoing brain activity?
   a. ESB   b. deep lesioning
   c. PET   d. surface ablation

10. Among animals and humans, greater corticalization is associated with increased
    a. muscular coordination   b. intelligence
    c. fight-or-flight responses d. conduction speed in the axon

11. In a "split-brain" operation, the _____ is cut, thereby separating the two cerebral _____.
    a. corpus callosum,   b. chiasm, medullas
       hemispheres
    c. motor cortex, lobes d. occipital region, reticulums

12. The left hemisphere of the brain processes information sequentially, and it is superior at
    a. recognizing patterns   b. holistic thinking
    c. expressing and detecting   d. analysis
       emotions

13. Damage to Broca's area causes
    a. a loss of coordination   b. disturbed sleep patterns
    c. aphasia   d. an inability to remember
                                    recent events

14. Impaired hearing could result from damage to the _____ lobes of the brain.
    a. frontal   b. temporal
    c. occipital   d. parietal

15. Structures in the brain that play a major role in producing emotion and motivating behavior are called the
    a. thalamic branch   b. cerebellar activating system
       of the RAS
    c. medial brainstem   d. limbic system

16. Which of the following parts of the brain is most involved in forming lasting memories?
    a. amygdala   b. hippocampus
    c. thalamus   d. hypothalamus

17. The endocrine gland that most influences the activities of other glands is the
    a. pituitary   b. adrenal
    c. pineal   d. thyroid

18. Dwarfism and gigantism can be caused by problems in the
    a. pituitary gland   b. adrenal glands
    c. pineal gland   d. thyroid gland

19. A majority of both right-handed and left-handed people produce speech from the
    a. right brain hemisphere   b. corpus callosum
    c. left brain hemisphere   d. hippocampus

20. One consistent finding about left-handed people is that they are
    a. less lateralized   b. more likely to die at an early age
    c. unable to use the right d. usually also ambidextrous
       brain to produce language

Answers   1. d 2. a 3. a 4. c 5. b 6. a 7. a 8. c 9. c 10. b 11. a 12. d 13. c 14. b 15. d 16. b 17. a 18. a 19. c 20. a

Human Development

Journey into Psychology: It's a Girl!

With those words, Carol catches her first glimpse of Samantha, her tiny newborn baby. Frankly, at the moment Samantha looks something like a prune, with pudgy arms, stubby legs, and lots of wrinkles. Yet she looks so perfect—at least in her parents' eyes. As Carol and her husband, David, look at Samantha, they wonder: How will her life unfold? What kind of a person will she be? Will Samantha be a happy teenager? Will she marry, become a mother, find an interesting career? David and Carol can only hope that by the time Samantha is 83, she will have lived a full and satisfying life.

What if we could skip ahead through Samantha's life and observe her at various ages? What could we learn? Seeing the world through her eyes would be fascinating and instructive. For example, a child's viewpoint can make us more aware of things we take for granted. Younger children, in particular, are very literal in their use of language. When Samantha was 3 years old, she thought her bath was too hot and said to David, "Make it warmer, Daddy." At first, David was confused. The bath was already fairly hot. But then he realized that what she really meant was, "Bring the water closer to the temperature we call *warm*." It makes perfect sense if you look at it that way.

Research tells a fascinating story about human growth and development. Let's let Carol, David, and Samantha represent parents and children everywhere, as we see what psychology can tell us about the challenges of growing up, maturing, aging, and facing death. Tracing Samantha's development might even help you answer two very important questions: "How did I become the person I am today?" and "Who will I become tomorrow?"

Journey Questions

3.1 How do heredity and environment affect development?

3.2 Of what significance is a child's emotional bond with adults?

3.3 How important are parenting styles?

3.4 How do children acquire language?

3.5 How do children learn to think?

3.6 Why is the transition from adolescence to adulthood especially challenging?

3.7 How do we develop morals and values?

3.8 What are the typical tasks and dilemmas through the life span?

3.9 What is involved in well-being during middle and later adulthood?

3.10 What factors contribute most to a happy and fulfilling life?

95

Nature and Nurture—It Takes Two to Tango

JOURNEY QUESTION 3.1 *How do heredity and environment affect development?*

When we think of development, we naturally think of children "growing up" into adults. But even as adults, we never really stop changing. **Developmental psychology**, the study of progressive changes in behavior and abilities, involves every stage of life from conception to death (or "the womb to the tomb"). Heredity and environment also affect us throughout our lifetimes. Some events, such as Samantha's achieving sexual maturity, are governed mostly by heredity. Others, such as Samantha's learning to swim, read, or drive a car, are matters primarily of environment.

But which is more important, heredity or environment? Actually, neither. Biopsychologist Donald Hebb once offered a useful analogy: To define the area of a rectangle, what is more important, height or width? Of course, both dimensions are absolutely essential. Without height *and* width, there is no rectangle. Similarly, if Samantha grows up to become a prominent civil rights lawyer, her success will be due to both heredity and environment.

Although heredity gives each of us a variety of potentials and limitations, these are, in turn, affected by environmental influences, such as learning, nutrition, disease, and culture. Ultimately, the person you are today reflects a continuous *interaction*, or interplay, between the forces of nature and nurture (Kalat, 2013). Let's look in more detail at this dance.

Heredity

Heredity ("nature") refers to the transmission of physical and psychological characteristics from parents to their children through genes. An incredible number of personal features are set at conception, when a sperm and an ovum (egg; *plural*, ova) unite.

How does heredity operate? The nucleus of every human cell contains **DNA, deoxyribonucleic acid** (dee-OX-see-RYE-bo-new-KLEE-ik). DNA is a long, ladder-like chain of pairs of chemical molecules (Figure 3.1). The order of these molecules, or organic bases, acts as a code for genetic information. The DNA in each cell contains a record of all the instructions needed to make a human—with room left over to spare. In 2003, a major scientific milestone was reached when the Human Genome Project completed sequencing all 3 billion chemical base pairs in human DNA (U.S. Department of Energy Office of Science, 2011).

Human DNA is organized into 46 **chromosomes**. (The word *chromosome* means "colored body.") These thread-like structures hold the coded instructions of heredity (Figure 3.2). Notable exceptions are sperm cells and ova, which contain only 23 chromosomes. Thus, Samantha received 23 chromosomes from Carol and 23 from David. This is her genetic heritage.

Genes are small segments of DNA that affect a particular process or personal characteristic. Sometimes, a single gene is responsible for an inherited feature, such as Samantha's eye color. Genes may be dominant or recessive. When a gene is **dominant**, the feature it controls will appear every time the gene is present. When a gene is **recessive**, it must be paired with a second recessive gene before its effect will be expressed. For example, if Samantha got a blue-eye gene from David and a brown-eye gene from Carol, Samantha will be brown eyed, because brown-eye genes are dominant.

If brown-eye genes are dominant, why do two brown-eyed parents sometimes have a blue-eyed child? If one or both parents have two brown-eye genes, the couple's children can only be brown eyed. But what if each parent has one brown-eye gene and one blue-eye gene? In that case, both parents would have brown eyes. Yet, there is one chance in four that their children will get two blue-eye genes and have blue eyes (Figure 3.3).

In actuality, few of our characteristics are controlled by single genes. Instead, most are **polygenic** (pol-ih-JEN-ik), or controlled by many genes working in combination. So, for example, there is no one "tall" or "short" gene; in fact, almost *two hundred* genes have

Twins who share identical genes (identical twins) demonstrate the powerful influence of heredity. Even when they are reared apart, identical twins are strikingly alike in motor skills, physical development, and appearance. At the same time, twins are less alike as adults than they were as children, which shows environmental influences are at work (Freberg, 2010; Larsson, Larsson, & Lichtenstein, 2004).

Developmental psychology The study of progressive changes in behavior and abilities from conception to death.

Heredity ("nature") The transmission of physical and psychological characteristics from parents to offspring through genes.

DNA (deoxyribonucleic acid) A molecular structure that contains coded genetic information.

Chromosomes Thread-like "colored bodies" in the nucleus of each cell that are made up of DNA.

Genes Specific areas on a strand of DNA that carry hereditary information.

Dominant gene A gene whose influence will be expressed each time the gene is present.

Recessive gene A gene whose influence will be expressed only when it is paired with a second recessive gene.

Polygenic characteristics Personal traits or physical properties that are influenced by many genes working in combination.

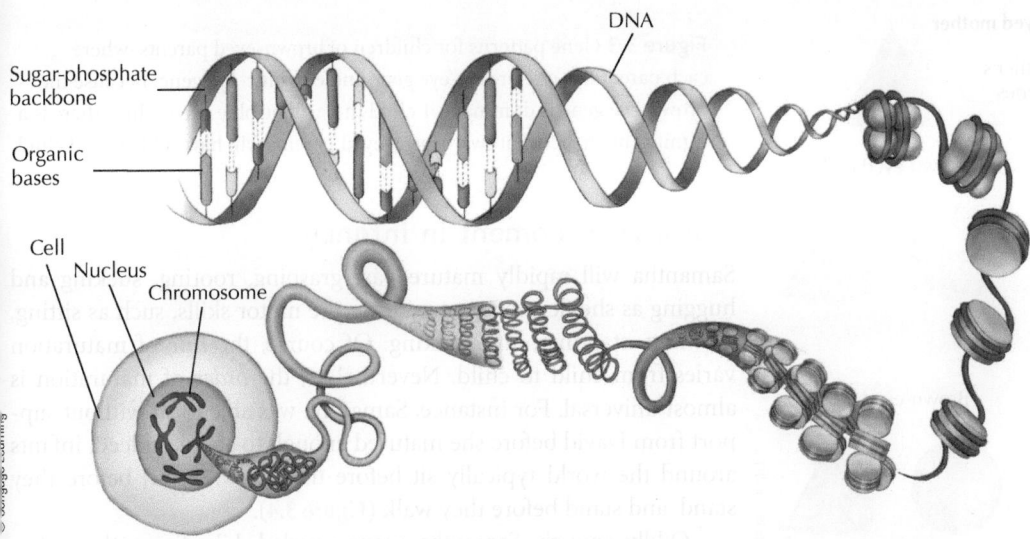

Sugar-phosphate backbone

Organic bases

DNA

Cell

Nucleus

Chromosome

Figure 3.1 *(Top left)* Linked molecules (organic bases) make up the "rungs" on DNA's twisted "molecular ladder." The order of these molecules serves as a code for genetic information. The code provides a genetic blueprint that is unique for each individual (except identical twins). The drawing shows only a small section of a DNA strand. An entire strand of DNA is composed of billions of smaller molecules. *(Bottom left)* The nucleus of each cell in the body contains chromosomes made up of tightly wound coils of DNA. (Don't be misled by the drawing: Chromosomes are microscopic, and the chemical molecules that make up DNA are even smaller.)

already been shown to play a role in determining height (Allen et al., 2010). Through the expression of genes, heredity determines eye color, skin color, and susceptibility to some diseases. Also, genes can switch on (or off) at certain ages or developmental stages. In this way, heredity continues to exert a powerful influence throughout **maturation**, the physical growth and development of the body, brain, and nervous system (Cummings, 2011). As the *human growth sequence* unfolds, genetic instructions influence body size and shape, height, intelligence, athletic potential, personality traits, sexual orientation, and a host of other details (**Table 3.1**).

Maturation in the Newborn

So human babies have already been "maturing" while in the womb? Don't be fooled. Even though human *neonates* (NEE-oh-NATE: newborn infant) will die if not cared for by adults, cannot lift their heads, turn over, or feed themselves, they are born with some basic survival skills and the capacity to continue to mature at breakneck speed.

For example, at birth Samantha has a number of adaptive infant reflexes (Siegler, DeLoache, & Eisenberg, 2011). To elicit the *grasping reflex*, press an object in a neonate's palm and she will grasp it with surprising strength. Many infants, in fact, can hang from a raised bar, like little trapeze artists. The grasping reflex aids survival by helping infants to avoid falling. You can observe the *rooting reflex* (reflexive head turning and nursing) by touching Samantha's cheek. Immediately, she will turn toward your finger, as if searching for something. The rooting reflex helps infants find a bottle or a breast. Then, when a nipple touches the infant's mouth, the *sucking reflex* (rhythmic nursing) helps her obtain needed food. Like other reflexes, this is a genetically programmed action.

The *Moro reflex* is also interesting. If Samantha's position is changed abruptly or if she is startled by a loud noise, she will make a hugging motion. This reaction has been compared to the movements baby monkeys use to cling to their mothers. (We leave it to the reader's imagination to decide if there is any connection.)

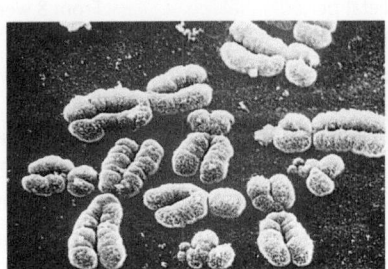

Figure 3.2 This image, made with a scanning electron microscope, shows several pairs of human chromosomes. (Colors are artificial.)

Maturation The physical growth and development of the body, brain, and nervous system.

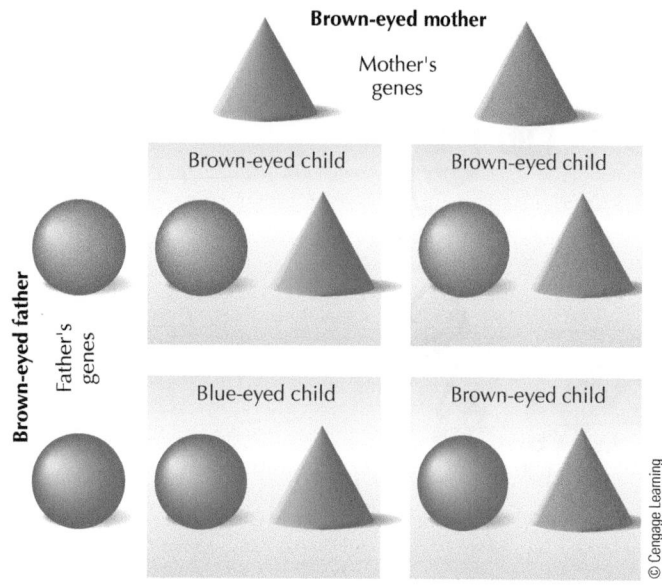

Brown-eyed mother

Mother's genes

Brown-eyed father
Father's genes

Brown-eyed child

Brown-eyed child

Blue-eyed child

Brown-eyed child

© Cengage Learning

Figure 3.3 Gene patterns for children of brown-eyed parents, where each parent has one brown-eye gene and one blue-eye gene. Because the brown-eye gene is dominant, 1 child in 4 will be blue eyed. Thus, there is a significant chance that two brown-eyed parents will have a blue-eyed child.

Motor Development in Infancy

Samantha will rapidly mature past grasping, rooting, sucking and hugging as she develops more and more motor skills, such as sitting, crawling, standing, and walking. Of course, the *rate* of maturation varies from child to child. Nevertheless, the *order* of maturation is almost universal. For instance, Samantha was able to sit without support from David before she matured enough to stand. Indeed, infants around the world typically sit before they crawl, crawl before they stand, and stand before they walk (**Figure 3.4**).

Oddly enough, Samantha never crawled. Like Samantha, a few children move directly from sitting to standing and walking. Even so, their motor development is orderly. In general, muscular control spreads in a pattern that is *cephalocaudal* (SEF-eh-lo-KOD-ul: from head to toe) and *proximodistal* (PROK-seh-moe-DIS-tul: from the center of the body to the extremities) (Piek, 2006).

Although maturation has a big impact, motor skills don't simply "emerge." Samantha must learn to control her actions. When babies are beginning to crawl or walk, they actively try new movements and select those that work. Samantha's first efforts may be flawed—wobbly sitting or some shaky first steps. However, with practice, babies "tune" their movements to be smoother and more effective. Such learning is evident from the very first months of life (Piek, 2006; see **Figure 3.5**).

Table 3.1 Human Growth Sequence

PERIOD	DURATION	DESCRIPTIVE NAME
PRENATAL PERIOD	From conception to birth	
Germinal period	First 2 weeks after conception	Zygote
Embryonic period	2–8 weeks after conception	Embryo
Fetal period	From 8 weeks after conception to birth	Fetus
NEONATAL PERIOD	From birth to a few weeks after birth	Neonate
INFANCY	From a few weeks after birth until child is walking securely; some children walk securely at less than a year, while others may not be able to until age 17–18 months	Infant
EARLY CHILDHOOD	From about 15–18 months until about 2–2½ years	Toddler
	From age 2–3 to about age 6	Preschool child
MIDDLE CHILDHOOD	From about age 6 to age 12	School-age child
PUBESCENCE	Period of about 2 years before puberty	
PUBERTY	Point of development at which biological changes of pubescence reach a climax marked by sexual maturity	
ADOLESCENCE	From the beginning of pubescence until full social maturity is reached (difficult to fix duration of this period)	Adolescent
ADULTHOOD	From adolescence to death; sometimes subdivided into other periods as shown at left	Adult
Young adulthood (18–34)		
Middle adulthood (35–64)		
Late adulthood or old age (65 plus)		
SENESCENCE	No defined limit that would apply to all people; extremely variable; characterized by marked physiological and psychological deterioration	Adult (senile), "old age"

*Note: There is no exact beginning or ending point for various growth periods. The ages are approximate, and each period may be thought of as blending into the next.
(Table courtesy of Tom Bond.)

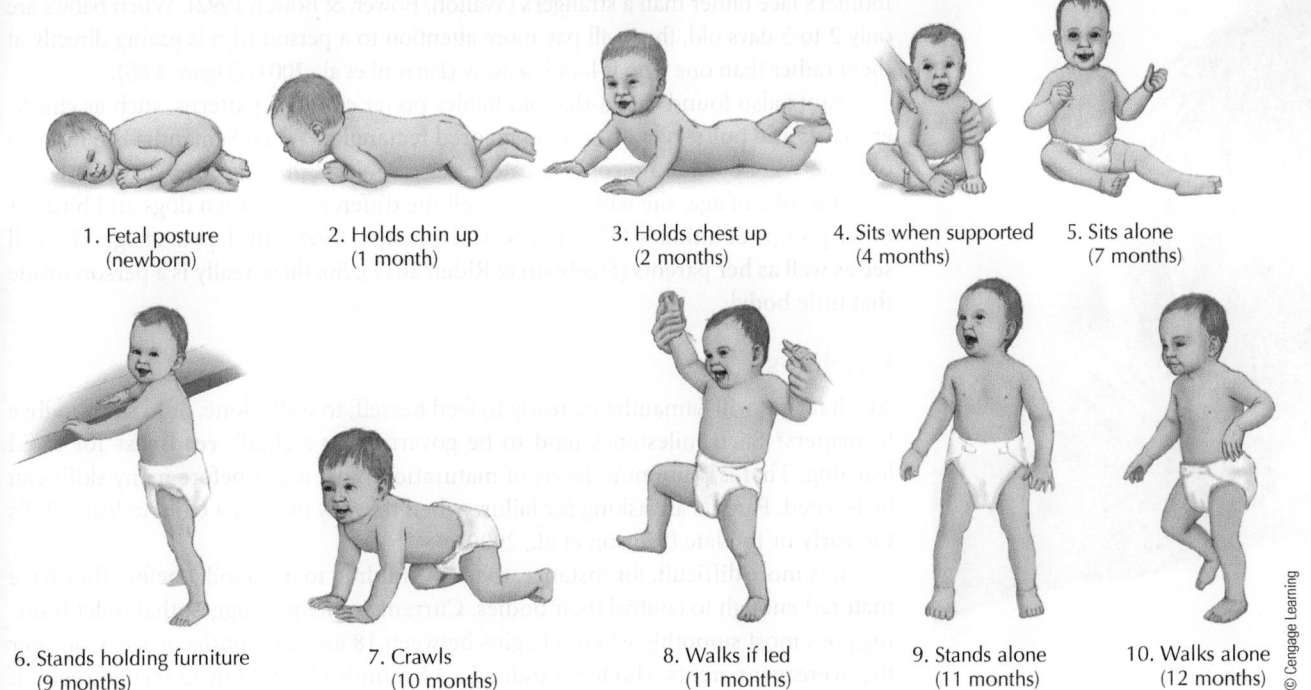

1. Fetal posture (newborn)
2. Holds chin up (1 month)
3. Holds chest up (2 months)
4. Sits when supported (4 months)
5. Sits alone (7 months)

6. Stands holding furniture (9 months)
7. Crawls (10 months)
8. Walks if led (11 months)
9. Stands alone (11 months)
10. Walks alone (12 months)

© Cengage Learning

Figure 3.4 Motor development. Most infants follow an orderly pattern of motor development. Although the order in which children progress is similar, there are large individual differences in the ages at which each ability appears. The ages listed are averages for American children. It is not unusual for many of the skills to appear 1 or 2 months earlier than average or several months later (Piek, 2006). Parents should not be alarmed if a child's behavior differs some from the average.

Sensory Development in Infancy

Contrary to common belief, newborn babies are not oblivious to their surroundings. Neonates can see, hear, smell, taste, and respond to pain and touch. Although their senses are less acute, babies are very responsive. From birth, Samantha could follow a moving object with her eyes and turn in the direction of sounds.

An interesting glimpse into world of infants comes from testing their vision. However, such testing is a challenge because infants cannot talk. Robert Fantz invented a device called a *looking chamber* to find out what infants can see and what holds their attention (**Figure 3.6a**). Imagine that Samantha is placed on her back inside the chamber, facing a lighted area above. Next, two objects are placed in the chamber. By observing the movements of Samantha's eyes and the images they reflect, we can tell what she is looking at.

Such tests show that neonate vision is not as sharp as that of adults; they can most clearly see objects about a foot away from them. It is as if they are best prepared to see the people who love and care for them (Gopnik, Meltzoff, & Kuhl, 2000; Leppänen, 2011). Perhaps that's why babies have a special fascination with human faces. Just *hours* after they are born, babies begin to prefer seeing their

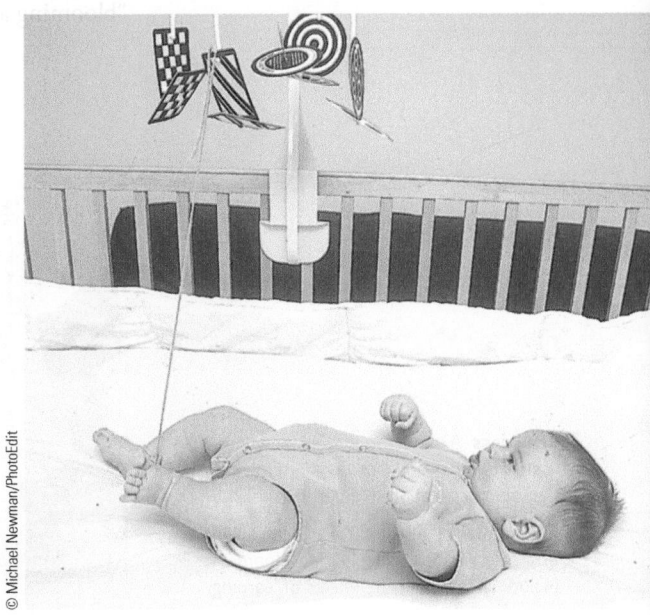

© Michael Newman/PhotoEdit

Figure 3.5 Psychologist Carolyn Rovee-Collier has shown that babies as young as 3 months old can learn to control their movements. In her experiments, babies lie on their backs under a colorful crib mobile. A ribbon is tied around the baby's ankle and connected to the mobile. Whenever babies spontaneously kick their legs, the mobile jiggles and rattles. Within a few minutes, infants learn to kick faster. Their reward for kicking is a chance to see the mobile move (Hayne & Rovee-Collier, 1995).

Newborn babies display a special interest in the human face. A preference for seeing their mother's face develops rapidly and encourages social interactions between mother and baby.

mother's face rather than a stranger's (Walton, Bower, & Bower, 1992). When babies are only 2 to 5 days old, they will pay more attention to a person who is gazing directly at them rather than one who is looking away (Farroni et al., 2004) (Figure 3.6*b*).

Fantz also found that 3-day-old babies prefer complex patterns, such as checkerboards and bull's-eyes, to simpler colored rectangles. When Samantha is 6 months old, she will be able to recognize categories of objects that differ in shape or color. By 9 months of age, she will be able to tell the difference between dogs and birds or other groups of animals (Mandler & McDonough, 1998). By 1 year of age, she will see as well as her parents (Sigelman & Rider, 2012). So, there really is a person inside that little body!

Readiness

At what ages will Samantha be ready to feed herself, to walk alone, or to say goodbye to diapers? Such milestones tend to be governed by a child's **readiness** for rapid learning. That is, minimum levels of maturation must occur before many skills can be learned. Parents are asking for failure when they try to force a child to learn skills too early or too late (Joinson et al., 2009).

It is more difficult, for instance, to teach children to use a toilet before they have matured enough to control their bodies. Current guidelines suggest that toilet training goes most smoothly when it begins between 18 and 24 months of age. Consider the overeager parents who toilet trained a 14-month-old child in 12 trying weeks of false alarms and "accidents." If they had waited until the child was 20 months old, they might have succeeded in just 3 weeks. Parents may control when toilet training starts, but maturation tends to dictate when it will be completed (Au & Stavinoha, 2008). On the other hand, parents who delay the onset of toilet training may fare no better. The older a child is before toilet training begins, the more likely he or she is to fail to develop full bladder control and become a daytime "wetter" (Joinson et al., 2009). So why fight nature?

Environment

Our environment also exerts a profound influence on our development. **Environment ("nurture")** refers to the sum of all external conditions that affect a person. For example, the brain of a newborn baby has fewer *dendrites* (nerve cell branches) and *synapses* (connections between nerve cells) than an adult brain. However, the newborn brain is highly *plastic* (capable of being altered by experience). During the first 3 years of life, millions of new connections form in the brain every day. At the same time, unused connections disappear. As a result, early learning environments literally shape the developing brain, through "blooming and pruning" of synapses (Nelson, 1999; Walker et al., 2011).

Readiness A condition that exists when maturation has advanced enough to allow the rapid acquisition of a particular skill.

Environment ("nurture") The sum of all external conditions affecting development, including especially the effects of learning.

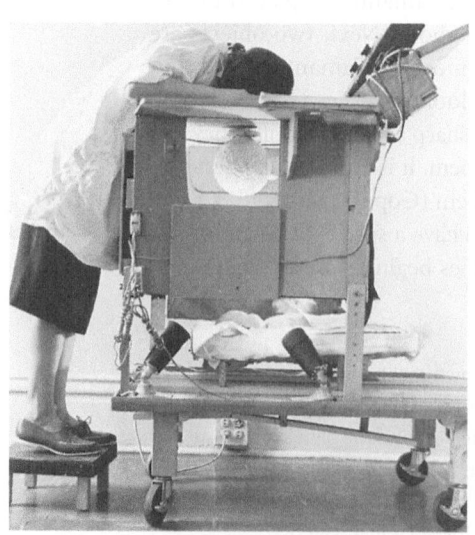

(b)

Figure 3.6 *(a)* Eye movements and fixation points of infants are observed in Fantz's "looking chamber." *(b)* When they are just days old, infants pay more attention to the faces of people who are gazing directly at them. (Photo *a* courtesy David Linton.)

(a)

Prenatal Influences

Environmental factors actually start influencing development before birth. Although the *intrauterine* environment (interior of the womb) is highly protected, environmental conditions can nevertheless affect the developing child. For example, when Carol was pregnant, Samantha's fetal heart rate and movements increased when loud sounds or vibrations penetrated the womb (Kisilevsky et al., 2004).

Had Carol experienced excess stress during her pregnancy, Samantha might have been a smaller, weaker baby at birth (Schetter, 2011). If Carol's health or nutrition had been poor or if she had had German measles, syphilis, or HIV, had used drugs, or had been exposed to X-rays or radiation, Samantha's growth sequence might have also have been harmed. In such cases, babies can suffer from **congenital problems**, or "birth defects." These environmental problems affect the developing fetus and become apparent at birth. In contrast, **genetic disorders** are inherited from parents. Examples are sickle-cell anemia, hemophilia, cystic fibrosis, muscular dystrophy, albinism, and some types of intellectual disability.

How is it possible for the embryo or the fetus to be harmed? No direct intermixing of blood takes place between a mother and her unborn child. Yet some substances—especially drugs—do reach the fetus. Anything capable of disturbing normal development in the womb is called a **teratogen** (teh-RAT-uh-jen). Sometimes women are exposed to powerful teratogens, such as radiation, lead, pesticides, or polychlorinated biphenyls (PCBs), without knowing it. But pregnant women do have direct control over many teratogens. For example, a woman who takes cocaine runs a serious risk of injuring her fetus (Dow-Edwards, 2011). In short, when a pregnant woman takes drugs, her unborn child does too.

Unfortunately, in the United States, drugs are one of the greatest risk factors facing unborn children (Coles & Black, 2006; Keegan et al., 2010). In fact, repeated heavy drinking during pregnancy is the most common cause of birth defects in the United States (Liles & Packman, 2009). Affected infants have *fetal alcohol syndrome (FAS)*, including low birth weight, a small head, bodily defects, and facial malformations. Many also suffer from emotional, behavioral, and mental disabilities (Golden, 2005; Jones & Streissguth, 2010).

If a mother is addicted to morphine, heroin, or methadone, her baby may be born with an addiction. Tobacco is also harmful. Smoking during pregnancy greatly reduces oxygen to the fetus. Heavy smokers risk miscarrying or having premature, underweight babies who are more likely to die soon after birth. Children of smoking mothers score lower on tests of language and mental ability (Huijbregts et al., 2006). In other words, an unborn child's future can go "up in smoke." That goes for smoking marijuana as well (Goldschmidt et al., 2011).

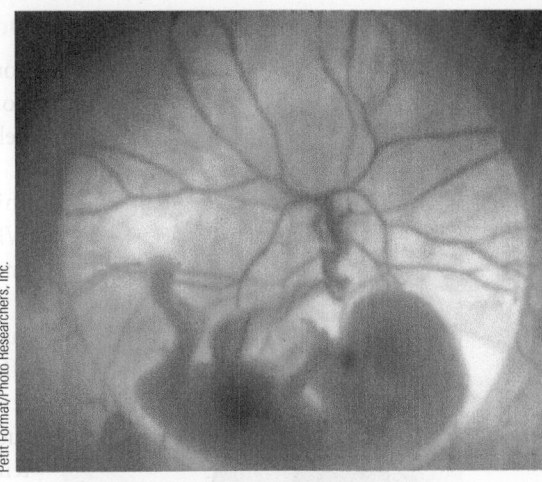

An 11-week-old fetus. Because of the rapid growth of basic structures, the developing fetus is sensitive to a variety of diseases, drugs, and sources of radiation. This is especially true during the first trimester (3 months) of gestation (pregnancy).

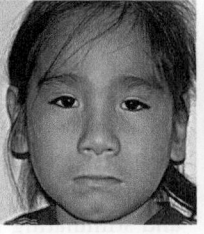 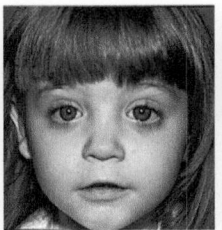 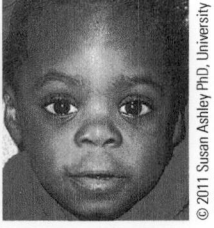

Some of the typical features of children suffering from fetal alcohol syndrome (FAS) include a small nonsymmetrical head, a short nose, a flattened area between the eyes, oddly shaped eyes, and a thin upper lip. Many of these features become less noticeable by adolescence. However, intellectual disability and other problems commonly follow the FAS child into adulthood. The children shown here represent moderate examples of FAS.

Sensitive Periods

Early experiences can have particularly lasting effects. For example, children who are abused may suffer lifelong emotional problems (Goodwin, Fergusson, & Horwood, 2005). At the same time, extra care can sometimes reverse the effects of a poor start in life (Bornstein & Tamis-LeMonda, 2001; Walker et al., 2011). In short, environmental forces guide human development, for better or worse, throughout life.

Why do some experiences have more lasting effects than others? Part of the answer lies in **sensitive periods**. These are times when children are more susceptible to particular types of environmental influences. Events that occur during a sensitive period can permanently alter the course of development (Michel & Tyler, 2005). For example, forming a loving bond with a caregiver early in life seems to be crucial for optimal development. Likewise, babies who don't hear normal speech during their first year may have impaired language abilities (Thompson & Nelson, 2001).

Congenital problems Problems or defects that originate during prenatal development in the womb.

Genetic disorders Problems caused by defects in the genes or by inherited characteristics.

Teratogen Anything capable of altering fetal development in noninheritable ways that cause birth defects.

Sensitive period During development, a period of increased sensitivity to environmental influences. Also, a time during which certain events must take place for normal development to occur.

Children who grow up in poverty run a high risk of experiencing many forms of deprivation. There is evidence that lasting damage to social, emotional, and cognitive development occurs when children must cope with severe early deprivation.

Deprivation and Enrichment

Some environments can be described as *deprived* or *enriched*. **Deprivation** refers to a lack of normal nutrition, stimulation, comfort, or love. **Enrichment** exists when an environment is deliberately made more stimulating, loving, and so forth.

What happens when children suffer severe deprivation? Tragically, a few mistreated children have spent their first years in closets, attics, and other restricted environments. When first discovered, these children are usually mute, intellectually disabled, and emotionally damaged (Wilson, 2003). Fortunately, such extreme deprivation is unusual.

Nevertheless, milder perceptual, intellectual, or emotional deprivation occurs in many families, especially those that must cope with poverty (Matthews & Gallo, 2011). Poverty can affect the development of children in at least two ways (Huston & Bentley, 2010; Sobolewski & Amato, 2005). First, poor parents may not be able to give their children needed resources such as nutritious meals, health care, or learning materials. As a result, impoverished children tend to be sick more often, their mental development lags, and they do poorly at school. Second, the stresses of poverty can also be hard on parents, leading to marriage problems, less positive parenting, and poorer parent-child relationships. The resulting emotional turmoil can damage a child's socioemotional development. In the extreme, it may increase the risk of mental illness and delinquent behavior.

Adults who grew up in poverty often remain trapped in a vicious cycle of continued poverty. Because over 45,000,000 Americans fell below the poverty line in 2010, this grim reality plays itself out in millions of American homes every day (U.S. Census Bureau, 2011).

Can an improved environment enhance development? To answer this question, psychologists have created *enriched environments* that are especially novel, complex, and stimulating. Enriched environments may be the "soil" from which brighter children grow. To illustrate, let's consider the effects of raising rats in a sort of "rat wonderland." The walls of their cages were decorated with colorful patterns, and each cage was filled with platforms, ladders, and cubbyholes. As adults, these rats were superior at learning mazes. In addition, they had larger, heavier brains, with a thicker cortex (Benloucif, Bennett, & Rosenzweig, 1995). Of course, it's a long leap from rats to people, but an actual increase in brain size is impressive. If extra stimulation can enhance the "intelligence" of a lowly rat, it's likely that human infants also benefit from enrichment. Many studies have shown that enriched environments improve abilities or enhance development (Phillips & Lowenstein, 2011). It would be wise for David and Carol to make a point of nourishing Samantha's mind as well as her body (Beeber et al., 2007).

What can parents do to enrich a child's environment? They can encourage exploration and stimulating play by paying attention to what holds the baby's interest. It is better to "child-proof" a house than to strictly limit what a child can touch. There is also value in actively enriching sensory experiences. Infants are not vegetables. Babies should be surrounded by colors, music, people, and things to see, taste, smell, and touch. It makes perfect sense to take them outside, to hang mobiles over their cribs, to place mirrors nearby, to play music for them, or to rearrange their rooms now and then. Children progress most rapidly when they have responsive parents and stimulating play materials at home (Beeber et al., 2007). In light of this, it is wise to view all of childhood as a *relatively sensitive period* (Nelson, 1999; Walker et al., 2011).

The Whole Human

Nurture often affects the expression of hereditary tendencies through ongoing reciprocal influences. A good example of such influences is the fact that growing infants influence their parents' behavior at the same time they are changed by it.

Newborn babies differ noticeably in **temperament**. This is the inherited, physical core of personality. It includes sensitivity, irritability, distractibility, and typical mood (Kagan, 2004). About 40 percent of all newborns are *easy children* who are relaxed and agreeable. Ten percent are *difficult children* who are moody, intense, and easily angered. *Slow-to-warm-up children* (about 15 percent) are restrained, unexpressive, or shy. The remaining children do not fit neatly into a single category (Chess & Thomas, 1986).

Deprivation In development, the loss or withholding of normal stimulation, nutrition, comfort, love, and so forth; a condition of lacking.

Enrichment In development, deliberately making an environment more stimulating, nutritional, comforting, loving, and so forth.

Temperament The physical core of personality, including emotional and perceptual sensitivity, energy levels, typical mood, and so forth.

Because of differences in temperament, some babies are more likely than others to smile, cry, vocalize, reach out, or pay attention. As a result, babies rapidly become active participants in their own development. For example, Samantha is an easy baby who smiles frequently and is easily fed. This encourages Carol to touch, feed, and sing to Samantha. Carol's affection rewards Samantha, causing her to smile more. Soon, a dynamic relationship blossoms between mother and child. Similarly, good parenting can reciprocally influence a very shy child who, in turn, becomes progressively less shy.

The reverse also occurs: Difficult children may make parents unhappy and elicit more negative parenting (Parke, 2004). Alternatively, negative parenting can turn a moderately shy child into a very shy one. This suggests that inherited temperaments are dynamically modified by learning (Bridgett et al., 2009; Kiff, Lengua, & Bush, 2011).

A person's **developmental level** is his or her current state of physical, emotional, and intellectual development. To summarize, three factors combine to determine your developmental level at any stage of life. These are *heredity, environment,* and your *own behavior,* each tightly interwoven with the others.

 study break The Interplay of Heredity and Environment

RECITE

1. Areas of the DNA molecule called *genes* are made up of dominant and recessive chromosomes. T or F?
2. Most inherited characteristics can be described as polygenic. T or F?
3. The orderly sequence observed in the unfolding of many basic responses can be attributed to _____
4. If an infant is startled, he or she will make movements similar to an embrace. This is known as the

    a. grasping reflex   *b.* rooting reflex
    c. Moro reflex   *d.* adaptive reflex

5. During infancy, a capacity for imitating others as they watch them first becomes evident at about 9 months of age. T or F?
6. A _____ _____ is a time of increased sensitivity to environmental influences.
7. As a child develops, there is a continuous _____ between the forces of heredity and environment.

REFLECT

THINK CRITICALLY

8. Environmental influences can interact with genetic programming in an exceedingly direct way. Can you guess what it is?

SELF-REFLECT

Can you think of clear examples of some ways in which heredity and environmental forces have combined to affect your development?

How would maturation affect the chances of teaching an infant to eat with a spoon?

What kind of temperament did you have as an infant? How did it affect your relationship with your parents or caregivers?

ANSWERS

1. F 2. T 3. maturation 4. c 5. F 6. sensitive period 7. Interaction or interplay 8. Environmental conditions sometimes turn specific genes on or off, thus directly affecting the expression of genetic tendencies (Keller, 2010; Lickliter & Honeycutt, 2010).

Emotional and Social Development in Infancy—Baby, I'm Stuck on You

JOURNEY QUESTION 3.2 *Of what significance is a child's emotional bond with adults?*

With dazzling speed, human infants are transformed from helpless babies to independent persons. Samantha will begin to develop relationships with her primary caretakers almost immediately. By her second year, she will show the full range of basic human emotions. By her third year, she will have a unique personality. During the same period, Samantha's relationships with other people will expand as well.

Developmental level An individual's current state of physical, emotional, and intellectual development.

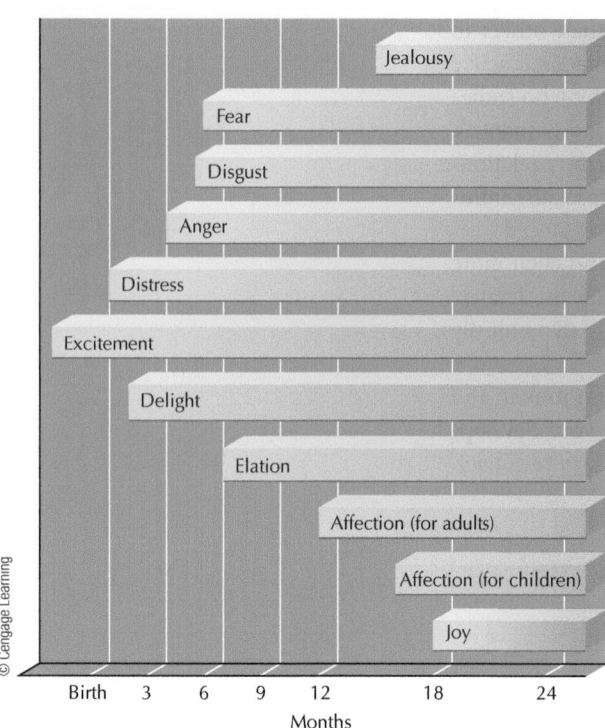

Jealousy

Fear

Disgust

Anger

Distress

Excitement

Delight

Elation

Affection (for adults)

Affection (for children)

Joy

Birth 3 6 9 12 18 24

Months

© Cengage Learning

Figure 3.7 The traditional view of infancy holds that emotions are rapidly differentiated from an initial capacity for excitement. (After K. M. B. Bridges, 1932. Reprinted by permission of the Society for Research in Child Development, Inc.)

Emotional Development in Infancy

Although experts do not yet agree on exactly how quickly emotions unfold (Oster, 2005), early emotional development also follows a pattern closely tied to maturation (Music, 2011; Panksepp & Pasqualini, 2005). Even the basic emotions of *anger*, *fear*, and *joy*—which appear to be unlearned—take time to develop. General *excitement* is the only emotion newborn infants clearly express. However, as David and Carol can tell you, a baby's emotional life blossoms rapidly. One researcher (Bridges, 1932) observed that all the basic human emotions appear before age 2. Bridges found that emotions appear in a consistent order and that the first basic split is between pleasant and unpleasant emotions (Figure 3.7).

Psychologist Carroll Izard thinks that infants can express several basic emotions as early as 10 weeks of age. When Izard looks carefully at the faces of babies, he sees abundant signs of emotion (Izard, Woodburn, & Finlon, 2010). The most common infant expression, he found, is not excitement, but *interest*—followed by *joy*, *anger*, and *sadness* (Izard et al., 1995).

If Izard is right, then emotions are "hardwired" by heredity and related to evolution. Perhaps that's why smiling is one of a baby's most common reactions. Smiling probably helps babies survive by inviting parents to care for them (Izard et al., 1995).

At first, a baby's smiling is haphazard. By the age of 8 to 12 months, however, infants smile more frequently when another person is nearby (Jones & Hong, 2001; Mcquaid, Bibok, & Carpendale, 2009). This **social smile** is especially rewarding to parents. Infants can even use their social smile to communicate interest in an object, like the time Samantha smiled when her mother held up her favorite teddy bear (Venezia et al., 2004). On the other hand, when new parents see and hear a crying baby, they feel annoyed, irritated, disturbed, or unhappy. Babies the world over, it seems, rapidly become capable of letting others know what they like and dislike. (Prove this to yourself sometime by driving a baby buggy.)

Social Development in Infancy

Like all humans, babies are social creatures. They rapidly begin to form **emotional attachments**, or close emotional bonds, with their primary caregivers (Music, 2011). As infants form their first emotional bond with an adult, usually a parent, they also begin to develop self-awareness and to become aware of others. This early **social development** lays a foundation for subsequent relationships with parents, siblings, friends, and relatives (Shaffer & Kipp, 2010).

To investigate mother–infant relationships, Harry Harlow separated baby rhesus monkeys from their mothers at birth. The real mothers were replaced with **surrogate** (substitute) **mothers**. Some were made of cold, unyielding wire. Others were covered with soft terry cloth (Figure 3.8).

When the infants were given a choice between the two mothers, they spent most of their time clinging to the cuddly terry-cloth mother. This was true even when the wire mother held a bottle, making her the source of food. The "love" and attachment displayed toward the cloth replicas was identical to that shown toward natural mothers. For example, when frightened by rubber snakes, wind-up toys, and other "fear stimuli," the infant monkeys ran to their cloth mothers and clung to them for security.

These classic studies suggest that attachment begins with **contact comfort**, the pleasant, reassuring feeling infants get from touching something soft and warm, especially their mother. There is a sensitive period (roughly the first year of life) during which this must

Social smile Smiling elicited by social stimuli, such as seeing a parent's face.

Emotional attachment An especially close emotional bond that infants form with their parents, caregivers, or others.

Social development The development of self-awareness, attachment to parents or caregivers, and relationships with other children and adults.

Surrogate mother A substitute mother (often an inanimate dummy in animal research).

Contact comfort A pleasant and reassuring feeling human and animal infants get from touching or clinging to something soft and warm, usually their mother.

occur for optimal development. Returning to Samantha's story, we find that attachment keeps her close to Carol, who provides safety, stimulation, and a secure "home base" from which Samantha can go exploring.

Mothers usually begin to feel attached to their baby before birth. For their part, as babies mature, they become more and more capable of bonding with their mothers. For the first few months, babies respond more or less equally to everyone. By 2 or 3 months, most babies prefer their mothers to strangers. By around 7 months, babies generally become truly attached to their mothers, crawling after them if they can. Shortly thereafter they begin to form attachments to other people as well, such as their father, grandparents, or siblings (Sigelman & Rider, 2012).

A direct sign that an emotional bond has formed appears around 8 to 12 months of age. At that time Samantha will display **separation anxiety** (crying and signs of fear) when she is left alone or with a stranger. Mild separation anxiety is normal. When it is more intense, it may reveal a problem. At some point in their lives, about 1 in 20 children suffer from *separation anxiety disorder* (Dick-Niederhauser & Silverman, 2006). These children are miserable when they are separated from their parents, whom they cling to or constantly follow. Some fear that they will get lost and never see their parents again. Many refuse to go to school, which can be a serious handicap. Children tend to grow out of the disorder (Kearney et al., 2003), but if separation anxiety is intense or lasts for more than a month, parents should seek professional help for their child (Allen et al., 2010).

Figure 3.8 An infant monkey clings to a cloth-covered surrogate mother. Baby monkeys become attached to the cloth "contact-comfort" mother but not to a similar wire mother. This is true even when the wire mother provides food. Contact comfort may also underlie the tendency of children to become attached to inanimate objects, such as blankets or stuffed toys.

Attachment Quality

According to psychologist Mary Ainsworth (1913–1999), the quality of attachment is revealed by how babies act when their mothers return after a brief separation. Infants who are **securely attached** have a stable and positive emotional bond. They are upset by the mother's absence and seek to be near her when she returns. **Insecure-avoidant** infants have an anxious emotional bond. They tend to turn away from the mother when she returns. **Insecure-ambivalent** attachment is also an anxious emotional bond. In this case, babies have mixed feelings: They both seek to be near the returning mother and angrily resist contact with her (**Figure 3.9**).

Attachment can have lasting effects (Bohlin & Hagekull, 2009; Morley & Moran, 2011). Infants who are securely attached at the age of 1 year show resiliency, curiosity, problem-solving ability, and social skills in preschool (Collins & Gunnar, 1990). In contrast, attachment failures can be quite damaging (Santelices et al., 2011). Consider, for example, the plight of children raised in severely overcrowded orphanages (Wilson, 2003). These children get almost no attention from adults for the first year or two of their lives. Once adopted, many are poorly attached to their new parents. Some, for instance, will wander off with strangers, are anxious and remote, and don't like to be touched or to make eye contact with others (O'Conner et al., 2003). In short, for some children, a lack of affectionate care early in life leaves a lasting emotional impact well into adulthood (see "What's Your Attachment Style?").

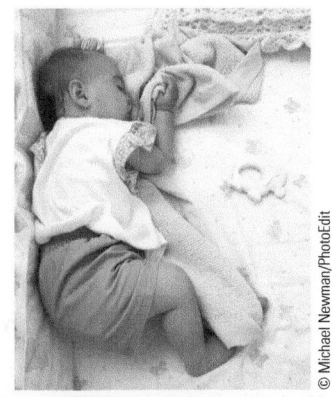

Most parents are familiar with the storm of crying that sometimes occurs when babies are left alone at bedtime. Bedtime distress can be a mild form of separation anxiety. As many parents know, it is often eased by the presence of "security objects," such as a stuffed animal or favorite blanket (Donate-Bartfield & Passman, 2004).

Promoting Secure Attachment

One key to secure attachment is a mother who is accepting and sensitive to her baby's signals and rhythms. Poor attachment occurs when a mother's actions are inappropriate, inadequate, intrusive, overstimulating, or rejecting. An example is a mother who tries to play with a drowsy infant or who ignores a baby who is looking at her and vocalizing. The link between sensitive caregiving and secure attachment appears to apply to all cultures (Posada et al., 2002; Santelices et al., 2011).

What about attachment to fathers? Fathers of securely attached infants tend to be outgoing, agreeable, and happy in their marriage. In general, a warm family atmosphere—one that includes sensitive mothering *and* fathering—produces secure children (Gomez & McLaren, 2007; Mattanah, Lopez, & Govern, 2011).

Separation anxiety Distress displayed by infants when they are separated from their parents or principal caregivers.

Secure attachment A stable and positive emotional bond.

Insecure-avoidant attachment An anxious emotional bond marked by a tendency to avoid reunion with a parent or caregiver.

Insecure-ambivalent attachment An anxious emotional bond marked by both a desire to be with a parent or caregiver and some resistance to being reunited.

Discovering Psychology

Do our first attachments continue to affect us as adults? Some psychologists believe they do, by influencing how we relate to friends and lovers (Bohlin & Hagekull, 2009; Sroufe et al., 2005). Read the following statements and see which best describes your adult relationships.

Secure Attachment Style

In general, I think most other people are well intentioned and trustworthy.

I find it relatively easy to get close to others.

I am comfortable relying on others and having others depend on me.

I don't worry much about being abandoned by others.

I am comfortable when other people want to get close to me emotionally.

Avoidant Attachment Style

I tend to pull back when things don't go well in a relationship.

I am somewhat skeptical about the idea of true love.

I have difficulty trusting my partner in a romantic relationship.

Other people tend to be too eager to seek commitment from me.

I get a little nervous if anyone gets too close emotionally.

Ambivalent Attachment Style

I have often felt misunderstood and unappreciated in my romantic relationships.

My friends and lovers have been somewhat unreliable.

I love my romantic partner but I worry that she or he doesn't really love me.

I would like to be closer to my romantic partner, but I'm not sure I trust her or him.

Do any of the preceding statements sound familiar? If so, they may describe your adult attachment style (Welch & Houser, 2010). Most adults have a secure attachment style that is marked by caring, supportiveness, and understanding. However, it's not unusual to have an avoidant attachment style that reflects a tendency to resist intimacy and commitment to others (Collins et al., 2002). An ambivalent attachment style is marked by mixed feelings about love and friendship (DeWall et al., 2011). Do you see any similarities between your present relationships and your attachment experiences as a child?

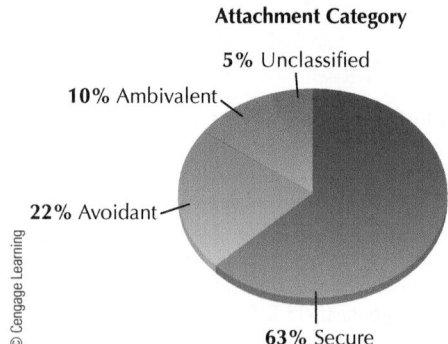

Attachment Category

5% Unclassified
10% Ambivalent
22% Avoidant
63% Secure

© Cengage Learning

Figure 3.9 In the United States, about two thirds of all children from middle-class families are securely attached. About 1 child in 3 is insecurely attached. (Percentages are approximate.) (From Kaplan, 1998.)

Affectional needs Emotional needs for love and affection.

Day Care

Does commercial day care interfere with the quality of attachment? It depends on the quality of day care. Overall, *high-quality* day care does not adversely affect attachment to parents. In fact, high-quality day care can actually improve children's social and mental skills (Mercer, 2006; National Institute of Child Health and Human Development, 2010a). Children in high-quality day care tend to have better relationships with their mothers and fewer behavior problems. They also have better cognitive skills and language abilities (Burchinal et al., 2000; Vandell, 2004).

However, all the positive effects just noted are *reversed* for low-quality day care. Low-quality day care *is* risky and *may* weaken attachment (Phillips & Lowenstein, 2011). Poor-quality day care can even create behavior problems that didn't exist beforehand (Pierrehumbert et al., 2002). Parents are wise to carefully evaluate and monitor the quality of day care their children receive.

What should parents look for when they evaluate the quality of child care? Parents seeking quality day care should look for responsive and sensitive caregivers who offer plenty of attention and verbal and cognitive stimulation (Phillips & Lowenstein, 2011). This is more likely to occur in daycares with *at least* the following: (1) a small number of children per caregiver, (2) small overall group size (12 to 15), (3) trained caregivers, (4) minimal staff turnover, and (5) stable, consistent care. (Also, avoid any child-care center with the words *zoo, menagerie,* or *stockade* in its name.)

Attachment and Affectional Needs

A baby's **affectional needs** (needs for love and affection) are every bit as important as more obvious needs for food, water, and physical care. All things considered, creating a bond of trust and affection between the infant and at least one other person is a key event during the first year of life. Parents are sometimes afraid of "spoiling" babies with too much attention, but for the first year or two this is nearly impossible. In fact, a later capacity to experience warm and loving relationships may depend on it.

Parental Influences—Life with Mom and Dad

JOURNEY QUESTION 3.3 *How important are parenting styles?*

From the first few years of life, when caregivers are the center of a child's world, through to adulthood, the style and quality of mothering and fathering are very important.

Parenting Styles

Psychologist Diana Baumrind (1991, 2005) has studied the effects of three major **parental styles**, which are identifiable patterns of parental caretaking and interaction with children. See if you recognize the styles she describes.

Authoritarian parents enforce rigid rules and demand strict obedience to authority. Typically they view children as having few rights but adult-like responsibilities. The child is expected to stay out of trouble and to accept, without question, what parents regard as right or wrong ("Do it because I say so"). Authoritarian parents tend to discipline their children through **power assertion**—physical punishment or a show of force, such as taking away toys or privileges. Power-oriented techniques—particularly harsh or severe physical punishment— are associated with fear, hatred of parents, and a lack of spontaneity and warmth (Hergenhahn & Olson, 2009).

As an alternative, authoritarian parents may use **withdrawal of love**, or withholding affection, by refusing to speak to a child, threatening to leave, rejecting the child, or otherwise acting as if the child is temporarily unlovable. The children of authoritarian parents are usually obe- dient and self-controlled. But they also tend to be emotionally stiff, withdrawn, apprehensive, lacking in curiosity, and dependent on adults for approval. They can also develop low *self-esteem*. If you regard yourself as a worthwhile person, you have **self-esteem**. Low self- esteem is related to physical punishment and the withholding of love. And why not? What message do children receive if a parent beats them or tells them they are not worthy of love?

"*Your father and I have come to believe that incarceration is sometimes the only appropriate punishment.*"

Overly permissive parents give little guidance, allow too much freedom, or don't hold children accountable for their actions. Typically, the child has rights similar to an adult's but few responsibilities. Rules are not enforced, and the child usually gets his or her way ("Do whatever you want"). Permissive parents tend to produce dependent, immature children who misbehave frequently. Such children are aimless and likely to "run amok."

Some overly permissive parents genuinely wish to "empower" their children by imposing few limits on their behavior, making them feel special, and giving them everything they want (Mamen, 2004). But such good intentions can backfire, leaving parents with children who have developed an artificially high level of self-esteem and a sense of entitlement. That is, overly "empowered" offspring are often spoiled, self-indulgent, and lack self-control (Crocker & Park, 2004).

Baumrind describes **authoritative parents** as those who supply firm and consistent guidance, combined with love and affection. Such parents balance their own rights with those of their children. They control their children's behavior through **management tech- niques**, which combine praise, recognition, approval, rules, reasoning, and the like to encourage desirable behavior. Effective parents are firm and consistent, not harsh or rigid. In general, they encourage the child to act responsibly, to think, and to make good deci- sions. This style produces children who are *resilient* (good at bouncing back after bad experiences) and develop the strengths they need to thrive even in difficult circumstances

Parental styles Identifiable patterns of parental caretaking and interaction with children.

Authoritarian parents Parents who enforce rigid rules and demand strict obedience to authority.

Power assertion The use of physical punishment or coercion to enforce child discipline.

Withdrawal of love Withholding affection to enforce child discipline.

Self-esteem Regarding oneself as a worthwhile person; a positive evaluation of oneself.

Overly permissive parents Parents who give little guidance, allow too much freedom, or do not require the child to take responsibility.

Authoritative parents Parents who supply firm and consistent guidance combined with love and affection.

Management techniques Combining praise, recognition, approval, rules, and reasoning to enforce child discipline.

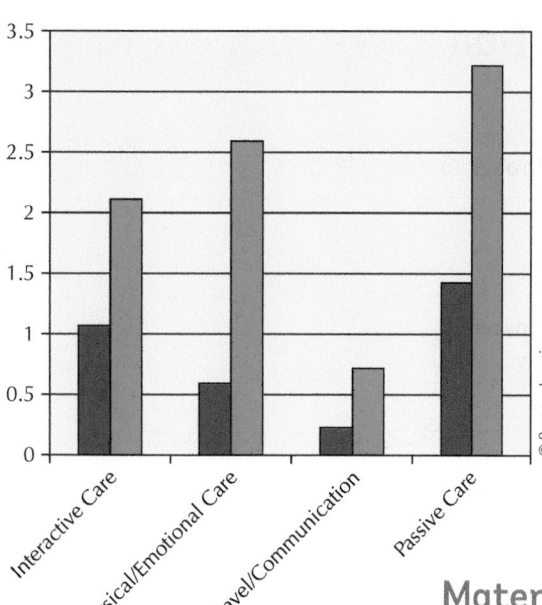

Figure 3.10 Mother–child and father–child interactions. This graph shows what occurred on routine days in a sample of more than 1,400 Australian homes. Mothers spend about twice as long each day on child care compared with fathers. Further, mothers spend more time on physical and emotional care (e.g., feeding, bathing, soothing) than on interactive care (e.g., playing, reading, activities); fathers show the reverse pattern. Finally, mothers spend more time on travel (e.g., driving children to sports or music lessons), communication (e.g., talking to teachers about their children), and passive care (e.g., supervising children while they play). (Adapted from Craig, 2006.)

Type of child care

■ Fathers
■ Mothers

(Bahr & Hoffmann, 2010; Kim-Cohen et al., 2004). The children of authoritative parents are competent, self-controlled, independent, assertive, and inquiring. They know how to manage their emotions and use positive coping skills (Eisenberg et al., 2003; Lynch, Geller, & Schmidt, 2004).

Maternal and Paternal Influences

Don't mothers and fathers parent differently? Yes. Although **maternal influences**—all the effects a mother has on her child—have a greater impact, fathers do make a unique contribution to parenting (Bjorklund & Hernández Blasi, 2012). Although fathers are spending more time with their children, mothers still do most of the nurturing and caretaking, especially of young children (Craig, 2006).

Studies of **paternal influences** (the sum of all effects a father has on his child) reveal that fathers are more likely to play with their children and tell them stories. In contrast, mothers are typically responsible for the physical and emotional care of their children (Figure 3.10).

It might seem that the father's role as a playmate makes him less important. Not so. Samantha's playtime with David is very valuable. From birth onward, fathers pay more visual attention to children than mothers do. Fathers are much more tactile (lifting, tickling, and handling the baby), more physically arousing (engaging in rough-and-tumble play), and more likely to engage in unusual play (imitating the baby, for example). In comparison, mothers speak to infants more, play more conventional games (such as peekaboo), and, as noted, spend much more time in caregiving. Young children who spend a lot of time playing with their fathers tend to be more competent in many ways (Paquette, 2004; Tamis-LeMonda et al., 2004).

Overall, fathers can be as affectionate, sensitive, and responsive as mothers are. Nevertheless, infants and children tend to get very different views of males and females. Females, who offer comfort, nurturance, and verbal stimulation, tend to be close at hand. Males come and go, and when they are present, action, exploration, and risk-taking prevail. It's no wonder, then, that the parental styles of mothers and fathers have a major impact on children's gender role development (Holmes & Huston, 2010; Videon, 2005).

Ethnic Differences: Four Flavors of Parenting

Do ethnic differences in parenting affect children in distinctive ways? Diana Baumrind's work provides a good overall summary of the effects of parenting. However, her conclusions are probably most valid for families whose roots lie in Europe. Child rearing in other ethnic groups often reflects different customs and beliefs. Cultural differences are especially apparent with respect to the meaning attached to a child's behavior. Is a particular behavior "good" or "bad"? Should it be encouraged or discouraged? The answer depends on parents' cultural values (Leyendecker et al., 2005).

Making generalizations about groups of people is always risky. Nevertheless, some typical differences in child-rearing patterns have been observed in North American ethnic communities, as we discuss here (Kaplan, 1998; Parke, 2004).

Fathering typically makes a contribution to early development that differs in emphasis from mothering.

Maternal influences The aggregate of all psychological effects mothers have on their children.

Paternal influences The aggregate of all psychological effects fathers have on their children.

African-American Families

Traditional African-American values emphasize loyalty and interdependence among family members, security, developing a positive identity, and not giving up in the face of adversity. African-American parents typically stress obedience and respect for elders (Dixon, Graber, & Brooks-Gunn, 2008). Child discipline tends to be fairly strict (Parke, 2004), but many African-American parents see this as a necessity, especially if they live in urban areas where safety is a concern. Self-reliance, resourcefulness, and an ability to take care of oneself in difficult situations are also qualities that African-American parents seek to promote in their children.

Hispanic Families

Like African-American parents, Hispanic parents tend to have relatively strict standards of discipline (Dixon, Graber, & Brooks-Gunn, 2008). They also place a high value on *familismo*: the centrality of the family, with a corresponding stress on family values, family pride, and loyalty (Glass & Owen, 2010). Hispanic families are typically affectionate and indulgent toward younger children. However, as children grow older, they are expected to learn social skills and to be calm, obedient, courteous, and respectful (Calzada, Fernandez, & Cortes, 2010). In fact, such social skills may be valued more than cognitive skills (Delgado & Ford, 1998). In addition, Hispanic parents tend to stress cooperation more than competition. Such values can put Hispanic children at a disadvantage in highly competitive, European-American culture.

Asian-American Families

Asian cultures tend to be group oriented, and they emphasize interdependence among individuals. In contrast, Western cultures value individual effort and independence. This difference is often reflected in Asian-American child-rearing practices (Chao & Tseng, 2002). Asian-American children are often taught that their behavior can bring either pride or shame to the family. Therefore, they are obliged to set aside their own desires when the greater good of the family is at stake (Parke, 2004). Parents tend to act as home-based teachers who encourage hard work, moral behavior, and achievement. For the first few years, parenting is lenient and permissive. However, after about age 5, Asian-American parents begin to expect respect, obedience, self-control, and self-discipline from their children.

Arab-American Families

In Middle Eastern cultures, children are expected to be polite, obedient, disciplined, and conforming (Erickson & Al-Timimi, 2001). Punishment may consist of spankings, teasing, or shaming in front of others. Arab-American fathers tend to be strong authority figures who demand obedience so that the family will not be shamed by a child's bad behavior. Success, generosity, and hospitality are highly valued in Arab-American culture. The pursuit of family honor encourages hard work, thrift, conservatism, and educational achievement. The welfare of the family is emphasized over individual identity. Thus, Arab-American children are raised to respect their parents, members of their extended family, and other adults as well (Medhus, 2001).

Implications

Children are reared in a remarkable variety of ways around the world. In fact, many of the things we do in North America, such as forcing young children to sleep alone, would be considered odd or wrong in other cultures. In the final analysis, parenting can be judged only if we know what culture or ethnic community a child is being prepared to enter (Leyendecker et al., 2005).

In ethnic communities, norms for effective parenting often differ in subtle ways from parenting styles in Euro-American culture.

RECITE

1. General excitement or interest is the clearest emotional response present in newborn infants, but meaningful expressions of delight and distress appear soon after. T or F?
2. Neonates display a social smile as early as 10 days after birth. T or F?
3. The development of separation anxiety in an infant corresponds to the formation of an attachment to parents. T or F?
4. High-quality day care can actually improve children's social and mental skills. T or F?
5. Fathers are more likely to act as playmates for their children rather than as caregivers. T or F?
6. According to Diana Baumrind's research, effective parents are authoritarian in their approach to their children's behavior. T or F?
7. Asian-American parents tend to be more individually oriented than parents whose ethnic roots are European. T or F?

REFLECT

THINK CRITICALLY

8. Can emotional bonding begin before birth?
9. Which parenting style do you think would be most likely to lead to eating disorders in children?

SELF-REFLECT

Do you think that your experiences as a child, such as your early attachment pattern, affect your life as an adult? Can you think of any examples from your own life?

Do you know any parents who have young children and who are authoritarian, permissive, or authoritative? What are their children like?

Do you think parenting depends on ethnicity? If so, why? If not, why not?

ANSWERS

1. T 2. F 3. T 4. T 5. T 6. F 7. F 8. It certainly can for parents. When a pregnant woman begins to feel fetal movements, she becomes aware that a baby is coming to life inside of her. Likewise, prospective parents who hear a fetal heartbeat at the doctor's office or see an ultrasound image of the fetus begin to become emotionally attached to the unborn child (Santrock, 2009). 9. Both authoritarian and permissive styles are more likely to lead to eating disorders in children. Parents who are too controlling about what their children eat or too willing to withdraw from conflicts over eating can create problems for their children (Haycraft & Blissett, 2010).

Language Development—Who Talks Baby Talk?

JOURNEY QUESTION 3.4 *How do children acquire language?*

There's something almost miraculous about a baby's first words. As infants, how did we manage to leap into the world of language? Even a quick survey like this one reveals that both maturation (nature) and social development (nurture) provide a foundation for language learning (Saxton, 2010).

Language development is closely tied to maturation (Gleason & Ratner, 2009). As every parent knows, babies can cry from birth on. By 1 month of age they use crying to gain attention. Typically, parents can tell if an infant is hungry, angry, or in pain from the tone of the crying (Nakayama, 2010). Around 6 to 8 weeks of age, babies begin *cooing* (the repetition of vowel sounds such as "oo" and "ah").

By 7 months of age, Samantha's nervous system will mature enough to allow her to grasp objects, to smile, laugh, sit up, and *babble*. In the babbling stage, the consonants *b*, *d*, *m*, and *g* are combined with the vowel sounds to produce meaningless language sounds: *dadadadada* or *bababa*. At first, babbling is the same around the world. But soon, the language spoken by parents begins to have an influence (Goldstein & Schwade, 2008). That is, Japanese babies start to babble in a way that sounds like Japanese, Mexican babies babble in Spanish-like sounds, and so forth (Kuhl, 2004).

At about 1 year of age, children respond to real words such as *no* or *hi*. Soon afterward, the first connection between words and objects forms, and children may address their parents as "Mama" or "Dada." By age 18 months to 2 years, Samantha's vocabulary may include a hundred words or more. At first there is a *single-word stage*, during which children use one word at a time, such as "go," "juice," or "up." Soon after, words are arranged in simple two-word sentences called *telegraphic speech*: "Want-Teddy," "Mama-gone."

Language and the Terrible Twos

At about the same time that children begin to put two or three words together they become much more independent. Two-year-olds understand some of the commands parents make, but they are not always willing to carry them out. A child like Samantha may assert her independence by saying, "No drink," "Me do it," "My cup, my cup," and the like. It can be worse, of course. A 2-year-old may look at you intently, make eye contact, listen as you shout "No, no," and still pour her juice on the cat.

During their second year, children become increasingly capable of mischief and temper tantrums. Thus, calling this time "the terrible twos" is not entirely inappropriate. One-year-olds can do plenty of things parents don't want them to do. However, it's usually 2-year-olds who do things *because* you don't want them to (Gopnik, Meltzoff, & Kuhl, 2000). Perhaps parents can take some comfort in knowing that a stubborn, negative 2-year-old is simply becoming more independent. When Samantha is 2 years old, Carol and David would be wise to remember that "This, too, shall pass."

After age 2, the child's comprehension and use of words takes a dramatic leap forward. From this point on, vocabulary and language skills grow at a phenomenal rate (Fernald, Perfors, & Marchman, 2006). By first grade, Samantha will be able to understand around 8,000 words and use about 4,000. She will have truly entered the world of language.

The Roots of Language

What accounts for this explosion of language development? Linguist Noam Chomsky (1975, 1986) has long claimed that humans have a **biological predisposition** or hereditary readiness to develop language. According to Chomsky, language patterns are inborn, much like a child's ability to coordinate walking. If such inborn language recognition does exist, it may explain why children around the world use a limited number of patterns in their first sentences. Typical patterns include (Mussen et al., 1979):

Identification:	"See kitty."
Nonexistence:	"All gone milk."
Possession:	"My doll."
Agent-Action:	"Mama give."
Negation:	"Not ball."
Question:	"Where doggie?"

Does Chomsky's theory explain why language develops so rapidly? It is certainly part of the story (Saxton, 2010). But many psychologists feel that Chomsky underestimates the importance of learning (Tomasello, 2003) and the social contexts that shape language development (Hoff, 2006, 2009). *Psycholinguists* (specialists in the psychology of language) have shown that imitation of adults and rewards for correctly using words (as when a child asks for a cookie) are an important part of language learning. Also, babies actively participate in language learning by asking questions, such as "What dis?" (Domingo & Goldstein-Alpern, 1999).

When a child makes a language error, parents typically repeat the child's sentence, with needed corrections (Hoff, 2006), or ask a clarifying question to draw the child's attention to the error (Saxton, Houston-Price, & Dawson, 2005). More important is the fact that parents

Biological predisposition The presumed hereditary readiness of humans to learn certain skills, such as how to use language, or a readiness to behave in particular ways.

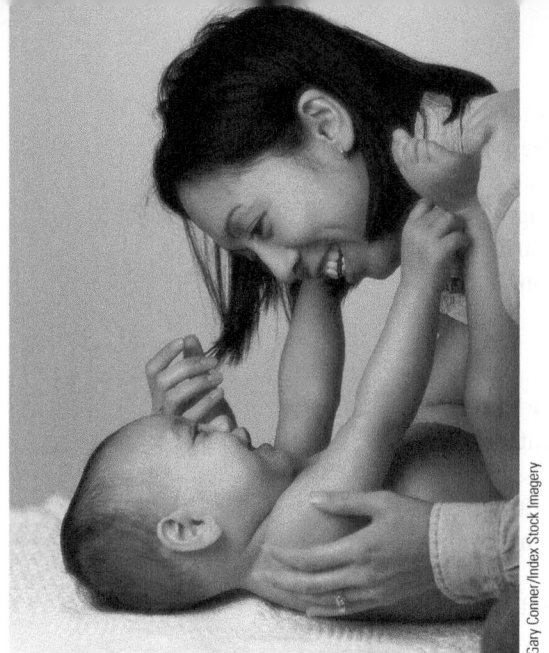

As with motherese, parents use a distinctive style when singing to an infant. Even people who speak another language can tell if a tape-recorded song was sung to an infant or an adult. Likewise, lullabies remain recognizable when electronic filtering removes words (Trehub et al., 1993a, 1993b).

and children begin to communicate long before the child can speak. A readiness to interact *socially* with parents may be as important as innate language recognition. The next section explains why.

Early Communication

How do parents communicate with infants before they can talk? Parents go to a great deal of trouble to get babies to smile and vocalize. In doing so, they quickly learn to change their actions to keep the infant's attention, arousal, and activity at optimal levels. A familiar example is the "I'm-Going-to-Get-You" game. In it, the adult says, "I'm gonna getcha. . . . I'm gonna getcha. . . . I'm gonna getcha. . . . Gotcha!" Through such games, adults and babies come to share similar rhythms and expectations (Carroll, 2008). Soon a system of shared **signals** is created, including touching, vocalizing, gazing, and smiling. These help lay a foundation for later language use (Tamis-LeMonda, Bornstein, & Baumwell, 2001). Specifically, signals establish a pattern of "conversational" *turn-taking* (alternate sending and receiving of messages).

From the outside, such exchanges may look meaningless. In reality, they represent real communication. One study found that 6-week-old babies gaze at an adult's face in rhythm with the adult's speech (Crown et al., 2002). Infants as young as 4 months engage in vocal turn-taking with adults (Jaffe et al., 2001). The more children interact with parents, the faster they learn to talk and the faster they learn thinking abilities (Hoff & Tian, 2005). Unmistakably, social relationships contribute to early language learning (Hoff, 2009; Vernon-Feagans et al., 2011).

Parentese

When they talk to infants, parents use an exaggerated pattern of speaking called **motherese** or **parentese**. Typically, they raise their tone of voice, use short, simple sentences, repeat themselves, and use frequent gestures (Gogate, Bahrick, & Watson, 2000). They also slow their rate of speaking and use exaggerated voice inflections: "Did Samantha eat it A-L-L UP?"

What is the purpose of such changes? Parents are apparently trying to help their children learn language (Soderstrom, 2007). When a baby is still babbling, parents tend to use long, adult-style sentences. But as soon as the baby says its first word, they switch to parentese. By the time babies are 4 months old, they prefer parentese over normal speech (Cooper et al., 1997).

In addition to being simpler, parentese has a distinct "musical" quality (Trainor & Desjardins, 2002). No matter what language mothers speak, the melodies, pauses, and inflections they use to comfort, praise, or give warning are universal. Psychologist Anne Fernald has found that mothers of all nations talk to their babies with similar changes in pitch. For instance, we praise babies with a rising, then falling pitch ("BRA-vo!" "GOOD girl!"). Warnings are delivered in a short, sharp rhythm ("Nein! Nein!" "Basta! Basta!" "Not! Dude!"). To give comfort, parents use low, smooth, drawn-out tones ("Oooh poor baaa-by." "Oooh pobrecito.") A high-pitched, rising melody is used to call attention to objects ("See the pretty BIRDIE?") (Fernald, 1989).

Parentese helps parents get babies' attention, communicate with them, and teach them language (Thiessen, Hill, & Saffran, 2005). Later, as a child's speaking improves, parents tend to adjust their speech to the child's language ability. Especially from 18 months to 4 years of age, parents seek to clarify what a child says and prompt the child to say more.

In summary, some elements of language are innate. Nevertheless, our inherited tendency to learn language does not determine if we will speak English or Vietnamese, Spanish or Russian. Environmental forces also influence whether a person develops simple or sophisticated language skills. The first 7 years of life are a sensitive period in language learning (Hoff, 2009). Clearly, a full flowering of speech requires careful cultivation.

Signal In early language development, any behavior, such as touching, vocalizing, gazing, or smiling, that allows nonverbal interaction and turn-taking between parent and child.

Motherese (or parentese) A pattern of speech used when talking to infants, marked by a higher-pitched voice; short, simple sentences; repetition, slower speech; and exaggerated voice inflections.

RECITE

1. The development of speech and language usually occurs in which order?

   a. crying, cooing, babbling, telegraphic speech
   b. cooing, crying, babbling, telegraphic speech
   c. babbling, crying, cooing, telegraphic speech
   d. crying, babbling, cooing, identification

2. Simple two-word sentences are characteristic of _____ speech.

3. Noam _____ has advanced the idea that language acquisition is built on innate patterns.

4. Pre-language turn-taking and social interactions would be of special interest to a psycholinguist. T or F?

5. The style of speaking known as _____ is higher in pitch and has a musical quality.

REFLECT

THINK CRITICALLY

6. The children of professional parents hear more words per hour than the children of welfare parents, and they also tend to score higher on tests of mental abilities. How else could their higher scores be explained?

SELF-REFLECT

See if you can name and imitate the language abilities you had as you progressed from birth to age 2 years in order of occurrence. Now see if you can label and imitate some basic elements of parentese.

You are going to spend a day with a person who speaks a different language than you do. Do you think you would be able to communicate with the other person? How does this relate to language acquisition?

ANSWERS

1. a 2. telegraphic 3. Chomsky 4. T 5. Parentese or motherese 6. Children in professional homes receive many educational benefits that are less common in welfare homes. Yet, even when such differences are taken into account, brighter children tend to come from richer language environments (Hart & Risley, 1999).

Cognitive Development in Children—Think Like a Child

JOURNEY QUESTION 3.5 *How do children learn to think?*

Now that we have Samantha talking, let's move on to a broader view of intellectual development. Babies are smarter than many people think. While they don't yet have any learned knowledge and skills (*crystallized intelligence*), they do have a remarkable capability for rapid learning (*fluid intelligence*). From an evolutionary perspective, a baby's mind is designed to soak up information, which it does at an amazing pace (Bjorklund, 2012). Although baby Samantha was a "sponge," soaking up new experiences, by the time she is 83 she will find it much harder to learn new skills (such as becoming fluent in a second language) and will find herself relying much more on what she already knows.

From the earliest days of life, babies are learning how the world works. They immediately begin to look, touch, taste, and otherwise explore their surroundings. In the first months of life, babies are increasingly able to think, to learn from what they see, to make predictions, and to search for explanations. For example, Jerome Bruner (1983) observed that 3- to 8-week-old babies seem to understand that a person's voice and body should be connected. If a baby hears his mother's voice coming from where she is standing, the baby will remain calm. If her voice comes from a loudspeaker several feet away, the baby will become agitated and begin to cry.

As another example, psychologist Andrew Meltzoff has found that babies are born mimics. **Figure 3.11** shows Meltzoff as he sticks out his tongue, opens his mouth, and purses his lips at a 20-day-old girl. Will she imitate him? Videotapes of babies confirm that they imitate adult facial gestures while they can see them (mirror neurons, anyone?). As early as 9 months of age, infants can remember and imitate actions a day after seeing them (Heimann & Meltzoff, 1996; Meltzoff, 2005). Such mimicry obviously aids rapid learning in infancy.

Swiss psychologist and philosopher Jean Piaget (Jahn pea-ah-ZHAY) (1896–1980) provided some of the first great insights into how children develop thinking abilities when

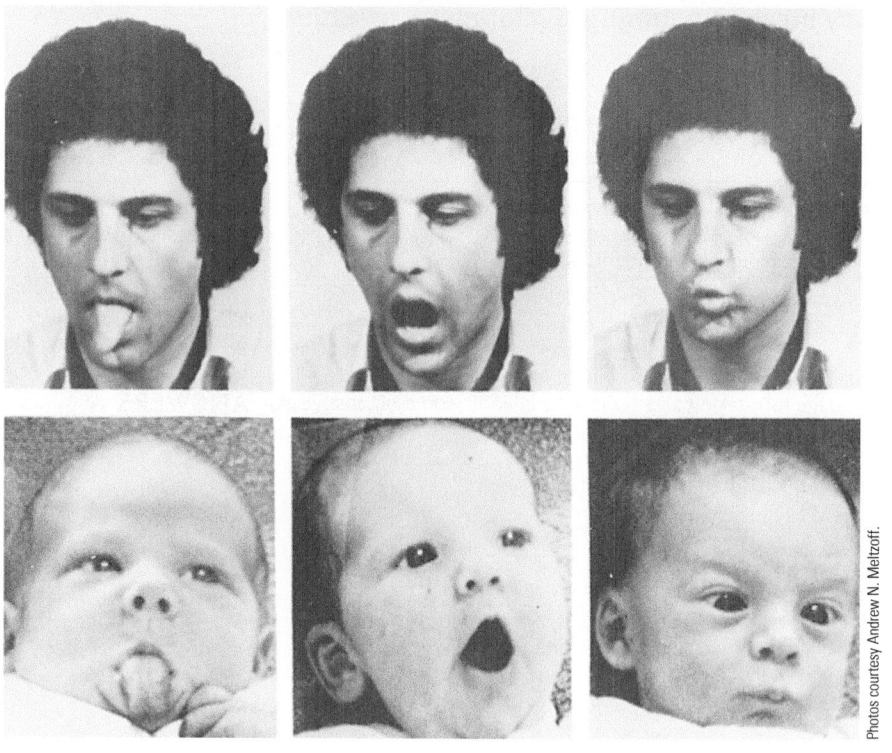

Figure 3.11 Infant imitation. In the top row of photos, Andrew Meltzoff makes facial gestures at an infant. The bottom row records the infant's responses. Videotapes of Meltzoff and of tested infants helped ensure objectivity.

he proposed that children's cognitive skills progress through a series of maturational stages. Also, many psychologists have become interested in how children learn the intellectual skills valued by their culture. Typically, children do this with guidance from skilled "tutors" (parents and others).

Piaget's Theory of Cognitive Development

Piaget's ideas have deeply affected our view of children (Miller, 2011). According to Piaget (1951, 1952), children's thinking is, generally speaking, less abstract that that of adults. They tend to base their understanding on particular examples and objects they can see or touch. Also, children use fewer generalizations, categories, and principles. Piaget also believed that all children mature through a series of distinct stages in intellectual development. Many of his ideas came from observing his own children as they solved various thought problems. (It is tempting to imagine that Piaget's illustrious career was launched one day when his wife said to him, "Watch the children for a while, will you, Jean?")

Mental Processes

Piaget was convinced that intellect grows through processes he called assimilation and accommodation. **Assimilation** refers to using existing mental patterns in new situations. Let's say that little Benjamin is taken for a drive in the country. He sees his first live horse in a field, points, and calls out, "Horse!" He has already seen horses on television and even has a stuffed toy horse. In this case, he adds this new experience to his existing concept of *horse*. Piaget would say it has been *assimilated* to an existing knowledge structure.

In **accommodation**, existing ideas are modified to fit new requirements. For instance, suppose a month later Benjamin goes to the zoo, where he sees his first zebra. Proudly, he again exclaims, "Horse!" This time, his mother replies, "No dear, that's a zebra." Little Benjamin has *failed to assimilate* the zebra to his horse concept. He must now *accommodate* by creating a new concept, *zebra*, and modifying his concept of horse (*not* black and white stripes).

Jean Piaget—philosopher, psychologist, and keen observer of children.

Assimilation In Piaget's theory, the application of existing mental patterns to new situations (that is, the new situation is assimilated to existing mental schemes).

Accommodation In Piaget's theory, the modification of existing mental patterns to fit new demands (that is, mental schemes are changed to accommodate new information or experiences).

The Sensorimotor Stage (0–2 Years)

Look up from this book until your attention is attracted to something else in the room. Now close your eyes. Is it still there? How do you know? As an adult, you can keep an image of the object in your "mind's eye." According to Piaget, newborn babies cannot create *internal representations* such as mental images. As a result, they lack **object permanence**, an understanding that objects continue to exist when they are out of sight.

For this reason, in the first 2 years of life, Samantha's intellectual development will be largely nonintellectual and nonverbal. She will be concerned mainly with learning to coordinate information from her senses with her motor movements. But sometime during their first year, babies begin to actively pursue disappearing objects. By age 2, they can anticipate the movement of an object behind a screen. For example, when watching a toy train, Samantha will look ahead to the end of a tunnel, rather than staring at the spot where the train disappeared.

In general, developments in this stage indicate that the child's conceptions are becoming more *stable*. Objects cease to appear and disappear magically, and a more orderly and predictable world replaces the confusing and disconnected sensations of infancy.

The Preoperational Stage (2–7 Years)

Close your eyes again. Imagine the room you sleep in. What would it look like if you were perched on the ceiling and your bed was missing? You have now mentally operated on your image by *transforming* it. According to Piaget, even though preoperational children can form mental images or ideas, they are preoperational because they cannot easily **transform** those images or ideas in their minds.

This is why, although children begin to think *symbolically* and use language before the age of 6 or 7, their thinking is still very concrete and **intuitive** (it makes little use of reasoning and logic). (Do you remember thinking as a child that the sun and the moon followed you when you took a walk?) Such thinking is also often labeled *superstitious*, especially when it persists into later childhood and adulthood (Wargo, 2008).

Let's visit Samantha at age 5: If you show her a short, wide glass full of milk and a taller, narrow glass full of milk, she will most likely tell you that the taller glass contains more milk (even if it doesn't). Samantha will tell you this even if she watches you pour milk from the short glass into an empty taller glass. Older children can easily mentally transform the pouring of the milk by mentally *reversing* it, to see that the shape of the container is irrelevant to the volume of milk it contains. But Samantha is preoperational; she cannot engage in the mental operation of transforming the tall, narrow glass of milk back into a short, wide glass. Thus she is not bothered by the fact that the milk appears to be transformed from a smaller to a larger amount. Instead, she responds only to the fact that *taller* seems to mean *more* (Figure 3.12).

After about age 7, children are no longer fooled by this situation. Perhaps that's why age 7 has been called the "age of reason." From age 7 on, we see a definite trend toward more logical, adult-like thought.

During the preoperational stage, the child is also quite **egocentric**, or unable to take the viewpoint of other people. The child's ego seems to stand at the center of his or her world. To illustrate, show a preoperational child a two-sided mirror. Then hold it between you and her, so she can see herself in it. If you ask her what she thinks *you* can see, she imagines that you see *her* face reflected in the mirror, instead of your own. She cannot mentally transform the view she sees into the view you must be seeing.

Such egocentrism explains why children can seem exasperatingly selfish or uncooperative at times. If Benjamin blocks your view by standing in front of the television, he assumes that you can see it if he can. If you ask him to move so you can see better, he may move so that *he* can see better! Benjamin is not being selfish in the ordinary sense. He just doesn't realize that your view differs from his.

Figure 3.12 Children under age 7 intuitively assume that a volume of liquid increases when it is poured from a short, wide container into a taller, thinner one. This boy thinks the tall container holds more than the short one. Actually, each holds the same amount of liquid. Children make such judgments based on the height of the liquid, not its volume.

Sensorimotor stage Stage of intellectual development during which sensory input and motor responses become coordinated.

Object permanence Concept, gained in infancy, in which objects continue to exist even when they are hidden from view.

Preoperational stage Period of intellectual development during which children begin to use language and think symbolically, yet remain intuitive and egocentric in their thought.

Transformation The mental ability to change the shape or form of a substance (such as clay or water) and to perceive that its volume remains the same.

Intuitive thought Thinking that makes little or no use of reasoning and logic.

Egocentric thought Thought that is self-centered and fails to consider the viewpoints of others.

In addition, the child's use of language is not as sophisticated as it might seem. Children have a tendency to confuse words with the objects they represent. If Benjamin calls a toy block a "car" and you use the block to make a "house," he may be upset. To children, the name of an object is as much a part of the object as its size, shape, and color. This seems to underlie a preoccupation with name-calling. To the preoperational child, insulting words may really hurt. Samantha was once angered by her older brother. Searching for a way to retaliate against her larger and stronger foe, she settled on, "You panty-girdle!" It was the worst thing she could think of saying.

Crossing a busy street can be dangerous for the preoperational child. Because their thinking is still egocentric, younger children cannot understand why the driver of a car can't see them if they can see the car. Children under the age of 7 also cannot consistently judge speeds and distances of oncoming cars. Adults can easily overestimate the "street smarts" of younger children. It is advisable to teach children to cross with a light, in crosswalks, or with assistance.

The Concrete Operational Stage (7–11 Years)

The hallmark of this stage is the ability to carry out mental operations such as *reversing* thoughts. A 4-year-old boy in the preoperational stage might have a conversation like this (showing what happens when a child's thinking *lacks* reversibility):

"Do you have a brother?"

"Yes."

"What's his name?"

"Billy."

"Does Billy have a brother?"

"No."

Reversibility of thought allows children in the concrete operational stage to recognize that if $4 \times 2 = 8$, then 2×4 does, too. Younger children must memorize each relationship separately.

The development of mental operations allows mastery of **conservation** (the concept that mass, weight, and volume remain unchanged when the shape of objects changes). Children have learned conservation when they understand that rolling a ball of clay into a "snake" does not increase the amount of clay. Likewise, pouring liquid from a tall, narrow glass into a shallow dish does not reduce the amount of liquid. In each case the volume remains the same despite changes in shape or appearance. The original amount is *conserved*. (See Figure 3.12.)

During the concrete operational stage, children begin to use concepts of time, space, and number. The child can think logically about very concrete objects or situations, categories, and principles. Such abilities help explain why children stop believing in Santa Claus when they reach this stage. Because they can conserve volume, they realize that Santa's sack couldn't possibly hold enough toys for millions of girls and boys.

The Formal Operational Stage (11 Years and Up)

After about the age of 11, children begin to break away from concrete objects and specific examples. Thinking is based more on abstract principles, such as "democracy," "honor," or "correlation." Children who reach this stage become self-reflective about their thoughts, and they become less egocentric. Older children and young adolescents also gradually become able to consider hypothetical possibilities (suppositions, guesses, or projections). For example, if you ask a younger child, "What do you think would happen if it suddenly became possible for people to fly?" the child might respond, "People can't fly." Older children are better able to consider such possibilities.

Full adult intellectual ability is attained during the stage of formal operations. Older adolescents are capable of inductive and deductive reasoning, and they can comprehend math, physics, philosophy, psychology, and other abstract systems. They can learn to test hypotheses in a scientific manner. Of course, not everyone reaches this level of thinking. Also, many adults can think formally about some topics, but their thinking becomes concrete when the topic is unfamiliar. This implies that formal thinking may be more a result of culture and learning than maturation. In any case, after late adolescence, improvements in intellect are based on gaining specific knowledge, experience, and wisdom, rather than on any leaps in basic thinking capacity.

Concrete operational stage Period of intellectual development during which children become able to use the concepts of time, space, volume, and number, but in ways that remain simplified and concrete, rather than abstract.

Conservation In Piaget's theory, mastery of the concept that the weight, mass, and volume of matter remains unchanged (is conserved) even when the shape or appearance of objects changes.

Formal operational stage Period of intellectual development characterized by thinking that includes abstract, theoretical, and hypothetical ideas.

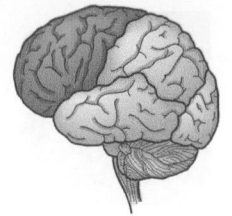
3 to 6 years

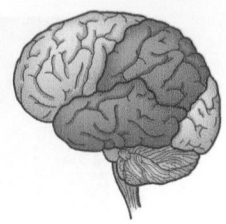
7 to 15 years

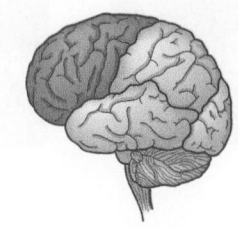

Growth

Pruning

16 to 20 years

Figure 3.13 Between the ages of 3 and 6, a tremendous wave of growth occurs in connections among neurons in the frontal areas of the brain. This corresponds to the time when children make rapid progress in their ability to think symbolically. Between the ages of 7 and 15, peak synaptic growth shifts to the temporal and parietal lobes. During this period, children become increasingly adept at using language, a specialty of the temporal lobes. In the late teens, the brain actively destroys unneeded connections, especially in the frontal lobes. This pruning of synapses sharpens the brain's capacity for abstract thinking (Restak, 2001). (Courtesy Dr. Paul Thompson, Laboratory of Neuro Imaging, UCLA School of Medicine.)

How can parents apply Piaget's ideas? Piaget's theory suggests that the ideal way to guide intellectual development is to provide experiences that are only slightly novel, unusual, or challenging. Remember, a child's intellect develops mainly through accommodation. It is usually best to follow a *one-step-ahead strategy*, in which your teaching efforts are aimed just beyond a child's current level of comprehension (Brainerd, 2003).

Parents should avoid *forced teaching*, or "hothousing," which is like trying to force plants to bloom prematurely. Forcing children to learn reading, math, gymnastics, swimming, or music at an accelerated pace can bore or oppress them. True intellectual enrichment respects the child's interests. It does not make the child feel pressured to perform.

Piaget Today

Today, Piaget's theory remains a valuable "road map" for understanding how children think. On a broad scale, many of Piaget's ideas have held up well. However, there has been disagreement about specific details. For example, according to learning theorists, children continuously gain specific knowledge; they do not undergo stage-like leaps in general mental ability (Miller, 2011; Siegler, 2005). On the other hand, the growth in connections between brain cells occurs in waves that parallel some of Piaget's stages (Figure 3.13). Thus, the truth may lie somewhere between Piaget's stage theory and modern learning theory.

In addition, it is now widely accepted that children develop cognitive skills somewhat earlier than Piaget originally thought (Bjorklund, 2012). For example, Piaget believed that infants under the age of 1 year cannot think (use internal representations). Such abilities, he believed, emerge only after a long period of sensorimotor development. Babies, he said, can have no memory of people and objects that are out of sight. Yet we now know that infants begin forming representations of the world very early in life. For example, babies as young as 3 months of age appear to know that objects are solid and do not disappear when out of view (Baillargeon, 2004).

Why did Piaget fail to detect the thinking skills of infants? Most likely, he mistook babies' limited *physical* skills for *mental* incompetence. Piaget's tests required babies to search for objects or reach out and touch them. Newer, more sensitive methods are uncovering abilities Piaget missed. One such method takes advantage of the fact that babies, like adults, act surprised when they see something "impossible" or unexpected occur. To use this effect, psychologist Renee Baillargeon (1991, 2004) puts on little "magic shows" for infants. In her "theater," babies watch as possible and impossible events occur with toys or other objects. Some 3-month-old infants act surprised and gaze longer at impossible events. An example is seeing two solid objects appear to pass through each other. By the time they are 8 months old, babies can remember where objects are (or should be) for at least 1 minute (Figure 3.14).

Similarly, Piaget thought that children remain egocentric during the preoperational stage, becoming aware of perspectives other than their own only at age 7. Researchers have since begun to refer to

"Young man, go to your room and stay there until your cerebral cortex matures."

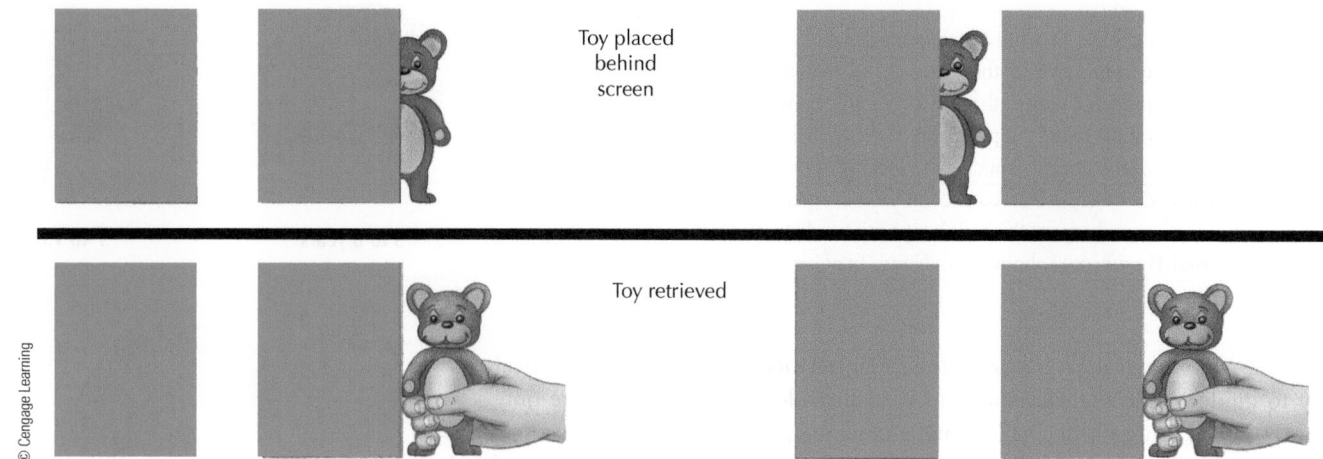

Figure 3.14 The panels on the left show a possible event, in which an infant watches as a toy is placed behind the right of two screens. After a delay of 70 seconds, the toy is brought into view from behind the right screen. In the two panels on the right, an impossible event occurs. The toy is placed behind the left screen and retrieved from behind the right. (A duplicate toy was hidden there before testing.) Eight-month-old infants react with surprise when they see the impossible event staged for them. Their reaction implies that they remember where the toy was hidden. Infants appear to have a capacity for memory and thinking that greatly exceeds what Piaget claimed is possible during the sensorimotor period. (Adapted with permission from Baillargeon, R., De Vos, J., & Graber, M. "Location memory in 8-month-old infants in a non-search AB task," *Cognitive Development, 4,* 345–367, (Figure 1, p. 351), Copyright © 1989, with permission from Elsevier.)

this development as **theory of mind**, the understanding that people have mental states, such as thoughts, beliefs, and intentions, and that other people's mental states can be different from one's own. Psychologists currently believe that children as young as age 4 can understand that other people's mental states differ from their own (Doherty, 2009). (To read more about this fascinating development, see "Theory of Mind: I'm a Me!... and You're a You!")

Another criticism of Piaget is that he underestimated the impact of culture on mental development. The next section tells how Samantha will master the intellectual tools valued by her culture.

Vygotsky's Sociocultural Theory

While Piaget stressed the role of maturation in cognitive development, Russian scholar Lev Vygotsky (1896–1934) focused on the impact of sociocultural factors. Many psychologists are convinced that Piaget gave too little credit to the effects of the learning environment. For example, children who grow up in villages where pottery is made can correctly answer questions about the conservation of clay at an earlier age than Piaget would have predicted. Vygotsky's (1962, 1978) key insight is that children's thinking develops through dialogues with more capable persons.

How does that relate to intellectual growth? So far, no one has published *A Child's Guide to Life on Earth.* Instead, children must learn about life from various "tutors," such as parents, teachers, and older siblings. Even if *A Child's Guide to Life on Earth* did exist, we would need a separate version for every culture. It is not enough for children to learn how to think. They must also learn specific intellectual skills valued by their culture.

Like Piaget, Vygotsky believed that children actively seek to discover new principles. However, Vygotsky emphasized that many of a child's most important "discoveries" are guided by skillful tutors. Psychologists David Shaffer and Katherine Kipp (2010) offer the following example:

Tonya, a 4-year-old, has just received her first jigsaw puzzle as a birthday present. She attempts to work the puzzle but gets nowhere until her father comes along, sits down beside her, and gives

Theory of mind The understanding that people have mental states, such as thoughts, beliefs, and intentions, and that other people's mental states can be different from one's own.

© Cengage Learning

Critical Thinking

A major step in human development is becoming aware of oneself as a person. When you look in a mirror, you recognize the image staring back as your own—except, perhaps, early on Monday mornings. Like many such events, initial self-awareness depends on maturation of the nervous system. In a typical test of self-recognition, infants are shown images of themselves on a television. Most infants have to be 18 months old before they recognize themselves (Nielsen & Dissanayake, 2004).

But just because a 2-year-old knows he is a *me* doesn't mean he knows you are a *you*. At age 3, Eric once put his hands over his eyes and exclaimed to his friend, Laurence, "You can't see me now!" He knew he had a point of view but did not know his friend's point of view could be different from his own.

Earlier, we saw that Piaget used the term *egocentrism* to refer to this endearing feature of young children and proposed that young children remain egocentric until they enter the concrete operational stage at about age 7. More recent evidence suggests that children become less egocentric beginning at about age 4 (Baron-Cohen, 1985; Doherty, 2009). As noted above, this developing capacity is called *theory of mind* (Gopnik, 2009).

One way to assess if a child understands that other people have their own mental states is the false-belief (or "Sally-Anne") task. A child is shown two dolls, Sally and Anne. Sally has a basket and Anne has a box. Sally puts a coin in her basket and goes out to play. In the meantime, Anne takes the coin from Sally's basket and puts it into her box. Sally comes back and looks for the coin. To assess theory of mind, the child is asked where Sally will look for her coin. Although the child knows the coin is in Anne's box, the correct answer is that Sally will look in her basket. To answer correctly, the child must understand that Sally's point of view did not include what the child saw (Baron-Cohen, 1985).

Theory of mind develops over time. It takes further development to appreciate that other people may lie, be sarcastic, make jokes, or use figures of speech. Some adults are not good at this. In fact, the available evidence suggests that children with autism spectrum disorders are particularly poor at this task (O'Hare et al., 2009).

A sense of self, or self-awareness, develops at about age 18 months. Before children develop self-awareness, they do not recognize their own image in a mirror. Typically, they think they are looking at another child. Some children hug the child in the mirror or go behind it looking for the child they see there (Lewis, 1995).

---

her some tips. He suggests that it would be a good idea to put together the corners first, points to the pink area at the edge of one corner piece, and says, "Let's look for another pink piece." When Tonya seems frustrated, he places two interlocking pieces near each other so that she will notice them, and when Tonya succeeds, he offers words of encouragement. As Tonya gradually gets the hang of it, he steps back and lets her work more and more independently (p. 283).

Interactions like this are most helpful when they take place within a child's **zone of proximal development**.

What did Vygotsky mean by that? The word *proximal* means close or nearby. Vygotsky realized that, at any given time, some tasks are just beyond a child's reach. The child is close to having the mental skills needed to do the task, but it is a little too complex to be mastered alone. However, children working within this zone can make rapid progress if they receive sensitive guidance from a skilled partner (Morrissey & Brown, 2009). (Notice that this is similar to the one-step-ahead strategy described earlier.)

Vygotsky also emphasized a process he called **scaffolding**. A scaffold is a framework or temporary support. Vygotsky believed that adults help children learn how to think by "scaffolding," or supporting, their attempts to solve problems or discover principles (Daniels, 2005). To be most effective, scaffolding must be responsive to a child's needs. For example, as Tonya's father helped her with the puzzle, he tailored his hints and guidance to match her evolving abilities. The two of them worked together, step by step, so that Tonya could better understand how to assemble a puzzle. In a sense, Tonya's father set up a series

Zone of proximal development Refers to the range of tasks a child cannot yet master alone, but that she or he can accomplish with the guidance of a more capable partner.

Scaffolding The process of adjusting instruction so that it is responsive to a beginner's behavior and supports the beginner's efforts to understand a problem or gain a mental skill.

of temporary bridges that helped her move into new mental territory. As predicted by Vygotsky's theory, the reading skills of 8- to 10-year-old children are closely related to the amount of verbal scaffolding their mothers provided at ages 3 and 4 (Dieterich et al., 2006).

During their collaborations with others, children learn important cultural beliefs and values. For example, imagine that a boy wants to know how many baseball cards he has. His mother helps him stack and count the cards, moving each card to a new stack as they count it. She then shows him how to write the number on a slip of paper so he can remember it. This teaches the child not only about counting, but also that writing is valued in our culture. In other parts of the world, a child learning to count might be shown how to make notches on a stick or tie knots in a cord.

Implications

Vygotsky saw that grown-ups play a crucial role in what children know. As they try to decipher the world, children rely on adults to help them understand how things work. Vygotsky further noticed that adults unconsciously adjust their behavior to give children the information they need to solve problems that interest the child. In this way, children use adults to learn about their culture and society (Gredler & Shields, 2008; Morrissey & Brown, 2009).

 study break Cognitive Development in Childhood

RECITE

Match each item with one of the following stages.

   A. Sensorimotor   B. Preoperational
   C. Concrete operational   D. Formal operations

1. _____ egocentric thought
2. _____ abstract or hypothetical
3. _____ purposeful movement
4. _____ intuitive thought
5. _____ conservation
6. _____ reversibility thought
7. _____ object permanence
8. _____ nonverbal development
9. *Assimilation* refers to applying existing thought patterns or knowledge to new situations. T or F?
10. Vygotsky called the process of providing a temporary framework of supports for learning new mental abilities _____ _____.

REFLECT

THINK CRITICALLY

11. In Western cultures, children as young as age 4 can understand that other people have mental states that differ from their own. In other words, they have developed a *theory of mind*. Is this ability uniquely Western, or might children from other cultures also develop a theory of mind?

SELF-REFLECT

You are going to make cookies with children of various ages. See if you can name each of Piaget's stages and give an example of what a child in that stage might be expected to do.

You have been asked to help a child learn to use a calculator to do simple addition. How would you go about identifying the child's zone of proximal development for this task? How would you scaffold the child's learning?

ANSWERS

1. B 2. D 3. A 4. B 5. C 6. C 7. A 8. A 9. T 10. scaffolding 11. All humans need to be able to base their actions on their understanding of the intentions, desires, and beliefs of others. For example, children from Micronesia, a group of small islands in the Pacific Ocean, also develop a theory of mind at around 4 years of age (Oberle, 2009).

Adolescence and Young Adulthood— The Best of Times, the Worst of Times

JOURNEY QUESTION 3.6 *Why is the transition from adolescence to adulthood especially challenging?*

Adolescence and young adulthood is a time of change, exploration, exuberance, and youthful searching. It can also be a time of worry and problems, especially in today's world. It might even be fair to describe this period as "the best of times, the worst of times." During adolescence, a person's identity and moral values come into sharper focus even as the transition to adulthood is occurring at ever-later ages.

Adolescence is the culturally defined period between childhood and adulthood (Bjorklund & Hernández Blasi, 2012). Socially, the adolescent is no longer a child, yet not quite an adult. Almost all cultures recognize this transitional status. However, the length of adolescence varies greatly from culture to culture. For example, most 14-year-old girls in North America live at home and go to school. In contrast, many 14-year-old females in rural villages of many poorer countries are married and have children. In our culture, 14-year-olds are adolescents. In others, they may be adults.

Is marriage the primary criterion for adult status in North America? No, it's not even one of the top three criteria. Today, the most widely accepted standards are (1) taking responsibility for oneself, (2) making independent decisions, and (3) becoming financially independent. In practice, this typically means breaking away from parents by taking a job and setting up a separate residence (Arnett, 2010).

Puberty

Many people confuse adolescence with puberty. However, puberty is a *biological* event, not a social status. During **puberty**, hormonal changes promote rapid physical growth and sexual maturity. Biologically, most people reach reproductive maturity in the early teens. Social and intellectual maturity, however, may lie years ahead. Young adolescents often make decisions that affect their entire lives, even though they are immature mentally and socially. The tragically high rates of teenage pregnancy and drug abuse are prime examples. Despite such risks, most people do manage to weather adolescence without developing any serious psychological problems (Rathus, 2011).

How much difference does the timing of puberty make? For boys, maturing early is generally beneficial. Typically, it enhances their self-image and gives them an advantage socially and athletically. Early-maturing boys tend to be more relaxed, dominant, self-assured, and popular. However, early puberty does carry some risks because early-maturing boys are also more likely to get into trouble with drugs, alcohol, and antisocial behavior (Steinberg, 2001).

For girls, the advantages of early maturation are less clearcut. In elementary school, fast-maturing girls are *less* popular and have poorer self-images, perhaps because they are larger and heavier than their classmates (Deardorff et al., 2007). This is a growing problem as more American girls are reaching puberty at earlier ages (Biro et al., 2010). By junior high, however, early development includes sexual features. This leads to a more positive body image, *greater* peer prestige, and adult approval. Early-maturing girls tend to date sooner and are more independent and more active in school. However, like their male counterparts, they are also more often in trouble at school and more likely to engage in early sex (Negriff & Trickett, 2010).

As you can see, there are costs and benefits associated with early puberty. One added cost of early maturation is that it may force premature identity formation. When Samantha is a teenager and she begins to look like an adult, she may be treated like an adult. Ideally, this change can encourage greater maturity and independence. However, if the search for identity ends too soon, it may leave Samantha with a distorted, poorly formed sense of self (Figure 3.15).

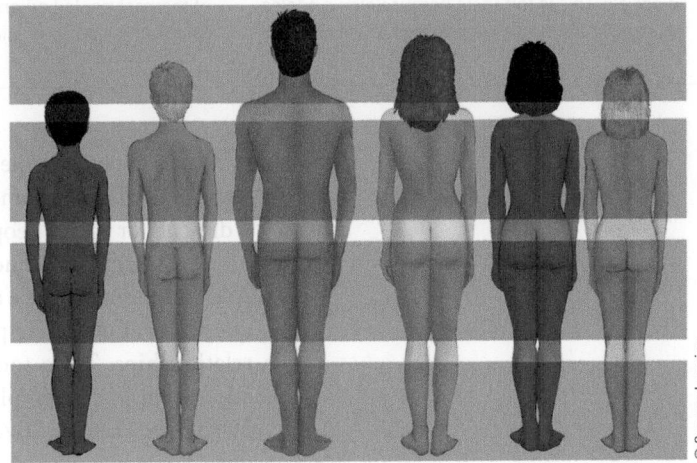

Figure 3.15 Dramatic differences in physical size and maturity are found in adolescents of the same age. The girls pictured are all 13, the boys 16. Maturation that occurs earlier or later than average can affect the "search for identity." (Adapted from "Growing Up" by J. M. Tanner. Copyright © September 1973 by Scientific American, Inc. All rights reserved.)

The Search for Identity

Identity formation is a key challenge faced by adolescents (Schwartz, 2008). Of course, problems of identity occur at other times too. But in a very real sense, puberty signals that it's time to begin forming a new, more mature self-image (Rathus, 2011). Many problems stem from unclear

Adolescence The culturally defined period between childhood and adulthood.

Puberty The biologically defined period during which a person matures sexually and becomes capable of reproduction.

Ethnic heritage is an important aspect of personal identity (Weisskirch, 2005). For adolescents of ethnic descent, the question is often not just "Who am I?" Rather, it is "Who am I at home? Who am I at school? Who am I with friends from my neighborhood?"

As ethnic minorities in America continue to grow in status and prominence, adolescents are less and less likely to feel rejected or excluded because of their ethnic heritage as they try to find their place in society. This is fortunate because ethnic adolescents have often faced degrading stereotypes concerning their intelligence, sexuality, social status, manners, and so forth. The result can be lowered self-esteem and confusion about roles, values, and personal identity (Charmaraman & Grossman, 2010). At the same time, the increasingly multicultural nature of contemporary American society raises new questions for adolescents about what it means to be American (Schwartz, 2008).

In forming an identity, adolescents of ethnic descent face the question of how they should think of themselves. Is Lori an American or a Chinese American or both? Is Jaime a Latino, a Chicano, or a Mexican American? The answer typically depends on how strongly adolescents identify with their family and ethnic community. Teens who take pride in their ethnic heritage have higher self-esteem, a better self-image, and a stronger sense of personal identity (Galliher, Jones, & Dahl, 2011; Roberts et al., 1999). They are also less likely to engage in drug use (Marsiglia et al., 2004) or violent behavior (French, Kim, & Pillado, 2006).

Group pride, positive models, and a more tolerant society could do much to keep a broad range of options open to *all* adolescents.

standards about the role adolescents should play within society. Are they adults or children? Should they be autonomous or dependent? Should they work or play? Such ambiguities make it difficult for young people to form clear images of themselves and of how they should act.

Answering the question "Who am I?" is also spurred by cognitive development. After adolescents have attained the stage of formal operations, they are better able to ask questions about their place in the world and about morals, values, politics, and social relationships. Then too, being able to think about hypothetical possibilities allows the adolescent to contemplate the future and ask more realistically, "Who will I be?" (Côté, 2006b; see "Ethnic Diversity and Identity.")

Emerging Adulthood

Today the challenge of identity formation is further complicated by the fact that more and more young people are deferring young adulthood, preferring to prolong identity explorations well into their twenties before they commit to long-term choices in love and work. Western industrialized societies, like the United States and Canada, have become increasingly tolerant of **emerging adulthood**, a socially accepted period of extended adolescence (Arnett, 2010; Côté, 2006a). (See "The Twixters.")

Samantha may live with Carol and David until her mid-twenties, delaying her transition to adulthood. Alternatively, she may make the transition to young adulthood during the traditional 18-to-21 period. Regardless, she will eventually face the primary adult issues of marriage, children, and career. How she manages, especially in her core relationships, will determine whether she feels a sense of intimacy or feels isolated from others.

Emerging adulthood A socially accepted period of extended adolescence now quite common in Western and Westernized societies.

As you read this text, we encourage you to reflect on new ideas and concepts by thinking critically about them. Consider, for example, the term *adulthood*. Is becoming an adult strictly a biological event? Meet 22-year old Kirsten:

"When our mothers were our age, they were engaged...They at least had some idea what they were going to do with their lives...I, on the other hand, will have a dual degree in majors that are ambiguous at best and impractical at worst (English and political science), no ring on my finger and no idea who I am, much less what I want to do...I realize that having nothing ahead to count on

means I now have to count on myself; that having no direction means forging one of my own" (Page, 1999).

Indeed, it is no longer uncommon to meet someone like Kirsten, a "twixter," or an emerging adult: twentysomething, still living at home, not yet married, with no children, and no settled career. Are such people still adolescents who are taking longer to find their identity? Or are they self-indulgent adults trapped in a "maturity gap" (Galambos, Barker, & Tilton-Weaver, 2003)? Either way, emerging adulthood is an unstable, "in-between," self-focused period of time to explore identities and life possibilities (Arnett, 2004).

According to psychologist Jeffrey Arnett, emerging adulthood is now becoming increasingly common in affluent Westernized cultures around the world (Arnett, 2011). However, in less affluent countries, as in poorer parts of every country, including America, most adolescents continue to "become adults" at much younger ages (Arnett & Galambos, 2003). Thus, words like *adolescent* or *adulthood* cannot be defined solely in terms of physical maturation. Sociocultural factors also play a role in defining when we stop being children or become adults (Arnett, 2010).

In many ways adolescence and young adulthood are more emotionally turbulent than midlife or old age. One important aspect of this period is the struggle with right and wrong—in other words, the need to develop moral values.

Moral Development—Growing a Conscience

JOURNEY QUESTION 3.7 *How do we develop morals and values?*

A person with a terminal illness is in great pain. She is pleading for death. Should extraordinary medical efforts be made to keep her alive? A friend of yours desperately needs to pass a test and asks you to help him cheat. Will you do it? These are *moral* questions, or questions of conscience.

Moral development starts in childhood and continues into adulthood (Nucci & Gingo, 2011). Through this process, we acquire values, beliefs, and thinking patterns that guide responsible behavior (King, 2009). Moral values are especially likely to come into sharper focus during adolescence and the transition to adulthood, as capacities for self-control and abstract thinking increase (Hart & Carlo, 2005). Let's take a brief look at this intriguing aspect of personal development.

Levels of Moral Development

How are moral values acquired? In an influential account, psychologist Lawrence Kohlberg (1981) held that we learn moral values through thinking and reasoning. To study moral development, Kohlberg posed dilemmas to children of different ages. The following is one of the moral dilemmas he used (Kohlberg, 1969, adapted):

A woman was near death from cancer and there was only one drug that might save her. It was discovered by a druggist who was charging 10 times what it cost to make the drug. The sick woman's husband could pay only $1,000, but the druggist wanted $2,000. He asked the druggist to sell it cheaper or to let him pay later. The druggist said no. So the husband became desperate and broke into the store to steal the drug for his wife. Should he have done that? Was it wrong or right? Why?

Each child was asked what action the husband should take. Kohlberg classified the reasons given for each choice and identified three levels of moral development. Each is based not so much on the choices made, but on the reasoning used to arrive at a choice.

Moral development The development of values, beliefs, and thinking abilities that act as a guide regarding what is acceptable behavior.

At the lowest, **preconventional level**, moral thinking is guided by the consequences of actions (punishment, reward, or an exchange of favors). For example, a person at this level might reason: "The man shouldn't steal the drug because he could get caught and sent to jail" (avoiding punishment) or "It won't do him any good to steal the drug because his wife will probably die before he gets out of jail" (self-interest).

At the second, **conventional level**, reasoning is based on a desire to please others or to follow accepted authority, rules, and values. For example, a person at this intermediate level might say: "He shouldn't steal the drug because others will think he is a thief. His wife would not want to be saved by thievery" (avoiding disapproval) or "Although his wife needs the drug, he should not break the law to get it. Everyone has to obey the law. His wife's condition does not justify stealing" (traditional morality of authority).

At the highest, **postconventional level**, moral behavior is directed by self-chosen ethical principles that tend to be general, comprehensive, or universal. People at this level place high value on justice, dignity, and equality. For example, a highly principled person might say: "He should steal the drug and then inform the authorities that he has done so. He will have to face a penalty, but he will have saved a human life" (self-chosen ethical principles).

Does everyone eventually reach the highest level? People advance at different rates, and many fail to reach the postconventional level of moral reasoning. In fact, some may not even reach the conventional level. For instance, a significant number of men in their first year of college think unwanted sexual aggression is acceptable (Tatum & Foubert, 2009).

The preconventional level is most characteristic of young children and delinquents (Forney, Forney, & Crutsinger, 2005). Conventional, group-oriented morals are typical of older children and most adults. Kohlberg estimated that only about 20 percent of the adult population achieves postconventional morality, representing self-direction and higher principles. (It would appear that few of these people enter politics!)

Developing a "moral compass" is an important part of growing up. Many of the choices we make every day involve fundamental questions of right and wrong. The ability to think clearly about such questions is essential to becoming a responsible adult.

Preconventional moral reasoning Moral thinking based on the consequences of one's choices or actions (punishment, reward, or an exchange of favors).

Conventional moral reasoning Moral thinking based on a desire to please others or to follow accepted rules and values.

Postconventional moral reasoning Moral thinking based on carefully examined and self-chosen moral principles.

🖐 **study break** Adolescence, Young Adulthood, and Moral Development

RECITE

1. In North America the primary criterion for the transition from adolescence to adulthood is marriage. T or F?
2. Identify formation is spurred by _____ and _____ _____.
3. According to Jeffrey Arnett, the trend in affluent Westernized cultures towards allowing young people to take longer to settle into their adult roles is best referred to as
   a. emerging adulthood
   b. hurried childhood
   c. a maturity gap
   d. extended adolescence
4. According to Lawrence Kohlberg, the conventional level of moral development is marked by a reliance on outside authority. T or F?
5. Self-interest and avoiding punishment are elements of postconventional morality. T or F?
6. About 80 percent of all adults function at the postconventional level of moral reasoning. T or F?

REFLECT

THINK CRITICALLY

7. Are labels like "adolescent" or "young adult" reflective of heredity or environment?

SELF-REFLECT

To what extent does the concept of identity formation apply to your own experience during adolescence?

Do you know any emerging adults? (Are you one?) Do you think emerging adults are adolescents taking longer to find their identity or young adults avoiding their need to establish themselves in the world of adults?

At what stage of moral development do you think most terrorists function?

ANSWERS

1. F 2. puberty, cognitive development 3. a 4. T 5. F 6. F 7. Environment, rather than heredity, is the better answer. Even better, the meanings of terms like "adolescence" or "adult" vary considerably from culture to culture, indicating that it is really a matter of definition (Arnett, 2011).

The Story of a Lifetime—Rocky Road or Garden Path?

JOURNEY QUESTION 3.8 *What are the typical tasks and dilemmas through the life span?*

Every life is marked by a number of developmental milestones (Kail & Cavanaugh, 2012). These are notable events, markers, or turning points in personal development. Some examples include graduating from school, voting for the first time, getting married, watching a child leave home (or move back!), burying a parent, becoming a grandparent, retiring, and, in the end, dying. Thus far, we have traced Samantha's progress through childhood, adolescence, and young adulthood. What challenges lie ahead for her?

Erikson's Psychosocial Theory

Perhaps the best way to get a preview of Samantha's life is to consider some of the major psychological milestones and challenges she is likely to encounter. Broad similarities between people can be found in the life stages of infancy, childhood, adolescence, young adulthood, middle adulthood, and old age. Each developmental stage confronts a person with new **developmental tasks**, specific challenges that must be mastered for optimal development. Examples are learning to read in childhood, adjusting to sexual maturity in adolescence, and establishing a vocation as an adult.

In a highly influential book entitled *Childhood and Society*, personality theorist Erik Erikson (1903–1994) suggests that we face a specific *psychosocial dilemma*, or "crisis," at each stage of life. A **psychosocial dilemma** is a conflict between personal impulses and the social world. Resolving each dilemma creates a new balance between a person and society. A string of "successes" produces healthy development and a satisfying life. Unfavorable outcomes throw us off balance, making it harder to deal with later crises. Life becomes a "rocky road," and personal growth is stunted. **Table 3.2** lists Erikson's (1963) dilemmas.

What are the major developmental tasks and life crises? A brief description of each psychosocial dilemma follows.

Stage One, First Year of Life: Trust Versus Mistrust

During the first year of life, children are completely dependent on others. Erikson believes that a basic attitude of trust or mistrust is formed at this time. **Trust** is established when babies are given warmth, touching, love, and physical care. **Mistrust** is caused by inadequate or unpredictable care and by parents who are cold, indifferent, or rejecting. Basic mistrust may later cause insecurity, suspiciousness, or an inability to relate to others. Notice that trust comes from the same conditions that help babies become securely attached to their parents.

Personality theorist Erik Erikson (1903–1994) is best known for his life-stage theory of human development.

© Ted Streshinsky/Corbis

Table 3.2 Erikson's Psychosocial Dilemmas

AGE	CHARACTERISTIC DILEMMA
Birth to 1 year	Trust versus mistrust
1 to 3 years	Autonomy versus shame and doubt
3 to 5 years	Initiative versus guilt
6 to 12 years	Industry versus inferiority
Adolescence	Identity versus role confusion
Young adulthood	Intimacy versus isolation
Middle adulthood	Generativity versus stagnation
Late adulthood	Integrity versus despair

© Cengage Learning

Developmental task Any skill that must be mastered, or personal change that must take place, for optimal development.

Psychosocial dilemma A conflict between personal impulses and the social world.

Trust versus mistrust A conflict early in life about learning to trust others and the world.

Stage Two, 1–3 Years: Autonomy Versus Shame and Doubt

In stage two, children express their growing self-control by climbing, touching, exploring, and trying to do things for themselves. David and Carol fostered Samantha's sense of **autonomy** by encouraging her to try new skills. However, her first efforts were sometimes crude, involving spilling, falling, wetting, and other "accidents." If David and Carol had ridiculed or overprotected Samantha, they might have caused her to feel **shameful** about her actions and **doubt** her abilities.

Stage Three, 3–5 Years: Initiative Versus Guilt

In stage three, children move beyond simple self-control and begin to take initiative. Through play, children learn to make plans and carry out tasks. Parents reinforce **initiative** by giving children freedom to play, ask questions, use imagination, and choose activities. Feelings of **guilt** about initiating activities are formed if parents criticize severely, prevent play, or discourage a child's questions.

Stage Four, 6–12 Years: Industry Versus Inferiority

Many events of middle childhood are symbolized by that fateful day when you first entered school. With dizzying speed your world expanded beyond your family, and you faced a whole series of new challenges.

The elementary school years are a child's "entrance into life." In school, children begin to learn skills valued by society, and success or failure can affect a child's feelings of adequacy. Children learn a sense of **industry** if they win praise for productive activities, such as building, painting, cooking, reading, and studying. If a child's efforts are regarded as messy, childish, or inadequate, feelings of **inferiority** result. For the first time, teachers, classmates, and adults outside the home become as important as parents in shaping attitudes toward oneself.

Stage Five, Adolescence: Identity Versus Role Confusion

As we have noted, adolescence is often a turbulent time. Erikson considers a need to answer the question "Who am I?" the primary task during this stage of life. As Samantha matures mentally and physically, she will have new feelings, a new body, and new attitudes. Like other adolescents, she will need to build a consistent **identity** out of her talents, values, life history, relationships, and the demands of her culture (Côté, 2006b). Her conflicting experiences as a student, friend, athlete, worker, daughter, lover, and so forth must be integrated into a unified sense of self. Persons who fail to develop a sense of identity suffer from **role confusion**, an uncertainty about who they are and where they are going.

Stage Six, Young Adulthood: Intimacy Versus Isolation

In stage six, the individual feels a need for *intimacy* in his or her life. After establishing a stable identity, a person is prepared to share meaningful love or deep friendship with others (Beyers & Seiffge-Krenke, 2010). By **intimacy**, Erikson means an ability to care about others and to share experiences with them. And yet, marriage or sexual involvement is no guarantee of intimacy: Many adult relationships remain shallow and unfulfilling. Failure to establish intimacy with others leads to a deep sense of **isolation**—feeling alone and uncared for in life. This often sets the stage for later difficulties.

Stage Seven, Middle Adulthood: Generativity Versus Stagnation

According to Erikson, an interest in guiding the next generation provides emotional balance in middle adulthood. Erikson called this quality **generativity**. It is expressed by caring about oneself, one's children, and future generations. Samantha may achieve generativity by guiding her own children or by helping other children, as a teacher or coach, for example (Hebblethwaite & Norris, 2011). Productive or creative work can also

Autonomy versus shame and doubt A conflict created when growing self-control (autonomy) is pitted against feelings of shame and doubt.

Initiative versus guilt A conflict between learning to take initiative and overcoming feelings of guilt about doing so.

Industry versus inferiority A conflict in middle childhood centered on lack of support for industrious behavior, which can result in feelings of inferiority.

Identity versus role confusion A conflict of adolescence, involving the need to establish a personal identity.

Intimacy versus isolation The challenge of overcoming a sense of isolation by establishing intimacy with others.

Generativity versus stagnation A conflict of middle adulthood in which self-interest is countered by an interest in guiding the next generation.

express generativity. In any case, a person must broaden his or her concerns and energies to include the welfare of others and society as a whole. Failure to do this is marked by a **stagnant** concern with one's own needs and comforts. Life loses meaning, and the person feels bitter, dreary, and trapped (Friedman, 2004).

Stage Eight, Late Adulthood: Integrity Versus Despair

What does Erikson see as the conflicts of old age? Late adulthood is a time of reflection. According to Erikson, when Samantha grows old she must be able to look back over her life with acceptance and satisfaction. People who have lived richly and responsibly develop a sense of **integrity**, or self-respect. This allows them to face aging and death with dignity. If previous life events are viewed with regret, the elderly person experiences **despair**, or heartache and remorse. In this case, life seems like a series of missed opportunities. The person feels like a failure, knowing it's too late to reverse what has been done. Aging and the threat of death then become sources of fear and depression.

According to Erikson, an interest in future generations characterizes optimal adult development.

The Whole Human

To squeeze a lifetime into a few pages, we had to ignore countless details. Although much is lost, the result is a clearer picture of an entire life cycle. Is Erikson's description, then, an exact map of Samantha's past and her future—or your own? Probably not. Still, psychosocial dilemmas are major events in many lives. Knowing about them may allow you to anticipate typical trouble spots in your own life. You may also be better prepared to understand the problems and feelings of friends and relatives at various points in the life cycle.

Middle and Late Adulthood: You're an Adult Now!

JOURNEY QUESTION 3.9 *What is involved in well-being during middle and later adulthood?*

Although Erikson's dilemmas extend into adulthood, they are not the only challenges adults face, as we'll discuss in this section.

Other Challenges of Adulthood

Middle-aged adults (those from about ages 35 to 64) and *later adults* (those age 65 and older) face life challenges such as financial pressures, legal conflicts, and personal tragedies, to name but a few. However, most challenges of adulthood revolve around health, careers, marriage, children, and parents (Damman, Henkens, & Kalmijn, 2011).

Health

Samantha's father, David, just came back from his physiotherapy appointment. He put his knee out in a game of touch football (he swears the other guy didn't just "touch" him!). A high school football star, 40-year old David has encountered the obvious: he is getting older. Although some adults face far more serious health issues, from heart attacks to cancer, every adult faces the routine wear and tear of aging. How one deals with the inevitable slow declines of adulthood strongly influences that adult's degree of life satisfaction (Lachman, 2004). Fortunately, most of the time, declines happen slowly enough that they can be offset by increased life experience. Most adults learn to work "smarter," both physically and mentally (Santrock, 2010).

Integrity versus despair A conflict in old age between feelings of integrity and the despair of viewing previous life events with regret.

Careers

The work adults do—as homemakers, volunteers, hourly workers, or in careers—is also critical to feeling successful (Sterns & Huyck, 2001). While peak earnings commonly occur during these years, growing expenses may continue to create financial pressures, from child care to tuition fees for children and from rent to mortgages. This is one reason why career difficulties and unemployment can pose such serious challenges to adult well-being. Another reason, of course, is that many adults derive much of their identity from their work (Santrock, 2010).

Marriage, Children, and Parents

Most adult Americans identify their social relationships—especially with children, spouses, and parents—as another important aspect of adult life (Markus et al., 2004). Creating and sustaining social relationships can involve working through the stresses of child-rearing, becoming "empty nesters" when children move away, becoming grandparents, experiencing marital strife or divorce, living as singles or in blended families, seeing parents grow old, need support, and die, to mention some of the more common social challenges faced by adults.

A Midlife Crisis?

Don't people face a "midlife crisis" at this point in their lives? Although adulthood brings its fair share of life's challenges, only about a quarter of men and women believe they have experienced a midlife crisis (Wethington, Kessler, & Pixley, 2004). It is more common to make a "midcourse correction" at midlife than it is to survive a "crisis" (Freund & Ritter, 2009; Lachman, 2004). Ideally, the midlife transition involves reworking old identities, achieving valued goals, finding one's own truths, and preparing for old age. Taking stock may be especially valuable at midlife, but reviewing past choices to prepare for the future is helpful at any age. For some people, difficult turning points in life can serve as "wake-up calls" that create opportunities for personal growth (Weaver, 2009; Wethington, 2003).

Facing the Challenges of Adulthood

How do people maintain a state of well-being as they run the gauntlet of modern life? Psychologist Carol Ryff believes that well-being during adulthood has six elements (Ryff & Singer, 2009; van Dierendonck et al., 2008):

1. Self-acceptance
2. Positive relations with others
3. Autonomy (personal freedom)
4. Environmental mastery
5. A purpose in life
6. Continued personal growth

Ryff found that, for many adults, age-related declines are offset by positive relationships and greater mastery of life's demands (Ryff & Singer, 2009). Thus, sharing life's joys and sorrows with others, coupled with a better understanding of how the world works, can help carry people through midlife and into their later years (Lachman et al., 2008; Ryff, Singer, & Palmersheim, 2004). It is important to note that despite the emphasis on youth in our culture, middle age and beyond can be a rich period of life in which people feel secure, happy, and self-confident (Rubenstein, 2002).

Old Age

After the late 50s, physical aging complicates personal development. However, it is wrong to believe that most elderly people are sickly, infirm, or senile. (Nowadays, 60 is the new 40, an idea with which both of your authors wholeheartedly agree!) Only about 5 percent of those older than 65 are in nursing homes. Mentally, many elderly persons are at least as capable as the average young adult. On intellectual tests, top scorers over the age of 65 match the average for men younger than 35. What sets these silver-haired stars apart? Typically they are people who have continued to work and remain intellectually active (Hooyman & Kiyak, 2011; Salthouse, 2004). *Gerontologist*—a psychologist who studies aging and the aged—Warner Schaie (1994, 2005) found that you are most likely to stay mentally sharp in old age if:

1. You remain healthy.
2. You live in a favorable environment. (You are educated and have a stimulating occupation, an above-average income, and an intact family.)
3. You are involved in intellectually stimulating activities (reading, travel, cultural events, continuing education, clubs, and professional associations).
4. You have a flexible personality.
5. You are married to an intelligent spouse.
6. You maintain your perceptual processing speed by staying active.
7. You were satisfied with your accomplishments in midlife.

A shorter summary of this list is "Those who live by their wit die with their wits."

Shown here at her star-studded 90th birthday party in 2012, Betty White's 70+ years as a popular entertainer show that aging does not inevitably bring an end to engaging in challenging activities

Successful Aging

What are the keys to successful aging? They are not unlike the elements of well-being at midlife. The psychological characteristics shared by the healthiest, happiest older people are (de Leon, 2005; Vaillant, 2002):

Optimism, hope, and an interest in the future

Gratitude and forgiveness; an ability to focus on what is good in life

Empathy; an ability to share the feelings of others and see the world through their eyes

Connection with others; an ability to reach out, to give and receive social support

Actually, these are excellent guidelines for well-being at any stage of adulthood.

In summary, enlightened views of aging call for an end to the forced obsolescence of the elderly. As a group, older people represent a valuable source of skill, knowledge, and energy that we can't afford to cast aside. As we face the challenges of this planet's uncertain future, we need all the help we can get!

Aging and Ageism

Ageism, which refers to discrimination or prejudice based on age, can oppress the young as well as the old (Bodner, 2009). For instance, a person applying for a job may just as well be told "You're too young" as "You're too old." In some societies, ageism is expressed as respect for the elderly. In Japan, for instance, aging is seen as positive, and greater age brings more status and respect. In most Western nations, however, ageism tends to have a negative impact on older individuals.

Ageism is often expressed through patronizing language. Older people are frequently spoken to in an overly polite, slow, loud, and simple way, implying that they are infirm, even when they are not (Nelson, 2005). Popular stereotypes of the "dirty old man," "meddling old woman," "senile old fool," and the like also help perpetuate myths about aging. But such stereotypes are clearly wrong: A tremendous diversity exists among the elderly—ranging from the infirm to aerobic-dancing grandmothers.

In many occupations, older workers perform well in jobs that require *both* speed and skill. Of course, people do experience a gradual loss of *fluid intelligence* (abilities requiring speed or rapid learning) as they age but, often, this can be offset by many *crystallized intelligence* (abilities involving already learned knowledge and skills), such as vocabulary and stored-up facts, which may actually improve—at least into the 60s (Schaie, 2005). (Remember, infants show just the opposite pattern, being high in fluid intelligence but

Ageism Discrimination or prejudice based on a person's age.

low in crystalized intelligence.) Overall, very little loss of job performance need occur as workers grow older (Agrigoroaei & Lachman, 2011). In the professions, wisdom and expertise can usually more than compensate for any loss of mental quickness (Ericsson, 2000). Basing retirement solely on a person's age makes little sense.

Death and Dying

We have seen throughout this chapter that it is valuable to understand major trends in the course of development. With this in mind, let's explore emotional responses to death, the inevitable conclusion of every life.

Reactions to Impending Death

An influential account of emotional responses to death comes from the work of Elisabeth Kübler-Ross (1926–2004) who spent hundreds of hours at the bedsides of the terminally ill, where she observed five basic emotional reactions to impending death (Kübler-Ross, 1975):

1. **Denial and isolation.** A typical first reaction is to deny death's reality and isolate oneself from information confirming that death is really going to occur. Initially, the person may be sure that "It's all a mistake." "Surely," she or he thinks, "the doctor made an error."
2. **Anger.** Many dying individuals feel anger and ask, "Why me?" As they face the ultimate threat of having life torn away, their anger may spill over into rage toward the living.
3. **Bargaining.** In another common reaction, the terminally ill bargain with themselves or with God. The dying person thinks, "Just let me live a little longer and I'll do anything to earn it."
4. **Depression.** As death draws near and the person begins to recognize that it cannot be prevented, feelings of futility, exhaustion, and deep depression may set in.
5. **Acceptance.** If death is not sudden, many people manage to come to terms with dying and accept it calmly. The person who accepts death is neither happy nor sad but at peace with the inevitable.

Not all terminally ill persons display all these reactions, nor do they always occur in this order. In general, one's approach to dying will mirror his or her style of living (Yedidia & MacGregor, 2001). It is a mistake to think that Kübler-Ross's list is a series of stages to go through in order or that there is something wrong if a person does not show all these emotions. Rather, the list describes typical reactions to impending death.

Implications

How can I make use of this information? First, it can help both the dying and survivors to recognize and cope with periods of depression, anger, denial, and bargaining. Second, it helps to realize that close friends or relatives may feel many of the same emotions before or after a person's death because they, too, are facing a loss.

Perhaps the most important thing to recognize is that dying persons need to share their feelings and to discuss death openly (Corr, Nabe, & Corr, 2012). Too often, dying persons feel isolated and separated from others. If someone in your life is dying, here's some advice (Dyer, 2001):

- Be yourself and relate person to person.
- Be ready to listen again and again.
- Be respectful.
- Be aware of feelings and nonverbal cues.
- Be comfortable with silence.
- Be genuine.
- Most of all, be there.

Death may be inevitable, but it can be faced with dignity and sometimes even humor. Mel Blanc's famous sign-off, "That's all folks," is engraved on a marble headstone over his grave. Blanc was the voice of Bugs Bunny, Porky Pig, and many other cartoon characters.

study break Challenges Across the Lifespan

RECITE

The first 8 questions are about Erikson's life stages and crises:

1. In the first year of life the crisis is trust vs. _____.
2. During ages 1–3 the crisis is _____ vs. shame and doubt.
3. During ages 3–5 the crisis is _____ vs. guilt.
4. The crisis is industry vs. _____ from ages 6–12.
5. The crisis is _____ vs. _____ during adolescence.
6. During young adulthood the crisis is _____ vs. isolation.
7. During middle adulthood the crisis is generativity vs. _____.
8. The crisis is _____ vs. _____ during late adulthood.
9. After age 65, a large proportion of older people show significant signs of mental disability and most require special care. T or F?
10. In the reaction that Kübler-Ross describes as bargaining, the dying individual asks, "Why me?" T or F?

REFLECT

THINK CRITICALLY

11. Trying to make generalizations about development throughout life is complicated by at least one major factor. What do you think it is?

SELF-REFLECT

See if you can think of a person you know who is facing one of Erikson's psychosocial dilemmas. Now see if you can think of specific people who seem to be coping with each of the other dilemmas.

Describe three instances of ageism you have witnessed.

ANSWERS

1. mistrust 2. autonomy 3. initiative 4. inferiority 5. identity, role confusion 6. intimacy 7. stagnation 8. integrity, despair 9. F 10. F. 11. Different cohorts (groups of people born in the same year) live in different historical times. People born in various decades may have very different life experiences. This makes it difficult to identify universal patterns (Stewart & Ostrove, 1998).

Psychology in Action

Well-Being and Happiness—What Makes a Good Life?

JOURNEY QUESTION 3.10 *What factors contribute most to a happy and fulfilling life?*

What makes you happy? Love? Money? Music? Sports? Partying? Religion? Clearly, there is no simple, universal formula for happiness. And what does it mean to have a good life? Is it a matter of health? Achievement? Friendship? Leisure? Personal growth? Again, there are no simple answers. Both happiness and living a "good life" depend greatly on individual needs and cultural values (Scollon, Koh, & Au, 2011). Nevertheless, psychologists are beginning to understand some aspects of what it means to be happy and live well. Their findings provide valuable hints about how to live a successful life.

Happiness

To study happiness, psychologist Ed Diener and his associates have focused on what they call **subjective well-being**. According to them, feelings of well-being, or happiness, occur when people are generally satisfied with their lives, have frequent positive emotions, and have relatively few negative emotions (Diener, Scollon, & Lucas, 2009; Tay & Diener, 2011).

Life Satisfaction *What does life satisfaction refer to?* You are high in life satisfaction if you strongly agree with the following statements (from the "Satisfaction with Life Scale," Diener, 2009):

1. In most ways my life is close to my ideal.
2. The conditions of my life are excellent.
3. I am satisfied with my life.
4. So far I have gotten the important things I want in life.
5. If I could live my life over, I would change almost nothing.

These statements seem to cover a lot of what it means to be happy. However, Diener and his colleagues believe day-to-day emotional experiences are also important.

Subjective well-being General life satisfaction combined with frequent positive emotions and relatively few negative emotions.

The way you perceive, interpret, and manage events is as important as the nature of the events themselves.

Emotions   Imagine that several pleasant or rewarding events have occurred today. These events caused you to experience moments of laughter, joy, delight, and satisfaction. As a result, you feel happy and life seems good. In contrast, imagine that your day was marred by a series of unpleasant or punishing events, which left you feeling sad. In reality, of course, we rarely have entirely good or bad days. Life is a mixture of rewarding and punishing events, so everyone feels both positive and negative emotions. It's possible for the same person to have lots of positive feelings *and* lots of negative feelings. That's why happiness is not just a matter of having good feelings. The happiest people are those who have many positive emotional experiences and relatively few negative experiences (Diener, Scollon, & Lucas, 2009).

Life Events

Then do good and bad events in life dictate whether a person is happy? Happiness is related to good and bad life events, but the impact is smaller than you might imagine. The reason for this is that happiness tends to come from within a person. Subjective well-being is affected by our goals, choices, emotions, values, and personality. The way events are perceived, interpreted, and managed is as important as the nature of the events themselves. People who are good at dodging life's hard knocks tend to create their own "luck." As a result, they are happier and seem to negotiate life's demands more smoothly (Wong, 2011).

Personal Factors

What about factors such as income, age, or marital status? Are they related to happiness? Personal characteristics have only a small connection with overall happiness. Let's see why.

Wealth   It is tempting to think that wealth brings happiness. And, up to a certain point, it's true: more resources can bring happiness to people living in poverty (Howell & Howell, 2008). However, the overall association between money and happiness is weak. In fact, people who win lotteries are often *less* happy than they were before (Lutter, 2007). New life stresses that instant riches usually bring into a person's life tend to cancel out any positive effects of wealth. While money may make it possible to meet your basic needs in life, it can't buy you a good life. Happiness must usually come from other sources (Diener et al., 2010; Scollon & King, 2011).

Education   More educated people tend to be a little happier than the less educated. However, this is most likely just another way of saying that there is a small connection between wealth and happiness. Higher education generally results in higher income and more social status.

Marriage   Married people report greater happiness than people who are divorced, separated, or single. It could be that happier people are simply more likely to get married. But a better explanation for this association is that happy people are more likely to get married and stay married. Most people get a small boost in happiness immediately after getting married. However, most eventually return to about the same level of happiness they had before they tied the knot (Lucas et al., 2003).

Religion   There is a small but positive association between happiness and holding spiritual beliefs (Diener, Tay, & Myers, 2011). Religious beliefs may add to feelings of purpose and meaning in life, resulting in greater happiness. Another possibility is that church membership may simply provide social support that softens the impact of life's negative events.

Age   The stereotype of the crotchety old person who is dissatisfied with everything is inaccurate (Sorrell, 2009). Life satisfaction and happiness generally *do not* decline with age. People are living longer and staying healthier, which has greatly delayed age-related declines. When declines do occur, older people today seem better able to cope with them.

Sex Overall, men and women do not differ in happiness (Brannon, 2011). However, women do have a tendency to experience higher emotional highs and lower lows than men do. Thus, more women are found among those rare individuals who are extremely happy or unhappy.

Work People who are satisfied with their jobs tend to be happier, but the association is weak. If fact, it probably just reflects the fact that job satisfaction is a large part of greater life satisfaction.

Personality To a degree, some people are more temperamentally disposed to be happy, regardless of life events. In general, happier people also tend to be extraverted (outgoing), optimistic, and worry-free. This combination probably influences the balance of positive and negative emotions a person feels (Lucas & Diener, 2009).

Goals and Happiness

The preceding account gives some insight into who is happy, but we can learn more by examining people's goals. To know if someone is happy, it is helpful to ask, "What is this person trying to do in life? How well is she or he succeeding at it?"

Do you want to be healthy and physically fit? To do well in school? To be liked by friends? To own a recording studio? A BMW? The goals people choose vary widely. Nevertheless, one generalization we can make is that people tend to be happy if they are meeting their personal goals. This is especially true if you feel you are making progress on a day-to-day basis on smaller goals that relate to long-term, life goals (King, Richards, & Stemmerich, 1998).

The importance of personal goals helps explain why specific circumstances tell us so little about happiness. It is often difficult to know if an event is good or bad without knowing what a person is trying to achieve in life (Diener, Scollon, & Lucas, 2009).

The Whole Human In summary, happier persons tend to be married, comfortable with their work, extraverted, religious, optimistic, and generally satisfied with their lives. They also are making progress toward their goals. However, attaining goals that do not express our deeper interests and values may add little to happiness (Scollon & King, 2011).

What, then, makes a good life? Earlier in this chapter we noted that purpose and meaning are important sources of well-being at mid-life (Ryff & Singer, 2009). Actually, this appears to be true at any point in life. As we have seen, a good life is one that is happy *and* meaningful (Shrira et al., 2011).

🖐 study break Well-Being and Happiness

RECITE

1. Subjective well-being consists of a mixture of _____ _____, positive emotions, and negative emotions.
2. People who experience many positive emotions are, by definition, very happy. T or F?
3. Happiness has only a small positive correlation with wealth. T or F?
4. Single persons are generally happier than those who are married. T or F?
5. Making progress day-by-day toward important _____ _____ is a major source of happiness.

REFLECT

THINK CRITICALLY

6. "To thine own self be true" may seem like a cliché, but it's actually not a bad place to begin a search for a happy and meaningful life. Explain.

SELF-REFLECT

How do you think you would rate on each of the three components of subjective well-being? What other factors discussed in this section are related to your own level of happiness?

It is common for students to pursue goals that are imposed on them. Which of your activities do you regard as most meaningful? How do they relate to your personal beliefs and values?

ANSWERS

1. life satisfaction 2. F 3. T 4. F 5. life goals 6. To be true to yourself is to live with *integrity*, by finding happiness through the pursuit of meaningful life goals (McGregor, McAdams, & Little, 2006).

Chapter in Review

Summary

3.1 How do heredity and environment affect development?

- 3.1.1 Heredity (nature) and environment (nurture) are interacting forces that are both necessary for human development. However, caregivers can only influence environment.

- 3.1.2 The chromosomes and genes in each cell of the body carry hereditary instructions. Most characteristics are polygenic and reflect the combined effects of dominant and recessive genes.

- 3.1.3 Maturation of the body and nervous system underlies the orderly development of motor and perceptual skills, cognitive abilities, emotions, and language. The rate of maturation varies from person to person.

- 3.1.4 The human neonate has a number of adaptive reflexes, including the grasping, rooting, sucking, and Moro reflexes.

- 3.1.5 Testing with a looking chamber reveals that neonates prefer complex patterns to simple ones and human face patterns, especially familiar faces.

- 3.1.6 Many early skills are subject to the principle of readiness.

- 3.1.7 Prenatal development is influenced by environmental factors, such as various teratogens, including diseases, drugs, and radiation, as well as the mother's diet, health, and emotions.

- 3.1.8 During sensitive periods in development, infants are more sensitive to specific environmental influences.

- 3.1.9 Early perceptual, intellectual, or emotional deprivation seriously retards development, whereas deliberate enrichment of the environment has a beneficial effect on infants.

- 3.1.10 Temperament is hereditary. Most infants fall into one of three temperament categories: easy children, difficult children, and slow-to-warm-up children.

- 3.1.11 A child's developmental level reflects heredity, environment, and the effects of the child's own behavior.

3.2 Of what significance is a child's emotional bond with adults?

- 3.2.1 Emotions develop in a consistent order, starting with generalized excitement in newborn babies. Three of the basic emotions—fear, anger, and joy—may be unlearned.

- 3.2.2 Emotional attachment of human infants is a critical early event.

- 3.2.3 Infant attachment is reflected by separation anxiety. The quality of attachment can be classified as secure, insecure-avoidant, or insecure-ambivalent.

- 3.2.4 High-quality day care does not appear to harm children. Low-quality day care can be risky.

- 3.2.5 Meeting a baby's affectional needs is as important as meeting needs for physical care.

3.3 How important are parenting styles?

- 3.3.1 Studies suggest that parental styles have a substantial impact on emotional and intellectual development.

- 3.3.2 Three major parental styles are authoritarian, permissive, and authoritative (effective). Authoritative parenting, relying more on management techniques rather than power assertion or withdrawal of love, appears to benefit children the most.

- 3.3.3 Whereas mothers typically emphasize caregiving, fathers tend to function as playmates for infants.

- 3.3.4 Parental styles vary across cultures.

3.4 How do children acquire language?

- 3.4.1 Language development proceeds from crying to cooing, then babbling, the use of single words, and then to telegraphic speech.

- 3.4.2 The underlying patterns of telegraphic speech suggest a biological predisposition to acquire language. This innate tendency is augmented by learning.

- 3.4.3 Prelanguage communication between parent and child involves shared rhythms, nonverbal signals, and turn-taking.

- 3.4.4 Motherese or parentese is a simplified, musical style of speaking that parents use to help their children learn language.

3.5 How do children learn to think?

- 3.5.1 Neonates begin to learn immediately and they appear to be aware of the effects of their actions.

- 3.5.2 The intellect of a child is less abstract than that of an adult. Jean Piaget theorized that intellectual growth occurs through a combination of assimilation and accommodation.

- 3.5.3 Piaget also held that children go through a fixed series of cognitive stages. The stages and their approximate age ranges are sensorimotor (0–2), preoperational (2–7), concrete operational (7–11), and formal operations (11–adult).

- 3.5.4 Caregivers should offer learning opportunities that are appropriate for a child's level of cognitive development.

- 3.5.5 Learning principles provide an alternate explanation that assumes that cognitive development is continuous; it does not occur in stages.

- 3.5.6 Studies of infants under the age of 1 year suggest that they are capable of thought well beyond that observed by Piaget. Similarly children begin to outgrow egocentrism as early as age 4.

- 3.5.7 Lev Vygotsky's sociocultural theory emphasizes that a child's mental abilities are advanced by interactions with more competent partners. Mental growth takes place in a child's zone of proximal development, where a more skillful person may scaffold the child's progress.

3.6 Why is the transition from adolescence to adulthood especially challenging?

- 3.6.1 The timing of puberty can complicate the task of identity formation, a major task of adolescence.
- 3.6.2 Identity formation is even more challenging for adolescents of ethnic descent.
- 3.6.3 In Western industrialized societies, the transition into adulthood is further complicated as it is increasingly delayed well into the 20s (emerging adulthood).

3.7 How do we develop morals and values?

- 3.7.1 Lawrence Kohlberg identified preconventional, conventional, and postconventional levels of moral reasoning.
- 3.7.2 Developing mature moral standards is also an important task of adolescence.
- 3.7.3 Most people function at the conventional level of morality, but some never get beyond the selfish, preconventional level. Only a minority of people attain the highest, or postconventional, level of moral reasoning.

3.8 What are the typical tasks and dilemmas through the life span?

- 3.8.1 Erik Erikson identified a series of challenges that occur across the life span. These range from a need to gain trust in infancy to the need to live with integrity in old age.
- 3.8.2 Successful resolution of the dilemmas produces healthy development, whereas unsuccessful outcomes make it harder to deal with later crises.

3.9 What is involved in well-being during middle and later adulthood?

- 3.9.1 Physical aging starts early in adulthood. Every adult must find ways to successfully cope with aging.
- 3.9.2 Only a minority of people have a midlife crisis, but midlife course corrections are more common.

- 3.9.3 Well-being during adulthood consists of six elements: self-acceptance, positive relations with others, autonomy, environmental mastery, having a purpose in life, and continued personal growth.
- 3.9.4 Intellectual declines associated with aging are limited, at least through one's 70s. This is especially true of individuals who remain mentally active.
- 3.9.5 Ageism refers to prejudice, discrimination, and stereotyping on the basis of age. It affects people of all ages but is especially damaging to older people. Most ageism is based on stereotypes, myths, and misinformation.
- 3.9.6 Typical emotional reactions to impending death include denial, anger, bargaining, depression, and acceptance, but not necessarily in that order or in every case.

3.10 What factors contribute most to a happy and fulfilling life?

- 3.10.1 Subjective well-being (happiness) is a combination of general life satisfaction, plus more positive emotions than negative emotions.
- 3.10.2 Life events and various demographic factors have relatively little influence on happiness.
- 3.10.3 People with extraverted (outgoing), optimistic, and worry-free personalities tend to be happier.
- 3.10.4 Making progress toward one's goals is associated with happiness.
- 3.10.5 Overall well-being is a combination of happiness and meaning in life, which comes from pursuing goals that express one's deeper interests and values.

Interactive Learning

Log in to CengageBrain to access the resources your instructor requires. For this book, you can access:

CourseMate Go to CengageBrain.com to access Psychology CourseMate, where you will find an interactive eBook, glossaries, flashcards, quizzes, videos, Virtual Psychology Labs, and more.

Aplia If your professor has assigned Aplia:

1. Sign in to your account.
2. Complete the corresponding exercises as required by your professor.
3. When finished, click "Grade It Now" to see which areas you have mastered, which areas need more work, and detailed explanations of every answer.

Test Your Knowledge

Human Development

1. If a personal trait is controlled by a single dominant gene, the trait cannot be
   a. hereditary
   b. related to DNA sequences
   c. influenced by chromosomes
   d. polygenic

2. Early in life, the learning of basic skills is most effective when parents respect the
   a. Mozart effect
   b. value of reactive maternal involvement
   c. principle of readiness
   d. fact that babies cannot imitate adult actions until they are 18 months old

3. Deprivation has an especially strong impact on development during
   a. the reciprocal stage
   b. sensitive periods
   c. the polygenic stage
   d. the social play phase

4. According to research using a looking chamber, infants begin to show a preference for complex over simple patterns within _____ after birth.
   a. three months
   b. three years
   c. three days
   d. three weeks

5. Cephalocaudal and proximodistal patterns show the effects of _____ on motor development.
   a. enriched environments
   b. maturation
   c. scaffolding
   d. sensitive periods

6. A clear sign that infant attachment is beginning to occur is found in the presence of
   a. a social smile
   b. separation anxiety
   c. social scaffolding
   d. affectional needs

7. A baby who turns away from his mother when she returns after a brief separation shows signs of having which type of attachment?
   a. insecure-avoidant
   b. insecure-ambivalent
   c. solitary-ambivalent
   d. maternal-disaffectional

8. Psychologist Diana Baumrind describes parents who enforce rigid rules and demand strict obedience as
   a. authoritative
   b. permissive-repressive
   c. proactive-reactive
   d. authoritarian

9. Turn-taking with nonverbal signals is a first step toward
   a. secure attachment
   b. motor development
   c. using language
   d. an ability to make transformations

10. Parents talk to young children with a raised tone of voice and an exaggerated pattern of speaking that is called
    a. transformational grammar
    b. telegraphic speech
    c. signal switching
    d. parentese

11. Piaget believed that a child's understanding of the world grows through the mental processes of assimilation and
    a. intuition
    b. accommodation
    c. egocentricism
    d. reversibility

12. According to Piaget, a child's mastery of conservation occurs during the
    a. formal operations stage
    b. preoperational stage
    c. concrete operational stage
    d. sensorimotor stage

13. Vygotsky believed that adults help children learn how to think by using a process he called
    a. reversible thinking
    b. scaffolding
    c. accommodation
    d. moral reasoning

14. The phenomenon of emerging adulthood teaches us that terms like *adolescent* or *adulthood* cannot be defined solely in terms of
    a. identity formation
    b. emotional turbulence
    c. moral development
    d. physical maturation

15. According to Kohlberg, the highest level of moral development involves being guided by
    a. self-chosen universal ethical principles
    b. the consequences of actions
    c. a desire to follow accepted authority
    d. choosing right rather than wrong

16. According to Erikson, the dilemma faced by most 3- to-5-year-olds is
    a. autonomy versus shame and doubt
    b. initiative versus guilt
    c. trust versus mistrust
    d. industry versus inferiority

17. Erikson's theory states that mature adults are best able to avoid stagnation when they express
    a. integrity
    b. generativity
    c. intimacy
    d. preconventional moral reasoning

18. In middle age, most adults experience
    a. a loss of crystallized abilities
    b. a midlife correction
    c. a midlife crisis
    d. ageism

19. Subjective well-being is high when people are
    a. generally satisfied with their lives
    b. have frequent positive emotions
    c. have relatively few negative emotions
    d. experiencing all of the above

20. Meeting personal goals generally makes people
    a. set new goals
    b. happy
    c. frustrated
    d. greedy

Answers

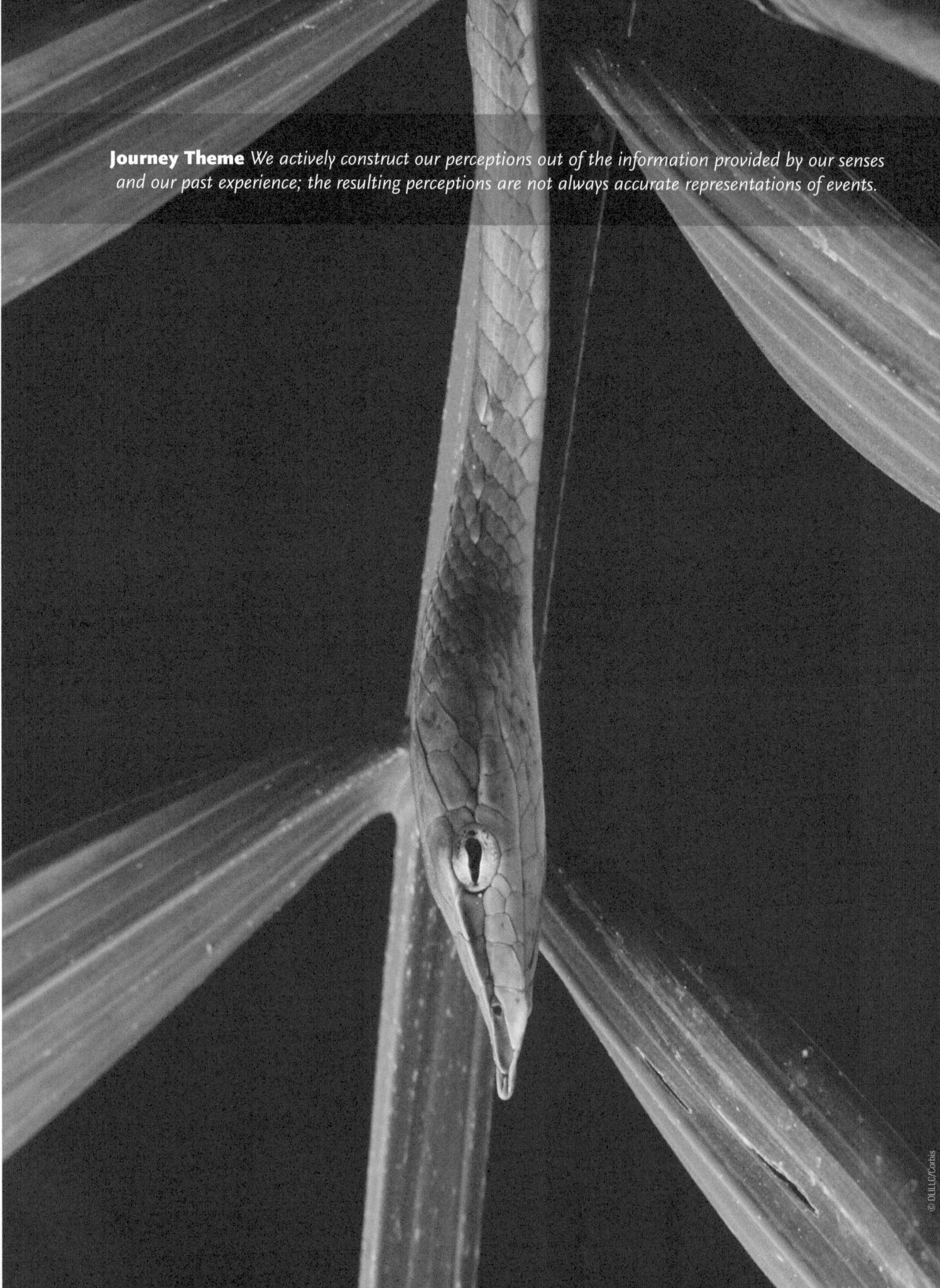

Journey Theme *We actively construct our perceptions out of the information provided by our senses and our past experience; the resulting perceptions are not always accurate representations of events.*

4

Sensation and Perception

Journey into Psychology: The Trees Have Eyes

Right now, you are bathed in a swirling kaleidoscope of electromagnetic radiation, heat, pressure, vibrations, molecules, and mechanical forces. However, unless your senses translate these forces into a form your brain can understand, you will experience only a void of silence and darkness. The next time you drink in the beauty of a sunset, a flower, or a friend, remember that sensation makes it all possible.

But are our senses enough to give us a completely accurate "picture" of reality? One of your authors was once admiring a flower in a beautiful tropical rainforest when he had the uncanny impression he was being watched. For several minutes he fruitlessly searched around, taking in the lush scene. Nothing. No, wait, there it was. Hanging not more than a foot from his own head was the head of a snake, staring straight at him. Yikes! How on earth could he have missed it? Slowly backing away, he marveled at how the snake was perfectly *camouflaged*, hanging motionless from an overhanging branch, looking for all the world like just another green vine (this species isn't called a green vine snake for nothing).

As this story shows, sensing the world is really just a first step in perceiving the world. Even though his eyes were picking up the basic visual information he needed to perceive the snake, his brain couldn't put the perceptual puzzle together. Sensory information can be interpreted (and misinterpreted) in various ways. That's step two in experiencing the world. We begin this chapter with the first step, sensation. Then we'll explore the second step, perception. Our perceptions create faces, melodies, works of art, illusions, and occasionally snakes out of the raw material of sensation.

Journey Questions

4.1 In general, how do sensory systems function?

4.2 How does the visual system function?

4.3 What are the mechanisms of hearing?

4.4 How do the chemical senses operate?

4.5 What are the somesthetic senses?

4.6 In general, how do we construct our perceptions?

4.7 Why are we more aware of some sensations than others?

4.8 How is it possible to see depth and judge distance?

4.9 How is perception altered by expectations, motives, emotions, and learning?

4.10 Is extrasensory perception possible?

4.11 How can I perceive events more accurately?

Sensory Processes—The First Step

Physical energy in the form of light or heat or sound strikes your senses. An instant later you notice a bumblebee whiz past or the warmth of the sun on your face or a catchy new tune on the radio. In that instant, a remarkable series of events will have transpired as you detect, analyze, and interpret sensory information. Before we examine specific senses in more detail, let's explore how the senses reduce the amount of information the brain must process.

The primary function of the senses is to act as biological **transducers**, devices that convert one kind of energy into another (Fain, 2003). Each sense translates a specific type of external energy into patterns of activity (action potentials) in neurons. Information arriving from the sense organs creates **sensations**. Then the brain processes these messages. When the brain organizes sensations into meaningful patterns, we speak of **perception**. It is fascinating to realize that "seeing" and "hearing" take place in your brain, not in your eyes or ears.

Let's explore sensation in more detail before we move on to perception. Consider, for example, vision, which gives us amazingly wide access to the world. In one instant, you can view a star light years away, and in the next, you can peer into the microscopic universe of a dewdrop. Yet, vision also narrows what we can possibly observe. Like the other senses, vision acts as a *data reduction system*. It selects and analyzes information in order to code and send to the brain only the most important data (Goldstein, 2010).

Selection

How does sensory data reduction take place? Considerable selection occurs because sensory receptors do not transduce all of the energies they encounter. For example, a guitar transduces string vibrations into sound waves. Pluck a string and the guitar will produce a sound. However, stimuli that don't cause the string to move will have no effect. If you shine a light on the string, or pour cold water on it, the guitar will remain silent. (The owner of the guitar, however, might get quite loud at this point!) In a similar way, the eye transduces electromagnetic radiation, the ear transduces sound waves, and so on. Many other types of stimuli cannot be sensed directly because we lack sensory receptors to transduce their energy. For example, humans cannot sense the bioelectric fields of other living creatures, but sharks have special organs that can (Fields, 2007). (Do they *hear* the fields or *feel* them or what?)

In the field of **psychophysics**, physical energy (such as sound waves or electromagnetic radiation) is measured and related to dimensions of the resulting sensations we experience (such as loudness or brightness). Psychophysical research has shown that sense receptors transduce only part of their target energy range (Fain, 2003). For example, your eyes transduce only a tiny fraction of the entire range of electromagnetic energies—the part we call the *visible spectrum*. The eyes of honeybees can transduce, and therefore see, parts of the electromagnetic spectrum invisible to us humans. Likewise, bats "shout" at a pitch too high for humans to transduce. But they can hear their own reflected echoes. This ability, called *echolocation*, allows bats to fly in total darkness while avoiding collisions and catching insects.

Similarly, energy below a certain minimum intensity is necessary for a sensation to occur. The necessary minimum defines the **absolute threshold** for a sensory system. For example, very soft sounds (which could be heard if they were just a little louder) fall below the absolute threshold for human hearing. Of course owls, who hunt at night, have much lower absolute thresholds for hearing. As you can see, our rich sensory experiences are only a small part of what *could* be sensed and what some animals *can* sense.

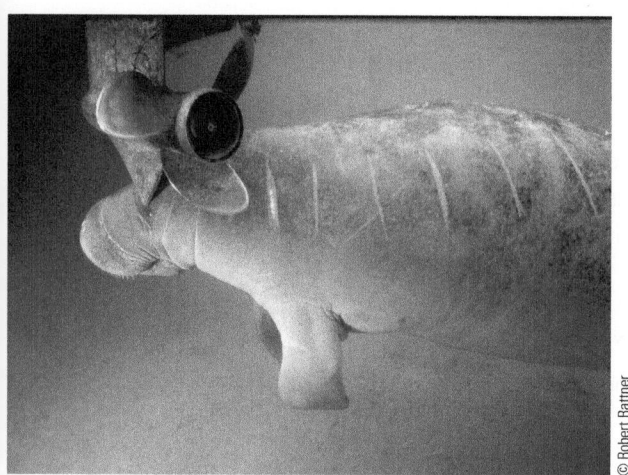

© Robert Rattner

Absolute thresholds define the sensory worlds of humans and animals, sometimes with serious consequences. The endangered Florida manatee ("sea cow") is a peaceful, plant-eating creature that can live for more than 60 years. For the last decade, the number of manatees killed by boats has climbed alarmingly. The problem? Manatees have poor sensitivity to the low-frequency sounds made by slow-moving boats. Current laws require boats to slow down in manatee habitats, which may actually increase the risk to these gentle giants (Gerstein, 2002).

Transducers Devices that convert one kind of energy into another.

Sensation A sensory impression; also, the process of detecting physical energies with the sensory organs.

Perception The mental process of organizing sensations into meaningful patterns.

Psychophysics Study of the relationship between physical stimuli and the sensations they evoke in a human observer.

Absolute threshold The minimum amount of physical energy necessary to produce a sensation.

Sensory Adaptation

The flow of sensations to the brain is reduced in another way. Think about walking into a house in which fried liver, sauerkraut, and head cheese were just prepared for dinner. (Some dinner!) While you might pass out at the door, people who had been in the house for some time wouldn't be aware of the food odors. Why? Because sensory receptors respond less to unchanging stimuli, a process called **sensory adaptation**.

Fortunately, the olfactory (smell) receptors adapt quickly. When exposed to a constant odor, they send fewer and fewer nerve impulses to the brain until the odor is no longer noticed. Adaptation to pressure from a wristwatch, waistband, ring, or glasses is based on the same principle. Since there is usually little reason to keep reminding the brain that a sensory input is unchanged, sensory receptors generally respond best to *changes* in stimulation. No one wants or needs to be reminded 16 hours a day that his or her shoes are on.

Sensory Analysis

What we experience is also influenced by **sensory analysis**. As they process information, the senses divide the world into important **perceptual features**, or basic stimulus patterns. The visual system, for example, has a set of *feature detectors* that are attuned to very specific stimuli, such as lines, shapes, edges, spots, colors, and other patterns (Hubel & Wiesel, 2005). Look at **Figure 4.1** and notice how eye-catching the single vertical line is among a group of slanted lines. This effect, which is called *visual pop-out*, occurs because your visual system is highly sensitive to these perceptual features (Hsieh, Colas, & Kanwisher, 2011).

Similarly, frog eyes are highly sensitive to small, dark, moving spots. In other words, they are basically "tuned" to detect bugs flying nearby (Lettvin, 1961). But the insect (spot) must be moving, or the frog's "bug detectors" won't work. A frog could starve to death surrounded by dead flies.

Although our sensitivity to perceptual features is an innate characteristic of the nervous system, it is also influenced by experiences early in life. For instance, Colin Blakemore and Graham Cooper of Cambridge University raised kittens in a room with only vertical stripes on the walls. Another set of kittens saw only horizontal stripes. When returned to normal environments, the "horizontal" cats could easily jump onto a chair, but when walking on the floor, they bumped into chair legs. "Vertical" cats, on the other hand, easily avoided chair legs, but they missed when trying to jump to horizontal surfaces. The cats raised with vertical stripes were "blind" to horizontal lines, and the "horizontal" cats acted as if vertical lines were invisible (Blakemore & Cooper, 1970). Other experiments show that there is an actual decrease in brain cells tuned to the missing features (Grobstein & Chow, 1975).

Sensory Coding

As they select and analyze information, sensory systems *code* it. **Sensory coding** refers to converting important features of the world into neural messages understood by the brain (Hubel & Wiesel, 2005). For example, not every difference between two stimuli can be coded; instead, the difference must be sufficiently large. Psychophysics also involves the study of **difference thresholds**. Here we are asking, "How different must two stimuli be before the difference becomes noticeable and, hence, codable?" For example, if you were to put one extra grain of sugar in your coffee, would you notice difference? How much would it take? A few grains? A half spoonful? A spoonful?

To see coding at work, try closing your eyes for a moment. Then take your fingertips and press firmly on your eyelids. Apply enough pressure to "squash" your eyes slightly. Do

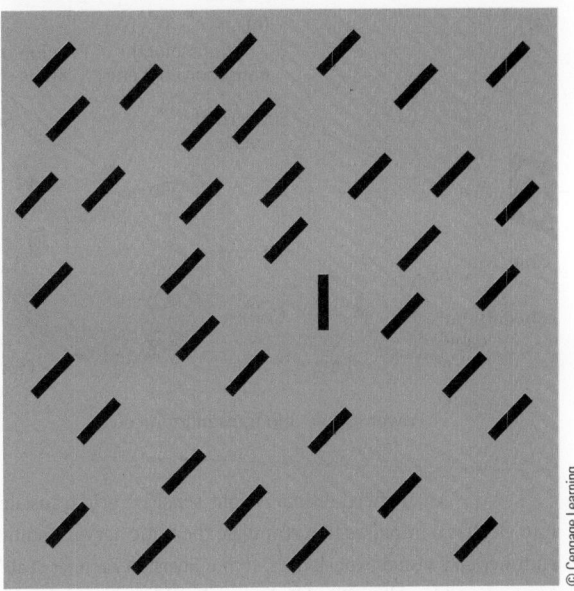

Figure 4.1 Visual pop-out. Pop-out is so basic that babies as young as 3 months respond to it. (Adapted from Adler & Orprecio, 2006.)

© Cengage Learning

Sensory adaptation A decrease in sensory response to an unchanging stimulus.

Sensory analysis Separation of sensory information into important elements.

Perceptual features Basic elements of a stimulus, such as lines, shapes, edges, or colors.

Sensory coding Codes used by the sense organs to transmit information to the brain.

Difference threshold The minimum difference between two stimuli that is detectable to an observer.

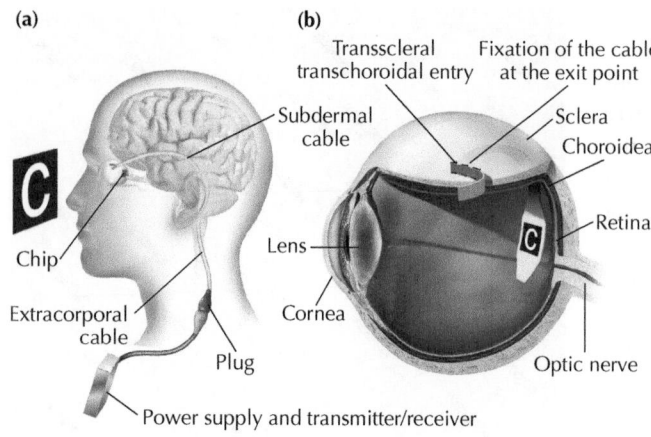

(a) Chip · Extracorporal cable · Plug · Power supply and transmitter/receiver · Subdermal cable

(b) Transscleral transchoroidal entry · Fixation of the cable at the exit point · Sclera · Choroidea · Retina · Optic nerve · Lens · Cornea

Figure 4.2 An artificial retina. A light-sensitive grid translates light into electrical impulses that stimulate the optic nerve, resulting in rudimentary visual experiences. (From Eberhart Zrenner et al. "Subretinal Electronic Chips Allow Blind Patients to Read Letters and Combine Them to Words (Figure 2, a & b)." *Proceedings of the Royal Society B.* Copyright © 2010 by The Royal Society. Reprinted by permission.)

this for about 30 seconds and observe what happens. (Readers with eye problems or contact lenses should not try this.)

Did you "see" stars, checkerboards, and flashes of color? These are called *phosphenes* (FOSS-feens), visual sensations caused by mechanical excitation of the retina. They occur because the eye's receptor cells, which normally respond to light, are also somewhat sensitive to pressure. Notice, though, that the eye is prepared to code stimulation—including pressure—only into visual features. As a result, you experience light sensations, not pressure. Also important in producing this effect is *sensory localization* in the brain.

Sensory localization means that the type of sensation you experience depends on which brain area is activated. Some brain areas receive visual information; others receive auditory information, and still others receive taste or touch. Knowing which brain areas are active tells us, in general, what kinds of sensations you are feeling.

Sensory localization is beginning to make it possible to artificially restore sight, hearing, or other senses. In one approach, researchers have used a miniature television camera to send electrical signals to directly stimulate to the brain (Warren & Normann, 2005). In another approach, a grid of light-sensitive elements is implanted into the retina so that it can electrically stimulate the optic nerve instead (Figure 4.2). Using such technologies, people who have lost their vision are now able to "see" letters, words, and some common objects like knives and forks (Zrenner et al., 2010).

Although the senses supply raw data to the brain, these data remain mostly meaningless until they are interpreted. It's as if the senses provide only the jumbled pieces of a complex puzzle. In the remaining sections of this chapter, we will further explore the various senses and how we put the puzzle together.

study break Sensory Processes

RECITE

1. Sensory receptors are biological _____, or devices for converting one type of energy to another.
2. As time passes, nerve endings in the skin under your clothes send fewer signals to the brain and you become unable to feel your clothes. This process is called
   a. transduction
   b. difference threshold
   c. reverse attention
   d. sensory adaptation
3. Lettvin found that a frog's eyes are especially sensitive to phosphenes. T or F?
4. Important features of the environment are transmitted to the brain through a process known as
   a. perception
   b. coding
   c. detection
   d. programming

REFLECT

THINK CRITICALLY

5. William James once said, "If a master surgeon were to cross the auditory and optic nerves, we would hear lightning and see thunder." Can you explain what James meant?

SELF-REFLECT

How does sensation affect what you are experiencing right now? Try to imagine how overwhelmed you would be if data reduction didn't occur.

What if, like some other animals, you could transduce other energies? What if your senses were tuned to detect different perceptual features? How would the sensory world you live in change? What would it be like to be a bat?

ANSWERS

1. transducers 2. d 3. F 4. b 5. The explanation is based on sensory localization: If a lightning flash caused rerouted messages from the eyes to activate auditory areas of the brain, we would experience a sound sensation. Likewise, if the ears transduced a thunderclap and sent impulses to the visual area, a sensation of light would occur. Amazingly, some people, called *synesthetes*, naturally experience sensory inputs in terms of other senses. For example, one synesthete experiences pain as the color orange, whereas for another the taste of spiced chicken is pointy (Dixon, Smilek, & Merikle, 2004).

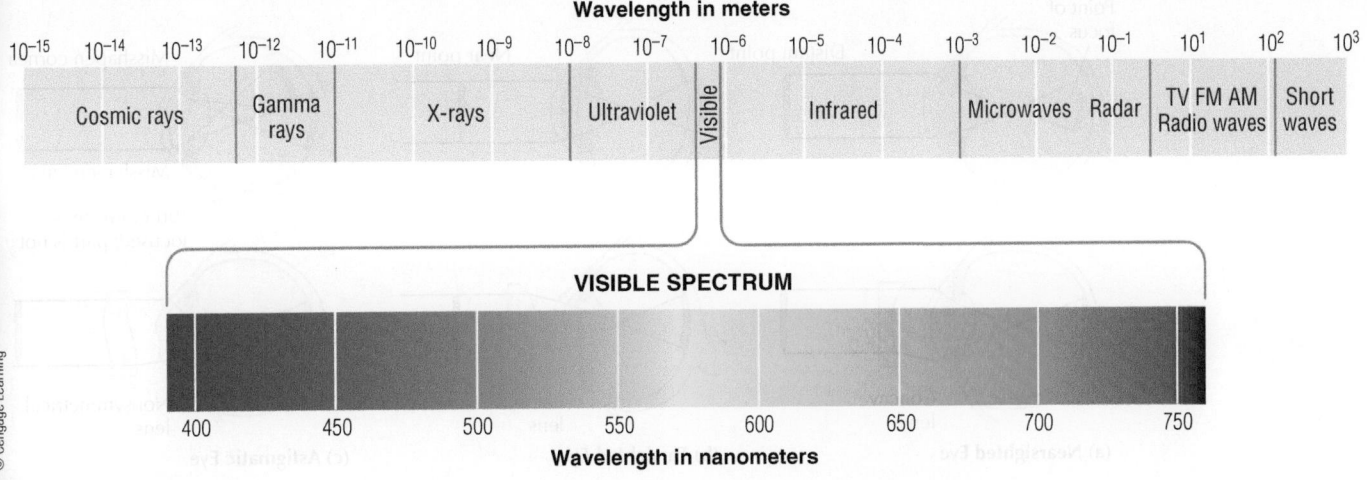

Wavelength in meters
10^{-15} 10^{-14} 10^{-13} 10^{-12} 10^{-11} 10^{-10} 10^{-9} 10^{-8} 10^{-7} 10^{-6} 10^{-5} 10^{-4} 10^{-3} 10^{-2} 10^{-1} 10^{1} 10^{2} 10^{3}
Cosmic rays
Gamma rays
X-rays
Ultraviolet
Visible
Infrared
Microwaves
Radar
TV FM AM Radio waves
Short waves
VISIBLE SPECTRUM
400 450 500 550 600 650 700 750
Wavelength in nanometers

Figure 4.3 The visible spectrum.

Vision—Catching Some Rays

JOURNEY QUESTION 4.2 *How does the visual system function?*

In the morning when you first open your eyes, you effortlessly become aware of the visual richness of the world around you. But the ease with which normally sighted people can *see* conceals incredible complexity. Vision is an impressive sensory system, worthy of a detailed discussion.

What are the basic dimensions of light and vision? The *visible spectrum*—the spread of electromagnetic energies to which the eyes respond—is made up of a narrow range of wavelengths of electromagnetic radiation. Visible light starts at "short" wavelengths of 400 *nanometers* (nan-OM-et-er: one billionth of a meter), which we sense as purple or violet. Longer light waves produce blue, green, yellow, orange, and red, which has a wavelength of 700 nanometers (Figure 4.3).

The term *hue* refers to the basic color categories of red, orange, yellow, green, blue, indigo, and violet. As just noted, various hues, or color sensations, correspond to the wavelength of the light that reaches our eyes (Mather, 2011). White light, in contrast, is a mixture of many wavelengths. Hues (colors) from a narrow band of wavelengths are very *saturated*, or "pure." (An intense "fire-engine" red is more saturated than a muddy "brick" red.) A third dimension of vision, *brightness*, corresponds roughly to the amplitude, or height, of light waves. Waves of greater amplitude are "taller," carry more energy, and cause the colors we see to appear brighter or more intense. For example, the same "brick" red would look bright under intense, high-energy illumination and drab under dim light.

Ciliary muscle
Aqueous humor
Iris
Pupillary opening
Cornea
Lens
Fovea
Blind spot
Optic nerve
Retinal arteries and veins
Retina

Figure 4.4 The human eye, a simplified view.

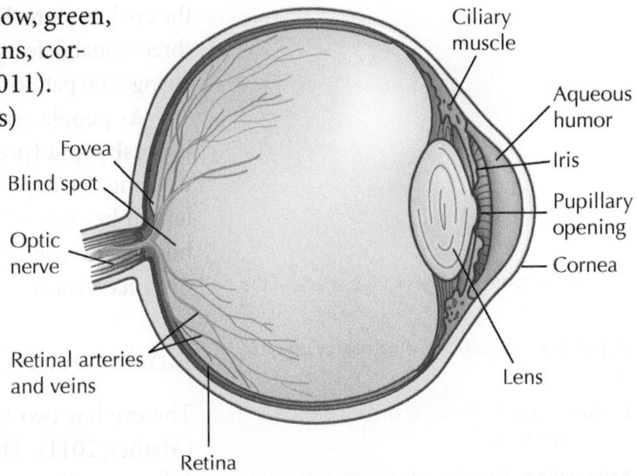

Structure of the Eye

Although the visual system is much more complex than any digital camera, both cameras and eyes have a *lens* to focus images on a light-sensitive layer at the back of an enclosed space. In a camera, it is a layer of light-sensitive pixels in the digital image sensor. In the eye, it is a layer of *photoreceptors* (light-sensitive cells) in the **retina**, an area about the size and thickness of a postage stamp (Figure 4.4).

How does the eye focus? Most focusing is done at the front of the eye by the *cornea*, a clear membrane that bends light inward. The lens makes additional, smaller adjustments.

Retina The light-sensitive layer of cells at the back of the eye.

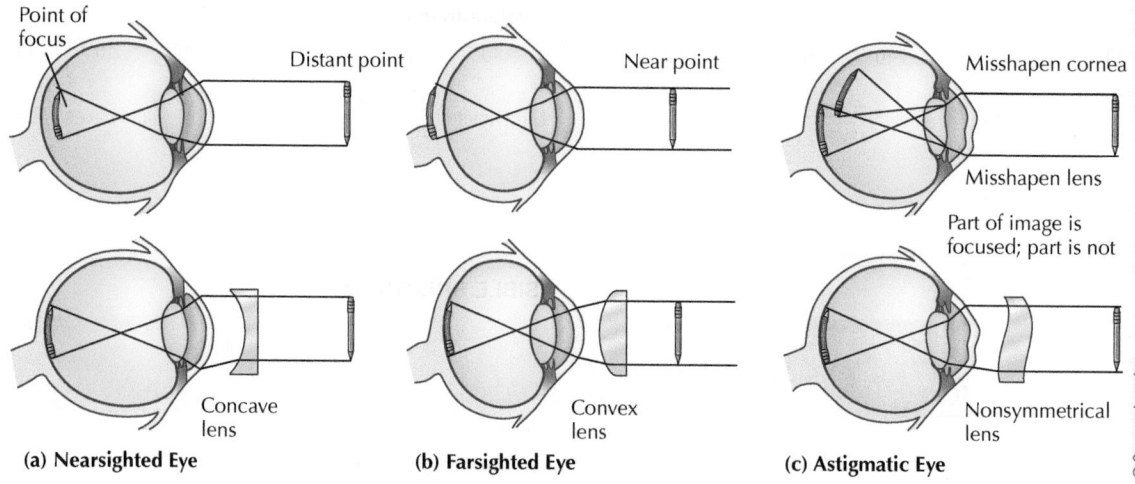

Point of focus	Distant point	Misshapen cornea
	Near point	Misshapen lens
		Part of image is focused; part is not
Concave lens	Convex lens	Nonsymmetrical lens
(a) Nearsighted Eye	**(b) Farsighted Eye**	**(c) Astigmatic Eye**

Figure 4.5 Visual defects and corrective lenses: *(a)* A myopic (longer than usual) eye. The concave lens spreads light rays just enough to increase the eye's focal length. *(b)* A hyperopic (shorter than usual) eye. The convex lens increases refraction (bending) to focus light on the retina. *(c)* An astigmatic (lens or cornea not symmetrical) eye. In astigmatism, parts of vision are sharp and parts are unfocused. Lenses that correct astigmatism are nonsymmetrical.

Your eye's focal point changes when muscles attached to the lens alter its shape. This process is called **accommodation**. In cameras, focusing is done more simply—by changing the distance between the lens and the image sensor.

Visual Problems

Focusing is also affected by the shape of the eye. If your eye is too short, nearby objects will be blurred but distant objects will be sharp. This is called **hyperopia** (HI-per-OPE-ee-ah), or farsightedness. If your eyeball is too long, images fall short of the retina and you won't be able to focus distant objects. This results in **myopia** (my-OPE-ee-ah), or nearsightedness. When the cornea or the lens is misshapen, part of vision will be focused and part will be fuzzy. In this case, the eye has more than one focal point, a problem called **astigmatism** (ah-STIG-mah-tiz-em). All three visual defects can be corrected by placing glasses (or contact lenses) in front of the eye to change the path of light (**Figure 4.5**).

As people age, the lens becomes less flexible and less able to accommodate. The result is **presbyopia** (prez-bee-OPE-ee-ah), from the Latin for "old vision," or farsightedness due to aging. Perhaps you have seen a grandparent or older friend reading a newspaper at arm's length because of presbyopia. If you now wear glasses for nearsightedness, you may need bifocals as you age. (Just like your authors. Sigh.) Bifocal lenses correct near vision *and* distance vision.

Rods and Cones

The eye has two types of "image sensors," consisting of receptor cells called *rods* and *cones* (Mather, 2011). The 5 million **cones** in each eye work best in bright light. They also produce color sensations and fine details. In contrast, the **rods**, numbering about 120 million, can't detect colors (**Figure 4.6**). Pure rod vision is black and white. However, the rods are much more sensitive to light than the cones are. The rods therefore allow us to see in very dim light.

Surprisingly, the retina has a "hole" in it: Each eye has a *blind spot* because there are no receptors where the optic nerve passes out of the eye and blood vessels enter (Lamb, 2011; **Figure 4.7a**). The blind spot shows that vision depends greatly on the brain. If you close one eye, some of the incoming light will fall on the blind spot of your open eye. Why isn't there a gap in your vision? The answer is that the visual cortex of the brain actively fills in the gap

Accommodation Changes in the shape of the lens of the eye.

Hyperopia Difficulty focusing nearby objects (farsightedness).

Myopia Difficulty focusing distant objects (nearsightedness).

Astigmatism Defects in the cornea, lens, or eye that cause some areas of vision to be out of focus.

Presbyopia Farsightedness caused by aging.

Cones Visual receptors for colors and daylight visual acuity.

Rods Visual receptors for dim light that produce only black and white sensations.

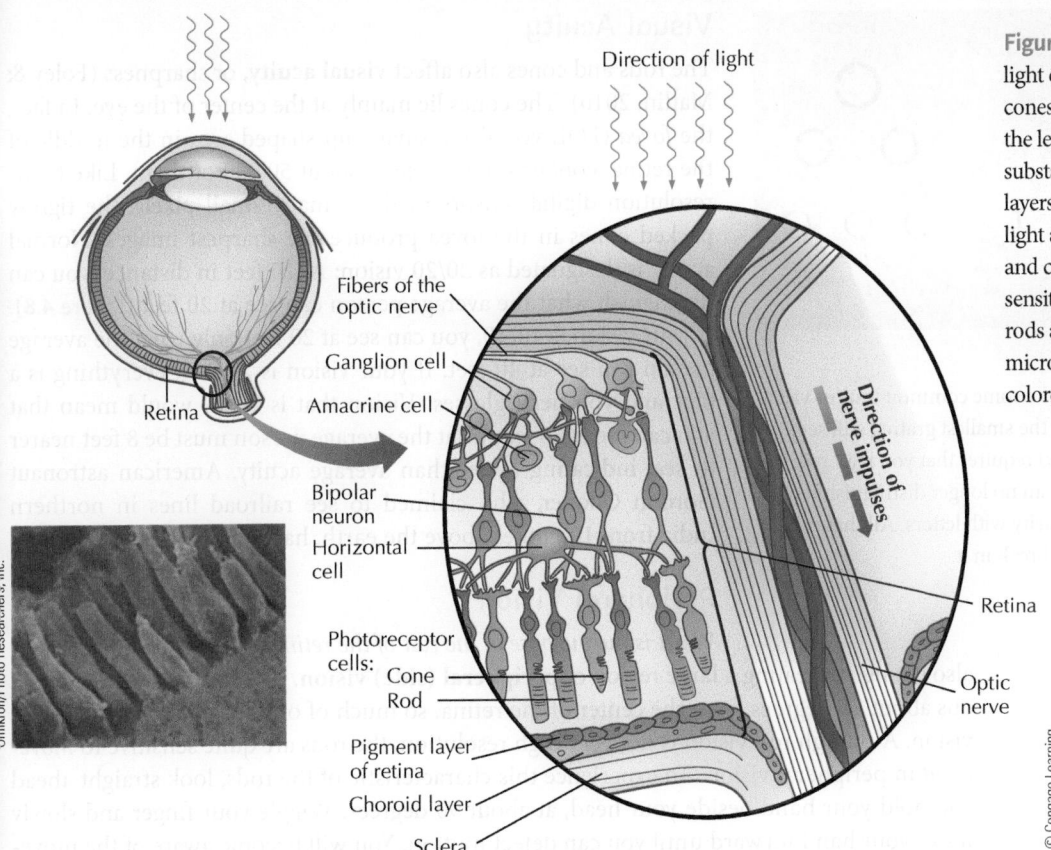

Direction of light

Fibers of the optic nerve
Ganglion cell
Amacrine cell
Bipolar neuron
Horizontal cell
Photoreceptor cells:
Cone
Rod
Pigment layer of retina
Choroid layer
Sclera

Retina

Direction of nerve impulses

Retina

Optic nerve

© Cengage Learning

Figure 4.6 Anatomy of the retina. Note that light does not fall directly on the rods and cones. It must first pass through the cornea, the lens, the vitreous humor (a jelly-like substance that fills the eyeball), and the outer layers of the retina. Only about one half of the light at the front of the eye reaches the rods and cones—testimony to the retina's amazing sensitivity. The lower left photograph shows rods and cones as seen through an electron microscope. In the photograph the cones are colored green and the rods blue.

with patterns from surrounding areas (**Figure 4.7b**). By closing one eye, you can visually "behead" other people by placing their images on your blind spot. (Just a hint for some classroom fun.) The brain can also "erase" distracting information. Roll your eyes all the way to the right and then close your right eye. You should clearly see your nose in your left eye's field of vision. Now, open your right eye again and your nose will nearly disappear as your brain disregards its presence.

(a)

(b)

© Cengage Learning

Figure 4.7 Experiencing the blind spot. *(a)* With your right eye closed, stare at the upper-right cross. Hold the book about 1 foot from your eye and slowly move it back and forth. You should be able to locate a position that causes the black spot to disappear. When it does, it has fallen on the blind spot. With a little practice you can learn to make people or objects you dislike disappear too! *(b)* Repeat the procedure described, but stare at the lower cross. When the white space falls on the blind spot, the black lines will appear to be continuous. This may help you understand why you do not usually experience a blind spot in your visual field.

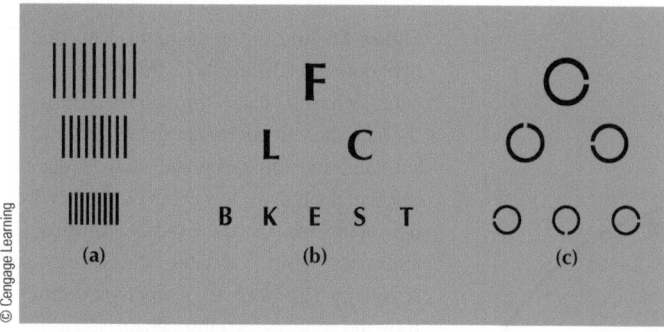

Figure 4.8 Tests of visual acuity. Here are some common tests of visual acuity. In *(a)*, sharpness is indicated by the smallest grating still seen as individual lines. The Snellen chart *(b)* requires that you read rows of letters of diminishing size until you can no longer distinguish them. The Landolt rings *(c)* require no familiarity with letters. All that is required is a report of which side has a break in it.

Visual Acuity

The rods and cones also affect **visual acuity**, or sharpness (Foley & Matlin, 2010). The cones lie mainly at the center of the eye. In fact, the *fovea* (FOE-vee-ah), a small cup-shaped area in the middle of the retina, contains only cones—about 50,000 of them. Like high-resolution digital sensors made of many small pixels, the tightly packed cones in the fovea produce the sharpest images. Normal acuity is designated as 20/20 vision: At 20 feet in distance, you can distinguish what the average person can see at 20 feet (Figure 4.8). If your vision is 20/40, you can see at 20 feet only what the average person can see at 40 feet. If your vision is 20/200, everything is a blur and you need glasses! Vision that is 20/12 would mean that you can see at 20 feet what the average person must be 8 feet nearer to see, indicating better than average acuity. American astronaut Gordon Cooper, who claimed to see railroad lines in northern India from 100 miles above the earth, had 20/12 vision.

Peripheral Vision

What is the purpose of the rest of the retina? Areas outside the fovea also get light, creating a large region of **peripheral (side) vision**. The rods are most numerous about 20 degrees from the center of the retina, so much of our peripheral vision is rod vision. Although rod vision is not very high resolution, the rods are quite sensitive to *movement* in peripheral vision. To experience this characteristic of the rods, look straight ahead and hold your hand beside your head, at about 90 degrees. Wiggle your finger and slowly move your hand forward until you can detect motion. You will become aware of the movement before you can actually "see" your finger. Seeing "out of the corner of the eye" is important for sports, driving, and walking down dark alleys. People who suffer from *tunnel vision* (a loss of peripheral vision) feel as if they are wearing blinders (Godnig, 2003).

The rods are also highly responsive to dim light. Because most rods are 20 degrees to each side of the fovea, the best night vision comes from looking *next to* an object you wish to see. Test this yourself some night by looking at, and next to, a very dim star.

Color Vision

How do the cones produce color sensations? The **trichromatic** (TRY-kro-MAT-ik) **theory** of color vision holds that there are three types of cones, each most sensitive to either red, green, or blue. Other colors result from combinations of these three.

A basic problem with the trichromatic theory is that four colors of light—red, green, blue, and yellow—seem to be primary (you can't get them by mixing other colors). Also, why is it impossible to have a reddish green or a yellowish blue? These problems led to the development of a second view, known as the **opponent-process theory**, which states that vision analyzes colors into "either-or" messages (Goldstein, 2010). That is, the visual system can produce messages for either red or green, yellow or blue, black or white. Coding one color in a pair (red, for instance) seems to block the opposite message (green) from coming through. As a result, a reddish green is impossible but a yellowish red (orange) can occur.

According to opponent-process theory, fatigue caused by making one response produces an afterimage of the opposite color as the system recovers. *Afterimages* are visual sensations that persist after a stimulus is removed—like seeing a spot after a flashbulb goes off. To see an afterimage of the type predicted by opponent-process theory, look at Figure 4.9 and follow the instructions there.

Which color theory is correct? Both! The three-color theory applies to the retina, in which three different types of cone have been found. Each contains a different type of *iodopsin* (i-oh-DOP-sin), a light-sensitive pigment that breaks down when struck by light. This triggers action potentials and sends neural messages to the brain. The three types of cones are most sensitive to red, green, or blue. Other colors result from combinations of these three. As

Visual acuity The sharpness of visual perception.

Peripheral (side) vision Vision at the edges of the visual field.

Trichromatic theory Theory of color vision based on three cone types: red, green, and blue.

Opponent-process theory Theory of color vision based on three coding systems (red or green, yellow or blue, black or white).

Figure 4.9 Negative afterimages. Stare at the dot near the middle of the flag for at least 30 seconds. Then look immediately at a plain sheet of white paper or a white wall. You will see the American flag in its normal colors. Reduced sensitivity to yellow, green, and black in the visual system, caused by prolonged staring, results in the appearance of complementary colors. Project the afterimage of the flag on other colored surfaces to get additional effects.

predicted, each form of iodopsin is most sensitive to light in roughly the red, green, or blue region. Thus, the three types of cones fire nerve impulses at different rates to produce various color sensations (Figure 4.10).

In contrast, the opponent-process theory better explains what happens in optic pathways and the brain *after* information leaves the eye. For example, some nerve cells in the brain are excited by the color red and inhibited by the color green. So both theories are "correct." One explains what happens in the eye itself. The other explains how colors are analyzed after messages leave the eye (Gegenfurtner & Kiper, 2003).

Color Blindness and Color Weakness

Do you know anyone who regularly draws hoots of laughter by wearing clothes of wildly clashing colors? Or someone who sheepishly tries to avoid saying what color an object is? If so, you probably know someone who is color-blind.

What is it like to be color-blind? What causes color blindness? A person who is **color-blind** cannot perceive colors. It is as if the world were a black-and-white movie. The color-blind person either lacks cones or has cones that do not function normally (Deeb, 2004; Neitz & Neitz, 2011). Such total color blindness is rare. In **color weakness**, or partial color blindness, a person can't see certain colors. Approximately 8 percent of Caucasian males (but fewer Asian, African, and Native American males and less than 1 percent of women) are red-green color-blind . These people see reds and greens as the same color, usually a yellowish brown (Figure 4.11). Another type of color weakness, involving yellow and blue, is extremely rare (National Institutes of Health, 2006).

Surprisingly, some people reach adulthood without knowing that some colors are missing (Gündogan et al., 2005). If you can't see the number 5 or follow the dots from X to X in Figure 4.12, you might be red-green color-blind.

How can color-blind individuals drive? Don't they have trouble with traffic lights? Red-green color-blind individuals have normal vision for yellow and blue, so the main problem is telling red lights from green. In practice, that's not difficult. The red light is always on top, and the green light is brighter than the red. Also, "red" traffic signals have yellow light mixed in with the red and a "green" light that is really blue-green.

Seeing in the Dark

What happens when the eyes adjust to a dark room? **Dark adaptation** is the dramatic increase in retinal sensitivity to light that occurs after a person enters the dark (Goldstein, 2010). Consider walking into a theater. If you enter from a brightly lit lobby, you practically need to be led to your seat. After a short time, however, you can see the entire room in detail (including the couple kissing over in the corner). It takes about 30 to 35 minutes of complete darkness to reach maximum visual sensitivity (Figure 4.13). At that point, your eye will be 100,000 times more sensitive to light.

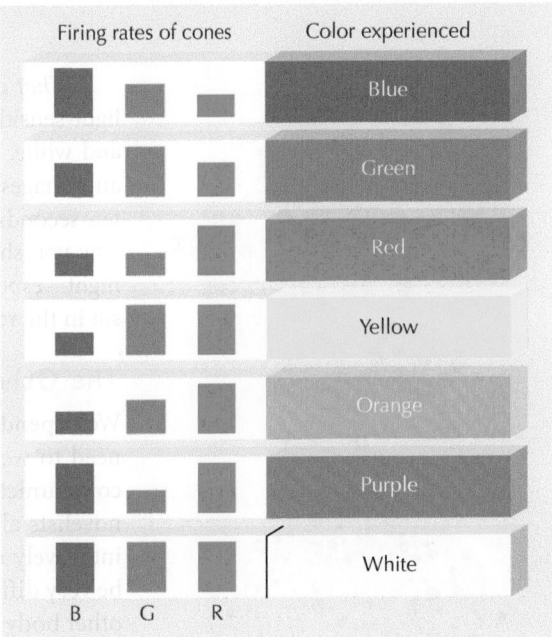

Figure 4.10 Firing rates of blue, green, and red cones in response to different colors. The taller the colored bar, the higher the firing rates for that type of cone. As you can see, colors are coded by differences in the activity of all three types of cones in the normal eye. (Adapted from Goldstein, 2010.)

Color blindness A total inability to perceive colors.

Color weakness An inability to distinguish some colors.

Dark adaptation Increased retinal sensitivity to light.

(a)

(b)

(c)

Figure 4.11 Color blindness and color weakness. *(a)* Photograph illustrates normal color vision. *(b)* Photograph is printed in blue and yellow and gives an impression of what a red-green color-blind person sees. *(c)* Photograph simulates total color blindness. If you are totally color-blind, all three photos will look nearly identical.

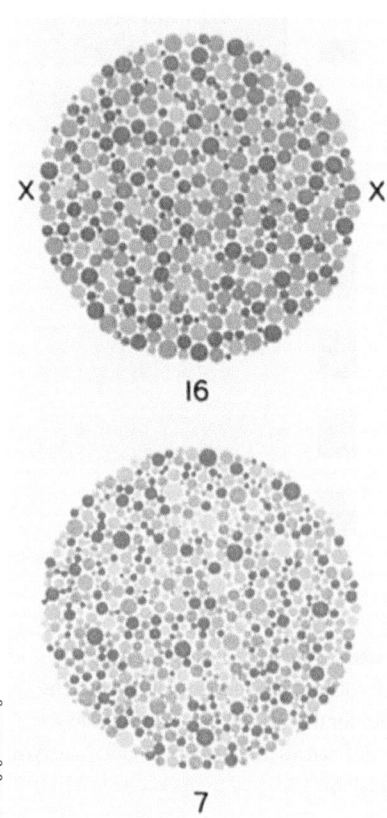

Figure 4.12 A replica of two images from the widely used Ishihara test for red-green color blindness.

What causes dark adaptation? Like cones, which contain iodopsin, rods also contain a light-sensitive visual pigment, *rhodopsin* (row-DOP-sin), which allows them to see in black and white. When struck by light, visual pigments *bleach*, or break down chemically. The afterimages you have seen after looking at a flashbulb are a result of this bleaching. In fact, a few seconds of exposure to bright white light can completely wipe out dark adaptation. That's why you should be sure to avoid looking at oncoming headlights when you are driving at night—especially the new bluish-white xenon lights. To restore light sensitivity, the rhodopsin in the rods must recombine, which takes time.

The Other Senses

We depend so much on vision that we sometimes neglect the other senses. But you only need to wear earplugs for a short time to appreciate how much we rely on hearing for communication, navigation, entertainment, and many other purposes. Similarly, skilled novelists always include descriptions of odors and tastes in their writings. Perhaps they intuitively realize that a scene is incomplete without smells and tastes. Further, it would be very difficult to move, stay upright, or even stay alive without touch, pain, balance, and other body senses. Like the other senses, the bodily senses are also an essential part of our sensory world. Before we examine the other senses in more detail, let's see if you have gained any insights into vision.

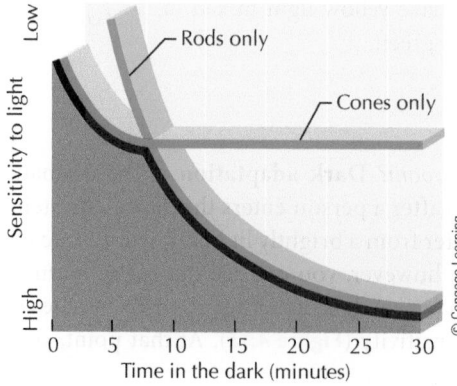

Figure 4.13 Typical course of dark adaptation. The dark line shows how the threshold for vision lowers as a person spends time in the dark. (A lower threshold means that less light is needed for vision.) The green line shows that the cones adapt first, but they soon cease adding to light sensitivity. Rods, shown by the red line, adapt more slowly. However, they continue to add to improved night vision long after the cones are fully adapted.

RECITE

1. Match:

_____ Myopia   A. Farsightedness
_____ Hyperopia   B. Elongated eye
_____ Presbyopia   C. Farsightedness due to aging
_____ Astigmatism   D. Lack of cones in the fovea
                            E. Misshapen cornea or lens

2. In dim light, vision depends mainly on the _____. In brighter light, color and fine detail are produced by the _____.
3. The fovea has the greatest visual acuity due to the large concentration of rods found there. T or F?
4. Colored afterimages are best explained by

    a. trichromatic theory   *b.* the effects of astigmatism
    c. sensory localization   *d.* opponent-process theory

REFLECT

THINK CRITICALLY

5. Sensory transduction in the eye takes place first in the cornea, then in the lens, then in the retina. True or false?

SELF-REFLECT

Pretend you are a beam of light. What will happen to you at each step as you pass into the eye and land on the retina? What will happen if the eye is not perfectly shaped? How will the retina know you've arrived? How will it tell what color of light you are? What will it tell the brain about you?

ANSWERS

1. B, A, C, E 2. rods, cones 3. F 4. d. 5. False. Although the cornea and lens prepare incoming light rays by bending them and focusing them on the retina, they do not change light to another form of energy. No change in the type of energy takes place until the retina converts light to nerve impulses.

Hearing—Good Vibrations

JOURNEY QUESTION 4.3 *What are the mechanisms of hearing?*

Rock, classical, jazz, blues, country, hip-hop—whatever your musical taste, you have undoubtedly been moved by the riches of sound. Hearing also collects information from all around the body, such as detecting the approach of an unseen car (Yost, 2007). Vision, in all its glory, is limited to stimuli in front of the eyes.

What is the stimulus for hearing? If you throw a stone into a quiet pond, a circle of waves will spread in all directions. In much the same way, sound travels as a series of invisible waves of *compression* (peaks) and *rarefaction* (RARE-eh-fak-shun: valleys) in the air. Any vibrating object—a tuning fork, the string of a musical instrument, or the vocal cords—will produce sound waves (rhythmic movement of air molecules). Other materials, such as fluids or solids, can also carry sound.

The *frequency* of sound waves (the number of waves per second) corresponds to the perceived *pitch* (higher or lower tone) of a sound. The *amplitude*, or physical "height," of a sound wave tells how much energy it contains. Psychologically, amplitude corresponds to sensed *loudness* (sound intensity) (Figure 4.14).

How We Hear Sounds

How are sounds converted to nerve impulses? Hearing involves a chain of events that begins with the *pinna* (PIN-ah), the visible, external part of the ear. In addition to being a good place to hang earrings or balance pencils, the pinna acts like a funnel to concentrate sounds. After they are guided into the ear canal, sound waves collide with the *tympanic membrane* (eardrum), setting it in motion. This, in turn, causes three small bones, the *auditory ossicles* (OSS-ih-kuls), to vibrate (Figure 4.15). The ossicles are the malleus (MAL-ee-us), incus, and stapes (STAY-peas). Their common names are the hammer, anvil, and stirrup. The ossicles link the eardrum with the *cochlea* (KOCK-lee-ah), a snail-shaped organ that makes up the inner ear. The stapes is attached to a membrane on the cochlea called the *oval window*. As the oval window moves back and forth, it makes waves in a fluid inside the cochlea.

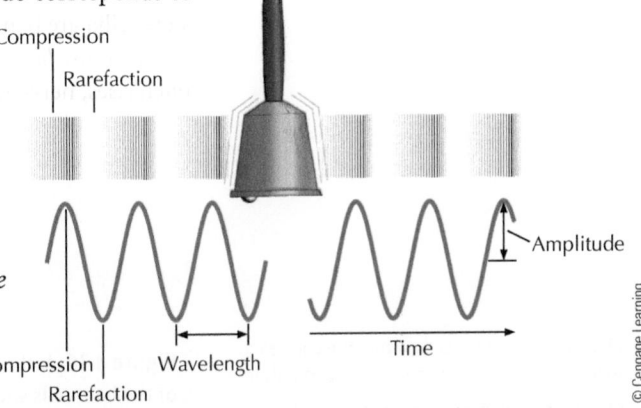

Figure 4.14 Waves of compression in the air, or vibrations, are the stimulus for hearing. The frequency of sound waves determines their pitch. The amplitude determines loudness.

© Cengage Learning

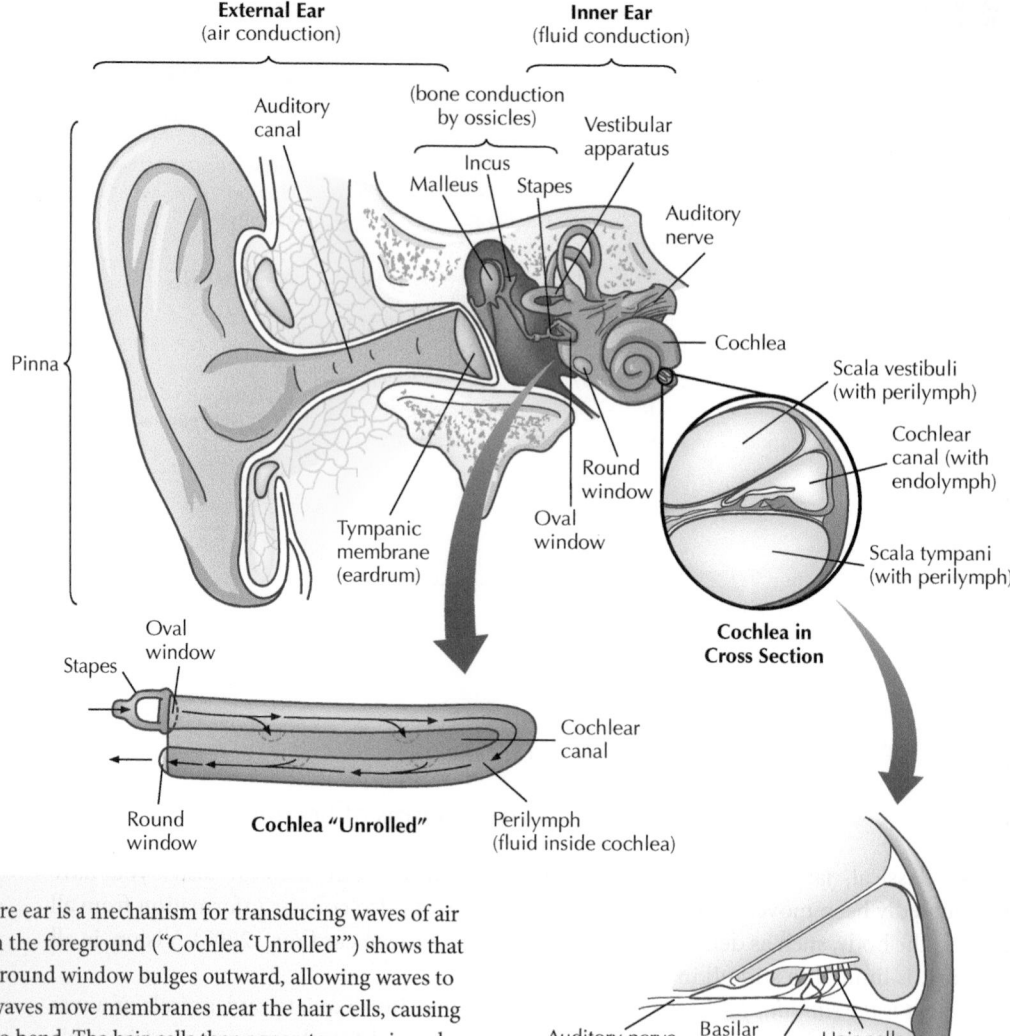

Figure 4.15 Anatomy of the ear. The entire ear is a mechanism for transducing waves of air pressure into nerve impulses. The inset in the foreground ("Cochlea 'Unrolled'") shows that as the stapes moves the oval window, the round window bulges outward, allowing waves to ripple through fluid in the cochlea. The waves move membranes near the hair cells, causing cilia, or "bristles," on the tips of the cells to bend. The hair cells then generate nerve impulses carried to the brain. (See an enlarged cross section of cochlea in Figure 4.16.)

Inside the cochlea tiny **hair cells** detect waves in the fluid. The hair cells are part of the **organ of Corti** (KOR-tee), which makes up the center part of the cochlea (Figure 4.16). A set of *stereocilia* (STER-ee-oh-SIL-ih-ah), or "bristles," atop each hair cell brush against the tectorial membrane when waves ripple through the fluid surrounding the organ of Corti. As the stereocilia are bent, nerve impulses are triggered, which then flow to the brain.

How are higher and lower sounds detected? The **frequency theory** of hearing states that as pitch rises, nerve impulses of a corresponding frequency are fed into the auditory nerve. That

Hair cells Receptor cells within the cochlea that transduce vibrations into nerve impulses.

Organ of Corti Center part of the cochlea, containing hair cells, canals, and membranes.

Frequency theory Holds that tones up to 4,000 hertz are converted to nerve impulses that match the frequency of each tone.

Figure 4.16 A closer view of the hair cells shows how movement of fluid in the cochlea causes the bristling "hairs," or cilia, to bend, generating a nerve impulse.

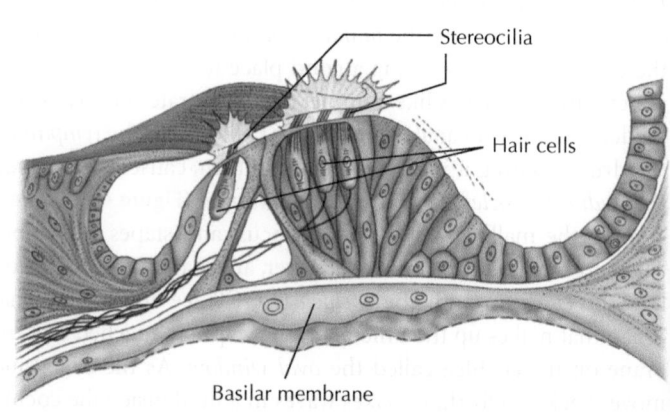

is, an 800-hertz tone produces 800 nerve impulses per second. (*Hertz* refers to the number of vibrations per second.) This explains how sounds up to about 4,000 hertz reach the brain. But what about higher tones? **Place theory** states that higher and lower tones excite specific areas of the cochlea. High tones register most strongly at the base of the cochlea (near the oval window). Lower tones, on the other hand, mostly move hair cells near the narrow outer tip of the cochlea (**Figure 4.17**). Pitch is signaled by the area of the cochlea most strongly activated. Place theory also explains why hunters sometimes lose hearing in a narrow pitch range. "Hunter's notch," as it is called, occurs when hair cells are damaged in the area affected by the pitch of gunfire.

Hearing Loss

Are there different types of hearing loss? The two most common types of hearing loss afflict some 270 million people worldwide (Tennesen, 2007). **Conductive hearing loss** occurs when the transfer of vibrations from the outer ear to the inner ear weakens. For example, the eardrums or ossicles may be damaged or immobilized by disease or injury. In many cases, conductive hearing loss can be overcome with a hearing aid, which makes sounds louder and clearer.

Sensorineural hearing loss results from damage to the inner ear hair cells or auditory nerve. Many jobs, hobbies, and pastimes can cause **noise-induced hearing loss**, a common form of sensorineural hearing loss that occurs when very loud sounds damage fragile hair cells (as in hunter's notch).

If you work in a noisy environment or enjoy loud music, motorcycling, snow-mobiling, hunting, or similar pursuits, you may be risking noise-induced hearing loss. Dead hair cells are never replaced: When you abuse them, you lose them. By the time you are 65, more than 40 percent of them will be gone, mainly those that transduce high pitches (Chisolm, Willott, & Lister, 2003; Lin et al., 2011). This explains why younger students are beginning to download very high-pitched ring tones for their cell phones: If their teacher has an aging ear, the students can hear the ring tone but their teacher cannot. (Your authors may have experienced this effect without knowing it!)

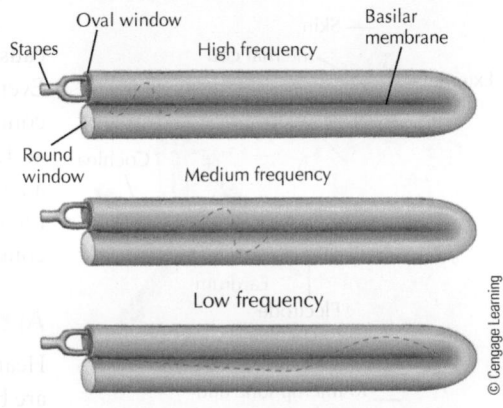

Figure 4.17 Here we see a simplified side view of the cochlea "unrolled." The basilar membrane is the elastic "roof" of the lower chamber of the cochlea. The organ of Corti, with its sensitive hair cells, rests atop the basilar membrane. The colored line shows where waves in the cochlear fluid cause the greatest deflection of the basilar membrane. (The amount of movement is exaggerated in the drawing.) Hair cells respond most in the area of greatest movement, which helps identify sound frequency.

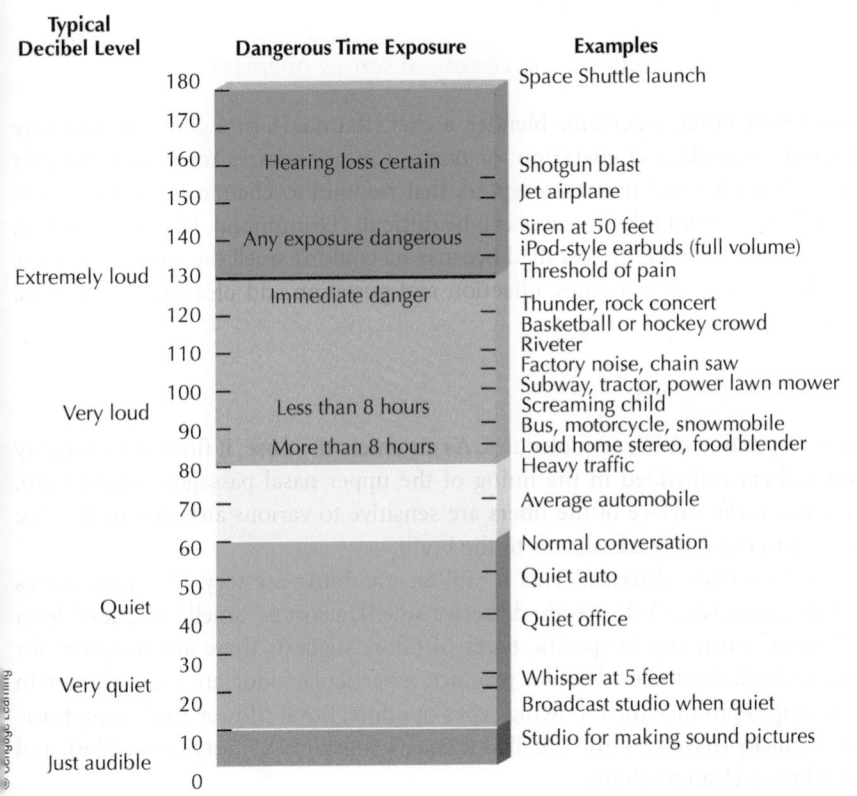

Figure 4.18 The loudness of sound is measured in decibels. Zero decibels is the faintest sound most people can hear. Sounds of 110 decibels are uncomfortably loud. Prolonged exposure to sounds above 85 decibels may damage the inner ear. Some rock concerts, which can reach 120 decibels, have caused hearing loss in musicians and may affect audiences as well. Sounds of 130 decibels pose an immediate danger to hearing.

Place theory Theory that higher and lower tones excite specific areas of the cochlea.

Conductive hearing loss Poor transfer of sounds from the eardrum to the inner ear.

Sensorineural hearing loss Loss of hearing caused by damage to the inner ear hair cells or auditory nerve.

Noise-induced hearing loss Damage caused by exposing the hair cells to excessively loud sounds.

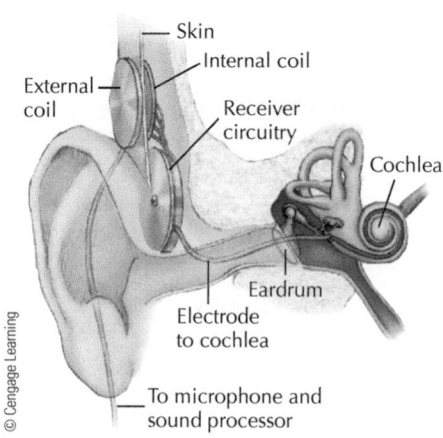

Figure 4.19 A cochlear implant, or "artificial ear."

How loud must a sound be to be hazardous? Daily exposure to 85 decibels or more may cause permanent hearing loss (Mather, 2011). *Decibels* are a measure of sound intensity. Every 20 decibels increases the sound pressure by a factor of 10. In other words, a rock concert at 120 decibels is 1,000 times stronger than a voice at 60 decibels. Even short periods at 120 decibels can cause temporary hearing loss. Brief exposure to 150 decibels (a jet airplane nearby) may cause permanent hearing loss. You might find it interesting to check the decibel ratings of some of your activities in Figure 4.18. Be aware that amplified music concerts, iPod-style earbuds, and car stereos can also damage your hearing.

Artificial Hearing

Hearing aids are of no help in cases of sensorineural hearing loss because auditory messages are blocked from reaching the brain. In many cases, however, the auditory nerve is actually intact. This finding has spurred the development of cochlear implants that bypass hair cells and stimulate the auditory nerves directly (Figure 4.19). Wires from a microphone carry electrical signals to an external coil. A matching coil under the skin picks up the signals and carries them to one or more areas of the cochlea. The latest implants make use of place theory to separate higher and lower tones into separate channels. This has allowed some formerly deaf persons to hear human voices, music, and other higher frequency sounds. About 60 percent of all multichannel implant patients can understand some spoken words and appreciate music (Leal et al., 2003; Foley & Matlin, 2010). Some deaf children with implants learn to speak. Those who receive a cochlear implant before age 2 have the best chance to learn spoken language at a near normal rate (Dorman & Wilson, 2004; Gordon et al., 2011).

At present, artificial hearing remains crude. All but the most successful cochlear implant patients describe the sound as "like a radio that isn't quite tuned in." But cochlear implants are improving. And even now, it is hard to argue with enthusiasts like Kristen Cloud. Shortly after Kristen received an implant, she was able to hear a siren and avoid being struck by a speeding car. She says simply, "The implant saved my life."

Smell and Taste—The Nose Knows When the Tongue Can't Tell

JOURNEY QUESTION 4.4 *How do the chemical senses operate?*

Unless you are a wine taster, a perfume blender, a chef (Ramsay?), or a gourmet, you may think of **olfaction**, or smell, and **gustation**, or taste, as minor senses. You could probably survive without these *chemical senses*—receptors that respond to chemical molecules. But don't be deceived—life without these senses can be difficult (Drummond, Douglas, & Olver, 2007). One person, for instance, almost died because he couldn't smell the smoke when his apartment building caught fire. Besides, olfaction and gustation add pleasure to our lives. Let's see how they operate.

The Sense of Smell

Smell receptors respond to airborne molecules. As air enters the nose, it flows over roughly 5 million nerve fibers embedded in the lining of the upper nasal passages (Figure 4.20). Receptor proteins on the surface of the fibers are sensitive to various airborne molecules. When a fiber is stimulated it sends signals to the brain.

How are different odors detected? This is still an unfolding mystery. One hint comes from a type of *dysosmia* (dis-OZE-me-ah: defective smell), a sort of "smell blindness" for a single odor. Loss of sensitivity to specific types of odors suggests there are receptors for specific odors. Indeed, the molecules that produce a particular odor are quite similar in shape. Specific shapes produce the following types of odors: floral (flower-like), camphoric (camphor-like), musky (have you ever smelled a sweaty musk ox?), minty (mint-like), and etherish (like ether or cleaning fluid).

Olfaction The sense of smell.

Gustation The sense of taste.

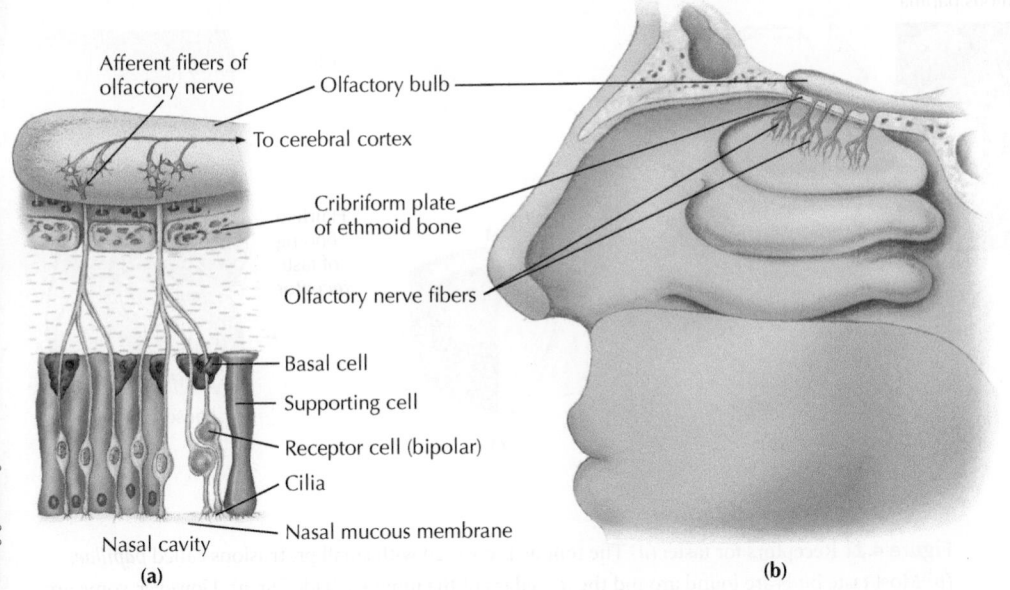

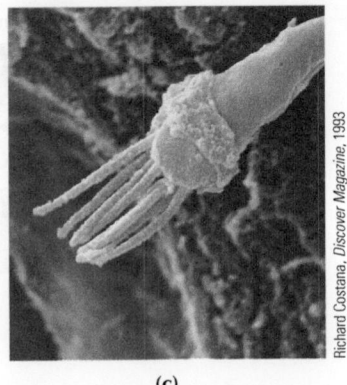

(c)

Richard Costana, *Discover Magazine*, 1993

Figure 4.20 Receptors for the sense of smell (olfaction). *(a)* Olfactory nerve fibers respond to gaseous molecules. Receptor cells are shown in cross section to the left. *(b)* Olfactory receptors are located in the upper nasal cavity. *(c)* On the right, an extreme close-up of an olfactory receptor shows fibers that sense gaseous molecules of various shapes.

Does this mean that there are five different types of olfactory receptors? Although humans carry genes for about 1,000 types of smell receptors, only about 400 of them are actually expressed (Sela & Sobel, 2010). It appears that different-shaped "holes," or "pockets," exist on the surface of olfactory receptors. Like a piece fits in a puzzle, chemicals produce odors when part of a molecule matches a hole of the same shape. This is the **lock and key theory of olfaction**.

Further, molecules trigger activity in different *combinations* of odor receptors. Thus, humans can detect at least 10,000 different odors. Just as you can make many thousands of words from the 26 letters of the alphabet, many combinations of the 400 types of receptors are possible, resulting in many different odors. Scents are also identified, in part, by the *location* of the receptors in the nose that are activated by a particular odor. And finally, the *number of activated receptors* tells the brain how strong an odor is (Bensafi et al., 2004). The brain uses these distinctive patterns of messages it gets from the olfactory receptors to recognize particular scents (Sela & Sobel, 2010).

What causes dysosmia? Five people out of 100 experience some degree of dysosmia, including *anosmia*, the total loss of smell (Bramerson et al., 2004). Risks include infections, allergies, and blows to the head (which may tear the olfactory nerves). Exposure to chemicals such as ammonia, paints, solvents, and hairdressing potions can also cause dysosmia. If you value your sense of smell, be careful what you sniff (Drummond, Douglas, & Olver, 2007).

Taste and Flavors

There are at least four basic taste sensations: *sweet, salt, sour,* and *bitter*. We are most sensitive to bitter, less sensitive to sour, even less sensitive to salt, and least sensitive to sweet. This order may have helped prevent poisonings when most humans foraged for food, because bitter and sour foods are more likely to be inedible.

Most experts now believe that a fifth taste quality exists (Nakamura et al., 2011). The Japanese word *umami* (oo-MAH-me) describes a pleasant savory or "brothy" taste associated with certain amino acids in chicken soup, some meat extracts, kelp, tuna, human milk, cheese, and soybeans. The receptors for *umami* are sensitive to glutamate, a substance found in monosodium glutamate (MSG) (Sugimoto & Ninomiya, 2005).

If there are only four or five tastes, how can there be so many different flavors? Flavors seem more varied because we tend to include sensations of texture, temperature, smell, and even pain ("hot" chili peppers) along with taste. Smell is particularly important in determining flavor (Shepherd, 2006). If you plug your nose and eat small bits of apple, potato, and onion, they will "taste" almost exactly alike. So do gourmet jelly beans! That's why food loses its "taste" when you have a cold. It is probably fair to say that subjective flavor is half smell.

Lock and key theory of olfaction Holds that odors are related to the shapes of chemical molecules.

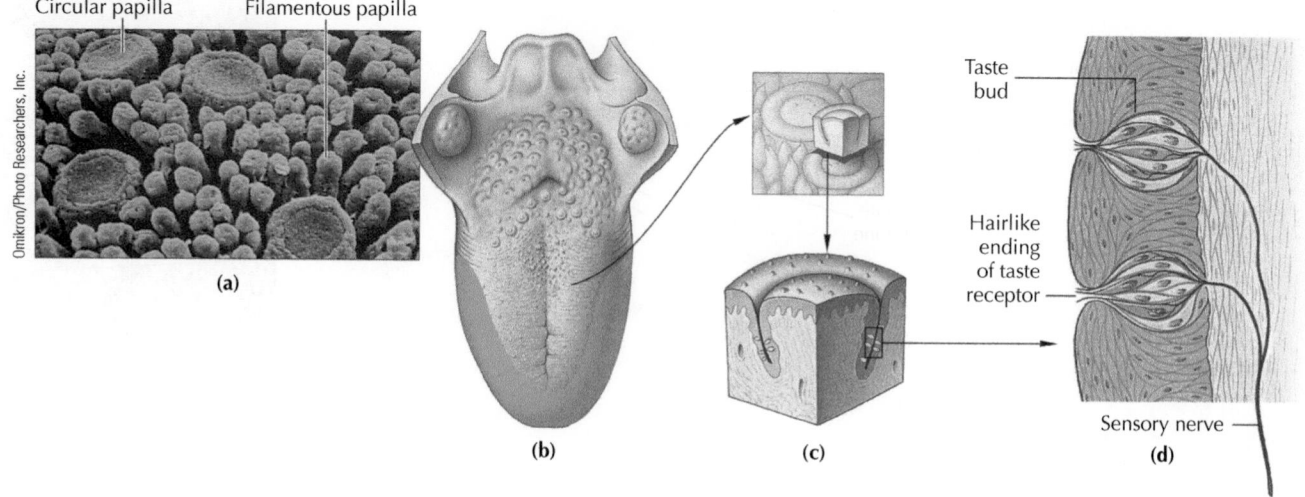

Circular papilla   Filamentous papilla

Omikron/Photo Researchers, Inc.

(a)

(b)   (c)   (d)

Taste bud

Hairlike ending of taste receptor

Sensory nerve

Figure 4.21 Receptors for taste: *(a)* The tongue is covered with small protrusions called *papillae.* *(b)* Most taste buds are found around the top edges of the tongue (shaded area). However, some are located elsewhere, including under the tongue. Stimulation of the central part of the tongue causes no taste sensations. All four primary taste sensations occur anywhere that taste buds exist. *(c)* An enlarged drawing shows that taste buds are located near the base of papillae. *(d)* Detail of a taste bud. These receptors also occur in other parts of the digestive system, such as the lining of the mouth.

Taste buds, or taste-receptor cells, are located mainly on the top side of the tongue, especially around the edges. However, a few are found elsewhere inside the mouth (Figure 4.21). As food is chewed, it dissolves and enters the taste buds, where it sets off nerve impulses to the brain (Northcutt, 2004). Much like smell, sweet and bitter tastes appear to be based on a lock-and-key match between molecules and intricately shaped receptors. Saltiness and sourness, however, are triggered by a direct flow of charged atoms into the tips of taste cells (Lindemann, 2001).

If smell and taste are seen as minor senses, then the somesthetic senses are the unnoticed senses. Let's see why they merit our careful attention.

The Somesthetic Senses—Flying by the Seat of Your Pants

JOURNEY QUESTION 4.5 *What are the somesthetic senses?*

A gymnast "flying" through a routine on the uneven bars may rely as much on the **somesthetic senses** as on vision (*soma* means "body," *esthetic* means "feel"). Even the most routine activities, such as walking, running, or passing a sobriety test, would be impossible without the **skin senses** (touch), the **kinesthetic senses** (receptors in muscles and joints that detect body position and movement), and the **vestibular senses** (receptors in the inner ear for balance, gravity, and acceleration). Because of their importance, let's begin with the skin senses.

The Skin Senses

It's difficult to imagine what life would be like without the sense of touch, but the plight of Ian Waterman gives a hint. After an illness, Waterman permanently lost all feeling below his neck. Now, in order to know what position his body is in he has to be able to see it. If he moves with his eyes closed, he has no idea where he is moving. If the lights go out in a room, he's in big trouble (Gallagher, 2004).

Skin receptors produce at least five different sensations: *light touch, pressure, pain, cold,* and *warmth.* Receptors with particular shapes appear to specialize somewhat in various

Taste bud The receptor organ for taste.

Somesthetic senses Sensations produced by the skin, muscles, joints, viscera, and organs of balance.

Skin senses The senses of touch, pressure, pain, heat, and cold.

Kinesthetic senses The senses of body movement and positioning.

Vestibular senses The senses of balance, gravity, and acceleration.

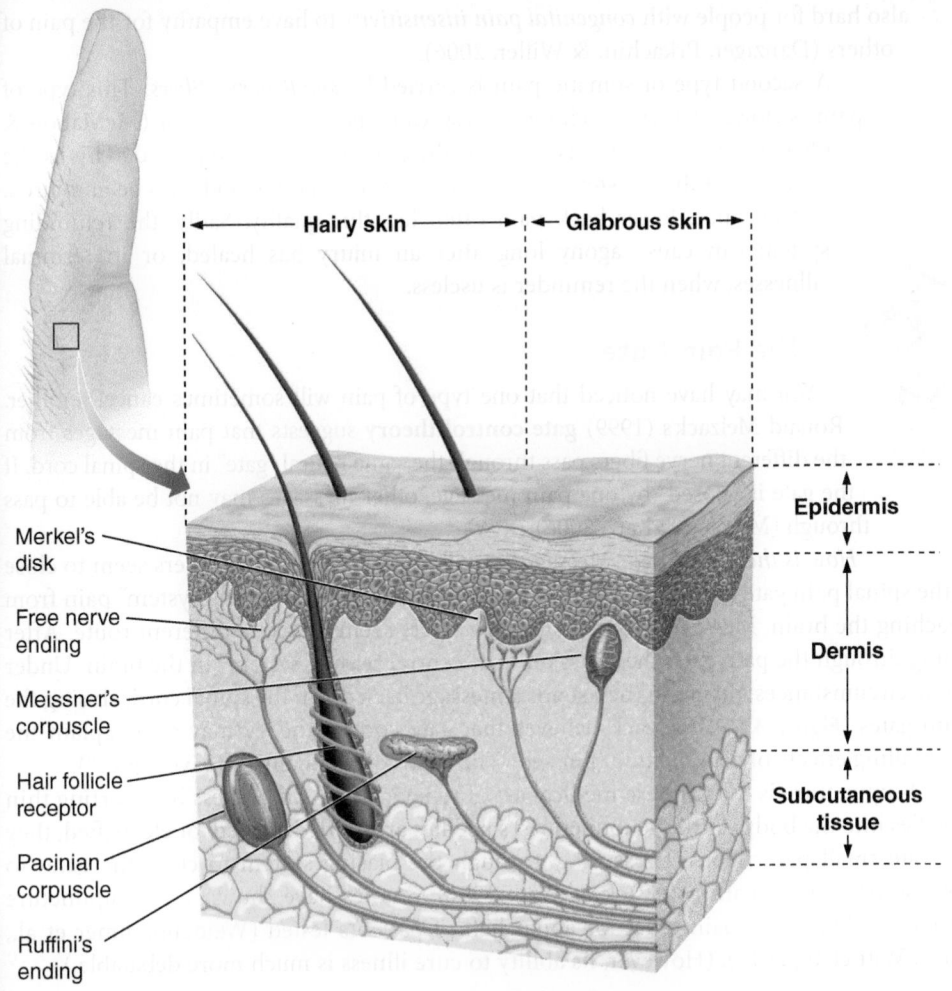

Hairy skin | Glabrous skin

Epidermis

Dermis

Subcutaneous tissue

Merkel's disk

Free nerve ending

Meissner's corpuscle

Hair follicle receptor

Pacinian corpuscle

Ruffini's ending

Figure 4.22 The skin senses include touch, pressure, pain, cold, and warmth. This drawing shows different forms the skin receptors can take. The functions of these receptors is likely as follows: Merkel's disks sense pressure on the skin; free nerve endings sense warmth, cold, and pain; Meissner's corpuscles sense pressure; hair follicle receptors sense hair movement; Pacinian corpuscles sense pressure and vibration; while Ruffini's endings sense skin stretching (Freberg, 2010; Kalat, 2013). The feeling of being touched is likely made up of a combination of varying degrees of activity in all of these receptors. (From Freberg, *Discovering Biological Psychology*, 2e, Copyright © 2010 Cengage Learning. Reproduced by permission.)

sensations (Figure 4.22). However, free nerve endings alone can produce all five sensations (Carlson, 2010). Altogether, the skin has about 200,000 nerve endings for temperature, 500,000 for touch and pressure, and 3 million for pain.

Does the number of receptors in an area of skin relate to its sensitivity? Yes. Your skin could be "mapped" by applying heat, cold, touch, pressure, or pain to points all over your body (Hollins, 2010). Such testing would show that the number of skin receptors varies and that sensitivity generally matches the number of receptors in a given area. Broadly speaking, important areas such as the lips, tongue, face, hands, and genitals have a higher density of receptors. Of course, the sensation you ultimately feel will depend on brain activity.

Pain

The number of pain receptors also varies, right? Yes, like the other skin senses, pain receptors vary in their distribution. About 230 pain points per square centimeter (about a half inch) are found behind the knee, 180 per centimeter on the buttocks, 60 on the pad of the thumb, and 40 on the tip of the nose. (Is it better then, to be pinched on the nose or behind the knee? It depends on what you like!)

Pain carried by *large nerve fibers* is sharp, bright, and fast and seems to come from specific body areas (McMahon & Koltzenburg, 2005). This is the body's **warning system**. Give yourself a small jab with a pin and you will feel this type of pain. As you do this, notice that warning pain quickly disappears. Much as we may dislike warning pain, it is usually a signal that the body has been, or is about to be, damaged. Without warning pain, we would be unable to detect or prevent injury. Children who are born with a rare inherited insensitivity to pain repeatedly burn themselves, break bones, bite off parts of their tongues, and become ill without knowing it (Erez et al., 2010). As you might imagine, it's

Warning system Pain based on large nerve fibers; warns that bodily damage may be occurring.

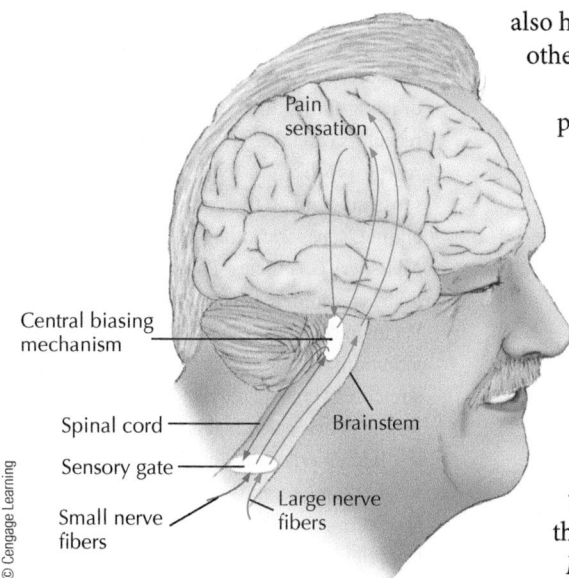

Pain sensation

Central biasing mechanism

Spinal cord

Sensory gate

Small nerve fibers

Brainstem

Large nerve fibers

© Cengage Learning

Figure 4.23 Diagram of a sensory gate for pain. A series of pain impulses going through the gate may prevent other pain messages from passing through. Or pain messages may relay through a "central biasing mechanism" that exerts control over the gate, closing it to other impulses.

Reminding system Pain based on small nerve fibers; reminds the brain that the body has been injured.

Gate control theory Proposes that pain messages pass through neural "gates" in the spinal cord.

also hard for people with *congenital pain insensitivity* to have empathy for the pain of others (Danziger, Prkachin, & Willer, 2006).

A second type of somatic pain is carried by *small nerve fibers*. This type of pain is slower, nagging, aching, widespread, and very unpleasant (McMahon & Koltzenburg, 2005). It gets worse if the pain stimulus is repeated. This is the body's **reminding system**. It reminds the brain that the body has been injured. For instance, lower back pain often has this quality. Sadly, the reminding system can cause agony long after an injury has healed, or in terminal illnesses, when the reminder is useless.

The Pain Gate

You may have noticed that one type of pain will sometimes cancel another. Ronald Melzack's (1999) **gate control theory** suggests that pain messages from the different nerve fibers pass through the same neural "gate" in the spinal cord. If the gate is "closed" by one pain message, other messages may not be able to pass through (Melzack & Katz, 2006).

How is the gate closed? Messages carried by large, fast nerve fibers seem to close the spinal pain gate directly. Doing so can prevent slower, "reminding system" pain from reaching the brain. Messages from small, slow fibers seem to take a different route. After going through the pain gate, they pass on to a "central biasing system" in the brain. Under some circumstances, the brain then sends a message back down the spinal cord, closing the pain gates (Figure 4.23). Melzack believes that gate control theory may also explain the painkilling effects of *acupuncture* (but see "The Matrix: Do Phantoms Live Here?").

Acupuncture is the Chinese medical art of relieving pain and illness by inserting thin needles into the body. As the acupuncturist's needles are twirled, heated, or electrified, they activate small pain fibers. These relay through the biasing system to close the gates to intense or chronic pain (Melzack & Wall, 1996). Studies have shown that acupuncture produces short-term pain relief for about half of patients tested (Weidenhammer et al., 2007; Witt et al., 2011). (However, its ability to cure illness is much more debatable.)

Pain Control

Gate control theory helps explain *counterirritation*, one widely used pain control technique. Pain clinics use it by applying a mild electrical current to the skin. This causes only a mild tingling, but it can greatly reduce more agonizing pain (Köke et al., 2004). For more extreme pain, the electrical current can be applied directly to the spinal cord (Linderoth & Foreman, 2006).

You can use counterirritation to control your own pain (Schmelz, 2010). For instance, if you are having a tooth filled, try itching or pinching yourself, or digging a fingernail into

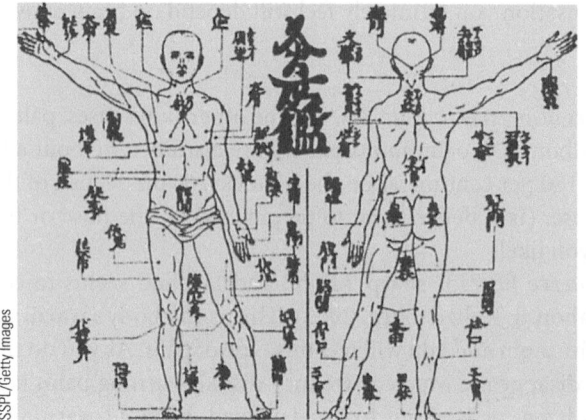

SSPL/Getty Images

(Left) An acupuncturist's chart. *(Right)* Thin stainless steel needles are inserted into areas defined by the chart. Modern research has begun to explain the painkilling effects of acupuncture (see text). Acupuncture's claimed ability to cure diseases is more debatable.

Brainwaves

In the popular *Matrix* films, Neo, as played by Keanu Reeves, discovers that machines have imprisoned humans in a phantom world called the Matrix, in order to steal human energy for their own use. Actually, the idea of a "matrix" is not totally farfetched. Your own brain may create a *neuromatrix* that allows you to perceive your own body (Iannetti & Mouraux, 2010).

Most amputees have *phantom limb* sensations, including pain, for months or years after losing a limb (Fraser, 2002; Murray et al., 2007). Because the phantom limb feels so "real," a patient with a recently amputated leg may inadvertently try to walk on it, risking further injury. Sometimes, phantom limbs feel like they are stuck in awkward positions. For instance, one man can't fall asleep on his back because his missing arm feels like it is twisted behind him.

What causes the experience of phantom limbs? Gate control theory cannot explain phantom limb pain (Hunter, Katz, & Davis, 2003). Since pain can't be coming from the missing limb (after all, it's missing!), it cannot pass through pain gates to the brain. Instead, according to Ronald Melzack (1999; Melzack & Katz, 2006), over time the brain creates a body image called the *neuromatrix*. This internal model of the body generates our sense of bodily self. Although amputation may remove a limb, it still exists as far as the neuromatrix is concerned.

In fact, amputees dream of intact, fully functional limbs without any phantom limb experiences at all. Evidently, during sleep, sensory inputs from the area of the missing limb are suppressed. In contrast, when amputees are awake, sensory inputs from the area of the missing limb conflict with the neuromatrix, which interprets the conflict as a phantom limb, complete with phantom limb pain (Alessandria et al., 2011; Giummarra et al., 2007). Functional magnetic resonance imaging (fMRI) confirms that sensory and motor areas of the brain are more active when a person feels a phantom limb (MacIver et al., 2008).

Sometimes the brain gradually reorganizes to adjust for the sensory loss (Schmalzl et al., 2011). For example, a person who loses an arm may at first have a phantom arm and hand. After many years, the phantom may shrink, until only a hand is felt at the shoulder. Perhaps more vividly than others, people with phantom limbs are reminded that the sensory world we experience is constructed, moment by moment, not by some futuristic machines but by our own brain activity.

---

a knuckle, while the dentist is working. Focus your attention on the pain you are creating, and increase it anytime the dentist's work becomes more painful. This strategy may seem strange, but it works. Generations of children have used it to take the edge off a spanking.

In some cultures, people endure tattooing, stretching, cutting, and burning with little apparent pain. How do they do it? Very likely the answer lies in a reliance on psychological factors that anyone can use to reduce pain, such as anxiety reduction, control, and attention (Mailis-Gagnon & Israelson, 2005).

In general, unpleasant emotions such as fear and anxiety increase pain; pleasant emotions decrease it (Kerns, Sellinger, & Goodin, 2011). Anytime you can anticipate pain (such as a trip to the doctor, dentist, or tattoo parlor), you can lower anxiety by making sure you are *fully informed*. Be sure everything that will happen is explained. In general, the more control you *feel* over a painful stimulus, the less pain is experienced (Vallerand, Saunders, & Anthony, 2007). To apply this principle, you might arrange a signal so your doctor, dentist, or body piercer will know when to start and stop a painful procedure. Finally, distraction also reduces pain. Instead of listening to the whirr of a dentist's drill, for example, you might imagine that you are lying in the sun at a beach, listening to the roar of the surf. Or take an iPod along and crank up your favorite MP3s (Bushnell, Villemure, & Duncan, 2004). At home, music can also be a good distractor from chronic pain (Mitchell et al., 2007).

The Vestibular System

Although space flight might look like fun, you are about 70 percent likely to throw up during your first experience in orbit.

But why? Weightlessness and space flight affect the vestibular system, often causing severe motion sickness. Within the vestibular system, fluid-filled sacs called *otolith* (OH-toe-lith) *organs* are sensitive to movement, acceleration, and gravity (**Figure 4.24**). The otolith organs contain tiny crystals in a soft, gelatin-like mass. The tug of gravity or rapid head movements can cause the mass to shift. This, in turn, stimulates hair-like receptor cells,

AP Photo/Zero Gravity Corp

Weightlessness presents astronauts with a real challenge in sensory adaptation. In 2007, world-famous physicist Steven Hawking, who suffers from amyotrophic lateral sclerosis (ALS, or Lou Gehrig's disease), fulfilled a lifelong dream of experiencing weightlessness. He took a flight on the "Weightless Wonder," NASA's official nickname for the high-flying airplane that provides short periods of weightlessness to train astronauts. (Unofficially it is called the "Vomit Comet.")

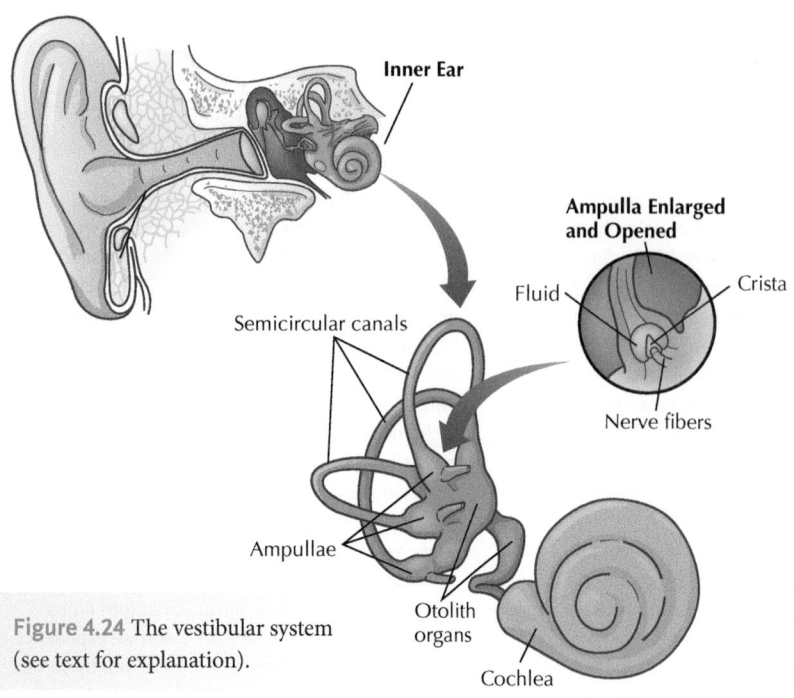

Inner Ear

Ampulla Enlarged and Opened

Fluid

Crista

Nerve fibers

Semicircular canals

Ampullae

Otolith organs

Cochlea

Figure 4.24 The vestibular system (see text for explanation).

© Cengage Learning

Sensory conflict theory Explains motion sickness as the result of a mismatch among information from vision, the vestibular system, and kinesthesis.

allowing us to sense gravity, acceleration, and movement through space (Lackner & DiZio, 2005).

Three fluid-filled tubes—called the *semicircular canals*—are the sensory organs for balance. If you could climb inside these tubes, you would find that head movements cause the fluid to swirl about. As the fluid moves, it bends a small "flap," or "float," called the *crista*, that detects movement in the semicircular canals. The bending of each crista again stimulates hair cells and signals head rotation.

What causes motion sickness? According to **sensory conflict theory**, dizziness and nausea occur when sensations from the vestibular system don't match sensations from the eyes and body (Flanagan, May, & Dobie, 2004). On solid ground, information from the vestibular system, vision, and kinesthesis usually matches. However, in a heaving, pitching boat, car, or airplane, or even playing a videogame, a serious mismatch can occur—causing disorientation and heaving of another kind (Merhi et al., 2007; Stoffregen et al., 2008).

Why would sensory conflict cause nausea? You can probably blame (or thank) evolution. Many poisons disturb the vestibular system, vision, and the body. Therefore, we may have evolved so that we react to sensory conflict by vomiting to expel poison. The value of this reaction, however, may be of little comfort to anyone who has ever been "green" and miserable with motion sickness. To minimize such conflicts, try to keep your head still, fix your vision on a distant immobile object, and lie down if you can (Harm, 2002).

✋ study break Hearing, the Chemical Senses, and the Somesthetic Senses

RECITE

1. The frequency of a sound wave corresponds to how loud it is. T or F?
2. Which of the following is not a part of the cochlea?

    a. ossicles
    b. pinna
    c. tympanic membrane
    d. all of the above

3. Sensorineural hearing loss occurs when the auditory ossicles are damaged. T or F?
4. Daily exposure to sounds with a loudness of _____ decibels may cause permanent hearing loss.
5. Olfaction appears to be at least partially explained by the _____ _____ _____ theory of molecule shapes and receptor sites.
6. Which of the following is a somesthetic sense?

    a. gustation
    b. olfaction
    c. rarefaction
    d. kinesthesis

7. Warning pain is carried by _____ nerve fibers.
8. Head movements are detected primarily in the semicircular canals, gravity by the otolith organs. T or F?

REFLECT

THINK CRITICALLY

9. Drivers are less likely to become carsick than passengers are. Why do you think drivers and passengers differ in susceptibility to motion sickness?

SELF-REFLECT

Close your eyes and listen to the sounds around you. As you do, try to mentally trace the events necessary to convert vibrations in the air into the sounds you are hearing.

What is your favorite food odor? What is your favorite taste? Can you explain how you are able to sense the aroma and taste of foods?

Stand on one foot with your eyes closed. Now touch the tip of your nose with your index finger. Which of the somesthetic senses did you use to perform this feat?

Can you think of any ways in which you have used counterirritation to lessen pain?

ANSWERS

1. F 2. d 3. F 4. 85 5. lock and key 6. d 7. large 8. T 9. Drivers experience less sensory conflict because they control the car's motion. This allows them to anticipate the car's movements and to coordinate their head and eye movements with those of the car.

Perception—The Second Step

JOURNEY QUESTION 4.6 *In general, how do we construct our perceptions?*

While driving at night, a woman slams on her brakes to avoid hitting a deer. As she skids to a stop, she realizes that the "deer" is actually a bush on the roadside. Such misperceptions are common. The brain must continuously find patterns in a welter of sensations. How do we organize sensations into meaningful perceptions? Our brain creates our perceptions by using preexisting knowledge such as the principles of perceptual grouping and perceptual constancies to help us make sense out of sensations.

Are you born able to create perceptions out of sensations? Imagine what it would be like to have your vision restored after a lifetime of blindness. Actually, a first look at the world can be disappointing because the newfound ability to *sense* the world does not guarantee that it can be *perceived*. Newly sighted persons must *learn* to identify objects, to read clocks, numbers, and letters, and to judge sizes and distances (Gregory, 2003). For instance, Mr. S. B. was a cataract patient who had been blind since birth. After an operation restored his sight at age 52, Mr. S. B. struggled to use his vision.

Mr. S. B. soon learned to tell time from a large clock and to read block letters he had known only from touch. At a zoo, he recognized an elephant from descriptions he had heard. However, handwriting meant nothing to him for more than a year after he regained sight, and many objects were meaningless until he touched them. Thus, Mr. S. B. slowly learned to organize his *sensations* into meaningful *perceptions*. Cases like those of Mr. S. B. show that your experiences are **perceptual constructions**, or mental models of external events, that *are actively created by your brain*.

Of course, perceptions can be misconstructed as they are filtered through our needs, expectations, attitudes, values, and beliefs (Figure 4.25). One of your authors was once approached in a supermarket by a young girl screaming, "Help! Someone is killing my father." He followed her to see two men struggling. The guy on top had his victim by the throat. There was blood everywhere. It was a murder in progress! Soon, however, it turned out that the "guy on the bottom" had passed out, hit his head, and was bleeding. The "guy on top" saw the first man fall and was loosening his collar.

Obviously, the girl had misperceived what was happening to her father. Because of the dramatic influence of her words, so did your author. As this story shows, sensory information can be interpreted in various ways. The girl's description completely shaped his own initial perceptions. This perhaps is understandable. But he'll never forget the added shock he felt when he met the "murderer." The man he had seen a few moments before as vicious and horrible-looking was not even a stranger. He was a neighbor whom your author had seen dozens of times before. Clearly, we don't just believe what we see. We also see what we believe.

Visual perception involves finding meaningful patterns in complex stimuli. If you look closely at this photomosaic by Robert Silver, you may see that it is entirely made up of small individual photos. An infant or newly sighted person might well see only a jumble of meaningless colors. But because the photos form a familiar pattern, you should easily see the American flag.

Figure 4.25 It is difficult to look at this simple drawing without perceiving depth. Yet the drawing is nothing more than a collection of flat shapes. Turn this page counterclockwise 90 degrees and you will see 3 Cs, one within another. When the drawing is turned sideways, it seems nearly flat. However, if you turn the page upright again, a sense of depth will reappear. Clearly, you have used your knowledge and expectations to *construct* an illusion of depth. The drawing itself would only be a flat design if you didn't invest it with meaning.

Perceptual construction A mental model of external events.

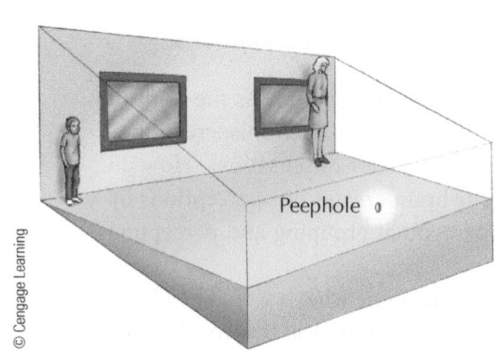 

Peephole

Figure 4.26 The Ames room. From the front, the room looks normal; actually, the right-hand corner is very short, and the left-hand corner is very tall. In addition, the left side of the room slants away from viewers. The diagram shows the shape of the room and reveals why people appear to get bigger as they cross the room toward the nearer, shorter right corner.

Illusions

Perceptual *mis*construction is responsible for many illusions. In an **illusion**, length, position, motion, curvature, or direction is consistently misjudged. For example, because we have seen thousands of rooms shaped roughly like a box, we habitually construct perceptions based on this assumption. This need not be true, however. An *Ames room* (named for the man who designed it) is a lopsided space that appears square when viewed from a certain angle (Figure 4.26). This illusion is achieved by carefully distorting the proportions of the walls, floor, ceiling, and windows. Because the left corner of the Ames room is farther from a viewer than the right, a person standing in that corner looks very small; one standing in the nearer, shorter right corner looks very large. A person who walks from the left to the right corner, will seem to "magically" grow larger.

Notice that illusions are distorted perceptions of stimuli that actually exist. In a **hallucination**, people perceive objects or events that have no external reality (Boksa, 2009). For example, they hear voices that are not there (see "Staying in Touch with Reality"). If you think you are experiencing an illusion or a hallucination, try engaging in some reality testing.

What do you mean by reality testing? In any situation having an element of doubt or uncertainty, **reality testing** involves obtaining additional information to check your perceptions (Landa et al., 2006). If you think you see a 3-foot-tall butterfly, you can confirm you are hallucinating by trying to touch its wings. To detect an illusion, you may have to measure a drawing or apply a straight-edge to it. Figure 4.27 shows a powerful illusion called Fraser's spiral. What appears to be a spiral is actually made up of a series of closed circles. Most people cannot spontaneously see this reality. Instead, they must carefully trace one of the circles to confirm what is "real" in the design.

Let's explore the process of perceptual construction and some factors that shape or even distort it.

Bottom-Up and Top-Down Processing

Moment by moment, our perceptions are typically constructed in both *bottom-up* and *top-down* fashion. Think about the process of building a house: Raw materials, such as lumber, doors, tiles, carpets, screws, and nails, must be painstakingly fit together. At the same time, a building plan guides how the raw materials are assembled.

Our brain builds perceptions in similar ways. In **bottom-up processing**, we start constructing at the "bottom," with raw materials. That is, we begin with small sensory units (features), and build upward to a complete perception. The reverse also occurs. In

Illusion A misleading or misconstructed perception.

Hallucination An imaginary sensation—such as seeing, hearing, or smelling something that does not exist in the external world.

Reality testing Obtaining additional information to check on the accuracy of perceptions.

Bottom-up processing Organizing perceptions by beginning with low-level features.

Just imagine that often, and without warning, you hear a voice shouting, "Buckets of blood!" or see blood spattering across the walls of your bedroom. Chances are people would think you are mentally disturbed. Hallucinations are a major symptom of psychosis, dementia, epilepsy, migraine headaches, alcohol withdrawal, and drug intoxication (Spence & David, 2004). They are also one of the clearest signs that a person has "lost touch with reality."

Yet consider the case of mathematician John Nash (the subject of *A Beautiful Mind*, the winner of the 2002 Oscar for best film). Even though Nash suffered from schizophrenia, he eventually learned to use his *reality testing* to sort out which of his experiences were perceptions and which were hallucinations. Unlike John Nash, most people who experience full-blown hallucinations have a limited ability to engage in reality testing (Hohwy & Rosenberg, 2005).

Curiously, "sane hallucinations" also occur. *Charles Bonnet syndrome* is a rare condition that afflicts mainly older people who are partially blind but not mentally disturbed (Cammaroto et al., 2008). Animals, buildings, plants, people, and other objects may seem to appear and disappear in front of their eyes. One older man suffering from partial blindness and leukemia complained of seeing animals in his house, including cattle and bears (Jacob et al., 2004). However, people experiencing "sane hallucinations" can more easily tell that their hallucinations aren't real because their capacity for reality testing is not impaired.

Such unusual experiences show how powerfully the brain seeks meaningful patterns in sensory input and the role that reality testing plays in our normal perceptual experience.

---

top-down processing, preexisting knowledge is used to rapidly organize features into a meaningful whole (Goldstein, 2010).

If you put together a picture puzzle you've never seen before, you are relying mainly on bottom-up processing: You must assemble small pieces until a recognizable pattern begins to emerge. Top-down processing is like putting together a puzzle you have solved many times: After only a few pieces are in place, your past experience gives you the plan to rapidly fill in the final picture.

Both types of processing are illustrated by **Figure 4.28**. Also, look ahead to Figure 4.31. The first time you see this photo you will probably process it bottom-up, picking out features until it becomes recognizable. The next time you see it, because of top-down processing, you should recognize it instantly.

An excellent example of perceptual construction is found in the Gestalt organizing principles.

Gestalt Organizing Principles

How are sensations organized into perceptions? The Gestalt psychologists proposed that the simplest organization involves grouping some sensations into an object, or figure, that stands out on a plainer background. **Figure-ground organization** is probably inborn, because it is

Top-down processing Applying higher-level knowledge to rapidly organize sensory information into a meaningful perception.

Figure-ground organization Organizing a perception so that part of a stimulus appears to stand out as an object (figure) against a less prominent background (ground).

Figure 4.27 The limits of pure perception. Even simple designs are easily misperceived. Fraser's spiral is actually a series of concentric circles. The illusion is so powerful that people who try to trace one of the circles sometimes follow the illusory spiral and jump from one circle to the next. (After Seckel, 2000.)

Figure 4.29 A reversible figure-ground design. Do you see two faces in profile, or a wineglass?

Figure 4.28 Check out this abstract design. If you process it "bottom-up," all you will likely see is three small dark geometric shapes near the edges. Would you like to try some top-down processing? Knowing the title of the design will allow you to apply your knowledge and see it in an entirely different way. The title? It's *Special K.* Can you see it now?

the first perceptual ability to appear after cataract patients like Mr. S. B. regain sight. In normal figure-ground perception, only one figure is seen. In *reversible figures*, however, figure and ground can be switched. In Figure 4.29 it is equally possible to see either a wineglass on a dark background or two facial profiles on a light background. As you shift from one pattern to the other, you should get a clear sense of what figure-ground organization means.

Are there other Gestalt organizing principles? The Gestalt psychologists identified several other principles that bring some order to your perceptions (Figure 4.30).

1. **Nearness.** All other things equal, stimuli that are near each other tend to be grouped together (Quinn, Bhatt, & Hayden, 2008). Thus, if three people stand near each other and a fourth person stands 10 feet away, the adjacent three will be seen as a group and the distant person as an outsider (see Figure 4.30*a*).
2. **Similarity.** "Birds of a feather flock together," and stimuli that are similar in size, shape, color, or form tend to be grouped together (see Figure 4.30*b*). Picture two bands marching side by side. If their uniforms are different colors, the bands will be seen as two separate groups, not as one large group.
3. **Continuation, or continuity.** Perceptions tend toward simplicity and continuity. In Figure 4.30*c* it is easier to visualize a wavy line on a squared-off line than it is to see a complex row of shapes.
4. **Closure.** Closure refers to the tendency to *complete* a figure, so that it has a consistent overall form. Each of the drawings in Figure 4.30*d* has one or more gaps, yet each is perceived as a recognizable figure. The "shapes" that appear in the two right drawings in Figure 4.30*d* are *illusory figures* (implied shapes that are not actually bounded by an edge or an outline). Even young children see these shapes, despite knowing that they are "not really there." Illusory figures reveal that our tendency to form shapes—even with minimal cues—is powerful.
5. **Contiguity.** A principle that can't be shown in Figure 4.30 is contiguity, or nearness in time *and* space. Contiguity is often responsible for the perception that one thing has *caused* another (Buehner & May, 2003). A psychologist friend of ours demonstrates this principle in class by knocking on his head with one hand while knocking on a wooden table (out of sight) with the other. The knocking sound is perfectly timed with the movements of his visible hand. This leads to the irresistible perception that his head is made of wood.

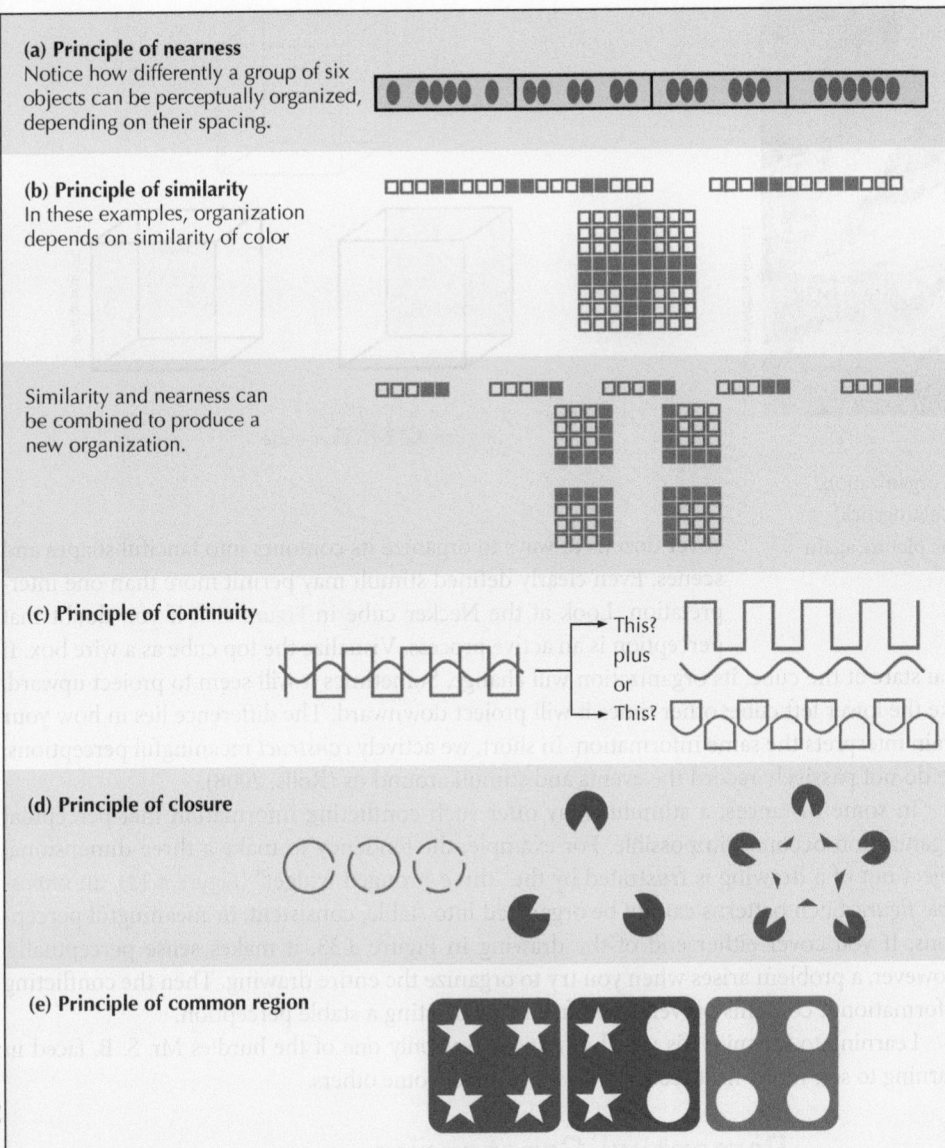

Figure 4.30 Some Gestalt organizing principles.

(a) Principle of nearness
Notice how differently a group of six objects can be perceptually organized, depending on their spacing.

(b) Principle of similarity
In these examples, organization depends on similarity of color

Similarity and nearness can be combined to produce a new organization.

(c) Principle of continuity

This?
plus
or
This?

(d) Principle of closure

(e) Principle of common region

6. **Common region.** As you can see in Figure 4.30*e*, stimuli that are found within a common area tend to be seen as a group (Palmer & Beck, 2007). On the basis of similarity and nearness, the stars in Figure 4.30*e* should be one group and the dots another. However, the colored backgrounds define regions that create three groups of objects (four stars, two stars plus two dots, and four dots).

Clearly, the Gestalt principles offer us some basic "plans" for organizing parts of our day-to-day perceptions in top-down fashion. Take a moment and look for the camouflaged animal pictured in Figure 4.31 (no, it's not a green vine snake). Since camouflage patterns break up figure-ground organization, Mr. S. B. would have been at a total loss to find meaning in such a picture.

In a way, we are all detectives, seeking patterns in what we see. In this sense, a meaningful pattern represents a **perceptual hypothesis**, or initial plan or guess about how to organize sensations. Have you ever seen a "friend" in the distance, only to have the person turn into a stranger as you drew closer? Preexisting ideas and expectations *actively* guide our interpretation of sensations (Most et al., 2005).

The active, constructive nature of perception is perhaps most apparent for *ambiguous stimuli* (patterns allowing more than one interpretation). If you look at a cloud, you may dis-

Perceptual hypothesis An initial guess regarding how to organize (perceive) a stimulus pattern.

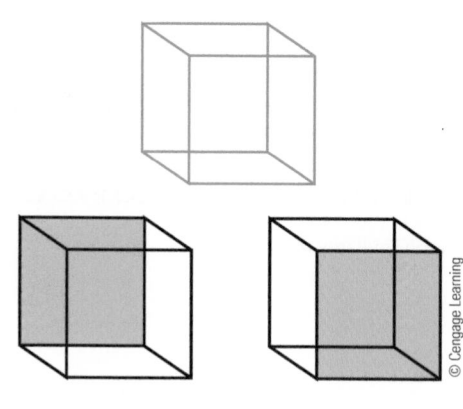

Figure 4.32 Necker cube.

Figure 4.31 A challenging example of perceptual organization. Once the camouflaged insect (known as a giant walkingstick) becomes visible, it is almost impossible to view the picture again without seeing the insect.

cover dozens of ways to organize its contours into fanciful shapes and scenes. Even clearly defined stimuli may permit more than one interpretation. Look at the Necker cube in Figure 4.32 if you doubt that perception is an active process. Visualize the top cube as a wire box. If you stare at the cube, its organization will change. Sometimes it will seem to project upward, like the lower left cube; other times it will project downward. The difference lies in how your brain interprets the same information. In short, we actively *construct* meaningful perceptions; we do not passively record the events and stimuli around us (Rolls, 2008).

In some instances, a stimulus may offer such conflicting information that perceptual organization becomes impossible. For example, the tendency to make a three-dimensional object out of a drawing is frustrated by the "three-pronged widget" (Figure 4.33), an *impossible figure*. Such patterns cannot be organized into stable, consistent, or meaningful perceptions. If you cover either end of the drawing in Figure 4.33, it makes sense perceptually. However, a problem arises when you try to organize the entire drawing. Then the conflicting information it contains prevents you from constructing a stable perception.

Learning to organize his visual sensations was only one of the hurdles Mr. S. B. faced in learning to see. In the next section, we will consider some others.

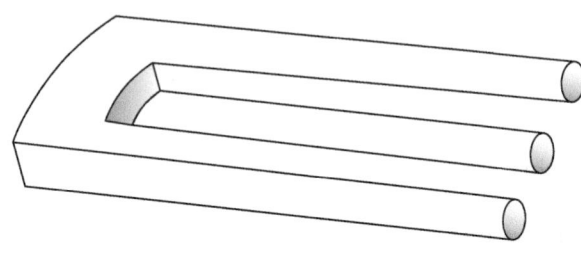

Figure 4.33 *(Left)* An impossible figure—the "three-pronged widget." © Cengage Learning

Perceptual Constancies

When Mr. S. B. first regained his vision, he could judge distance only in familiar situations (Gregory, 1990). One day he was found crawling out of a hospital window to get a closer look at traffic on the street. It's easy to understand his curiosity, but he had to be restrained. His room was on the fourth floor!

Why would Mr. S. B. try to crawl out of a fourth-story window? Couldn't he at least tell distance from the size of the cars? No, you must be visually familiar with objects to use their size to judge distance. Try holding your left hand a few inches in front of your nose and your right hand at arm's length. Your right hand should appear to be about half the size of your left hand. Still, you know your right hand did not suddenly shrink, because you have seen it many times at various distances. We call this **size constancy**: The perceived size of an object remains the same, even though the size of its image on the retina changes.

To perceive your hand accurately, you had to draw on past experience to provide a top-down plan for constructing your perception. Some of these plans are so basic they seem to be *native*, or inborn. An example is the ability to see a line on a piece of paper. Likewise, even newborn babies show some evidence of size constancy (Granrud, 2006). However, many of our perceptions are *empirical*, or based on prior experience. For instance, cars, houses, and people look like toys when seen from a great distance or from an unfamiliar perspective, such as from the top of a skyscraper. This suggests that although some size constancy is innate, it is also affected by learning (Granrud, 2009).

Size constancy The perceived size of an object remains constant, despite changes in its retinal image.

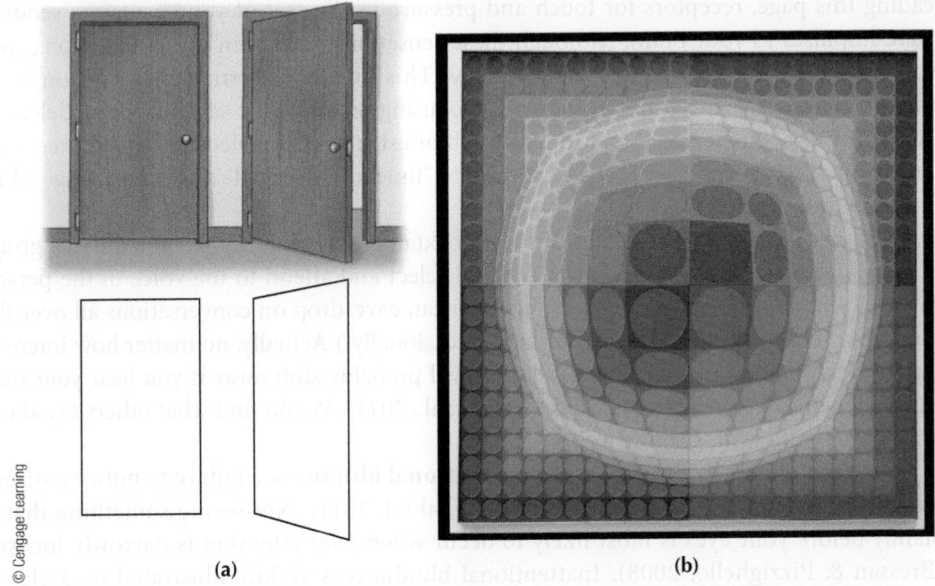

(a)　　　　　　　　　　　　(b)

© Cengage Learning

Figure 4.34 Shape constancy. *(a)* When a door is open, its image actually forms a trapezoid. Shape constancy is indicated by the fact that it is still perceived as a rectangle. *(b)* With great effort you may be able to see this design as a collection of flat shapes. However, if you maintain shape constancy, the distorted pentagrams strongly suggest the surface of a sphere. (Paz-Ket [oil on canvas], Vasarely, Victor [1908–1997]/ Museo de Bellas Artes, Bilbao, Spain/ © DACS/The Bridgeman Art Library International.)

In **shape constancy** the shape of an object remains stable, even though the shape of its retinal image changes. You can demonstrate shape constancy by looking at this page from directly overhead and then from an angle. Obviously, the page is rectangular, but most of the images that reach your eyes are distorted. Yet, though the book's image changes, your perception of its shape remains constant (for additional examples, see Figure 4.34). On the highway, alcohol intoxication impairs size and shape constancy, adding to the accident rate among drunk drivers (Goldstein, 2010).

Let's say that you are outside in bright sunlight. Beside you, a friend is wearing a gray skirt and a white blouse. Suddenly a cloud shades the sun. It might seem that the blouse would grow dimmer, but it still appears to be bright white. This happens because the blouse continues to reflect a greater *proportion* of light than nearby objects. **Brightness constancy** refers to the fact that the brightness of objects appears to stay the same as lighting conditions change. However, this holds true only if the blouse and other objects are all illuminated by the same amount of light. You could make an area on your friend's gray skirt look whiter than the shaded blouse by shining a bright spotlight on the skirt.

To summarize, the energy patterns reaching our senses are constantly changing, even when they come from the same object. Size, shape, and brightness constancy rescue us from a confusing world in which objects would seem to shrink and grow, change shape as if made of rubber, and light up or fade like neon lamps.

Selective Attention—Tuning In and Tuning Out

JOURNEY QUESTION 4.7 *Why are we more aware of some sensations than others?*

Although the senses reduce a mixture of sights, sounds, odors, tastes, and touch sensations to more manageable amounts, they are still too much for the brain to handle. That's why the brain further filters sensory information through *selective attention*. For example, as you sit

Shape constancy The perceived shape of an object is unaffected by changes in its retinal image.

Brightness constancy The apparent (or relative) brightness of objects remains the same as long as they are illuminated by the same amount of light.

reading this page, receptors for touch and pressure in the seat of your pants are sending nerve impulses to your brain. Although these sensations have been present all along, you were probably not aware of them until just now. This "seat-of-the-pants phenomenon" is an example of **selective attention**—voluntarily focusing on a specific sensory input. Selective attention appears to be based on the ability of brain structures to select and divert incoming sensory messages (Mather, 2011). We are able to "tune in on" a single sensory message while excluding others.

Another familiar example of this is the "cocktail party effect." When you are in a group of people, surrounded by voices, you can still select and attend to the voice of the person you are facing. Or if that person gets dull, you can eavesdrop on conversations all over the room. (Be sure to smile and nod your head occasionally!) Actually, no matter how interesting your companion may be, your attention will probably shift away if you hear your own name spoken somewhere in the room (Koch et al., 2011). We do find what others say about us to be very interesting, don't we?

At times, we can even suffer from **inattentional blindness**, a failure to notice a stimulus because attention is focused elsewhere (Thakral, 2011). Not seeing something that is plainly before your eyes is most likely to occur when your attention is narrowly focused (Bressan & Pizzighello, 2008). Inattentional blindness is vividly illustrated by a classic study in which participants were shown a film of two basketball teams, one wearing black shirts and the other wearing white. Observers were asked to watch the film closely and count how many times a basketball passed between members of one of the teams, while ignoring the other team. As observers watched and counted, a person wearing a gorilla suit walked into the middle of the basketball game, faced the camera, thumped its chest, and walked out of view. Half the observers failed to notice this rather striking event (Simons & Chabris, 1999).

In a similar way, using a cell phone while driving can cause inattentional blindness. Instead of ignoring a gorilla, you might miss seeing another car, a motorcyclist, or a pedestrian while your attention is focused on the phone. It probably goes without saying, but the more engaged you are with your cell phone while driving (like texting instead of just having a conversation), the greater the problem (Fougnie & Marois, 2007).

You might find it helpful to think of selective attention as a *bottleneck*, or narrowing in the information channel linking the senses to perception. When one message enters the bottleneck, it seems to prevent others from passing through (Figure 4.35). Imagine, for instance, that you are driving a car and approaching an intersection. You need to be sure the traffic light is still green. Just as you are about to check it, your passenger points to a friend at the side of the road. If you then fail to notice the light just changed to red, an accident may be seconds away.

Are some stimuli more attention getting than others? Yes. Very *intense* stimuli usually command attention. Stimuli that are brighter, louder, or larger tend to capture attention: A gunshot in a library would be hard to ignore. If a brightly colored hot-air balloon ever lands at your college campus, it will almost certainly draw a crowd.

Repetitious stimuli, repetitious stimuli, repetitious stimuli, repetitious stimuli, repetitious stimuli, repetitious stimuli are also attention getting. A dripping faucet at night makes little noise by normal standards, but because of repetition, it may become as attention getting as a single sound many times louder. This effect is used repeatedly, so to speak, in television and radio commercials.

ATTENTION IS ALSO **FREQUENTLY** RELATED TO contrast OR *change* IN STIMULATION. The contrasting type styles in the preceding sentence draw attention because they are *unexpected*.

One of the most amazing perceptual feats is our capacity to create three-dimensional space from flat retinal images. We'll explore that topic in the next section, but first here's a chance to pay some attention to what you've learned.

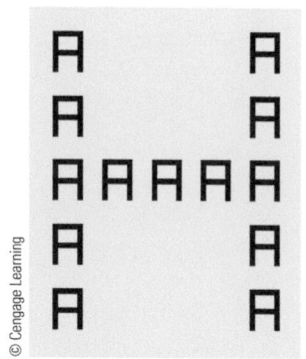

Figure 4.35 The attentional "bottleneck," or "spotlight," can be widened or narrowed. If you focus on local details in this drawing you will see the letter *A* repeated 13 times. If you broaden your field of attention to encompass the overall pattern, you see the letter *H*.

Selective attention Giving priority to a particular incoming sensory message.

Inattentional blindness A failure to notice a stimulus because attention is focused elsewhere.

RECITE

1. In top-down processing of information, individual features are analyzed and assembled into a meaningful whole. T or F?
2. The first and most basic perceptual organization to emerge when sight is restored to a blind person is

   a. continuity
   b. nearness constancy
   c. recognition of numbers and letters
   d. figure-ground

3. At times, meaningful perceptual organization represents a _____, or "guess," held until the evidence contradicts it.
4. The design known as the Necker cube is a good example of an impossible figure. T or F?
5. Which among the following are subject to basic perceptual constancy?

   a. figure-ground organization
   b. size
   c. ambiguity
   d. brightness
   e. continuity
   f. closure
   g. shape
   h. nearness

6. Which of the following stimuli are more effective at getting attention?

   a. unexpected stimuli
   b. repetitious stimuli
   c. intense stimuli
   d. all of the above

REFLECT

THINK CRITICALLY

7. People who have taken psychedelic drugs, such as LSD or mescaline, often report that the objects and people they see appear to be changing in size, shape, and brightness. This suggests that such drugs disrupt which perceptual process?

SELF-REFLECT

As you look around the area in which you are now, how are the Gestalt principles helping to organize your perceptions? Try to find a specific example for each principle.

If you needed to explain the perceptual constancies to a friend, what would you say? Why are the constancies important for maintaining a stable perceptual world?

Can you pay attention to more than one sensory input at once?

ANSWERS

1. F 2. d 3. hypothesis 4. F 5. b, d, g 6. d 7. Perceptual constancies (size, shape, and brightness).

Depth Perception—What If the World Were Flat?

JOURNEY QUESTION 4.8 *How is it possible to see depth and judge distance?*

Cross your eyes, hold your head very still, and stare at a single point across the room; your surroundings may appear to be almost flat, like a 2-D painting or photograph. This is the world that neuroscientist Susan Barry, cross-eyed from birth, lived with until, at the age of 48, she learned to see in 3-D (Barry & Sacks, 2009). Now, uncross your eyes. Suddenly, the three-dimensional perceptual world returns. Let's explore the mechanisms that underlie our ability to perceive depth and space.

Depth perception is the ability to see space and to accurately judge distances. Without 3-D depth perception, another form of perceptual construction, the world would look like a flat surface. You would have great difficulty driving a car or riding a bicycle, shooting baskets, threading a needle, or simply navigating around a room (Harris & Jenkin, 2011).

Mr. S. B. had trouble with depth perception after his sight was restored. Is depth perception learned? Studies done with a visual cliff suggest that depth perception is partly learned and partly innate (Witherington et al., 2005). Basically, a visual cliff is a glass-topped table (**Figure 4.36**). On one side, a checkered surface lies directly beneath the glass. On the other side, the checkered surface is 4 feet below. This makes the glass look like a tabletop on one side and a cliff, or drop-off, on the other.

To test for depth perception, 6- to 14-month-old infants were placed in the middle of the visual cliff. This gave them a choice of crawling to the shallow side or the deep side. (The glass prevented them from doing any "skydiving" if they chose the deep side.) Most infants chose the shallow side. In fact, most refused the deep side even when their mothers tried to call them toward it (Gibson & Walk, 1960).

If the infants were at least 6 months old when they were tested, isn't it possible that they learned to perceive depth? Yes. More recent research has shown that depth perception begins

Depth perception The ability to see three-dimensional space and to accurately judge distances.

"I can't go on living with such lousy depth perception!"

to develop as early as 2 weeks of age (Yonas, Elieff, & Arterberry, 2002). It is very likely that at least a basic level of depth perception is innate. Yet, the development of depth perception is not complete until about 6 months, suggesting that it depends on both brain maturation and individual experience.

But don't some older babies crawl off tables or beds? As soon as infants become active crawlers, they refuse to cross the deep side of the visual cliff. However, older infants who have just learned to walk must again learn to avoid the "deep" side of the visual cliff (Witherington et al., 2005). Besides, even babies who perceive depth may not be able to catch themselves if they slip. A lack of coordination—not an inability to see depth—probably explains most "crash landings" after about 4 months of age.

We learn to construct our perception of three-dimensional space by integrating information from a variety of *depth cues* (Schiller et al., 2011). **Depth cues** are features of the environment and messages from the body that supply information about distance and space. Some cues require two eyes (*binocular depth cues*), whereas others will work with just one eye (*monocular depth cues*).

Binocular Depth Cues

The most basic source of depth perception is *retinal disparity* (a discrepancy in the images that reach the right and left eyes). Retinal disparity is based on the fact that the eyes are about 2.5 inches apart. Because of this, each eye receives a slightly different view of the world. Try this: put a finger in front of your eyes and as close to your nose as you can. First close one eye and then the other, over and over again. You should notice that your finger seems to jump back and forth as you view the different images reaching each eye. However, when the two different images are fused into one overall image, **stereoscopic vision** (3-D sight) occurs (Harris & Jenkin, 2011). The result is a powerful sensation of depth (**Figure 4.37** and **Figure 4.38**).

Convergence is a second binocular depth cue. When you look at a distant object, the lines of vision from your eyes are parallel. You are normally not aware of it, but whenever

Depth cues Features of the environment and messages from the body that supply information about distance and space.

Stereoscopic vision Perception of space and depth due to the fact that the eyes receive different images.

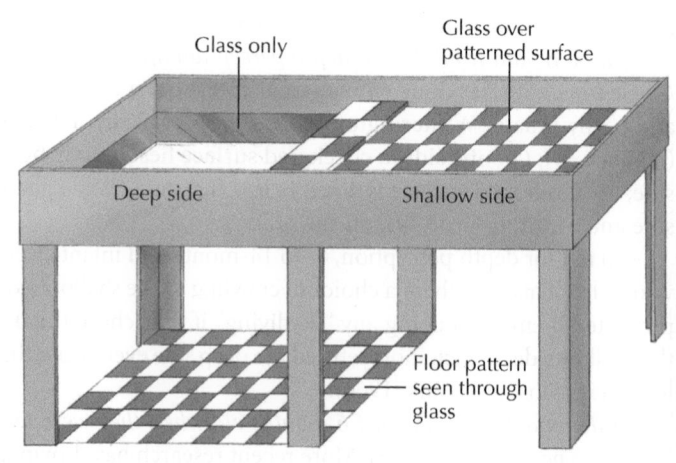

Glass only

Glass over patterned surface

Deep side

Shallow side

Floor pattern seen through glass

Figure 4.36 Human infants and newborn animals refuse to go over the edge of the visual cliff.

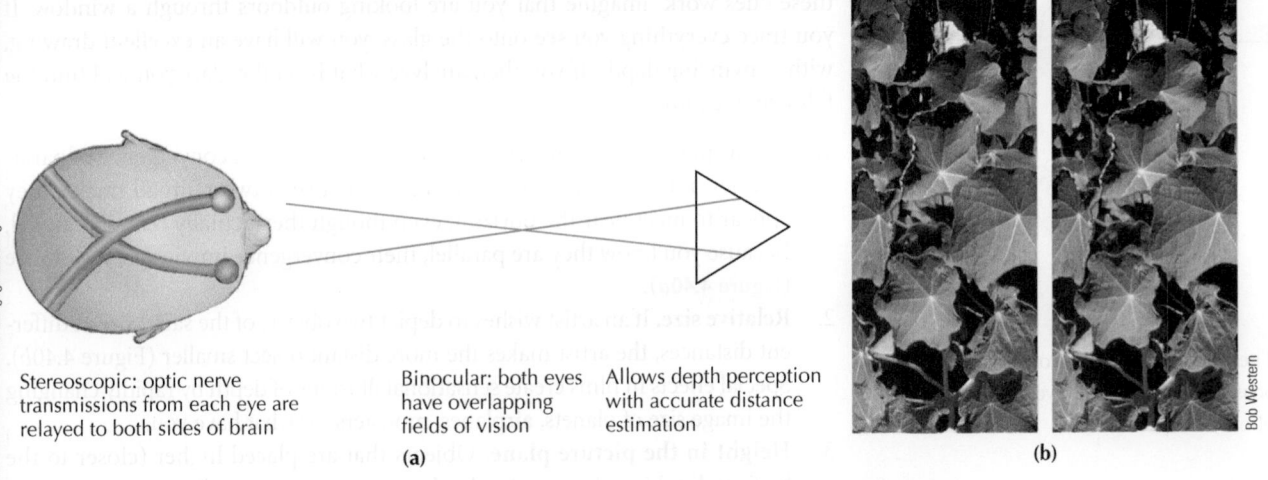

Stereoscopic: optic nerve transmissions from each eye are relayed to both sides of brain

Binocular: both eyes have overlapping fields of vision

Allows depth perception with accurate distance estimation

(a)

(b)

Bob Western

Figure 4.37 *(a)* Stereoscopic vision. *(b)* The photographs show what the right and left eyes would see when viewing a plant. Hold the page about 6 to 8 inches from your eyes. Allow your eyes to cross and focus on the overlapping image between the two photos. Then try to fuse the leaves into one image. If you are successful the third dimension will appear like magic.

you estimate a distance under 50 feet (as when you play catch or shoot trash can hoops with the first draft of your essay), you are using convergence. How? Muscles attached to the eyeball feed information on eye position to the brain to help it judge distance (Figure 4.39).

You can feel convergence by exaggerating it: Focus on your fingertip and bring it toward your eyes until they almost cross. You can actually feel the muscles that control eye movement working harder and harder as your fingertip gets closer.

Can a person with one eye perceive depth? Yes, but not nearly as well as a person with two eyes. Try driving a car or riding a bicycle with one eye closed. You will find yourself braking too soon or too late, and you will have difficulty estimating your speed. ("But officer, my psychology text said to . . .") Despite this, you will be able to drive, although it will be more difficult than usual. This is possible because your single eye can still make use of monocular depth cues.

Monocular Depth Cues

As their name implies, monocular depth cues can be perceived with just one eye. One such cue is *accommodation*, the bending of the lens to focus on nearby objects. Sensations from muscles attached to each lens flow back to the brain. Changes in these sensations help us judge distances within about 4 feet of the eyes. This information is available even if you are just using one eye, so accommodation is a monocular cue. Beyond 4 feet, accommodation has limited value. Obviously, it is more important to a watchmaker or a person trying to thread a needle than it is to a basketball player or someone driving an automobile. Other monocular depth cues are referred to as pictorial depth cues, because a good movie, painting, or photograph can create a convincing sense of depth where none exists.

How is the illusion of depth created on a two-dimensional surface? **Pictorial depth cues** are features that impart information about space, depth, and distance. To understand how

Figure 4.38 *Avatar*, released in 2009, is the most successful 3-D film to date. One of the tools director James Cameron developed specially for this film was a stereoscopic camera that simulates retinal disparity and creates a sensation of depth. When viewed through polarized goggles, the resulting film appears fully three-dimensional.

Pictorial depth cues Monocular depth cues found in paintings, drawings, and photographs that impart information about space, depth, and distance.

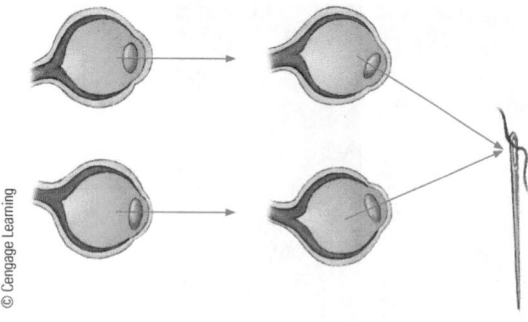

Figure 4.39 The eyes must converge, or turn in toward the nose, to focus close objects. The eyes shown are viewed from above the head.

these cues work, imagine that you are looking outdoors through a window. If you trace everything you see onto the glass, you will have an excellent drawing, with convincing depth. If you then analyze what is on the glass you will find the following features:

1. **Linear perspective.** This cue is based on the apparent convergence of parallel lines in the environment. If you stand between two railroad tracks, they appear to meet near the horizon, even though they actually remain parallel. Because you know they are parallel, their convergence implies great distance (Figure 4.40a).

2. **Relative size.** If an artist wishes to depict two objects of the same size at different distances, the artist makes the more distant object smaller (Figure 4.40b). Special effects in films create sensational illusions of depth by rapidly changing the image size of planets, airplanes, monsters, or what have you.

3. **Height in the picture plane.** Objects that are placed higher (closer to the horizon line) in a drawing tend to be perceived as more distant. In the upper frame of Figure 4.40b, the black columns look like they are receding into the distance partly because they become smaller but also because they move higher in the drawing.

4. **Light and shadow.** Most objects are lighted in ways that create clear patterns of light and shadow. Copying such patterns of light and shadow can give a two-dimensional design a three-dimensional appearance (Figure 4.40c). (Also, look ahead to Figure 4.41 for more information on light and shadow.)

5. **Overlap.** Overlap (or *interposition*) occurs when one object partially blocks another object. Hold your hands up and ask a friend across the room which is nearer. Relative size will give the answer if one hand is much nearer to your friend than the other. But if one hand is only slightly closer than the other, your friend may not be able to tell—until you slide one hand in front of the other. Overlap then removes any doubt (Figure 4.40d).

6. **Texture gradients.** Changes in texture also contribute to depth perception. If you stand in the middle of a cobblestone street, the street will look coarse near your feet. However, its texture will get smaller and finer as you look into the distance (Figure 4.40e).

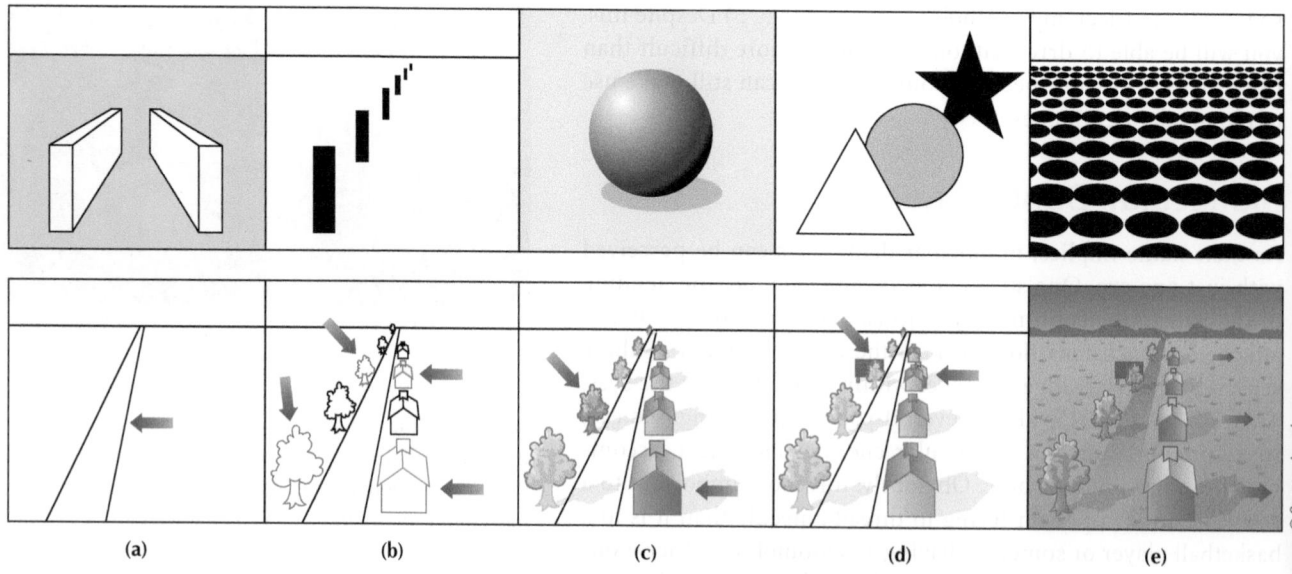

(a)   (b)   (c)   (d)   (e)

Figure 4.40 (a) Linear perspective. (b) Relative size. (c) Light and shadow. (d) Overlap. (e) Texture gradients. Drawings in the top row show fairly "pure" examples of each of the pictorial depth cues. In the bottom row, the pictorial depth cues are used to assemble a more realistic scene.

Figure 4.41 *(Above)* When judging depth we usually assume that light comes mainly from one direction, usually from above. Squint a little to blur the image you see here. You should perceive a collection of globes projecting outward. If you turn this page upside down, the globes should become cavities. (After Ramachandran, 1995.) *(Below)* The famed Dutch artist M. C. Escher violated our assumptions about light to create the dramatic illusions of depth found in his 1953 lithograph *Relativity*. In this print, light appears to come from all sides of the scene.

7. **Aerial perspective.** Smog, fog, dust, and haze add to the apparent distance of an object. Because of aerial perspective, distant objects tend to be hazy, washed out in color, and lacking in detail. Aerial haze is often most noticeable when it is missing. If you have ever seen a distant mountain range on a crystal-clear day, it might have looked like it was only a few miles away. In reality, you could have been viewing them through 50 miles of crystal-clear air.

8. **Relative motion.** Relative motion, also known as *motion parallax* (PAIR-ah-lax), can be seen by looking out a window and moving your head from side to side. Notice that nearby objects appear to move a sizable distance as your head moves. Trees, houses, and telephone poles that are farther away appear to move slightly in relation to the background. Distant objects like hills, mountains, or clouds don't seem to move at all.

When combined, pictorial cues can create a powerful illusion of depth. (See **Table 4.1** for a summary of all the depth cues we have discussed.)

Is motion parallax really a pictorial cue? Strictly speaking, it is not—except in the world of two-dimensional movies, television, or animated cartoons. However, when parallax is present, we almost always perceive depth (Yoonessi & Baker, 2011). Much of the apparent depth of a good movie comes from relative motion captured by the camera. **Figure 4.42** illustrates the defining feature of motion parallax. Imagine that you are in a bus and watching the passing scenery (with your gaze at a right angle to the road). Under these conditions, nearby objects will appear to rush *backward*. Those farther away, such as distant mountains, will seem to move very little or not at all. Objects that are more remote, such as the sun or moon, will appear to move in the *same* direction you are traveling. (That's why the sun appears to "follow" you when you take a stroll.)

Table 4.1 Summary of Visual Depth Cues

Binocular Depth Cues
- Retinal disparity
- Convergence

Monocular Depth Cues
- Accommodation
- Pictorial depth cues (listed below)
    - Linear perspective
    - Relative size
    - Height in the picture plane
    - Light and shadow
    - Overlap
    - Texture gradients
    - Aerial perspective
    - Relative motion (motion parallax)

© Cengage Learning

◀ Direction of travel

Figure 4.42 The apparent motion of objects viewed during travel depends on their distance from the observer. Apparent motion can also be influenced by an observer's point of fixation. At middle distances, objects closer than the point of fixation appear to move backward; those beyond the point of fixation appear to move forward. Objects at great distances, such as the sun or moon, always appear to move forward.

The Moon Illusion

How do the depth perception cues relate to daily experience? We constantly use both pictorial cues and bodily cues to sense depth and judge distances. Consider an intriguing effect called the *moon illusion* (perceiving the moon as larger when it is low in the sky). When the moon is on the horizon, it tends to look like a silver dollar. When it is directly overhead, it looks more like a dime. Contrary to what some people believe, the moon is not magnified by the atmosphere. But the moon *looks* nearly twice as large when it's low in the sky (Ross & Plug, 2002). This occurs, in part, because the moon's *apparent distance* is greater when it is near the horizon than when it is overhead (Jones & Wilson, 2009).

But if it seems farther away, shouldn't it look smaller? No. When the moon is overhead, few depth cues surround it. In contrast, when you see the moon on the horizon, it is behind houses, trees, telephone poles, and mountains. These objects add numerous depth cues, which cause the horizon to seem more distant than the sky overhead. Picture two balloons, one 10 feet away and the second 20 feet away. Suppose the more distant balloon is inflated until its image matches the image of the nearer balloon. How do we know the more distant balloon is larger? Because its image is the same size as a balloon that is closer. Similarly, the moon makes the same-size image on the horizon as it does overhead. However, the horizon seems more distant because more depth cues are present. As a result, the horizon moon must be perceived as larger (Kaufman & Kaufman, 2000; see Figure 4.43).

This explanation is known as the **apparent-distance hypothesis** (the horizon seems more distant than the night sky). You can test it by removing depth cues while looking at a horizon moon. Try looking at the moon through a rolled-up paper tube, or make your hands into a "telescope" and look at the next large moon you see. It will immediately appear to shrink when viewed without depth cues (Ross & Plug, 2002).

Apparent-distance hypothesis An explanation of the moon illusion stating that the horizon seems more distant than the night sky.

Figure 4.43 The Ponzo illusion may help you understand the moon illusion. Picture the two white bars as resting on the railroad tracks. In the drawing, the upper bar is the same length as the lower bar. However, because the upper bar appears to be farther away than the lower bar, we perceive it as longer. The same logic applies to the moon illusion.

1. The visual cliff is used to test for infant sensitivity to linear perspective. T or F?
2. Write an *M* or a *B* after each of the following to indicate whether it is a monocular or binocular depth cue.

   accommodation _____ convergence _____ retinal disparity _____ linear perspective _____ motion parallax _____ overlap _____ relative size _____

3. Which of the depth cues listed in Question 2 are based on muscular feedback? _____.
4. Interpretation of pictorial depth cues requires no prior experience. T or F?
5. The moon's image is greatly magnified by the atmosphere near the horizon. T or F?

REFLECT

THINK CRITICALLY

6. What hearing ability would you say is most closely related to stereoscopic vision?

Part of the rush of excitement produced by action movies and video games is based on the sense of depth they create. Return to the list of pictorial depth cues. What cues have you seen used to portray depth? Try to think of specific examples in a movie or game you have seen recently.

ANSWERS

1. F 2. accommodation (M), convergence (M), retinal disparity (B), linear perspective (M), motion parallax (M), overlap (M), relative size (M) 3. accommodation and convergence 4. F 5. F 6. If you close your eyes, you can usually tell the direction and perhaps the location of a sound source, such as a hand-clap. Locating sounds in space is heavily dependent on having two ears, just as stereoscopic vision depends on having two eyes.

Perceptual Learning—Believing Is Seeing

JOURNEY QUESTION 4.9 *How is perception altered by expectations, motives, emotions, and learning?*

Various processes distort our perceptions, which are far from a perfect model of the world. Let's investigate some factors that affect the accuracy of our perceptual experiences. As we just saw, we use Gestalt organizing principles, perceptual constancies, and depth cues to construct our visual perceptions. All these processes and others make up the common, partly inborn core of our perceptual abilities. In addition, we each have specific life experiences that can, in top-down fashion, affect our perceptions. For instance, what you perceive can be altered by *perceptual expectancies*, motives, emotions, and *perceptual habits*.

Perceptual Expectancies

What is a perceptual expectancy? If you are a runner in the starting blocks at a track meet, you are *set* to respond in a certain way. If a car backfires, runners at a track meet may jump the gun. Likewise, past experience, motives, context, or suggestions may create a **perceptual expectancy (or set)** that prepares you to perceive in a certain way. As a matter of fact, we all frequently jump the gun when perceiving. In essence, an expectancy is a perceptual hypothesis we are *very likely* to apply to a stimulus—even if applying it is inappropriate.

Perceptual sets often lead us to see what we *expect* to see. For example, let's say while driving you just made an illegal lane change (or texted on your cell phone!?). You then see a flashing light. "Rats," you think, "busted," and wait for the police car to pull you over. But as the car draws nearer, you see it was just a car with a vivid turn signal. Most people have had similar experiences in which expectations altered their perceptions. To observe perceptual expectancies firsthand, perform the demonstration described in **Figure 4.44**.

Perceptual expectancies are frequently created by *suggestion*. In one study (wine snobs take note), participants given a taste of a $90 wine reported that it tasted better

Perceptual expectancy (or set) A readiness to perceive in a particular manner, induced by strong expectations.

View I   View II   View III

Figure 4.44 "Young woman/old woman" illustrations. As an interesting demonstration of perceptual expectancy, show some of your friends view I and some view II (cover all other views). Next show your friends view III and ask them what they see. Those who saw view I should see the old woman in view III; those who saw view II should see the young woman in view III. Can you see both? (After Leeper, 1935.)

than a $10 wine. Functional MRI images confirmed that brain areas related to pleasure were indeed more active when participants tasted the more expensive wine (Plassmann et al., 2008). The twist is that exactly the same wine was served in both cases. Suggesting that the wine was expensive created a perceptual expectancy that it would taste better. And so it did (advertisers also take note). In the same way, labeling people as "gang members," "mental patients," "queers," "illegal immigrants," "bitches," and so on, is very likely to distort perceptions.

Motives, Emotions, and Perception

Our motives and emotions also play a role in shaping our perceptions. For example, if you are hungry, food and even food-related words are more likely to gain your attention than non–food-related words (Mogg et al., 1998; Werthmann et al., 2011). Advertisers take advantage of two motives that are widespread in our society: *anxiety* and *sex*. Everything from automobile tires to cosmetic surgery is merchandised by using sex to gain attention (Hennink-Kaminski & Reichert, 2011). Other ads combine sex with anxiety. Deodorant, soaps, toothpaste, and countless other products are pushed in ads that play on desires to be attractive, to have "sex appeal," or to avoid embarrassment.

Our emotions can also shape our perceptions (Yiend, 2010). According to psychologist Barbara Frederickson, negative emotions generally narrow our perceptual focus, or "spotlight," increasing the likelihood of inattentional blindness. In contrast, positive emotions can actually broaden the scope of attention (Fredrickson & Branigan, 2005). For example, positive emotions can affect how well people recognize people from other races. In recognizing faces, a consistent *other-race effect* occurs. This is a sort of "They all look alike to me" bias in perceiving persons from other racial and ethnic groups. In tests of facial recognition, people are much better at recognizing faces of their own race than others. But when people are in positive moods, their ability to recognize people from other races improves (Johnson & Fredrickson, 2005).

The main reason for the other-race effect is that we typically have more experience with people from our own race. As a result, we become very familiar with the features that help us recognize different persons. For other groups, we lack the perceptual expertise needed to accurately separate one face from another (Megreya, White, & Burton, 2011; Sporer, 2001). Such differences indicate the importance of perceptual learning, a topic we turn to next.

Human Diversity

According to psychologist Richard Nisbett and his colleagues, people from different cultures do, in fact, perceive the world differently. European Americans are individualistic people who tend to focus on themselves and their sense of personal control. In contrast, East Asians are collectivist people who tend to focus on their interpersonal relationships and social responsibilities. As a consequence, European Americans tend to perceive actions in terms of internal factors ("She did it because she chose to do it"). In comparison, East Asians tend to perceive actions in terms of their social context ("He did it because it was his responsibility to his family") (Henrich, Heine, & Norenzayan, 2010; Norenzayan & Nisbett, 2000).

Do such cultural differences affect our everyday perception of objects and events? Apparently they do. In one study, American and Japanese participants were shown drawings of everyday scenes, such as a farm. Later, they saw a slightly changed version of the scene. Some of the changes were made to the focal point, or figure of the scene. Other changes altered the surrounding context, or ground of the scene. Americans, it turns out, were better at detecting changes in the figure of a scene. Japanese participants were better at finding alterations in the background (Nisbett & Miyamoto, 2005).

To explain this difference, Chua, Boland, and Nisbett (2005) presented American and Chinese participants with pictures of a figure (such as a tiger) placed on a ground (such as a jungle) and monitored their eye-movement patterns. The Americans focused their eye movements on the figure; Chinese participants made more eye movements around the ground. In other words, Westerners have a relatively narrow focus of attention, whereas Easterners have a broader focus of attention (Boduroglu, Shah, & Nisbett, 2009). Apparently, the society we live in can indeed influence even our most basic perceptual habits (Hedden et al., 2008). This difference in perceptual style even influences the artistic and aesthetic preferences expressed in Eastern and Western art (Masuda et al., 2008).

Okay, so maybe members of different races or ethnic groups have developed perceptual sets that lead them to see in-group faces differently, but we all see everything else the same, right? For an answer, see "Do They See What We See?"

Perceptual Habits

England is one of the few countries in the world where people drive on the left side of the road. Because of this reversal, it is not unusual for visitors to step off curbs in front of cars—after carefully looking for traffic in the *wrong* direction. As this example suggests, learning has a powerful impact on top-down processing in perception.

How does learning affect perception? The term **perceptual learning** refers to changes in the brain that alter how we construct sensory information into perceptions (Moreno et al., 2009). For example, to use a computer, you must learn to pay attention to specific stimuli, such as icons and cursors. We also learn to tell the difference between stimuli that seemed identical at first. An example is the novice chef who discovers how to tell the difference between dried basil, oregano, and tarragon. In other situations, we learn to focus on just one part of a group of stimuli. This saves us from having to process all the stimuli in the group. For instance, a linebacker in football may be able to tell if the next play will be a run or a pass by watching one or two key players, rather than the entire opposing team (Seitz & Watanabe, 2005).

In general, learning creates *perceptual habits*—ingrained patterns of organization and attention—that affect our daily experience. Stop for a moment and look at **Figure 4.45.** The left face looks somewhat unusual, to be sure. But the distortion seems mild—until you turn the page upside down. Viewed normally, the face looks quite grotesque. Why is there a difference? Apparently, most people have little experience with upside-down faces. Perceptual learning, therefore, has less impact on our perceptions of an upside-down face. With a face in the normal position, you know what to expect and where to look. Also, you tend to see the entire face as a recognizable pattern. When a face is inverted, we are forced to perceive its individual features separately (Caharel et al., 2006).

Lars Baron/Getty Images

In many sports, expert players are much better than beginners at paying attention to key information. Compared with novices, experts scan actions and events more quickly and they focus on only the most meaningful information. This helps experts to make decisions and react more quickly (Gorman, Abernethy, & Farrow, 2011).

Perceptual learning Changes in perception that can be attributed to prior experience; a result of changes in how the brain processes sensory information.

Figure 4.45 The effects of prior experience on perception. The doctored face looks far worse when viewed right side up because it can be related to past experience.

The Müller-Lyer Illusion

Can perceptual habits explain other illusions? Perceptual habits play a role in explaining some illusions. In general, size and shape constancy, habitual eye movements, continuity, and perceptual habits combine in various ways to produce the illusions in Figure 4.46. Rather than attempt to explain all of them, let's focus on one deceptively simple example.

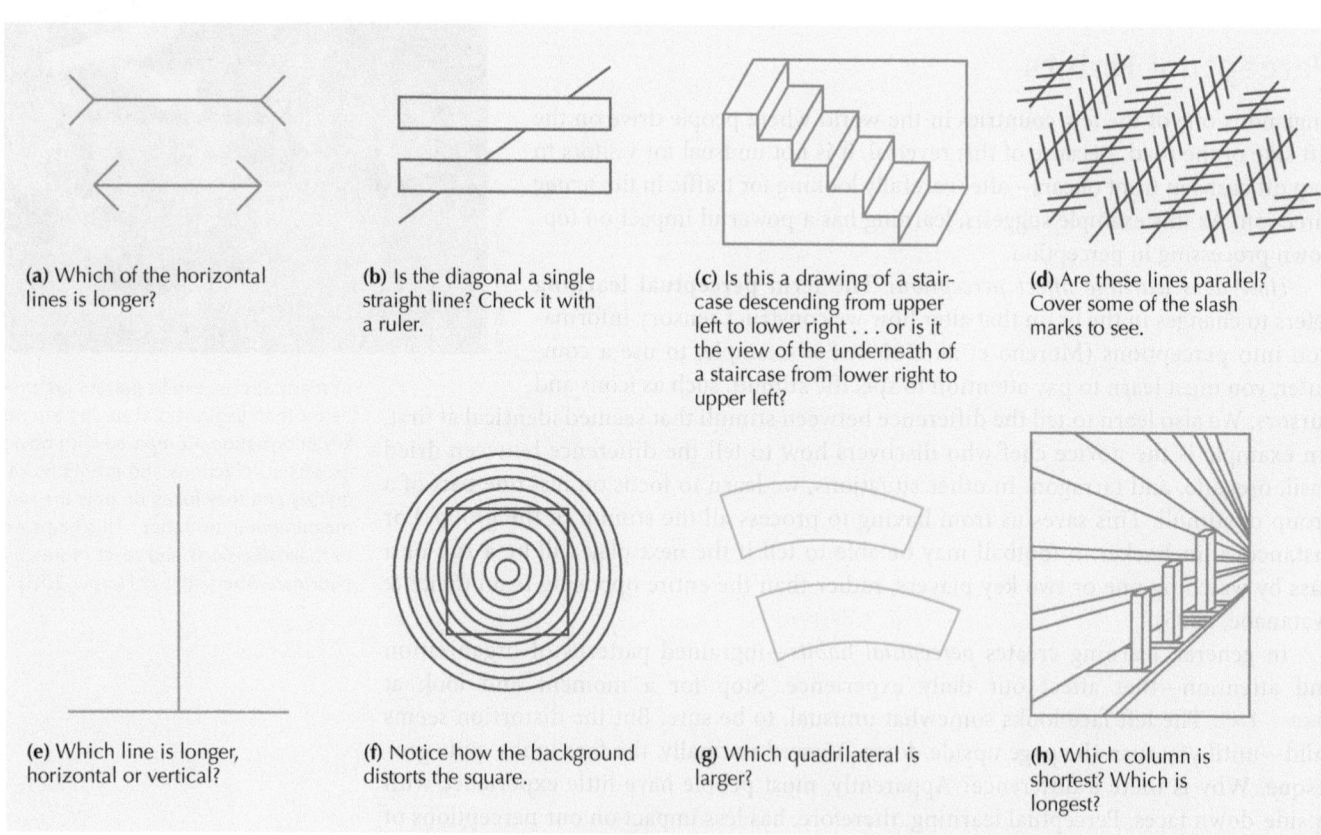

(a) Which of the horizontal lines is longer?

(b) Is the diagonal a single straight line? Check it with a ruler.

(c) Is this a drawing of a staircase descending from upper left to lower right . . . or is it the view of the underneath of a staircase from lower right to upper left?

(d) Are these lines parallel? Cover some of the slash marks to see.

(e) Which line is longer, horizontal or vertical?

(f) Notice how the background distorts the square.

(g) Which quadrilateral is larger?

(h) Which column is shortest? Which is longest?

Figure 4.46 Some interesting perceptual illusions. Such illusions reveal that perceptual misconstructions are a normal part of visual perception.

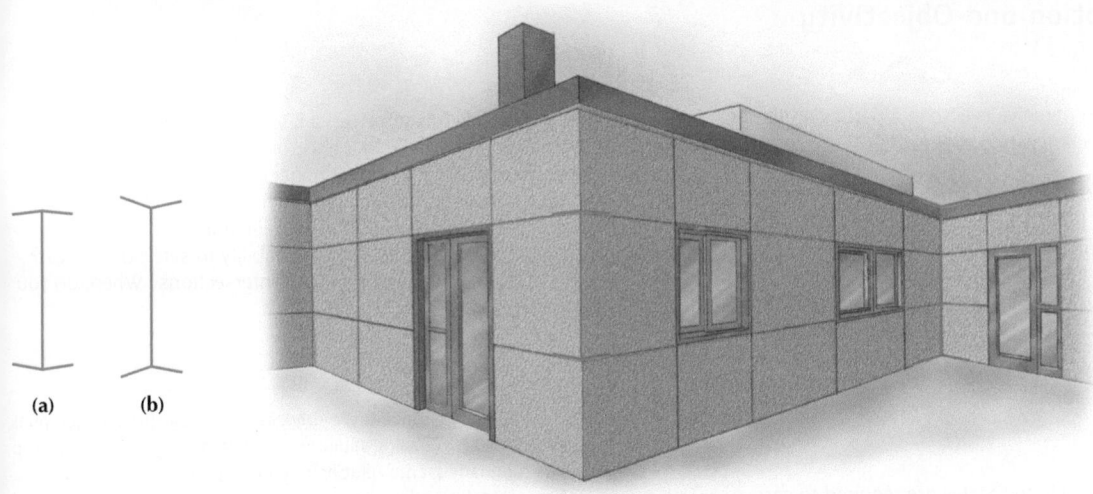

(a)   (b)

© Cengage Learning

Figure 4.47 Why does line *(b)* in the Müller-Lyer illusion look longer than line *(a)*? Probably because it looks more like a distant corner than a nearer one. Because the vertical lines form images of the same length, the more "distant" line must be perceived as larger. As you can see in the drawing on the right, additional depth cues accentuate the Müller-Lyer illusion.

Consider the drawing in Figure 4.46*a*. This is the familiar **Müller-Lyer** (MEOO-ler-LIE-er) **illusion** in which the horizontal line with arrowheads appears shorter than the line with Vs. A quick measurement will show that they are the same length. How can we explain this illusion? Evidence suggests it is based on a lifetime of experience with the edges and corners of rooms and buildings. Richard Gregory (2000) believes you see the horizontal line with the Vs as if it were the corner of a room viewed from inside (**Figure 4.47**). The line with arrowheads, on the other hand, suggests the corner of a room or building seen from outside. In other words, cues that suggest a three-dimensional space alter our perception of a two-dimensional design.

Earlier, to explain the moon illusion, we said that if two objects make images of the same size, the more distant object must be larger. This is known formally as *size-distance invariance* (the size of an object's image is precisely related to its distance from the eyes). Gregory believes the same concept explains the Müller-Lyer illusion. If the V-tipped line looks farther away than the arrowhead-tipped line, you must compensate by seeing the V-tipped line as longer. This explanation presumes that you have had years of experience with straight lines, sharp edges, and corners—a pretty safe assumption in our culture.

Is there any way to show that past experience causes the illusion? If we could test someone who saw only curves and wavy lines as a child, we would know if experience with a "square" culture is important. Fortunately, a few San bushmen, a culture from the Kalahari desert in Africa, still live a traditional hunter-gathering life in the "round." Traditional San rarely encounter a straight line in their daily lives: Their temporary dwellings are semicircular, and there are few straight roads or square buildings.

What happens if a San looks at the Müller-Lyer design? The typical traditional San does not experience the illusion. At most, she or he sees the V-shaped line as *slightly* longer than the other (Henrich, Heine, & Norenzayan, 2010). This seems to confirm the importance of perceptual habits in determining our view of the world.

In the next section, we will go beyond normal perception to ask, "Is extrasensory perception possible?" Before we do that, here's a chance to answer the question, "Is remembering the preceding discussion possible?"

Müller-Lyer illusion Two equal-length lines tipped with inward or outward pointing Vs that appear to be of different lengths.

study break Perception and Objectivity

RECITE

1. When a person is prepared to perceive events in a particular way, it is said that a perceptual expectancy or _____ _____ exists.
2. People around the world perceive in the same way regardless of culture. T or F?
3. Perceptual habits may become so ingrained that they lead us to misperceive a stimulus. T or F?
4. Perceptual learning seems to program the brain for sensitivity to important _____ of the environment.

REFLECT

THINK CRITICALLY

5. Cigarette advertisements in the United States are required to carry a warning label about the health risks of smoking. How have tobacco companies made these labels less visible?

SELF-REFLECT

You have almost certainly misperceived a situation at some time because of a perceptual expectancy or the influence of your motives and emotions. How were your perceptions influenced?

If you spent a year hiking the Amazon River Basin, what effect might it have on your perception of the Müller-Lyer illusion?

How has perceptual learning affected your ability to safely drive a car? For example, what do you pay attention to at intersections? Where do you habitually look as you are driving?

ANSWERS

1. set 2. F 3. T 4. features 5. Advertisers place health warnings in the corners of ads, where they attract the least possible attention. Also, the labels are often placed on "busy" backgrounds so that they are partially camouflaged. Finally, the main images in ads are designed to strongly attract attention. This further distracts readers from seeing the warnings. Over time, perceptual learning (and habituation) renders these warnings practically invisible.

Extrasensory Perception—Do You Believe in Ghosts?

JOURNEY QUESTION 4.10 *Is extrasensory perception possible?*

About half of the general public believes in the existence of extrasensory perception (Wiseman & Watt, 2006). Yet very few psychologists share this belief. Actually, it's surprising that even more people aren't believers. ESP and other paranormal events are treated as accepted facts in many movies and television programs. Stage entertainers routinely "astound" their audiences. What is the evidence for and against extrasensory perception?

Let's consider an actual example. Once, during the middle of the night, a woman away for a weekend visit suddenly had a strong impulse to return home. When she arrived, she found the house on fire with her husband asleep inside (Rhine, 1953). How could she have known? Could she have used **extrasensory perception (ESP)**—the purported ability to perceive events in ways that cannot be explained by known sensory capacities?

The field of *parapsychology* studies ESP and other **psi phenomena**—events that seem to defy accepted scientific laws. (Psi is pronounced like "sigh.") Parapsychologists seek answers to the questions raised by three basic forms that ESP could take. These are:

1. **Telepathy.** The purported ability to communicate directly with another person's mind. When the other person is dead, the communications are called *mediumship*.
2. **Clairvoyance.** The purported ability to perceive events or gain information in ways that appear unaffected by distance or normal physical barriers.
3. **Precognition.** The purported ability to perceive or accurately predict future events. Precognition may take the form of prophetic dreams that foretell the future.

An Appraisal of ESP

Why don't psychologists also believe in ESP? Regardless of all the popular enthusiasm, psychologists as a group are highly skeptical about psi abilities. Let's have a look at the evidence for and against extrasensory perception. The formal investigation of psi events owes much to the late J. B. Rhine, who tried to study ESP objectively. Many of Rhine's experiments made use of *Zener cards* (a deck of 25 cards, each bearing one of five symbols) (**Figure 4.48**). In a typical clairvoyance test, people try to guess the symbols on the cards as they are turned

Extrasensory perception The purported ability to perceive events in ways that cannot be explained by known capacities of the sensory organs.

Psi phenomena Events that seem to lie outside the realm of accepted scientific laws.

up from a shuffled deck. In a typical telepathy test, a *receiver* tries to guess the correct symbol by reading the mind of a *sender* looking at a card. Pure guessing in these tests will produce an average score of 5 "hits" out of 25 cards. Rhine and others since have reported results much greater than might be expected by chance alone.

Doesn't evidence like that settle the issue? No, it doesn't, for a number of reasons, including fraud, poorly designed experiments, and chance.

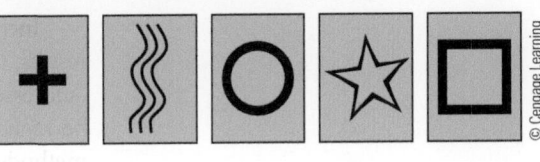

Figure 4.48 ESP cards used by J. B. Rhine, an early experimenter in parapsychology.

Fraud

Fraud continues to plague parapsychology. The need for skepticism is especially great any time there's money to be made from purported psychic abilities. Stage demonstrations of ESP are based on deception and tricks, as are other "for profit" enterprises. For example, in 2002 the owners of the "Miss Cleo" television-psychic operation were convicted of felony fraud. "Miss Cleo," supposedly a Jamaican-accented psychic, was really just an actress from Los Angeles. People who paid $4.99 a minute for a "reading" from "Miss Cleo" actually reached one of several hundred operators. These people were hired to do "cold readings" through ads that read, "No experience necessary." Despite being entirely faked, the "Miss Cleo" scam brought in more than $1 billion before it was shut down.

Anyone can learn to do "cold readings" well enough to produce satisfied customers (Wood et al., 2003). *Cold reading* is a set of techniques that are used to lead people to believe in the truth of what a psychic or medium is saying about them. These include a reliance on many of the same techniques used by astrologers, such as uncritical acceptance, confirmation bias, and the Barnum effect. (Remember Chapter 1?)

The "psychic" begins a "reading" by making general statements about a person. The psychic then plays "hot and cold" by attending to the person's facial expressions, body language, or tone of voice. When the psychic is "hot" (on the right track), he or she continues to make similar statements about the person. If the person's reactions signal that the psychic is "cold," the psychic drops that topic or line of thought and tries another (Hyman, 2007).

Poorly Designed Experiments

Unfortunately, some of Rhine's most dramatic early experiments used badly printed Zener cards that allowed the symbols to show faintly on the back. It is also very easy to cheat, by marking cards with a fingernail or by noting marks on the cards caused by normal use. There is also evidence that early experimenters sometimes unconsciously gave people cues about cards with their eyes or facial gestures. In short, none of the early studies in parapsychology were done in a way that eliminated the possibility of deliberate fraud or the accidental "leakage" of helpful information (Alcock, Burns, & Freeman, 2003).

Modern parapsychologists are now well aware of the need for double-blind experiments, security and accuracy in record keeping, meticulous control, and repeatability of experiments (Milton & Wiseman, 1997; O'Keeffe & Wiseman, 2005). In the last 10 years, hundreds of experiments have been reported in parapsychological journals. Many of them seem to support the existence of psi abilities (Aldhous, 2010).

Chance

Then why do most psychologists still remain skeptical about psi abilities? The most important reason has to do with chance. Remember the woman who had a premonition that something bad was about to happen to her husband? She returned home early to find her house on fire with him sleeping inside. An apparent clairvoyant or telepathic experience like this is certainly striking, but it does not confirm the existence of ESP. Such *coincidences* occur quite often. On any given night, many thousands of people around the world might act on a "premonition." If, by coincidence, one person's hunch turns out to be correct, it may be *reinterpreted* as clairvoyance (Marks, 2000; Wiseman & Watt, 2006). Then you read about it in the news the next day. No one reports the vast majority of false premonitions, which are simply forgotten.

Inconsistency in psi research is a related problem. For every published study with positive results, there are others that fail and are never reported (Alcock, 2010). Even experimental "successes" are weak. Many of the most spectacular findings in parapsychology simply cannot be *replicated* (reproduced or repeated) (Hyman, 1996a). Furthermore, improved research methods usually result in fewer positive results (Hyman, 1996b; O'Keeffe & Wiseman, 2005).

Even when a person does seem to show evidence of psi ability, it is rare—in fact, almost unheard of—for him or her to maintain that ability over any sustained period of time (Alcock, Burns, & Freeman, 2003). This is likely because a person who only temporarily scores above chance has just received credit for a **run of luck**—a statistically unusual outcome that could occur by chance alone.

To understand the run-of-luck criticism, imagine that you flip a coin 100 times and record the results. You then flip another coin 100 times, again recording the results. The two lists are compared. For any 10 pairs of flips, we would expect heads or tails to match 5 times. Let's say you go through the list and find a set of 10 pairs in which 9 out of 10 matched. This is far above chance expectation. But does it mean that the first coin "knew" what was going to come up on the second coin? The idea is obviously silly. Now, what if a person guesses 100 times what will come up on a coin? Again, we might find a set of 10 guesses that matches the results of flipping the coin. Does this mean that the person, for a time, had precognition—then lost it?

You may be surprised to learn that some ESP researchers believe this "decline effect" shows that parapsychological skills are very fragile, like a weak cell phone connection, fading in and out over time. If a person has a good short run of guessing, it is assumed that the person, for a time, had precognition. A subsequent run of poor guesses is interpreted to mean the person's precognition has temporarily faded out.

In fact, creative interpretation is a common problem when it comes to psi. For example, former astronaut Edgar Mitchell claimed he did a successful telepathy experiment from space. Yet, news accounts never mentioned that on some trials Mitchell's "receivers" scored above chance, whereas on others they scored *below* chance. Although you might assume that below-chance trials were failures to find telepathy, Mitchell reinterpreted them as "successes," claiming that they represented intentional "psi missing." But, as skeptics have noted, if both high scores and low scores count as successes, how can you lose?

Implications

After close to 130 years of investigation, it is still impossible to say conclusively whether psi events occur. As we have seen, a close look at psi experiments often reveals serious problems of evidence, procedure, and scientific rigor (Alcock, Burns, & Freeman, 2003; Hyman, 2007; Stokes, 2001). The more closely psi experiments are examined, the more likely it is that claimed successes will evaporate (Alcock, 2010; Stokes, 2001). As one critic put it, positive ESP results usually mean "Error Some Place" (Marks, 2000).

What would it take to scientifically demonstrate the existence of ESP? Quite simply, a set of instructions that would allow any competent, unbiased observer to produce a psi event under standardized conditions that rule out any possibility of fraud or chance (Schick & Vaughn, 2010). In fact, professional magician and skeptic James Randi even offers a $1 million prize to anyone who can demonstrate evidence of psi events under standardized conditions. No one has yet tried for the prize. (Go ahead, claim your cool million by Googling the James Randi Educational Foundation.)

Undoubtedly, researchers will continue their attempts to supply irrefutable evidence. Others remain skeptics and consider 130 years of inconclusive efforts reason enough to abandon the concept of ESP (Marks, 2000). Yet, being a skeptic does not mean a person is against something. It means that you are unconvinced. The purpose of this discussion, then, has been to counter the *uncritical* acceptance of psi events that is reported in the popular press or by researchers who are uncritical "true believers." (But then, you already knew we were going to say that, didn't you?)

Of course, in many ESP tests, the outcome is beyond debate. A good example is provided by ESP experiments done through newspapers, radio, and television. The results

Run of luck A statistically unusual outcome (as in getting five heads in a row when flipping a coin) that could still occur by chance alone.

of more than 1.5 million ESP trials done through the mass media are easy to summarize: There was no significant ESP effect (Milton & Wiseman, 1999). Clearly, lottery organizers have nothing to fear!

A Look Ahead

In these last few sections we have moved from basic sensations to the complexities of perceiving people and events. We have also probed some of the controversies concerning ESP. In the *Psychology in Action* section, we will return to "everyday" perception, for a look at perceptual awareness.

 study break Extrasensory Perception

RECITE

1. Three purported psi events investigated by parapsychologists are clairvoyance, telepathy, and _____.
2. The _____ cards were used by J. B. Rhine in early tests of ESP.
3. Natural, or "real life," occurrences are regarded as the best evidence for the existence of ESP. T or F?
4. Skeptics attribute positive results in psi experiments to statistical runs of luck. T or F?
5. Replication rates are very high for ESP experiments. T or F?

REFLECT

THINK CRITICALLY

6. What would you estimate is the chance that two people will have the same birthday (day and month, but not year) in a group of 30 people?
7. A "psychic" on television offers to fix broken watches for viewers. Moments later, dozens of viewers call the station to say that their watches miraculously started running again. What have they overlooked?

SELF-REFLECT

Let's say that a friend of yours is an avid fan of television shows that feature paranormal themes. See if you can summarize for her or him what is known about ESP. Be sure to include evidence for and against the existence of ESP and some of the thinking errors associated with nonskeptical belief in the paranormal.

ANSWERS

1. precognition 2. Zener 3. F 4. T 5. F 6. Most people assume that this would be a relatively rare event. Actually there is a 71 percent chance that two people will share a birthday in a group of 30. Most people probably underestimate the natural rate of occurrence of many seemingly mysterious coincidences (Alcock, Burns, & Freeman, 2003). 7. When psychologists handled watches awaiting repair at a store, 57 percent began running again, with no help from a "psychic." Believing the psychic's claim also overlooks the impact of big numbers: If the show reached a large audience, at least a few "broken" watches would start working merely by chance.

Psychology in Action

Pay Attention!—Becoming a Better Eyewitness to Life

JOURNEY QUESTION 4.11 *How can I perceive events more accurately?*

In the courtroom, eyewitness testimony can be a key to proving guilt or innocence. The claim "I saw it with my own eyes" still carries a lot of weight with a jury. Too many jurors (unless they have taken a psychology course) tend to assume that eyewitness testimony is nearly infallible (Brewer & Wells, 2006). Even U.S. judges are vulnerable to over-optimism about eyewitness testimony (Wise et al., 2010; Wise & Safer, 2010). But, to put it bluntly, eyewitness testimony is frequently wrong (Shermer, Rose, & Hoffman, 2011). Recall, for instance, that one of your authors would have sworn in court that he had seen a murder taking place at the supermarket—*if* he hadn't received more information to correct his misperceptions.

What about witnesses who are certain that their perceptions were accurate? Should juries believe them? Actually, having confidence in your testimony has almost no bearing on its accuracy (Brewer & Wells, 2006)! Psychologists are gradually convincing lawyers, judges,

Even in broad daylight, eyewitness testimony is untrustworthy. In 2001 an airliner crashed near Kennedy International Airport in New York. Hundreds of people saw the plane go down. Half of them said the plane was on fire. Flight recorders showed there was no fire. One witness in five saw the plane make a right turn. An equal number saw it make a left turn! As one investigator noted, the best witness may be a "kid under 12 years old who doesn't have his parents around." Adults, it seems, are easily swayed by their expectations.

and police that eyewitness errors are common (Yarmey, 2010). Even so, thousands of people have been wrongfully convicted (Scheck, Neufeld, & Dwyer, 2000).

Unfortunately, perception rarely provides an "instant replay" of events. Impressions formed when a person is surprised, threatened, or under stress are especially prone to distortion (Yuille & Daylen, 1998). One study of eyewitness cases found that the *wrong person* was chosen from police lineups 25 percent of the time (Levi, 1998).

Wouldn't the victim of a crime remember more than a mere witness? Not necessarily. A classic study found that eyewitness accuracy is virtually the same for witnessing a crime (seeing a pocket calculator stolen) as it is for being a victim (seeing one's own watch stolen) (Hosch & Cooper, 1982). Placing more weight on the testimony of victims may be a serious mistake. In many crimes, victims fall prey to *weapon focus*. Understandably, they fix their entire attention on the knife, gun, or other weapon used by an attacker. In doing so, they fail to notice details of appearance, dress, or other clues to identity (Pickel, French, & Betts, 2003). Additional factors that consistently lower eyewitness accuracy are summarized in **Table 4.2**.

Implications

Since DNA testing became available, almost 300 people who were convicted of murder, rape, and other crimes in the United States have been exonerated. About 75 percent of these innocent people were convicted mainly on the basis of eyewitness testimony. Each also spent *years* in prison before being cleared (Innocence Project, 2012). How often are everyday perceptions as inaccurate or distorted as those of an emotional eyewitness? The answer we have been moving toward is very frequently. Bearing this in mind may help you be more tolerant of the views of others and more cautious about your own objectivity. It may also encourage more frequent *reality testing* on your part.

If you have ever concluded that someone was angry, upset, or unfriendly without checking the accuracy of your perceptions, you have fallen into a subtle trap. Personal objectivity is an elusive quality, requiring frequent reality testing to maintain. At the very least, it pays to ask a person what she or he is feeling when you are in doubt. Clearly, most of us could learn to be better "eyewitnesses" to daily events (Siegel, 2010).

Table 4.2 Factors Affecting the Accuracy of Eyewitness Perceptions

SOURCES OF ERROR	SUMMARY OF FINDINGS
1. Wording of questions	An eyewitness's testimony about an event can be affected by how questions put to the witness are worded.
2. Postevent information	Eyewitness testimony about an event often reflects not only what was actually seen but also information obtained later.
3. Attitudes, expectations	An eyewitness's perception and memory for an event may be affected by his or her attitudes and expectations.
4. Alcohol intoxication	Alcohol intoxication impairs later ability to recall events.
5. Cross-racial perceptions	Eyewitnesses are better at identifying members of their own race than they are at identifying people of other races.
6. Weapon focus	The presence of a weapon impairs an eyewitness's ability to identify the culprit's face.
7. Accuracy-confidence	An eyewitness's confidence is not a good predictor of his or her accuracy.
8. Exposure time	The less time an eyewitness has to observe an event, the less well she or he will perceive and remember it.
9. Unconscious transference	Eyewitnesses sometimes identify as a culprit someone they have seen in another situation or context.
10. Color perception	Judgments of color made under monochromatic light (such as an orange street light) are highly unreliable.
11. Stress	Very high levels of stress impair the accuracy of eyewitness perceptions.

Source: Adapted from Wells & Olson, 2003; Yarmey, 2010. © Cengage Learning

The Whole Human: Perceptual Awareness

Do some people perceive things more accurately than others? Humanistic psychologist Abraham Maslow (1969) believed that some people perceive themselves and others with unusual accuracy. Maslow characterized these people as especially alive, open, aware, and mentally healthy. He found that their perceptual styles were marked by immersion in the present; a lack of self-consciousness; freedom from selecting, criticizing, or evaluating; and a general "surrender" to experience. The kind of perception Maslow described is like that of a mother with her newborn infant, a child at Christmas, or two people in love.

In daily life, we quickly **habituate**, or respond less, to predictable and unchanging stimuli. Habituation is a type of learning—basically, we learn to cease paying attention to familiar stimuli. For instance, when you download a new song from iTunes, the music initially holds your attention all the way through. But when the song becomes "old," it may play without your really attending to it. When a stimulus is repeated *without change*, our response to it habituates, or decreases. Interestingly, creative people habituate *more slowly* than average. We might expect that they would rapidly become bored with a repeated stimulus. Instead, it seems that creative people actively attend to stimuli, even those that are repeated (Colin, Moore, & West, 1996).

The Value of Paying Attention

Whereas the average person has not reached perceptual restriction of the "if you've seen one tree, you've seen them all" variety, the fact remains that most of us tend to look at a tree and classify it into the perceptual category of "trees in general" without really appreciating the miracle standing before us. How, then, can we bring about **dishabituation**—a reversal of habituation—on a day-to-day basis? The deceptively simple key to dishabituation is this: Pay attention. The following story summarizes the importance of attention:

> One day a man of the people said to Zen Master Ikkyu: "Master, will you please write for me some maxims of the highest wisdom?"
> Ikkyu immediately took his brush and wrote the word "Attention."
> "Is that all?" asked the man. "Will you not add something more?"
> Ikkyu then wrote twice running: "Attention. Attention."
> "Well," remarked the man rather irritably, "I really don't see much depth or subtlety in what you have just written."
> Then Ikkyu wrote the same word three times running: "Attention. Attention. Attention."
> Half angered, the man demanded, "What does that word 'Attention' mean anyway?"
> And Ikkyu answered gently: "Attention means attention." (Kapleau, 1966)

How to Become a Better "Eyewitness" to Life

Here's a summary of ideas from this chapter to help you maintain and enhance perceptual awareness and accuracy:

1. *Remember that perceptions are constructions of reality.* Learn to regularly question your own perceptions. Are they accurate? Could another interpretation fit the facts? What assumptions are you making? How might your assumptions be distorting your perceptions?
2. *Break perceptual habits and interrupt habituation.* Each day, try to get away from habitual, top-down processing and do some activities in new ways. For example, take different routes when you travel to work or school. Do routines, such as brushing your teeth or combing your hair, with your nonpreferred hand. Try to look at friends and family members as if they are persons you just met for the first time.
3. *Seek out-of-the-ordinary experiences.* The possibilities here range from trying foods you don't normally eat to reading opinions very different from your own. Experiences ranging from a quiet walk in the woods to a trip to an amusement park may be perceptually refreshing.

Habituation A decrease in perceptual response to a repeated stimulus.

Dishabituation A reversal of habituation.

4. *Beware of perceptual sets.* Anytime you pigeonhole people, objects, or events, there is a danger that your perceptions will be distorted by expectations or preexisting categories. Be especially wary of labels and stereotypes. Try to see people as individuals and events as unique, one-time occurrences.

5. *Be aware of the ways in which motives and emotions influence perceptions.* It is difficult to avoid being swayed by your own interests, needs, desires, and emotions. But be aware of this trap and actively try to see the world through the eyes of others. Taking the other person's perspective is especially valuable in disputes or arguments.

6. *Make a habit of engaging in reality testing.* Actively look for additional evidence to check the accuracy of your perceptions. Ask questions, seek clarifications, and find alternate channels of information. Remember that perception is not automatically accurate. You could be wrong—we all are frequently.

7. *Pay attention.* Make a conscious effort to pay attention to other people and your surroundings. Try to get in the habit of approaching perception as if you are going to have to testify later about what you saw and heard.

 study break Perceptual Awareness

RECITE

1. Most perceptions can be described as active constructions of external reality. T or F?
2. Inaccuracies in eyewitness perceptions obviously occur in real life, but they cannot be reproduced in psychology experiments. T or F?
3. Accuracy scores for facts provided by witnesses to staged crimes may be as low as 25 percent correct. T or F?
4. Victims of crimes are more accurate eyewitnesses than are impartial observers. T or F?
5. *Reality testing* is another term for dishabituation. T or F?
6. A good antidote to perceptual habituation can be found in conscious efforts to

   a. reverse sensory gating   *b.* pay attention
   c. achieve visual   *d.* counteract shape constancy
       accommodation

REFLECT

THINK CRITICALLY

7. Return for a moment to the snake incident described at the beginning of this chapter. What perceptual factors were involved? Why was it so hard for your author to see the snake?

SELF-REFLECT

Because perceptions are constructions or models of external events, we should all engage in more frequent reality testing. Can you think of a recent event when a little reality testing would have saved you from misjudging a situation?

In order to improve your own perceptual awareness and accuracy, which strategies would you emphasize first?

ANSWERS

1. T 2. F 3. T 4. F 5. F 6. b 7. Your author's inexperience with green vine snakes made it harder for him to quickly construct a more accurate perception. Besides, the snake's camouflage evolved precisely to make it harder for potential predators and prey (for a long instant your author wasn't sure which he was) to see it.

Chapter in Review

Summary

4.1 In general, how do sensory systems function?

- 4.1.1 The senses act as selective data reduction systems in order to prevent the brain from being overwhelmed by sensory input.
- 4.1.2 Sensation begins with transduction in a receptor organ; other data reduction processes are sensory adaptation, analysis, and coding.
- 4.1.3 Sensation can be partially understood in terms of sensory localization in the brain.

4.2 How does the visual system function?

- 4.2.1 The eye is a visual system, not a photographic one. The entire visual system is structured to analyze visual information.
- 4.2.2 Four common visual defects are myopia, hyperopia, presbyopia, and astigmatism.
- 4.2.3 The rods and cones are photoreceptors in the retina of the eye.
- 4.2.4 The rods specialize in peripheral vision, night vision, seeing black and white, and detecting movement. The cones specialize in color vision, acuity, and daylight vision.
- 4.2.5 Color vision is explained by the trichromatic theory in the retina and by the opponent-process theory in the visual system beyond the eyes.
- 4.2.6 Total color blindness is rare, but 8 percent of males and 1 percent of females are red-green color-blind or color-weak.
- 4.2.7 Dark adaptation is caused mainly by an increase in the amount of rhodopsin in the rods.

4.3 What are the mechanisms of hearing?

- 4.3.1 Sound waves are the stimulus for hearing. They are transduced by the eardrum, auditory ossicles, oval window, cochlea, and ultimately the hair cells.
- 4.3.2 Frequency theory explains how we hear tones up to 4,000 hertz; place theory explains tones above 4,000 hertz.
- 4.3.3 Two basic types of hearing loss are conductive hearing loss and sensorineural hearing loss. Noise-induced hearing loss is a common form of sensorineural hearing loss caused by exposure to loud noise.

4.4 How do the chemical senses operate?

- 4.4.1 Olfaction (smell) and gustation (taste) are chemical senses that respond to airborne or liquefied molecules.
- 4.4.2 The lock and key theory of olfaction partially explains smell. In addition, the location of the olfactory receptors in the nose helps identify various scents.
- 4.4.3 Sweet and bitter tastes are based on a lock-and-key coding of molecule shapes. Salty and sour tastes are triggered by a direct flow of ions into taste receptors.

4.5 What are the somesthetic senses?

- 4.5.1 The somesthetic senses include the skin senses, vestibular senses, and kinesthetic senses (receptors that detect muscle and joint positioning).
- 4.5.2 The skin senses are touch, pressure, pain, cold, and warmth. Sensitivity to each is related to the number of receptors found in an area of skin.
- 4.5.3 Distinctions can be made between warning pain and reminding pain.
- 4.5.4 Selective gating of pain messages takes place in the spinal cord, as explained by gate control theory.
- 4.5.5 Pain can be reduced through counterirritation and by controlling anxiety and attention.
- 4.5.6 According to sensory conflict theory, motion sickness is caused by a mismatch of visual, kinesthetic, and vestibular sensations. Motion sickness can be avoided by minimizing sensory conflict.

4.6 In general, how do we construct our perceptions?

- 4.6.1 Perception is an active process of constructing sensations into a meaningful mental representation of the world.
- 4.6.2 Perceptions are based on simultaneous bottom-up and top-down processing. Complete percepts are assembled out of small sensory features in "bottom-up" fashion guided by preexisting knowledge applied "top-down" to help organize features into a meaningful whole.
- 4.6.3 Separating figure and ground is the most basic perceptual organization.
- 4.6.4 The following Gestalt principles also help organize sensations: nearness, similarity, continuity, closure, contiguity, and common region.
- 4.6.5 A perceptual organization may be thought of as a hypothesis held until evidence contradicts it.
- 4.6.6 In vision, the image projected on the retina is constantly changing, but the external world appears stable and undistorted because of size, shape, and brightness constancy.

4.7 Why are we more aware of some sensations than others?

- 4.7.1 Incoming sensations are affected by selective attention, a brain-based process that allows some sensory inputs to be selected for further processing while others are ignored.
- 4.7.2 Don't use your cell phone while driving!

4.8 How is it possible to see depth and judge distance?

- 4.8.1 A basic, innate capacity for depth perception is present soon after birth.
- 4.8.2 Depth perception depends on binocular cues of retinal disparity and convergence.
- 4.8.3 Depth perception also depends on the monocular cue of accommodation.
- 4.8.4 Monocular "pictorial" depth cues also underlie depth perception. They are linear perspective, relative size, height in the picture plane, light and shadow, overlap, texture gradients, aerial haze, and motion parallax.

- 4.8.5 The moon illusion can be explained by the apparent-distance hypothesis, which emphasizes that many depth cues are present when the moon is near the horizon and few are present when it is overhead.

4.9 How is perception altered by expectations, motives, emotions, and learning?

- 4.9.1 Suggestion, motives, emotions, attention, and prior experience combine in various ways to create perceptual sets, or expectancies.

- 4.9.2 Personal motives and values often alter perceptions by changing the evaluation of what is seen or by altering attention to specific details.

- 4.9.3 Perceptual learning influences the top-down organization and interpretation of sensations.

- 4.9.4 One of the most familiar of all illusions, the Müller-Lyer illusion, seems to be related to perceptual learning, linear perspective, and size–distance invariance relationships.

4.10 Is extrasensory perception possible?

- 4.10.1 Parapsychology is the study of purported psi phenomena, including telepathy (including mediumship), clairvoyance, and precognition.

- 4.10.2 Research in parapsychology remains controversial because of a variety of problems and shortcomings. The bulk of the evidence to date is against the existence of ESP.

- 4.10.3 The more carefully controlled an ESP experiment is, the less likely it is to produce evidence that ESP occurs.

4.11 How can I perceive events more accurately?

- 4.11.1 Eyewitness testimony is surprisingly unreliable. Eyewitness accuracy is further damaged by weapon focus and a number of similar factors.

- 4.11.2 When a stimulus is repeated without change, our response to it undergoes habituation.

- 4.11.3 Perceptual accuracy is enhanced by reality testing, dishabituation, and conscious efforts to pay attention.

- 4.11.4 It is also valuable to break perceptual habits, to broaden frames of reference, to beware of perceptual sets, and to be aware of the ways in which motives and emotions influence perceptions.

Interactive Learning

CourseMate Go to CengageBrain.com to access Psychology CourseMate, where you will find an interactive eBook, glossaries, flashcards, quizzes, videos, Virtual Psychology Labs, and more.

Aplia If your professor has assigned Aplia:

1. Sign in to your account.
2. Complete the corresponding exercises as required by your professor.
3. When finished, click "Grade It Now" to see which areas you have mastered, which areas need more work, and detailed explanations of every answer.

Test Your Knowledge

Sensation and Perception

1. The senses divide the world into basic perceptual features, or basic stimulus patterns, a process known as
   a. sensory localization   b. sensory analysis
   c. accommodation   d. phosphenation

2. If you press on your closed eyelids, you will experience phosphenes. This illustrates the concept of
   a. visual saturation   b. sensory coding
   c. accommodation   d. hyperopia

3. People who become farsighted as they get older have the condition known as
   a. hyperopia   b. myopia
   c. astigmatism   d. presbyopia

4. The greatest visual acuity is associated with the _____ and the _____.
   a. periphery, rods   b. periphery, cones
   c. fovea, cones   d. nanometer, rods

5. Black-and-white vision and a high degree of sensitivity to movement are characteristic of
   a. rod vision   b. cone vision
   c. the blind spot   d. the fovea

6. Opponent-process theory best explains
   a. inattentional blindness   b. astigmatism
   c. sensory coding   d. colored afterimages

7. Dark adaptation is directly related to an increase in
   a. visual pigments in the rods   b. astigmatism
   c. accommodation   d. saturation

8. The loudness of a sound is determined by the _____ of sound waves.
   a. frequency   b. amplitude
   c. rarefaction   d. complexity

9. Sounds are ultimately transduced by movements of the
   a. pinna   b. malleus
   c. cochlea   d. hair cells

10. We are most sensitive to _____ tastes.
    a. umami   b. sweet
    c. salty   d. bitter

11. The lock and key theory appears to partly explain
    a. motion sickness   b. olfaction and gustation
    c. dark adaptation   d. color blindness

12. Which of the following is NOT a somesthetic sense?
    a. taste   b. touch
    c. balance   d. kinesthesis

13. As time passes, nerve endings in the skin under a wristwatch send fewer signals to the brain and you become less able to feel the watch. This process is called
    a. sensory gating   b. the sensory bottleneck
    c. reverse attention   d. sensory adaptation

14. The fact that a mild surface pain can greatly reduce more agonizing pain is consistent with
    a. gate control theory   b. the concept of sensory adaptation
    c. sensory conflict theory   d. perceptual constancy theory

15. Which of the following is LEAST likely to contribute to the formation of a perceptual figure?
    a. continuity   b. closure
    c. similarity   d. separation

16. The clearest example of a binocular depth cue is
    a. linear perspective   b. retinal disparity
    c. aerial perspective   d. motion parallax

17. The apparent distance hypothesis provides a good explanation of the
    a. moon illusion   b. horizontal-vertical illusion
    c. San illusion   d. effects of inattentional blindness

18. Top-down perceptual processing is closely related to
    a. perceptual expectancies   b. the Müller-Lyer illusion
    c. size-distance invariances   d. precognition

19. Psychics often make use of
    a. cold reading   b. Zener cards
    c. precognition   d. clairvoyance

20. Eyewitness testimony is vulnerable to distortion because of
    a. habituation   b. weapon focus
    c. a failure to pay attention   d. all of these reasons

Answers   1. b   2. b   3. d   4. c   5. a   6. d   7. a   8. b   9. d   10. d   11. b   12. a   13. d   14. a   15. d   16. b   17. a   18. a   19. a   20. d

Journey Theme *Understanding states of consciousness can promote self-awareness and enhance personal effectiveness.*

States of Consciousness—The Many Faces of Awareness

5

States of Consciousness

Journey into Psychology: Grand, Indeed!

- At the Grand Canyon, a college student spends a day exploring, in a fully conscious state of mindfulness meditation.
- In New York City, an aspiring actor consults a hypnotist for help in reducing her stage fright.
- In a Rio de Janeiro hospital, a man lies deep in a coma after surviving a horrendous traffic accident.
- In Minnesota, a college student drifts into a pleasant daydream while sitting at the back of class.
- In New Zealand, a Maori tohunga (priest) performs a nightlong ritual to talk to the spirits who created the world in the mythical period the Aborigines call "Dreamtime."
- In Montreal, Canada, three businesswomen head for a wine bar after a particularly stressful day.
- In the American Southwest, a Navajo elder gives his congregation peyote tea, a sacrament in the Native American Church, as a drumbeat resounds in the darkness.
- At a park in Amsterdam, a group of street musicians smoke a joint and sing for spare change.
- In Tucson, Arizona, one of your authors brews himself another cup of cappuccino.

Each of these people is experiencing a different state of consciousness. Some have no choice, and some are deliberately seeking to bend their minds—to alter consciousness—in different ways, to different degrees, and for different reasons. As these examples suggest, consciousness can take many forms, some grand and some not so grand. In the discussion that follows, we will begin with the familiar realms of sleep and dreaming and then move on to more exotic states of consciousness.

Journey Questions

5.1 What is consciousness?

5.2 What are the effects of sleep loss or changes in sleep patterns?

5.3 What are some functions of sleep?

5.4 What are some sleep disorders and unusual sleep events?

5.5 Do dreams have meaning?

5.6 What is hypnosis?

5.7 Do meditation and mindfulness have any benefits?

5.8 What are the effects of the more commonly used psychoactive drugs?

5.9 How can dreams be used to promote personal understanding?

States of Consciousness—The Many Faces of Awareness

JOURNEY QUESTION 5.1 *What is consciousness?*

To be *conscious* means to be aware. **Consciousness** consists of your sensations and perceptions of external events as well as your self-awareness of mental events, including thoughts, memories, and feelings about your experiences and yourself (Morin, 2006; Robinson, 2008). Take, for example, Eric's profound moment at the Grand Canyon. As he first looked over the rim he was "blown away" by deep feelings of insignificance and awe. In that instant, he was also fully aware that he *was* experiencing a deeply moving moment.

Although this definition of consciousness may seem obvious, it is based on your own subjective, *first person* experience. You are the expert on what it feels like to be you. But what about other people? What does it feel like to be your mother? Or someone in a coma? What runs through a dog's mind when it sniffs other dogs? Does it feel joy?

You simply can't answer these questions about *other minds* through your own first-person perspective. The difficulty of knowing other minds is one reason why the early behaviorists distrusted introspection. (Remember Chapter 1?) Instead, psychologists adopt an objective, *third person* point of view. A key challenge for psychology is to use objective studies of the brain and behavior to help us understand the mind and consciousness, which are basically private phenomena (Robinson, 2008). This chapter summarizes some of what we have learned about different states of consciousness.

Altered States of Consciousness

We spend most of our lives in *waking consciousness*, a state of clear, organized alertness. In waking consciousness, we perceive times, places, and events as real, meaningful, and familiar. But states of consciousness related to fatigue, delirium, hypnosis, drugs, and euphoria may differ markedly from "normal" awareness (Chalmers, 2010). Everyone experiences at least some altered states, such as sleep, dreaming, and daydreaming (Blackmore, 2004). Some people experience dramatically altered states, such as the lower levels of awareness associated with strokes and other forms of brain damage (Morin, 2006). In everyday life, changes in consciousness may even accompany long-distance running, listening to music, making love, or other circumstances.

How are altered states distinguished from normal awareness? During an **altered state of consciousness (ASC)**, changes occur in the *quality* and *pattern* of mental activity. Typically there are distinct shifts in our perceptions, emotions, memories, time sense, thoughts, feelings of self-control, and suggestibility (Siegel, 2005). Definitions aside, most people know when they have experienced an ASC. In fact, heightened self-awareness is an important feature of many ASCs (Revonsuo, Kallio, & Sikka, 2009).

Are there other causes of ASCs? In addition to the ones mentioned, we could add sensory overload (a rave, Mardi Gras crowd, or mosh pit), monotonous stimulation (such as "highway hypnotism" on long drives), unusual physical conditions (high fever, hyperventilation, dehydration, sleep loss, near-death experiences), restricted sensory input (extended periods of isolation), and many other possibilities. In some instances, altered states have important cultural meanings (see "Consciousness and Culture" for more information).

An unconscious person will die without constant care. Yet as crucial as consciousness is, we can't really explain how it occurs (Robinson, 2008; Schwitzgebel, 2011). Nevertheless, it is possible to identify various states of consciousness and to explore the role they play in our lives. Let's begin with a look at the most common altered state, sleep and dreaming.

Consciousness Mental awareness of sensations and perceptions of external events as well as self-awareness of internal events including thoughts, memories, and feelings about experiences and the self.

Altered state of consciousness (ASC) A condition of awareness distinctly different in quality or pattern from waking consciousness.

Human Diversity

Throughout history, people everywhere have found ways to alter consciousness (Siegel, 2005). A dramatic example is the sweat lodge ceremony of the Sioux Indians. During the ritual, several men sit in total darkness inside a small chamber heated by coals. Cedar smoke, bursts of steam, and sage fill the air. The men chant rhythmically. The heat builds. At last they can stand it no more. The door is thrown open. Cooling night breezes rush in. And then? The cycle begins again—often to be repeated four or five times more.

Like Buddhist meditation practices or the dances of the Whirling Dervishes of Turkey, the ritual "sweats" of the Sioux are meant to cleanse the mind and body. When they are especially intense, they bring altered awareness and personal revelation.

People seek some altered states purely for pleasure or escape, as is often true of drug intoxication. Yet, as the Sioux illustrate, many cultures regard altered consciousness as a pathway to personal enlightenment. Indeed, all cultures and most religions recognize and accept some alterations of consciousness. However, the meaning given to these states varies greatly—from signs of "madness" and "possession" by spirits to life-enhancing breakthroughs. Thus, cultural conditioning greatly affects what altered states we recognize, seek, consider normal, and attain (de Rios & Grob, 2005).

In many cultures, rituals of healing, prayer, meditation, purification, or personal transformation at sites like this Buddhist temple near Hong Kong are accompanied by altered states of consciousness.

John Mitterer

Sleep—Catching a Few ZZZs

JOURNEY QUESTION 5.2 *What are the effects of sleep loss or changes in sleep patterns?*

Each of us will spend some 25 years of life asleep. Because sleep is familiar, many people think they know all about it. But many common-sense beliefs about sleep are false. For example, you are not totally unresponsive during sleep. A sleeping mother may ignore a jet thundering overhead but wake at the slightest whimper of her child. Likewise, you are more likely to awaken if you hear your own name spoken instead of another. It's even possible to do simple tasks while asleep. In one experiment, people learned to avoid an electric shock by touching a switch each time a tone sounded. Eventually, they could do it without waking. (This is much like the basic survival skill of turning off your alarm clock without waking.) Of course, sleep does impose limitations. Don't expect to learn math, a foreign language, or other complex skills while asleep—especially if the snooze takes place in class (Froufe & Schwartz, 2001; González-Vallejo et al., 2008). But do expect that a good sleep will help you remember what you learned the day before (Fenn, Nusbaum, & Margoliash, 2003; Saxvig et al., 2008).

Timothy Ross/The Image Works

The Need for Sleep

How strong is the need for sleep? Sleep is an innate **biological rhythm** that can never be entirely ignored (Mistlberger, 2005; **Figure 5.1**). Of course, sleep will give way temporarily, especially at times of great danger. As comedian and filmmaker Woody Allen once put it, "The lion and the lamb shall lie down together, but the lamb will not be very sleepy." However, there are limits to how long humans can go without sleep. A rare disease that prevents sleep always ends with stupor, coma, and death (Zhang et al., 2010).

How long could a person go without sleep? With few exceptions, 4 days or more without sleep becomes hell for everyone. The world record is held by Randy Gardner, who at age 17 went 264 hours (11 days) without sleep. (Although others have gone even longer without

Figure 5.1 Not all animals sleep, but like humans, those that do have powerful sleep needs. For example, dolphins must voluntarily breathe air, which means they face the choice of staying awake or drowning. The dolphin solves this problem by sleeping on just one side of its brain at a time! The other half of the brain, which remains awake, controls breathing (Jouvet, 1999).

Biological rhythm Any repeating cycle of biological activity, such as sleep and waking cycles or changes in body temperature.

sleep, Randy still holds the "official" record because *Guinness World Records* no longer recognizes sleep deprivation competitions due to possible health risks.) Surprisingly, Randy needed only 14 hours of sleep to recover. As Randy found, most symptoms of **sleep deprivation**, or sleep loss, are reversed by a single night's rest (Sallinen et al., 2008).

What are the costs of sleep loss? At various times, Randy's speech was slurred, and he couldn't concentrate, remember clearly, or name common objects (Coren, 1996). Sleep loss also typically causes trembling hands, drooping eyelids, inattention, irritability, staring, increased pain sensitivity, and general discomfort (Doran, Van Dongen, & Dinges, 2001).

Most people experience *hypersomnia* (hi-per-SOM-nee-ah), or excessive daytime sleepiness, after even a few hours of sleep loss. Hypersomnia is a common problem during adolescence (Carskadon, Acebo, & Jenni, 2004). Rapid physical changes during puberty increase the need for sleep. However, the quality and quantity of sleep time tends to decrease during the teen years (Fukuda & Ishihara, 2001).

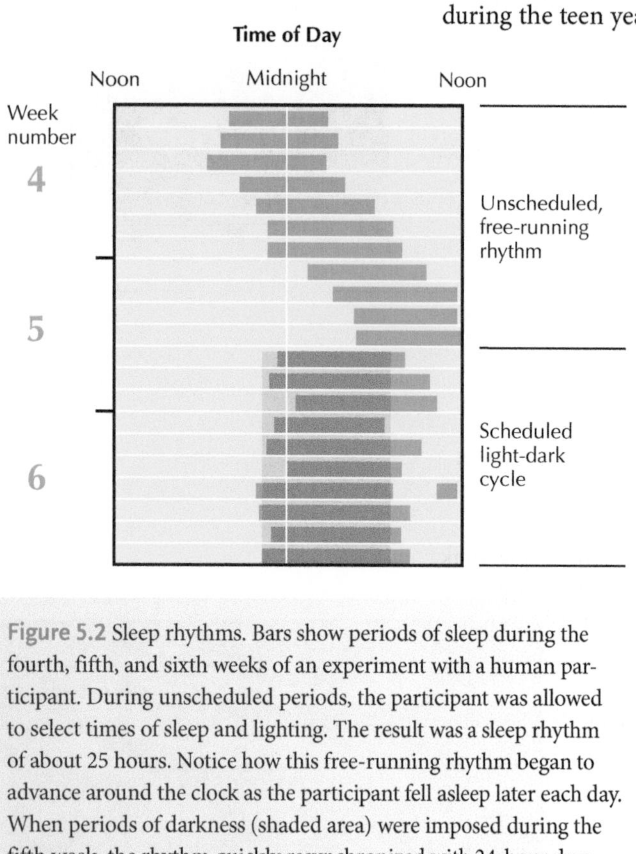

Most people who have not slept for a day or two can still do interesting or complex mental tasks. But they have trouble paying attention, staying alert, and doing simple or boring routines (Trujillo, Kornguth, & Schnyer, 2009). They are also susceptible to **microsleeps**, which are brief shifts in brain activity to the pattern normally recorded during sleep. Imagine placing an animal on a moving treadmill, over a pool of water. Even under these conditions, animals soon drift into repeated microsleeps. For a pilot or machine operator, this can spell disaster (Hardaway & Gregory, 2005). If a task is monotonous (such as factory work or air traffic control), no amount of sleep loss is safe. In fact, if you lose just 1 hour of sleep a night, it can affect your mood, memory, ability to pay attention, and even your health (Maas, 1999). When you drive, remember that microsleeps can lead to macro-accidents. Even if your eyes are open, you can fall asleep for a few seconds. A hundred thousand crashes every year are caused by sleepiness (Rau, 2005). Although coffee helps (Kamimori et al., 2005), if you are struggling to stay awake while driving, you should stop, quit fighting it, and take a short nap.

Sleep also helps keep the body, including the brain, healthy by regulating its temperature and immune system, conserving energy, and aiding development and repair (Faraut et al., 2011; Freberg, 2010). According to **repair/restorative theories of sleep**, lowering body and brain activity and metabolism during sleep may help conserve energy and lengthen life. Biologically, sleep is a necessity, not a luxury.

Severe sleep loss can even cause a temporary **sleep-deprivation psychosis**—a loss of contact with reality. Confusion, disorientation, delusions, and hallucinations are typical of this reaction. Fortunately, such "crazy" behavior is uncommon. Hallucinations and delusions rarely appear before 60 hours of wakefulness (Naitoh, Kelly, & Englund, 1989).

How can I tell how much sleep I really need? Pick a day when you feel well rested. Then sleep that night until you wake without an alarm clock. If you feel rested when you wake up, that's your natural sleep need. If you're sleeping fewer hours than you need, you're building up a sleep debt (Basner & Dinges, 2009).

Figure 5.2 Sleep rhythms. Bars show periods of sleep during the fourth, fifth, and sixth weeks of an experiment with a human participant. During unscheduled periods, the participant was allowed to select times of sleep and lighting. The result was a sleep rhythm of about 25 hours. Notice how this free-running rhythm began to advance around the clock as the participant fell asleep later each day. When periods of darkness (shaded area) were imposed during the fifth week, the rhythm quickly resynchronized with 24-hour days. (Adapted from Czeisler et al., 1981. Czeisler, C. A., Richardson, G. S., Zimmerman, J. C., Moore-Ede, M. C., et al. (1981.) Entrainment of human circadian rhythms by light-dark cycles: A reassessment. *Photochemistry, Photobiology, 34,* 239–247. Fig 2.)

Sleep deprivation Being prevented from getting desired or needed amounts of sleep.

Microsleep A brief shift in brain-wave patterns to those of sleep.

Repair/restorative theories of sleep Propose that lowering body and brain activity and metabolism during sleep may help conserve energy and lengthen life.

Sleep-deprivation psychosis A major disruption of mental and emotional functioning brought about by sleep loss.

Sleep Patterns

Sleep was described as an innate biological rhythm. What does that mean? Daily sleep and waking periods create a variety of sleep patterns. Rhythms of sleep and waking are so steady that they continue for many days, even when clocks and light–dark cycles are removed. However, under such conditions, humans eventually shift to a sleep–waking cycle that averages slightly more than 24 hours (Czeisler et al., 1999; Figure 5.2). This suggests that external time markers, especially light and dark, help tie our sleep rhythms to days that are exactly

24 hours long. Otherwise, many of us would drift into our own unusual sleep cycles (Duffy & Wright, 2005).

What is the normal range of sleep? A few rare individuals can get by on an hour or two of sleep a night—and feel perfectly fine. Only a small percentage of the population are *short sleepers*, averaging 5 hours of sleep or less per night. On the other end of the scale we find *long sleepers*, who doze 9 hours or more (Grandner & Kripke, 2004). The majority of us sleep on a familiar 7- to 8-hour-per-night schedule. Urging everyone to sleep 8 hours would be like advising everyone to wear medium-size shoes.

We need less sleep as we get older, right? Yes, total sleep time declines throughout life. Those older than 50 average only 6 hours of sleep a night. In contrast, infants spend up to 20 hours a day sleeping, usually in 2- to 4-hour cycles. As they mature, most children go through a "nap" stage and eventually settle into a steady cycle of sleeping once a day. Perhaps we should all continue to take an afternoon "siesta." Midafternoon sleepiness is a natural part of the sleep cycle. Brief, well-timed naps can help maintain alertness in people like truck drivers and hospital interns, who often must fight to stay alert (Ficca et al., 2010).

Busy people may be tempted to sleep less. However, people on *shortened* cycles—for example, 3 hours of sleep to 6 hours awake—often can't get to sleep when the cycle calls for it. That's why astronauts continue to sleep on their normal earth schedule while in space. Adapting to *longer* than normal days is more promising. Such days can be tailored to match natural sleep patterns, which have a ratio of 2 to 1 between time awake and time asleep (16 hours awake and 8 hours asleep). For instance, one study showed that 28-hour "days" work for some people. Overall, sleep patterns may be bent and stretched, but they rarely yield entirely to human whims (Åkerstedt, 2007).

Stages of Sleep—The Nightly Roller-Coaster

JOURNEY QUESTION 5.3 *What are some functions of sleep?*

What causes sleep? Whether you are awake or asleep right now depends on the *balance* between separate sleep and waking systems. Brain circuits and chemicals in one of the systems promote sleep (Lagos et al., 2009; Steiger, 2007). A network of brain cells in the other system responds to chemicals that inhibit sleep. The two systems seesaw back and forth, switching the brain between sleep and wakefulness. Note that the brain does not "shut down" during sleep. Rather, the *pattern* of activity changes.

Sleep Stages

How does brain activity change when you fall asleep? Changes in tiny electrical signals (brainwaves) generated by the brain can be amplified and recorded with an **electroencephalograph** (eh-LEK-tro-en-SEF-uh-lo-graf), or **EEG**. When you are awake and alert, the EEG reveals a pattern of small, fast waves called **beta waves** (Figure 5.3). Immediately before sleep, the pattern shifts to larger and slower waves called **alpha waves**. (Alpha waves also occur when you are relaxed and allow your thoughts to drift.) As the eyes close, breathing becomes slow and regular, the pulse rate slows, and body temperature drops. Soon after, we descend into *slow-wave sleep* through four distinct **sleep stages**.

Stage 1

As you enter **light sleep** (Stage 1 sleep), your heart rate slows even more. Breathing becomes more irregular. The muscles of your body relax. This may trigger a reflex muscle twitch called a *hypnic* (HIP-nik: sleep) *jerk*. (This is quite normal, so have no fear about admitting to your friends that you fell asleep with a hypnic jerk.) In Stage 1 sleep, the EEG is made up mainly of small, irregular waves with some alpha waves. Persons awakened at this time may or may not say they were asleep.

Electroencephalograph (EEG) A device designed to detect, amplify, and record electrical activity in the brain.

Beta waves Small, fast brainwaves associated with being awake and alert.

Alpha waves Large, slow brainwaves associated with relaxation and falling asleep.

Sleep stages Levels of sleep identified by brain-wave patterns and behavioral changes.

Light sleep Stage 1 sleep, marked by small, irregular brainwaves and some alpha waves.

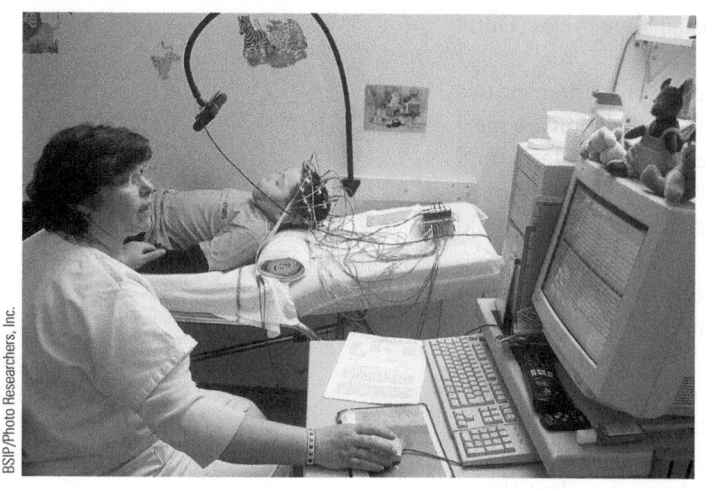

(a)

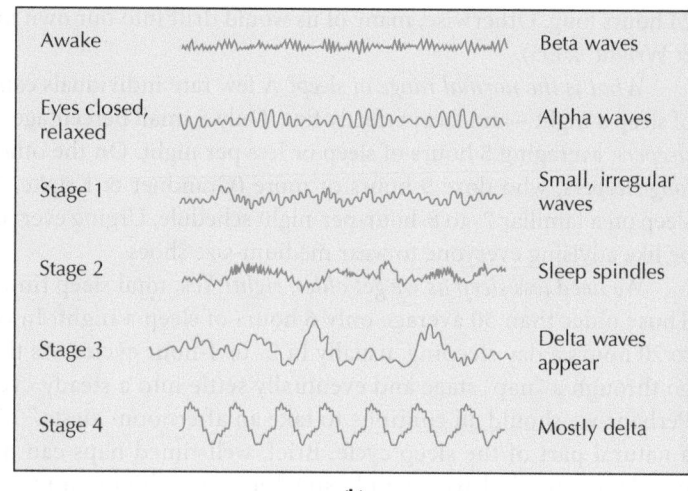

(b)

Figure 5.3 (a) Photograph of an EEG recording session. The boy in the background is asleep. (b) Changes in brainwave patterns associated with various stages of sleep. Actually, most wave types are present at all times, but they occur more or less frequently in various sleep stages.

Stage 2

As sleep deepens, body temperature drops further. Also, the EEG begins to include **sleep spindles**, which are short bursts of distinctive brainwave activity generated by the thalamus (Fogel et al., 2007). Sleep spindles may help prevent the sleeping brain from being aroused by external stimuli, thus marking the true boundary of sleep (Dang-Vu et al., 2010). Within 4 minutes after spindles appear, most people will say they were asleep.

Stage 3

In Stage 3, a new brain wave called delta begins to appear. **Delta waves** are very large and slow. They signal a move to deeper slow-wave sleep and a further loss of consciousness.

Stage 4

Most people reach **deep sleep** (the deepest level of normal sleep) in about 1 hour. Stage 4 brainwaves are almost pure slow-wave delta, and the sleeper is in a state of oblivion. If you make a loud noise during Stage 4, the sleeper will wake up in a state of confusion and may not remember the noise.

The Dual Process Hypothesis of Sleep

There is much more to a night's sleep than a simple descent into Stage 4. Fluctuations in sleep hormones cause recurring cycles of deeper and lighter sleep throughout the night (Steiger, 2007). During these repeated periods of lighter sleep, a curious thing happens: The sleeper's eyes occasionally move under the eyelids. (If you ever get a chance to watch a sleeping child, roommate, or spouse, you may see these eye movements.) **Rapid eye movements**, or **REMs**, are associated with dreaming (Figure 5.4). In addition, **REM sleep** is marked by a return of fast, irregular EEG patterns similar to Stage 1 sleep. In fact, the brain is so active during REM sleep that it looks as if the person is awake (Rock, 2004).

The two most basic states of sleep, then, are **non-REM (NREM) sleep**, which occurs during Stages 1, 2, 3, and 4, and REM sleep, with its associated dreaming (Rock, 2004). Earlier, we noted some of the biological benefits of sleep. According to the **dual process hypothesis of sleep**, REM and NREM sleep have two added purposes: They help "refresh" the brain and store memories (Ficca & Salzarulo, 2004).

Sleep spindles Distinctive bursts of brainwave activity that indicate a person is asleep.

Delta waves Large, slow brainwaves that occur in deeper sleep (Stages 3 and 4).

Deep sleep Stage 4 slow-wave sleep; the deepest form of normal sleep.

Rapid eye movements (REMs) Swift eye movements during sleep.

REM sleep Sleep marked by rapid eye movements and a return to Stage 1 EEG patterns.

Non-REM (NREM) sleep Non–rapid eye movement sleep characteristic of Stages 2, 3, and 4.

Dual process hypothesis of sleep Proposes that NREM sleep reduces the overall level of brain activation, allowing unimportant memories to be forgotten while REM sleep sharpens memory for important events from the previous day.

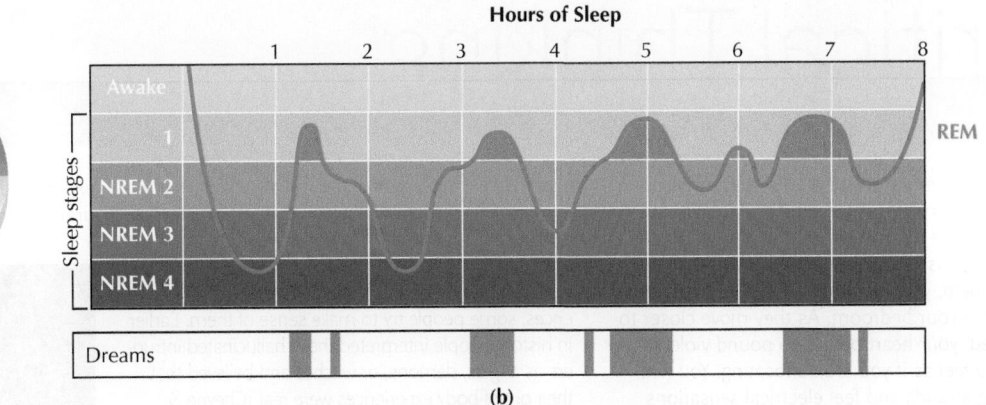

Figure 5.4 *(a)* Average proportion of time adults spend daily in REM sleep and NREM sleep. REM periods add up to about 20 percent of total sleep time. *(b)* Typical changes in stages of sleep during the night. Notice that dreams mostly coincide with REM periods.

The Function of NREM Sleep

What is the function of NREM sleep? NREM sleep is dream free about 90 percent of the time and is deepest early in the night during the first few Stage 4 periods. Your first period of Stage 1 sleep usually lacks REMs and dreams. Later Stage 1 periods typically include a shift into REM sleep. Dreamless, slow-wave NREM sleep increases after physical exertion and may help us recover from bodily fatigue. It also appears to "calm" the brain during the earlier part of a night's sleep (Tononi & Cirelli, 2003).

According to the dual process hypothesis, we are bombarded by information throughout the day, which causes our neural networks to become more and more active. As a result, your brain requires more and more energy to continue functioning. Slow-wave sleep early in the night brings overall brain activation levels back down, allowing a "fresh" approach to the next day.

Consider for a moment the rich jumble of events that make up a day. Some experiences are worth remembering (like what you are reading right now, of course), and others are not so important (like which sock you put on first this morning). As slow-wave sleep reduces overall activation in the brain, less important experiences may fade away and be forgotten. If you wake up feeling clearer about what you studied the previous night, it might be because your brain doesn't "sweat the small stuff"!

The Function of REM Sleep

What, then, is the purpose of REM sleep? According to the dual process hypothesis, whereas NREM sleep "calms" the brain, REM sleep appears to "sharpen" our memories of the previous day's more important experiences (Saxvig et al., 2008). Daytime stress tends to increase REM sleep, which may rise dramatically when there is a death in the family, trouble at work, a marital conflict, or other emotionally charged events. The value of more REM sleep is that it helps us sort and retain memories, especially memories about strategies for solving problems (Walker & Stickgold, 2006). This is why, after studying for a long period, you may remember more if you go to sleep, rather than pulling an all-nighter. (REMember to get some REM!)

Early in life, REM sleep may stimulate the developing brain. Newborn babies have lots of new experiences to process, so they spend a hearty 8 or 9 hours a day in REM sleep. That's about 50 percent of their total sleep time.

REM Sleep and Dreaming

Roughly 85 percent of the time, people awakened during REMs report vivid dreams. Some eye movements correspond to dream activities. Dream that you are watching a tennis match, and you will probably move your eyes from side to side. However, people who were

Critical Thinking

"Imagine opening your eyes shortly before dawn, attempting to roll over in your bed, and suddenly realizing that you are entirely paralyzed. While lying helplessly on your back and unable to cry out for help, you become aware of sinister figures lurking in your bedroom. As they move closer to your bed, your heart begins to pound violently and you feel as if you are suffocating. You hear buzzing sounds and feel electrical sensations shooting throughout your body. Within moments, the visions vanish and you can move once again. Terrified, you wonder what has just happened" (McNally & Clancy, 2005).

Sleep paralysis, which normally prevents us from moving during REM sleep, can also occur just as you begin to wake up. During such episodes, people sometimes have *hypnopompic* (hip-neh-POM-pik: "upon awakening") hallucinations. According to psychologist Al Cheyne (2005), these hallucinations may include bizarre experiences, such as sensing that an alien being is in your bedroom; feeling something pressing on your chest, suffocating you; or feeling like you are floating out of your body.

Although most of us shrug off these weird experiences, some people try to make sense of them. Earlier in history, people interpreted these hallucinated intruders as angels, demons, or witches and believed that their out-of-body experiences were real (Cheyne & Girard, 2009; Cheyne, Rueffer, & Newby-Clark, 1999). However, as our culture changes, so do our interpretations of sleep experiences. Today, for example, some people who have sleep-related hallucinations believe they have been abducted by space aliens or sexually abused (McNally & Clancy, 2005).

Superstitions and folklore often develop as attempts to explain human experiences, including some of the stranger aspects of sleep. By studying hypnopompic hallucinations, psychologists hope to offer natural explanations for many experiences that might otherwise seem supernatural or paranormal (Cheyne & Girard, 2009).

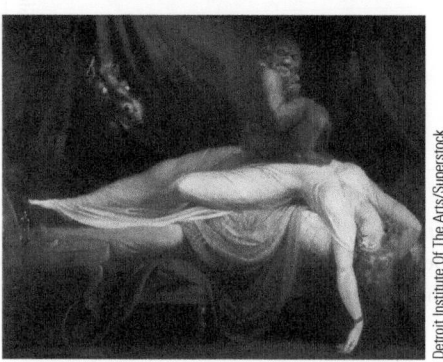

Swiss artist Henry Fuseli drew on hypnopompic imagery as an inspiration for his famous painting *The Nightmare*.

born blind still have REMs, so eye movements are not just a result of "watching" dream images (Shafton, 1995). REM sleep is easy to observe in pets, such as dogs and cats. Watch for eye and face movements and irregular breathing. (You can forget about your pet iguana, though. Reptiles show no signs of REM sleep.)

Dreams during REM sleep tend to be longer, clearer, more detailed, more bizarre, and more "dream-like" than thoughts and images that occur in NREM sleep (Hobson, Pace-Schott, & Stickgold, 2000). Also, brain areas associated with imagery and emotion become more active during REM sleep. This may explain why REM dreams tend to be more vivid than NREM dreams (Rock, 2004).

Speaking very loosely, it's as if the dreaming brain were reviewing messages left on a telephone answering machine to decide which are worth keeping. During the day, when information is streaming in, the brain may be too busy to efficiently select useful memories. When the conscious brain is "off-line," we are better able to identify and solidify important new memories.

What happens to the body when a person dreams? REM sleep is a time of high emotion. The heart beats irregularly. Blood pressure and breathing waver. Both males and females appear to be sexually aroused: Men usually have an erection, and genital blood flow increases in women. This occurs for all REM sleep, so it is not strictly related to erotic dreams (Jouvet, 1999).

During REM sleep, your body becomes quite still, as if you were paralyzed. Imagine for a moment the results of acting out some of your recent dreams. Very likely, REM-sleep paralysis prevents some hilarious—and dangerous—nighttime escapades. When it fails, some people thrash violently, leap out of bed, and may attack their bed partners. A lack of muscle paralysis during REM sleep is called *REM behavior disorder* (Ochoa & Pulido, 2005). One patient suffering from the disorder tied himself to his bed every night. That way, he couldn't jump up and crash into furniture or walls (Shafton, 1995). And yet sometimes sleep paralysis can go a little too far. See "They Came from Outer Space?" to find out why.

In a moment, we will survey some additional sleep problems—if you are still awake. First, here are a few questions to check your memory of our discussion so far.

RECITE

1. Changes in the quality and pattern of mental activity define a(n)

   a. EEG
   b. REM
   c. SIDS
   d. ASC

2. Delusions and hallucinations typically continue for several days after a sleep-deprived individual returns to normal sleep. T or F?

3. Alpha waves are to presleep drowsiness as _____ _____ are to Stage 4 sleep.

4. Rapid eye movements indicate that a person is in deep sleep. T or F?

5. Sharpening memories and facilitating their storage is one function of

   a. activation-synthesis cycles
   b. REM sleep
   c. deep sleep
   d. NREM sleep

REFLECT

THINK CRITICALLY

6. In addition to helping restore the body and store memories, what direct evolutionary advantage might sleeping provide?

SELF-REFLECT

Make a quick list of some altered states of consciousness you have experienced. What do they have in common? How are they different? What conditions caused them?

Imagine that you are a counselor at a sleep clinic. You must explain the basics of sleep and dreaming to a new client who knows little about these topics. Can you do it?

ANSWERS

1. d 2. F 3. delta waves 4. F 5. b 6. Natural selection may have favored sleep because animals that remained active at night probably had a higher chance of being killed (Freberg, 2010). (We'll bet they had more fun, though.)

Sleep Disturbances—The Sleepy Time Blues

JOURNEY QUESTION 5.4 *What are some sleep disorders and unusual sleep events?*

Sleep quality has taken a beating in North America. Artificial lighting, frenetic schedules, exciting pastimes, smoking, drinking, overstimulation, and many other factors have contributed to a near epidemic of sleep problems. Sleep disturbances are a serious risk to health and happiness (Shneerson, 2005). Sleep clinics treat thousands of people each year who suffer from sleep disorders or complaints. Let's explore some of the more interesting problems these people face. These disturbances range from daytime sleep attacks to sleepwalking and terrifying nightmares (Table 5.1).

Table 5.1 Sleep Disturbances—Things That Go Wrong in the Night

Hypersomnia	Excessive daytime sleepiness. This can result from depression, insomnia, narcolepsy, sleep apnea, sleep drunkenness, periodic limb movements, drug abuse, and other problems.
Insomnia	Difficulty in getting to sleep or staying asleep; also, not feeling rested after sleeping.
Narcolepsy	Sudden, irresistible, daytime sleep attacks that may last anywhere from a few minutes to a half hour. Victims may fall asleep while standing, talking, or even driving.
Nightmare disorder	Vivid, recurrent nightmares that significantly disturb sleep.
Periodic limb movement syndrome	Muscle twitches (primarily affecting the legs) that occur every 20 to 40 seconds and severely disturb sleep.
REM behavior disorder	A failure of normal muscle paralysis, leading to violent actions during REM sleep.
Restless legs syndrome	An irresistible urge to move the legs to relieve sensations of creeping, tingling, prickling, aching, or tension.

Continued

Table 5.1 Sleep Disturbances—Things That Go Wrong In The Night—cont'd

Sleep apnea	During sleep, breathing stops for 20 seconds or more until the person wakes a little, gulps in air, and settles back to sleep; this cycle may be repeated hundreds of times per night.
Sleep drunkenness	A slow transition to clear consciousness after awakening; sometimes associated with irritable or aggressive behavior.
Sleep terror disorder	The repeated occurrence of night terrors that significantly disturb sleep.
Sleep–wake schedule disorder	A mismatch between the sleep–wake schedule demanded by a person's bodily rhythm and that demanded by the environment.
Sleepwalking disorder	Repeated incidents of leaving bed and walking about while asleep.

Adapted from Carney, Geyer, & Berry, 2005; Shneerson, 2005.

© Cengage Learning

Insomnia

Staring at the ceiling at 2 AM is pretty low on most people's list of favorite pastimes. Yet about 60 million Americans have frequent or chronic insomnia (National Institute of Neurological Disorders and Stroke, 2007). **Insomnia** includes difficulty in falling to sleep, frequent nighttime awakenings, waking too early, or a combination of these problems. Insomnia can harm people's work, health, and relationships (Ebben & Spielman, 2009).

Types and Causes of Insomnia

Worry, stress, and excitement can cause *temporary insomnia* and a self-defeating cycle. First, excess mental activity ("I can't stop turning things over in my mind") and heightened arousal block sleep. Then, frustration and anger over not being able to sleep cause more worry and arousal. This further delays sleep, which causes more frustration, and so on (Sateia & Nowell, 2004). A good way to beat this cycle is to avoid fighting it. Get up and do something useful or satisfying when you can't sleep. (Reading a textbook might be a good choice of useful activities.) Return to bed only when you begin to feel that you are struggling to stay awake. If sleeping problems last for more than 3 weeks, then a diagnosis of *chronic insomnia* can be made.

Drug-dependency insomnia (sleep loss caused by withdrawal from sleeping pills) can also occur. There is real irony in the billion dollars a year North Americans spend on sleeping pills. Nonprescription sleeping pills such as Sominex, Nytol, and Sleep-Eze have little sleep-inducing effect. Barbiturates are even worse. These prescription sedatives decrease both Stage 4 sleep and REM sleep, drastically lowering sleep quality. In addition, many users become "sleeping-pill junkies" who need an ever-greater number of pills to get to sleep. Victims must be painstakingly weaned from their sleep medicines. Otherwise, terrible nightmares and "rebound insomnia" may drive them back to drug use.

It's worth remembering that although alcohol and other depressant drugs may help a person get to sleep, they greatly reduce sleep quality (Nau & Lichstein, 2005). Even newer drugs, such as Ambien and Lunesta, which induce sleep, have drawbacks. Possible side effects include amnesia, impaired judgment, increased appetite, decreased sex drive, depression, and even sleepwalking, sleep eating, and sleep driving. Rebound insomnia is also a risk, making these drugs at best a temporary remedy for insomnia.

"It's only insomnia if there's nothing good on."

B. Smaller

Insomnia Difficulty in getting to sleep or staying asleep.

Behavioral Remedies for Insomnia

If sleeping pills are a poor way to treat insomnia, what can be done? Sleep specialists prefer to treat insomnia with lifestyle changes and behavioral techniques (Montgomery & Dennis, 2004). Treatment for chronic insomnia usually begins with a careful analysis of a patient's sleep habits, lifestyle, stress levels, and medical problems. All the approaches discussed in the following list are helpful for treating insomnia (Ebben & Spielman, 2009; Nau & Lichstein, 2005):

1. **Stimulus control.** Insisting on a regular schedule helps establish a firm body rhythm, greatly improving sleep. This is best achieved by exercising **stimulus control**, which refers to linking a response with specific stimuli. It is important to get up and go to sleep at the same time each day, including weekends (Bootzin & Epstein, 2000). In addition, insomniacs are told to avoid doing anything but sleeping when they are in bed. They are not to study, eat, watch television, read, pay the bills, worry, or even think in bed. (Lovemaking is okay, however.) In this way, only sleeping and relaxation become associated with going to bed at specific times.

2. **Sleep restriction.** Even if an entire night's sleep is missed, it is important not to sleep late in the morning, nap more than an hour, sleep during the evening, or go to bed early the following night. Instead, restricting sleep to normal bedtime hours avoids fragmenting sleep rhythms (Shneerson, 2005).

3. **Paradoxical intention.** Another helpful approach is to remove the pressures of trying to go to sleep. Instead, the goal becomes trying to keep the eyes open (in the dark) and stay awake as long as possible (Nau & Lichstein, 2005). This allows sleep to come unexpectedly and lowers performance anxiety (Taylor & Roane, 2010).

4. **Relaxation.** Some insomniacs lower their arousal before sleep by using a physical or mental strategy for relaxing, such as progressive muscle relaxation, meditation, or blotting out worries with calming images. It is also helpful to schedule time in the early evening to write down worries or concerns and plan what to do about them the next day in order to set them aside before going to bed.

5. **Exercise.** Strenuous exercise during the day promotes sleep (Brand et al., 2010). However, exercise within 3 to 6 hours of sleep is helpful only if it is very light.

6. **Food intake.** What you eat can affect how easily you get to sleep. Eating starchy foods increases the amount of *tryptophan* (TRIP-tuh-fan: an amino acid) reaching the brain. More tryptophan, in turn, increases the amount of serotonin in the brain, which is associated with relaxation, a positive mood, and sleepiness (Silber & Schmitt, 2010). Thus, to promote sleep, try eating a starchy snack, such as cookies, bread, pasta, oatmeal, pretzels, or dry cereal. If you really want to drop the bomb on insomnia, try eating a baked potato (which may be the world's largest sleeping pill!).

7. **Stimulant avoidance.** Stimulants, such as coffee and cigarettes, should be avoided. It is also worth remembering that alcohol, although not a stimulant, impairs sleep quality.

Sleepwalking, Sleeptalking, and Sleepsex

Sleepsex? As strange as it may seem, many waking behaviors can be engaged in while asleep, such as driving a car, cooking, playing a musical instrument, and eating (Plazzi et al., 2005). The most famous, sleepwalking, is eerie and fascinating in its own right. **Somnambulists** (som-NAM-bue-lists: those who sleepwalk) avoid obstacles, descend stairways, and on rare occasions may step out of windows or in front of automobiles. Sleepwalkers have been observed jumping into lakes, urinating in garbage pails or closets (phew!), shuffling furniture around, and even brandishing weapons (Schenck & Mahowald, 2005).

The sleepwalker's eyes are usually open, but a blank face and shuffling feet reveal that the person is still asleep. If you find someone sleepwalking, you should gently guide the person back to bed. Awakening a sleepwalker does no harm, but it is not necessary.

Does sleepwalking occur during dreaming? No. Remember that people are normally immobilized during REM sleep. EEG studies have shown that somnambulism occurs during NREM Stages 3 and 4 (Stein & Ferber, 2001). *Sleeptalking* also occurs mostly during

Stimulus control Linking a particular response with specific stimuli.

Somnambulists People who sleepwalk; occurs during NREM sleep.

NREM sleep. The link with deep sleep explains why sleeptalking makes little sense and why sleepwalkers are confused and remember little when awakened.

Oh, yes, you're curious about sleepsex. There is, of course, an official name for it: *sexsomnia* (Klein & Houlihan, 2010). Sexsomnia is not as exciting as it might sound: Just imagine being startled wide awake by your bed partner, who is asleep but attempting to have sex with you (Andersen et al., 2007; Mangan, 2004).

Nightmares and Night Terrors

Stage 4 sleep is also the realm of night terrors. These frightening episodes are quite different from ordinary nightmares. A **nightmare** is simply a bad dream that takes place during REM sleep. Frequently occurring nightmares (one a week or more) are associated with higher levels of psychological distress (Levin & Fireman, 2002). During Stage 4 **night terrors**, a person suffers total panic and may hallucinate frightening dream images into the bedroom. An attack may last 15 or 20 minutes. When it is over, the person awakens drenched in sweat but only vaguely remembers the terror. Because night terrors occur during NREM sleep (when the body is not immobilized), victims may sit up, scream, get out of bed, or run around the room. Victims remember little afterward. (Other family members, however, may have a story to tell.) Although night terrors are more common in childhood, they are not uncommon in adulthood (Belicki, Chambers, & Ogilvie, 1997; Kataria, 2004).

How to Eliminate a Nightmare

Is there any way to stop a recurring nightmare? A bad nightmare can be worse than any horror movie. It's easy to leave a theater, but we often remain trapped in terrifying dreams. Nevertheless, most nightmares can be banished by following three simple steps. First, write down your nightmare, describing it in detail. Next, change the dream any way you wish, making sure to spell out the details of the new dream. The third step is *imagery rehearsal*, in which you mentally rehearse the changed dream before you fall asleep again (Krakow & Zadra, 2006). Imagery rehearsal may work because it makes upsetting dreams familiar while a person is awake and feeling safe. Or perhaps it mentally "reprograms" future dream content. In any case, the technique has helped many people.

Sleep Apnea

Some sage once said, "Laugh and the whole world laughs with you; snore and you sleep alone." Nightly "wood sawing" is often harmless, but it can signal a serious problem. A person who snores loudly, with short silences and loud gasps or snorts, may suffer from apnea (AP-nee-ah: interrupted breathing). In **sleep apnea**, breathing stops for periods of 20 seconds to 2 minutes. As the need for oxygen becomes intense, the person wakes a little and gulps in air. She or he then settles back to sleep. But soon, breathing stops again. This cycle is repeated hundreds of times a night. Although snoring might be funny, sleep apnea is no joke. As you might guess, apnea victims are extremely sleepy during the day (Collop, 2005). They can also have a harder time functioning during the day (Grenèche et al., 2011) and, in the long run, may suffer damage to their oxygen-hungry brains (Jo et al., 2010).

What causes sleep apnea? Some cases occur because the brain stops sending signals to the diaphragm to maintain breathing. Another cause is blockage of the upper air passages. One of the most effective treatments is the use of a continuous positive airway pressure (CPAP) mask to aid breathing during sleep. The resulting improvement in sleep will often result in improved daytime function (Tregear et al., 2010). Other treatments include weight loss and surgery for breathing obstructions (Collop, 2005).

SIDS

Sleep apnea is suspected as one cause of **sudden infant death syndrome (SIDS)**, or "crib death." In the "typical" crib death, a slightly premature or small baby with some signs of a cold or cough is bundled up and put to bed. A short time later, parents find the child has died. A baby deprived of air will normally struggle to begin breathing again. However, SIDS babies

Nightmare A bad dream that occurs during REM sleep.

Night terror A state of panic during NREM sleep.

Sleep apnea Repeated interruption of breathing during sleep.

Sudden infant death syndrome (SIDS) The sudden, unexplained death of an apparently healthy infant.

seem to have a weak arousal reflex. This prevents them from changing positions and resuming breathing after an episode of apnea (Horne et al., 2001). SIDS is the leading cause of death in children between 1 month and 1 year of age (National Institute of Child Health and Human Development, 2010b).

Babies at risk for SIDS must be carefully watched for the first 6 months of life. To aid parents in this task, a special monitor may be used that sounds an alarm when breathing or pulse becomes weak (**Figure 5.5**). Babies at risk for SIDS are often premature; have a shrill, high-pitched cry; engage in "snoring," breath-holding, or frequent awakening at night; breathe mainly through an open mouth; or remain passive when their face rolls into a pillow or blanket.

"*Back* to Sleep"

Sleeping position is another major risk factor for SIDS. Healthy infants are best off sleeping on their backs (sides are not as good but much better than facedown) (Shapiro-Mendoza et al., 2009). (Premature babies, those with respiratory problems, and those who often vomit may need to sleep facedown. Ask a pediatrician for guidance.) It is also worth noting that up to 15 percent of all SIDS cases can be attributed to accidental suffocation and strangulation in bed, which includes suffocation by overly soft bedding or pillows; strangulation, such as an infant's head being caught in crib railings; and *overlaying* (which occurs when a sleeping adult rolls over on top of an infant) (Shapiro-Mendoza et al., 2009).

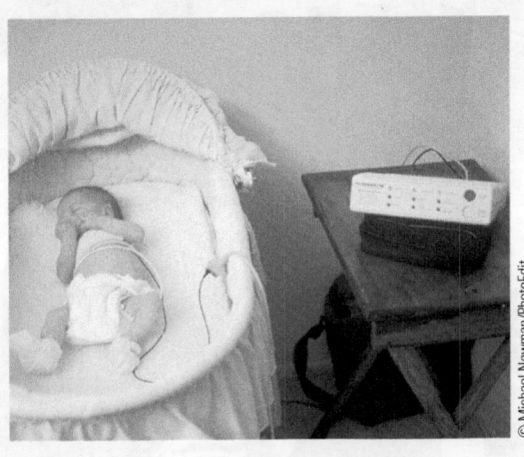

Figure 5.5 Infants at risk for SIDS are often attached to devices that monitor breathing and heart rate during sleep. An alarm sounds to alert parents if either pulse or respiration falters. SIDS rarely occurs after an infant is 1 year old. Babies at risk for SIDS should be placed on their sides or backs.

Narcolepsy

One of the most dramatic sleep problems is **narcolepsy** (NAR-koe-lep-see), or sudden, irresistible sleep attacks. These last anywhere from a few minutes to a half hour. Victims may fall asleep while standing, talking, or even driving. Emotional excitement, especially laughter, commonly triggers narcolepsy. (Tell an especially good joke and a narcoleptic may fall asleep.) Many victims also suffer from *cataplexy* (CAT-uh-plex-see), a sudden temporary paralysis of the muscles, leading to complete body collapse (Peterson & Husain, 2008). Sleep attacks and paralysis appear to occur when REM sleep intrudes into the waking state (Mignot, 2001). It's easy to understand why narcolepsy can devastate careers and relationships (Thorpy, 2006).

Fortunately, narcolepsy is rare. It runs in families, which suggests that it is hereditary (Chabas et al., 2003). In fact, this has been confirmed by breeding several generations of narcoleptic dogs. (These dogs, by the way, are simply outstanding at learning the trick "Roll over and play dead.") There is no known cure for narcolepsy, but a drug named sodium oxybate reduces the frequency and intensity of attacks (Lammers et al., 2010).

Dreams—A Separate Reality?

JOURNEY QUESTION 5.5 *Do dreams have meaning?*

When REM sleep was discovered in 1952, it ushered in a "golden era" of dream inquiry. To conclude our discussion of sleep, let's consider some age-old questions about dreaming.

Does everyone dream? Do dreams occur in an instant? Most people dream four or five times a night, but not all people remember their dreams. "Nondreamers" are often surprised by their dreams when first awakened during REM sleep. Dreams are usually spaced about 90 minutes apart. The first dream lasts only about 10 minutes; the last averages 30 minutes and may run as long as 50. Dreams, therefore, occur in real time, not as "flashes" (Shafton, 1995).

REM Rebound

How important is REM sleep for dreaming? To answer this question, sleep expert William Dement awakened volunteers each time they entered REM sleep. Soon, their need for "dream time" grew more urgent. By the fifth night, many had to be awakened 20 or 30 times to prevent REM sleep.

Narcolepsy A sudden, irresistible sleep attack.

According to psychodynamic theory, dream imagery often has symbolic meaning. How would you interpret Italian artist Mimmo Paladino's dream-like image, titled *Vespero*? The fact that dreams don't have a single unambiguous meaning is one of the short-comings of Freudian dream theory.

When the volunteers were finally allowed to sleep undisturbed, they dreamed extra amounts. This effect, called a **REM rebound**, explains why alcoholics have horrible nightmares after they quit drinking. Alcohol reduces sleep quality by suppressing REM sleep, thus setting up a powerful rebound when it is withdrawn (Stein & Friedmann, 2005).

Dement's volunteers complained of memory lapses, poor concentration, and anxiety. For a while, it was thought that people deprived of REM sleep might go crazy. But later experiments showed that missing *any* sleep stage can cause a rebound for that stage. In general, daytime disturbances are related to the *total amount* of sleep lost, not to the *type* of sleep lost (Devoto et al., 1999).

Dream Theories

How meaningful are dreams? Some theorists believe that dreams have deeply hidden meanings. Others regard dreams as nearly meaningless. Yet others hold that dreams reflect our waking thoughts, fantasies, and emotions. Let's examine all three views.

Psychodynamic Dream Theory

Psychodynamic theories of dreaming emphasize internal conflicts and unconscious forces (Jones, 2007). Sigmund Freud's (1900) landmark book, *The Interpretation of Dreams*, first advanced the idea that many dreams are based on *wish fulfillment* (an expression of unconscious desires). One of Freud's key proposals was that dreams express unconscious desires and conflicts as disguised **dream symbols**—images that have deeper symbolic meaning. Understanding a dream, then, requires analyzing the dream's **manifest content**, or obvious, visible meaning, to uncover its **latent content**, or hidden, symbolic meaning.

For instance, a woman who dreams of stealing her best friend's wedding ring and placing it on her own hand may be unwilling to consciously admit that she is sexually attracted to her best friend's husband. Similarly, a journey might symbolize death, and horseback riding or dancing, sexual intercourse.

Do all dreams have hidden meanings? Probably not. Freud realized that some dreams are trivial "day residues" or carryovers from ordinary waking events. On the other hand, dreams do tend to reflect a person's current concerns, so Freud wasn't entirely wrong.

The Activation-Synthesis Hypothesis

Psychiatrists Allan Hobson and Robert McCarley have a radically different view of dreaming, called the **activation-synthesis hypothesis**. They believe that during REM sleep several lower brain centers are "turned on" *(activated)* in more or less random fashion. However, messages from those cells are blocked from reaching the body, so no movement occurs. Nevertheless, the cells continue to tell higher brain areas of their activities. Struggling to interpret this random information, the brain searches through stored memories and manufactures *(synthesizes)* a dream (Hobson, 2000, 2005). Because frontal areas of the cortex, which control higher mental abilities, are mostly shut down during REM sleep, the resulting dreams are more primitive and more bizarre than daytime thoughts (Hobson, 2000).

How does that help explain dream content? According to the activation-synthesis hypothesis, dreams are usually meaningless. Let's use the classic chase dream as an example. In such dreams we feel we are running but not going anywhere. This occurs because the brain is told the body is running, but it gets no feedback from the motionless legs. To try to make sense of this information, the brain creates a chase drama. A similar process probably explains dreams of floating or flying.

So dreams have no meaning? The activation-synthesis hypothesis rejects the idea that dreams are deliberate, meaningful messages from our unconscious. It does not rule out the possibility that we can find meaning in some dreams. Because dreams are created from memories and past experiences, parts of dreams can sometimes reflect each person's mental life, emotions, and concerns (Hobson, 2000).

REM rebound The occurrence of extra rapid eye movement sleep following REM sleep deprivation.

Psychodynamic theory Any theory of behavior that emphasizes internal conflicts, motives, and unconscious forces.

Dream symbols Images in dreams that serve as visible signs of hidden ideas, desires, impulses, emotions, relationships, and so forth.

Manifest content (of dreams) The surface, "visible" content of a dream; dream images as they are remembered by the dreamer.

Latent content (of dreams) The hidden or symbolic meaning of a dream, as revealed by dream interpretation and analysis.

Activation-synthesis hypothesis An attempt to explain how dream content is affected by motor commands in the brain that occur during sleep but are not carried out.

Neurocognitive Dream Theory

Can't dreams just be about normal day-to-day stuff? Yes they can. According to William Domhoff's **neurocognitive dream theory**, dreams actually have much in common with waking thoughts and emotions. Domhoff believes this is true because many brain areas that are active when we are awake remain active during dreaming (Domhoff, 2001, 2003). From this perspective, our dreams are a conscious expression of REM sleep processes that are sorting and storing daily experiences. Thus, we shouldn't be surprised if a student who is angry at a teacher dreams of embarrassing the teacher in class, a lonely person dreams of romance, or a hungry child dreams of food. It is not necessary to seek deep symbolic meanings to understand these dreams.

Dream Worlds

Which dream theory is the most widely accepted? Each theory has strengths and weaknesses (MacDuffie & Mashour, 2010). However, studies of dream content tend to support neurocognitive theory's focus on the continuity between dreams and waking thought. Rather than seeming exotic or bizarre, most dreams reflect everyday events (Domhoff & Schneider, 2008; Pesant & Zadra, 2006). For example, athletes tend to dream about the previous day's athletic activities (Erlacher & Schredl, 2004). In general, the favorite dream setting is a familiar room in a house. Action usually takes place between the dreamer and two or three other emotionally important people—friends, enemies, loved ones, or employers. Dream actions are also mostly familiar: running, jumping, riding, sitting, talking, and watching. About half of all dreams have sexual elements. Dreams of flying, floating, and falling occur less frequently. However, note that such dreams lend some support to the activation-synthesis hypothesis, because they are not everyday events (unless you are a trapeze artist).

Even if many dreams can be viewed as just a different form of thought, many psychologists continue to believe that some dreams have deeper meaning (Halliday, 2010; Wilkinson, 2006). There seems to be little doubt that dreams can make a difference in our lives: Veteran sleep researcher William Dement once dreamed that he had lung cancer. In the dream, a doctor told Dement he would die soon. At the time, Dement was smoking two packs of cigarettes a day. He says, "I will never forget the surprise, joy, and exquisite relief of waking up. I felt reborn." Dement quit smoking the following day. (For more information about dreaming, see the Psychology in Action section later in this chapter.)

Neurocognitive dream theory Proposal that dreams reflect everyday waking thoughts and emotions.

 study break Sleep Disturbances and Dreaming

RECITE

1. Which of the following is *not* a behavioral remedy for insomnia?
   a. daily hypersomnia
   b. stimulus control
   c. progressive relaxation
   d. paradoxical intention

2. Eating a snack that is nearly all starch can promote sleep because it increases _____ in the brain.
   a. beta waves
   b. tryptophan
   c. EEG activity
   d. hypnic cycling

3. Night terrors, sleepwalking, and sleeptalking all occur during Stage 1, NREM sleep. T or F?

4. Sleep _____ is suspected as one cause of SIDS.

5. According to the activation-synthesis hypothesis of dreaming, dreams are constructed from _____ to explain messages received from nerve cells controlling eye movement, balance, and bodily activity.

6. The favored setting for dreams is
   a. work
   b. school
   c. outdoors or unfamiliar places
   d. familiar rooms

REFLECT

THINK CRITICALLY

7. Even without being told that somnambulism is an NREM event, you could have predicted that sleepwalking doesn't occur during dreaming. Why?

SELF-REFLECT

Almost everyone suffers from insomnia at least occasionally. Are any of the techniques for combating insomnia similar to strategies you have discovered on your own?

Do you think the activation-synthesis theory provides an adequate explanation of your own dreams? Have you had dreams that seem to reflect Freudian wish fulfillment? Do you think your dreams have symbolic meaning or reflect everyday concerns?

ANSWERS

1. a 2. b 3. F 4. apnea 5. memories 6. d 7. Because people are immobilized during REM sleep and REM sleep is strongly associated with dreaming. This makes it unlikely that sleepwalkers are acting out dreams.

Hypnosis—Look into My Eyes

JOURNEY QUESTION 5.6 *What is hypnosis?*

"Your body is becoming heavy. You can barely keep your eyes open. You are so tired you can't move. Relax. Let go. Relax. Close your eyes and relax." These are the last words a textbook should ever say to you, and the first a hypnotist might say.

Interest in hypnosis began in the 1700s with Austrian doctor Franz Mesmer, whose name gave us the term *mesmerize* (to hypnotize). Mesmer believed he could cure disease with magnets. Mesmer's strange "treatments" are related to hypnosis because they actually relied on the power of suggestion, not magnetism (Benjafield, 2010; Waterfield, 2002). For a time, Mesmer enjoyed quite a following. In the end, however, his theories of "animal magnetism" were rejected and he was branded a fraud.

Ever since, stage hypnotists have entertained us with a combination of little or no hypnosis and a bit of deception. On stage, people are unusually cooperative because they don't want to "spoil the act." As a result, they will readily follow almost any instruction given by the entertainer. After volunteers loosen up and respond to a few suggestions, they find that they are suddenly the stars of the show. Audience response to the antics on stage brings out the "ham" in many people. No hypnosis is required; all the "hypnotist" needs to do is direct the action.

Like stage magicians, stage hypnotists also make liberal use of deception. One of the more impressive stage tricks is to rigidly suspend a person between two chairs. This is astounding only because the audience does not question it. Anyone can do it, as is shown in the photographs and instructions in Figure 5.6. Try it!

Entertainment aside, hypnosis is a real phenomenon. The term *hypnosis* was later coined by English surgeon James Braid. The Greek word *hypnos* means "sleep," and Braid used it to describe the hypnotic state. Today, we know that hypnosis is *not* sleep. Confusion about this point remains because some hypnotists give the suggestion, "Sleep, sleep." However, brain activity recorded during hypnosis is different from that observed when a person is asleep or pretending to be hypnotized (Oakley & Halligan, 2010).

Theories of Hypnosis

If hypnosis isn't sleep, then what is it? That's a good question. **Hypnosis** is often defined as an altered state of consciousness, characterized by narrowed attention and an increased openness to suggestion (Kallio & Revonsuo, 2003). Notice that this definition assumes hypnosis is a distinct *state* of consciousness.

The best-known *state theory* of hypnosis was proposed by Ernest Hilgard (1904–2001), who argued that hypnosis causes a *dissociative state*, or "split" in awareness. To illustrate, he

Hypnosis An altered state of consciousness characterized by narrowed attention and increased suggestibility.

Figure 5.6 Arrange three chairs as shown. Have someone recline as shown. Ask him to lift slightly while you remove the middle chair. Accept the applause gracefully! (Concerning hypnosis and similar phenomena, the moral, of course, is "Suspend judgment until you have something solid to stand on.")

Discovering Psychology

Here's a demonstration you can use to gain insight into hypnosis. Tie a short length of string (about 6 inches) to a small, heavy object, such as a ring or a small metal nut. Hold the ring at eye level, about a foot from your face. Concentrate on the ring and notice that it will begin to move, ever so slightly. As it does, focus all your attention on the ring. Narrow your attention to a beam of energy and mentally push the ring away from you. Each time the ring swings away, push on it, using only mental force. Then release it and let it swing back toward you. Continue to mentally push and release the ring until it is swinging freely. For the best results, try this now, before reading more.

Did the ring move? If it did, you used *autosuggestion* to influence your own behavior in a subtle way. Suggestions that the ring would swing caused your hand to make tiny micromuscular movements. These, in turn, caused the ring to move—no special mental powers or supernatural forces are involved.

As is true of hypnotic suggestion, the ring's movement probably seemed to be automatic. Obviously, you could just intentionally swing the ring. However, if you responded to suggestion, the movement seemed to happen without any effort on your part. In the same way, when people are hypnotized, their actions seem to occur without any voluntary intent. Incidentally, autosuggestion likely underlies other phenomena, such as how Ouija boards answer questions without any conscious movements by the person using the pointer. Autosuggestion also plays a role in many forms of self-therapy (Yapko, 2011).

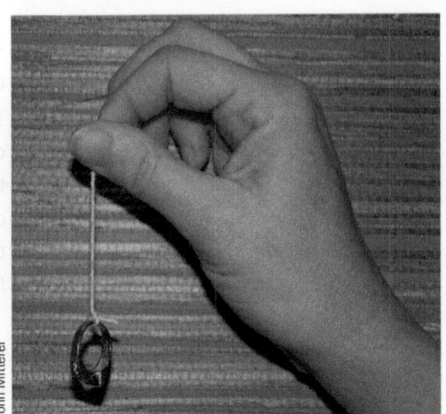

John Mitterer

---

asked hypnotized participants to plunge one hand into a painful bath of ice water. Participants told to feel no pain said they felt none. The same participants were then asked if there was any part of their mind that did feel pain. With their free hand, many wrote, "It hurts," or "Stop it, you're hurting me," while they continued to act pain free (Hilgard, 1977, 1994). Thus, one part of the hypnotized person says there is no pain and acts as if there is none. Another part, which Hilgard calls the *hidden observer*, is aware of the pain but remains in the background. The **hidden observer** is a detached part of the hypnotized person's awareness that silently observes events.

In contrast, *nonstate theorists* argue that hypnosis is not a distinct state at all. Instead it is merely a blend of conformity, relaxation, imagination, obedience, and role-playing (Kirsch, 2005; Lynn & O'Hagen, 2009). For example, many theorists believe that all hypnosis is really self-hypnosis (autosuggestion). From this perspective, a hypnotist merely helps another person to follow a series of suggestions. These suggestions, in turn, alter sensations, perceptions, thoughts, feelings, and behaviors (Lynn & Kirsch, 2006; see "Swinging Suggestions").

The Reality of Hypnosis

How is hypnosis done? Could I be hypnotized against my will? Hypnotists use many different methods. Still, all techniques encourage a person (1) to focus attention on what is being said; (2) to relax and feel tired; (3) to "let go" and accept suggestions easily; and (4) to use vivid imagination (Barabasz & Watkins, 2005). Basically, you must cooperate to become hypnotized.

What does it feel like to be hypnotized? You might be surprised at some of your actions during hypnosis. You also might have mild feelings of floating, sinking, anesthesia, or separation from your body. Personal experiences vary widely. A key element in hypnosis is the **basic suggestion effect**—a tendency of hypnotized persons to carry out suggested actions as if they were involuntary. Hypnotized persons feel like their actions and experiences are *automatic*—they seem to happen without effort. Here is how one person described his hypnotic session:

> "I felt lethargic, my eyes going out of focus and wanting to close. My hands felt real light ... I felt I was sinking deeper into the chair ... I felt like I wanted to relax more and more ... My responses were more automatic. I didn't have to *wish* to do things so much or *want* to do them ... I just did them ... I felt floating ... very close to sleep." (Hilgard, 1968)

Hidden observer A detached part of the hypnotized person's awareness that silently observes events.

Basic suggestion effect The tendency of hypnotized persons to carry out suggested actions as if they were involuntary.

Contrary to the way hypnosis is portrayed in movies, hypnotized people generally remain in control of their behavior and aware of what is going on. For instance, most people will not act out hypnotic suggestions that they consider immoral or repulsive (such as disrobing in public or harming someone) (Kirsch & Lynn, 1995).

Hypnotic Susceptibility

Can everyone be hypnotized? About 8 people out of 10 can be hypnotized, but only 4 out of 10 will be good hypnotic participants. People who are imaginative and prone to fantasy are often highly responsive to hypnosis (Kallio & Revonsuo, 2003). But people who lack these traits may also be hypnotized. If you are willing to be hypnotized, chances are good that you could be. Hypnosis depends more on the efforts and abilities of the hypnotized person than the skills of the hypnotist. But make no mistake: People who are hypnotized are not merely faking their responses.

Hypnotic susceptibility refers to how easily a person can become hypnotized. It is measured by giving a series of suggestions and counting the number of times a person responds. A typical hypnotic test is the *Stanford Hypnotic Susceptibility Scale*, shown in Table 5.2. In the test, various suggestions are made, and the person's response is noted. For instance, you might be told that your left arm is becoming more and more rigid and that it will not bend. If you can't bend your arm during the next 10 seconds, you have shown susceptibility to hypnotic suggestions.

Effects of Hypnosis

What can (and cannot) be achieved with hypnosis? Many abilities have been tested during hypnosis, leading to the following conclusions:

1. **Strength.** Hypnosis has no more effect on physical strength than instructions that encourage a person to make his or her best effort (Chaves, 2000).
2. **Memory.** There is some evidence that hypnosis can enhance memory (Wagstaff et al., 2004). However, it frequently increases the number of false memories as well. For this reason, many states now bar persons from testifying in court if they were hypnotized to improve their memory of a crime they witnessed.
3. **Amnesia.** A person told not to remember something heard during hypnosis may claim not to remember. In some instances this may be nothing more than a deliberate attempt to avoid thinking about specific ideas. However, brief memory loss of this type actually does seem to occur (Barnier, McConkey, & Wright, 2004).

Table 5.2 Stanford Hypnotic Susceptibility Scale

Suggested Behavior	Criterion of Passing
1. Postural sway	Falls without forcing
2. Eye closure	Closes eyes without forcing
3. Hand lowering (left)	Lowers at least 6 inches by end of 10 seconds
4. Immobilization (right arm)	Arm rises less than 1 inch in 10 seconds
5. Finger lock	Incomplete separation of fingers at end of 10 seconds
6. Arm rigidity (left arm)	Less than 2 inches of arm bending in 10 seconds
7. Hands moving together	Hands at least as close as 6 inches after 10 seconds
8. Verbal inhibition (name)	Name unspoken in 10 seconds
9. Hallucination (fly)	Any movement, grimacing, acknowledgment of effect
10. Eye catalepsy	Eyes remain closed at end of 10 seconds
11. Posthypnotic (changes chairs)	Any partial movement response
12. Amnesia test	Three or fewer items recalled

Adapted From Weitzenhoffer & Hilgard, 1959.

© Cengage Learning

Hypnotic susceptibility One's capacity for becoming hypnotized.

4. **Pain relief.** Hypnosis can relieve pain (Hammond, 2008; Keefe, Abernethy, & Campbell, 2005). It can be especially useful when chemical painkillers are ineffective. For instance, hypnosis can reduce phantom limb pain (Oakley, Whitman, & Halligan, 2002). (As discussed in Chapter 4, amputees sometimes feel phantom pain that seems to come from a missing limb.)

5. **Age regression.** Given the proper suggestions, some hypnotized people appear to "regress" to childhood. However, most theorists now believe that "age-regressed" participants are only acting out a suggested role.

6. **Sensory changes.** Hypnotic suggestions concerning sensations are among the most effective. Given the proper instructions, a person can be made to smell a small bottle of ammonia and respond as if it were a wonderful perfume. It is also possible to alter color vision, hearing sensitivity, time sense, perception of illusions, and many other sensory responses.

Like meditation, which we will explore next, hypnosis is a valuable tool in a variety of settings (Yapko, 2011). It can help people relax, feel less pain, and make better progress in therapy (Chapman, 2006). Generally, hypnosis is more successful at changing subjective experience than it is at modifying behaviors such as smoking or overeating.

Meditation and Mindfulness—Chilling, the Healthy Way

JOURNEY QUESTION 5.7 *Do meditation and mindfulness have any benefits?*

Throughout history, meditation has been widely used as a means of altering consciousness through deep relaxation. Let's see how meditation works.

Meditation

Meditation is a mental exercise used to alter consciousness. In general, meditation focuses attention and interrupts the typical flow of thoughts, worries, and analysis. People who use meditation to reduce stress often report less daily physical tension and anxiety (Andresen, 2000; Sears & Kraus, 2009). Brain scans (PET and fMRI) reveal changes in the activity of the frontal lobes during meditation, which suggests that it may be a distinct state of consciousness (Cahn & Polich, 2006; Farb et al., 2007).

Meditation takes two major forms. In **concentrative meditation**, you attend to a single focal point, such as an object, a thought, or your own breathing. In contrast, **mindfulness meditation** is "open," or expansive. In this case, you widen your attention to embrace a total, nonjudgmental awareness of the world (Lazar, 2005). An example is losing all self-consciousness while walking in the wilderness with a quiet and receptive mind. Although it may not seem so, mindfulness meditation is more difficult to attain than concentrative meditation. For this reason, we will discuss concentrative meditation as a practical self-control method.

Performing Concentrative Meditation

How is concentrative meditation done? The basic idea is to sit still and quietly focus on some external object or on a repetitive internal stimulus, such as your own breathing or humming (Blackmore, 2004). As an alternative, you can silently repeat a *mantra* (a word used as the focus of attention in concentrative meditation). Typical mantras are smooth, flowing sounds that are easily repeated. A widely used mantra is the word "om." A mantra could also be any pleasant word or a phrase from a familiar song, poem, or prayer. If other thoughts arise as you repeat a mantra, just return attention to it as often as necessary to maintain meditation.

Meditation A mental exercise for producing relaxation or heightened awareness.

Concentrative meditation Mental exercise based on attending to a single object or thought.

Mindfulness meditation Mental exercise based on widening attention to become aware of everything experienced at any given moment.

The Relaxation Response

Medical researcher Herbert Benson believes that the core of meditation is the **relaxation response**—an innate physiological pattern that opposes your body's fight-or-flight mechanisms. Benson feels, quite simply, that most of us have forgotten how to relax deeply. People in his experiments learned to produce the relaxation response by following these instructions:

> Sit quietly and comfortably. Close your eyes. Relax your muscles, beginning at your feet and progressing up to your head. Relax them deeply. Become aware of breathing through your nose. As you breathe out, say a word like "peace" silently to yourself. Don't worry about how successful you are in relaxing deeply. Just let relaxation happen at its own pace. Don't be surprised by distracting thoughts. When they occur, ignore them and continue repeating "peace." (Adapted from Benson, 1977; Lazar et al., 2000)

As a stress-control technique, meditation may be a good choice for people who find it difficult to "turn off" upsetting thoughts when they need to relax. In one study, a group of college students who received just 90 minutes of training in the relaxation response experienced greatly reduced stress levels (Deckro et al., 2002). The physical benefits of meditation include lowered heart rate, blood pressure, muscle tension, and other signs of stress (Zeidan et al., 2010), as well as improved immune system activity (Davidson et al., 2003).

According to Shauna Shapiro and Roger Walsh (2006), meditation has benefits beyond relaxation. Practiced regularly, meditation may foster mental well-being and positive mental skills such as clarity, concentration, and calm. In this sense, meditation may share much in common with psychotherapy. Indeed, research has shown that mindfulness meditation relieves a variety of psychological disorders, from insomnia to excessive anxiety. It can also reduce aggression and the use of psychoactive drugs (Brewer et al., 2011; Shapiro & Walsh, 2006). Regular meditation may even help people develop better control over their attention, heightened self-awareness, and maturity (Hodgins & Adair, 2010; Travis, Arenander, & DuBois, 2004). For a curious way to meditate, see "Tranquility in a Tank."

Summary

To summarize, research suggests that meditation, including mild sensory deprivation, is a way to elicit the relaxation response. For many people, sitting quietly and "resting" can be as effective. Similar stress reduction occurs when people set aside time daily to engage in other restful activities, such as muscle relaxation, positive daydreaming, and even leisure reading. However, if you are the type of person who finds it difficult to ignore upsetting thoughts, then concentrative meditation might be a good way to promote relaxation. Practiced regularly, meditation and mild sensory isolation may even help improve overall mental health—something almost everyone could use in our fast-paced society.

The Whole Human: Mindfulness and Well-Being

Did you "space out" anytime today? Most of us have occasional moments of reduced awareness. **Mindfulness** is the opposite of such mindless moments: It involves an open, nonjudgmental awareness of current experience. In other words, mindfulness is similar to the state that people who practice mindfulness receptive meditation are trying to achieve. A person who is mindful is fully present, moment by moment (Hölzel et al., 2011). She or he is acutely aware of every thought, emotion, or sensation, but does not judge it or react to it. The person is fully "awake" and attuned to immediate reality, just like Eric that day at the Grand Canyon.

Psychologists interested in positive mental states have begun to study the effects of mindfulness. For example, cancer patients who are taught mindfulness meditation have lower levels of distress and a greater sense of well-being. Similarly, being mindful makes it easier to quit smoking (Brewer et al., 2011). Such benefits apply to healthy people, too. In general, mindfulness is associated with self-knowledge and well-being (Friese, Messner, & Schaffner, 2012; Siegel, 2010). Anyone who has a tendency to sleepwalk through life—and that's most of us at times—would be wise to be mindful of the value of mindfulness.

Relaxation response The pattern of internal bodily changes that occurs at times of relaxation.

Mindfulness A state of open, nonjudgmental awareness of current experience.

Clinical File

Tranquility in a Tank

Imagine floating in a tank of warm water, for a short while, without the least bit of muscle tension (**Figure 5.7**). You cannot hear anything, and it is pitch dark. You are experiencing brief *sensory deprivation*, a major reduction in the amount or variety of sensory stimulation.

What happens when stimulation is greatly reduced? A hint comes from reports by prisoners in solitary confinement, Arctic explorers, high-altitude pilots, long-distance truck drivers, and radar operators. When faced with limited or monotonous stimulation, people sometimes have bizarre sensations, dangerous lapses in attention, and wildly distorted perceptions. Intense or prolonged sensory deprivation is stressful and disorienting.

Yet, oddly enough, brief periods of sensory restriction can produce a strong relaxation response (Bood et al., 2006). An hour or two spent in a flotation tank can cause a large drop in blood pressure, muscle tension, chronic pain, and other signs of stress (Bood et al., 2006; Kjellgren, Buhrkall, & Norlander, 2011).

Like other forms of meditation, mild sensory deprivation may also help with more than relaxation. Deep relaxation makes people more open

to suggestion, and sensory deprivation interrupts habitual behavior patterns. This can "loosen" belief systems, making it easier for people to quit smoking, lose weight, and reduce their use of alcohol and drugs (Suedfeld & Borrie, 1999; van Dierendonck & Te Nijenhuis, 2005).

Mild sensory deprivation even shows promise as a way to stimulate creative thinking and enhance sports and music performance skills (Norlander, Bergman, & Archer, 1998, 1999; Vartanian & Suedfeld, 2011). Clearly, there is much yet to be learned from studying "nothingness."

Figure 5.7 A sensory deprivation chamber. Small flotation tanks like the one pictured have been used by psychologists to study the effects of mild sensory deprivation. Participants float in darkness and silence. The shallow body-temperature water contains hundreds of pounds of Epsom salts, so that participants float near the surface.

Pixtal/SuperStock

---

study break Hypnosis and Meditation

RECITE

1. In Ernest Hilgard's dissociative state theory of hypnosis, awareness is split between normal consciousness and
   - *a.* disinhibition
   - *b.* autosuggestion
   - *c.* memory
   - *d.* the hidden observer

2. Tests of hypnotic susceptibility measure a person's tendency to respond to
   - *a.* suggestion
   - *b.* imagery rehearsal
   - *c.* stimulus control techniques
   - *d.* the activation-synthesis effect

3. Which of the following can most definitely be achieved with hypnosis?
   - *a.* unusual strength
   - *b.* pain relief
   - *c.* improved memory
   - *d.* sleeplike brainwaves

4. The focus of attention in concentrative meditation is "open," or expansive. T or F?
5. The most immediate benefit of meditation appears to be its capacity for producing the relaxation response. T or F?

REFLECT

THINK CRITICALLY

6. What kind of control group would you need in order to identify the true effects of hypnosis?

7. Regular meditators report lower levels of stress and a greater sense of well-being. What other explanations must we eliminate before this effect can be regarded as genuine?

SELF-REFLECT

How have your beliefs about hypnosis changed after reading the preceding section? Can you think of specific examples in which hypnosis was misrepresented? For example, in high school assemblies, stage acts, movies, or television dramas?

Various activities can produce the relaxation response. When do you experience states of deep relaxation, coupled with a sense of serene awareness? What similarities do these occurrences have to meditation?

ANSWERS

1. d 2. a 3. b 4. F 5. T 6. Most experiments on hypnosis include a control group in which people are asked to simulate being hypnotized. Without such controls, the tendency of participants to cooperate with experimenters makes it difficult to identify true hypnotic effects. 7. Studies on the effects of meditation must control for the placebo effect and the fact that those who choose to learn meditation may not be a representative sample of the general population.

Drug-Altered Consciousness—The High and Low of It

JOURNEY QUESTION 5.8 *What are the effects of the more commonly used psychoactive drugs?*

Another common way to alter human consciousness is to administer a **psychoactive drug**—a substance capable of altering attention, judgment, memory, time sense, self-control, emotion, or perception. In fact, most Americans regularly use consciousness-altering drugs (don't forget that caffeine, alcohol, and nicotine are mildly psychoactive). Psychoactive drugs alter consciousness by directly influencing brain activity (Maisto, Galizio, & Connors, 2011; see "How Psychoactive Drugs Affect the Brain"). Many psychoactive drugs can be placed on a scale ranging from stimulation to depression (Figure 5.8). A **stimulant**, or *upper*, is a substance that increases activity in the body and nervous system. A **depressant**, or *downer*, does the reverse.

Because drugs that can ease pain, induce sleep, or end depression have a high potential for abuse, the more powerful psychoactive drugs are controlled substances (Goldberg, 2010). Regardless, almost 23 million Americans use illicit drugs (Substance Abuse and Mental Health Services Administration, 2011). Drug abuse has been one of the most persistent of all social problems in Western nations.

Why is drug abuse so common? People seek drug experiences for many reasons, ranging from curiosity and a desire to belong to a group to a search for meaning or an escape from feelings of inadequacy. Many abusers turn to drugs in a self-defeating attempt to cope with life. All the frequently abused drugs produce immediate feelings of pleasure. The negative consequences follow much later. This combination of immediate pleasure and delayed punishment allows abusers to feel good on demand. In time, of course, most of the pleasure goes out of drug abuse and the abuser's problems get worse. But if an abuser merely feels better (however briefly) after taking a drug, drug taking can become compulsive (Higgins, Heil, & Lussier, 2004).

Adolescents are more likely to use and abuse drugs if they believe that the risks of drug use are low, that drugs are readily available, and that drug use by their peers is okay (Substance Abuse and Mental Health Services Administration, 2011). Additional predictors include parental drug use, delinquency, parental maladjustment, poor self-esteem, social nonconformity, and stressful life changes. One study found that many adolescents who abuse drugs tend to be maladjusted, alienated, impulsive, and emotionally distressed (Masse & Tremblay, 1997). Antisocial behavior, school failure, and risky sexual behavior are also commonly associated with drug abuse (Ary et al., 1999). Such patterns make it clear that taking drugs is a symptom, rather than a cause, of personal and social maladjustment (Hart, Ksir, & Ray, 2009).

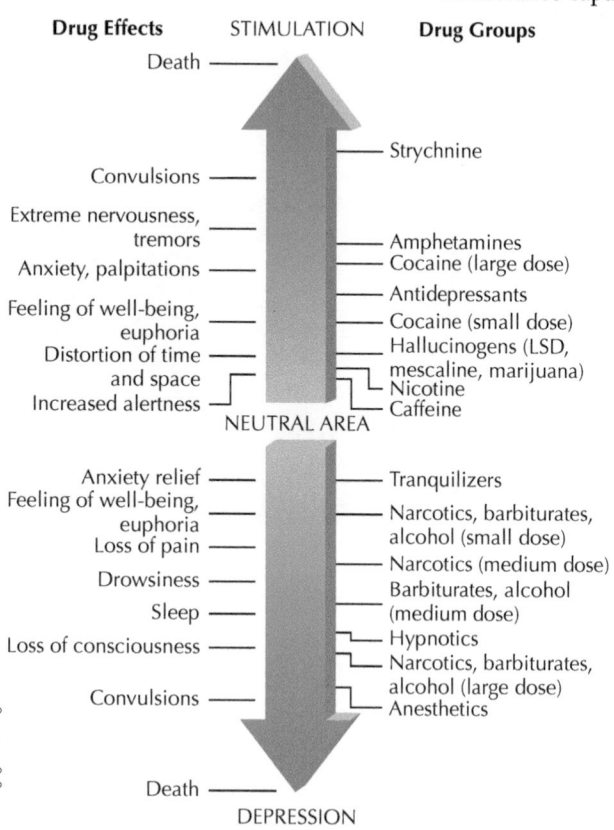

© Cengage Learning

Figure 5.8 Spectrum and continuum of drug action. Many drugs can be rated on a stimulation–depression scale according to their effects on the central nervous system. Although LSD, mescaline, and marijuana are listed here, the stimulation-depression scale is less relevant to these drugs. The principal characteristic of such hallucinogens is their mind-altering quality.

Psychoactive drug A substance capable of altering attention, memory, judgment, time sense, self-control, mood, or perception.

Stimulant (Upper) A substance that increases activity in the body and nervous system.

Depressant (Downer) A substance that decreases activity in the body and nervous system.

Physical dependence (Addiction) Physical addiction, as indicated by the presence of drug tolerance and withdrawal symptoms.

Withdrawal symptoms Physical illness and discomfort following the withdrawal of a drug.

Drug Dependence

Another reason why drug abuse is so common is that taking most psychoactive drugs tends to create dependencies. Once you get started, it can be very hard to stop (Calabria et al., 2010). Drug dependence falls into two broad categories (Maisto, Galizio, & Connors, 2011). When a person compulsively uses a drug to maintain bodily comfort, a **physical dependence** (addiction) exists. Addiction occurs most often with drugs that cause **withdrawal symptoms** (physical illness that follows removal of a drug). Withdrawal from drugs such as alcohol, barbiturates, and opiates can cause violent flu-like symptoms of nausea, vomiting, diarrhea,

Psychoactive drugs influence the activity of brain cells (Kalat, 2013). Typically, drugs imitate or alter the effects of neurotransmitters, the chemicals that carry messages between brain cells. Some drugs, such as Ecstasy, amphetamines, and some antidepressants, cause more neurotransmitters to be released, increasing the activity of brain cells. Other drugs, such as cocaine, slow the removal of neurotransmitters after they are released. This prolongs the action of transmitter chemicals and typically has a stimulating effect. Other drugs, such as nicotine and opiates, directly stimulate brain cells by mimicking neurotransmitters. Another possibility is illustrated by alcohol and tranquilizers. These drugs affect certain types of brain cells that cause relaxation and relieve anxiety. Some drugs fill receptor sites on brain cells and block incoming messages. Other possibilities also exist, which is why drugs can have such a wide variety of effects on the brain (Julien, 2011).

Nearly all addictive drugs stimulate the brain's reward circuitry, producing feelings of pleasure (Freberg, 2010). In particular, addictive drugs stimulate a brain region called the *nucleus* *accumbens* to release the neurotransmitter dopamine, which results in intensified feelings of pleasure (**Figure 5.9**). As one expert put it, addictive drugs fool brain-reward pathways. As a result, the reward pathway signals, "That felt good. Let's do it again. Let's remember exactly how we did it." This creates a compulsion to repeat the drug experience. It's the hook that eventually snares the addict (National Institute on Drug Abuse, 2010b). In the end, the addictive drug physically changes the brain's reward circuitry, making it even harder for the addict to overcome his or her addiction (Henry et al., 2010; Niehaus, Cruz-Bermúdez & Kauer, 2009). Adolescents are especially susceptible to addiction because brain systems that restrain their risk taking are not as mature as those that reward pleasure seeking (Chambers, Taylor, & Potenza, 2003).

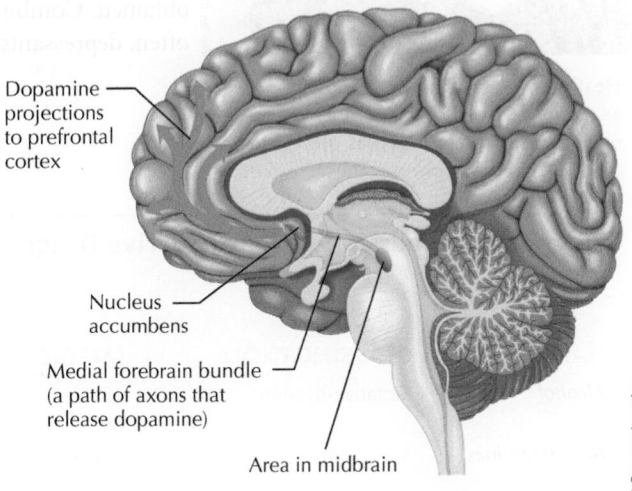

Dopamine projections to prefrontal cortex

Nucleus accumbens

Medial forebrain bundle (a path of axons that release dopamine)

Area in midbrain

© Cengage Learning

Figure 5.9 Addictive drugs increase dopamine activity in the medial forebrain bundle and the nucleus accumbens, stimulating the frontal cortex and giving rise to intensified feelings of pleasure.

chills, sweating, and cramps. Addiction is often accompanied by a **drug tolerance** (reduced response to a drug). This leads users to take larger and larger doses to get the desired effect.

Persons who develop a **psychological dependence** feel that a drug is necessary to maintain their comfort or well-being. Usually, they intensely crave the drug and its rewarding qualities (Winger et al., 2005). Psychological dependence can be just as powerful as physical addiction. That's why some psychologists define addiction as any compulsive habit pattern. By this definition, a person who has lost control over drug use, for whatever reason, is addicted. In fact, most people who answer yes to both of the following questions have an alcohol or drug problem and should seek professional help:

- In the last year, did you ever drink or use drugs more than you meant to?
- Have you felt you wanted or needed to cut down on your drinking or drug use in the last year?

Patterns of Abuse

Some drugs, of course, have a higher potential for abuse than others. Heroin is certainly more dangerous than caffeine. However, this is only one side of the picture. It can be as useful to classify drug-taking *behavior* as it is to rate drugs. For example, some people remain social drinkers for life, whereas others become alcoholics within weeks of taking their first drink (Robinson & Berridge, 2003). In this sense, drug use can be classified as *experimental* (short-term use based on curiosity), *social-recreational* (occasional social use for pleasure or relaxation), *situational* (use to cope with a specific problem, such as needing to stay awake), *intensive* (daily use with elements of dependence), or *compulsive* (intense use and extreme dependence). The last three categories of drug taking tend to be damaging no matter what drug is used.

Drug tolerance A reduction in the body's response to a drug.

Psychological dependence Drug dependence that is based primarily on emotional or psychological needs.

Polydrug Abuse

There is one more pattern of drug abuse that bears mentioning: the abuse of more than one drug at the same time. According to the Florida Medical Examiners Commission (2010), polydrug abuse accounts for the "vast majority" of deaths due to drug overdose. When mixed, the effects of different drugs can be multiplied by **drug interactions**—one drug enhances the effect of another—that are responsible for thousands of fatal drug overdoses every year (Goldberg, 2010). This is true whether the mixed drugs were legally or illegally obtained. Combining barbiturates or tranquilizers with alcohol is especially risky. All too often, depressants are gulped down with alcohol or added to a spiked punch bowl.

Heath Ledger's Oscar-winning performance as the Joker in one of the *Batman* films was one of his last. His career was one of many to be cut short by polydrug abuse.

Table 5.3 Comparison of Psychoactive Drugs

NAME	CLASSIFICATION	MEDICAL USE	USUAL DOSE	DURATION OF EFFECT
Alcohol	Sedative-hypnotic	Solvent, antiseptic, sedative	Varies	1–4 hours
Amphetamines	Stimulant	Relief of mild depression, control of narcolepsy and hyperactivity	2.5–5 milligrams	4 hours
Barbiturates	Sedative-hypnotic	Sedation, relief of high blood pressure, anticonvulsant, antianxiety	50–100 milligrams	1–16 hours
Benzodiazepines	Anxiolytic (antianxiety drug)	Tranquilizer	2–100 milligrams	10 minutes–8 hours
Caffeine	Stimulant	Counteract depressant drugs, treatment of migraine headaches	Varies	Varies
Cocaine	Stimulant, local anesthetic	Local anesthesia	Varies	Varied, 1–4 hours
Codeine	Narcotic	Ease pain and coughing	30 milligrams	3–6 hours
GHB	Sedative-hypnotic	Experimental treatment of narcolepsy, alcoholism	1–3 grams (powder)	1–3 hours
Heroin	Narcotic	Pain relief	Varies	3–6 hours
LSD	Hallucinogen	Experimental study of mental function, alcoholism	100–500 milligrams	8–12 hours
Marijuana (THC)	Relaxant, euphoriant; in high doses, hallucinogen	Treatment of glaucoma and side effects of chemotherapy	1–2 cigarettes	2–4 hours
MDMA	Stimulant/hallucinogen	None	125 milligrams	4–6 hours
Mescaline	Hallucinogen	None	350 micrograms	8–12 hours
Methadone	Narcotic	Pain relief	10 milligrams	12–24 hours
Morphine	Narcotic	Pain relief	15 milligrams	3–6 hours
PCP	Anesthetic	None	2–10 milligrams	4–6 hours, plus 12-hour recovery
Psilocybin	Hallucinogen	None	25 milligrams	Varies
Tobacco (nicotine)	Stimulant	Emetic (nicotine)	Varies	Varies

Question marks indicate conflict of opinion. It should be noted that illicit drugs are frequently adulterated and thus pose unknown hazards to the user. © Cengage Learning

Drugs of Abuse

Many, if not all, of the drugs discussed in this section have legitimate uses (Hart, Ksir, & Ray, 2009). Some have been used for centuries in various cultures, in search of insight. Others were developed specifically to treat various mental illnesses. Still others have a variety of health benefits. The key to healthy drug use is moderation and it is truly unfortunate that it is so very hard to keep "the monkey off your back." That is why so many people make a special effort to never get started.

Be that as it may, Table 5.3 reveals that the drugs most likely to lead to physical dependence are alcohol, amphetamines, barbiturates, cocaine, codeine, heroin, methadone, morphine, and tobacco (nicotine). Using *any* of the drugs listed in Table 5.3 can result in

Drug interaction A combined effect of two drugs that exceeds the addition of one drug's effects to the other.

EFFECTS SOUGHT	LONG-TERM SYMPTOMS	PHYSICAL DEPENDENCE POTENTIAL	PSYCHOLOGICAL DEPENDENCE POTENTIAL	ORGANIC DAMAGE POTENTIAL
Sense alteration, anxiety reduction, sociability	Cirrhosis, toxic psychosis, neurologic damage, addiction	Yes	Yes	Yes
Alertness, activeness, relieve fatigue	Loss of appetite, delusions, hallucinations, toxic psychosis	Yes	Yes	Yes
Anxiety reduction, euphoria	Addiction with severe withdrawal symptoms, possible convulsions, toxic psychosis	Yes	Yes	Yes
Anxiety relief	Irritability, confusion, depression, sleep disorders	Yes	Yes	No, but can affect fetus
Wakefulness, alertness	Insomnia, heart arrhythmias, high blood pressure	No?	Yes	Yes
Excitation, talkativeness	Depression, convulsions	Yes	Yes	Yes
Euphoria, prevent withdrawal discomfort	Addiction, constipation, loss of appetite	Yes	Yes	No
Intoxication, euphoria, relaxation	Anxiety, confusion, insomnia, hallucinations, seizures	Yes	Yes	No?
Euphoria, prevent withdrawal discomfort	Addiction, constipation, loss of appetite	Yes	Yes	No*
Insightful experiences, exhilaration, distortion of senses	May intensify existing psychosis, panic reactions	No	No?	No?
Relaxation; increased euphoria, perceptions, sociability	Possible lung cancer, other health risks	Yes	Yes	Yes?
Excitation, euphoria	Personality change, hyperthermia, liver damage	No	Yes	Yes
Insightful experiences, exhilaration, distortion of senses	May intensify existing psychosis, panic reactions	No	No?	No?
Prevent withdrawal discomfort	Addiction, constipation, loss of appetite	Yes	Yes	No
Euphoria, prevent withdrawal discomfort	Addiction, constipation, loss of appetite	Yes	Yes	No*
Euphoria	Unpredictable behavior, suspicion, hostility, psychosis	Debated	Yes	Yes
Insightful experiences, exhilaration, distortion of senses	May intensify existing psychosis, panic reactions	No	No?	No?
Alertness, calmness, sociability	Emphysema, lung cancer, mouth and throat cancer, cardiovascular damage, loss of appetite	Yes	Yes	Yes

*Persons who inject drugs under nonsterile conditions run a high risk of contracting AIDS, hepatitis, abscesses, or circulatory disorders.

psychological dependence. Note also that people who take drugs intravenously are at high risk for developing hepatitis and AIDS (see Chapter 11). The discussion that follows focuses on the drugs most often abused by students.

Uppers—Amphetamines, Cocaine, MDMA, Caffeine, Nicotine

Let's begin with *uppers*, including amphetamines, cocaine, MDMA, caffeine, and nicotine.

Amphetamines

Amphetamines are synthetic stimulants. Some common street names for amphetamine are "speed," "bennies," "dexies," "amp," and "uppers." These drugs were once widely prescribed for weight loss or depression. Today, the main legitimate medical use of amphetamines is to treat childhood hyperactivity and overdoses of depressant drugs. Illicit use of amphetamines is widespread, however, especially by people seeking to stay awake and by those who rationalize that such drugs can improve mental or physical performance (DeSantis & Hane, 2010; Iversen, 2006).

Adderall and Ritalin, two popular "study drugs," are both mixes of amphetamines used to treat **attention deficit/hyperactivity disorder (ADHD)**. People with ADHD have difficulty controlling their attention and are prone to displaying hyperactive and impulsive behavior (American Psychiatric Association, 2012). Increasing numbers of normal college students are illegally taking these drugs in the hopes they will also be able to focus better while doing school work (McCabe et al., 2005).

Is it true that those drugs actually can help students study? Taking "study drugs" may produce slight improvements in problem-solving performance (Elliott et al., 1997); however, this may be offset by a slight loss of creativity (Farah et al., 2009). Most importantly, the side effects of all amphetamines are worrisome, as we will see shortly.

Methamphetamine is a more potent variation of amphetamine. It can be snorted, injected, or eaten. Of the various types of amphetamine, methamphetamine has created the largest drug problem. "Bergs," "glass," "meth," "crank," or "crystal," as it is known on the street, can be made cheaply in backyard labs and sold for massive profits. In addition to ruining lives through addiction, it has fueled a violent criminal subculture.

Amphetamines rapidly produce a drug tolerance. Most abusers end up taking ever-larger doses to get the desired effect. Eventually, some users switch to injecting methamphetamine directly into the bloodstream. True speed freaks typically go on binges lasting several days, after which they "crash" from lack of sleep and food.

Abuse

How dangerous are amphetamines? Large doses can cause nausea, vomiting, extremely high blood pressure, fatal heart attacks, and disabling strokes. It is important to realize that amphetamines speed up the use of the body's resources; they do not magically supply energy. After an amphetamine binge, people suffer from crippling fatigue, depression, confusion, uncontrolled irritability, and aggression. Repeated amphetamine use damages the brain. Amphetamines can also cause *amphetamine psychosis*, a loss of contact with reality. Affected users have paranoid delusions that someone is out to get them. Acting on these delusions, they may become violent, resulting in suicide, self-injury, or injury to others (Iversen, 2006).

A potent smokable form of crystal methamphetamine has added to the risks of stimulant abuse. This drug, known as "ice" on the street, is highly addictive. Like "crack," the smokable form of cocaine, it produces an intense high. But also like crack (discussed in a moment), crystal methamphetamine very rapidly leads to compulsive abuse and severe drug dependence.

Attention deficit/hyperactivity disorder (ADHD) A behavioral problem characterized by short attention span, restless movement, and impaired learning capacity.

Cocaine

Cocaine ("coke," "snow," "blow," "snuff," "flake") is a powerful central nervous system stimulant extracted from the leaves of the coca plant. Cocaine produces feelings of alertness, euphoria, well-being, power, boundless energy, and pleasure (Julien, 2011). At the turn of the 20th century, dozens of nonprescription potions and cure-alls contained cocaine. It was during this time that Coca-Cola was indeed the "real thing." From 1886 until 1906, when the U.S. Pure Food and Drug Act was passed, Coca-Cola contained cocaine (which has since been replaced with caffeine).

How does cocaine differ from amphetamines? The two are very much alike in their effects on the central nervous system. The main difference is that amphetamine effects typically lasts longer than those of cocaine, which is more quickly metabolized.

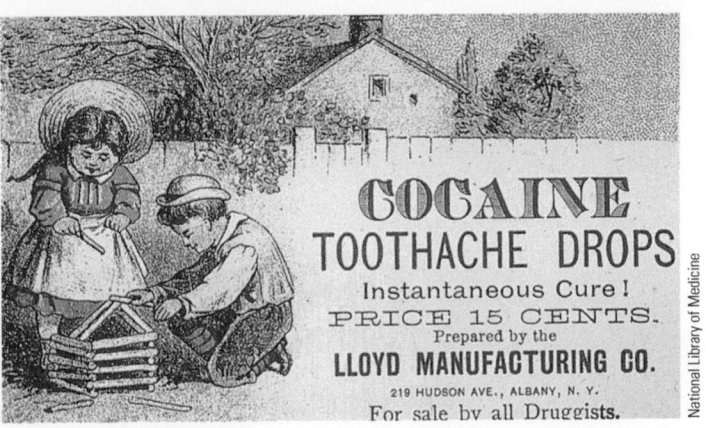

Cocaine was the main ingredient in many nonprescription elixirs before the turn of the 20th century. Today cocaine is recognized as a powerful and dangerous drug. Its high potential for abuse has damaged the lives of countless users.

Abuse

How dangerous is cocaine? Cocaine's capacity for abuse and social damage rivals that of heroin. Rats and monkeys given free access to cocaine find it irresistible. Many, in fact, end up dying of convulsions from self-administered overdoses of the drug. Even casual or first-time users risk having convulsions, a heart attack, or a stroke (Lacayo, 1995). Cocaine increases the chemical messengers dopamine (DOPE-ah-meen) and noradrenaline (nor-ah-DREN-ah-lin). Noradrenaline arouses the brain, and dopamine produces a "rush" of pleasure. This combination is so powerfully rewarding that cocaine users run a high risk of becoming compulsive abusers (Ridenour et al., 2005).

A person who stops using cocaine does not experience heroin-like withdrawal symptoms. Instead, the brain adapts to cocaine abuse in ways that upset its chemical balance, causing depression when cocaine is withdrawn. First, there is a jarring "crash" of mood and energy. Within a few days, the person enters a long period of fatigue, anxiety, paranoia, boredom, and **anhedonia** (an-he-DAWN-ee-ah), an inability to feel pleasure. Before long, the urge to use cocaine becomes intense. So, although cocaine does not fit the classic pattern of addiction, it is ripe for compulsive abuse. Even a person who gets through withdrawal may crave cocaine months or years later (Washton & Zweben, 2009). If cocaine were cheaper, 9 out of 10 users would progress to compulsive abuse. In fact, rock cocaine ("crack," "rock," or "*roca*"), which is cheaper, produces very high abuse rates.

Anyone who thinks she or he has a cocaine problem should seek advice at a drug clinic or a Cocaine Anonymous meeting. Although quitting cocaine is extremely difficult, three out of four abusers who remain in treatment do succeed in breaking their coke dependence (Simpson et al., 1999; Sinha et al., 2006). There is also hope on the horizon in the form of a vaccine currently undergoing clinical trials that prevents cocaine from stimulating the nervous system (Kampman, 2005).

MDMA ("Ecstasy")

The drug *MDMA* (methylenedioxymethamphetamine, or "Ecstasy") is also chemically similar to amphetamine. In addition to producing a rush of energy, users say it makes them feel closer to others and heightens sensory experiences. Ecstasy causes brain cells to release extra amounts of serotonin as well as prolonging its effects. The physical effects of MDMA include dilated pupils, elevated blood pressure, jaw clenching, loss of appetite, and elevated body temperature (National Institute on Drug Abuse, 2010a). Although some users believe that Ecstasy increases sexual pleasure, it *diminishes* sexual performance, impairing erection in 40 percent of men and retarding orgasm in both men and women (Zemishlany, Aizenberg, & Weizman, 2001).

Anhedonia An inability to feel pleasure.

Abuse

Ecstasy use in North America has declined slightly from a peak around 2002, perhaps because of widespread negative publicity. Regardless, in 2010, almost 700,000 Americans tried Ecstasy for the first time (Substance Abuse and Mental Health Services Administration, 2011). Every year, emergency room doctors see many MDMA cases, including MDMA-related deaths. Some of these incidents are caused by elevated body temperature (hyperthermia) or heart arrhythmias, which can lead to collapse. Ecstasy users at "rave" parties try to prevent overheating by drinking water to cool themselves. This may help to a small degree, but the risk of fatal heat exhaustion is real.

MDMA can also cause severe liver damage, which can be fatal (National Institute on Drug Abuse, 2010a). In addition, Ecstasy users are more likely to abuse alcohol and other drugs, to neglect studying, to party excessively, and to engage in risky sex (Strote, Lee, & Wechsler, 2002). Ironically, Ecstasy use at "rave" parties actually does intensify the impact of the music. We say ironically because the end result is often overstimulation of the brain, which can result in a "rebound" depression (Iannone et al., 2006).

Enough time has passed to assess the long-term effects of Ecstasy use. Feelings of anxiety or depression can persist for months after a person stops taking Ecstasy. In addition, heavy users typically do not perform well in tests of learning and memory and show some signs of underlying brain damage (National Institute on Drug Abuse, 2010a; Quednow et al., 2006). Fortunately, however, the long-term consequences are not as severe as once feared (Advisory Council on the Misuse of Drugs, 2009).

Caffeine

Caffeine is the most frequently used psychoactive drug in North America. (And that's not counting Seattle!) Many people have a hard time starting a day (or writing another paragraph) without a cup, since caffeine suppresses drowsiness and increases alertness (Wesensten et al., 2002), especially when combined with sugar (Adan & Serra-Grabulosa, 2010). Physically, caffeine causes sweating, talkativeness, tinnitus (ringing in the ears), and hand tremors (Nehlig, 2004). Caffeine stimulates the brain by blocking chemicals that normally inhibit or slow nerve activity (Maisto, Galizio, & Connors, 2011). Its effects become apparent with doses as small as 50 milligrams, the amount found in about one-half cup of brewed coffee.

How much caffeine did you consume today? It is common to think of coffee as the major source of caffeine, but there are many others. Caffeine is found in tea, many soft drinks (especially colas), chocolate, and cocoa. Thousands of nonprescription drugs also contain caffeine, including stay-awake pills, cold remedies, and many name-brand aspirin products.

Abuse

Are there any serious drawbacks to using caffeine? Overuse of caffeine may result in an unhealthy dependence known as **caffeinism**. Insomnia, irritability, loss of appetite, chills, racing heart, and elevated body temperature are all signs of caffeinism. Many people with these symptoms drink 15 or 20 cups of coffee a day. However, even as few as 2.5 cups of coffee a day (or the equivalent) can intensify anxiety and other psychological problems (Hogan, Hornick, & Bouchoux, 2002). People who consume even such modest amounts may experience anxiety, depression, fatigue, headaches, and flu-like symptoms during withdrawal (Juliano & Griffiths, 2004).

Caffeine poses a variety of other health risks. Caffeine encourages the growth of breast cysts in women, and it may contribute to bladder cancer, heart problems, and high blood pressure. Pregnant women who consume as little as two cups of coffee a day increase the risk of having a miscarriage (Cnattingius et al., 2000). It is wise to remember that caffeine *is* a drug and to use it in moderation.

Caffeinism Excessive consumption of caffeine, leading to dependence and a variety of physical and psychological complaints.

Nicotine

Next to caffeine and alcohol, *nicotine* is the most widely used psychoactive drug (Julien, 2011). A natural stimulant found mainly in tobacco, nicotine is so toxic that it is sometimes used to kill insects! In large doses it causes stomach pain, vomiting and diarrhea, cold sweats, dizziness, confusion, and muscle tremors. In very large doses, nicotine may cause convulsions, respiratory failure, and death. For a nonsmoker, 50 to 75 milligrams of nicotine taken in a single dose could be lethal. (Chain-smoking a pack of cigarettes can produce this dosage.) Most first-time smokers get sick on one or two cigarettes. In contrast, regular smokers build a tolerance for nicotine. A heavy smoker may inhale several packs a day without feeling ill.

Abuse

How addictive is nicotine? A vast array of evidence confirms that nicotine is very addictive (Dani & Balfour, 2011; Spinella, 2005). Most smokers begin when they are teenagers, which is unfortunate because young people are even more vulnerable to addiction than are adults (Baker, Brandon, & Chassin, 2004). Although 35 million Americans each year want to quit smoking, more than 85 percent of them relapse, many within a week (National Institute on Drug Abuse, 2009). As humorist Mark Twain once whimsically lamented, "Giving up smoking is the easiest thing in the world. I know because I've done it thousands of times."

This should come as no surprise since withdrawal from nicotine causes headaches, sweating, cramps, insomnia, digestive upset, irritability, and a sharp craving for cigarettes. These symptoms may last from 2 to 6 weeks and may even be worse than heroin withdrawal. Just a few puffs will make that all go away until the next time the smoker works up the courage to quit.

Impact on Health

How serious are the health risks of smoking? Smoking is the leading cause of preventable deaths worldwide. Every year 6 million people around the globe, including almost 450,000 Americans, die from tobacco use (National Center for Chronic Disease Prevention and Health Promotion, 2011; World Health Organization, 2011). Tens of millions more live diminished lives because they smoke.

A burning cigarette releases a large variety of potent *carcinogens* (car-SIN-oh-jins: cancer-causing substances). Smoking causes widespread damage to the body, leading to an increased risk of many cancers (such as lung cancer), cardiovascular diseases (such as stroke), respiratory diseases (such as chronic bronchitis), and reproductive disorders (such as decreased fertility). Together, these health risks combine to reduce the life expectancy of the average smoker by 10 to 15 years.

By the way, urban cowboys and Skoal bandits, the same applies to chewing tobacco and snuff. A 30-minute exposure to one pinch of smokeless tobacco is equivalent to smoking three or four cigarettes. Along with all the health risks of smoking, users of smokeless tobacco also run a higher risk of developing oral cancer (Centers for Disease Control, 2012a).

Smokers don't just risk their own health; they also endanger those who live and work nearby. Secondary smoke causes about 3,500 lung cancer deaths and as many as 70,000 heart disease deaths each year in the United States alone. It is particularly irresponsible of smokers to expose young children, who are especially vulnerable, to secondhand smoke (American Lung Association, 2012).

Quitting Smoking

If it is so hard to quit, how do some people manage to succeed? Whatever approach is taken, quitting smoking is not easy. It is especially difficult to try quitting alone, without any support.

"Not for me thanks, mate - I'm only a passive smoker."

Clive Goddard/www.CartoonStock.com

AP Photo/The News Tribune, Dean J. Koepfler

E-cigarettes are electrical devices that look and feel like cigarettes as they vaporize a smokeless mist that can mimic tobacco smoke. When they deliver no nicotine, or a reduced dose, they may help people quitting smoking by allowing the smoker to enjoy the ritual of smoking while withdrawing from nicotine. However, when they are used as a smokeless way to deliver the usual dose, they become just another delivery device that must be medically regulated (Cobb & Abrams, 2011).

Many people find that using nicotine patches or gum and/or other medications, such as *bupropion*, helps them suppress their cravings during the withdrawal period (Bolt et al., 2012). The best chance of success comes when the smoker combines the desire to quit with both medication and some sort of counseling (Centers for Disease Control, 2011b).

Some smokers try to quit cold turkey, whereas others try to taper down gradually. Although going cold turkey has its advocates, gradually quitting works better for more people. Going cold turkey makes quitting an all-or-nothing proposition. Smokers who smoke even one cigarette after "quitting forever" tend to feel they've failed. Many figure they might just as well resume smoking. Those who quit gradually accept that success may take many attempts, spread over several months. Either way, you will have a better chance of success if you decide to quit *now* rather than at some time in the future and don't delay your quit date too often (Hughes & Callas, 2011).

The best way to taper off is *scheduled gradual reduction* (Riley et al., 2002). There are many ways in which smoking can be gradually reduced. For example, the smoker can (1) delay having a first cigarette in the morning and then try to delay a little longer each day; (2) gradually reduce the total number of cigarettes smoked each day; or (3) quit completely, but for just 1 week, then quit again, a week at a time, for as many times as necessary to make it stick. Deliberately scheduling and then gradually stretching the length of time between cigarettes is a key part of this program. Scheduled smoking apparently helps people learn to cope with the urge to smoke.

It is also worth noting that smoking is more than a nicotine delivery system for most smokers. The entire ritual of smoking is itself a positive experience. Just holding a cigarette, dangling it between the lips, or even seeing a favorite smoking chair, can give a smoker pleasure. For this reason, behavioral self-management techniques can be very useful for breaking habits such as smoking (see Chapters 6 and 11). In recent years, *e-cigarettes* have become popular as a way to simulate smoking either with or without delivering any nicotine.

Anyone trying to quit should be prepared to make several attempts before succeeding. But the good news is that tens of millions of people have quit.

Downers—Narcotics, Sedatives, Tranquilizers, and Alcohol

While narcotics, like *heroin* and *morphine*, may be more powerful, both as drugs of abuse and as painkillers, the most widely used downers, or depressant drugs, are alcohol, barbiturates, GHB, and benzodiazepine (ben-zoe-die-AZ-eh-peen) tranquilizers. These drugs are much alike in their effects. In fact, barbiturates and tranquilizers are sometimes referred to as "solid alcohol." Let's examine the properties of each.

Narcotics

Opium poppies have been cultivated throughout recorded history (Dikotter, Laamann, & Xun, 2008). Raw opium, secreted by poppy seedpods, has been used for centuries to produce pain relief. Two narcotics refined from opium, morphine and codeine, are still widely used for that purpose. That narcotics are highly addictive has also long been recognized; *heroin* ("big H," "dope," "horse"), derived by further refining morphine, is widely thought to be the most addictive drug of all.

Narcotics can produce a powerful feeling of euphoria ("rush") accompanied by a reduction of anxiety, relaxation, and, of course, pain relief. At higher doses, breathing can be impaired, leading to death. A new wave of narcotics addiction, notable for the number of younger abusers involved, has followed the more recent introduction of oxycodone (Oxycontin), another opium derivative (Substance Abuse and Mental Health Services Administration, 2011).

Another narcotic, *methadone*, also bears mentioning. Narcotics addicts are often treated with methadone, which reduces the narcotics "rush," making it much easier to go through withdrawal. Methadone is often freely given to addicts as part of a *harm reduction strategy* meant to reduce the negative consequences of addiction without requiring drug abstinence (Tober & Strang, 2003). Harm reduction programs are controversial because it can seem as if they merely support substance abusers in their addiction (supplying clean needles for drug injections is another example); in reality, they are often the only hope for addicts who would otherwise cause more harm to themselves and to others (Centre for Addiction and Mental Health, 2011).

Barbiturates

Barbiturates are sedative drugs that depress brain activity. Common barbiturates include amobarbital, pentobarbital, secobarbital, and tuinal. On the street they are known as "downers," "blue devils," "yellow jackets," "lows," "goof balls," "reds," "pink ladies," "rainbows," or "tooies." Medically, barbiturates are used to calm patients or to induce sleep.

Abuse

At mild dosages, barbiturates have an effect similar to alcohol intoxication. Higher dosages can cause severe mental confusion or even hallucinations. Barbiturates are often taken in excess amounts because a first dose may be followed by others, as the user becomes uninhibited or forgetful. Overdoses first cause a loss of consciousness. Then they severely depress brain centers that control heartbeat and breathing. The result is often death (Grilly & Salamone, 2012).

GHB

Would you swallow a mixture of degreasing solvent and drain cleaner to get high? Apparently, a lot of people would. A mini-epidemic of GHB (gamma-hydroxybutyrate) use has taken place in recent years, especially at nightclubs and raves. GHB ("goop," "scoop," "max," "Georgia Home Boy") is a central nervous system depressant that relaxes and sedates the body. Users describe its effects as similar to those of alcohol. Mild GHB intoxication tends to produce euphoria, a desire to socialize, and a mild loss of inhibitions. GHB's intoxicating effects typically last a few hours, depending on the dosage.

Abuse

At lower dosages, GHB can relieve anxiety and produce relaxation. However, as the dose increases, its sedative effects may result in nausea, a loss of muscle control, and either sleep or a loss of consciousness. Potentially fatal doses of GHB are only three times the amount typically taken by users. This narrow margin of safety has led to numerous overdoses, especially when GHB was combined with alcohol. An overdose causes coma, breathing failure, and death. GHB also inhibits the gag reflex, so some users choke to death on their own vomit.

In 2000, the U.S. government classified GHB as a controlled substance, making possession a felony. Evidence increasingly suggests that GHB is addictive and a serious danger to users. Two out of three frequent users have lost consciousness after taking GHB. Chronic use leads to brain damage (Pedraza, García, & Navarro, 2009). Heavy users who stop taking GHB have withdrawal symptoms that include anxiety, agitation, tremor, delirium, and hallucinations (Miotto et al., 2001).

As if the preceding weren't reason enough to be leery of GHB, here's one more to consider: GHB is often manufactured in homes with recipes and ingredients purchased on the Internet. As mentioned earlier, it can be produced by combining degreasing solvent with drain cleaner (Falkowski, 2000). If you want to degrease your brain, GHB will do the trick.

Tranquilizers

Tranquilizers lower anxiety and reduce tension. Doctors prescribe benzodiazepine tranquilizers to alleviate nervousness and stress. Valium is the best-known drug in this family; others are Xanax, Halcion, and Librium. Even at normal dosages these drugs can cause drowsiness, shakiness, and confusion. When used at too high a dosage or for too long, benzodiazepines are addictive (McKim, 2007).

Abuse

Repeated use of barbiturates can cause physical dependence. Some abusers suffer severe emotional depression that may end in suicide. Similarly, when tranquilizers are used at too high a dosage or for too long, addiction can occur. Many people have learned the hard way that their legally prescribed tranquilizers are as dangerous as many illicit drugs (Goldberg, 2010).

Alcohol

Alcohol is the common name for ethyl alcohol, the intoxicating element in fermented and distilled liquors. Contrary to popular belief, alcohol is not a stimulant. The noisy animation at drinking parties is due to alcohol's effect as a *depressant*. Small amounts of alcohol reduce inhibitions and produce feelings of relaxation and euphoria. Larger amounts cause greater impairment of the brain until the drinker loses consciousness. Alcohol is also not an aphrodisiac. Rather than enhancing sexual arousal, it usually impairs performance, especially in males. As William Shakespeare observed long ago, drink "provokes the desire, but it takes away the performance."

Some people become relaxed and friendly when they are drunk. Others become aggressive and want to argue or fight. How can the same drug have such different effects? Some people drink for pleasure while others drink to cope with negative emotions, such as anxiety and depression. That's why alcohol abuse increases with the level of stress in people's lives. People who drink to relieve bad feelings are at great risk of becoming alcoholics (Kenneth, Carpenter, & Hasin, 1998).

Also, when a person is drunk, thinking and perception become dulled or shortsighted, a condition that has been called *alcohol myopia* (my-OH-pea-ah) (Giancola et al., 2010). Only the most obvious and immediate stimuli catch a drinker's attention. Worries and "second thoughts" that would normally restrain behavior are banished from the drinker's mind. That's why many behaviors become more extreme when a person is drunk. On college campuses, drunken students tend to have accidents, get into fights, sexually assault others, or engage in risky sex. They also destroy property and disrupt the lives of students who are trying to sleep or study (Brower, 2002).

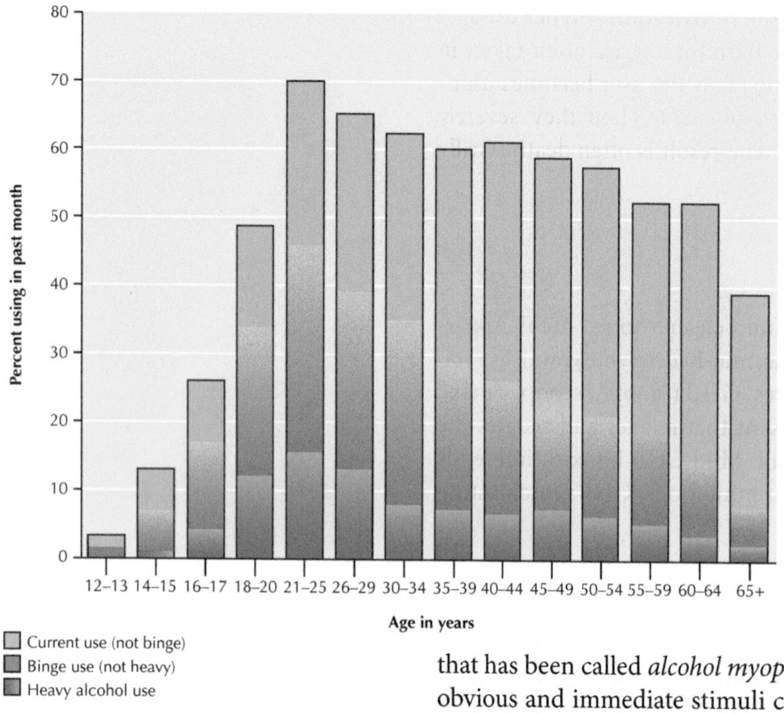

Figure 5.10 Many Americans of all ages abuse alcohol. According to this 2010 survey, about 40 percent of young adults aged 18–29 admitted to heavy alcohol use or binge drinking in the month before the survey was administered (Substance Abuse and Mental Health Services Administration, 2011). © Cengage Learning

Tranquilizer A drug that lowers anxiety and reduces tension.

Binge drinking Consuming five or more drinks in a short time (four for women).

Abuse

Alcohol, the world's favorite depressant, breeds our biggest drug problem. More than 20 million people in the United States and Canada have serious drinking problems. One American dies every 20 minutes in an alcohol-related car crash. Significant percentages of Americans of all ages abuse alcohol (**Figure 5.10**).

It is especially worrisome to see binge drinking among adolescents and young adults. **Binge drinking** is defined as downing five or more drinks (four drinks for women) in a short time. Apparently, many students think it's entertaining to get completely wasted and throw up on their friends. However, binge drinking is a serious sign of alcohol abuse

(Beseler, Taylor, & Leeman, 2010). It is responsible for 1,800 college student deaths each year and thousands of trips to the emergency room (Mitka, 2009).

Binge drinking is of special concern because the brain continues to develop into the early twenties. Research has shown that teenagers and young adults who drink too much may lose as much as 10 percent of their brain power—especially their memory capacity (Brown et al., 2000). Such losses can have a long-term impact on a person's chances for success in life. In short, getting drunk is a slow but sure way to get stupid (Wechsler & Wuethrich, 2002).

At Risk

Children of alcoholics and those who have other relatives who abuse alcohol are at greater risk for becoming alcohol abusers themselves. The increased risk appears to be partly genetic. It is based on the fact that some people have stronger cravings for alcohol after they drink (Hutchison et al., 2002). Women also face some special risks. For one thing, alcohol is absorbed faster and metabolized more slowly by women's bodies. As a result, women get intoxicated from less alcohol than men do. Women who drink are also more prone to liver disease, osteoporosis, and depression. Each extra drink per day adds 7 percent to a woman's risk of breast cancer (Aronson, 2003).

Recognizing Problem Drinking

What are the signs of alcohol abuse? Because alcohol abuse is such a common problem, it is important to recognize the danger signals. If you can answer yes to even one of the following questions, you may have a problem with drinking (adapted from the College Alcohol Problems Scale, revised; Maddock et al., 2001):

Binge drinking and alcohol abuse have become serious problems among college students (Tewksbury, Higgins, & Mustaine, 2008).

As a result of drinking alcoholic beverages I. . . .

1. engaged in unplanned sexual activity.

2. drove under the influence.

3. did not use protection when engaging in sex.

4. engaged in illegal activities associated with drug use.

5. felt sad, blue, or depressed.

6. was nervous or irritable.

7. felt bad about myself.

8. had problems with appetite or sleeping.

Moderated Drinking

Almost everyone has been to a party spoiled by someone who drank too much too fast. Those who avoid overdrinking have a better time, and so do their friends. But how do you avoid drinking too much? After all, as one wit once observed, "The conscience dissolves in alcohol." It takes skill to regulate drinking in social situations, where the temptation to drink can be strong. If you choose to drink, here are some guidelines that may be helpful (adapted from Miller & Munoz, 2005; National Institute on Alcohol Abuse and Alcoholism, 2008):

Paced Drinking

1. Think about your drinking beforehand, plan how you will manage it, and keep track of how much you drink.

2. Drink slowly (no more than one drink an hour), eat while drinking or drink on a full stomach, and make every other drink (or more) a nonalcoholic beverage.

3. Limit drinking primarily to the first hour of a social event or party.

4. Practice how you will politely but firmly refuse drinks.

5. Learn how to relax, meet people, and socialize without relying on alcohol.

And remember, research has shown that you are likely to overestimate how much your fellow students are drinking (Maddock & Glanz, 2005). So don't let yourself be lured into overdrinking just because you have the (probably false) impression that other students are drinking more than you. Limiting your own drinking may help others as well. When people are tempted to drink too much, their main reason for stopping is that "other people were quitting and deciding they'd had enough" (Johnson, 2002).

Treatment

Treatment for alcohol dependence begins with sobering up the person and cutting off the supply. This phase is referred to as **detoxification** (literally, "to remove poison"). It frequently produces all the symptoms of drug withdrawal and can be extremely unpleasant. The next step is to try to restore the person's health. Heavy abuse of alcohol usually causes severe damage to body organs and the nervous system. After alcoholics have "dried out" and some degree of health has been restored, they may be treated with tranquilizers, antidepressants, or psychotherapy. Unfortunately, the success of these procedures has been limited.

One mutual-help approach that has been fairly successful is Alcoholics Anonymous (AA). AA takes a spiritual approach while acting on the premise that it takes a former alcoholic to understand and help a current alcoholic. Participants at AA meetings admit that they have a problem, share feelings, and resolve to stay "dry" one day at a time. Other group members provide support for those struggling to end dependency (Vaillant, 2005). (Other "12-step" programs, such as Cocaine Anonymous and Narcotics Anonymous, use the same approach.)

Other groups offer a rational, nonspiritual approach to alcohol abuse that better fits the needs of some people. Examples include Rational Recovery and Secular Organizations for Sobriety (SOS). Other alternatives to AA include medical treatment, group therapy, mindfulness meditation, and individual psychotherapy (Buddie, 2004; Jacobs-Stewart, 2010). There is a strong tendency for abusive drinkers to deny they have a problem. The sooner they seek help, the better.

Hallucinogens—Tripping the Light Fantastic

Marijuana is the most popular illicit drug in America (Substance Abuse and Mental Health Services Administration, 2011). The main active chemical in marijuana is tetrahydrocannabinol (tet-rah-hydro-cah-NAB-ih-nol), or THC for short. THC is a mild **hallucinogen** (hal-LU-sin-oh-jin: a substance that alters sensory impressions). Other hallucinogenic drugs include LSD and PCP.

LSD and PCP

The drug LSD (lysergic acid diethylamide, or "acid") is perhaps the best-known hallucinogen. Even when taken in tiny amounts, LSD can produce hallucinations and psychotic-like disturbances in thinking and perception. Two other common hallucinogens are mescaline (peyote) and psilocybin ("magic mushrooms," or "shrooms"). Incidentally, the drug PCP (phencyclidine, or "angel dust") can have hallucinogenic effects. However, PCP, which is an anesthetic, also has stimulant and depressant effects. This potent combination can cause extreme agitation, disorientation, violence—and too often, tragedy. Like other psychoactive drugs, all of the hallucinogens, including marijuana, typically affect neurotransmitter systems that carry messages between brain cells (Maisto, Galizio, & Connors, 2011).

Marijuana

Marijuana and hashish are derived from the hemp plant *Cannabis sativa*. Marijuana ("pot," "grass," "reefer," "MJ") consists of the dried leaves and flowers of the hemp plant. Hashish is a resinous material scraped from cannabis buds. Marijuana's psychological effects include a

Detoxification In the treatment of alcoholism, the withdrawal of the patient from alcohol.

Hallucinogen A substance that alters or distorts sensory impressions.

sense of euphoria or well-being, relaxation, altered time sense, and perceptual distortions. At high dosages, however, paranoia, hallucinations, and delusions can occur (Hart, Ksir, & Ray, 2009). All considered, marijuana intoxication is relatively subtle by comparison to drugs such as LSD or alcohol. Despite this, driving a car while high on marijuana can be extremely hazardous. As a matter of fact, driving under the influence of any intoxicating drug is dangerous.

No overdose deaths from marijuana have been reported. However, marijuana cannot be considered harmless. Particularly worrisome is the fact that THC accumulates in the body's fatty tissues, especially in the brain and reproductive organs. Even if a person smokes marijuana just once a week, the body is never entirely free of THC. Scientists have located a specific receptor site on the surface of brain cells where THC binds to produce its effects (**Figure 5.11**). These receptor sites are found in several parts of the brain, including prefrontal cortex, which is the seat of human consciousness (Julien, 2011). In addition, THC receptors are found in areas involved in the control of skilled movement. Naturally occurring chemicals similar to THC may help the brain cope with pain and stress. However, when THC is used as a drug, high doses can cause paranoia, hallucinations, and dizziness (Maisto, Galizio, & Connors, 2011).

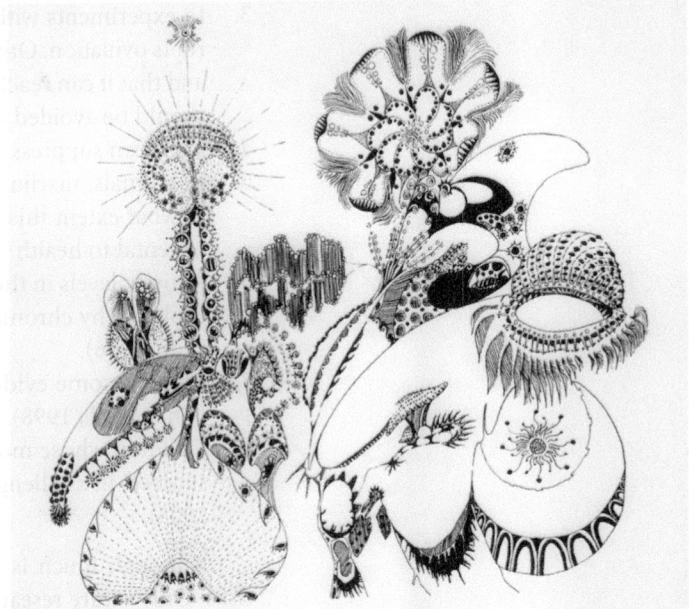

Artists have tried at times to capture the effects of hallucinogens. Here, the artist depicts visual experiences he had while under the influence of LSD.

Abuse

Does marijuana produce physical dependence? Yes, according to recent studies (Filbey et al., 2009; Lichtman & Martin, 2006). Frequent users of marijuana find it very difficult to quit, so dependence is a risk (Budney & Hughes, 2006). But marijuana's potential for abuse lies primarily in the realm of psychological dependence, not physical addiction.

For about a day after a person smokes marijuana, his or her attention, coordination, and short-term memory are impaired. Frequent marijuana users show small declines in learning, memory, attention, and thinking abilities (Solowij et al., 2002). When surveyed at age 29, nonusers are healthier, earn more, and are more satisfied with their lives than people who smoke marijuana regularly (Ellickson, Martino, & Collins, 2004). In fact, marijuana use is associated with mental health problems (Buckner, Ecker, & Cohen, 2010).

People who smoke five or more "joints" a week score 4 points lower on IQ tests. This is enough to dull their learning capacity. In fact, many people who have stopped using marijuana say they quit because they were bothered by short-term memory loss and concentration problems. Fortunately, IQ scores and other cognitive measures rebound in about a month after a person quits using marijuana (Grant et al., 2001). In other words, people who smoke dope may act like dopes, but if they quit, there's a good chance they will regain their mental abilities.

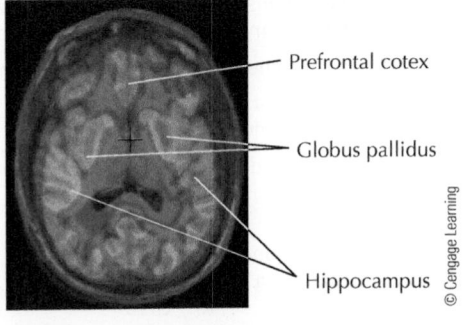

Prefrontal cotex

Globus pallidus

Hippocampus

Long-Term Health Risks

Marijuana's long-term effects include the following health risks:

1. Marijuana smoke contains 50 percent more cancer-causing hydrocarbons and 16 times more tar than tobacco smoke does. Thus, smoking several "joints" a week may be the equivalent of smoking a dozen cigarettes a day. In regular users, marijuana increases the risk of a variety of cancers, including prostate and cervical cancer (Hashibe et al., 2005).
2. Marijuana temporarily lowers sperm production in males, and users produce more abnormal sperm. This could be a problem for a man who is marginally fertile and wants to have a family (Schuel et al., 1999).

Figure 5.11 The red and yellow areas in this PET scan show where the brain is rich in THC receptors. The prefrontal cortex plays a role in human consciousness, the globus pallidus is involved in the control of coordinated movement, and the hippocampus plays a role in memory (Freberg, 2010). This may explain why marijuana use negatively affects memory and coordination (but what about the munchies?).

3. In experiments with female monkeys, THC causes abnormal menstrual cycles and disrupts ovulation. Other animal studies show that THC causes a higher rate of miscarriages and that it can reach the developing fetus. As is true for so many other drugs, marijuana should be avoided during pregnancy.
4. THC can suppress the body's immune system, increasing the risk of disease.
5. In animals, marijuana causes genetic damage within cells of the body. It is not known to what extent this happens in humans, but it does suggest that marijuana can be detrimental to health.
6. Activity levels in the cerebellum are lower than normal in marijuana abusers. This may explain why chronic marijuana users tend to show some loss of coordination (Volkow et al., 1996).
7. There is some evidence that THC damages parts of the brain important for memory (Chan et al., 1998).
8. Children whose mothers smoked marijuana during pregnancy show lowered ability to succeed in challenging, goal-oriented activities (Fried & Smith, 2001; Noland et al., 2005).

Although much is still unknown, marijuana appears to pose a wide range of health risks. Only future research will tell for sure "what's in the pot."

A Look Ahead

Of the many states of consciousness we have discussed, dreaming remains one of the most familiar—and the most surprising. Are there lessons to be learned from dreams? What personal insights lie hidden in the ebb and flow of your dream images? Let's find out in the upcoming Psychology in Action section.

---

study break Psychoactive Drugs

RECITE

1. Addictive drugs stimulate the brain's reward circuitry by affecting
   a. neurotransmitters   b. alpha waves
   c. tryptophan levels   d. delta spindles
2. Drug interaction is a special danger when a person combines
   a. marijuana and amphetamine   b. barbiturates and alcohol
   c. alcohol and cocaine   d. marijuana and THC
3. Which of the drugs listed below are known to cause a physical dependence?
   a. heroin   b. morphine   c. codeine
   d. methadone   e. barbiturates   f. alcohol
   g. marijuana   h. amphetamines   i. nicotine
   j. cocaine   k. GHB
4. Amphetamine psychosis is similar to extreme _____, in which the individual feels threatened and suffers from delusions.
5. Cocaine is very similar to which of the following in its effects on the central nervous system?
   a. Seconal   b. codeine
   c. cannabis   d. amphetamine
6. Treatment for alcohol dependence begins with sobering up the person and cutting off the supply. This is referred to as
   a. "hitting bottom"   b. the crucial phase
   c. detoxification   d. clinical anhedonia

REFLECT

THINK CRITICALLY

7. The U.S. government, which helps fund antismoking campaigns and smoking-related health research, also continues to subsidize tobacco growers. Can you explain this contradiction?
8. Why do you think there is such a contrast between the laws regulating marijuana and those regulating alcohol and tobacco?

SELF-REFLECT

What legal drugs did you use in the last year? Did any have psychoactive properties? How do psychoactive drugs differ from other substances in their potential for abuse?

ANSWERS

1. a 2. b 3. All of them do. 4. paranoia 5. d 6. c 7. Neither can we. 8. Drug laws in Western societies reflect cultural values and historical patterns of use. Inconsistencies in the law can often be justified on the basis of pharmacology, health risks, or abuse potential.

Psychology in Action

Exploring and Using Dreams

JOURNEY QUESTION 5.9 *How can dreams be used to promote personal understanding?*

No matter what theory of dreaming we favor, dreams can be thought of as a message *from* yourself *to* yourself. Thus, the way to understand dreams is to remember them, write them down, look for the messages they contain, and become deeply acquainted with *your own* symbol system. Here's how:

How to Catch a Dream

1. Before going to sleep, plan to remember your dreams. Keep a pen and paper or a digital recorder beside your bed.
2. If possible, arrange to awaken gradually without an alarm. Natural awakening almost always follows soon after an REM period.
3. If you rarely remember your dreams, you may want to set an alarm clock to go off an hour before you usually awaken. Although less desirable than awakening naturally, this may let you catch a dream.
4. Upon awakening, lie still and review the dream images with your eyes closed. Try to recall as many details as possible.
5. If you can, make your first dream record (whether by writing or by recording) with your eyes closed. Opening your eyes will disrupt dream recall.
6. Review the dream again and record as many additional details as you can remember. Dream memories disappear quickly. Be sure to describe feelings as well as the plot, characters, and actions of the dream.
7. Put your dreams into a permanent dream diary. Keep dreams in chronological order and review them periodically. This procedure will reveal recurrent themes, conflicts, and emotions. It almost always produces valuable insights.
8. Remember, a number of drugs suppress dreaming by interfering with REM sleep (including alcohol, amphetamines, barbiturates, cocaine, marijuana, and opiates).

Dream Work

At one time or another, almost everyone has had a dream that seemed to have deep meaning (Rock, 2004). Exploring everyday dream life can be a source of personal enrichment and personal growth (Halliday, 2010). What strategies do psychologists use to interpret dreams? Let's start with Sigmund Freud's pioneering approach.

To unlock dreams, Freud identified four **dream processes**, or mental filters, that disguise the meanings of dreams. The first is **condensation**, in which several people, objects, or events are combined into a single dream image. A dream character that looks like a teacher, acts like your father, talks like your mother, and is dressed like your employer might be a condensation of authority figures in your life.

Displacement is a second way of disguising dream content. Displacement may cause important emotions or actions of a dream to be redirected toward safe or seemingly unimportant images. Thus, a student angry at his parents might dream of accidentally wrecking their car instead of directly attacking them.

A third dream process is **symbolization**. As mentioned earlier, Freud believed that dreams are often expressed in images that are symbolic rather than literal. That's why it helps to ask what feelings or ideas a dream image might symbolize. Let's say, for example, that a

Dream processes Mental filters that hide the true meanings of dreams.

Condensation Combining several people, objects, or events into a single dream image.

Displacement Directing emotions or actions toward safe or unimportant dream images.

Symbolization The nonliteral expression of dream content.

How would you try to find the meaning of a dream? A traditional approach is to look for symbolic messages, as well as literal meanings. If you find yourself wearing a mask in a dream, for instance, it could relate to important roles that you play at school, work, or home. It could also mean that you want to hide or that you are looking forward to a costume party. However, to accurately interpret a dream, it is important to learn your own "vocabulary" of dream images and meanings. Keeping a dream diary is the first step toward gaining valuable insights.

student dreams of coming to class naked. A literal interpretation would be that the student is an exhibitionist. A more likely symbolic meaning is that the student feels vulnerable or unprepared in the class.

Secondary elaboration is the fourth method by which dream meanings are disguised. **Secondary elaboration** is the tendency to make a dream more logical and to add details when remembering it. The fresher a dream memory is, the more useful it is likely to be.

Looking for condensation, displacement, symbolization, and secondary elaboration may help you unlock your dreams. But there are other techniques that may be more effective. Fritz Perls, the originator of Gestalt therapy, considered most dreams a special message about what's missing in our lives, what we avoid doing, or feelings that need to be "re-owned." Perls believed that dreams are a way of filling in gaps in personal experience (Perls, 1969).

An approach that Perls found helpful is to "take the part of" or "speak for" each of the characters and objects in the dream. In other words, if you dream about a strange man standing behind a doorway, you would speak aloud to the man, then answer for him. To use Perls' method, you would even speak for the door, perhaps saying something like, "I am a barrier. I keep you safe, but I also keep you locked inside. The stranger has something to tell you. You must risk opening me to learn it."

Another theorist, Ernest Hartmann, suggests that dreams arise as our brains seek to make creative connections. Ignoring the elements of a dream which merely replay a day's events and focusing instead on unusual dream elements is central to unlocking the dream's meaning (Hartmann, 2010). Hartmann adds that our emotions guide making of dream connections. Thus, the overall *emotional tone* (underlying mood) of a dream is a major clue to its meaning (Hartmann, 2008). Is the dream comical, threatening, joyous, or depressing? Were you lonely, jealous, frightened, in love, or angry?

Because each dream has several possible meanings or levels of meaning, there is no fixed way to work with it (Halliday, 2010). Telling the dream to others and discussing its meaning can be a good start. Describing it may help you relive some of the feelings in the dream. Also, family members or friends may be able to offer interpretations to which you would be blind. Watch for verbal or visual puns and other playful elements in dreams. For example, if you dream that you are in a wrestling match and your arm is pinned behind your back, it may mean that you feel someone is "twisting your arm" in real life.

The meaning of most dreams will yield to a little detective work. Try asking a series of questions about dreams you would like to understand:

Probing Dreams

1. Who was in the dream? Were there humans, animals, or mythical characters? Do you recognize any of the characters?
2. What social interactions were taking place? Were those interactions friendly? Aggressive? Sexual?
3. What activities were taking place? Were they physical activities or not?
4. Was there striving? Was the striving successful or not?
5. Was the dream about good fortune or misfortune?
6. What emotions were present in the dream? Was there anger, apprehension, confusion, happiness, or sadness?
7. What were the physical surroundings like? What was the setting? Were there any physical objects present? (Adapted from the Hall-Van de Castle system of dream content analysis; Domhoff, 2003.)

A particularly interesting dream exercise is to continue a dream as waking fantasy so that it may be concluded or carried on to a more meaningful ending. As the world of dreams and your personal dream language become more familiar, you will doubtless find many answers, paradoxes, intuitions, and insights into your own behavior.

Secondary elaboration Making a dream more logical and complete while remembering it.

Using Your Dreams

It is possible to learn to use dreams for our own purposes. For example, as mentioned previously, nightmare sufferers can use imagery rehearsal to modify their own nightmares (Germain et al., 2004; Krakow & Zadra, 2006). Similarly, it is possible to use your dreams to enhance creativity (Stickgold & Walker, 2004).

Dreams and Creativity   History is full of cases in which dreams have been a pathway to creativity and discovery. A striking example is provided by Dr. Otto Loewi, a pharmacologist and winner of a Nobel Prize. Loewi had spent years studying the chemical transmission of nerve impulses. A tremendous breakthrough in his research came when he dreamed of an experiment three nights in a row. On the third night, he got up after having the dream, went straight to his laboratory and performed the crucial experiment. Loewi later said that if the experiment had occurred to him while awake, he would have rejected it.

Loewi's experience gives some insight into using dreams to produce creative solutions. Inhibitions are reduced during dreaming, which may be especially useful in solving problems that require a fresh point of view. Even unimaginative people may create amazing worlds each night in their dreams. For many of us, this rich ability to create is lost in the daily rush of sensory input.

The ability to take advantage of dreams for problem solving is improved if you "set" yourself before retiring. Before you go to bed, try to visualize or think intently about a problem you wish to solve. Steep yourself in the problem by stating it clearly and reviewing all relevant information. Then use the suggestions listed previously to catch your dreams. Although this method is not guaranteed to produce a novel solution or a new insight, it is certain to be an adventure. About half of a group of college students using the method for one week recalled a dream that helped them solve a personal problem (Barrett, 1993).

Lucid Dreaming   If you would like to press further into the territory of dreams, you may want to learn lucid dreaming, a relatively rare, but fascinating, experience. During a **lucid dream** a person feels as if she or he is fully awake within the dream world and capable of normal thought and action. If you ask yourself, "Could this be a dream?" and answer "Yes," you are having a lucid dream (Holzinger, LaBerge, & Levitan, 2006; LaBerge, 2000).

Stephen LaBerge has used a unique approach to show that lucid dreams are real and that they occur during REM sleep. In the sleep lab, lucid dreamers agree to make prearranged signals when they become aware they are dreaming. One such signal is to look up abruptly in a dream, causing a distinct upward eye movement. Another signal is to clench the right and left fists (in the dream) in a prearranged pattern. In other words, lucid dreamers can partially overcome REM sleep paralysis. Such signals show very clearly that lucid dreaming and voluntary action in dreams is possible (LaBerge, 2000).

How can a person learn to have lucid dreams? Try following this simple routine: When you awaken spontaneously from a dream, take a few minutes to try to memorize it. Next, engage in 10 to 15 minutes of reading or any other activity requiring full wakefulness. Then while lying in bed and returning to sleep, say to yourself, "Next time I'm dreaming, I want to remember I'm dreaming." Finally, visualize yourself lying in bed asleep while in the dream you just rehearsed. At the same time, picture yourself realizing that you are dreaming. Follow this routine each time you awaken (substitute a dream memory from another occasion if you don't awaken from a dream).

Why would anyone want to have more lucid dreams? Researchers are interested in lucid dreams because they provide a tool for understanding dreaming (Paulsson & Parker, 2006). Using participants who can signal when they are dreaming makes it possible to explore dreams with firsthand data from the dreamer's world itself.

On a more personal level, lucid dreaming can convert dreams into a nightly "workshop" for emotional growth. Consider, for example, a recently divorced woman who kept dreaming that she was being swallowed by a giant wave. The woman was asked to try

Lucid dream A dream in which the dreamer feels awake and capable of normal thought and action.

swimming the next time the wave engulfed her. She did, with great determination, and the nightmare lost its terror. More important, her revised dream made her feel that she could cope with life again. For reasons such as this, people who have lucid dreams tend to feel a sense of emotional well-being (Wolpin et al., 1992). Dream expert Allan Hobson believes that learning to voluntarily enter altered states of consciousness (through lucid dreaming or self-hypnosis, for example) has allowed him to have enlightening experiences without the risks of taking mind-altering drugs (Hobson, 2001). So, day or night, don't be afraid to dream a little.

 study break Exploring and Using Dreams

RECITE

1. Which is NOT one of the four dream processes identified by Freud?

    a. condensation   *b.* lucidity
    c. displacement   *d.* symbolization

2. In secondary elaboration, one dream character stands for several others. T or F?
3. Fritz Perls' approach to dream interpretation emphasizes taking the part of characters and even objects portrayed in a dream. T or F?
4. Ernest Hartmann stresses that dreaming is a relatively mechanical process having little personal meaning. T or F?
5. Recent research shows that lucid dreaming occurs primarily during NREM sleep or micro-awakenings. T or F?

REFLECT

THINK CRITICALLY

6. The possibility of having a lucid dream raises an interesting question: If you were dreaming right now, how could you prove it?

SELF-REFLECT

Some people are very interested in remembering and interpreting their dreams. Others pay little attention to dreaming. What importance do you place on dreams? Do you think dreams and dream interpretation can increase self-awareness?

ANSWERS

1. b 2. F 3. T 4. F 5. F 6. In waking consciousness, our actions have consequences that produce immediate sensory feedback. Dreams lack such external feedback. Thus, trying to walk through a wall or doing similar tests would reveal if you were dreaming.

Chapter in Review

Summary

5.1 What is consciousness?

- 5.1.1 Consciousness is a core feature of mental life consisting of sensations and perceptions of external events as well as self-awareness of mental events including thoughts, memories, and feelings about experiences and the self.
- 5.1.2 States of awareness that differ from normal, alert, waking consciousness are called altered states of consciousness (ASCs). Altered states are especially associated with sleep and dreaming, hypnosis, sensory deprivation, and psychoactive drugs.
- 5.1.3 Cultural conditioning greatly affects what altered states a person recognizes, seeks, considers normal, and attains.

5.2 What are the effects of sleep loss or changes in sleep patterns?

- 5.2.1 Sleep is an innate biological rhythm essential for survival.
- 5.2.2 Moderate sleep loss mainly affects vigilance and performance on routine or boring tasks.
- 5.2.3 Higher animals and people deprived of sleep experience involuntary microsleeps.
- 5.2.4 Lowering body and brain activity and metabolism during sleep may help conserve energy and lengthen life.
- 5.2.5 Extended sleep loss can (somewhat rarely) produce a temporary sleep-deprivation psychosis.
- 5.2.6 Sleep patterns show some flexibility, but 7 to 8 hours remains average. The amount of daily sleep decreases steadily from birth to old age.

5.3 What are some functions of sleep?

- 5.3.1 Sleep occurs in four stages. Stage 1 is light sleep, and Stage 4 is deep sleep. The sleeper alternates between Stages 1 and 4 (passing through Stages 2 and 3) several times each night.
- 5.3.2 According to the dual process hypothesis, non-REM (NREM) sleep "refreshes" the body and brain and rapid eye movement (REM) sleep helps form lasting memories.
- 5.3.3 NREM sleep brings overall brain activation levels down, "calming" the brain.
- 5.3.4 REM sleep is strongly associated with dreaming. REM sleep and dreaming help us store important memories.

5.4 What are some sleep disorders and unusual sleep events?

- 5.4.1 Sleep disorders can be serious health problems that should be corrected when they persist.
- 5.4.2 Insomnia may be temporary or chronic. Behavioral approaches to managing insomnia, such as sleep restriction and stimulus control, are quite effective.
- 5.4.3 Sleepwalking, sleeptalking, and sleepsex occur during NREM sleep.
- 5.4.4 Night terrors occur in NREM sleep, whereas nightmares occur in REM sleep.
- 5.4.5 Sleep apnea (interrupted breathing) is one source of insomnia and daytime hypersomnia (sleepiness).
- 5.4.6 Apnea is suspected as one cause of sudden infant death syndrome (SIDS). With only a few exceptions, healthy infants should sleep on their backs.
- 5.4.7 Narcolepsy (sleep attacks) and cataplexy are caused by a sudden shift to Stage 1 REM patterns during normal waking hours.

5.5 Do dreams have meaning?

- 5.5.1 The Freudian, or psychodynamic, view is that dreams express unconscious wishes, frequently hidden by dream symbols.
- 5.5.2 Many theorists have questioned Freud's view of dreams. For example, the activation-synthesis model portrays dreaming as a random physiological process.
- 5.5.3 The neurocognitive view of dreams holds that dreams are continuous with waking thoughts and emotions.
- 5.5.4 Dreams are at least as meaningful as waking thoughts. Most dream content is about familiar settings, people, and actions.

5.6 What is hypnosis?

- 5.6.1 Although not all psychologists agree, hypnosis is usually defined as an altered state characterized by narrowed attention and increased suggestibility.
- 5.6.2 Hypnosis appears capable of producing relaxation, controlling pain, and altering perceptions. It is also more capable of changing subjective experiences more than habits, such as smoking.

5.7 Do meditation and mindfulness have any benefits?

- 5.7.1 Concentrative meditation can be used to focus attention, alter consciousness, and reduce stress. Mindfulness meditation widens attention to achieve similar outcomes.
- 5.7.2 Major benefits of meditation are its ability to interrupt anxious thoughts and to elicit the relaxation response.
- 5.7.3 Brief exposure to sensory deprivation can also elicit the relaxation response.
- 5.7.4 Mindfulness is a positive mental state which involves an open, nonjudgmental awareness of current experience.

5.8 What are the effects of the more commonly used psychoactive drugs?

- 5.8.1 Psychoactive drugs affect the brain in ways that alter consciousness. Most psychoactive drugs can be placed on a scale ranging from stimulation to depression.
- 5.8.2 Psychoactive drugs are highly prone to abuse.
- 5.8.3 Drug abuse is related to personal maladjustment, the reinforcing qualities of drugs, peer group influences, and expectations about drug effects.

- 5.8.4 Drugs may cause a physical dependence (addiction), a psychological dependence, or both. The physically addicting drugs are alcohol, amphetamines, barbiturates, cocaine, codeine, GHB, heroin, marijuana, methadone, morphine, nicotine, and tranquilizers. All psychoactive drugs can lead to psychological dependence.
- 5.8.5 Drug use can be classified as experimental, recreational, situational, intensive, and compulsive. Drug abuse is most often associated with the last three.
- 5.8.6 Stimulant drugs are readily abused because of the period of depression that often follows stimulation. The greatest risks are associated with amphetamines (especially methamphetamine), cocaine, MDMA, and nicotine, but even caffeine can be a problem. Nicotine includes the added risk of lung cancer, heart disease, and other health problems.
- 5.8.7 Narcotics are highly addictive because they produce intense feelings of euphoria. Narcotics addiction is often treated with a harm reduction strategy.
- 5.8.8 Barbiturates and tranquilizers are depressant drugs whose action is similar to that of alcohol. The overdose level for barbiturates and GHB is close to the intoxication dosage, making them dangerous drugs. Mixing barbiturates, tranquilizers, or GHB and alcohol may result in a fatal drug interaction.

- 5.8.9 Alcohol is the most heavily abused drug in common use today. Binge drinking is a problem among college students. It is possible to pace the consumption of alcohol.
- 5.8.10 Marijuana is subject to an abuse pattern similar to alcohol. Studies have linked chronic marijuana use with lung cancer, various mental impairments, and other health problems.

5.9 How can dreams be used to promote personal understanding?

- 5.9.1 Collecting and interpreting your dreams can promote self-awareness.
- 5.9.2 Freud held that the meaning of dreams is hidden by condensation, displacement, symbolization, and secondary elaboration. Perls emphasized the technique of speaking for dream elements, and Hartmann's view of dreams as creative connections guided by emotions suggests focusing on unusual dream elements and emotions.
- 5.9.3 Dreams may be used for creative problem solving, especially when dream awareness is achieved through lucid dreaming.

Interactive Learning

Log in to CengageBrain to access the resources your instructor requires. For this book, you can access:

CourseMate Go to CengageBrain.com to access Psychology CourseMate, where you will find an interactive eBook, glossaries, flashcards, quizzes, videos, Virtual Psychology Labs, and more.

aplia™

Aplia If your professor has assigned Aplia:

1. Sign in to your account.
2. Complete the corresponding exercises as required by your professor.
3. When finished, click "Grade It Now" to see which areas you have mastered, which areas need more work, and detailed explanations of every answer.

Test Your Knowledge

States of Consciousness

1. We can only know the consciousness of other minds through a(n) _____ point of view.
- a. introspective
- b. third-person
- c. psychodynamic
- d. first-person

2. If you are sleep deprived as you read this question, you may well be experiencing
- a. mostly alpha waves
- b. pain insensitivity
- c. hyposomnia
- d. microsleeps

3. A person in deep sleep produces mostly
- a. beta waves
- b. alpha waves
- c. delta waves
- d. REMs

4. Which of the following would normally be most incompatible with moving your arms and legs while asleep?
- a. REM sleep
- b. sleep spindles
- c. delta waves
- d. NREM sleep

5. Which of the following is NOT a form of insomnia?
- a. NREM insomnia
- b. temporary insomnia
- c. drug-dependency insomnia
- d. chronic insomnia

6. Nightmares differ from night terrors because they occur during _____ sleep.
- a. NREM
- b. REM
- c. Stage 1
- d. Stage 4

7. Sleep restriction and stimulus control are techniques used to treat
- a. sleep apnea
- b. sleeptalking
- c. night terrors
- d. insomnia

8. If REM sleep is interrupted, a person will experience REM
- a. nightmares
- b. rebound
- c. disturbance
- d. forgetfulness

9. Wish fulfillment and dream symbols are important concepts in which explanation of dream content?
- a. activation-synthesis
- b. neurocognitive
- c. imagery rehearsal
- d. psychodynamic

10. Suggestible people are more likely to be
- a. more hypnotizable
- b. unimaginative
- c. hidden observers
- d. less hypnotizable

11. Research has shown that hypnosis cannot produce
- a. unusual strength
- b. improved memory
- c. pain relief
- d. sensory changes

12. Which terms DO NOT belong together?
- a. concentrative meditation—relaxation response
- b. mindfulness meditation— relaxation response
- c. mindfulness meditation—mantra
- d. concentrative meditation—mantra

13. Addictive drugs trigger
- a. physical dependence
- b. drug tolerance
- c. psychological dependence
- d. all of the above

14. Drug tolerance is most closely associated with
- a. psychological dependence
- b. marijuana
- c. withdrawal symptoms
- d. anhedonia

15. When rats and monkeys are given free access to cocaine, they
- a. avoid it
- b. prefer it
- c. excrete it
- d. find it irresistible

16. Hyperthermia, heart arrhythmias, and severe liver damage are major risks in the use of
- a. marijuana
- b. benzodiazepine
- c. MDMA
- d. GHB

17. Polydrug abuse accounts for _____ deaths due to drug overdose.
- a. very few
- b. almost all
- c. quite a few
- d. all

18. _____ refers to cutting a person off from his or her supply of an addictive substance.
- a. "hitting bottom"
- b. recovery
- c. detoxification
- d. staying "clean"

19. Drug abuse is partly explained by the fact that psychoactive drugs produce immediate pleasure and
- a. somnambulism
- b. enhanced self-esteem
- c. delayed punishment
- d. brain carcinogens

20. Freud's four dream processes _____ dreams.
- a. elaborate
- b. disguise
- c. disrupt
- d. clarify

Journey Theme *The principles of learning can be used to understand and manage behavior.*

Conditioning and Learning

Journey into Psychology: Rats!

Larry vividly remembers his mother describing how a rat had terrified her. She gestured excitedly as she recounted the horror of seeing the creature scamper out of a camp stove. Although everyone else laughed, 6-year-old Larry shivered as he imagined the attacking rodent. That's the day he learned to fear rats.

Years later, while studying gorillas in Africa, he encountered his first live rat. Larry was shocked by his own reaction. Despite being a respected scientist, he ran away shrieking like a little child. After failing to control his fear a few more times (and being good-naturedly ribbed about it by others), he resolved to conquer it.

Back home, Larry read about irrational fears and realized that a form of learning called *vicarious classical conditioning* explained how he had come to dread rats. After reading several more books, he returned to the jungle, certain that he could cope with his next close encounter. However, he was shocked to discover that his newfound knowledge was no help at all.

Larry had bumped into a strange truth: All his abstract "book learning," a form of *cognitive learning*, was powerless to protect him in the presence of a rat. Chastened, he went to a therapist who used classical conditioning to help him overcome his fear. Larry eventually came to like rats and now has a pet rat named Einstein. Larry also went on to study how baby gorillas learn by observing others—much as he did when he observed his mother's story about the rat.

Different forms of learning reach into every corner of our lives. Are you ready to learn more? If so, let's begin!

Journey Questions

6.1   What is learning?

6.2   How does classical conditioning occur?

6.3   Does conditioning affect emotions?

6.4   How does operant conditioning occur?

6.5   Are there different kinds of operant reinforcement?

6.6   How are we influenced by patterns of reward?

6.7   What does punishment do to behavior?

6.8   What is cognitive learning?

6.9   Does learning occur by imitation?

6.10 How does conditioning apply to everyday problems?

What Is Learning—Does Practice Make Perfect?

JOURNEY QUESTION 6.1 *What is learning?*

Almost all human behavior is learned. Imagine if you suddenly lost all you had ever learned. What could you do? You would be unable to read, write, or speak. You couldn't feed yourself, find your way home, drive a car, play the clarinet, or "party." Needless to say, you would be totally incapacitated. (Dull, too!)

Learning is a relatively permanent change in behavior due to experience (Domjan, 2010). Notice that this definition excludes both temporary changes and more permanent changes caused by motivation, fatigue, maturation, disease, injury, or drugs. Each of these can alter behavior, but none qualifies as learning.

Types of Learning

As Larry's rat experience illustrates, there are different types of learning (Shanks, 2010). **Associative learning** occurs whenever a person or an animal forms a simple association among various stimuli and/or behaviors. Humans share the capacity for associative learning with many other species. In a moment, we will explore two types of associative learning called classical conditioning and operant conditioning.

Humans also engage in **cognitive learning**, which refers to understanding, knowing, anticipating, or otherwise making use of information-rich higher mental processes. More complex forms of cognitive learning, such as learning from written language, are unique to humans. However, some animals do engage in simpler forms of cognitive learning, which we will describe later in this chapter.

Associative Learning

Unlocking the secrets of associative learning begins with noting what happens before and after a particular behavior. Events that precede a behavior are **antecedents**. For example, Ashleigh, who is 3, runs to the front door whenever Daddy gets home. She has recently begun running as soon as she hears his truck pull into the driveway. She has associated running to the door with the antecedent sound of the truck. Effects that follow a behavior are **consequences**. The hug she gets from her father strengthens Ashleigh's tendency to run to the door. As this suggests, paying careful attention to the "before and after" of associative learning is a key to understanding it.

Classical conditioning is based on what happens before we respond. It begins with a stimulus that reliably triggers a behavior as a response. Imagine, for example, that a puff of air (the stimulus) is aimed at your eye. The air puff will make you blink (a response) every time. The eyeblink is a **reflex** (automatic, nonlearned response). Now, assume that we sound a horn (another stimulus) just before each puff of air hits your eye. If the horn and the air puff occur together many times, what happens? Soon, the horn alone will make you blink. Clearly, you've learned something. Before, the horn didn't make you blink. Now it does.

In **classical conditioning**, an antecedent stimulus that doesn't produce a response is linked with one that does (a horn is associated with a puff of air to the eye, for example). We can say that learning has occurred when the new stimulus will also elicit (bring forth) responses (**Figure 6.1**).

In **operant conditioning**, learning is based on the consequences of responding. A behavior may be followed by a positive consequence, or *reinforcer*, such as food; or by a negative consequence, or *punisher*, such as a slap; or by nothing. These results determine whether the behavior is likely to be made again (see Figure 6.1). For example, if you wear a particular hat and get lots of compliments (reward or reinforcement), you are likely to wear it more often. If people snicker, insult you, call the police, or scream (punishment), you will probably wear it less often.

Now that you have an idea of what happens in the two basic kinds of associative learning, let's look at classical conditioning in more detail.

Learning Any relatively permanent change in behavior that can be attributed to experience.

Associative learning The formation of simple associations between various stimuli and responses.

Cognitive learning Higher-level learning involving thinking, knowing, understanding, and anticipation.

Antecedents Events that precede a response.

Consequences Effects that follow a response.

Reflex An innate, automatic response to a stimulus; for example, an eyeblink.

Classical conditioning A form of learning in which reflex responses are associated with new stimuli.

Operant conditioning Learning based on the consequences of responding.

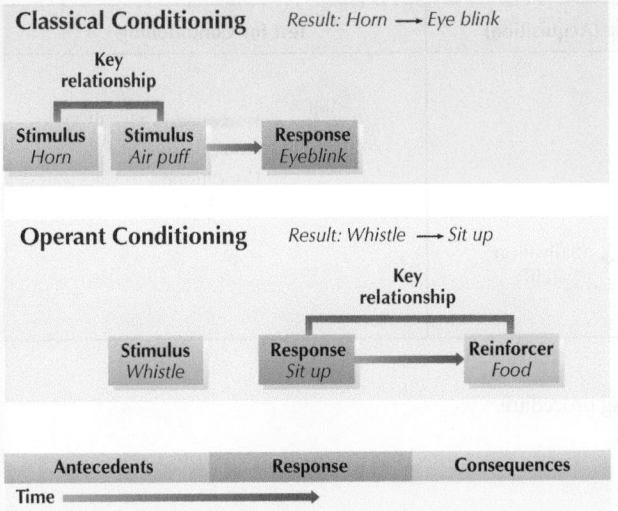

Classical Conditioning   Result: Horn → Eye blink

Key relationship

| Stimulus *Horn* | Stimulus *Air puff* | → | Response *Eyeblink* |

Operant Conditioning   Result: Whistle → Sit up

Key relationship

| Stimulus *Whistle* | Response *Sit up* | → | Reinforcer *Food* |

| Antecedents | Response | Consequences |

Time →

© Cengage Learning

Figure 6.1 In classical conditioning, a stimulus that does not produce a response is paired with a stimulus that does elicit a response. After many such pairings, the stimulus that previously had no effect begins to produce a response. In the example shown, a horn precedes a puff of air to the eye. Eventually the horn alone will produce an eyeblink. In operant conditioning, a response that is followed by a reinforcing consequence becomes more likely to occur on future occasions. In the example shown, a dog learns to sit up when it hears a whistle.

Classical Conditioning—Does the Name Pavlov Ring a Bell?

JOURNEY QUESTION 6.2 *How does classical conditioning occur?*

At the beginning of the 20th century, something happened in the lab of Russian physiologist Ivan Pavlov that brought him the Nobel Prize: His subjects drooled at him. Actually, Pavlov was studying digestion. To observe salivation, he placed meat powder or some tidbit on a dog's tongue and measured the resulting flow of saliva. However, after repeating his procedure many times, Pavlov noticed that his dogs began salivating *before* the food reached their mouths. Later, the dogs even began to salivate when they saw Pavlov enter the room (Schultz & Schultz, 2011).

Pavlov believed that salivation is an automatic, inherited reflex. It really shouldn't change from one day to the next. His dogs were *supposed* to salivate when he put food in their mouths, but they were *not supposed* to salivate when they merely saw him. This was a change in behavior due to experience. Pavlov realized that some type of learning had occurred and soon began investigating "conditioning," as he called it (Figure 6.2). Because of its place in history, this form of learning is now called *classical conditioning* (also known as *Pavlovian conditioning* or *respondent conditioning*) (Bitterman, 2006).

Pavlov's Experiment

How did Pavlov study conditioning? To begin, he rang a bell. At first, the bell was a neutral stimulus (the dogs did not respond to it by salivating). Immediately after, he placed meat powder on the dogs' tongues, which caused reflex salivation. This sequence was repeated a number of times: bell, meat powder, salivation; bell, meat powder, salivation. Eventually (as conditioning took place), the dogs began to salivate when they heard the bell (Figure 6.3). By association, the bell, which before had no effect, began to evoke the same response that food did. This was shown by sometimes ringing the bell alone. Then the dogs salivated, even though no food had been placed in their mouths.

Figure 6.2 An apparatus for Pavlovian conditioning. A tube carries saliva from the dog's mouth to a lever that activates a recording device *(far left)*. During conditioning, various stimuli can be paired with a dish of food placed in front of the dog. The device pictured here is more elaborate than the one Pavlov used in his early experiments.

© Cengage Learning

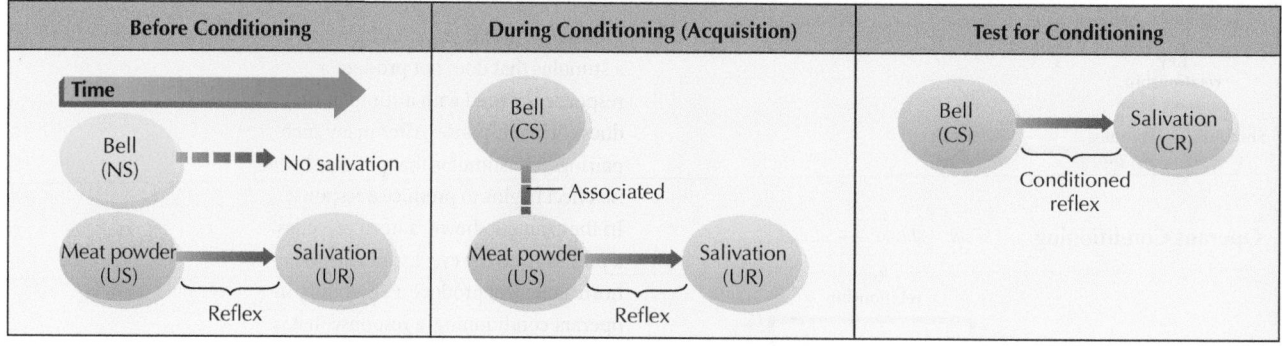

Figure 6.3 The classical conditioning procedure.

Psychologists use several terms to describe these events. The meat powder is an **unconditioned stimulus (US)**—a stimulus innately capable of producing a response (salivation in this case). Notice that the dog did not have to learn to respond to the US. Such stimuli naturally trigger reflexes or emotional reactions. Because a reflex is innate, or "built in," it is called an **unconditioned** (nonlearned) **response (UR)**. Reflex salivation was the UR in Pavlov's experiment.

The bell starts out as a **neutral stimulus (NS)**. In time, the bell becomes a **conditioned stimulus (CS)**—a stimulus that, because of learning, will elicit a response. When Pavlov's bell also produced salivation, the dog was making a new response. Thus, salivation had also become a **conditioned** (learned) **response (CR)** (see Figure 6.3). **Table 6.1** summarizes the important elements of classical conditioning.

Are all these terms really necessary? Yes, because they help us recognize similarities in various instances of learning. Let's summarize the terms using an earlier example:

Before Conditioning	Example
US → UR	Puff of air → eyeblink
NS → no effect	Horn → no effect

After Conditioning	Example
CS → CR	Horn → eyeblink

See "In the Blink of an Eye" for an example of how classical conditioning is used to solve a clinical problem.

Unconditioned stimulus (US) A stimulus innately capable of eliciting a response.

Unconditioned response (UR) An innate reflex response elicited by an unconditioned stimulus.

Neutral stimulus (NS) A stimulus that does not evoke a response.

Conditioned stimulus (CS) A stimulus that evokes a response because it has been repeatedly paired with an unconditioned stimulus.

Conditioned response (CR) A learned response elicited by a conditioned stimulus.

Table 6.1 Elements of Classical Conditioning

ELEMENT	SYMBOL	DESCRIPTION	EXAMPLE
Unconditioned stimulus	US	A stimulus innately capable of eliciting a response	Meat powder
Unconditioned response	UR	An innate reflex response elicited by an unconditioned stimulus	Reflex salivation *to the US*
Neutral stimulus	NS	A stimulus that does not evoke the unconditioned response	Bell *before conditioning*
Conditioned stimulus	CS	A stimulus that evokes a response because it has been repeatedly paired with an unconditioned stimulus	Bell *after conditioning*
Conditioned response	CR	A learned response elicited by a conditioned stimulus	Salivation *to the CS*

© Cengage Learning

Did you notice the eyeblink example earlier in this chapter? Good. Many instructors use it because it's fairly easy for students to grasp.

OK, but is it useful for anything else? As trivial as using classical conditioning to condition blinking might seem, it has great clinical potential. Remember Kate Adamson, the courageous woman with locked-in syndrome, who we met in Chapter 2? Because she was totally paralyzed, doctors assumed she was brain dead. Fortunately, Kate discovered she could communicate by deliberately blinking her eyes. But what if she couldn't do even that? Worse still, what if she was only *minimally conscious* instead of brain dead (in a *vegetative state*)?

One exciting possibility is that eyeblink conditioning may be useful for distinguishing locked-in individuals from those with more severe brain damage and even severely brain-damaged

individuals who are minimally conscious from those who are in a vegetative state (Bekinschtein et al., 2009). Patients who are at least minimally conscious can be conditioned and may recover some mental functions, whereas patients in a vegetative state likely cannot be conditioned or recover. Currently, some minimally conscious patients are misdiagnosed and are not offered appropriate therapy.

Eyeblink conditioning may also help make earlier diagnoses. For example, psychologist Diana Woodruff-Pak (2001) noticed disordered eyeblink conditioning in a patient 6 years before other tests showed any signs of dementia (duh-MEN-sha). (Eventually, people with dementia suffer major declines in memory, judgment, language, and thinking abilities.)

More clinical applications may be developed since the details of eyeblink conditioning,

including which brain areas are involved, are now fairly well understood (Freeman & Steinmetz, 2011). Knowing, for example, that the cerebellum is involved in eyeblink conditioning and suspecting that cerebellar dysfunction may be involved in, say, autism, we can study eyeblink conditioning in autistic people. When psychologist Joseph Steinmetz and his colleagues did exactly that, they found that people with autism show unusual eyeblink conditioning. So do people with obsessive-compulsive disorder, fetal alcohol syndrome, and schizophrenia (Bolbecker et al., 2011; Jacobson et al., 2011; Woodruff-Pak, 2001). This relationship now gives us another way to diagnose such disorders as well as to learn more about them.

Who would have thought so much could be seen "in the blink of an eye"?

Principles of Classical Conditioning—Leonard Studies Lemon Juice

Suppose a scientist named Leonard wants to study conditioning by conditioning his friend Sheldon. To observe conditioning, he could ring a bell and squirt lemon juice into Sheldon's mouth. By repeating this procedure several times, he could condition Sheldon to salivate to the bell. Sheldon might then be used to explore other aspects of classical conditioning.

Acquisition

During **acquisition**, or training, a conditioned response must be established and strengthened (**Figure 6.4**). Classical conditioning occurs when the NS is followed by, or associated with, a US. As this association is strengthened, the NS increasingly elicits the UR; it is becoming a CS capable of eliciting a CR. For Sheldon, the bell is an NS on the way to becoming a CS, the sour lemon juice is a US, and salivating is a UR on the way to becoming a CR. For the bell to elicit salivation, we must link the bell with the lemon juice. Conditioning will be most rapid if the US (lemon juice) follows *immediately* after the CS (the bell). With most classical conditioning, the optimal delay between CS and US is from $\frac{1}{2}$ second to about 5 seconds (Chance, 2009).

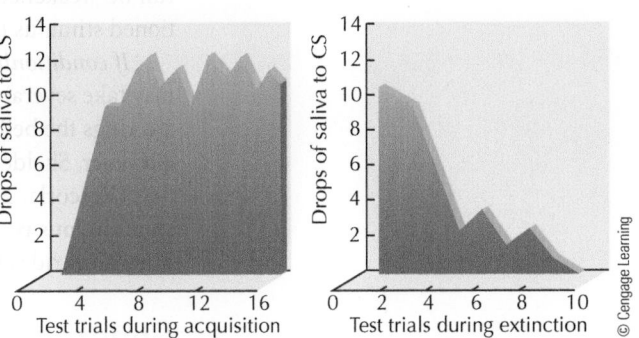

Figure 6.4 Acquisition and extinction of a conditioned response. (After Pavlov, 1927.)

Higher Order Conditioning

Once a response is learned, it can bring about **higher order conditioning**. In this case, a well-learned CS is used to condition further learning (Lefrançois, 2012). That is, the CS has become strong enough to be used like an unconditioned stimulus. Let's illustrate again with Sheldon.

As a result of earlier learning, the bell now makes Sheldon salivate. (No lemon juice is needed.) To go a step further, Leonard could clap his hands and then ring the bell. (Again, no lemon juice would be used.) Through higher order conditioning, Sheldon would soon learn to salivate when Leonard clapped his hands (**Figure 6.5**). (This little trick could be a real hit with Leonard's colleagues.)

Acquisition The period in conditioning during which a response is strengthened.

Higher order conditioning Classical conditioning in which a conditioned stimulus is used to reinforce further learning; that is, a CS is used as if it were a US.

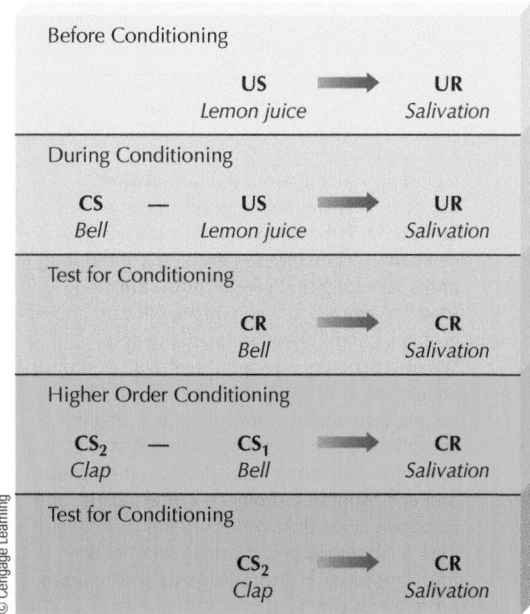

Before Conditioning		
	US *Lemon juice* →	**UR** *Salivation*
During Conditioning		
CS *Bell* —	**US** *Lemon juice* →	**UR** *Salivation*
Test for Conditioning		
	CR *Bell* →	**CR** *Salivation*
Higher Order Conditioning		
CS₂ *Clap* —	**CS₁** *Bell* →	**CR** *Salivation*
Test for Conditioning		
	CS₂ *Clap* →	**CR** *Salivation*

Figure 6.5 Higher order conditioning takes place when a well-learned conditioned stimulus is used as if it were an unconditioned stimulus. In this example, Sheldon is first conditioned to salivate to the sound of a bell. In time, the bell will elicit salivation. At that point, Leonard could clap his hands and then ring the bell. Soon, after repeating the procedure, Sheldon would learn to salivate when Leonard clapped his hands.

Higher order conditioning extends learning one or more steps beyond the original conditioned stimulus. Many advertisers use this effect by pairing images that evoke good feelings (such as people, including celebrities, smiling and having fun) with pictures of their products. They hope that you will learn, by association, to feel good when you see their products (Priluck & Till, 2004; Till, Stanley, & Priluck, 2008).

Expectancies

Pavlov believed that classical conditioning does not involve any higher mental processes. Today, many psychologists think that classical conditioning does have cognitive origins because it is related to information that might aid survival. According to this **informational view** we look for associations among events (Schultz & Helmstetter, 2010). Doing so creates new mental **expectancies**, or thoughts about how events are interconnected.

How does classical conditioning alter expectancies? Notice that the conditioned stimulus reliably precedes the unconditioned stimulus. Because it does, the CS *predicts* the US (Rescorla, 1987). During conditioning, the brain learns to *expect* that the US will follow the CS. As a result, the brain prepares the body to respond to the US. Here's an example: When you are about to get a shot with a hypodermic needle, your muscles tighten and there is a catch in your breathing. Why? Because your body is preparing for pain. You have learned to expect that getting poked with a needle will hurt. This expectancy, which was acquired during classical conditioning, changes your behavior.

Extinction and Spontaneous Recovery

Once an association has been classically conditioned, will it ever go away? If the US stops following the CS, conditioning will fade away, or extinguish. Let's return to Sheldon. If Leonard rings the bell many times and does not follow it with lemon juice, Sheldon's expectancy that "bell precedes lemon juice" will weaken. As it does, he will lose his tendency to salivate when he hears the bell. Thus, we see that classical conditioning can be weakened by removing the connection between the conditioned and the unconditioned stimulus (see Figure 6.4). This process is called **extinction**.

If conditioning takes a while to build up, shouldn't it take time to reverse? Yes. In fact, it may take several extinction sessions to completely reverse conditioning. Let's say that Leonard rings the bell until Sheldon quits responding. It might seem that extinction is complete. However, Sheldon will probably respond to the bell again on the following day, at least at first (Rescorla, 2004). The return of a learned response after apparent extinction is called **spontaneous recovery**. It explains why people who have had a car accident may need many slow, calm rides before their fear of driving completely extinguishes.

Generalization

After conditioning, other stimuli similar to the CS may also trigger a response. This is called **stimulus generalization**. For example, Leonard might find that Sheldon salivates to the sound of a ringing telephone or doorbell, even though they were never used as conditioning stimuli.

It is easy to see the value of stimulus generalization. Consider the child who burns her finger while playing with matches. Most likely, lighted matches will become conditioned fear stimuli for her. Because of stimulus generalization, she may also have a healthy fear of flames from lighters, fireplaces, stoves, and so forth. It's fortunate that generalization extends learning to related situations. Otherwise, we would all be far less adaptable.

As you may have guessed, stimulus generalization has limits. As stimuli become less like the original CS, responding decreases. If you condition a person to blink each time you play a particular note on a piano, blinking will decline as you play higher or lower notes. If the notes are *much* higher or lower, the person will not respond at all (Figure 6.6). Stimulus

Informational view (of conditioning) Perspective that explains learning in terms of information imparted by events in the environment.

Expectancy An anticipation concerning future events or relationships.

Extinction The weakening of a conditioned response through removal of reinforcement.

Spontaneous recovery The reappearance of a learned response after its apparent extinction.

Stimulus generalization The tendency to respond to stimuli similar to, but not identical to, a conditioned stimulus.

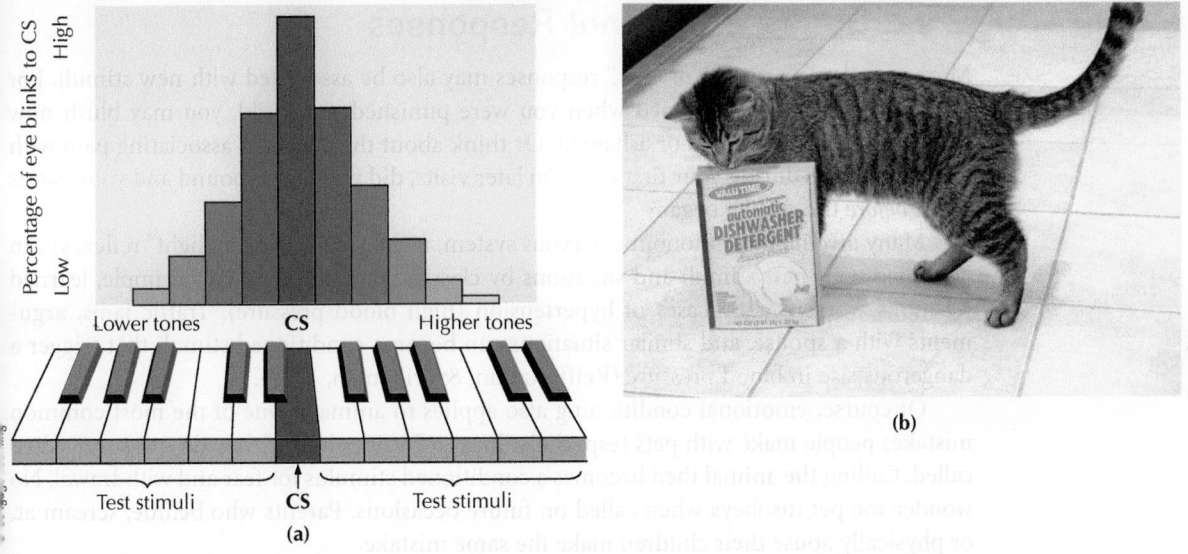

Percentage of eye blinks to CS — High / Low

Lower tones — CS — Higher tones

Test stimuli — CS — Test stimuli

(a)

(b)

Dennis Coon

Figure 6.6 *(a)* Stimulus generalization. Stimuli similar to the CS also elicit a response. *(b)* This cat has learned to salivate when it sees a cat food box. Because of stimulus generalization, it also salivates when shown a similar-looking detergent box.

generalization partly explains why many stores carry imitations of nationally known products. For many customers, positive attitudes conditioned to the original products tend to generalize to the cheaper knockoffs (Till & Priluck, 2000).

Discrimination

Let's consider one more idea with Sheldon (who by now must be ready to explode in a big bang). Suppose Leonard again conditions Sheldon, with a bell as the CS. As an experiment, he also occasionally sounds a buzzer instead of ringing the bell. However, the buzzer is never followed by the US (lemon juice). At first, Sheldon salivates when he hears the buzzer (because of generalization). But after Leonard sounds the buzzer several times more, Sheldon will stop responding to it. Why? In essence, Sheldon's generalized response to the buzzer has extinguished. As a result, he has learned to *discriminate*, or respond differently, to the bell and the buzzer.

Stimulus discrimination is the ability to respond differently to various stimuli. As an example, you might remember the feelings of anxiety or fear you had as a child when your mother's or father's voice changed to the dreaded put-away-that-PlayStation-controller tone. Most children quickly learn to discriminate voice tones associated with punishment from those associated with praise or affection.

Classical Conditioning in Humans—An Emotional Topic

JOURNEY QUESTION 6.3 *Does conditioning affect emotions?*

Is much human learning actually based on classical conditioning? At its simplest, classical conditioning depends on unconditioned reflex responses. As mentioned earlier, a reflex is a dependable, inborn stimulus-and-response connection. For example, your hand reflexively draws back from pain. Bright light causes the pupil of your eye to narrow. A puff of air directed at your eye will make you blink. Various foods elicit salivation. Any of these reflexes, and others as well, can be associated with a new stimulus. At the very least, you have probably noticed how your mouth waters when you see or smell a bakery. Even pictures of food may make you salivate (a photo of a sliced lemon is great for this).

Stimulus discrimination The learned ability to respond differently to similar stimuli.

Conditioned Emotional Responses

More complex *emotional*, or "gut," responses may also be associated with new stimuli. For instance, if your face reddened when you were punished as a child, you may blush now when you are embarrassed or ashamed. Or think about the effects of associating pain with a dentist's office during your first visit. On later visits, did your heart pound and your palms sweat *before* the dentist began?

Many *involuntary*, autonomic nervous system, responses ("fight-or-flight" reflexes) can be linked with new stimuli and situations by classical conditioning. For example, learned reactions worsen many cases of hypertension (high blood pressure). Traffic jams, arguments with a spouse, and similar situations can become conditioned stimuli that trigger a dangerous rise in blood pressure (Reiff, Katkin, & Friedman, 1999).

Of course, emotional conditioning also applies to animals. One of the most common mistakes people make with pets (especially dogs) is hitting them if they do not come when called. Calling the animal then becomes a conditioned stimulus for fear and withdrawal. No wonder the pet disobeys when called on future occasions. Parents who belittle, scream at, or physically abuse their children make the same mistake.

Learned Fears

In 1920, pioneering psychologist John Watson reported classically conditioning a young child named Little Albert to fear rats (Beck, Levinson, & Irons, 2009). Since then, it has been widely accepted that that many phobias (FOE-bee-ahs) begin as a **conditioned emotional response (CER)**, or learned emotional reaction to a previously neutral stimulus (Laborda & Miller, 2011). A *phobia* is a fear that persists even when no realistic danger exists. Fears of animals, water, heights, thunder, fire, bugs, elevators, and the like are common.

People who have phobias can often trace their fears to a time when they were frightened, injured, or upset by a particular stimulus, especially in childhood (King, Muris, & Ollendick, 2005). One bad experience in which you were frightened or disgusted by a spider may condition fears that last for years (de Jong & Muris, 2002). Stimulus generalization and higher order conditioning can spread CERs to other stimuli. As a result, what began as a limited fear may become a disabling phobia (Figure 6.7).

During a CER, an area of the brain called the amygdala becomes more active, producing feelings of fear (Schweckendiek et al., 2011). The amygdala is part of the limbic system, which is responsible for other emotions as well (see Chapter 2). Cognitive learning has little effect on these lower brain areas (Olsson, Nearing, & Phelps, 2007). Perhaps that's why fears and phobias cannot be readily eased by merely reading about how to control fears—as our friend Larry discovered with his rat phobia. However, conditioned fears do respond to a therapy called **systematic desensitization**. This is done by gradually exposing the phobic person to feared stimuli while she or he remains calm and relaxed. For example, people who fear heights can be slowly taken to ever-higher elevations until their fears extinguish. Similarly, people can overcome their fear of spiders by slowly getting closer and closer to actual spiders. Systematic desensitization even works when computer graphics are used to simulate the experience of the phobic object or event (Michaliszyn et al., 2010; Price et al., 2011). (See Chapter 13 for more information about therapies based on learning principles.)

Undoubtedly, we acquire many of our likes, dislikes, and fears as conditioned emotional responses. As noted before, advertisers try to achieve the same effect by pairing products with pleasant images and music. So do many students on a first date.

(a)

(b)

(c)

(d)

© Cengage Learning

Figure 6.7 Hypothetical example of a CER becoming a phobia. A child approaches a dog *(a)* and is frightened by it *(b)*. This fear generalizes to other household pets *(c)* and later to virtually all furry animals *(d)*.

Conditioned emotional response (CER) An emotional response that has been linked to a previously nonemotional stimulus by classical conditioning.

Systematic desensitization Reducing fear or anxiety by repeatedly exposing a person to emotional stimuli while the person is deeply relaxed.

Vicarious, or Secondhand, Conditioning

Conditioning can also occur indirectly. Let's say, for example, that you watch another person get an electric shock. Each time, a signal light comes on before the shock is delivered. Even if you don't receive a shock yourself, you will soon develop a CER to the light. Children who learn to fear thunder by watching their parents react to it have undergone similar conditioning. Many Americans were traumatized as a consequence of watching media coverage of the September 11, 2001, terrorist attacks in New York and Washington (Blanchard et al., 2004). Similarly, people who counsel traumatized victims of sexual abuse can themselves develop vicarious trauma (Jordan, 2010).

Vicarious classical conditioning occurs when we learn to respond emotionally to a stimulus by observing another person's emotional reactions (Olsson, Nearing, & Phelps, 2007). Such "secondhand" learning affects feelings in many situations. Being told that "snakes are dangerous" may not explain the child's *emotional* response. More likely, the child has observed others reacting fearfully to the word *snake* or to snake images on television (King, Muris, & Ollendick, 2005). That is exactly how Larry, the researcher we met at the beginning of this chapter, developed his fear of rats. As children grow up, the emotions of parents, friends, and relatives undoubtedly add to fears of snakes, caves, spiders, heights, and other terrors. Even "horror" movies filled with screaming actors can have a similar effect.

The emotional attitudes we develop toward foods, political parties, ethnic groups, escalators—whatever—are probably conditioned not only by direct experiences but vicariously as well. No one is born prejudiced—all attitudes are learned. Parents may do well to look in a mirror if they wonder how or where a child "picked up" a particular fear or emotional attitude.

Vicarious classical conditioning Classical conditioning brought about by observing another person react to a particular stimulus.

---

 study break Classical Conditioning

RECITE

1. The concept of forming an association applies to both
   a. antecedents and consequences
   b. neutral stimuli and rewards
   c. classical and operant conditioning
   d. acquisition and spontaneous recovery

2. You smell the odor of cookies being baked and your mouth waters. Apparently, the odor of cookies is a _____ and your salivation is a _____.
   a. CR, CS
   b. CS, CR
   c. consequence, neutral stimulus
   d. reflex, CS

3. The informational view says that classical conditioning is based on changes in mental _____ about the CS and US.

4. After you have acquired a conditioned response, it may be weakened by repeated
   a. spontaneous recovery
   b. stimulus generalization
   c. presentation of the CS alone
   d. presentation of the CS followed by the US

5. When a conditioned stimulus is used to reinforce the learning of a second conditioned stimulus, higher order conditioning has occurred. T or F?

6. Psychologists theorize that many phobias begin when a CER generalizes to other, similar situations. T or F?

7. Three-year-old Josh sees his 5-year-old sister get chased by a neighbor's dog. Now Josh is as afraid of the dog as his sister is. Josh's fear is a result of
   a. stimulus discrimination
   b. vicarious conditioning
   c. spontaneous recovery
   d. higher order conditioning

REFLECT

THINK CRITICALLY

8. Lately you have been getting a shock of static electricity every time you touch a door handle. Now there is a hesitation in your door-opening movements. Can you analyze this situation in terms of classical conditioning?

SELF-REFLECT

US, CS, UR, CR—How will you remember these terms? First, you should note that we are interested in either a stimulus (S) or a response (R). What else do we need to know? Each S or R can be either conditioned (C) or unconditioned (U).

Can a stimulus provoke a response before any learning has occurred? If it can, then it's a US. Do you have to learn to respond to the stimulus? Then it's a CS. Does a response occur without being learned? Then it's a UR. If it has to be learned, then it's a CR.

ANSWERS

1. c. 2. b 3. expectancies 4. c 5. T 6. T 7. b 8. Door handles have become conditioned stimuli that elicit the reflex withdrawal and muscle tensing that normally follows getting a shock. This conditioned response may also have generalized to other handles.

Operant Conditioning—Ping-Pong-Playing Pigeons

JOURNEY QUESTION 6.4 *How does operant conditioning occur?*

The principles of *operant conditioning*, another form of associative learning, are among the most powerful tools in psychology. You won't regret learning how to use them. Operant conditioning applies to all living creatures and explains much day-to-day behavior. Operant conditioning can be used to alter the behavior of pets, children, other adults, and your own behavior too.

As stated earlier, in **operant conditioning** (also known as *instrumental learning*), we associate responses with their consequences. The basic principle is simple: Acts that are followed by a positive consequence tend to be repeated (Chance, 2009). Pioneer learning theorist Edward L. Thorndike called this the **law of effect**: The probability of a response is altered by the effect it has (Benjafield, 2010). Learning is strengthened each time a response is followed by a satisfying state of affairs. You are much more likely to keep telling a joke if people laugh at it. If the first three people frown when they hear the joke, you may not tell it again.

In operant conditioning, the learner actively "operates on" the environment. Thus, operant conditioning refers mainly to learning *voluntary* responses. For example, pushing buttons on a television remote control is a learned operant response. Pushing a particular button is reinforced by gaining the consequence you desire, such as changing channels or muting an obnoxious commercial. In contrast, classical conditioning is passive. It simply "happens to" the learner when a US follows a CS. (See **Table 6.2** for a further comparison of classical and operant conditioning.)

Positive Reinforcement

Isn't reinforcement *another term for* reward? Not exactly. To be correct, it is better to say *reinforcer*. Why? Because rewards do not always increase responding. If you give chocolate to a child as a "reward" for good behavior, it will work only if the child likes chocolate. What is reinforcing for one person may not be for another. As a practical rule of thumb, psychologists define an **operant reinforcer** as any event that follows a response and increases its probability of occurring again (**Figure 6.8**).

Acquiring an Operant Response

Many studies of operant conditioning in animals make use of an **operant conditioning chamber**, or **Skinner box**, after B. F. Skinner, who invented it (Skinner, 1938; **Figure 6.9**). The walls are bare except for a

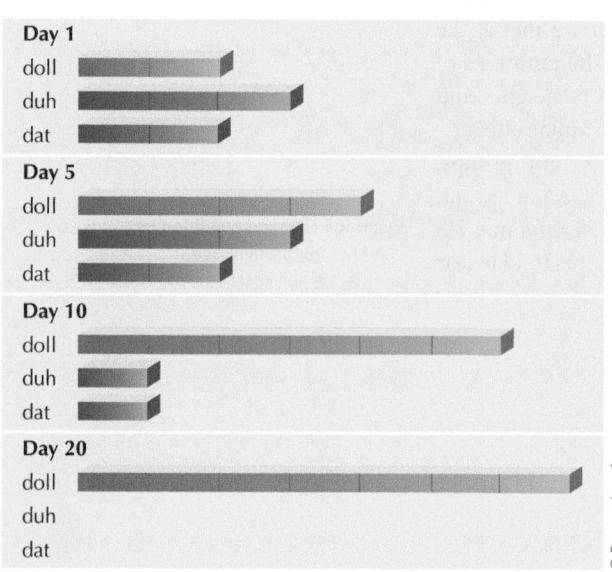

Day 1
doll
duh
dat

Day 5
doll
duh
dat

Day 10
doll
duh
dat

Day 20
doll
duh
dat

© Cengage Learning

Figure 6.8 Assume that a child who is learning to talk points to her favorite doll and says either "doll," "duh," or "dat" when she wants it. Day 1 shows the number of times the child uses each word to ask for the doll (each block represents one request). At first, she uses all three words interchangeably. To hasten learning, her parents decide to give her the doll only when she names it correctly. Notice how the child's behavior shifts as operant reinforcement is applied. By day 20, saying "doll" has become the most probable response.

Operant conditioning Learning based on the consequences of responding.

Law of effect Responses that lead to desirable effects are repeated; those that produce undesirable results are not.

Operant reinforcer Any event that reliably increases the probability or frequency of responses it follows.

Operant conditioning chamber (Skinner box) An apparatus designed to study operant conditioning in animals.

Table 6.2 Comparison of Classical and Operant Conditioning

	CLASSICAL CONDITIONING	OPERANT CONDITIONING
Nature of response	Involuntary, reflex	Spontaneous, voluntary
Timing of learning	Occurs *before* response (CS paired with US)	Occurs *after* response (response is followed by reinforcing stimulus or event)
Role of learner	Passive (response is *elicited* by US)	Active (response is emitted)
Nature of learning	Neutral stimulus becomes a CS through association with a US	Probability of making a response is altered by consequences that follow it
Learned expectancy	US will follow CS	Response will have a specific effect

metal lever and a tray into which food pellets can be dispensed. The fact that there's not much to do in a Skinner box increases the chances that a subject will make the desired response, which is pressing the bar. Also, hunger keeps the animal motivated to seek food and actively *emit*, or freely give off, a variety of responses. A look into a typical Skinner box will clarify the process of operant conditioning:

Einstein Snags a Snack

A smart and hungry rat (yes, it's Larry's rat) is placed in an operant conditioning chamber. For a while, Einstein walks around, grooms, sniffs at the corners, or stands on his hind legs—all typical rat behaviors. Then it happens. He places his paw on the lever to get a better view of the top of the cage. *Click!* The lever depresses, and a food pellet drops into the tray. The rat scurries to the tray, eats the pellet, and then grooms himself. Up and exploring the cage again, he leans on the lever. *Click!* After a trip to the food tray, he returns to the bar and sniffs it, then puts his foot on it. *Click!* Soon Einstein settles into a smooth pattern of frequent bar pressing.

Notice that the rat did not acquire a new skill in this situation. He was already able to press the bar. Reinforcement alters only how *frequently* he presses the bar. In operant conditioning, new behavior patterns are molded by changing the probability that various responses will be made.

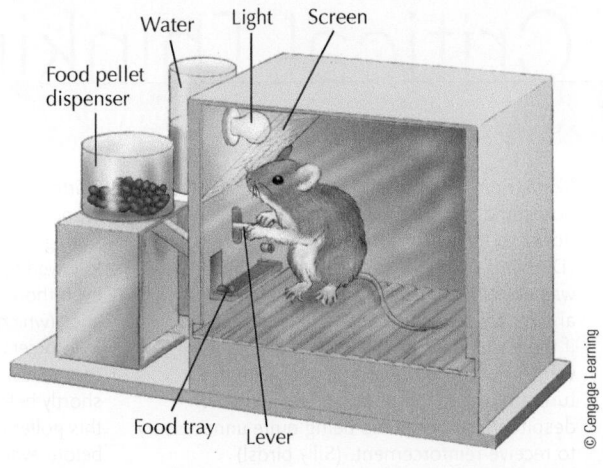

Figure 6.9 The Skinner box. This simple device allows careful study of operant conditioning. When the rat presses the bar, a pellet of food or a drop of water is automatically released. (A photograph of a Skinner box appears in Chapter 1.)

Information and Contingency

Like classical conditioning, we can think of operant learning as based on information and expectancies (Chance, 2009). In operant conditioning, *we learn to expect that a certain response will have a certain effect at certain times.* That is, we learn that a particular response is associated with reinforcement. Further, operant reinforcement works best when it is *response contingent* (kon-TIN-jent). That is, it must be given only after a desired response has occurred. From this point of view, a reinforcer tells a person or an animal that a response was "right" and worth repeating.

For example, reinforcement was used to teach, Jay, a 3-year-old autistic child, to answer questions with a "Yes" or a "No" (Shillingsburg et al., 2009). (Recall from Chapter 2 that autistic children have an impaired ability to communicate with other people.) If he answered "Yes" to questions like "Do you want a cookie?" (a preferred food), he was reinforced with a cookie and verbal praise. Similarly, if he answered "No" to questions like "Do you want corn?" (a non-preferred food), he was reinforced with verbal praise. Additionally, he was praised if he answered "Yes" to questions like "Does a cow say 'moo'?" or "No" to a question like (upon seeing a photo of a boat) "Is this a shoe?"

In similar ways, operant principles greatly affect behavior in homes, schools, and businesses. It is always worthwhile to arrange reinforcers so that they encourage productive and responsible behavior.

The Timing of Reinforcement

Operant reinforcement is most effective when it rapidly follows a correct response (Powell & Honey, 2012). For rats in a Skinner box, little or no learning occurs if the delay between bar pressing and receiving food exceeds 50 seconds (Figure 6.10). In general, you will be most successful if you present a reinforcer *immediately* after a response you wish to change. Thus, a child who is helpful or courteous should be immediately praised for her good behavior. In fact, tight timing is all that is required for learning to occur. (See "Are We Less Superstitious Than Pigeons?")

Let's say I work hard all semester in a class to get an A. Wouldn't the delay in reinforcement keep me from learning anything? No, for several reasons. First, as a mature human you can anticipate future reward. Second, you get reinforced by quiz and test grades all through the semester. Third, a single

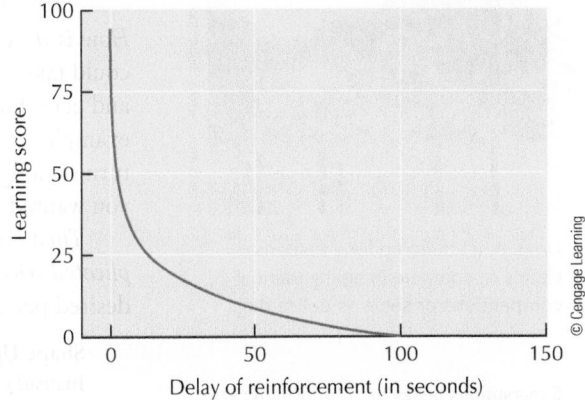

Figure 6.10 The effect of delay of reinforcement. Notice how rapidly the learning score drops when reward is delayed. Animals learning to press a bar in a Skinner box showed no signs of learning if food reward followed a bar press by more than 100 seconds. (Adapted from Perin, 1943.)

Critical Thinking

Skinner once placed some pigeons in Skinner boxes and reinforced them with food every now and then no matter what they were doing (Domjan, 2010). Despite the fact that there was no real connection between their behavior and its consequences, each pigeon acted as if there was. One bird began to flap its left wing, another to hop on one leg, a third to turn around in complete circles, and so on, despite these behaviors being quite unnecessary to receive reinforcement. (Silly birds!)

But humans wouldn't behave that way, right? Don't bet on it. When Skinner did this research, he had in mind human behavior like that of a golfer who always taps her club on the ground three times before hitting a shot. This probably started because once, by chance, the golfer tapped her club three times immediately before hitting a great shot. The tapping behavior was followed by success, and was hence reinforced, even though it had nothing to do with the great shot (which was due to her correct swing). Reinforcers affect not only the specific response they follow but also other responses that occur shortly before. After happening a few more times, this golfer ended up tapping her club three times before every shot. (Silly human!)

Skinner even used the term **superstitious behavior** to describe a behavior that is repeated because it appears to produce reinforcement, even though it is actually unnecessary. Some examples of actual superstitious behaviors of professional baseball players include drawing four lines in the dirt before getting in the batter's box, eating chicken before each game, and always playing in the same athletic supporter—for 4 years (phew!) (Burger & Lynn, 2005; Wright & Erdal, 2008).

Skinner's idea helps explain many human superstitions. If you walk under a ladder and then hurt yourself, you may avoid ladders in the future. Each time you avoid a ladder and nothing bad happens, your superstitious action is reinforced. Belief in magic can also be explained along such lines. Rituals to bring rain, ward off illness, or produce abundant crops very likely earn the faith of participants because they occasionally appear to succeed (Abbott & Sherratt, 2011; Jahoda, 2007). So keep your fingers crossed!

---

reinforcer can often maintain a long **response chain**—a linked series of actions that lead to reinforcement.

An example of response chaining is provided by the sport of dog agility training. Dogs are taught to navigate a variety of obstacles. These include jumping over hurdles, walking over seesaws, climbing up and jumping off inclined walls, and running through tunnels made out of cloth (Helton, 2007, 2009). During competitions, a trainer can reinforce a dog with a snack or a hug only after the dog completes the entire response chain. The winning dog is the one who finishes the course with the fewest mistakes and the fastest time. (Good dog!)

Many of the things we do every day involve similar response chains. The long series of events necessary to prepare a meal is rewarded by the final eating. A violinmaker may carry out thousands of steps for the final reward of hearing a first musical note. And as a student, you have built up long response chains for the final reward of getting good grades (right?).

Shaping

How is it possible to reinforce responses that rarely occur? Even in a barren Skinner box, it could take a long time for a rat (even one as smart as Einstein) to accidentally press the bar and get a food pellet. We might wait forever for more complicated responses to occur. For example, you would have to wait a long time for a duck to accidentally walk out of its cage, turn on a light, play a toy piano, turn off the light, and walk back to its cage. If this is what you wanted to reward, you would never get the chance.

Then how are the animals on television and at amusement parks taught to perform complicated tricks? The answer lies in **shaping**, which is the gradual molding of responses to a desired pattern. Let's look again at our favorite rat, Einstein.

Shape Up, Einstein

Instead of waiting for Einstein's first accidental bar press, which might have taken a long time, we could have shaped his behavior. Assume that Einstein has not yet learned to press the bar. At first, we settle for just getting him to face the bar. Any time he turns toward the bar, he is reinforced with a bit of food. Soon, Einstein spends much of his time facing the bar. Next, we reinforce him every time he takes a step toward the bar. If he turns toward the bar and walks away, nothing happens. But when he faces the bar and takes a step forward, *click!* His responses are being shaped.

By changing the rules about what makes a successful response, we can gradually train the rat to approach the bar and press it. In other words, *successive approximations* (ever-closer

Dogs must build up long response chains to compete in agility training competitions or serve as police dogs.

Superstitious behavior A behavior repeated because it seems to produce reinforcement, even though it is actually unnecessary.

Response chaining The assembly of separate responses into a series of actions that lead to reinforcement.

Shaping Gradually molding responses to a final desired pattern.

matches) to a desired response are reinforced during shaping. B. F. Skinner once taught two pigeons to play Ping-Pong in this way (**Figure 6.11**). Humans can also be shaped (Lamb et al., 2010). Let's say you want to study more, clean the house more often, or exercise more. In each case, it would be best to set a series of gradual, daily goals. Then you can reward yourself for small steps in the right direction (Watson & Tharp, 2007).

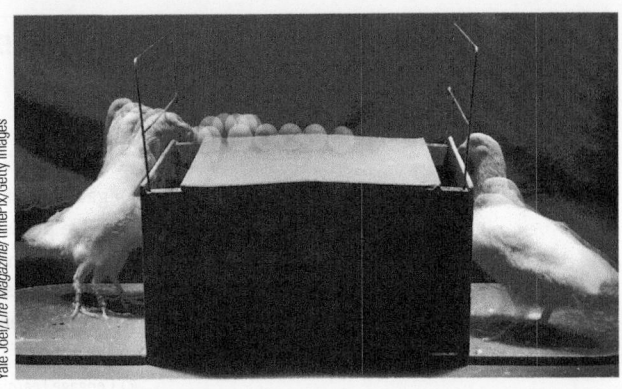

Yale, Joel/*Life Magazine*/TimePix/Getty Images

Figure 6.11 Operant conditioning principles were used to train these pigeons to play Ping-Pong.

Operant Extinction

Would a rat stop bar pressing if no more food arrived? Yes, but not immediately. Through **operant extinction**, learned responses that are not reinforced fade away gradually. Just as acquiring an operant response takes time, so does extinction. For example, if a television program repeatedly bores you, watching the program will likely extinguish over time.

Even after extinction seems complete, the previously reinforced response may return. If a rat is removed from a Skinner box after extinction and given a short rest, the rat will press the bar again when returned to the box. Similarly, a few weeks after they give up on buying lottery tickets, many people are tempted to try again.

Does extinction take as long the second time? If reinforcement is still withheld, a rat's bar pressing will extinguish again, usually more quickly. The brief return of an operant response after extinction is another example of *spontaneous recovery* (mentioned earlier regarding classical conditioning). Spontaneous recovery is very adaptive. After a rest period, the rat responds again in a situation that produced food in the past: "Just checking to see if the rules have changed!"

Marked changes in behavior occur when reinforcement and extinction are combined. For example, parents often unknowingly reinforce children for *negative attention seeking* (using misbehavior to gain attention). Children are generally ignored when they are playing quietly. They get attention when they become louder and louder, yell "Hey, Mom!" at the top of their lungs, throw tantrums, show off, or break something. Granted, the attention they get is often a scolding, but attention is a powerful reinforcer nevertheless. Parents report dramatic improvements when they praise or attend to a child who is quiet or playing constructively and *ignore* their children's disruptive behavior.

Negative Reinforcement

Until now, we have stressed **positive reinforcement**, which occurs when a pleasant or desirable event follows a response. How else could operant learning be reinforced? The time has come to consider **negative reinforcement**, which occurs when making a response removes an unpleasant event. Don't be fooled by the word *negative*. Negative reinforcement also increases responding. However, it does so by ending (*negating*, or taking away) discomfort.

Let's say that you have a headache and take an aspirin. Your aspirin taking will be negatively reinforced if the headache stops. Likewise, a rat could be taught to press a bar to get food (positive reinforcement), or the rat could be given a continuous mild shock (through the floor of its cage) that is turned off by a bar press (negative reinforcement). Either way, the rat will learn to press the bar more often. Why? Because it leads to a desired state of affairs (food or an end to pain). Here's another example of negative reinforcement: While walking outside, your hands get so cold they hurt. You take a pair of gloves out of your backpack and put them on, ending the pain. (You are *more likely* to put gloves on in the future because putting on the gloves was negatively reinforced.)

Punishment

Many people mistake negative reinforcement for punishment. However, **punishment** usually refers to following a response with an *aversive* (unpleasant) consequence. This form of punishment is also known as **positive punishment**. Again, don't be fooled by the

Operant extinction The weakening or disappearance of a nonreinforced operant response.

Positive reinforcement Occurs when a response is followed by a reward or other positive event.

Negative reinforcement Occurs when a response is followed by an end to discomfort or by the removal of an unpleasant event.

Positive punishment (Punishment) Any event that follows a response and *decreases* its likelihood of occurring again; the process of suppressing a response.

Table 6.3 Behavioral Effects of Various Consequences

	CONSEQUENCE OF MAKING A RESPONSE	EXAMPLE	EFFECT ON RESPONSE PROBABILITY
Positive reinforcement	Good event begins	Food given	Increase
Negative reinforcement	Bad event ends	Pain stops	Increase
Positive punishment	Bad event begins	Pain begins	Decrease
Negative punishment (response cost)	Good event ends	Food removed	Decrease
Nonreinforcement	Nothing	—	Decrease

© Cengage Learning

word *positive*. Positive punishment *decreases* the likelihood that the response will occur again. However, it does so by initiating *(adding)* discomfort. As noted, negative reinforcement *increases* responding.

The difference can be seen in a hypothetical example. Let's say you live in an apartment and your neighbor's stereo is blasting so loudly that you can't concentrate on reading this book. If you pound on the wall and the volume suddenly drops (negative reinforcement), future wall pounding will be more likely. But if you pound on the wall and the volume increases (punishment) or if the neighbor comes over and pounds on you (more punishment), wall pounding becomes less likely. Here's another example of punishment, in which an unpleasant result follows a response: You are driving your car too fast. You are caught in a radar trap and given a speeding ticket. Henceforth, you will be less likely to speed. (You are *less likely* to speed next time because speeding was punished by a fine.)

Isn't it also punishing to have privileges, money, or other positive things taken away for making a particular response? Yes. Punishment also occurs when a reinforcer or positive state of affairs is removed, such as losing privileges. This second type of punishment is called **negative punishment** or **response cost**. One more time, don't be fooled by the word *negative*. Negative punishment also decreases responding. However, it does so by ending (*negating*, or taking away) something pleasant.

The best-known form of response cost is *time out*, in which children are removed from situations that normally allow them to gain reinforcement. When your parents put you on time out by sending you to your room, they denied you the reinforcement of being with the rest of your family or hanging out with your friends. For your convenience, **Table 6.3** summarizes five basic consequences of making a response.

Operant Reinforcers—What's Your Pleasure?

JOURNEY QUESTION 6.5 *Are there different kinds of operant reinforcement?*

For humans, learning may be reinforced by anything from a candy bar to a word of praise. In categorizing reinforcers, a useful distinction can be made between *primary reinforcers* and *secondary reinforcers*. It is also important to distinguish *reinforcement*, which exerts its effect through associative learning, from *feedback*, a key component of cognitive learning. Let's examine reinforcement and feedback in more detail.

Primary Reinforcers

Primary reinforcers produce comfort, end discomfort, or fill an immediate physical need: They are natural, nonlearned, and rooted in biology. Food, water, and sex are obvious examples. Every time you open the refrigerator, walk to a drinking fountain, turn up the heat, or order a double latte, your actions reflect primary reinforcement.

Negative punishment (Response cost) Removal of a positive reinforcer after a response is made.

Primary reinforcers Nonlearned reinforcers; usually those that satisfy physiological needs.

Brainwaves

Suppose you could have an electrode implanted in your brain and connected to a remote control. Slide the controller upwards and electrical impulses stimulate one of your brain's "pleasure centers." The very few humans who have ever had a chance to try direct brain stimulation report feeling intense pleasure that is better than food, water, sex, drugs, or any other primary reinforcer (Heath, 1963; **Figure 6.12**.)

Most of what we know about such intracranial self-stimulation comes from studying rats with similar implants (Vlachou & Markou, 2011). A rat "wired for pleasure" can be trained to press the bar in a Skinner box to deliver electrical stimulation to its own limbic system (refer back to Figure 2.26). Some rats will press the bar thousands of times per hour to obtain brain stimulation. After 15 or 20 hours of constant pressing, animals sometimes collapse from exhaustion. When they revive, they begin pressing again. If the reward circuit is not turned off,

an animal will ignore food, water, and sex in favor of bar pressing.

Many natural primary reinforcers activate the same pleasure pathways in the brain that make intracranial self-stimulation so powerful (Powell & Honey, 2012). So do psychoactive drugs, such as alcohol and cocaine (Galankin, Shekunova, & Zvartau, 2010; Rodd et al., 2005). In fact, rats will also self-administer nicotine. When they do, they are even more likely to engage in intracranial self-stimulation (Kenny & Markou, 2006). Apparently, nicotine further increases the sensitivity of pleasure pathways in the brain.

One shudders to think what might happen if brain implants were easy and practical to do. (They are not.) Every company from *Playboy* to *Microsoft* would have a device on the market, and we would have to keep a closer watch on politicians than usual!

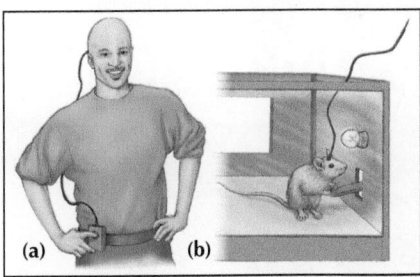

Figure 6.12 Humans have been "wired" for brain stimulation, as shown in *(a)*. However, in humans, this has been done only as an experimental way to restrain uncontrollable outbursts of violence. Implants have not been done merely to produce pleasure. Most research has been carried out with rats. Using the apparatus shown in *(b)*, the rat can press a bar to deliver mild electric stimulation to a "pleasure center" in the brain.

In addition to obvious examples, there are other, less obvious, primary reinforcers, such as psychoactive drugs. One of the most powerful reinforcers is *intracranial self-stimulation*, which involves the direct activation of "pleasure centers" in the brain. (See "Tickling Your Own Fancy.")

Secondary Reinforcers

Although human learning is still strongly tied to food, water, and other primary reinforcers, humans also respond to a much broader range of rewards and reinforcers. Money, praise, attention, approval, success, affection, grades, and the like all serve as learned or **secondary reinforcers**.

How does a secondary reinforcer gain its ability to promote learning? Some secondary reinforcers are simply associated with a primary reinforcer. For example, if you would like to train a dog to follow you ("heel") when you take a walk, you could reward the dog with small food treats for staying near you. If you praise the dog each time you give it a treat, praise will become a secondary reinforcer. In time, you will be able to skip giving treats and simply praise your pup for doing the right thing. The same principle applies to children. One reason that parents' praise becomes a secondary reinforcer is because it is frequently associated with food, candy, hugs, and other primary reinforcers.

Tokens and Token Economies

Secondary reinforcers that can be *exchanged* for primary reinforcers gain their value more directly (Powell & Honey, 2012). Printed money obviously has little or no value of its own. You can't eat it, drink it, or sleep with it. However, it can be exchanged for food, water, lodging, and other necessities.

A **token reinforcer** is a tangible secondary reinforcer, such as money, gold stars, poker chips, and the like. In a series of classic experiments, chimpanzees were taught to work for tokens. The chimps were first trained to put poker chips into a vending machine (**Figure 6.13**).

Secondary reinforcer A learned reinforcer; often one that gains reinforcing properties by association with a primary reinforcer.

Token reinforcer A tangible secondary reinforcer such as money, gold stars, poker chips, and the like.

Figure 6.13 Poker chips normally have little or no value for chimpanzees, but this chimp will work hard to earn them once he learns that the "Chimp-O-Mat" will dispense food in exchange for them.

Each chip dispensed a few grapes or raisins. Once the animals had learned to exchange tokens for food, they would learn new tasks to earn the chips. To maintain the value of the tokens, the chimps were occasionally allowed to use the "Chimp-O-Mat" (Cowles, 1937).

A major advantage of tokens is that they don't lose reinforcing value as quickly as primary reinforcers do. For instance, if you use candy to reinforce a developmentally disabled child for correctly naming things, the child might lose interest once he is satiated (fully satisfied) or no longer hungry. It would be better to use tokens as immediate rewards for learning. Later, the child can exchange his tokens for candy, toys, or other treats.

Token economies, systems for managing and altering behavior through reinforcement of selected responses, have been used with troubled children and adults in special programs, and even in ordinary school classrooms (Alberto & Troutman, 2009; Maggin et al., 2011; Figure 6.14). In each case the goal is to provide an immediate reward for learning. Typically, tokens may be exchanged for food, special privileges, or trips to movies, amusement parks, and so forth. Many parents find that tokens greatly reduce discipline problems with younger children. For example, children can earn points or gold stars during the week for good behavior. If they earn enough tokens, they are allowed on the weekend to choose one item out of a "grab bag" of small prizes.

Social Reinforcers

As we have noted, learned desires for attention and approval, which are called **social reinforcers**, often influence human behavior. This fact can be used in a classic, if somewhat mischievous, demonstration.

Shaping a Teacher

For this activity, about one half (or more) of the students in a classroom must participate. First, select a target behavior. This should be something like "lecturing from the right side of the room." (Keep it simple, in case your teacher is a slow learner.) Begin training in this way: Each time the instructor turns toward the right or takes a step in that direction, participating students should look *really* interested. Also, smile, ask questions, lean forward, and make eye contact. If the teacher turns to the left or takes a step in that direction, participating students should lean back, yawn, check out their split ends, close their eyes, or generally look bored. Soon, without being aware of why, the instructor should be spending most of his or her time each class period lecturing from the right side of the classroom.

This trick has been a favorite of psychology graduate students for decades. For a time, one of your author's professors delivered all her lectures from the right side of the room while toying with the cords on the window shades. (The students added the cords the second week!) The point to remember from this example is that attention and approval can change the behavior of children, family members, friends, roommates, and coworkers. Be aware of what you are reinforcing. And be aware that you may be unaware of some of the reinforcers that are changing your own behavior! (In fact, such automatic associative learning is a hallmark of experiential processing; but more about that in Chapter 8.)

Feedback

His eyes are driven and blazing and his body contorts. One hand jerks up and down while the other one furiously spins in circular motions. Does this describe some strange neurological disorder? Actually, it depicts our friend Sheldon (still occasionally salivating at the thought of a lemon) as he plays a Wii animated fishing adventure.

How did Sheldon learn the complex movements needed to excel at virtual fishing? After all, he was not rewarded with food or money. The answer lies in the fact that Sheldon's video game provides **feedback**, a key element that underlies learning. Feedback—information about the effect a response had—is particularly important in human cognitive learning (Lefrançois, 2012).

Social reinforcer Reinforcement based on receiving attention, approval, or affection from another person.

Feedback Information returned to a person about the effects a response has had; also known as knowledge of results.

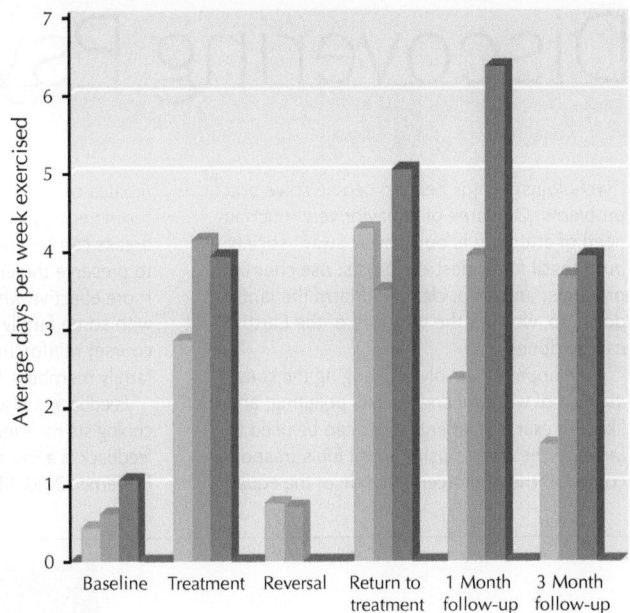

Figure 6.14 Reinforcement in a token economy. Children with cystic fibrosis (a hereditary lung disease) benefit from exercise that clears blocked airways. This graph shows the effects of using tokens to reward aerobic exercise in three children with cystic fibrosis. The number of minutes of aerobic exercise each day was measured. Tokens earned could be exchanged for rewards such as going to see a movie or staying up past bedtime. The graph shows that all three children exercised relatively infrequently without the reinforcement (*baseline* and *reversal* phases) and relatively more when the reinforcement was in place (*training* and return to *treatment* phases). It is encouraging to note that exercise rates remained heightened for months after the token economy was first implemented. (Bernard, R. S., Cohen, L. L., Moffett, K. (2009). A token economy for exercise adherence in pediatric cystic fibrosis: A single-subject analysis. *Journal of Pediatric Psychology, 34(4)*, 354–365. Copyright © 2009, Oxford University Press. Reprinted by permission.)

Every time a player does something, a video game responds instantly with sounds, animated actions, and a higher or lower score. The machine's responsiveness and the information flow it provides can be very motivating if you want to win. The same principle applies to many other learning situations: If you are trying to learn to use a computer, to play a musical instrument, to cook, to play a sport, or to solve math problems, feedback that you achieved a desired result can be reinforcing in its own right.

The adaptive value of feedback helps explain why much human learning occurs in the absence of obvious reinforcers, such as food or water. Humans readily learn responses that merely have a desired effect or that bring a goal closer. Let's explore this idea further.

Knowledge of Results

Imagine that you are asked to throw darts at a target. Each dart must pass over a screen that prevents you from telling if you hit the target. If you threw 1,000 darts, we would expect little improvement in your performance because no feedback is provided. Sheldon's video game did not explicitly reward him for correct responses. Yet, because it provided feedback, rapid learning took place.

How can feedback be applied? Increased feedback—also called **knowledge of results (KR)**—almost always improves learning and performance (Snowman & McCown, 2011; Vojdanoska, Cranney, & Newell, 2010). If you want to learn to play a musical instrument, to sing, to speak a second language, or to deliver a speech, recorded feedback can be very helpful. In sports, video replays are used to provide feedback on everything from tennis serves to pick-off moves in baseball. Whenever you are trying to learn a complex skill, it pays to get more feedback (Eldridge, Saltzman, & Lahav, 2010; Jaehnig & Miller, 2007). (Also see "Learning and Conservation.")

Learning Aids

How can feedback be applied? Since increased feedback almost always improves learning and performance, it makes sense to design learning aids to supply effective feedback (Snowman & McCown, 2011). Feedback is most effective when it is *frequent*, *immediate*, and *detailed*. **Programmed instruction** teaches students in a format that presents information in small amounts, gives immediate practice, and provides continuous feedback to learners. Frequent feedback keeps learners from practicing errors. It also lets students work at their own pace.

To get a sense of the programmed instruction format, finish reading the next few paragraphs and complete the Study Break when you encounter it (just like you do with *all* of the Study Breaks you come across, right?). Work through the Recite questions one at a time, checking your answer before moving on. (You can find the correct answers upside down at the end of the Study Break.) In this way, your correct (or incorrect) responses will be followed by immediate feedback.

Knowledge of results (KR) Informational feedback.

Programmed instruction Any learning format that presents information in small amounts, gives immediate practice, and provides continuous feedback to learners.

Psychologists enjoy helping people solve practical problems. One area of behavior very much in need of attention is our "throw-away" society. We burn fossil fuels; destroy forests; use chemical products; and strip, clear, and farm the land. In doing so, we alter the very face of the Earth. What can be done?

One approach involves changing the *consequences* of wasteful energy use, polluting, and the like. For example, energy taxes can be used to increase the cost of using fossil fuels (response cost). On the reinforcement side of the equation,

rebates can be offered for installing insulation or buying energy-efficient appliances or cars, and tax breaks can be given to companies that take steps to preserve the environment. Recycling is also more effective when entire families participate, with some family members (usually Mom, of course) reinforcing the recycling behavior of other family members (Meneses & Beerlipalacio, 2005).

Feedback is also important. Environmental psychologists have long known that a lack of prompt feedback is a major barrier to conservation (Carrico & Riemer, 2010; McCalley, de Vries, & Midden, 2011).

When families, work groups, factories, and dorms receive feedback, on a weekly basis, about how much they recycled, they typically recycle more.

New tools, such as *ecological footprint calculators*, make it a lot easier for individuals to get feedback about their individual resource consumption (Global Footprint Network, 2011). With growing public concern over global warming, many people are now calculating their individual *carbon footprint*, the volume of greenhouse gases individual consumption adds to the atmosphere (The Nature Conservancy, 2012).

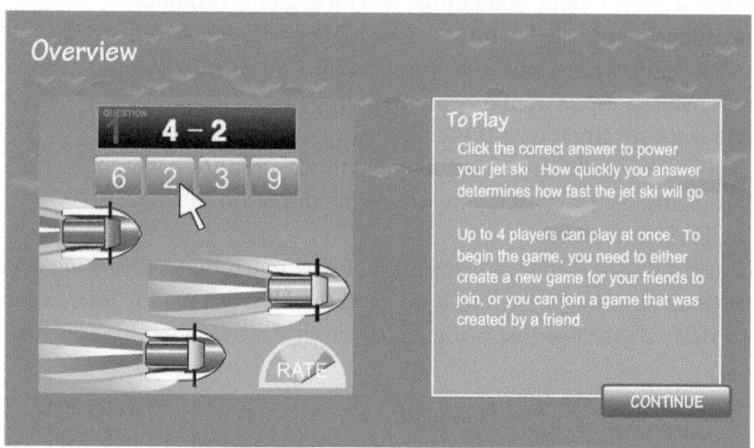

Figure 6.15 Computer-assisted instruction. In order to increase interest and motivation, this math game allows students to compete in a speedboat race rather than just completing a series of subtraction problems. The faster correct answers are selected, the faster the student's boat speeds toward the finish line. (Screenshot from "Island Chase Subtraction." http://www.arcademicskillbuilders.com/games/island_chase/island_chase.html. Copyright © 2012, Arcademics. Reprinted by permission.)

Michael Dunning/Getty Images

Figure 6.16 Boeing 747 Airline Training Simulator. Student pilots can learn all the ins and outs of flying a jumbo jet in this flight simulator. Aren't you glad they don't have to do that with real planes (and passengers)? Your authors sure are!

Today programmed instruction is often presented via computer (Mayer, 2011; Springer & Pear, 2008). You may know it as CAI *(computer-assisted instruction)* or drill-and-practice (or, affectionately, drill-and-kill). In addition to giving learners immediate feedback, the computer can give hints about why an answer was wrong and what is needed to correct it (Timmerman & Kruepke, 2006). Increasingly, CAI programs called *serious games* are making use of game formats such as stories, competition with a partner, sound effects, and rich computer graphics to increase interest and motivation (Charsky, 2010; Westera, et al., 2008; see Figure 6.15).

Educational *simulations*, the most complex serious games, allow students to explore an imaginary situation or "microworld" to learn to solve real-world problems (Figure 6.16). By seeing the effects of their choices, students discover basic principles of physics, biology, psychology, or other subjects (Grabe, 2006; Herold, 2010).

CAI software can save teachers and learners much time and effort, although the final level of skill or knowledge gained is not necessarily higher. In addition, people often do better with feedback from a computer because they can freely make mistakes and learn from them (Mayer, 2011; Ward & Parr, 2010). Let's pause now for some learning exercises (remember?) so that you can get some feedback about your mastery of the preceding ideas.

RECITE

1. Responses in operant conditioning are _____ or _____, whereas those in classical conditioning are passive, _____, or _____ responses.
2. Extinction in operant conditioning is also subject to _____ of a response.

    a. successive approximations b. shaping
    c. automation d. spontaneous recovery

3. Positive reinforcers increase the rate of responding and negative reinforcers decrease it. T or F?
4. Which is a correct match?

    a. social reinforcer–primary reinforcement b. token reinforcer–secondary reinforcement
    c. intracranial stimulation–secondary reinforcement d. negative reinforcer–punishment

5. Superstitious responses are those that are

    a. shaped by secondary reinforcement b. extinguished
    c. prepotent d. unnecessary to obtain reinforcement

REFLECT

THINK CRITICALLY

6. Can you imagine different forms of feedback?
7. Can you think of any reasons why engaging in superstitious behaviors might actually improve performance?

SELF-REFLECT

Can you explain the difference between positive reinforcement, negative reinforcement, and punishment? Can you give an example of each concept from your own experience?

A friend of yours punishes his dog all the time. What advice would you give him about how to use reinforcement, extinction, and shaping, instead of punishment?

ANSWERS

1. voluntary or emitted, involuntary or elicited 2. d 3. F 4. b 5. d 6. Knowledge of results means you find out if your response was right or wrong. Knowledge of correct response also tells you what the correct response should have been. Elaboration feedback adds additional information, such as an explanation of the correct answer. Adding knowledge of correct response and/or some elaboration is more effective than knowledge of results alone (Jaehnig & Miller, 2007). 7. Even though you know tapping your club on the ground three times is not causing a better golf shot, it might nevertheless help settle you down or help you focus your attention on your swing (Damisch, Stoberock, & Mussweiler, 2010).

Partial Reinforcement—Las Vegas, a Human Skinner Box?

JOURNEY QUESTION 6.6 *How are we influenced by patterns of reward?*

If you would like to influence operant learning, you will need to know how patterns of reinforcement affect behavior. Imagine, for example, that a mother wants to reward her child for turning off the lights when he leaves a room. Contrary to what you might think, it is better to reinforce only some of her son's correct responses. Why should this be so? You'll find the answer in the following discussion.

Until now, we have treated operant reinforcement as if it were continuous. *Continuous reinforcement* means that a reinforcer follows every correct response. At the start, continuous reinforcement is useful for learning new responses (Domjan, 2010). To teach your dog to come to you, it is best to reinforce your dog every time it comes when called. Curiously, once your dog has learned to come when called, it is best to shift to **partial reinforcement**, in which reinforcers do not follow every response. Responses acquired by partial reinforcement are highly resistant to extinction, a phenomenon known as the *partial reinforcement effect* (Domjan, 2010; Svartdal, 2003).

How does getting reinforced part of the time make a habit stronger? If you have ever visited a casino, you have probably seen row after row of people playing slot machines. To gain insight into the distinction between continuous and partial reinforcement, imagine that you put a dollar in a slot machine and pull the handle. Ten dollars spills into the tray. Let's say this continues for several minutes. Every pull is followed by a payoff. Because you are being reinforced on a continuous schedule, you quickly "get hooked" (and begin to plan your retirement).

Partial reinforcement A pattern in which only a portion of all responses are reinforced.

The one-armed bandit (slot machine) is a dispenser of partial reinforcement.

But, alas, suddenly each pull is followed by nothing. Obviously, you would respond several times more before giving up. However, when continuous reinforcement is followed by extinction, the message quickly becomes clear: No more payoffs (or early retirement).

Contrast this with partial reinforcement. This time, imagine that you put a dollar in a slot machine five times without a payoff. You are just about to quit, but decide to play once more. Bingo! The machine returns $20. After this, payoffs continue on a partial schedule; some are large, and some are small. All are unpredictable. Sometimes you hit two in a row, and sometimes 20 or 30 pulls go unrewarded.

Now let's say the payoff mechanism is turned off again. How many times do you think you would respond this time before your handle-pulling behavior is extinguished? Because you have developed the expectation that any play may be "the one," it will be hard to resist just one more play. . . . and one more. . . . and one more. Also, because partial reinforcement might include long periods of nonreward, it will be harder to distinguish between periods of reinforcement and extinction. It is no exaggeration to say that the partial reinforcement effect has left many people penniless. Even psychologists visiting a casino may get "cleaned out." (Not your authors, of course!)

To return to our examples, after using continuous reinforcement to teach a child to turn off the lights or a dog to come when called, it is best to shift to partial reinforcement. That way, the new behavior will become more resistant to extinction.

Schedules of Partial Reinforcement

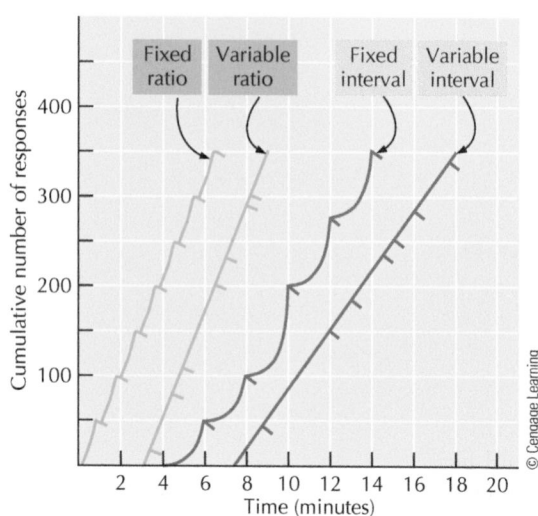

Figure 6.17 Typical response patterns for reinforcement schedules.

Partial reinforcement can be given in several patterns, or partial **schedules of reinforcement**—plans for determining which responses will be reinforced (Domjan, 2010). Let's consider the four most basic, which have some interesting effects on us. Typical responses to each pattern are shown in Figure 6.17. Results such as these are obtained when a *cumulative recorder* is connected to a Skinner box. The device consists of a moving strip of paper and a mechanical pen that jumps upward each time a response is made. Rapid responding causes the pen to draw a steep line; a horizontal line indicates no response. Small tick marks on the lines show when a reinforcer was given.

Fixed Ratio (FR)

What would happen if a reinforcer followed only every other response? Or what if we followed every third, fourth, fifth, or other number of responses with reinforcement? Each of these patterns is a **fixed ratio (FR) schedule**—a set number of correct responses must be made to obtain a reinforcer. Notice that in an FR schedule the ratio of reinforcers to responses is fixed: FR-3 means that every third response is reinforced; FR-10 means that 10 responses must be made to obtain a reinforcer.

Fixed ratio schedules produce *very high response rates* (Figure 6.17). A hungry rat on an FR-10 schedule will quickly run off 10 responses, pause to eat, and then run off 10 more. A similar situation occurs when factory or farm workers are paid on a piecework basis. When a fixed number of items must be produced for a set amount of pay, work output is high.

Variable Ratio (VR)

In a **variable ratio (VR) schedule** a varied number of correct responses must be made to get a reinforcer. Instead of reinforcing every fourth response (FR-4), for example, a person or animal on a VR-4 schedule gets rewarded *on average* every fourth response. Sometimes 2 responses must be made to obtain a reinforcer; sometimes it's 5; sometimes 4; and so on. The actual number varies, but it averages out to 4 (in this example). Variable ratio schedules also produce high response rates.

VR schedules seem less predictable than FR. Does that have any effect on extinction? Yes. Because reinforcement is less predictable, VR schedules tend to produce greater resistance to extinction than fixed ratio schedules. Playing a slot machine is an example of behavior

Schedule of reinforcement A rule or plan for determining which responses will be reinforced.

Fixed ratio (FR) schedule A set number of correct responses must be made to get a reinforcer. For example, a reinforcer is given for every four correct responses.

Variable ratio (VR) schedule A varied number of correct responses must be made to get a reinforcer. For example, a reinforcer is given after three to seven correct responses; the actual number changes randomly.

Critical Thinking

We humans are *cognitive time travelers*, regularly zooming back and forth through time in our minds. You can, for example, think about past events, such as what you had for breakfast this morning. We can also imagine events in the future. Brides-to-be are famous for planning their weddings down to the last detail. But what about animals? Are they cognitive time travelers, or are they less cognitive and hence "stuck in time" (Clayton, Russell, & Dickinson, 2009)? Do dogs ever think about how hot it was yesterday or what they plan to do tomorrow? To answer such questions, psychologists have used operant conditioning as a research tool.

Conditioning studies have repeatedly shown that animals are sensitive to the passage of time (Zentall, 2010). For example, pigeons and rats reinforced on fixed interval schedules stop responding immediately after they receive a reinforcer and do not start again until just before the next scheduled reinforcement (Roberts, 2002). In one study, pigeons were put

in a Skinner box with a pecking key on each wall. They quickly learned to peck only at Key 1 if it was 9:30 in the morning and at Key 3 if it was 4:00 in the afternoon (Saksida & Wilkie, 1994).

Another study focused on scrub jays. These birds are hoarders; they store excess food at different locations and then go back later to eat it. Scrub jays were allowed to hoard some nuts in one location and some worms in another. If they were released 4 hours later, they went directly to the worms. However, if they were released 5 days later, they went straight for the nuts. Worms are a scrub jay's favorite food, which explains their choice after 4 hours. But worms decay after a day or so, whereas nuts stay edible. It seems that the jays knew exactly where they stored each type of food and how much time had passed (Clayton, Yu, & Dickinson, 2001).

Although these studies are suggestive, they are part of an ongoing debate about animal cognition, including whether animals are stuck in time (Roberts & Roberts, 2002; Zentall, 2010).

George McCarthy/NPL/Minden Pictures

Florida scrub jays are food hoarders. Does their food hoarding behavior prove they are not "trapped in time"?

---

maintained by a variable ratio schedule. Another would be our plan to only occasionally reward a child for turning off the lights, once he has learned to do so. Golf, tennis, baseball, and many other sports are also reinforced on a variable ratio basis: Even the best batters in baseball rarely get a hit more than an average of 3 out of every 10 times they are at bat.

Fixed Interval (FI)

In another pattern, reinforcement is given only when a correct response is made after a fixed amount of time has passed. This time interval is measured from the last reinforced response. Responses made during the time interval are not reinforced. In a **fixed interval (FI) schedule** the first correct response made after the time period has passed is reinforced. Thus, a rat on an FI-30-second schedule has to wait 30 seconds after the last reinforced response before a bar press will pay off again. The rat can press the bar as often as it wants during the interval, but it will not be rewarded.

Fixed interval schedules produce *moderate response rates*. Animals working on an FI schedule seem to develop a keen sense of the passage of time (Eckerman, 1999). Few responses occur just after a reinforcement is delivered and a spurt of activity occurs just before the next reinforcement is due. (See "Are Animals Stuck in Time?")

Is getting paid weekly an FI schedule? Pure examples of fixed interval schedules are rare, but getting paid each week at work does come close. Notice, however, that most people do not work faster just before payday, as an FI schedule predicts. A closer parallel would be having a report due every 2 weeks for a class. Right after turning in a paper, your work would probably drop to zero for a week or more (Chance, 2009).

Variable Interval (VI)

Variable interval (VI) schedules are a variation on fixed intervals. Here, reinforcement is given for the first correct response made after a varied amount of time. On a VI-30-second schedule, reinforcement is available after an interval that *averages* 30 seconds.

VI schedules produce *slow, steady response rates* and tremendous resistance to extinction (Lattal, Reilly, & Kohn, 1998). When you dial a phone number and get a busy signal,

Fixed interval (FI) schedule A reinforcer is given only when a correct response is made after a set amount of time has passed since the last reinforced response. Responses made during the time interval are not reinforced.

Variable interval (VI) schedule A reinforcer is given for the first correct response made after a varied amount of time has passed since the last reinforced response. Responses made during the time interval are not reinforced.

reward (getting through) is on a VI schedule. You may have to wait 30 seconds or 30 minutes. If you are like most people, you will doggedly dial over and over again until you get a connection. Success in fishing is also on a VI schedule—which may explain the bulldog tenacity of many anglers (Chance, 2009).

Stimulus Control—Red Light, Green Light

When you are driving, your behavior at intersections is controlled by the red or green light. In similar fashion, many of the stimuli we encounter each day act like stop or go signals that guide our behavior. To state the idea more formally, stimuli that consistently precede a rewarded response tend to influence when and where the response will occur. This effect is called **stimulus control**. Notice how it works with our friend Einstein:

Lights Out for Einstein

While learning the bar-pressing response, Einstein has been in a Skinner box illuminated by a bright light. During several training sessions, the light is alternately turned on and off. When the light is on, a bar press will produce food. When the light is off, bar pressing goes unrewarded. We soon observe that the rat presses vigorously when the light is on and ignores the bar when the light is off.

In this example, the light signals what consequences will follow if a response is made. A similar example of stimulus control would be a child learning to ask for candy when her mother is in a good mood, but not asking at other times. Evidence for stimulus control could be shown by turning the food delivery *on* when the light is *off*. A well-trained animal might never discover that the rules had changed (Powell & Honey, 2012). Likewise, we pick up phones that are ringing but rarely answer phones that are silent.

Generalization

Two important aspects of stimulus control are generalization and discrimination. Let's return to dogs to illustrate these concepts. First, generalization.

Is generalization the same in operant conditioning as it is in classical conditioning? Basically, yes. **Operant stimulus generalization** is the tendency to respond to stimuli similar to those that preceded operant reinforcement. That is, a reinforced response tends to be made again when similar antecedents are present.

Assume, for instance, that your dog has begun to jump up at you whenever you are eating dinner at the kitchen table. (Bad dog!) Mind you, that's because you have been rewarding its behavior with table scraps. (Bad master!) Then your dog begins to jump any time you sit at the kitchen table. The dog has learned that reinforcement tends to occur when you are at the kitchen table. The dog's behavior has come under stimulus control. Now let's say that there are some other tables in your house. Because they are similar, your dog will likely jump up if you sit at any of them because the jumping response *generalized* to other tables. Similar generalization explains why children may temporarily call all men *Daddy*—much to the embarrassment of their parents.

Discrimination

Meanwhile, back at the table. . . . As stated earlier, to discriminate means to respond differently to varied stimuli. Because one table signaled the availability of reinforcement to your dog, it began jumping up while you sat at other tables as well (generalization). If you do not feed your dog while sitting at any other table, the jumping response that originally generalized to them will extinguish because of nonreinforcement. Thus, your dog's jumping response is consistently rewarded in the presence of a specific table. The same response to different tables is extinguished. Through **operant stimulus discrimination**, your dog has learned to differentiate between antecedent stimuli that signal reward and nonreward. As a result, the dog's response pattern will shift to match these **discriminative stimuli**—stimuli that precede reinforced and nonreinforced responses.

Stimulus control Stimuli present when an operant response is acquired tend to control when and where the response is made.

Operant stimulus generalization The tendency to respond to stimuli similar to those that preceded operant reinforcement.

Operant stimulus discrimination The tendency to make an operant response when stimuli previously associated with reward are present and to withhold the response when stimuli associated with nonreward are present.

Discriminative stimuli Stimuli that precede rewarded and nonrewarded responses in operant conditioning.

Stimulus discrimination is aptly illustrated by the "sniffer" dogs that locate drugs and explosives at airports and border crossings. Operant discrimination is used to teach these dogs to recognize contraband. During training, they are reinforced only for approaching containers baited with drugs or explosives.

Stimulus discrimination also has a tremendous impact on human behavior. Learning to recognize different automobile brands, birds, animals, wines, types of music, and even the answers on psychology tests all depends, in part, on operant discrimination learning.

A discriminative stimulus that most drivers are familiar with is a police car on the freeway. This stimulus is a clear signal that a specific set of reinforcement contingencies applies. As you have probably observed, the presence of a police car brings about rapid reductions in driving speed, lane changes, and tailgating.

Would using different ringtones on my cellphone be an example of using discriminative stimuli? Excellent! Suppose you use one ringtone for people you want to speak to, one for people you don't, and yet another for calls from strangers. In no time at all you will be showing different telephone answering behavior in response to different ringtones.

Carleton Ray/Photo Researchers, Inc.

Stimulus control. Operant shaping was used to teach this whale to "bow" to an audience. Fish were used as reinforcers. Notice the trainer's hand signal, which serves as a discriminative stimulus to control the performance.

---

study break Partial Reinforcement and Stimulus Control

RECITE

1. Two aspects of stimulus control are _____ and _____.
2. Responding tends to occur in the presence of discriminative stimuli associated with reinforcement and tends not to occur in the presence of discriminative stimuli associated with nonreinforcement. T or F?
3. *Stimulus generalization* refers to making an operant response in the presence of stimuli similar to those that preceded reinforcement. T or F?
4. Moderate response rates that are marked by spurts of activity and periods of inactivity are characteristic of
   a. FR schedules   b. VR schedules
   c. FI schedules   d. VI schedules
5. Partial reinforcement tends to produce slower responding and reduced resistance to extinction. T or F?
6. The schedule of reinforcement associated with playing slot machines and other types of gambling is _____ _____.

REFLECT

THINK CRITICALLY

7. A business owner who pays employees an hourly wage wants to increase productivity. How could the owner make more effective use of reinforcement?

SELF-REFLECT

Think of something you do that is reinforced only part of the time. Do you pursue this activity persistently? How have you been affected by partial reinforcement?

See if you can think of at least one everyday example of the five basic schedules of reinforcement (continuous reinforcement and the four types of partial reinforcement).

Doors that are meant to be pushed outward have metal plates on them. Those that are meant to be pulled inward have handles. Do these discriminative stimuli affect your behavior?

ANSWERS

1. generalization, discrimination 2. T 3. T 4. c 5. F 6. variable ratio 7. Continuing to use fixed interval rewards (hourly wage or salary) would guarantee a basic level of income for employees. To reward extra effort, the owner could add some fixed ratio reinforcement (such as incentives, bonuses, commissions, or profit sharing) to employees' pay.

Punishment—Putting the Brakes on Behavior

JOURNEY QUESTION 6.7 *What does punishment do to behavior?*

Spankings, reprimands, fines, jail sentences, firings, failing grades, and the like are commonly used to control behavior. Clearly, the story of instrumental learning is unfinished without a return to the topic of punishment. Recall that **punishment** lowers the probability that a response will occur again. To be most effective, punishment must be given contingently (only after an undesired response occurs).

Punishment Any event that follows a response and *decreases* its likelihood of occurring again; the process of suppressing a response.

Punishers are consequences that lower the probability that a response will be made again. Receiving a traffic citation is directly punishing because the driver is delayed and reprimanded. Paying a fine and higher insurance rates add to the punishment in the form of response cost.

Punishers, like reinforcers, are defined by observing their effects on behavior. A **punisher** is any consequence that reduces the frequency of a target behavior. It is not always possible to know ahead of time what will act as a punisher for a particular person. For example, when Jason's mother reprimanded him for throwing toys, he stopped doing it. In this instance, the reprimand was a punisher. However, Chris is starved for attention of any kind from his parents, who both work full-time. For Chris, a reprimand, or even a spanking, might actually reinforce toy throwing. Remember, too, that a punisher can be either the onset of an unpleasant event (positive punishment) or the removal of a pleasant state of affairs (negative punishment or response cost).

Variables Affecting Punishment

How effective is punishment? The effectiveness of punishers depends greatly on their *timing*, *consistency*, and *intensity*. Punishment works best when it occurs as the response is being made, or *immediately* afterward (timing), and when it is given *each time* a response occurs (consistency). Thus, if simply refusing to feed your dog table scraps is not enough to stop it from jumping at you when you sit at a table, you could effectively (and humanely) punish it by spraying water on its nose each time it jumps up. About 10 to 15 such treatments are usually enough. This would not be the case if you applied punishment haphazardly or long after the jumping stopped. If you discover that your dog dug up a tree and ate it while you were gone, punishing the dog hours later will do little good. Likewise, the commonly heard childhood threat, "Wait 'til your father comes home, then you'll be sorry," just makes the father a feared brute; it doesn't effectively punish an undesirable response.

Severe punishment (following a response with an intensely aversive or unpleasant stimulus) can be extremely effective in stopping behavior. If 3-year-old Beavis sticks his finger in a light socket and gets a shock, that may be the last time he *ever* tries it. Intense punishment may permanently suppress responding, even for actions as basic as eating.

However, mild punishment only temporarily *suppresses* a response. If the response is still reinforced, punishment may be particularly ineffective. This fact was demonstrated by slapping rats on the paw as they were bar pressing in a Skinner box. Two groups of well-trained rats were placed on extinction. One group was punished with a slap for each bar press, and the other group was not. It might seem that the slap would cause bar pressing to extinguish more quickly. Yet, this was not the case, as you can see in Figure 6.18. Punishment temporarily slowed responding, but it did not cause more rapid extinction. Slapping the paws of rats or children has little permanent effect on a reinforced response.

Figure 6.18 The effect of punishment on extinction. Immediately after punishment, the rate of bar pressing is suppressed, but by the end of the second day, the effects of punishment have disappeared. (After B. F. Skinner, 1938.)

The Downside of Punishment

Are there drawbacks to using punishment? There are several, all of which become more of a problem as punishment increases in severity. Basically, punishment is *aversive* (painful or uncomfortable). As a result, people and situations associated with punishment tend, through classical conditioning, to become feared, resented, or disliked. The aversive nature of punishment makes it especially poor to use when teaching children to eat politely or in toilet training (Miltenberger, 2011).

Escape and Avoidance

A second major problem is that aversive stimuli encourage escape and avoidance learning, a regular part of daily experience (Schlund & Cataldo, 2010). In **escape learning**, we learn to make a response in order to end an aversive stimulus. For example, if you work with a loud and obnoxious person, you may at first escape from conversations with him to obtain

Punisher Any event that decreases the probability or frequency of responses it follows.

Escape learning Learning to make a response in order to end an aversive stimulus.

relief. (Notice that escape learning is based on negative reinforcement.) Later you may dodge him altogether. This is an example of **avoidance learning**—making a response in order to postpone or prevent discomfort. Each time you sidestep him, your avoidance is again reinforced by a sense of relief. In many situations involving frequent punishment, similar desires to escape and avoid are activated. For example, children who run away from punishing parents (escape) may soon learn to lie about their behavior (avoidance) or to spend as much time away from home as possible (also an avoidance response).

Aggression

A third problem with punishment is that it can greatly increase *aggression*. Animals react to pain by attacking whomever or whatever else is around. A common example is the faithful dog that nips its owner during a painful procedure at the veterinarian's office. Likewise, humans who are in pain have a tendency to lash out at others. When spanked, a child may feel angry, frustrated, and hostile. What if that child then goes outside and hits a brother, a sister, or a neighbor? The danger is that aggressive acts may feel good because they release anger and frustration. If so, aggression has been rewarded and will tend to occur again in other frustrating situations.

Several studies have found that children who are physically punished are more likely to engage in aggressive, impulsive, antisocial behavior (Taylor et al., 2010; Thomas, 2004). Similarly, a classic study of angry adolescent boys found that they were severely punished at home. This suppressed their misbehavior at home but made them more aggressive elsewhere. Parents were often surprised to learn that their "good boys" were in trouble for fighting at school (Bandura & Walters, 1959; Simons & Wurtele, 2010). Fortunately, at least for younger children, if parents change to less punitive parenting, their children's levels of aggression will decline (Thomas, 2004).

In the classroom, physical punishment, yelling, and humiliation are also generally ineffective. Positive reinforcement, in the form of praise, approval, and reward, is much more likely to quell classroom disruptions, defiance, and inattention (Alberto & Troutman, 2009).

Using Punishment Wisely

In light of its limitations and drawbacks, should punishment be used to control behavior? Parents, teachers, animal trainers, and the like have three basic tools to control simple learning: (1) Reinforcement strengthens responses; (2) Nonreinforcement causes responses to extinguish; (3) Punishment suppresses responses. (Consult Figure 6.19 to refresh your memory about the different types of reinforcement and punishment.) These tools work best in combination. It is usually best to begin by making liberal use of positive reinforcement, especially praise, to encourage good behavior (Martin & Pear, 2011). Also, try extinction first: See what happens if you ignore a problem behavior, or shift attention to a desirable activity and then reinforce it with praise. Remember, it is much more effective to strengthen and encourage desirable behaviors than it is to punish unwanted behaviors (Gershoff, 2002; Olson & Hergenhahn, 2009). When all else fails, it may be necessary to use punishment to help manage the behavior of an animal, child, or even another adult. For those times, here are some tips to keep in mind:

1. *Avoid harsh punishment.* Harsh or excessive punishment has serious negative drawbacks (never slap a child's face, for instance). "Sparing the rod" will not spoil a child. In fact, the reverse is true. As we just discussed, harsh punishment can lead to negative emotional reactions, avoidance and escape behaviors, and increased aggression (Aucoin, Frick, & Bodin, 2006; Simons & Wurtele, 2010). It can even lead to long-term mental health problems (Afifi et al., 2006).

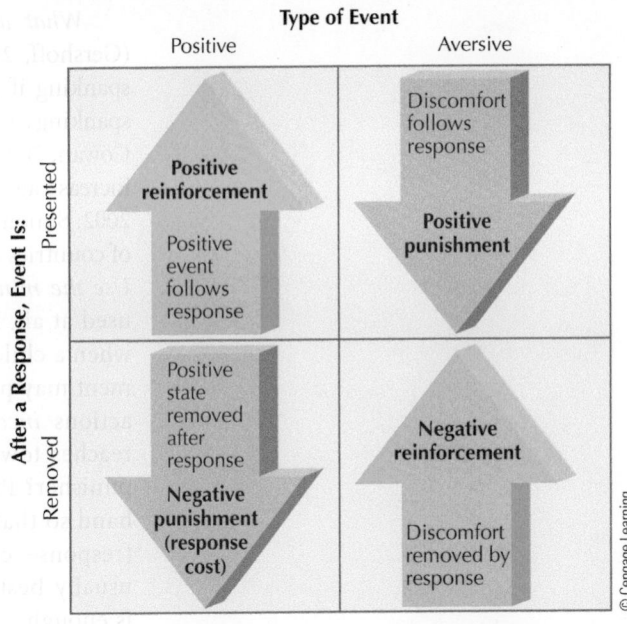

Figure 6.19 Types of reinforcement and punishment. The impact of an event depends on whether it is presented or removed after a response is made. Each square defines one possibility: Arrows pointing upward indicate that responding is increased; downward-pointing arrows indicate that responding is decreased.

Avoidance learning Learning to make a response in order to postpone or prevent discomfort.

What about spanking? Parents should minimize spanking or avoid it entirely (Gershoff, 2002). Although most children show no signs of long-term damage from spanking if it is backed up by supportive parenting, emotional damage does occur if spankings are severe, frequent, or coupled with harsh parenting (Baumrind, Larzelere, & Cowan, 2002; Stacks et al., 2009). Like all harsh punishment, frequent spanking tends to increase aggression and leads to more problem behaviors, not fewer (McLoyd & Smith, 2002; Simons & Wurtele, 2010). In fact, antispanking laws have been passed in a number of countries around the world (Isaacs, 2011).

2. *Use the minimum punishment necessary to suppress misbehavior.* If punishment is used at all, it should be mild. In a situation that poses immediate danger, such as when a child reaches for something hot or a dog runs into the street, mild punishment may prevent disaster. Punishment in such cases works best when it produces actions *incompatible* with the response you want to suppress. Let's say a child reaches toward a stove burner. Would a swat on the bottom serve as an effective punisher? Probably so. It would be better, however, to slap the child's outstretched hand so that it will be *withdrawn* from the source of danger. Negative punishment (response cost) such as taking away privileges or other positive reinforcers is usually best for older children and adults. Often, a verbal rebuke or a scolding is enough.

3. *Apply punishment during, or immediately after, misbehavior.* Of course, immediate punishment is not always possible. With older children and adults, you can bridge the delay by clearly stating what act you are punishing. If you cannot punish an animal or young child immediately, wait for the next instance of misbehavior.

4. *Be consistent.* Be very clear about what you regard as misbehavior. Punish every time the misbehavior occurs. Don't punish for something one time and ignore it the next. If you are usually willing to give a child three chances, don't change the rule and explode without warning after a first offense. Both parents should try to punish their children for the same things and in the same way.

5. *Use counterconditioning.* Mild punishment tends to be ineffective if reinforcers are still available in the situation. That's why it is best to also reward an alternate, desired response. For example, Sally, who has a habit of taking toys from her sister, should not just be reprimanded for it. She should be *counterconditioned*, or rewarded, for displaying any behavior that is counter to the unacceptable behavior, such as cooperative play or sharing her toys. As desired behaviors become more frequent, undesired behaviors become less frequent. Sally can't very well share her toys and take them from her sister at the same time. Remember, punishment tells a person or an animal only that a response was "wrong." Punishment does not say what the "right" response is, so it *does not teach new behaviors.* If reinforcement is missing, punishment becomes less effective (Gershoff, 2002).

6. *Expect anger from a punished person.* Briefly acknowledge this anger, but be careful not to reinforce it. Be willing to admit your mistake if you wrongfully punish someone or if you punished too severely.

7. *Punish with kindness and respect.* Avoid punishing when you are angry. It is easy to get carried away and become abusive (Gershoff & Bitensky, 2007; Gonzalez et al., 2008). Two-thirds of child abuse cases start out as attempts at physical punishment (Trocmé et al., 2001). One way to guard against doing harm is to punish with kindness and respect. Doing so also allows the punished person to retain self-respect. For instance, do not punish a person in front of others, if possible. A strong, trusting relationship tends to minimize behavior problems. Ideally, others should want to behave well to get your praise, not because they fear punishment.

To summarize, an unfortunately common error is to rely too much on punishment for training or discipline. The overall emotional adjustment of a child or pet disciplined mainly by reward is usually superior to one disciplined mainly by punishment. Frequent punishment makes a person or an animal unhappy, confused, anxious, aggressive, and fearful (Gershoff, 2002; Hergenhahn & Olson, 2009).

Parents and teachers should also be aware that using punishment can be "habit forming." When children are noisy, messy, disrespectful, or otherwise misbehave, the temptation to punish them can be strong. The danger is that punishment often works. When it does, a sudden end to the adult's irritation acts as a negative reinforcer. This encourages the adult to use punishment more often in the future (Alberto & Troutman, 2009). Immediate silence may be "golden," but its cost can be very high in terms of a child's emotional health.

 study break Punishment

RECITE

1. Negative reinforcement increases responding; punishment suppresses responding. T or F?
2. Three factors that greatly influence the effects of punishment are timing, consistency, and _____.
3. Mild punishment tends to only temporarily _____ a response that is also reinforced.
   a. enhance   b. aggravate
   c. replace   d. suppress
4. Three undesired side effects of punishment are (1) conditioning of fear and resentment, (2) encouragement of aggression, and (3) the learning of escape or _____ responses.
5. Using punishment can be "habit forming" because putting a stop to someone else's irritating behavior can _____ _____ the person who applies the punishment.

REFLECT

THINK CRITICALLY

6. Using the concept of partial reinforcement, can you explain why inconsistent punishment is especially ineffective?

7. Escape and avoidance learning have been applied to encourage automobile seat belt use. Can you explain how?

SELF-REFLECT

Think of how you were punished as a child. Was the punishment immediate? Was it consistent? What effect did these factors have on your behavior? Was the punishment effective? Which of the side effects of punishment have you witnessed or experienced?

ANSWERS

1. T 2. intensity 3. d 4. avoidance 5. negatively reinforce 6. An inconsistently punished response will continue to be reinforced on a partial schedule, which can make it even more resistant to extinction. 7. Many automobiles have an unpleasant buzzer that sounds if the ignition key is turned before the driver's seat belt is fastened. Most drivers quickly learn to fasten the belt to stop the annoying sound. This is an example of escape conditioning. Avoidance conditioning is evident when a driver learns to buckle up before the buzzer sounds.

Cognitive Learning—Beyond Conditioning

JOURNEY QUESTION 6.8 *What is cognitive learning?*

Is all learning just an association between stimuli and responses? Much learning can be explained by classical and operant conditioning. But, as we have seen, even basic conditioning has "mental" elements. As a human, you can anticipate future reward or punishment and react accordingly. (You may wonder why this doesn't seem to work when a doctor or dentist says, "This won't hurt a bit." Here's why: They lie!) There is no doubt that human learning includes a large *cognitive*, or mental, dimension (Goldstein, 2011; Lefrançois, 2012). As humans, we are greatly affected by information, expectations, perceptions, mental images, and the like.

As we mentioned at the beginning of this chapter, loosely speaking, *cognitive learning* refers to understanding, knowing, anticipating, or otherwise making use of information-rich higher mental processes. Cognitive learning extends beyond basic conditioning into the realms of memory, thinking, problem solving, and language. Because these topics are covered in later chapters, our discussion here is limited to a first look at learning beyond conditioning.

Cognitive Maps

How do you navigate around the town you live in? Have you simply learned to make a series of right and left turns to get from one point to another? More likely, you have an overall mental picture of how the town is laid out. This *cognitive map* acts as a guide even when you

must detour or take a new route (Foo et al., 2005; Lew, 2011). A **cognitive map** is an internal representation of an area, such as a maze, city, or campus. Even the lowly rat—not exactly a mental giant (well, except for our Einstein)—learns *where* food is found in a maze, not just which turns to make to reach the food (Tolman, Ritchie, & Kalish, 1946). If you have ever learned your way through some of the levels found in many video games, you will have a good idea of what a cognitive map is. In a sense, cognitive maps also apply to other kinds of knowledge. For instance, it could be said that you have been developing a "map" of psychology while reading this book. That's why students sometimes find it helpful to draw pictures or diagrams of how they envision concepts fitting together.

Latent Learning

Cognitive learning is also revealed by latent (hidden) learning. **Latent learning** occurs without obvious reinforcement and remains hidden until reinforcement is provided (Davidson, 2000; Gershman & Niv, 2010). Here's an example from a classic animal study: Two groups of rats were allowed to explore a maze. The animals in one group found food at the far end of the maze. Soon, they learned to rapidly make their way through the maze when released. Rats in the second group were unrewarded and showed no signs of learning. But later, when the "uneducated" rats were given food, they ran the maze as quickly as the rewarded group (Tolman & Honzik, 1930). Although there was no outward sign of it, the unrewarded animals had learned their way around the maze. Their learning, therefore, remained latent at first (Figure 6.20).

How did they learn if there was no reinforcement? Just satisfying curiosity can be enough to reward learning (Harlow & Harlow, 1962). In humans, latent learning is related to higher-level abilities, such as anticipating future reward. For example, if you give an attractive classmate a ride home, you may make mental notes about how to get to his or her house, even if a date is only a remote future possibility.

Discovery Learning

Much of what is meant by cognitive learning is summarized by the word *understanding*. Each of us has, at times, learned ideas by **rote** (mechanical repetition and memorization). Although rote learning can be efficient, many psychologists believe that learning is more lasting and flexible when people *discover* facts and principles on their own. In **discovery learning,** skills are gained by insight and understanding instead of by rote (Snowman & McCown, 2011).

Cognitive map Internal images or other mental representations of an area (maze, city, campus, and so forth) that underlie an ability to choose alternative paths to the same goal.

Latent learning Learning that occurs without obvious reinforcement and that remains unexpressed until reinforcement is provided.

Rote learning Learning that takes place mechanically, through repetition and memorization, or by learning rules.

Discovery learning Learning based on insight and understanding.

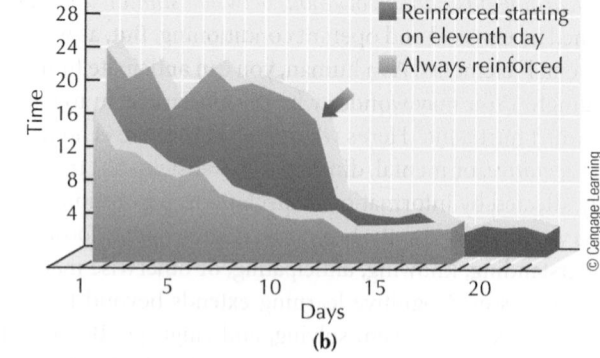

(a)   **(b)**

Figure 6.20 Latent learning. *(a)* The maze used by Tolman and Honzik to demonstrate latent learning by rats. *(b)* Results of the experiment. Notice the rapid improvement in performance that occurred when food was made available to the previously unreinforced animals. This indicates that learning had occurred but that it remained hidden or unexpressed. (Adapted from Tolman & Honzik, 1930.)

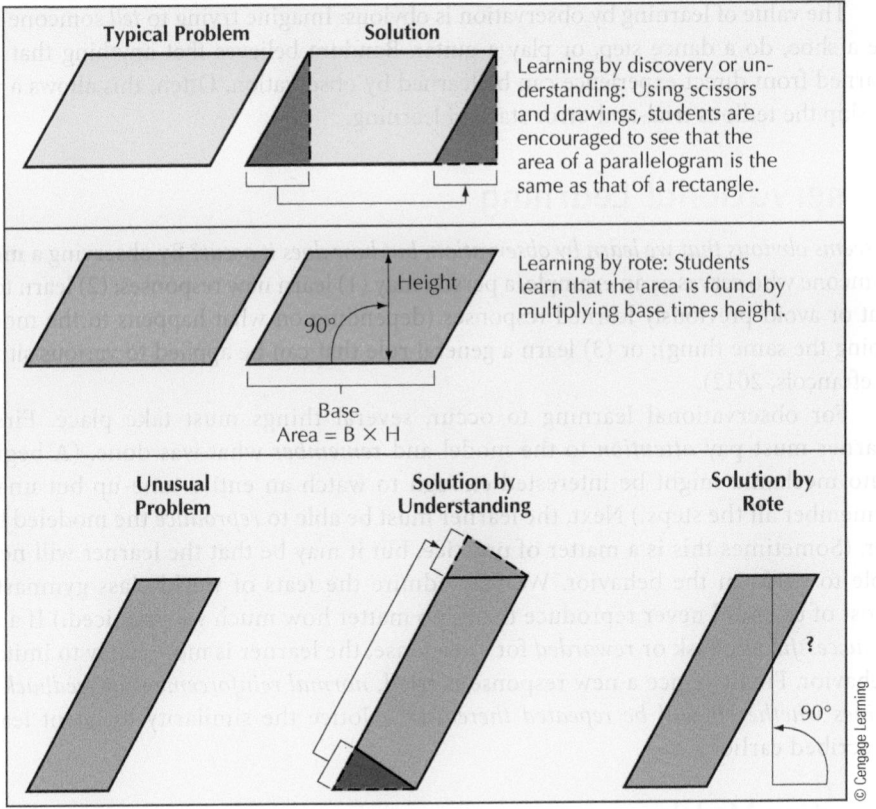

Typical Problem   **Solution**

Learning by discovery or understanding: Using scissors and drawings, students are encouraged to see that the area of a parallelogram is the same as that of a rectangle.

Learning by rote: Students learn that the area is found by multiplying base times height.

Height

90°

Base
Area = B × H

Unusual Problem   **Solution by Understanding**   **Solution by Rote**

?

90°

© Cengage Learning

Figure 6.21 Learning by understanding and by rote. For some types of learning, understanding may be superior, although both types of learning are useful. (After Wertheimer, 1959.)

As long as learning occurs, what difference does it make if it is by discovery or by rote? Figure 6.21 illustrates the difference. Two groups of students were taught to calculate the area of a parallelogram by multiplying the height by the length of the base. Some were encouraged to see that a "piece" of a parallelogram could be "moved" to create a rectangle. Later, they were better able to solve unusual problems in which the height times base formula didn't seem to work. Students who simply memorized a rule were confused by the similar problems (Wertheimer, 1959). As this implies, discovery can lead to a better understanding of new or unusual problems. When possible, people should try new strategies and discover new solutions during learning. However, this doesn't mean that students are supposed to stumble around and rediscover the principles of math, physics, or chemistry. The best teaching strategies are based on *guided discovery*, in which students are given enough freedom to actively think about problems and enough guidance so that they gain useful knowledge (Mayer, 2004, 2011).

Modeling—Do as I Do, Not as I Say

JOURNEY QUESTION 6.9 *Does learning occur by imitation?*

Many skills are learned by what Albert Bandura (1971) calls **observational learning**, or **modeling**—watching and imitating the actions of another person or noting the consequences of those actions. We humans share the capacity for observational learning with many mammals, like Larry's gorillas (Zentall, 2011; Tennie et al., 2010).

Observational learning (modeling) Learning achieved by watching and imitating the actions of another or noting the consequences of those actions.

The value of learning by observation is obvious: Imagine trying to *tell* someone how to tie a shoe, do a dance step, or play a guitar. Bandura believes that anything that can be learned from direct experience can be learned by observation. Often, this allows a person to skip the tedious trial-and-error stage of learning.

Observational Learning

It seems obvious that we learn by observation, but how does it occur? By observing a **model**—someone who serves as an example, a person may (1) learn new responses; (2) learn to carry out or avoid previously learned responses (depending on what happens to the model for doing the same thing); or (3) learn a general rule that can be applied to various situations (Lefrançois, 2012).

For observational learning to occur, several things must take place. First, the learner must pay *attention* to the model and *remember* what was done. (A beginning auto mechanic might be interested enough to watch an entire tune-up but unable to remember all the steps.) Next, the learner must be able to *reproduce* the modeled behavior. (Sometimes this is a matter of practice, but it may be that the learner will never be able to perform the behavior. We may admire the feats of world-class gymnasts, but most of us could never reproduce them, no matter how much we practiced.) If a model is *successful* at a task or *rewarded* for a response, the learner is more likely to imitate the behavior. Finally, once a new response is tried, *normal reinforcement or feedback determines whether it will be repeated thereafter.* (Notice the similarity to latent learning, described earlier.)

Imitating Models

Modeling has a powerful effect on behavior. In a classic experiment, children watched an adult attack a large blow-up "Bo-Bo the Clown" doll. Some children saw an adult sit on the doll, punch it, hit it with a hammer, and kick it around the room. Others saw a movie of these actions. A third group saw a cartoon version of the aggression. Later, the children were frustrated by having some attractive toys taken away from them. Then, they were allowed to play with the Bo-Bo doll. Most imitated the adult's attack (**Figure 6.22**). Some even added new aggressive acts of their own! Interestingly, the cartoon was only slightly less effective in encouraging aggression than the live adult model and the filmed model (Bandura, Ross, & Ross, 1963).

Then do children blindly imitate adults? No. Remember that observational learning only prepares a person to duplicate a response. Whether it is actually imitated depends on whether the model was rewarded or punished for what was done. Nevertheless, when parents tell a child to do one thing but model a completely different response, children tend to imitate what the parents *do*, and *not* what they *say*.

Consider a typical situation: Little Raymond has just been irritated by his older brother, Robert. Angry and frustrated, he swats Robert. This behavior interrupts his father Frank

Observational learning often imparts large amounts of information that would be difficult to obtain by reading instructions or memorizing rules.

Model (in learning) A person who serves as an example in observational learning.

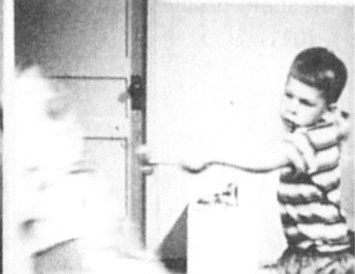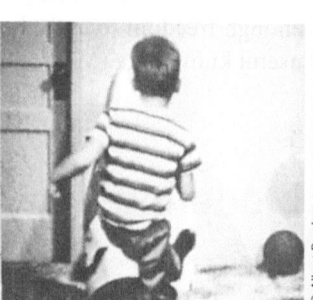

Figure 6.22 A nursery school child imitates the aggressive behavior of an adult model he has just seen in a movie. (Courtesy Albert Bandura/Stanford University.)

Today's kids can experience more gore in a day than most people used to experience in a lifetime, even during military combat. For example, one video game begins as zombies graphically attack a little girl, turning her into one of them. She viciously attacks her father only to be flung several stories to her death.

What effects do such experiences have on people who play violent video games? Many reviews have concluded that violent video games increase aggressive behavior in children and young adults (Anderson, 2004; Krahé & Möller, 2010). As with television, younger children appear to be especially susceptible to fantasy violence in video games (Anderson et al., 2003; Bensley & Van Eenwyk, 2001). In fact, the more personalized, intimate experience of video games may heighten their impact (Fischer, Kastenmüller, & Greitemeyer, 2010).

Unfortunately, much of the early research may have led to overly strong conclusions (Adachi & Willoughby, 2011a; Valadez & Ferguson, 2012). For example, in one earlier study, college students played a violent *(Mortal Kombat)* or nonviolent *(PGA Tournament Golf)* video game. Next, they competed with another student (actually an actor) in a task that allowed aggression and retaliation to take place. Students who played the violent game were much more likely to aggress by punishing their competitor (Bartholow & Anderson, 2002). However, these two games differed not only in their degree of violence, they also differed in degree of competitiveness, difficulty, and pace of action.

A more recent study compared a violent action game *(Conan)* and a nonviolent racing game *(Fuel)* that were equally competitive, difficult, and fast-paced. In a subsequent task, college students who played the violent game were no more likely to be aggressive than those who played the nonviolent game (Adachi & Willoughby, 2011b). In other words, it is entirely possible that the competitiveness, difficulty, or pacing of a game influences aggression levels just as much, if not more, than the violent content of the game.

Until further research can more definitively disentangle these issues, the question of whether playing violent videogames triggers aggression toward others remains unresolved. Regardless, before you write off video games altogether, read "You Mean Video Games Might Be Good for Me?" in Chapter 8.

---

watching television. Father promptly spanks little Raymond, saying, "This will teach you to hit your big brother." And it will. The message Frank has given the child is clear: "You have frustrated me; therefore, I will hit you." The next time little Raymond is frustrated, it won't be surprising if he imitates his father and hits his brother. (So why does everybody love Raymond, anyway?)

Thus, through modeling, children learn not only attitudes, gestures, emotions, and personality traits, but fears, anxieties, and bad habits as well. For example, adolescents are much more likely to begin smoking if their parents, siblings, and friends smoke (Wilkinson & Abraham, 2004). More tragically, children who witness domestic violence are more likely to commit it themselves (Murrell, Christoff, & Henning, 2007).

Modeling and the Media

Much of what we learn, good and bad, comes from media. Today's children and young adults spend less time in the classroom than they do engaged with various media, including television, video games, movies, the Internet, music, and print (Rideout, Foehr, & Roberts, 2010). It should come as no surprise, then, that many parents and educators have worried about the effects of experiencing high levels of media violence.

Media Violence

By the time the average American has graduated from high school, she or he will have "witnessed" thousands of murders and countless acts of robbery, arson, bombing, torture, and beatings. Even G-rated cartoons average 10 minutes of violence per hour (Yokota & Thompson, 2000). But does all of this media mayhem promote the observational learning of aggression? Early studies appeared to confirm that children who watch a great deal of televised violence are more prone to behave aggressively (Anderson, Gentile, & Buckley, 2007; Miller et al., 2012).

Does the same conclusion apply to video games? Children tend to imitate what they observe in all media (Kirsh, 2010). From professional wrestling (Bernthal, 2003) to rap music (Wingood et al., 2003) to video games (Carnagey & Anderson, 2004), children have

Media regularly portray violent and often incredible feats. Fortunately, only a few "jackasses" actually try to imitate them despite the usual warning "Do not try this at home."

plenty of opportunity to observe and imitate both the good and the bad (and the ugly?). (See "You Mean Video Games Might Be Bad for Me?")

How might media violence increase aggressive behavior? We have already suggested that experiencing media violence may teach people how to be more aggressive in real life (Kirsh, 2010; Unsworth & Ward, 2001). Another possibility is that repeated exposure to media violence may desensitize people, making them less likely to react negatively to violence and hence more prone to engage in it (Funk, 2005; Krahé et al., 2011).

Either way, according to clinical psychologist Christopher Ferguson, experiencing media violence does not invariably "cause" any given person to become more aggressive. At best it can make aggression more *likely* (Ferguson & Dyck, 2012). Many other factors, such as personality characteristics, family conflict, depression, and negative peer influences, also affect the chances that hostile thoughts will be turned into actions (Ferguson, Miguel, & Hartley, 2009).

Parents and educators who worry that violent media are turning young people into a generation of sadistic criminals can take heart from the data shown in Figure 6.23. In recent years, the violent crime rate among youth has declined even as sales of violent video games have risen. However, none of this is to say that we should be unconcerned about the long-term effects of experiencing violent media, including imitation, desensitization, and vicarious traumatization. This is especially true for younger children, who are more likely to be influenced because they don't always fully recognize that media characters and stories are fantasies (McKenna & Ossoff, 1998).

A Look Ahead

Conditioning principles are often derived from animal experiments. However, it should be apparent that the same principles apply to human behavior. Perhaps the best way to appreciate this fact is to observe how reinforcement affects your own behavior. With this in mind, the upcoming Psychology in Action section proposes a personal experiment in operant conditioning. Don't miss this coming attraction!

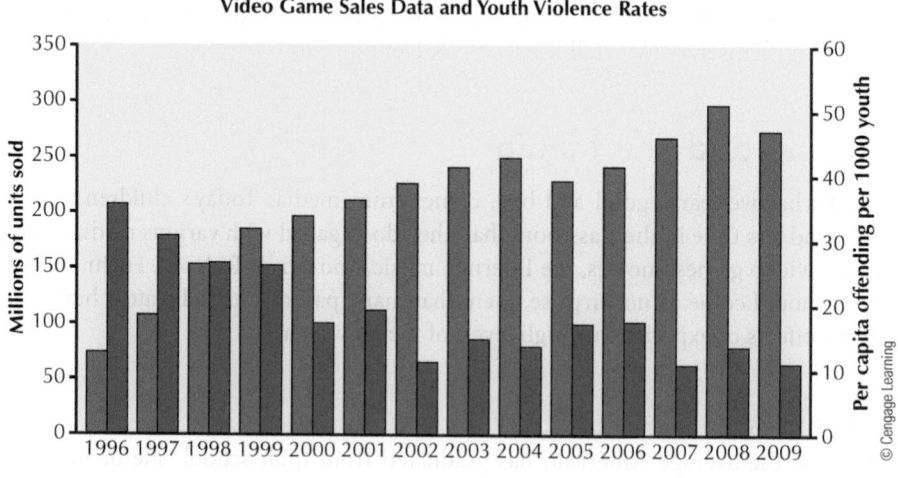

Figure 6.23 This graph shows that the rate of violent crimes among youth declined between the years 1996 to 2007. Yet during the same period, sales of violent video games increased. While correlational data such as these are not by themselves conclusive, they do help us put the issue of violence in video games into perspective. (Data adapted from Ferguson & Garza, 2011.)

study break Cognitive Learning and Imitation

RECITE

1. An internal representation of spatial relationships is referred to as a _____.
2. Learning that suddenly appears when a reward or incentive for performance is given is called

    a. discovery learning
    b. latent learning
    c. rote learning
    d. reminiscence

3. If a model is successful, or rewarded, the model's behavior is

    a. less difficult to reproduce
    b. less likely to be attended to
    c. more likely to be imitated
    d. more subject to positive transfer

4. Children who observed a live adult behave aggressively became more aggressive; those who observed movie and cartoon aggression did not. T or F?
5. Children are most likely to imitate media characters with whom they identify. T or F?
6. Children who watch a great deal of media violence are more prone to be aggressive, an effect that is best explained by

    a. negative reinforcement
    b. shaping and successive approximations
    c. observational learning
    d. vicarious classical conditioning

REFLECT

THINK CRITICALLY

7. Draw a map of your school's campus as you picture it now. Draw a map of the campus as you pictured it after your first visit. Why do the maps differ?
8. Children who watch many aggressive programs on television tend to be more aggressive than average. Why doesn't this observation prove that televised aggression causes aggressive behavior?

SELF-REFLECT

Try to think of at least one personal example of each of these concepts: cognitive map, latent learning, discovery learning.

Describe a skill you have learned primarily through observational learning. How did modeling help you learn?

ANSWERS

1. cognitive map 2. b 3. c 4. F 5. T 6. c 7. Your cognitive map of the campus has undoubtedly become more accurate and intricate over time as you have added details to it. Your drawings should reflect this change. 8. Because the observation is based on a correlation. Children who are already aggressive may choose to watch more aggressive programs, rather than being made aggressive by them. It took experimental studies to verify that televised aggression promotes aggression by viewers.

Psychology in Action

Behavioral Self-Management—A Rewarding Project

JOURNEY QUESTION 6.10 *How does conditioning apply to everyday problems?*

Would you like to exercise more, attend more classes, cut down on smoking, concentrate longer, or read more books? This is an invitation to carry out a self-management project of your own. As such, this could be the start of one of the most personal applications of psychology in this book.

Self-Managed Behavior

The principles of operant conditioning can be adapted to manage your own behavior (Miltenberger, 2011; Watson & Tharp, 2007). Here's how:

1. **Choose a target behavior.** Identify the activity you want to change.
2. **Record a baseline.** Record how much time you currently spend performing the target activity or count the number of desired or undesired responses you make each day.
3. **Establish goals.** Remember the principle of shaping and set realistic goals for gradual improvement on each successive week. Also, set daily goals that add up to the weekly goal.
4. **Choose reinforcers.** If you meet your daily goal, what reward will you allow yourself? Daily rewards might be watching television, eating a candy bar, socializing with friends, listening to your iPod, or whatever you enjoy. Also establish a weekly reward. If you reach your weekly goal, what reward will you allow yourself? A movie? A dinner out? Some time playing a game like *Guitar Hero*? A weekend hike?

"This is your last warning, Wilson, shape up!"

5. **Record your progress.** Keep accurate records of the amount of time spent each day on the desired activity or the number of times you make the desired response.
6. **Reward successes.** If you meet your daily goal, collect your reward. If you fall short, be honest with yourself and skip the reward. Do the same for your weekly goal.
7. **Adjust your plan as you learn more about your behavior.** Overall progress will reinforce your attempts at self-management.

If you have trouble thinking of rewards, remember that anything done often can serve as reinforcement. This is known as the **Premack principle**, named after David Premack, the psychologist who popularized its use. For example, if you like to watch television every night and want to study more, make it a rule not to turn on the set until you have studied for an hour (or whatever length of time you choose). Then lengthen the requirement each week. Here is a sample of one student's plan:

1. *Target behavior:* number of hours spent studying.
2. *Recorded baseline:* an average of 25 minutes per day for a weekly total of 3 hours.
3. *Goal for the first week:* an increase in study time to 40 minutes per day; weekly goal of 5 hours total study time. *Goal for second week:* 50 minutes per day and 6 hours per week. *Goal for third week:* 1 hour per day and 7 hours per week. *Ultimate goal:* to reach and maintain 14 hours per week study time.
4. *Daily reward for reaching goal:* 1 hour of guitar playing in the evening; no playing if the goal is not met. *Weekly reward for reaching goal:* going to a movie or buying a DVD.

Self-Recording Even if you find it difficult to give and withhold rewards, **self-recording**—keeping records of response frequencies, a form of feedback—can make a difference all by itself. This is because we tend to react to being observed, even when we are the ones watching our own behavior. In general, when you systematically (and honestly) observe yourself, you are more likely to engage in desired behaviors and less likely to perform undesired behaviors (Fireman, Kose, & Solomon, 2003; Watson & Tharp, 2007).

Keep track of the number of times that you exercise, arrive late to class, eat vegetables, smoke a cigarette, study, watch television, drink a cappuccino, swear, or whatever you are interested in changing. A simple tally on a piece of paper will do, or you can get a small mechanical counter like those used to keep golf scores or count calories. Record keeping helps break patterns, and the feedback can be motivating as you begin to make progress.

Good Ways to Break Bad Habits

Are there any extra tips for breaking bad habits? By using the methods we have discussed, you can *decrease* unwanted behaviors, such as swearing, biting your nails, criticizing others, smoking, drinking coffee, watching television too much, or engaging in any other behavior you choose to target. However, breaking bad habits may require some additional techniques. Here are four strategies to help you change bad habits.

Alternate Responses A good strategy for change is to try to get the same reinforcement with a new response.

Example: Marta often tells jokes at the expense of others. Her friends sometimes feel hurt by her sharp-edged humor. Marta senses this and wants to change. What can she do? Usually, Marta's joke telling is reinforced by attention and approval. She could just as easily get the same reinforcement by giving other people praise or compliments. Making a

Premack principle Any high-frequency response can be used to reinforce a low-frequency response.

Self-recording Self-management based on keeping records of response frequencies.

change in her behavior should be easy because she will continue to receive the reinforcement she seeks.

Extinction   Try to discover what is reinforcing an unwanted response and remove, avoid, or delay the reinforcement.

Example: Fatima has developed a habit of taking longer and longer "breaks" to watch television when she should be studying. Obviously, television watching is reinforcing her break-taking. To improve her study habits, Fatima could delay reinforcement by studying at the library or some other location a good distance from her television.

Response Chains   Break up response chains that precede an undesired behavior; this will help break the bad habit. The key idea is to scramble the chain of events that leads to an undesired response (Watson & Tharp, 2007).

Example: Most nights Ignacio comes home from work, turns on the television, and eats a whole bag of cookies or chips. He then takes a shower and changes clothes. By dinnertime he has lost his appetite. Ignacio realizes he is substituting junk food for dinner. Ignacio could solve the problem by breaking the response chain that precedes dinner. For instance, he could shower immediately when he gets home, or avoid turning on the television until after dinner.

Cues and Antecedents   Try to avoid, narrow down, or remove stimuli that elicit the bad habit.

Example: Brent wants to cut down on smoking. He can take many smoking cues out of his surroundings by removing ashtrays, matches, and extra cigarettes from his house, car, and office. Drug cravings are strongly related to cues conditioned to the drug, such as the odor of cigarettes. Brent can narrow antecedent stimuli even more. He could begin by smoking only in the lounge at work, never in his office or in his car. He could then limit his smoking to home. Then to only one room at home. Then to one chair at home. If he succeeds in getting this far, he may want to limit his smoking to only one unpleasant place, such as a bathroom, basement, or garage (Riley et al., 2002).

Contracting   If you try the techniques described here and have difficulty sticking with them, you may want to try behavioral contracting. In a **behavioral contract**, you state a specific problem behavior you want to control, or a goal you want to achieve. Also, state the rewards you will receive, privileges you will forfeit, or punishments you must accept. The contract should be signed by you and a person you trust.

A behavioral contract can be quite motivating, especially when mild punishment is part of the agreement. Here's a classic example reported by Nurnberger and Zimmerman (1970): A student working on his Ph.D. had completed all requirements but his dissertation, yet for 2 years had not written a single page. A contract was drawn up for him in which he agreed to meet weekly deadlines on the number of pages he would complete. To make sure he would meet the deadlines, he wrote postdated checks. These were to be forfeited if he failed to reach his goal for the week. The checks were made out to organizations he despised (the Ku Klux Klan and American Nazi Party). From the time he signed the contract until he finished his degree, the student's work output was greatly improved.

Getting Help

Attempting to manage or alter your own behavior may be more difficult than it sounds. If you feel you need more information, consult the books listed below. You will also find helpful advice in the Psychology in Action section of Chapter 13. If you do try a self-modification project but find it impossible to reach your goals, be aware that professional advice is available.

Behavioral contract A formal agreement stating behaviors to be changed and consequences that apply.

Where to Obtain More Information.

Watson, D. L., & Tharp, R. G. (2007). *Self-directed behavior* (9th ed.). Belmont, CA: Wadsworth.

Miltenberger, R. G. (2011). *Behavior modification: Principles and procedures* (5th ed.). Belmont, CA: Cengage Learning/Wadsworth.

 study break Behavioral Self-Management

RECITE

1. After a target behavior has been selected for reinforcement, it's a good idea to record a baseline so that you can set realistic goals for change. T or F?
2. Self-recording, even without the use of extra rewards, can bring about desired changes in target behaviors. T or F?
3. The Premack principle states that behavioral contracting can be used to reinforce changes in behavior. T or F?
4. A self-management plan should make use of the principle of shaping by setting a graduated series of goals. T or F?
5. Eleni plays solitaire on her computer each time she tries to work on a term paper. To break this habit, Eleni removes the solitaire icon from her computer screen so that she won't see it when she begins work. Eleni has used which strategy for breaking bad habits?

   a. alternative responses   *b.* extinction
   c. avoid cues   *d.* contracting

REFLECT

THINK CRITICALLY

6. How does setting daily goals in a behavioral self-management program help maximize the effects of reinforcement?

SELF-REFLECT

Even if you don't expect to carry out a self-management project right now, outline a plan for changing your own behavior. Be sure to describe the behavior you want to change, set goals, and identify reinforcers.

ANSWERS

1. T 2. T 3. F 4. T 5. c 6. Daily performance goals and rewards reduce the delay of reinforcement, which maximizes its impact.

Chapter in Review

Summary

6.1 What is learning?

- 6.1.1 Learning is a relatively permanent change in behavior due to experience.
- 6.1.2 Associative learning is a simple type of learning that affects many aspects of daily life.
- 6.1.3 Cognitive learning involves making use of information-rich higher mental processes.
- 6.1.4 Classical (or respondent) conditioning and instrumental (or operant) conditioning are two basic types of associative learning.
- 6.1.5 In classical conditioning, a neutral stimulus is followed by an unconditioned stimulus. With repeated pairings, the neutral stimulus begins to elicit a response.
- 6.1.6 In operant conditioning, responses that are followed by reinforcement occur more frequently.

6.2 How does classical conditioning occur?

- 6.2.1 Classical conditioning, studied by Pavlov, occurs when a neutral stimulus (NS) is associated with an unconditioned stimulus (US).
- 6.2.2 The US causes a reflex called the unconditioned response (UR). If the NS is consistently paired with the US, it becomes a conditioned stimulus (CS) capable of producing a conditioned (learned) response (CR).
- 6.2.3 When the conditioned stimulus is repeatedly followed by the unconditioned stimulus, an association between the two is established and strengthened.
- 6.2.4 Higher order conditioning occurs when a well-learned conditioned stimulus is used as if it were an unconditioned stimulus, bringing about further learning.
- 6.2.5 From an informational view, conditioning creates expectancies, which alter response patterns. In classical conditioning, the CS creates an expectancy that the US will follow.
- 6.2.6 When the CS is repeatedly presented alone, conditioning is extinguished (weakened or inhibited). After extinction seems to be complete, a rest period may lead to the temporary reappearance of a conditioned response. This is called spontaneous recovery.
- 6.2.7 Through stimulus generalization, stimuli similar to the conditioned stimulus will also produce a response. Generalization gives way to stimulus discrimination when an organism learns to respond to one stimulus but not to similar stimuli.

6.3 Does conditioning affect emotions?

- 6.3.1 Conditioning applies to visceral or emotional responses as well as simple reflexes. As a result, conditioned emotional responses (CERs) also occur.
- 6.3.2 Irrational fears called phobias may begin as CERs. Conditioning of emotional responses can occur vicariously (secondhand) as well as directly.

6.4 How does operant conditioning occur?

- 6.4.1 Operant conditioning occurs when a voluntary action is followed by a reinforcer (which increases the frequency of the response) or a punisher (which decreases the frequency of the response).
- 6.4.2 Delaying reinforcement greatly reduces its effectiveness, but long chains of responses may be maintained by a single reinforcer.
- 6.4.3 Superstitious behaviors often become part of response chains because they appear to be associated with reinforcement.
- 6.4.4 By rewarding successive approximations to a particular response, behavior can be shaped into desired patterns.
- 6.4.5 If an operant response is not reinforced, it may extinguish (disappear). But after extinction seems complete, it may temporarily reappear (spontaneous recovery).
- 6.4.6 Both positive reinforcement and negative reinforcement increase the likelihood that a response will be repeated. Punishment decreases the likelihood that the response will occur again.

6.5 Are there different kinds of operant reinforcement?

- 6.5.1 Operant learning may be based on primary reinforcers (which are rooted in biology), secondary reinforcers (such as tokens and social reinforcers), and feedback (knowledge of results).
- 6.5.2 Primary reinforcers are "natural," physiologically based rewards. Intracranial stimulation of "pleasure centers" in the brain can also serve as a primary reinforcer.
- 6.5.3 Secondary reinforcers are learned. They typically gain their reinforcing value by direct association with primary reinforcers or because they can be exchanged for primary reinforcers. Tokens and money gain their reinforcing value in this way.
- 6.5.4 Feedback, or knowledge of results, also aids learning and improves performance. It is most effective when it is immediate, detailed, and frequent.
- 6.5.5 Programmed instruction breaks learning into a series of small steps and provides immediate feedback. Computer-assisted instruction (CAI) does the same but has the added advantage of providing alternative exercises and information when needed.

6.6 How are we influenced by patterns of reward?

- 6.6.1 Reward or reinforcement may be given continuously (after every response) or on a schedule of partial reinforcement. Partial reinforcement produces greater resistance to extinction.
- 6.6.2 The four most basic partial schedules of reinforcement are fixed ratio, variable ratio, fixed interval, and variable interval. Each produces a distinct pattern of responding.
- 6.6.3 Stimuli that precede a reinforced response tend to control the response on future occasions (stimulus control). Two aspects of stimulus control are generalization and discrimination.

6.6.4 In generalization, an operant response tends to occur when stimuli similar to those preceding reinforcement are present.

6.6.5 In discrimination, responses are given in the presence of discriminative stimuli associated with reinforcement and withheld in the presence of stimuli associated with nonreinforcement.

6.7 What does punishment do to behavior?

6.7.1 Punishment decreases response frequency.

6.7.2 Punishment occurs when a response is followed by the onset of an aversive event (positive punishment) or by the removal of a positive event (negative punishment or response cost).

6.7.3 Punishment is most effective when it is immediate, consistent, and intense.

6.7.4 Although severe punishment can virtually eliminate a particular behavior, mild punishment usually only temporarily suppresses responding. Reinforcement must be used to make lasting changes in the behavior of a person or an animal.

6.7.5 The undesirable side effects of punishment include the conditioning of fear to punishing agents and situations associated with punishment, the learning of escape and avoidance responses, and the encouragement of aggression.

6.8 What is cognitive learning?

6.8.1 Cognitive learning involves higher mental processes, such as memory, thinking, problem solving, understanding, knowing, and anticipating.

6.8.2 Even in relatively simple learning situations, animals and people seem to form cognitive maps (internal representations of spatial relationships).

6.8.3 In latent learning, learning remains hidden or unseen until a reward or incentive for performance is offered.

6.8.4 Discovery learning emphasizes insight and understanding, in contrast to rote learning.

6.9 Does learning occur by imitation?

6.9.1 Learning can occur by merely observing and imitating the actions of another person or by noting the consequences of the person's actions.

6.9.2 Observational learning is influenced by the success or failure of the model's behavior. Aggression is readily learned and released by modeling.

6.9.3 Media characters can act as powerful models for observational learning. Media violence increases the likelihood of aggression by viewers.

6.10 How does conditioning apply to everyday problems?

6.10.1 By applying operant conditioning principles, it is possible to change or manage your own behavior.

6.10.2 Four strategies that can help change bad habits are reinforcing alternative responses, promoting extinction, breaking response chains, and avoiding antecedent cues.

6.10.3 When managing behavior, self-reinforcement, self-recording, feedback, and behavioral contracting are all helpful.

Interactive Learning

Log in to CengageBrain to access the resources your instructor requires. For this book, you can access:

CourseMate Go to CengageBrain.com to access Psychology CourseMate, where you will find an interactive eBook, glossaries, flashcards, quizzes, videos, Virtual Psychology Labs, and more.

Aplia If your professor has assigned Aplia:

1. Sign in to your account.
2. Complete the corresponding exercises as required by your professor.
3. When finished, click "Grade It Now" to see which areas you have mastered, which areas need more work, and detailed explanations of every answer.

Test Your Knowledge

Conditioning and Learning

1. Classical and operant conditioning can be distinguished by paying attention to which aspects of a response?
   a. associative and cognitive
   b. neutral stimuli and rewards
   c. antecedents and consequences
   d. acquisition and spontaneous recovery

2. You once got sick on a roller coaster. Now the sight of a roller coaster makes you feel queasy. Apparently, the sight of a roller coaster is a _____ and your queasiness is a _____.
   a. CR, CS
   b. CS, CR
   c. consequence, neutral stimulus
   d. reflex, CS

3. According to the informational view, classical conditioning creates new
   a. expectancies
   b. unconditioned responses
   c. unconditioned stimuli
   d. generalizations

4. After you have extinguished a conditioned response, it may recur because of
   a. removing reinforcement
   b. stimulus generalization
   c. spontaneous recovery
   d. following the CS with a US

5. At least some phobias can be thought of as
   a. NS-CR connections
   b. desensitization gradients
   c. extinction responses
   d. CERs

6. Conditioned fears respond to a therapy called
   a. systematic desensitization
   b. CER
   c. spontaneous recovery
   d. conditioning

7. Mary watched her brother fall off a bike and hurt himself. Now she is afraid to ride her bike. Mary's fear is a result of
   a. stimulus discrimination
   b. vicarious conditioning
   c. spontaneous recovery
   d. higher order conditioning

8. The law of effect defines the role of _____ in learning.
   a. antecedent stimuli
   b. stimulus generalization
   c. operant reinforcers
   d. stimulus approximations

9. Operant reinforcement works best when it is
   a. delayed
   b. an antecedent
   c. response contingent
   d. aversive

10. Negative reinforcement _____ responding.
    a. increases
    b. decreases
    c. reverses
    d. extinguishes

11. Response cost is one form of
    a. discrimination conditioning
    b. generalization
    c. higher order conditioning
    d. punishment

12. Tokens are
    a. primary reinforcers
    b. secondary reinforcers
    c. social reinforcers
    d. a form of feedback

13. Programmed instruction presents information in small amounts, gives immediate practice, and provides _____ feedback to learners.
    a. negative
    b. continuous
    c. positive
    d. delayed

14. Studies have shown that animals are _____ to the passage of time.
    a. insensitive
    b. stuck
    c. sensitive
    d. stop responding

15. The "sniffer" dogs that locate drugs and explosives at airports learn to identify contraband through _____ _____ training.
    a. classical extinction
    b. classical desensitization
    c. vicarious feedback
    d. operant discrimination

16. Punishment tends to encourage escape learning, avoidance learning, and
    a. rapid extinction
    b. aggression
    c. correct responses
    d. the partial reinforcement effect

17. Discovery learning is often superior to its opposite:
    a. rote learning
    b. negative reinforcement
    c. observational learning
    d. cognitive learning

18. For observational learning to occur, the learner must pay attention to a model, remember what was done, and _____ the modeled behavior.
    a. reinforce
    b. reinvent
    c. reproduce
    d. repress

19. As a behavioral management strategy, self-recording applies _____ to change personal habits.
    a. vicarious conditioning
    b. feedback
    c. behavioral contracting
    d. the Premack principle

20. Bad habits can be altered by finding ways to remove, avoid, or delay the reinforcement that follows unwanted responses. This strategy is best described as
    a. seek alternate responses
    b. use operant extinction
    c. break up response chains
    d. narrow cues and antecedents

Answers   1. c 2. b 3. a 4. c 5. d 6. a 7. b 8. c 9. c 10. a 11. d 12. b 13. b 14. c 15. d 16. b 17. a 18. c 19. b 20. b

Journey Theme *Memory is not like a tape recorder or a video camera: Memories change as they are stored and retrieved.*

7

Memory

Journey into Psychology: Fuhgeddaboudit

That advice, offered New York City style, may not seem helpful at exam time. After all, the less you forget, the better, right?

Not always. Consider what Jill Price thinks about her "perfect" memory: "My memory has ruled my life...Whenever I see a date flash on the television (or anywhere else for that matter) I automatically go back to that day and remember where I was, what I was doing, what day it fell on and on and on and on and on. It is nonstop, uncontrollable, and totally exhausting...Most have called it a gift, but I call it a burden. I run my entire life through my head every day and it drives me crazy!!!" (Parker, Cahill, & McGaugh, 2006; Price & Davis, 2009).

Another person with an amazing memory, known as Mr. S., even made a living as a professional memorizer, or *mnemonist* (Luria, 1968). He regularly wowed audiences with his ability to memorize, with equal ease, long strings of digits, meaningless consonants, mathematical formulas, and poems in foreign languages. Don't be too quick to envy Mr. S.'s abilities either. He remembered so much that he couldn't separate important facts from trivia or facts from fantasy. His memory was so powerful that he had to devise ways to *forget*—such as writing information on a piece of paper and then burning it.

On the one hand, most people would be quite upset if they found they could no longer, for example, remember their mother. On the other hand, consider the woman pictured here. Although she lost her mother to cancer five years ago, she has been unable to "let go" and move on with her life. In a very real sense, who we are is determined by what we remember *and* what we forget. As you read this chapter on memory and forgetting, you'll almost certainly discover ways to improve your memory.

Journey Questions

7.1	How does memory work?
7.2	What are the features of short-term memory?
7.3	What are the features of long-term memory?
7.4	How is memory measured?
7.5	Why do we forget?
7.6	How does the brain form and store memories?
7.7	What are "photographic" memories?
7.8	How can I improve my memory?
7.9	What are mnemonics?

Stages of Memory—Do You Have a Mind Like a Steel Trap? Or a Sieve?

JOURNEY QUESTION 7.1 *How does memory work?*

Do you remember what you had for breakfast this morning? Or any of what happened last month? The last friend you texted? Of course you do. But how is it possible for us to so easily travel back in time? Let's begin with a look at some basic memory concepts. An interesting series of events must occur before we can say "I remember."

Many people think of memory as "a dusty storehouse of facts." In reality, human **memory** is an active system that receives, stores, organizes, alters, and recovers information (Baddeley, Eysenck, & Anderson, 2009). To be stored for a long time (like, say, between when you study and when you need to remember for an exam), information must pass through sensory memory, short-term memory, and long-term memory.

In some general ways, each of these three memory systems acts like a computer. Incoming information is first **encoded**, or changed into a usable form. This step is like entering data into a computer. Next, information is **stored**, or held, in the memory system. Finally, information must be **retrieved**, or taken out of storage, to be useful. If you're going to remember all of the 9,856 new terms on your next psychology exam, you must successfully encode them in sensory memory, move them through short-term memory, and eventually retrieve them from long-term memory.

These stages are summarized by the Atkinson-Shiffrin model of memory, shown in Figure 7.1 (Atkinson & Shiffrin, 1968). Let's trace the interesting series of memory events that must occur before you can pass that exam.

Sensory Memory

Let's say you sit down to memorize a few terms from this textbook for your exam next month. How will you remember them? As you read, information is first encoded in **sensory memory**, which can hold an exact copy of what you are seeing for a few seconds or less. We are normally unaware of the functioning of our sensory memories, which hold information just long enough for it to be retrieved and encoded into short-term memory (Radvansky, 2011).

For instance, look at a definition in this book and then quickly close your eyes. If you are lucky, a fleeting visual image of the letters will persist. **Iconic** (eye-KON-ick) **memories**—visual sensory images—are typically stored for about a half second (Keysers et al., 2005). Similarly, when you hear information, sensory memory stores it for up to 2 seconds as an **echoic memory**, a brief flurry of activity in the auditory system (Cheng & Lin, 2012).

If you are *selectively attending* (focusing on a selected portion of sensory input) to the terms you are trying to study, they will most likely be automatically retrieved from sensory

Memory The mental system for receiving, encoding, storing, organizing, altering, and retrieving information.

Encoding Converting information into a form in which it will be retained in memory.

Storage Holding information in memory for later use.

Retrieval Recovering information from storage in memory.

Sensory memory The first, normally unconscious, stage of memory, which holds an exact record of incoming information for a few seconds or less.

Iconic memory A mental image or visual representation.

Echoic memory A brief continuation of sensory activity in the auditory system after a sound is heard.

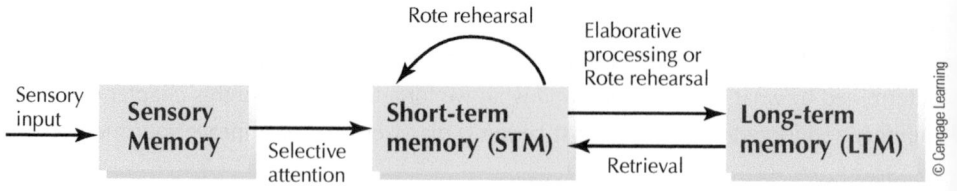

Figure 7.1 The Atkinson-Shiffrin model. Successful long-term remembering involves three stages of memory. Sensory memory encodes and stores sensory information for a second or two. Selectively attending to that information encodes small amounts in short-term memory, where it may be processed. Any resulting meaningful information may be encoded in long-term memory, where it may be stored until it is needed, at which time it may be retrieved as needed. The preceding is a useful, but highly simplified, *model* of memory; it may not be literally true of what happens in the brain.

memory and encoded in short-term memory. Background events, such as a voice on the television announcing a new episode of *Toddlers and Tiaras*, will not. However, if you are just looking at the words on the page but not paying attention (maybe you are too busy sneaking peeks at the television), that does not bode well for your exam. (As your elementary teacher might have commented, reading is more than just passing your eyes over the page.)

Short-Term Memory

Even though you might normally be unaware of your sensory memory, you cannot fail to be aware of your short-term memory. Carefully read the definition contained in the next two sentences. **Short-term memory (STM)** stores small amounts of information. We are consciously aware of short-term memories for a dozen seconds or so (Jonides et al., 2008). That's right, what you're aware of right now *is* in your short-term memory. So, as you encode information in short-term memory, you become consciously aware of it. Back to those definitions you are studying. You pay attention to what you are reading and so become aware of the definitions as you encode them in STM.

How are short-term memories encoded? Short-term memories can be encoded as images. But more often they are encoded *phonetically* (by sound), especially when it comes to words and letters (Page et al., 2007; Reed, 2010). If you are introduced to Tim at a party and you forget his name, you are more likely to call him by a name that sounds like Tim (Jim, Kim, or Slim, for instance), rather than a name that sounds different, such as Bob or Mike. If a friend interrupts to ask what you are studying, you may be lucky if you don't say "axon potential" instead of "action potential," or "depression" instead of "repression"!

One nice feature of short-term memory is that it prevents our minds from more permanently storing useless names, dates, telephone numbers, and other trivia. Supposed you use STM to dial a phone number or briefly remember a shopping list. Notice that unless you *rehearse* information (silently say it over and over to yourself; see Figure 7.1), it is quickly "dumped" from STM and forever lost. Unfortunately, as you may have noticed when dialing a telephone, STM is very sensitive to *interruption*, or *displacement*. You've probably had something like this happen: Someone gives you a phone number to call. You repeat the number to yourself as you start to dial. He or she then asks you a question. You answer, turn back to the phone, and find that your memory of the number was displaced by processing the question. Notice again that STM can handle only small amounts of information. It is very difficult to do more than one task at a time in STM (Mercer & McKeown, 2010; Oberauer & Göthe, 2006).

Working Memory

Short-term memory is often used for more than just storing information. When STM is combined with other mental processes, it acts more like a sort of "mental scratchpad," or **working memory**, in which we do much of our thinking (Chein & Fiez, 2010). That is, working memory briefly holds the information we need when we are thinking and solving problems (Holmes & Adams, 2006). Whenever you read a book, do mental arithmetic, put together a puzzle, plan a meal, or follow directions, you are using working memory (Baddeley, 2012; Prime & Jolicoeur, 2010).

Long-Term Memory

If STM is so limited, how do we remember for longer periods? Information that is important or meaningful is retrieved from STM and encoded in **long-term memory (LTM)**, which acts as a lasting storehouse for knowledge. LTM contains everything you know about the world—from aardvark to zebra, math to *The Walking Dead*, facts to fantasy. Yet, there appears to be no danger of running out of room. LTM can store nearly limitless amounts of information. In fact, the more you know, the easier it becomes to add new information to memory. This is the reverse of what we would expect if LTM could be "filled up" (Goldstein, 2011). It is also one of many reasons for getting an education.

Short-term memory (STM) The memory system used to hold small amounts of information in our conscious awareness for about a dozen seconds.

Working memory Another name for short-term memory, especially as it is used for thinking and problem solving.

Long-term memory (LTM) The memory system used for relatively permanent storage of meaningful information.

Are long-term memories also encoded as sounds? They can be. But typically, long-term memories are encoded on the basis of *meaning*, not sound. If you make an error in LTM, it will probably be related to meaning. For example, if you are trying to recall the phrase *test anxiety* for your psychology exam, you are more likely to mistakenly write down *test nervousness* or *test worry* than *text anxiety* or *tent anxiety*.

Back to your exam. If you can link information currently in STM to knowledge already stored in LTM, it gains meaning. This makes it easier to encode in LTM and, hence, remember. If you can relate the definition of *test anxiety* to a memory of a time when you or a friend were nervous about taking a test, you are more likely to remember the definition. As another example, try to memorize this story:

> With hocked gems financing him, our hero bravely defied all scornful laughter. "Your eyes deceive," he had said. "An egg, not a table, correctly typifies this unexplored planet." Now three sturdy sisters sought proof. Forging along, days became weeks as many doubters spread fearful rumors about the edge. At last from nowhere welcome winged creatures appeared, signifying momentous success. (Adapted from Dooling & Lachman, 1971.)

This odd story emphasizes the impact that meaning has on memory. People given the title of the story were able to remember it far better than those not given a title. See if the title helps you as much as it did them: "Columbus Discovers America."

Now that my understanding of the definitions has been encoded in LTM, all I have to do is store them until the exam, right? While you do have to retain your understanding in LTM, don't forget about the need to be able to retrieve those definitions if you are asked to. Tune in later in this chapter for more on retrieval from LTM.

The Relationship Between STM and LTM

Although sensory memory is involved every time we store information, we are most likely to notice STM and LTM. To summarize their connection, picture a small desk (STM) at the front of a huge warehouse full of filing cabinets (LTM). As information enters the warehouse, it is first placed on the desk. Because the desk is small, it must be quickly cleared off to make room for new information. Unimportant items are simply tossed away. Meaningful or personally important information is placed in the files (LTM). When we want to use knowledge from LTM to answer a question, the information is returned to STM. Or, in our analogy, a folder is taken out of the files (LTM) and moved to the desk (STM), where it can be used.

Now that you have a general picture of memory, it is time to explore STM and LTM in more detail. But first, here's a chance to rehearse what you've learned.

 study break Memory Systems

RECITE

Match: A. Sensory memory B. STM C. LTM
1. _____ Information tends to be stored phonetically
2. _____ Holds information for a few seconds or less
3. _____ Stores an iconic memory or echoic memory
4. _____ Permanent, unlimited capacity
5. _____ Temporarily holds small amounts of information
6. _____ Selective attention determines its contents
7. STM is improved by interruption, or displacement, because attention is more focused at such times. T or F?

REFLECT

THINK CRITICALLY

8. Why is sensory memory important to filmmakers?

SELF-REFLECT

Think of a time today when you used short-term memory (such as briefly remembering a phone number, a URL, or someone's name). How long did you retain the information? How did you encode it? How much do you remember now?

How is long-term memory helping you read this sentence? If your understanding of the meanings of the words weren't already stored in LTM, could you read at all? How else have you used LTM today?

ANSWERS

1. B 2. A 3. A 4. C 5. B 6. B 7. F 8. Without sensory memory, a movie would look like a series of still pictures. The split-second persistence of visual images helps blend one motion-picture frame into the next.

Short-Term Memory—Do You Know the Magic Number?

JOURNEY QUESTION 7.2 *What are the features of short-term memory?*

To make good use of your memory, it is valuable to know more about the quirks and characteristics of both STM and LTM. Let's dig deeper into their inner workings.

How much information can be held in short-term memory? For an answer, read the following numbers once. Then close the book and write as many as you can in the correct order.

8 5 1 7 4 9 3

This is called a digit-span test. It is a measure of attention and short-term memory. If you were able to correctly repeat seven digits, you have an average short-term memory. Now try to memorize the following list, again reading it only once.

7 1 8 3 5 4 2 9 1 6 3 4

This series was probably beyond your short-term memory capacity. Psychologist George Miller found that short-term memory is limited to the "magic number" seven (plus or minus two) **information bits** (Miller, 1956). A bit is a single meaningful "piece" of information, such as a digit. It is as if short-term memory has seven "slots" or "bins" into which separate items can be placed. Actually, a few people can remember up to nine bits, and for some types of information five bits is the limit. Thus, an *average* of seven information bits can be stored in short-term memory (Radvansky, 2011).

When all of the "slots" in STM are filled, there is no room for new information. Picture how this works at a party: Let's say your hostess begins introducing everyone who is there, "Chun, Dasia, Sandra, Roseanna, Cholik, Shawn, Kyrene. . ." *Stop*, you think to yourself. But she continues, "Nelia, Jay, Frank, Patty, Amit, Ricky." The hostess leaves, satisfied that you have met everyone. And you spend the evening talking with Chun, Dasia, and Ricky, the only people whose names you remember!

Chunking

Before we continue, try your short-term memory again, this time on letters. Read the following letters once, then look away and try to write them in the proper order.

T V I B M U S N Y M C A

Notice that there are 12 letters, or "bits" of information. If you studied the letters one at a time, this should be beyond the 7-item limit of STM. However, you may have noticed that some of the letters can be grouped, or *chunked*, together. For example, you may have noticed that NY is the abbreviation for New York. If so, the two bits N and Y became one chunk. **Information chunks** are made up of bits of information grouped into larger units.

Does chunking make a difference? Yes. Chunking *recodes* (reorganizes) information into units that are already in LTM. In a classic experiment that used lists like this one, people remembered best when the letters were read as familiar meaningful chunks: TV, IBM, USN, YMCA (Bower & Springston, 1970). If you recoded the letters this way, you organized them into four *chunks* of information and probably remembered the entire list. If you didn't, go back and try it again; you'll notice a big difference.

Chunking suggests that STM holds about five to seven of whatever units we are using. A single chunk could be made up of numbers, letters, words, phrases, or familiar sentences. Picture STM as a small desk again. Through chunking, we combine several items into one "stack" of information. This allows us to place seven stacks on the desk, whereas before there was only room for seven separate items. While you are studying, try to find ways to link two, three, or more separate facts or ideas into larger chunks, and your

Information bits Meaningful units of information, such as numbers, letters, words, or phrases.

Information chunks Information bits grouped into larger units.

short-term memory will improve. In fact, some psychologists believe that STM may actually hold only four items, unless some chunking has occurred (Jonides et al., 2008; Mathy & Feldman, 2012).

The clear message is that creating information chunks is the key to making good use of your short-term memory (Gilchrist, Cowan, & Naveh-Benjamin, 2009; Gobet, 2005). Remember, good memory results from finding or creating meaningful chunks in what you study. When meaningful organizations are elusive, even artificial ones (mnemonics—see the Psychology in Action section) are better than none at all.

Rehearsing Information

How long are short-term memories stored? They disappear very rapidly. However, you can prolong a memory by silently repeating it, a process called **maintenance rehearsal**. In a sense, rehearsing information allows you to "hear" it many times, not just once (Tam et al., 2010). You have probably used maintenance rehearsal to keep a phone number active in your mind while looking at your cell phone and dialing it.

Isn't saying stuff to yourself over and over also a way of studying? It *is* true that the more times a short-term memory is rehearsed, the greater its chances of being stored in LTM (Goldstein, 2011; refer back to Figure 7.1). This is **rote rehearsal** or **rote learning**—learning by simple repetition. But rote learning is not a very effective way to study.

Elaborative processing, which makes information more meaningful, is a far better way to form lasting memories. When encoding information for the first time, it is best to elaborate on links between that information and memories that are already in LTM. When you are studying, you will remember more if you elaborate on the meaning of the information (Raposo, Han, & Dobbins, 2009). As you read, try to reflect frequently. Ask yourself "why" questions, such as, "Why would that be true?" (Toyota & Kikuchi, 2005). Also, try to relate new ideas to your own experiences and knowledge (Hartlep & Forsyth, 2000). If you recognize this advice from "The Psychology of Studying—Reflective Learning" at the front of this book, good. If not, consider reading about reflective learning if only to elaborate on your processing of the idea of elaborative processing.

What if rehearsal is prevented, so a memory cannot be recycled or moved to LTM? Without maintenance rehearsal, STM storage is quite brief. In one experiment, participants heard meaningless syllables like "xar," followed by a number like 67. As soon as participants heard the number, they began counting backward by threes (to prevent them from repeating the syllable). After a delay of between 12 and 18 seconds, their memory for the syllables fell to zero (Peterson & Peterson, 1959). That's why if you are introduced to someone and that person's name slips out of STM, it is gone forever. To avoid embarrassment, pay careful attention to the name, repeat it to yourself several times, and try to use it in the next sentence or two—before you lose it (Radvansky, 2011).

Long-Term Memory—A Blast from the Past

JOURNEY QUESTION 7.3 *What are the features of long-term memory?*

An electrode touched the patient's brain. Immediately she said, "Yes, sir, I think I heard a mother calling her little boy somewhere. It seemed to be something happening years ago. It was somebody in the neighborhood in which I live." A short time later the electrode was applied to the same spot. Again the patient said, "Yes, I hear the same familiar sounds. It seems to be a woman calling, the same lady" (Penfield, 1958). A woman made these statements while she was undergoing brain surgery. There are no pain receptors in the brain, so the patient was awake as her brain was electrically stimulated (Figure 7.2). When activated, some brain areas seemed to produce vivid memories of long-forgotten events (Jacobs, Lega, & Anderson, 2012).

Maintenance rehearsal Silently repeating or mentally reviewing information to hold it in short-term memory.

Rote rehearsal (rote learning) Learning by simple repetition.

Elaborative processing Making memories more meaningful through processing that encodes links between new information and existing memories and knowledge, either at the time of the original encoding or on subsequent retrievals.

Permanence

Are all our experiences permanently recorded in memory? Results like those described led neurosurgeon Wilder Penfield to propose that the brain records the past like a "strip of movie film, complete with sound track" (Penfield, 1957). But as you already know, this is an exaggeration, since many events never get past sensory or short-term memory. Also, brain stimulation produces memory-like experiences in only about 3 percent of cases. Most reports resemble dreams more than memories, and many are clearly imaginary. Memory experts now believe that, except for a few rare individuals like Jill Price and Mr. S., who we met at the beginning of this chapter (remember?), long-term memories are only relatively permanent (Goldstein, 2011; Parker, Cahill, & McGaugh, 2006; Price & Davis, 2009).

Try It Yourself: How's Your Memory?
To better appreciate the next topic, pause for a moment and read the words you see here. Read through the list once. Then continue reading the next section of this chapter.

| bed | dream | blanket | doze | pillow | nap | snore | mattress | alarm |
| clock | rest | slumber | nod | sheet | bunk | cot | cradle | groggy |

Elaborating False Memories

There's another reason for doubting that all our experiences are permanently recorded. Through elaborative processing, as new long-term memories are stored, older memories are often updated, changed, lost, or *revised* (Baddeley, Eysenck, & Anderson, 2009). To illustrate this point, Elizabeth Loftus and John Palmer (1974) showed people a filmed automobile accident. Afterward, some participants were asked to estimate how fast the cars were going when they "smashed" into one another. For others the words "bumped," "contacted," or "hit" replaced "smashed." One week later, each person was asked, "Did you see any broken glass?" Those asked earlier about the cars that "smashed" into one another were more likely to say yes, even though no broken glass was shown in the film. The new information ("smashed") was included in memories and revised them, producing a **false memory**, a memory that can seem accurate but is not.

Try It Yourself: Old or New?
Now, without looking back to the list of words you read a few minutes ago, see if you can tell which of the following are "old" words (items from the list you read) and which are "new" words (items that weren't on the list). Mark each of the following words as old or new:

| sofa | sleep | lamp | kitchen |

Gaps in memory, which are common, may be filled in by logic, guessing, or new information (Schacter & Addis, 2008). Although elaboration is helpful when you're making meaningful connections between new information and what you already know, it can also lead to false memories. Indeed, it is possible to have "memories" for things that never happened (such as remembering broken glass at an accident when there was none) (Loftus, 2003; Weinstein & Shanks, 2010).

In one study, people who had visited a Disney resort were shown several fake ads for Disney that featured Bugs Bunny. Later, about 16 percent of the people who saw these fake ads claimed that they had met Bugs at Disneyland. This is impossible, of course, because Bugs Bunny is a Warner Brothers character who would never show his face at Disneyland (Braun, Ellis, & Loftus, 2002). In another study, even people who were exposed to repeated warnings about a product nevertheless ended up with a more favorable impression of the product (Skurnik et al., 2005).

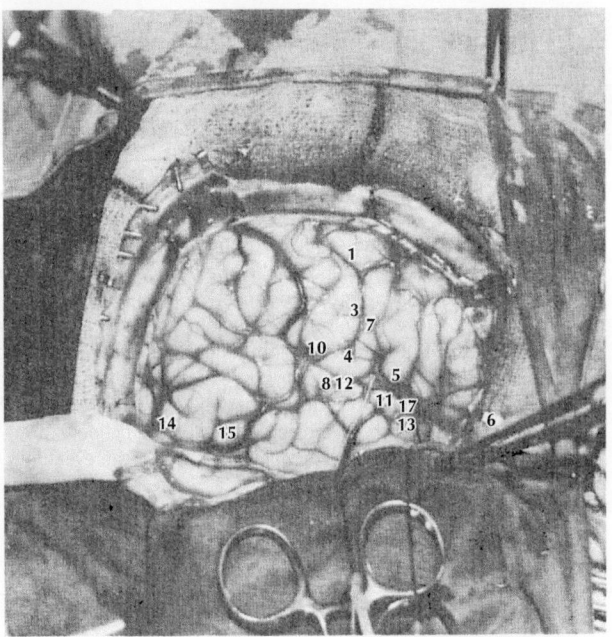

Figure 7.2 Exposed cerebral cortex of a patient undergoing brain surgery. Numbers represent points that reportedly produced "memories" when electrically stimulated. A critical evaluation of such reports suggests that they are more like dreams than memories. This fact raises questions about claims that long-term memories are permanent. (From Penfield, 1958. Courtesy the author and Charles C Thomas, Publisher, Springfield, Illinois.)

False memory A memory that can seem accurate but is not.

Have you ever wondered why well-known companies that already sell huge quantities of familiar products (such as soft drinks or beer) continue to advertise as heavily as they do? If you believe that the point of the advertising is to familiarize people with a product or to inform them about it, this *is* a mystery. But if you think about the elaborative nature of memory, the mystery is solved. According to economist Jesse Shapiro (2006), the intent of much advertising is to "jam" your memory with positive impressions of a product.

How does "memory jamming" work? How many times have you had a bottle or can of your favorite beer or soft drink? And how many commercials for those beverages have you watched? Every extra commercial adds one more positive memory of the beverage to your long-term memory. Here's a typical commercial: Boy goes to cool party, sees a hot girl, flashes favorite beer, gets the girl. (Yes, beer commercials mainly target young men.) Because we cannot always easily tell which recollection is fact and which is fiction, storing enough of these commercials can eventually create "memories" that never happened. For example, you might remember that you enjoy drinking a particular beverage more than you actually do in reality.

According to Shapiro (2006), the more positive fictional commercials we see, the less likely we are to remember an actual negative experience with a product. In effect, the positive, fictional memories "jam," or block, our ability to remember actual negative memories when deciding whether to buy a product. Kathryn Braun-LaTour and Michael LaTour (2004) add that long-term advertising campaigns create a "brand" memory that can be remarkably strong. This appears to be especially true when the ads are first viewed in early childhood. So perhaps you have been having jam with your memories ever since you were a baby.

So elaborative processing could be used to deliberately manipulate memory? Yup. According to one theory, advertisers do it all the time. (See "Do You Like Jam with Your Memory?" for more information.)

Try It Yourself: And Now, the Results

Return now and look at the labels you wrote on the "old or new" word list. Contrary to what you may think you "remembered," all of the listed words are "new." None was on the original list!

If you thought you "remembered" that "sleep" was on the original list, you had a false memory. The word *sleep* is associated with most of the words on the original list, which creates a strong impression that you saw it before (Roediger & McDermott, 1995).

Eyewitness memories are notoriously inaccurate. By the time witnesses are asked to testify in court, information they learned after an incident may blend into their original memories.

As the preceding examples show, thoughts, inferences, and mental associations may be mistaken for true memories (Scoboria et al., 2012). People in Elizabeth Loftus's experiments who had false memories were often quite upset to learn they had given false "testimony" (Loftus & Ketcham, 1994; Loftus & Bernstein, 2005).

False memories are a common problem in police work. For example, a witness may select a photo of a suspect from police files or see a photo in the news. Later, the witness identifies the suspect in a lineup or in court. Did the witness really remember the suspect from the scene of the crime? Or was it from the more recently seen photograph?

Does new information "overwrite" existing memories? No, the real problem is that elaborative processing makes us vulnerable to **source confusion**, which occurs when the origins of a memory are misremembered (Rosa & Gutchess, 2011; Woroch & Gonsalves, 2010). This can, for example, lead witnesses to "remember" a face that they actually saw somewhere other than the crime scene (Ruva, McEvoy, & Bryant, 2007). Many tragic cases of mistaken identity occur this way. One famous example involved memory expert Donald Thomson. After appearing live on Australian television, he was accused of rape. It turns out that the victim was watching him on television when the actual rapist broke into her apartment (Schacter, 1996). She correctly remembered his face but attributed it to the wrong *source*.

Is there any way to avoid such problems? Forensic psychologists have tried a variety of techniques to help improve the memory of witnesses. "Telling Wrong from Right in Forensic Memory" examines research on this important question.

Source confusion (in memory) Occurs when the origins of a memory are misremembered.

Imagine you are a forensic psychologist, investigating a crime. Unfortunately, your witness can't remember much of what happened. As a "memory detective," what can you do to help?

Could hypnosis improve the witness's memory? It might seem so. In one case in California, 26 children were abducted from a school bus and held captive for ransom. Under hypnosis, the bus driver recalled the license plate number of the kidnappers' van. This memory helped break the case. Such successes seem to imply that hypnosis can improve memory. But does it?

Research has shown that hypnosis increases false memories more than it does true ones. Eighty percent of the new memories produced by hypnotized participants in one classic experiment were *incorrect* (Dywan & Bowers, 1983). This is in part because a hypnotized person is more likely than normal to use imagination to fill in gaps in memory. Also, if a questioner asks misleading or suggestive questions, hypnotized persons tend to weave the information into their memories (Scoboria et al., 2002). To make matters worse, even when a memory is completely false, the hypnotized person's confidence in it can be unshakable (Burgess & Kirsch, 1999). Thus, hypnosis sometimes uncovers more information, as it did with the bus driver (Schreiber & Schreiber, 1999). However, in the absence of corroborating evidence, there is no sure way to tell which of these memories are false and which are true (Mazzoni, Heap, & Scoboria, 2010).

Is there a better way to improve eyewitness memory? To help police detectives, R. Edward Geiselman and Ron Fisher created the **cognitive interview**, a technique for jogging the memory of eyewitnesses (Fisher & Geiselman, 1987). The key to this approach is recreating the crime scene. Witnesses revisit the scene in their imaginations or in person. That way, aspects of the crime scene, such as sounds, smells, and objects, provide helpful retrieval cues (stimuli associated with a memory). Back in the context of the crime, the witness is encouraged to recall events in different orders and from different viewpoints. Every new memory, no matter how trivial it may seem, can serve as a cue to trigger the retrieval of yet more memories. (Later in this chapter, we will see why such cues are so effective for jogging memories.)

When used properly, the cognitive interview produces 35 percent more correct information than standard questioning (Davis, McMahon, & Greenwood, 2005; Geiselman et al., 1986). This improvement comes without adding to the number of false memories elicited, as occurs with hypnosis (Centofanti & Reece, 2006). The result is a procedure that is more effective in actual police work and in different cultures (Memon, Meissner, & Fraser, 2010; Stein & Memon, 2006).

To summarize, forming and using long-term memories is an active, creative, highly personal process. Our memories are colored by emotions, judgments, and quirks of personality. If you and a friend were joined at the hip and you went through life side by side, you would still have different memories. What we remember depends on what we pay attention to, what we regard as meaningful or important, how we elaborate our memory, and what we feel strongly about.

Organizing Memories

Long-term memory stores huge amounts of information during a lifetime. How are we able to quickly find specific memories? The answer is that each person's "memory index" is highly organized.

Does that mean that information is arranged alphabetically, as in a dictionary? Not a chance! If we ask you to name a black and white animal that lives on ice, is related to a chicken, and cannot fly, you don't have to go from aardvark to zebra to find the answer. You will probably think of only black-and-white birds living in the Antarctic. *Voilá*—the answer is a penguin.

Information in LTM may be arranged according to rules, images, categories, symbols, similarity, formal meaning, or personal meaning (Baddeley, Eysenck, & Anderson, 2009). Psychologists have begun to develop a picture of the *structure*, or organization, of memories. *Memory structure* refers to the pattern of associations among items of information. For example, assume that you are given two statements, to which you must answer yes or no: (1) *A canary is an animal.* (2) *A canary is a bird.* Which do you answer more quickly? Most people can say that *A canary is a bird* faster than they can recognize that *A canary is an animal* (Collins & Quillian, 1969).

Why should this be so? Psychologists believe that a **network model** of memory explains why. According to this view, LTM is organized as a network of linked ideas (**Figure 7.3**). When ideas are "farther" apart, it takes a longer chain of associations to connect them. The more two items are separated, the longer it takes to answer. In terms of information links, *canary* is probably "close" to *bird* in your "memory files." *Animal* and *canary* are farther

Cognitive interview Use of various cues and strategies to improve the memory of eyewitnesses.

Network model (of memory) A model of memory that views it as an organized system of linked information.

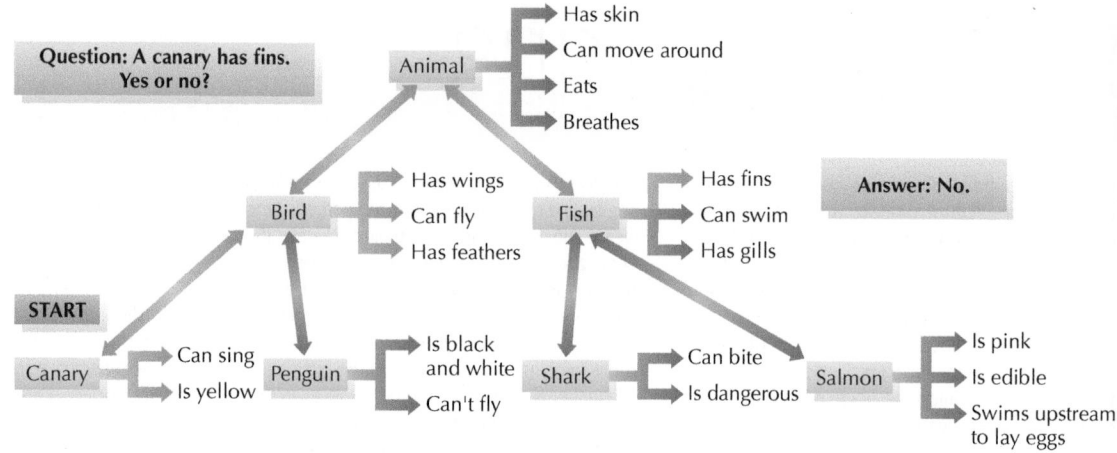

Figure 7.3 A hypothetical network of facts about animals shows what is meant by the structure of memory. Small networks of ideas such as this are probably organized into larger and larger units and higher levels of meaning. (Adapted from *Journal of Verbal Learning and Verbal Behavior, 8*, Allan M. Collins & M. Ross Quillian, "Retrieval time from semantic memory," 240–247, Copyright © 1969 with permission from Elsevier.)

apart. Remember, though, this has nothing to do with alphabetical order. We are talking about a system of linked meanings.

Redintegration

Networks of associated memories may also help explain a common experience: Imagine finding a picture taken on your sixth birthday or at your high school graduation. As you look at the photo, one memory leads to another, which leads to another, and another. Soon you have unleashed a flood of seemingly forgotten details. This process is called *redintegration* (reh-DIN-tuh-GRAY-shun).

Redintegration seems to spread through the "branches" of memory networks. The key idea in redintegration is that one memory serves as a cue to trigger another. As a result, an entire past experience may be reconstructed from one small recollection. Many people find that redintegration can be touched off by distinctive odors from the past—from a farm visited in childhood, Grandma's kitchen, the seashore, the perfume or aftershave of a former lover, and so on (Willander & Larsson, 2006).

From Encoding to Retrieval in Long-Term Memory

Let's get back to passing that psychology exam. On one recent exam, Jerry studied using rote learning whereas Erica made extensive use of elaborative processing. Figure 7.4 shows what their memory networks might look like for the concept of reinforcement (see Chapter 6).

Because Jerry spent most of his time in rote rehearsal, his memory network for the concept of reinforcement is quite sparse. He managed to get the definition right. Also, during rote learning, it occurred to him that extra soldiers joining a battle were also reinforcements. In contrast, while studying, Erica asked herself how reinforcement and punishment differ, what kinds of reinforcement (and punishment) there are, and tried to think of personal examples. She also checked out the difference between operant and respondent learning.

That must mean Erica has a better chance of doing well on the psychology exam, right? You bet. To begin, because Jerry used rote learning, his memories will be weaker since he cannot be as sure as Erica that he actually understood the concept of reinforcement. Also, suppose Jerry cannot directly retrieve the definition of reinforcement during his exam. His only other hope is to remember soldiers so that redintegration might pop up the needed definition.

Redintegration Process by which memories are reconstructed or expanded by starting with one memory and then following chains of association to other, related memories.

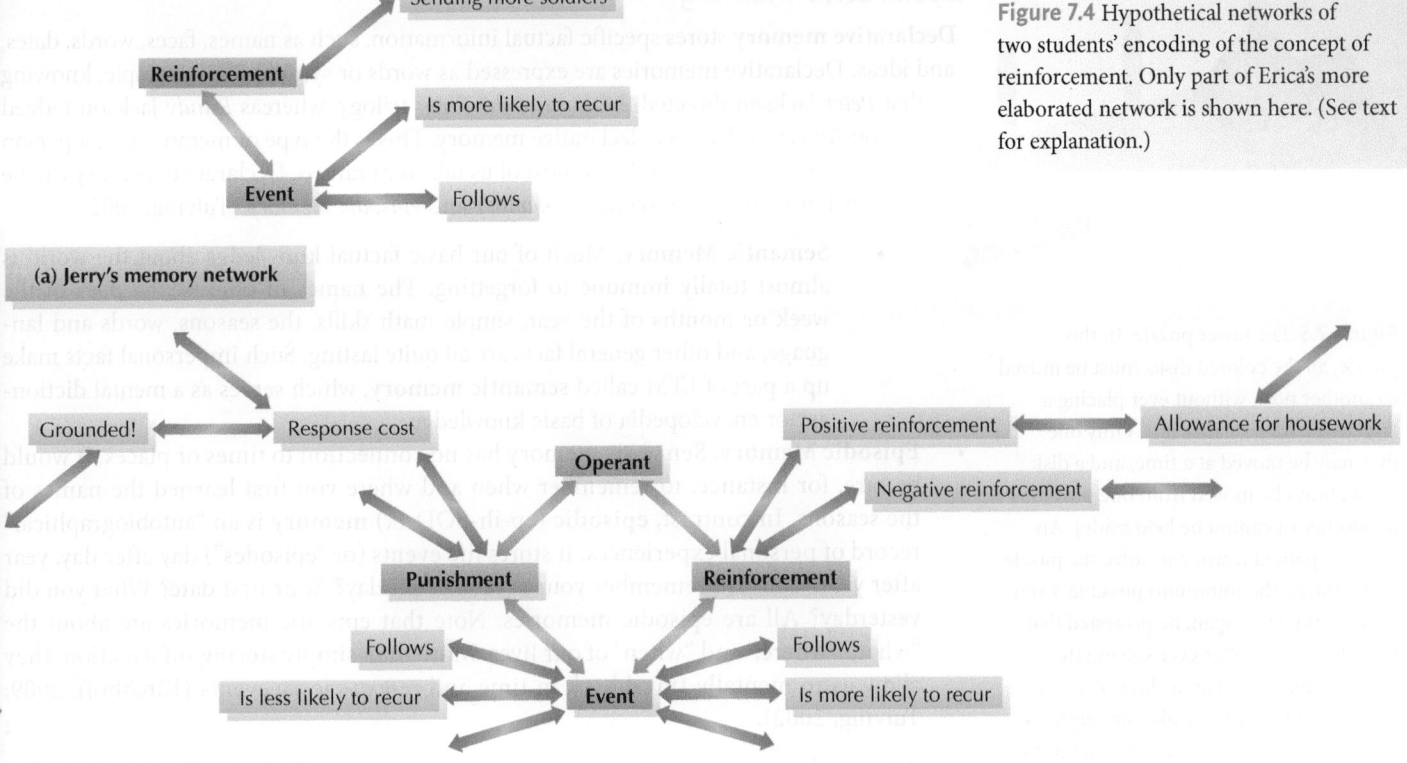

(a) Jerry's memory network

(b) Erica's memory network

In sharp contrast, for Erica to successfully encode her more elaborated network she *had* to understand the concept of reinforcement. Hence, she is more likely than Jerry to directly retrieve that information if she needs to. On the off-chance Erica does not immediately remember the needed definition, she has many retrieval cues to help her. Remembering punishment, or an example of reinforcement, or even the time she got grounded, could well trigger redintegration of "reinforcement."

In summary, more elaborative processing results in more elaborate memory networks and, hence, more retrieval cues to help with redintegration. Time spent in elaborative processing is time well spent, at least if you want to do well on exams.

Types of Long-Term Memory

How many types of long-term memory are there? It is becoming clear that more than one type of long-term memory exists. For example, a curious thing happens to many people who develop amnesia. Amnesic patients may be unable to learn a telephone number, an address, or a person's name. Yet the same patients can learn to solve complex puzzles in a normal amount of time (Cavaco et al., 2004; Figure 7.5). These and other observations have led many psychologists to conclude that long-term memories fall into at least two categories (Lum & Bleses, 2012). One is called *procedural memory* (or skill memory). The other is *declarative memory* (also sometimes called fact memory).

Procedural Memory

Procedural memory includes basic conditioned responses and learned actions, such as those involved in typing, driving, or swinging a golf club. Memories such as these can be fully expressed only as actions (or "know-how"). It is likely that skill memories register in "lower" brain areas, especially the basal ganglia and the cerebellum. They represent the more basic "automatic" elements of conditioning, learning, and memory (Freberg, 2010; Lum & Bleses, 2012).

Procedural memory Long-term memories of conditioned responses and learned skills.

Declarative Memory

Declarative memory stores specific factual information, such as names, faces, words, dates, and ideas. Declarative memories are expressed as words or symbols. For example, knowing that *Peter* Jackson directed the *Lord of the Rings* trilogy, whereas *Randy* Jackson judged on *American Idol*, is a declarative memory. This is the type of memory that a person with amnesia lacks and that most of us take for granted. Declarative memory can be further divided into *semantic memory* and *episodic memory* (Tulving, 2002):

- **Semantic Memory.** Much of our basic factual knowledge about the world is almost totally immune to forgetting. The names of objects, the days of the week or months of the year, simple math skills, the seasons, words and language, and other general facts are all quite lasting. Such impersonal facts make up a part of LTM called **semantic memory**, which serves as a mental dictionary or encyclopedia of basic knowledge.

- **Episodic Memory.** Semantic memory has no connection to times or places. It would be rare, for instance, to remember when and where you first learned the names of the seasons. In contrast, **episodic** (ep-ih-SOD-ik) **memory** is an "autobiographical" record of personal experiences. It stores life events (or "episodes") day after day, year after year. Can you remember your seventh birthday? Your first date? What you did yesterday? All are episodic memories. Note that episodic memories are about the "what," "where," and "when" of our lives. More than simply storing information, they allow us to mentally travel back in time and *re-experience* events (Kirchhoff, 2009; Tulving, 2002).

Are episodic memories as lasting as semantic memories? Either type of memory can last indefinitely. However, unless episodic memories are important, they are more easily forgotten than semantic memories. In fact, it is the forgetting of episodic information that results in the formation of semantic memories. At first, you remembered when and where you were when you learned the names of the seasons. (Mommy, Mommy, guess what I learned in preschool today!) Over time, you forgot the episodic details but will likely remember the names for the rest of your life.

How Many Types of Long-Term Memory?

In answer to the question posed at the beginning of this section, it is very likely that three kinds of long-term memories exist: procedural memory and two types of declarative memory, semantic and episodic (Figure 7.6).

Figure 7.5 The tower puzzle. In this puzzle, all the colored disks must be moved to another post, without ever placing a larger disk on a smaller one. Only one disk may be moved at a time, and a disk must always be moved from one post to another (it cannot be held aside). An amnesic patient learned to solve the puzzle in 31 moves, the minimum possible. Even so, each time he began, he protested that he did not remember ever solving the puzzle before and that he did not know how to begin. Evidence like this suggests that memories for skills are distinct from memories for facts.

Declarative memory That part of long-term memory containing specific factual information.

Semantic memory A subpart of declarative memory that records impersonal knowledge about the world.

Episodic memory A subpart of declarative memory that records personal experiences that are linked with specific times and places.

Figure 7.6 In the model shown here, long-term memory is divided into procedural memory (learned actions and skills) and declarative memory (stored facts). Declarative memories can be either semantic (impersonal knowledge) or episodic (personal experiences associated with specific times and places).

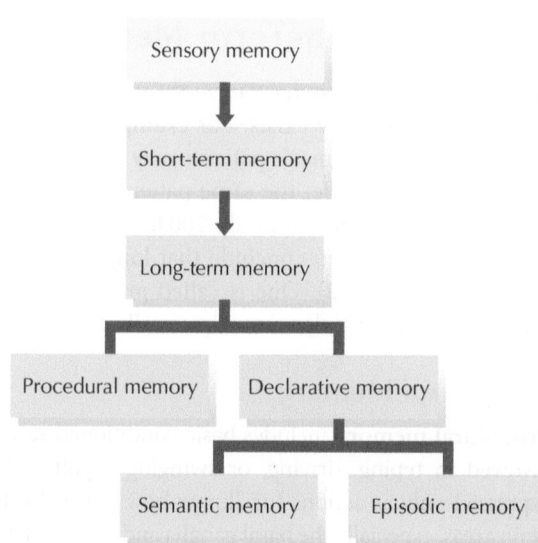

study break STM and LTM

RECITE

1. Information is best transferred from STM to LTM when a person engages in
   a. maintenance chunking   b. maintenance recoding
   c. elaborative networking   d. elaborative processing
2. Elaborative processing is often responsible for creating false memories. T or F?
3. Electrical stimulation of the brain has shown conclusively that all memories are stored permanently but not all memories can be retrieved. T or F?
4. The existence of redintegration is best explained by _____ models of memory.
   a. network   b. integrative
   c. implicit   d. chunking
5. Which of the following is a synonym for skill memory?
   a. semantic memory   b. declarative memory
   c. episodic memory   d. procedural memory

REFLECT

THINK CRITICALLY

6. Parents sometimes warn children not to read comic books, fearing that they will learn less in school if they "fill their heads up with junk." Why is this warning unnecessary?

SELF-REFLECT

In the United States, telephone numbers are divided into an area code (three digits) and a seven-digit number that is divided into three digits plus four more. Can you relate this practice to STM? How about to chunking and recoding?

Think about how you've used your memory in the last hour. See if you can identify an example of each of the following: a procedural memory, a declarative memory, a semantic memory, and an episodic memory.

ANSWERS

1. d 2. T 3. F 4. a 5. d 6. Because the more information you have in long-term memory, the greater the possibilities for linking new information to it. Generally, the more you know, the more you can learn—even if some of what you know is "junk."

Measuring Memory—The Answer Is on the Tip of My Tongue

JOURNEY QUESTION 7.4 *How is memory measured?*

You either remember something or you don't, right? Wrong. Partial memories are common. For instance, have you ever tried to remember something only to find yourself stuck in a **tip-of-the-tongue (TOT) state**? This is the feeling that a memory is available but not quite retrievable (Brown, 2012). It is as if an answer or a memory is just out of reach—on the "tip of your tongue."

In a classic TOT study, university students read the definitions of words such as *sextant*, *sampan*, and *ambergris*. Students who "drew a blank" and couldn't name a defined word were asked to give any other information they could. Often, they could guess the first and last letter and the number of syllables of the word they were seeking. They also gave words that sounded like or meant the same thing as the defined word (Brown & McNeill, 1966).

Closely related to the TOT state is the fact that people can often tell beforehand if they are likely to remember something. This is called the *feeling of knowing* (Thomas, Bulevich, & Dubois, 2011; Widner, Otani, & Winkelman, 2005). Feeling-of-knowing reactions are easy to observe on television game shows, where they occur just before contestants are allowed to answer.

Oddly enough, having a TOT state or a feeling of knowing is no guarantee of memory retrieval. You may have experienced this yourself, perhaps during an exam. You read a question and immediately the answer is on the tip of your tongue or, at the very least, you know you know the answer. Either way, the required answer doesn't come to mind. You know what often happens next, right? After you leave the exam, the answer "pops" into your head. (Professor, I *knew* my stuff!)

Tip-of-the-tongue (TOT) state The feeling that a memory is available but not quite retrievable.

MEMORY **285**

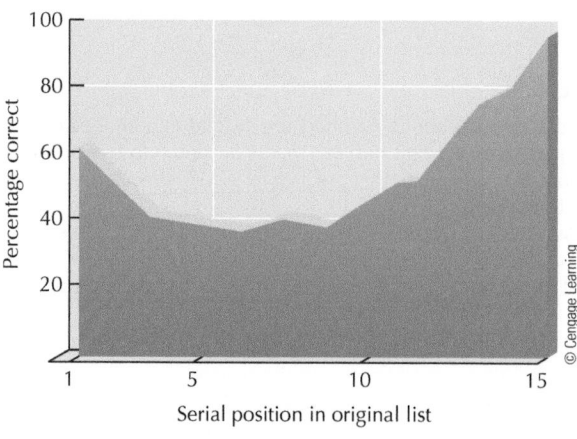

Percentage correct (y-axis): 100, 80, 60, 40, 20

Serial position in original list (x-axis): 1, 5, 10, 15

Figure 7.7 The serial position effect. The graph shows the percentage of participants correctly recalling each item in a 15-item list. Recall is best for the first and last items. (Data from Craik, 1970.)

Déjà vu, the feeling that you have already experienced a situation that you are actually experiencing for the first time, may be another example of partial memory (Brown & Marsh, 2010). If a new experience triggers vague memories of a past experience, without yielding *any* details at all, you might be left saying to yourself, "I feel like I've seen it before." The new experience seems familiar even though the older memory is too weak to rise to the level of awareness.

Because memory is not an all-or-nothing event, there are several ways of measuring it. Three commonly used methods of measuring memory are *recall*, *recognition*, and *relearning*. Let's see how they differ.

Recalling Information

What is the name of the first song on your favorite playlist? Who won the World Series last year? Who wrote *Hamlet*? If you can answer these questions, you are using **recall**, a direct retrieval of facts or information. Tests of recall often require *verbatim* (word-for-word) memory. If you study a poem until you can recite it without looking at it, you are recalling it. If you complete a fill-in-the-blank question, you are using recall. When you answer an essay question by providing facts and ideas, you are also using recall, even though you didn't learn your essay verbatim.

The order in which information is memorized has an interesting effect on recall. To experience it, try to memorize the following list, reading it only once:

> bread, apples, soda, ham, cookies, rice, lettuce, beets, mustard, cheese, oranges, ice cream, crackers, flour, eggs

If you are like most people, it will be hardest for you to recall items from the middle of the list. Figure 7.7 shows the results of a similar test. Notice that most errors occur with middle items of an ordered list. This is the **serial position effect** (Bonk & Healy, 2010). You can remember the last items on a list because they are still in STM. The first items are also remembered well because they entered an "empty" short-term memory. This allows you to rehearse the items so they move into long-term memory (Addis & Kahana, 2004). The middle items are neither held in short-term memory nor moved to long-term memory, so they are often lost.

Recognizing Information

Try to write down everything you can remember learning from a class you took last year. If you actually did this, you might conclude that you had learned very little. However, a more sensitive test based on recognition could be used. In **recognition**, previously learned material is correctly identified. For instance, you could take a multiple-choice test on facts and ideas from the course. Because you would have to recognize only correct answers, you would probably find that you had learned a lot.

Recognition can be amazingly accurate for pictures and photographs (Whitehouse, Maybery, & Durkin, 2006). In one classic study, people viewed 2,560 photographs at a rate of one every 10 seconds. Each person was then shown 280 pairs of photographs. Each pair included an "old" picture (from the first set of photos) and a similar "new" image. Participants could tell 85 to 95 percent of the time which photograph they had seen before (Haber, 1970). This finding may explain why we rarely need to see our friends' vacation photos more than once.

Recognition is usually superior to recall. That's why people so often say, "I may forget a name, but I never forget a face." (You can't recall the name but can recognize the face.) That's also why police departments use photographs or a lineup to identify criminal suspects. Witnesses who disagree when they try to recall a suspect's height, weight, age, or eye color often agree completely when they merely need to recognize the person.

Is recognition always superior? It depends greatly on the kind of *distractors* used (Flowe & Ebbese, 2007). These are false items included with an item to be recognized. If distractors

Recall To supply or reproduce memorized information with a minimum of external cues.

Serial position effect The tendency to make the most errors in remembering the middle items of an ordered list.

Recognition An ability to correctly identify previously learned information.

are very similar to the correct item, memory may be poor. A reverse problem occurs when only one choice looks like it could be correct. This can produce a *false positive*, or false sense of recognition, like the false memory you had earlier when you thought you remembered seeing the word *sleep*.

Many hundreds of people have been put in jail on the basis of mistaken eyewitness memories (Lampinen, Neuschatz, & Cling, 2012; Wade, Green, & Nash, 2010). There have been instances in which witnesses described a criminal as black, tall, or young. Then a lineup was held in which a suspect was the only African American among whites, the only tall suspect, or the only young person. In such cases, a false identification is very likely. To avoid tragic mistakes, it's better to have *all* the distractors look like the person witnesses described. Also, to reduce false positives, witnesses should be warned that the culprit *may not be present*. It's also better to show witnesses one photo at a time (a sequential lineup). For each photo, the witness must decide whether the person is the culprit before another photo is shown (Wells, 2001; Wells & Olsen, 2003).

Police lineups make use of the sensitivity of recognition memory. However, unless great care is taken, false identifications are still possible (Wells, 2001). Is this a fair or an unfair lineup? What problems may be created with this lineup?

Relearning Information

In another classic experiment, a psychologist read a short passage in Greek to his son every day when the boy was between 15 months and 3 years of age. At age 8, the boy was asked if he remembered the Greek passage. He showed no evidence of recall. He was then shown selections from the passage he heard and selections from other Greek passages. Could he recognize the one he heard as an infant? "It's all Greek to me!" he said, indicating a lack of recognition (and drawing a frown from everyone in the room).

Had the psychologist stopped, he might have concluded that no memory of the Greek remained. However, the child was then asked to memorize the original quotation and others of equal difficulty. This time, his earlier learning became evident. The boy memorized the passage he had heard in childhood 25 percent faster than the others (Burtt, 1941). As this experiment suggests, **relearning** is typically the most sensitive measure of memory.

When a person is tested by relearning, how do we know a memory still exists? As with the boy described, relearning is measured by a *savings score* (the amount of time saved when relearning information). Let's say it takes you 1 hour to memorize all the names in a telephone book. (It's a small town.) Two years later you relearn them in 45 minutes. Because you "saved" 15 minutes, your savings score would be 25 percent (15 divided by 60 times 100). Savings of this type are a good reason for studying a wide range of subjects. It may seem that learning algebra, history, or a foreign language is wasted if you don't use the knowledge immediately. But when you do need such information, you will be able to relearn it quickly.

Explicit and Implicit Memories

Who were the last three presidents of the United States? What did you have for breakfast today? What is the title of Taylor Swift's latest album? Explicit memory is used in answering each of these questions. **Explicit memories** are past experiences that are consciously brought to mind. Recall, recognition, and the tests you take in school rely on explicit memories.

In contrast, **implicit memories** lie outside of awareness (Roediger & Amir, 2005; Gopie, Craik, & Hasher, 2011). That is, we are not aware that a memory exists. For example, if you know how to type, it is apparent that you know where the letters are on the keyboard. But how many typists could correctly label blank keys in a drawing of a keyboard? Many people find that they cannot directly remember such information, even though they "know" it. Nevertheless, implicit memories—such as unconsciously knowing where the letters are on a keyboard—greatly influence our behavior (Radvansky, 2011).

Relearning Learning again something that was previously learned. Used to measure memory of prior learning.

Explicit memory A memory that a person is aware of having; a memory that is consciously retrieved.

Implicit memory A memory that a person does not know exists; a memory that is retrieved unconsciously.

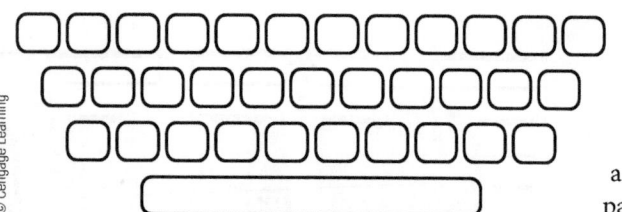

Can you label the letter keys on this blank keyboard? If you can, you probably used implicit memory to do it.

© Cengage Learning

Priming

How is it possible to show that a memory exists if it lies outside of awareness? Psychologists first noticed implicit memory while studying memory loss caused by brain injuries. Let's say, for example, that a patient is shown a list of common words, such as *chair, tree, lamp, table,* and so on. Later, the patient fails to recall any words from the list.

Now, instead of asking the patient to explicitly recall the list, we could "prime" his memory by giving him the first two letters of each word. "Just say whatever word comes to mind that begins with these letters," we tell him. Of course, many words could be made from each pair of letters. For example, the first item (from "chair") would be the letters CH. The patient could say "child," "chalk," "chain," "check," or many other words. Instead, he says "chair," a word from the original list. The patient is not aware that he is remembering the list, but as he gives a word for each letter pair, almost all are from the list. Apparently, the letters **primed** (activated) hidden memories, which then influenced his answers.

Similar effects have been found for people with normal memories. As the preceding example implies, implicit memories are often revealed by giving a person limited cues, such as the first letter of words or partial drawings of objects. Typically, the person believes that he or she is just saying whatever comes to mind. Nevertheless, information previously seen or heard affects his or her answers (Rueckl & Galantucci, 2005).

🖐 study break Measuring Memory

RECITE

1. Four techniques for measuring or demonstrating memory are
   _____ _____
   _____ _____
2. Essay tests require _____ of facts or ideas.
3. As a measure of memory, a savings score is associated with
   a. recognition   b. priming
   c. relearning   d. reconstruction
4. Priming is used to reveal which type of memories?
   a. explicit   b. sensory
   c. skill   d. implicit

REFLECT

THINK CRITICALLY

5. When asked to explain why they may have failed to recall some information, people often claim it must be because the information is no longer in their memory. Why does the existence of implicit memories challenge this explanation?

SELF-REFLECT

Have you experienced a TOT state recently? Were you able to retrieve the word you were searching for? If not, what could you remember about it?

Do you prefer tests based primarily on recall or recognition? Have you observed a savings effect while relearning information you studied in the past (such as in high school)?

Can you think of things you do that are based on implicit memories? For instance, how do you know which way to turn various handles in your house, apartment, or dorm?

ANSWERS

1. recall, recognition, relearning, priming 2. recall 3. c 4. d 5. It is possible to have an implicit memory that cannot be consciously recalled. Memories like these (*available*) in memory even though they are not consciously *accessible*) show that failing to recall something does not guarantee it is no longer in memory (Landau & Leynes, 2006).

Forgetting—Why We, Uh, Let's See; Why We, Uh . . . Forget!

JOURNEY QUESTION 7.5 *Why do we forget?*

We don't expect sensory memories and short-term memories to remain with us for long. But when you deliberately encode and store information in long-term memory, you want it to stay there (after all, it's supposed to be *long*-term). For example, when you study for an exam, you count on your long-term memory to retain the information at least until you take your exam.

Priming Facilitating the retrieval of an implicit memory by using cues to activate hidden memories.

Why do we forget long-term memories? The more you know about how we "lose" memories, the better you will be able to hang on to them. Most forgetting tends to occur immediately after memorization. Herman Ebbinghaus (1885) famously tested his own memory at various intervals after learning. To be sure he would not be swayed by prior learning, he memorized *nonsense syllables*. These are meaningless three-letter words such as "cef," "wol," and "gex." The importance of using meaningless words is shown by the fact that "Vel," "Fab," and "Duz" are no longer used on memory tests. People who recognize these words as detergent names find them very easy to remember. This is another reminder that relating new information to what you already know can improve memory.

By waiting various lengths of time before testing himself, Ebbinghaus plotted a **curve of forgetting**. This graph shows the amount of information remembered after varying lengths of time (**Figure 7.8**). Notice that forgetting is rapid at first and is then followed by a slow decline (Hintzman, 2005). The same applies to meaningful information, but the forgetting curve is stretched over a longer time. As you might expect, recent events are recalled more accurately than those from the remote past (O'Connor et al., 2000). Thus, you are more likely to remember that *The Artist* won the "Best Picture" Academy Award for 2011 than you are to remember that *The Departed* won it for 2006.

As a student, you should note that a short delay between studying and taking a test minimizes forgetting. However, this is no reason for cramming. Most students make the error of *only* cramming. If you cram, you don't have to remember for very long, but you may not learn enough in the first place. If you use short, daily study sessions and review intensely before a test, you will get the benefit of good preparation and a minimum time lapse.

The Ebbinghaus curve shows less than 30 percent remembered after only 2 days have passed. Is forgetting really that rapid? No, not always. Meaningful information is not lost nearly as quickly as nonsense syllables. After 3 years, students who took a university psychology course had forgotten about 30 percent of the facts they learned. After that, little more forgetting occurred (Conway, Cohen, & Stanhope, 1992). Actually, as learning grows stronger, some knowledge may become nearly permanent (Berntsen & Thomsen, 2005).

Although the Ebbinghaus curve gives a general picture of forgetting from long-term memory, it doesn't explain it. For explanations, we must search further. (Before we do, look at "Card Magic!," in which you will find an interesting demonstration.) Earlier in this chapter, we pointed out that three processes are involved in successfully remembering: encoding, storage, and retrieval. Conversely, forgetting can be due to the failure of any one of these three processes.

When Memory Encoding Fails

Whose head is on a U.S. penny? Which way is it facing? What is written at the top of a penny? Can you accurately draw and label a penny? In an interesting experiment, Ray Nickerson and Marilyn Adams (1979) asked a large group of students to draw a penny. Few could. In fact, few could even recognize a drawing of a real penny among fakes (**Figure 7.11**). Can you?

The most obvious reason for forgetting is also the most commonly overlooked. Obviously, few of us ever encode the details of a penny. Similarly, we may not encode the details of what we are reading in a book or studying for an exam. In such cases, we "forget" because of **encoding failure**. That is, a memory was never formed in the first place (the card trick you just saw is another example). If you are bothered by frequent forgetting or

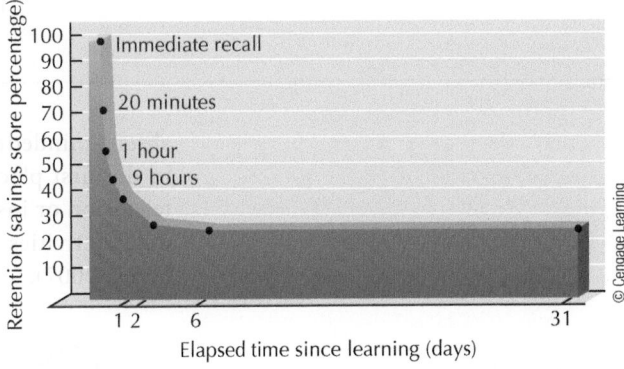

Figure 7.8 The curve of forgetting. This graph shows the amount remembered (measured by relearning) after varying lengths of time. Notice how rapidly forgetting occurs. The material learned was nonsense syllables. Forgetting curves for meaningful information also show early losses followed by a long gradual decline, but overall, forgetting occurs much more slowly. (After Ebbinghaus, 1885.)

Curve of forgetting A graph that shows the amount of memorized information remembered after varying lengths of time.

Encoding failure Failure to store sufficient information to form a useful memory.

Discovering Psychology

Figure 7.9

Pick a card from the six shown in **Figure 7.9** above. Look at it closely and be sure you can remember which card is yours. Now, snap your fingers and look at the cards in **Figure 7.10** below. Poof! Only five cards remain, and the card you chose has disappeared. Obviously, you could have selected any one of the six cards in Figure 7.9. How did we know which one to remove?

This trick is based entirely on an illusion of memory. Recall that you were asked to concentrate on one card among the six cards in Figure 7.9. That prevented you from paying attention to the other cards, so they weren't stored in your memory (Mangels, Picton, & Craik, 2001; Naveh-Benjamin, Guez, & Sorek, 2007).

The five cards you see below are all new (none is shown in Figure 7.9). Because you couldn't find it in the "remaining five," your card seemed to disappear. What looked like "card magic" is actually memory magic. Now return to "When Memory Encoding Fails" and continue reading to learn more about forgetting.

Figure 7.10

absent-mindedness, it is wise to ask yourself, "Have I been encoding the information in the first place?" (Kirchhoff, 2009). By the way, if you like to study while watching television or instant messaging, beware. Dividing your attention between studying and other activities increases the likelihood of encoding failure (Naveh-Benjamin, Guez, & Sorek, 2007).

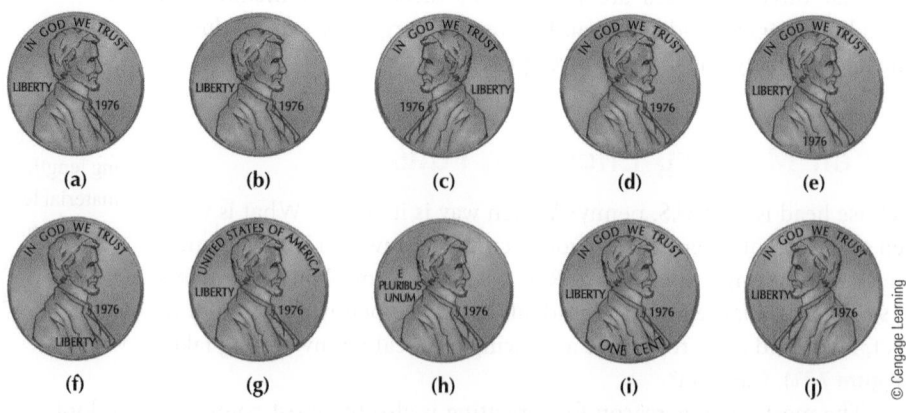

Figure 7.11 Some of the distractor items used in a study of recognition memory and encoding failure. Penny A is correct but was seldom recognized. Pennies G and J were popular wrong answers. (Adapted from Nickerson & Adams, 1979.)

Actively focusing on the information you are learning (elaborative processing) is a good way to prevent encoding failure (Hall et al., 2007). You'll find more memory strategies in "The Psychology of Studying—Reflective Learning" at the beginning of this book. Check it out, if you haven't already.

College Students: They're All Alike!

Encoding failures can even affect our memories of people. Imagine yourself in this situation: As you are walking on campus, a young man, who looks like a college student, approaches you and asks for directions. While you are talking, two workers carrying a door pass between you and the young man. While your view is blocked by the door, another man takes the place of the first. Now you are facing a different person than the one who was there just seconds earlier. If this happened to you, do you think you would notice the change? Remarkably, only half the people tested in this way noticed the switch (Simons & Levin, 1998)!

How could anyone fail to notice that one stranger had been replaced by another? The people who didn't remember the first man were all older adults. College students weren't fooled by the switch. Apparently, older adults encoded the first man in very general terms as a "college student." As a result, that's all they remembered about him. Because his replacement also looked like a college student, they thought he was the same person (Simons & Levin, 1998).

Actually, we all tend to categorize strangers in general terms: Is the person young or old, male or female, a member of my ethnic group or another? This tendency is one reason why eyewitnesses are better at identifying members of their own ethnic group than persons from other groups (Burgess & Weaver, 2003; Michel, Caldara, & Rossion, 2006). It may seem harsh to say so, but during brief social contacts, people really do act as if members of other ethnic groups "all look alike." Of course, this bias disappears when people get acquainted and learn more about one another as individuals (Bukach et al., 2012).

When Memory Storage Fails

One view of forgetting holds that **memory traces** (changes in nerve cells or brain activity) decay (fade or weaken) over time. **Memory decay** does appears to be a factor in the loss of sensory memories. Such fading also applies to short-term memory. Information stored in STM seems to initiate a brief flurry of activity in the brain that quickly dies out. Sensory memory and short-term memory, therefore, operate like "leaky buckets": New information constantly pours in, but it rapidly fades away and is replaced by still newer information.

Disuse

Does decay also occur in long-term memory? There is evidence that memories not retrieved and "used" or rehearsed become weaker over time. That is, some long-term memory traces may fade from **disuse** (infrequent retrieval) and eventually become too weak to retrieve. However, disuse alone cannot fully explain forgetting (Della Sala, 2010). Disuse doesn't seem to account for our ability to recover seemingly forgotten memories through redintegration, relearning, and priming. It also fails to explain why some unused memories fade, whereas others are carried for life.

A third contradiction will be recognized by anyone who has spent time with the elderly. People growing senile may become so forgetful that they can't remember what happened a week ago. Unfortunately, this is often due to diseases like *Alzheimer's disease* and other *dementias*, which slowly strangle the brain's ability to process and store information (Hanyu et al., 2010). Yet at the same time that your Uncle Oscar's recent memories are fading, he may have vivid memories of trivial and long-forgotten events from the past. "Why, I remember it as clearly as if it were yesterday," he will say, forgetting that the story he is about to tell is one he told earlier the same day (twice). In short, disuse offers no more than a partial explanation of long-term forgetting.

Memory traces Physical changes in nerve cells or brain activity that take place when memories are stored.

Memory decay The fading or weakening of memories assumed to occur when memory traces become weaker.

Disuse Theory that memory traces weaken when memories are not periodically used or retrieved.

External cues like those found in a photograph, in a scrapbook, or during a walk through an old neighborhood often aid recall of seemingly lost memories. For many veterans, finding a familiar name engraved in the Vietnam Veterans Memorial unleashes a flood of memories.

When Memory Retrieval Fails

If encoding failure and storage failure don't fully explain forgetting from long-term memory, what does? If you have encoded and stored information, that leaves retrieval failure as a likely cause of forgetting (Della Sala, 2010). Even if memories are **available** (stored in your memory), you still have to be able to **access** them (locate or retrieve them) in order to remember. For example, as we mentioned earlier, you might have had the experience of knowing you know the answer to an exam question (you knew it was *available*) but being unable to retrieve it during the exam (it was *inaccessible*) (Landau & Leynes, 2006).

Cue-Dependent Forgetting

One reason retrieval may fail is because **retrieval cues**—stimuli associated with a memory—are missing when the time comes to retrieve information. For instance, if you were asked, "What were you doing on Monday afternoon of the third week in May, two years ago?" your reply might be, "Come on, how should I know?" However, if you were reminded, "That was the day the courthouse burned," or "That was the day Stacy had her automobile accident," you might remember immediately.

The presence of appropriate cues almost always enhances memory. As we saw previously, more elaborately encoded memories are more likely to be remembered because more retrieval cues are associated with any particular piece of information. Memory will even tend to be better if you study in the same room where you will be tested. Because this is often impossible, when you study, try to visualize the room where you will be tested. Doing so can enhance memory later (Jerabek & Standing, 1992). Similarly, people even remember better if the same odor (such as lemon or lavender) is present both when they study and are tested (Parker, Ngu, & Cassaday, 2001). If you wear a particular perfume or cologne while you prepare for a test, it might be wise to wear it when you take the test (or go "odorless" on both occasions).

State-Dependent Learning

Have you heard the one about the drunk who misplaced his wallet and had to get drunk again to find it? Actually, this is not too farfetched. The bodily state that exists during learning can also be a strong retrieval cue for later memory, an effect known as **state-dependent learning** (Radvansky, 2011). Being very thirsty, for instance, might prompt you to remember events that took place on another occasion when you were thirsty. Because of such effects, information learned under the influence of a drug is best remembered when the drugged state occurs again (Slot & Colpaert, 1999). However, this is a laboratory finding. In school, it's far better to study with a clear mind in the first place.

A similar effect applies to emotional states (Wessel & Wright, 2004). For instance, Gordon Bower (1981) found that people who learned a list of words while in a happy mood recalled them better when they were again happy. People who learned while they felt sad remembered best when they were sad (Figure 7.12). Similarly, if you are in a happy mood you

Availability (in memory) Memories currently stored in memory are available.

Accessibility (in memory) Memories currently stored in memory that can be retrieved when necessary are both available and accessible.

Retrieval cue Stimulus associated with a memory. Retrieval cues usually enhance memory.

State-dependent learning Memory influenced by one's physical state at the time of learning and at the time of retrieval. Improved memory occurs when the physical states match.

Figure 7.12 The effect of mood on memory. Participants best remembered a list of words when their mood during testing was the same as their mood was when they learned the list. (Adapted from Bower, 1981.)

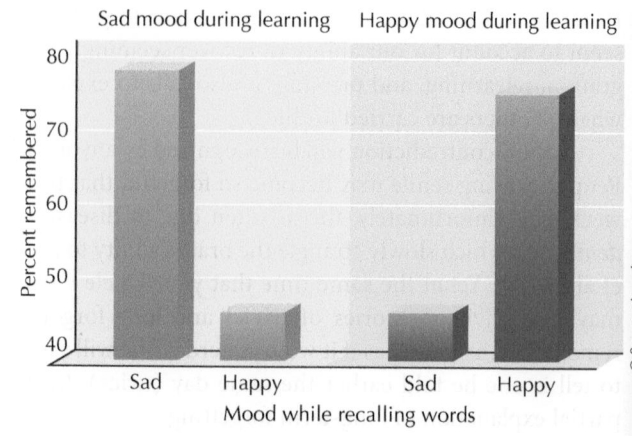

are more likely to remember recent happy events. If you are in a bad mood you will tend to have unpleasant memories. Such links between emotional cues and memory could explain why couples who quarrel often end up remembering—and rehashing—old arguments.

Interference

Further insight into forgetting comes from a classic experiment in which college students learned lists of nonsense syllables. After studying, students in one group slept for 8 hours and were then tested for memory of the lists. A second group stayed awake for 8 hours and went about business as usual. When members of the second group were tested, they remembered *less* than the group that slept (**Figure 7.13**). This difference is based on the fact that new learning can interfere with the ability to retrieve previous learning. (Sleep can improve memory in another way: REM sleep and dreaming appear to help us form certain types of memories. See Chapter 5.) **Interference** refers to the tendency for new memories to impair retrieval of older memories (and the reverse). It seems to apply to both short-term and long-term memory (Jonides et al., 2008; Radvansky, 2011).

It is not completely clear whether new memories alter existing memory traces or whether they make it harder to retrieve (or "locate") earlier memories. In any case, there is no doubt that interference is a major cause of forgetting (Radvansky, 2011). College students who memorized 20 lists of words (one list each day) were able to recall only 15 percent of the last list. Students who learned only one list remembered 80 percent (Underwood, 1957) (**Figure 7.14**).

The sleeping college students who studied nonsense syllables remembered more because the type of interference called retroactive (RET-ro-AK-tiv) interference was held to a minimum. **Retroactive interference** refers to the tendency for new learning to inhibit retrieval of old learning. Avoiding new learning prevents retroactive interference. This doesn't exactly mean you should hide in a closet after you study for an exam. However, you should, if possible, avoid studying other subjects until the exam. Sleeping after study can help you retain memories, and reading, writing, or even watching television may cause interference.

Retroactive interference is easily demonstrated in the laboratory by this arrangement:

Experimental group:	Learn A	Learn B	Test A
Control group:	Learn A	Rest	Test A

Imagine yourself as a member of the experimental group. In task A, you learn a list of telephone numbers. In task B, you learn a list of Social Security numbers. How do you score on a test of task A (the telephone numbers)? If you do not remember as much as the control group that learns *only* task A, then retroactive interference has occurred. The second thing learned interfered with memory of the first thing learned; the interference went "backward," or was "retroactive" (**Figure 7.15**).

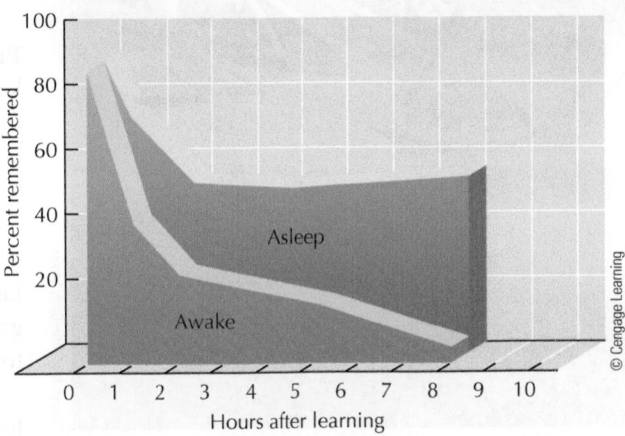

Figure 7.13 The amount of forgetting after a period of sleep or of being awake. Notice that sleep causes less memory loss than activity that occurs while one is awake. (After Jenkins & Dallenbach, 1924.)

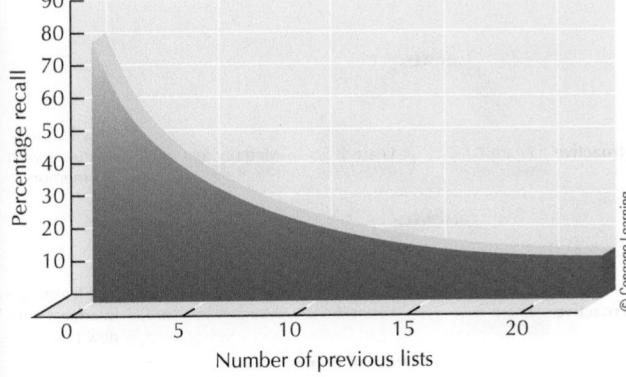

Figure 7.14 Effects of interference on memory. A graph of the approximate relationship between percentage recalled and number of different word lists memorized. (Adapted from Underwood, 1957.)

Interference The tendency for new memories to impair retrieval of older memories, and the reverse.

Retroactive interference The tendency for new memories to interfere with the retrieval of old memories.

How could anyone lose something as large as a car? If you park your car in a different place every day, you may have experienced forgetting caused by interference. Today's memory about your car's location is easily confused with memories from yesterday, and the day before, and the day before that.

Proactive (pro-AK-tiv) interference is the second type of interference. **Proactive interference** occurs when prior learning inhibits recall of later learning. A test for proactive interference would take this form:

Experimental group:	Learn A	Learn B	Test B
Control group:	Rest	Learn B	Test B

Let's assume that the experimental group remembers less than the control group on a test of task B. In that case, learning task A interfered with memory for task B.

Then proactive interference goes "forward"? Yes. For instance, if you cram for a psychology exam and then later the same night cram for a history exam, your memory for the second subject studied (history) will be less accurate than if you had studied only history. (Because of retroactive interference, your memory for psychology would probably also suffer.) The greater the similarity in the two subjects studied, the more interference takes place. The moral, of course, is don't procrastinate in preparing for exams. The more you can avoid competing information, the more likely you are to recall what you want to remember (Wixted, 2004).

Repression and Suppression of Memories

Take a moment and scan over the events of the last few years of your life. What kinds of things most easily come to mind? Many people remember happy, positive events better than disappointments and irritations (Moore & Zoellner, 2007). This tendency is called **repression**, or motivated forgetting. Through repression, painful, threatening, or embarrassing memories are held out of consciousness. An example is provided by soldiers who have repressed some of the horrors they saw during combat (Anderson et al., 2004).

The forgetting of past failures, upsetting childhood events, the names of people you dislike, or appointments you don't want to keep may reveal repression (Goodman, Quas, & Ogle, 2010). People prone to repression tend to be extremely sensitive to emotional events. As a result, they use repression to protect themselves from threatening thoughts (McNally, Clancy, & Barrett, 2004). See "The Recovered Memory/False Memory Debate" for further cautions.

If I try to forget a test I failed, am I repressing it? Probably not. Repression can be distinguished from **suppression**, an active, conscious attempt to put something out of mind (Anderson et al., 2011). By not thinking about the test, you have merely suppressed a memory. If you choose to, you can remember the test. Clinicians consider true repression an *unconscious* event and one of the major psychological defenses we use against emotional threats. (See Chapter 11.) When a memory is repressed, we may be unaware that forgetting has even occurred.

Although some psychologists have questioned whether repression exists (Court & Court, 2001), evidence suggests that we can choose to actively suppress upsetting memories (Neufeind et al., 2009). If you have experienced a painful emotional event, you will probably avoid all thoughts associated with it. This tends to keep cues out of mind that could trigger a painful memory. In time, your active suppression of the memory may become true repression (Anderson & Green, 2001).

Proactive interference The tendency for old memories to interfere with the retrieval of newer memories.

Repression Unconsciously pushing unwanted memories out of awareness.

Suppression A conscious effort to put something out of mind or to keep it from awareness.

Figure 7.15 Retroactive and proactive interference. The order of learning and testing shows whether interference is retroactive (backward) or proactive (forward). © Cengage Learning

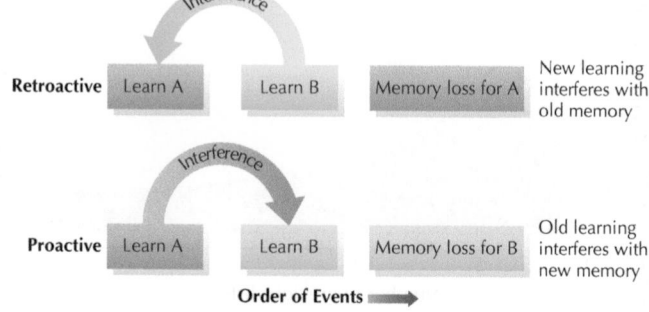

Many sexually abused children develop problems that persist into adulthood. In some instances, they repress all memory of the abuse. According to some psychologists, uncovering these hidden memories can be an important step toward regaining emotional health (Colangelo, 2007; Haaken & Reavey, 2010).

Although the preceding may be true, the search for repressed memories of sexual abuse has itself been a problem. Families have been torn apart by accusations of sexual abuse that later turned out to be completely false. For example, when Meridith Maran thought she had recovered vivid memories of being molested by her father, she withdrew herself and her children from any further contact with him. It was not until nine years later that she realized that her "memories" were not true and finally apologized to her father (Maran, 2010). Things have gotten much worse for other people as some cases have

gone to court, some innocent people have gone to jail, and some actual sexual abuse victims have been accused of making false claims about their very real memories.

Why would anyone have false memories about such disturbing events? Several popular books and a few misguided therapists have actively encouraged people to find repressed memories of abuse. Hypnosis, guided visualization, suggestion, age regression, administering the so-called truth drug Amytal, and similar techniques can elicit fantasies that are mistaken for real memories. As we saw earlier, it is easy to create false memories, especially by using hypnosis (Loftus & Bernstein, 2005; Weinstein & Shanks, 2010).

In an effort to illustrate how easy it is to create false memories, and to publicize *false memory syndrome*, memory expert Elizabeth Loftus once deliberately implanted a false memory in actor Alan Alda. As the host of the television series

Scientific American Frontiers, he was scheduled to interview Loftus. Before the interview, Alda was asked to fill out a questionnaire about his tastes in food. When he arrived, Loftus told Alda that his answers revealed that he must once have gotten sick after eating hard-boiled eggs (which was false). Later that day, at a picnic, Alda would not eat hard-boiled eggs (Loftus, 2003).

Certainly, some memories of abuse that return to awareness are genuine and must be dealt with. However, there is little doubt that some "recovered" memories are pure fantasy. No matter how real a recovered memory may seem, it could be false, unless it can be verified by others or by court or medical records (Bernstein & Loftus, 2009; Otgaar & Smeets, 2010). The saddest thing about such claims is that they deaden public sensitivity to actual abuse. Childhood sexual abuse is widespread. Awareness of its existence must not be repressed.

Memory and the Brain—Some "Shocking" Findings

JOURNEY QUESTION 7.6 *How does the brain form and store memories?*

One possibility overlooked in our discussion of forgetting is that memories may be lost as they are being formed (Papanicolaou, 2006). For example, a head injury may cause a "gap" in memories preceding the accident. **Retrograde amnesia**, as this is called, involves forgetting events that occurred before an injury or trauma (MacKay & Hadley, 2009). In contrast, **anterograde amnesia** involves forgetting events that follow an injury or trauma (Behrend, Beike, & Lampinen, 2004). (We will discuss an example of this type of amnesia in a moment.)

Consolidation

We can explain retrograde amnesia by assuming that it takes time to form a lasting memory, a process called **consolidation** (Vogel, Woodman, & Luck, 2006). You can think of consolidation as being somewhat like writing your name in wet concrete. Once the concrete is set, the information (your name) is fairly lasting. But while the concrete is setting, the information can be wiped out (amnesia) or scribbled over (interference).

Consider a classic experiment on consolidation, in which a rat is placed on a small platform. The rat steps down to the floor and receives a painful electric shock. After one shock, the rat can be returned to the platform repeatedly, but it will not step down. Obviously, the rat remembers the shock. Would it remember if consolidation were disturbed?

Curiously, one way to prevent consolidation is to give a different kind of shock called *electroconvulsive shock (ECS)*. ECS is a mild electric shock to the brain. It does not harm the animal, but it does destroy any memory that is being formed. If each painful shock (the one the animal remembers) is followed by ECS (which wipes out memories during consolidation), the rat will step down over and over. Each time, ECS will erase the

Retrograde amnesia Loss of memory for events that preceded a head injury or other amnesia-causing event.

Anterograde amnesia Loss of the ability to form or retrieve memories for events that occur after an injury or trauma.

Consolidation Process by which relatively permanent memories are formed in the brain.

Do you have a flashbulb memory for the massive April 2011 earthquake and tsunami that devastated Japan, resulting in some 18,000 deaths and triggering a nuclear emergency at a Japanese nuclear power plant? You do if someone alerted you about the news and you remember that person's call. You do if you saw the news on television and you have clear memories of how you reacted.

memory of the painful shock. (ECS is employed as a psychiatric treatment for severe depression in humans.)

What would happen if ECS were given several hours after the learning? Recent memories are more easily disrupted than older memories. If enough time is allowed to pass between learning and ECS, the memory will be unaffected because consolidation is already complete. That's why people with mild head injuries lose only memories from just before the accident, whereas older memories remain intact (Baddeley, Eysenck, & Anderson, 2009). Likewise, you would forget more if you studied, stayed awake 8 hours, and then slept 8 hours than you would if you studied, slept 8 hours, and were awake for 8 hours. Either way, 16 hours would pass. However, less forgetting would occur in the second instance, because more consolidation would occur before interference begins (Wixted, 2005).

Where does consolidation take place in the brain? Actually, many parts of the brain are responsible for memory, but the **hippocampus** is particularly important (Squire & Wixted, 2011). The hippocampus acts as a sort of "switching station" between short-term and long-term memory (Hardt, Einarsson, & Nader, 2010). The hippocampus does this, in part, by growing new neurons (nerve cells) and by making new connections within the brain (Leuner & Gould, 2010).

If the hippocampus is damaged, patients usually develop anterograde amnesia and show a striking inability to consolidate new memories. A man described by Brenda Milner (1965) provides a dramatic example. Two years after an operation damaged his hippocampus, the 29-year-old H. M. continued to give his age as 27 and reported that the operation had just taken place. His memory of events before the operation remained clear, but he found forming new long-term memories almost impossible. When his parents moved to a new house a few blocks away on the same street, he could not remember the new address. Month after month, he read the same magazines over and over without finding them familiar. If you were to meet this man, he would seem fairly normal because he still has short-term memory. But if you were to leave the room and return 15 minutes later, he would act as if he had never seen you before. Lacking the ability to form new lasting memories, he lived eternally in the present until his death in 2008 at the age of 82 (Bohbot & Corkin, 2007).

Memory, Stress, and Emotion

Do you remember when you first learned about the terrorist attacks on New York City's World Trade Center in 2001? Can you recall lots of detail, including how you reacted? If so, you have a **flashbulb memory** for 9/11. A flashbulb memory is an especially vivid image that seems to be frozen in memory at times of emotionally significant personal or public events (Lanciano, Curci, & Semin, 2010). Depending on your age, you may also have a flashbulb memory for the assassinations of John F. Kennedy or Martin Luther King, Jr., the *Challenger* or *Columbia* space shuttle disasters, or the death of Princess Diana (Curci & Luminet, 2006).

Are flashbulb memories handled differently by the brain? Powerfully exciting or stressful experiences activate the limbic system, a part of the brain that processes emotions. Heightened activity in the limbic system, in turn, appears to intensify memory consolidation (Kensinger, 2007; LaBar, 2007). As a result, flashbulb memories tend to form at times of intense emotion.

Although flashbulb memories are often related to public tragedies, memories of both positive and negative events can have "flashbulb" clarity (Paradis et al., 2004). Would you consider any of the following to be a flashbulb memory: Your first kiss, a special date, or your prom night? How about a time you had to speak in front of a large audience? A car accident you were in or witnessed?

The term *flashbulb memories* was first used to describe recollections that seemed to be unusually vivid and permanent (Brown & Kulik, 1977). It has become clear, however,

Hippocampus A brain structure associated with emotion and the transfer of information from short-term memory to long-term memory.

Flashbulb memory Memory created at times of high emotion that seems especially vivid.

that flashbulb memories are not always accurate (Greenberg, 2004; Kensinger, 2007). More than anything else, what sets flashbulb memories apart is that we tend to place great *confidence* in them—even when they are wrong (Niedzwienska, 2004). Perhaps that's because we review emotionally charged events over and over and tell others about them. Also, public events such as wars, earthquakes, and elections reappear many times in the news, which highlights them in memory. Over time, flashbulb memories tend to crystallize into consistent, if not entirely accurate, landmarks in our lives (Lanciano, Curci, & Semin, 2010).

Some memories go beyond flashbulb clarity and become so intense that they may haunt a person for years. Extremely traumatic experiences, such as military combat or maltreatment as a child, can produce so much limbic system activation that the resulting memories and "flashbacks" leave a person emotionally handicapped (Goodman, Quas, & Ogle, 2010; Nemeroff et al., 2006).

Long-Term Memory and the Brain

Somewhere within the 3-pound mass of the human brain lies all we know: ZIP codes, faces of loved ones, history, favorite melodies, the taste of an apple, and much, much more. Where is this information? According to neuroscientists, many parts of the brain become active when we form and retrieve long-term memories, but some areas are more important for different types of memory and memory process (Squire & Wixted, 2011; Thompson, 2005).

For example, patterns of blood flow in the cerebral cortex (the wrinkled outer layer of the brain) can be used to map brain activity. Figure 7.16 shows the results of measuring blood flow while people were thinking about a semantic memory or an episodic memory. The resulting pattern indicates that we use the front of the cortex for episodic memory. Back areas are more associated with semantic memory (Tulving, 1989, 2002). As another example, different parts of cortex are activated when we are engaging in memory retrieval and suppression (Mecklinger, 2010).

Let's summarize (and simplify greatly). Earlier we noted that the hippocampus handles memory consolidation (Wang & Morris, 2010). Once declarative long-term memories are

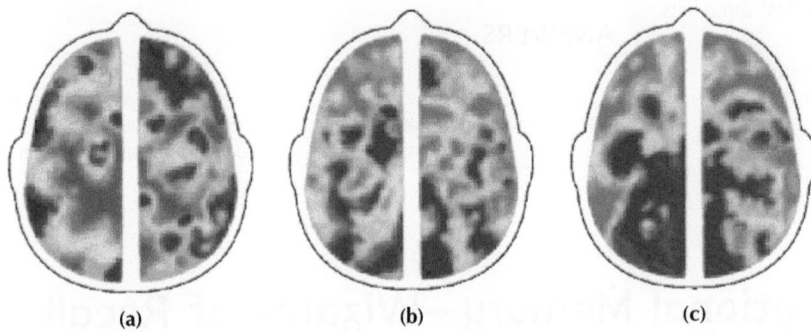

(a)   (b)   (c)

Figure 7.16 Patterns of blood flow in the cerebral cortex (wrinkled outer layer of the brain) change as areas become more or less active. Thus, blood flow can be used to draw "maps" of brain activity. This drawing, which views the brain from the top, shows the results of measuring cerebral blood flow while people were thinking about a semantic memory (a) or an episodic memory (b). In the map, green indicates areas that are more active during semantic thinking. Reds show areas of greater activity during episodic thinking. The brain in view c shows the difference in activity between views a and b. The resulting pattern suggests that the front of the cortex is related to episodic memory. Areas toward the back and sides of the brain, especially the temporal lobes, are more associated with semantic memory (Tulving, 1989, 2002). (Copyright © Tulving, E. (1989). "Remembering and knowing the past." *American Scientist, 77*(4), 361–367. Reprinted by permission.)

An *aplysia*. The relatively simple nervous system of this sea animal allows scientists to study memory as it occurs in single nerve cells.

formed, they appear to be stored and retrieved in the cortex of the brain (episodic in the front, semantic in the back) (Mecklinger, 2010; Squire, 2004). Long-term procedural (skill) memories are stored in the basal ganglia and cerebellum, parts of the brain that are also responsible for muscular coordination (Freberg, 2010; Lum & Bleses, 2012).

How are memories recorded in the brain? Scientists are beginning to identify the exact ways in which nerve cells record information. For example, Eric Kandel and his colleagues have studied learning in the marine snail *aplysia* (ah-PLEEZ-yah). Learning in *aplysia* occurs when certain nerve cells in a circuit alter the amount of transmitter chemicals they release (Bailey & Kandel, 2004). Learning also alters the activity, structure, and chemistry of brain cells. Such changes determine which connections get stronger and which become weaker. This "reprograms" the brain and records information (Abraham, 2006).

Scientists continue to study various chemicals, especially neurotransmitters, that affect memory (Xu & Yao, 2010). Their research may eventually help the millions of persons who suffer from memory impairment (Elli & Nathan, 2001).

✋ study break Forgetting

RECITE

1. According to the Ebbinghaus curve of forgetting, we forget slowly at first and then a rapid decline occurs. T or F?
2. Which explanation(s) seem(s) to account for the loss of short-term memories?

   a. decay   b. disuse
   c. repression   d. displacement

3. When memories are available but not accessible, forgetting may be cue dependent. T or F?
4. When learning one thing makes it more difficult to recall another, forgetting may be caused by _____.
5. You are asked to memorize long lists of telephone numbers. You learn a new list each day for 10 days. When tested on list 3, you remember less than a person who learned only the first three lists. Your larger memory loss is probably caused by

   a. disuse   b. retroactive interference
   c. regression   d. proactive interference

6. Retrograde amnesia results when consolidation is speeded up. T or F?

REFLECT

THINK CRITICALLY

7. You must study French, Spanish, psychology, and biology in one evening. (Poor thing!) What do you think would be the best order in which to study these subjects so as to minimize interference?

SELF-REFLECT

Do you know someone whose name you have a hard time remembering? Do you like or dislike that person? Do you think your difficulty is an instance of repression? Suppression? Interference? Retrieval failure?

Have you had a flashbulb memory? How vivid is the memory today? How accurate do you think it is?

ANSWERS

1. F 2. a and d 3. T 4. interference 5. b 6. F 7. Any order that separates French from Spanish and psychology from biology would be better (for instance: French, psychology, Spanish, biology).

Exceptional Memory—Wizards of Recall

JOURNEY QUESTION 7.7 *What are "photographic" memories?*

In this section we will explore exceptional memories. Is superior memory a biological gift, such as having a "photographic" memory? Or do excellent memorizers merely make strategic use of normal memory capacities?

Whether or not you have an exceptional memory, odds are you make use of mental imagery. Can you remember how many doors there are in your house or apartment? To answer a question like this, many people form **mental images** (mental pictures) of each room and count the doorways they visualize. As this example implies, many memories are processed and stored as mental images (Shorrock & Isaac, 2010).

Stephen Kosslyn, Thomas Ball, and Brian Reiser (1978) found an interesting way to show that memories do exist as images. Participants first memorized a sort of treasure map

Mental images Mental pictures or visual depictions used in memory and thinking.

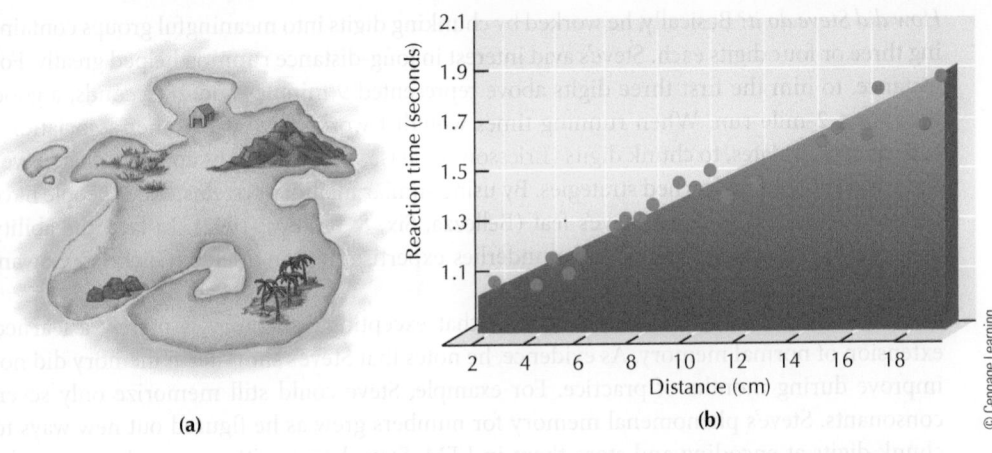

Figure 7.17 *(a)* "Treasure map" similar to the one used by Kosslyn, Ball, and Reiser (1978) to study images in memory. *(b)* This graph shows how long it took participants to move a visualized spot various distances on their mental images of the map. (See text for explanation.)

similar to the one shown in Figure 7.17a. They were then asked to picture a black dot moving from one object, such as one of the trees, to another, such as the hut at the top of the island. Did people really form an image to do this task? It seems they did. As shown in Figure 7.17b, the time it took to "move" the dot was directly related to actual distances on the map.

Photographic Memory and Eidetic Imagery

Is the "treasure map" task an example of photographic memory? In some ways, internal mental images do have "photographic" qualities. In rare instances, such images may be so vivid that it is reasonable to say that a person has "photographic memory." However, the term *photographic memory* is more often used to describe an uncommon memory ability called eidetic imagery.

Eidetic (eye-DET-ik) **imagery** occurs when a person has visual images clear enough to be "scanned" or retained for at least 30 seconds. Internal mental images can be "viewed" mentally with the eyes closed. In contrast, eidetic images are "projected" out in front of a person. That is, they are best "seen" on a plain surface, such as a blank piece of paper. In this respect, eidetic images are somewhat like the afterimages you might have after looking at a flashbulb or a brightly lit neon sign (Haber & Haber, 2000). Eidetic memory is more common in childhood and becomes rare by adulthood (Haber & Haber, 2000).

Strategies for Remembering

Few adults possess naturally amazing memory abilities, such as photographic memory, eidetic imagery, or the near perfect recall of Jill Price and Mr. S., who we met at the beginning of this chapter. Instead, most people with good memories are selective in what and how they choose to remember (unlike, say, Mr. S., who actually had to develop strategies to forget). If you didn't have selective memory, you would recall all the ingredients on your cereal box, every street number you've seen, and countless other scraps of information. In other words, most good memorizers have learned effective strategies for remembering. Let's investigate further.

Learning to Chunk

As an example of an effective strategy for remembering, consider Steve. At first, this intrepid student volunteer could remember 7 digits. Could he improve with practice? For 20 months (!), Steve practiced memorizing ever-longer lists of digits. Ultimately, he was able to memorize approximately 80 digits, like this sample:

92842048050842268953990190252912807999706606574717310601080585269726026357332135

Eidetic imagery The ability to retain a "projected" mental image long enough to use it as a source of information.

```
8 7 3 7 9 2 6 8
2 0 1 1 7 4 9 5
0 1 7 5 8 7 8 3
1 9 4 7 6 0 6 9
3 6 1 6 8 1 5 4
4 5 2 4 0 2 9 7
```

This number matrix is similar to the ones contestants in the World Memory Championship had to memorize. To be scored as correct, digits had to be recalled in their proper positions (Wilding & Valentine, 1994).

How did Steve do it? Basically, he worked by chunking digits into meaningful groups containing three or four digits each. Steve's avid interest in long-distance running helped greatly. For instance, to him the first three digits above represented 9 minutes and 28 seconds, a good time for a 2-mile run. When running times wouldn't work, Steve used other associations, such as ages or dates, to chunk digits (Ericsson & Chase, 1982). It seems apparent that Steve's success was based on learned strategies. By using similar memory systems, other people have trained themselves to equal Steve's feat (Bellezza, Six, & Phillips, 1992). In fact, the ability to organize information into chunks underlies expertise in many fields (Gilchrist, Cowan, & Naveh-Benjamin, 2009; Gobet, 2005).

Psychologist Anders Ericsson believes that exceptional memory is merely a learned extension of normal memory. As evidence, he notes that Steve's short-term memory did not improve during months of practice. For example, Steve could still memorize only seven consonants. Steve's phenomenal memory for numbers grew as he figured out new ways to chunk digits at encoding and store them in LTM. Steve began with a normal memory for digits. He extended his memory by diligent practice. Clearly, exceptional memory can be learned (Ericsson et al., 2004). However, we still have to wonder, do some people have naturally superior memories?

Memory Champions

Each year the World Memory Championship is held in England. Contestants must rapidly memorize daunting amounts of information, such as long lists of unrelated words and numbers. Psychologists John Wilding and Elizabeth Valentine saw this event as an opportunity to study exceptional memory and persuaded the contestants to take some additional memory tests. These ranged from ordinary (recall a story), to challenging (recall the telephone numbers of six different people), to diabolical (recall 48 numerals arranged in rows and columns) (Maguire et al., 2003; Wilding & Valentine, 1994).

Exceptional memorizers were found to:

- Use memory strategies and techniques
- Have specialized interests and knowledge that make certain types of information easier to encode and recall
- Have naturally superior memory abilities, often including vivid mental images
- Not have superior intellectual abilities or different brains

The first two points confirm what we learned from Steve's acquired memory ability. Many of the contestants, for example, actively used memory strategies, including special memory "tricks" called *mnemonics* (nee-MON-iks). Specialized interests and knowledge also helped for some tasks. For example, one contestant, a mathematician, was exceedingly good at memorizing numbers (Wilding & Valentine, 1994).

Several of the memory contestants were able to excel on tasks that prevented the use of learned strategies and techniques. This observation implies that superior memory ability can be a "gift" as well as a learned skill (Yi & Qian, 2009). Wilding and Valentine conclude that exceptional memory may be based on either natural ability or learned strategies. Usually it requires both.

Improving Memory—Keys to the Memory Bank

JOURNEY QUESTION 7.8 *How can I improve my memory?*

Let's see how you can improve your memory. To begin, there is very little you can do to improve your brain's ability to store long-term memories. The jury is still out on the use of drugs, herbs (such as *Ginkgo biloba*), and vitamins (such as vitamin E) to improve human memory (McDaniel, Maier, & Einstein, 2002; McGaugh & Roozendaal, 2009). However, until there's a memory pill, you can immediately use meaning-based strategies to improve memory encoding and memory retrieval (Fry, 2012; Hancock, 2011). Most super-memorizers use these strategies to augment whatever natural talents they have. Some of their strategies are described in the remainder of this section. Later, mnemonics are explored in this chapter's Psychology in Action section. Please do remember to read it.

Memory Encoding Strategies

One way to improve your memory is to be sure to fully encode information. That way you can avoid forgetting due to encoding failure. Following are some steps you can take to become a better encoder:

Elaborative Processing

Let us reiterate one more time. The more you *rehearse* (mentally review) information as you read, the better you will remember it. Even repeatedly thinking about facts helps link them together in memory. But remember that maintenance rehearsal alone is not very effective. Elaborative processing, in which you rehearse by looking for connections to existing knowledge, is far better. To learn college-level information, you must make active use of more reflective study strategies (Santrock & Halonen, 2010).

Selection

The Dutch scholar Erasmus said that a good memory should be like a fish net: It should keep all the big fish and let the little ones escape. If you boil down the paragraphs in most textbooks to one or two important terms or ideas, your memory chores will be more manageable. Practice very selective marking in your texts and use marginal notes to further summarize ideas. Most students mark their texts too much instead of too little. If everything is underlined, you haven't been selective. And, very likely, you didn't pay much attention in the first place.

Organization

Assume that you must memorize the following list of words: north, man, red, spring, woman, east, autumn, yellow, summer, boy, blue, west, winter, girl, green, south. This rather difficult list could be reorganized into *chunks* as follows: north-east-south-west, spring-summer-autumn-winter, red-yellow-green-blue, man-woman-boy-girl. Organizing class notes and summarizing chapters can be quite helpful (Hettich, 2005). You may even want to summarize your summaries, so that the overall network of ideas becomes clearer and simpler. Summaries improve memory by encouraging better encoding of information (Anderson, 2010).

Whole versus Part Learning

If you have to memorize a speech, is it better to try to learn it from beginning to end? Or in smaller parts like paragraphs? It depends. For fairly short, organized information it is usually better to practice whole packages of information rather than smaller parts *(whole learning)*. Learning parts is usually better for extremely long, complicated information. In *part learning*, subparts of a larger body of information are studied (such as sections of a textbook chapter). To decide which approach to use, remember to study the *largest meaningful amount of information* you can at one time.

For very long or complex material, try the *progressive-part method* by breaking a learning task into a series of short sections. At first, you study part A until it is mastered. Next, you study parts A and B; then A, B, and C; and so forth. This is a good way to learn the lines of a play, a long piece of music, or a poem (Ash & Holding, 1990). After the material is learned, you should also practice by starting at points other than A (at C, D, or B, for example). This helps prevent getting "lost" or going blank in the middle of a performance.

Figure 7.18 Actors can remember large amounts of complex information for many months, even when learning new roles in between. During testing, they remember their lines best when they are allowed to move and gesture as they would when performing. Apparently their movements supply cues that aid recall (Noice & Noice, 1999).

Serial Position

Whenever you must learn something in order, be aware of the serial position effect. As you will recall, this is the tendency to make the most errors in remembering the middle of a list. If you are introduced to a long line of people, the names you are likely to forget will be those in the middle, so you should make an extra effort to attend to them. You should also give extra practice to the middle of a list, poem, or speech. Try to break long lists of information into short sublists, and make the middle sublists the shortest of all.

Cues

The best *retrieval cues* (stimuli that aid retrieval) are those that were present during encoding (Anderson, 2010). For example, students in one classic study had the daunting task of trying to recall a list of 600 words. As they read the list (which they did not know they would be tested on), the students gave three other words closely related in meaning to each listed word. In a test given later, the words each student supplied were used as cues to jog memory. The students recalled an astounding 90 percent of the original word list (Mantyla, 1986).

Now read the following sentence:

The fish bit the swimmer.

If you were tested a week from now, you would be more likely to recall the sentence if you were given a retrieval cue. And, surprisingly, the word *shark* would work better as a reminder than *fish* would. The reason for this is that most people think of a shark when they read the sentence. As a result, *shark* becomes a potent retrieval cue.

The preceding example shows, once again, that it often helps to *elaborate* information as you learn. When you study, try to use new names, ideas, or terms in several sentences. Also, form images that include the new information and relate it to knowledge you already have. Your goal should be to knit meaningful cues into your memory code to help you retrieve information when you need it (Figure 7.18).

Overlearning

Numerous studies have shown that memory is greatly improved when you *overlearn*, or continue to study beyond bare mastery. After you have learned material well enough to remember it once without error, you should continue studying. Overlearning is your best insurance against going blank on a test because of nervousness.

Spaced Practice

To keep boredom and fatigue to a minimum, try alternating short study sessions with brief rest periods. This pattern, called **spaced practice**, is generally superior to **massed practice**, in which little or no rest is given between learning sessions (Radvansky, 2011). By improving attention and consolidation, three 20-minute study sessions can produce more learning than 1 hour of continuous study.

Perhaps the best way to make use of spaced practice is to *schedule* your time. To make an effective schedule, designate times during the week before, after, and between classes when you will study particular subjects. Then treat these times just as if they are classes you have to attend.

Memory Retrieval Strategies

Once you have successfully encoded information, you still have to retrieve it. Following are some strategies to help you avoid retrieval failure:

Spaced practice A practice schedule that alternates study periods with brief rests.

Massed practice A practice schedule in which studying continues for long periods, without interruption.

Retrieval Practice

Learning proceeds best when feedback allows you to check your progress. Feedback can help you identify ideas that need extra practice. In addition, knowing that you have remembered or answered correctly is rewarding. A prime way to provide feedback for yourself while studying is *recitation*. If you are going to remember something, eventually you will have to retrieve it. *Recitation* refers to summarizing aloud while you are learning. Recitation forces you to practice retrieving information. When you are reading a text, you should stop frequently and try to remember what you have just read by restating it in your own words. In one classic experiment, the best memory score was earned by a group of students who spent 80 percent of their time reciting and only 20 percent reading (Gates, 1917). Maybe students who talk to themselves aren't crazy after all.

If you have spaced your practice and overlearned, retrieval practice in the form of review will be like icing on your study cake. Reviewing shortly before an exam cuts down the time during which you must remember details that may be important for the test. When reviewing, hold the amount of new information you try to memorize to a minimum. It may be realistic to take what you have actually learned and add a little more to it at the last minute by cramming. But remember that more than a little new learning may interfere with what you already know.

Using a Strategy to Aid Recall

Successful retrieval is usually the result of a planned *search* of memory (Herrmann et al., 2006). For example, one study found that students were most likely to recall names that eluded them if they made use of partial information to trigger redintegration (Reed & Bruce, 1982). The students were trying to answer questions such as, "He is best remembered as the scarecrow in the Judy Garland movie *The Wizard of Oz*." (The answer is Ray Bolger.) Partial information that helped students remember included impressions about the length of the name, letter sounds within the name, similar names, and related information (such as the names of other characters in the movie). A similar helpful strategy is to go through the alphabet, trying each letter as the first sound of a name or word you are seeking.

The *cognitive interview* described earlier in this chapter (see "Telling Wrong from Right in Forensic Memory") offers some further hints for recapturing context and jogging memories:

1. Say or write down *everything* you can remember that relates to the information you are seeking. Don't worry about how trivial any of it seems; each bit of information you remember can serve as a cue to bring back others.
2. Try to recall events or information in different orders. Let your memories flow out backward or out of order, or start with whatever impressed you the most.
3. Recall from different viewpoints. Review events by mentally standing in a different place. Or try to view information as another person would remember it. When taking a test, for instance, ask yourself what other students or your professor would remember about the topic.
4. Mentally put yourself back in the situation where you learned the information. Try to mentally recreate the learning environment or relive the event. As you do, include sounds, smells, details of the weather, nearby objects, other people present, what you said or thought, and how you felt as you learned the information (Milne & Bull, 2002).

Extend How Long You Remember

When you are learning new information, practice retrieval repeatedly. As you do, gradually lengthen the amount of time that passes before you test yourself again. For example, if you are studying German words on flash cards, look at the first card and then move it a few cards back in the stack. Do the same with the next few cards. When you get to the first "old" card, test yourself on it and check the answer. Then, move it farther back in the stack. Do the same with other "old" cards as they come up. When "old" cards come up for the third time, put them clear to the back of the stack.

Sleep and Memory

Remember that sleeping after study reduces interference. However, unless you are a "night person," late evening may not be a very efficient time for you to study. Also, you obviously can't sleep after every study session or study everything just before you sleep. That's why your study schedule should include ample breaks between subjects as described earlier (see "Spaced Practice"). The breaks and free time in your schedule are as important as your study periods.

Hunger and Memory

People who are hungry almost always score lower on memory tests. So Mother was right, it's a good idea to make sure you've had a good breakfast or lunch before you take tests at school (Smith, Clark, & Gallagher, 1999). And a cup of coffee won't hurt your test performance, either (Smith, 2005).

A Look Ahead

Psychologists still have much to learn about the nature of memory and how to improve it. For now, one thing stands out clearly: People who have good memories excel at organizing meaningful information. Sometimes, however, you are faced with the need to memorize information without much inherent meaning. For example, a shopping list is just a list of more or less unrelated items. There isn't much of a meaningful relationship between carrots, rolls of toilet paper, TV dinners, and Twinkies except that you need more of them. With this in mind, the Psychology in Action discussion for this chapter tells how you can use mnemonics to better memorize when meaning-based memory strategies, like those described in this section, are not helpful.

 **study break** Improving Memory

RECITE

1. For most people, having an especially good memory is based on
   a. maintenance rehearsal
   b. elaborative processing
   c. phonetic imagery
   d. learned strategies
2. As new information is encoded, it is helpful to elaborate on its meaning and connect it to other information. T or F?
3. Organizing information while studying has little effect on memory because long-term memory is already highly organized. T or F?
4. The progressive-part method of study is best suited to long and complex learning tasks. T or F?
5. The cognitive interview helps people remember more by providing
   a. retrieval cues
   b. a serial position effect
   c. phonetic priming
   d. massed practice

REFLECT

THINK CRITICALLY

6. Mr. S. had great difficulty remembering faces. Can you guess why?

7. What advantages would there be to taking notes as you read a textbook, as opposed to underlining words in the text?

SELF-REFLECT

What kinds of information are you good at remembering? Why do you think your memory is better for those topics?

Return to the topic headings in the preceding pages that list techniques for improving memory. Review any you didn't mark and think of a specific example of how you could use each technique at school, at home, or at work.

ANSWERS

1. d 2. T 3. F 4. T 5. a 6. Mr. S.'s memory was so specific that faces seemed different and unfamiliar if he saw them from a new angle or if a face had a different expression on it than when Mr. S. last saw it. 7. Properly done, note-taking is a form of elaborative processing; it encourages active reflection and facilitates the organization and selection of important ideas, and your notes can be used for review.

Psychology in Action

Mnemonics—Memory Magic

JOURNEY QUESTION 7.9 *What are mnemonics?*

Just imagine the poor biology or psychology student who is required to learn the names of the 12 cranial nerves (in order, of course). Although the spinal nerves connect the brain to the body through the spinal cord, the cranial nerves do so directly. Just in case you wanted to know, their names are: olfactory, optic, oculomotor, trochlear, trigeminal, abducens, facial, vestibulocochlear, glossopharyngeal, vagus, spinal accessory, and hypoglossal.

As you might imagine, most of us find it difficult to successfully encode this list. In the absence of any obvious meaningful relationship among these terms, it is difficult to apply the memory strategies we discussed earlier in the chapter and tempting to resort to *rote* learning (learning by simple repetition). Fortunately, there *is* an alternative: mnemonics (nee-MON-iks) (Baddeley, Eysenck, & Anderson, 2009; Radvansky, 2011). A **mnemonic** is any kind of memory system or aid. The superiority of mnemonic learning as opposed to rote learning has been demonstrated many times (Saber & Johnson, 2008; Worthen & Hunt, 2010).

Some mnemonic systems are so common that almost everyone knows them. If you are trying to remember how many days there are in a month, you may find the answer by reciting, "Thirty days hath September. . . ." Physics teachers often help students remember the colors of the spectrum by giving them the mnemonic "Roy G. Biv": **R**ed, **O**range, **Y**ellow, **G**reen, **B**lue, **I**ndigo, **V**iolet. The budding sailor who has trouble telling port from starboard may remember that "port" and "left" both have four letters or may remind herself, "I *left* port." And what beginning musician hasn't remembered the notes represented by the lines and spaces of the musical staff by learning "F-A-C-E" and "**E**very **G**ood **B**oy **D**oes **F**ine."

Generations of students have learned the names of the spinal nerves by memorizing the sentence "**O**n **O**ld **O**lympus' **T**owering **T**op **A** **F**amous **V**ocal **G**erman **V**iewed **S**ome **H**ops." This mnemonic, which uses the first letter of each of the cranial nerves to generate a nonsense sentence, indeed produces better recall of the cranial nerves. Such *acrostics* are even more effective if you make up your own (Fry, 2012). By practicing mnemonics, you should be able to greatly improve your memory with little effort.

Here, then, are some basic principles of mnemonics:

1. **Make things meaningful.** In general, transferring information from short-term memory to long-term memory is aided by making it meaningful. If you encounter technical terms that have little or no immediate meaning for you, *give* them meaning, even if you have to stretch the term to do so. (This point is clarified by the examples following this list.)
2. **Make information familiar.** Another way to get information into long-term memory is to connect it to information already stored there. If some facts or ideas in a chapter seem to stay in your memory easily, associate other more difficult facts with them.
3. **Use mental pictures.** Visual pictures, or images, are generally easier to remember than words. Turning information into mental pictures is therefore very helpful. Make these images as vivid as possible (Radvansky, 2011).
4. **Form bizarre, unusual, or exaggerated mental associations.** Forming images that make sense is better in most situations. However, when associating two ideas, terms, or especially mental images, you may find that the more outrageous and exaggerated the association, the more likely you are to remember. Bizarre images make stored information more *distinctive* and therefore easier to retrieve (Worthen & Marshall, 1996). Imagine, for example, that you have just been introduced to Mr. Rehkop. To remember his name, you could picture him wearing a police uniform. Then replace his nose with a ray gun. This bizarre image will provide two hints when you want to remember Mr. Rehkop's name: *ray* and *cop*.

Mnemonics can be an aid in preparing for tests. However, because mnemonics help most in the initial stages of storing information, it is important to follow through with other elaborative learning strategies.

Mnemonic Any kind of memory system or aid.

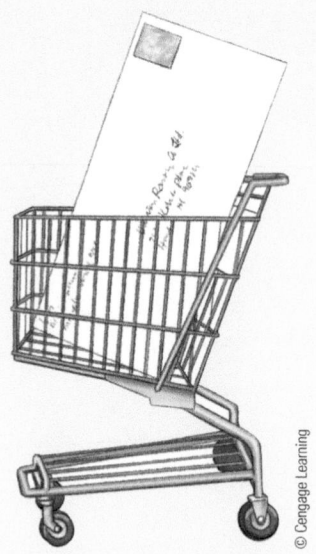

Exaggerated mental images can link two words or ideas in ways that aid memory. Here, the keyword method is used to link the English word *letter* with the Spanish word *carta*.

This technique works for other kinds of information, too. College students who used exaggerated mental associations to remember the names of unfamiliar animals outperformed students who just used rote memory (Carney & Levin, 2001). Bizarre images help improve mainly immediate memory, and they work best for fairly simple information (Fritz et al., 2007). Nevertheless, they can be a first step toward learning.

A sampling of typical applications of mnemonics should make these four points clearer to you:

Example 1   Let's say you have some new vocabulary words to memorize in Spanish. You can proceed by rote memorization (repeat them over and over until you begin to get them), or you can learn them with little effort by using the **keyword method**, in which a familiar word or image is used to link two other words or items (Fritz et al., 2007; Pressley, 1987). To remember that the word *pajaro* (pronounced PAH-hah-ro) means bird, you can link it to a "key" word in English: *Pajaro* sounds a bit like "parked car-o." Therefore, to remember that *pajaro* means bird, you might visualize a parked car jam-packed full of birds. You should try to make this image as vivid and exaggerated as possible, with birds flapping and chirping and feathers flying everywhere. Similarly, for the word *carta* (which means "letter"), you might imagine a shopping *cart* filled with postal letters.

If you link similar keywords and images for the rest of the list, you may not remember them all, but you will get most without much more practice. As a matter of fact, if you have formed the *pajaro* and *carta* images just now, it is going to be almost impossible for you to see these words again without remembering what they mean.

What about a year from now? How long do keyword memories last? Mnemonic memories work best in the short run. Later, they may be more fragile than conventional memories. That's why it's usually best to use mnemonics during the initial stages of learning (Carney & Levin, 2003; Fry, 2012). To create more lasting memories, you'll need to use the techniques discussed earlier in this chapter.

Example 2   Suppose you have to learn the names of all the bones and muscles in the human body. To remember that the jawbone is the *mandible*, you can associate it to a *man nibbling*, or maybe you can picture a *man dribbling* a basketball with his jaw (make this image as ridiculous as possible). If the muscle name *latissimus dorsi* gives you trouble, familiarize it by turning it into "*the ladder misses the door, sigh.*" Then picture a ladder glued to your back where the muscle is found. Picture the ladder leading up to a small door at your shoulder. Picture the ladder missing the door. Picture the ladder sighing like an animated character in a cartoon.

This seems like more to remember, not less; and it seems like it would cause you to misspell things. Mnemonics are an aid, not a complete substitute for normal memory. Mnemonics are not likely to be helpful unless you make extensive use of *images* (Worthen & Hunt, 2010). Your mental pictures will come back to you easily. As for misspellings, mnemonics can be thought of as a built-in hint in your memory. Often, when taking a test, you will find that the slightest hint is all you need to remember correctly. A mnemonic image is like having someone leaning over your shoulder who says, "Psst, the name of that muscle sounds like 'ladder misses the door, sigh.'" If misspelling continues to be a problem, try to create memory aids for spelling, too.

Here are two more examples to help you appreciate the flexibility of a mnemonic approach to studying.

Example 3   Your art history teacher expects you to be able to name the artist when you are shown slides as part of exams. You have seen many of the slides only once before in class. How will you remember them? As the slides are shown in class, make each artist's name into an object or image. Then picture the object *in* the paintings done by the artist. For example, you can picture Van Gogh as a *van* (automobile) *going* through the middle of each Van Gogh painting. Picture the van running over things and knocking things over. Or, if you remember that Van Gogh cut off his ear, picture a giant bloody ear in each of his paintings.

Example 4   If you have trouble remembering history, try to avoid thinking of it as something from the dim past. Picture each historical personality as a person you know right now (a friend, teacher, parent, and so on). Then picture these people doing whatever the

Keyword method As an aid to memory, using a familiar word or image to link two items.

historical figures did. Also, try visualizing battles or other events as if they were happening in your town, or make parks and schools into countries. Use your imagination.

How can mnemonics be used to remember things in order? Here are three techniques that are helpful:

1. **Form a story or a chain.** To remember lists of ideas, objects, or words in order, try forming an exaggerated association (mental image) connecting the first item to the second, then the second to the third, and so on. To remember the following short list in order—elephant, doorknob, string, watch, rifle, oranges—picture a full-size *elephant* balanced on a *doorknob* playing with a *string* tied to him. Picture a *watch* tied to the string, and a *rifle* shooting *oranges* at the watch. This technique can be used quite successfully for lists of 20 or more items. In one test, people who used a linking mnemonic did much better at remembering lists of 15 and 22 errands (Higbee et al., 1990). Try it next time you go shopping and leave your list at home. Another helpful strategy is to make up a short story that links all the items on a list you want to remember (McNamara & Scott, 2001).

2. **Take a mental walk.** Ancient Greek orators had an interesting way to remember ideas in order when giving a speech. Their method was to take a mental walk along a familiar path. As they did, they associated topics with the images of statues found along the walk. You can do the same thing by "placing" objects or ideas along the way as you mentally take a familiar walk (Radvansky, 2011).

3. **Use a system.** As we have already seen, many times, the first letters or syllables of words or ideas can be formed into another word that will serve as a reminder of order. "Roy G. Biv" is an example. As an alternative, learn the following: 1 is a bun, 2 is a shoe, 3 is a tree, 4 is a door, 5 is a hive, 6 is sticks, 7 is heaven, 8 is a gate, 9 is a line, 10 is a hen. To remember a list in order, form an image associating bun with the first item on your list. For example, if the first item is *frog*, picture a "frog-burger" on a bun to remember it. Then, associate shoe with the second item, and so on.

If you have never used mnemonics, you may still be skeptical, but give this approach a fair trial. Most people find they can greatly extend their memory through the use of mnemonics. But remember, like most things worthwhile, remembering takes effort (Hancock, 2011).

study break Mnemonics

RECITE

1. Memory systems and aids are referred to as
   _____.
2. Which of the following is least likely to improve memory?
   a. using exaggerated mental images
   b. forming a chain of associations
   c. turning visual information into verbal information
   d. associating new information to information that is already known or familiar
3. Bizarre images make stored information more distinctive and therefore easier to retrieve. T or F?
4. In general, mnemonics improve only memory for related words or ideas. T or F?

REFLECT

THINK CRITICALLY

5. How are elaborative processing and mnemonics alike?

SELF-REFLECT

The best mnemonics are your own. As an exercise, see if you can create a better acrostic for the 12 cranial nerves. One student generated **O**ld **O**tto **O**ctavius **T**ried **T**rigonometry **A**fter **F**acing **V**ery **G**rim **V**irgin's **S**ad **H**usbands (Bloom & Lamkin, 2006).

Go through the glossary items in this chapter and make up mnemonics for any terms you have difficulty remembering. Here is an example to help you get started. An iconic memory is a visual image: Picture an *eye* in a *can* to remember that iconic memories store visual information.

ANSWERS

Chapter in Review

Summary

7.1 How does memory work?

- 7.1.1 Memory is an active system that encodes, stores, and retrieves information.
- 7.1.2 The Atkinson-Shiffrin model of memory includes three stages of memory (sensory memory, short-term or working memory, and long-term memory) that hold information for increasingly longer periods.
- 7.1.3 Sensory memories are encoded as iconic memories or echoic memories.
- 7.1.4 Selective attention determines what information moves from sensory memory, which is exact but very brief, on to STM.
- 7.1.5 Short-term memories tend to be encoded by sound and are sensitive to interruption, or displacement.
- 7.1.6 Long-term memories are encoded by meaning.

7.2 What are the features of short-term memory?

- 7.2.1 STM has a capacity of about 5 to 7 bits of information, but this limit can be extended by chunking.
- 7.2.2 Short-term memories are brief; however, they can be prolonged by maintenance rehearsal.
- 7.2.3 For transferring information to LTM, rote rehearsal is less effective than elaborative processing.

7.3 What are the features of long-term memory?

- 7.3.1 Long-term memories are relatively permanent. LTM seems to have an almost unlimited storage capacity.
- 7.3.2 Elaborative processing can have the effect of altering memories. Remembering is an active process. Our memories are frequently lost, altered, revised, or distorted.
- 7.3.3 LTM is highly organized. The structure of memory networks is the subject of current research.
- 7.3.4 In redintegration, memories are reconstructed, as one bit of information leads to others, which then serve as cues for further recall.
- 7.3.5 LTM contains procedural (skill) and declarative (fact) memories. Declarative memories can be semantic or episodic.

7.4 How is memory measured?

- 7.4.1 The tip-of-the-tongue state shows that memory is not an all-or-nothing event. Memories may be revealed by recall, recognition, relearning, or priming.
- 7.4.2 In recall, memories are retrieved without explicit cues, as in an essay exam. Recall of listed information often reveals a serial position effect.
- 7.4.3 A common test of recognition is the multiple-choice question.
- 7.4.4 In relearning, material that seems to be forgotten is learned again, and memory is revealed by a savings score.
- 7.4.5 Recall, recognition, and relearning mainly measure explicit memories. Other techniques, such as priming, are necessary to reveal implicit memories.

7.5 Why do we forget?

- 7.5.1 Herman Ebbinghaus found that forgetting is most rapid immediately after learning, as shown by the curve of forgetting.
- 7.5.2 Forgetting can occur because of failures of encoding, of storage, or of retrieval.
- 7.5.3 Failure to encode information is a common cause of "forgetting."
- 7.5.4 Forgetting in sensory memory and STM is due to a failure of storage through a weakening (decay) of memory traces. STM forgetting also occurs through displacement. Decay of memory traces due to disuse may also explain some LTM losses.
- 7.5.5 Failures of retrieval occur when information that resides in memory is nevertheless not retrieved. A lack of retrieval cues can produce retrieval failure. State-dependent learning is related to the effects of retrieval cues.
- 7.5.6 Much forgetting in LTM is caused by interference. In retroactive interference, new learning interferes with the ability to retrieve earlier learning. Proactive interference occurs when old learning interferes with the retrieval of new learning.
- 7.5.7 Memories can be consciously suppressed and they may be unconsciously repressed.
- 7.5.8 Extreme caution is warranted when "recovered" memories are the only basis for believing that traumatic events, such as childhood sexual abuse, happened in the past.

7.6 How does the brain form and store memories?

- 7.6.1 It takes time to consolidate memories. In the brain, memory consolidation takes place in the hippocampus. Until they are consolidated, long-term memories are easily destroyed, resulting in retrograde amnesia.
- 7.6.2 Intensely emotional experiences can result in flashbulb memories.
- 7.6.3 After memories have been consolidated, they appear to be stored in the cortex of the brain.
- 7.6.4 Lasting memories are recorded by changes in the activity, structure, and chemistry of nerve cells as well as how they interconnect.

7.7 What are "photographic" memories?

- 7.7.1 Eidetic imagery (photographic memory) occurs when a person is able to project an image onto a blank surface. Eidetic imagery is rarely found in adults. However, many adults have internal mental images, which can be very vivid.
- 7.7.2 Exceptional memory may be based on natural ability or learned strategies. Usually it involves both.

7.8 How can I improve my memory?

- 7.8.1 Excellent memory abilities are based on using strategies and techniques that make learning efficient and that compensate for natural weaknesses in human memory.

- 7.8.2 Memory can be improved through better encoding strategies, such as elaborating, selecting, and organizing information as well as whole learning, the progressive part method, encoding retrieval cues, overlearning, and spaced practice.
- 7.8.3 Memory can also be improved through better retrieval strategies, such as retrieval practice, which involves feedback, recitation, and review and active search strategies.
- 7.8.4 When you are studying or memorizing, you should also keep in mind the effects of serial position, sleep, and hunger.

7.9 What are mnemonics?

- 7.9.1 Memory systems (mnemonics) greatly improve immediate memory. However, conventional learning tends to create the most lasting memories.
- 7.9.2 Mnemonic systems use mental images and unusual associations to link new information with familiar memories already stored in LTM.
- 7.9.3 Effective mnemonics tend to rely on mental images and bizarre or exaggerated mental associations.

Interactive Learning

Log in to CengageBrain to access the resources your instructor requires. For this book, you can access:

CourseMate Go to CengageBrain.com to access Psychology CourseMate, where you will find an interactive eBook, glossaries, flashcards, quizzes, videos, Virtual Psychology Labs, and more.

Aplia If your professor has assigned Aplia:

1. Sign in to your account.
2. Complete the corresponding exercises as required by your professor.
3. When finished, click "Grade It Now" to see which areas you have mastered, which areas need more work, and detailed explanations of every answer.

Test Your Knowledge

Memory

1. The first step in forming a memory is
   a. retrieval
   b. storage
   c. rehearsal
   d. encoding

2. Storing information as an iconic or an echoic memory is most characteristic of
   a. sensory memory
   b. short-term memory
   c. long-term memory
   d. procedural memory

3. Selective attention controls which information moves from sensory memory to
   a. phonetic memory
   b. iconic memory
   c. STM
   d. LTM

4. Information in LTM is stored mainly on the basis of
   a. meaning
   b. sounds and phonetics
   c. icons and echoes
   d. how it will be retrieved

5. The digit-span test is primarily a measure of
   a. LTM
   b. elaborative processing
   c. recoding
   d. STM

6. Elaborative processing while encoding is especially useful for forming
   a. memory icons
   b. long-term memories
   c. skill memories
   d. retroactive memories

7. Redintegration can be said to occur when one memory
   a. leads to another
   b. blocks retrieval
   c. is transferred to LTM
   d. is forgotten

8. Which of the following is a type of declarative memory?
   a. long-term memory
   b. redintegrative memory
   c. procedural memory
   d. episodic memory

9. The least sensitive test of memory is
   a. redintegration
   b. relearning
   c. recall
   d. recognition

10. Which type of memory test would be most likely to reveal a serial position effect?
    a. recall
    b. recognition
    c. relearning
    d. implicit

11. Implicit memories are which type of memories?
    a. factual
    b. conscious
    c. skill
    d. unconscious

12. The fact that most people cannot correctly draw a U.S. penny is best explained by
    a. storage failure
    b. retrieval failure
    c. financial failure
    d. encoding failure

13. Decay of memory traces appears to apply most to the forgetting of
    a. sensory and short-term memories
    b. procedural memories
    c. semantic memories
    d. state-dependent memories

14. A saxophone player learns three new pieces of music, one after the other, in a single afternoon. The next day he is least able to remember the third piece because of
    a. retroactive interference
    b. the time decay of memory traces
    c. proactive interference
    d. disuse of retrieval cues

15. If you can't remember putting a painful memory out of mind, you may have used
    a. redintegration
    b. suppression
    c. negative rehearsal
    d. repression

16. Repressed memories could be thought of as the reverse of
    a. flashbulb memories
    b. proactive memories
    c. retroactive memories
    d. episodic memories

17. Memory consolidation would most likely be disrupted by
    a. rehearsal
    b. ECS
    c. massed practice
    d. sleep

18. Which of the following is BAD advice for improving memory?
    a. Select and organize information.
    b. Use spaced practice.
    c. Take tests when you are hungry.
    d. Sleep after you study.

19. The cognitive interview is superior to hypnosis for helping people remember because it
    a. does not lead to more false memories
    b. leads to more false memories
    c. leads to less correct information
    d. uses fewer retrieval cues

20. The keyword method is a commonly used
    a. cognitive interviewing technique
    b. massed practice strategy
    c. mnemonic technique
    d. first step in the progressive-part method

Answers   1. d   2. a   3. c   4. a   5. d   6. b   7. a   8. d   9. c   10. a   11. d   12. d   13. a   14. c   15. d   16. a   17. b   18. c   19. a   20. c

Journey Theme *Our behavior is energized and directed by motives and emotions.*

Michael Caulfield/WireImage/Getty Images

Motivation and Emotion

Journey into Psychology: No Need to Tell Lady Gaga

Russian novelist Leo Tolstoy once commented, "Music is the shorthand of emotion." So true, as any American-born, Grammy award–winning glam rocker with a wicked fashion sense could tell you. But there is more to motivation and emotion than getting you all gaga about an upcoming concert. The words *motivation* and *emotion* both derive from the Latin word *movere* (to move). Even getting out of bed in the morning can be difficult if you are unmotivated. And if you are unaware of your emotions, you will be vulnerable to health problems such as depression or addiction.

In this chapter, you will learn how motives provide the drumbeat of human behavior and emotions color its rhythms. As we will see, both play complex roles in our daily lives. Even "simple" motivated activities, such as eating, are not solely under the control of the body. In many instances, external cues, expectations, learning, cultural values, and other factors influence our motives and emotions.

Let's begin with basic motives, such as hunger and thirst, and then explore how emotions affect us. Although emotions can be the music of life, they are sometimes the music of death as well. Read on to find out why.

Journey Questions

9.1 What is motivation and are there different types of motives?

9.2 What causes hunger and thirst?

9.3 What are the typical patterns of human sexual response?

9.4 How does arousal relate to motivation?

9.5 What are learned and social motives and why are they important?

9.6 Are some motives more basic than others?

9.7 What happens during emotion?

9.8 What physiological changes underlie emotion and can "lie detectors" really detect lies?

9.9 How accurately are emotions expressed by the face and "body language"?

9.10 How do psychologists explain emotions?

9.11 What does it mean to have "emotional intelligence"?

Motivation—Forces That Push and Pull

JOURNEY QUESTION 9.1 *What is motivation and are there different types of motives?*

What are your goals? Why do you pursue them? When are you satisfied? These are questions about motivation, or why we act as we do. Let's begin with a basic model of motivation and an overview of types of motives. **Motivation** refers to the dynamics of behavior—the ways in which our actions are *initiated*, *sustained*, *directed*, and *terminated* (Deckers, 2010; Petri & Govern, 2013).

Can you clarify that? Yes. Imagine that Stefani is studying biology in the library. Her stomach begins to growl. She can't concentrate. She grows restless and decides to go to the cafeteria. Closed. Stefani drives to a nearby fast food outlet, where she finally eats. Her hunger satisfied, she resumes studying. Notice how Stefani's food seeking was *initiated* by a physical need. Her search was *sustained* because her need was not immediately met, and her actions were *directed* by possible sources of food. Finally, achieving her goal *terminated* her food seeking.

A Model of Motivation

Many motivated activities begin with a **need**, or internal deficiency. The need that initiated Stefani's search was a shortage of key nutrients in her body. Needs cause a **drive** (an energized motivational state) to develop. In Stefani's case, the drive was hunger. Drives activate a **response** (an action or series of actions) designed to push us toward a **goal** (the "target" of motivated behavior). Reaching a goal that satisfies the need will end the chain of events. Thus, a simple model of motivation can be shown in this way:

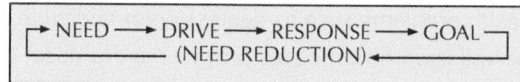

Aren't needs and drives the same thing? No, because the strength of needs and drives can differ (Deckers, 2010). For example, it is not uncommon for older people to suffer from dehydration (a physical need for water) despite experiencing a lack of thirst (the drive to drink) (Farrell et al., 2008).

Now, let's observe Stefani again. It's a holiday weekend and she's home from school. For dinner, Stefani has soup, salad, a large steak, a baked potato, two pieces of cheesecake, and three cups of coffee. After dinner, she complains that she is "too full to move." Soon after, Stefani's aunt arrives with a strawberry pie. Stefani exclaims that strawberry pie is her favorite and eats three large pieces! Is this hunger? Certainly, Stefani's dinner already satisfied her biological needs for food.

How does that change the model of motivation? Stefani's "pie lust" illustrates that motivated behavior can be energized by the "pull" of external stimuli, as well as by the "push" of internal needs.

Incentives

The "pull" of a goal is called its **incentive value** (the goal's appeal beyond its ability to fill a need). Some goals are so desirable (strawberry pie, for example) that they can motivate behavior in the absence of an internal need. Other goals are so low in incentive value that they may be rejected even if they meet the internal need. Fresh silkworms, for instance, are highly nutritious. However, it is doubtful that you would eat one no matter how hungry you might be. Regardless, because they are also easy to grow and produce few waste products, silkworms may become the preferred food on long space voyages (Yang et al., 2009).

Usually, our actions are energized by a mixture of internal needs *and* external incentives. That's why a strong need may change an unpleasant incentive into a desired goal. Perhaps you've never eaten a silkworm, but we'll bet you've eaten some pretty horrible

Motivation Internal processes that initiate, sustain, direct, and terminate activities.

Need An internal deficiency that may energize behavior.

Drive The psychological expression of internal needs or valued goals. For example, hunger, thirst, or a drive for success.

Response Any action, glandular activity, or other identifiable behavior.

Goal The target or objective of motivated behavior.

Incentive value The value of a goal above and beyond its ability to fill a need.

leftovers when the refrigerator was bare. The incentive value of goals also helps explain motives that don't seem to come from internal needs, such as drives for success, status, or approval (**Figure 9.1**).

Types of Motives

For our purposes, motives can be divided into three major categories:

1. **Biological motives** are based on biological needs that must be met for survival. The most important biological motives are hunger, thirst, pain avoidance, and needs for air, sleep, elimination of wastes, and regulation of body temperature. Biological motives are innate.
2. **Stimulus motives** express our needs for stimulation and information. Examples include activity, curiosity, exploration, manipulation, and physical contact. Although such motives also appear to be innate, they are not strictly necessary for survival.
3. **Learned motives** are based on learned needs, drives, and goals. Learned motives, which are often social in nature, help explain many human activities, such as standing for election or auditioning for *America's Got Talent*. Many learned motives are related to learned needs for power, affiliation (the need to be with others), approval, status, security, and achievement.

Biological Motives and Homeostasis

How important is air in your life? Water? Sleep? Food? Temperature regulation? Finding a public rest room? For most of us, satisfying biological needs is so routine that we tend to overlook how much of our behavior these needs direct. But exaggerate any of these needs through famine, shipwreck, poverty, near drowning, bitter cold, or drinking 10 cups of coffee, and their powerful grip on behavior becomes evident.

Biological drives are essential because they maintain *homeostasis* (HOE-me-oh-STAY-sis), or bodily equilibrium (Cooper, 2008). The term **homeostasis** means "standing steady" or "steady state." Optimal levels exist for body temperature, chemicals in the blood, blood pressure, and so forth (Franken & Dijk, 2009; Levin, 2006). When the body deviates from these "ideal" levels, automatic reactions begin to restore equilibrium (Deckers, 2010). Thus, it might help to think of homeostasis as similar to a thermostat set at a particular temperature.

A (Very) Short Course on Thermostats

The thermostat in your house constantly compares the actual room temperature to a *set point*, or ideal temperature, which you can control. When room temperature falls below the set point, the heat is automatically turned on to warm the room. When the heat equals or slightly exceeds the set point, it is automatically turned off or the air conditioning is turned on. In this way room temperature is kept in a state of equilibrium hovering around the set point.

The first reactions to disequilibrium in the human body are also automatic. For example, if you become too hot, more blood will flow through your skin and you will begin to perspire, thus lowering body temperature. We are often unaware of such changes unless continued disequilibrium drives us to seek shade, warmth, food, or water.

Circadian Rhythms

Our needs and drives can change from moment to moment. After eating, our motivation to eat more food tends to diminish, and a few minutes in the hot sun can leave us feeling thirsty. But our motivation can also vary over longer cycles, guided by internal "biological clocks." Every 24 hours, your body undergoes a cycle of changes called **circadian** (SUR-kay-dee-AN) **rhythms** (*circa*: about; *diem*: a day) (Beersma & Gordijn, 2007; Franken & Dijk, 2009). Throughout the day, activities in the liver, kidneys, and endocrine

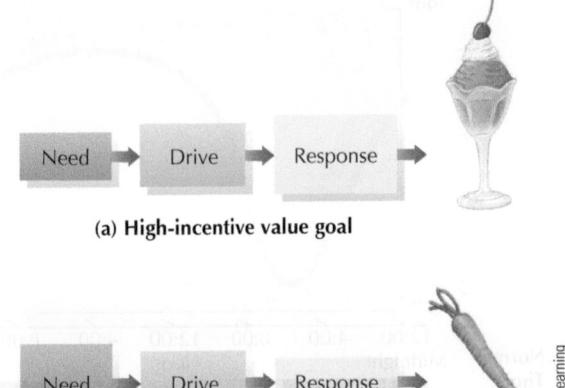

(a) High-incentive value goal

(b) Low-incentive value goal

© Cengage Learning

© Anna Clopet/Corbis

Figure 9.1 Needs and incentives interact to determine drive strength. *(a)* Moderate need combined with a high-incentive goal produces a strong drive. *(b)* Even when a strong need exists, drive strength may be moderate if a goal's incentive value is low. It is important to remember, however, that incentive value lies "in the eye of the beholder." No matter how hungry, few people would be able to eat the pictured silkworms.

Biological motives Innate motives based on biological needs.

Stimulus motives Innate needs for stimulation and information.

Learned motives Motives based on learned needs, drives, and goals.

Homeostasis A steady state of body equilibrium.

Circadian rhythms Cyclical changes in body functions and arousal levels that vary on a schedule approximating a 24-hour day.

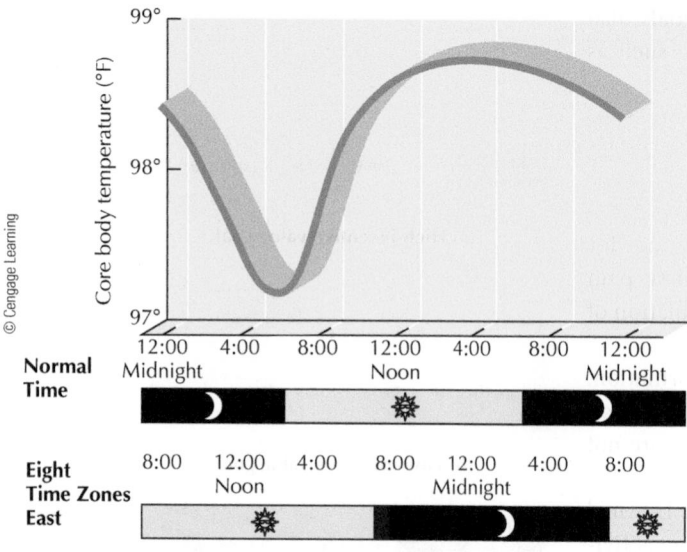

Figure 9.2 Core body temperature is a good indicator of a person's circadian rhythm. Rapid travel to a different time zone, shift work, depression, and illness can throw sleep and waking patterns out of synchronization with the body's core rhythm. Mismatches of this kind are very disruptive (Reinberg & Ashkenazi, 2008). Most people reach a low point 2 to 3 hours before their normal waking time. It's no wonder that both the Chernobyl and Three-Mile Island nuclear power plant accidents occurred around 4 AM.

Tolerance for pain and the strength of a person's motivation to avoid discomfort are greatly affected by cultural practices and beliefs, such as this penitent at a Hindu ceremony.

Episodic drive A drive, like pain, that occurs in distinct episodes.

glands undergo large changes. Body temperature, blood pressure, and amino acid levels also shift from hour to hour. These activities, and many others, peak once a day (Figure 9.2). People are usually more motivated and alert at the high point of their circadian rhythms (Bass & Takahashi, 2010; Chipman & Jin, 2009).

People with early peaks in their circadian rhythms are "day people" who wake up alert, are energetic early in the day, and fall asleep early in the evening. People with later peaks are "night people," who wake up groggy, are lively in the afternoon or early evening, and stay up late (Martynhak et al., 2010).

Jet Lag and Shift Work

Circadian rhythms are most noticeable after a major change in time schedules. Businesspeople, athletes, and other time zone travelers tend to perform poorly when their body rhythms are disturbed. If you travel great distances east or west, the peaks and valleys of your circadian rhythms will be out of phase with the sun and clocks (Sack, 2010). For example, you might be wide awake at midnight and feel like you're sleepwalking during the day (see Figure 9.2). Shift work has the same effect, causing fatigue, irritability, upset stomach, and depression (Shen et al., 2006; Smith et al., 2011).

Adjusting to "jet lag" is slowest when you stay indoors, where you can sleep and eat on "home time." Getting outdoors speeds adaptation. A few intermittent 5-minute periods of exposure to bright light early in the morning are also helpful for resetting your circadian rhythm (Dodson & Zee, 2010; Duffy & Wright, 2005). Bright light affects the timing of body rhythms by reducing the amount of melatonin produced by the pineal gland. When melatonin levels rise late in the evening, it's bedtime as far as the brain is concerned.

How does this affect those of us who are not world travelers? There are few college students who have not at one time or another "burned the midnight oil." At such times, it is wise to remember that departing from your regular schedule usually costs more than it's worth. You may be motivated to do as much during 1 hour in the morning as you could have done in 3 hours of work after midnight. You might just as well go to sleep 2 hours earlier.

Pain

Not all drives are governed by circadian rhythms. While hunger, thirst, and sleepiness come and go in a fairly regular cycle each day, pain avoidance is an **episodic** (ep-ih-SOD-ik) **drive**. That is, it occurs in distinct episodes when bodily damage takes place or is about to occur. Most drives prompt us to actively seek a desired goal (food, drink, warmth, and so forth). Pain prompts us to *avoid* or *eliminate* sources of discomfort.

Some people feel they must be "tough" and not show any distress. Others complain loudly at the smallest ache or pain. The first attitude raises pain tolerance, and the second lowers it. As this suggests, the drive to avoid pain is partly learned. That's why members of some societies endure cutting, burning, whipping, tattooing, and piercing of the skin that would agonize most people (Chang, 2009). (But apparently not devotees of piercing and "body art.") In general, we learn how to react to pain by observing family members, friends, and other role models (McMahon & Koltzenburg, 2005).

RECITE

1. Motives _____, sustain, _____, and terminate activities.
2. Needs provide the _____ of motivation, whereas incentives provide the _____.

Classify the following needs or motives by placing the correct letter in the blank.

   a. Biological motive   *b.* Stimulus motive
   c. Learned motive

3. _____ curiosity   6. _____ thirst
4. _____ status   7. _____ achievement
5. _____ sleep   8. _____ physical contact
9. A goal high in incentive value may create a drive in the absence of any internal need. T or F?
10. Pain avoidance is a(n) _____ drive.

REFLECT

THINK CRITICALLY

11. Many people mistakenly believe that they suffer from "hypoglycemia" (low blood sugar), which is often blamed for fatigue, difficulty concentrating, irritability, and other symptoms. Why is it unlikely that many people actually have hypoglycemia?

SELF-REFLECT

See if you can think of something you do that illustrates the concepts of need, drive, response, and goal. Does the goal in your example vary in incentive value? What effects do high- and low-incentive-value goals have on your behavior?

Reflect on some biological, stimulus, and learned motives you have satisfied today. How did each influence your behavior?

ANSWERS

1. initiate, direct 2. push, pull 3. b 4. c 5. a 6. a 7. c 8. b 9. T 10. episodic 11. Because of homeostasis: Blood sugar is normally maintained within narrow bounds. Although blood sugar levels fluctuate enough to affect hunger, true hypoglycemia is an infrequent medical problem.

Hunger and Thirst—Eat, Drink, and Be Merry

JOURNEY QUESTION 9.2 *What causes hunger and thirst?*

You get hungry, you find food, and you eat. Hunger might seem like a "simple" motive, but we have only recently begun to understand it. Hunger provides a good example of how internal and external factors direct our behavior. And, as we will see later, many of the principles that explain hunger also apply to thirst. Like other human motives, our hunger levels are affected by both internal physiological factors and external environmental and social ones. To understand how this works, let's begin with a survey of some of the internal factors controlling our hunger.

Internal Factors in Hunger

Don't feelings of hunger originate in the stomach? To find out, Walter Cannon and A. L. Washburn (1912) decided to see whether stomach contractions cause hunger. In an early study, Washburn trained himself to swallow a balloon, which could be inflated through an attached tube. (You, too, will do anything for science, right?) This allowed Cannon to record the movements of Washburn's stomach (**Figure 9.3**). When Washburn's stomach contracted, he reported that he felt "hunger pangs." In view of this, the two scientists concluded that hunger is nothing more than the contractions of an empty stomach. (This, however, proved to be an inflated conclusion.)

For many people, hunger produces an overall feeling of weakness or shakiness, rather than a "growling"

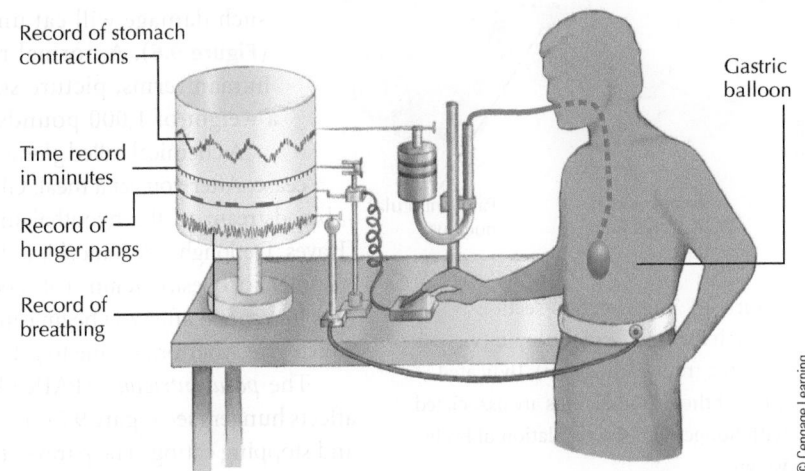

Record of stomach contractions

Time record in minutes

Record of hunger pangs

Record of breathing

Gastric balloon

© Cengage Learning

Figure 9.3 In Walter Cannon's early study of hunger, a simple apparatus was used to simultaneously record hunger pangs and stomach contractions. (Adapted from Cannon, 1934.)

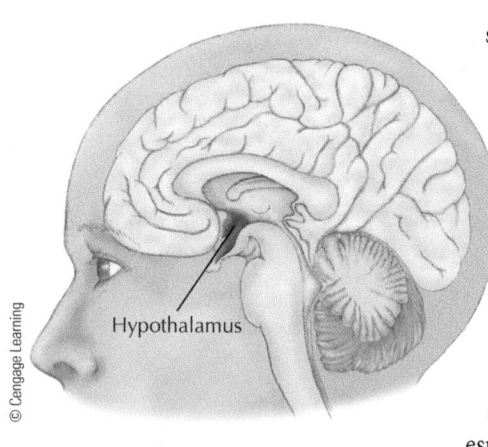

Figure 9.4 Location of the hypothalamus in the human brain.

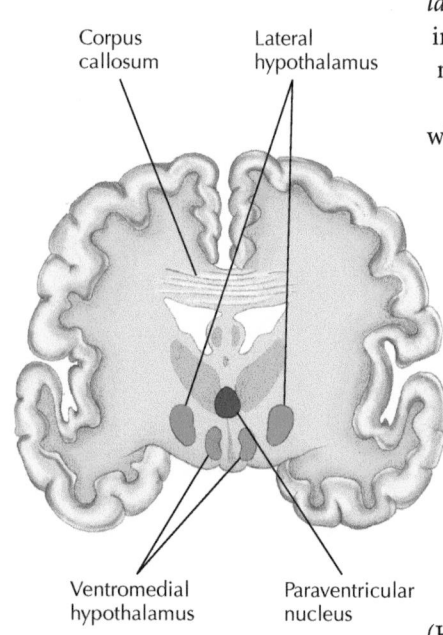

Figure 9.5 This is a cross-section through the middle of the brain (viewed from the front of the brain). Indicated areas of the hypothalamus are associated with hunger and the regulation of body weight.

Hypothalamus A small area at the base of the brain that regulates many aspects of motivation and emotion, especially hunger, thirst, and sexual behavior.

stomach. Of course, eating *does* slow when the stomach is stretched or distended (full). (Remember last Thanksgiving?) However, we now know that the stomach is not essential for feeling hunger. Even people who have had their stomachs removed for medical reasons continue to feel hungry and eat regularly (Woods et al., 2000).

Then what does cause hunger? Many different factors combine to promote and suppress hunger (Ribeiro et al., 2009). The brain receives many signals from parts of the digestive system, ranging from the tongue and stomach to the intestines and the liver.

Brain Mechanisms

What part of the brain controls hunger? Although no single "hunger thermostat" exists, a small subcortical area of the brain called the **hypothalamus** (HI-po-THAL-ah-mus) is especially important because it regulates many motives, including hunger, thirst, and the sex drive (**Figure 9.4**).

The hypothalamus is sensitive to levels of a variety of substances in the blood, such as sugar. It also receives neural messages from the digestive system. For example, as the levels of blood sugar (glucose) drop, the liver responds by sending nerve impulses to the brain. When combined, these signals determine whether you are hungry (Freberg, 2010; Woods & Ramsay, 2011).

One part of the hypothalamus acts as a feeding system that initiates eating. If the *lateral hypothalamus* is "turned on" with an electrified probe, even a well-fed animal will immediately begin eating. (The term *lateral* simply refers to the *sides* of the hypothalamus. See **Figure 9.5**.) If the same area is destroyed, the animal may never eat again.

The lateral hypothalamus is normally activated in a variety of ways. For example, when you are hungry, your stomach lining produces *ghrelin* (GREL-in), a hormone that activates your lateral hypothalamus (Castañeda et al., 2010; Olszewski et al., 2003). Ghrelin also activates parts of your brain involved in learning. This means you should consider studying before you eat, not immediately afterward (Diano et al., 2006).

How do we know when to stop eating? A second area in the hypothalamus is part of a satiety system, or "stop mechanism" for eating. If the *ventromedial* (VENT-ro-MEE-dee-al) *hypothalamus* is destroyed, dramatic overeating results. (*Ventromedial* refers to the bottom middle of the hypothalamus.) Rats with such damage will eat until they balloon up to weights of 1,000 grams or more (**Figure 9.6**). A normal rat weighs about 180 grams. To put this weight gain in human terms, picture someone you know who weighs 180 pounds growing to a weight of 1,000 pounds.

A chemical called *glucagon-like peptide 1* (GLP-1) is also involved in causing eating to cease. After you eat a meal, GLP-1 is released by the intestines. From there, it travels in the bloodstream to the hypothalamus. When enough GLP-1 arrives, your desire to eat ends (Hayes, De Jonghe, & Kanoski, 2010). As you might imagine, GLP-1 pills show promise in the treatment of obesity (Raun et al., 2007). By the way, it takes at least 10 minutes for the hypothalamus to respond after you begin eating. That's why you are less likely to overeat if you eat slowly, which gives your brain time to get the message that you've had enough (Liu et al., 2000).

The *paraventricular* (PAIR-uh-ven-TRICK-you-ler) *nucleus* of the hypothalamus also affects hunger (see Figure 9.5). This area helps keep blood sugar levels steady by both starting and stopping eating. The paraventricular nucleus is sensitive to a substance called *neuropeptide Y (NPY)*. If NPY is present in large amounts, an animal will eat until it cannot hold another bite (Williams et al., 2004). Incidentally, the hypothalamus also responds to a chemical in marijuana, which can produce intense hunger (the "munchies") (Di Marzo et al., 2001).

In addition to knowing when to start eating and when meals are over, your brain also controls your weight over long periods of time. (See "Your Brain's 'Fat Point.'")

The substances we have reviewed are only some of the chemical and neural signals that start and stop eating (Geary, 2004; Turenius et al., 2009). Others continue to be discovered.

Brainwaves

Your Brain's "Fat Point"

Like a thermostat, your brain maintains a **set point** in order to control your weight over the long term. It does this by monitoring the amount of fat stored in your body in specialized *fat cells* (Ahima & Osei, 2004; Gloria-Bottini, Magrini, & Bottini, 2009).

Your set point is the weight you maintain when you are making no effort to gain or lose weight. When your body weight goes below its set point, you will feel hungry most of the time. On the other hand, fat cells release a substance called *leptin* when your "spare tire" is well inflated. Leptin is carried in the bloodstream to the hypothalamus, where it tells us to eat less (Williams et al., 2004; Woods & Ramsay, 2011).

Can you change your fat set point? Your leptin levels are partly under genetic control. In rare cases mice (and we humans) inherit a genetic defect that reduces leptin levels in the body, leading to obesity. In such cases, taking leptin can help (Williamson et al., 2005).

For the rest of us, the news is not so encouraging because there is currently no known way to lower your set point for fat, since the number of fat cells remains unchanged throughout adult life (Spalding et al., 2008). To make matters worse, radical diets do not help. (But you knew that already, didn't you?) They may even raise the set point for fat, resulting in *diet-induced obesity* (Ahima & Osei, 2004). You may not be able to lose weight by resetting your hypothalamus, but psychologists have studied more effective approaches to weight loss. We will examine some later in this chapter.

In time, they may make it possible to artificially control hunger. If so, better treatments for extreme obesity and self-starvation could follow (Batterham et al., 2003).

External Factors in Hunger and Obesity

As we have seen, "hunger" is affected by more than just the "push" of our biological needs for food. In fact, if internal needs alone controlled eating, fewer people would overeat (Stroebe, Papies, & Aarts, 2008). Nevertheless, roughly 65 percent of adults in the United States are currently overweight and more than one third are obese (extremely overweight) (Flegal et al., 2010; Ogden & Carroll, 2010; Figure 9.7). Childhood obesity has also shown a dramatic rise. As a result, obesity is overtaking smoking as a major cause of needless deaths (Freedman, 2011). Let's consider some external influences on hunger and their role in obesity, a major health risk and, for many, a source of social stigma and low self-esteem.

External Eating Cues

Most of us are sensitive to the "pull" of *external eating cues*, signs and signals linked with food. For example, do you tend to eat more when food is highly visible and easy to get? In cultures like ours, in which food is plentiful, eating cues add greatly to the risk of overeating (Casey et al., 2008). Many college freshmen gain weight rapidly during their first 3 months on campus (the famous "Frosh 15"). All-you-can-eat dining halls in the dorms and nighttime snacking appear to be the culprits (Kapinos & Yakusheva, 2011). The presence of others can also affect whether people overeat (or undereat), depending on how much everyone else is eating and how important it is to impress them (Pliner & Mann, 2004).

Taste

The availability of a variety of tasty foods can also lead to overeating and obesity in societies in which such foods are plentiful. Normally, tastes for foods vary considerably. For example, if you are well fed, leptin dulls the tongue's sensitivity to sweet tastes (Kawai et al., 2000). If you have noticed that you lose your "sweet tooth" when you are full, you

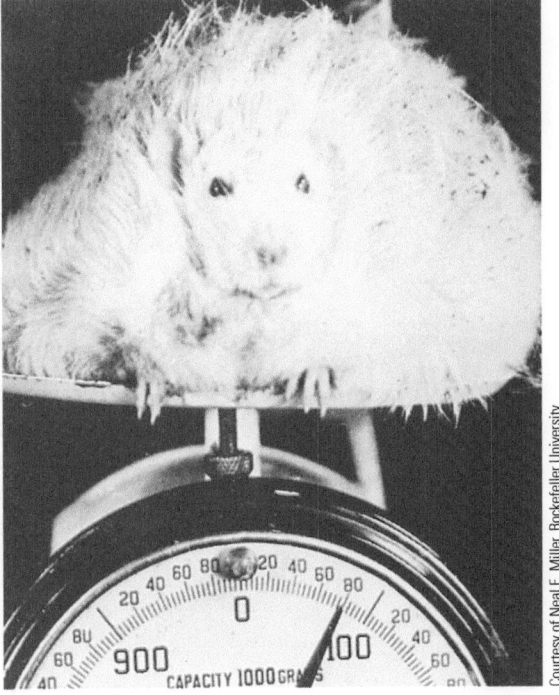

Courtesy of Neal E. Miller, Rockefeller University

Figure 9.6 Damage to the hunger satiety system in the hypothalamus can produce a very fat rat, a condition called hypothalamic *hyperphagia* (Hi-per-FAGE-yah: overeating). This rat weighs 1,080 grams. (The pointer has gone completely around the dial and beyond.)

Set point (for fat) The proportion of body fat that tends to be maintained by changes in hunger and eating.

Childhood obesity has reached epidemic proportions in the United States, having tripled in prevalence since 1980 (Ogden et al., 2010). In 2010, First Lady Michelle Obama launched "Let's Move," her national program to confront this problem head on.

may have observed this effect. Actually, if you eat too much of any particular food, it will become less appealing. This probably helps us maintain variety in our diets. However, it also encourages obesity. If you overdose on hamburgers or French fries, moving on to some cookies or chocolate cheesecake certainly won't do your body much good (Pinel, Assanand, & Lehman, 2000).

Emotional Eating

Is it true that people also overeat when they are emotionally upset? Yes. People with weight problems are prone to overeat when they are anxious, angry, or sad (Macht & Simons, 2011). Furthermore, obese individuals are often unhappy in our fat-conscious culture. The result is overeating that leads to emotional distress and still more overeating (Davis & Carter, 2009).

Cultural Factors

Learning to think of some foods as desirable and others as revolting has a large impact on what we eat. In North America, we would never consider eating the eyes out of the steamed head of a monkey, but in some parts of the world they are considered a delicacy. By the same token, vegans and vegetarians think it is barbaric to eat any kind of meat. In short, cultural values greatly affect the *incentive value* of foods.

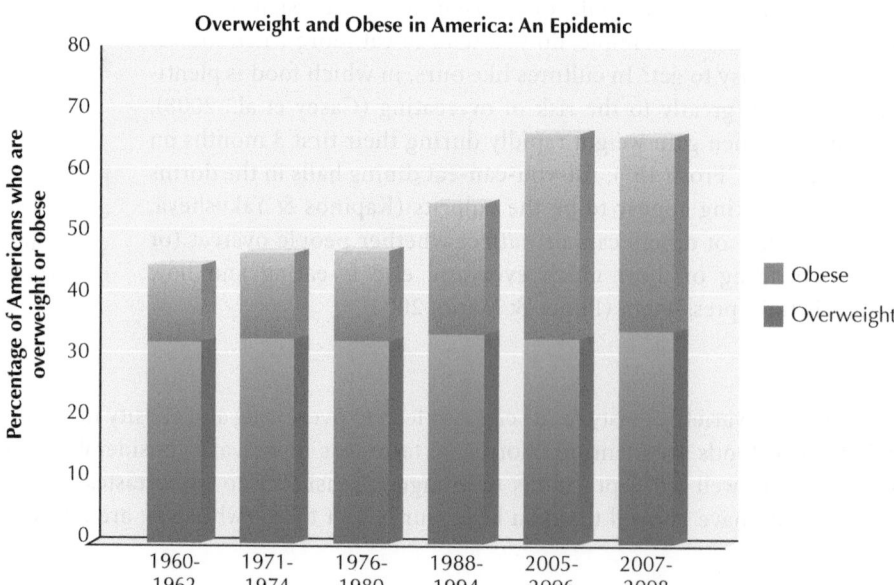

Figure 9.7 A near epidemic of obesity has occurred in the United States during the last 20 years, with more than 65 percent of all Americans now classified as overweight or obese. (Adapted from Ogden & Carroll, 2010; Flegal et al., 2010.)

Dieting

A diet is not just a way to lose weight. Your current diet is defined by the types and amounts of food you regularly eat. Some diets actually encourage overeating. For instance, placing animals on a "supermarket" diet leads to gross obesity. In one classic experiment, rats were given meals of chocolate chip cookies, salami, cheese, bananas, marshmallows, milk chocolate, peanut butter, and fat. These pampered rodents overate, gaining almost three times as much weight as rats that ate only laboratory chow (Sclafani & Springer, 1976). (Rat chow is a dry mixture of several bland grains. If you were a rat, you'd probably eat more cookies than rat chow, too.)

People are also sensitive to dietary content. In general, *sweetness*, high *fat content*, and *variety* tend to encourage overeating. Unfortunately, North American culture provides the worst kinds of foods for people who suffer from obesity. For example, restaurant and fast food tends to be higher in fat and calories than meals made at home (Kessler, 2009).

"Supersized" meals are another problem. Food portions at restaurants in the United States are 25 percent larger, or more, than they are in France. Far fewer people are obese in France, most likely because they simply eat less. The French also take longer to eat a meal, which discourages overeating (Rozin et al., 2003).

An added problem faced by people who want to control their weight concerns "yo-yo" dieting.

Singer Jennifer Hudson has been a lifelong dieter who tried many different diets and experienced weight swings. As a spokeswoman for a national weight-loss program, Jennifer lost about 80 pounds. Will she maintain her weight loss over time?

The Paradox of Yo-Yo Dieting

If dieting works, why are hundreds of "new" diets published each year? The answer is that although dieters do lose weight, most regain it soon after they stop dieting. In fact, many people end up weighing even more than before (Freedman, 2011). Why should this be so? Dieting (starving) slows the body's rate of metabolism (the rate at which energy is used up). In effect, a dieter's body becomes highly efficient at *conserving* calories and storing them as fat (Pinel, Assanand, & Lehman, 2000).

Apparently, evolution prepared us to save energy when food is scarce and to stock up on fat when food is plentiful. Briefly starving yourself, therefore, may have little lasting effect on weight. "Yo-yo dieting," or repeatedly losing and gaining weight, is especially dangerous. Frequent changes in weight can dramatically slow the body's metabolic rate. As noted earlier, this may raise the body's set point for fat and make it harder to lose weight each time a person diets and easier to regain weight when the diet ends. Frequent weight changes also increase the risk for heart disease and premature death (Wang & Brownell, 2005). To avoid bouncing between feast and famine, a *permanent* change in eating habits and exercise is required.

To summarize, eating and overeating are related to internal and external influences, diet, emotions, genetics, exercise, and many other factors. We live in a culture that provides inexpensive, good-tasting food everywhere, and have a brain that evolved to say "Eat whenever food is available." People become obese in different ways and for different reasons. Nevertheless, many people have learned to take control of eating by applying psychological principles. (See "Behavioral Dieting.")

Anorexia nervosa is far more dangerous than many people realize. This haunting Italian anti-anorexia poster shows 68-pound model Isabelle Caro, who suffered from anorexia for years up until her death in 2010 at age 28. Many celebrities have struggled with eating disorders, including Karen Carpenter (who died of starvation-induced heart failure), Paula Abdul, Kirstie Alley, Fiona Apple, Victoria Beckham (Posh Spice), Princess Diana, Tracey Gold, Janet Jackson, and Mary-Kate Olsen.

Eating Disorders

Under the sheets of her hospital bed, Krystal looks like a skeleton. Victims of anorexia suffer devastating weight losses from severe, self-inflicted dieting. If she cannot overcome her **anorexia nervosa** (AN-uh-REK-see-yah ner-VOH-sah: self-starvation), Krystal may die of malnutrition.

Anorexia nervosa Active self-starvation or a sustained loss of appetite that has psychological origins.

Discovering Psychology

If you really want to lose weight and keep it off, you must overhaul your eating and exercise habits, an approach called **behavioral dieting** (Freedman, 2011; Roizen & Oz, 2006). Here are some helpful behavioral techniques:

1. **Get yourself committed to weight loss.** Involve other people in your efforts. Programs such as Overeaters Anonymous or Take Off Pounds Sensibly can be good sources of social support (Mitchell et al., 2010).

2. **Exercise.** No diet can succeed for long without an increase in exercise. To lose weight, you must use more calories than you take in. Burning just 200 extra calories a day can help prevent rebound weight gains. Add activity to your routine in every way you can think of. Stop saving steps and riding elevators. Buy a *step counter* to track the number of steps you take every day. Walking 10,000 steps per day will burn between 2,000 and 3,500 calories a week (depending on your weight). The more frequently and vigorously you exercise, the more weight you will lose (Annesi & Marti, 2011; Jeffery & Wing, 2001).

3. **Learn your eating habits by observing yourself and keeping a "diet diary."** Begin by making a complete, 2-week record of when and where you eat, what you eat, and the feelings and events that occur just before and after eating. Is a roommate, relative, or spouse encouraging you to overeat? What are your most "dangerous" times and places for overeating?

4. **Learn to weaken your personal eating cues.** When you have learned when and where you do most of your eating, avoid these situations. Try to restrict your eating to one room, and do not read, watch television, study, or talk on the phone while eating. Require yourself to interrupt what you are doing in order to eat.

5. **Count calories, but don't starve yourself.** To lose weight, you must eat less, and calories allow you to keep a record of your food intake. If you have trouble eating less every day, try dieting 4 days a week. People who diet intensely every other day lose as much as those who diet moderately every day.

6. **Develop techniques to control the act of eating.** Whenever you can, check for nutritional information and buy groceries and meals lower in calories and fats. Begin to take smaller portions. Carry to the table only what you plan to eat. Put all other food away before leaving the kitchen. Eat slowly, sip water between bites of food, leave food on your plate, and stop eating before you are completely full. Be especially wary of the extra large servings at fast-food restaurants; they can, indeed, leave you supersized.

7. **Avoid snacks.** It is generally better to eat more small meals a day than fewer large ones because more calories are burned (Roizen & Oz, 2006). (No, we don't mean high-calorie snacks *in addition to* meals.) If you have an impulse to snack, set a timer for 20 minutes and see if you are still hungry then. Delay the impulse to snack several times if possible. Dull your appetite by filling up on raw carrots, bouillon, water, coffee, or tea.

8. **Chart your daily progress.** Record your weight, the number of calories eaten, and whether you met your daily goal. Set realistic goals by cutting down calories gradually. Losing about a pound per week is realistic, but remember, you are changing habits, not just dieting. "Diets" don't work!

9. **Set a "threshold" for weight control.** Maintaining weight loss can be even more challenging than losing weight. It is easier to maintain weight loss if you set a regain limit of 3 pounds or less. In other words, if you gain more than 2 or 3 pounds, you immediately begin to make corrections in your eating habits and amount of exercise (Kessler, 2009).

Be patient. It takes years to develop eating habits. You can expect it to take at least several months to change them. If you are unsuccessful at losing weight with these techniques, you might find it helpful to seek the aid of a psychologist familiar with behavioral weight-loss techniques.

Adam@Home © by Universal Press Syndicate. Reprinted with permission. All rights reserved.

Do anorexics lose their appetite? Although a compulsive attempt to lose weight causes them to not seek or desire food, they usually still feel physical hunger. Often, anorexia starts with "normal" dieting that slowly begins to dominate the person's life. In time, anorexics suffer debilitating health problems, including the highest mortality rates of all the mental illnesses (Krantz et al., 2012). Table 9.1 lists the symptoms of anorexia nervosa.

Bulimia nervosa (bue-LIHM-ee-yah) is a second major eating disorder (Bardone-Cone et al., 2008; Koda & Sugawara, 2009). Bulimic persons gorge on food, then vomit or take laxatives to avoid gaining weight. (See Table 9.1.) Bingeing and purging can seriously damage health. Typical risks include sore throat, hair loss, muscle spasms, kidney damage, dehydration, tooth erosion, swollen salivary glands, menstrual irregularities, loss of sex drive, and even heart attack.

About 1 percent of all adults suffer from anorexia, along with 3 percent who are bulimic. But these are only the most serious cases. As many as 14 to 22 percent of all adolescents experience some form of disordered eating (Swanson et al., 2011). While women are more prone to develop eating disorders, they are on the rise among men.

Behavioral dieting Weight reduction based on changing exercise and eating habits, rather than temporary self-starvation.

Bulimia nervosa Excessive eating (gorging) usually followed by self-induced vomiting and/or taking laxatives.

Table 9.1 Recognizing Eating Disorders

ANOREXIA NERVOSA

- Refusal to maintain body weight in normal range. Body weight below 85 percent of normal for one's height and age.
- Intense fear of becoming fat or gaining weight, even though underweight.
- Disturbance in one's body image or perceived weight. Self-evaluation is unduly influenced by body weight. Denial of seriousness of abnormally low body weight.
- Absence of menstrual periods (may be removed from DSM-5).
- Purging behavior (vomiting or misuse of laxatives or diuretics).

BULIMIA NERVOSA

- Recurring binge eating. Eating within an hour or two an amount of food that is much larger than most people would consume. Feeling a lack of control over eating.
- Purging behavior (vomiting or misuse of laxatives or diuretics). Excessive exercise to prevent weight gain. Fasting to prevent weight gain.
- Self-evaluation is unduly influenced by body weight.

Adapted from *American Psychiatric Association*, 2000, 2012. The DSM content has been adapted for the particular audience and is intended for educational purposes only.

Men and Eating Disorders

More and more men are experiencing *muscle dysmorphia*, or excessive worry about not being muscular enough (Darcy, 2011; Mosley, 2009). Currently, one third of men say they want less body fat and another third want more muscles (McCabe & Ricciardelli, 2004). As a result, many men are altering what they eat and exercising excessively. Some are going too far: About 10 to 20 percent of anorexics and bulimics are now males (Jones & Morgan, 2010; Weltzin et al., 2005).

Causes

What causes anorexia and bulimia? People who suffer from eating disorders are extremely dissatisfied with their bodies (Crisp et al., 2006). Usually, they have distorted views of themselves. Women have low self-esteem and exaggerated fears of becoming fat. Many overestimate their body size by 25 percent or more. As a result, they think they are disgustingly "fat" when they are actually wasting away (**Figure 9.8**) (Polivy & Herman, 2002). Men generally think they are not muscular enough if they are not "cut" or have a "six-pack" (Jones & Morgan, 2010).

Many of these problems are related to the idealized body images presented in the media (Levine & Harrison, 2004). Some websites even go so far as to celebrate anorexia and bulimia (referred to by "fans" as "Ana" and "Mia"; Borzekowski et al., 2010; Tierney, 2008). Girls

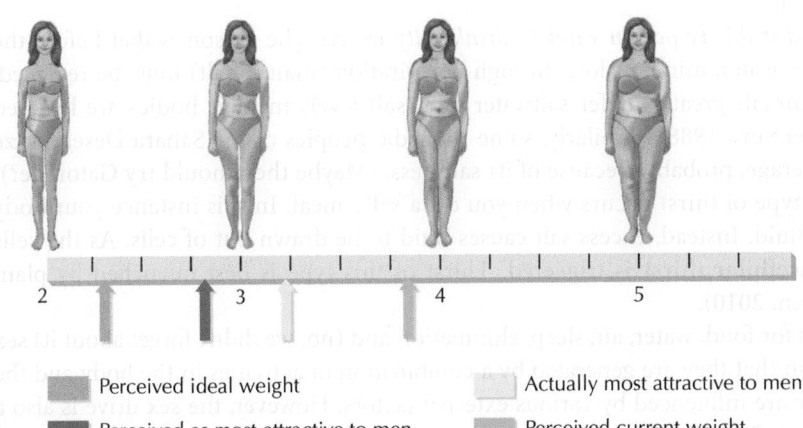

Perceived ideal weight
Perceived as most attractive to men
Actually most attractive to men
Perceived current weight

Figure 9.8 Women with abnormal eating habits were asked to rate their body shape on a scale similar to the one you see here. As a group, they chose ideal figures much thinner than what they thought their current weights were. (Most women say they want to be thinner than they currently are, but to a lesser degree than women with eating problems.) Notice that the women with eating problems chose an ideal weight that was even thinner than what they thought men prefer. This is not typical of most women. In this classic study, only women with eating problems wanted to be thinner than what they thought men find attractive (Zellner, Harner, & Adler, 1989).

who spend a lot of time reading fashion magazines or visiting these websites are more likely to have distorted body images and unrealistic ideas about how they compare with others (Martinez-Gonzalez et al., 2003).

The popularity of fitness, exercise, and sports has also contributed to eating disorders. Today, more people are changing their diets in search of a lean, muscular look. People engaged in sports that require low body fat or extreme weight loss (such as wrestling, gymnastics, pole vaulting, high jumping, and even cycling) are particularly likely to develop eating disorders (Weltzin et al., 2005).

People with eating disorders appear to be trying to gain some measure of control. Anorexic teen girls are usually described as "perfect" daughters—helpful, considerate, conforming, and obedient. They seem to be rewarded by seeking perfect control in their lives by being perfectly slim (Castro et al., 2004; Keating, 2010). People suffering from bulimia are also concerned with control (Bardone-Cone et al., 2008). Typically, they are obsessed with thoughts of weight, food, eating, and ridding themselves of food. As a result, they feel guilt, shame, self-contempt, and anxiety. Vomiting reduces their anxiety, which makes purging highly reinforcing.

Treatment

Most people suffering from eating disorders will not seek help on their own. This is especially true for men, because eating disorders are still widely perceived to be a female problem (Jones & Morgan, 2010; Weltzin et al., 2005). Typically, it takes strong urging by family or friends to get victims into treatment.

Treatment for anorexia usually begins with giving drugs to relieve obsessive fears of gaining weight. Then a medical diet is used to restore weight and health. Next, a counselor may help patients work on the emotional conflicts that led to weight loss. For bulimia, behavioral counseling may include self-monitoring of food intake. A related cognitive-behavioral approach focuses on changing the thinking patterns and beliefs about weight and body shape that perpetuate eating disorders (Cooper, 2005; Goldstein et al., 2011).

Thirst

Most biological motives work in ways that are similar to hunger. For example, thirst is only partially controlled by dryness of the mouth. If you were to take a drug that made your mouth constantly wet, or dry, your water intake would remain normal. Like hunger, thirst is regulated by separate *thirst* and *thirst satiety* systems in the hypothalamus. Also like hunger, thirst is strongly affected by learning and cultural values.

You may not have noticed, but there are actually two kinds of thirst (Thornton, 2010). **Extracellular thirst** occurs when water is lost from the fluids surrounding the cells of your body. Bleeding, vomiting, diarrhea, sweating, and drinking alcohol cause this type of thirst (Petri & Govern, 2013). When a person loses both water and minerals in any of these ways—especially by perspiration—a slightly salty liquid may be more satisfying than plain water.

Why would a thirsty person want to drink salty water? The reason is that before the body can retain water, minerals lost through perspiration (mainly salt) must be replaced. In lab tests, animals greatly prefer saltwater after salt levels in their bodies are lowered (Strickler & Verbalis, 1988). Similarly, some nomadic peoples of the Sahara Desert prize blood as a beverage, probably because of its saltiness. (Maybe they should try Gatorade?)

A second type of thirst occurs when you eat a salty meal. In this instance your body does not lose fluid. Instead, excess salt causes fluid to be drawn out of cells. As the cells "shrink," **intracellular thirst** is triggered. Thirst of this type is best quenched by plain water (Thornton, 2010).

The drives for food, water, air, sleep, elimination and (no, we didn't forget about it) sex are all similar in that they are generated by a combination of activities in the body and the brain, and they are influenced by various external factors. However, the sex drive is also a bit different. Let's find out why.

Extracellular thirst Thirst caused by a reduction in the volume of fluids found between body cells.

Intracellular thirst Thirst triggered when fluid is drawn out of cells due to an increased concentration of salts and minerals outside the cell.

Sex—Mapping the Erogenous Zones

JOURNEY QUESTION 9.3 *What are the typical patterns of human sexual response?*

Sex is unlike other biological motives for two reasons. First, sex (contrary to anything your personal experience might suggest) is not necessary for *individual* survival. It is necessary, of course, for *group* survival. Second, the **sex drive**—the strength of one's motivation to engage in sexual behavior—is largely *non-homeostatic* (relatively independent of bodily need states). In humans, the sex drive can be aroused at virtually any time by almost anything. Therefore it shows no clear relationship to deprivation (the amount of time since the drive was last satisfied). Certainly, an increase in desire may occur as time passes. But recent sexual activity does not prevent sexual desire from occurring again. Notice, too, that people may seek to arouse the sex drive as well as to reduce it. This unusual quality makes the sex drive capable of motivating a wide range of behaviors. It also explains why sex is used to sell almost everything imaginable.

In lower animals, the sex drive is directly related to hormones. Female mammals (other than humans) are interested in mating only when their fertility cycles are in the stage of **estrus**, or "heat." Estrus is caused by a release of **estrogen** (a female sex hormone) into the bloodstream. Hormones are important in males as well. In most animals, castration will abolish the sex drive. But in contrast to females, the normal male animal is almost always ready to mate. His sex drive is aroused primarily by the behavior and scent of a receptive female. Therefore, in many species, mating is closely tied to female fertility cycles.

How much do hormones affect human sex drives? Hormones affect the human sex drive, but not as directly as in animals (Rosenthal, 2013). The sex drive in men is related to the amount of **androgens** (male hormones such as testosterone) provided by the testes. When the supply of androgens dramatically increases at puberty, so does the male sex drive. Likewise, the sex drive in women is related to their estrogen levels (Hyde & DeLamater, 2011). However, "male" hormones also affect the female sex drive. In addition to estrogen, a woman's body produces small amounts of androgens. When their androgen levels increase, many women experience a corresponding increase in sex drive. Testosterone levels decline with age, and various medical problems can lower sexual desire. In some instances, taking testosterone supplements can restore the sex drive in both men and women (Rosenthal, 2013).

Does alcohol increase the sex drive? In general, no. Alcohol is a *depressant*. As such, it may, in small doses, stimulate erotic desire by lowering inhibitions. This effect no doubt accounts for alcohol's reputation as an aid to seduction. (Humorist Ogden Nash once summarized this bit of folklore by saying "Candy is dandy, but liquor is quicker.") However, in larger doses, alcohol suppresses orgasm in women and erection in men. Getting drunk *decreases* sexual desire, arousal, pleasure, and performance (McKay, 2005).

Numerous other drugs are reputed to be *aphrodisiacs* (af-ruh-DEEZ-ee-aks: substances that increase sexual desire or pleasure). However, like alcohol, many other drugs actually impair sexual response, rather than enhance it (McKay, 2005). Some examples are amphetamines, amyl nitrite, barbiturates, cocaine, Ecstasy, LSD, and marijuana. In the end, love is the best aphrodisiac (Crooks & Baur, 2011).

Sexual Arousal

Human sexual arousal is complex. It may, of course, be produced by direct stimulation of the body's **erogenous** (eh-ROJ-eh-nus: productive of pleasure or erotic desire) **zones**. Human erogenous zones include the genitals, mouth, breasts, ears, anus, and to a lesser degree, the entire surface of the body. It is clear, however, that more than physical contact is involved: A urological or gynecological exam rarely results in any sexual arousal. Likewise, an unwanted sexual advance may produce only revulsion. Human sexual arousal obviously includes a large mental element.

Are men more easily sexually aroused than women? Overall, women and men have equal potential for sexual arousal, and women are no less *physically* responsive than men. However,

Sex drive The strength of one's motivation to engage in sexual behavior.

Estrus Changes in the sexual drives of animals that create a desire for mating; particularly used to refer to females in heat.

Estrogen Any of a number of female sex hormones.

Androgen Any of a number of male sex hormones, especially testosterone.

Erogenous zones Areas of the body that produce pleasure and/or provoke erotic desire.

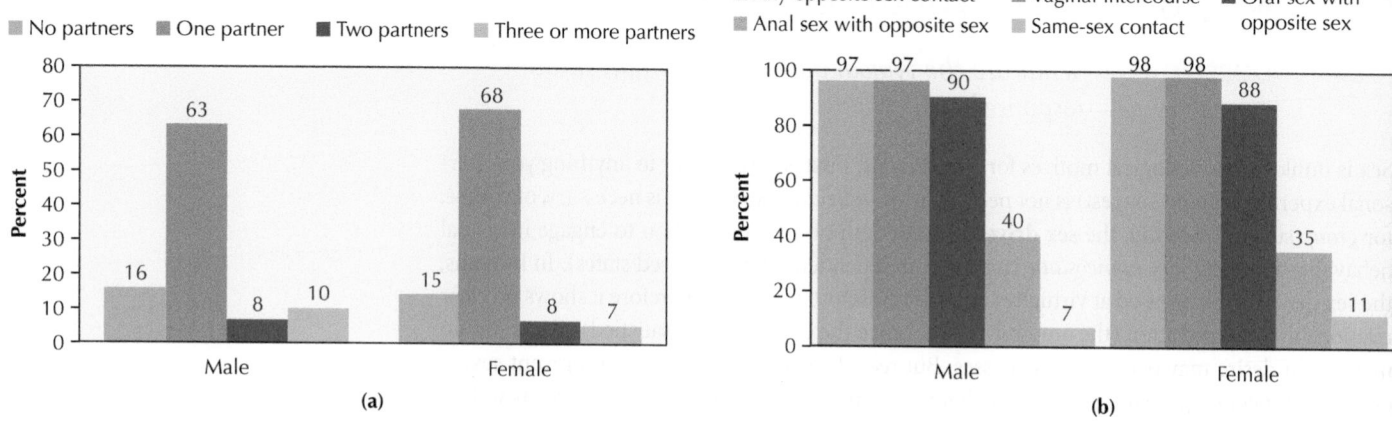

Figure 9.9 These graphs show the pattern of sexual behavior for American adults. *(a)* Men and women do not differ in their average number of sexual partners or *(b)* in their overall pattern of sexual activity. (Adapted from Mosher, Chandra, & Jones, 2005.)

women tend to place more emphasis on emotional closeness with a lover than men do (Basson et al., 2005; Peplau, 2003).

Based on the frequency of orgasm (from masturbation or intercourse), the peak of male sexual activity is at age 18. The peak rate of female sexual activity appears to occur a little later (Janus & Janus, 1993). However, male and female sexual patterns are rapidly becoming more alike. **Figure 9.9** presents some of the data on sexual behavior from a major national health survey of American men and women ages 25 to 44. As you can see, in any given year men and women do not differ in their average number of opposite-sex partners or in their overall pattern of sexual activity (Mosher, Chandra, & Jones, 2005). Exaggerating the differences between male and female sexuality is not only inaccurate; it can also create artificial barriers to sexual satisfaction (Wiederman, 2001). For example, assuming that men should always initiate sex denies the fact that women have comparable sexual interests and needs.

Human Sexual Response

The pioneering work of gynecologist William Masters and psychologist Virginia Johnson greatly expanded our understanding of sexual response (Masters & Johnson, 1966, 1970). In a series of experiments, interviews, and controlled observations, Masters and Johnson directly studied sexual intercourse and masturbation in nearly 700 males and females. This objective information has given us a much clearer picture of human sexuality.

According to Masters and Johnson, sexual response can be divided into four phases: (1) *excitement*, (2) *plateau*, (3) *orgasm*, and (4) *resolution* (**Figures 9.10** and **9.11**). These four phases, which are the same for people of all sexual orientations (Carroll, 2013; Garnets & Kimmel, 1991), can be described as follows:

Excitement phase: The first level of sexual response, indicated by initial signs of sexual arousal.

Plateau phase: The second level of sexual response, during which physical arousal intensifies.

Orgasm: A climax and release of sexual excitement.

Resolution: The final phase of sexual response, involving a return to lower levels of sexual tension and arousal.

Excitement phase The first phase of sexual response, indicated by initial signs of sexual arousal.

Plateau phase The second phase of sexual response, during which physical arousal is further heightened.

Orgasm The third phase of sexual response; a climax and release of sexual excitement.

Resolution The fourth phase of sexual response, involving a return to lower levels of sexual tension and arousal.

Female Response

In women, the excitement phase is marked by a complex pattern of changes in the body. The vagina is prepared for intercourse, the nipples become erect, pulse rate rises, and the skin may become flushed or reddened. If sexual stimulation ends, the excitement phase will gradually subside. If a woman moves into the plateau phase, physical changes and subjective feelings of arousal become more intense. Sexual arousal that ends during this phase tends to ebb more slowly, which may produce considerable frustration. Occasionally, women skip the plateau phase. (See Figure 9.10.) For some women, this is almost always the case. Orgasm is usually followed by resolution, a return to lower levels of sexual tension and arousal. After orgasm, about 15 percent of all women return to the plateau phase and may have one or more additional orgasms (Mah & Binik, 2001).

Male Response

Sexual arousal in the male is signaled by erection of the penis during the excitement phase. A rise in heart rate, increased blood flow to the genitals, enlargement of the testicles, erection of the nipples, and numerous other body changes also occur. As is true of female sexual response, continued stimulation moves the male into the plateau phase. Again, physical changes and subjective feelings of arousal become more intense. Further stimulation during the plateau phase brings about a reflex release of sexual tension, resulting in orgasm.

In the mature male, orgasm is usually accompanied by *ejaculation* (release of sperm and seminal fluid). Afterward, it is followed by a short *refractory period*, during which a second orgasm is impossible. (Many men cannot even have an erection until the refractory phase has passed.) Only rarely is the male refractory period immediately followed by a second orgasm. Both orgasm and resolution in the male usually do not last as long as they do for females.

Comparing Male and Female Responses

Although male and female sexual responses are generally quite similar, the differences that do exist can affect sexual compatibility. For example, women typically go through the sexual phases more slowly than do men. However, during masturbation, 70 percent of females reach orgasm in 4 minutes or less. This is quite comparable to male response times. It suggests again that women are no less physically responsive than men.

In one regard, women are clearly more responsive. Only about 5 percent of males are capable of multiple orgasm (and then only after an unavoidable refractory period). Most men are limited to a second orgasm at best. In contrast, Masters and Johnson's findings suggest that most women who regularly experience orgasm are capable of multiple orgasm. According to one survey, 48 percent of all women have had multiple orgasms (Darling, Davidson, & Passarello, 1992). Remember though, that only about 15 percent regularly have multiple orgasms. A woman should not automatically assume that something is wrong if she isn't orgasmic or multiorgasmic. Many women have satisfying sexual experiences even when orgasm is not involved (Komisaruk, Beyer-Flores, & Whipple, 2006; Zietsch et al., 2011).

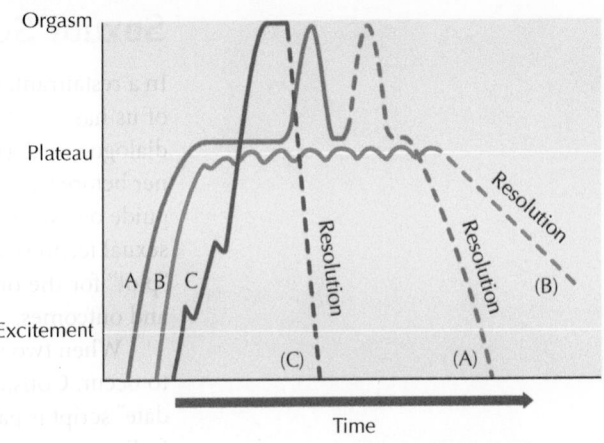

Figure 9.10 Female sexual response cycle. The green line shows that sexual arousal rises through the excitement phase and levels off for a time during the plateau phase. Arousal peaks during orgasm and then returns to pre-excitement levels. In pattern A, arousal rises from excitement through the plateau phase and peaks in orgasm. Resolution may be immediate, or it may first include a return to the plateau phase and a second orgasm (dotted line). In pattern B, arousal is sustained at the plateau phase and slowly resolved without sexual climax. Pattern C shows a fairly rapid rise in arousal to orgasm. Little time is spent in the plateau phase, and resolution is fairly rapid. (Adapted from W. Masters, V. Johnson, R. Kolodny, *Heterosexuality*, pp. 51–52. Copyright 1994 by William H. Masters, Virginia E. Johnson, and Robert E. Kolodny. Reprinted by permission of HarperCollins Publishers, Inc.

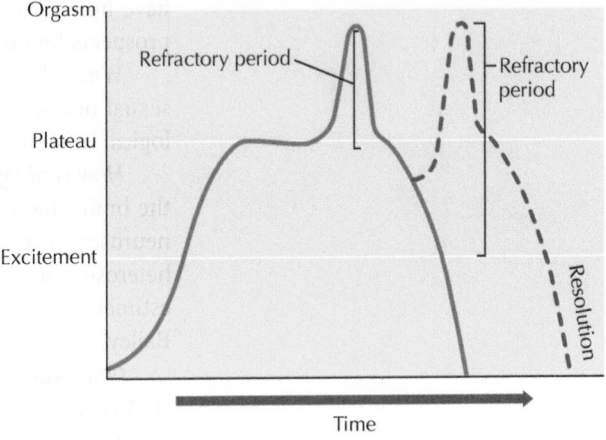

Figure 9.11 Male sexual response cycle. The green line shows that sexual arousal rises through the excitement phase and levels off for a time during the plateau phase. Arousal peaks during orgasm and then returns to pre-excitement levels. During the refractory period, immediately after orgasm, a second sexual climax is typically impossible. However, after the refractory period has passed, there may be a return to the plateau phase, followed by a second orgasm (dotted line). (Adapted from W. Masters, V. Johnson, R. Kolodny, *Heterosexuality*, pp. 51–52. Copyright 1994 by William H. Masters, Virginia E. Johnson, and Robert E. Kolodny. Reprinted by permission of HarperCollins Publishers, Inc.

Sexual Scripts

In a restaurant, we commonly expect certain things to occur. It could even be said that each of us has a restaurant "script" that defines a plot (eating dinner outside of the home), the dialogue (ordering from the menu), and actions that should take place (paying for the dinner before leaving). We also learn a variety of **sexual scripts**, or unspoken mental plans that guide our sexual behavior. Such scripts determine when and where we are likely to express sexual feelings, and with whom (Lenton & Bryan, 2005; McCormick, 2010). They provide a "plot" for the order of events in lovemaking and they outline "approved" actions, motives, and outcomes.

When two people follow markedly different scripts, misunderstandings are almost sure to occur. Consider, for instance, what happens when a woman acting out a "romantic first date" script is paired with a man following a "hook-up" script: The result is often anger, hurt feelings, or worse (Schleicher & Gilbert, 2005). Even newlyweds may find that their sexual "agendas" differ. In such cases, considerable "rewriting" of scripts is often needed for sexual compatibility. For humans the mind (or brain) is the ultimate erogenous zone. (To read more about contemporary sexual scripts, see "What's Love Got to Do with It?")

Sexual Orientation—Who Do You Love?

Another aspect of sexuality is **sexual orientation**, your degree of emotional and erotic attraction to members of the same sex, opposite sex, or both sexes. *Heterosexuals* are romantically and erotically attracted to members of the opposite sex. *Homosexuals* are attracted to people whose sex matches their own. *Bisexuals* are attracted to both men and women. *Asexuals* are attracted to neither.

Sexual orientation is a deep part of personal identity and is usually quite stable. Starting with their earliest erotic feelings, most people remember being attracted to either the opposite sex or the same sex. The chances are practically nil of an exclusively heterosexual or homosexual person being "converted" from one orientation to the other (Glassgold et al., 2009). If you are heterosexual, you are probably certain that nothing could ever make you have homoerotic feelings. If so, then you know how homosexual persons feel about the prospects for changing *their* sexual orientation.

What determines a person's sexual orientation? The available evidence suggests that sexual orientation is mainly genetic and hormonal, although social, cultural, and psychological influences are also involved (LeVay, 2011; LeVay & Baldwin, 2008).

How could genes and biology affect sexual orientation? Possibly, heredity shapes areas of the brain that orchestrate sexual behavior. Support for this idea comes from the work of neuroscientists who have shown that various brain structures and brain chemicals differ in heterosexuals and homosexuals (Balthazart, 2012; Kinnunen et al., 2004). Some researchers estimate that sexual orientation is from 30 to 70 percent genetic (Mustanski, Chivers, & Bailey, 2002).

One popular theory holds that prenatal hormone levels influence the developing fetus (LeVay, 2011). According to the *prenatal hormonal theory of homosexuality*, some male fetuses are exposed to too little testosterone. Similarly, some female fetuses are exposed to too much testosterone. These differences, in turn, can impact sexual orientation (Balthazart, 2012). Regardless, homosexuality is not caused by hormone imbalances in adulthood; the hormone levels of most gay men and lesbians are within the normal range (Banks & Gartrell, 1995).

Consistent with the genetic and biological view of sexual orientation, it is unlikely that parenting makes children homosexual. There is little difference in the development of children with gay or lesbian parents and those who have heterosexual parents (Patterson, 2002; Wainwright, Russell, & Patterson, 2004).

It appears that nature strongly prepares people to be either homosexual or heterosexual. In view of this, discriminating against homosexuals is much like rejecting a person for being blue-eyed or left-handed (Rathus, Nevid, & Fichner-Rathus, 2010). Homosexual people are found in all walks of life, at all social and economic levels, and in all cultural groups. More than 10 million people in the United States alone are gay, lesbian, or bisexual

Sexual script An unspoken mental plan that defines a "plot," dialogue, and actions expected to take place in a sexual encounter.

Sexual orientation One's degree of emotional and erotic attraction to members of the same sex, opposite sex, both sexes, or neither sex.

Younger Americans are shifting toward scripts favoring casual sex (Hughes, Morrison, & Asada, 2005; Wentland & Reissing, 2011). One such script includes sex in a friendship, without traditional romance. According to one survey, more than half of all college students have been *friends with benefits* (friends who have sex but aren't romantically involved) (Puentes, Knox, & Zusman, 2008). Even more casual is the *hook-up* script, in which two people having sex are more or less strangers (Bradshaw, Kahn, & Saville, 2010; Holman & Sillars, 2012). (Seek pleasure first, ask questions later?) In contrast, traditional sexual scripts stress courtship, romance, and marriage. Sex in such relationships might be premarital, but it is still romantic (Roese et al., 2006).

As casual sexual scripts become more common, the traditional focus on intercourse is fading in favor of oral sex, which tends to be seen as less risky, more acceptable, and "not a big deal." Casual sexual scripts are also spreading to younger children. One study found that 20 percent of American ninth graders have already had oral sex and more than 30 percent intend to try it soon (Halpern-Felsher et al., 2005).

Casual sex is often viewed as easier than facing the challenges of romantic attachment and finding a lifelong partner. However, it is not without its own risks. Casual sex is usually associated with alcohol use and unsafe sexual behaviors, such as unprotected sex (Fortunato et al., 2010; Grello, Welsh, & Harper, 2006). Although oral sex is safer than intercourse, a significant chance of getting a sexually transmitted disease remains (Boskey, 2011). Another downside of casual sex is the letdown that can occur when one person follows a romantic script and the other follows a casual script ("He [or she] is just not that into you"). For example, young women who are having casual sex are more likely to be depressed (Grello, Welsh, & Harper, 2006).

Adolescents and young adults have always engaged in experimentation and exploration. Most young people emerge unscathed from their explorations if they clearly understand that their encounters are casual and practice safe sex. Most eventually also "graduate" to a more traditional search for love.

(Conron, Mimiaga, & Landers, 2010). Perhaps as more people come to see gay and lesbian people in terms of their humanity, rather than their sexuality, the prejudices they have faced will wane.

Healthy Sexual Relationships

Regardless of sexual responsiveness or sexual orientation, as a shared pleasure, a form of intimacy, a means of communication, and a haven from everyday tensions, a positive sexual relationship can do much to enhance a couple's mutual understanding and caring. People are most likely to value their sexuality when they put some effort into developing a respectful, trusting, and intimate relationship with their partner (Strong, DeVault, & Cohen, 2011). A sense of closeness and intimacy with one's partner helps maintain sexual desire, especially in long-term relationships (Impett et al., 2008, 2010; McCarthy & Fucito, 2005).

Sexual Problems—When Pleasure Fades

Even the best-intentioned people may nevertheless experience sexual dysfunction, which is far more common than many people realize. Most people who seek sexual counseling have one or more of the following types of problems (Crooks & Baur, 2011; American Psychiatric Association, 2000, 2012):

Desire Disorders: The person has little or no sexual motivation or desire.

Arousal Disorders: The person desires sexual activity but does not become sexually aroused.

Orgasm Disorders: The person does not have orgasms or experiences orgasm too soon or too late.

Sexual Pain Disorders: The person experiences pain that makes lovemaking uncomfortable or impossible.

There was a time when people suffered such problems in silence. However, in recent years, effective treatments have been found for many complaints (Carroll, 2013). Medical treatments or drugs (such as Viagra for men) may be helpful for sexual problems that clearly have physical causes. In other cases, counseling or psychotherapy may be the best approach.

For example, many patients benefit from a technique called *sensate focus*. In sensate focus, distressed couples begin by taking turns caressing each other in nonsexual ways.

They are told to concentrate on giving pleasure and on signaling what feels good to them. This relieves the pressure to perform and builds communication skills. Slowly, the couple moves on to mutually satisfying lovemaking, as natural arousal begins to replace fear and anger. Similar solutions exist for many sexual problems. In most communities, professional help can be obtained from appropriately trained psychologists, physicians, or counselors (Rosenthal, 2013).

 study break Hunger, Thirst, and Sex

RECITE

1. The hunger satiety system in the hypothalamus signals the body to start eating when it receives signals from the liver or detects changes in blood sugar. T or F?
2. People who diet frequently tend to benefit from practice: They lose weight more quickly each time they diet. T or F?
3. Bulimia nervosa is also known as the binge–purge syndrome. T or F?
4. In addition to burning calories, physical exercise can lower the body's set point for fat. T or F?
5. Thirst may be either intracellular or _____.
6. Sexual behavior in animals is largely controlled by estrogen levels in the female and the occurrence of estrus in the male. T or F?
7. List the four phases of sexual response identified by Masters and Johnson:

   _____, _____, _____, _____.

REFLECT

THINK CRITICALLY

8. Kim, who is overweight, is highly sensitive to external eating cues. How might her wristwatch contribute to her overeating?

SELF-REFLECT

How sensitive are you to external eating cues? How were you influenced by portion size?

A friend of yours seems to be engaging in yo-yo dieting. Can you tell your friend why such dieting is ineffective and summarize how behavioral dieting is done?

In what ways are sexual responses of members of the opposite sex similar to your own? In what ways are they different?

ANSWERS

1. F 2. F 3. T 4. F 5. extracellular 6. F 7. excitement, plateau, orgasm, resolution 8. The time of day can influence eating, especially for externally cued eaters, who tend to get hungry at mealtimes, irrespective of their internal needs for food.

Stimulus Motives—Monkey Business

JOURNEY QUESTION 9.4 *How does arousal relate to motivation?*

Are you full of energy right now? Or are you tired? Clearly, the level of arousal you are experiencing is closely linked with your motivation. Are there ideal levels of arousal for different people and different activities? Let's find out.

Most people enjoy a steady "diet" of new movies, novels, music, fashions, games, news, websites, and adventures. Yet as we noted earlier, *stimulus motives*, which reflect needs for information, exploration, manipulation, and sensory input, go beyond mere entertainment. Stimulus motives also help us survive. As we scan our surroundings, we constantly identify sources of food, danger, shelter, and other key details. The drive for stimulation is already present during infancy. By the time a child can walk, there are few things in the home that have not been tasted, touched, viewed, handled, or, in the case of toys, destroyed!

Stimulus motives are readily apparent in animals as well as humans. For example, monkeys will quickly learn to solve a mechanical puzzle made up of interlocking metal pins, hooks, and latches (Butler, 1954) (**Figure 9.12**). No food treats or other external rewards are needed to get them to explore and manipulate their surroundings. The monkeys seem to work for the sheer fun of it.

Arousal Theory

Are stimulus motives homeostatic? Yes. According to **arousal theory**, we try to keep arousal at an optimal level (Hancock & Ganey, 2003; Petri & Govern, 2013). In other words, when your level of arousal is too low or too high, you will seek ways to raise or lower it.

What do you mean by arousal? Arousal refers to activation of the body and nervous system. Arousal is zero at death, low during sleep, moderate during normal daily activities, and high at times of excitement, emotion, or panic. Arousal theory assumes that we become uncomfortable when arousal is too low ("I'm bored") or when it is too high, as in fear, anxiety, or panic ("The dentist will see you now"). Most adults vary music, parties, sports, conversation, sleep, surfing the Web, and the like to keep arousal at moderate levels. The right mix of activities prevents boredom *and* overstimulation (Csikszentmihalyi, Abuhamdeh, & Nakamura, 2005).

Courtesy Harry F. Harlow.

Figure 9.12 Monkeys happily open locks that are placed in their cage. Because no reward is given for this activity, it provides evidence for the existence of stimulus needs.

Sensation Seekers

Do people vary in their needs for stimulation? Arousal theory also suggests that people learn to seek particular levels of arousal (Lynne-Landsman et al., 2011). Where would you prefer to go on your next summer vacation? Your backyard? How about a week with your best friends at a cottage on a nearby lake? Or a shopping and museum trip to New York City? Better yet, how about diving with sharks? If the shark adventure attracts you, you are probably high in sensation seeking and would be interested in a vacation that includes activities like bungee-jumping, scuba diving, skiing, skydiving, and white-water rafting (Pizam et al., 2004).

Sensation seeking is a trait of people who prefer high levels of stimulation (Gray & Wilson, 2007). Whether you are high or low in sensation seeking is probably based on how your body responds to new, unusual, or intense stimulation (Harden, Quinn, & Tucker-Drob, 2012; Zuckerman, 2002). People high in sensation seeking tend to be bold, independent, and value change. They also report more sexual partners, are more likely to smoke, and prefer spicy, sour, and crunchy foods over bland foods. Low sensation seekers are orderly, nurturant, and giving, and enjoy the company of others.

Exciting lives aside, there is a dark side to sensation seeking (Dunlop & Romer, 2010). High sensation seekers are more likely to engage in high-risk behaviors such as substance abuse and casual unprotected sex (Gullette & Lyons, 2005; Harden, Quinn, & Tucker-Drob, 2012; Horvath et al., 2004).

Levels of Arousal

Is there an ideal level of arousal for peak performance? If we set aside individual differences, most people perform best when their arousal level is *moderate*. Let's say that you have to take an essay exam. If you are feeling sleepy or lazy (arousal level too low), your performance will suffer. If you are in a state of anxiety or panic about the test (arousal level too high), you will also perform below par. Thus, the relationship between arousal and performance forms an *inverted U function* (a curve in the shape of an upside-down U; Figure 9.13) (Petri & Govern, 2013).

The inverted U tells us that at very low levels of arousal, you're not sufficiently energized to perform well. Performance will improve as your arousal level increases, up to the middle of the curve. Then it begins to drop off as you become emotional, frenzied, or disorganized. For example, imagine trying to start a car stalled on a railroad track, with a speeding train bearing down on you. That's what the high-arousal end of the curve feels like.

Is performance always best at moderate levels of arousal? No, the ideal level of arousal depends on the complexity of a task. If a task is relatively simple, it is best for arousal to be high. When a task is more complex, your best performance will occur at lower levels of arousal. This relationship is called the **Yerkes-Dodson law**. (See Figure 9.13.) It applies to a wide variety of tasks and to measures of motivation other than arousal.

For example, at a track meet it is almost impossible for sprinters to get too aroused for a race. The task is direct and simple: Run as fast as you can for a short distance. On the other hand, a

F. Schneider/DPA/Landow

Sensation seeking is a trait of people who prefer high levels of stimulation.

Arousal theory Assumes that people prefer to maintain ideal, or comfortable, levels of arousal.

Yerkes-Dodson law A summary of the relationships among arousal, task complexity, and performance.

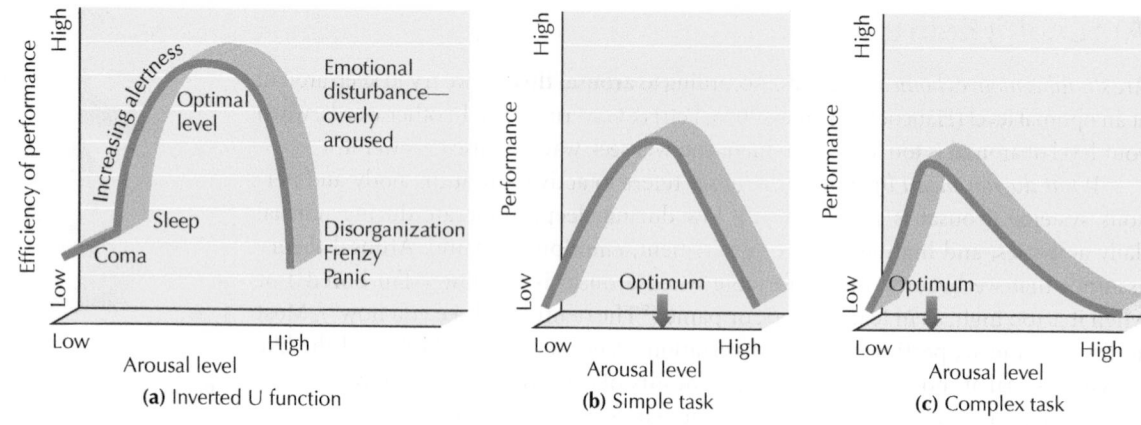

(a) Inverted U function

(b) Simple task

(c) Complex task

Figure 9.13 (a) The general relationship between arousal and efficiency can be described by an inverted U curve. The optimal level of arousal or motivation is higher for a simple task (b) than for a complex task (c).

golfer making a tournament-deciding putt faces a more sensitive and complex task. Excessive arousal is almost certain to hurt his or her performance. In school, most students have had experience with "test anxiety," a familiar example of how too much arousal can lower performance.

Coping with Test Anxiety

Then is it true that by learning to calm down, a person would do better on tests? Usually, but not always. To begin with, some arousal is healthy; it focuses us on the task at hand. It is only when arousal interferes with performance that we refer to anxiety. **Test anxiety** is a mixture of *heightened physiological arousal* (nervousness, sweating, pounding heart) and *excessive worry*. This combination—arousal plus worry—tends to distract students with a rush of upsetting thoughts and feelings (Conley & Lehman, 2012; Eysenck et al., 2007). Here are some suggestions for coping with test anxiety.

Preparation

Hard work is the most direct antidote for test anxiety. Many test-anxious students simply study too little, too late. That's why improving your study skills is a good way to reduce test anxiety (Cassady, 2004). If test anxiety is a problem for you, it would be wise to return to the Introduction in this book and review the learning and test-taking skills described there. The best solution is to *overprepare* by studying long before the "big day." Well-prepared students score higher, worry less, and are less likely to panic (Kaplan, 2008; Santrock & Halonen, 2013).

Relaxation

Learning to relax is another way to lower test anxiety (Bradley et al., 2010; Powell, 2004). You can learn self-relaxation skills by looking at Chapter 11, where a relaxation technique is described. Emotional support also helps (Stöber, 2004). If you are test anxious, discuss the problem with your professors or study for tests with a supportive classmate.

Rehearsal

To reduce nervousness, rehearse how you will cope with upsetting events. Before taking a test, imagine yourself going blank, running out of time, or feeling panicked. Then calmly plan how you will handle each situation—by keeping your attention on the task, by focusing on one question at a time, and so forth (Watson & Tharp, 2007).

Restructuring Thoughts

Another helpful strategy involves listing the upsetting thoughts you have during exams. Then you can learn to combat these worries with calming, rational replies (Jones & Petruzzi, 1995; Olpin & Hesson, 2010). (These are called *coping statements*; see Chapter 11 for more

Test anxiety High levels of arousal and worry that seriously impair test performance.

information.) Let's say you think, "I'm going to fail this test and everybody will think I'm stupid." A good reply to this upsetting thought would be to say, "If I prepare well and control my worries, I will probably pass the test. Even if I don't, it won't be the end of the world. My friends will still like me, and I can try to improve on the next test."

Students who cope well with exams usually try to do the best they can, even under difficult circumstances. Becoming a more confident test taker can actually increase your scores because it helps you remain calm. With practice, most people can learn to be less testy at test-taking time.

Learned Motives—The Pursuit of Excellence

JOURNEY QUESTION 9.5 *What are learned and social motives and why are they important?*

Some of your friends are more interested than others in success, achievement, competition, money, possessions, status, love, approval, grades, dominance, power, or belonging to groups—all of which are **social motives** or goals. We acquire social motives in complex ways, through socialization and cultural conditioning (Deckers, 2010). The behavior of outstanding artists, scientists, athletes, educators, and leaders is best understood in terms of such learned needs, particularly the need for achievement.

The Need for Achievement

To many people, being "motivated" means, like Lady Gaga, being interested in achievement (Petri & Govern, 2013; Wigfield & Eccles, 2002). In a later chapter, we will investigate aggression, helping, affiliation, seeking approval, and other social motives. For now, let's focus on the **need for achievement (nAch)**, which is a desire to meet an internal standard of excellence (McClelland, 1961). People with a high need for achievement strive to do well any time they are evaluated (Steinmayr & Spinath, 2009).

Is that like the aggressive businessperson who strives for success? Not necessarily. Needs for achievement may lead to wealth and prestige, but people who are high achievers in art, music, science, or amateur sports may excel without seeking riches. Such people typically enjoy challenges and relish a chance to test their abilities. (See "True Grit" for more information about the characteristics of people high in achievement motivation.)

Power

The need for achievement differs from the **need for power**, which is a desire to have impact or control over others (McClelland, 1975; Wirth, Welsh, & Schultheiss, 2006). People with strong needs for power want their importance to be visible: They buy expensive possessions, wear prestigious clothes, and exploit relationships. In some ways the pursuit of power and financial success is the dark side of the American dream. People whose main goal in life is to make lots of money tend to be poorly adjusted and unhappy (Kasser & Ryan, 1993).

Motives in Perspective—A View from the Pyramid

JOURNEY QUESTION 9.6 *Are some motives more basic than others?*

Are all motives equally important? Abraham Maslow proposed a **hierarchy of human needs**, in which some needs are more basic or powerful than others. (As you may recall from Chapter 1, Maslow called the full use of personal potential *self-actualization*.)

Social motives Learned motives acquired as part of growing up in a particular society or culture.

Need for achievement (nAch) The desire to excel or meet some internalized standard of excellence.

Need for power The desire to have social impact and control over others.

Hierarchy of human needs Abraham Maslow's ordering of needs, based on their presumed strength or potency.

Discovering Psychology

So you want to be a success. To best achieve your goals, would it be better to be naturally talented or determined? (Yes, we know you would definitely prefer to have it *both* ways. So would we.) It probably will not surprise you to learn that, in general, drive and determination, not great natural talent, lead to exceptional success (Duckworth et al., 2007). Elite performance in music, sports, chess, the arts, and many other pursuits requires at least 10 years of dedicated practice (Ericsson & Charness, 1994; Ross, 2006). The old belief that "talent will surface" on its own is largely a myth.

How can this be? When people high in need for achievement (nAch) tackle a task, they do so with perseverance, passion, and self-confidence (Duckworth et al., 2007; Munroe-Chandler, Hall, & Fishburne, 2008). They tend to complete difficult tasks, they earn better grades, and they tend to excel in their occupations. College students high in nAch attribute success to their own ability, and failure to insufficient effort. Thus, high nAch students are more likely to renew their efforts when they perform poorly. When the going gets tough, high achievers get going.

You may be able to improve your achievement motivation by increasing your self-confidence (Hanton, Mellalieu, & Hall, 2004). It is easier to perform an activity or reach a goal with perseverance and passion when you believe you can be successful. When you tackle an important task, how many of the items on the following list can you check off? To enhance self-confidence, you would be wise to do as many as possible (Druckman & Bjork, 1994; Munroe-Chandler, Hall, & Fishburne, 2008):

- Set goals that are specific and challenging but attainable.
- Visualize the steps you need to take to reach your goal.
- Advance in small steps.
- When you first acquire a skill, your goal should be to make progress in learning. Later, you can concentrate on improving your performance compared with other people.
- Get expert instruction that helps you master the skill.
- Find a skilled model (someone good at the skill) to emulate.
- Get support and encouragement from an observer.
- If you fail, regard it as a sign that you need to try harder, not that you lack ability.

Self-confidence affects motivation by influencing the challenges you will undertake, the effort you will make, and how long you will persist when things don't go well. You can be confident that self-confidence is worth cultivating.

The Williams sisters possess high achievement motivation. They have become professional tennis champions by playing with perseverance, passion, and self-confidence.

Wheelchair athletes engage in vigorous competition. Maslow considered such behavior an expression of the need for self-actualization.

Basic needs The first four levels of needs in Maslow's hierarchy; lower needs tend to be more potent than higher needs.

Growth needs In Maslow's hierarchy, the higher-level needs associated with self-actualization.

Meta-needs In Maslow's hierarchy, needs associated with impulses for self-actualization.

Think about the needs that influence your own behavior. Which seem strongest? Which do you spend the most time and energy satisfying? Now look at Maslow's hierarchy (**Figure 9.14**).

Note that biological needs are at the base of the pyramid. Because these needs must be met if we are to survive, they tend to be *prepotent*, or dominant over the higher needs. Maslow believed that higher, more fragile needs are expressed only after we satisfy our biological needs. That's why, when you are really hungry, you can think of little else but food. This is also true of needs for safety and security. Until they are met, we may have little interest in higher pursuits. For instance, a person who is feeling threatened might have little interest in writing poetry or even talking with friends. For this reason, Maslow described the first four levels of the hierarchy as **basic needs**. Other basic needs are for love and belonging (family, friendship, caring) and esteem and self-esteem (recognition and self-respect).

All the basic needs are *deficiency* motives. That is, they are activated by a *lack* of food, water, security, love, esteem, or other basic needs. At the top of the hierarchy we find **growth needs**, which are expressed as a need for self-actualization. The need for self-actualization is not based on deficiencies. Rather, it is a positive, life-enhancing force for personal growth (Reiss & Havercamp, 2005). Like other humanistic psychologists, Maslow believed that people are basically good. If our basic needs are met, he said, we will tend to move on to actualizing our potentials (Tay & Diener, 2011).

How are needs for self-actualization expressed? Maslow also called the less powerful but humanly important actualization motives meta-needs (Maslow, 1970). **Meta-needs** are an

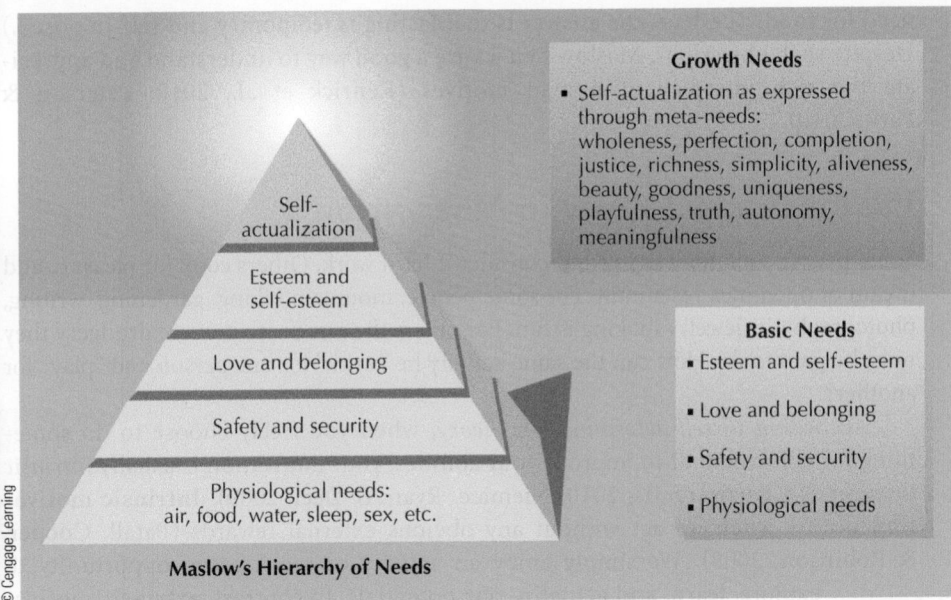

Maslow's Hierarchy of Needs

Growth Needs
- Self-actualization as expressed through meta-needs: wholeness, perfection, completion, justice, richness, simplicity, aliveness, beauty, goodness, uniqueness, playfulness, truth, autonomy, meaningfulness

Basic Needs
- Esteem and self-esteem
- Love and belonging
- Safety and security
- Physiological needs

Figure 9.14 Maslow believed that lower needs in the hierarchy are dominant. Basic needs must be satisfied before growth motives are fully expressed. Desires for self-actualization are reflected in various meta-needs (see Table 9.2).

expression of tendencies to fully develop your personal potentials (Table 9.2). According to Maslow, we tend to move up through the hierarchy of needs toward the meta-needs. When the meta-needs are unfulfilled, people fall into a "syndrome of decay" marked by despair, apathy, and alienation. Maslow's point is that mere survival or comfort is usually not enough to make a full and satisfying life. It's interesting to note, in this regard, that college students who are concerned primarily with money, personal appearance, and social recognition score lower than average in vitality, self-actualization, and general well-being (Kasser & Ryan, 1996; Nickerson, Diener, & Schwarz, 2011).

Maslow's hierarchy is not well documented by research, and parts of it are questionable. How, for instance, do we explain the actions of a person who fasts as part of a social protest? How can the meta-need for justice overcome the more basic

Table 9.2 Maslow's Meta-Needs

1. Wholeness (unity)
2. Perfection (balance and harmony)
3. Completion (ending)
4. Justice (fairness)
5. Richness (complexity)
6. Simplicity (essence)
7. Aliveness (spontaneity)
8. Beauty (rightness of form)
9. Goodness (benevolence)
10. Uniqueness (individuality)
11. Playfulness (ease)
12. Truth (reality)
13. Autonomy (self-sufficiency)
14. Meaningfulness (values)

Adapted from Maslow, 1970.

© Cengage Learning

need for food? (Perhaps the answer is that fasting is temporary and self-imposed.) Despite such objections, Maslow's views are a good way to understand and appreciate the rich interplay of human motives (Kenrick et al., 2010; Peterson & Park, 2010).

Intrinsic and Extrinsic Motivation

Some people cook for a living and consider it hard work. Others cook for pleasure and dream of opening a restaurant. For some people, mountain biking, gardening, writing, photography, or jewelry making is fun. For others the same activities are drudgery they must be paid to do. How can the same activity be "work" for one person and "play" for another?

According to *self-determination theory*, when you freely choose to do something for enjoyment or to improve your abilities, your motivation is usually *intrinsic* (Hagger & Chatzisarantis, 2010; Niemiec, Ryan, & Deci, 2009). **Intrinsic motivation** occurs when we act without any obvious external rewards (Patall, Cooper, & Robinson, 2008). We simply enjoy an activity or see it as an opportunity to explore, learn, and actualize our potentials. In contrast, **extrinsic motivation** stems from external factors, such as pay, grades, rewards, obligations, and approval. Most of the activities we think of as "work" are extrinsically rewarded (Baard, Deci, & Ryan, 2004).

Turning Play into Work

Don't extrinsic incentives strengthen motivation? Yes, they can, but not always. In fact, *excessive* rewards can decrease intrinsic motivation and spontaneous interest. For instance, in one classic study, children who were lavishly rewarded for drawing with felt-tip pens later showed little interest in playing with the pens again (Greene & Lepper, 1974). Apparently, "play" can be turned into "work" by *requiring* people to do something they would otherwise enjoy (Patall, Cooper, & Robinson, 2008). When we are coerced or "bribed" to act, we tend to feel as if we are "faking it." Employees who lack initiative and teenagers who reject school and learning are good examples of those who have such a reaction (Niemiec, Ryan, & Deci, 2009).

People who are intrinsically motivated feel free to explore creative solutions to problems. *(top)* The late Steve Jobs, one of the founders of Apple, and one of his many innovative products. *(bottom)* "Extreme Makeover," an entrant in The Great Arcata to Ferndale World Championship Cross Country Kinetic Sculpture Race.

Creativity

People are more likely to be creative when they are intrinsically motivated. At work, it is valuable for managers to find out what each employee's interests and career goals are. Although salaries and bonuses may increase the amount of work done, people are not motivated solely by money. A chance to do challenging, interesting, and intrinsically rewarding work is often just as important. Work *quality* is affected more by intrinsic factors, such as personal interest and freedom of choice (Nakamura & Csikszentmihalyi, 2003). When a person is intrinsically motivated, a certain amount of challenge, surprise, and complexity makes a task rewarding. When extrinsic motivation is stressed, people are less likely to solve tricky problems and come up with innovative ideas (Amabile, Hadley, & Kramer, 2002; Hennessey & Amabile, 2010).

Should extrinsic motivation always be avoided? No, but extrinsic motivation shouldn't be overused, especially with children. In general, (1) if there's no intrinsic interest in an activity to begin with, you have nothing to lose by using extrinsic rewards; (2) if basic skills are lacking, extrinsic rewards may be necessary at first; (3) extrinsic rewards can focus attention on an activity so that real interest will develop; and (4) if extrinsic rewards are used, they should be small and phased out as soon as possible (Buckworth et al., 2007; Cameron & Pierce, 2002).

Intrinsic motivation Motivation that comes from within, rather than from external rewards; motivation based on personal enjoyment of a task or activity.

Extrinsic motivation Motivation based on obvious external rewards, obligations, or similar factors.

RECITE

1. Exploration, manipulation, and curiosity provide evidence for the existence of _____ motives.
2. Sensation seekers tend to be extroverted, independent, and individuals who value change. T or F?
3. Two key elements of test anxiety that must be controlled are _____ and excessive _____.
4. People high in nAch show high levels of perseverance, passion, and _____.

   a. control
   b. intelligence
   c. self-confidence
   d. sensation seeking

5. According to Maslow, meta-needs are the most basic and prepotent sources of human motivation. T or F?
6. Intrinsic motivation is often undermined in situations in which obvious external rewards are applied to a naturally enjoyable activity. T or F?

REFLECT

THINK CRITICALLY

7. Many U.S. college freshmen say that "being well-off financially" is an essential life goal and that "making more money" was a very important factor in their decision to attend college. Which meta-needs are fulfilled by "making more money"?

SELF-REFLECT

Does arousal theory seem to explain any of your own behavior? Think of at least one time when your performance was impaired by arousal that was too low or too high.

   Are you high or low in your need for stimulation?
   Which levels of Maslow's hierarchy of needs occupy most of your time and energy?
   Name an activity you do that is intrinsically motivated and one that is extrinsically motivated. How do they differ?

ANSWERS

1. stimulus 2. T 3. arousal, worry 4. c 5. F 6. T 7. None of them.

Inside an Emotion—Caught in That Feeling?

JOURNEY QUESTION 9.7 *What happens during emotion?*

Picture the faces of terrified people fleeing a tornado in the Midwest and it's easy to see that motivation and emotion are closely related. As mentioned earlier, the word *emotion* also derives from the Latin word meaning "to move." **Emotion** is characterized by physiological arousal and changes in facial expressions, gestures, posture, and subjective feelings.

What "moves" during an emotion? First of all, your body is physically aroused during emotion. Such bodily stirrings are what cause us to say we were "moved" by a play, a funeral, or an act of kindness. Second, we are often motivated, or moved to take action, by emotions. Many of the goals we seek make us feel good. Many of the activities we avoid make us feel bad. We feel happy when we succeed and sad when we fail (Kalat & Shiota, 2012).

Emotions are linked to many basic **adaptive behaviors**, such as attacking, fleeing, seeking comfort, helping others, and reproducing. Such behaviors help us survive and adjust to changing conditions (Freberg, 2010). However, it is also apparent that emotions can have negative effects. Stage fright or "choking" in sports can spoil performances. Hate, anger, contempt, disgust, and fear disrupt behavior and relationships. But more often, emotions aid survival. As social animals, it would be impossible for humans to live in groups, cooperate in raising children, and defend one another without emotions (Buss, 2012).

A pounding heart, sweating palms, "butterflies" in the stomach, and other bodily reactions are major elements of fear, anger, joy, and other emotions. Typical **physiological changes** take place in heart rate, blood pressure, perspiration, and other bodily stirrings. Most are caused by activity in the sympathetic nervous system and by the hormones *adrenaline* and *noradrenaline*, which the adrenal glands release into the bloodstream.

Emotional expressions, or outward signs of what a person is feeling, are another ingredient of emotion. For example, when you are intensely afraid, your hands tremble, your face contorts, your posture becomes tense and defensive, and your voice changes. In general, these expressions serve to tell others what emotions we are experiencing (Hortman, 2003). **Emotional feelings** (a person's private emotional experience) are a final major element of emotion. This is the part of emotion with which we are usually most familiar.

Emotion A state characterized by physiological arousal, changes in facial expression, gestures, posture, and subjective feelings.

Adaptive behaviors Actions that aid attempts to survive and adapt to changing conditions.

Physiological changes (in emotion) Alterations in heart rate, blood pressure, perspiration, and other involuntary responses.

Emotional expression Outward signs that an emotion is occurring.

Emotional feelings The private, subjective experience of having an emotion.

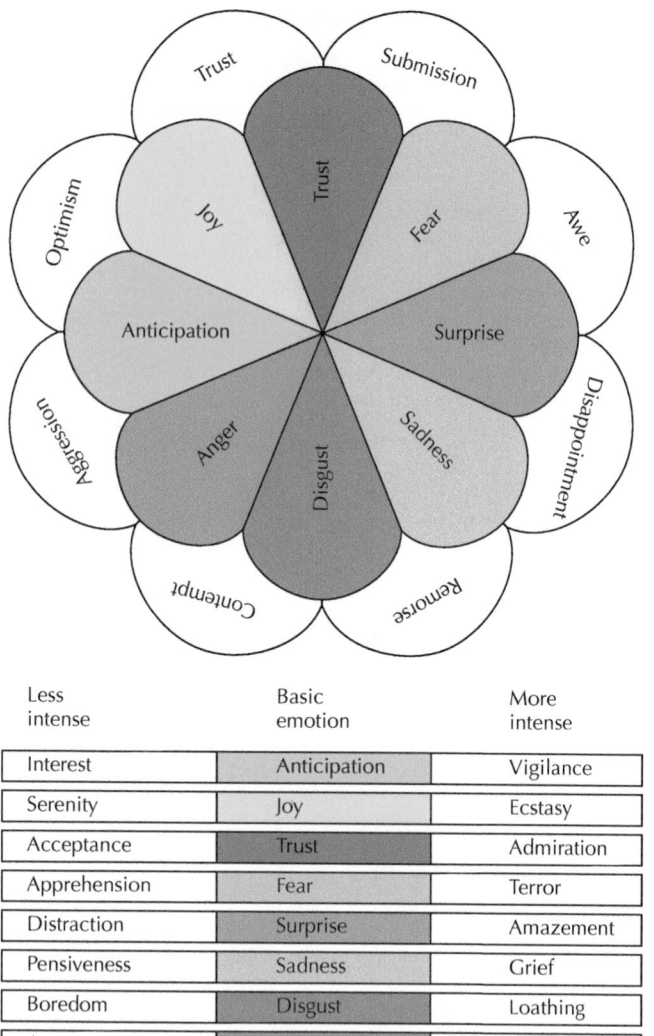

Less intense	Basic emotion	More intense
Interest	Anticipation	Vigilance
Serenity	Joy	Ecstasy
Acceptance	Trust	Admiration
Apprehension	Fear	Terror
Distraction	Surprise	Amazement
Pensiveness	Sadness	Grief
Boredom	Disgust	Loathing
Annoyance	Anger	Rage

Figure 9.15 Basic and mixed emotions. In Robert Plutchik's model, there are eight basic emotions, as listed in the inner areas. Adjacent emotions (*top part of figure*) may combine to give the emotions listed around the perimeter. Mixtures involving more widely separated emotions are also possible. For example, fear plus anticipation produces anxiety. (Copyright © 2002 by the American Psychological Association. Adapted with permission. The official citation that should be used in referencing this material is Robert Plutchik, *Emotions and Life: Perspectives from Psychology, Biology, and Evolution*. The use of APA information does not imply endorsement by APA.)

Basic emotions According to Robert Plutchik's theory, the most fundamental emotions are fear, surprise, sadness, disgust, anger, anticipation, joy, and acceptance.

Mood A low-intensity, long-lasting emotional state.

Basic Emotions

How many different emotions are there? That's actually a tough question to answer. Let's start by noting that some emotions may be more basic than others (Ekman & Cordaro, 2011). For example, Robert Plutchik (2003) has identified eight **basic emotions** (Figure 9.15). These are anticipation, joy, trust (acceptance), fear, surprise, sadness, disgust, and anger.

What makes these emotions "basic"? In general, our basic emotions can arise quickly and without much thought. They mature early, suggesting they are relatively unlearned. All humans, and many mammals, share these basic biological processes (Ekman & Cordaro, 2011; Izard, 2011; Panksepp & Watt, 2011). To better understand what this means, imagine you're hiking in the woods and a bear steps onto the trail right in front of you. What happens next?

- **Basic emotions are fast and automatic:** Chances are your fear level will arise rather quickly and without much reflective processing. (Who thinks to herself, *Hmm, a bear. Maybe I should be afraid?*) This is an example of experiential processing. (Refer back to Chapter 8.) As we'll shortly see, basic emotions like fear are likely first processed by subcortical brain structures in the limbic system (Arnsten, Mazure, & Sinha, 2012).

- **Basic emotions develop early:** Recall from Chapter 3 that basic emotions develop early in infancy, unfolding mainly because of maturation (Music, 2011). Simply put, even young children show fast, automatic basic emotional responses.

- **Basic emotions are universal among humans:** It appears that people the world around, more or less independent of their cultures, experience the same basic emotions. As we will see later in the chapter, all humans make the same facial expressions. You would know instantly, just by looking, if someone from, say, the island of Java, is afraid. (It's that pesky bear again.)

- **Basic emotions are shared with other mammals:** It is highly likely that we share the experience of basic emotions with other mammals. Being chased by a bear wouldn't feel like fun to a deer, either.

There must be more than eight emotions, right? If eight seems too few, it's because each emotion can vary in *intensity*. When you're angry, for instance, you may feel anything from rage to simple annoyance. As shown in the top part of Figure 9.15, each pair of adjacent basic emotions can be mixed to yield a third, more complex emotion. For example, mixing anger and disgust produces contempt. Other mixtures are also possible. For example, 5-year-old Tupac feels both joy and fear as he eats a cookie he stole from Mom's cookie jar. The result? Guilt—as you may recall from your own childhood. Likewise, jealousy could be a mixture of love, anger, and fear.

A **mood** is the mildest form of emotion (Figure 9.16). Moods are low-intensity emotional states that can last for many hours, or even days. Moods often affect day-to-day behavior by preparing us to act in certain ways. For example, when your neighbor Roseanne is in an irritable mood, she may react angrily to almost anything you say. When she is in a happy mood, she can easily laugh off an insult. Happy, positive moods tend to make us more adaptable in several ways. For example, when you are in a good mood, you are likely to make better decisions and you will be more helpful, efficient, creative, and peaceful (Compton, 2005; Fredrickson & Branigan, 2005).

Like our motives, our moods are closely tied to circadian rhythms. When your body temperature is at its daily low point, you are more likely to feel "down" emotionally. When body temperature is at its peak, your mood is likely to be positive—even if you missed a night of sleep (Boivin, Czeisler, & Waterhouse, 1997; McClung, 2011).

Emotion and the Brain

Imagine this test of willpower: Go to a zoo and place your face close to the glass in front of a rattlesnake display. Suddenly, the rattlesnake strikes at your face. Do you flinch? Even though you know you are safe, Joseph LeDoux predicts that you will recoil from the snake's attack (LeDoux, 2000).

According to LeDoux, the **amygdala** (ah-MIG-duh-la), a part of the *limbic system*, specializes in producing fear (**Figure 9.17**). (See Chapter 2 for more information.) These subcortical areas of the brain receive sensory information directly and quickly, bypassing the cortex, allowing us to respond to potential danger before we really know what's happening (Walker & Davis, 2008). This primitive fear response is not under the control of higher brain centers; it is a form of experiential processing. Other basic emotions may also be processed first in the limbic system. The role of the limbic system in emotion may explain why people who suffer from phobias and disabling anxiety often feel afraid without knowing why (Schlund & Cataldo, 2010).

People who suffer damage to the amygdala become "blind" to emotion. An armed robber could hold a gun to a person's head and the person wouldn't feel fear. Such people are also unable to "read" or understand other people's emotional expressions, especially as conveyed by their eyes (Adolphs, 2008). Many lose their ability to relate normally to friends, family, and coworkers.

Even if they are basic emotions and processed first in the limbic system, all emotions are eventually sent to the cortex for reflective processing, where they give rise to more or less complicated emotional feelings. Several interesting, and very human, curiosities arise because of this "two-layer" processing. For example, you can *feel* very afraid, and yet clearly *think* you have nothing to be afraid of. You can even, as Tupac's "cookie guilt" implies, have positive and negative emotions at the same time.

How is that possible? Positive emotions are processed mainly in the left hemisphere of the brain. In contrast, negative emotions are processed in the right hemisphere (Hofman, 2008; Simon-Thomas, Role, & Knight, 2005). In one study, people watching their favorite

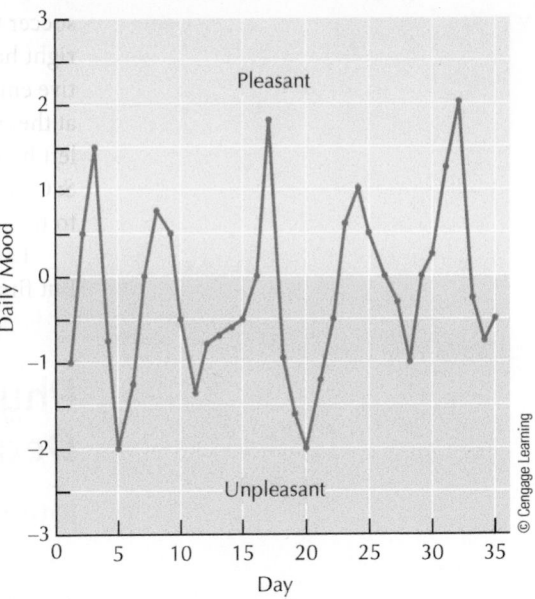

Figure 9.16 Folklore holds that people who work or attend school on a weekly schedule experience their lowest moods on "Blue Monday." Actually, moods tend to be generally lower for *most* weekdays than they are on weekends. The graph shown here plots the average daily moods of a group of college students over a 5-week period. As you can see, many people find that their moods rise and fall on a 7-day cycle. For most students, a low point tends to occur around Monday or Tuesday and a peak on Friday or Saturday. In other words, moods are shaped by weekly schedules. (Adapted from Larsen & Kasimatis, 1990.)

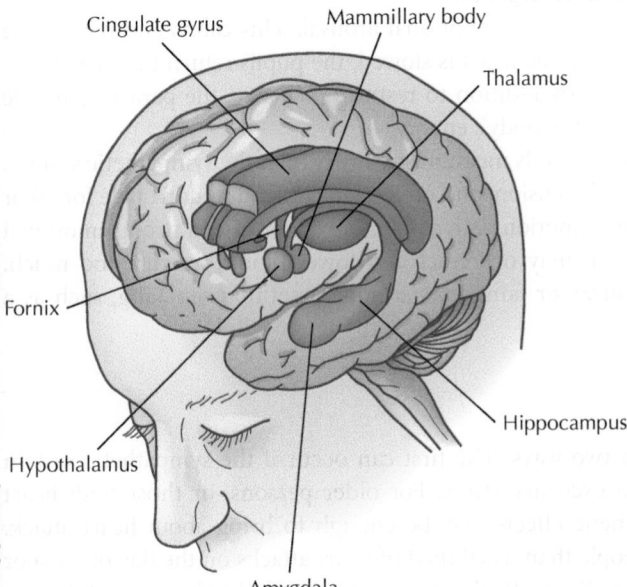

Figure 9.17 Parts of the limbic system. An amygdala can be found buried beneath the temporal lobes on each side of the brain. (See Chapter 2.) The amygdala appears to provide "quick and dirty" processing of emotional stimuli that allows us to react involuntarily to danger. The subcortical limbic system is a sort of "primitive core" of the brain strongly associated with emotion.

Amygdala A part of the limbic system (within the brain) that produces fear responses.

soccer team play well showed activity in both hemispheres but showed activity only in the right hemisphere when they were losing (Park et al, 2009). The fact that positive and negative emotions are based in different brain areas helps explain why we can feel happy and sad at the same time. It also explains why your right foot is more ticklish than your left foot! The left hemisphere controls the right side of the body and processes positive emotions (Smith & Cahusac, 2001). Thus, most people are more ticklish on their right side. If you really want to tickle someone, be sure to "do it right."

Later we will attempt to put all the elements of emotion together into a single picture. But first, we need to look more closely at physiological arousal and emotional expressions.

Physiology and Emotion—Arousal, Sudden Death, and Lying

JOURNEY QUESTION 9.8 *What physiological changes underlie emotion and can "lie detectors" really detect lies?*

An African Bushman frightened by a lion and a city dweller frightened by a prowler will react in much the same way. Such encounters usually produce muscle tension, a pounding heart, irritability, dryness of the throat and mouth, sweating, butterflies in the stomach, frequent urination, trembling, restlessness, sensitivity to loud noises, and numerous other body changes. These reactions are nearly universal because they are innate. Specifically, they are caused by the **autonomic nervous system (ANS)**—the neural system that connects the brain with internal organs and glands. As you may recall from Chapter 2, activity of the ANS is *automatic* rather than voluntary (Freberg, 2010).

Fight or Flight

The ANS has two divisions, the sympathetic branch and the parasympathetic branch. The two branches are active at all times. Whether you are relaxed or aroused at any moment depends on the relative activity of both branches.

What does the ANS do during emotion? In general, the **sympathetic branch** activates the body for emergency action—for "fighting or fleeing." It does this by arousing some body systems and inhibiting others (**Figure 9.18**). Sugar is released into the bloodstream for quick energy, the heart beats faster to supply blood to the muscles, digestion is temporarily slowed, blood flow in the skin is restricted to reduce bleeding, and so forth. Such reactions improve the chances of surviving an emergency.

The **parasympathetic branch** reverses emotional arousal. This calms and relaxes the body. After a period of high emotion, the heart is slowed, the pupils return to normal size, blood pressure drops, and so forth. In addition to restoring balance, the parasympathetic system helps build up and conserve the body's energy.

The parasympathetic system responds much more slowly than the sympathetic system. That's why a pounding heart, muscle tension, and other signs of arousal don't fade for 20 or 30 minutes after you feel an intense emotion such as fear. Moreover, after a strong emotional shock, the parasympathetic system may overreact and lower blood pressure too much. This can cause you to become dizzy or faint after seeing something shocking, such as a horrifying accident.

Sudden Death

Strong emotions can kill you in two ways. The first can occur if the sympathetic system becomes too active, resulting in excessive stress. For older persons, or those with heart problems, stress-related sympathetic effects may be enough to bring about heart attack. For example, five times more people than usual died of heart attacks on the day of a major 1994 earthquake in Los Angeles (Leor, Poole, & Kloner, 1996). Similarly, in Asia, the

Autonomic nervous system (ANS) The system of nerves that connects the brain with the internal organs and glands.

Sympathetic branch A part of the ANS that activates the body at times of stress.

Parasympathetic branch A part of the autonomic system that quiets the body and conserves energy.

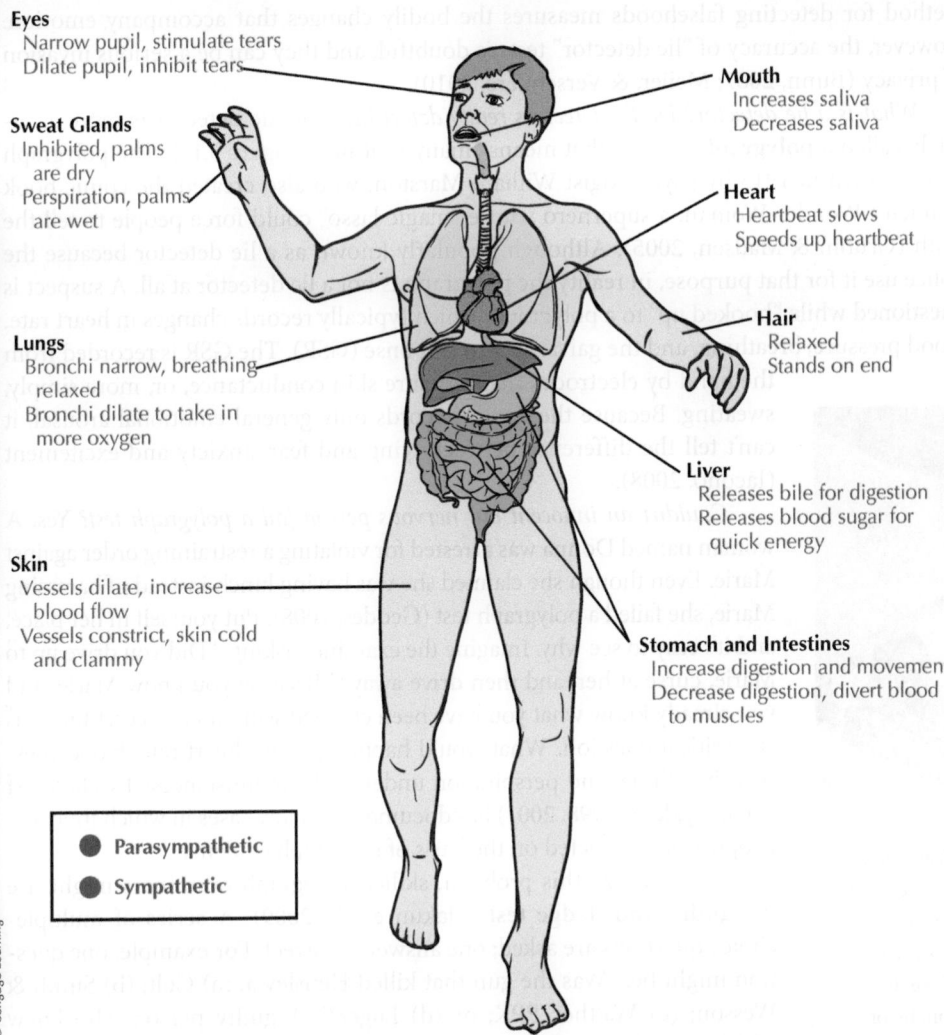

Eyes
Narrow pupil, stimulate tears
Dilate pupil, inhibit tears

Sweat Glands
Inhibited, palms
  are dry
Perspiration, palms
  are wet

Lungs
Bronchi narrow, breathing
  relaxed
Bronchi dilate to take in
  more oxygen

Skin
Vessels dilate, increase
  blood flow
Vessels constrict, skin cold
  and clammy

Mouth
Increases saliva
Decreases saliva

Heart
Heartbeat slows
Speeds up heartbeat

Hair
Relaxed
Stands on end

Liver
Releases bile for digestion
Releases blood sugar for
  quick energy

Stomach and Intestines
Increase digestion and movement
Decrease digestion, divert blood
  to muscles

● **Parasympathetic**
● **Sympathetic**

Figure 9.18 The parasympathetic branch of the ANS calms and quiets the body. The sympathetic branch arouses the body and prepares it for emergency action.

number "4" is considered unlucky, and more heart patients die on the fourth day of the month than any other day. Because of the extra stress due to the fear that they will die on an "unlucky day," their chance of dying actually increases (Phillips et al., 2001).

Second, the **parasympathetic rebound** to sympathetic arousal can also be severe enough to cause death. In times of war, for instance, combat can be so savage that some soldiers literally die of fear (Moritz & Zamchech, 1946). Apparently, such deaths occur because the parasympathetic nervous system overreacts to the sympathetic arousal, slowing the heart to a stop. Even in civilian life this is possible. In one case, a terrified young woman was admitted to a hospital because she felt she was going to die. A backwoods midwife had predicted that the woman's two sisters would die before their 16th and 21st birthdays. Both died as predicted. The midwife also predicted that this woman would die before her 23rd birthday. She was found dead in her hospital bed the day after she was admitted. It was 2 days before her 23rd birthday (Seligman, 1989). The woman was an apparent victim of her own terror.

Lie Detectors

You undoubtedly know that criminals are not always truthful. But what you may not know is that up to 25 percent of all wrongful convictions include false confessions as evidence (Kassin, 2005). If you can't count on someone's word, what can you trust? The most popular

Parasympathetic rebound Excess activity in the parasympathetic nervous system following a period of intense emotion.

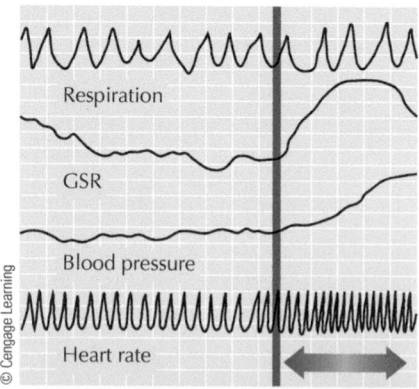

Respiration

GSR

Blood pressure

Heart rate

© Cengage Learning

© Bob Daemmrich/The Image Works

Figure 9.19 *(top)* A typical polygraph measures heart rate, blood pressure, respiration, and galvanic skin response. Pens mounted on the top of the machine record bodily responses on a moving strip of paper. *(bottom)* Changes in the area marked by the arrow indicate emotional arousal. If such responses appear when a person answers a question, he or she may be lying, but arousal may have other causes.

Polygraph A device for recording heart rate, blood pressure, respiration, and galvanic skin response; commonly called a "lie detector."

Guilty knowledge test Polygraph procedure involving testing people with knowledge only a guilty person could know.

method for detecting falsehoods measures the bodily changes that accompany emotion. However, the accuracy of "lie detector" tests is doubtful, and they can be a serious invasion of privacy (Bunn, 2007; Meijer, & Verschuere, 2010).

What is a lie detector? Do lie detectors really detect lies? The lie detector is more accurately called a **polygraph**, a word that means "many writings" (**Figure 9.19**). The polygraph was invented in 1915 by psychologist William Marston, who also created the comic book character Wonder Woman, a superhero whose "magic lasso" could force people to tell the truth (Grubin & Madsen, 2005). Although popularly known as a lie detector because the police use it for that purpose, in reality the polygraph is not a lie detector at all. A suspect is questioned while "hooked up" to a polygraph, which typically records changes in heart rate, blood pressure, breathing, and the galvanic skin response (GSR). The GSR is recorded from the hand by electrodes that measure skin conductance, or, more simply, sweating. Because the device records only general emotional arousal, it can't tell the difference between lying and fear, anxiety and excitement (Iacono, 2008).

Couldn't an innocent but nervous person fail a polygraph test? Yes. A woman named Donna was arrested for violating a restraining order against Marie. Even though she claimed she was having lunch instead of harassing Marie, she failed a polygraph test (Geddes, 2008). Put yourself in her place, and it's easy to see why. Imagine the examiner asking, "Did you drive up to Marie, curse at her, and then drive away?" Because you know Marie, and you already know what you have been charged with, it's no secret that this is a critical question. What would happen to *your* heart rate, blood pressure, breathing, and perspiration under such circumstances? Psychologist David Lykken (1998, 2001) has documented many cases in which innocent people were convicted on the basis of polygraph evidence.

To minimize this problem, skilled polygraph examiners might use the **guilty knowledge test** (Hakun et al., 2009). A series of multiple-choice questions are asked; one answer is correct. For example, one question might be: "Was the gun that killed Hensley a: (a) Colt; (b) Smith & Wesson; (c) Walther PPK; or (d) Luger?" A guilty person who knew which gun she had used may show an elevated response to the correct answer. Since an innocent person couldn't know which gun was involved, she could only respond similarly to all four alternatives (Iacono, 2008).

Although proponents of lie detection claim it is 95 percent accurate, errors may occur even when questioning is done properly (Grubin & Madsen, 2005). But in one study, accuracy was dramatically lowered when people thought about past emotional experiences as they answered irrelevant questions (Ben-Shakhar & Dolev, 1996). Similarly, the polygraph may be thrown off by self-inflicted pain, by tranquilizing drugs, or by people who can lie without anxiety. Worst of all, the test is much more likely to label an innocent person guilty rather than a guilty person innocent. In studies involving real crimes, an average of one innocent person in five was rated as guilty by the lie detector (Lykken, 2001). For such reasons, the National Academy of Sciences (2003) has concluded that polygraph tests should not be used to screen employees.

Despite the lie detector's flaws, you may be tested for employment or for other reasons. Should this occur, the best advice is to remain calm; then actively challenge the results if the machine wrongly questions your honesty.

Isn't there a better way to detect lies? Possibly. Harassment charges against Donna were dropped when a functional magnetic resonance imaging (fMRI) scan revealed she was indeed telling the truth. Brain scans like fMRI directly measure brain activity, thus bypassing the traditional approach of measuring indirect signs of emotional arousal (Hakun et al., 2009; Lefebvre et al., 2007). For example, researchers have found that different brain areas are involved in telling a lie (Abe et al., 2007). Psychiatrist Daniel Langleben (2008) theorizes that a liar must inhibit telling the truth in order to lie. Thus, extra brain areas must be activated to tell a lie, which can be seen in brain images when people are lying. (See Chapter 2.)

Even if new methods are used, the key problem remains: How can we avoid falsely classifying liars as truth tellers and truth tellers as liars? Until that can be done with acceptable accuracy, any new technique may have no more value than the polygraph does.

🖐 study break Emotion and Physiological Arousal

RECITE

1. Many of the physiological changes associated with emotion are caused by secretion of the hormone

   a. atropine
   b. adrenaline
   c. attributine
   d. insulin

2. Emotional _____ often serve to communicate a person's emotional state to others.

3. Awe, remorse, and disappointment are among the basic emotions listed by Robert Plutchik. T or F?

4. Emotional arousal is closely related to activity of the _____ nervous system.

5. The sympathetic system prepares the body for "fight or flight" by activating the parasympathetic system. T or F?

6. What body changes are measured by a polygraph?

REFLECT

THINK CRITICALLY

7. In Chapter 6 we met Larry, who understood his rat phobia after reading about it and yet still needed classical conditioning to overcome his fear. Why?

SELF-REFLECT

How did your most emotional moment of the past week affect your behavior, expressions, feelings, and physical state? Could you detect both sympathetic and parasympathetic effects?

Make a list of the emotions you consider to be most basic. To what extent do they agree with Plutchik's list?

What did you think about lie detectors before reading this chapter? What do you think now?

ANSWERS

1. b 2. expressions 3. F 4. autonomic 5. F 6. heart rate, blood pressure, breathing rate, galvanic skin response 7. Reading about phobias is a form of cognitive learning or reflective processing. Classical conditioning is a form of associative learning, which seems to operate mainly at the level of experiential processing. This could be why the best thing you can do after falling off a horse or getting in an automobile accident is get back on the horse or in a car.

Expressing Emotions—Making Faces and Talking Bodies

JOURNEY QUESTION 9.9 *How accurately are emotions expressed by the face and "body language"?*

Next to our own feelings, the expressions of others are the most familiar part of emotion. Are emotional expressions a carryover from human evolution? Charles Darwin thought so. Darwin (1872) observed that angry tigers, monkeys, dogs, and humans all bare their teeth in the same way. Psychologists believe that emotional expressions evolved to communicate our feelings to others, which aids survival. Such messages give valuable hints about what other people are likely to do next (Kalat & Shiota, 2012). For instance, in one study, people were able to detect angry and scheming faces faster than happy, sad, or neutral faces (Figure 9.20). Presumably, we are especially sensitive to threatening faces because they warn us of possible harm (Adolphs, 2008; Panksepp & Watt, 2011).

Facial Expressions

Are emotional expressions the same for all people? Basic expressions appear to be fairly universal (Figure 9.21). Facial expressions of fear, anger, disgust, sadness, surprise, and happiness (enjoyment) are recognized around the world (Smith et al., 2005). Expressions of contempt and interest may also be universal (Ekman, 1993). Notice that this list covers most of the basic emotions described earlier. Children who are born blind have little opportunity to learn emotional expressions from others. Even so, they also display basic expressions in

Angry   Sad   Happy   Scheming   Neutral

Figure 9.20 When shown groups of simplified faces (without labels), the angry and scheming faces "jumped out" at people faster than sad, happy, or neutral faces. An ability to rapidly detect threatening expressions probably helped our ancestors survive. (Copyright © 2002 by the American Psychological Association. Adapted with permission. The official citation that should be used in referencing this material is Tipples, J., Young, A., & Atkinson, A. P. (2002). "The raised eyebrow: A salient social signal." *Emotion, 2*, 288–296. The use of APA information does not imply endorsement by APA.)

Bernd Klumpp/Getty Images

Figure 9.21 Is anger expressed the same way in different cultures? Masks that are meant to be frightening or threatening are strikingly similar around the world. Most have an open, downward-curved mouth and diagonal or triangular eyes, eyebrows, nose, cheeks, and chin. (Keep this list in mind next Halloween.) Obviously, the pictured mask is not meant to be warm and cuddly. Your ability to "read" its emotional message suggests that basic emotional expressions have universal biological roots (Adolphs, 2008).

Alexithymia A learned difficulty expressing emotions; more common in men.

the same way sighted people do (Galati, Scherer, & Ricci-Bitti, 1997). It's also nice to note that a smile is the most universal and easily recognized facial expression of emotion.

There are more than a few facial expressions, aren't there? Yes. Your face can produce some 20,000 different expressions, which makes it the most expressive part of your body. Most of these are *facial blends* (a mixture of two or more basic expressions). Imagine, for example, that you just received an "F" on an unfair test. Quite likely, your eyes, eyebrows, and forehead would reveal anger, and your mouth would be turned downward in a sad frown.

Most of us believe we can fairly accurately tell what others are feeling by observing their facial expressions. If thousands of facial blends occur, how do we make such judgments? The answer is that facial expressions can be boiled down to three basic dimensions: *pleasantness–unpleasantness, attention–rejection,* and *activation* (or arousal) (Schlosberg, 1954). By smiling when you give a friend a hard time, you add an emotional message of acceptance to the verbal insult, which changes its meaning. As they say in movie Westerns, it makes a big difference to "Smile when you say that, pardner."

Cultural Differences in Expressing Emotion

Some facial expressions are shaped by learning and may be found only in specific cultures. Among the Chinese, for example, sticking out the tongue is a gesture of surprise, not of disrespect or teasing. If a person comes from another culture, it is wise to remember that you may easily misunderstand his or her expressions. At such times, knowing the social *context* in which an expression occurs helps clarify its meaning (Carroll & Russell, 1996; Kalat & Shiota, 2012).

How many times have you expressed anger this week? If it was more than once, you're not unusual. In Western cultures, expressing anger is widely viewed as a "natural" reaction to feeling that you have been treated unfairly. Very likely this is because our culture emphasizes personal independence and free expression of individual rights and needs. In contrast, many Asian cultures place a high value on group harmony. In Asia, expressing anger in public is less common and anger is regarded as less "natural." The reason for this is that anger tends to separate people. Thus, being angry is at odds with a culture that values cooperation.

Culture also influences positive emotions. In America, we tend to have positive feelings such as pride, happiness, and superiority, which emphasize our role as *individuals*. In Japan, positive feelings are more often linked with membership in groups (friendly feelings, closeness to others, and respect) (Kitayama, Markus, & Kurokawa, 2000; Markus et al., 2006).

It is common to think of emotion as an individual event. However, as you can see, emotion is shaped by cultural ideas, values, and practices.

Gender and Emotion

Women have a reputation for being "more emotional" than men. Are they? Compared with women, men in Western cultures are more likely to have difficulty expressing their emotions. In fact, Western men are more likely than women to experience **alexithymia** (a-LEX-ih-THIGH-me-ah), from the Latin for "can't name emotions."

According to psychologist Ronald Levant and colleagues (2006, 2009), although male babies start out life more emotionally expressive than female babies, little boys soon learn to "toughen up," beginning in early childhood. As a result, men have learned to curtail the expression of most of their emotions. Whereas girls are encouraged to express sadness, fear, shame, and guilt, boys are more likely to be allowed to express only anger and hostility (Fischer et al., 2004).

But does this mean that men experience emotions less than women? Levant believes that men who fail to express emotions over time become less aware of their own emotions and, hence, less able to name them (Reker et al., 2010). For many men, a learned inability to express feelings or to even be aware of them is a major barrier to having close, satisfying relationships with others and can also lead to health problems, such as depression or addictive behaviors (Lumley, 2004; Ogrodniczuk, Piper, & Joyce, 2011; Vanheule et al., 2010). Blunted emotions may even contribute to tragedies like all too common school shootings. For many young males, anger is the only emotion they can freely feel and express.

The expression of emotion is strongly influenced by learning. As you have no doubt observed, women cry more often, longer, and more intensely than men do. Men begin learning early in childhood to suppress crying—possibly to the detriment of their emotional health (Williams & Morris, 1996). Many men are especially unwilling to engage in public displays of emotion, in contrast to this woman, who is grieving for victims of the devastating 2010 earthquake in Haiti.

Body Language

If a friend walked up to you and said, "Hey, ugly, what are you doing?" would you be offended? Probably not, because such remarks are usually delivered with a big grin. The facial and body gestures of emotion speak a language all their own and add to what a person says.

Kinesics (kih-NEEZ-iks) is the study of communication through body movement, posture, gestures, and facial expressions (Goman, 2008; Harrigan, 2006). Informally, we call it body language. To see a masterful use of body language, turn off the sound on a television and watch a popular entertainer or politician at work.

What kinds of messages are sent with body language? It is important to realize cultural learning also affects the meaning of gestures. What, for instance, does it mean if you touch your thumb and first finger together to form a circle? In North America, it means "Everything is fine" or "A-okay." In France and Belgium, it means "You're worth zero." In southern Italy, it means "You're an ass!" When the layer of culturally defined meanings is removed, it is more realistic to say that body language reveals an overall emotional tone (underlying emotional state).

The body telegraphs other feelings. The most general "messages" involve *relaxation* or *tension*, and *liking* or *disliking*. Relaxation is expressed by casually positioning the arms and legs, leaning back (if sitting), and spreading the arms and legs. Liking is expressed mainly by leaning toward a person or object. Thus, body positioning can reveal feelings that would normally be concealed. Who do you "lean toward"?

Theories of Emotion—Several Ways to Fear a Bear

JOURNEY QUESTION 9.10 *How do psychologists explain emotions?*

Is it possible to explain what takes place during emotion? Theories of emotion offer different answers to this question. Let's explore some prominent views. Each appears to have a part of the truth, so we will try to put them all together in the end.

The James-Lange Theory

Let's not keep that bear waiting. Remember, you're hiking in the woods when a bear steps onto the trail. What will happen next? Common sense tells us that we will then feel fear, become aroused, and run (and sweat and yell). But is this the true order of events? In the 1880s, William James and Carl Lange (LON-geh) proposed that common sense had it

Emotions are often unconsciously revealed by gestures and body positioning.

Kinesics Study of the meaning of body movements, posture, hand gestures, and facial expressions; commonly called body language.

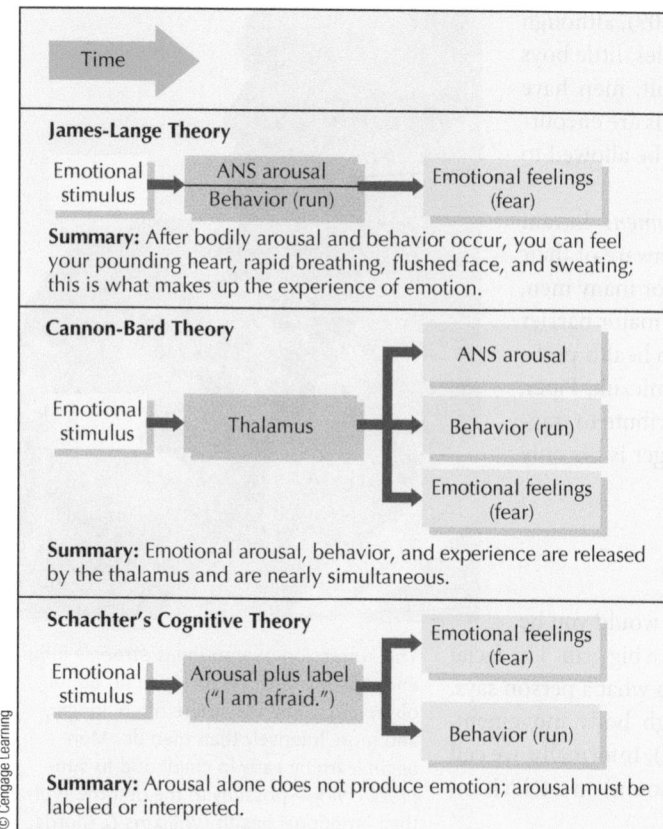

Figure 9.22 Theories of emotion.

backward (Hergenhahn, 2009). According to the **James-Lange theory**, physical arousal (such as increased heart rate) does not *follow* a feeling such as fear. Instead, they argued, *emotional feelings follow physical arousal*. Thus, we see a bear, run, are aroused, and *then* feel fear as we become aware of our body reactions (**Figure 9.22**).

In support, James pointed out that we often do not experience an emotion until after reacting. For example, imagine that you are driving. Suddenly, a car pulls out in front of you. You swerve and skid to an abrupt halt. Only then do you notice your pounding heart, rapid breathing, and tense muscles—and recognize your fear.

The Cannon-Bard Theory

Walter Cannon (1932) and Phillip Bard disagreed with the James-Lange theory. According to the **Cannon-Bard theory**, emotional feelings and physical arousal *occur at the same time*. Cannon and Bard believed that seeing a bear activates limbic structures in the brain, like the thalamus. The thalamus, in turn, alerts the hypothalamus and amygdala for action and the cortex for further reflection. The hypothalamus and amygdala trigger a chain of events that arouses the body. The cortex produces our emotional feelings and emotional behavior. Thus, if you see a dangerous-looking bear, brain activity will simultaneously produce body arousal, running, and a feeling of fear. (See Figure 9.22.)

Schachter's Cognitive Theory of Emotion

The previous theories are concerned mostly with our physical responses. Stanley Schachter realized that cognitive (mental) factors also enter into emotion, even basic emotions. According to **Schachter's cognitive theory**, emotion occurs when we apply a particular *label* to general physiological *arousal*. We likely choose the appropriate label through a process of **attribution**, by deciding which source is leading to the arousal (Valins, 1966).

Assume, for instance, that someone sneaks up behind you on a dark street and says, "Boo!" Your body is now aroused (pounding heart, sweating palms, and so on). If you attribute your arousal to a total stranger, you might label your arousal as fear; if you attribute your arousal to a close friend, you may experience surprise or delight. The label (such as anger, fear, or happiness) you apply to body arousal is influenced by your past experiences, the situation, and the reactions of others. (See Figure 9.22.)

Support for the cognitive theory of emotion comes from an experiment in which people watched a slapstick movie (Schachter & Wheeler, 1962). Before viewing the movie, everyone got an injection but no one was told what he or she was injected with. One third of the people received an arousing injection of adrenaline, one third got a placebo (salt water) injection, and one third were given a tranquilizer. People who received the adrenaline rated the movie funniest and laughed the most while watching it. In contrast, those given the tranquilizer were least amused. The placebo group fell in between.

According to the cognitive theory of emotion, individuals who received adrenaline had a stirred-up body but no explanation for what they were feeling. By attributing their arousal to the movie, they became happy and amused. This and similar experiments make it clear that emotion is much more than just an agitated body. Perception, experience, attitudes, judgment, and many other mental factors also affect the emotions we feel. Schachter's theory would predict, then, that if you met a bear, you would be aroused and might suddenly find yourself at full gallop. An instant later,

James-Lange theory States that emotional feelings follow physical arousal and come from awareness of such arousal.

Cannon-Bard theory States that activity in the thalamus causes emotional feelings and bodily arousal to occur simultaneously.

Schachter's cognitive theory States that emotions occur when physical arousal is labeled or interpreted on the basis of experience and situational cues.

Attribution The mental process of assigning causes to events. In emotion, the process of attributing arousal to a particular source.

if the bear seemed unfriendly, you might confirm your arousal as fear, and if the bear was offering to shake your "paw," you might experience happiness, amazement, and relief!

Misattribution

There is, of course, no guarantee that we always make the correct attributions about our emotions. To see this, let's shift from a fear of bear bodies to an appreciation of bare bodies. In one study, male college students viewed a series of photographs of nude females while listening to an amplified heartbeat that each student believed was his own (Valins, 1967). In reality, students were listening to a recorded heartbeat carefully designed to beat *louder* and *stronger* when some (but not all) of the photos were shown.

After watching the photos, each student was asked to say which was most attractive. Students who heard the false heartbeat consistently rated photos paired with a "pounding heart" as the most attractive. In other words, when a student saw a photo and heard his heart beat louder, he (falsely) attributed his "emotion" to the photo. His attribution seems to have been, "Now that one I like!"

That seems somewhat artificial. Does it really make any difference what arousal is attributed to? Yes. Attribution theory predicts that you are most likely to "love" someone who gets you stirred up emotionally (Foster et al., 1998). This is true even when fear, anger, frustration, or rejection is part of the formula. Thus, if you want to successfully propose marriage, take your intended to the middle of a narrow, windswept suspension bridge over a deep chasm and look deeply into his or her eyes. As your beloved's heart pounds wildly (from being on the bridge, not from your irresistible charms), say, "I love you." Attribution theory predicts that your companion will conclude, "Oh wow, I must love you too."

Really? The preceding is not as farfetched as it may seem. In an ingenious classic study, a female psychologist interviewed men in a park. Some were on a swaying suspension bridge, 230 feet above a river. The rest were on a solid wooden bridge just 10 feet above the ground. After the interview, the psychologist gave each man her telephone number, so he could "find out about the results" of the study. Men interviewed on the suspension bridge were much more likely to give the "lady from the park" a call (Dutton & Aron, 1974). Apparently, these men experienced heightened arousal, which they misinterpreted as attraction to the experimenter—a clear case of love at first fright!

Emotional Appraisal

According to Richard Lazarus (1991a, 1991b), the role of cognition in experiencing emotions is not restricted to making causal attributions about why arousal has occurred. The emotions you experience are also greatly influenced by your **emotional appraisal**, how you evaluate the personal meaning of a stimulus: Is it good/bad, threatening/supportive, relevant/irrelevant, and so on (León & Hernández, 1998). Emotional appraisals can be experiential and occur quickly, as with startling fear stimuli, or they can be more reflective.

Our discussion suggests that emotion is greatly influenced by how you think about an event. For example, if another driver "cuts you off" on the highway, you could become very angry. But if you do, you will add 15 minutes of emotional upset to your day. By changing your attribution ("He probably didn't mean it") and/or your emotional appraisal ("No big deal, anyway"), you could just as easily choose to brush off the other driver's behavior—and minimize your emotional wear-and-tear (Deutschendorf, 2009; Gross, 2001).

The Facial Feedback Hypothesis

Schachter and Lazarus added thinking and interpretation (cognition) to our view of emotion, but the picture still seems incomplete. What about expressions? How do they influence emotion? As Charles Darwin observed, the face is very central to emotion—perhaps it is more than just an "emotional billboard."

Which theory of emotion best describes the reactions of these people? Given the complexity of emotion, each theory appears to possess an element of truth.

Emotional appraisal Evaluating the personal meaning of a stimulus or situation.

Psychologist Carrol Izard (1990) was among the first to suggest that the face does, indeed, affect emotion. According to Izard, emotions cause innately programmed changes in facial expression. Sensations from the face then provide cues to the brain that help us determine what emotion we are feeling. This idea is known as the **facial feedback hypothesis** (Hennenlotter et al., 2009). Stated another way, it says that having facial expressions in turn influences our private emotional experience.

Psychologist Paul Ekman takes this idea one step further. He believes that "making faces" can actually *cause* emotion (Ekman, 1993). In one study, participants were guided as they arranged their faces, muscle by muscle, into expressions of surprise, disgust, sadness, anger, fear, and happiness (Figure 9.23). At the same time, each person's bodily reactions were monitored.

Contrary to what you might expect, "making faces" can affect the autonomic nervous system, as shown by changes in heart rate and skin temperature. In addition, each facial expression produces a different pattern of activity. An angry face, for instance, raises heart rate and skin temperature, whereas disgust lowers both (Ekman, Levenson, & Friesen, 1983). Other studies have confirmed that posed expressions alter emotions and bodily activity (Dimberg & Söderkvist, 2011; Soussignan, 2002).

In a fascinating experiment, people rated how funny they thought cartoons were while holding a pen crosswise in their mouths. Those who held the pen in their teeth thought the cartoons were funnier than did people who held the pen in their lips. Can you guess why? If you hold a pen with your teeth, you are forced to form a smile. Holding it with the lips makes a frown. As predicted by the facial feedback hypothesis, emotional experiences were influenced by the facial expressions that people made (Strack, Martin, & Stepper, 1988). Next time you're feeling sad, bite a pen! Or, at least, make yourself smile. It appears, then, that not only do emotions influence expressions, but expressions influence emotions.

Do people who have Botox injected into their faces experience any less emotion? It can certainly be uncanny to watch celebrities whose faces have been injected with Botox. (Ain't nothin' gonna move!) And it is indeed possible they feel less emotion as a consequence. In one study, compared with normal participants, participants injected with Botox showed less brain activity as they imitated angry faces (Hennenlotter et al., 2009).

If smiling can improve a person's mood, is it a good idea to inhibit negative emotions? For an answer, see "Suppressing Emotion—Don't Turn Off the Music."

A Contemporary Model of Emotion

To summarize, James and Lange were right that feedback from arousal and behavior adds to our emotional experiences. Cannon and Bard were right about the timing of events. Schachter showed us that cognitive attribution is important. Richard Lazarus

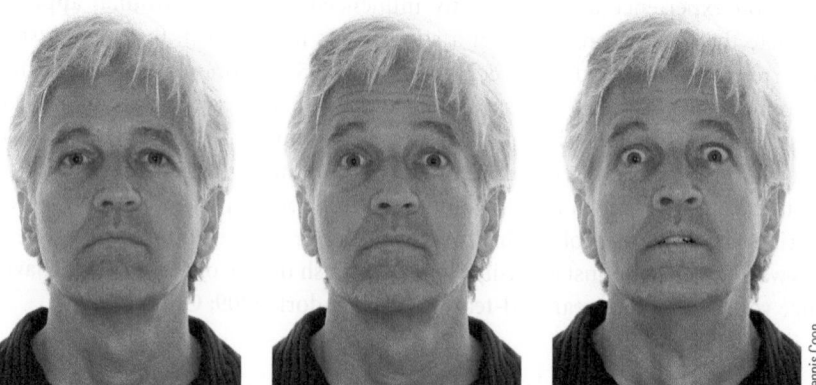

Figure 9.23 Facial feedback and emotion. Participants in Ekman's study formed facial expressions like those normally observed during emotion. When they did this, emotion-like changes took place in their bodily activity. (Adapted from Ekman, Levenson, & Friesen, 1983.)

Facial feedback hypothesis States that sensations from facial expressions help define what emotion a person feels.

Suppressing Emotion—Don't Turn Off the Music

According to popular media, we are supposed to be happy all the time (Hecht, 2007). However, real emotional life has its ups and downs. Have you ever been angry with a friend in public? Embarrassed by someone's behavior at a party? Disgusted by someone's table manners? Often we try to appear less emotional than we really are, especially when we are feeling negative emotions. In such circumstances, people are quite good at suppressing outward signs of emotion.

However, restraining emotion can actually increase activity in the sympathetic nervous system. In other words, hiding emotion requires a lot of effort. Suppressing emotions can also impair thinking and memory, as you devote energy to self-control. Thus, although suppressing emotion allows us to appear calm and collected on the outside, this cool appearance comes at a high cost (Richards & Gross, 2000). People who constantly suppress their emotions cope poorly with life and are prone to depression and other problems (Haga, Kraft, & Corby, 2010; Lynch et al., 2001).

Conversely, people who express their emotions generally experience better emotional and physical health (Lumley, 2004; Pennebaker, 2004). Paying attention to our negative emotions can also lead us to think more clearly about the positive *and* the negative. The end result is better decision making, which can increase our overall happiness in the long run (Deutschendorf, 2009; Norem, 2002). Usually, it's better to manage emotions than it is to suppress them. You will find some suggestions for managing emotions in the upcoming Psychology in Action section.

---

stressed the importance of emotional appraisal. In fact, psychologists are increasingly aware that both the *attributions* you make and how you *appraise* a situation greatly affects your emotions (León & Hernández, 1998; Strongman, 2003). Carrol Izard focused on facial expressions. Let's put these ideas together in a single model of emotion (**Figure 9.24**).

Imagine that a large, snarling dog lunges at you with its teeth bared. A modern view of your emotional reactions goes something like this: An *emotional stimulus* (the dog) is *appraised* (judged, probably experientially and quickly in this example) as a threat or other cause for emotion. Your appraisal gives rise to *ANS arousal* (your heart pounds and your body becomes stirred up). At the same time, your appraisal leads to *adaptive behavior* (you run from the dog) as it releases *innate emotional expressions* (your face twists into a mask of fear and your posture becomes tense). In addition, it triggers *cognitive labeling* and a change in consciousness that you recognize as the subjective experience of fear. (You think to yourself, *Uh oh, big trouble!* The intensity of this *emotional feeling* is directly related to the amount of ANS arousal taking place in your body.)

Each element of emotion—ANS arousal, labeling, adaptive behavior, subjective experience, and your emotional expressions—may further alter your emotional appraisal of the situation, as well as your attributions, thoughts, judgments, and perceptions. Thus, according to the facial feedback hypothesis, your facial expression may further influence your emotion. Such changes affect each of the other reactions, which again alters your appraisal and interpretation of events. Thus, emotion may blossom, change course, or diminish as it proceeds. Note too that the original emotional stimulus can be external, like the attacking dog, or internal, such as a memory of being chased by a dog, rejected by a lover, or praised by a friend. That's why mere thoughts and memories can make us fearful, sad, or happy (Strongman, 2003).

A Look Ahead

In the Psychology in Action section of this chapter we will look at *emotional intelligence*. Before we continue, you might want to appraise your learning with the exercises that follow.

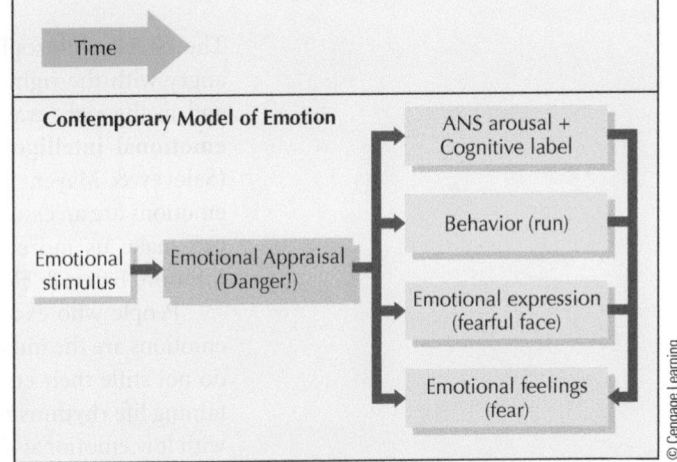

Figure 9.24 A contemporary model of emotion. Appraisal gives rise to arousal and cognitive labeling, behavior, facial/postural expressions, and emotional feelings. Arousal, attribution, behavior, and expressions add to emotional feelings. Emotional feelings influence appraisal, which further affects arousal, behavior, expressions, and feelings.

study break Emotional Expression and Theories of Emotion

RECITE

1. Charles Darwin held that emotional expressions aid survival for animals. T or F?
2. Which three dimensions of emotion are communicated by facial expressions?

    a. pleasantness–unpleasantness   b. complexity
    c. attention–rejection   d. anger
    e. curiosity–disinterest   f. activation

3. A formal term for "body language" is _____.
4. According to the James-Lange theory, emotional experience precedes physical arousal and emotional behavior. (We see a bear, are frightened, and run.) T or F?
5. The Cannon-Bard theory of emotion says that physical arousal and emotional experience occur _____.
6. According to Schachter's cognitive theory, physical arousal must be labeled or interpreted for an emotional experience to occur. T or F?

REFLECT

THINK CRITICALLY

7. People with upper spinal injuries may feel almost no signs of physiological arousal from their bodies. Nevertheless they still feel emotion, which can be intense at times. What theory of emotion does this observation contradict?

Psychology in Action

Emotional Intelligence—The Fine Art of Self-Control

JOURNEY QUESTION 9.11 *What does it mean to have "emotional intelligence"?*

The Greek philosopher Aristotle had a recipe for handling relationships smoothly: "Be angry with the right person, to the right degree, at the right time, for the right purpose, and in the right way." Psychologists Peter Salovey and John Mayer call such self-control **emotional intelligence**, the ability to perceive, use, understand, and manage emotions (Salovey & Mayer, 1997). In general, being emotionally intelligent means accepting that emotions are an essential part of who we are and how we survive. Being emotionally skilled can make us more flexible, adaptable, and emotionally mature (Bonanno et al., 2004; Johnson, Batey, & Holdsworth, 2009).

People who excel in life tend to be emotionally intelligent (Mehrabian, 2000). If our emotions are the music of life, then emotionally intelligent people are good musicians. They do not stifle their emotions or overindulge in them. Instead, they compose them into sustaining life rhythms that mesh well with other people. They are more *agreeable* than people with low emotional skills (Haas et al., 2007).

Indeed, the costs of poor emotional skills can be high. They range from problems in marriage and parenting to poor physical health. A lack of emotional intelligence can ruin careers and sabotage achievement (Zampetakis & Moustakis, 2011). Perhaps the greatest toll falls on children and teenagers (Alegre, 2011; Frederickson, Petrides, & Simmonds, 2012). For them, having poor emotional skills can contribute to depression, eating disorders, unwanted pregnancy, aggression, violent crime, and poor academic performance. Thus, in many life circumstances emotional intelligence is as important as IQ (Parker, 2005).

Emotional intelligence The ability to perceive, use, understand, and manage emotions.

Are there specific skills that make up emotional intelligence? Many elements contribute to emotional intelligence (Deutschendorf, 2009; Larsen & Prizmic, 2004; Mayer et al., 2001). A description of some of the most important skills follows:

AP Photo/Camay Sungu

Perceiving Emotions The foundation of emotional intelligence is the ability to perceive emotions in yourself and others. Unlike alexithymic people, emotionally intelligent people are tuned in to their own feelings (Taylor & Taylor-Allan, 2007). They are able to recognize quickly if they are angry, envious, feeling guilty, or depressed. This is valuable because many people have disruptive emotions without being able to pinpoint why they are uncomfortable. At the same time, emotionally intelligent people have *empathy* (Engelen & Röttger-Rössler, 2012). They accurately perceive emotions in others and sense what others are feeling. They are good at "reading" facial expressions, tone of voice, and other signs of emotion.

Using Emotions People who are emotionally intelligent use their feelings to enhance thinking and decision making. For example, if you can remember how you reacted emotionally in the past, it can help you react better to new situations. You can also use emotions to promote personal growth and improve relationships with others. For instance, you may have noticed that helping someone else makes you feel better, too. Likewise, when good fortune comes their way, people who are emotionally smart share the news with others. Almost always, doing so strengthens relationships and increases emotional well-being (Gable et al., 2004).

Understanding Emotions Emotions contain useful information. For instance, anger is a cue that something is wrong; anxiety indicates uncertainty; embarrassment communicates shame; depression means we feel helpless; enthusiasm tells us we're excited. People who are emotionally intelligent know what causes various emotions, what they mean, and how they might affect behavior (Hoerger et al., 2012).

Managing Emotions Emotional intelligence involves an ability to manage your own emotions and those of others. For example, you know how to calm down when you are angry and you also know how to calm others. As Aristotle noted so long ago, people who are emotionally intelligent have an ability to amplify or restrain emotions, depending on the situation (Bonanno et al., 2004).

Becoming Emotionally Smart

Often, the "right" choices in life can only be defined by taking personal values, needs, and emotions into account. Extremely rational approaches to making choices can produce sensible but emotionally empty decisions. In short, emotional intelligence is the ability to consciously make your emotions work for you (Dacre Pool & Qualter, 2012).

There are many valuable lessons to learn from paying close attention to your emotions and the emotions of others. It's a good bet that many of the people you admire the most are not just smart but also emotionally smart. (Lady Gaga?) They are people who know how to offer a toast at a wedding, tell a joke at a roast, comfort the bereaved at a funeral, add to the fun at a party, or calm a frightened child. These are skills worth cultivating (Deutschendorf, 2009).

The Whole Person

There is a natural tendency to welcome positive emotions, such as joy, but to treat negative emotions, such as anger, as unwelcome misery. Make no mistake, though, negative emotions are also part of the whole human. They can also be valuable and constructive. Negative emotions tend to narrowly focus attention on actions that helped our ancestors survive: escaping, attacking, expelling poison, and the like. Similarly, persistent distress may focus a person on seeking help, mending a relationship, or finding a new direction in life (Izard, 2011).

In contrast, positive emotions are not just a pleasant side effect of happy circumstances; they tend to broaden our focus (Fredrickson & Branigan, 2005). For instance, emotions such as joy, interest, and contentment create an urge to play, to be creative, to explore, to savor life, to seek new experiences, to integrate, and to grow. This opens up new possibilities and encourages personal growth and social connection (Izard, 2011).

Happiness can be cultivated by using the strengths we already possess—including kindness, originality, humor, optimism, and generosity. Such strengths are natural buffers against misfortune, and they can help people live more positive, genuinely happy lives (Ong, Zautra, & Reid, 2010; Seligman, 2002). A capacity for having positive emotions is a basic human strength, and cultivating good feelings is a part of emotional intelligence (Fredrickson, 2003).

 study break Emotional Intelligence

RECITE

1. People who rate high in emotional intelligence tend to be highly aware of their own feelings and unaware of emotions experienced by others. T or F?
2. Using the information imparted by emotional reactions can enhance thinking and decision making. T or F?
3. Positive emotions may be pleasant, but they tend to narrow our focus of attention and limit the range of possible actions we are likely to consider. T or F?
4. Which of the following is *not* an element of emotional intelligence?

   a. empathy   *b.* self-control
   c. self-centeredness   *d.* self-awareness

REFLECT

THINK CRITICALLY

5. You are angry because a friend borrowed money from you and hasn't repaid it. What would be an emotionally intelligent response to this situation?

SELF-REFLECT

Think of a person you know who is smart but low in emotional intelligence. Think of another person who is smart cognitively *and* emotionally. How does the second person differ from the first? Which person do you think would make a better parent, friend, supervisor, roommate, or teacher?

ANSWERS

1. F 2. T 3. F 4. c 5. There's no single right answer. Rather than being angry, it might be better to reflect on whether friendship or money is more important in life. If you appreciate your friend's virtues, accept that no one is perfect, and reappraise the loan as a gift, you could save a valued relationship and reduce your anger at the same time. Alternately, if you become aware that your friend persistently manipulates other people with emotional appeals for support, it may be worth reappraising your friendship.

Chapter in Review

Summary

9.1 What is motivation and are there different types of motives?

- 9.1.1 Motives initiate, sustain, direct, and terminate activities. Motivation typically involves the sequence: need, drive, goal, and goal attainment (need reduction).
- 9.1.2 Behavior can be activated either by needs (push) or by goals (pull).
- 9.1.3 The attractiveness of a goal and its ability to initiate action are related to its incentive value.
- 9.1.4 Three principal types of motives are biological motives, stimulus motives, and learned motives.
- 9.1.5 Most biological motives operate to maintain homeostasis.
- 9.1.6 Circadian rhythms of body activity are closely tied to sleep, activity, and energy cycles. Time zone travel and shift work can seriously disrupt sleep and body rhythms.
- 9.1.7 Pain avoidance is unusual because it is episodic as opposed to cyclic. Pain avoidance and pain tolerance are partially learned.

9.2 What causes hunger and thirst?

- 9.2.1 Hunger, thirst, and other basic motives are affected by a number of body factors but are primarily under the central control of the hypothalamus.
- 9.2.2 Hunger is influenced by a complex interplay between fullness of the stomach, blood sugar levels, metabolism in the liver, and fat stores in the body.
- 9.2.3 The hypothalamus exerts the most direct control of eating, through areas that act like feeding and satiety systems. The hypothalamus is sensitive to both neural and chemical messages, which affect eating.
- 9.2.4 Other factors influencing hunger are the body's set point, external eating cues, the attractiveness and variety of diet, emotions, and cultural values.
- 9.2.5 Obesity is the result of internal and external influences, diet, emotions, genetics, and exercise.
- 9.2.6 The most effective way to lose weight is behavioral dieting, which is based on techniques that change eating patterns and exercise habits.
- 9.2.7 Anorexia nervosa and bulimia nervosa are two prominent eating disorders. Both tend to involve conflicts about self-image, self-control, and anxiety.
- 9.2.8 Thirst may be either intracellular or extracellular.

9.3 What are the typical patterns of human sexual response?

- 9.3.1 The sex drive is unusual in that it is non-homeostatic.
- 9.3.2 Sexual arousal is related to the body's erogenous zones, but mental and emotional reactions are the ultimate source of sexual responsiveness.

- 9.3.3 Human sexual response can be divided into four phases: excitement, plateau, orgasm, and resolution.
- 9.3.4 Overall, male and female sexual responses are similar. However, males experience a refractory period after orgasm, and women are more likely than men to be multiorgasmic.
- 9.3.5 *Sexual orientation* refers to one's degree of emotional and erotic attraction to members of the opposite sex (heterosexuality), same sex (homosexuality, both sexes (bisexuality), or neither sex (asexuality). All four sexual orientations are part of the normal range of human variability.
- 9.3.6 Similar factors (heredity, biology, and socialization) underlie all sexual orientations.

9.4 How does arousal relate to motivation?

- 9.4.1 Drives for stimulation are partially explained by arousal theory, which states that an ideal level of body arousal will be maintained if possible.
- 9.4.2 The desired level of arousal or stimulation varies from person to person.
- 9.4.3 Optimal performance on a task usually occurs at *moderate* levels of arousal. This relationship is described by an inverted U function. The Yerkes-Dodson law further states that for simple tasks the ideal arousal level is higher, and for complex tasks it is lower.

9.5 What are learned and social motives and why are they important?

- 9.5.1 Learned motives, including social motives, account for much of the diversity of human motivation.
- 9.5.2 Social motives are learned through socialization and cultural conditioning.
- 9.5.3 People high in need for achievement (nAch) are successful in many situations due to their perseverance, passion, and self-confidence.
- 9.5.4 Self-confidence greatly affects motivation in everyday life.

9.6 Are some motives more basic than others?

- 9.6.1 Maslow's hierarchy of motives categorizes needs as either basic or growth oriented. Lower needs in the hierarchy are assumed to be prepotent (dominant) over higher needs. Self-actualization, the highest and most fragile need, is reflected in meta-needs.
- 9.6.2 Meta-needs are closely related to intrinsic motivation. In some situations, external rewards can undermine intrinsic motivation, enjoyment, and creativity.

9.7 What happens during emotion?

- 9.7.1 An emotion consists of physiological changes, adaptive behavior, emotional expressions, and emotional feelings.
- 9.7.2 The basic emotions of anticipation, joy, trust (acceptance), fear, surprise, sadness, disgust, and anger can be mixed to produce more complex emotional experiences.

9.7.3 The amygdala provides a "quick and dirty" pathway for the arousal of fear that bypasses the cerebral cortex.

9.7.4 The left hemisphere of the brain primarily processes positive emotions. Negative emotions are processed in the right hemisphere.

9.8 What physiological changes underlie emotion and can "lie detectors" really detect lies?

9.8.1 Physical changes associated with emotion are caused by activity in the autonomic nervous system (ANS).

9.8.2 The sympathetic branch of the ANS is responsible primarily for arousing the body, the parasympathetic branch for quieting it.

9.8.3 The polygraph, or "lie detector," measures emotional arousal (rather than lying) by monitoring heart rate, blood pressure, breathing rate, and the galvanic skin response (GSR). The accuracy of the lie detector can be quite low.

9.8.4 Newer brain imaging methods, such as fMRI, are showing great promise in lie detection.

9.9 How accurately are emotions expressed by the face and "body language"?

9.9.1 Basic facial expressions of fear, anger, disgust, sadness, surprise, and happiness are universally recognized. Facial expressions of contempt and interest may be universal as well.

9.9.2 Facial expressions reveal pleasantness versus unpleasantness, attention versus rejection, and a person's degree of emotional activation.

9.9.3 The formal study of body language is known as *kinesics*. Body gestures and movements (body language) also express feelings, mainly by communicating emotional tone rather than specific universal messages.

9.9.4 Body positioning expresses relaxation or tension and liking or disliking.

9.10 How do psychologists explain emotions?

9.10.1 Contrary to common sense, the James-Lange theory says that emotional experience follows bodily reactions. In contrast, the Cannon-Bard theory says that bodily reactions and emotional experiences occur at the same time.

9.10.2 Schachter's cognitive theory emphasizes that labeling bodily arousal can determine what emotion you feel. Appropriate labels are chosen by attribution (ascribing arousal to a particular source).

9.10.3 Contemporary views of emotion place greater emphasis on the effects of cognitive appraisals. Also, our feelings and actions change as each element of emotion interacts with others. One of the best ways to manage emotion is to change your emotional appraisal of a situation.

9.10.4 The facial feedback hypothesis holds that facial expressions help define the emotions we feel.

9.10.5 Contemporary views of emotion emphasize that all the elements of emotion are interrelated and interact with one another.

9.11 What does it mean to have "emotional intelligence"?

9.11.1 Emotional intelligence is the ability to consciously make your emotions work for you in a wide variety of life circumstances.

9.11.2 People who are "smart" emotionally are able to perceive, use, understand, and manage emotions. They are self-aware and empathetic; know how to use emotions to enhance thinking, decision making, and relationships; and have an ability to understand and manage emotions.

9.11.3 Positive emotions are valuable because they tend to broaden our focus and they encourage personal growth and social connection.

Interactive Learning

Log in to CengageBrain to access the resources your instructor requires. For this book, you can access:

CourseMate Go to CengageBrain.com to access Psychology CourseMate, where you will find an interactive eBook, glossaries, flashcards, quizzes, videos, Virtual Psychology Labs, and more.

Aplia If your professor has assigned Aplia:

1. Sign in to your account.
2. Complete the corresponding exercises as required by your professor.
3. When finished, click "Grade It Now" to see which areas you have mastered, which areas need more work, and detailed explanations of every answer.

Test Your Knowledge

Motivation and Emotion

1. Human needs for activity and exploration are an expression of
   a. learned motives
   b. biological motives
   c. incentive values
   d. stimulus motives

2. Desirable goals are motivating because they are high in
   a. secondary value
   b. stimulus value
   c. homeostatic value
   d. incentive value

3. The term *jet lag* is commonly used to refer to disruptions of
   a. the inverted U function
   b. circadian rhythms
   c. any of the episodic drives
   d. the body's set point

4. A feeding system exists in the _____ _____ of the brain.
   a. medial hyperthalamus
   b. ventral paraventriculum
   c. lateral hypothalamus
   d. thalamic nucleus

5. Maintaining your body's set point for fat is closely linked with the amount of _____ in the bloodstream.
   a. hypothalamic factor-1
   b. ventromedial peptide-1
   c. NPY
   d. leptin

6. Chronic self-starvation is most characteristic of people who have
   a. taste aversions
   b. anorexia
   c. bulimia
   d. strong sensitivity to external eating cues

7. In addition to changing eating habits, a key element of behavioral dieting is
   a. exercise
   b. well-timed snacking
   c. better eating cues
   d. commitment to "starving" every day

8. One thing that men and women have in common is that their sex drive is
   a. affected by androgens
   b. extracellular
   c. controlled by estrogen
   d. homeostatic and episodic

9. The typical phases of human sexual arousal are
   a. estrus, refractory period, orgasm, resolution
   b. excitement, orgasm, resolution, refractory period
   c. estrus, orgasm, plateau, resolution
   d. excitement, plateau, orgasm, resolution

10. Sensate focus is a technique used to treat
    a. estrus disorders in men
    b. bulimia nervosa
    c. excessive weight cycling
    d. sexual disorders

11. Which of the following is NOT a characteristic of people who are sensation seekers?
    a. boredom susceptibility
    b. experience seeking
    c. inhibition
    d. thrill seeking

12. Complex tasks, such as taking a classroom test, tend to be disrupted by high levels of arousal, an effect predicted by
    a. the Sensation-Seeking Scale
    b. the Yerkes-Dodson law
    c. studies of circadian arousal patterns
    d. studies of the need for achievement

13. People high in nAch do not necessarily show
    a. perseverance
    b. self-confidence
    c. great talent
    d. passion

14. The highest level of Maslow's hierarchy of needs involves
    a. meta-needs
    b. needs for safety and security
    c. needs for love and belonging
    d. extrinsic needs

15. Polygraph operators try to use which component of emotion to detect deception?
    a. adaptive behaviors
    b. physiological changes
    c. emotional expressions
    d. the parasympathetic rebound

16. Preparing the body for "fighting or fleeing" is largely the job of the
    a. paraventricular nucleus
    b. sympathetic branch
    c. GSR
    d. androgens

17. The idea that labeling arousal helps define what emotions we experience is associated with
    a. the James-Lange theory
    b. Schachter's cognitive theory
    c. the Cannon-Bard theory
    d. Darwin's theory of innate emotional expressions

18. Holding a pen crosswise in your mouth is likely to improve your mood, a result predicted by
    a. the Cannon-Bard theory
    b. attribution theory
    c. the facial-feedback hypothesis
    d. Schachter's cognitive theory

19. Emotionally intelligent people have which of the following skills?
    a. empathy
    b. self-awareness
    c. understanding of emotions
    d. all three of the previously mentioned skills

20. One benefit of positive emotions is the capacity to
    a. broaden our focus
    b. limit our ideas about possible actions
    c. narrow our focus
    d. help our ancestors escape attack

Journey Theme *Personality refers to the consistency we see in personal behavior patterns. Measures of personality reveal individual differences and help predict future behavior.*

Personality

Journey into Psychology: Even Cowgirls Get the Blues

Rural Wyoming. The car banged over one last, brain-jarring rut and lurched toward the dilapidated farmhouse. Sissy awaited one of your authors on the porch, hooting and whooping and obviously happy to see an old friend arrive.

If anyone was suited for a move to the "wilds" of Wyoming, it was Sissy, a strong and resourceful woman. Still, it was hard to imagine a more radical change. After going through a bout of the "blues" when she separated from her husband, she had traded a comfortable life in the city for rough times in the high country. Sissy was working as a cowgirl, trying to make it through some hard winters. The changes in Sissy's life were radical and we worried that she might be entirely different. She was, on the contrary, more her "old self" than ever. We howled with laughter as she described recently decking a guy twice her size who was harassing her in a tavern.

Perhaps you have had a similar experience. After several years of separation, it is always intriguing to see an old friend. At first you may be struck by how the person has changed ("Where did you get that haircut!?"). Soon, however, you will probably be delighted to discover that the semi-stranger before you is still the person you once knew. It is exactly this core of consistency that psychologists have in mind when they use the term *personality*.

What is personality? How does it differ from character, temperament, or attitudes? Is it possible to measure personality? Can we change our personality? We'll address these questions and more in this chapter.

Journey Questions

10.1 How do psychologists use the term *personality*?

10.2 Are some personality traits more basic or important than others?

10.3 How do psychodynamic theories explain personality?

10.4 What are humanistic theories of personality?

10.5 What do behaviorists and social learning theorists emphasize in their approach to personality?

10.6 How do heredity and environment affect personality?

10.7 How do psychologists measure personality?

10.8 What causes shyness and what can be done about it?

Does this man have personality? Do you?

The Psychology of Personality—Do You Have Personality?

JOURNEY QUESTION 10.1 *How do psychologists use the term personality?*

"Sissy has a very optimistic personality." "Ramiro's not handsome, but he has a great personality." "My father's business friends think he's a nice guy. They should see him at home where his real personality comes out." "It's hard to believe Tanya and Nikki are sisters. They have such opposite personalities."

It's obvious that we all frequently use the term *personality*. But if you think that personality means "charm," "charisma," or "style," you have misused the term. Many people also confuse personality with the term **character**, which implies that a person has been *evaluated* as possessing positive qualities, not just *described* (Bryan & Babelay, 2009). If, by saying someone has "personality," you mean the person is friendly, outgoing, and upstanding, you might be describing what we regard as good character in our culture. But in some cultures, it is deemed good for people to be fierce, warlike, and cruel.

Psychologists regard **personality** as a person's unique long-term pattern of thinking, emotions, and behavior (Burger, 2011; Ewen, 2009). In other words, *personality* refers to the consistency in who you are, have been, and will become. It also refers to the special blend of talents, values, hopes, loves, hates, and habits that makes each of us a unique person. So, everyone in a particular culture has personality, whereas not everyone has character—or at least not good character. (Do you know any good characters?)

Psychologists use a large number of concepts and theories to explain personality. It might be wise, therefore, to start with a few key ideas to help you keep your bearings as you read more about personality.

Traits

We use the idea of traits every day to talk about personality. For instance, Daryl is *sociable*, *orderly*, and *intelligent*. His sister Hollie is *shy*, *sensitive*, and *creative*. As we observed in our reunion with Sissy, personality traits like these can be quite stable (Rantanen et al., 2007; Schultz & Schultz, 2013). Think about how little your best friends have changed in the last 5 years. It would be strange indeed to feel like you were talking with a different person every time you met a friend or an acquaintance. In general, then, **personality traits** like these are stable qualities that a person shows in most situations (Matthews, Deary, & Whiteman, 2009). As you will see when you read further into this chapter, there is considerable debate about just *why* traits are stable qualities. But more about that later.

Psychologists and employers are especially interested in the personality traits of individuals who hold high-risk, high-stress positions involving public safety, such as police, firefighters, air-traffic controllers, and nuclear power plant employees.

Typically, traits are inferred from behavior. If you see Daryl talking to strangers—first at a supermarket and later at a party—you might deduce that he is "sociable." Once personality traits are identified, they can be used to predict future behavior. For example, noting that Daryl is outgoing might lead you to predict that he will be sociable at school or at work. In fact, such consistencies can span many years (Caspi, Roberts, & Shiner, 2005; Harker & Keltner, 2001). Traits even influence our health as well as our marital and occupational success (Roberts et al., 2007). For example, who do you think will be more successful in her chosen career: Jane, who is conscientious, or Sally, who is not (Brown et al., 2011; Chamorro-Premuzic & Furnham, 2003)?

Types

Have you ever asked the question, "What type of person is she (or he)?" A **personality type** refers to people who have *several traits in common* (Larsen & Buss, 2010). Informally, your own thinking might include categories such as the executive type, the

Character Personal characteristics that have been judged or evaluated; a person's desirable or undesirable qualities.

Personality A person's unique and relatively stable patterns of thinking, emotions, and behavior.

Personality trait A stable, enduring quality that a person shows in most situations.

Personality type A style of personality defined by a group of related traits.

athletic type, the motherly type, the hip-hop type, the techno geek, and so forth. If you tried to define these informal types, you would probably list a different collection of traits for each one.

How valid is it to speak of personality "types"? Over the years, psychologists have proposed many ways to categorize personalities into types. For example, Swiss psychiatrist Carl Jung (pronounced yoong) proposed that people are either *introverts* or *extroverts*. An **introvert** is a shy, reserved person whose attention is usually focused inward. An **extrovert** is a bold, outgoing person whose attention is usually directed outward. These terms are so widely used that you may think of yourself and your friends as being one type or the other. However, knowing if someone is extroverted or introverted tells you little about how conscientious she is, or how kind or open to new ideas he is. In short, two categories (or even several) are often inadequate to fully capture differences in personality. That's why rating people on a list of traits tends to be more informative than classifying them into two or three types (Engler, 2009).

Even though types tend to oversimplify personality, they do have value. Most often, types are a shorthand way of labeling people who have several key traits in common. For example, in the next chapter we will discuss Type A and Type B personalities. Type A's are people who have personality traits that increase their chance of suffering a heart attack; Type B's take a more laid-back approach to life (**Figure 10.1**). Similarly, you will read in Chapter 12 about unhealthy personality types such as the paranoid personality, the dependent personality, and the antisocial personality. Each problem type is defined by a specific collection of traits that are not adaptive.

Self-Concept

Self-concepts provide another way of understanding personality. Your **self-concept** consists of all your ideas, perceptions, stories, and feelings about who you are. It is the mental "picture" you have of your own personality (Ritchie et al., 2011; Swann, Chang-Schneider, & Larsen McClarty, 2007).We creatively build our self-concepts out of daily experiences. Then we slowly revise them as we have new experiences. Once a stable self-concept exists, it tends to guide what we pay attention to, remember, and think about. Because of this, self-concepts can greatly affect our behavior and personal adjustment—especially when they are inaccurate (Ryckman, 2013). For instance, Alesha is a student who thinks she is stupid, worthless, and a failure, despite getting good grades. With such an inaccurate self-concept, she tends to be depressed regardless of how well she does.

Self-Esteem

Note that in addition to having a faulty self-concept, Alesha has low **self-esteem** (a negative self-evaluation). A person with high self-esteem is confident, proud, and self-respecting. One who has low self-esteem is insecure, lacking in confidence, and

Self-concepts can be remarkably consistent. In an interesting study, old people were asked how they had changed over the years. Almost all thought they were essentially the same person they were when they were young (Troll & Skaff, 1997). Well over 90 years old, Nelson Mandela, for example, has been a highly committed human rights activist for his entire adult life.

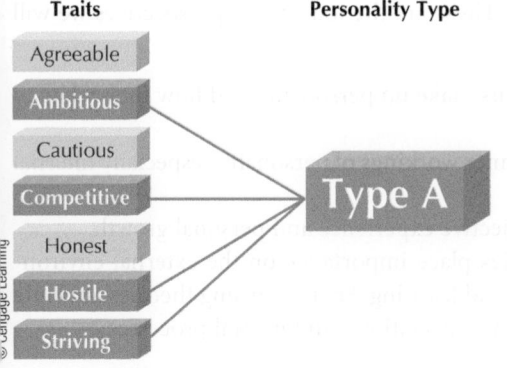

Figure 10.1 Personality types are defined by the presence of several specific traits. For example, several possible personality traits are shown in the left column. A person who has a Type A personality typically possesses all or most of the highlighted traits. Type A persons are especially prone to heart disease. (See Chapter 11.)

Introvert A person whose attention is focused inward; a shy, reserved, self-centered person.

Extrovert A person whose attention is directed outward; a bold, outgoing person.

Self-concept A person's perception of his or her own personality traits.

Self-esteem Regarding oneself as a worthwhile person; a positive evaluation of oneself.

You and some friends are playing soccer. Your team wins, in part because you make some good plays. After the game, you bask in the glow of having performed well. You don't want to brag about being a hotshot, but your self-esteem gets a boost from your personal success.

In Japan, Shinobu and some of his friends are playing soccer. His team wins, in part because he makes some good plays. After the game, Shinobu is happy because his team did well. However, Shinobu also dwells on the ways in which he let his team down. He thinks about how he could improve, and he resolves to be a better team player.

These sketches illustrate a basic difference in Eastern and Western psychology. In individualistic cultures such as the United States, self-esteem is based on personal success and outstanding performance (Buss, 2012; Lay & Verkuyten, 1999). For us, the path to higher self-esteem lies in self-enhancement. We are pumped up by our successes and tend to downplay our faults and failures (Ross et al., 2005).

Japanese and other Asian cultures place a greater emphasis on collectivism or interdependence among people. For them, self-esteem is based on a secure sense of belonging to social groups. As a result, people in Asian cultures are

more apt to engage in self-criticism (Ross et al., 2005). By correcting personal faults, they add to the well-being of the group (Kitayama, Markus, & Kurokawa, 2000). And, when the *group* succeeds, individual members feel better about themselves, which raises their self-esteem.

Perhaps self-esteem is still based on success in both Eastern and Western cultures (Brown et al., 2009). However, it is fascinating that cultures define success in such different ways (Buss, 2012; Schmitt & Allik, 2005).

---

self-critical. Like Alesha, people with low self-esteem are usually anxious and unhappy. People who have low self-esteem typically also suffer from poor self-knowledge. Their self-concepts are inconsistent, inaccurate, and confused. Problems of this type are explored later in this chapter.

Self-esteem tends to rise when we experience success or praise. It also buffers us against negative experiences (Brown, 2010). A person who is competent and effective and who is loved, admired, and respected by others will almost always have high self-esteem (Baumeister et al., 2003; Buss, 2012). The reasons for having high self-esteem, however, can vary in different cultures. See "Self-Esteem and Culture" for more information.

What if you "think you're hot," but you're not? Genuine self-esteem is based on an accurate appraisal of your strengths and weaknesses. A positive self-evaluation that is bestowed too easily may not be healthy (Kernis & Lakey, 2010; Twenge & Campbell, 2001). People who think very highly of themselves (and let others know it) may at first seem confident, but their arrogance quickly turns off other people (Paulhus, 1998).

The Whole Human: Personality Theories

As you can already see, it would be easy to get lost without a framework for understanding the richness of human personality. How do our thoughts, actions, and feelings relate to one another? How does personality develop? Why do some people suffer from psychological problems? How can they be helped? To answer such questions, psychologists have created a dazzling array of theories. A **personality theory** is a system of concepts, assumptions, ideas, and principles proposed to explain personality (Figure 10.2). In this chapter, we can explore only a few of the many personality theories. These are the four major perspectives we will consider:

1. **Trait theories** attempt to learn what traits make up personality and how they relate to actual behavior.
2. **Psychodynamic theories** focus on the inner workings of personality, especially internal conflicts and struggles.
3. **Humanistic theories** stress private, subjective experience and personal growth.
4. **Behaviorist and social learning theories** place importance on the external environment and on the effects of conditioning and learning. Social learning theories attribute differences in personality to socialization, expectations, and mental processes.

With these broad perspectives in mind, let's take a deeper look at personality.

Personality theory A system of concepts, assumptions, ideas, and principles used to understand and explain personality.

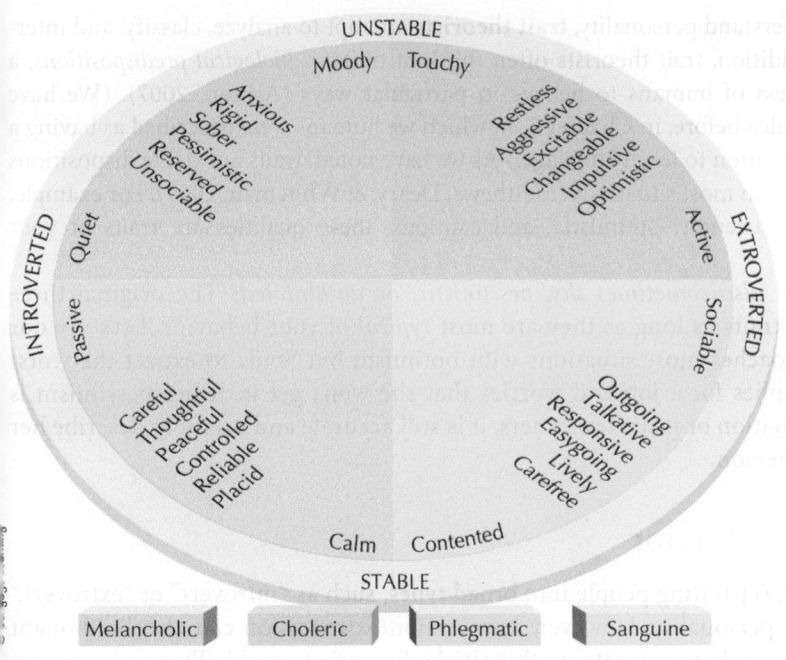

Figure 10.2 English psychologist Hans Eysenck (1916–1997) proposed the personality theory that many personality traits are related to whether you are mainly introverted or extroverted and whether you tend to be emotionally stable or unstable (highly emotional). These characteristics, in turn, are related to four basic types of temperament first recognized by the early Greeks. The types are: *melancholic* (sad, gloomy), *choleric* (hot-tempered, irritable), *phlegmatic* (sluggish, calm), and *sanguine* (cheerful, hopeful). (Adapted from Eysenck, 1981.)

The Trait Approach—Describe Yourself in 18,000 Words or Less

JOURNEY QUESTION 10.2 *Are some personality traits more basic or important than others?*

The *trait approach* is currently the dominant method for studying personality. Trait theorists seek to describe personality with a small number of key traits or factors. Take a moment to check the traits in Table 10.1 that describe your personality. Don't worry if some of your key traits weren't in the table. More than 18,000 English words refer to personal characteristics. Are the traits you checked of equal importance? Are some stronger or more basic than others? Do any overlap? For example, if you checked "dominant," did you also check "confident" and "bold"? Answers to these questions would interest a trait theorist.

Table 10.1 Adjective Checklist

Check the traits you feel are characteristic of your personality. Are some more basic than others?

aggressive	organized	ambitious	clever
confident	loyal	generous	calm
warm	bold	cautious	reliable
sensitive	mature	talented	jealous
sociable	honest	funny	religious
dominant	dull	accurate	nervous
humble	uninhibited	visionary	cheerful
thoughtful	serious	helpful	emotional
orderly	anxious	conforming	good-natured
liberal	curious	optimistic	kind
meek	neighborly	passionate	compulsive

© Cengage Learning

To better understand personality, **trait theorists** attempt to analyze, classify, and interrelate traits. In addition, trait theorists often think of traits as *biological predispositions*, a hereditary readiness of humans to behave in particular ways (Ashton, 2007). (We have encountered this idea before, in Chapter 3, in which we humans were described as having a biological predisposition to learn language.) As we have noted, traits are stable dispositions that a person shows in most situations (Matthews, Deary, & Whiteman, 2009). For example, if you are usually friendly, optimistic, and cautious, these qualities are traits of your personality.

What if I am also sometimes shy, pessimistic, or uninhibited? The original three qualities are still traits as long as they are most *typical* of your behavior. Let's say our friend Sissy approaches most situations with optimism but tends to expect the worst each time she applies for a job and worries that she won't get it. If her pessimism is limited to this situation or just a few others, it is still accurate and useful to describe her as an optimistic person.

Predicting Behavior

As we have noted, separating people into broad types, such as "introvert" or "extrovert," may oversimplify personality. However, introversion/extroversion can also be thought of as a trait. Knowing how you rate on this single dimension would allow us to predict how you will behave in a variety of settings. How, for example, do you prefer to meet people—face-to-face or through the Internet? Researchers have found that students high in the trait of introversion are more likely to prefer the Internet because they find it easier to talk with people online (Koch & Pratarelli, 2004; Rice & Markey, 2009). Other interesting links exist between traits and behavior. See "What's Your Musical Personality?"

Classifying Traits

Are there different types of traits? Yes, psychologist Gordon Allport (1961) identified several kinds. **Common traits** are characteristics shared by most members of a culture. Common traits tell us how people from a particular nation or culture are similar, or which traits a culture emphasizes. In America, for example, competitiveness is a fairly common trait. Among the Hopi of northern Arizona, however, it is relatively rare.

Of course, common traits don't tell us much about individuals. Although many people are competitive in American culture, various people you know may rate high, medium, or low in this trait. Usually we are also interested in **individual traits**, which describe a person's unique qualities.

Here's an analogy to help you separate common traits from individual traits: If you decide to buy a pet dog, you will want to know the general characteristics of the dog's breed (its common traits). In addition, you will want to know about the "personality" of a specific dog (its individual traits) before you decide to take it home.

Allport also made distinctions between *cardinal traits*, *central traits*, and *secondary traits*. **Cardinal traits** are so basic that all of a person's activities can be traced to the trait. For instance, compassion was an overriding trait of Mother Teresa's personality. Likewise, Abraham Lincoln's personality was dominated by the cardinal trait of honesty. According to Allport, few people have cardinal traits.

Central Traits

How do central and secondary traits differ from cardinal traits? **Central traits** are the basic building blocks of personality. A surprisingly small number of central traits can capture the essence of a person. For instance, just six traits would provide a good description of Sissy's personality: dominant, sociable, honest, cheerful, intelligent, and optimistic. When college students were asked to describe someone they knew well, they mentioned an average of seven central traits (Allport, 1961).

Trait theorist A psychologist interested in classifying, analyzing, and interrelating traits to understand personality.

Common traits Personality traits that are shared by most members of a particular culture.

Individual traits Personality traits that define a person's unique individual qualities.

Cardinal trait A personality trait so basic that all of a person's activities relate to it.

Central traits The core traits that characterize an individual personality.

Discovering Psychology

Even if you like all kinds of music, you probably prefer some styles to others. Of the styles listed here, which three do you enjoy the most? (Circle your choices.)

blues   jazz   classical   folk   rock   alternative   heavy metal   country   soundtrack   religious   pop   rap/hip-hop   soul/funk   electronic/dance

In one study, Peter Rentfrow and Samuel Gosling found that the types of music people prefer tend to be associated with their personality characteristics (Rentfrow & Gosling, 2003). See if your musical tastes match their findings (Rentfrow & Gosling, 2007):

- People who value aesthetic experiences, have good verbal abilities, and are liberal and tolerant of others tend to like music that is reflective and complex (blues, jazz, classical, and folk music).

- People who are curious about new experiences, enjoy taking risks, and are physically active prefer intense, rebellious music (rock, alternative, and heavy metal music).

- People who are cheerful, conventional, extroverted, reliable, helpful, and conservative tend to enjoy upbeat conventional music (country, soundtrack, religious, and pop music).

- People who are talkative, full of energy, forgiving, and physically attractive, and who reject conservative ideals tend to prefer energetic, rhythmic music (rap/hip-hop, soul/funk, and electronic/dance music).

Unmistakably, personality traits are related to our everyday behavior (Rentfrow, Goldberg, & Levitin, 2011).

Secondary traits are more superficial personal qualities, such as food preferences, attitudes, political opinions, musical tastes, and so forth. In Allport's terms, a personality description might therefore include the following items:

Name: Jane Doe

Age: 22

Cardinal traits: None

Central traits: Possessive, autonomous, artistic, dramatic, self-centered, trusting

Secondary traits: Prefers colorful clothes, likes to work alone, politically liberal, always late

Source Traits

How can you tell whether a personality trait is central or secondary? Raymond Cattell (1906–1998) tried to answer this question by directly studying the traits of a large number of people. Cattell began by measuring visible features of personality, which he called **surface traits**. Soon, Cattell noticed that these surface traits often appeared together in groups. In fact, some traits clustered together so often that they seemed to represent a single more basic trait. Cattell called these deeper characteristics, or dimensions, **source traits** (or **factors**) (Cattell, 1965). They are the core of each individual's personality.

How do source traits differ from Allport's central traits? Allport classified traits subjectively, and it's possible that he was wrong at times. To look for connections among traits, Cattell used *factor analysis*, a statistical technique used to correlate multiple measurements and identify general underlying factors. For example, he found that imaginative people are almost always inventive, original, curious, creative, innovative, and ingenious. If you are an imaginative person, we automatically know that you have several other traits, too. Thus, *imaginative* is a source trait or factor.

Cattell (1973) identified 16 source traits. According to him, all 16 are needed to fully describe a personality. Source traits are measured by a test called the *Sixteen Personality Factor Questionnaire* (often referred to as the 16 PF). Like many personality tests, the 16 PF can be used to produce a **trait profile**, or graph of a person's score on each trait. Trait profiles draw a "picture" of individual personalities, which makes it easier to compare them (**Figure 10.3**).

Secondary traits Traits that are inconsistent or relatively superficial.

Surface traits The visible or observable traits of one's personality.

Source traits (factors) Basic underlying traits, or dimensions, of personality; each source trait is reflected in a number of surface traits.

Trait profile A graph of the scores obtained on several personality traits.

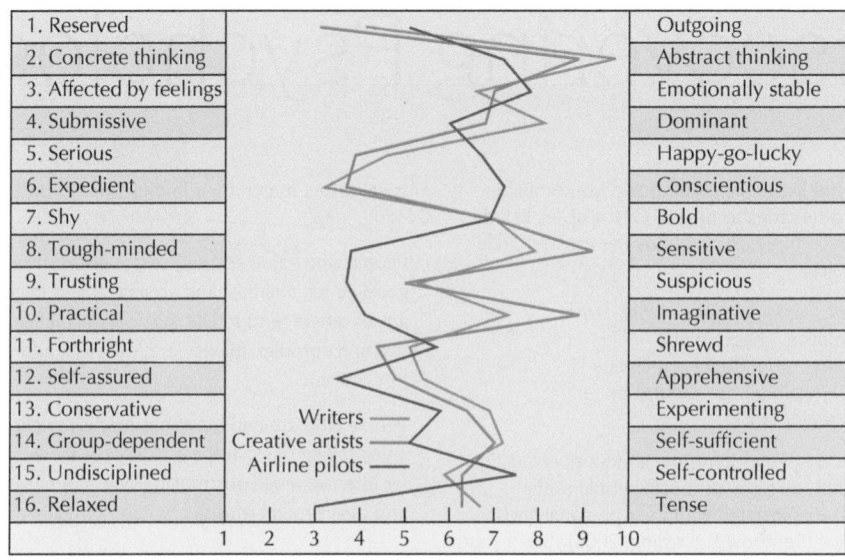

1. Reserved		Outgoing
2. Concrete thinking		Abstract thinking
3. Affected by feelings		Emotionally stable
4. Submissive		Dominant
5. Serious		Happy-go-lucky
6. Expedient		Conscientious
7. Shy		Bold
8. Tough-minded		Sensitive
9. Trusting		Suspicious
10. Practical		Imaginative
11. Forthright		Shrewd
12. Self-assured		Apprehensive
13. Conservative		Experimenting
14. Group-dependent	Writers / Creative artists / Airline pilots	Self-sufficient
15. Undisciplined		Self-controlled
16. Relaxed		Tense

Figure 10.3 The 16 source traits measured by Cattell's 16 PF are listed beside the graph. Scores can be plotted as a profile for an individual or a group. The profiles shown here are group averages for airline pilots, creative artists, and writers. Notice the similarity between artists and writers and the difference between these two groups and pilots. (Figure depicting data relating to personality profiles for source traits for writers, artists and airline pilots and as developed by Cattell, Eber, and Tatsuoka: Handbook for the Sixteen Personality Factor Questionnaire (16PF®), Copyright © 1970, 1988, 1992 by the Institute for Personality and Ability Testing (IPAT) Inc., Champaign, Illinois, USA. All rights reserved. 16PF is a registered trademark of IPAT Inc. Reproduced with permission of the copyright holder.)

Knowing where a person stands on the "Big Five" personality factors helps predict his or her behavior. For example, people who score high on conscientiousness tend to be safe drivers who are unlikely to have automobile accidents.

Five-factor model Proposes that there are five universal dimensions of personality.

The Big Five

Noel is outgoing and friendly, conscientious, even-tempered, and curious. His brother Joel is reserved, hostile, irresponsible, temperamental, and disinterested in ideas. You will be spending a week in a space capsule with either Noel or Joel. Who would you choose? If the answer seems obvious, it's because Noel and Joel were described with the **five-factor model**, a system that identifies the five most basic dimensions of personality.

Five Key Dimensions

The "Big Five" factors listed in Figure 10.4 attempt to further reduce Cattell's 16 factors to just five universal dimensions, or source traits (Costa & McCrae, 2006; Noftle & Fleeson, 2010). The Big Five may be the best answer of all to the question, What is the essence of human personality?

If you would like to compare the personalities of two people, try rating them informally on the five dimensions shown in Figure 10.4. For Factor 1, *extroversion*, rate how introverted or extroverted each person is. Factor 2, *agreeableness*, refers to how friendly, nurturant, and caring a person is, as opposed to cold, indifferent, self-centered, or spiteful. A person who is *conscientious* (Factor 3) is self-disciplined, responsible, and achieving. People low on this factor are irresponsible, careless, and undependable. Factor 4, *neuroticism*, refers to negative, upsetting emotions. People who are high in neuroticism tend to be anxious, emotionally "sour," irritable, and unhappy. Finally, people who rate high on Factor 5, *openness to experience*, are intelligent and open to new ideas (Ashcraft, 2012).

The beauty of the Big Five model is that almost any trait you can name will be related to one of the five factors. If you were selecting a college roommate, hiring an employee, or answering a singles ad, you would probably like to know all the personal dimensions covered by the Big Five. Now, try rating yourself as you read "Which Personality Are You (and Which Is Best)?"

Discovering Psychology

According to the *five-factor model*, your rating on each of five basic personality dimensions, or factors, gives a good overall description of your personality. Try rating yourself (see Figure 10.4). How well do you think your ratings describe you?

When you were rating yourself, did you notice that some of the traits in Figure 10.4 don't seem very attractive? After all, who would want to score low in *extroversion*? What could be good about being a quiet, passive, and reserved loner? In other words, aren't some personality patterns better than others?

OK, so what is the best personality pattern? You might be surprised to learn that there is no one "best" personality pattern. For example, extroverts tend to earn more during their careers than introverts and they have more sexual partners. But they are also more likely to take risks than introverts (and to land in the hospital with an injury). Extroverts are also more likely to

divorce. Because of this, extroverted men are less likely to live with their children. In other words, extroversion tends to open the doors to some life experiences and close doors to others (Cain, 2012; Nettle, 2005).

The same is true for *agreeableness*. Agreeable people attract more friends and enjoy strong social support from others. But agreeable people often put the interests of friends and family ahead of their own. This leaves agreeable people at a disadvantage. To do creative, artistic work or to succeed in the business world often involves putting your own interests first (Nettle, 2008).

How about conscientiousness? Up to a point, conscientiousness is associated with high achievement. However, having impossibly high standards, a trait called *perfectionism*, can be a problem. As you might expect, college students who are perfectionists tend to get good

grades. Yet, some students cross the line into maladaptive perfectionism, which typically *lowers* performance at school and elsewhere (Weiner & Carton, 2012). Authentic Navajo rugs always have a flaw in their intricate designs. Navajo weavers intentionally make a "mistake" in each rug as a reminder that humans are not perfect. There is a lesson in this: It is not always necessary, or even desirable, to be "perfect." To learn from your experiences you must feel free to make mistakes (Castro & Rice, 2003). Success, in the long run, is more often based on seeking "excellence" rather than "perfection" (Enns, Cox, & Clara, 2005).

Except for very extreme personality patterns, which are often maladaptive, most "personalities" involve a mix of costs and benefits. We all face the task of pursuing life experiences that best suit our own unique personality patterns (Nettle, 2008).

Extroversion										
Loner Quiet Passive Reserved	**Low**	1	2	3	4	5	6	7	**High**	Joiner Talkative Active Affectionate

Agreeableness										
Suspicious Critical Ruthless Irritable	**Low**	1	2	3	4	5	6	7	**High**	Trusting Lenient Soft-hearted Good-natured

Conscientiousness										
Negligent Lazy Disorganized Late	**Low**	1	2	3	4	5	6	7	**High**	Conscientious Hard-working Well-organized Punctual

Neuroticism										
Calm Even-tempered Comfortable Unemotional	**Low**	1	2	3	4	5	6	7	**High**	Worried Temperamental Self-conscious Emotional

Openness to Experience										
Down-to-earth Uncreative Conventional Uncurious	**Low**	1	2	3	4	5	6	7	**High**	Imaginative Creative Original Curious

Figure 10.4 The Big Five. According to the five-factor model, basic differences in personality can be "boiled down" to the dimensions shown here. Rate yourself on each factor. The five-factor model answers these essential questions about a person: Is she/he extroverted or introverted? Agreeable or difficult? Conscientious or irresponsible? Emotionally stable or unstable? Smart or unintelligent? These questions cover a large measure of what we might want to know about someone's personality. (Trait descriptions adapted from McCrae & Costa, 2001.)

The Big Five traits have been related to different brain systems and chemicals (Ashton, 2007; Nettle, 2008). They also predict how people will act in various circumstances (Sutin & Costa, 2010). For example, people who score high in conscientiousness tend to perform well at work, do well in school, and rarely have automobile accidents (Arthur & Doverspike, 2001; Brown et al., 2010; Chamorro-Premuzic & Furnham, 2003). They even live longer (Martin, Friedman, & Schwartz, 2007).

study break Personality and Trait Theories

RECITE

1. The term _____ refers to the presence or absence of desirable personal qualities.
   a. personality   b. source trait
   c. character   d. temperament

2. A system that classifies all people as either introverts or extroverts is an example of a _____ approach to personality.

3. An individual's perception of his or her own personality constitutes that person's _____.

4. Central traits are those shared by most members of a culture. T or F?

5. Cattell believes that clusters of _____ traits reveal the presence of underlying _____ traits.

6. Which of the following is *not* one of the Big Five personality factors?
   a. submissiveness   b. agreeableness
   c. extroversion   d. neuroticism

REFLECT

THINK CRITICALLY

7. Can you think of a Big Five trait besides conscientiousness that might be related to academic achievement?

SELF-REFLECT

See if you can define or describe the following terms in your own words: personality, character, trait, type, self-concept, self-esteem.

List six or seven traits that best describe your personality. Which system of traits seems to best match your list, Allport's, Cattell's, or the Big Five?

ANSWERS

1. c 2. type 3. self-concept 4. F 5. surface, source 6. a 7. In one study, conscientiousness was positively related to academic performance, as you might expect. Students high in neuroticism were also better academic performers, but only if they were not too stressed (Kappe & van der Flier, 2010).

Psychoanalytic Theory—Id Came to Me in a Dream

JOURNEY QUESTION 10.3 *How do psychodynamic theories explain personality?*

Psychodynamic theorists are not content with studying traits. Instead, they try to probe under the surface of personality—to learn what drives, conflicts, and energies animate us. Psychodynamic theorists believe that many of our actions are based on hidden, or unconscious, thoughts, needs, and emotions. What psychodynamic theorists tend to share in common with trait theorists is the view that human personality is based on a set of biological dispositions.

As we discussed in Chapter 1, **psychoanalytic theory**, the first, and best-known psychodynamic approach, grew out of the work of Sigmund Freud, a Viennese physician. As a doctor, Freud was fascinated by patients whose problems seemed to be more emotional than physical. From about 1890 until his death in 1939, Freud evolved a theory of personality that deeply influenced modern thought (Schultz & Schultz, 2013; Tauber, 2010). Let's consider some of its main features.

The Structure of Personality

How did Freud view personality? Freud's model portrays personality as a dynamic system directed by three mental structures: the *id*, the *ego*, and the *superego*. According to Freud, most behavior involves activity of all three systems. (Freud's theory includes a large number of concepts. For your convenience, they are defined in Table 10.2 rather than in glossary boxes.)

Psychoanalytic theory Freudian theory of personality that emphasizes unconscious forces and conflicts.

Table 10.2 Key Freudian Concepts

Anal stage The psychosexual stage corresponding roughly to the period of toilet training (ages 1 to 3).

Anal-expulsive personality A disorderly, destructive, cruel, or messy person.

Anal-retentive personality A person who is obstinate, stingy, or compulsive, and who generally has difficulty "letting go."

Conscience The part of the superego that causes guilt when its standards are not met.

Conscious The region of the mind that includes all mental contents a person is aware of at any given moment.

Ego The executive part of personality that directs rational behavior.

Ego ideal The part of the superego representing ideal behavior; a source of pride when its standards are met.

Electra conflict A girl's sexual attraction to her father and feelings of rivalry with her mother.

Erogenous zone Any body area that produces pleasurable sensations.

Eros Freud's name for the "life instincts."

Fixation A lasting conflict developed as a result of frustration or overindulgence.

Genital stage Period of full psychosexual development, marked by the attainment of mature adult sexuality.

Id The primitive part of personality that remains unconscious, supplies energy, and demands pleasure.

Latency According to Freud, a period in childhood when psychosexual development is more or less interrupted.

Libido In Freudian theory, the force, primarily pleasure oriented, that energizes the personality.

Moral anxiety Apprehension felt when thoughts, impulses, or actions conflict with the superego's standards.

Neurotic anxiety Apprehension felt when the ego struggles to control id impulses.

Oedipus conflict A boy's sexual attraction to his mother, and feelings of rivalry with his father.

Oral stage The period when infants are preoccupied with the mouth as a source of pleasure and means of expression.

Oral-aggressive personality A person who uses the mouth to express hostility by shouting, cursing, biting, and so forth. Also, one who actively exploits others.

Oral-dependent personality A person who wants to passively receive attention, gifts, love, and so forth.

Phallic personality A person who is vain, exhibitionistic, sensitive, and narcissistic.

Phallic stage The psychosexual stage (roughly ages 3 to 6) when a child is preoccupied with the genitals.

Pleasure principle A desire for immediate satisfaction of wishes, desires, or needs.

Preconscious An area of the mind containing information that can be voluntarily brought to awareness.

Psyche The mind, mental life, and personality as a whole.

Psychosexual stages The oral, anal, phallic, and genital stages, during which various personality traits are formed.

Reality principle Delaying action (or pleasure) until it is appropriate.

Superego A judge or censor for thoughts and actions.

Thanatos The death instinct postulated by Freud.

Unconscious The region of the mind that is beyond awareness, especially impulses and desires not directly known to a person.

The Id

The **id** is made up of innate biological instincts and urges. The id operates on the **pleasure principle**. It is self-serving, irrational, impulsive, and totally unconscious. That is, it seeks to freely express pleasure-seeking urges of all kinds. If we were solely under control of the id, the world would be chaotic beyond belief.

The id acts as a power source for the entire **psyche** (sigh-KEY), or personality. This energy, called **libido** (lih-BEE-doe), flows from the **life instincts** (or **Eros**). According to Freud, libido underlies our efforts to survive, as well as our sexual desires and pleasure seeking. Freud also described a **death instinct** (although today it is more often thought of as an impulse toward aggression). **Thanatos**, as he called it, produces aggressive and destructive urges. Freud offered humanity's long history of wars and violence as evidence of such urges. Most id energies, then, are aimed at discharging tensions related to sex and aggression.

The Ego

The **ego** is sometimes described as the "executive," because it directs energies supplied by the id. The id is like a blind warrior whose power is awesome but who must rely on others to carry out orders. The id can only form mental images of things it desires. The ego wins power to direct behavior by relating the desires of the id to external reality.

Are there other differences between the ego and the id? Yes. Recall that the id operates on the pleasure principle. The ego, in contrast, is guided by the **reality principle**. The ego is the system of thinking, planning, problem solving, and deciding. It is in conscious control of the personality and often delays action until it is practical or appropriate.

The Superego

What is the role of the superego? The **superego** acts as a judge or censor for the thoughts and actions of the ego. One part of the superego, called the **conscience**, reflects actions for which a person has been punished. When standards of the conscience are not met, you are punished internally by *guilt* feelings.

A second part of the superego is the **ego ideal**. The ego ideal reflects all behavior one's parents approved of or rewarded. The ego ideal is a source of goals and aspirations. When its standards are met, we feel *pride*.

The superego acts as an "internalized parent" to bring behavior under control. In Freudian terms, a person with a weak superego will be a delinquent, criminal, or antisocial personality. In contrast, an overly strict or harsh superego may cause inhibition, rigidity, or unbearable guilt.

The Dynamics of Personality

How do the id, ego, and superego interact? Freud didn't picture the id, ego, and superego as parts of the brain or as "little people" running the human psyche. Instead, they are conflicting mental processes. Freud theorized a delicate balance of power among the three. For example, the id's demands for immediate pleasure often clash with the superego's moral restrictions. Perhaps an example will help clarify the role of each part of the personality:

> **Freud in a Nutshell**
> Let's say you are sexually attracted to an acquaintance. The id clamors for immediate satisfaction of its sexual desires but is opposed by the superego (which finds the very thought of sex shocking). The id says, "Go for it!" The superego icily replies, "Never even think that again!" And what does the ego say? The ego says, "I have a plan!"

This is, of course, a drastic simplification, but it does capture the core of Freudian thinking. To reduce tension, the ego could begin actions leading to friendship, romance, courtship, and marriage. If the id is unusually powerful, the ego may give in and attempt a seduction. If the superego prevails, the ego may be forced to *displace* or *sublimate* sexual energies to other activities (sports, music, dancing, push-ups, cold showers). According to Freud, internal struggles and rechanneled energies typify most personality functioning.

Is the ego always caught in the middle? Basically yes, and the pressures on it can be intense. In addition to meeting the conflicting demands of the id and superego, the overworked ego must deal with external reality.

According to Freud, you feel anxiety when your ego is threatened or overwhelmed. Impulses from the id cause **neurotic anxiety** when the ego can barely keep them under

Freud considered personality an expression of two conflicting forces, life instincts and the death instinct. Both are symbolized in this drawing by Allan Gilbert. (If you don't immediately see the death symbolism, stand farther from the drawing.)

© Rykoff Collection/Corbis

control. Threats of punishment from the superego cause **moral anxiety**. Each person develops habitual ways of calming these anxieties, and many resort to using *ego-defense mechanisms* to lessen internal conflicts. Defense mechanisms are mental processes that deny, distort, or otherwise block out sources of threat and anxiety. (The ego-defense mechanisms that Freud identified are used as a form of protection against stress, anxiety, and threatening events. See Chapter 11.)

Levels of Awareness

Like other psychodynamic theorists, Freud believed that our behavior often expresses unconscious (or hidden) forces. The **unconscious** holds repressed memories and emotions, plus the instinctual drives of the id. Interestingly, modern scientists have found that the brain's limbic system does, in fact, seem to trigger unconscious emotions and memories (LeDoux, 2000).

Even though they are beyond awareness, unconscious thoughts, feelings, or urges may slip into behavior in disguised or symbolic form (Reason, 2000; yes, these are *Freudian slips*). For example, if you meet someone you would like to know better, you may unconsciously leave a book or a jacket at that person's house to ensure another meeting.

Are the actions of the ego and superego also unconscious, like the id? At times, yes, but they also operate on two other levels of awareness (Figure 10.5). The **conscious** level includes everything you are aware of at a given moment, including thoughts, perceptions, feelings, and memories. The **preconscious** contains material that can be easily brought to awareness. If you stop to think about a time when you felt angry or rejected, you will be moving this memory from the preconscious to the conscious level of awareness.

The superego's activities also reveal differing levels of awareness. At times we consciously try to live up to moral codes or standards. Yet, at other times a person may feel guilty without knowing why. Psychoanalytic theory credits such guilt to unconscious workings of the superego. Indeed, Freud believed that the unconscious origins of many feelings cannot be easily brought to awareness.

Personality Development

How does psychoanalytic theory explain personality development? Freud theorized that the core of personality is formed before age 6 in a series of **psychosexual stages**. Freud believed that erotic urges in childhood have lasting effects on development (Ashcraft, 2012). As you might expect, this is a controversial idea. However, Freud used the terms *sex* and *erotic* very broadly to refer to many physical sources of pleasure.

A Freudian Fable?

Freud identified four psychosexual stages: **oral, anal, phallic,** and **genital**. (He also described a period of "latency" between the phallic and genital stages. Latency is explained in a moment.) At each stage, a different part of the body becomes a child's primary **erogenous zone** (an area capable of producing pleasure). Each area then serves as the main source of pleasure, frustration, and self-expression. Freud believed that many adult personality traits can be traced to fixations in one or more of the stages.

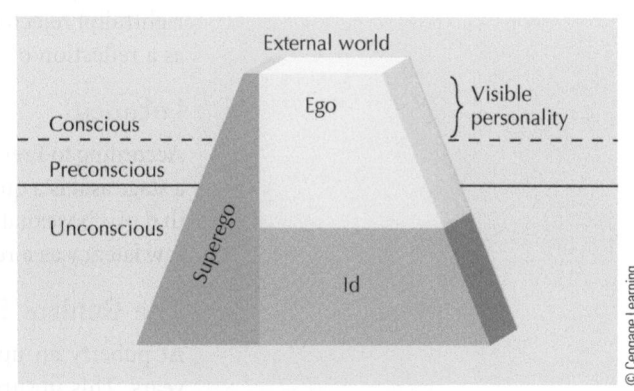

Figure 10.5 The approximate relationship between the id, ego, and superego, and the levels of awareness.

Was Freud's ever-present cigar a sign of an oral fixation? Was it a phallic symbol? Was it both? Or was it neither? Once, when he was asked, Freud himself apparently replied, "Sometimes a cigar is just a cigar." An inability to say for sure is one of the shortcomings of psychoanalytic theory.

What is a fixation? A **fixation** is an unresolved conflict or emotional hang-up caused by overindulgence or by frustration. As we describe the psychosexual stages, you'll see why Freud considered fixations important.

The Oral Stage

During the first year of life, most of an infant's pleasure comes from stimulation of the mouth. If a child is overfed or frustrated, oral traits may be created. Adult expressions of oral needs include gum chewing, nail biting, smoking, kissing, overeating, and alcoholism.

What if there is an oral fixation? Fixation early in the oral stage produces an **oral-dependent personality**. Oral-dependent persons are gullible (they swallow things easily!) and passive and need lots of attention (they want to be mothered and showered with gifts). Frustrations later in the oral stage may cause aggression, often in the form of biting. Fixations here create cynical, **oral-aggressive** adults who exploit others. They also like to argue. ("Biting sarcasm" is their forte!)

The Anal Stage

Between the ages of 1 and 3, the child's attention shifts to the process of elimination. When parents attempt toilet training, the child can gain approval or express rebellion or aggression by "holding on" or by "letting go." Therefore, harsh or lenient toilet training can cause an anal fixation that may lock such responses into personality. Freud described the **anal-retentive** (holding-on) **personality** as obstinate, stingy, orderly, and compulsively clean. (If someone accuses you of being "anal," blame Freud.) The **anal-expulsive** (letting-go) **personality** is disorderly, destructive, cruel, or messy.

The Phallic Stage

Adult traits of the **phallic personality** are vanity, exhibitionism, sensitive pride, and narcissism (self-love). Freud theorized that phallic fixations develop between the ages of 3 and 6. At this time, increased sexual interest causes the child to be physically attracted to the parent of the opposite sex. In males, this attraction leads to an **Oedipal conflict**. In it, the boy feels a rivalry with his father for the affection of his mother. Freud believed that the male child feels threatened by the father (specifically, the boy fears castration). To ease his anxieties, the boy must identify with the father. Their rivalry ends when the boy seeks to become more like his father. As he does, he begins to accept the father's values and forms a conscience.

What about the female child? Girls experience an **Electra conflict**. In this case, the girl loves her father and competes with her mother. However, according to Freud, the girl identifies with the mother more gradually.

Freud believed that females already feel castrated. Because of this, they are less driven to identify with their mothers than boys are with their fathers. This, he said, is less effective in creating a conscience. This particular part of Freudian thought has been thoroughly (and rightfully) rejected by modern experts in the psychology of women. It is better understood as a reflection of the male-dominated times in which Freud lived.

Latency

According to Freud, there is a period of latency from age 6 to puberty. **Latency** is not so much a stage as it is a quiet time during which psychosexual development is dormant. Freud's belief that psychosexual development is "on hold" at this time is hard to accept. Nevertheless, Freud saw latency as a relatively quiet time compared with the stormy first 6 years of life.

The Genital Stage

At puberty an upswing in sexual energies activates all the unresolved conflicts of earlier years. This upsurge, according to Freud, is the reason why adolescence can be filled with emotion and turmoil. The genital stage begins at puberty. It is marked, during adolescence, by a growing capacity for responsible social–sexual relationships. The genital stage ends with a mature capacity for love and the realization of full adult sexuality.

Critical Comments

Is Freudian theory still widely accepted? Although few psychologists wholeheartedly embrace Freud's theory today, it remains influential for several reasons. First, it pioneered the general idea of unconscious processes. Contemporary psychodynamic theorists generally agree that some part of the human mind is unconscious and yet plays an important role in shaping human behavior, even if they do not share Freud's (over?)focus on the motivating power of sex and death (Epstein, 2003). Other motives and cognitive factors are today seen as of equal importance.

Second, the general idea that critical events during the first years of life help shape adult personality remains widely accepted. For example, Freud was among the first to propose that development proceeds through a series of stages (Shaffer, 2009). (Erik Erikson's psycho-*social* stages, which cover development from birth to old age, are a modern offshoot of Freudian thinking. See Chapter 3.)

However, when it comes to the details, Freud was clearly often wrong. His portrayal of the elementary school years (latency) as free from sexuality and unimportant for personality development is hard to believe. His idea of the role of a stern or threatening father in the development of a strong conscience in males has also been challenged. Studies show that a son is more likely to develop a strong conscience if his father is affectionate and accepting, rather than stern and punishing.

In addition, Freud's ideas on the development of women have been thoroughly discredited (Hyde & Else-Quest, 2013). For example, Freud has been heavily criticized for his views of patients who believed they were sexually molested as children (Marcel, 2005). Freud assumed that such events were merely childhood fantasies. This view led to a long-standing tendency to disbelieve children who have been molested and women who have been raped (Brannon, 2011).

Another important criticism is that Freud's concepts are almost impossible to verify scientifically. The theory provides numerous ways to explain almost any thought, action, or feeling *after* it has occurred. However, it leads to few predictions, which makes its claims difficult to test. Although more criticisms of Freud could be listed, the fact remains that there is an element of truth to much of what he said (Moran, 2010; Tauber, 2010).

 study break Psychodynamic Theory

RECITE

1. List the three divisions of personality postulated by Freud. _____
   _____
2. Which division is totally unconscious?
3. Which division is responsible for moral anxiety?
4. Freud proposed the existence of a life instinct known as Thanatos. T or F?
5. Freud's view of personality development is based on the concept of _____ stages.
6. Arrange these stages in the proper order: phallic, anal, genital, oral, latency.
   _____

REFLECT

THINK CRITICALLY

7. Many adults would find it embarrassing or humiliating to drink from a baby bottle. Can you explain why?

SELF-REFLECT

Try to think of at least one time when your thoughts, feelings, or actions seemed to reflect the workings of each of the following: the id, the ego, and the superego.

Do you know anyone who seems to have oral, anal, or phallic personality traits? Do you think Freud's concept of fixation explains their characteristics?

Do any of your personal experiences support the existence of an Oedipus conflict or an Electra conflict? If not, is it possible that you have repressed feelings related to these conflicts?

ANSWERS

1. id, ego, superego 2. id 3. superego 4. F 5. psychosexual 6. oral, anal, phallic, genital, latency 7. A psychoanalytic theorist would say that it is because the bottle rekindles oral conflicts and feelings of vulnerability and dependence.

Humanistic Theory—Peak Experiences and Personal Growth

JOURNEY QUESTION 10.4 *What are humanistic theories of personality?*

At the beginning of this chapter, you met Sissy. Before they split up, Sissy and her husband spent a year riding mules across the country as a unique way to see America and get to know themselves better. From where do such desires for personal growth come? Humanistic theories pay special attention to the fuller use of human potentials, and they help bring balance to our overall views of personality.

Humanism focuses on human experience, problems, potentials, and ideals. As we saw in Chapter 1, the core of humanism is a positive image of humans as creative beings capable of *free will*—an ability to choose that is not determined by genetics, learning, or unconscious forces. In short, humanists seek ways to encourage our potentials to blossom.

Humanism is sometimes called a "third force" in that it is opposed to both psychoanalytic and behaviorist theories of personality. Humanism is a reaction to the pessimism of psychoanalytic theory. It rejects the Freudian view of personality as a battleground for instincts and unconscious forces. Instead, humanists view *human nature*—the traits, qualities, potentials, and behavior patterns most characteristic of the human species—as inherently good. Humanists also oppose the machine-like overtones of the behaviorist view of human nature, which we will encounter shortly. We are not, they say, merely a bundle of moldable responses.

To a humanist, the person you are today is largely the product of all the choices you have made. Humanists also emphasize immediate *subjective experience* (private perceptions of reality), rather than prior learning. They believe that there are as many "real worlds" as there are people. To understand behavior, we must learn how a person subjectively views the world—what is "real" for her or him.

Who are the major humanistic theorists? Many psychologists have added to the humanistic tradition. Of these, the best known are Abraham Maslow (1908–1970) and Carl Rogers (1902–1987). Because Maslow's idea of self-actualization was introduced in Chapter 1, let's begin with a more detailed look at this facet of his thinking.

Maslow and Self-Actualization

Abraham Maslow became interested in people who were living unusually effective lives (Hoffman, 2008). He studied only people of obvious creativity or high achievement until it became clear that anyone can live a rich, creative, and satisfying life (Davidson, Bromfield, & Beck, 2007). Maslow referred to the process of fully developing personal potentials as **self-actualization** (Maslow, 1954). The heart of self-actualization is a continuous search for personal fulfillment (Ewen, 2009; Peterson & Park, 2010; Reiss & Havercamp, 2005).

Characteristics of Self-Actualizers

A *self-actualizer* is a person who is living creatively and fully using his or her potentials. Maslow found that self-actualizers tend to fit the following profile:

1. **Efficient perceptions of reality.** Self-actualizers are able to judge situations correctly and honestly. They are very sensitive to the fake and dishonest.
2. **Comfortable acceptance of self, others, and nature.** Self-actualizers accept their own human nature with all its flaws. The shortcomings of others and the contradictions of the human condition are accepted with humor and tolerance.
3. **Spontaneity.** Maslow's subjects extended their creativity into everyday activities. Actualizers tend to be unusually alive, engaged, and spontaneous.
4. **Task centering.** Most of Maslow's subjects had a mission to fulfill in life or some task or problem outside of themselves to pursue. Humanitarians such as Albert Schweitzer and Mother Teresa represent this quality.

Humanism An approach that focuses on human experience, problems, potentials, and ideals.

Self-actualization The process of fully developing personal potentials.

5. **Autonomy.** Self-actualizers are free from reliance on external authorities or other people. They tend to be resourceful and independent.

6. **Continued freshness of appreciation.** The self-actualizer seems to constantly renew appreciation of life's basic goodness. A sunset or a flower will be experienced as intensely time after time as it was at first. There is an "innocence of vision," like that of an artist or child.

7. **Fellowship with humanity.** Maslow's subjects felt a deep identification with others and the human situation in general.

8. **Profound interpersonal relationships.** The interpersonal relationships of self-actualizers are marked by deep, loving bonds (Hanley & Abell, 2002).

9. **Comfort with solitude.** Despite their satisfying relationships with others, self-actualizing persons value solitude and are comfortable being alone (Sumerlin & Bundrick, 1996).

10. **Nonhostile sense of humor.** This refers to the wonderful capacity to laugh at oneself. It also describes the kind of humor a man like Abraham Lincoln had. Lincoln probably never made a joke that hurt anybody. His wry comments were a gentle prodding of human shortcomings.

11. **Peak experiences.** All of Maslow's subjects reported the frequent occurrence of **peak experiences** (temporary moments of self-actualization). These occasions were marked by feelings of ecstasy, harmony, and deep meaning. Self-actualizers reported feeling at one with the universe, stronger and calmer than ever before, filled with light, beautiful and good, and so forth.

What steps can be taken to promote self-actualization? For Maslow, there is no magic formula for leading a more creative life. Undoubtedly there are many ways to make full use of personal potential. Maslow's primary contribution was to draw our attention to the possibility of lifelong personal growth (Peterson & Park, 2010). Self-actualization is primarily a *process*, not a goal or an end point. Nevertheless, some helpful suggestions can be gleaned from his writings (Maslow, 1954, 1967, 1971). Here are some ways to begin:

1. **Be willing to change.** Continually ask yourself, "Am I living in a way that is deeply satisfying to me and that truly expresses me?" If not, be prepared to make changes in your life.

2. **Take responsibility.** You can become an architect of self by acting as if you are personally responsible for every aspect of your life. Avoid the habit of blaming others for your own shortcomings.

3. **Examine your motives.** Self-discovery involves an element of risk. If your behavior is restricted by a desire for safety or security, it may be time to test some limits.

4. **Experience honestly and directly.** Wishful thinking is another barrier to personal growth. Self-actualizers trust themselves enough to accept all kinds of information without distorting it to fit their fears and desires. Try to see yourself as others do.

5. **Make use of positive experiences.** Maslow considered peak experiences temporary moments of self-actualization. Therefore, you might actively repeat activities that have caused feelings of awe, amazement, exaltation, renewal, reverence, humility, fulfillment, or joy.

6. **Be prepared to be different.** Maslow felt that everyone has a potential for "greatness," but most fear becoming what they might. As part of personal growth, be prepared to trust your own impulses and feelings; don't automatically judge yourself by the standards of others.

7. **Get involved.** With few exceptions, self-actualizers tend to have a mission or "calling" in life. For these people, "work" is not done just to fill deficiency needs, but to satisfy higher yearnings for truth, beauty, community, and meaning. Turn your attention to problems outside yourself.

8. **Assess your progress.** There is no final point at which one becomes self-actualized. It's important to gauge your progress frequently and to renew your efforts. If you feel bored at school, at a job, or in a relationship, consider it a challenge. Have you been taking responsibility for your own personal growth?

Peak experiences Temporary moments of self-actualization.

The Whole Person: Thriving

It could be said that self-actualizing people are thriving, not just surviving. Like Maslow, proponents of positive psychology have tried to scientifically study positive personality traits that contribute to happiness and well-being (Keyes & Haidt, 2003; Seligman, 2003). Although their work does not always fall within the humanistic tradition, their findings are relevant here.

Martin Seligman, Christopher Peterson, and others have identified six human strengths that contribute to well-being and life satisfaction. Each strength is expressed by the positive personality traits listed here (Peterson & Seligman, 2004):

- **Wisdom and knowledge:** Creativity, curiosity, open-mindedness, love of learning, perspective
- **Courage:** Bravery, persistence, integrity, vitality
- **Humanity:** Love, kindness, social intelligence
- **Justice:** Citizenship, fairness, leadership
- **Temperance:** Forgiveness, humility, prudence, self-control
- **Transcendence:** Appreciation of beauty and excellence, gratitude, hope, humor, spirituality

Which of the positive personality traits are most closely related to happiness? One study found that traits of hope, vitality, gratitude, love, and curiosity are strongly associated with life satisfaction (Park, Peterson, & Seligman, 2004). These characteristics, in combination with Maslow's descriptions of self-actualizers, provide a good guide to the characteristics that help people live happy, meaningful lives.

Carl Rogers' Self Theory

Carl Rogers, another well-known humanist, also emphasized the human capacity for inner peace and happiness (Elliott & Farber, 2010). The *fully functioning person*, he said, lives in harmony with his or her deepest feelings and impulses. Such people are open to their experiences, and they trust their inner urges and intuitions (Rogers, 1961). Rogers believed that this attitude is most likely to occur when a person receives ample amounts of love and acceptance from others.

Personality Structure and Dynamics

Rogers' theory emphasizes the **self**, a flexible and changing perception of personal identity. Much behavior can be understood as an attempt to maintain consistency between our *self-image* and our actions. (Your **self-image** is a total subjective perception of your body and personality.) For example, people who think of themselves as kind tend to be considerate in most situations.

Let's say I know a person who thinks she is kind, but she really isn't. How does that fit Rogers' theory? According to Rogers, we allow experiences that match our self-image into awareness, where they gradually change the self. Information or feelings inconsistent with the self-image are said to be incongruent. Thus, a person who thinks she is kind but really isn't is in a state of **incongruence**. In other words, there is a discrepancy between her experiences and her self-image. As another example, it would be incongruent to believe that you are a person who "never gets angry" if you spend much of each day seething inside.

Experiences seriously incongruent with the self-image can be threatening, and are often distorted or denied conscious recognition. Blocking, denying, or distorting experiences prevents the self from changing. This creates a gulf between the self-image and reality (Ryckman, 2013). As the self-image grows more unrealistic, the *incongruent person* becomes confused, vulnerable, dissatisfied, or seriously maladjusted (**Figure 10.6**). In line with Rogers' observations, a study of college students confirmed that being

Joe McBride/Getty Images

Humanists consider self-image a central determinant of behavior and personal adjustment.

Self A continuously evolving conception of one's personal identity.

Self-image Total subjective perception of one's body and personality (another term for self-concept).

Incongruence A state that exists when there is a discrepancy between one's experiences and self-image or between one's self-image and ideal self.

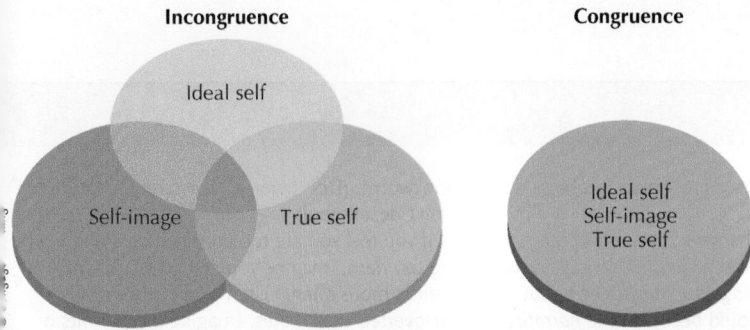

Incongruence

Ideal self

Self-image   True self

Congruence

Ideal self
Self-image
True self

Figure 10.6 Incongruence occurs when there is a mismatch between any of these three entities: the ideal self (the person you would like to be), your self-image (the person you think you are), and the true self (the person you actually are). Self-esteem suffers when there is a large difference between one's ideal self and self-image. Anxiety and defensiveness are common when the self-image does not match the true self.

authentic is vital for healthy functioning. That is, we need to feel that our behavior accurately expresses who we are (Sheldon et al., 1997). Please note, however, that being authentic doesn't mean you can do whatever you want. Being true to yourself is no excuse for acting irresponsibly or ignoring the feelings of others (Kernis & Goldman, 2005).

When your self-image is consistent with what you really think, feel, do, and experience, you are best able to actualize your potentials. Rogers also considered it essential to have congruence between the self-image and the **ideal self**. The ideal self is similar to Freud's ego ideal. It is an image of the person you would most like to be (Zentner & Renaud, 2007).

Is it really incongruent not to live up to your ideal self? Rogers was aware that we never fully attain our ideals. Nevertheless, the greater the gap between the way you see yourself and the way you would like to be, the more tension and anxiety you will experience.

Rogers emphasized that to maximize our potentials, we must accept information about ourselves as honestly as possible. In accord with his thinking, researchers have found that people with a close match between their self-image and ideal self tend to be socially poised, confident, and resourceful. Those with a poor match tend to be depressed, anxious, and insecure (Boldero et al., 2005).

According to psychologists Hazel Markus and Paula Nurius (1986), our ideal self is only one of a number of **possible selves** (persons we could become or are afraid of becoming). Sissy, who was described earlier, is an interesting personality, to say the least. Sissy is one of those people who seems to have lived many lives in the time that most of us manage only one. Like Sissy, you may have pondered many possible personal identities. (See "Telling Stories about Ourselves.")

Possible selves translate our hopes, fears, fantasies, and goals into specific images of who we *could* be. Thus, a beginning law student might picture herself as a successful attorney, an enterprising college student might imagine himself as an Internet entrepreneur, and a person on a diet might imagine both slim and grossly obese possible selves. Such images tend to direct our future behavior (Oyserman et al., 2004).

Of course, almost everyone over age 30 has probably felt the anguish of realizing that some cherished possible selves will never be realized. Nevertheless, there is value in asking yourself not just "Who am I?" but also "Who would I like to become?" As you do, remember Maslow's advice that everyone has a potential for "greatness," but most fear becoming what they might.

Humanistic View of Development

Why do mirrors, photographs, video cameras, and the reactions of others hold such fascination and threat for many people? Carl Rogers' theory suggests it is because they provide information about one's self. The development of a self-image depends greatly on information from the environment. It begins with a sorting of perceptions and

Ideal self An idealized image of oneself (the person one would like to be).

Possible self A collection of thoughts, beliefs, feelings, and images concerning the person one could become.

Clinical File

You know these two student types: the carefree party animal and the conscientious bookworm. College life often creates a conflict between opportunities for fun with friends and the need to study hard. Perhaps you even think of yourself as one or the other. Is there any truth to these (stereo)types? Can you change your type?

In general, our personality traits are relatively stable characteristics (McAdams & Pals, 2006). As a result, a person high in the Big Five traits of extroversion and agreeableness will tend to embrace a carefree college lifestyle. In comparison, someone high in conscientiousness will find it easier to hit the books (McGregor, McAdams, & Little, 2006).

Does that mean a partier can't become a bookworm (or vice versa)? It depends: Do you mean over a week? Or a lifetime? Personality traits do slowly change as we age. In particular, we tend to become more agreeable, conscientious, and emotionally stable as we grow older (Roberts & Mroczek, 2008).

Oh, you need to change by the end of the semester? That's a taller order. In that case, you might want to try telling yourself stories about possible selves you could become. The *narrative approach* to personality asserts that our personalities are shaped by the stories we tell about ourselves (Lodi-Smith et al., 2009; Pals, 2006). In other words, alternate life stories are not just fantasies or daydreams. They actually influence who we are and who we become.

So, if you feel that you are being too careless and carefree at school, start imagining yourself studying more, getting to classes on time, and getting good grades. Listen to the stories of successful students and use them to revise your own story. Visit your campus counseling center to learn more about how to succeed at school. In other words, imagine yourself as a bit more of a bookworm. (Don't worry, your carefree nature won't desert you!)

If you feel you are too conscientious and working too hard, imagine yourself going out with friends more often. Listen to the stories of your extroverted classmates. Imagine the benefits of balancing work and play in your life. If you are shy or perfectionistic, visit your campus counseling center to learn how to become more sociable or relaxed. And, again, don't worry: Having more fun won't make you irresponsible.

Whatever possible self you choose to pursue, you are more likely to become what you imagine if you elaborate your story, making it more detailed and "real" as you gradually adopt new patterns. You *can* create a new narrative identity for yourself (Bauer, McAdams, & Pals, 2008; Nelson et al., 2012).

---

feelings: my body, my toes, my nose, I want, I like, I am, and so on. Soon, it expands to include self-evaluation: I am a good person, I did something bad just now, and so forth.

How does development of the self contribute to later personality functioning? Rogers believed that positive and negative evaluations by others cause children to develop internal standards of evaluation called **conditions of worth**. In other words, we learn that some actions win our parents' love and approval, whereas others are rejected. More important, parents may label some *feelings* as bad or wrong. For example, a child might be told that it is wrong to feel angry toward a brother or sister—even when anger is justified. Likewise, a little boy might be told that he must not cry or show fear, two very normal emotions.

Learning to evaluate some experiences or feelings as "good" and others as "bad" is directly related to a later capacity for self-esteem, positive self-evaluation, or **positive self-regard**, to use Rogers' term. To think of yourself as a good, lovable, worthwhile person, your behavior and experiences must match your internal conditions of worth. The problem is that this can cause incongruence by leading to the denial of many true feelings and experiences.

To put it simply, Rogers blamed many adult emotional problems on attempts to live by the standards of others (Ashcraft, 2012). He believed that congruence and self-actualization are encouraged by replacing conditions of worth with **organismic valuing** (a natural, undistorted, full-body reaction to an experience). Organismic valuing is a direct, gut-level response to life that avoids the filtering and distortion of incongruence. It involves trusting one's own feelings and perceptions. Organismic valuing is most likely to develop, Rogers felt, when children (or adults) receive **unconditional positive regard** (unshakable love and approval) from others. That is, when they are "prized" as worthwhile human beings, just for being themselves, without any conditions or strings attached. Although this may be a luxury few people enjoy, we are more likely to move toward our ideal selves if we receive affirmation and support from a close partner (Drigotas et al., 1999).

Conditions of worth Internal standards used to judge the value of one's thoughts, actions, feelings, or experiences.

Positive self-regard Thinking of oneself as a good, lovable, worthwhile person.

Organismic valuing A natural, undistorted, full-body reaction to an experience.

Unconditional positive regard Unshakable love and approval given without qualification.

Learning Theories of Personality—Habit I Seen You Before?

JOURNEY QUESTION 10.5 *What do behaviorists and social learning theorists emphasize in their approach to personality?*

Unlike psychodynamic and humanistic theories, behavioral theorists explain personality through straightforward concepts, such as learning, reinforcement, and imitation. Behavioral and social learning theories are also based on more scientific research, which makes them powerful ways of looking at personality.

How do behaviorists approach personality? According to some critics, as if people are robots. Actually, the behaviorist position is not nearly that mechanistic, and its value is well established. Behaviorists have shown repeatedly that children can *learn* things like kindness, hostility, generosity, or destructiveness. What does this have to do with personality? Everything, according to the behavioral viewpoint.

Behavioral personality theories emphasize that personality is no more (or less) than a collection of relatively stable learned behavior patterns. Personality, like other learned behavior, is acquired through classical and operant conditioning, observational learning, reinforcement, extinction, generalization, and discrimination. When Mother says, "It's not nice to make mud pies with Mommy's blender. If we want to grow up to be a big girl, we won't do it again, will we?" she serves as a model and in other ways shapes her daughter's personality.

Strict learning theorists reject the idea that personality is made up of traits. They would assert, for instance, that there is no such thing as a trait of "honesty" (Mischel, 2004).

Certainly some people are honest and others are not. How can honesty not be a trait? Remember, for many trait theorists, traits are biological dispositions. According to learning theorists, they are, instead, stable learned responses. If his parents consistently reward little Alexander for honesty, he is more likely to become an honest adult. If his parents are less scrupulous, Alexander might well grow up differently.

Learning theorists also stress the **situational determinants** (external causes) of actions. Knowing that someone is honest does not automatically allow us to predict whether that person will be honest in a specific situation. It would not be unusual, for example, to find

Freud believed that aggressive urges are "instinctual." In contrast, behavioral theories assume that personal characteristics such as aggressiveness are learned. Is this boy's aggression the result of observational learning, harsh punishment, or prior reinforcement?

Behavioral personality theory Any model of personality that emphasizes learning and observable behavior.

Situational determinants External conditions that strongly influence behavior.

Seventy-five percent of American college students admit that they have been academically dishonest in one way or another. What can be done about these high rates of dishonesty? The behavioral perspective holds that honesty is determined as much by circumstances as it is by personality. In line with this, simple measures like announcing in classes that integrity codes will be enforced can significantly reduce cheating. Using multiple forms of exams and web-based plagiarism software and educating students about plagiarism also tend to deter dishonesty (Altschuler, 2001; McKeever, 2006).

that a person honored for returning a lost wallet had cheated on a test, bought a term paper, or broken the speed limit. If you were to ask a learning theorist, "Are you an honest person?" the reply might be, "In what situation?"

A good example of how situations can influence behavior is a study in which people were intentionally overpaid for doing an assigned task. Under normal circumstances, 80 percent kept the extra money without mentioning it. But as few as 17 percent were dishonest if the situation was altered. For instance, if people thought the money was coming out of the pocket of the person doing the study, far fewer were dishonest (Bersoff, 1999). Thus, situations always interact with our prior learning to activate behavior.

How Situations Affect Behavior

Situations vary greatly in their impact. Some are powerful. Others are trivial and have little effect on behavior. The more powerful the situation, the easier it is to see what is meant by *situational determinants*. For example, each of the following situations would undoubtedly have a strong influence on your behavior: An armed person walks into your classroom; you accidentally sit on a lighted cigarette; you find your lover in bed with your best friend. Yet even these situations could provoke very different reactions from different personalities. That's why behavior is always a product of both prior learning and the situations in which we find ourselves (Mischel, Shoda, & Smith, 2008; Mischel & Shoda, 2010).

Ultimately, what is predictable about personality is that we respond in fairly consistent ways to certain types of situations. Consider, for example, two people who are easily angered: One person might get angry when she is delayed (for example, in traffic or a checkout line), but not when she misplaces something at home; the other person might get angry whenever she misplaces things, but not when she is delayed. Overall, the two women are equally prone to anger, but their anger tends to occur in different patterns and different types of situations (Mischel, 2004).

Personality = Behavior

How do learning theorists view the structure of personality? The behavioral view of personality can be illustrated with an early theory proposed by John Dollard and Neal Miller (1950). In their view, *habits* (learned behavior patterns) make up the structure of personality. As for the dynamics of personality, habits are governed by four elements of learning: *drive, cue, response,* and *reward*. A *drive* is any stimulus strong enough to goad a person to action (such as hunger, pain, lust, frustration, or fear). *Cues* are signals from the environment. These signals guide *responses* (actions) so that they are most likely to bring about *reward* (positive reinforcement).

How does that relate to personality? Let's say a child named Amina is frustrated by her older brother Kelvin, who takes a toy from her. Amina could respond in several ways: She could throw a temper tantrum, hit Kelvin, tell her mother, and so forth. The response she chooses is guided by available cues and the previous effects of each response. If telling her mother has paid off in the past, and her mother is present, telling again may be Amina's immediate response. If a different set of cues exists (if her mother is absent or if Kelvin looks particularly menacing), Amina may select some other response. To an outside observer, Amina's actions seem to reflect her personality. To a learning theorist, they simply express the combined effects of drive, cue, response, and reward. Behavioral theories have contributed greatly to the creation of therapies for various psychological problems and disorders. See the discussion of behavior therapy in Chapter 13.

Doesn't this analysis leave out a lot? Yes. Learning theorists originally set out to provide a simple, clear model of personality. But they eventually had to face a fact that they previously tended to set aside: People think. Contemporary behavioral psychologists—whose views include perception, thinking, expectations, and other mental events—are called social learning theorists. Learning principles, modeling, thought patterns, perceptions, expectations, beliefs, goals, emotions, and social relationships are combined in **social learning theory** to explain personality (Mischel, Shoda, & Smith, 2008; Santrock, 2010).

Social learning theory An explanation of personality that combines learning principles, cognition, and the effects of social relationships.

Social Learning Theory

The "cognitive behaviorism" of social learning theory can be illustrated by three concepts proposed by Julian Rotter: the psychological situation, expectancy, and reinforcement value (Rotter & Hochreich, 1975). Let's examine each.

Someone trips you. How do you respond? Your reaction probably depends on whether you think it was planned or an accident. It is not enough to know the setting in which a person responds. We also need to know the person's **psychological situation** (how the person interprets or defines the situation). As another example, let's say you score low on an exam. Do you consider it a challenge to work harder, a sign that you should drop the class, or an excuse to get drunk? Again, your interpretation is important.

Our actions are affected by an **expectancy**, or anticipation, that making a response will lead to reinforcement. To continue the example, if working harder has paid off in the past, it is a likely reaction to a low test score. But to predict your response, we would also have to know if you *expect* your efforts to pay off in the present situation. In fact, expected reinforcement may be more important than actual past reinforcement. And what about the *value* you attach to grades, school success, or personal ability? The third concept, **reinforcement value**, states that we attach different subjective values to various activities or rewards. You will likely choose to study harder if passing your courses and obtaining a degree is highly valued. This, too, must be taken into account to understand personality.

Self-Efficacy

An ability to control your own life is the essence of what it means to be human (Corey & Corey, 2010). Because of this, Albert Bandura believes that one of the most important expectancies we develop concerns **self-efficacy** (EF-uh-keh-see: a capacity for producing a desired result). Believing that our actions will produce desired results influences the activities and environments we choose (Bandura, 2001; Schultz & Schultz, 2013). You're attracted to someone in your anthropology class. Will you ask him or her out? You're beginning to consider a career in psychology. Will you take the courses you need to get into graduate school? You'd like to exercise more on the weekends. Will you join a hiking club? In these and countless other situations, efficacy beliefs play a key role in shaping our lives (Byrne, Barry, & Petry, 2012; Prat-Sala & Redford, 2012).

John Mitterer

Spring break in Key West. We can reward ourselves through self-reinforcement for personal achievements and other "good" behavior. (At least that's the theory, right?)

Self-Reinforcement

One more idea deserves mention. At times, we all evaluate our actions and may reward ourselves with special privileges or treats for "good behavior." With this in mind, social learning theory adds the concept of self-reinforcement to the behaviorist view. **Self-reinforcement** refers to praising or rewarding yourself for having made a particular response (such as completing a school assignment). Thus, habits of self-praise and self-blame become an important part of personality (Schultz & Schultz, 2013). In fact, self-reinforcement can be thought of as the social learning theorist's counterpart to the superego.

Self-reinforcement is closely related to high self-esteem. The reverse is also true: Mildly depressed college students tend to have low rates of self-reinforcement. It is not known if low self-reinforcement leads to depression, or the reverse. In either case, higher rates of self-reinforcement are associated with less depression and greater life satisfaction (Seybolt & Wagner, 1997). From a behavioral viewpoint, there is value in learning to be "good to yourself."

Behaviorist View of Development

How do learning theorists account for personality development? Many of Freud's ideas can be restated in terms of learning theory. John Dollard and Neal Miller (1950) agree with Freud that the first 6 years are crucial for personality development, but for different reasons.

Psychological situation A situation as it is perceived and interpreted by an individual, not as it exists objectively.

Expectancy Anticipation about the effect a response will have, especially regarding reinforcement.

Reinforcement value The subjective value a person attaches to a particular activity or reinforcer.

Self-efficacy Belief in your capacity to produce a desired result.

Self-reinforcement Praising or rewarding oneself for having made a particular response (such as completing a school assignment).

Rather than thinking in terms of psychosexual urges and fixations, they ask, "What makes early learning experiences so lasting in their effects?" Their answer is that childhood is a time of urgent drives, powerful rewards and punishments, and crushing frustrations. Also important is *social reinforcement*, which is based on praise, attention, or approval from others. These forces combine to shape the core of personality (Shaffer, 2009).

Critical Situations

Dollard and Miller believe that during childhood, four **critical situations** are capable of leaving a lasting imprint on personality. These are (1) feeding, (2) toilet or cleanliness training, (3) sex training, and (4) learning to express anger or aggression. (Does this remind you of Freud?)

Why are these of special importance? Feeding serves as an illustration. If children are fed when they cry, it encourages them to actively manipulate their parents. The child allowed to cry without being fed learns to be passive. Thus, a basic active or passive orientation toward the world may be created by early feeding experiences. Feeding can also affect later social relationships because the child learns to associate people with pleasure or with frustration and discomfort.

Toilet and cleanliness training can be a particularly strong source of emotion for both parents and children. Rashad's parents were aghast the day they found him smearing feces about with joyful abandon. They reacted with sharp punishment, which frustrated and confused Rashad. Many attitudes toward cleanliness, conformity, and bodily functions are formed at such times. Studies have also long shown that severe, punishing, or frustrating toilet training can have undesirable effects on personality development (Christophersen & Mortweet, 2003). Because of this, toilet and cleanliness training demand patience and a sense of humor.

What about sex and anger? When, where, and how a child learns to express anger and sexual feelings can leave an imprint on personality. Specifically, permissiveness for sexual and aggressive behavior in childhood is linked to adult needs for power (McClelland & Pilon, 1983). This link probably occurs because permitting such behaviors allows children to get pleasure from asserting themselves. Sex training also involves learning socially defined "male" and "female" gender roles—which, in turn, affects personality (Cervone & Pervin, 2010).

Adult personality is influenced by identification with parents and imitation of their behavior.

Critical situations Situations during childhood that are capable of leaving a lasting imprint on personality.

Gender role The pattern of behaviors that are regarded as "male" or "female" by one's culture; sometimes also referred to as a sex role.

Identification Feeling emotionally connected to a person and seeing oneself as like him or her.

Imitation An attempt to match one's own behavior to another person's behavior.

Personality and Gender

What does it mean to have a "masculine" or "feminine" personality? From birth onward, children are labeled as boys or girls and encouraged to learn appropriate **gender roles**—the favored pattern of behavior expected of each sex (Fine, 2010; Orenstein, 2011). According to social learning theory, identification and imitation contribute greatly to personality development and to sex training. **Identification** refers to the child's emotional attachment to admired adults, especially those who provide love and care. Identification typically encourages **imitation**, a desire to act like the admired person. Many "male" or "female" traits come from children's attempts to imitate a same-sex parent with whom they identify (Helgeson, 2009).

If children are around parents of both sexes, why don't they imitate behavior typical of the opposite sex as well as of the same sex? You may recall from Chapter 6 that learning takes place vicariously as well as directly. This means that we can learn without direct reward by observing and remembering the actions of others. But the actions we choose to imitate depend on their outcomes. For example, boys and girls have equal chances to observe adults and other children acting aggressively. However, girls are less likely than boys to imitate directly aggressive behavior (shouting at or hitting another person). Instead, girls are more likely to rely on indirectly aggressive behavior (excluding others from friendship, spreading rumors). This may well be because the expression of direct aggression is thought to be inappropriate for girls.

As a consequence, girls do not as often see direct female aggression rewarded or approved (Field et al., 2009). In others words, "girlfighting" is likely a culturally reinforced pattern (Brown, 2005). Intriguingly, over the last few years, girls have become more willing to engage in direct aggression as popular culture presents more and more images of directly aggressive women (Artz, 2005).

We have considered only a few examples of the links between social learning and personality. Nevertheless, the connection is unmistakable. When parents accept their children and give them affection, the children become sociable, positive, and emotionally stable, and they have high self-esteem. When parents are rejecting, punishing, sarcastic, humiliating, or neglectful, their children become hostile, unresponsive, unstable, and dependent and have impaired self-esteem (Triandis & Suh, 2002).

Historically, parents and other adults in Western countries like the United States tended to encourage boys to engage in **instrumental** (goal-directed) **behaviors**, to be directly aggressive, to hide their emotions, and to prepare for the world of work. Girls, on the other hand, were encouraged in **expressive** (emotion-oriented) **behaviors** and, to a lesser degree, were socialized for indirect aggression and for motherhood (Eagly, 2009). Thus, from an early age, males and females tended to grow up in different, gender-defined cultures (Fine, 2010; Shaffer & Kipp, 2010). But these differences are becoming less and less noticeable as traditional male and female gender roles have been called into question.

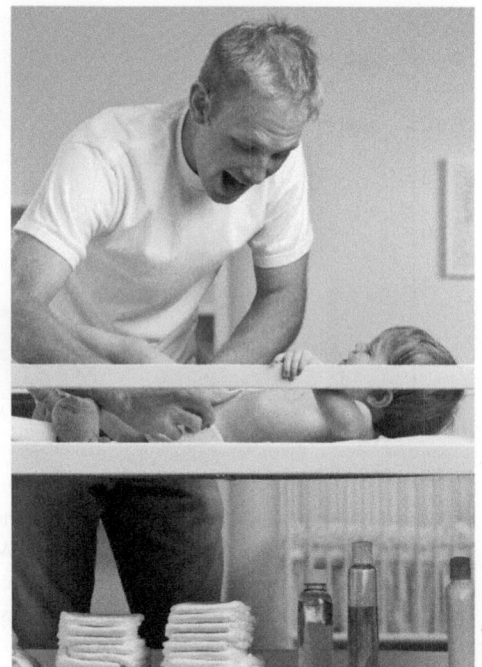

Androgyny

Are you aggressive, ambitious, analytical, assertive, athletic, competitive, decisive, dominant, forceful, independent, individualistic, self-reliant, and willing to take risks? If so, you are quite "masculine." Are you affectionate, cheerful, childlike, compassionate, flatterable, gentle, gullible, loyal, sensitive, shy, soft-spoken, sympathetic, tender, understanding, warm, and yielding? If so, then you are quite "feminine." What if you have traits from both lists? In that case, you may be *androgynous* (an-DROJ-ih-nus).

The two lists you just read are from the seminal work of psychologist Sandra Bem (1974). By combining 20 traditionally "masculine" traits (self-reliant, assertive, and so forth), 20 traditionally "feminine" traits (affectionate, gentle), and 20 neutral traits (truthful, friendly), Bem created the *Bem Sex Role Inventory* (BSRI). (Some psychologists prefer to use the term *sex role* instead of gender role.) Next, she and her associates gave the BSRI to thousands of people, asking them to say whether each trait applied to them. Of those surveyed, 50 percent fell into traditional feminine or masculine categories, 15 percent scored higher on traits of the opposite sex, and 35 percent were androgynous, getting high scores on both feminine and masculine items.

The word **androgyny** (an-DROJ-ih-nee) literally means "man-woman" and refers to having both masculine and feminine traits (Helgeson, 2009). Bem is convinced that our complex society requires flexibility with respect to gender roles. She believes that it is necessary for men to also be gentle, compassionate, sensitive, and yielding and for women to also be forceful, self-reliant, independent, and ambitious—*as the situation requires*. In short, Bem feels that more people should be androgynous and has shown that androgynous individuals are more adaptable. They seem especially to be less hindered by images of "feminine" or "masculine" behavior. In contrast, rigid gender stereotypes and gender roles can seriously restrict behavior.

For example, in one study people were given the choice of doing either a "masculine" activity (oil a hinge, nail boards together, and so forth) or a "feminine" activity (prepare a baby bottle, wind yarn into a ball, and so on). Masculine men and feminine women consistently chose to do gender-appropriate activities, even when the opposite choice paid more!

Bem has concluded that masculine males have great difficulty expressing warmth, playfulness, and concern—even when they are appropriate (Bem, 1975, 1981). Masculine men, it seems, tend to view such feelings as unacceptably "feminine." Masculine men (let's call

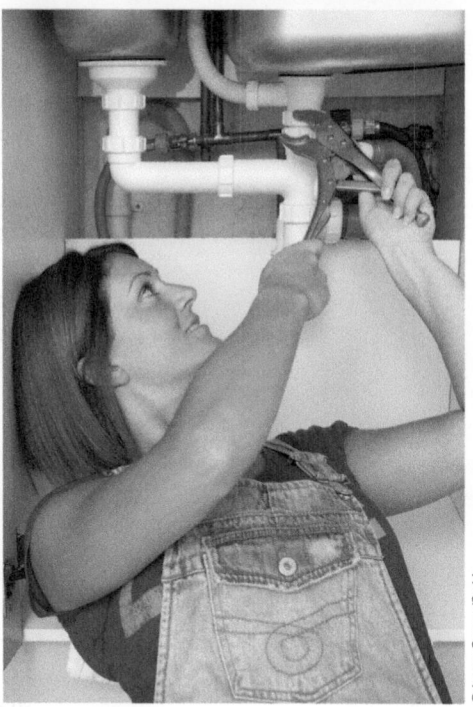

Androgynous individuals adapt easily to both traditionally "feminine" and "masculine" situations.

Instrumental behaviors Behaviors directed toward the achievement of some goal; behaviors that are instrumental in producing some effect.

Expressive behaviors Behaviors that express or communicate emotion or personal feelings.

Androgyny The presence of both "masculine" and "feminine" traits in a single person (as masculinity and femininity are defined within one's culture).

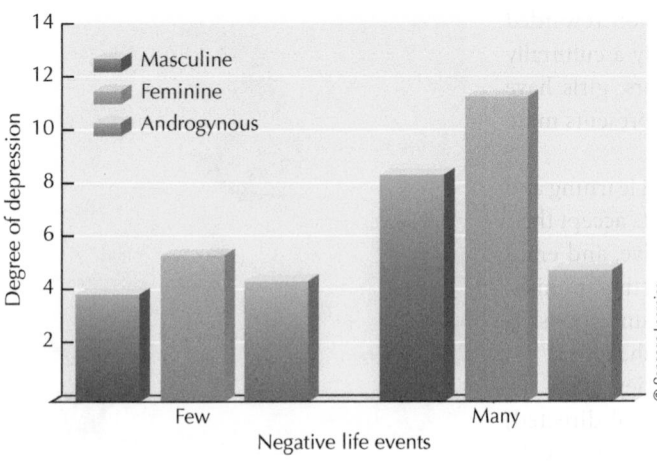

Figure 10.7 Another indication of the possible benefits of androgyny is found in a study of reactions to stress. When confronted with an onslaught of negative events, strongly masculine or feminine persons become more depressed than androgynous individuals do. (Adapted from Roos & Cohen, 1987.)

them "manly men") also find it hard to accept emotional support from others, particularly from women (Levant, 2001, 2003).

Problems faced by highly feminine women are the reverse of those faced by masculine men. Such women have trouble being independent and assertive, even when these qualities are desirable. In contrast, more androgynous individuals are higher in emotional intelligence (Guastello & Guastello, 2003). (Remember Chapter 9?)

Gender in Perspective

Over the years, androgyny has been variously supported, attacked, and debated. Now, as the dust begins to settle, the picture looks like this:

- Having "masculine" traits means primarily that a person is independent and assertive. Scoring high in "masculinity," therefore, is related to high self-esteem and to success in many situations (Long, 1989).
- Having "feminine" traits means primarily that a person is nurturing and interpersonally oriented. People who score high in "femininity," therefore, are more likely to seek and receive social support. They tend to experience greater social closeness with others and more happiness in marriage (Reevy & Maslach, 2001).

In sum, there are advantages to possessing both "feminine" and "masculine" traits (Guastello & Guastello, 2003; Lefkowitz & Zeldow, 2006). In general, androgynous persons are more flexible when it comes to coping with difficult situations (Crooks & Baur, 2011; Woodhill & Samuels, 2004) (Figure 10.7). Androgynous persons also tend to be more satisfied with their lives. Apparently, they can use both instrumental and emotionally expressive capacities to enhance their lives and relationships (Lefkowitz & Zeldow, 2006).

It is worth saying again that many people remain comfortable with traditional views of gender. Nevertheless, "feminine" traits and "masculine" traits can exist in the same person, and androgyny can be a highly adaptive balance.

Nature and Nurture—The Great Personality Debate

JOURNEY QUESTION 10.6 *How do heredity and environment affect personality?*

Personality theorists have long grappled with the relative roles of nature and nurture in shaping personalities. Some theories, such as trait theory and psychoanalytic theory, stress the role of inherited biological predispositions, whereas others, including humanist and behavioral theories, stress the role of learning and life experiences. Let's look at the roles that heredity and biological predispositions (nature) and environmental situations (nurture) play in forming personality.

Do We Inherit Personality?

Even newborn babies differ in **temperament**, the "raw material" from which personalities are formed, such as biological predispositions to be sensitive, irritable, and distractible and to display a typical mood (Rothbart, 2007). Temperament, which refers to the hereditary aspects of your personality, has a large impact on how infants interact with their parents. Judging from Sissy's adult personality, you might guess that she was an active, happy baby.

Temperament The hereditary aspects of personality, including sensitivity, activity levels, prevailing mood, irritability, and adaptability.

At what age are personality traits firmly established? Personality starts to stabilize at around age 3 and continues to "harden" through age 50 (Caspi, Roberts, & Shiner, 2005; Hopwood et al., 2011). However, as mentioned earlier, personality slowly matures during old age as most people continue to become more conscientious, agreeable, and emotionally stable (Roberts & Mroczek, 2008). It appears that stereotypes of the "grumpy old man" and "cranky old woman" are largely unfounded.

Does the stability of personality traits mean that they are affected by heredity? Some breeds of dogs have reputations for being friendly, aggressive, intelligent, calm, or emotional. Such differences fall in the realm of **behavioral genetics**, the study of inherited behavioral traits. We know that facial features, eye color, body type, and many other physical characteristics are inherited. So are many of our behavioral dispositions (Bouchard, 2004; Kalat, 2013). Genetic studies have shown that intelligence, language, some mental disorders, temperament, and other complex qualities are influenced by heredity. In view of such findings, it wouldn't be a surprise to find that genes affect personality as well (Nettle, 2006).

Wouldn't comparing the personalities of identical twins help answer the question? It would indeed—especially if the twins were separated at birth or soon after.

Studying Traits

For several decades, psychologists at the University of Minnesota have been studying identical twins who grew up in different homes. Medical and psychological tests reveal that reunited twins are very much alike, even when they are reared apart (Bouchard, 2004; Bouchard et al., 1990). If one twin excels at art, music, dance, drama, or athletics, the other is likely to as well—despite wide differences in childhood environment. They may even be similar in voice quality, facial gestures, hand movements, and nervous tics, such as nail biting. However, as "The Amazing Twins" explains, it's wise to be cautious about some reports of extraordinary similarities in reunited twins.

Summary

Studies of twins make it clear that heredity has a sizable effect on each of us. All told, it seems reasonable to conclude that heredity is responsible for about 25 to 50 percent of the variation in many personality traits (Caspi, Roberts, & Shiner, 2005; Loehlin et al., 1998). Notice, however, that the same figures imply that personality is shaped as much, or more, by environment as it is by biological predispositions.

Each personality, then, is a unique blend of heredity and environment, nature and nurture, biology and culture. We are not—thank goodness—genetically programmed robots whose behavior and personality traits are "wired in" for life. Where you go in life is the result of the choices you make. Although these choices are influenced by inherited tendencies, they are not merely a product of your genes (Funder, 2006).

Personality and Environment

Remember Sissy? When we heard she actually decked a man who was harassing her, we were surprised. The Sissy we had known was always quite calm and peaceful. Had she changed so much? Before we try to provide an answer, take a moment to answer the questions that follow. Doing so will add to your understanding of a long-running controversy in the psychology of personality.

Rate Yourself: How Do You View Personality?
1. My friends' actions are fairly consistent from day to day and in different situations. T or F?
2. Whether a person is honest or dishonest, kind or cruel, a hero or a coward depends mainly on circumstances. T or F?
3. Most people I have known for several years have pretty much the same personalities now as they did when I first met them. T or F?

Behavioral genetics The study of inherited behavioral traits and tendencies.

Critical Thinking

Many reunited twins in the Minnesota study (the Minnesota Twins?) have displayed similarities far beyond what would be expected on the basis of heredity. The "Jim twins," James Lewis and James Springer, are one famous example. Both Jims had married and divorced women named Linda. Both had undergone police training. One named his firstborn son James Allan, the other named *his* firstborn son James Alan. Both drove Chevrolets and vacationed at the same beach each summer. Both listed carpentry and mechanical drawing among their hobbies. Both had built benches around trees in their yards. And so forth (Holden, 1980).

Are all identical twins so, well, identical? No, they aren't. Consider identical twins Carolyn Spiro and Pamela Spiro Wagner, who, unlike the "Jim Twins," lived together throughout their childhood. While in sixth grade, they found out that President Kennedy had been assassinated. Carolyn wasn't sure why everyone was so upset. Pamela heard voices announcing that she was responsible for his death. After years of hiding her voices from everyone, Pamela tried to commit suicide while the twins were attending Brown University. She was diagnosed with schizophrenia. Never to be cured, she has gone on to write award-winning poetry. Carolyn eventually became a Harvard psychiatrist (Spiro Wagner & Spiro, 2005). Some twins reared apart appear very similar; some reared together appear rather different.

So why are some identical twins, like the Jim Twins, so much alike even if they were reared apart? Although genetics is important, it is preposterous to suggest that there are child-naming genes and bench-building genes. How, then, do we explain the eerie similarities? Imagine that you were separated at birth from a twin brother or sister. If you were reunited with your twin today, what would you do? Quite likely, you would spend the next several days comparing every imaginable detail of your lives. Under such circumstances, it is virtually certain that you and your twin would notice and compile a long list of similarities ("Wow! I use the same brand of toothpaste you do!"). Yet, two unrelated persons of the same age, sex, and race could probably rival your list—*if* they were as motivated to find similarities.

In fact, one study compared twins with unrelated pairs of students. The unrelated pairs, who were the same age and sex, were almost as alike as the twins. They had highly similar political beliefs, musical interests, religious preferences, job histories, hobbies, favorite foods, and so on (Wyatt et al., 1984). Why were the unrelated students so similar? Basically, it's because people of the same age and sex live in the same historical times and select from similar societal options. As just one example, in nearly every elementary school classroom, you will find several children with the same first name.

It appears then that many of the seemingly "astounding" coincidences shared by reunited twins may be yet another example of confirmation bias, described in Chapter 1. Reunited twins tend to notice the similarities and ignore the differences.

---

4. The reason people in some professions (such as teachers, lawyers, or doctors) seem so much alike is because their work requires that they act in particular ways. T or F?

5. One of the first things I would want to know about a potential roommate is what the person's personality is like. T or F?

6. I believe that immediate circumstances usually determine how people act at any given time. T or F?

7. To be comfortable in a particular job, a person's personality must match the nature of the work. T or F?

8. Almost anyone would be polite at a wedding reception; it doesn't matter what kind of personality the person has. T or F?

Now count the number of times you marked true for the odd-numbered items. Do the same for the even-numbered items.

If you agreed with most of the odd-numbered items, you tend to view behavior as strongly influenced by personality traits or lasting personal dispositions, whether biological or learned.

If you agreed with most of the even-numbered items, you view behavior as strongly influenced by external situations and circumstances.

What if I answered true about equally for odd and even items? Then you place equal weight on traits and situations as ways to explain behavior. This is the view now held by many personality psychologists (Funder, 2006; Mischel, Shoda, & Smith, 2008).

Traits, Consistency, and Situations

Does that mean that to predict how a person will act, it is better to focus on both personality traits and external circumstances? Yes, it's best to take both into account. Because personality *traits* are consistent, they can predict such things as job performance, dangerous driving, or a successful marriage (Burger, 2011). Yet, as we mentioned earlier in the chapter, *situations* also greatly influence our behavior. Sissy's normally calm demeanor became aggressive only because the situation was unusual and extreme: The man in the bar seriously harassed her, making her uncharacteristically angry and afraid.

Can all unusual behaviors be "blamed" on unusual situations? Great question. Consider Fred Cowan, a model student in school and described by those who knew him as quiet, gentle, and a man who loved children. Despite his size (6 feet tall, 250 pounds), Fred was described by a coworker as "someone you could easily push around." Two weeks after he was suspended from his job, Fred returned to work determined to get even with his supervisor. Unable to find the man, he killed four coworkers and a policeman before taking his own life (Lee, Zimbardo, & Bertholf, 1977).

Sudden murderers like Fred Cowan tend to be quiet, overcontrolled individuals. They are likely to be especially violent if they ever lose control. Although their attacks may be triggered by a minor irritation or frustration, the attack reflects years of unexpressed feelings of anger and belittlement. When sudden murderers finally release the strict controls they have maintained on their overcontrolled behavior, a furious and frenzied attack ensues (Cartwright, 2002). Usually it is totally out of proportion to the offense against them, and many have amnesia for their violent actions. So, unlike Sissy, who reacted in an unexpected way to an unusual situation, Fred Cowan's overreaction was typical of people who share his personality pattern.

Trait–Situation Interactions

It would be unusual for you to dance at a movie or read a book at a football game. Likewise, few people sleep in roller coasters or tell off-color jokes at funerals. However, your personality traits may predict whether you choose to read a book, go to a movie, or attend a football game in the first place. Typically, traits *interact* with situations to determine how we will act (Mischel, 2004).

In a **trait–situation interaction**, external circumstances influence the expression of a personality trait. For instance, imagine what would happen if you moved from a church to a classroom to a party to a football game. As the setting changed, you would probably become louder and more boisterous. This change would show situational effects on behavior. At the same time, your personality traits would also be apparent: If you were quieter than average in church and class, you would probably be quieter than average in the other settings, too.

Overview and Comparison of Personality Theories

Which of the personality theories is right? To date, each major personality theory has added to our understanding by providing a sort of lens through which human behavior can be viewed. Nevertheless, theories can't be fully proved or disproved. We can only ask, "Does the evidence tend to support this theory or disconfirm it?" Yet, although theories are neither true nor false, their implications or predictions may be. The best way to judge a theory, then, is in terms of its *usefulness*. Does the theory adequately explain behavior? Does it stimulate new research? Does it suggest how to treat psychological disorders? Each theory has fared differently in these areas (Cervone & Pervin, 2010). Table 10.3 provides an overview of the four principal approaches to personality. In the final analysis, the challenge now facing personality theorists is how to integrate the four major perspectives into a unified, systematic explanation of personality (Mayer, 2005; McAdams & Pals, 2006).

Table 10.3 Comparison of Personality Theories

	TRAIT THEORIES	PSYCHOANALYTIC THEORY	HUMANISTIC THEORIES	BEHAVIORIST AND SOCIAL LEARNING THEORIES
Role of inheritance (genetics)	Maximized	Stressed	Minimized	Minimized
Role of environment	Recognized	Recognized	Maximized	Maximized

Continued

Trait–situation interaction The influence that external settings or circumstances have on the expression of personality traits.

Table 10.3 Comparison of Personality Theories—cont'd

	TRAIT THEORIES	PSYCHOANALYTIC THEORY	HUMANISTIC THEORIES	BEHAVIORIST AND SOCIAL LEARNING THEORIES
View of human nature	Neutral	Negative	Positive	Neutral
Is behavior free or determined?	Determined	Determined	Free will	Determined
Principal motives	Depends on one's traits	Sex and aggression	Self-actualization	Drives of all kinds
Personality structure	Traits	Id, ego, superego	Self	Habits, expectancies
Role of unconscious	Minimized	Maximized	Minimized	Practically nonexistent
Conception of conscience	Traits of honesty, etc.	Superego	Ideal self, valuing process	Self-reinforcement, punishment history
Developmental emphasis	Combined effects of heredity and environment	Psychosexual stages	Development of self-image	Critical learning situations, identification, and imitation
Barriers to personal growth	Unhealthy traits	Unconscious conflicts, fixations	Conditions of worth, incongruence	Maladaptive habits, unhealthy environment

© Cengage Learning

🖐 **study break** Behavioral and Social Learning Theories

RECITE

1. Learning theorists believe that personality "traits" really are _____ acquired through prior learning.
2. Which of the following is *not* a "critical situation" in the behaviorist theory of personality development?

   a. feeding   *b.* sex training
   c. language training   *d.* anger training
3. Social learning theories of development emphasize the impact of identification and _____.
4. A person who is aggressive, ambitious, analytical, and assertive would be rated as androgynous on the BSRI. T or F?
5. _____ refers to the hereditary aspects of a person's emotional nature.
6. To understand personality, it is wise to remember that traits and situations _____ to determine our behavior.

REFLECT

THINK CRITICALLY

7. The concept of *reinforcement value* is closely related to a motivational principle discussed in Chapter 9. Can you name it?
8. Are situations equally powerful in their impact on behavior?

SELF-REFLECT

Some people love to shop. Others hate it. How have the psychological situation, expectancy, and reinforcement value affected your willingness to "shop 'til you drop"?

Who did you identify with as a child? What aspects of that person's behavior did you imitate?

Think of three people you know, one who is androgynous, one who is traditionally feminine, and one who is traditionally masculine. What advantages and disadvantages do you see in each collection of traits? How do you think you would be classified if you took the BSRI?

Which of the four views of personality has most helped you reflect on your own personality? Have the others helped at all?

ANSWERS

1. habits 2. c 3. imitation 4. F 5. Temperament 6. Interact 7. incentive value 8. No. Circumstances can have a strong or weak influence. In some situations, almost everyone will act the same, no matter what their personality traits may be. In other situations, traits may be of greater importance.

Personality Assessment—Psychological Yardsticks

JOURNEY QUESTION 10.7 *How do psychologists measure personality?*

Measuring personality can help predict how people will behave at work, at school, and in therapy. However, painting a detailed picture can be a challenge. In many instances, it requires several of the techniques described in this section. To capture a personality as unique as Sissy's, it might take all of them!

How is personality "measured"? Psychologists use interviews, observation, questionnaires, and projective tests to assess personality (Burger, 2011). Each method has strengths and limitations. For this reason, they are often used in combination.

Formal personality measures are refinements of more casual ways of judging a person. At one time or another, you have probably "sized up" a potential date, friend, or roommate by engaging in conversation (interview). Perhaps you have asked a friend, "When I am delayed I get angry. Do you?" (questionnaire). Maybe you watch your professors when they are angry or embarrassed to learn what they are "really" like when they're caught off-guard (observation). Or possibly you have noticed that when you say, "I think people feel...," you may be expressing your own feelings (projection). Let's see how psychologists apply each of these methods to probe personality.

Interviews

In an **interview**, direct questioning is used to learn about a person's life history, personality traits, or current mental state (Murphy & Dillon, 2011; Sommers-Flanagan & Sommers-Flanagan, 2008). In an *unstructured interview*, conversation is informal and topics are taken up freely as they arise. In a *structured interview*, information is gathered by asking a planned series of questions.

How are interviews used? Interviews are used to identify personality disturbances; to select people for jobs, college, or special programs; and to study the dynamics of personality. Interviews also provide information for counseling or therapy. For instance, a counselor might ask a depressed person, "Have you ever contemplated suicide? What were the circumstances?" The counselor might then follow by asking, "How did you feel about it?" or, "How is what you are now feeling different from what you felt then?"

In addition to providing information, interviews make it possible to observe a person's tone of voice, hand gestures, posture, and facial expressions. Such "body language" cues are important because they may radically alter the message sent, as when a person claims to be "completely calm" but trembles uncontrollably.

What is your impression of the person wearing the beige suit? If you think that she looks friendly, attractive, or neat, your other perceptions of her might be altered by that impression. Interviewers are often influenced by the halo effect (see text).

Limitations

Interviews give rapid insight into personality, but they have limitations. For one thing, interviewers can be swayed by preconceptions. A person identified as a "housewife," "college student," "high school athlete," "punk," "geek," or "ski bum" may be misjudged because of an interviewer's personal biases. Second, an interviewer's own personality, gender, or ethnicity may influence a client's behavior. When this occurs, it can accentuate or distort the person's apparent traits (Pollner, 1998). A third problem is that people sometimes try to deceive interviewers. For example, a person accused of a crime might try to avoid punishment by pretending to be mentally disabled.

A fourth problem is the **halo effect**, which is the tendency to generalize a favorable (or unfavorable) impression to an entire personality (Hartung et al., 2010). Because of the halo effect, a person who is likable or physically attractive may be rated more mature, intelligent, or mentally healthy than she or he actually is. The halo effect is something to keep in mind at job interviews.

Interview (personality) A face-to-face meeting held for the purpose of gaining information about an individual's personal history, personality traits, current psychological state, and so forth.

Halo effect The tendency to generalize a favorable or unfavorable particular impression to unrelated details of personality.

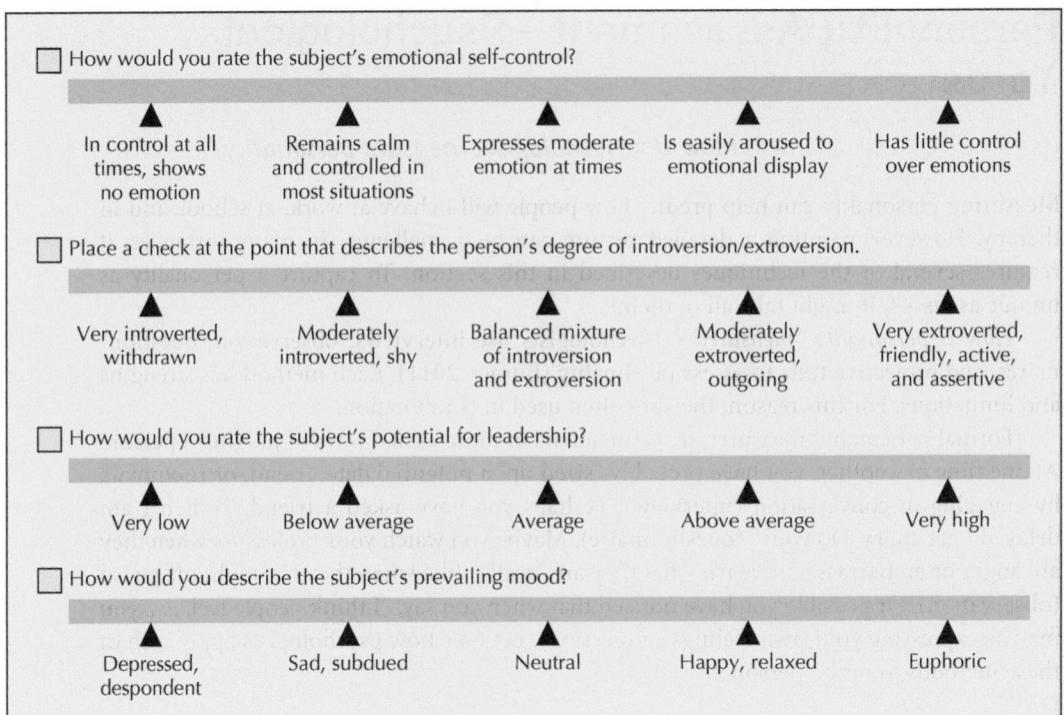

□ How would you rate the subject's emotional self-control?

| In control at all times, shows no emotion | Remains calm and controlled in most situations | Expresses moderate emotion at times | Is easily aroused to emotional display | Has little control over emotions |

□ Place a check at the point that describes the person's degree of introversion/extroversion.

| Very introverted, withdrawn | Moderately introverted, shy | Balanced mixture of introversion and extroversion | Moderately extroverted, outgoing | Very extroverted, friendly, active, and assertive |

□ How would you rate the subject's potential for leadership?

| Very low | Below average | Average | Above average | Very high |

□ How would you describe the subject's prevailing mood?

| Depressed, despondent | Sad, subdued | Neutral | Happy, relaxed | Euphoric |

Figure 10.8 Sample rating scale items. To understand how the scale works, imagine someone you know well. Where would you place check marks on each of the scales to rate that person's characteristics?

Even with their limitations, interviews are a respected method of assessment. In many cases, interviews are the first step in evaluating personality and an essential prelude to therapy. Nevertheless, interviews are usually not enough and must be supplemented by other measures and tests (Murphy & Dillon, 2011; Meyer et al., 2001).

Direct Observation and Rating Scales

Are you fascinated by airports, bus depots, parks, taverns, subway stations, or other public places? Many people relish a chance to observe the actions of others. When used for assessment, **direct observation** (looking at behavior) is a simple extension of this natural interest in "people watching." For instance, a psychologist might arrange to observe a disturbed child as she plays with other children. Is the child withdrawn? Does she become hostile or aggressive without warning? By careful observation, the psychologist can identify the girl's personality traits and clarify the nature of her problems.

Wouldn't observation be subject to the same problems of misperception as an interview? Yes. Misperceptions can be a difficulty, which is why rating scales are sometimes used (Figure 10.8). A **rating scale** is a list of personality traits or aspects of behavior that can be used to evaluate a person (Siefert, 2010). Rating scales limit the chance that some traits will be overlooked while others are exaggerated (Synhorst et al., 2005). Perhaps they should be a standard procedure for choosing a roommate, spouse, or lover!

An alternative approach is to do a **behavioral assessment** by counting the frequency of specific behaviors (Cipani & Schock, 2007). In this case, observers record *actions*, not what traits they think a person has (Ramsay, Reynolds, & Kamphaus, 2002). For example, a psychologist working with hospitalized mental patients might note the frequency of a patient's aggression, self-care, speech, and unusual behaviors. Behavioral assessments can also be used to probe thought processes. In one study, for example, couples were assessed while talking with each other about their sexuality. Couples with sexual difficulties were less likely

Direct observation Assessing behavior through direct surveillance.

Rating scale A list of personality traits or aspects of behavior on which a person is rated.

Behavioral assessment Recording the frequency of various behaviors.

to be receptive to discussing their sexuality and more likely to blame each other than were couples with no sexual difficulties (Kelly, Strassberg, & Turner, 2006).

Situational Testing

In **situational testing,** a type of direct observation, real-life conditions are simulated so that a person's spontaneous reactions can be observed. Such tests assume that the best way to learn how people react is to put them in realistic situations and watch what happens. Situational tests expose people to frustration, temptation, pressure, boredom, or other conditions capable of revealing personality characteristics (Weekley & Polyhart, 2006). Some popular "reality TV" programs, such as *American Idol, Survivor,* and *The Amazing Race,* bear some similarity to situational tests—which may account for their ability to attract millions of viewers.

How are situational tests done? An interesting example of situational testing is the judgmental firearms training provided by many police departments. At times, police officers must make split-second decisions about using their weapons. A mistake could be fatal. In a typical shoot/don't-shoot test, actors play the part of armed criminals. As various high-risk scenes are acted out live, or on videotape, or by computer, officers must decide to shoot or hold fire.

A police special tactics team undergoes judgmental firearms training. Variations on this situational test are used by many police departments. All officers must score a passing grade.

Personality Questionnaires

Personality questionnaires are paper-and-pencil tests that reveal personality characteristics. Questionnaires are more objective than interviews or observation. (An *objective test* gives the same score when different people correct it.) Questions, administration, and scoring are all standardized so that scores are unaffected by any biases an examiner may have. However, this is not enough to ensure accuracy. A good test must also be reliable and valid (Kaplan & Saccuzzo, 2013). A test is **reliable** if it yields close to the same score each time it is given to the same person. A test has **validity** if it measures what it claims to measure. Unfortunately, many personality tests you will encounter, such as those in magazines or on the Internet, have little or no validity.

Dozens of personality tests are available, including the *Guilford-Zimmerman Temperament Survey,* the *California Psychological Inventory,* the *Allport-Vernon Study of Values,* the *16 PF,* and many more. One of the best-known and most widely used objective tests is the **Minnesota Multiphasic Personality Inventory-2 (MMPI-2)** (Butcher, 2011). The MMPI-2 is composed of 567 items to which a test taker must respond "true" or "false." Items include statements such as the following:

Everything tastes the same.
I am very normal, sexually.
I like birds.
I usually daydream in the afternoon.
Mostly I stay away from other people.
Someone has been trying to hurt me.
Sometimes I think strange thoughts.*

How can these items show anything about personality? For instance, what if a person has a cold so that "everything tastes the same"? For an answer (and a little bit of fun), read the following items. Answer "Yes," "No," or "Don't bother me, I can't cope!"

I have a collection of 1,243 old pizza cartons.
I enjoy the thought of eating liver-flavored ice cream.

MMPI-2 statements themselves cannot be reproduced, to protect the validity of the test.

Situational test Simulating real-life conditions so that a person's reactions may be directly observed.

Personality questionnaire A paper-and-pencil test consisting of questions that reveal aspects of personality.

Reliability The ability of a test to yield nearly the same score each time it is given to the same person.

Validity The ability of a test to measure what it purports to measure.

Minnesota Multiphasic Personality Inventory-2 (MMPI-2) One of the best-known and most widely used objective personality questionnaires.

I love the smell of napalm in the morning.

I hate the movie *Apocalypse Now*.

I can't add numbers correctly.

Bathing sucks.

I like rats and dry hand towels.

I absolutely adore this textbook.

These items were written by your authors to satirize personality questionnaires. (Why not try writing some of your own?) Such questions may seem ridiculous, but they are not very different from the real thing. How, then, do the items on tests such as the MMPI-2 reveal anything about personality? The answer is that a single item tells little about personality. For example, a person who agrees that "Everything tastes the same" might simply have a cold. It is only through *patterns* of response that personality dimensions are revealed.

Items on the MMPI-2 were selected for their ability to correctly identify persons with particular psychological problems (Butcher, 2011). For instance, if depressed persons consistently answer a series of items in a particular way, it is assumed that others who answer the same way are also prone to depression. As silly as the gag items in the preceding list may seem, it is possible that some could actually work in a legitimate test. But before an item could be part of a test, it would have to be shown to correlate highly with some trait or dimension of personality.

The MMPI-2 measures 10 major aspects of personality (listed in Table 10.4). After the MMPI-2 is scored, results are charted graphically as an *MMPI-2 profile* (Figure 10.9). By comparing a person's profile with scores produced by typical, normal adults, a psychologist can identify various personality disorders. Additional scales can identify substance abuse, eating disorders, Type A (heart-attack prone) behavior, repression, anger, cynicism, low self-esteem, family problems, inability to function in a job, and other problems (Butcher, 2011).

How accurate is the MMPI-2? Personality questionnaires are accurate only if people tell the truth about themselves. Because of this, the MMPI-2 has additional **validity scales** that reveal whether a person's scores should be discarded. The validity scales detect attempts by test takers to "fake good" (make themselves look good) or "fake bad" (make it look like they have problems). Other scales uncover defensiveness or tendencies to exaggerate shortcomings and troubles. When taking the MMPI-2, it is best to answer honestly, without trying to second-guess the test.

Table 10.4 MMPI-2 Basic Clinical Subscales

1. **Hypochondriasis** (HI-po-kon-DRY-uh-sis). Exaggerated concern about one's physical health.
2. **Depression.** Feelings of worthlessness, hopelessness, and pessimism.
3. **Hysteria.** The presence of physical complaints for which no physical basis can be established.
4. **Psychopathic deviate.** Emotional shallowness in relationships and a disregard for social and moral standards.
5. **Masculinity/femininity.** One's degree of traditional "masculine" aggressiveness or "feminine" sensitivity.
6. **Paranoia.** Extreme suspiciousness and feelings of persecution.
7. **Psychasthenia** (sike-as-THEE-nee-ah). The presence of obsessive worries, irrational fears (phobias), and compulsive (ritualistic) actions.
8. **Schizophrenia.** Emotional withdrawal and unusual or bizarre thinking and actions.
9. **Mania.** Emotional excitability, manic moods or behavior, and excessive activity.
10. **Social introversion.** One's tendency to be socially withdrawn.

MMPI®-2 (Minnesota Multiphasic Personality Inventory®-2) Manual for Administration, Scoring, and Interpretation, Revised Edition. Copyright © 2001 by the Regents of the University of Minnesota. Used by permission of the University of Minnesota Press. All rights reserved. "MMPI" and "Minnesota Multiphasic Personality Inventory" are trademarks owned by the Regents of the University of Minnesota. © Cengage Learning

Validity scales Scales that tell whether test scores should be invalidated for lying, inconsistency, or "faking good."

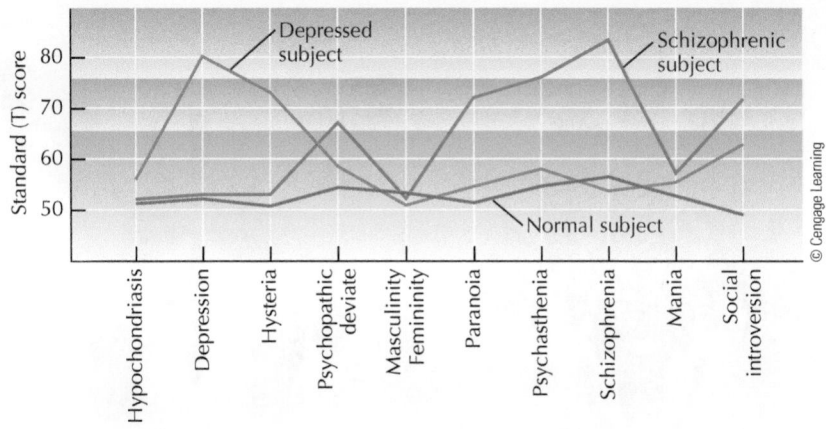

Figure 10.9 An MMPI-2 profile showing hypothetical scores indicating normality, depression, and psychosis. High scores begin at 66 and very high scores at 76. An unusually low score (40 and below) may also reveal personality characteristics or problems.

A clinical psychologist trying to decide whether a person has emotional problems would be wise to take more than the MMPI-2 into account. Test scores are informative, but they can incorrectly label some people (Kaplan & Saccuzzo, 2013). Fortunately, clinical judgments usually rely on information from interviews, tests, and other sources. Also, despite their limitations, it is reassuring to note that psychological assessments are at least as accurate as commonly used medical tests (Neukrug & Fawcett, 2010).

Projective Tests of Personality

Projective tests take a different approach to personality. Interviews, observation, rating scales, and inventories try to directly identify overt, observable traits. By contrast, projective tests seek to uncover deeply hidden or *unconscious* wishes, thoughts, and needs (Burger, 2011; McGrath & Carroll, 2012).

As a child you may have delighted in finding faces and objects in cloud formations. Or perhaps you have learned something about your friends' personalities from their reactions to movies or paintings. If so, you will have some insight into the rationale for projective tests. In a **projective test**, a person is asked to describe ambiguous stimuli or make up stories about them. Describing an unambiguous stimulus (a picture of an automobile, for example) tells little about your personality. But when you are faced with an unstructured stimulus, you must organize what you see in terms of your own life experiences. Everyone sees something different in a projective test, and what is perceived can reveal the inner workings of personality.

Projective tests have no right or wrong answers, which makes them difficult to fake. Moreover, projective tests can be a rich source of information, because responses are not restricted to simple true/false or yes/no answers.

The Rorschach Inkblot Test

Is the inkblot test a projective technique? The inkblot test, or **Rorschach** (ROAR-shock) **Inkblot Test** is one of the oldest and most widely used projective tests. Developed by Swiss psychologist Hermann Rorschach in the 1920s, it consists of 10 standardized inkblots. These vary in color, shading, form, and complexity.

How does the test work? First, a person is shown each blot and asked to describe what she or he sees in it (Figure 10.10). Later the psychologist may return to a blot, asking the person to identify specific sections of it, to expand previous descriptions, or to give new impressions about what it contains. Obvious differences in content—such as "blood

Projective tests Psychological tests making use of ambiguous or unstructured stimuli.

Rorschach Inkblot Test A projective test comprising 10 standardized inkblots.

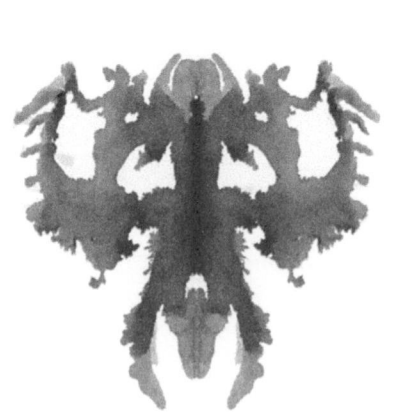  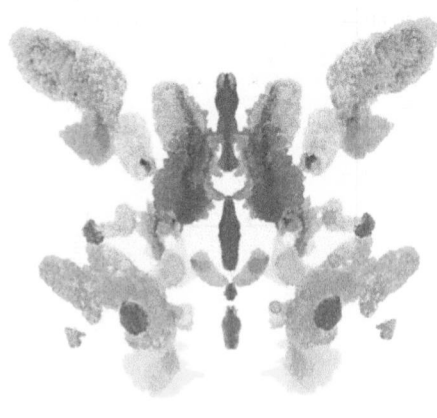

Figure 10.10 Inkblots similar to those used on the Rorschach. What do you see?

Figure 10.11 This is a picture like those used for the Thematic Apperception Test. If you wish to simulate the test, tell a story that explains what led up to the pictured situation, what is happening now, and how the action will end.

Thematic Apperception Test (TAT) A projective test consisting of 20 different scenes and life situations about which respondents make up stories.

dripping from a dagger" versus "flowers blooming in a basket"—are important for identifying personal conflicts and fantasies. But surprisingly, content is less important than what parts of the inkblot are used to organize images. These factors allow psychologists to detect emotional disturbances by observing how a person perceives the world (Bornstein, 2012; Hilsenroth, 2000). Schizophrenia and other psychotic disorders are associated with severe disturbances in thinking and perception. Such disturbances are usually readily apparent during projective testing. (See Chapter 12.)

The Thematic Apperception Test

Another popular projective test is the **Thematic Apperception Test (TAT)** developed by personality theorist Henry Murray (1893–1988).

How does the TAT differ from the Rorschach? The TAT consists of 20 sketches depicting various scenes and life situations (Figure 10.11). During testing, a person is shown each sketch and asked to make up a story about the people in it. Later, the person looks at each sketch a second or a third time and elaborates on previous stories or creates new stories.

To score the TAT, a psychologist analyzes the content of the stories. Interpretations focus on how people feel, how they interact, what events led up to the incidents depicted in the sketch, and how the story will end. For example, TAT stories told by bereaved college students typically include themes of death, grief, and coping with loss (Balk et al., 1998).

A psychologist might also count the number of times the central figure in a TAT story is angry, overlooked, apathetic, jealous, or threatened. Here is a story written by a student to describe Figure 10.11:

> The girl has been seeing this guy her mother doesn't like. The mother is telling her that she better not see him again. The mother says, "He's just like your father." The mother and father are divorced. The mother is smiling because she thinks she is right. But she doesn't really know what the girl wants. The girl is going to see the guy again, anyway.

As this example implies, the TAT is especially good at revealing feelings about a person's social relationships (Aronow et al, 2001; Teglasi, 2010).

Limitations of Projective Testing

Although projective tests have been popular, their validity is open to question (Bornstein, 2012; Wood et al., 2003). Objectivity and reliability (consistency) are also low for different users of the TAT and Rorschach. Note that after a person interprets an ambiguous stimulus, the scorer must interpret the person's (sometimes) ambiguous responses. In a sense, the interpretation of a projective test may be a projective test for the scorer!

Despite their drawbacks, projective tests still have value (Hilsenroth, 2000; McGrath & Carroll, 2012). This is especially true when they are used as part of a *test battery* (collection of assessment devices and interviews). In the hands of a skilled clinician, projective tests can be a good way to detect major conflicts, to get clients to talk about upsetting topics, and to set goals for therapy (O'Roark, 2001; Teglasi, 2010).

A Look Ahead

The Psychology in Action section that follows should add balance to your view of personality. Don't be shy. Read on!

 **study break** Personality Assessment

RECITE

1. The halo effect is the tendency of an interviewer to influence what is said by the interviewee. T or F?
2. Situational testing allows direct _____ of personality characteristics.
3. A psychotic person would probably score highest on which MMPI-2 scale?

   a. depression   b. hysteria
   c. schizophrenia   d. mania

4. The use of ambiguous stimuli is most characteristic of

   a. interviews   b. projective tests
   c. personality inventories   d. direct observation

5. The content of one's responses to the MMPI-2 is considered an indication of unconscious wishes, thoughts, and needs. T or F?
6. A test is considered valid if it consistently yields the same score when the same person takes it on different occasions. T or F?

REFLECT

THINK CRITICALLY

7. Can you think of one more reason why personality traits may not be accurately revealed by interviews?

SELF-REFLECT

How do *you* assess personality? Do you informally make use of any of the methods described in this chapter?

    You are a candidate for a desirable job. Your personality is going to be assessed by a psychologist. What method (or methods) would you prefer that she or he use? Why?

ANSWERS

1. F 2. observation 3. c 4. b 5. F 6. F 7. Because of trait–situation interactions, a person may not behave in a normal fashion while being evaluated in an interview.

Psychology in Action

Barriers and Bridges—Understanding Shyness

JOURNEY QUESTION 10.8 *What causes shyness and what can be done about it?*

Do you find it hard to talk to strangers? Lack confidence around people? Feel uncomfortable in social situations? Feel nervous with people who are not close friends? As a personality trait, **shyness** refers to a tendency to avoid others, accompanied by feelings of anxiety, preoccupation, and social inhibition (uneasiness and strain when socializing) (Flowers, 2011). Shy persons fail to make eye contact, retreat when spoken to, speak too quietly, and display little interest or animation in conversations (Brunet, Mondloch, & Schmidt, 2010). Mild shyness may be no more than a nuisance. However, extreme shyness (which may be diagnosed as *social anxiety disorder*) is often associated with depression, loneliness, fearfulness, social anxiety, inhibition, and low self-esteem (Baker & McNulty, 2010; Stein & Stein, 2008).

Joshua Rainey Photography/Shutterstock

Elements of Shyness

What causes shyness? To begin, shyness is often rooted in **social anxiety** (a feeling of apprehension in the presence of others). Almost everyone feels nervous in some social situations (such as meeting an attractive stranger). Typically, this is a reaction to *evaluation fears* (fears of being inadequate, embarrassed, ridiculed, or rejected). Although fears of rejection are common, they are much more frequent or intense for shy persons (Bradshaw, 2006; Jackson, Towson, & Narduzzi, 1997). Also, shy people can, over time, develop a *self-defeating bias* (distortion) in their thinking. Specifically, shy persons almost always blame themselves when a social encounter doesn't go well. To compound matters further, since shy people tend to avoid social situations, they fail to develop *social skills* (proficiency at interacting with others). Many simply have not learned how to meet people or how to start a conversation and keep it going.

Dynamics of Shyness   Shyness is most often triggered by *novel* or *unfamiliar* social situations. A person who does fine with family or close friends may become socially anxious and awkward when meeting a stranger. Shyness is also magnified by formality, meeting someone of higher status, being noticeably different from others, or being the focus of attention (as in giving a speech) (Larsen & Buss, 2010).

Don't most people become cautious and inhibited in such circumstances? That's why we need to see how the personalities of shy and not-shy persons differ. There is a tendency to think that shy persons are wrapped up in their own feelings and thoughts. But surprisingly, researchers Jonathan Cheek and Arnold Buss (1979) found no connection between shyness and **private self-consciousness** (attention to inner feelings, thoughts, and fantasies). Instead, they discovered that shyness is linked to **public self-consciousness** (acute awareness of oneself as a social object).

Persons who rate high in public self-consciousness are intensely concerned about what others think of them (Cowden, 2005; Fenigstein, 2009). They are unnecessarily self-critical in social situations (Lundh et al., 2002). They worry about saying the wrong thing or appearing foolish. In public, they may feel "naked" or as if others can "see through them." Such feelings trigger anxiety or outright fear during social encounters, leading to awkwardness and inhibition (Cowden, 2005). The shy person's anxiety, in turn, often causes her or him to misperceive others in social situations (Schroeder, 1995).

Self-Defeating Bias and Shyness   As mentioned, almost everyone feels anxious in at least some social situations. But there is a key difference in the way shy and not-shy persons *label* this anxiety. Shy persons tend to consider their social anxiety a *lasting personality trait*. Shyness, in other words, becomes part of their self-concept. In contrast, not-shy persons believe that *external situations* cause their occasional feelings of shyness. When not-shy persons feel anxiety or "stage fright," they assume that almost anyone would feel as they do under the same circumstances (Zimbardo, Pilkonis, & Norwood, 1978).

Labeling is important because it affects *self-esteem*. In general, not-shy persons tend to have higher self-esteem than shy persons. This is because not-shy persons give themselves credit for their social successes and recognize that failures are often due to circumstances. In contrast, shy people blame themselves for social failures, never give themselves credit for successes, and expect to be rejected (Jackson et al., 2002).

What can be done to reduce shyness? Shyness is often maintained by a number of unrealistic or self-defeating beliefs (Antony & Swinson, 2008; Butler, 2001). Becoming mindful of these beliefs is an important first step in reducing their impact (Flowers, 2011). Here's a sample of such beliefs:

1. *If you wait around long enough at a social gathering, something will happen.*
   Comment: This is really a cover-up for fear of starting a conversation. For two people to meet, at least one has to make an effort, and it might as well be you.

Shyness A tendency to avoid others plus uneasiness and strain when socializing.

Social anxiety A feeling of apprehension in the presence of others.

Private self-consciousness Preoccupation with inner feelings, thoughts, and fantasies.

Public self-consciousness Intense awareness of oneself as a social object.

2. *Other people who are popular are just lucky when it comes to being invited to social events or asked out.*

   Comment: Except for times when a person is formally introduced to someone new, this is false. People who are more active socially typically make an effort to meet and spend time with others. They join clubs, invite others to do things, strike up conversations, and generally leave little to luck.

3. *The odds of meeting someone interested in socializing are always the same, no matter where I am.*

   Comment: This is another excuse for inaction. It pays to seek out situations that have a higher probability of leading to social contact, such as clubs, teams, and school events.

4. *If someone doesn't seem to like you right away, they really don't like you and never will.*

   Comment: This belief leads to much needless shyness. Even when a person doesn't show immediate interest, it doesn't mean the person dislikes you. Liking takes time and opportunity to develop.

Unproductive beliefs like the preceding can be replaced with statements such as the following (adapted from Antony & Swinson, 2008; Butler, 2001):

1. I've got to be active in social situations.
2. I can't wait until I'm completely relaxed or comfortable before taking a social risk.
3. I don't need to pretend to be someone I'm not; it just makes me more anxious.
4. I may think other people are harshly evaluating me, but actually I'm being too hard on myself.
5. I can set reasonable goals for expanding my social experience and skills.
6. Even people who are very socially skillful are never successful 100 percent of the time. I shouldn't get so upset when an encounter goes badly.

Social Skills and Shyness   Because shy people avoid social encounters, they have fewer opportunities to learn and practice social skills (Carducci & Fields, 2007). There is nothing "innate" about knowing how to meet people or start a conversation. Social skills can be directly practiced in a variety of ways. It can be helpful, for instance, to get a tape recorder and listen to several of your conversations. You may be surprised by the way you pause, interrupt, miss cues, or seem disinterested. Similarly, it can be useful to look at yourself in a mirror and exaggerate facial expressions of surprise, interest, dislike, pleasure, and so forth. By such methods, most people can learn to put more animation and skill into their self-presentation. (For a discussion of related skills, see the section on self-assertion in Chapter 14.)

One of the easiest social skills to develop is how to ask questions during conversation. A good series of questions shifts attention to the other person and shows you are interested. Nothing fancy is needed. You can do fine with questions such as, "Where do you (work, study, live)? Do you like (dancing, travel, music)? How long have you (been at this school, worked here, lived here)?" After you've broken the ice, the best questions are often those that are *open ended* (they can't be answered yes or no):

"What parts of the country have you seen?" (as opposed to, "Have you ever been to Florida?")

"What's it like living on the West Side?" (as opposed to, "Do you like living on the West Side?")

"What kinds of food do you like?" (as opposed to, "Do you like Chinese cooking?")

It's easy to see why open-ended questions are helpful. In replying to open-ended questions, people often give "free information" about themselves. This extra information can be used to ask other questions or to lead into other topics of conversation.

This brief sampling of ideas is no substitute for actual practice. Overcoming shyness requires a real effort to test old beliefs and attitudes and learn new skills. It may even require the help of a counselor or therapist. At the very least, a shy person must be willing to take social risks. Breaking down the barriers of shyness will always include some awkward or unsuccessful encounters. Nevertheless, the rewards are powerful: human companionship and personal freedom.

RECITE

1. Social anxiety and evaluation fears are seen almost exclusively in shy individuals; the not-shy rarely have such experiences. T or F?
2. Public self-consciousness plus a tendency to label oneself as shy are major characteristics of the shy personality. T or F?
3. Shy persons tend to consider their social anxiety to be a

   a. situational reaction   b. personality trait
   c. public efficacy   d. habit

4. Changing personal beliefs and practicing social skills can be helpful in overcoming shyness. T or F?

REFLECT

THINK CRITICALLY

5. Shyness is a trait of Vonda's personality. Like most shy people, Vonda is most likely to feel shy in unfamiliar social settings. Vonda's shy behavior demonstrates that the expression of traits is governed by what concept?

SELF-REFLECT

If you are shy, see if you can summarize how social skills, social anxiety, evaluation fears, self-defeating thoughts, and public self-consciousness contribute to your social inhibition. If you're not shy, imagine how you would explain these concepts to a shy friend.

ANSWERS

1. F 2. T 3. b 4. T 5. trait-situation interactions (again)

Chapter in Review

Summary

10.1 How do psychologists use the term personality?

- 10.1.1 *Personality* refers to a person's consistent and unique patterns of thinking, emotion, and behavior.
- 10.1.2 Character is personality evaluated, or the possession of desirable qualities.
- 10.1.3 Personality traits are lasting personal qualities that are inferred from behavior.
- 10.1.4 Personality types group people into categories on the basis of shared traits.
- 10.1.5 Behavior is influenced by self-concept, which is a perception of one's own personality traits.
- 10.1.6 A positive self-evaluation leads to high self-esteem. Low self-esteem is associated with stress, unhappiness, and depression.
- 10.1.7 Each of the four major theories of personality—trait, psychodynamic, humanistic, and behaviorist and social learning—combines interrelated assumptions, ideas, and principles to explain personality.

10.2 Are some personality traits more basic or important than others?

- 10.2.1 Trait theories identify qualities that are most lasting or characteristic of a person.
- 10.2.2 Allport made useful distinctions between common traits and individual traits and among cardinal, central, and secondary traits.
- 10.2.3 Cattell's theory attributes visible surface traits to the existence of 16 underlying source traits.
- 10.2.4 Source traits are measured by the *Sixteen Personality Factor Questionnaire* (16 PF).
- 10.2.5 The five-factor model identifies five universal dimensions of personality: extroversion, agreeableness, conscientiousness, neuroticism, and openness to experience.

10.3 How do psychodynamic theories explain personality?

- 10.3.1 Like other psychodynamic approaches, Sigmund Freud's psychoanalytic theory emphasizes unconscious forces and conflicts within the personality.
- 10.3.2 In Freud's theory, personality is made up of the id, ego, and superego.
- 10.3.3 Libido, derived from the life instincts, is the primary energy running the personality. Conflicts within the personality may cause neurotic anxiety or moral anxiety and motivate us to use ego-defense mechanisms.
- 10.3.4 The personality operates on three levels: the conscious, preconscious, and unconscious.
- 10.3.5 The Freudian view of personality development is based on a series of psychosexual stages: the oral, anal, phallic, and genital stages. According to Freud, fixation at any stage can leave a lasting imprint on personality.

10.4 What are humanistic theories of personality?

- 10.4.1 Humanistic theories stress subjective experience, free choice, self-actualization, and positive models of human nature.
- 10.4.2 Abraham Maslow found that self-actualizers share traits that range from efficient perceptions of reality to frequent peak experiences.
- 10.4.3 Positive psychologists have identified six human strengths that contribute to well-being and life satisfaction: wisdom and knowledge, courage, humanity, justice, temperance, and transcendence.
- 10.4.4 Carl Rogers viewed the self as an entity that emerges from personal experience. We tend to become aware of experiences that match our self-image and exclude those that are incongruent with it.
- 10.4.5 The incongruent person has a highly unrealistic self-image and/or a mismatch between the self-image and the ideal self. The congruent or fully functioning person is flexible and open to experiences and feelings.
- 10.4.6 As parents apply conditions of worth to children's behavior, thoughts, and feelings, children begin to do the same. Internalized conditions of worth then contribute to incongruence and disrupt the organismic valuing process.

10.5 What do behaviorists and social learning theorists emphasize in their approach to personality?

- 10.5.1 Behavioral theories of personality emphasize learning, conditioning, and immediate effects of the environment (situational determinants).
- 10.5.2 Learning theorists John Dollard and Neal Miller consider habits the basic core of personality. Habits express the combined effects of drive, cue, response, and reward.
- 10.5.3 Social learning theory adds cognitive elements, such as perception, thinking, and understanding to the behavioral view of personality.
- 10.5.4 Social learning theory is exemplified by Julian Rotter's concepts of the psychological situation, expectancies, and reinforcement value.
- 10.5.5 The behaviorist view of personality development holds that social reinforcement in four situations is critical: feeding, toilet or cleanliness training, sex training, and anger or aggression training.
- 10.5.6 Identification and imitation are of particular importance in learning male or female gender roles.
- 10.5.7 Psychological androgyny is related to greater behavioral adaptability and flexibility.

10.6 How do heredity and environment affect personality?

- 10.6.1 Temperament refers to the hereditary and physiological aspects of one's emotional nature.
- 10.6.2 Behavioral genetics and studies of identical twins suggest that heredity contributes significantly to adult personality traits.

- 10.6.3 Biological predispositions (traits) interact with environment (situations) to explain our behavior.
- 10.6.4 Each of the four major theories of personality—trait, psychodynamic, humanistic, and behaviorist and social learning—is useful for understanding some aspects of personality.

10.7 How do psychologists measure personality?

- 10.7.1 Techniques typically used for personality assessment are interviews, observation, questionnaires, and projective tests.
- 10.7.2 Structured and unstructured interviews provide much information, but they are subject to interviewer bias and misperceptions. The halo effect may also lower the accuracy of an interview.
- 10.7.3 Direct observation, sometimes involving situational tests, behavioral assessment, or rating scales, allows psychologists to evaluate a person's actual behavior.
- 10.7.4 Personality questionnaires, such as the *Minnesota Multiphasic Personality Inventory-2 (MMPI-2)*, are objective and reliable, but their validity is open to question.

- 10.7.5 Projective tests ask a person to project thoughts or feelings to an ambiguous stimulus or unstructured situation.
- 10.7.6 The *Rorschach Technique,* or inkblot test, is a well-known projective technique. A second is the *Thematic Apperception Test* (TAT).
- 10.7.7 Projective tests are low in validity and objectivity. Nevertheless, they are considered useful by many clinicians, particularly as part of a test battery.

10.8 What causes shyness and what can be done about it?

- 10.8.1 Shyness typically involves social anxiety, evaluation fears, heightened public self-consciousness, self-defeating bias, a tendency to regard one's shyness as a lasting trait, and a lack of social skills.
- 10.8.2 Shyness can be reduced by replacing self-defeating beliefs with more supportive thoughts and by learning social skills.

Interactive Learning

Log in to CengageBrain to access the resources your instructor requires. For this book, you can access:

CourseMate Go to CengageBrain.com to access Psychology CourseMate, where you will find an interactive eBook, glossaries, flashcards, quizzes, videos, Virtual Psychology Labs, and more.

Aplia If your professor has assigned Aplia:

1. Sign in to your account.
2. Complete the corresponding exercises as required by your professor.
3. When finished, click "Grade It Now" to see which areas you have mastered, which areas need more work, and detailed explanations of every answer.

Test Your Knowledge

Personality

1. When someone's personality has been *evaluated*, we are making a judgment about his or her
   a. temperament
   b. character
   c. extroversion
   d. self-esteem

2. A personality type is usually defined by the presence of
   a. all five personality dimensions
   b. a stable self concept
   c. several specific traits
   d. a source trait

3. Personality theorist Raymond Cattell used factor analysis to identify 16
   a. common traits
   b. source traits
   c. cardinal traits
   d. trait–situation interactions

4. Which of the following is NOT one of the Big Five personality dimensions?
   a. extroversion
   b. agreeableness
   c. neuroticism
   d. androgyny

5. According to Freud, which division of personality is governed by the reality principle?
   a. ego
   b. id
   c. ego ideal
   d. superego

6. Freud stated that the mind functions on three levels: the conscious, the unconscious, and the
   a. psyche
   b. preconscious
   c. superego
   d. subconscious

7. Freudian theory states that a person who is passive and dependent and needs lots of attention has a fixation in the
   a. oral stage
   b. anal stage
   c. Oedipal stage
   d. genital stage

8. Maslow thought of peak experiences as temporary moments of
   a. congruence
   b. positive self-regard
   c. self-actualization
   d. self-reinforcement

9. Carl Rogers believed that personal growth is encouraged when conditions of worth are replaced by
   a. self-efficacy
   b. instrumental worth
   c. latency
   d. organismic valuing

10. The situational determinants of our actions are of special interest and importance to
    a. psychodynamic theorists
    b. humanistic theorists
    c. learning theorists
    d. behavioral geneticists

11. Which of the following is NOT a concept of social learning theory?
    a. incongruence
    b. expectancy
    c. self-efficacy
    d. reinforcement value

12. The research methods of _____ have been used to study the extent to which we inherit personality characteristics.
    a. behavioral genetics
    b. social learning theory
    c. factor analysis
    d. trait profiling

13. The halo effect can be a serious problem in accurate personality assessment that is based on
    a. projective testing
    b. behavioral recording
    c. interviewing
    d. the TAT

14. Situational testing is primarily an example of using _____ to assess personality.
    a. direct observation
    b. structured interviewing
    c. cardinal traits
    d. projective techniques

15. Which of the following is an objective personality questionnaire?
    a. the TAT
    b. the In-basket Test
    c. the NDE-16
    d. the MMPI-2

16. Which MMPI-2 scale is designed to detect phobias and compulsive actions?
    a. Hysteria
    b. Paranoia
    c. Psychasthenia
    d. Mania

17. Which of the following items DOES NOT belong with the others?
    a. Rorschach technique
    b. TAT
    c. MMPI-2
    d. projective testing

18. By definition, a test that measures what it claims to measure is
    a. valid
    b. situational
    c. objective
    d. reliable

19. Contrary to what many people think, shyness is NOT related to
    a. private self-consciousness
    b. social anxiety
    c. self-esteem
    d. blaming oneself for social failures

20. Shy persons tend to consider their social anxiety to be a
    a. situational reaction
    b. personality trait
    c. public efficacy
    d. habit

Answers

1. b 2. c 3. b 4. d 5. a 6. b 7. a 8. c 9. d 10. c 11. a 12. a 13. c 14. a 15. d 16. c 17. c 18. a 19. a 20. b

Journey Theme *Health is affected greatly by lifestyle and behavior patterns, especially those related to stress.*

11

Health, Stress, and Coping

Journey into Psychology: Mee Jung's Amazing Race

What a year! Mee Jung had barely managed to survive the rush of make-or-break term papers, projects, and classroom presentations. Then, it was on to the last leg of her race: final exams. Perfectly timed to inflict as much suffering as possible, her two hardest exams fell on the same day! Great.

On the last day of finals, Mee Jung got caught in a traffic jam on her way to school. Two drivers cut her off, and another gave her a one-finger salute. When Mee Jung finally got to campus, the parking lot was swarming with frantic students. Most of them, like her, were within minutes of missing a final exam. At last, Mee Jung spied an empty space. As she started toward it, a Mini Cooper darted around the corner and into "her" place. The driver of the car behind her began to honk impatiently. For a moment, Mee Jung was seized by a colossal desire to karate chop anything in sight.

Finally, after a week and a half of stress, pressure, and frustration, Mee Jung had crossed the finish line. Sleep deprivation, gallons of coffee, junk food, and equal portions of cramming and complaining had carried her through finals. She was off for a summer of karate. At last, she could kick back, relax, and have some fun. Or could she? Just 4 days after the end of school, Mee Jung got a bad cold, followed by bronchitis that lasted for nearly a month.

Mee Jung's experience illustrates what happens when stress, emotion, personal habits, and health collide. Though the timing of her cold *might* have been a coincidence, odds are it wasn't. Periods of stress are frequently followed by illness.

In the first part of this chapter, we will explore a variety of behavioral health risks. Then, we will look more closely at what stress is and how it affects us. After that, we will emphasize ways of coping with stress so you can do a better job of staying healthy than Mee Jung did.

Journey Questions

11.1 What is health psychology and how do cognition and behavior affect health?

11.2 What impacts have sexually transmitted diseases had on sexual behavior?

11.3 What is stress and what factors determine its severity?

11.4 What causes frustration and what are typical reactions to it?

11.5 Are there different types of conflict and how do people react to conflict?

11.6 What are defense mechanisms?

11.7 What do we know about coping with feelings of helplessness and depression?

11.8 How is stress related to health and disease?

11.9 What are the best strategies for managing stress?

Health Psychology—Here's to Your Good Health

JOURNEY QUESTION 11.1 *What is health psychology and how do cognition and behavior affect health?*

For centuries, the *medical model* has dominated Western thinking (Ghaemi, 2010). From this perspective, health is an absence of illness and your body is a complex biological machine that can break down and become ill. Sometimes an external cause, such as a virus, is the culprit. Sometimes you inflict the damage yourself through poor lifestyle choices, such as smoking or overeating. In either event, the problem is physical or biological, and your "mind" has little to do with it. Moreover, physical problems call for physical treatments ("Take your medicine."), so your mind also has little to do with your recovery. In the medical model, *any* impact of the mind on health is dismissed as a mere placebo effect. (To remind yourself about placebo effects, see Chapter 1.)

Over the last 50 years, the medical model has slowly begun to give way to the **biopsychosocial model**, which states that diseases are caused by a combination of biological, psychological, and social factors (Suls, Luger, & Martin, 2010). More often than you might think, psychological and social processes play a role in influencing the progress and outcome of "biological" diseases. It is becoming clear that medicine works best when doctors help people *make sense* of their medical condition to maximize healing (Benedetti, 2009; Moerman, 2002). Further, the biopsychosocial model defines health as a state of well-being that we can *actively* attain and maintain (Oakley, 2004). So, as you take responsibility for your own well-being, remember that in some ways health *is* all in your mind.

Health psychology, then, aims to use cognitive and behavioral principles to prevent illness and death and to promote health (Harrington, 2013). Psychologists working in the allied field of **behavioral medicine** apply psychology to manage medical problems, such as diabetes or asthma. Their interests include pain control, helping people cope with chronic illness, stress-related diseases, self-screening for diseases (such as breast cancer), and similar topics (Brannon & Feist, 2010).

Most of us agree that our health is priceless. Yet, many diseases, and well over half of all deaths each year in North America, can be traced to our unhealthy behaviors (Danaei et al., 2009).

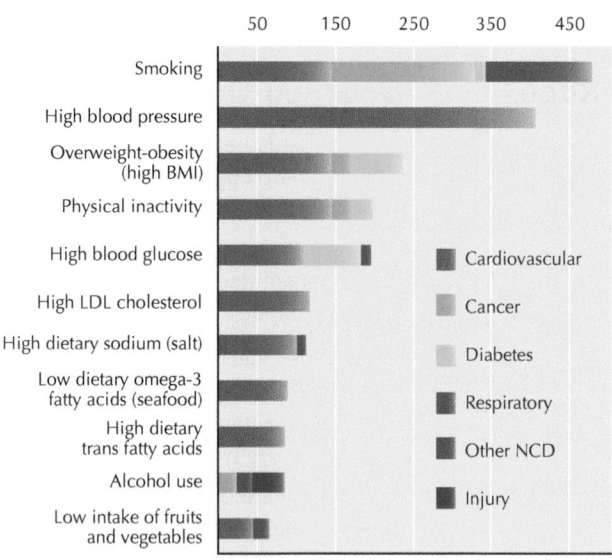

Deaths attributable to individual risks (thousands) in both sexes

	50	150	250	350	450

Smoking
High blood pressure
Overweight-obesity (high BMI)
Physical inactivity
High blood glucose
High LDL cholesterol
High dietary sodium (salt)
Low dietary omega-3 fatty acids (seafood)
High dietary trans fatty acids
Alcohol use
Low intake of fruits and vegetables

Cardiovascular
Cancer
Diabetes
Respiratory
Other NCD
Injury

© Cengage Learning

Figure 11.1 The leading causes of preventable deaths in the United States are tobacco and alcohol consumption, along with poor diet and exercise habits. Together they account for over half of all premature deaths and cause no end of day-to-day health problems. (Data adapted from Danaei et al., 2009.)

Behavioral Risk Factors

A century ago, people died primarily from infectious diseases and accidents. Today, people generally die from **lifestyle diseases**, which are related to health-damaging personal habits (Dombrowski et al., 2007). Examples include heart disease, stroke, HIV/AIDS, and lung cancer (Figure 11.1). Clearly, some lifestyles promote health, whereas others lead to illness and death (Hales, 2013). As one observer put it, "If you don't take care of yourself, the undertaker will overtake that responsibility for you."

What are some unhealthy behaviors? Some causes of illness are beyond our control, but many behavioral risks can be reduced. **Behavioral risk factors** are actions that increase the chances of disease, injury, or early death. For example, about 450,000 Americans die every year from smoking-related diseases—about 20 percent of all deaths, regardless of the cause (Centers for Disease Control, 2011). Similarly, roughly two-thirds of all American adults are overweight. Of those, half are extremely overweight, or *obese* (Flegal et al., 2010). Being fat is not just a matter of fashion—in the long run, it could kill you. Being overweight may soon

Biopsychosocial model Approach to which acknowledges that biological, psychological, and social factors interact to influence illness and health.

Health psychology Study of the ways in which cognitive and behavioral principles can be used to prevent illness and promote health.

Behavioral medicine The study of behavioral factors in medicine, physical illness, and medical treatment.

Lifestyle disease A disease related to health-damaging personal habits.

Behavioral risk factors Behaviors that increase the chances of disease, injury, or premature death.

overtake smoking as the main cause of preventable death (Danaei et al., 2009). A person who is overweight at age 20 can expect to lose 5 to 20 years of life expectancy (Fontaine et al., 2003).

Each of the following factors is a major behavioral risk (Brannon & Feist, 2010): high levels of stress, untreated high blood pressure, cigarette smoking, abuse of alcohol or other drugs, overeating, inadequate exercise, unsafe sexual behavior, exposure to toxic substances, violence, excess sun exposure, reckless driving, and disregarding personal safety (avoidable accidents). Seventy percent of all medical costs are related to just six of the listed factors—smoking, alcohol abuse, drug abuse, poor diet, insufficient exercise, and risky sexual practices (Brannon & Feist, 2010; Orleans, Gruman, & Hollendonner, 1999). (Unsafe sex is discussed in the next section.)

The personal habits you have by the time you are 18 or 19 greatly affect your health, happiness, and life expectancy years later (Gurung, 2010; Hales, 2013). Table 11.1 shows how many American high school students engage in various kinds of risky behaviors.

Specific risk factors are not the only concern. Some people have a general **disease-prone personality** that leaves them depressed, anxious, hostile, and frequently ill. In contrast, people who are intellectually resourceful, compassionate, optimistic, and nonhostile tend to enjoy good health (Li et al., 2009; Taylor, 2012). Depression, in particular, is likely to damage health (Luppa et al., 2007). People who are depressed eat poorly, sleep poorly, rarely exercise, fail to use seat belts in cars, smoke more, and so on.

Lifestyle

In your mind's eye, fast-forward an imaginary film of your life all the way to old age. Do it twice—once with a lifestyle including a large number of behavioral risk factors, and again without them. It should be obvious that many small risks can add up, dramatically raising the chance of illness. If stress is a frequent part of your life, visualize your body seething with emotion, day after day. If you smoke, picture a lifetime's worth of cigarette smoke blown through your lungs in a week. If you drink, take a lifetime of alcohol's assaults on the brain, stomach, and liver and squeeze them into a month: Your body would be poisoned, ravaged, and soon dead. If you eat a high-fat, high-cholesterol diet, fast-forward a lifetime of heart-killing plaque clogging your arteries.

We don't mean to sermonize. We just want to remind you that risk factors make a difference. To make matters worse, unhealthy lifestyles almost always create multiple risks. That is, people who smoke are also likely to drink excessively. Those who overeat usually do not get enough exercise, and so on (Lippke, Nigg, & Maddock, 2012). Even infectious diseases are often linked to behavioral risks. For example, pneumonia and other infections occur at higher rates in people who have cancer, heart disease, lung disease, or liver disease. Thus, many deaths attributed to infections can actually be traced back to smoking, poor diet, or alcohol abuse (Mokdad et al., 2004).

In the long run, behavioral risk factors and lifestyles do make a difference in health and life expectancy.

Table 11.1 Percentage of U.S. High School Students Who Engaged in Health-Endangering Behaviors

RISKY BEHAVIOR IN THE PREVIOUS 30 DAYS	PERCENTAGE
Rode with drinking driver	28
Were in a physical fight	32
Carried a weapon	18
Drank alcohol	42
Used marijuana	20
Engaged in sexual intercourse	34
Did not use condom during last sexual intercourse	39
Smoked cigarettes	20
Did not eat enough fruits and vegetables	78
Did not get enough physical exercise	81

Source: Eaton et al., 2010.

© Cengage Learning

Disease-prone personality A personality type associated with poor health; marked by persistent negative emotions, including anxiety, depression, and hostility.

Health-Promoting Behaviors

To prevent disease, health psychologists first try to reduce behavioral risk factors. All the medicine in the world may not be enough to restore health without changes in behavior. We all know someone who has had a heart attack or lung disease who couldn't change the habits that led to his or her illness.

In some cases, lifestyle diseases can be treated or prevented by making specific, minor changes in behavior. For example, hypertension (high blood pressure) can be deadly. Yet, consuming less sodium (salt) can help fend off this "silent killer." Losing weight, using alcohol sparingly, and getting more exercise will also help (Edenfield & Blumenthal, 2011; Hales, 2013).

In addition to removing specific risk factors, psychologists are interested in getting people to increase behaviors that promote health. *Health-promoting behaviors* include such obvious practices as getting regular exercise, controlling smoking and alcohol use, maintaining a balanced diet, getting good medical care, and managing stress (Zarcadoolas, Pleasant, & Greer, 2006). In one study, the risk of dying during a 10-year period was cut by 65 percent for adults who were careful about diet, alcohol, exercise, and smoking (Knoops et al., 2004).

Health-promoting behaviors don't have to be restrictive or burdensome. For instance, maintaining a healthy diet doesn't mean surviving on tofu and wheatgrass. The healthiest people in the study just described ate a tasty "Mediterranean diet" higher in fruit, vegetables, and fish and lower in red meat and dairy products. Likewise, you don't need to exercise like an Olympic athlete to benefit from physical activity. All you need is 30 minutes of exercise (the equivalent of a brisk walk) three or four times a week. Almost everyone can fit such "lifestyle physical activity" into his or her schedule (Pescatello, 2001).

What about alcohol? Moderation in drinking doesn't mean that you must be a teetotaler. Consuming one or two alcoholic drinks per day is generally safe for most people, especially if you remain alcohol free 2 or 3 days a week. A glass of red wine daily may even be healthy (Anekonda, 2006). However, having three or more drinks a day greatly increases the risk for stroke, cirrhosis of the liver, cancer, high blood pressure, heart disorders, and other diseases (Knoops et al., 2004; Lamont et al., 2011).

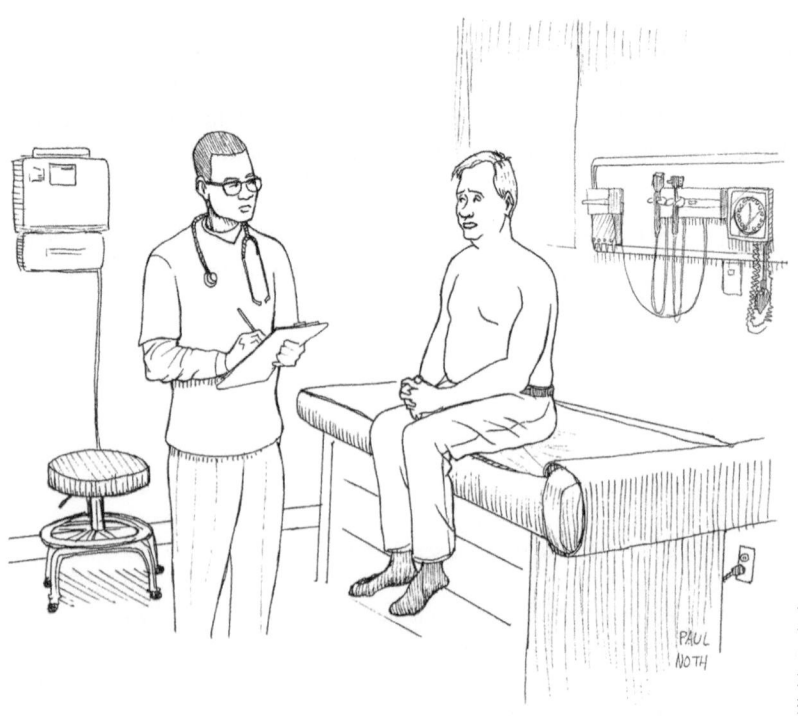

"Will I still be able to not exercise?"

To summarize, a small number of behavioral patterns accounts for many common health problems (Eaton et al., 2010; Straub, 2012). **Table 11.2** lists several major ways to promote good health. (To explore an interesting social factor that may underlie common health problems, see "Unhealthy Birds of a Feather.")

Early Prevention

Of the behavioral risks we have discussed, smoking is the largest preventable cause of death and the single most lethal factor (National Center for Chronic Disease Prevention and Health Promotion, 2011). As such, it illustrates the prospect for preventing illness.

What have health psychologists done to lessen the risks of smoking? Attempts to "immunize" youths against pressures to start smoking are a good example. When humorist Mark Twain said, "Giving up smoking is the easiest thing in the world. I know because I've done it thousands of times," he stated a basic truth—only 1 smoker in 10 has long-term success at quitting (Krall, Garvey, & Garcia, 2002). Thus, the best way to deal with smoking is to prevent it before it becomes a lifelong habit. For example, prevention programs in schools discourage smoking with quizzes about smoking, multimedia presentations, antismoking art contests, poster and T-shirt giveaways, antismoking pamphlets for parents, and questions for students to ask their parents (Flynn et al., 2011; Prokhorov et al., 2010). Such efforts are designed to persuade kids that smoking is dangerous and "uncool."

Some antismoking programs include **refusal skills training**. In this case, youths learn to resist pressures to begin smoking (or using other drugs). For example, junior high students can role-play ways to resist smoking pressures from peers, adults, and cigarette ads. Similar methods can be applied to other health risks, such as sexually transmitted diseases and teen pregnancy (Wandersman & Florin, 2003).

Many health programs also teach students general life skills. The idea is to give kids skills that will help them cope with day-to-day stresses. That way, they will be less tempted to escape problems through drug use or other destructive behaviors. **Life skills training** includes practice in stress reduction, self-protection, decision making, goal setting, self-control, and social skills (Corey & Corey, 2010; Tobler et al., 2000).

Community Health

In addition to early prevention, health psychologists have had some success with **community health campaigns**. These are community-wide education projects designed to lessen major risk factors (Lounsbury & Mitchell, 2009; Orleans, 2000). Health campaigns inform people

Celebrities can also help persuade young people to not start smoking in the first place.

Table 11.2 Major Health-Promoting Behaviors

SOURCE	DESIRABLE BEHAVIORS
Tobacco	Do not smoke; do not use smokeless tobacco.
Nutrition	Eat a balanced, low-fat diet; have appropriate caloric intake; maintain healthy body weight.
Exercise	At least 30 minutes of aerobic exercise, 5 days per week.
Blood pressure	Lower blood pressure with diet and exercise or medicine if necessary.
Alcohol and drugs	No more than 2 drinks per day; abstain from using drugs.
Sleep and relaxation	Avoid sleep deprivation; provide for periods of relaxation every day.
Sex	Practice safer sex; avoid unplanned pregnancy.
Injury	Curb dangerous driving habits; use seat belts; minimize sun exposure; forgo dangerous activities.
Stress	Learn stress management; lower hostility.

© Cengage Learning

Refusal skills training Program that teaches youths how to resist pressures to begin smoking. (Can also be applied to other drugs, and health risks.)

Life skills training A program that teaches stress reduction, self-protection, decision making, self-control, and social skills.

Community health campaign A community-wide education program that provides information about how to lessen risk factors and promote health.

Discovering Psychology

Would you like to eat better, exercise more, or quit smoking? Researchers Nicholas Christakis and James Fowler believe they know why it can be difficult to alter unhealthy behaviors. Often, social factors are a barrier to change. If you are a smoker, do your friends also smoke? Are your family members fast-food junkies just like you? Are your friends all drinkers? Unhealthy behaviors such as overeating or smoking seem to spread almost like a "mental virus" (Christakis & Fowler, 2009; Lyons, 2011).

One study of social contagion found that people were 57 percent more likely to become obese if they had a friend who became fat first (Christakis & Fowler, 2007). Similarly, smokers tend to "hang out" with other smokers (Christakis & Fowler, 2008). Another study found that spending time with drinkers increases alcohol consumption (Ali & Dwyer, 2010). Apparently, we tend to flock together with like-minded people and adopt many of their habits.

Does that mean I am doomed to be unhealthy if my family and friends have unhealthy habits? Not necessarily. Social networks can also spread healthy behaviors (Fowler & Christakis, 2010). If one smoker in a group of smokers quits, others are more likely to follow suit. If your spouse quits smoking, you are 67 percent more likely to quit. If a good friend quits smoking, your chances of abandoning tobacco go up by 36 percent (Christakis & Fowler, 2008). The growing social unpopularity of smoking may be the best explanation of why fewer and fewer American adults (now only 19 percent) still smoke (Schroeder, 2008).

The implication? Don't wait for your friends or family to adopt healthier habits. Take the lead and get them to join you. Failing that, start hanging out with a healthier crowd. You might catch something healthy.

---

of risks such as stress, alcohol abuse, high blood pressure, high cholesterol, smoking, sexually transmitted diseases, or excessive sun exposure. This is followed by efforts to motivate people to change their behavior. Campaigns sometimes provide *role models* (positive examples) who show people how to improve their own health. They also direct people to services for health screening, advice, and treatment. Health campaigns may reach people through the mass media, public schools, health fairs, workplaces, or self-help programs.

The Whole Human: Subjective Well-Being

Health is not just an absence of disease (Allen, Carlson, & Ham, 2007; Diener & Chan, 2011; Tay & Diener, 2011). People who are truly healthy enjoy a positive state of **subjective well-being**. Maintaining subjective well-being is a lifelong pursuit and, hopefully, a labor of love. People who attain optimal subjective well-being are both physically and psychologically healthy. They are happy, optimistic, self-confident individuals who can bounce back emotionally from adversity. People who enjoy a sense of well-being also have supportive relationships with others, do meaningful work, and live in a clean environment. Many of these aspects of subjective well-being are addressed elsewhere in this book.

One major risk factor young people are likely to face is the danger of contracting a sexually transmitted disease. Yet this serious, and possibly fatal, health risk can be dramatically reduced by making some changes in behavior. Let's apply your new understanding of health psychology to this important topic.

STDs and Safer Sex—Choice, Risk, and Responsibility

JOURNEY QUESTION 11.2 *What impacts have sexually transmitted diseases had on sexual behavior?*

In general, most adults favor greater freedom of choice for themselves. When it comes to sex, however, greater choice is accompanied by greater risk. This is especially true for younger people who are exploring their sexual identities in an era of more casual sex (Wentland & Reissing, 2011).

Risk in sexual behavior often comes in the form of a **sexually transmitted disease (STD)**, an infection passed from one person to another by intimate physical contact. Sexually active people run higher risks for chlamydia (klah-MID-ee-ah),

Subjective well-being A positive state of good health; more than the absence of disease.

Sexually transmitted disease (STD) A disease that is typically passed from one person to the next by intimate physical contact; a venereal disease.

gonorrhea, hepatitis B, herpes, syphilis, and other STDs. For example, about 3 million new cases of chlamydia and gonorrhea are estimated to occur each year in the United States, only about half of which are reported (Centers for Disease Control, 2012).

Despite such statistics, many sexually active people underestimate their risk for a variety of reasons. One study of sexually active teenage girls engaging in risky sex is a case in point. Nearly 90 percent of the girls thought that they had virtually no chance of getting an STD. In reality, over the next 18 months, 1 in 4 got chlamydia or gonorrhea (Ethier et al., 2003).

One reason for underestimating sexual risk is that people who are sexually active may have indirect contact with many other people. One study of sexual relationships at a high school in a Midwestern city found long chains of sexual contact between students. Thus, a student at the end of the chain might have had sex with only one person, but in reality she or he had indirect contact with dozens or even hundreds of others (Bearman, Moody, & Stovel, 2004).

Another reason people underestimate their risk is that many individuals who carry STDs remain *asymptomatic* (a-SIMP-teh-mat-ik: lacking obvious symptoms). It is easy to have an infection without knowing it. Likewise, it is often impossible to tell whether a sexual partner is infectious.

Also, because most of the more common STDs are treatable, it is easy to dismiss their impact on health. But STDs such as chlamydia or gonorrhea produce a variety of painful and embarrassing symptoms. Chlamydia can even "silently" (without symptoms) damage a woman's reproductive organs, resulting in infertility. Gonorrhea can damage the fertility of both men and women (Centers for Disease Control, 2012).

HIV/AIDS

For many sexually active people, the human immunodeficiency virus (HIV) adds a whole new level of risk. Whereas most other STDs are treatable, HIV infections lead to acquired immune deficiency syndrome (AIDS), which can be lethal. As the immune system weakens, other "opportunistic" diseases invade the body. Most people with AIDS eventually die of multiple infections (although newer multidrug therapies have greatly improved the odds of survival).

HIV/AIDS became a worldwide epidemic in the 1980s and is still going strong. World-wide, 1.8 million people still die each year from HIV/AIDS, and 2.6 million new infections occur. Around the world, about half of all cases are female (United Nations Programme on HIV/AIDS, 2010). In the United States, 1.2 million people are now infected (of whom one quarter are women) and each passing year adds about 50,000 new cases (Centers for Disease Control, 2011).

In North America, those who are at greatest risk for HIV infection remain men who have had sex with other men (homosexual and bisexual men), people who have shared needles (for tattoos or for intravenous drug use), hemophiliacs (who require frequent blood transfusions), sexual partners of people in the preceding groups, and heterosexuals with a history of multiple partners. Regardless, HIV can be spread by all forms of sexual inter-course, and it has affected persons of all sexual orientations. Almost thirty percent of new HIV infections in the United States are transmitted through heterosexual sex (Centers for Disease Control, 2011).

The first symptoms of AIDS may show up as little as 2 months after infection, but they typically don't appear for 10 years. Because of this long incubation period, infected persons often pass the AIDS virus on to others without knowing it. Medical testing can detect an HIV infection. However, for at least the first 6 months after becoming infected, a person can test negative while carrying the virus. Even a negative test result, therefore, is no guarantee that a person is a "safe" sex partner. In fact, 25 percent of HIV infected individuals are unaware of their infections (Nguyen, 2008).

It remains worth noting that HIV infections are spread by direct contact with body fluids—especially blood, semen, and vaginal secretions. The HIV virus cannot be transmitted by casual contact. People do not get HIV from shaking hands, touching or using objects touched by a person with AIDS, eating food prepared by an infected person, or from social kissing, sweat or tears, sharing drinking glasses, sharing towels, and so forth.

Behavioral Risk Factors for STDs

Sexually active people can do much to protect their own health. The behaviors listed here are risky when performed with an infected person:

Risky Behaviors
- Unprotected vaginal, oral, or anal sex (without a condom) with an infected partner
- Having two or more sex partners (additional partners further increase the risk)
- Sex with someone you don't know well, or with someone you know has several partners
- Sex with someone you know injects drugs or sharing drug needles and syringes (HIV/AIDS)

It's important to remember that you can't tell from appearance if a person is infected. Many people would be surprised to learn that their partners have engaged in behavior that places them both at risk. The preceding high-risk behaviors can be contrasted with the following list of safer sexual practices. Note, however, that unless a person completely abstains, sex can be made safer but not risk free.

Safer Sex Practices
- Not having sex
- Sex with one mutually faithful, uninfected partner
- Using a condom
- Discussing contraception with partner
- Discussing partner's sexual health prior to engaging in sex
- Being selective regarding sexual partners
- Reducing the number of sexual partners
- Not engaging in sex while intoxicated
- Not injecting drugs (HIV/AIDS)

Sexually active persons should practice safer sex until their partner's sexual history and/or health has been clearly established. Unfortunately, this message is not always getting through to those who most need to hear it. The HIV/AIDS epidemic initially triggered a sharp decrease in risky sex and an increase in monogamous relationships among gay men. Unfortunately, this trend has begun to reverse. Once again, rates for many STDs are rising among gay men. In part, this may be due to the fact that new medical treatments are helping people with HIV live longer. Many victims simply do not look or act sick. This gives a false impression about the dangers of HIV infection and encourages foolish risk taking (Handsfield, 2001). The focus on HIV/AIDS prevention may also have deemphasized the health impact of the other STDs.

High school and college age students also remain too willing to engage in risky behavior (casual sex) and yet unwilling to use condoms (Bauman, Karasz, & Hamilton, 2007). A study of heterosexual adults also found that the majority did not practice safer sex with their last partner. Most of these "gamblers" knew too little about their partners to be sure they were not taking a big risk. For many people, drinking alcohol greatly increases the likelihood of taking sexual risks (Corbin & Fromme, 2002).

Isn't it possible that practicing safer sex would be interpreted as a sign that you mistrust your lover? Those who do not ensure their own safety, or that of their partners, are gambling with their health. As is the case with other behavioral risk factors, taking precautions could, instead, be defined as a way of showing that you really care about your own health as well as that of your partner (Essien et al., 2010).

We'll next turn our attention to the effect that stress has on health and sickness. Understanding stress and learning to control it can improve not only your health but the quality of your life as well (Harrington, 2013; Suinn, 2001). For these reasons, a discussion of stress and stress management follows (right after you pause for a healthy study break).

1. With respect to health, which of the following is *not* a major behavioral risk factor?

   a. overexercise   *b.* cigarette smoking
   c. stress   *d.* high blood pressure

2. Health psychologists tend to prefer _____ rather than modifying habits (like smoking) that become difficult to break once they are established.

3. The disease-prone personality is marked by _____, anxiety, and hostility.

4. For at least the first 6 months after becoming infected with HIV, a person can test negative while carrying the virus. T or F?

5. Wanting to practice safe sex is an insult to your lover. T or F?

REFLECT

THINK CRITICALLY

6. The general public is increasingly well informed about health risks and healthful behavior. Can you apply the concept of reinforcement to explain why so many people fail to act on this information?

7. Which do you think would be better suited to reducing STDs and unwanted pregnancies among adolescents: abstinence-only education programs or more comprehensive sex education programs?

SELF-REFLECT

Make a list of the major behavioral risk factors that apply to you. Are you laying the foundation for a lifestyle disease?

Which of the health-promoting behaviors listed in Table 11.2 would you like to increase?

As a counselor, you are working with a young person who seems to be sexually active. What can you tell this person about STDs and safer sex practices?

ANSWERS

1. a 2. prevention 3. depression 4. T 5. F 6. Many of the health payoffs are delayed by months or years, greatly lessening the immediate rewards for healthful behavior (Watson & Tharp, 2007). 7. More comprehensive programs are actually more effective at reducing STDs and unwanted pregnancies among adolescents (Kirby, 2008).

Stress—Threat or Thrill?

JOURNEY QUESTION 11.3 *What is stress and what factors determine its severity?*

Stress can be a major behavioral risk factor if it is prolonged or severe, but it isn't always bad. As Canadian stress research pioneer Hans Selye (SEL-yay) (1978) observed, "To be totally without stress is to be dead." That's because **stress** is the mental and physical condition that occurs when we adjust or adapt to the environment. Unpleasant events such as work pressures, marital problems, or financial woes naturally produce stress. But so do travel, sports, a new job, rock climbing, dating, and other positive activities. Even if you aren't a thrill seeker, a healthy lifestyle may include a fair amount of *eustress* (good stress). Activities that provoke "good stress" are usually challenging, rewarding, and energizing.

Regardless of whether it is triggered by a pleasant or an unpleasant event, a **stress reaction** begins with the same autonomic nervous system (ANS) arousal that occurs during emotion. Imagine you are standing at the top of a wind-whipped ski jump for the first time. Internally, you would experience a rapid surge in your heart rate, blood pressure, respiration, muscle tension, and other ANS responses. *Short-term* stresses of this kind can be uncomfortable, but they rarely do any damage. (Your landing might, however.) *Long-term* stresses are another matter entirely.

General Adaptation Syndrome

The impact of long-term stresses can be understood by examining the body's defenses against stress, a pattern known as the **general adaptation syndrome (GAS)**. The GAS is a series of bodily reactions to prolonged stress. Selye (1978) noticed that the first symptoms of almost any disease or trauma (poisoning, infection, injury, or stress) are almost identical. The body responds in the same way to any stress, be it infection, failure, embarrassment, a new job, trouble at school, or a stormy romance.

How does the body respond to stress? The GAS consists of three stages: an alarm reaction, a stage of resistance, and a stage of exhaustion (**Figure 11.2**) (Selye, 1978).

Stress The mental and physical condition that occurs when a person must adjust or adapt to the environment.

Stress reaction The physical response to stress, consisting mainly of bodily changes related to autonomic nervous system arousal.

General adaptation syndrome (GAS) A series of bodily reactions to prolonged stress; occurs in three stages: alarm, resistance, and exhaustion.

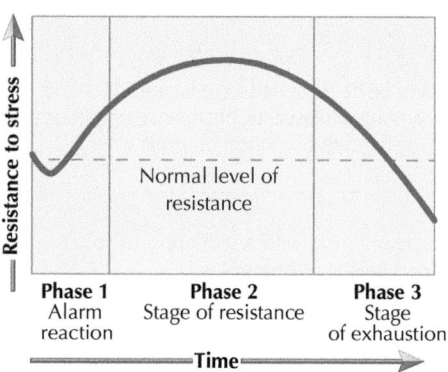

Figure 11.2 The general adaptation syndrome. During the initial alarm reaction to stress, resistance falls below normal. It rises again as bodily resources are mobilized, and it remains high during the stage of resistance. Eventually, resistance falls again as the stage of exhaustion is reached. (From Weiten, W., *Psychology: Themes and Variations, Briefer Edition*, 9e. Copyright © 2014 Wadsworth, a part of Cengage Learning, Inc.)

In the **alarm reaction**, your body mobilizes its resources to cope with added stress. The pituitary gland signals the adrenal glands to produce more adrenaline, noradrenaline, and cortisol. As these stress hormones are dumped into the bloodstream, some body processes are speeded up and others are slowed. This allows body resources to be applied where they are needed.

We should all be thankful that our bodies automatically respond to emergencies. But brilliant as this emergency system is, it can also cause problems. In the first phase of the alarm reaction, people have such symptoms as headache, fever, fatigue, sore muscles, shortness of breath, diarrhea, upset stomach, loss of appetite, and a lack of energy. Notice that these are also the symptoms of being sick, of stressful travel, of high-altitude sickness, of final exams week, and (possibly) of falling in love!

During the **stage of resistance**, body adjustments to stress stabilize. As the body's defenses come into balance, symptoms of the alarm reaction disappear. Outwardly, everything seems normal. However, this appearance of normality comes at a high cost. The body is better able to cope with the original stressor, but its resistance to other stresses is lowered. For example, animals placed in extreme cold become more resistant to the cold, but more susceptible to infection. It is during the stage of resistance that the first signs of psychosomatic disorders (physical disorders triggered by psychological factors) begin to appear.

Continued stress leads to the **stage of exhaustion**, in which the body's resources are drained and stress hormones are depleted. Some of the typical signs or symptoms of impending exhaustion include the following (Friedman, 2002; Gurung, 2010):

Emotional signs: Anxiety, apathy, irritability, mental fatigue.

Behavioral signs: Avoidance of responsibilities and relationships, extreme or self-destructive behavior, self-neglect, poor judgment.

Physical signs: Excessive worry about illness, frequent illness, exhaustion, overuse of medicines, physical ailments and complaints.

The GAS may sound melodramatic if you are young and healthy or if you've never endured prolonged stress. However, you should not take stress lightly. Unless a way of relieving stress is found, the result will be a psychosomatic disease, a serious loss of health, or complete collapse. When Selye examined animals in the later stages of the GAS, he found that their adrenal glands were enlarged and discolored. There was intense shrinkage of internal organs, such as the thymus, spleen, and lymph nodes, and many animals had stomach ulcers. In addition to such direct effects, stress can disrupt the body's immune system, as described next.

Stress, Illness, and Your Immune System

How can prolonged stress result in a physical illness? An answer can be found in your body's immune system, which mobilizes defenses (such as white blood cells) against invading microbes and other disease agents. The immune system is regulated, in part, by the brain. Because of this link, stress and upsetting emotions can affect the immune system in ways that increase susceptibility to disease (Miller, Cohen, & Ritchey, 2002; Zachariae, 2009). By the way, the study of links among behavior, stress, disease, and the immune system is called **psychoneuroimmunology** (Daruna, 2012; Kendall-Tackett, 2010). (Try dropping that into a conversation sometime if you want to see a stress reaction!)

Studies show that the immune system is weakened in students during major exam times, as Mee Jung found out during her mad dash to the end of term. Immunity is also lowered by divorce, bereavement, a troubled marriage, job loss, poor sleep, depression, and similar stresses (Motivala & Irwin, 2007; Segerstrom & Miller, 2004). Lowered immunity explains why the "double whammy" of getting sick when you are trying to cope with

Alarm reaction First stage of the GAS, during which bodily resources are mobilized to cope with a stressor.

Stage of resistance Second stage of the GAS, during which bodily adjustments to stress stabilize, but at a high physical cost.

Stage of exhaustion Third stage of the GAS, at which time the body's resources are exhausted and serious health consequences occur.

Psychoneuroimmunology Study of the links among behavior, stress, disease, and the immune system.

prolonged or severe stress is so common (Pedersen, Bovbjerg, & Zachariae, 2011). Stress causes the body to release substances that increase inflammation. This is part of the body's self-protective response to threats, but it can prolong infections and delay healing (Kiecolt-Glaser, 2010).

It's also worth noting again the value of positive emotions. Happiness, laughter, and delight tend to strengthen immune system response. Doing things that make you happy can also protect your health (Diener & Chan, 2011; Rosenkranz et al., 2003).

Could reducing stress help prevent illness? Yes. Various psychological approaches, such as support groups, relaxation exercises, guided imagery, and stress management training, can actually boost immune system functioning (Kottler & Chen, 2011). By doing so, they help promote and restore health. For example, stress management reduced the severity of cold and flu symptoms in a group of university students (Reid, Mackinnon, & Drummond, 2001).

There is even evidence that stress management can improve the chances of survival in people with life-threatening diseases, such as cancer, heart disease, and HIV/AIDS (Schneiderman et al., 2001). With some successes to encourage them, psychologists are now searching for the best combination of treatments to help people resist disease (Miller & Cohen, 2001).

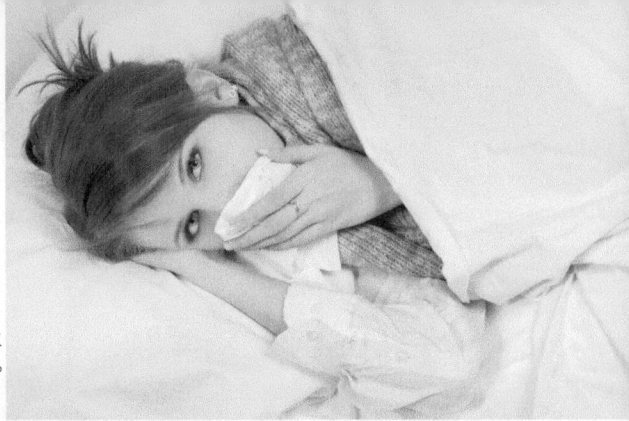

Stress and negative emotions lower immune system activity and increase inflammation. This, in turn, raises our vulnerability to infection, worsens illness, and delays recovery.

When Is Stress a Strain?

It goes almost without saying that some events are more likely to cause stress than others. A **stressor** is a condition or event that challenges or threatens a person. Police officers, for instance, suffer from a high rate of stress-related diseases. The threat of injury or death—plus occasional confrontations with angry, drunk, or hostile citizens—takes a toll. A major factor is the *unpredictable* nature of police work. An officer who stops a car to issue a traffic ticket never knows if a cooperative citizen or an armed gang member is waiting inside.

A revealing study shows how unpredictability adds to stress. In a series of 1-minute trials, college students breathed air through a mask. In some trials, the air contained 20 percent more carbon dioxide (CO_2) than normal. If you were to inhale this air, you would feel anxious, stressed, and a little like you were suffocating. Students tested this way hated the "surprise" doses of CO_2. They found it much less stressful to be told in advance which trials would include a choking whiff of CO_2 (Lejuez et al., 2000).

Air traffic control is stressful work. Employees must pay intense attention for long periods and have little control over the pace of work, and the consequences of making a mistake can be dire.

Pressure is another element of stress, especially job stress. **Pressure** occurs when a person must meet *urgent* external demands or expectations (Szollos, 2009). For example, we feel pressured when activities must be speeded up, when deadlines must be met, when extra work is added, or when we must work near maximum capacity for long periods. Most students who have survived final exams are familiar with the effects of pressure.

What if I set deadlines for myself? Does it make a difference where the pressure comes from? Yes. People generally feel more stress in situations over which they have little or no control (Leiter, Gascón, & Martínez-Jarreta, 2010; Taris et al., 2005). In one study, nurses with a high sense of control (e.g., over the pacing of work and the physical arrangement of the working environment) were less likely to get sick, either physically or mentally, than nurses with a low sense of control (Ganster, Fox, & Dwyer, 2001).

To summarize, when emotional "shocks" are *intense* or *repeated, unpredictable, uncontrollable,* and linked to *pressure,* stress will be magnified, and damage is likely to result. At work, people face many of these sources of stress every day. (See **Table 11.3** for a list of the most common sources of stress at work.) In fact, chronic job stress sometimes results in *burnout.*

Stressor A specific condition or event in the environment that challenges or threatens a person.

Pressure A stressful condition that occurs when a person must meet urgent external demands or expectations.

Table 11.3 The Top 10 Work Stressors

WORK STRESSOR	RANK
Workload	1
Feeling undervalued	2
Deadlines	3
Type of work people have to do	4
Having to take on other people's work	5
Lack of job satisfaction	6
Lack of control over the working day	7
Having to work long hours	8
Frustration with the working environment	9
Performance targets	10

Source: Data from Skillsoft, 2006.

© Cengage Learning

Burnout

Burnout occurs when workers are physically, mentally, and emotionally drained (Leiter, Gascón, & Martínez-Jarreta, 2010). When people become burned out, they experience emotional exhaustion, cynicism or detachment, and feelings of reduced personal accomplishment (Maslach, Schaufeli, & Leiter, 2001).

Burnout may occur in any job, but it is a special problem in emotionally demanding helping professions, such as nursing, teaching, social work, childcare, counseling, or police work. Also, people who are more passionate about their work are more vulnerable to burnout (Garrosa et al., 2008; Vallerand et al., 2010). If we wish to keep caring people in the helping professions, it may be necessary to adjust workloads, rewards, and the amount of control people have in their jobs (Leiter & Maslach, 2005).

Can college students experience burnout? Yes, they can (Parker & Salmela-Aro, 2011). If you have a negative attitude toward your studies and feel that your college workload is too heavy, you may be vulnerable to burnout (Jacobs & Dodd, 2003). On the other hand, if you have a positive attitude toward your studies, participate in extracurricular activities, and enjoy good social support from your friends, rock on!

Appraising Stressors

It might seem that stressful events "happen to" us. Sometimes this is true, but as noted in Chapter 9, our emotions are greatly affected by how we appraise situations. That's why some people are distressed by events that others view as a thrill or a challenge (eustress). Ultimately, stress depends on how you perceive a situation. Our friend Akihito would find it stressful to listen to five of his son's hip-hop CDs in a row. His son Takashi would find it stressful to listen to *one* of his father's opera CDs. To know if you are stressed, we must know what meaning you place on events. As we will see in a moment, whenever a stressor is appraised as a *threat* (potentially harmful), a powerful stress reaction follows (Lazarus, 1991a; Smith & Kirby, 2011).

"Am I Okay or in Trouble?"

You have been selected to give a speech to 300 people. Or a doctor tells you that you must undergo a dangerous and painful operation. Or the one true love of your life walks out the door. What would your emotional response to these events be? How do you cope with a threat?

According to Richard Lazarus (1991a), there are two important steps in managing a threat. The first is a **primary appraisal**, in which you decide whether a situation is relevant

Burnout A work-related condition of mental, physical, and emotional exhaustion.

Primary appraisal Deciding if a situation is relevant to oneself and if it is a threat.

Human Diversity

Being poor is no fun. It will probably not surprise you to learn it's no good for your health, either (Sapolsky, 2005). In general, the poorer people are, the more their health suffers and the lower their life expectancy. According to the World Health Organization, 1.2 *billion* people around the world live in *absolute poverty*, surviving on less than a dollar a day. Tragically, absolute poverty wreaks havoc with people's health. But that's not the whole story. For example, physician Stephen Bezruchka has shown that Greeks earn, on average, less than half of what Americans earn and yet have a longer life expectancy (Bezruchka as cited in Sapolsky, 2005).

How could this be? One possible answer is hinted at in a study that found poorer women in California are more likely to die if they live in better-off neighborhoods than if they live in poorer neighborhoods (Winkleby, Ahn, & Cubbin, 2006). Apparently, being constantly reminded that you are *relatively poor* piles on an extra measure of stress (Bjornstrom, 2011; Wilkinson & Pickett, 2006, 2007). Add to that the fact that the United States currently has the largest income inequalities in the developed world. Constantly living with an awareness of their relative poverty, then, may help explain why Americans have shorter life expectancies than Greeks.

No one should pretend that relative poverty in the United States is anywhere near as big a problem as absolute poverty around the world.

Nevertheless, it is a growing problem in the United States as the gap between rich and poor continues to widen (Emerson, 2009; Oishi, Kesebir, & Diener, 2011).

What should I do if I always feel poor? That may be part of the reason you are reading this book. First, commit to changing your circumstances through education and hard work. That's called *problem-focused coping* (you'll read about it in a few paragraphs). In the meantime, remember Lazarus's (1991a,b) point about appraisal: It's only a stressor if you appraise it as one. A realistic appraisal of your situation may reveal that you are actually "richer" than you think you are. Maybe the best things in life are not all free. But why make yourself sick comparing yourself to people much better off than you (Wilkinson & Pickett, 2009)?

Although being poor in the United States may mean living above an absolute poverty level, it also means constantly living with stress of dramatic income inequality (Wilkinson & Pickett, 2009).

---

or irrelevant, positive or threatening. In essence, this step answers the question "Am I okay or in trouble?" Then you make a **secondary appraisal**, in which you assess your resources and choose a way to meet the threat or challenge ("What can I do about this situation?"). Thus, the way a situation is "sized up" greatly affects our ability to cope with it (Figure 11.3). Public speaking, for instance, can be appraised as an intense threat or as a chance to perform. Emphasizing the threat—by imagining failure, rejection, or embarrassment—obviously invites disaster (Strongman, 2003). (For an example of how changing your appraisal may make a big difference in your life, see "So You Think You're Poor.")

The Nature of Threat

What does it mean to feel threatened by a stressor? Certainly in most day-to-day situations it doesn't mean you think your life is in danger. (Unless, of course, you owe money to Tony Soprano.) Threat has more to do with the idea of control. We are particularly prone to feel stressed when we can't—or think we can't—control our immediate environment. In short, a *perceived* lack of control is just as threatening as an actual lack of control. For example, college students who *feel* overloaded experience stress even though their workload may not actually be heavier than that of their classmates (Jacobs & Dodd, 2003).

A sense of control also comes from believing you can reach desired goals. It is threatening to feel that we lack *competence* to cope with life's demands (Bandura, 2001; Leiter, Gascón, & Martínez-Jarreta, 2010). Because of this, the intensity of your body's stress reaction often depends on what you think and tell yourself about a stressor. That's why it's

Secondary appraisal Deciding how to cope with a threat or challenge.

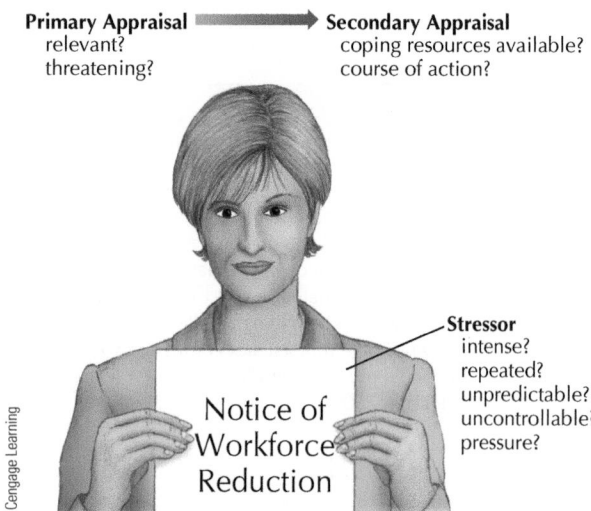

Primary Appraisal ➡ **Secondary Appraisal**
relevant?   coping resources available?
threatening?   course of action?

Stressor
intense?
repeated?
unpredictable?
uncontrollable?
pressure?

Notice of Workforce Reduction

Figure 11.3 Stress is the product of an interchange between a person and the environment.

valuable to learn to think in ways that ward off the body's stress response. (Some strategies for controlling upsetting thoughts are described in the Psychology in Action section of this chapter.)

Coping with Threat

You have appraised a situation as threatening. What will you do next? You have two major choices. Both involve thinking and acting in ways that help us handle stressors. In **emotion-focused coping**, we try to control our emotional reactions to the situation. For example, a distressed person may distract herself by listening to music, taking a walk to relax, or seeking emotional support from others. In contrast, **problem-focused coping** is aimed at managing or correcting the distressing situation itself. Some examples are making a plan of action or concentrating on your next step (Herman & Tetrick, 2009; Smith & Kirby, 2011).

Couldn't both types of coping occur together? Yes. Sometimes the two types of coping aid one another. For instance, quieting your emotions may make it easier for you to find a way to solve a problem. Say, for example, that you feel anxious as you step in front of your class to give a presentation. If you take a few deep breaths to reduce your anxiety (emotion-focused coping), you will be better able to glance over your notes to improve your delivery (problem-focused coping).

It is also possible for coping efforts to clash. For instance, if you have to make a difficult decision, you may suffer intense emotional distress. In such circumstances there is a temptation to make a quick, unreflective choice, just to end the suffering (Arnsten, Mazure, & Sinha, 2012). Doing so may allow you to cope with your emotions, but it shortchanges problem-focused coping.

In general, problem-focused coping tends to be especially useful when you are facing a controllable stressor—that is, a situation you can actually do something about. Emotion-focused efforts are best suited to managing your reaction to stressors you cannot control (Folkman & Moskowitz, 2004; Smith & Kirby, 2011). To improve your chances of coping effectively, the stress-fighting strategies described in this chapter include a mixture of both techniques.

So far, our discussion has focused on everyday stresses. How do people react to the extreme stresses imposed by war, violence, or disaster? "Coping with Traumatic Stress" discusses this important topic.

Frustration—Blind Alleys and Lead Balloons

JOURNEY QUESTION 11.4 *What causes frustration and what are typical reactions to it?*

Do you remember how frustrated Mee Jung was when she couldn't find a parking place? **Frustration** is a negative emotional state that occurs when people are prevented from reaching desired goals. In Mee Jung's case, the goal of finding a parking space was blocked by another car.

Obstacles of many kinds cause frustration. A useful distinction can be made between external and personal sources of frustration. *External frustration* is based on conditions outside a person that impede progress toward a goal. All the following are external frustrations: getting stuck with a flat tire; having a marriage proposal rejected; finding the cupboard bare when you go to get your poor dog a bone; being chased out of the house by your starving dog. In other words, external frustrations are based on *delays, failure, rejection, loss,* and other direct blocking of motivated behavior.

Notice that external obstacles can be either *social* (slow drivers, tall people in theaters, people who cut into lines) or *nonsocial* (stuck doors, a dead battery, rain on the day of

Emotion-focused coping Managing or controlling one's emotional reaction to a stressful or threatening situation.

Problem-focused coping Directly managing or remedying a stressful or threatening situation.

Frustration A negative emotional state that occurs when one is prevented from reaching a goal.

Traumatic experiences produce psychological injury or intense emotional pain. Victims of **traumatic stresses**, such as war, torture, rape, assassination, plane crashes, natural disasters, and street violence, may suffer from nightmares, flashbacks, insomnia, irritability, nervousness, grief, emotional numbing, and depression (Durand & Barlow, 2013). For example, the 2011 earthquake, tsunami, and resulting nuclear crisis in Japan, along with the resulting chaos, was a traumatically stressful event.

People who personally witness or survive a disaster are most affected by traumatic stress. Twenty percent of the people who lived close to the World Trade Center in New York City suffered serious stress disorders after the 9/11 terrorist attack (Galea et al., 2002). Yet even those who experience horror at a distance may be traumatized (Galea & Resnick, 2005). Forty-four percent of U.S. adults who only saw the 9/11 attacks on television had at least some stress symptoms (Schuster et al., 2001). For example, Americans faced elevated risks of hypertension and heart problems for 3 years after 9/11 (Holman et al., 2008). Indirect exposure to such terrorist attacks, coupled with the ongoing risk of more attacks, has ensured that many people will suffer ongoing stress into the foreseeable future (Marshall et al., 2007).

Traumatic stress produces feelings of helplessness and vulnerability (Fields & Margolin, 2001). Victims realize that disaster could strike again without warning. In addition to feeling threatened, many victims sense that they are losing control of their lives (Scurfield, 2002).

What can people do about such reactions? Psychologists recommend the following:

- Identify what you are feeling and talk to others about your fears and concerns.

- Think about the skills that have helped you overcome adversity in the past and apply them to the present situation.

- Continue to do the things that you enjoy and that make life meaningful (LeDoux & Gorman, 2001).

- Get support from others. This is a major element in recovery from all traumatic events.

- Give yourself time to heal. Fortunately, most people are more resilient than they think.

When traumatic stresses are severe or repeated, some people have even more serious symptoms (Durand & Barlow, 2013). They suffer from crippling anxiety or become emotionally numb. Typically, they can't stop thinking about the disturbing event, they anxiously avoid anything associated with the event, and they are constantly fearful or nervous. (These are the symptoms of *stress disorders*, which are discussed in Chapter 12.) Such reactions can leave victims emotionally handicapped for months or years after a disaster. The consequences can last a lifetime for children who are the victims of trauma (Gillespie & Nemeroff, 2007). If you feel that you are having trouble coping with a severe emotional shock, consider seeking help from a psychologist or other professional (Bisson et al., 2007).

AP Photo/E. Pablo Kosmicki

There can be no doubt that mountain climber Aron Ralston experienced a trauma. After suffering a fall, his arm became impossibly wedged between two boulders. Left with no choice, he amputated his own arm with a dull knife. Remarkably, he survived to overcome his trauma, and the resulting disability, to climb again. Ralston (2004) told his story in his book, *Between a Rock and a Hard Place*, which inspired the 2010 film *127 Hours*.

---

the game). If you ask your friends what has frustrated them recently, most will probably mention someone's behavior ("My sister wore one of my dresses when I wanted to wear it," "My supervisor is unfair," "My history teacher grades too hard"). As social animals, we humans are highly sensitive to social sources of frustration (Taylor, 2012). That's probably why unfair treatment associated with racial or ethnic prejudice is a major source of frustration and stress in the lives of many African Americans and other minority group members (Clark et al., 1999; Gurung, 2010).

Frustration usually increases as the *strength, urgency,* or *importance* of a blocked motive increases. Mee Jung was especially frustrated in the parking lot because she was late for an exam. (Likewise, an escape artist submerged in a tank of water and bound with 200 pounds of chain would become *quite* frustrated if a trick lock jammed.) Remember, too, that motivation becomes stronger as we near a goal. As a result, frustration is more intense when a person runs into an obstacle very close to a goal. If you've ever missed an A grade by five points, you were probably very frustrated. If you've missed an A by one point—well, frustration builds character, right?

A final factor affecting frustration is summarized by the old phrase "the straw that broke the camel's back." The effects of *repeated* frustrations can accumulate until a small irritation sets off an unexpectedly violent response. A case in point is the fact that people

Traumatic stresses Extreme events that cause psychological injury or intense emotional pain.

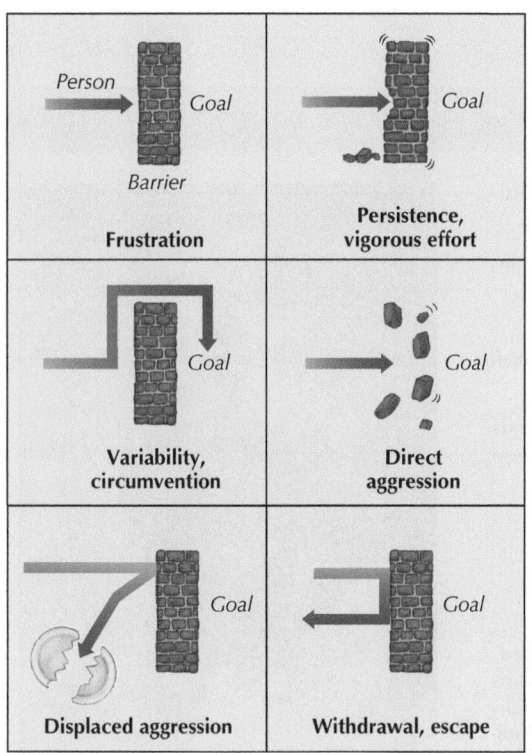

Figure 11.4 Frustration and common reactions to it.

with long daily commutes are more likely to display "road rage" (angry, aggressive driving) (Sansone & Sansone, 2010).

Personal frustrations are based on personal characteristics. If you are 4 feet tall and aspire to be a professional basketball player, you very likely will be frustrated. If you want to go to medical school but can earn only D grades, you will likewise be frustrated. In both examples, frustration is actually based on personal limitations. Yet, failure may be *perceived* as externally caused. We will return to this point in a discussion of stress management. In the meantime, let's look at some typical reactions to frustration.

Reactions to Frustration

Aggression is any response made with the intent of harming a person or an object. It is one of the most persistent and frequent responses to frustration (Anderson & Bushman, 2002; Shaver & Mikulincer, 2011).

Does frustration always cause aggression? Aren't there other reactions? Although the connection is strong, frustration does not always incite aggression. More often, frustration is met first with *persistence,* often in the form of more vigorous efforts and varied responses (Figure 11.4). For example, if you put your last dollar in a vending machine and pressing the button has no effect, you will probably press harder and faster (vigorous effort). Then you will press all the other buttons (varied response). Persistence may help you reach your goal by getting *around* a barrier. However, if the machine *still* refuses to deliver, or return your dollar, you may become aggressive and kick the machine (or at least tell it what you think of it).

Persistence can be very adaptive. Overcoming a barrier ends the frustration and allows the need or motive to be satisfied. The same is true of aggression that removes or destroys a barrier. Picture a small band of nomadic humans, parched by thirst but separated from a water hole by a menacing animal. It is easy to see that attacking the animal may ensure their survival. In modern society such direct aggression is seldom acceptable. If you find a long line at the drinking fountain, aggression is hardly appropriate. Because direct aggression is discouraged, it is frequently *displaced.*

How is aggression displaced? Directing aggression toward a source of frustration may be impossible, or it may be too dangerous. If you are frustrated by your boss at work or by a teacher at school, the cost of direct aggression may be too high (losing your job or failing a class). Instead, the aggression may be displaced, or redirected, toward whomever or whatever is available. Targets of **displaced aggression** tend to be safer, or less likely to retaliate, than the original source of frustration. At one time or another, you have probably lashed out at a friend or relative who was not the real cause of your annoyance. As this suggests, excessive anger over a minor irritation is a common form of displaced aggression (Miller et al., 2003).

Psychologists attribute much hostility to displaced aggression. A disturbing example is the finding that unemployment and divorce are associated with increased child abuse (Weissman, Jogerst, & Dawson, 2003). In a pattern known as **scapegoating**, a person or a group is blamed for conditions not of their making. A *scapegoat* is a person who has become a habitual target of displaced aggression. Despite recent progress, many minority groups continue to face hostility based on scapegoating (Vasquez, Lickel, & Hennigan, 2010). Think, for example, about the hostility expressed toward illegal immigrants during times of economic hardship. In many communities, layoffs and job losses are closely linked to increased violence (Glick, 2008). Or think about the hostility expressed toward anyone in the United States who looked even vaguely "foreign" right after the 9/11 terrorist attacks.

I have a friend who dropped out of school to hitchhike around the country. He seemed very frustrated before he quit. What type of response to frustration is that? Another major reaction to frustration is escape, or withdrawal. It is stressful and unpleasant to be frustrated. If other reactions do not reduce frustration, a person may try to escape. **Escape** may mean actually leaving a source of frustration (dropping out of school, quitting a job, leaving an unhappy

Aggression Any response made with the intent of causing harm.

Displaced aggression Redirecting aggression to a target other than the actual source of one's frustration.

Scapegoating Blaming a person or a group of people for conditions not of their making.

Escape Reducing discomfort by leaving frustrating situations or by psychologically withdrawing from them.

marriage), or it may mean psychologically escaping. Two common forms of psychological escape are feigned apathy (pretending not to care) and the use of drugs such as cocaine, alcohol, marijuana, or narcotics. Notice that these are examples of ineffective emotion-focused coping. (See Figure 11.4 for a summary of common reactions to frustration.)

Coping with Frustration

In a classic experiment, a psychologist studying frustration placed rats on a small platform at the top of a tall pole. Then, he forced them to jump off the platform toward two elevated doors, one locked and the other unlocked. If the rat chose the correct door, it swung open and the rat landed safely on another platform. Rats that chose the locked door bounced off it and fell into a net far below.

The problem of choosing the open door was made unsolvable and very frustrating by randomly alternating which door was locked. After a time, most rats adopted a stereotyped response. That is, they chose the same door every time. This door was then permanently locked. All the rat had to do was jump to the other door to avoid a fall, but time after time the rat bounced off the locked door (Maier, 1949).

Isn't that an example of persistence? No. Persistence that is *inflexible* can turn into "stupid," stereotyped behavior like that of a rat on a jumping platform. When dealing with frustration, you must know when to quit and establish a new direction. Here are some suggestions to help you avoid needless frustration:

1. Try to identify the source of your frustration. Is it external or personal?
2. Is the source of frustration something that can be changed? How hard would you have to work to change it? Is it under your control at all?
3. If the source of your frustration can be changed or removed, are the necessary efforts worth it?

The answers to these questions help determine whether persistence will be futile. There is value in learning to accept gracefully those things that cannot be changed.

Paintball seems to bring out aggressive impulses in many players. Wild shoot-outs are part of the fun, but are some players displacing aggressive urges related to frustration in other areas of their lives?

Conflict—Yes, No, Yes, No, Yes, No, Well, Maybe

JOURNEY QUESTION 11.5 *Are there different types of conflict and how do people react to conflict?*

Conflict occurs whenever a person must choose between contradictory needs, desires, motives, or demands. Choosing between college and work, marriage and single life, or study and failure are common conflicts. There are three basic forms of conflict. As we will see, each has its own properties (**Figures 11.5** and **11.6**).

Figure 11.5 Three basic forms of conflict. For this woman, choosing between pie and ice cream is a minor approach-approach conflict; choosing between paying higher rent or moving is an avoidance-avoidance conflict; and deciding whether to take a job that will require weekend work is an approach-avoidance conflict.

Conflict A stressful condition that occurs when a person must choose between incompatible or contradictory alternatives.

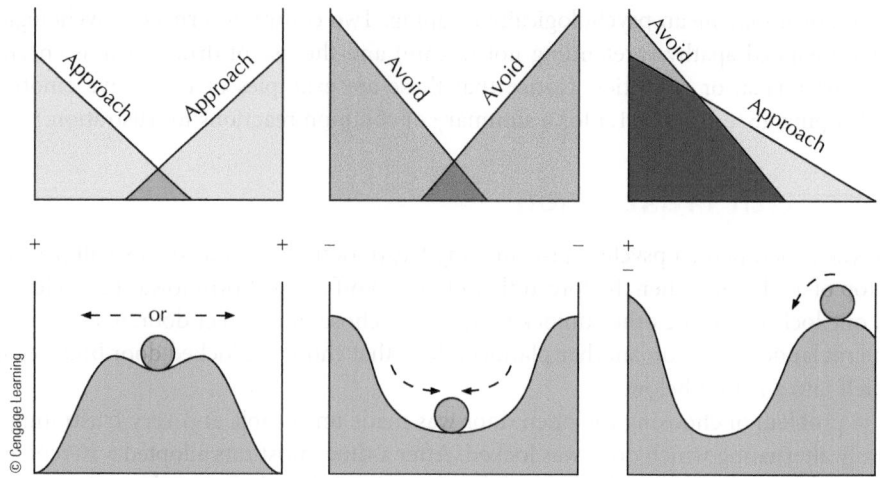

Figure 11.6 Conflict diagrams. As shown by the colored areas in the graphs, desires to approach and to avoid increase near a goal. The effects of these tendencies are depicted below each graph. The "behavior" of the ball in each example illustrates the nature of the conflict above it. An approach conflict *(left)* is easily decided. Moving toward one goal will increase its attraction *(graph)* and will lead to a rapid resolution. (If the ball moves in either direction, it will go all the way to one of the goals.) In an avoidance conflict *(center),* tendencies to avoid are deadlocked, resulting in inaction. In an approach-avoidance conflict *(right),* approach proceeds to the point where desires to approach and avoid cancel each other. Again, these tendencies are depicted *(below)* by the action of the ball. (Graphs after Miller, 1944.)

Approach Conflicts

An **approach-approach conflict** comes from having to choose between two positive, or desirable, alternatives. Choosing between tutti-frutti-coconut-mocha-champagne ice and orange-marmalade-peanut butter-coffee swirl at the ice cream parlor may throw you into a temporary conflict. However, if you really like both choices, your decision will be quickly made. Even when more important decisions are at stake, approach-approach conflicts tend to be the easiest to resolve. The old fable about the mule that died of thirst and starvation while standing between a bucket of water and a bucket of oats is obviously unrealistic. When both options are positive, the scales of decision are easily tipped one direction or the other.

Avoidance-Avoidance Conflicts

Being forced to choose between two negative, or undesirable, alternatives creates an **avoidance-avoidance conflict**. A person in an avoidance conflict is caught between "the devil and the deep blue sea," "the frying pan and the fire," or "a rock and a hard place." In real life, double-avoidance conflicts involve dilemmas such as choosing between unwanted pregnancy and abortion, the dentist and tooth decay, a monotonous job and poverty, or dorm food and starvation.

Suppose that I consider any pregnancy sacred and not to be tampered with. Or suppose I don't object to abortion. Like many other stressful situations, these examples can be defined as conflicts only on the basis of personal needs and values. If a woman would not consider abortion under any circumstances, she experiences no conflict. If she wants to end a pregnancy and does not object to abortion, there is also no conflict.

Avoidance conflicts often have a "damned if you do, damned if you don't" quality. In other words, both choices are negative, but *not choosing* may be impossible or equally undesirable. To illustrate, imagine the plight of a person trapped in a hotel fire 20 stories from the ground. Should she jump from the window and almost surely die on the pavement? Or should she try to dash through the flames and almost surely die of smoke inhalation and burns? When faced with a choice such as this, it is easy to see why people often *freeze,* finding it impossible to decide or take action. In actual disasters of this sort, people are often found dead in their rooms, victims of an inability to take action.

Indecision, inaction, and freezing are not the only reactions to double-avoidance conflicts. Because avoidance conflicts are stressful and difficult to solve, people sometimes pull out of them entirely. This reaction, called *leaving the field,* is another form of escape. It may explain the behavior of a student who could not attend school unless he worked. However, if he worked, he could not earn passing grades. His solution after much conflict and indecision? He joined the Navy.

Approach-Avoidance Conflicts

Approach-avoidance conflicts are also difficult to resolve. In some ways they are more troublesome than avoidance conflicts because people seldom escape them. A person in an **approach-avoidance conflict** is "caught" by being attracted to, and repelled by, the same goal or activity. Attraction keeps the person in the situation, but its negative aspects cause turmoil and distress. For example, a high school student arrives to pick up his date for the first time. He is met at the door by her father, who is a professional wrestler—7 feet tall, 300 pounds, and entirely covered with hair. The father gives the boy a crushing handshake and growls that he will break him in half if the girl is not home on time. The student considers the girl attractive and has a good time. But does he ask her out again? It depends on the relative strength of his attraction and his fear. Almost certainly he will feel *ambivalent* about asking her out again, knowing that another encounter with her father awaits him.

Ambivalence (mixed positive and negative feelings) is a central characteristic of approach-avoidance conflicts. Ambivalence is usually translated into *partial approach* (Miller, 1944). Because our student is still attracted to the girl, he may spend time with her at school and elsewhere. But he may not actually date her again. Some more realistic examples of approach-avoidance conflicts are planning to marry someone your parents strongly disapprove of, wanting to be in a play but suffering stage fright, wanting to buy a car but not wanting to make monthly payments, and wanting to eat when you're already overweight. Many of life's important decisions have approach-avoidance dimensions.

Multiple Conflicts

Aren't real-life conflicts more complex than the ones described here? Yes. Conflicts are rarely as clear-cut as those described. People in conflict are usually faced with several dilemmas at once, so several types of conflict may be intermingled. In real life, it is common to face **multiple approach-avoidance conflicts,** in which you are simultaneously attracted to and repelled by each of several alternatives. For example, you are offered two jobs: One is in a good city and pays well but offers poor hours and dull work; the other is in a city you don't like so much and pays poorly but offers very interesting work and excellent hours. Which do you select? These situations are more typical of the choices we must usually make. There are neither completely positive nor completely negative options.

As with single approach-avoidance conflicts, people faced with multiple approach-avoidance conflicts tend to feel ambivalent about each choice. This causes them to *vacillate,* or waver between, the alternatives. Just as you are about to choose one such alternative, its undesirable aspects tend to loom large. So, what do you do? You swing back toward the other choice. When multiple approach-avoidance conflicts involve major life decisions, such as choosing a career, a school, a mate, or a job, they can add greatly to the amount of stress we experience.

Managing Conflicts

How can I handle conflicts more effectively? Most of the suggestions made earlier concerning frustration also apply to conflicts. However, here are some additional things to remember when you are in conflict or must make a difficult decision:

1. Don't be hasty when making important decisions. Hasty decisions are often regretted. Even if you do make a faulty decision, it will trouble you less if you know that you did everything possible to avoid a mistake.

Approach-avoidance conflict Being attracted to and repelled by the same goal or activity.

Multiple approach-avoidance conflict Being simultaneously attracted to and repelled by each of several alternatives.

2. Try out important decisions *partially* when possible. If you are thinking about moving to a new town, try to spend a few days there first. If you are choosing between colleges, do the same. If classes are in progress, sit in on some. If you want to learn to scuba dive, rent equipment for a reasonable length of time before buying.

3. Look for workable compromises. Again, it is important to get all available information. If you think that you have only one or two alternatives and they are undesirable or unbearable, seek the aid of a teacher, counselor, minister, or social service agency. You may be overlooking possible alternatives these people will know about.

4. When all else fails, make a decision and live with it. Indecision and conflict exact a high cost. Sometimes it is best to select a course of action and stick with it unless it is very obviously wrong after you have taken it.

Conflicts are a normal part of life. With practice, you can learn to manage many of the conflicts you will face.

study break Stress, Frustration, and Conflict

RECITE

1. The first stage of the GAS is called the _____ reaction.
2. Emotional exhaustion, cynicism, and reduced accomplishment are characteristics of job _____.
3. Stress tends to be greatest when a situation is appraised as a _____ and a person does not feel _____ to cope with the situation.
4. According to Lazarus, coping with threatening situations can be both problem focused and _____ focused.
5. Which of the following is *not* a common reaction to frustration?

   a. ambivalence   b. aggression
   c. displaced aggression   d. persistence

6. Inaction and freezing are most characteristic of avoidance-avoidance conflicts. T or F?

REFLECT

THINK CRITICALLY

7. Which do you think would produce more stress: (a) appraising a situation as mildly threatening but feeling like you are totally incompetent to cope with it, or (b) appraising a situation as very threatening but feeling that you have the resources and skills to cope with it?

SELF-REFLECT

What impact did pressure, control, predictability, repetition, and intensity have on your last stress reaction?

What type of coping do you tend to use when you face a stressor such as public speaking or taking an important exam?

Think of a time when you were frustrated. What was your goal? What prevented you from reaching it? Was your frustration external or personal?

Have you ever displaced aggression? Why did you choose another target for your hostility?

ANSWERS

1. alarm 2. burnout 3. threat, competent 4. emotion 5. a 6. T 7. There is no correct answer here because individual stress reactions vary greatly. However, the secondary appraisal of a situation often determines just how stressful it is. Feeling incapable of coping is very threatening.

Psychological Defense—Mental Karate?

JOURNEY QUESTION 11.6 *What are defense mechanisms?*

Threatening situations tend to produce **anxiety**. When you are anxious, you feel tense, uneasy, apprehensive, worried, and vulnerable. This unpleasant state can lead to emotion-focused coping that is defensive in nature (Kramer et al., 2010; Lazarus, 1991b). Psychodynamic psychologists have identified various defense mechanisms that allow us to reduce anxiety caused by stressful situations or our own shortcomings. You might not always be aware of it, but you have probably used several of the defenses described here.

What are psychological defense mechanisms, and how do they reduce anxiety? A **defense mechanism** is any mental process used to avoid, deny, or distort sources of threat or anxiety, especially threats to one's self-image. Many of the defenses were first identified by Sigmund Freud, who assumed they operate *unconsciously*. Often, defense mechanisms create large

Anxiety Apprehension, dread, or uneasiness similar to fear but based on an unclear threat.

Defense mechanism A habitual and often unconscious psychological process used to reduce anxiety.

blind spots in awareness. For instance, you might know an extremely stingy person who is completely unaware that he is a tightwad. Let's consider some of the most common; a more complete listing is given in Table 11.4.

Denial

One of the most basic defenses is **denial** (protecting oneself from an unpleasant reality by refusing to accept it or believe it). We are prone to deny death, illness, and similar painful and threatening events. For instance, if you were told that you had only 3 months to live, how would you react? Your first thoughts might be, "Aw, come on, someone must have mixed up the X-rays," or, "The doctor must be mistaken," or simply, "It can't be true!" Similar denial and disbelief are common reactions to the unexpected death of a friend or relative: "It's just not real. I don't believe it!"

Repression

Freud noticed that his patients had tremendous difficulty recalling shocking or traumatic events from childhood. It seemed that powerful forces were holding these painful memories from awareness. Freud called this **repression**, and said we use it to protect ourselves by blocking out threatening thoughts and impulses. Feelings of hostility toward a family member, the names of people we dislike, and past failures are common targets of repression. Research suggests that you are most likely to repress information that threatens your self-image (Axmacher et al., 2010; Mendolia, 2002).

Reaction Formation

In a **reaction formation**, impulses are not just repressed; they are also held in check by exaggerating opposite behavior. For example, a mother who unconsciously resents her children may, through reaction formation, become absurdly overprotective and overindulgent. Her real thoughts of "I hate them" and "I wish they were gone" are replaced by "I love them" and "I don't know what I would do without them." The mother's hostile impulses are traded for "smother" love, so that she won't have to admit she hates her children. Thus, the basic idea in a reaction formation is that the individual acts out an opposite behavior to block threatening impulses or feelings.

Table 11.4 Psychological Defense Mechanisms

Compensation Counteracting a real or imagined weakness by emphasizing desirable traits or seeking to excel in the area of weakness or in other areas.

Denial Protecting oneself from an unpleasant reality by refusing to perceive it.

Fantasy Fulfilling unmet desires in imagined achievements or activities.

Identification Taking on some of the characteristics of an admired person, usually as a way of compensating for perceived personal weaknesses or faults.

Intellectualization Separating emotion from a threatening or anxiety-provoking situation by talking or thinking about it in impersonal "intellectual" terms.

Isolation Separating contradictory thoughts or feelings into "logic-tight" mental compartments so that they do not come into conflict.

Projection Attributing one's own feelings, shortcomings, or unacceptable impulses to others.

Rationalization Justifying your behavior by giving reasonable and "rational," but false, reasons for it.

Reaction formation Preventing dangerous impulses from being expressed in behavior by exaggerating opposite behavior.

Regression Retreating to an earlier level of development or to earlier, less demanding habits or situations.

Repression Unconsciously preventing painful or dangerous thoughts from entering awareness.

Sublimation Working off unmet desires, or unacceptable impulses, in activities that are constructive.

© Cengage Learning

Regression

In its broadest meaning, **regression** refers to any return to earlier, less demanding situations or habits. Most parents who have a second child have to put up with at least some regression by the older child. Threatened by a new rival for affection, an older child may regress to childish speech, bed-wetting, or infantile play after the new baby arrives. If you've ever seen a child get homesick at summer camp or on a vacation, you've observed regression. The child wants to go home, where it's "safe." An adult who throws a temper tantrum or a married adult who "goes home to mother" is also regressing.

Projection

Projection is an unconscious process that protects us from the anxiety we would feel if we were to discern our faults. A person who is projecting tends to see his or her own feelings, shortcomings, or unacceptable impulses in others. **Projection** lowers anxiety by exaggerating negative traits in others. This justifies one's own actions and directs attention away from personal failings.

One of your authors once worked for a greedy shop owner who cheated many of his customers. This same man considered himself a pillar of the community and very moral and religious. How did he justify to himself his greed and dishonesty? He believed that everyone who entered his store was bent on cheating *him* any way they could. In reality, few, if any, of his customers shared his motives, but he projected his own greed and dishonesty onto them.

Rationalization

Every teacher is familiar with this strange phenomenon: On the day of an exam, an incredible wave of disasters sweeps through the city. Mothers, fathers, sisters, brothers, aunts, uncles, grandparents, friends, relatives, and pets of students become ill or die. Motors suddenly fall out of cars. Books are lost or stolen. Alarm clocks go belly-up and ring no more. All manner of computer equipment malfunctions.

The making of excuses comes from a natural tendency to explain our behavior. **Rationalization** refers to justifying personal actions by giving "rational" but false reasons for them. When the explanation you give for your behavior is reasonable and convincing— but not the real reason—you are *rationalizing*. For example, Mee Jung failed to turn in an assignment made at the beginning of the semester in one of her classes. Here's the explanation she gave her professor:

> My car broke down 2 days ago, and I couldn't get to the library until yesterday. Then I couldn't get all the books I needed because some were checked out, but I wrote what I could. Then last night, as the last straw, the ink cartridge in my printer ran out, and since all the stores were closed, I couldn't finish the paper on time.

When asked why she left the assignment until the last minute (the real reason it was late), Mee Jung offered another set of rationalizations. Like many people, Mee Jung had difficulty seeing herself without the protection of her rationalizations.

All the defense mechanisms described seem pretty undesirable. Do they have a positive side? People who overuse defense mechanisms become less adaptable, because they consume great amounts of emotional energy to control anxiety and maintain an unrealistic self-image. Defense mechanisms do have value, though. Often, they help keep us from being overwhelmed by immediate threats. This can provide time for a person to learn to cope in a more effective, problem-focused manner. If you recognize some of your own behavior in the descriptions here, it is hardly a sign that you are hopelessly defensive. As noted earlier, most people occasionally use defense mechanisms.

Two defense mechanisms that have a decidedly more positive quality are compensation and sublimation.

Compensation

Compensatory reactions are defenses against feelings of inferiority. A person who has a defect or weakness (real or imagined) may go to unusual lengths to overcome the weakness or to *compensate* for it by excelling in other areas. One of the pioneers of "pumping iron" is Jack LaLanne, who opened the first modern health club in America. LaLanne made a successful career out of bodybuilding in spite of the fact that he was thin and sickly as a young man. Or perhaps it would be more accurate to say *because* he was thin and sickly. You can find dozens of examples of **compensation** at work. A childhood stutterer may excel in debate at college. As a child, Helen Keller was unable to see or hear, but she became an outstanding thinker and writer. Perhaps Ray Charles, Stevie Wonder, Andrea Bocelli, and other blind entertainers were drawn to music because of their handicap.

For some players—and fans—football probably allows sublimation of aggressive urges. *Call of Duty, Mass Effect*, and similar computer games may serve the same purpose.

Sublimation

The defense called **sublimation** (sub-lih-MAY-shun) is defined as working off frustrated desires (especially sexual desires) through socially acceptable activities. Freud believed that art, music, dance, poetry, scientific investigation, and other creative activities could serve to rechannel sexual energies into productive behavior. Freud also felt that almost any strong desire could be sublimated. For example, a very aggressive person may find social acceptance as a professional soldier, boxer, or football player. Greed may be refined into a successful business career. Lying may be sublimated into storytelling, creative writing, or politics.

Sexual motives appear to be the most easily and widely sublimated (Moran, 2010). Freud would have had a field day with such modern pastimes as surfing, motorcycle riding, drag racing, and dancing to or playing rock music, to name but a few. People enjoy each of these activities for a multitude of reasons, but it is hard to overlook the rich sexual symbolism apparent in each.

Learned Helplessness and Depression—Is There Hope?

JOURNEY QUESTION 11.7 *What do we know about coping with feelings of helplessness and depression?*

What would happen if a person's defenses failed or if the person appraised a threatening situation as hopeless? Martin Seligman studied the case of a young Marine who seemed to have adapted to the stresses of being held prisoner during the Vietnam War. The Marine's health was related to a promise made by his captors: If he cooperated, they said, he would be released on a certain date. As the date approached, his spirits soared. Then came a devastating blow. He had been deceived. His captors had no intention of ever releasing him. He immediately lapsed into a deep depression, refused to eat or drink, and died shortly thereafter.

That seems like an extreme example. Does anything similar occur outside of concentration camps? Apparently so. For example, researchers in San Antonio, Texas, asked older people if they were hopeful about the future. Those who answered "No" died at elevated rates (Stern, Dhanda, & Hazuda, 2001).

Learned Helplessness

To explain such patterns psychologists have focused on the concept of **learned helplessness**, an acquired inability to overcome obstacles and avoid aversive stimuli (Seligman, 1989). To observe learned helplessness, let's see what happens when animals are tested in a shuttle box (**Figure 11.7**). If placed in one side of a divided box, dogs will quickly learn to leap to the

Learned helplessness A learned inability to overcome obstacles or to avoid punishment; learned passivity and inaction to aversive stimuli.

(a)

(b)

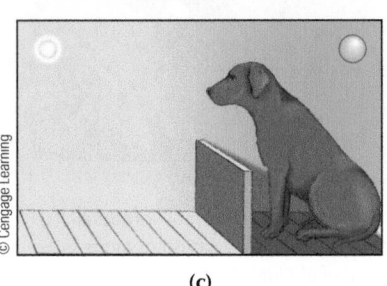

(c)

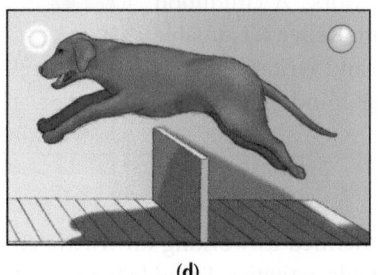

(d)

© Cengage Learning

Figure 11.7 In the normal course of escape and avoidance learning, a light dims shortly before the floor is electrified *(a)*. Because the light does not yet have meaning for the dog, the dog receives a shock (non-injurious, by the way) and leaps the barrier *(b)*. Dogs soon learn to watch for the dimming of the light *(c)* and to jump before receiving a shock *(d)*. Dogs made to feel "helpless" rarely even learn to escape shock, much less to avoid it.

other side to escape an electric shock. If they are given a warning before the shock occurs (for example, a light that dims), most dogs learn to avoid the shock by leaping the barrier before the shock arrives. This is true of most dogs, but not those who have learned to feel helpless (Overmier & LoLordo, 1998).

How is a dog made to feel helpless? Before being tested in the shuttle box, a dog can be placed in a harness (from which the dog cannot escape) and then given several painful shocks. The animal is helpless to prevent these shocks. When placed in the shuttle box, dogs prepared this way react to the first shock by crouching, howling, and whining. None of them try to escape. They helplessly resign themselves to their fate. After all, they have already learned that there is nothing they can do about shock.

As the shuttle box experiments suggest, helplessness is a psychological state that occurs when events *appear to be uncontrollable* (Seligman, 1989). Helplessness also afflicts humans (Domjan, 2010; Reivich et al., 2005). It is a common reaction to repeated failure and to unpredictable or unavoidable punishment. A prime example is college students who feel helpless about their schoolwork. Such students tend to procrastinate, give up easily, and drop out of school (Perry, 2003).

Where humans are concerned, attributions (discussed in Chapter 9) have a large effect on helplessness. Persons who are made to feel helpless in one situation are more likely to act helpless in other situations if they attribute their failure to *lasting, general* factors. An example would be concluding "I must be stupid" after doing poorly on a test in a biology class. In contrast, attributing a low score to specific factors in the situation ("I'm not too good at the type of test my biology professor uses" or "I'm not very interested in biology") tends to prevent learned helplessness from spreading (Peterson & Vaidya, 2001; Prochaska & Norcross, 2010).

Depression

Seligman and others have pointed out the similarities between learned helplessness and **depression**. Both are marked by feelings of despondency, powerlessness, and hopelessness. "Helpless" animals display decreased activity, lowered aggression, blunted appetite, and a loss of sex drive. Humans suffer from similar effects and also tend to see themselves as failing, even when they're not (Brown & Barlow, 2011; LoLordo, 2001).

Depression is one of the most widespread emotional problems, and it undoubtedly has many causes. However, learned helplessness seems to explain many cases of depression and hopelessness. For example, Seligman (1972) describes the fate of Archie, a 15-year-old boy. For Archie, school is an unending series of shocks and failures. Other students treat him as if he's stupid; in class he rarely answers questions because he doesn't know some of the words. He feels knocked down everywhere he turns. These may not be electric shocks, but they are certainly emotional "shocks," and Archie has learned to feel helpless to prevent them. When he leaves school his chances of success will be poor. He has learned to passively endure whatever shocks life has in store for him. Archie is not alone in this regard. Hopelessness is almost always a major element of depression (Durand, & Barlow, 2013; Reivich et al., 2005).

Recognizing Depression

Most people know, obviously enough, when they are "down." You should assume that more than a minor fluctuation in mood is involved when these conditions exist (National Institute of Mental Health, 2012a):

1. Persistent sad, anxious, or "empty" feelings.
2. Feelings of guilt, worthlessness, and/or helplessness.

Depression A state of despondency marked by feelings of powerlessness and hopelessness.

3. Difficulty concentrating, remembering details, and making decisions.
4. Feelings of hopelessness and/or pessimism.
5. Loss of interest in activities or hobbies once pleasurable, including sex.

Hope

Does Seligman's research give any clues about how to "unlearn" helplessness? With dogs, an effective technique is to forcibly drag them away from shock into the "safe" compartment. After this is done several times, the animals regain "hope" and feelings of control over the environment. Just how this can be done with humans is a question psychologists are exploring. It seems obvious, for instance, that someone like Archie would benefit from an educational program that would allow him to "succeed" repeatedly.

In **mastery training**, responses that lead to mastery of a threat or control over one's environment are reinforced. Animals that undergo such training become more resistant to learned helplessness (Volpicelli et al., 1983). For example, animals that first learn to escape shock become more persistent in trying to flee inescapable shock. In effect, they won't give up, even when the situation really is "hopeless."

Such findings suggest that we might be able to "immunize" people against helplessness and depression by allowing them to master difficult challenges (Miltenberger, 2012). The Outward Bound schools, in which people pit themselves against the rigors of mountaineering, white-water canoeing, and wilderness survival, might serve as a model for such a program.

The value of hope should not be overlooked. As fragile as this emotion seems, it is a powerful antidote to depression and helplessness (Weingarten, 2010). As an individual, you may find hope in religion, nature, human companionship, or even technology. Wherever you find it, remember its value: Hope is among the most important of all human emotions. Having positive beliefs, such as optimism, hope, and a sense of meaning and control, is closely related to overall well-being (Diener & Chan, 2011; Taylor et al., 2003).

The College Blues

During the school year, many college students suffer symptoms of depression, which can exert a toll on academic performance (Lindsey, Fabiano, & Stark, 2009). In one study, students diagnosed with depression scored half a grade point below nondepressed students (Hysenbegasi, Hass, & Rowland, 2005). Why do students get "blue"? Various problems contribute to depressive feelings. Here are some of the most common:

1. Stresses from college work and pressures to choose a career can leave students feeling that they are missing out on fun or that all their hard work is meaningless.
2. Isolation and loneliness are common when students leave their support groups behind. In the past, family, a circle of high school friends, and often a boyfriend or girlfriend could be counted on for support and encouragement.
3. Problems with studying and grades frequently trigger depression. Many students start college with high aspirations and little prior experience with failure. At the same time, many lack basic skills necessary for academic success and are afraid of failure (Martin & Marsh, 2003).
4. Depression can be triggered by the breakup of an intimate relationship, either with a former boyfriend or girlfriend or with a newly formed college romance.
5. Students who find it difficult to live up to their idealized images of themselves are especially prone to depression (Enns, Cox, & Clara, 2005).
6. An added danger is that depressed students are more likely to abuse alcohol, which is a depressant (Gonzalez, Reynolds, & Skewes, 2011).

Coping with the College Blues

Bouts of the college blues are closely related to stressful events. Learning to manage college work and to challenge reflective, self-critical thinking can help alleviate mild school-related depression (Santrock & Halonen, 2013). For example, if you don't do well on a test or a class

Mastery training Reinforcement of responses that lead to mastery of a threat or control over one's environment.

assignment, how do you react? If you see it as a small, isolated setback, you probably won't feel too bad. However, if you feel like you have "blown it" in a big way, depression may follow. Students who strongly link everyday events to long-term goals (such as a successful career or high income) tend to overreact to day-to-day disappointments (McIntosh, Harlow, & Martin, 1995; Santrock & Halonen, 2013).

What does the preceding tell us about the college blues? The implication is that it's important to take daily tasks one step at a time and chip away at them (Watson & Tharp, 2007). That way, you are less likely to feel overwhelmed, helpless, or hopeless. When you feel "blue," you should make a *daily schedule* for yourself (Burka & Yuen, 2008). Try to schedule activities to fill up every hour during the day. It is best to start with easy activities and progress to more difficult tasks. Check off each item as it is completed. That way, you will begin to break the self-defeating cycle of feeling helpless and falling further behind. (Depressed students spend much of their time sleeping.) A series of small accomplishments, successes, or pleasures may be all that you need to get going again. However, if you are lacking skills needed for success in college, ask for help in getting them. Don't remain "helpless."

Feelings of worthlessness and hopelessness are usually supported by self-critical or negative thoughts. Consider writing down such thoughts as they occur, especially those that immediately precede feelings of sadness (Pennebaker, 2004). After you have collected these thoughts, write a rational answer to each. For example, the thought "No one loves me" should be answered with a list of those who do care. One more point to keep in mind is this: When events begin to improve, try to accept it as a sign that better times lie ahead. Positive events are most likely to end depression if you view them as stable and continuing, rather than temporary and fragile.

Attacks of the college blues are common and should be distinguished from more serious cases of depression. Severe depression is a serious problem that can lead to suicide or a major impairment of emotional functioning. In such cases, it would be wise to seek professional help (Hollon, Stewart, & Strunk, 2006).

study break Defense Mechanisms, Helplessness, and Depression

RECITE

1. Fulfilling frustrated desires in imaginary achievements or activities defines the defense mechanism of
   a. compensation   b. isolation
   c. fantasy   d. sublimation

2. Of the defense mechanisms, two that are considered relatively constructive are
   a. compensation   b. denial
   c. isolation   d. projection
   e. regression   f. rationalization
   g. sublimation

3. Depression in humans is similar to _____ _____ observed in animal experiments.

4. College students suffering from depression have lower grades than nondepressed students. T or F?

5. Frequent self-criticism and self-blame are a natural consequence of doing college work. T or F?

REFLECT

THINK CRITICALLY

6. Learned helplessness is closely related to which of the factors that determine the severity of stress?

SELF-REFLECT

We tend to be blind to our own reliance on defense mechanisms. See if you can think of one example of each defense that you have observed yourself or someone else using.

Have you ever felt helpless in a particular situation? Does any part of Seligman's description of learned helplessness match your own experience?

Imagine that a friend of yours is suffering from the college blues. What advice would you give your friend?

ANSWERS

1. c 2. a, g 3. learned helplessness 4. T 5. F 6. Feelings of incompetence and lack of control.

Stress and Health—Unmasking a Hidden Killer

JOURNEY QUESTION 11.8 *How is stress related to health and disease?*

At the beginning of this chapter you read about Mee Jung, our intrepid student who became ill after a stressful final exam period. Was Mee Jung's illness a coincidence? Psychologists have now firmly established *that* stress affects our health. Let's see *how* this occurs. We will also explore some factors that limit the health risks we face. Because we live in a fast-paced and often stressful society, these are topics worth stressing.

Life Events and Stress

Disaster, depression, and sorrow often precede illness (Harrington, 2013). As Mee Jung learned after finals week, stressful events reduce the body's natural defenses against disease. More surprising is the finding that *life changes*—both good and bad—can increase susceptibility to accidents or illness. Major changes in our surroundings or routines require us to be on guard and ready to react. Over long periods, this can be quite stressful (Sternberg, 2009).

How can I tell if I am subjecting myself to too much stress? Psychiatrist Thomas Holmes and graduate student Richard Rahe developed the first rating scale to estimate the health hazards we face when stresses add up (Holmes & Rahe, 1967). Still widely used today, a version of the **Social Readjustment Rating Scale (SRRS)** is reprinted in Table 11.5 (Miller & Rahe, 1997; Woods, Racine, & Klump, 2010). Notice that the impact of life events is expressed in *life change units (LCUs)* (numerical values assigned to each life event).

Why is going on vacation on the list? Positive life events can be stressful as well. (For example, marriage rates a 50 and Christmas a 30, even though they are usually happy events.) Even a change in social activities rates 27 LCUs, whether the change is due to an improvement or a decline. A stressful adjustment may be required in either case.

To use the scale shown in Table 11.5, add up the LCUs for all life events you have experienced during the last year and compare the total to the following standards:

> 0–150: No significant problems
> 150–199: Mild life crisis (33 percent chance of illness)
> 200–299: Moderate life crisis (50 percent chance of illness)
> 300 or more: Major life crisis (80 percent chance of illness)

There is a higher chance of illness or accident when your LCU total exceeds 300 points. A more conservative rating of stress can be obtained by totaling LCU points for only the previous 6 months. The health of college students is also affected by stressful events, such as entering college, changing majors, or breaking up in a steady relationship. (For a student-oriented rating of stress, see Table 11.8 in the Psychology in Action section.)

Evaluation

People differ greatly in their reactions to the same event. For this reason, stress scales like the SRRS at best provide a rough index of stress. Nevertheless, research has shown that if your stress level is too high, an adjustment in your activities or lifestyle may be needed. In one classic study, people were deliberately exposed to the virus that causes common colds. The results were nothing to sneeze at: If a person had a high stress score, she or he was much more likely to actually get a cold (Cohen, Tyrrell, & Smith, 1993). In view of such findings, higher levels of stress should be taken seriously (Hales, 2013). Remember, "To be forewarned is to be forearmed."

The Hazards of Hassles

There must be more to stress than major life changes. Isn't there a link between ongoing stresses and health? In addition to having a direct impact, major life events spawn countless daily frustrations and irritations (Henderson, Roberto, & Kamo, 2010). Also, many of us face

Marriage is usually a positive life event. Nevertheless, the many changes it brings can be stressful.

Social Readjustment Rating Scale (SRRS) A scale that rates the impact of various life events on the likelihood of illness.

Table 11.5 Social Readjustment Rating Scale

RANK	LIFE EVENT	LIFE CHANGE UNITS	RANK	LIFE EVENT	LIFE CHANGE UNITS
1	Death of spouse or child	119	23	Mortgage or loan greater than $10,000	44
2	Divorce	98	24	Change in responsibilities at work	43
3	Death of close family member	92	25	Change in living conditions	42
4	Marital separation	79	26	Change in residence	41
5	Fired from work	79	27	Begin or end school	38
6	Major personal injury or illness	77	28	Trouble with in-laws	38
7	Jail term	75	29	Outstanding personal achievement	37
8	Death of close friend	70	30	Change in work hours or conditions	36
9	Pregnancy	66	31	Change in schools	35
10	Major business readjustment	62	32	Christmas	30
11	Foreclosure on a mortgage or loan	61	33	Trouble with boss	29
12	Gain of new family member	57	34	Change in recreation	29
13	Marital reconciliation	57	35	Mortgage or loan less than $10,000	28
14	Change in health or behavior of family member	56	36	Change in personal habits	27
15	Change in financial state	56	37	Change in eating habits	27
16	Retirement	54	38	Change in social activities	27
17	Change to different line of work	51	39	Change in number of family get-togethers	26
18	Change in number of arguments with spouse	51	40	Change in sleeping habits	26
19	Marriage	50	41	Vacation	25
20	Spouse begins or ends work	46	42	Change in church activities	22
21	Sexual difficulties	45	43	Minor violations of the law	22
22	Child leaving home	44			

Source: Reprinted from M. A. Miller & R. H. Rahe, 'Life scaling for the 1990s' in *Journal of Psychosomatic Research:* 43(3): pp. 279–292, Table II, copyright © 1997 Elsevier Ltd., with permission from Elsevier.

ongoing stresses at work or at home that do not involve major life changes (Pett & Johnson, 2005). Such minor but frequent stresses are called **hassles**, or **microstressors**. (See Table 11.6 for some examples of hassles faced by college students.)

In a yearlong study, 100 men and women recorded the hassles they endured. Participants also reported on their physical and mental health. Frequent and severe hassles turned out to be better predictors of day-to-day health than major life events were. However, major life events did predict changes in health 1 or 2 years after the events took place. It appears that daily hassles are closely linked to immediate health and psychological well-being

Table 11.6 Examples of Common Hassles Faced by College Students

Too many things to do
Not enough money for housing
Feeling discriminated against
People making gender jokes
Communication problems with friends
Driving to school
People making fun of my religion
Fear of losing valuables
Work schedule
Getting into shape
Parents' expectations

Source: Pett & Johnson, 2005.

© Cengage Learning

Hassle (microstressor) Any distressing, day-to-day annoyance.

Human Diversity

Around the world, an increasing number of emigrants and refugees must adapt to dramatic changes in language, dress, values, and social customs. For many, the result is a period of culture shock or **acculturative stress**—stress caused by adapting to a foreign culture. Typical reactions to acculturative stress are anxiety, hostility, depression, alienation, physical illness, or identity confusion (Rummens, Beiser, & Noh, 2003). For many young immigrants, acculturative stress is a major source of mental health problems (Choi & Dancy, 2009; Mejía & McCarthy, 2010; Yeh, 2003).

The severity of acculturative stress is related, in part, to how a person adapts to a new culture. Here are four main patterns (Berry et al., 2005; Sam & Berry, 2010):

Integration—maintain your old cultural identity but participate in the new culture.

Separation—maintain your old cultural identity and avoid contact with the new culture.

Assimilation—adopt the new culture as your own and have contact with its members.

Marginalization—reject your old culture but suffer rejection by members of the new culture.

To illustrate each pattern, let's consider a family that has immigrated to the United States from the imaginary country of Heinleinia:

The father favors integration. He is learning English and wants to get involved in American life. At the same time, he is a leader in the Heinleinian American community and spends much of his leisure time with other Heinleinian Americans. His level of acculturative stress is low.

The mother speaks only the Heinleinian language and interacts only with other Heinleinian Americans. She remains almost completely separate from American society. Her stress level is high.

The teenage daughter is annoyed by hearing Heinleinian spoken at home, by her mother's serving only Heinleinian food, and by having to spend her leisure time with her extended Heinleinian family. She would prefer to speak English and to be with her American friends. Her desire to assimilate creates moderate stress.

The son doesn't particularly value his Heinleinian heritage, yet his schoolmates reject him because he speaks with a Heinleinian accent. He feels trapped between two cultures. His position is marginal, and his stress level is high.

To summarize, those who feel marginalized tend to be highly stressed; those who seek to remain separate are also highly stressed; those who pursue integration into their new culture are minimally stressed; and those who assimilate are moderately stressed.

As you can see, integration and assimilation are the best options. However, a big benefit of assimilating is that people who embrace their new culture experience fewer social difficulties. For many, this justifies the stress of adopting new customs and cultural values (Gurung, 2010; Sam & Berry, 2010).

One of the best antidotes for acculturative stress is a society that tolerates or even celebrates ethnic diversity. Although some people find it hard to accept new immigrants, the fact is, nearly everyone's family tree includes people who were once strangers in a strange land.

(Crowther et al., 2001). Major life changes have more of a long-term impact as well as exacerbating the effects of daily hassles (Woods, Racine, & Klump, 2010).

One way to guarantee that you will experience a large number of life changes and hassles is to live in a foreign culture. "Acculturative Stress—Stranger in a Strange Land" offers a brief glimpse into some of the consequences of culture shock.

What can be done about a high LCU score or feeling excessively hassled?

A good response is to use stress management skills. For serious problems, stress management should be learned directly from a therapist or a stress clinic. When ordinary stresses are involved, there is much you can do on your own. An upcoming discussion of stress management will give you a start. In the meantime, take it easy!

Psychosomatic Disorders

As we have seen, chronic or repeated stress can damage physical health, as well as upset emotional well-being. Prolonged stress reactions are closely related to a large number of psychosomatic (SIKE-oh-so-MAT-ik) illnesses. In **psychosomatic disorders** (*psyche:* mind; *soma:* body), psychological factors contribute to actual bodily damage or to damaging changes in

Acculturative stress Stress caused by the many changes and adaptations required when a person moves to a foreign culture.

Psychosomatic disorders Illnesses in which psychological factors contribute to bodily damage or to damaging changes in bodily functioning.

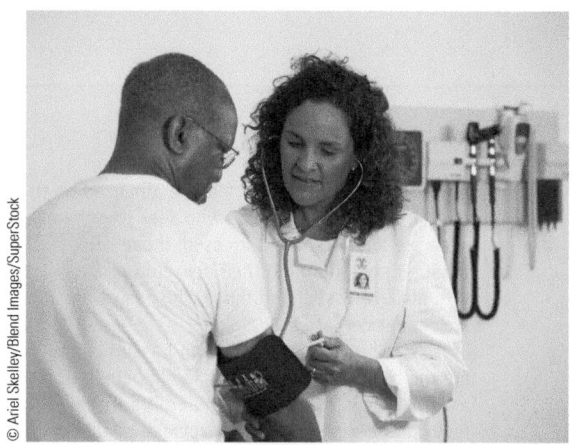

It is estimated that at least half of all patients who see a doctor have a psychosomatic disorder or an illness that is complicated by psychosomatic symptoms.

bodily functioning (Asmundson & Taylor, 2005; Bourgeois et al., 2009). Psychosomatic problems, therefore, are *not* the same as hypochondria. **Hypochondriacs** (HI-po-KON-dree-aks) imagine that they have diseases. There is nothing imaginary about asthma, a migraine headache, or high blood pressure.

The most common psychosomatic problems are gastrointestinal and respiratory (stomach pain and asthma, for example), but many others exist. Typical problems include eczema (skin rash), hives, migraine headaches, rheumatoid arthritis, hypertension (high blood pressure), colitis (ulceration of the colon), and heart disease. Actually, these are only the major problems. Many lesser health complaints are also stress related. Typical examples include sore muscles, headaches, neckaches, backaches, indigestion, constipation, chronic diarrhea, fatigue, insomnia, premenstrual problems, and sexual dysfunctions (Taylor, 2012).

Severe psychosomatic disorders can even be fatal. Thus, the person who says, "Oh it's *just* psychosomatic" doesn't understand how serious stress-related diseases really are. For some of these problems, biofeedback may be helpful. The next section explains how.

Biofeedback

Psychologists have discovered that people can learn to control bodily activities once thought to be involuntary. This is done by applying informational feedback to bodily control, a process called **biofeedback**. If you were asked to raise the temperature of your right hand, you probably couldn't, because you wouldn't know if you were succeeding. To make your task easier, a sensitive thermometer could be attached to your hand. The thermometer could be wired so that an increase in temperature would activate a signal light. Then, all you would have to do is try to keep the light on as much as possible. With practice and the help of biofeedback, you could learn to raise your hand temperature at will.

Biofeedback holds promise as a way to treat some psychosomatic problems (Figure 11.8). For instance, people have been trained to prevent migraine headaches with biofeedback. Sensors are taped to patients' hands and foreheads. Patients then learn to redirect blood flow away from the head to their extremities. Because migraine headaches involve excessive blood

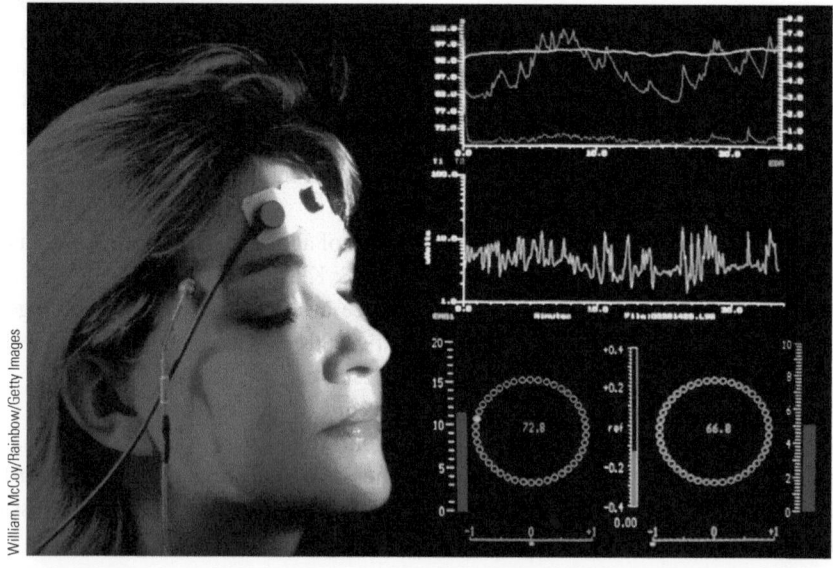

Figure 11.8 In biofeedback training, bodily processes are monitored and processed electronically. A signal is then routed back to the patient through headphones, signal lights, or other means. This information helps the patient alter bodily activities not normally under voluntary control. This woman is learning to control her brainwaves in order to relax.

Hypochondriac A person who complains about illnesses that appear to be imaginary.

Biofeedback Information given to a person about his or her ongoing bodily activities; aids voluntary regulation of physical states.

flow to the head, biofeedback helps patients reduce the frequency of their headaches (Larsson et al., 2005; Stokes & Lappin, 2010).

Biofeedback can also help relieve muscle-tension headaches and chronic pain (Middaugh & Pawlick, 2002; Sousa et al., 2009). It shows promise for lowering blood pressure and controlling heart rhythms (Olsson et al., 2010; Wheat & Larkin, 2010). The technique has been used with some success to control epileptic seizures and hyperactivity in children (Demos, 2005). Insomnia also responds to biofeedback therapy (Gathchel & Oordt, 2003; McLay & Spira, 2009).

How does biofeedback work? Some researchers believe that many of its benefits arise from *general relaxation.* Others stress that the method simply acts as a "mirror" to help a person perform tasks involving *self-regulation.* Just as a mirror does not comb your hair, biofeedback does not do anything by itself. It can, however, help people make desired changes in their behavior.

The Cardiac Personality

It would be a mistake to assume that stress is the sole cause of psychosomatic diseases. Genetic differences, organ weaknesses, and learned reactions to stress combine to do damage. Personality also enters the picture. As mentioned earlier, a general disease-prone personality type exists. To a degree, there are also "headache personalities," "asthma personalities," and so on. The best documented of such patterns is the "cardiac personality"—a person at high risk for heart disease.

In a landmark study of heart problems, two cardiologists, Meyer Friedman and Ray Rosenman, classified people as either **Type A personalities** (those who run a high risk for heart attack) or **Type B personalities** (those who are unlikely to have a heart attack). In an 8-year follow-up, they found more than twice the rate of heart disease in Type A's than in Type B's (Friedman & Rosenman, 1983).

Type A

What is the Type A personality like? Type A people are hard driving, ambitious, highly competitive, achievement oriented, and striving. Type A people believe that with enough effort they can overcome any obstacle, and they "push" themselves accordingly. Perhaps the most telltale signs of a Type A personality are *time urgency* and chronic *anger* or *hostility* (Allan, 2011).

Type A's hurry from one activity to another, racing the clock in self-imposed urgency. As they do, they feel a constant sense of frustration and anger. Feelings of anger and hostility, in particular, are strongly related to increased risk for heart attack (Boyle et al., 2004; Bunde & Suls, 2006). One study found that 15 percent of a group of 25-year-old doctors and lawyers who scored high on a hostility test were dead by age 50. The most damaging pattern may occur in hostile persons who keep their anger "bottled up." Such people seethe with anger but don't express it outwardly. This increases their pulse rate and blood pressure and puts a tremendous strain on the heart (Bongard, al'Absi, & Lovallo, 1998). To summarize, there is growing evidence that anger or hostility may be the core lethal factor of Type A behavior (Lemogne et al., 2010; Smith & Traupman. 2011). In view of this, Type A's would be wise to take their increased health risks seriously.

How are Type A people identified? Characteristics of Type A people are summarized in the short self-identification test presented in Table 11.7. If most of the list applies to you, you might be a Type A. However, confirmation of your type would require more powerful testing methods. Also, remember that the original definition of Type A behavior was probably too broad. The key psychological factors that increase heart disease risk appear to be anger, hostility, and mistrust (Myrtek, 2007; Smith et al., 2004). Also, although Type A behavior appears to promote heart disease, depression or distress may be what finally triggers a heart attack (Denollet & Van Heck, 2001; Dinan, 2001).

TYPE Z BEHAVIOR.

© Donald Reilly/www.cartoonbank.com

Type A personality A personality type with an elevated risk of heart disease; characterized by time urgency, anger, and hostility.

Type B personality All personality types other than Type A; a low-cardiac-risk personality.

Table 11.7 Characteristics of the Type A Person

Check the items that apply to you. Do you:

_____ Try to get five things done in the time other people take to do four, creating overly tight schedules?

_____ Impatiently interrupt other people to finish their sentences yourself?

_____ Read only the headlines and summaries in newspapers rather than the entire articles?

_____ Feel road rage and "line rage" when traffic or lineups move slowly?

_____ Usually feel events are unfolding too slowly?

_____ Never stop to "smell the roses" or enjoy a beautiful sunset?

_____ Frequently try to be more efficient by doing several things at the same time?

_____ Tend to overstress key words in your speech even when you don't need to (You are really BUGGING me. GO AWAY)?

_____ Usually feel a bit guilty if you do try to relax, go on vacation, or have nothing in particular that you need to get done?

_____ Focus on achievement (your income, how much you win at sports, your academic average at school) rather than enjoyment?

_____ Always fidget (repetitively bounce your leg, twirl a ring or a lock of hair, tap your fingers)?

_____ Have difficulty *listening* to other people talk to you instead of thinking about other things?

_____ Always end up overloading yourself by taking on too much?

_____ Never take time for a casual meal or a calm stroll?

© Cengage Learning

Because our society places a premium on achievement, competition, and mastery, it is not surprising that many people develop Type A personalities. The best way to avoid the self-made stress this causes is to adopt behavior that is the opposite of that listed in Table 11.7 (Williams, Barefoot, & Schneiderman, 2003). It is entirely possible to succeed in life without sacrificing your health or happiness in the process.

Hardy Personality

How do Type A people who do not develop heart disease differ from those who do? Psychologist Salvatore Maddi has studied people who have a **hardy personality**. Such people seem to be unusually resistant to stress (Maddi et al., 2009; Stix, 2011). The first study of hardiness began with two groups of managers at a large utility company. All the managers held high-stress positions. Yet some tended to get sick after stressful events, whereas others were rarely ill. How did the people who were thriving differ from their "stressed-out" colleagues? Both groups seemed to have traits typical of the Type A personality, so that wasn't the explanation. They were also quite similar in most other respects. The main difference was that the hardy group seemed to hold a worldview that consisted of three traits (Maddi, 2006; Maddi et al., 2009):

1. They had a sense of personal *commitment* to self, work, family, and other stabilizing values.
2. They felt that they had *control* over their lives and their work.
3. They had a tendency to see life as a series of *challenges,* rather than as a series of threats or problems.

How do such traits protect people from the effects of stress? Persons strong in *commitment* find ways of turning whatever they are doing into something that seems interesting and important. They tend to get involved rather than feeling alienated.

Persons strong in *control* believe that they can more often than not influence the course of events around them. This prevents them from passively seeing themselves as victims of circumstance.

Hardy personality A personality style associated with superior stress resistance.

Finally, people strong in *challenge* find fulfillment in continual growth. They seek to learn from their experiences, rather than accepting easy comfort, security, and routine. Indeed, many "negative" experiences can actually enhance personal growth—if you have support from others and the skills needed to cope with challenge (Garrosa et al., 2008; Stix, 2011).

The Whole Human: Hardiness, Optimism, and Happiness

Good and bad events occur in all lives. What separates happy people from those who are unhappy is largely a matter of attitude. Happy people tend to see their lives in more positive terms, even when trouble comes their way. For example, happier people tend to find humor in disappointments. They look at setbacks as challenges. They are strengthened by losses (Lyubomirsky & Tucker, 1998). In short, happiness tends to be related to hardiness (Cohn et al., 2009; Maddi et al, 2009).

Why is there a connection? As psychologist Barbara Fredrickson has pointed out, positive emotions tend to broaden our mental focus. Emotions such as joy, interest, and contentment create an urge to play, to be creative, to explore, to savor life, to seek new experiences, to integrate, and to grow. When you are stressed, experiencing positive emotions can make it more likely that you will find creative solutions to your problems. Positive emotions also tend to reduce the bodily arousal that occurs when we are stressed, possibly limiting stress-related damage (Diener & Chan, 2011; Fredrickson, 2003).

Elsewhere in this chapter, we have noted the value of optimism, which goes hand in hand with hardiness and happiness. Optimists tend to expect that things will turn out well. This motivates them to actively cope with adversity. They are less likely to be stopped by temporary setbacks and more likely to deal with problems head-on. Pessimists are more likely to ignore or deny problems. The result of such differences is that optimists are less stressed and anxious than pessimists. They are also in better health than pessimists. In general, optimists tend to take better care of themselves because they believe that their efforts to stay healthy will succeed (Peterson & Chang, 2003; Taylor, 2011).

A Look Ahead

The work we have reviewed here has drawn new attention to the fact that each of us has a personal responsibility for maintaining and promoting health. In the Psychology in Action section that follows, we will look at what you can do to better cope with stress and the health risks that it entails. But first, the following questions may help you maintain a healthy grade on your next psychology test.

 study break Stress and Health

RECITE

1. The SRRS appears to predict long-range changes in health, whereas the frequency and severity of daily microstressors is closely related to immediate ratings of health. T or F?
2. Ulcers, migraine headaches, and hypochondria are all frequently psychosomatic disorders. T or F?
3. Two major elements of biofeedback training appear to be relaxation and self-regulation. T or F?
4. Evidence suggests that the most important feature of the Type A personality is a sense of time urgency rather than feelings of anger and hostility. T or F?
5. A sense of commitment, challenge, and control characterizes the hardy personality. T or F?

REFLECT

THINK CRITICALLY

6. People with a hardy personality type appear to be especially resistant to which of the problems discussed earlier in this chapter?

SELF-REFLECT

Use the SRRS to find your LCU score for the past year. Do you think there is a connection between your LCU score and your health? Or have you observed more of a connection between microstressors and your health?

Suppose you moved to a foreign country. How much acculturative stress do you think you would face? Which pattern of adaptation do you think you would adopt?

Do you think you are basically a Type A or a Type B personality? To what extent do you possess traits of the hardy personality?

ANSWERS

1. T 2. F 3. T 4. F 5. T 6. Learned helplessness.

Psychology in Action

Stress Management—Winning the Stress Game

JOURNEY QUESTION 11.9 *What are the best strategies for managing stress?*

Stress management is the use of cognitive and behavioral strategies to reduce stress and improve coping skills. As promised, this section describes strategies for managing stress. Before you continue reading, you may want to assess your level of stress again, this time using a scale developed for undergraduate students (Table 11.8). Like the SRRS, high scores on the *Undergraduate Stress Questionnaire* suggest that you have been exposed to health-threatening levels of stress (Crandall, Preisler, & Aussprung, 1992). But remember, stress is an internal state. If you are good at coping with stressors, a high score may not be a problem for you.

Now that you have a picture of your current level of stress, what can you do about it? The simplest way of coping with stress is to modify or remove its source—by leaving a stressful job, for example. Obviously this is often impossible, which is why learning to manage stress is so important.

As shown in **Figure 11.9**, stress triggers *body effects, upsetting thoughts,* and *ineffective behavior.* Also shown is the fact that each element worsens the others in a vicious cycle. Indeed, the basic idea of the "Stress Game" is that once it begins, *you lose*—unless you take action to break the cycle. The information that follows tells how.

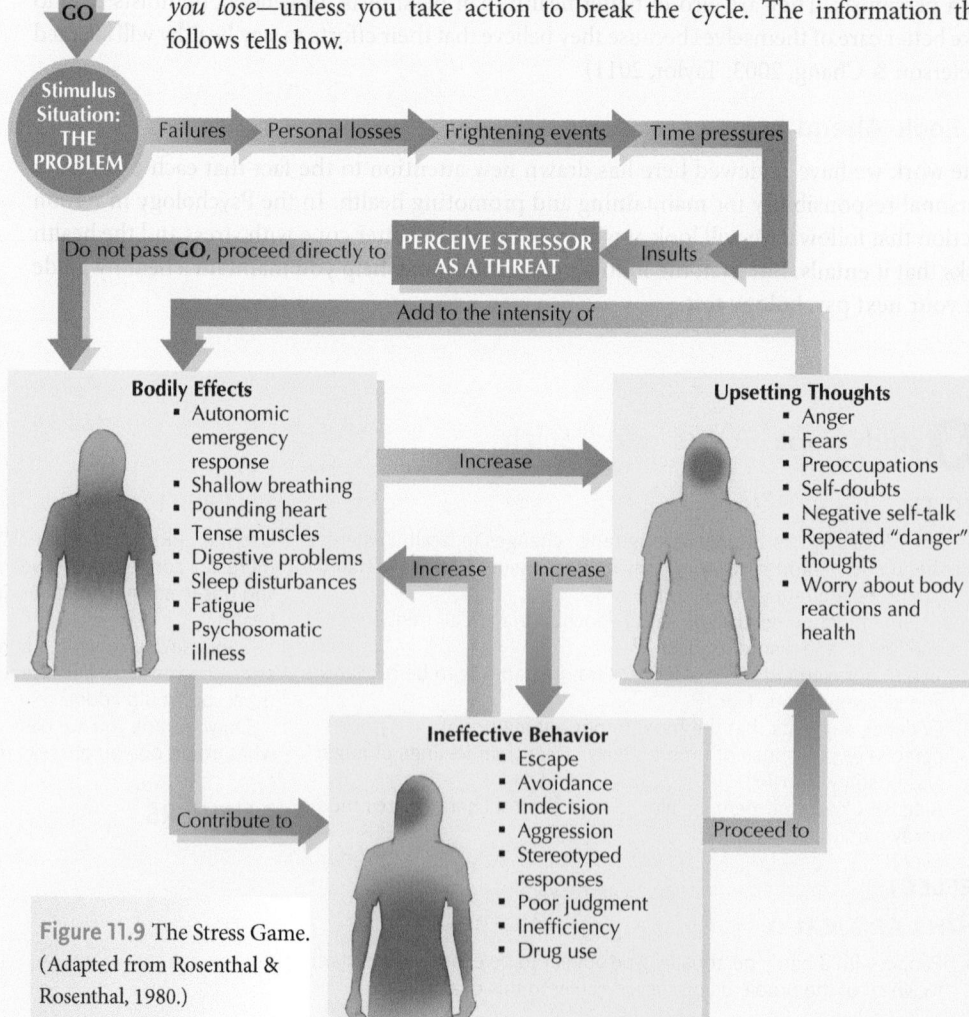

Figure 11.9 The Stress Game. (Adapted from Rosenthal & Rosenthal, 1980.)

Stress management The application of cognitive and behavioral strategies to reduce stress and improve coping skills.

Table 11.8 Undergraduate Stress Questionnaire

Has this stressful event happened to you at any time during the last 2 weeks? If it has, please check the box next to it. If it has not, then leave it blank.

- ☐ Death (of a family member or friend)
- ☐ Death of a pet
- ☐ Working while in school
- ☐ Parents getting a divorce
- ☐ Registration for classes
- ☐ Trying to decide on a major
- ☐ Talked with a professor
- ☐ Trying to get into college
- ☐ Had a class presentation
- ☐ Had projects, research papers due
- ☐ Had a lot of tests
- ☐ It's finals week
- ☐ Applying to graduate school
- ☐ You have a hard upcoming week
- ☐ Lots of deadlines to meet
- ☐ Missed your period and waiting
- ☐ Had an interview
- ☐ Applying for a job
- ☐ Sat through a boring class
- ☐ Can't understand your professor
- ☐ Did badly on a test
- ☐ Went into a test unprepared
- ☐ Crammed for a test
- ☐ Used a fake ID
- ☐ Breaking up with boy-/girlfriend
- ☐ Holiday
- ☐ Bad haircut today
- ☐ Victim of a crime
- ☐ Can't concentrate

- ☐ Coping with addictions
- ☐ Found out boy-/girlfriend cheated on you
- ☐ Did worse than expected on a test
- ☐ Stayed up late writing a paper
- ☐ Problems with your computer
- ☐ Favorite sporting team lost
- ☐ Problems with printing things out
- ☐ Change of environment (new doctor, dentist, etc.)
- ☐ Bothered by having no social support of family
- ☐ Arguments, conflict of value with friends
- ☐ Visit from relatives and entertaining them
- ☐ Noise disturbed you while trying to study
- ☐ Maintaining a long-distance boy-/girlfriend
- ☐ Assignments in all classes due at the same time
- ☐ Dealt with incompetence at the registrar's office
- ☐ Someone borrowed something without your permission
- ☐ Exposed to upsetting TV show, book, or movie
- ☐ Problem getting home from bar when drunk
- ☐ Had confrontation with an authority figure
- ☐ Got to class late
- ☐ Parents controlling with money
- ☐ Feel isolated
- ☐ Decision to have sex on your mind
- ☐ No sex in a while
- ☐ Living with boy-/girlfriend
- ☐ Felt some peer pressure
- ☐ Felt need for transportation

- ☐ Couldn't find a parking space
- ☐ Property stolen
- ☐ Car/bike broke down, flat tire, etc.
- ☐ Got a traffic ticket
- ☐ No time to eat
- ☐ Having roommate conflicts
- ☐ Had to ask for money
- ☐ Lack of money
- ☐ Checkbook didn't balance
- ☐ You have a hangover
- ☐ Someone you expected to call did not
- ☐ Lost something (especially wallet)
- ☐ Erratic schedule
- ☐ Thoughts about future
- ☐ Dependent on other people
- ☐ No sleep
- ☐ Sick, injured
- ☐ Fought with boy-/girlfriend
- ☐ Performed poorly at a task
- ☐ Heard bad news
- ☐ Thought about unfinished work
- ☐ Feel unorganized
- ☐ Someone cut ahead of you in line
- ☐ Job requirements changed
- ☐ Someone broke a promise
- ☐ Someone did a "pet peeve" of yours
- ☐ Couldn't finish everything you needed to do

Add together the number of check marks. Students with higher scores are more likely to need health care (as measured by going to the student health center or infirmary) than students with lower scores.

With kind permission from Springer Science + Business Media: Journal of Behavioral Medicine, Measuring life event stress in the lives of college students: The Undergraduate Stress Questionnaire (USQ), 15(6), 1992, Christian S. Crandall.

Managing Body Reactions

Much of the immediate discomfort of stress is caused by fight-or-flight emotional responses. The body is ready to act, with tight muscles and a pounding heart. If action is prevented, we merely remain "uptight." A sensible remedy is to learn a reliable, drug-free way of relaxing.

Exercise   Stress-based arousal can be dissipated by using the body. Any full-body exercise can be effective. Our intrepid student, Mee Jung, enjoys karate. Swimming, dancing, jumping rope, yoga, most sports, and especially walking are valuable outlets. Regular exercise alters hormones, circulation, muscle tone, and a number of other aspects of physical functioning. Together, such changes can reduce anxiety and lower the risks for disease (Edenfield & Blumenthal, 2011; Linden, 2005).

Be sure to choose activities that are vigorous enough to relieve tension, yet enjoyable enough to be done repeatedly. Exercising for stress management is most effective when it is done daily. As little as 30 minutes of total exercise per day, even if it occurs in short 10- to 20-minute sessions, can improve mood and energy (Hansen, Stevens, & Coast, 2001).

Meditation   Many stress counselors recommend meditation for quieting the body and promoting relaxation. Meditation is one of the most effective ways to relax (Deckro et al., 2002; Sears & Kraus, 2009). But be aware that listening to or playing music, taking nature walks, enjoying hobbies, and the like can be meditative. Anything that reliably interrupts upsetting thoughts and promotes relaxation can be helpful. For now, it is enough to state that meditation is easy to learn—taking an expensive commercial course is unnecessary. To learn more about meditation and its effects, read Chapter 5.

Progressive Relaxation   It is possible to relax systematically, completely, and by choice. The basic idea of **progressive relaxation** is to tighten all the muscles in a given area of your body (the arms, for instance) and then voluntarily relax them. By first tensing and relaxing each area of the body (also called the *tension-release method*), you can learn what muscle tension feels like. Then when each area is relaxed, the change is more noticeable and more controllable. In this way it is possible, with practice, to greatly reduce tension. To learn the details of how this is done, consult Chapter 13.

Guided Imagery   In a technique called **guided imagery**, people visualize images that are calming, relaxing, or beneficial in other ways. Relaxation, for instance, can be promoted by visualizing peaceful scenes. Pick several places where you feel safe, calm, and at ease. Typical locations might be a beach or lake, the woods, floating on an air mattress in a warm pool, or lying in the sun at a quiet park. To relax, vividly imagine yourself in one of these locations. In the visualized scene, you should be alone and in a comfortable position. It is important to visualize the scene as realistically as possible. Try to feel, taste, smell, hear, and see what you would actually experience in the calming scene. Practice forming such images several times a day for about 5 minutes each time. When your scenes become familiar and detailed, they can be used to reduce anxiety and encourage relaxation (Rosenthal, 1993). Remember, too, imagining that a supportive friend or a loving pet is nearby can also reduce tension and anxiety (Allen, Blascovich, & Mendes, 2002; Smith, Ruiz, & Uchino, 2004).

Modifying Ineffective Behavior

Stress is often made worse by our misguided responses to it. The following suggestions may help you deal with stress more effectively.

Slow Down   Remember that stress can be self-generated. Try to deliberately do things at a slower pace—especially if your pace has speeded up over the years. Tell yourself, "What counts most is not if I get there first, but if I get there at all," or "My goal is distance, not speed."

Organize   Disorganization creates stress. Try to take a fresh look at your situation and get organized. Setting priorities can be a real stress fighter. Ask yourself what's really important and concentrate on the things that count. Learn to let go of trivial but upsetting irritations. And above all, when you are feeling stressed, remember to K.I.S.: Keep It Simple. (Some people prefer K.I.S.S.: Keep It Simple, Stupid.)

Strike a Balance   Work, school, family, friends, interests, hobbies, recreation, community, church—there are many important elements in a satisfying life. Damaging stress often comes from letting one element—especially work or school—get blown out of proportion. Your goal should be quality in life, not quantity. Try to strike a balance between challenging "good stress" and relaxation. Remember, when you are "doing nothing" you are actually doing something very important: Set aside time for "me acts" such as loafing, browsing, puttering, playing, and napping.

Progressive relaxation A method for producing deep relaxation of all parts of the body.

Guided imagery Intentional visualization of images that are calming, relaxing, or beneficial in other ways.

Recognize and Accept Your Limits   Many of us set unrealistic and perfectionist goals. Given that no one can ever be perfect, this attitude leaves many people feeling inadequate, no matter how well they have performed. Set gradual, achievable goals for yourself. Also, set realistic limits on what you try to do on any given day. Learn to say no to added demands or responsibilities.

Seek Social Support **Social support**—close, positive relationships with others—facilitates good health and morale (Manne, 2003; Winfree & Jiang, 2010). People with close, supportive relationships have better immune responses and better health (Smith, Ruiz, & Uchino, 2004; Taylor & Master, 2011). Apparently, support from family, friends, and even pets serves as a buffer to cushion the impact of stressful events (Allen, Blascovich, & Mendes, 2002).

Women tend to make better use of social support than men do. Women who are stressed seek support, and they nurture others. Men are more likely to become aggressive or to withdraw emotionally (Taylor, 2012). This may be why "manly men" won't ask for help, whereas women in trouble call their friends! Where stress is concerned, many men could benefit from adopting women's tendency to tend and befriend others.

How else might social support help? Most people share positive events, such as marriages, births, graduations, and birthdays, with others. When things go well, we like to tell others. Sharing such events tends to amplify positive emotions and to further increase social support. In many ways, the sharing of good news is an important means by which positive events contribute to individual well-being (Gable et al., 2004).

Support from family and friends acts as a major buffer against stress.

Write about Your Feelings If you don't have someone you can talk to about stressful events, you might try expressing your thoughts and feelings in writing. Several studies have found that students who write about their upsetting experiences, thoughts, and feelings are better able to cope with stress. They also experience fewer illnesses, and they get better grades (Pennebaker, 2004; Smyth & Pennebaker, 2008). Writing about your feelings tends to leave your mind clearer. This makes it easier to pay attention to life's challenges and come up with effective coping strategies (Klein & Boals, 2001a,b). Thus, after you write about your feelings, it helps to make specific plans for coping with upsetting experiences (Pennebaker & Chung, 2007).

As an alternative, you might want to try writing about positive experiences. In one study, college students who wrote about intensely positive experiences had fewer illnesses over the next 3 months. Writing just 20 minutes a day for 3 days improved the students' moods and had a surprisingly long-lasting effect on their health (Burton & King, 2004).

Avoiding Upsetting Thoughts

Assume you are taking a test. Suddenly, you realize that you are running short of time. If you say to yourself, "Oh no, this is terrible, I've blown it now," your body's response will probably be sweating, tenseness, and a knot in your stomach. On the other hand, if you say, "I should have watched the time, but getting upset won't help; I'll just take one question at a time," your stress level will be much lower.

As stated earlier, stress is greatly affected by the views we take of events. Physical symptoms and a tendency to make poor decisions are increased by negative thoughts or "self-talk." In many cases what you say to yourself can be the difference between coping and collapsing (Smith & Kirby, 2011).

Coping Statements Psychologist Donald Meichenbaum has popularized a technique called **stress inoculation**. In it, clients learn to fight fear and anxiety with an internal monologue of positive coping statements. First, clients learn to identify and monitor **negative self-statements** (self-critical thoughts that increase anxiety). Negative thoughts are a problem because they tend to directly elevate physical arousal. To counter this effect, clients learn to replace negative statements with coping statements from a supplied list. Eventually they are encouraged to make their own lists (Saunders et al., 1996).

How are coping statements applied? **Coping statements** are reassuring and self-enhancing. They are used to block out, or counteract, negative self-talk in stressful situations. Before giving a short speech, for instance, you would replace "I'm scared," "I can't do this," "My mind

Social support Close, positive relationships with other people.

Stress inoculation Use of positive coping statements to control fear and anxiety.

Negative self-statements Self-critical thoughts that increase anxiety and lower performance.

Coping statements Reassuring, self-enhancing statements that are used to stop self-critical thinking.

will go blank and I'll panic," or "I'll sound stupid and boring" with "I'll give my speech on something I like," or "I'll breathe deeply before I start my speech," or "My pounding heart just means I'm psyched up to do my best." Additional examples of coping statements follow:

Preparing for Stressful Situation
- I'll just take things one step at a time.
- If I get nervous, I'll just pause a moment.
- Tomorrow, I'll be through it.
- I've managed to do this before.
- What exactly do I have to do?

Confronting the Stressful Situation
- Relax now; this can't really hurt me.
- Stay organized; focus on the task.
- There's no hurry; take it step by step.
- Nobody's perfect; I'll just do my best.
- It will be over soon; just be calm.

Meichenbaum cautions that saying the "right" things to yourself may not be enough to improve stress tolerance. You must practice this approach in actual stress situations. Also, it is important to develop your own personal list of coping statements by finding what works for you. Ultimately, the value of learning this and other stress management skills ties back into the idea that much stress is self-generated. Knowing that you can manage a demanding situation is in itself a major antidote for stress. In one study, college students who learned stress inoculation not only had less anxiety and depression, but better self-esteem as well (Schiraldi & Brown, 2001).

Lighten Up   Humor is worth cultivating as a way to reduce stress. A good sense of humor can lower your distress/stress reaction to difficult events (Lefcourt, 2003). In addition, an ability to laugh at life's ups and downs is associated with better immunity to disease (McClelland & Cheriff, 1997). Don't be afraid to laugh at yourself and at the many ways in which we humans make things difficult for ourselves. You've probably heard the following advice about everyday stresses: "Don't sweat the small stuff" and "It's all small stuff." Humor is one of the best antidotes for anxiety and emotional distress because it helps put things into perspective (Kuiper & McHale, 2009; Szabo, 2003). The vast majority of events are only as stressful as you allow them to be. Have some fun. It's perfectly healthy.

 study break Coping with Stress

RECITE

1. Exercise, meditation, and progressive relaxation are considered effective ways of countering negative self-statements. T or F?
2. Research shows that social support from family and friends has little effect on the health consequences of stress. T or F?
3. One element of stress inoculation is training in the use of positive coping statements. T or F?
4. While taking a stressful classroom test you say to yourself, "Stay organized, focus on the task." It's obvious that you are using
   a. guided imagery
   b. coping statements
   c. LCUs
   d. guided relaxation

REFLECT

THINK CRITICALLY

5. Steve always feels extremely pressured when the due date arrives for his major term papers. How could he reduce stress in such instances?

SELF-REFLECT

If you were going to put together a "tool kit" for stress management, what items would you include?

ANSWERS

1. F 2. F 3. T 4. b 5. The stress associated with doing term papers can be almost completely eliminated by breaking up a long-term assignment into many small daily or weekly assignments (Anderson, 2010a; Ariely & Wertenbroch, 2002). Students who habitually procrastinate are often amazed at how pleasant college work can be once they renounce "brinkmanship" (pushing things off to the limits of tolerance).

Summary

11.1 What is health psychology and how do cognition and behavior affect health?

- 11.1.1 Health psychologists are interested in how cognition and behavior help maintain and promote health.
- 11.1.2 Studies of health and illness have identified a number of behavioral risk factors that have a major effect on general health and life expectancy.
- 111.1.3 At the minimum, it is important to maintain health-promoting cognitions and behaviors with respect to diet, alcohol, exercise, and smoking.
- 11.1.4 Health psychologists have pioneered efforts to prevent the development of unhealthy habits and to improve well-being through community health campaigns.

11.2 What impacts have sexually transmitted diseases had on sexual behavior?

- 11.2.1 Many sexually active people continue to take unnecessary risks with their health by failing to follow safer sex practices.
- 11.2.2 Safe-sex practices help protect your own health and they show that you care about the welfare of your partner.

11.3 What is stress and what factors determine its severity?

- 11.3.1 Stress is a normal part of life occurring when demands are placed on an organism to adjust or adapt. However, it is also a major risk factor for illness and disease.
- 11.3.2 The body reacts to stress in a series of stages called the general adaptation syndrome (GAS).
- 11.3.3 The stages of the GAS are alarm, resistance, and exhaustion. Bodily reactions in the GAS follow the pattern observed in the development of psychosomatic disorders.
- 11.3.4 Studies of psychoneuroimmunology show that stress lowers the body's resistance to disease by weakening the immune system.
- 11.3.5 Stress is more damaging in situations involving pressure, a lack of control, unpredictability of the stressor, and intense or repeated emotional shocks.
- 11.3.6 In work settings, prolonged stress can lead to burnout.
- 11.3.7 Making a primary appraisal greatly affects our emotional responses to a situation. Stress is intensified when a situation is appraised as a threat
- 11.3.8 During a secondary appraisal, we select problem-focused coping or emotion-focused coping (or both) as a way of managing stress. Stress is also intensified when a person does not feel competent to cope with it.

11.4 What causes frustration and what are typical reactions to it?

- 11.4.1 Frustration is the negative emotional state that occurs when progress toward a goal is blocked.
- 11.4.2 External frustrations are based on delay, failure, rejection, loss, and other direct blocking of motives. Personal frustration is related to personal characteristics over which one has little control.
- 11.4.3 Frustrations of all types become more intense as the strength, urgency, or importance of the blocked motive increases.
- 11.4.4 Major behavioral reactions to frustration include persistence, more vigorous responding, circumvention, direct aggression, displaced aggression (including scapegoating), and escape or withdrawal.

11.5 Are there different types of conflict and how do people react to conflict?

- 11.5.1 Conflict occurs when one must choose between contradictory alternatives.
- 11.5.2 Four major types of conflict are approach-approach, avoidance-avoidance, approach-avoidance, and multiple approach-avoidance.
- 11.5.3 Approach-approach conflicts are usually the easiest to resolve.
- 11.5.4 Avoidance conflicts are difficult to resolve and are characterized by inaction, indecision, freezing, and a desire to escape (called leaving the field).
- 11.5.5 People usually remain in approach-avoidance conflicts but fail to fully resolve them. Approach-avoidance conflicts are associated with ambivalence and partial approach.
- 11.5.6 Vacillation is a common reaction to multiple approach-avoidance conflicts.

11.6 What are defense mechanisms?

- 11.6.1 Defense mechanisms are mental processes used to avoid, deny, or distort sources of threat or anxiety, including threats to one's self-image.
- 11.6.2 Overuse of defense mechanisms makes people less adaptable.
- 11.6.3 A large number of defense mechanisms have been identified, including compensation, denial, fantasy, intellectualization, isolation, projection, rationalization, reaction formation, regression, repression, and sublimation.

11.7 What do we know about coping with feelings of helplessness and depression?

- 11.7.1 Learned helplessness can be used as a model for understanding depression. Depression is a major, and surprisingly common, emotional problem.

- 11.7.2 Actions and thoughts that counter feelings of helplessness tend to reduce depression. Mastery training, optimism, and hope all act as antidotes for learned helplessness.
- 11.7.3 The college blues are a relatively mild form of depression. Learning to manage college work and to challenge self-critical thinking can help alleviate the college blues.

11.8 How is stress related to health and disease?

- 11.8.1 Work with stress scales like the Social Readjustment Rating Scale indicates that multiple life changes tend to increase long-range susceptibility to accident or illness.
- 11.8.2 Immediate physical and mental health is more closely related to the intensity and severity of daily hassles (microstressors).
- 11.8.3 Intense or prolonged stress may cause damage in the form of psychosomatic problems.
- 11.8.4 During biofeedback training, bodily processes are monitored and converted to a signal that tells what the body is doing. Biofeedback allows people to alleviate some psychosomatic illnesses by altering bodily activities.

- 11.8.5 People with Type A personalities are competitive, striving, hostile, impatient, and prone to having heart attacks.
- 11.8.6 People who have traits of the hardy personality seem to be unusually resistant to stress.
- 11.8.7 Optimism and positive emotions tend to buffer stress.

11.9 What are the best strategies for managing stress?

- 11.9.1 Stress management techniques focus on one of three areas: bodily effects, ineffective behavior, and upsetting thoughts.
- 11.9.2 All of the following are good ways to manage bodily reactions to stress: exercise, meditation, progressive relaxation, and guided imagery.
- 11.9.3 To minimize ineffective behavior when you are stressed, you can slow down, get organized, balance work and relaxation, accept your limits, seek social support, and write about your feelings.
- 11.9.4 Learning to use coping statements is a good way to combat upsetting thoughts.

Interactive Learning

Log in to CengageBrain to access the resources your instructor requires. For this book, you can access:

CourseMate Go to CengageBrain.com to access Psychology CourseMate, where you will find an interactive eBook, glossaries, flashcards, quizzes, videos, Virtual Psychology Labs, and more.

aplia

Aplia If your professor has assigned Aplia:

1. Sign in to your account.
2. Complete the corresponding exercises as required by your professor.
3. When finished, click "Grade It Now" to see which areas you have mastered, which areas need more work, and detailed explanations of every answer.

Test Your Knowledge

Health Psychology

1. Actions that increase the chances of disease, injury, or early death are termed behavioral
   a. health factors
   b. personalities
   c. risk factors
   d. habits

2. People who have a disease-prone personality style are anxious and hostile. These traits can also be observed in the _____ personality.
   a. emotion-focused
   b. problem-focused
   c. SRRS-prone
   d. Type A

3. Health promoting behaviors that combat hypertension include the following: lose weight, consume less sodium, use alcohol sparingly, and get more
   a. sleep
   b. exercise
   c. LCUs
   d. cholesterol

4. Which of the following is NOT an STD?
   a. herpes
   b. eczema
   c. chlamydia
   d. hepatitis B

5. For the first _____ after infection, a negative test result for the HIV virus is no guarantee that a person is a "safe" sex partner.
   a. 3 weeks
   b. 6 weeks
   c. 6 months
   d. 3 years

6. The first signs of psychosomatic disorders begin to appear during the stage of
   a. alarm
   b. exhaustion
   c. resistance
   d. appraisal

7. Students taking stressful final exams are more susceptible to the cold virus, a pattern best explained by the concept of
   a. the disease-prone personality
   b. psychoneuroimmunology
   c. emotion-focused coping
   d. reaction formation

8. A good indication that stress is a normal part of life is provided by the existence of
   a. learned helplessness
   b. hypochondria
   c. sublimation
   d. eustress

9. According to Richard Lazarus, choosing a way to meet a threat or challenge takes place during the
   a. primary stress reaction
   b. secondary stress reaction
   c. primary appraisal
   d. secondary appraisal

10. Aggression is an especially common reaction to
    a. frustration
    b. scapegoating
    c. approach conflicts
    d. ambivalence

11. Displaced aggression is closely related to the pattern of behavior known as
    a. scapegoating
    b. leaving the field
    c. stereotyped responding
    d. burnout

12. You would be most likely to experience vacillation if you found yourself in
    a. an approach-approach conflict
    b. an avoidance-avoidance conflict
    c. a multiple approach-avoidance conflict
    d. the condition called emotion-focused coping

13. Justifying your actions by making excuses that appear to explain your behavior is called
    a. sublimation
    b. reaction formation
    c. compensation
    d. rationalization

14. Learned helplessness tends to occur when events appear to be
    a. frustrating
    b. in conflict
    c. uncontrollable
    d. problem-focused

15. Ratings on the SRRS are based on the total number of _____ a person has for the preceding year.
    a. hassles
    b. LCUs
    c. STDs
    d. psychosomatic illnesses

16. Anger, hostility, and mistrust appear to be the core lethal factors in
    a. hypochondria
    b. learned helplessness
    c. the GAS
    d. Type A behavior

17. In many ways, a person who has a hardy personality is the opposite of a person who has
    a. a high STD score
    b. a low LCU score
    c. Type A traits
    d. Type B traits

18. A person using progressive relaxation for stress management is most likely trying to control which component of stress?
    a. bodily reactions
    b. upsetting thoughts
    c. ineffective behavior
    d. the primary appraisal

19. Exercise, meditation, progressive relaxation, and guided imagery would be least likely to help a person who is in the GAS stage of
    a. alarm
    b. resistance
    c. exhaustion
    d. adaptation

20. While taking a stressful classroom test, you say to yourself, "Stay organized, focus on the task." It's obvious that you are using
    a. guided imagery
    b. a coping statement
    c. LCUs
    d. guided relaxation

Answers 1. c 2. d 3. b 4. b 5. c 6. c 7. b 8. d 9. d 10. a 11. a 12. c 13. d 14. c 15. b 16. d 17. c 18. a 19. c 20. b

Journey Theme *While judgments of abnormality are difficult to make and are relative, psychological disorders nevertheless clearly exist and need to be classified, explained, and treated.*

12

Psychological Disorders

Journey into Psychology: At Least She Didn't Give Him Any Soda

Her son was sick and the doctors didn't know why. His mother said she desperately wanted him to be healed. She sought numerous tests and never missed an appointment. At 14, Ben was in the hospital again for his sinus problem. He was taking 19 different medications, had been diagnosed at various times with bipolar disorder, oppositional defiant disorder, and attention deficit disorder, and had already undergone 40 surgeries. Finally left alone with doctors, Ben complained he was "sick of being sick."

In reality, it was Ben's mother who was sick. She was eventually diagnosed as suffering from *Munchausen by proxy syndrome,* a pattern in which a person fakes the medical problems of someone in his or her care (Awadallah et al., 2005). (In *Munchausen syndrome,* the person fakes his or her *own* medical problems.) As in Ben's case, most people with the syndrome are mothers who fabricate their children's illnesses (Day & Moseley, 2010). Sometimes, they even deliberately harm their children. One mother injected her son with 7-Up (Reisner, 2006).

Ben's mother's case is but one hint of the scope of mental health problems. More than a quarter of American adults suffer from a diagnosable mental disorder in any given year (Kessler, 2010). In 2007, more than 34,500 Americans committed suicide, of whom about 90 percent had a diagnosable mental disorder (National Institute of Mental Health, 2010c).

What does it mean to be "crazy"? To draw the line between normal and abnormal, we must weigh some complex issues. We'll explore some of them in this chapter, as well as an array of psychological problems.

Journey Questions

12.1 How is abnormality defined?

12.2 What are the major psychological disorders?

12.3 How can psychiatric labeling be misused?

12.4 What are the general characteristics of psychotic disorders?

12.5 What is the nature of a delusional disorder?

12.6 What is schizophrenia and what causes it?

12.7 What are mood disorders and what causes them?

12.8 What problems result when a person suffers high levels of anxiety?

12.9 How do psychologists explain anxiety-based disorders?

12.10 What is a personality disorder?

12.11 Why do people commit suicide and can they be stopped?

Normality—What's Normal?

JOURNEY QUESTION 12.1 *How is abnormality defined?*

It can be quite amusing to hear or use phrases like "That guy is really wacko. His porch lights are dimming" or "The butter's sliding off his waffle. He's ready to go postal." A hundred years ago, doctors and nonprofessionals alike used terms such as "crazy," "insane," "cracked," and "lunatic" quite freely. Today, our understanding of psychological disorders is more sophisticated. The scientific study of mental, emotional, and behavioral disorders is known as **psychopathology**. The term also refers to mental disorders themselves, such as schizophrenia or depression, and to behavior patterns that make people unhappy and impair their personal growth (Butcher, Mineka, & Hooley, 2010).

Even though this definition may seem obvious, to seriously classify people as psychologically unhealthy raises complex and age-old issues (Luyten & Blatt, 2011). The conservative, churchgoing housewife down the street might be flagrantly psychotic and a lethal danger to her children. The reclusive eccentric who hangs out at the park could be the sanest person in town.

Let's begin with the idea of statistical abnormality, which some psychologists use to define normality more objectively. **Statistical abnormality** refers to scoring very high or low on some dimension, such as intelligence, anxiety, or depression. Anxiety, for example, is a feature of several psychological disorders. To measure it, we could create a test to learn how many people show low, medium, or high levels of anxiety. Usually, the results of such tests will form a *normal* (bell-shaped) *curve*. (*Normal* in this case refers only to the *shape* of the curve.) Notice that most people score near the middle of a normal curve; very few have extremely high or low scores (Figure 12.1). A person who deviates from the average by being anxious all the time (high anxiety) might be abnormal. So, too, might a person who never feels anxiety.

Then statistical abnormality tells us nothing about the meaning of deviations from the norm? Right. It is as statistically "abnormal" (unusual) for a person to score above 145 on an IQ test as it is to score below 55. However, only the lower score is regarded as "abnormal" or undesirable. In the same sense, it is unusual for a person to speak four languages or to win an event at the Olympics, but these are desirable, if rare, accomplishments.

Statistical definitions also can't tell us *where to draw the line* between normality and abnormality. For example, we could obtain the average frequency of sexual intercourse for persons of a particular age, sex, sexual orientation, and marital status. Clearly, a person who feels driven to have sex dozens of times a day has a problem. But as we move back toward the norm, we face the problem of drawing lines. How often does a normal behavior have to occur before it becomes abnormal? As you can see, statistical boundary lines tend to be somewhat arbitrary (Comer, 2013).

Another approach is to focus on the nonconformity that may be associated with some disorders. **Social nonconformity** refers to disobeying public standards for acceptable conduct. Extreme nonconformity can lead to destructive or self-destructive behavior. (Think, for instance, of a drug abuser or a prostitute.) However, we must be careful to separate unhealthy nonconformity from creative lifestyles. Many eccentric "characters" are charming and emotionally stable. Note, too, that strictly following social norms is no guarantee of mental health. In some cases, psychopathology involves rigid conformity (see "Crazy for a Day").

Further, before we can even begin to judge a behavior as abnormal or nonconforming, we must also consider the *situational context* (social situation, behavioral setting, or general circumstances) in which it occurs. A young woman ties a thick rubber cord around her ankles, screams hysterically, and jumps headfirst off a bridge. Thirty years ago, the woman's

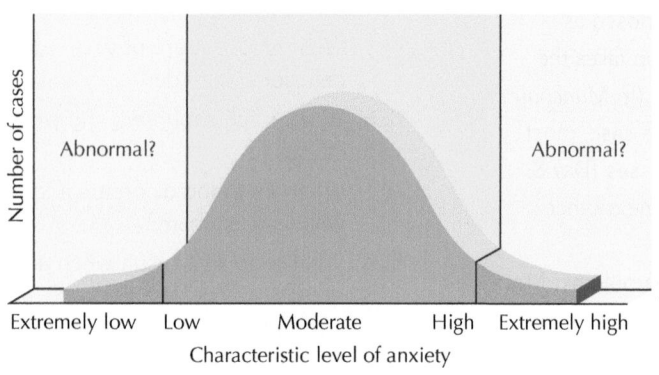

Figure 12.1 The number of people displaying a personal characteristic may help define what is statistically abnormal.

Psychopathology The scientific study of mental, emotional, and behavioral disorders; also, abnormal or maladaptive behavior.

Statistical abnormality Abnormality defined on the basis of an extreme score on some dimension, such as IQ or anxiety.

Social nonconformity Failure to conform to societal norms or the usual minimum standards for social conduct.

Discovering Psychology

Performing a mildly abnormal behavior is a good way to get a sense of how social norms define "normality" in daily life. Here's your assignment: Do something strange in public and observe how people react to you. (Please don't do anything dangerous, harmful, or offensive—and don't get arrested!) Here are some deviant behaviors that other students have staged:

- Sit in the dining area of a fast-food restaurant and loudly carry on a conversation with an imaginary companion.
- Stand in a busy hallway on campus and adopt a kung fu stance. Remain in that position for 10 minutes.
- Walk around campus on a sunny day wearing a raincoat and carrying an open umbrella. Keep the umbrella over your head when you are inside buildings.
- Stick one finger in your nose and another in your ear. Walk through a busy shopping mall.
- Wear a *Planet of the Apes* mask for a day.

Does the idea of performing any of these actions make you uncomfortable? If so, you may not need to do anything more to appreciate how powerfully social norms constrain our actions. As we have noted, social nonconformity is just one facet of abnormal behavior. Nevertheless, actions that are regarded as "strange" within a particular culture are often the first sign to others that a person has a problem.

© mikeledray/Shutterstock

behavior might have seemed completely crazy. Today, it is a routine form of entertainment—bungee jumping. Is it abnormal to stand outside and water a lawn with a hose? It depends on whether it is raining. Is it nonconforming for a grown man to remove his pants and expose himself to another man or woman in a place of business? It depends on whether the other person is a bank clerk or a doctor.

Almost any imaginable behavior can be considered normal in some contexts. For example, in 2003, a man sawed off his own arm. Mind you, he was a mountain climber who had fallen into a crevasse, trapping his arm between two boulders. After 5 days of trying to free his arm, and nearing unconsciousness, he did what he needed to do to survive (Ralston, 2004).

As implied by our earlier discussion of social norms, culture is one of the most influential contexts in which any behavior is judged (Fabrega, 2004). In some cultures, it is considered normal to defecate or urinate in public or to appear naked in public. In our culture, such behaviors would be considered unusual or abnormal. In some Muslim cultures, women who remain completely housebound are considered normal or even virtuous. In some Western cultures, they might be diagnosed as suffering from a disorder called agoraphobia. (Agoraphobia is described later in this chapter.)

Thus, *cultural relativity* (the idea that judgments are made relative to the values of one's culture) can affect the diagnosis of psychological disorders. Still, *all* cultures classify people as abnormal if they fail to communicate with others or are consistently unpredictable in their actions.

Yet another approach is to characterize psychopathology by *subjective discomfort* (private feelings of pain, unhappiness, or emotional distress).

But couldn't a person experience serious distress without psychopathology and couldn't someone be seriously disturbed without feeling discomfort? Yes on both counts. People who have, for example, lost a loved one or lived through a natural disaster like a hurricane will normally take some time to overcome their distress. Also, psychopathology doesn't always cause personal anguish. A person suffering from mania might feel elated and "on top of the world." A *lack* of discomfort may actually reveal a problem. For example, if you showed no signs of grief or distress after the violent death of a close friend, we might suspect psychopathology. In practice, though, subjective discomfort explains most instances in which people voluntarily seek professional help.

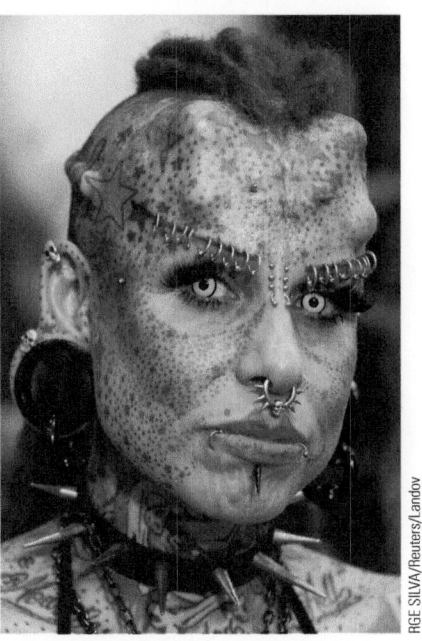

RGE SILVA/Reuters/Landov

Social nonconformity does not automatically indicate psychopathology.

Core Feature of Disordered Behavior

If abnormality is so hard to define, how are judgments of psychopathology made? Although the standards we have discussed thus far are *relative,* psychopathological behavior does have a core feature: It is **maladaptive**. Rather than helping people cope successfully, maladaptive behavior arises from an underlying psychological or biological dysfunction that makes it more difficult for them to meet the demands of day-to-day life (American Psychiatric Association, 2000; 2012). Maladaptive behavior most often results in serious psychological discomfort, disability, and/or *loss of control* of thoughts, behaviors, or feelings.

For example, gambling is not a problem if people bet for entertainment and can maintain self-control. However, compulsive gambling is a sign of psychopathology. Hearing uncontrollable voices is a prime example of what it means to lose control of one's thoughts. In the most extreme cases, people become a danger to themselves or others, which is clearly maladaptive (Bennett, 2011).

In practice, deciding that a person needs help usually occurs when the person *does something* (assaults a person, hallucinates, stares into space, collects too many old pizza cartons, and so forth) that *annoys* or *gains the attention* of a person in a *position of power* in the person's life (an employer, teacher, parent, spouse, or the person himself or herself). That person then does something about it. The person may voluntarily seek help, the person may be urged to see a psychologist, a police officer may be called, or a relative may start commitment proceedings.

Legal Insanity and the Insanity Defense

What are commitment proceedings? Commitment proceedings are legal proceedings that may result in the finding of **insanity**, which is a legal, not psychological, term (Hiday & Burns, 2010). It refers to an inability to manage one's affairs or foresee the consequences of one's actions. People who are declared insane are not legally responsible for their actions. If necessary, they can be involuntarily committed to a mental hospital.

Legally, insanity is established by testimony from *expert witnesses* (psychologists and psychiatrists) recognized by a court of law as qualified to give opinions on a specific topic. Involuntary commitments happen most often when people are brought to emergency rooms or are arrested for committing a crime. People who are involuntarily committed are usually judged to be a danger to themselves or to others, or they are severely intellectually disabled.

What is the insanity defense? Someone accused of a crime may argue that he or she is *not guilty by reason of insanity.* In practice, this means that the accused, due to a diagnosable psychological disorder, was unable to appreciate that what he or she did was wrong (Knoll & Resnick, 2008). This may be distinguished from *not guilty by reason of diminished responsibility,* which is more likely to apply in other situations, such as cases of intellectual disability, like Down syndrome or brain damage.

You may be surprised to learn that being diagnosed with a psychological disorder does not automatically imply a successful insanity defense (Martin & Weiss, 2010). For example, someone diagnosed with, say, an anxiety disorder who commits murder might nevertheless be well aware that murder is against the law. In fact, very few criminal trials end with this verdict (Hiday & Burns, 2010).

Classifying Mental Disorders—Problems by the Book

JOURNEY QUESTION 12.2 *What are the major psychological disorders?*

Psychological problems are classified by using the *Diagnostic and Statistical Manual of Mental Disorders* (DSM). The current edition is the DSM-IV-TR (the fourth edition, text revision) although a new edition, the DSM-5, is due to be published in 2013 (American

Maladaptive behavior Behavior arising from an underlying psychological or biological dysfunction that makes it difficult to adapt to the environment and meet the demands of day-to-day life.

Insanity A legal term that refers to a mental inability to manage one's affairs or to be aware of the consequences of one's actions.

Table 12.1 Some Selected DSM-IV-TR Categories of Psychopathology

PROBLEM	PRIMARY SYMPTOM	TYPICAL SIGNS OF TROUBLE
Schizophrenia and other psychotic disorders[1]	Loss of contact with reality	You hear or see things that others don't; your mind has been playing tricks on you.
Mood disorders[2]	Mania or depression	You feel sad and hopeless; or you talk too loud and too fast and have a rush of ideas and feelings that others think are unreasonable.
Anxiety disorders	High anxiety or anxiety-based distortions of behavior	You have anxiety attacks and feel like you are going to die; or you are afraid to do things that most people can do; or you spend unusual amounts of time doing things like washing your hands or counting your heartbeats.
Somatoform disorders[3]	Body complaints without an organic (physical) basis	You feel physically sick, but your doctor says nothing is wrong with you; or you suffer from pain that has no physical basis; or you are preoccupied with thoughts about being sick.
Dissociative disorders	Amnesia, feelings of unreality, multiple identities	There are major gaps in your memory of events; you feel like you are a robot or a stranger to yourself; others tell you that you have done things that you don't remember doing.
Personality disorders	Unhealthy personality patterns	Your behavior patterns repeatedly cause problems at work, at school, and in your relationships with others.
Sexual and gender identity disorders[4]	Disturbed gender identity, deviant sexual behavior, problems in sexual adjustment	You feel that you are a man trapped in a woman's body (or the reverse); or you can only gain sexual satisfaction by engaging in highly atypical sexual behavior; or you have problems with sexual desire, arousal, or performance.
Substance-related disorders[5]	Disturbances related to drug abuse or dependence	You have been drinking too much, using illegal drugs, or taking prescription drugs more often than you should.

Source: American Psychiatric Association (2000).

The DSM-5 may revise these categories and their labels in the following ways: 1. May be renamed *Schizophrenia spectrum and other psychotic disorders.* 2. May be split into *Bipolar and related disorders* and *Depressive disorders.* 3. May be renamed *Somatic symptom disorders.* 4. May be split into *Sexual dysfunctions* and *Gender dysphoria.* 5. May be renamed *Substance use and addictive disorders* (American Psychiatric Association, 2012). The DSM content has been adapted for the particular audience and is intended for educational purposes only.

Psychiatric Association, 2000; 2012). Regardless of the edition, the DSM influences most activities in mental health settings—from diagnosis to therapy to insurance company billing (First & Pincus, 2002).

A **mental disorder** is a significant impairment in psychological functioning. If you were to glance through the DSM, you would see many disorders described. It's impossible here to discuss all these problems. However, a simplified list of some major DSM-IV-TR disorders can be found in Table 12.1. Those disorders are further described in the next section.

An Overview of Psychological Disorders

People suffering from **psychotic disorders** have "retreated from reality." That is, they suffer from hallucinations and delusions and are socially withdrawn. Psychotic disorders are severely disabling and often lead to hospitalization. Typically, psychotic patients cannot control their thoughts and actions. For example, David often heard the voice of his Uncle Bill: "He told me to turn off the TV. He said, 'It's too damn loud, turn it down, turn it down.' Other times he talks about fishing. 'Good day for fishing. Got to go fishing'" (Durand & Barlow, 2013). Psychotic symptoms occur in schizophrenia, delusional disorders, and some mood disorders. Also, psychosis may be related to medical problems, drug abuse, and other conditions.

Mood disorders are defined primarily by the presence of extreme, intense, and long-lasting emotions. Afflicted persons may be *manic,* meaning agitated, elated, and hyperactive, or they may be *depressed.* Some people with mood disorders alternate between mania and depression and may have psychotic symptoms as well (Ellison-Wright & Bullmore, 2010).

Anxiety disorders are marked by fear or anxiety and by distorted behavior. Some anxiety disorders involve feelings of panic. Others take the form of phobias (irrational fears) or just overwhelming anxiety and nervousness. Two additional anxiety disorders are acute stress disorder and post-traumatic stress disorder. Obsessive-compulsive behavior patterns are also associated with high anxiety.

Mental disorder A significant impairment in psychological functioning.

Psychotic disorder A severe mental disorder characterized by a retreat from reality, by hallucinations and delusions, and by social withdrawal.

Mood disorder A major disturbance in mood or emotion, such as depression or mania.

Anxiety disorder Disruptive feelings of fear, apprehension, or anxiety, or distortions in behavior that are anxiety related.

Human Diversity

Every culture recognizes the existence of psychopathology, and most have at least a few folk names for afflictions you won't find in the DSM. Here are some examples of *culture-bound syndromes* from around the world (Durand & Barlow, 2013; López & Guarnaccia, 2000; Teo & Gaw, 2010):

- **Amok:** Men in Malaysia, Laos, the Philippines, and Polynesia who believe they have been insulted are sometimes known to go *amok*. After a period of brooding, they erupt into an outburst of violent, aggressive, or homicidal behavior randomly directed at people and objects.

- **Susto:** Among Latin Americans, the symptoms of *susto* include insomnia, irritability, phobias, and an increase in sweating and heart rate. Susto can result if someone is badly frightened by a black magic curse. In extreme cases, *voodoo death* can result, as the person is literally scared to death.

- **Ghost sickness:** Among many Native American tribes, people who become preoccupied with

death and the deceased are said to suffer from *ghost sickness*. The symptoms of ghost sickness include bad dreams, weakness, loss of appetite, fainting, dizziness, fear, anxiety, hallucinations, loss of consciousness, confusion, feelings of futility, and a sense of suffocation.

- **Koro:** In South Asia and East Asia, a man may experience sudden and intense anxiety that his penis (or, in females, the vulva and nipples) will recede into the body. In addition to the terror this incites, victims also believe that advanced cases of *koro* can cause death. A similar fear of shrinking genitals has also been reported from West Africa (Dzokoto & Adams, 2005).

- **Zar:** In North African and Middle Eastern societies, *zar* is said to occur when spirits possess an individual. Zar is marked by shouting, laughing, hitting the head against a wall, singing, or weeping. Victims may become apathetic or withdrawn and may refuse to eat or carry out daily tasks.

- **Hikikomori:** In Japanese society, adolescents or young adults who refuse to leave their parents' homes for months at a time are experiencing an extreme form of social withdrawal called *hikikomori*.

It is clear that people everywhere have a need to label and categorize troubled behavior. With some cultural sensitivity, it is often possible to understand these unusual experiences (Flaskerud, 2009). Regardless, the terms listed here provide little guidance about the true nature of a person's problems or the best ways to treat them. That's why the DSM is based on empirical data and clinical observations. Otherwise, psychologists and psychiatrists would be no better than folk healers when making diagnoses (Ancis, Chen, & Schultz, 2004).

By the way, culture-bound syndromes occur in all societies. For example, American psychologists Pamela Keel and Kelly Klump believe that the eating disorder bulimia is primarily a syndrome of Western cultures like the United States (Keel & Klump, 2003).

Somatoform disorder Physical symptoms that mimic disease or injury for which there is no identifiable physical cause.

Dissociative disorder Temporary amnesia, multiple personality, or depersonalization.

Personality disorder A maladaptive personality pattern.

Sexual and gender identity disorders Any of a wide range of difficulties with sexual identity, deviant sexual behavior, or sexual adjustment.

Substance-related disorder Abuse of, or dependence on, a mood- or behavior-altering drug.

Somatoform (so-MAT-oh-form) **disorders** occur when a person has physical symptoms that mimic disease or injury (e.g., paralysis, blindness, illness, chronic pain) for which there is no identifiable physical cause. In such cases, psychological factors appear to explain the symptoms.

A person with a **dissociative disorder** may have temporary amnesia or multiple personalities. Also included in this category are frightening episodes of depersonalization, in which people feel like they are outside of their bodies, are behaving like robots, or are lost in a dream world.

Personality disorders are deeply ingrained, unhealthy personality patterns. Such patterns usually appear in adolescence and continue through much of adult life. They include paranoid (overly suspicious), narcissistic (self-loving), dependent, borderline, and antisocial personality types, as well as others.

Sexual and gender identity disorders include any of a wide range of difficulties with sexual identity, deviant sexual behavior, or sexual adjustment. In *gender identity disorders*, sexual identity does not match a person's physical sex, and the person may seek a sex-change operation. Deviations in sexual behavior known as *paraphilias* include pedophilia, exhibitionism, fetishism, voyeurism, and so on. Also found in this category are a variety of *sexual dysfunctions* (problems in sexual desire, arousal, or response).

Substance-related disorders involve abuse of, or dependence on, psychoactive drugs. Typical culprits include alcohol, barbiturates, opiates, cocaine, amphetamines, hallucinogens, marijuana, and nicotine. A person with a substance-related disorder cannot stop using the drug and may also suffer from withdrawal symptoms, delirium, dementia, amnesia, psychosis, emotional outbursts, sexual problems, and sleep disturbances. (Problems with drug abuse and dependence are discussed in Chapter 5.)

In addition to the formal mental disorders we have reviewed, many cultures have names for "unofficial" psychological "disorders." See "Running Amok with Cultural Maladies" for some examples.

Comorbidity

When Ben's mother, who we met at the beginning of this chapter, was diagnosed with Munchausen by proxy syndrome, she was also diagnosed with schizoaffective disorder and borderline personality disorder. Like Ben's mother, many disturbed people are **comorbid**—that is, they suffer from more than one mental disorder at the same time. One way comorbidity develops is when a *primary* problem causes *secondary* problems. For example, someone experiencing severe anxiety might turn to drugs, legal or otherwise, for treatment and become addicted, complicating the primary disorder with a secondary, substance-related disorder (Fenton et al., 2012).

According to sociologist Ronald Kessler, comorbidity is quite common; more than 40 percent of all people with mental disorders are comorbid (Kessler, 2010). Not only does comorbidity increase these people's misery, it makes it much more difficult for health care providers to diagnose and treat them.

DSM-5

Isn't neurosis a psychological disorder? You might be surprised to learn that definitions of mental disorders change over time. When the DSM was first published in 1952, *neurosis* was included. The term was dropped in later editions because it is too imprecise. Even though **neurosis** is an outdated term, you may still hear it used to loosely refer to problems involving excessive anxiety.

As mentioned previously, a new edition, the DSM-5, is due in 2013. Like previous editions, it will reflect updated research and, hopefully, lead to better diagnosis and treatment (Birgegård, Norring, & Clinton, 2012). The revision process has already been controversial and full of disagreement (Maisel, 2011; Thomas, 2009). For example, *gender identity disorder* may continue to be included in the DSM-5 as *gender dysphoria* (American Psychiatric Association, 2012; Gever, 2009). Opponents of this term believe that many people whose physical sex does not match their gender identity are well adjusted and should not be labeled as "disordered" (Zucker & Spitzer, 2005).

New mental disorders may also be added to the DSM-5. One possibility being considered is *post-traumatic embitterment disorder*, which occurs when a person is left so bitter after a perceived injustice that he or she cannot let it go (Dobricki & Maercker, 2010). For example, Jack's wife left him 3 years ago. He is bitter, angry, and humiliated. He cannot forget or forgive her. Jack sits at home alone every night, is not seeing anyone else, is having troubles at work, and is estranged from his children.

If added, post-traumatic embitterment disorder would join an ever-growing list of recognized disorders. Other possibilities include *apathy syndrome, Internet addiction disorder,* and one every parent of a teenager will instantly recognize, *parental alienation syndrome* (American Psychiatric Association, 2012). Such proliferation has led some to worry that more and more behavior previously considered normal is being redefined as problematic (Lane, 2009). Yet each of the problems listed here can seriously disrupt a person's life, so others argue that they should be part of the next DSM.

General Risk Factors

What causes psychological disorders like those listed in Table 12.1? Here are some general risk factors that contribute to psychopathology:

- **Biological/organic factors:** genetic defects or inherited vulnerabilities, poor prenatal care, very low birth weight, chronic physical illness or disability, exposure to toxic chemicals or drugs, head injuries (**Figure 12.2**)
- **Psychological factors:** stress, low intelligence, learning disorders, lack of control or mastery
- **Family factors:** parents who are immature, mentally disturbed, criminal, or abusive; severe marital strife; extremely poor child discipline; disordered family communication patterns

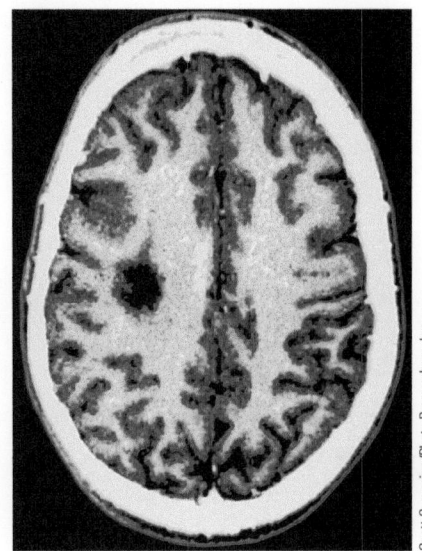

Scott Camazine/Photo Researchers, Inc.

Figure 12.2 This MRI scan of a human brain (viewed from the top) reveals a tumor (dark spot). Mental disorders sometimes have organic causes of this sort. However, in many instances, no obvious organic damage can be found.

Comorbidity (in mental disorders) The simultaneous presence in a person of two or more mental disorders.

Neurosis An outdated term once used to refer, as a group, to anxiety disorders, somatoform disorders, dissociative disorders, and some forms of depression.

- **Social conditions:** poverty, stressful living conditions, homelessness, social disorganization, overcrowding

Before we go on to explore some specific problems and their causes, let's take a detour into the issues involved in psychiatric labeling.

Disorders in Perspective—Psychiatric Labeling

JOURNEY QUESTION 12.3 *How can psychiatric labeling be misused?*

Before we go any further, a caution is in order. The terms we will encounter in this chapter are meant to aid communication about human problems. But if used maliciously or carelessly, they can hurt people. (See "A Disease Called Freedom" on p. 494) Everyone has felt or acted "crazy" during brief periods of stress or high emotion. People with psychological disorders have problems that are more severe or long lasting than most of us experience. Otherwise, they may not be that different from the rest of us.

A fascinating classic study carried out by psychologist David Rosenhan illustrates the impact of psychiatric labeling. Rosenhan and several colleagues had themselves committed to mental hospitals with a diagnosis of "schizophrenia" (Rosenhan, 1973). After being admitted, each of these "pseudo-patients" dropped all pretense of mental illness. Yet, even though they acted completely normal, none of the researchers was ever recognized by hospital *staff* as a phony patient. Real patients were not so easily fooled. It was not unusual for a patient to say to one of the researchers, "You're not crazy, you're checking up on the hospital!" or "You're a journalist."

To record his observations, Rosenhan took notes by carefully jotting things on a small piece of paper hidden in his hand. However, he soon learned that stealth was totally unnecessary. Rosenhan simply walked around with a clipboard, recording observations. No one questioned this behavior. Rosenhan's note taking was just regarded as another symptom of his "illness." This observation clarifies why staff members failed to detect the fake patients. Because they were in a mental ward, and because they had been *labeled* schizophrenic, anything the pseudo-patients did was seen as a symptom of psychopathology.

As Rosenhan's study implies, it is better to label *problems* than to label people. Think of the difference in impact between saying, "You are experiencing a serious psychological disorder" and, "You're a schizophrenic." Which statement would you prefer to have said about yourself?

Social Stigma

An added problem with psychiatric labeling is that it frequently leads to prejudice and discrimination. That is, the mentally ill in our culture are often *stigmatized* (rejected and disgraced). People who have been labeled mentally ill (at any time in their lives) are less likely to be hired. They also tend to be denied housing and they are more likely to be falsely accused of crimes. Sadly, the fear of stigmatization, including self-stigmatization, is one major reason why many people do not seek help for their mental illness (Mojtabai et al., 2011). Thus, people who are grappling with mental illness may be harmed by social stigma as well as by their immediate psychological problems (Elkington et al., 2012).

An Important Note—You're Okay, Really!

In upcoming sections, we will explore some disorders in more detail, beginning with psychotic disorders. (See Table 12.2 for a more detailed list of disorders, including those in Table 12.1. You needn't memorize all of them.) As you read further, we hope that you will not fall prey to "medical student's disease." Medical students, it seems, have a predictable tendency to notice in themselves the symptoms of each dreaded disease they study.

Table 12.2 Major DSM-IV-TR Categories

DISORDERS USUALLY FIRST DIAGNOSED IN INFANCY, CHILDHOOD, OR ADOLESCENCE[D]

Mental retardation (Intellectual disability)[MR]
  Example: Mild mental retardation (intellectual disability)[D]
Learning disorders[R]
  Example: Reading disorder (dyslexia)
Motor skills disorders[R]
  Example: Developmental coordination disorder
Communication disorders[R]
  Example: Stuttering (childhood-onset fluency disorder)
Pervasive developmental disorders[MR]
  Example: Autistic disorder (Autism spectrum disorder)[M]
Attention-deficit and disruptive behavior disorders[R]
  Example: Attention-deficit/hyperactivity disorder
Feeding and eating disorders of infancy or early childhood[M]
  Example: Pica (eating inedible substances)[R]
Tic disorders[M]
  Example: Tourette's disorder[R]
Elimination disorders[R]
  Example: Enuresis (bedwetting)[R]
Other disorders of infancy, childhood, or adolescence[M]
  Example: Separation anxiety disorder[R]

DELIRIUM, DEMENTIA, AMNESTIC, AND OTHER COGNITIVE DISORDERS[M]

Delirium
  Example: Delirium due to a general medical condition[M]
Dementia
  Example: Dementia of the Alzheimer's type
Amnestic disorders (memory loss)[D]
  Example: Amnestic disorder due to a general medical condition[MR]

MENTAL DISORDERS DUE TO A GENERAL MEDICAL CONDITION NOT ELSEWHERE CLASSIFIED[R]

Catatonic disorder due to a general medical condition[R]
Personality change due to a general medical condition[R]
Mental disorder not otherwise specified due to a general medical condition[R]

SUBSTANCE-RELATED DISORDERS[M]

Cocaine-related disorders[M]
  Example: Cocaine intoxication[R]

SCHIZOPHRENIA AND OTHER PSYCHOTIC DISORDERS[M]

Schizophrenia
  Example: Schizophrenia, paranoid type[D]
Schizophreniform disorder
Schizoaffective disorder
Delusional disorder
  Example: Delusional disorder, grandiose type
Brief psychotic disorder
Shared psychotic disorder (folie à deux)[D]
Psychotic disorder due to a general medical condition
Psychotic disorder not otherwise specified

MOOD DISORDERS[M]

Depressive disorders[MR]
  Example: Major depressive disorder
Bipolar disorders[MR]
  Example: Bipolar I disorder
Mood disorder due to a general medical condition[MR]
Substance-induced mood disorder[MR]
Depressive disorder not otherwise specified[MR]

ANXIETY DISORDERS

Example: Panic disorder

SOMATOFORM DISORDERS

Example: Conversion disorder

FACTITIOUS DISORDERS (FAKED DISABILITY OR ILLNESS)[R]

Example: Factitious disorder[R]

DISSOCIATIVE DISORDERS

Example: Dissociative identity disorder

SEXUAL AND GENDER IDENTITY DISORDERS[MR]

Sexual dysfunctions[R]
  Example: Hypoactive sexual desire disorder[M]
Paraphilias[R]
  Example: Voyeurism
Gender identity disorders[MR]
  Example: Gender identity disorder (Gender Incongruence)[M]

EATING DISORDERS[M]

Example: Anorexia nervosa

SLEEP DISORDERS

Primary sleep disorders
  Example: Primary insomnia
Parasomnias[R]
  Example: Nightmare disorder
Sleep disorders related to another mental disorder[R]
  Example: Insomnia related to a general medical condition[R]

IMPULSE CONTROL DISORDERS NOT ELSEWHERE CLASSIFIED[M]

Example: Kleptomania

ADJUSTMENT DISORDERS[R]

Example: Adjustment disorder[R]

PERSONALITY DISORDERS[M]

Example: Antisocial personality disorder[M]

Source: American Psychiatric Association (2000).

The DSM-5 may revise these categories and their labels in the following ways: *M,* May be modified in a major way; *R,* may be reclassified; *D,* may be deleted (American Psychiatric Association, 2012). The DSM content has been adapted for the particular audience and is intended for educational purposes only.

Human Diversity

A Disease Called Freedom

The year is 1840. You are a slave who has tried repeatedly to escape from a cruel and abusive master. You want to be free. An expert is consulted about your "abnormal" behavior. His conclusion? You are suffering from "drapetomania," a mental "disorder" that causes slaves to run away (Wakefield, 1992). Your "cure"? The expert will cut off your toes.

As this example suggests, psychiatric terms are easily abused. Historically, some have been applied to culturally disapproved behaviors that are not really disorders. Another of our personal favorites is the long-outdated diagnosis of "anarchia," a form of insanity that leads one to seek a more democratic society (Brown, 1990).

All of the following were also once considered disorders: childhood masturbation, lack of vaginal orgasm, self-defeating personality (applied mainly to women), homosexuality, and nymphomania (a woman with a healthy sexual appetite) (Wakefield, 1992). Even today, race, gender, and social class continue to affect the diagnosis of various disorders (Kearney & Trull, 2012; Poland & Caplan, 2004).

Gender is probably the most common source of bias in judging normality because standards tend to be based on males (Fine, 2010; Nolen-Hoeksema, 2011). According to psychologist Paula Caplan (1995) and others, women are penalized both for conforming to female stereotypes and for ignoring them. If a woman is independent, aggressive, and unemotional, she may be considered "unhealthy." Yet at the same time, a woman who is vain, emotional, irrational, and dependent on others (all "feminine" traits in our culture) may be classified as having a personality disorder (Bornstein, 1996). Indeed, a majority of persons classified as having dependent personality disorder are women. In view of this, Paula Caplan asks, why isn't there a category called "delusional dominating personality disorder" for obnoxious men (Caplan, 1995)?

Because biases can influence perceptions of disorder and normality, it is worth being cautious before you leap to conclusions about or label the mental health of others (American Psychiatric Association, 2000; 2012). (*Ape mask wearing disorder*? They might be doing an assignment for their psychology class!)

As a psychology student, you may notice what seem to be abnormal tendencies in your own behavior. If so, don't panic. In most instances, this only shows that pathological behavior is an *exaggeration* of normal defenses and reactions, not that your behavior is abnormal. Before we go on, though, here's a study break to help you diagnose your grasp of psychopathology.

 study break Normality and Psychopathology

RECITE

1. The core feature of abnormal behavior is that it is
   a. statistically unusual
   b. maladaptive
   c. socially nonconforming
   d. a source of subjective discomfort

2. One of the most powerful contexts in which judgments of normality and abnormality are made is
   a. the family
   b. occupational settings
   c. religious systems
   d. culture

3. Which of the following is a legal concept?
   a. neurosis
   b. psychosis
   c. drapetomania
   d. insanity

4. People are said to have "retreated from reality" when they suffer from
   a. psychotic disorders
   b. mood disorders
   c. somatoform disorders
   d. personality disorders

5. *Koro* and *hikikomori* are
   a. somatoform disorders
   b. forms of psychosis
   c. folk terminology
   d. DSM-5 disorders

6. It is far better to label _____ than to label people.

REFLECT

THINK CRITICALLY

7. At the beginning of this chapter, we met Ben's mother, who was deliberately faking her son's "illnesses." How could someone get away with Munchausen by proxy syndrome? Wouldn't doctors figure out that something was fishy with Ben long before he had 40 surgeries for a faked sinus disorder?

SELF-REFLECT

Think of an instance of abnormal behavior you have witnessed. By what formal standards would the behavior be regarded as abnormal? In every society? Was the behavior maladaptive in any way?

ANSWERS

1. b 2. d 3. d 4. a 5. c 6. problems 7. No one doctor tolerates false symptoms for long. Once a doctor refuses further treatment, the Munchausen sufferer will move on to another. Also, often more than one doctor is being seen at one time.

Psychotic Disorders—The Dark Side of the Moon

JOURNEY QUESTION 12.4 *What are the general characteristics of psychotic disorders?*

Psychotic disorders are among the most dramatic and serious of all mental problems. Imagine that a member of your family (Floyd?) has been hearing voices, is talking strangely, has covered his head with aluminum foil, and believes that houseflies are speaking to him in code. If you observed such symptoms, would you be concerned? Of course you would, and rightly so.

A person who is psychotic undergoes striking changes in thinking, behavior, and emotion. Basic to all these changes is the fact that **psychosis** reflects a loss of contact with shared views of reality (psycho*sis*, singular; psycho*ses*, plural). The following comments, made by a psychotic patient, illustrate what is meant by a break with reality (Durand & Barlow, 2013):

> "When you do the 25 of the clock, it means that you leave the house 25 after 1 to mail letters so they can check on you...and they know where you're at. That's the Eagle."

The Nature of Psychosis

What are the major symptoms of psychotic disorders? You might find it helpful to distinguish between *positive* and *negative symptoms* (Rollins et al., 2010).

Positive symptoms, such as delusions and hallucinations, are excesses or exaggerations compared to normal behavior. People who suffer from **delusions** hold exaggerated false beliefs that they insist are true, regardless of how much the facts contradict them. An example is a 43-year-old schizophrenic man who was convinced he was pregnant (Mansouri & Adityanjee, 1995). Some common types of delusions are: (1) *depressive* delusions, in which people feel that they have committed horrible crimes or sinful deeds; (2) *somatic* delusions, in which people believe their bodies are "rotting away" or emitting foul odors; (3) delusions of *grandeur,* in which people think they are extremely important; (4) delusions of *influence,* in which people feel they are being controlled or influenced by others or by unseen forces; (5) delusions of *persecution,* in which people believe that others are "out to get them"; and (6) delusions of *reference,* in which people give great personal meaning to unrelated events (Kearney & Trull, 2012).

Hallucinations are imaginary sensations, such as seeing, hearing, or smelling things that don't exist in the real world. The most common psychotic hallucination is hearing voices. Sometimes these voices command patients to hurt themselves. Unfortunately, sometimes people obey (Barrowcliff & Haddock, 2006). More rarely, psychotic people may feel "insects crawling under their skin," taste "poisons" in their food, or smell "gas" their "enemies" are using to "get" them. Sensory changes, such as anesthesia (numbness, or a loss of sensation) or extreme sensitivity to heat, cold, pain, or touch, can also occur.

In contrast, *negative symptoms* are absences or deficiencies compared to normal behavior. During a psychotic episode, emotions are often severely disturbed. For instance, the psychotic person may be wildly elated or hyperemotional. But sometimes psychotic patients may be depressed or apathetic and display a lack of emotion, or *flat affect,* a condition in which the face is frozen in a blank expression. Brain images from psychotic patients with "frozen faces" reveal that their brains process emotions abnormally (Fahim et al., 2005).

A psychotic individual in a state mental hospital.

Psychosis A withdrawal from reality marked by hallucinations and delusions, disturbed thought and emotions, and personality disorganization.

Delusion A false belief held against all contrary evidence.

Hallucination An imaginary sensation, such as seeing, hearing, or smelling things that don't exist in the real world.

Table 12.3 Warning Signs of Psychotic Disorders and Major Mood Disorders

- You express bizarre thoughts or beliefs that defy reality.
- You have withdrawn from family members and other relationships.
- You hear unreal voices or see things others don't.
- You are extremely sad, persistently despondent, or suicidal.
- You are excessively energetic and have little need for sleep.
- You lose your appetite, sleep excessively, and have no energy.
- You exhibit extreme mood swings.
- You believe someone is trying to get you.
- You have engaged in antisocial, destructive, or self-destructive behavior.

Sources: American Psychiatric Association (2000); Durand & Barlow (2013).

Similarly, a reduced capacity to communicate verbally is a nearly universal symptom of psychosis. In fact, psychotic speech can be so garbled and chaotic that it sometimes sounds like a "word salad." For this reason, psychotic symptoms are sometimes thought of as a primitive type of communication. That is, many patients may be using their actions to say "I need help" or "I can't handle it anymore."

Major disturbances such as those just described—as well as added problems with thinking, memory, and attention—bring about personality disintegration and a break with reality. *Personality disintegration* occurs when a person's thoughts, actions, and emotions are no longer coordinated. When psychotic disturbances and a fragmented personality are evident for weeks or months, the person has suffered a psychosis (American Psychiatric Association, 2000; 2012) (Table 12.3).

Dementia

There are several types of psychotic disorder. In a sense, all psychoses (and most, if not all, other mental illnesses) are partly organic—that is, involving physical changes in the brain. However, problems involving clear-cut brain injuries or diseases are often labeled *organic mental disorders*.

For example, poisoning by lead or mercury can damage the brain, causing hallucinations, delusions, and a loss of emotional control (Figure 12.3). Children who eat leaded paint flakes or breathe leaded paint powder can become psychotic or intellectually disabled (Mielke, 1999). Children with higher levels of lead in their blood are more likely

© Visions of America/Superstock

Former U.S. president Ronald Reagan was diagnosed with Alzheimer's disease in 1995. Like many Alzheimer's victims, Reagan slipped into a slow mental decline. He died in 2004.

Figure 12.3 The Mad Hatter, from Lewis Carroll's *Alice's Adventures in Wonderland*. History provides numerous examples of psychosis caused by toxic chemicals. Carroll's Mad Hatter character is modeled after an occupational disease of the eighteenth and nineteenth centuries. In that era, hatmakers were heavily exposed to mercury used in the preparation of felt. Consequently, many suffered brain damage and became psychotic, or "mad" (Kety, 1979).

© Bettmann/Corbis

to be arrested as adults for criminal offenses (Wright et al., 2008). On a much larger scale, "poisoning" of another type, in the form of drug abuse, can also produce deviant behavior and psychotic symptoms (American Psychiatric Association, 2000; 2012).

The most common *organic psychosis* is **dementia** (duh-MEN-sha), a serious mental impairment in old age caused by deterioration of the brain (Treves & Korczyn, 2012). In dementia, we see major disturbances in memory, reasoning, judgment, impulse control, and personality. This combination usually leaves people confused, suspicious, apathetic, or withdrawn. Some common causes of dementia are circulatory problems, repeated strokes, or general shrinkage and atrophy of the brain. The most common form of dementia is **Alzheimer's** (ALLS-hi-merz) **disease**. Alzheimer's victims slowly lose the ability to work, cook, drive, read, write, or do arithmetic. Eventually they are mute and bedridden. Alzheimer's disease appears to be caused by unusual webs and tangles in the brain that damage areas important for memory and learning (Hanyu et al., 2010; Stix, 2010). Genetic factors can increase the risk of developing this devastating disease (Treves & Korczyn, 2012).

Are there specific kinds of psychotic disorders? Two major types of psychosis are *delusional disorders* and *schizophrenia*.

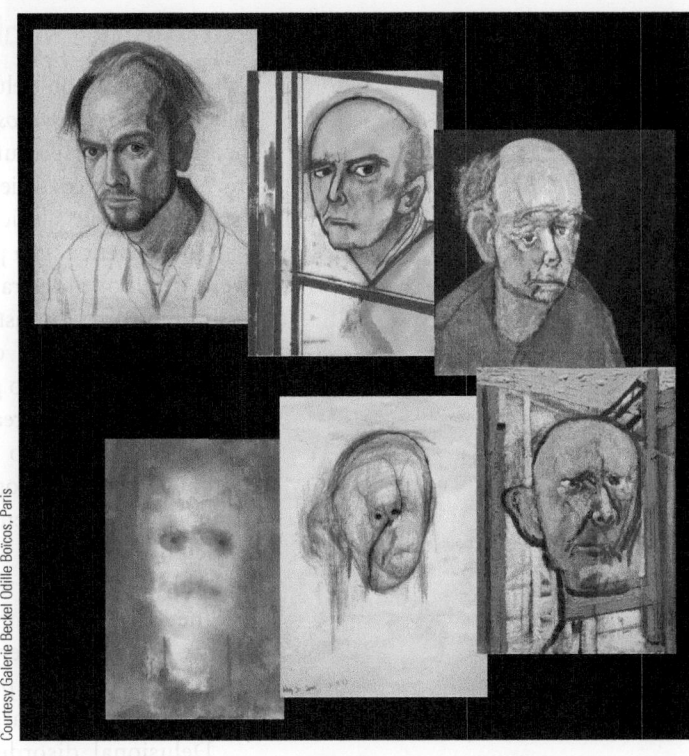

Courtesy Galerie Beckel Odille Boïcos, Paris

Artist William Utermohlen painted haunting images portraying his decline into the grasp of Alzheimer's disease.

Delusional Disorders—An Enemy Behind Every Tree

JOURNEY QUESTION 12.5 *What is the nature of a delusional disorder?*

People with delusional disorders usually do not suffer from hallucinations, emotional excesses, or personality disintegration. Even so, their break with reality is unmistakable. The main feature of **delusional disorders** is the presence of deeply held false beliefs, which may take the following forms (American Psychiatric Association, 2000; 2012):

- **Erotomanic type:** In this disorder, people have erotic delusions that they are loved by another person, especially by someone famous or of higher status. As you might imagine, some celebrity stalkers suffer from erotomania.
- **Grandiose type:** In this case, people suffer from the delusion that they have some great, unrecognized talent, knowledge, or insight. They may also believe that they have a special relationship with an important person or with God or that they are a famous person. (If the famous person is alive, the deluded person regards her or him as an imposter.)
- **Jealous type:** An example of this type of delusion would be having an all-consuming, but unfounded, belief that your spouse or lover is unfaithful.
- **Persecutory type:** Delusions of persecution involve belief that you are being conspired against, cheated, spied on, followed, poisoned, maligned, or harassed.
- **Somatic type:** People suffering from somatic delusions typically believe that their bodies are diseased or rotting, or infested with insects or parasites, or that parts of their bodies are defective.

Although they are false, and sometimes far-fetched, all these delusions are about experiences that could occur in real life. In other types of psychosis, delusions tend to be more bizarre (Brown & Barlow, 2011; Manschreck, 1996). For example, a person with schizophrenia might believe that space aliens have replaced all his internal organs with electronic monitoring devices. In contrast, people with ordinary delusions merely believe that someone is trying to steal their money, that they are being deceived by a lover, that the FBI is watching them, and the like.

Dementia A serious mental impairment in old age caused by deterioration of the brain.

Alzheimer's disease An age-related disease characterized by memory loss, mental confusion, and, in its later stages, a nearly total loss of mental abilities.

Delusional disorder A psychosis marked by severe delusions of grandeur, jealousy, persecution, or similar preoccupations.

Paranoid Psychosis

The most common delusional disorder centers on delusions of persecution and is often called *paranoid psychosis*. Many self-styled reformers, crank letter writers, conspiracy theorists, and the like suffer paranoid delusions. Paranoid individuals often believe that they are being cheated, spied on, followed, poisoned, harassed, or plotted against. Usually they are intensely suspicious, believing they must be on guard at all times.

The evidence such people find to support their beliefs usually fails to persuade others. Every detail of the paranoid person's existence is woven into a private version of "what's really going on." For instance, buzzing during a telephone conversation may be interpreted as "someone listening," or a stranger who comes to the door asking for directions may be seen as "really trying to get information."

It is difficult to treat people suffering from paranoid delusions because it is almost impossible for them to accept that they need help. Anyone who suggests that they have a problem simply becomes part of the "conspiracy" to "persecute" them. Consequently, paranoid people frequently lead lonely, isolated, and humorless lives dominated by constant suspicion and hostility.

Although they are not necessarily dangerous to others, they can be. People who believe that the Mafia, "government agents," terrorists, or a street gang is slowly closing in on them may be moved to violence by their irrational fears. Imagine that a stranger comes to the door to ask a paranoid person for directions. If the stranger has his hand in his coat pocket, he could become the target of a paranoid attempt at "self-defense."

Delusional disorders are rare. By far, the most common form of psychosis is schizophrenia. Let's explore schizophrenia in more detail and see how it differs from a delusional disorder.

Schizophrenia—Shattered Reality

JOURNEY QUESTION 12.6 *What is schizophrenia and what causes it?*

Schizophrenia (SKIT-soh-FREN-ee-uh) is marked by delusions, hallucinations, apathy, thinking abnormalities, and a disintegration or "splitting" apart of the normally integrated personality.

Do people with schizophrenia have two personalities? No. How many times have you heard people say something like, "Laurence was so warm and friendly yesterday, but today he's as cold as ice. He's so schizophrenic that I don't know how to react." Such statements show how often the term *schizophrenic* is misused. As we will see later on in this chapter, a person who displays two or more *integrated* personalities has a dissociative disorder and is not "schizophrenic." Neither, of course, is a person like Laurence, whose behavior is merely inconsistent.

In schizophrenia, emotions may become blunted or very inappropriate. For example, if a person with schizophrenia is told his mother just died, he might smile, giggle, or show no emotion at all. Schizophrenic delusions may include the idea that the person's thoughts and actions are being controlled, that thoughts are being broadcast (so others can hear them), that thoughts have been "inserted" into the person's mind, or that thoughts have been removed. In addition, schizophrenia involves withdrawal from contact with others, a loss of interest in external activities, a breakdown of personal habits, and an inability to deal with daily events (Neufeld et al., 2003; Ziv, Leiser, & Levine, 2011). One person in 100 has schizophrenia in any given year (National Institute of Mental Health, 2011a).

Many schizophrenic symptoms appear to be related to problems with *selective attention*. In other words, it is hard for people with schizophrenia to focus on one item of information at a time. Having an impaired "sensory filter" in their brains may be why they are overwhelmed by a jumble of thoughts, sensations, images, and feelings (Cellard et al., 2010; Heinrichs, 2001).

Schizophrenia A psychosis characterized by delusions, hallucinations, apathy, and a personality that disintegrates or "splits" apart.

Is there more than one type of schizophrenia? Schizophrenia appears to be a group of related disturbances. It currently has four major types, although these types may be removed from the DSM-5 (American Psychiatric Association, 2012):

- **Disorganized type:** Schizophrenia marked by incoherence, grossly disorganized behavior, bizarre thinking, and flat or grossly inappropriate emotions
- **Catatonic type:** Schizophrenia marked by stupor, rigidity, unresponsiveness, posturing, mutism, and sometimes agitated, purposeless behavior
- **Paranoid type:** Schizophrenia marked by a preoccupation with delusions or by frequent auditory hallucinations related to a single theme, especially grandeur or persecution
- **Undifferentiated type:** Schizophrenia in which there are prominent psychotic symptoms, but none of the specific features of catatonic, disorganized, or paranoid types

In disorganized schizophrenia, behavior is marked by silliness, laughter, and bizarre or obscene behavior.

Disorganized Schizophrenia

The disorder known as **disorganized schizophrenia** (sometimes called *hebephrenic* schizophrenia) comes close to matching the stereotyped images of "madness" seen in movies. In disorganized schizophrenia, personality disintegration is almost complete: Emotions, speech, and behavior are all highly disorganized. The result is silliness, laughter, and bizarre or obscene behavior, as shown by this intake interview of a patient named Edna:

Dr. Tell me, how do you feel?

Patient London's bell is a long, long dock. Hee! Hee! (Giggles uncontrollably.)

Dr. Do you know where you are now?

Patient D_____n! S_____t on you all who rip into my internals! The grudgerometer will take care of you all! (Shouting) I am the Queen, see my magic, I shall turn you all into smidgelings forever!

I. . . . I. . . . I. . . . I! (Makes grotesque faces.)

Edna was placed in the women's ward where she proceeded to masturbate. . . . Occasionally, she would scream or shout obscenities. At other times she giggled to herself. She was known to attack other patients. She began to complain that her uterus was attached to a "pipeline to the Kremlin" and that she was being "infernally invaded" by Communism (Suinn, 1975*).

Disorganized schizophrenia typically develops in adolescence or young adulthood. Chances of improvement are limited, and social impairment is usually extreme (American Psychiatric Association, 2000).

Catatonic Schizophrenia

Catatonic schizophrenics may remain *mute* (they do not speak) while holding odd postures for hours or even days at a time. These periods of stupor may be similar to the tendency to "freeze" at times of great emergency or panic. Catatonic individuals appear to be struggling desperately to control their inner turmoil (Fink, Shorter, & Taylor, 2010; Fink & Taylor, 2003). One sign of this is the fact that stupor may occasionally give way to agitated outbursts or violent behavior. As you might imagine, patients with catatonic schizophrenia are difficult to "reach." Fortunately, this bizarre disorder has become rare in Europe and North America (American Psychiatric Association, 2000).

Disorganized schizophrenia Schizophrenia marked by incoherence, grossly disorganized behavior, bizarre thinking, and flat or grossly inappropriate emotions.

Catatonic schizophrenia Schizophrenia marked by stupor, rigidity, unresponsiveness, posturing, mutism, and, sometimes agitated, purposeless behavior.

*Quotes from *Fundamentals of Behavior Pathology* by R. M. Suinn. Copyright © 1975. Reprinted by permission of John Wiley & Sons, Inc.

Paranoid Schizophrenia

Paranoid schizophrenia is the most common schizophrenic disorder (**Figure 12.4**). As in paranoid delusional disorders, **paranoid schizophrenia** centers on delusions of grandeur and persecution. However, paranoid schizophrenics also hallucinate, and their delusions are more bizarre and unconvincing than those in a delusional disorder (Corcoran, 2010; Freeman & Garety, 2004).

Thinking that God, the government, or "cosmic rays from space" are controlling their minds or that someone is trying to poison them, people suffering from paranoid schizophrenia may feel forced into violence to "protect" themselves. An example is James Huberty, who brutally murdered 21 people at a McDonald's restaurant in San Ysidro, California. Huberty, who had paranoid schizophrenia, felt persecuted and cheated by life. Shortly before he announced to his wife that he was "going hunting humans," Huberty had been hearing hallucinated voices.

How dangerous are the mentally ill? Horrific crimes, like the San Ysidro murders, lead many people to believe that the mentally ill are dangerous. Although sensationalized media reports tend to exaggerate the connection between mental illness and violence, the reality is just the opposite (Hiday & Burns, 2010; Markowitz, 2011). According to the largest study ever conducted on this question, mentally ill individuals who are not also substance abusers are no more prone to violence than are normal individuals (Monahan et al., 2001). In general, only persons who are *actively psychotic* and *currently* experiencing psychotic symptoms are at increased risk for violence. In fact, the risk of violence from mental patients is actually many times lower than that from persons who have the following attributes: young, male, poor, and intoxicated (Corrigan & Watson, 2005).

Undifferentiated Schizophrenia

The three types of schizophrenia just described occur most often in textbooks. In reality, patients may shift from one pattern to another at different times. Many patients, therefore, are simply classified as suffering from **undifferentiated schizophrenia**, in which the specific features of catatonic, disorganized, or paranoid types are missing. Diagnosing types of schizophrenia is fairly subjective, which is why the DSM-5 may no longer make those distinctions (American Psychiatric Association, 2012). Regardless, there is no doubt that schizophrenia is real or that its treatment is a major challenge.

The Causes of Schizophrenia

What causes schizophrenia? Former British prime minister Winston Churchill once described a question that perplexed him as "a riddle wrapped in a mystery inside an enigma." The same words might describe the causes of schizophrenia.

Environment

An increased risk of developing schizophrenia may begin at birth or even before. Women who are exposed to the influenza (flu) virus or to rubella (German measles) during the middle of pregnancy have children who are more likely to become schizophrenic (Durand & Barlow, 2013; Vuillermot et al., 2010). Malnutrition during pregnancy and complications at the time of birth can have a similar impact. Possibly, such events disturb brain development, leaving people more vulnerable to a psychotic break with reality (Walker et al., 2004).

Early **psychological trauma** (a psychological injury or shock) may also add to the risk. Often, the victims of schizophrenia were exposed to violence, sexual abuse, death, divorce, separation, or other stresses in childhood (Walker et al., 2004). Living in a troubled family is a related risk factor. In a disturbed family environment, stressful relationships, communication patterns, and negative emotions prevail. Deviant communication patterns cause

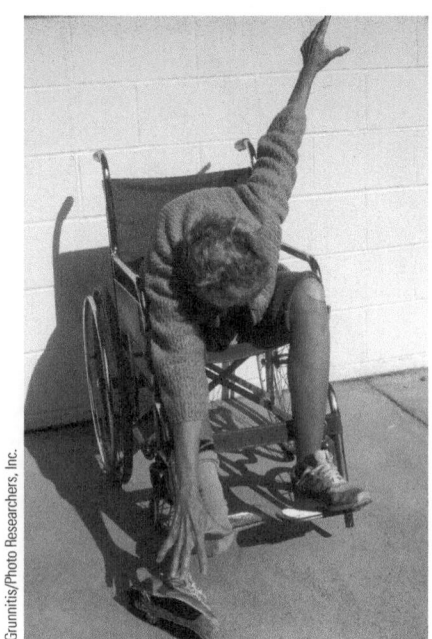

Can the catatonic's rigid postures and stupor be understood in terms of abnormal body chemistry? Environment? Heredity? As is true of other forms of schizophrenia, the answer appears to be all three factors.

Grumitis/Photo Researchers, Inc.

Paranoid schizophrenia Schizophrenia marked by a preoccupation with delusions or by frequent auditory hallucinations related to a single theme, especially grandeur or persecution.

Undifferentiated schizophrenia Schizophrenia lacking the specific features of catatonic, disorganized, or paranoid types.

Psychological trauma A psychological injury or shock, such as that caused by violence, abuse, neglect, separation, and so forth.

anxiety, confusion, anger, conflict, and turmoil. Typically, disturbed families interact in ways that are laden with guilt, prying, criticism, negativity, and emotional attacks (Bressi, Albonetti, & Razzoli, 1998; Davison & Neale, 2006).

Although they are attractive, environmental explanations alone are not enough to account for schizophrenia. For example, when the children of schizophrenic parents are raised away from their chaotic home environment, they are still more likely to become psychotic (Walker et al., 2004).

Heredity

Does that mean that heredity affects the risk of developing schizophrenia? There is now little doubt that heredity is a factor in schizophrenia. It appears that some individuals inherit a *potential* for developing schizophrenia (Levy et al., 2010). They are, in other words, more *vulnerable* to the disorder (Harrison & Weinberger, 2005; Walker et al., 2004).

How has that been shown? If one identical twin becomes schizophrenic (remember, identical twins have identical genes), then the other twin has a *48 percent* chance of also becoming schizophrenic (Insel, 2010; Lenzenweger & Gottesman, 1994). The figure for twins can be compared with the risk of schizophrenia for the population in general, which is 1 percent. (See Figure 12.5 for other relationships.) In general, schizophrenia is clearly more common among close relatives and tends to run in families. There's even a case on record of *four* identical quadruplets *all* developing schizophrenia (Mirsky et al., 2000). In light of such evidence, researchers are now beginning to search for specific genes related to schizophrenia (Curtis et al., 2011; Hyman, 2011; Roffman et al., 2011).

A problem exists with current genetic explanations of schizophrenia: Very few people with schizophrenia have children (Bundy, Stahl, & MacCabe, 2011). How could a genetic defect be passed from one generation to the next if afflicted people don't reproduce? One possibility is suggested by the fact that the older a man is (even if he doesn't suffer from schizophrenia) when he fathers a child, the more likely it is that the child will develop schizophrenia. Apparently, genetic mutations occur in aging male reproductive cells and increase the risk of schizophrenia (as well as other medical problems) (Malaspina et al., 2005; Sipos et al., 2004).

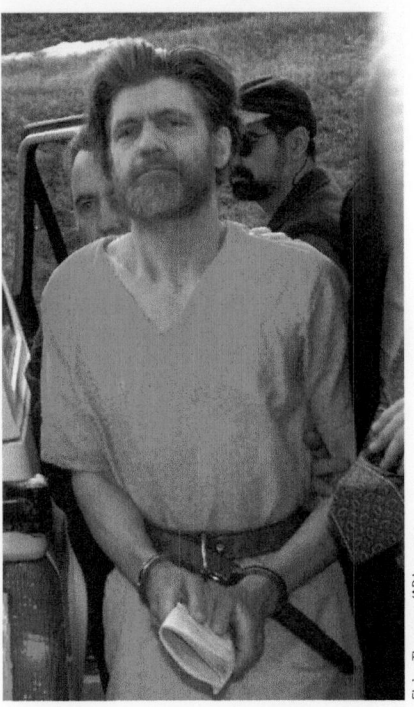

Figure 12.4 Over a period of years, Theodore Kaczynski mailed bombs to unsuspecting victims, many of whom were maimed or killed. As a young adult, Kaczynski was a brilliant mathematician. At the time of his arrest, he had become the Unabomber—a reclusive "loner" who deeply mistrusted other people and modern technology. After his arrest, Kaczynski was judged to be suffering from paranoid schizophrenia.

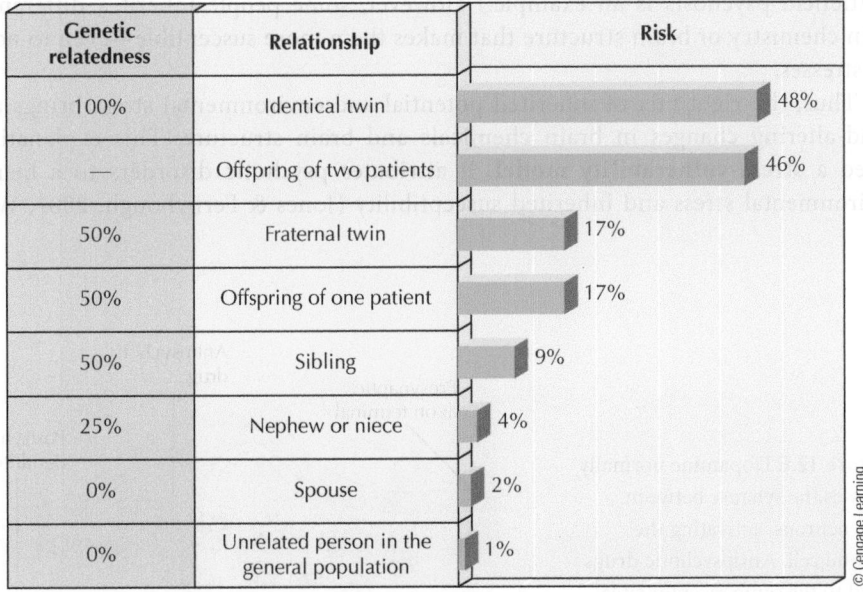

Genetic relatedness	Relationship	Risk
100%	Identical twin	48%
—	Offspring of two patients	46%
50%	Fraternal twin	17%
50%	Offspring of one patient	17%
50%	Sibling	9%
25%	Nephew or niece	4%
0%	Spouse	2%
0%	Unrelated person in the general population	1%

Figure 12.5 Lifetime risk of developing schizophrenia is associated with how closely a person is genetically related to a schizophrenic person. A shared environment also increases the risk. (Estimates from Lenzenweger & Gottesman, 1994.)

Brain Chemistry

Amphetamine, LSD, PCP ("angel dust"), and similar drugs produce effects that partially mimic the symptoms of schizophrenia. Also, the same drugs (phenothiazines) used to treat LSD overdoses tend to alleviate psychotic symptoms. Facts such as these suggest that biochemical abnormalities (disturbances in brain chemicals or neurotransmitters) may occur in schizophrenic people. It is possible that the schizophrenic brain produces some substance similar to a *psychedelic* (mind-altering) drug.

Many researchers believe that schizophrenia is related to disturbances in brain dopamine (DOPE-ah-meen) systems (Citrome, 2011). Dopamine receptors in one part of the brain appear to become super-responsive to normal amounts of dopamine, triggering a flood of unrelated thoughts, feelings, and perceptions, which may account for the positive symptoms (voices, hallucinations, and delusions) of schizophrenia. The implication is that schizophrenic people may be on a sort of drug trip caused by their own bodies (Figure 12.6).

Dopamine is not the only brain chemical that has caught scientists' attention. The neurotransmitter glutamate also appears to be related to schizophrenia (van Elst et al., 2005). People who take the hallucinogenic drug PCP, which affects glutamate, have symptoms that closely mimic schizophrenia (Murray, 2002). This occurs because glutamate influences brain activity in areas that control emotions and sensory information (Citrome, 2011; Tsai & Coyle, 2002). Another tantalizing connection is the fact that stress alters glutamate levels, which in turn alter dopamine systems (Moghaddam, 2002). The story is far from complete, but it appears that dopamine, glutamate, and other brain chemicals partly explain the devastating symptoms of schizophrenia (Walker et al., 2004). See "The Schizophrenic Brain" to learn how brain imaging techniques are improving our understanding of this condition.

Implications

In summary, the emerging picture of psychotic disorders such as schizophrenia takes this form: Anyone subjected to enough stress may be pushed to a psychotic break. (Battlefield psychosis is an example.) However, some people inherit a difference in brain chemistry or brain structure that makes them more susceptible—even to normal life stresses.

Thus, the right mix of inherited potential and environmental stress brings about mind-altering changes in brain chemicals and brain structure. This explanation is called a **stress-vulnerability model**. It attributes psychotic disorders to a blend of environmental stress and inherited susceptibility (Jones & Fernyhough, 2007; Walker

Stress-vulnerability model Attributes mental illness to a combination of environmental stress and inherited susceptibility.

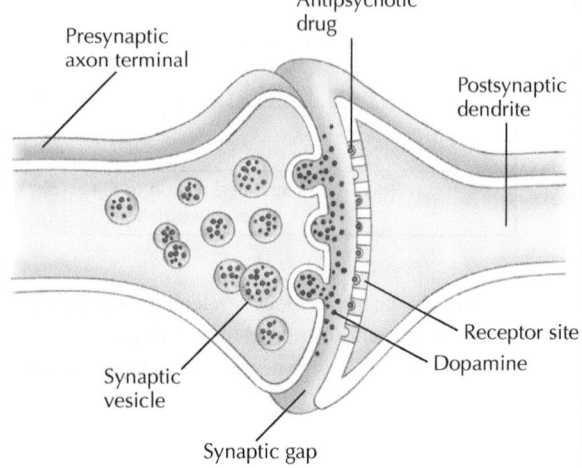

Figure 12.6 Dopamine normally crosses the synapse between two neurons, activating the second cell. Antipsychotic drugs bind to the same receptor sites as dopamine does, blocking its action. In people suffering from schizophrenia, a reduction in dopamine activity can quiet a person's agitation and psychotic symptoms.

Brainwaves

The Schizophrenic Brain

Several brain imaging methods (remember Chapter 2?) have made it possible to directly observe the living schizophrenic brain. Computed tomography (CT) scans and magnetic resonance imaging (MRI) scans, which can reveal brain structure, suggest that the brains of schizophrenics have shrunk, or atrophied (Bora et al., 2011). For example, **Figure 12.7** shows a CT scan (a computer-enhanced X-ray image) of the brain of John Hinkley, Jr., who shot former U.S. president Ronald Reagan and three other men in 1981. In the ensuing trial, Hinkley was declared insane. As you can see, his brain had wider than normal surface fissuring.

Similarly, MRI scans indicate that schizophrenic people tend to have enlarged ventricles (fluid-filled spaces within the brain), again suggesting that surrounding brain tissue has withered (Andreasen et al., 2011; Barkataki et al., 2006). One possible explanation is that the schizophrenic brain may be unable to continually create new neurons to replace old ones that have died. In contrast, normal brains continue to produce new neurons (a process referred to as neurogenesis) throughout life (DeCarolis & Eisch, 2010; Toro & Deakin, 2007). It is telling that the affected areas are crucial for regulating motivation, emotion, perception, actions, and attention (Kawada et al., 2009).

Other methods provide images of brain activity, including positron emission tomography (PET) scans. To make a PET scan, a radioactive sugar solution is injected into a vein. When the sugar reaches the brain, an electronic device measures how much is used in each area. These data are then translated into a color map, or scan, of brain activity (**Figure 12.8**). Researchers are finding patterns in such scans that are consistently linked with schizophrenia, affective disorders, and other problems. For instance, activity tends to be abnormally low in the frontal lobes of the schizophrenic brain (Durand & Barlow, 2013; Roffman et al., 2011). In the future, PET scans may be used to accurately diagnose schizophrenia. For now, such scans show that there is a clear abnormality in schizophrenic brain activity.

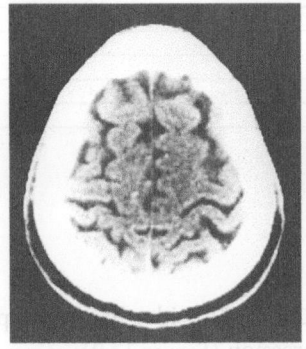
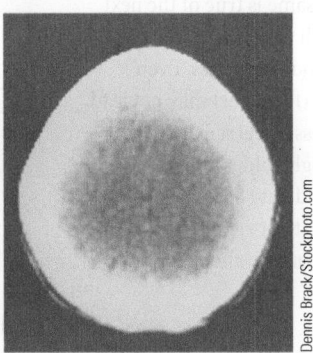

Figure 12.7 *(left)* CT scan of would-be presidential assassin John Hinkley, Jr., taken when he was 25. The X-ray image shows widened fissures in the wrinkled surface of Hinkley's brain. *(right)* CT scan of a normal 25-year-old's brain. In most young adults, the surface folds of the brain are pressed together too tightly to be seen. As a person ages, surface folds of the brain normally become more visible. Pronounced brain fissuring in young adults may be a sign of schizophrenia, chronic alcoholism, or other problems.

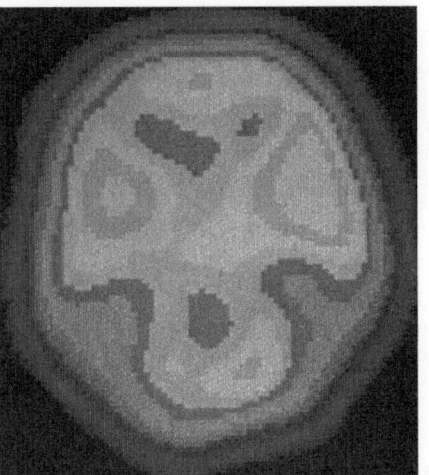

Normal

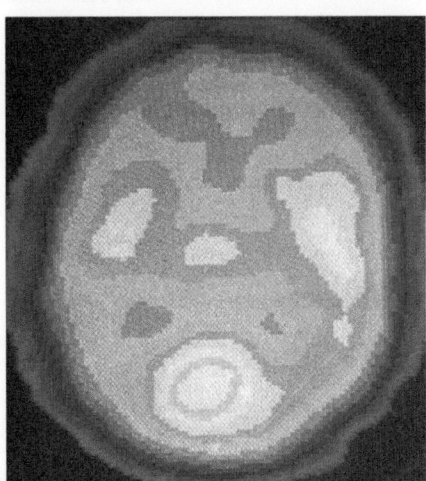

Schizophrenic

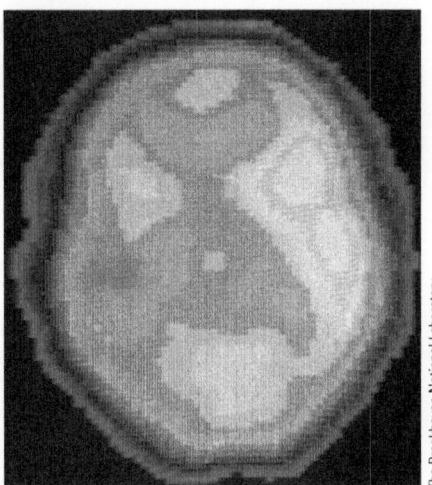

Manic Depressive

Figure 12.8 Positron emission tomography produces PET scans of the human brain. In the scans shown here, red, pink, and orange indicate lower levels of brain activity; white and blue indicate higher activity levels. Notice that activity in the schizophrenic brain is quite low in the frontal lobes (top area of each scan) (Velakoulis & Pantelis, 1996). Activity in the manic-depressive brain is low in the left brain hemisphere and high in the right brain hemisphere. The reverse is more often true of the schizophrenic brain. Researchers are trying to identify consistent patterns like these to aid diagnosis of mental disorders.

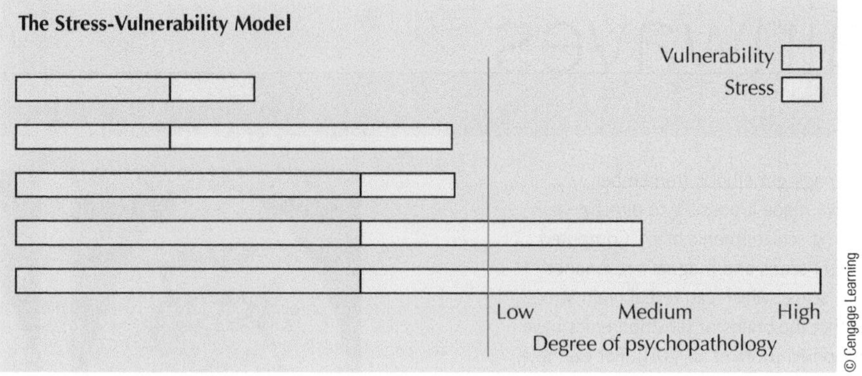

Figure 12.9 Various combinations of vulnerability and stress may produce psychological problems. The top bar shows low vulnerability and low stress. The result? No problem. The same is true of the next bar down, in which low vulnerability is combined with moderate stress. Even high vulnerability (third bar) may not lead to problems if stress levels remain low. However, when high vulnerability combines with moderate or high stress (bottom two bars), the person "crosses the line" and suffers from psychopathology.

The Stress-Vulnerability Model

Vulnerability ☐
Stress ☐

Low   Medium   High
Degree of psychopathology

© Cengage Learning

et al., 2004). This idea has been applied to other forms of psychopathology as well, such as depression (**Figure 12.9**).

Despite advances in our understanding, psychosis remains "a riddle wrapped in a mystery inside an enigma." Let's hope that recent progress toward a cure for schizophrenia will continue.

✋ study break Psychosis, Delusional Disorders, and Schizophrenia

RECITE

1. Angela wrongly believes that her body is "rotting away." She is suffering from
   a. depressive hallucinations   b. a delusion
   c. flat affect   d. Alzheimer's disease

2. Colin, who has suffered a psychotic break, is hearing voices. This symptom is referred to as
   a. flat affect   b. a hallucination
   c. a word salad   d. an organic delusion

3. A psychosis caused by lead poisoning would be regarded as an organic disorder. T or F?

4. Hallucinations and personality disintegration are the principal features of paranoid psychosis. T or F?

5. Environmental explanations of schizophrenia emphasize emotional trauma and
   a. manic parents   b. schizoaffective interactions
   c. psychedelic interactions   d. disturbed family relationships

REFLECT

THINK CRITICALLY

6. Enlarged surface fissures and ventricles are frequently found in the brains of chronic schizophrenics. Why is it a mistake to conclude that such features cause schizophrenia?

RELATE

If you were writing a "recipe" for psychosis, what would the main "ingredients" be?

If you were asked to play the role of a paranoid person for a theater production, what symptoms would you emphasize?

You have been asked to explain the causes of schizophrenia to the parents of a schizophrenic teenager. What would you tell them?

ANSWERS

1. b 2. b 3. T 4. F 5. d 6. Because correlation does not confirm causation. Structural brain abnormalities are merely *correlated* with schizophrenia. They could be additional symptoms, rather than causes, of the disorder.

Mood Disorders—Peaks and Valleys

JOURNEY QUESTION 12.7 *What are mood disorders and what causes them?*

For some people, minor bouts of depression are as common as colds. But extreme swings of mood can be as disabling as a serious physical illness. In fact, depression can be deadly, because depressed persons may be suicidal. It is difficult to imagine how bleak and hopeless the world looks to a person who is deeply depressed, or how "crazy" it can be to ride a wave of mania. Let's explore mood disorders and their causes.

Table 12.4 DSM-IV-TR Classification of Mood Disorders[1]

PROBLEM	PRIMARY SYMPTOM	TYPICAL SIGNS OF TROUBLE
DEPRESSIVE DISORDERS		
Major depressive disorder	Extreme emotional depression for at least 2 weeks	You feel extremely sad, worthless, fatigued, and empty; you are unable to feel pleasure; you are having thoughts of suicide.
Dysthymic disorder[2]	Moderately depressed mood on most days during the last 2 years	You feel down and depressed more days than not; your self-esteem and energy levels have been low for many months.
BIPOLAR DISORDERS		
Bipolar I disorder	Extreme mania and depression	At times you have little need for sleep, can't stop talking, your mind races, and everything you do is of immense importance; at other times you feel extremely sad, worthless, and empty.
Bipolar II disorder	Emotional depression and at least one episode of mild mania	Most of the time you feel extremely sad, worthless, fatigued, and empty; however, at times you feel unusually good, cheerful, energetic, or "high."
Cyclothymic disorder	Periods of moderate depression and moderate mania for at least 2 years	You have been experiencing upsetting emotional ups and downs for many months.

Sources: American Psychiatric Association (2000); Durand & Barlow (2013).

The DSM-5 may revise these categories and their labels in the following ways: *1,* May be split into *Bipolar and related disorders* and *Depressive disorders*; *2,* may be renamed *chronic depressive disorder* (American Psychiatric Association, 2012). The DSM content has been adapted for the particular audience and is intended for educational purposes only.

Nobody loves you when you're down and out—or so it seems. Psychologists have come to realize that **mood disorders** (major disturbances in emotion) are among the most serious of all psychological conditions. In any given year, roughly 9.5 percent of the U.S. population suffers from a mood disorder (National Institute of Mental Health, 2011a).

Two general types of mood disorder are depressive disorders and bipolar disorders (Table 12.4). In **depressive disorders**, sadness and despondency are exaggerated, prolonged, or unreasonable. Signs of a depressive disorder are dejection, hopelessness, and an inability to feel pleasure or to take interest in anything. Other common symptoms are fatigue, disturbed sleep and eating patterns, feelings of worthlessness, a very negative self-image, and thoughts of suicide. In **bipolar disorders**, people go both "up" and "down" emotionally (American Psychiatric Association, 2000; 2012).

Some mood disorders are long lasting but relatively moderate. If a person is mildly depressed for at least 2 years, the problem is called a **dysthymic disorder** (dis-THY-mik). If depression alternates with periods when the person's mood is cheerful, expansive, or irritable, the problem is a **cyclothymic disorder** (SIKE-lo-THY-mik). Even at this level, mood disorders can be debilitating. However, major mood disorders are much more damaging.

Major Mood Disorders

Major mood disorders are characterized by emotional extremes. The person who only goes "down" emotionally suffers from a **major depressive disorder**. During major depressive episodes, everything looks bleak and hopeless. The person has feelings of failure, worthlessness, and total despair. Suffering is intense and the person may become extremely subdued, withdrawn, or intensely suicidal. Suicide attempted during a major depression is rarely a "plea for help." Usually, the person intends to succeed and may give no prior warning.

In a **bipolar I disorder**, people experience both extreme mania and deep depression. During manic episodes, the person is loud, elated, hyperactive, grandiose, and energetic. Manic patients may go bankrupt in a matter of days, get arrested, or go on a binge of promiscuous sex. During periods of depression, the person is deeply despondent and possibly suicidal.

In a **bipolar II disorder** the person is mostly sad and guilt ridden, but has had one or more mildly manic episodes (called *hypomania*). That is, in a bipolar II disorder both elation and depression occur, but the person's mania is not as extreme as in a bipolar I disorder. Bipolar II patients who are hypomanic usually just manage to irritate everyone around them. They are excessively cheerful, aggressive, or irritable, and they may brag, talk too fast, interrupt conversations, or spend too much money (Nolen-Hoeksema, 2011).

Mood disorder Major disturbances in mood or emotion, such as depression or mania.

Depressive disorders Emotional disorders primarily involving sadness, despondency, and depression.

Bipolar disorders Emotional disorders involving both depression and mania or hypomania.

Dysthymic disorder Moderate depression that persists for 2 years or more.

Cyclothymic disorder Moderate manic and depressive behavior that persists for 2 years or more.

Major mood disorders Disorders marked by lasting extremes of mood or emotion and sometimes accompanied by psychotic symptoms.

Major depressive disorder A mood disorder in which the person has suffered one or more intense episodes of depression.

Bipolar I disorder A mood disorder in which a person has episodes of mania (excited, hyperactive, energetic, grandiose behavior) and also periods of deep depression.

Bipolar II disorder A mood disorder in which a person is mostly depressed (sad, despondent, guilt ridden) but has also had one or more episodes of mild mania (hypomania).

In major depressive disorders, suicidal impulses can be intense and despair total.

In serious cases of depression it is impossible for a person to function at work or at school. Sometimes, depressed individuals cannot even feed or dress themselves. In cases of depression and/or mania that are even more severe, the person may also lose touch with reality and display psychotic symptoms.

How do major mood disorders differ from dysthymic and cyclothymic disorders? As mentioned, the major mood disorders involve more severe emotional changes. Also, major mood disorders more often appear to be **endogenous** (en-DODGE-eh-nus: produced from within) rather than a reaction to external events.

What Causes Mood Disorders?

Depression and other mood disorders have resisted adequate explanation and treatment. Some scientists are focusing on the biology of mood changes. They are interested in brain chemicals and transmitter substances, especially serotonin, noradrenaline, and dopamine levels. Their findings are incomplete, but progress has been made. For example, the chemical lithium carbonate can be effective for treating some cases of bipolar depression (Malhi et al., 2012).

Other researchers seek psychological explanations. Psychoanalytic theory, for instance, holds that depression is caused by repressed anger. This rage is displaced and turned inward as self-blame and self-hate. As discussed in Chapter 11, behavioral theories of depression emphasize learned helplessness (LoLordo, 2001; Reivich et al., 2005). Cognitive psychologists believe that self-criticism and negative, distorted, or self-defeating thoughts underlie many cases of depression. (This view is discussed in Chapter 13.) Clearly, life stresses trigger many mood disorders (Calabrese et al., 2009). This is especially true for people who have personality traits and thinking patterns that make them vulnerable to depression (Dozois & Dobson, 2002).

Gender and Depression

Overall, women are 50 percent more likely than men to experience depression (National Institute of Mental Health, 2011a). Hormonal fluctuations likely play a role in cases of depression involving pregnancy, menstruation, and menopause (Lokuge et al., 2011). Nevertheless, researchers believe that social and environmental conditions are the main reason for this difference (Cambron, Acitelli, & Pettit, 2009; Jack & Ali, 2010).

Psychosocial factors that contribute to women's greater risk for depression include conflicts about birth control and pregnancy, work and parenting, and the strain of providing emotional support for others. Marital strife, sexual and physical abuse, and poverty are also factors. Nationwide, women and children are most likely to live in poverty. As a result, poor women frequently suffer the stresses associated with single parenthood, loss of control over their lives, poor housing, and dangerous neighborhoods (Stoppard & McMullen, 2003). One study found that women in the United States were most likely to be depressed if they lacked education, were unmarried, were Latina, had high stress levels, and experienced feelings of hopelessness (Myers et al., 2002).

Biology and Depression

Is heredity involved in the major mood disorders? Yes, especially in bipolar disorders (Curtis et al., 2011; Scharinger et al., 2010). As a case in point, if one identical twin is depressed, the other has a 67 percent chance of suffering depression, too. For fraternal twins the probability is 19 percent. This difference may be related to the finding that people who have a particular version of a gene are more likely to become depressed when they are stressed (Caspi et al., 2003). As we have noted, psychological causes are important in many cases of depression. But for major mood disorders, biological factors seem to play a larger role. Surprisingly, one additional source of depression is related to the seasons.

Endogenous depression Depression that appears to be produced from within (perhaps by chemical imbalances in the brain), rather than as a reaction to life events.

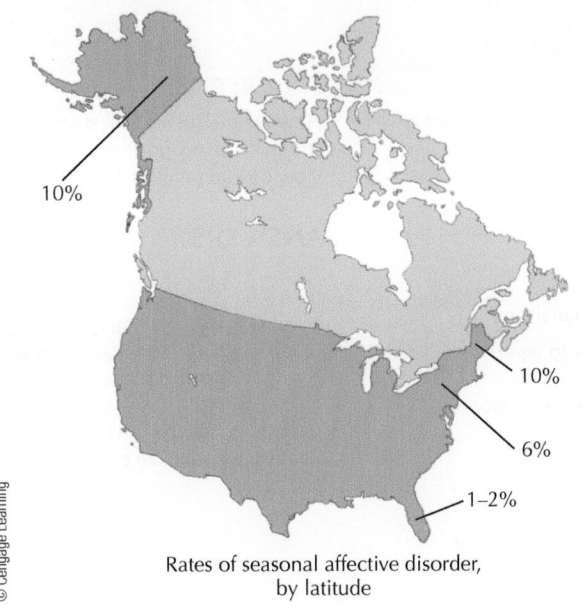

Figure 12.10 Seasonal affective disorder (SAD) appears to be related to reduced exposure to daylight during the winter. SAD affects 1 to 2 percent of Florida's population, about 6 percent of the people living in Maryland and New York City, and nearly 10 percent of the residents of New Hampshire and Alaska (Booker & Hellekson, 1992).

10%

10%

6%

1–2%

Rates of seasonal affective disorder, by latitude

© Cengage Learning

Seasonal Affective Disorder

Unless you have experienced a winter of "cabin fever" in the far north, you may be surprised to learn that the rhythms of the seasons underlie **seasonal affective disorder (SAD)**, or depression that occurs only during the fall and winter months. Almost anyone can get a little depressed when days are short, dark, and cold. But when a person's symptoms are lasting and disabling, the problem may be SAD.

Starting in the fall, people with SAD sleep longer but more poorly. During the day they feel tired and drowsy, and they tend to overeat. With each passing day, they become sadder, anxious, irritable, and socially withdrawn (Westrin & Lam, 2007a). Although their depressions are usually not severe, many victims of SAD face each winter with a sense of foreboding. SAD is especially prevalent in northern latitudes (think of countries like Sweden and Canada), where days are very short during the winter (Kegel et al., 2009; Michalak & Lam, 2002) (Figure 12.10). For instance, one study found that 13 percent of college students living in northern New England showed signs of suffering from SAD (Low & Feissner, 1998). The students most likely to be affected were those who had moved from the South to attend college!

Seasonal depressions are related to the release of more melatonin during the winter. This hormone, which is secreted by the pineal gland in the brain, regulates the body's response to changing light conditions (Wehr et al., 2001). That's why 80 percent of SAD patients can be helped by a remedy called phototherapy (Figure 12.11). **Phototherapy** involves exposing SAD patients to 1 or more hours of very bright fluorescent light each day (Vandewalle et al., 2011; Westrin & Lam, 2007b).

Figure 12.11 An hour or more of bright light a day can dramatically reduce the symptoms of seasonal affective disorder. Treatment is usually necessary from fall through spring. Light therapy is best done early in the morning, when it simulates dawn in the summer (Avery et al., 2001). For many SAD sufferers, a hearty dose of morning "sunshine" appears to be the next best thing to vacationing in the tropics.

Seasonal affective disorder (SAD) Depression that occurs only during fall and winter; presumably related to decreased exposure to sunlight.

Phototherapy A treatment for seasonal affective disorder that involves exposure to bright, full-spectrum light.

Anxiety-Based Disorders—When Anxiety Rules

JOURNEY QUESTION 12.8 *What problems result when a person suffers high levels of anxiety?*

Imagine that you are waiting to take an extremely important test, waiting to give a speech to a large audience, or waiting to find out whether you or a loved one has a serious illness. You've almost certainly felt *anxiety*—feelings of apprehension, dread, or uneasiness—in similar situations.

If anxiety is a normal emotion, when does it signify a problem? Anxiety only becomes a problem when it becomes so intense that it prevents people from doing what they want or need to do. Also, their anxieties are out of control—they simply cannot stop worrying. An example is a college student named Jian, who became unbearably anxious when he took exams. By the time Jian went to see a counselor, he had skipped several tests and was in danger of dropping out of school. In general, people with anxiety-related problems like Jian's display the following characteristics:

- High levels of anxiety and/or restrictive, self-defeating behavior patterns
- A tendency to use elaborate defense mechanisms or avoidance responses to get through the day
- Pervasive feelings of stress, insecurity, inferiority, and dissatisfaction with life

People with anxiety-related problems feel threatened and often can't do anything constructive about it (Cisler & Koster, 2010). They struggle to control themselves but remain ineffective and unhappy (Cisler et al., 2010). In any given year, roughly 18 percent of the adult population suffers from an anxiety disorder (National Institute of Mental Health, 2011a).

Adjustment Disorders

Do such problems cause a "nervous breakdown"? People suffering from anxiety-based problems may be miserable, but they rarely experience a "breakdown." Actually, the term *nervous breakdown* has no formal meaning. Nevertheless, a problem known as an *adjustment disorder* does come close to being something of a "breakdown."

Adjustment disorders occur when ordinary stresses push people beyond their ability to cope with life. Examples of such stresses are a job loss, intense marital strife, and chronic physical illness. People suffering from an adjustment disorder may be extremely irritable, anxious, apathetic, or depressed. They also have trouble sleeping, lose their appetite, and

Adjustment disorder An emotional disturbance caused by ongoing stressors within the range of common experience.

suffer from various physical complaints. Often, their problems can be relieved by rest, sedation, supportive counseling, and a chance to "talk through" their fears and anxieties (American Psychiatric Association, 2000; 2012).

How is an adjustment disorder different from an anxiety disorder? The outward symptoms are similar. However, adjustment disorders disappear when a person's life circumstances improve (Jones, Yates, & Zhou, 2002; Kramer et al., 2010). People suffering from anxiety disorders seem to generate their own misery, regardless of what's happening around them. They feel that they must be on guard against *future* threats that *could happen* at any time (Sue, Sue, et al., 2013).

Anxiety Disorders

In most anxiety disorders, distress seems greatly out of proportion to a person's circumstances. For example, consider the following description of Adrian H:

> She becomes very anxious that her children "might have been hurt or killed if they were out of the neighborhood playing and she hadn't heard from them in a couple of hours." She also worries all the time about her job performance and her relationships with men. Adrian believes that men rarely call back after a date or two because "they can sense I'm not a fun person." She never really relaxes, has difficulty focusing at work, has frequent headaches, and suffers from insomnia. (Adapted from Brown & Barlow, 2011)

Distress like Adrian H's is a key ingredient in anxiety disorders. It also may underlie dissociative and somatoform disorders, where maladaptive behavior serves to reduce anxiety and discomfort. To deepen your understanding, let's first examine the anxiety disorders themselves (Table 12.5). Then we will see how anxiety contributes to other problems.

Generalized Anxiety Disorder

A person with a **generalized anxiety disorder** has been extremely anxious and worried for at least 6 months. Sufferers typically complain of sweating, a racing heart, clammy hands, dizziness, upset stomach, rapid breathing, irritability, and poor concentration. Overall, more women than men have these symptoms (Brown & Barlow, 2011).

Was Adrian H's problem a generalized anxiety disorder? Yes. However, if she also experienced *anxiety attacks,* then she would likely be diagnosed with panic disorder (Batelaan et al., 2010).

Table 12.5 DSM-IV-TR Classification of Anxiety Disorders

TYPE OF DISORDER	TYPICAL SIGNS OF TROUBLE
Generalized anxiety disorder	You have been extremely anxious or worried for 6 months.
Panic disorder (without agoraphobia)[1]	You are anxious much of the time and have sudden panic attacks.
Panic disorder (with agoraphobia)[1]	You have panic attacks and are afraid that they might occur in public places, so you rarely leave home.
Agoraphobia (without a history of panic disorder)	You fear that something extremely embarrassing will happen if you leave home (but you don't have panic attacks).
Specific phobia	You have an intense fear of specific objects, activities, or locations.
Social phobia	You fear social situations in which people can watch, criticize, embarrass, or humiliate you.
Obsessive-compulsive disorder[2]	Your thoughts make you extremely nervous and compel you to rigidly repeat certain actions or routines.
Acute stress disorder	You are tormented for less than a month by the emotional after-effects of horrible events you have experienced.
Post-traumatic stress disorder	You are tormented for more than a month by the emotional after-effects of horrible events you have experienced.

Sources: American Psychiatric Association (2000); Durand & Barlow (2013).

The DSM-5 may revise these categories and their labels in the following ways: *1, Panic disorder with* and *without agoraphobia* may be combined. *2,* A new category, *obsessive-compulsive and related disorders,* may be created (American Psychiatric Association, 2012). The DSM content has been adapted for the particular audience and is intended for educational purposes only.

Generalized anxiety disorder A chronic state of tension and worry about work, relationships, ability, or impending disaster.

Shown here watching a basketball game, war hero Senator John McCain is no fan of the number 13. Apparently he always carries 31 cents with him (the opposite of 13). Once, when a campaign office was located on the 13th floor of a building, the floor was quickly renamed the "Mth floor" (Wargo, 2008).

Panic Disorder

In a **panic disorder (without agoraphobia)**, people are highly anxious and also feel sudden, intense, unexpected panic. During a panic attack, victims experience chest pain, a racing heart, dizziness, choking, feelings of unreality, trembling, or fears of losing control. Many believe that they are having a heart attack, are going insane, or are about to die. Needless to say, this pattern leaves victims unhappy and uncomfortable much of the time. Again, the majority of people who suffer from panic disorder are women (Foot & Koszycki, 2004).

To get an idea of how a panic attack feels, imagine that you are trapped in your stateroom on a sinking ocean liner (the Titanic?). The room fills with water. When only a small air space remains near the ceiling and you are gasping for air, you'll know what a panic attack feels like.

In a **panic disorder (with agoraphobia)**, people suffer from chronic anxiety and sudden panic. In addition, they have agoraphobia (ah-go-rah-FOBE-ee-ah), which is an intense *fear that a panic attack will occur* in a public place or unfamiliar situation. That is, agoraphobics intensely fear leaving their home and familiar surroundings. Typically, they find ways of avoiding places that frighten them—such as crowds, open roads, supermarkets, automobiles, and so on. As a result, some agoraphobics are prisoners in their own homes (American Psychiatric Association, 2000; 2012).

Agoraphobia

The problem known as **agoraphobia** can also occur without panic. In this case, people *fear that something extremely embarrassing will happen* if they leave home or enter an unfamiliar situation. For example, an agoraphobic person may refuse to go outside because he or she fears having a sudden attack of dizziness, diarrhea, or shortness of breath. Going outside the home alone, being in a crowd, standing in line, crossing a bridge, or riding in a car can be impossible for an agoraphobic person (American Psychiatric Association, 2000; 2012). About 4.2 percent of all adults suffer from agoraphobia (with or without panic) during their lifetime (Grant et al., 2006).

Specific Phobia

As we noted earlier, phobias are intense, irrational fears that a person cannot shake off, even when there is no real danger. In a **specific phobia**, the person's fear, anxiety, and avoidance are focused on particular objects, activities, or situations. People affected by phobias recognize that their fears are unreasonable, but they cannot control them. For example, a person with a spider phobia would find it impossible to ignore a picture of a spider, even though a photograph can't bite anyone (Lipka, Miltner, & Straube, 2011). Specific phobias can be linked to nearly any object or situation (Stinson et al., 2007). In descending order of prevalence, the most common specific phobias among Americans are:

Fear of insects, birds, snakes, or other animals (including, of course, arachnophobia, the fear of spiders, and zoophobia, fear of animals)

Acrophobia—fear of heights

Astraphobia—fear of storms, thunder, lightning

Aquaphobia—fear of being on or in water

Aviophobia—fear of airplanes

Claustrophobia—fear of closed spaces

Agoraphobia—fear of crowds

By combining the appropriate root word with the word "phobia," any number of fears can be named. Some are: triskaidekaphobia, fear of the number 13; xenophobia, fear of strangers; and hematophobia, fear of blood. One of your authors' favorites is coulrophobia, fear of clowns. Another is arachibutyrophobia, fear of peanut butter sticking to the roof of the mouth.

Panic disorder (without agoraphobia) A chronic state of anxiety and also brief moments of sudden, intense, unexpected panic.

Panic disorder (with agoraphobia) A chronic state of anxiety and brief moments of sudden panic. The person fears that these panic attacks will occur in public places or unfamiliar situations.

Agoraphobia (without panic) The fear that something extremely embarrassing will happen if one leaves the house or enters unfamiliar situations.

Specific phobia An intense, irrational fear of specific objects, activities, or situations.

Almost everyone has a few mild phobias, such as fear of heights, closed spaces, or bugs and crawly things. True phobias may lead to overwhelming fear, vomiting, wild climbing and running, or fainting. For a phobic disorder to exist, the person's fear must disrupt his or her daily life. Phobic persons are so threatened that they will go to almost any length to avoid the feared object or situation, such as driving 50 miles out of the way to avoid crossing a bridge. About 8.7 percent of all adults have a specific phobic disorder in any given year (National Institute of Mental Health, 2011a).

Hoarders are obsessive about collecting things, which they also have great difficulty discarding (Hayward & Coles, 2009).

Social Phobia

In **social phobia**, people fear situations in which they can be observed, evaluated, embarrassed, or humiliated by others. This leads them to avoid certain social situations, such as eating, writing, using the rest room, or speaking in public. When such situations cannot be avoided, people endure them with intense anxiety or distress. It is common for them to have uncomfortable physical symptoms, such as a pounding heart, shaking hands, sweating, diarrhea, mental confusion, and blushing. Social phobias greatly impair a person's ability to work, attend school, and form personal relationships (American Psychiatric Association, 2000). About 6.8 percent of all adults are affected by social phobias in a given year (National Institute of Mental Health, 2011a).

Obsessive-Compulsive Disorder

People who suffer from **obsessive-compulsive disorder** are preoccupied with certain distressing thoughts and feel compelled to perform certain behaviors. You have probably experienced a mild obsessional thought, such as a song or stupid commercial jingle that repeats over and over in your mind. This may be irritating, but it's usually not terribly disturbing. True obsessions are images or thoughts that force their way into awareness against a person's will. They are so disturbing that they cause intense anxiety. The most common obsessions are about violence or harm (such as one's spouse being poisoned or hit by a car), about being "dirty" or "unclean," about whether one has performed some action (such as locking the door), and about committing immoral acts (Grabill et al., 2008).

Obsessions usually give rise to compulsions. These are irrational acts that a person feels driven to repeat. Often, compulsive acts help control or block out anxiety caused by an obsession. For example, a minister who finds profanities popping into her mind might start compulsively counting her heartbeat. Doing this would prevent her from thinking "dirty" words.

Some compulsive people become *hoarders*, excessively collecting various things (Hayward & Coles, 2009). Other compulsive people are *checkers* or *cleaners*. For instance, a young mother who repeatedly pictures a knife plunging into her baby might check once an hour to make sure all the knives in her house are locked away. Doing so may reduce her anxieties, but it will probably also take over her life. Likewise, a person who feels "contaminated" from touching ordinary objects because "germs are everywhere" may be driven to wash his hands hundreds of times a day.

Of course, not all obsessive-compulsive disorders are so dramatic. Many simply involve extreme orderliness and rigid routine. Compulsive attention to detail and rigid following of rules help keep activities totally under control and make the highly anxious person feel more secure (Challacombe, Oldfield, & Salkovskis, 2011). (If such patterns are long-standing but less intense, they are classified as personality disorders, which we will discuss later in more detail.)

Stress Disorders

If a situation causes distress, anxiety, or fear, we tend to "put it behind us" and avoid it in the future. This is a normal survival instinct. **Stress disorders** occur when people experience unavoidable stresses outside the range of normal human experience, such as floods, tornadoes, earthquakes, or horrible accidents. They affect many political hostages; combat veterans; prisoners of war; victims of terrorism, torture, violent crime, child molestation, rape, or domestic violence; and people who have witnessed a death or serious injury (Hughes et al., 2011; Polusny et al., 2011).

Social phobia An intense, irrational fear of being observed, evaluated, embarrassed, or humiliated by others in social situations.

Obsessive-compulsive disorder An extreme preoccupation with certain thoughts and compulsive performance of certain behaviors.

Stress disorder A significant emotional disturbance caused by stresses outside the range of normal human experience.

The annual U.S. tornado season kills many people and upsets the lives of many more. In the aftermath of such disasters, many survivors suffer from acute stress reactions. For some, the flare-up of anxiety and distress occurs months or years after the stressful event, an example of a post-traumatic stress reaction.

Symptoms of stress disorders include repeated reliving of the traumatic event, avoidance of reminders of the event, and blunted emotions. Also common are insomnia, nightmares, wariness, poor concentration, irritability, and explosive anger or aggression. If such reactions last *less* than a month after a traumatic event, the problem is called an **acute stress disorder**. If they last *more* than a month, the person is suffering from **post-traumatic stress disorder (PTSD)** (Nemeroff et al., 2006; Sue, Sue, et al., 2013).

About 3.5 percent of American adults suffer from post-traumatic stress in any given year (National Institute of Mental Health, 2011a). And yet 10 to 20 percent of military veterans returning from combat develop PTSD (Salisbury & Burker, 2011). The constant threat of death and the gruesome sights and sounds of war take a terrible toll. Psychologists are already seeing high rates of PTSD among soldiers involved in combat in Iraq and Afghanistan (Hoge et al., 2004; Marx, 2009). Sadly, 8 percent of military veterans still suffer from PTSD decades after they were in combat (Dirkzwager, Bramsen, & Van Der Ploeg, 2001).

Dissociative Disorders

In dissociative reactions, we see striking episodes of *amnesia, fugue,* or *multiple identity.* **Dissociative amnesia** is an inability to recall one's name, address, or past. **Dissociative fugue** (fewg) involves sudden, unplanned travel away from home and confusion about personal identity. In such cases, forgetting personal identity and fleeing unpleasant situations appear to be defenses against intolerable anxiety. A person suffering from a **dissociative identity disorder** has two or more separate identities or personality states. (Don't forget that identity disorders are not the same as schizophrenia. Schizophrenia, which is a psychotic disorder, was discussed earlier in this chapter.)

One famous and dramatic example of multiple identities is described in the book *Sybil* (Schreiber, 1973). Sybil reportedly had 16 different personality states. Each identity had a distinct voice, vocabulary, and posture. One personality could play the piano (not Sybil), but the others could not. When an identity other than Sybil was in control, Sybil experienced a "time lapse," or memory blackout. Sybil's amnesia and alternate identities first appeared during childhood. As a girl she was beaten, locked in closets, perversely tortured, sexually abused, and almost killed. Sybil's first dissociations allowed her to escape by creating another person who would suffer torture in her place. Identity disorders often begin with unbearable childhood experiences, like those that Sybil endured. A history of childhood trauma, especially sexual abuse, is found in a high percentage of persons whose personalities split into multiple identities (McLewin & Muller, 2006; Simeon et al., 2002).

Flamboyant cases like Sybil's have led some experts to question the existence of multiple personalities (Casey, 2001; Piper, 2008). However, a majority of psychologists continue to believe that multiple identity is a real, if rare, problem (Boysen, 2011; Dell, 2009).

Therapy for dissociative identity disorders may make use of hypnosis, which allows contact with the various personality states. The goal of therapy is *integration* and *fusion* of the identities into a single, balanced personality. Fortunately, multiple identity disorders are far rarer in real life than they are in TV dramas!

Somatoform Disorders

Have you ever known someone who appeared to be healthy but seemed to constantly worry about disease? These people are preoccupied with bodily functions, such as their heartbeat or breathing or digestion. Minor physical problems—even a small sore or an occasional cough—may convince them that they have cancer or some other dreaded disease. Typically, they can't give up their fears of illness, even if doctors can find no medical basis for their complaints (Dimsdale, 2011; Korol, Craig, & Firestone, 2003).

Are you describing hypochondria? Yes. In **hypochondriasis** (HI-po-kon-DRY-uh-sis), people interpret normal bodily sensations as proof that they have a terrible disease. In a

Acute stress disorder A psychological disturbance lasting up to 1 month following stresses that would produce anxiety in anyone who experienced them.

Post-traumatic stress disorder (PTSD) A psychological disturbance lasting more than 1 month following stresses that would produce anxiety in anyone who experienced them.

Dissociative amnesia Loss of memory (partial or complete) for important information related to personal identity.

Dissociative fugue Sudden travel away from home, plus confusion about one's personal identity.

Dissociative identity disorder The presence of two or more distinct personalities (multiple personality).

Hypochondriasis A preoccupation with fears of having a serious disease. Ordinary physical signs are interpreted as proof that the person has a disease, but no physical disorder can be found.

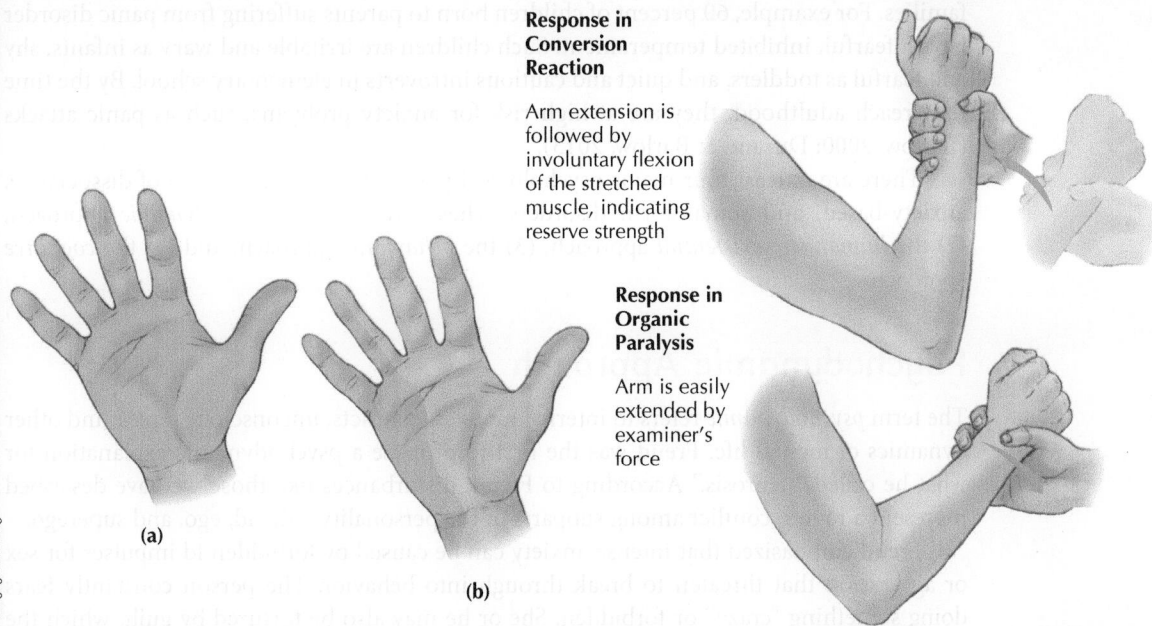

Response in Conversion Reaction

Arm extension is followed by involuntary flexion of the stretched muscle, indicating reserve strength

Response in Organic Paralysis

Arm is easily extended by examiner's force

(a)

(b)

Figure 12.12 *(left)* "Glove" anesthesia is a conversion reaction involving loss of feeling in areas of the hand that would be covered by a glove *(a)*. If the anesthesia were physically caused, it would follow the pattern shown in *(b)*. *(right)* To test for organic paralysis of the arm, an examiner can suddenly extend the arm, stretching the muscles. A conversion reaction is indicated if the arm pulls back involuntarily.

problem called **somatization disorder** (som-ah-tuh-ZAY-shun), people express their anxieties through various bodily complaints. That is, they suffer from problems such as vomiting or nausea, shortness of breath, difficulty swallowing, or painful menstrual periods. Typically, the person feels ill much of the time and visits doctors repeatedly. Most sufferers take medicines or other treatments, but no physical cause can be found for their distress. Similarly, a person with **pain disorder** is disabled by pain that has no identifiable physical basis.

A rarer somatoform disorder ("body-form" disorder) is called a *conversion reaction*. In a **conversion disorder**, severe emotional conflicts are "converted" into symptoms that actually disturb physical functioning or closely resemble a physical disability. For instance, a soldier might become deaf or lame or develop "glove anesthesia" just before a battle.

What is "glove anesthesia"? Glove anesthesia is a loss of sensitivity in the areas of the skin that would normally be covered by a glove. Glove anesthesia shows that conversion symptoms often contradict known medical facts. The system of nerves in the hands does not form a glove-like pattern and could not cause such symptoms (**Figure 12.12**).

If symptoms disappear when a victim is asleep, hypnotized, or anesthetized, a conversion reaction must be suspected (Russo et al., 1998). Another sign to watch for is that victims of conversion reactions are strangely unconcerned about suddenly being disabled.

Anxiety and Disorder—Four Pathways to Trouble

JOURNEY QUESTION 12.9 *How do psychologists explain anxiety-based disorders?*

What causes anxiety disorders? Anxiety disorders may also be best explained by the stress-vulnerability model. Susceptibility to anxiety-based disorders appears to be partly inherited (Rachman, 2004). Studies show that being high strung, nervous, or emotional runs in

Uncontrollable sneezing, which may continue for days or weeks, is often a conversion disorder. In such cases, sneezing is atypical in rate and rhythm. In addition, the person's eyes do not close during a sneeze and sneezing does not occur during sleep. (A normal sneeze is shown here.) All these signs suggest that the cause of the sneezing is psychological, not physical (Fochtmann, 1995).

Somatization disorder Afflicted persons have numerous physical complaints. Typically, they have consulted many doctors, but no organic cause for their distress can be identified.

Pain disorder Pain that has no identifiable physical cause and appears to be of psychological origin.

Conversion disorder A bodily symptom that mimics a physical disability but is actually caused by anxiety or emotional distress.

families. For example, 60 percent of children born to parents suffering from panic disorder have a fearful, inhibited temperament. Such children are irritable and wary as infants, shy and fearful as toddlers, and quiet and cautious introverts in elementary school. By the time they reach adulthood, they are at high risk for anxiety problems, such as panic attacks (Barlow, 2000; Durand & Barlow, 2013).

There are at least four major psychological perspectives on the causes of dissociative, anxiety-based, and somatoform disorders. These are (1) the *psychodynamic* approach, (2) the *humanistic-existential* approach, (3) the *behavioral* approach, and (4) the *cognitive* approach.

Psychodynamic Approach

The term *psychodynamic* refers to internal motives, conflicts, unconscious forces, and other dynamics of mental life. Freud was the first to propose a psychodynamic explanation for what he called "neurosis." According to Freud, disturbances like those we have described represent a raging conflict among subparts of the personality—the id, ego, and superego.

Freud emphasized that intense anxiety can be caused by forbidden id impulses for sex or aggression that threaten to break through into behavior. The person constantly fears doing something "crazy" or forbidden. She or he may also be tortured by guilt, which the superego uses to suppress forbidden impulses. Caught in the middle, the ego is eventually overwhelmed. This forces the person to use rigid defense mechanisms and misguided, inflexible behavior to prevent a disastrous loss of control (see Chapter 10).

Humanistic-Existential Approaches

Humanistic theories emphasize subjective experience, human problems, and personal potentials. Humanistic psychologist Carl Rogers regarded emotional disorders as the end product of a faulty self-image or self-concept (Rogers, 1959). Rogers believed that anxious individuals have built up unrealistic mental images of themselves. This leaves them vulnerable to contradictory information. Let's say, for example, that an essential part of Cheyenne's self-image is the idea that she is highly intelligent. If Cheyenne does poorly in school, she may begin to deny or distort her perceptions of herself and the situation. Should Cheyenne's anxiety become severe, she may resort to using defense mechanisms. A conversion reaction, anxiety attacks, or similar symptoms may also result from threats to her self-image. These symptoms, in turn, might become new threats that provoke further distortions. Soon, she could fall into a vicious cycle of maladjustment and anxiety that feeds on itself once started.

Existentialism focuses on the elemental problems of existence, such as death, meaning, choice, and responsibility. Psychologists who take a more existential view stress that unhealthy anxiety reflects a loss of *meaning* in one's life. According to them, we must show *courage* and *responsibility* in our choices if life is to have meaning. Too often, they say, we give in to "existential anxiety" and back away from life-enhancing choices. Existential anxiety is the unavoidable anguish that comes from knowing we are personally responsible for our lives. Hence, we have a crushing need to choose wisely and courageously as we face life's empty and impersonal void. Adolescents may experience considerable existential anxiety as they develop their identity (Berman, Weems, & Stickle, 2006).

From the existential view, people who are anxious are living in "bad faith"; that is, they have collapsed in the face of the awesome responsibility to choose a meaningful existence. In short, they have lost their way in life. From this point of view, making choices that don't truly reflect what you value, feel, and believe can make you sick.

Behaviorist Approaches

Behaviorist approaches emphasize overt, observable behavior and the effects of learning and conditioning. Behaviorists assume that the "symptoms" we have discussed are learned, just as other behaviors are. You might recall from Chapter 6, for instance, that phobias can be acquired through classical conditioning. Similarly, anxiety attacks may reflect conditioned emotional responses that generalize to new situations, and the hypochondriac's "sickness behavior" may be reinforced by the sympathy and attention he or she gets. One point that all theorists agree on is that disordered behavior is ultimately self-defeating because it makes the person more miserable in the long run, even though it temporarily lowers anxiety.

But if the person becomes more miserable in the long run, how does the pattern get started? The behavioral explanation is that self-defeating behavior begins with avoidance learning (described in Chapter 6). Avoidance learning occurs when making a response delays or prevents the onset of a painful or unpleasant stimulus. Here's a quick review to refresh your memory:

> An animal is placed in a special cage. After a few minutes a light comes on, followed a moment later by a painful shock. Quickly, the animal escapes into a second chamber. After a few minutes, a light comes on in this chamber, and the shock is repeated. Soon the animal learns to avoid pain by moving before the shock occurs. Once an animal learns to avoid the shock, it can be turned off altogether. A well-trained animal may avoid the nonexistent shock indefinitely.

The same analysis can be applied to human behavior. A behaviorist would say that the powerful reward of immediate relief from anxiety keeps self-defeating avoidance behaviors alive. This view, known as the **anxiety reduction hypothesis**, seems to explain why the behavior patterns we have discussed often look very "stupid" to outside observers.

Cognitive Approach

The cognitive view is that distorted thinking causes people to magnify ordinary threats and failures, which leads to distress (Provencher, Dugas, & Ladouceur, 2004). For example, Bonnie, who is socially phobic, constantly has upsetting thoughts about being evaluated at school. One reason for this is that people with social phobias tend to be perfectionists. Like other social phobics, Bonnie is excessively concerned about making mistakes. She also perceives criticism when none exists. If Bonnie expects that a social situation will focus too much attention on her, she avoids it (Brown & Barlow, 2011). Even when socially phobic persons are successful, distorted thoughts lead them to believe they have failed (Barlow, 2002). In short, changing the thinking patterns of anxious individuals like Bonnie can greatly lessen their fears (Hall, 2006).

Implications

All four psychological explanations probably contain a core of truth. For this reason, understanding anxiety-based disorders may be aided by combining parts of each perspective. Each viewpoint also suggests a different approach to treatment. Because many possibilities exist, therapy is discussed later, in Chapter 13.

Personality Disorders—Blueprints for Maladjustment

JOURNEY QUESTION 12.10 *What is a personality disorder?*

"Get out of here and leave me alone so I can die in peace," Judy screamed at her nurses in the seclusion room of the psychiatric hospital. On one of her arms, long dark-red marks mingled with the scars of previous suicide attempts. Judy once bragged that her record was 67 stitches. Today, the nurses had to strap her into restraints to keep her from gouging her own eyes. She was given a sedative and slept for 12 hours. She woke calmly and asked for her therapist—even though her latest outburst began when he canceled a morning appointment and changed it to afternoon.

Anxiety reduction hypothesis Explains the self-defeating nature of avoidance responses as a result of the reinforcing effects of relief from anxiety.

Judy has a condition called *borderline personality disorder*. Although she is capable of working, Judy has repeatedly lost jobs because of her turbulent relationships with other people. At times she can be friendly and a real charmer. At other times she is extremely unpredictable, moody, and even suicidal. Being a friend to Judy can be a fearsome challenge. Canceling an appointment, forgetting a special date, uttering a wrong turn of phrase—these and similar small incidents may trigger Judy's rage or a suicide attempt. Like other people with borderline personality disorder, Judy is extremely sensitive to ordinary criticism, which leaves her feeling rejected and abandoned. Typically, she reacts with anger, self-hatred, and impulsive behavior. These "emotional storms" damage her personal relationships and leave her confused about who she is (Siever & Koenigsberg, 2000).

Maladaptive Personality Patterns

As stated earlier, a person with a personality disorder has maladaptive personality traits. For example, people with a paranoid personality disorder are suspicious, hypersensitive, and wary of others. Narcissistic persons need constant admiration, and they are lost in fantasies of power, wealth, brilliance, beauty, or love. Celebrities appear more likely to be narcissistic than noncelebrities, perhaps because they receive so much attention (Young & Pinsky, 2006). The dependent personality suffers from extremely low self-confidence. Dependent persons allow others to run their lives, and they place everyone else's needs ahead of their own. People with a histrionic personality disorder constantly seek attention by dramatizing their emotions and actions.

Typically, patterns such as the ones just described begin during adolescence or even childhood. Thus, personality disorders are deeply rooted and usually span many years. The list of personality disorders is long (Table 12.6), so let us focus on the antisocial personality.

Table 12.6 DSM-IV-TR Classification of Personality Disorders[1]

MODERATE IMPAIRMENT

Dependent	You lack confidence, and you are extremely submissive and dependent on others (clinging).
Histrionic	You are dramatic and flamboyant; you exaggerate your emotions to get attention from others.
Narcissistic	You think you are wonderful, brilliant, important, and worthy of constant admiration.
Antisocial	You are irresponsible, lack guilt or remorse, and engage in antisocial behavior, such as aggression, deceit, or recklessness.

HIGH IMPAIRMENT

Obsessive-compulsive	You demand order, perfection, control, and rigid routine at all times.
Schizoid	You feel very little emotion and can't form close personal relationships with others.
Avoidant	You are timid, uncomfortable in social situations, and fear evaluation.

SEVERE IMPAIRMENT

Borderline	Your self-image, moods, and impulses are erratic, and you are extremely sensitive to any hint of criticism, rejection, or abandonment by others.
Paranoid	You deeply distrust others and are suspicious of their motives, which you perceive as insulting or threatening.
Schizotypal	You are a loner, you engage in extremely odd behavior, and your thought patterns are bizarre, but you are not actively psychotic.

Sources: American Psychiatric Association (2000); Durand & Barlow (2013).

The DSM-5 may revise these categories and their labels in the following ways: *1*, All of the personality disorders will be reformulated in the upcoming DSM-5 (American Psychiatric Association, 2012). The DSM content has been adapted for the particular audience and is intended for educational purposes only.

Antisocial Personality

What are the characteristics of an antisocial personality? A person with an **antisocial personality (antisocial/psychopathic personality)** lacks a conscience. Such people are impulsive, selfish, dishonest, emotionally shallow, and manipulative (Visser et al., 2010). Antisocial persons, who are sometimes called *sociopaths* or *psychopaths,* are poorly socialized and seem to be incapable of feeling guilt, shame, fear, loyalty, or love (American Psychiatric Association, 2000).

Are sociopaths dangerous? Sociopaths tend to have a long history of conflict with society. Many are delinquents or criminals who may be a threat to the general public (Ogloff, 2006). However, sociopaths are rarely the crazed murderers you may have seen portrayed in the media. In fact, many sociopaths are "charming" at first. Their "friends" only gradually become aware of the sociopath's lying and self-serving manipulation. One study found that psychopaths are "blind" to signs of disgust in others. This may add to their capacity for cruelty and their ability to use others (Kosson et al., 2002). Many successful businesspersons, entertainers, politicians, and other seemingly normal people have sociopathic leanings. Basically, antisocial persons coldly use others and cheat their way through life (Ogloff, 2006).

Causes

What causes sociopathy? Typically, people with antisocial personalities showed similar problems in childhood (Burt et al., 2007). Adult sociopaths also display subtle neurological problems (Figure 12.13). For example, they have unusual brain-wave patterns that suggest underarousal of the brain. This may explain why sociopaths tend to be thrill seekers. Quite likely, they are searching for stimulation strong enough to overcome their chronic underarousal and feelings of "boredom" (Hare, 2006).

In a revealing study, sociopaths were shown extremely grisly and unpleasant photographs of mutilations. The photos were so upsetting that they visibly startled normal people. The sociopaths, however, showed no startle response to the photos (Levenston et al., 2000). (They didn't "bat an eyelash.") Those with antisocial personalities might therefore be described as *emotionally cold.* They simply do not feel normal pangs of conscience, guilt, or anxiety (Blair et al., 2006). Again, this coldness seems to account for an unusual ability to calmly lie, cheat, steal, or take advantage of others.

Many prison inmates have been diagnosed with antisocial personality disorder (Bateman & Fonagy, 2012).

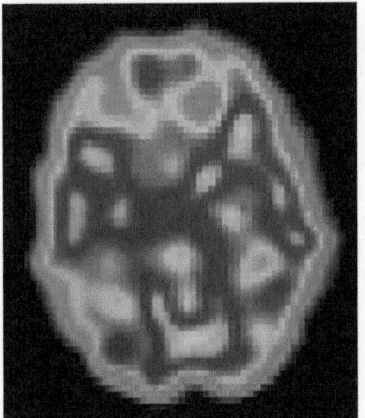 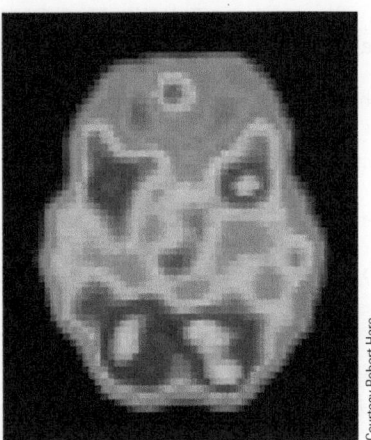

Figure 12.13 Using PET scans, Canadian psychologist Robert Hare found that the normally functioning brain *(left)* lights up with activity when a person sees emotion-laden words such as "maggot" or "cancer." But the brain of a psychopath *(right)* remains inactive, especially in areas associated with feelings and self-control. When Dr. Hare showed the right image to several neurologists, one asked, "Is this person from Mars?"

Antisocial personality (antisocial/psychopathic personality) A person who lacks a conscience; is emotionally shallow, impulsive, and selfish; and tends to manipulate others.

Can sociopathy be treated? Antisocial personality disorders are rarely treated with success (Bateman & Fonagy, 2012). All too often, sociopaths manipulate therapy, just like any other situation. If it is to their advantage to act "cured," they will do so. However, they return to their former behavior patterns as soon as possible. On a more positive note, antisocial behavior does tend to decline somewhat after age 40, even without treatment, because people tend to become more "mellow" as they age (Laub & Sampson, 2003).

A Look Ahead

Treatments for psychological problems range from counseling and psychotherapy to mental hospitalization and drug therapy. Because they vary greatly, a complete discussion of therapies is found in the next chapter. For now, it's worth noting that many milder mental disorders can be treated successfully. Even major disorders may respond well to drugs and other techniques. It is wrong to fear "former mental patients" or to exclude them from work, friendships, and other social situations. A struggle with major depression or a psychotic episode does not inevitably lead to lifelong dysfunction. Too often, however, it does lead to unnecessary rejection based on groundless fears (Elkington et al., 2012; Sarason & Sarason, 2005).

Let's conclude with a look at a widely misunderstood problem: By the time you finish reading this page, someone in the United States will have attempted suicide. What can be done about suicide? The upcoming Psychology in Action section provides some answers.

---

study break Anxiety-Based Disorders and Personality Disorders

RECITE

1. Excessive anxiety over ordinary life stresses is characteristic of which of the following disorders?

    a. PTSD
    b. agoraphobia
    c. hypochondriasis
    d. adjustment disorder

2. Panic disorder can occur with or without agoraphobia, but agoraphobia cannot occur alone, without the presence of a panic disorder. T or F?

3. "Hoarders," "checkers," and "cleaners" suffer from which disorder?

    a. acarophobia
    b. panic disorder with agoraphobia
    c. generalized anxiety disorder
    d. obsessive-compulsive disorder

4. Which of the following is NOT a dissociative disorder?

    a. fugue
    b. amnesia
    c. conversion reaction
    d. multiple identity

5. Which of the following personality disorders is associated with an inflated sense of self-importance and a constant need for attention and admiration?

    a. narcissistic
    b. antisocial
    c. paranoid
    d. manipulative

6. Antisocial personality disorders are difficult to treat, but there is typically a decline in antisocial behavior a year or two after adolescence. T or F?

REFLECT

THINK CRITICALLY

7. Many of the physical complaints associated with anxiety disorders are closely related to activity of what part of the nervous system?

SELF-REFLECT

Which of the anxiety disorders would you *least* want to suffer from? Why?

What minor obsessions or compulsions have you experienced? Many of the qualities that define personality disorders exist to a minor degree in normal personalities. Try to think of a person you know who has some of the characteristics described for each type of personality disorder.

ANSWERS

1. d 2. F 3. d 4. c 5. a 6. F 7. The autonomic nervous system (ANS), especially the sympathetic branch of the ANS.

Psychology in Action

JOURNEY QUESTION 12.11 *Why do people commit suicide and can they be stopped?*

Talk show host Phil Donahue once commented that "suicide is a permanent solution to a temporary problem." If this is so obvious, then why is suicide so distressingly common? In North America, for every three people who die by homicide, five will kill themselves. And there may be as many as 11 attempts for every "successful" suicide (National Institute of Mental Health, 2010c). Sooner or later you are likely to be affected by the suicide attempt of someone you know.

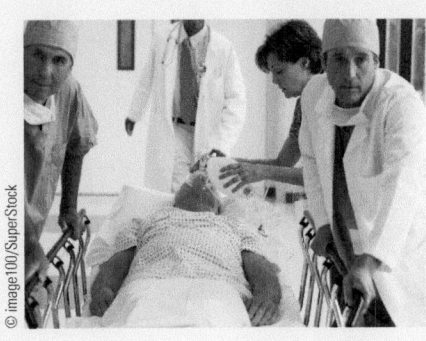

What factors affect suicide rates? Suicide rates vary greatly, but some general patterns do emerge.

Sex   Men are "better" at suicide than women. Four times as many men *complete* suicide, but women make more attempts (Denney et al., 2009; National Institute of Mental Health, 2010c). Male suicide attempts are more lethal because men typically use a gun or an equally fatal method. Women most often attempt a drug overdose, so there's a better chance of help arriving before death occurs. Sadly, women are beginning to use more deadly methods and may soon equal men in their likelihood of death by suicide.

Ethnicity   Suicide rates vary dramatically from country to country. The rate in the United States is almost ten times higher than the rate in Azerbaijan, and, in turn, the rate in Hungary is more than three times the U.S. rate (Lester & Yang, 2005). Within the United States, Caucasians generally have higher suicide rates than non-Caucasians (**Figure 12.14**), although rates have increased among African Americans in recent years (Griffin-Fennell & Williams, 2006; National Institute of Mental Health, 2010c). Sadly, the suicide rate among Native Americans is by far the highest in the country (suicide rates are also elevated among the aboriginal peoples of other countries) (Goldston et al., 2008; Sveticic, Milner, & De Leo, 2012).

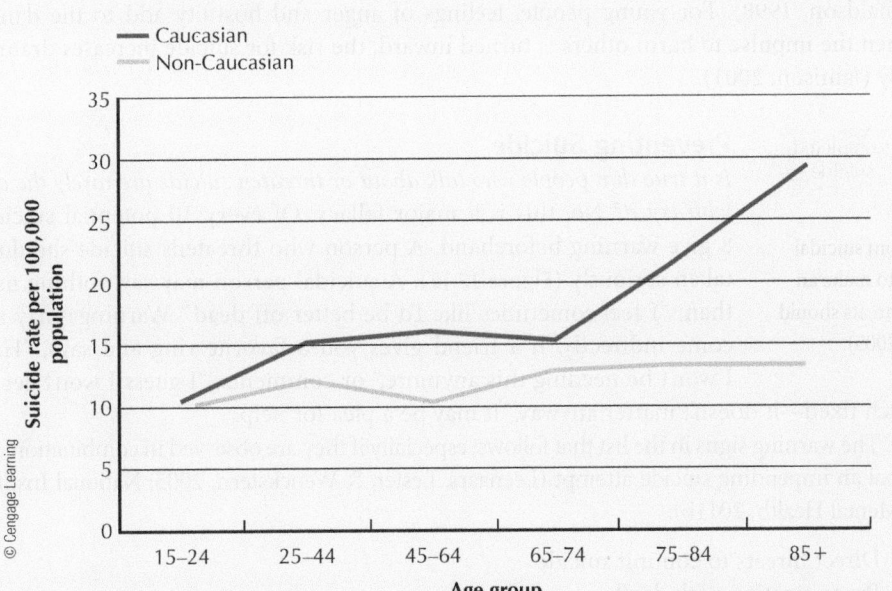

Figure 12.14 In the United States, in general, suicide rates for Caucasians are higher than those for non-Caucasians. Also, older people have higher suicide rates than younger people (Centers for Disease Control, 2003; National Institute of Mental Health, 2010c).

Age   Suicide rates increase with advancing age. More than half of all suicide victims are over 45 years old (see Figure 12.14). White males 65 years and older are particularly at risk. Of special concern is the rate of suicide among younger people. Between 1950 and 1990, suicide rates for adolescents and young adults doubled (Durand & Barlow, 2013). In fact, suicide is the third leading cause of death among 15- to 24-year-olds (National Institute of Mental Health, 2010c). School is a factor in some suicides, but only in the sense that suicidal students were not living up to their own extremely high standards. Many were good students. Other important factors in student suicide are cocaine or alcohol use (Garlow, Purselle, & Heninger, 2007), chronic health problems (real or imagined), and interpersonal difficulties (some who commit suicide are rejected lovers, but others are simply withdrawn and friendless people).

Marital Status   Marital status is also related to suicide rates. Married individuals have lower rates than divorced, widowed, or single persons (Yip & Thorburn, 2004), at least among men (Denney et al., 2009).

Immediate Causes of Suicide

Why do people try to kill themselves? The best explanation for suicide may simply come from a look at the conditions that precede it. A diagnosable mental disorder (usually depression or substance abuse disorder) is a factor in 90 percent of all suicides (National Institute of Mental Health, 2011a). Suicidal people usually have a history of trouble with family, a lover, or a spouse. Often they have drinking or drug abuse problems, sexual adjustment problems, or job difficulties.

The following are all major risk factors for suicide (National Institute of Mental Health, 2010c, 2011b; Rudd, Joiner, & Rajab, 2001): drug or alcohol abuse; a prior suicide attempt; depression or other mood disorder; feelings of hopelessness or worthlessness; antisocial, impulsive, or aggressive behavior; severe anxiety; panic attacks; a family history of suicidal behavior; shame, humiliation, failure, or rejection; and the availability of a firearm. Among ethnic adolescents, loss of face, acculturative stress, racism, and discrimination have been identified as additional risk factors (Goldston et al., 2008).

Typically, suicidal people isolate themselves from others; feel worthless, helpless, and misunderstood; and want to die. An extremely negative self-image and severe feelings of hopelessness are warnings that the risk for suicide is very high (Britton et al., 2008; Heisel, Flett, & Hewitt, 2003). However, a long history of such conditions is not always necessary to produce a desire for suicide. Anyone may temporarily reach a state of depression severe enough to impulsively attempt suicide. Most dangerous for the average person are times of divorce, separation, rejection, failure, and bereavement. Such situations can seem intolerable and motivate an intense desire to escape, to obtain relief, or to die (Boergers, Spirito, & Donaldson, 1998). For young people, feelings of anger and hostility add to the danger. When the impulse to harm others is turned inward, the risk for suicide increases dramatically (Jamison, 2001).

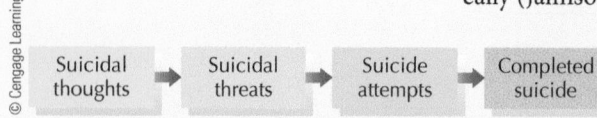

Figure 12.15 Suicidal behavior usually progresses from suicidal thoughts to threats to attempts. A person is unlikely to make an attempt without first making threats. Thus, suicide threats should be taken seriously (Leenaars, Lester, & Wenckstern, 2005).

Preventing Suicide

Is it true that people who talk about or threaten suicide are rarely the ones who try it? No, this is a major fallacy. Of every 10 potential suicides, 8 give warning beforehand. A person who threatens suicide should be taken seriously (Figure 12.15). A suicidal person may say nothing more than, "I feel sometimes like I'd be better off dead." Warnings may also come indirectly. If a friend gives you a favorite ring and says, "Here, I won't be needing this anymore," or comments, "I guess I won't get my watch fixed—it doesn't matter anyway," it may be a plea for help.

The warning signs in the list that follows, especially if they are observed in combination, can signal an impending suicide attempt (Leenaars, Lester, & Wenckstern, 2005; National Institute of Mental Health, 2011b):

- Direct threats to commit suicide
- Preoccupation with death

- Depression/hopelessness
- Rage/anger or seeking revenge
- Aggression and/or risk taking
- Alcohol/drug use
- Withdrawal from contact with others
- No sense of purpose in life
- Sudden swings in mood
- Personality change
- Gift giving of prized possessions
- Recent occurrence of life crisis or emotional shock

Is it true that suicide can't be prevented, that the person will find a way to do it anyway? No. Suicide attempts usually come when a person is alone, depressed, and unable to view matters objectively. You *should* intervene if someone seems to be threatening suicide.

It is estimated that about two thirds of all suicide attempts are made by people who do not really want to die. Almost a third more are *ambivalent* or undecided about dying. Only 3 to 5 percent of suicide cases involve people who really want to die. Most people, therefore, are relieved when someone comes to their aid. Remember that suicide is almost always a cry for help and that you *can* help.

How to Help

What is the best thing to do if someone hints at thinking about suicide? It helps to know some of the common characteristics of suicidal thoughts and feelings (Leenaars, Lester, & Wenckstern, 2005; Shneidman, 1987b):

1. **Escape.** At times, everyone feels like running away from an upsetting situation. Running away from home, quitting school, abandoning a marriage—these are all departures. Suicide, of course, is the ultimate escape. It helps when suicidal persons see that the natural wish for escape doesn't have to be expressed by ending it all.
2. **Unbearable psychological pain.** Emotional pain is what the suicidal person is seeking to escape. A goal of anyone hoping to prevent suicide should be to reduce the pain in any way possible. Ask the person, "Where does it hurt?" Suicide occurs when pain exceeds a person's resources for coping with pain.
3. **Frustrated psychological needs.** Often, suicide can be prevented if a distressed person's frustrated needs can be identified and eased. Is the person deeply frustrated in his or her search for love, achievement, trust, security, or friendship?
4. **Constriction of options.** The suicidal person feels helpless and decides that death is the *only* solution. The person has narrowed all his or her options solely to death. The rescuer's goal, then, is to help broaden the person's perspective. Even when all the choices are unpleasant, suicidal persons can usually be made to see that their *least unpleasant option* is better than death.

Knowing these patterns will give some guidance in talking to a suicidal person. In addition, your most important task may be to establish *rapport* (a harmonious connection) with the person. You should offer support, acceptance, and legitimate caring.

Remember that a suicidal person feels misunderstood. Try to accept and understand the feelings the person is expressing. Acceptance should also extend to the idea of suicide itself. It is completely acceptable to ask, "Are you thinking of suicide?"

Establishing communication with suicidal persons may be enough to carry them through a difficult time. You may also find it helpful to get day-by-day commitments from them to meet for lunch, share a ride, and the like. Let the person know you *expect* her or him to be there. Such commitments, even though small, can be enough to tip the scales when a person is alone and thinking about suicide.

Don't end your efforts too soon. A dangerous time for suicide is when a person suddenly seems to get better after a severe depression. This often means the person has finally decided to end it all. The improvement in mood is deceptive because it comes from an anticipation that suffering is about to end.

Crisis Intervention   Most cities have mental health crisis intervention teams or centers for suicide prevention trained to talk with suicidal persons over the phone (Spencer-Thomas & Jahn, 2012). Give a person who seems to be suicidal the number of one of these services. Urge the person to call you or the other number if she or he becomes frightened or impulsive. Or better yet, help the person make an appointment to get psychological treatment (Weishaar, 2006).

The preceding applies mainly to persons who are having mild suicidal thoughts. If a person actually threatens suicide, or if a suicide attempt seems to be imminent, don't worry about overreacting. Immediately seek professional assistance by calling the police, crisis intervention, or a rescue unit. If that is infeasible, ask how the person plans to carry out the suicide. A person who has a *specific, workable plan,* and the means to carry it out, should be asked to accompany you to the emergency ward of a hospital.

Needless to say, you should call immediately if a person is in the act of attempting suicide or if a drug has already been taken. The majority of suicide attempts come at temporary low points in a person's life and may never be repeated. Get involved—you may save a life!

study break Suicide and Suicide Prevention

RECITE

1. More women than men use guns in their suicide attempts. T or F?
2. While the overall suicide rate has remained about the same, there has been a decrease in adolescent suicides. T or F?
3. The highest suicide rates are found among the divorced. T or F?
4. The majority (two thirds) of suicide attempts are made by people who do not want to die. T or F?

REFLECT

THINK CRITICALLY

5. If you follow the history of popular music, see if you can answer this question: What two major risk factors contributed to the 1994 suicide of Kurt Cobain, lead singer for the rock group Nirvana?

SELF-REFLECT

You're working a suicide hotline and you take a call from a very distressed young man. What risk factors will you look for as he tells you about his anguish?

What are the common characteristics of suicidal thoughts and feelings? If a friend of yours were to express any of these thoughts or feelings, how would you respond?

ANSWERS

1. F 2. F 3. T 4. T 5. Drug or alcohol abuse and availability of a firearm.

Chapter in Review

Summary

12.1 How is abnormality defined?

- 12.1.1 *Psychopathology* refers to the scientific study of mental disorders and to maladaptive behavior.
- 12.1.2 Factors that typically affect judgments of abnormality include statistical abnormality, nonconformity, context, culture, and subjective discomfort.
- 12.1.3 The key element in judgments of disorder is that a person's behavior is maladaptive. The result is usually serious psychological discomfort or disability and loss of control.
- 12.1.4 *Insanity* is a legal term defining whether a person may be held responsible for his or her actions. Sanity is determined in court on the basis of testimony by expert witnesses.

12.2 What are the major psychological disorders?

- 12.2.1 Psychological problems are classified by using the *Diagnostic and Statistical Manual of Mental Disorders (DSM)*. The current edition is the DSM-IV-TR; a new edition, the DSM-5, is currently scheduled for publication in 2013.
- 12.2.2 Major mental problems include psychotic disorders, mood disorders, anxiety disorders, somatoform disorders, dissociative disorders, personality disorders, sexual and gender identity disorders, and substance-related disorders.
- 12.2.3 Culture-bound syndromes are not found in the DSM and are unique to every culture.
- 12.2.4 General risk factors that contribute to psychopathology include biological/organic factors, psychological factors, family factors, and social conditions.

12.3 How can psychiatric labeling be misused?

- 12.3.1 Psychiatric labels can be misused to harm and stigmatize people.

12.4 What are the general characteristics of psychotic disorders?

- 12.4.1 Psychosis is a break in contact with reality that is marked by delusions, hallucinations, sensory changes, disturbed emotions, disturbed communication, and personality disintegration.
- 12.4.2 Some psychotic disorders are informally labeled *organic psychoses* based on known injuries or diseases of the brain. Some common causes of organic psychosis are poisoning, drug abuse, and dementia (especially Alzheimer's disease).

12.5 What is the nature of a delusional disorder?

- 12.5.1 Delusional disorders are almost totally based on the presence of deeply held false beliefs of grandeur, persecution, infidelity, romantic attraction, or physical disease.
- 12.5.2 The most common delusional disorder is paranoid psychosis. Paranoid persons may be violent if they believe they are threatened.

12.6 What is schizophrenia and what causes it?

- 12.6.1 The varieties of schizophrenia all involve positive symptoms (delusions, hallucinations), negative symptoms (flat affect, communication difficulties), and a disintegrated personality.
- 12.6.2 Disorganized schizophrenia is marked by extreme personality disintegration and silly, bizarre, or obscene behavior.
- 12.6.3 Catatonic schizophrenia is associated with stupor, mutism, and odd postures. Sometimes violent and agitated behavior also occurs.
- 12.6.4 In paranoid schizophrenia (the most common type), outlandish delusions of grandeur and persecution are coupled with psychotic symptoms and personality breakdown.
- 12.6.5 Environmental factors that increase the risk for schizophrenia include viral infection or malnutrition during the mother's pregnancy, birth complications, early psychological trauma, and a disturbed family environment.
- 12.6.6 Heredity is a major factor in schizophrenia. Recent biochemical studies have focused on the neurotransmitters glutamate and dopamine and their receptor sites.
- 12.6.7 The dominant explanation of schizophrenia, and other problems as well, is the stress-vulnerability model, which emphasizes a combination of inherited susceptibility and environmental stress.

12.7 What are mood disorders and what causes them?

- 12.7.1 Mood disorders primarily involve disturbances of mood or emotion, producing manic or depressive states. Severe mood disorders may include psychotic features.
- 12.7.2 In a dysthymic disorder, depression is long lasting, though moderate. In a cyclothymic disorder, people suffer from long-lasting, though moderate, swings between depression and elation.
- 12.7.3 Bipolar disorders combine mania and depression. In bipolar I disorder the person swings between severe mania and severe depression. In bipolar II disorder the person is mostly depressed but has had periods of mild mania.
- 12.7.4 A major depressive disorder involves extreme sadness and despondency but no signs of mania.
- 12.7.5 Major mood disorders are partially explained by psychological factors such as loss, anger, learned helplessness, stress, and self-defeating thinking patterns.
- 12.7.6 Women are more likely than men to become depressed. Risk factors include hormonal fluctuations and stressful social and environmental conditions.
- 12.7.7 Major mood disorders are also partially explained by genetic vulnerability and changes in brain chemistry.
- 12.7.8 Seasonal affective disorder (SAD), which occurs during the winter months, is another common form of depression. SAD is typically treated with phototherapy.

12.8 What problems result when a person suffers high levels of anxiety?

- 12.8.1 Anxiety disorders, dissociative disorders, and somatoform disorders are characterized by high levels of anxiety, rigid defense mechanisms, and self-defeating behavior patterns.

- 12.8.2 In an adjustment disorder, ordinary stresses push people beyond their ability to cope with life.

- 12.8.3 Anxiety disorders include generalized anxiety disorder, panic disorder with or without agoraphobia, agoraphobia (without panic), specific phobias, social phobia, obsessive-compulsive disorders, acute stress disorder, and post-traumatic stress disorder.

- 12.8.4 Dissociative disorders may take the form of amnesia, fugue, or multiple identities.

- 12.8.5 Somatoform disorders center on physical complaints that mimic disease or disability. Four examples of somatoform disorders are hypochondriasis, somatization disorder, somatoform pain disorder, and conversion disorder.

12.9 How do psychologists explain anxiety-based disorders?

- 12.9.1 Susceptibility to anxiety-based disorders appears to be partly inherited.

- 12.9.2 The psychodynamic approach emphasizes unconscious conflicts as the cause of disabling anxiety.

- 12.9.3 The humanistic approach emphasizes the effects of a faulty self-image.

- 12.9.4 The behaviorists emphasize the effects of previous learning, particularly avoidance learning.

- 12.9.5 Cognitive theories of anxiety focus on distorted thinking and being fearful of others' attention and judgments.

12.10 What is a personality disorder?

- 12.10.1 Personality disorders are persistent, maladaptive personality patterns.

- 12.10.2 Sociopathy is a common personality disorder. Antisocial persons seem to lack a conscience. They are emotionally unresponsive, manipulative, shallow, and dishonest.

12.11 Why do people commit suicide and can they be stopped?

- 12.11.1 Suicide is a relatively frequent cause of death that can, in many cases, be prevented.

- 12.11.2 Suicide is statistically related to such factors as sex, ethnicity, age, and marital status.

- 12.11.3 In individual cases, the potential for suicide is best identified by a desire to escape, unbearable psychological pain, and frustrated psychological needs. People contemplating suicide narrow their options until death seems like the only way out.

- 12.11.4 The impulse to attempt suicide is usually temporary. Efforts to prevent suicide are worthwhile.

Interactive Learning

Log in to CengageBrain to access the resources your instructor requires. For this book, you can access:

CourseMate Go to CengageBrain.com to access Psychology CourseMate, where you will find an interactive eBook, glossaries, flashcards, quizzes, videos, Virtual Psychology Labs, and more.

Aplia If your professor has assigned Aplia:

1. Sign in to your account.
2. Complete the corresponding exercises as required by your professor.
3. When finished, click "Grade It Now" to see which areas you have mastered, which areas need more work, and detailed explanations of every answer.

Test Your Knowledge

Psychological Disorders

1. The main feature of abnormal behavior is that it is
a. statistically unusual
b. uncomfortable
c. socially nonconforming
d. maladaptive

2. In North America, the most widely used standard for classifying mental disorders is the
a. ICD
b. *Schedule of Personality Dysfunctions*
c. DSM
d. *Psychiatrist's Desk Reference*

3. People are said to have "retreated from reality" when they suffer from
a. psychotic disorders
b. mood disorders
c. somatoform disorders
d. personality disorders

4. A person who has periods of extreme mania suffers from
a. a somatoform disorder
b. a mood disorder
c. an anxiety disorder
d. a neurosis

5. Like amok and susto, bulimia may be a
a. paraphilia
b. somatoform
c. culture-bound syndrome
d. personality disorder

6. Which of the following is *not* a psychiatric concept?
a. schizophrenia
b. psychosis
c. anxiety
d. insanity

7. Delusions and hallucinations are most characteristic of
a. neurosis
b. psychosis
c. Alzheimer's disease
d. dysthymic disorder

8. Paranoid psychosis is the most common type of
a. catatonic schizophrenia
b. delusional disorder
c. personality disorder
d. dementia

9. Which of the following is NOT one of the subtypes of schizophrenia?
a. erotomanic type
b. catatonic type
c. paranoid type
d. disorganized type

10. Biochemical explanations of schizophrenia have focused on excessive amounts of _____ in the brain.
a. neurons
b. webs and tangles
c. PCP
d. dopamine and glutamate

11. The stress-vulnerability model of psychosis explains mental disorders as a product of environmental stresses and
a. psychological trauma
b. deviant communication
c. exposure to the flu virus during pregnancy
d. heredity

12. Bipolar disorders that are not too severe are called
a. endogenous disorders
b. cyclothymic disorders
c. seasonal affective disorders
d. dysthymic disorders

13. The fact that lithium carbonate is effective in treating some cases of bipolar depression suggests that the causes of bipolar disorders are at least partly _____.
a. biological
b. existential
c. environmental
d. neurotic

14. Depression that occurs only in the winter is likely to be classified as
a. SAD
b. PTSD
c. bipolar
d. endogenous

15. When prolonged unemployment, a bad marriage, or physical illness pushes a person beyond his or her ability to cope, it is most likely that which of the following problems will occur?
a. a dissociative disorder
b. agoraphobia
c. an adjustment disorder
d. a conversion disorder

16. Agoraphobia is most often a feature of
a. adjustment disorder
b. panic disorder
c. DSM
d. obsessive-compulsive disorder

17. According to the _____ view, anxiety disorders are the end result of a faulty self-image.
a. psychodynamic
b. humanistic
c. behaviorist
d. cognitive

18. Which of the following is NOT a type of personality disorder?
a. schizoid
b. borderline
c. neurotic
d. dependent

19. A person who is impulsive, dishonest, emotionally cold, and manipulative may suffer from
a. antisocial personality disorder
b. histrionic personality disorder
c. dependent personality disorder
d. obsessive-compulsive personality disorder

20. The risk that a person may attempt suicide is greatest if the person has
a. a concrete, workable plan
b. had a recent life crisis
c. withdrawn from contact with others
d. frustrated psychological needs

Answers 1. d 2. c 3. a 4. b 5. c 6. d 7. b 8. b 9. a 10. d 11. d 12. b 13. a 14. a 15. c 16. b 17. d 18. c 19. a 20. a

Journey Theme *Psychotherapies are based on a common core of therapeutic principles. Medical therapies treat the physical causes of psychological disorders. In many cases, these approaches are complementary.*

13

Therapies

Journey into Psychology: Paddle Like a Duck

Joe stared through the curtains in his professor's office at the ducks, quacking away as they explored the campus pond. As psychologists, we meet many students with personal problems. Still, Joe's teacher was surprised. His excellent work in class and his healthy, casual appearance left her unprepared when he murmured, "I feel like I'm losing my mind." As Joe described his own personal hell, it became clear he was like the ducks outside, appearing peaceful on the surface, but madly paddling underneath.

He was working hard to hide a world of crippling fear, anxiety, and depression. At work, he was deathly afraid to talk to coworkers and customers. His social phobia led to frequent absenteeism and embarrassing behavior. At school, Joe felt "different" and was sure that other students could tell he was "weird." Several disastrous romances had left him terrified of women. Lately, he had been so depressed that he thought of suicide.

At a time when he was becoming his own worst enemy, Joe realized he needed help. In Joe's case, that person was a talented clinical psychologist to whom his teacher referred him. With psychotherapy (and some temporary help from antidepressant medication), the psychologist was able to help Joe come to grips with his emotions and regain his balance.

This chapter discusses methods used to alleviate problems like Joe's. We will begin with a look at the origins of modern therapy before describing therapies that emphasize the value of viewing personal problems with *insight* and *changing thought patterns*. Then, we will focus on *behavior therapies*, which directly change troublesome actions. After that, we will explore *medical therapies*, which are based on psychiatric drugs and other physical treatments. We conclude with a look at some contemporary issues in therapy.

Journey Questions

13.1 How did psychotherapy originate?

13.2 Is Freudian psychoanalysis still used?

13.3 How do psychotherapies differ?

13.4 What are the major humanistic therapies?

13.5 How does cognitive therapy change thoughts and emotions?

13.6 What is behavior therapy?

13.7 What role do operant principles play in behavior therapy?

13.8 How do psychiatrists treat psychological disorders?

13.9 Are various psychotherapies effective and what do they have in common?

13.10 What will therapy be like in the future?

13.11 How are behavioral principles applied to everyday problems and how could a person find professional help?

Origins of Therapy—Bored Out of Your Skull

JOURNEY QUESTION 13.1 *How did psychotherapy originate?*

Fortunately, the odds are that you will *not* experience problems as serious as those of Joe, the student we just met. But if you did, what help is available? In most cases, it would be some form of **psychotherapy**, a psychological technique that can bring about positive changes in personality, behavior, or personal adjustment (Trull & Prinstein, 2013). It might, as with Joe, also include a medical therapy. Let's begin with a brief history of mental health care, including a discussion of psychoanalysis, the first fully developed psychotherapy.

Early treatments for mental problems give good reasons to appreciate modern therapies (Sharf, 2012). Archaeological findings dating to the Stone Age suggest that most premodern approaches were marked by fear and superstitious belief in spirits, demons, witchcraft, and magic (McNamara, 2011). If Joe was unlucky enough to have been born several thousand years ago, his "treatment" might have left him feeling "bored." One of the more dramatic "cures" practiced by primitive "therapists" was a process called *trepanning* (treh-PAN-ing), also sometimes spelled *trephining* (Terry, 2006). In modern usage, trepanning is any surgical procedure in which a hole is bored in the skull. In the hands of primitive therapists, it meant boring, chipping, or bashing holes in a patient's head. Presumably, this was done to relieve pressure or release the spirits "possessing" him (Figure 13.1).

Joe would not have been much better off during the Middle Ages. Then, treatments for mental illness in Europe focused on **demonology**, the study of demons and persons plagued by them. Medieval "therapists" commonly blamed abnormal behavior on supernatural forces, such as possession by the devil, or on curses from witches and wizards. As a cure, they used exorcism to "cast out evil spirits." For the fortunate, exorcism was a religious ritual. More often, physical torture was used to make the body an inhospitable place for the devil to reside.

One reason for the rise of demonology may lie in *ergot poisoning*. In the Middle Ages, rye (grain) fields were often infested with ergot fungus, a natural source of LSD and other mind-altering chemicals. Eating tainted bread could have caused symptoms that were easily mistaken for bewitchment or madness. Pinching sensations, muscle twitches, facial spasms, delirium, and hallucinations are all signs of ergot poisoning (Matossian, 1982). In addition, modern analyses of "demonic possession" suggest that many victims may have been suffering from epilepsy, schizophrenia, dissociative disorders, and depression (McNamara, 2011; Mirsky & Duncan, 2005; Thase, 2006; van der Hart, Lierens, & Goodwin, 1996). Thus, many people "treated" by demonologists may have been doubly victimized.

Then, in 1793, a French doctor named Philippe Pinel changed the Bicêtre Asylum in Paris from a squalid "madhouse" into a mental hospital by unchaining the inmates (Schuster, Hoertel, & Limosin, 2011). Finally, the emotionally disturbed were regarded as

Psychotherapy Any psychological technique used to facilitate positive changes in a person's personality, behavior, or adjustment.

Demonology In medieval Europe, the study of demons and the treatment of persons "possessed" by demons.

Figure 13.1 Primitive "treatment" for mental disorders sometimes took the form of boring a hole in the skull. This example shows signs of healing, which means the "patient" actually survived the treatment. Many didn't.

"mentally ill" and given compassionate treatment. Although it has been more than 200 years since Pinel began more humane treatment, the process of improving care continues today.

When was psychotherapy developed? The first true psychotherapy was created by Sigmund Freud little more than 100 years ago (Borch-Jacobsen & Shamdasani, 2011). As a physician in Vienna, Freud was intrigued by cases of *hysteria*. People suffering from hysteria have physical symptoms (such as paralysis or numbness) for which no physical causes can be found. (Such problems are now called somatoform disorders, as discussed in Chapter 12.) Slowly, Freud became convinced that hysteria was related to deeply hidden unconscious conflicts and developed psychoanalysis to help patients gain insight into those conflicts (Knafo, 2009). Because it is the "granddaddy" of more modern therapies, let's examine psychoanalysis in some detail.

Psychoanalysis—The Talking Cure

JOURNEY QUESTION 13.2 *Is Freudian psychoanalysis still used?*

How did Freud treat psychological problems? Freud's theory stressed that "neurosis" and "hysteria" are caused by repressed memories, motives, and conflicts—particularly those stemming from instinctual drives for sex and aggression. Although they are hidden, these forces remain active in the personality and cause some people to develop rigid ego defenses and compulsive, self-defeating behavior. Thus, the main goal of **psychoanalysis** is to reduce internal conflicts that lead to emotional suffering (Fayek, 2010).

Freud developed four basic techniques to uncover the unconscious roots of neurosis (Freud, 1949). These are *free association, dream analysis, analysis of resistance,* and *analysis of transference.*

Free Association

The basis for **free association** is saying whatever comes to mind without worrying whether ideas are painful, embarrassing, or illogical. Thoughts are simply allowed to move freely from one idea to the next, without self-censorship. The purpose of free association is to lower defenses so that unconscious thoughts and feelings can emerge (Hoffer & Youngren, 2004; Spence et al., 2009).

Dream Analysis

Freud believed that dreams disguise consciously unacceptable feelings and forbidden desires in dream form (Fischer & Kächele, 2009; Rock, 2004). The psychoanalyst can use this "royal road to the unconscious" to help the patient work past the obvious, visible meaning of the dream (its *manifest content*) to uncover the hidden, symbolic meaning (its *latent content*). This is achieved by analyzing *dream symbols* (images that have personal or emotional meanings; see Chapter 5).

Suppose that a young man dreams of pulling a pistol from his waistband and aiming at a target as his wife watches. The pistol repeatedly fails to discharge, and the man's wife laughs at him. Freud might have seen this as an indication of repressed feelings of sexual impotence, with the gun serving as a disguised image of the penis.

Analysis of Resistance

A central concern of psychoanalysis is the fact that patients who come to analysis for help nevertheless often *resist* changing in order to become healthier (Levenson, 2012). For example, when free associating or describing dreams, patients may resist talking about or thinking about certain topics. Such **resistances** (blockages in the flow of insights and ideas) reveal particularly important unconscious conflicts. As analysts become aware of resistances, they bring them to the patient's awareness so the patient can deal with them realistically. Rather than being roadblocks in therapy, resistances can be clues and challenges (Engle & Arkowitz, 2006).

Mary Evans Picture Library/Photo Researchers, Inc.

© Bettmann/Corbis

(top) Many early asylums were no more than prisons, with inmates held in chains. *(bottom)* One late 19th-century "treatment" was based on swinging the patient in a harness—presumably to calm the patient's nerves.

Psychoanalysis A Freudian therapy that emphasizes the use of free association, dream interpretation, resistances, and transference to uncover unconscious conflicts.

Free association In psychoanalysis, the technique of having a client say anything that comes to mind, regardless of how embarrassing or unimportant it may seem.

Resistance A blockage in the flow of insight and ideas during analysis; topics the client resists thinking or talking about.

Analysis of Transference

Transference is the tendency to "transfer" feelings to a therapist similar to those the patient had for important persons in his or her past. At times, the patient may act as if the analyst is a rejecting father, an unloving or overprotective mother, or a former lover, for example. As the patient re-experiences repressed emotions, the therapist can help the patient recognize and understand them. Troubled persons often provoke anger, rejection, boredom, criticism, and other negative reactions from others. Effective therapists learn to avoid reacting as others do and playing the patient's habitual resistance and transference games. This, too, contributes to therapeutic change (Fayek, 2010).

Psychoanalysis Today

What is the status of psychoanalysis today? Traditional psychoanalysis was open-ended, calling for three to five therapy sessions a week, often for many years. Today, most patients are seen only once or twice per week, but treatment may still go on for years. Because of the huge amounts of time and money this requires, psychoanalysts have become relatively rare. Nevertheless, psychoanalysis made a major contribution to modern therapies by highlighting the importance of unconscious conflicts (Borch-Jacobsen & Shamdasani, 2011; Friedman, 2006).

Many therapists have switched to doing time-limited **brief psychodynamic therapy**, which uses direct questioning to reveal unconscious conflicts (Binder, 2004). Modern therapists also actively provoke emotional reactions that will lower defenses and provide insights. Interestingly, brief therapy appears to accelerate recovery. Patients seem to realize that they need to get to the heart of their problems quickly (Lemma, Target, & Fonagy, 2011).

Interpersonal Psychotherapy

One example of a brief dynamic therapy is **interpersonal psychotherapy (IPT)**, which was first developed to help depressed people improve their relationships with others (Teyber & McClure, 2011). Research has confirmed that IPT is effective for depressive disorders, as well as eating disorders, substance abuse, social phobias, and personality disorders (Cuijpers et al., 2011; Fiore et al., 2008; Hoffart, 2005; Talbot & Gamble, 2008).

Liona's therapy is a good example of IPT (Brown & Barlow, 2011). Liona was suffering from depression that a therapist helped her trace to a conflict with her parents. When her father was absent, Liona adopted the role of her mother's protector and friend. However, when her father was home, she was expected to resume her role as a daughter. She was angry with her father for frequently abandoning her mother and upset about having to switch roles so often. Liona's IPT sessions (which sometimes included her mother) focused on clarifying Liona's family roles. Her mood improved a lot after her mother urged her to "stick to being herself."

Is Traditional Psychoanalysis Effective?

The development of newer, more streamlined dynamic therapies is in part due to questions about whether traditional psychoanalysis "works." In a classic criticism, Hans Eysenck (1994) suggested that psychoanalysis simply takes so long that patients experience a **spontaneous remission** of symptoms (improvement due to the mere passage of time).

How seriously should the possibility of spontaneous remission be taken? It's true that problems ranging from hyperactivity to anxiety do improve with the passage of time. Regardless, researchers have confirmed that psychoanalysis and related psychotherapies do, in fact, produce improvement in a majority of patients (Doidge, 1997; Shedler, 2010).

The real value of Eysenck's critique is that it encouraged psychologists to try new ideas and techniques. Researchers began to ask, "When psychoanalysis works, why does it work? Which parts of it are essential and which are unnecessary?" Modern therapists have given surprisingly varied answers to these questions. Let's move on to survey some of the ways modern therapies differ. Later, we will acquaint you with some of the therapies currently in use.

Transference The tendency of patients to transfer feelings to a therapist that correspond to those the patient had for important persons in his or her past.

Brief psychodynamic therapy A modern therapy based on psychoanalytic theory but designed to produce insights more quickly.

Interpersonal psychotherapy (IPT) A brief dynamic psychotherapy designed to help people by improving their relationships with other people.

Spontaneous remission Improvement of symptoms due to the mere passage of time.

Psychotherapy—Let Me Count the Ways

JOURNEY QUESTION 13.3 *How do psychotherapies differ?*

In contrast to *medical therapies*, which are physical in nature, *psychotherapy* refers to any psychological technique that can bring about positive changes in personality, behavior, or personal adjustment. Psychotherapy is usually based on a dialogue between therapists and their clients, although some therapists also use learning principles to directly alter troublesome behaviors (Corsini & Wedding, 2011).

Therapists have many approaches to choose from: psychoanalysis, which we just discussed, as well as client-centered therapy, Gestalt therapy, cognitive therapy, and behavior therapy—to name but a few. As we will see throughout the chapter, each therapy emphasizes different concepts and methods. For this reason, the best approach for a particular person or problem may vary (Prochaska & Norcross, 2010).

Dimensions of Psychotherapy

The terms in the list that follows describe some basic aspects of various psychotherapies (Prochaska & Norcross, 2010; Sharf, 2012). Notice that more than one term may apply to a particular therapy. For example, it is possible to have a directive, action-oriented, open-ended group therapy or a nondirective, individual, insight-oriented, time-limited therapy:

- **Insight versus action therapy:** Does the therapy aim to bring clients to a deeper understanding of their thoughts, emotions, and behavior? Or is it designed to bring about direct changes in troublesome thoughts, habits, feelings, or behavior without seeking insight into their origins or meanings?
- **Directive versus nondirective therapy:** Does the therapist provide strong guidance and advice? Or does the therapist assist clients, who are responsible for solving their own problems?
- **Individual versus group therapy:** Does the therapy involve one therapist with one client? Or do several clients participate at the same time?
- **Open-ended versus time-limited therapy:** Is the therapy open-ended? Or is it begun with the expectation that it will last only a limited number of sessions?

Myths about Psychotherapy

Psychotherapy has often been depicted as a complete personal transformation—a sort of "major overhaul" of the psyche. But therapy is *not* equally effective for all problems. Chances of improvement are fairly good for phobias, low self-esteem, some sexual problems, and marital conflicts. More complex problems can be difficult to solve and may, as in Joe's case, require medical treatment as well. The most extreme cases may not respond to psychotherapy at all, leaving a medical therapy as the only viable treatment option.

In short, it is often unrealistic to expect psychotherapy to undo a person's entire past. For many people, the major benefit of psychotherapy is that it provides comfort, support, and a way to make constructive changes (Bloch, 2006; Burns, 2010). Yet, even when problems are severe, therapy may help a person gain a new perspective or learn behaviors to better cope with life. Psychotherapy can be hard work for both clients and therapists, but when it succeeds, few activities are more worthwhile.

It's also a mistake to think that psychotherapy is used only to solve problems or end a crisis. Even if a person is already doing well, therapy can be a way to promote personal growth (Bloch, 2006). Therapists in the positive psychology movement are developing ways to help people make use of their personal strengths. Rather than trying to fix what is "wrong" with a person, they seek to nurture positive traits and actively solve problems (Compton & Hoffman, 2013). Before we dig deeper into some of the different types of psychotherapy, let's enhance your positive academic health with a short review.

study break Treating Psychological Distress

Humanistic Therapies—Liberating Human Potential

JOURNEY QUESTION 13.4 *What are the major humanistic therapies?*

When most people picture psychotherapists at work, they imagine them talking with their clients. Let's sample a variety of talk-oriented approaches. *Humanistic therapies* tend to be insight therapies intended to help clients gain deeper insight into their thoughts, emotions, and behavior. In contrast, *cognitive therapies* tend to be action therapies less concerned with insight than with helping people change harmful thinking patterns. Let's start with some insight.

Better self-knowledge was the goal of traditional psychoanalysis. However, Freud claimed that his patients could expect only to change their "hysterical misery into common unhappiness"! Humanistic therapists are more optimistic, believing that humans have a natural urge to seek health and self-growth. Most assume that it is possible for people to use their potentials fully and live rich, rewarding lives. In this section, we'll discuss three of the most common humanistic therapies: client-centered therapy, existential therapy, and Gestalt therapy.

Client-Centered Therapy

What is client-centered therapy? How is it different from psychoanalysis? Whereas psychoanalysis is directive and based on insights from the *unconscious*, **client-centered therapy** (also called **person-centered therapy**) is *non*directive and based on insights from *conscious* thoughts and feelings (Brodley, 2006). The psychoanalyst tends to take a position of authority, stating what dreams, thoughts, or memories "mean." In contrast, Carl Rogers (1902–1987), who originated client-centered therapy, believed that what is right or valuable for the therapist may be wrong for the client. (Rogers preferred the term *client* to *patient* because *patient* implies that a person is sick and needs to be cured.) Consequently, in client-centered therapy, therapists do not try to "fix" clients. Instead, client must actively seek to solve their problems as they determine what will be discussed during each session (Cooper & McLeod, 2011). The therapist's job is to create a safe "atmosphere of growth" by providing opportunities for change.

How do therapists create such an atmosphere? Rogers believed that effective therapists maintain four basic conditions. First, the therapist offers the client **unconditional positive regard** (unshakable personal acceptance). The therapist refuses to react with shock, dismay, or disapproval to anything the client says or feels. Total acceptance by the therapist is the first step to self-acceptance by the client.

Client-centered (or person-centered) therapy A nondirective therapy based on insights gained from conscious thoughts and feelings; emphasizes accepting one's true self.

Unconditional positive regard An unqualified, unshakable acceptance of another person.

Second, the therapist attempts to achieve genuine **empathy** by trying to see the world through the client's eyes and feeling some part of what the client is feeling (Grant, 2010).

As a third essential condition, the therapist strives to be **authentic** (genuine and honest). The therapist must not hide behind a professional role. Rogers believed that phony fronts destroy the growth atmosphere sought in client-centered therapy.

Fourth, the therapist does not make interpretations, propose solutions, or offer advice. Instead, the therapist **reflects** (rephrases, summarizes, or repeats) the client's thoughts and feelings. This enables the therapist to act as a psychological "mirror" so clients can see themselves more clearly. Rogers theorized that a person armed with a realistic self-image and greater self-acceptance will gradually discover solutions to life's problems.

Existential Therapy

According to the existentialists, "being in the world" (existence) creates deep anxiety. Each of us must deal with the realities of death. We must face the fact that we create our private world by making choices. We must overcome isolation on a vast and indifferent planet. Most of all, we must confront feelings of meaninglessness (Craig, 2012; Schneider, Galvin, & Serlin, 2009).

What do these concerns have to do with psychotherapy? **Existential therapy** focuses on the problems of existence, such as meaning, choice, and responsibility. Like client-centered therapy, it promotes self-knowledge. However, there are important differences. Client-centered therapy seeks to uncover a "true self" hidden behind a screen of defenses. In contrast, existential therapy emphasizes free will—the human ability to make choices. Accordingly, existential therapists believe you can *choose to become* the person you want to be.

Existential therapists try to give clients the *courage* to make rewarding and socially constructive choices. Typically, therapy focuses on death, freedom, isolation, and meaninglessness, the "ultimate concerns" of existence (Claessens, 2009). These universal human challenges include an awareness of one's mortality, the responsibility that comes with freedom to choose, being alone in your own private world, and the need to create meaning in your life.

One example of existential therapy is Victor Frankl's *logotherapy*, which emphasizes the need to find and maintain meaning in life. Frankl (1904–1997) based his approach on experiences he had as a prisoner in a Nazi concentration camp. In the camp, Frankl saw countless prisoners break down as they were stripped of all hope and human dignity (Frankl, 1955). Those who survived with their sanity did so because they managed to hang on to a sense of meaning *(logos)*. Even in less dire circumstances, a sense of purpose in life adds greatly to psychological well-being (Prochaska & Norcross, 2010).

What does the existential therapist do? The therapist helps clients discover self-imposed limitations in personal identity. To be successful, the client must fully accept the challenge of changing his or her life (Bretherton & Orner, 2004). A key aspect of existential therapy is *confrontation*, in which clients are challenged to be mindful of their values and choices and to take responsibility for the quality of their existence (Claessens, 2009). An important part of confrontation is the unique, intense, here-and-now *encounter* between two human beings. When existential therapy is successful, it brings about a renewed sense of purpose and a reappraisal of what's important in life. Some clients even experience an emotional rebirth, as if they had survived a close brush with death. As Marcel Proust wrote, "The real voyage of discovery consists not in seeing new landscapes but in having new eyes."

Gestalt Therapy

Gestalt therapy is based on the idea that perception, or *awareness*, is disjointed and incomplete in maladjusted persons. The German word *Gestalt* means "whole," or "complete." **Gestalt therapy** helps people rebuild thinking, feeling, and acting into connected wholes. This is achieved by expanding personal awareness; by accepting responsibility for one's thoughts, feelings, and actions; and by filling in gaps in experience (Masquelier, 2006).

What are "gaps in experience"? Gestalt therapists believe that we often shy away from expressing or "owning" upsetting feelings. This creates a gap in self-awareness that may become a barrier to personal growth. For example, a person who feels anger after the death

Psychotherapist Carl Rogers, who originated client-centered therapy.

Courtesy Dr. Natalie Rogers

Empathy A capacity for taking another's point of view; the ability to feel what another is feeling.

Authenticity In Carl Rogers' terms, the ability of a therapist to be genuine and honest about his or her own feelings.

Reflection In client-centered therapy, the process of rephrasing or repeating thoughts and feelings expressed by clients so they can become aware of what they are saying.

Existential therapy An insight therapy that focuses on the elemental problems of existence, such as death, meaning, choice, and responsibility; emphasizes making courageous life choices.

Gestalt therapy An approach that focuses on immediate experience and awareness to help clients rebuild thinking, feeling, and acting into connected wholes; emphasizes the integration of fragmented experiences.

of a parent might go for years without fully expressing it. This and similar threatening gaps may impair emotional health.

The Gestalt approach is more directive than client-centered or existential therapy, and it is less insight-oriented, instead emphasizing immediate experience. Working either one-to-one or in a group setting, the Gestalt therapist encourages clients to become more aware of their moment-to-moment thoughts, perceptions, and emotions (Levin, 2010). Rather than discussing *why* clients feel guilt, anger, fear, or boredom, the therapist encourages them to have these feelings in the "here and now" and become fully aware of them. The therapist promotes awareness by drawing attention to a client's posture, voice, eye movements, and hand gestures. Clients may also be asked to exaggerate vague feelings until they become clear. Gestalt therapists believe that expressing such feelings allows people to "take care of unfinished business" and break through emotional impasses (O'Leary, 2006).

Gestalt therapy is often associated with the work of Fritz Perls (1969). According to Perls, emotional health comes from knowing what you *want* to do, not dwelling on what you *should* do, *ought* to do, or *should want* to do (Brownell, 2010). In other words, emotional health comes from taking full responsibility for one's feelings and actions. For example, it means changing "I can't" to "I won't," or "I must" to "I choose to."

How does Gestalt therapy help people discover their real wants? Above all else, Gestalt therapy emphasizes *present* experience (Levin, 2010; Yontef, 2007). Clients are urged to stop intellectualizing and talking *about* feelings. Instead, they learn to live now; live here; stop imagining; experience the real; stop unnecessary thinking; taste and see; express rather than explain, justify, or judge; give in to unpleasantness and pain just as to pleasure; and surrender to being as you are. Gestalt therapists believe that, paradoxically, the best way to change is to become who you really are (Brownell, 2010).

Cognitive Therapy—Think Positive!

JOURNEY QUESTION 13.5 *How does cognitive therapy change thoughts and emotions?*

Whereas humanistic therapies usually seek to foster insight, cognitive therapies usually try to directly change what people think, believe, and feel, and, as a consequence, how they act (Rosner, 2012). In general, **cognitive therapy** helps clients change thinking patterns that lead to troublesome emotions or behaviors (Davey, 2008; Power, 2010).

For example, Janice is a hoarder whose home is crammed full with things she has acquired over two decades. If she seeks help from a therapist concerned with insight, she will try to better understand why she began collecting stuff. In contrast, if she seeks help from a cognitive therapist, she may spend little time examining her past. Instead, she will work to actively change her thoughts and beliefs about hoarding. With either approach, the goal is to give up hoarding. Further, in practice, humanistic therapies often also result in active change and cognitive therapies often also yield deeper insight.

Cognitive therapy has been successfully used as a remedy for many problems, ranging from generalized anxiety disorder and posttraumatic stress disorder to marital distress and anger (Butler et al., 2006). For example, compulsive hand washing can be greatly reduced by changing a client's thoughts and beliefs about dirt and contamination (Jones & Menzies, 1998). Cognitive therapy has been especially successful in treating depression (Hollon, Stewart, & Strunk, 2006). Joe's clinical psychologist relied on cognitive therapy to help lift Joe (who could forget Joe?) out of his depression.

Cognitive Therapy for Depression

Cognitive therapy A therapy directed at changing the maladaptive thoughts, beliefs, and feelings that underlie emotional and behavioral problems.

As you may recall from Chapter 12, cognitive psychologists believe that negative, self-defeating thoughts underlie depression. According to Aaron Beck (1991), depressed persons see themselves, the world, and the future in negative terms because of major distortions in thinking. The first is **selective perception**, which refers to perceiving only certain stimuli in a larger array. If five good things and three bad things happen during the day, depressed people focus only on the bad. A second thinking error in depression is **overgeneralization**, the tendency to think that an upsetting event applies to other, unrelated situations. An example would be Joe's considering himself a total failure, or completely worthless, if he were to lose a part-time job or fail a test. To complete the picture, depressed persons tend to magnify the importance of undesirable events by engaging in **all-or-nothing thinking**: They see events as completely good or bad, right or wrong, and themselves as either successful or failing miserably (Lam & Mok, 2008).

How do cognitive therapists alter such patterns? Cognitive therapists make a step-by-step effort to correct negative thoughts that lead to depression or similar problems. At first, clients are taught to recognize and keep track of their own thoughts. The client and therapist then look for ideas and beliefs that cause depression, anger, and avoidance. For example, here's how Joe's therapist began to challenge his all-or-nothing thinking:

> **Joe:** I'm feeling really depressed today. No one wants to hire me, and I can't even get a date. I feel completely incompetent!
>
> **Therapist:** I see. The fact that you are currently unemployed and don't have a girlfriend proves that you are completely and utterly incompetent?
>
> **Joe:** Well…I can see that doesn't add up.

Next, clients are asked to gather information to test their beliefs. For instance, a depressed person might list his or her activities for a week. The list is then used to challenge all-or-nothing thoughts, such as "I had a terrible week" or "I'm a complete failure." With more coaching, clients learn to alter their thoughts in ways that improve their moods, actions, and relationships.

Cognitive therapy is at least as effective as drugs for treating many cases of depression (Butler et al., 2006; Eisendrath, Chartier, & McLane, 2011). More importantly, people who have adopted new thinking patterns are less likely to become depressed again—a benefit that drugs can't impart (Dozois & Dobson, 2004; Hollon, Stewart, & Strunk, 2006).

In an alternate approach, cognitive therapists look for an *absence* of effective coping skills and thinking patterns, not for the *presence* of self-defeating thoughts (Dobson, Backs-Dermott, & Dozois, 2000). The aim is to teach clients how to cope with anger, depression, shyness, stress, and similar problems. Stress inoculation, which was described in Chapter 11, is a good example of this approach. Joe used it to help weaken his social phobia.

Cognitive therapy is a rapidly expanding specialty. Before we leave the topic, let's explore another widely used cognitive therapy.

Rational-Emotive Behavior Therapy

Rational-emotive behavior therapy (REBT) attempts to change irrational beliefs that cause emotional problems. According to Albert Ellis (1913–2007), the basic idea of REBT is as easy as A-B-C (Ellis, 1995, Ellis & Ellis, 2011). Ellis assumes that people become unhappy and develop self-defeating habits because they have unrealistic or faulty *beliefs*.

How are beliefs important? Ellis analyzes problems in this way: The letter *A* stands for an *activating experience*, which the person assumes to be the cause of *C*, an *emotional consequence*. For instance, a person who is rejected (the activating experience) feels depressed, threatened, or hurt (the consequence). Rational-emotive behavior therapy shows the client that the real problem is what comes between *A* and *C*: In between is *B*, the client's irrational and unrealistic *beliefs*. In this example, an unrealistic belief leading to unnecessary suffering is: "I must be loved and approved by everyone at all times." REBT holds that events do not *cause* us to have feelings. We feel as we do because of our beliefs (Dryden, 2011; Kottler & Shepard, 2011). (For some examples, see "Ten Irrational Beliefs—Which Do You Hold?")

Ellis (1979, Ellis & Ellis, 2011) says that most irrational beliefs come from three core ideas, each of which is unrealistic:

1. I *must* perform well and be approved of by significant others. If I don't, then it is awful, I cannot stand it, and I am a rotten person.

Selective perception Perceiving only certain stimuli among a larger array of possibilities.

Overgeneralization Blowing a single event out of proportion by extending it to a large number of unrelated situations.

All-or-nothing thinking Classifying objects or events as absolutely right or wrong, good or bad, acceptable or unacceptable, and so forth.

Rational-emotive behavior therapy (REBT) An approach that states that irrational beliefs cause many emotional problems and that such beliefs must be changed or abandoned.

Discovering Psychology

Rational-emotive behavior therapists have identified numerous beliefs that commonly lead to emotional upsets and conflicts. See if you recognize any of the following irrational beliefs:

1. I must be loved and approved by almost every significant person in my life or it's awful and I'm worthless.

   Example: "One of my classmates doesn't seem to like me. I must be a big loser."

2. I should be completely competent and achieving in all ways to be a worthwhile person.

   Example: "I don't understand my physics class. I guess I really am just stupid."

3. It's terribly upsetting when things don't go my way.

   Example: "I should have gotten a B in that class. The teacher is a total creep."

4. It's not my fault I'm unhappy; I can't control my emotional reactions.

   Example: "You make me feel awful. I would be happy if it weren't for you."

5. I should never forget it if something unpleasant happens.

   Example: "I'll never forget the time my boss insulted me. I think about it every day at work."

6. It is easier to avoid difficulties and responsibilities than to face them.

   Example: "I don't know why my girlfriend is angry. Maybe it will just pass if I ignore it."

7. A lot of people I have to deal with are bad. I should severely punish them for it.

   Example: "The students renting next door are such a pain. I'm going to play my stereo even louder the next time they complain."

8. I should depend on others who are stronger than me.

   Example: "I couldn't survive if she left me."

9. Because something once strongly affected me, it will do so forever.

   Example: "My girlfriend dumped me during my junior year in college. I can never trust a woman again."

10. There is always a perfectly obvious solution to human problems, and it is immoral if this solution is not put into practice.

    Example: "I'm so depressed about politics in this country. It all seems hopeless."*

If any of the listed beliefs sound familiar, you may be creating unnecessary emotional distress for yourself by holding on to unrealistic expectations.

*Adapted from Dryden, 2011; Ellis & Ellis, 2011; Teyber & McClure, 2011.

---

2. You *must* treat me fairly. When you don't, it is horrible, and I cannot bear it.
3. Conditions *must* be the way I want them to be. It is terrible when they are not, and I cannot stand living in such an awful world.

It's easy to see that such beliefs can lead to much grief and needless suffering in a less than perfect world. Rational-emotive behavior therapists are very directive in their attempts to change a client's irrational beliefs and "self-talk." The therapist may directly attack clients' logic, challenge their thinking, confront them with evidence contrary to their beliefs, and even assign "homework." Here, for instance, are some examples of statements that dispute irrational beliefs (adapted from Dryden, 2011; Ellis & Ellis, 2011; Kottler & Shepard, 2011):

- "Where is the evidence that you are a loser just because you didn't do well this one time?"
- "Who said the world should be fair? That's your rule."
- "What are you telling yourself to make yourself feel so upset?"
- "Is it really terrible that things aren't working out as you would like? Or is it just inconvenient?"

Many of us would probably do well to give up our irrational beliefs. Improved self-acceptance and a better tolerance of daily annoyances are the benefits of doing so. (See "Overcoming the Gambler's Fallacy.")

Cognitive Behavior Therapy

One last point, before we go on to explore behavior therapies: Did you notice that the B in REBT stands for "behavior"? Today, most therapists realize that changing maladaptive thoughts and doing the same for maladaptive behaviors can be done simultaneously. **Cognitive behavior therapy (CBT)** combines cognitive and behavioral therapies to optimize treatment outcomes (Mahoney & McEvoy, 2012). For example, compulsive hoarders respond well to therapy when it *both* corrects distorted thinking about hoarding *and* actively modifies hoarding behavior (Steketee et al., 2010). In fact, CBT is currently the most popular approach to nonmedical therapy (Pilgrim, 2011). Anyway, onward to the behavior therapies.

Cognitive behavior therapy (CBT) An approach combining cognitive and behavioral therapies to optimize treatment outcomes.

Clinical File

Overcoming the Gambler's Fallacy

Seventeen-year-old Jonathan just lost his shirt again. This time, he did it playing online blackjack. Jonathan started out making $5 bets and then doubled his bet over and over. Surely, he thought, his luck would eventually change. However, he ran out of money after just eight straight hands, having lost more than $1,000. Last week, he lost a lot of money playing Texas hold 'em. Now Jonathan is in tears—he has lost most of his summer earnings, and he is worried about having to drop out of school and tell his parents about his losses. Jonathan has had to admit that he is part of the growing ranks of underage gambling addicts (LaBrie & Shaffer, 2007; Wilber & Potenza, 2006).

Like many problem gamblers, Jonathan suffers from several cognitive distortions related to gambling. Here are some mistaken beliefs about gambling (adapted from Toneatto, 2002; Wickwire, Whelan, & Meyers, 2010):

Magnified gambling skill: Your self-confidence is exaggerated, despite the fact that you lose persistently.

Attribution errors: You ascribe your wins to skill but blame losses on bad luck.

Gambler's fallacy: You believe that a string of losses soon must be followed by wins.

Selective memory: You remember your wins but forget your losses.

Overinterpretation of cues: You put too much faith in irrelevant cues such as bodily sensations or a feeling that your next bet will be a winner.

Luck as a trait: You believe that you are a lucky person in general.

Probability biases: You have incorrect beliefs about randomness and chance events.

Do you have any of these mistaken beliefs? Taken together, Jonathan's cognitive distortions created an illusion of control. That is, he believed that if he worked hard enough, he could figure out how to win. Fortunately, a cognitive therapist helped Jonathan *cognitively restructure* his beliefs. He now no longer believes he can control chance events. Jonathan still gambles a bit, but he does so only recreationally, keeping his losses within his budget and enjoying himself in the process.

© Ocean/Corbis

Gambling addiction is a growing problem among young people (LaBrie & Shaffer, 2007).

---

study break Humanistic and Cognitive Therapies

RECITE

Match:

_____ 1. Client-centered therapy   A. Changing thought patterns
_____ 2. Gestalt therapy   B. Unconditional positive regard
_____ 3. Existential therapy   C. Gaps in awareness
_____ 4. REBT   D. Choice and becoming

5. Confrontation and encounter are concepts of existential therapy. T or F?

6. The Gestalt therapist tries to reflect a client's thoughts and feelings. T or F?

7. The B in the A-B-C of REBT stands for
   a. behavior   *b.* belief
   c. being   *d.* Beck

REFLECT

THINK CRITICALLY

8. How might using the term *patient* affect the relationship between an individual and a therapist?

SELF-REFLECT

You are going to play the role of a therapist for a classroom demonstration. How would you act if you were a client-centered therapist? A Gestalt therapist? A rational-emotive behavior therapist? A cognitive behavior therapist?

We all occasionally engage in negative thinking. Can you remember a time recently when you engaged in selective perception? Overgeneralization? All-or-nothing thinking?

ANSWERS

1. B 2. C 3. D 4. A 5. T 6. T 7. a 8. The terms *doctor* and *patient* imply a large gap in status and authority between the individual and his or her therapist. Client-centered therapy attempts to narrow this gap by making the person the final authority concerning solutions to his or her problems. Also, the word *patient* implies that a person is "sick" and needs to be "cured." Many regard this as an inappropriate way to think about human problems.

Behavior Therapies Based on Classical Conditioning—Healing by Learning

JOURNEY QUESTION 13.6 *What is behavior therapy?*

Jay repeatedly and vividly imagined himself going into a store to steal something. He then pictured himself being caught and turned over to the police, who handcuffed him and hauled him off to jail. Once there, he imagined calling his wife to tell her he had been arrested for shoplifting. He became very distressed as he faced her anger and his son's disappointment (Kohn & Antonuccio, 2002).

Why would anyone imagine such a thing? Jay's behavior is not as strange as it may seem. His goal was self-control: Jay is a *kleptomaniac* (a compulsive thief). The method he chose (called *covert sensitization*) is a form of behavior therapy (Prochaska & Norcross, 2010).

In general, how does behavior therapy work? A breakthrough occurred when psychologists realized they could use learning principles to solve human problems. **Behavior therapy** is an action therapy that uses learning principles to make constructive changes in behavior. Behavior therapists believe that deep insight into one's problems is often unnecessary for improvement. Instead, they try to directly alter troublesome actions and thoughts. Jay didn't need to probe into his past or his emotions and conflicts; he simply wanted to break his shoplifting habit. This and the next section describe some innovative—and very successful—behavioral therapies.

Behavior therapists assume that people have *learned* to be the way they are. If they have learned responses that cause problems, then they can change them by *relearning* more appropriate behaviors. Broadly speaking, **behavior modification** refers to any use of classical or operant conditioning to directly alter human behavior (Miltenberger, 2012; Spiegler & Guevremont, 2010). (Some therapists prefer to call this approach *applied behavior analysis.*) Behavioral approaches include aversion therapy, systematic desensitization, token economies, and other techniques (Forsyth & Savsevitz, 2002).

How does classical conditioning work? I'm not sure I remember. Perhaps a brief review would be helpful. Classical conditioning is a form of learning in which simple responses (especially reflexes) are associated with new stimuli. In classical conditioning, a neutral stimulus is followed by an *unconditioned stimulus (US)* that consistently produces an unlearned reaction, called the *unconditioned response (UR)*. Eventually, the previously neutral stimulus begins to produce this response directly. The response is then called a *conditioned response (CR)*, and the stimulus becomes a *conditioned stimulus (CS)*. Thus, for a child the sight of a hypodermic needle (CS) is followed by an injection (US), which causes anxiety or fear (UR). Eventually the sight of a hypodermic (the conditioned stimulus) may produce anxiety or fear (a conditioned response) *before* the child gets an injection. (For a more thorough review of classical conditioning, return to Chapter 6.)

What does classical conditioning have to do with behavior modification? Classical conditioning can be used, for example, to associate discomfort with a bad habit, as Jay did to deal with his kleptomania. More powerful versions of this approach are called aversion therapy.

Aversion Therapy

In **aversion therapy**, an individual learns to associate a strong aversion to an undesirable habit such as smoking, drinking, or gambling. Aversion therapy has been used to treat hiccups, sneezing, stuttering, vomiting, nail-biting, bed-wetting, compulsive hair-pulling, alcoholism, and the smoking of tobacco, marijuana, or crack cocaine.

Imagine, for example, that you want to quit smoking cigarettes. So, of course, you *start* to smoke—but very rapidly, for a long time, at a forced pace. During *rapid smoking*,

Behavior therapy Any therapy designed to actively change behavior.

Behavior modification The application of learning principles to change human behavior, especially maladaptive behavior.

Aversion therapy Suppressing an undesirable response by associating it with aversive (painful or uncomfortable) stimuli.

clients are told to smoke continuously, taking a puff every 6 to 8 seconds. Rapid smoking continues until the smoker is miserable and can stand it no more. After a few sessions, many smokers cannot smoke again without feeling a little ill (Gifford & Shoenberger, 2009). They have developed a conditioned aversion to cigarettes, which makes it easier for them to "kick the habit." (A *conditioned aversion* is a learned dislike or negative emotional response to some stimulus.)

Rapid smoking has long been known as an effective behavior therapy for smoking (McRobbie & Hajek, 2007). Nevertheless, anyone tempted to try rapid smoking should realize that it is very unpleasant. Without the help of a therapist, most people quit too soon for the procedure to succeed. In addition, rapid smoking can be dangerous. It should be done only with professional supervision. (An alternative method that is more practical is described in the Psychology in Action section of this chapter.)

Actually, aversive conditioning happens every day. For example, not many physicians who treat lung cancer patients are smokers, nor do many emergency room doctors drive without using their seat belts (Eifert & Lejuez, 2000).

Systematic Desensitization

Can behavior therapy be used to treat phobias, fears, and anxieties? Another behavioral technique, *systematic desensitization*, is used primarily to help people unlearn phobias (intense, unrealistic fears) or strong anxieties. For example, each of these people might be a candidate: a teacher with stage fright; a student with test anxiety; a salesperson who fears people; or a newlywed with an aversion to sexual intimacy.

Suppose a behavior therapist wanted to help Curtis overcome his fear of heights (acrophobia). How might she proceed? Simply forcing Curtis to go out onto a balcony on the top (35th) floor of his apartment building could be a psychological disaster (after all, Curtis is a ground floor kinda guy). The behavior therapist (and Curtis) would be better off using **systematic desensitization**—a guided reduction in fear, anxiety, or aversion attained by gradually approaching a feared stimulus while maintaining relaxation.

Performing Systematic Desensitization

How is systematic desensitization done? Curtis and the therapist begin by constructing his **fear hierarchy**—a list of fear-provoking situations, arranged from least disturbing to most frightening. In addition, Curtis is taught exercises that produce deep relaxation. (See "Feeling a Little Tense? Relax!") Then, once Curtis is relaxed, he tries to perform the least disturbing item on his fear of heights hierarchy, which might be: "(1) Stand on a chair." The first item is repeated until Curtis feels no anxiety. Any change from complete relaxation is a signal that Curtis must relax again before continuing. Slowly, Curtis moves up the hierarchy: "(2) Climb to the top of a small stepladder"; "(3) Look down one flight of stairs"; and so on, until the last item is performed without fear: "(20) Stand on the balcony on the top floor."

How does systematic desensitization work? Working through his fear hierarchy allows Curtis to gradually undergo *adaptation*. Systematic desensitization is also based on **reciprocal inhibition** (using one emotional state to block another) (Heriot & Pritchard, 2004). For instance, it is impossible to be anxious and relaxed at the same time. If we can get Curtis onto the building staircase in a relaxed state, his anxiety and fear will be inhibited. Repeated visits to the staircase should cause fear to disappear in this situation. When Curtis has conquered his fear, we can say that *desensitization* has occurred (Spiegler & Guevremont, 2010).

For many phobias, desensitization works best when people are directly exposed to the stimuli and situations they fear (Bourne, 2010; Miltenberger, 2012). For something like a simple spider phobia, this exposure can even be done in groups. Also, for some fears (such as fear of riding an elevator or fear of spiders) desensitization may be completed in a single session (Müller et al., 2011; Sturges & Sturges, 1998).

Programs for treating fears of flying combine relaxation, systematic desensitization, group support, and lots of direct and indirect exposure to airliners. Many such programs conclude with a brief flight, so that participants can "test their wings."

Systematic desensitization A reduction in fear, anxiety, or aversion brought about by planned exposure to aversive stimuli.

Fear hierarchy A list of fears, arranged from least fearful to most fearful, for use in systematic desensitization.

Reciprocal inhibition The presence of one emotional state can inhibit the occurrence of another, such as joy preventing fear or anxiety inhibiting pleasure.

Discovering Psychology

The key to desensitization is relaxation. To inhibit fear, you must *learn* to relax. One way to voluntarily relax is by using the **tension-release method**. To achieve deep-muscle relaxation, try the following exercise:

Tense the muscles in your right arm until they tremble. Hold them tight as you slowly count to ten and then let go. Allow your hand and arm to go limp and to relax completely. Repeat the procedure. Releasing tension two or three times will allow you to feel whether your arm muscles have relaxed. Repeat the tension-release procedure with your left arm. Compare it with your right arm. Repeat until the left arm is equally relaxed. Apply the tension-release technique to your right leg; to your left leg; to your abdomen; to your chest and shoulders. Clench and release your chin, neck, and throat. Wrinkle and release your forehead and scalp. Tighten and release your mouth and face muscles. As a last step, curl your toes and tense your feet. Then release.

If you carried out these instructions, you should be noticeably more relaxed than you were before you began. Practice the tension-release method until you can achieve complete relaxation quickly (5 to 10 minutes). After you have practiced relaxation once a day for a week or two, you will begin to be able to tell when your body (or a group of muscles) is tense. Also, you will begin to be able to relax on command. This is a valuable skill that you can apply in any situation that makes you feel tense or anxious.

Vicarious Desensitization

What if it's not practical to directly act out the steps of a fear hierarchy? For a fear of heights, the steps of the fear hierarchy might be acted out, just as Curtis did. However, if this is impractical, as it might be in the case of a fear of flying, the problem can be handled by having clients observe *models* who are performing the feared behavior (Eifert & Lejuez, 2000; Bourne, 2010) (Figure 13.2). A model is a person (either live or filmed) who serves as an example for observational learning. If such **vicarious desensitization** (secondhand learning) can't be used, there is yet another option. Fortunately, desensitization works almost as well when a person *vividly imagines* each step in the hierarchy (Yahnke, Sheikh, & Beckman, 2003). If the steps can be visualized without anxiety, fear in the actual situation is reduced. Because imagining feared stimuli can be done at a therapist's office, it is the most common way of doing desensitization.

Tension-release method A procedure for systematically achieving deep relaxation of the body.

Vicarious desensitization A reduction in fear or anxiety that takes place vicariously ("secondhand") when a client watches models perform the feared behavior.

Photos courtesy Albert Bandura

Figure 13.2 Treatment of a snake phobia by vicarious desensitization. These classic photographs show models interacting with snakes. To overcome their own fears, phobic subjects observed the models (Bandura, Blanchard, & Ritter, 1969).

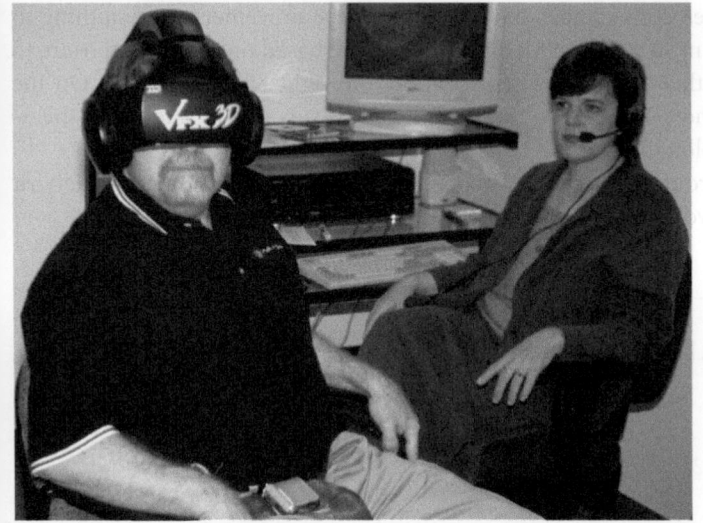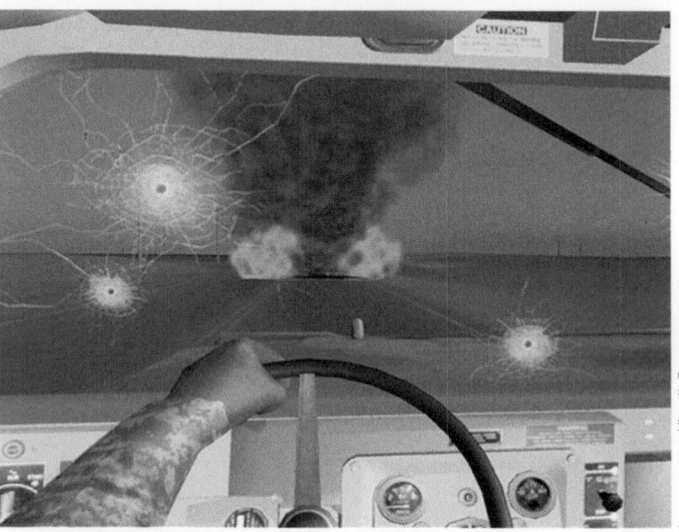

Images courtesy Virtually Better

Figure 13.3 *(left)* Dr. Larry Hodges (in the head-mounted display) and Dr. Page Anderson show how a virtual reality system is used to expose people to feared stimuli. *(right)* A computer image from a virtual Iraq or Afghanistan. Veterans suffering from post-traumatic stress disorder (PTSD) can re-experience their traumas. For example, someone whose Humvee was destroyed by an improvised explosive device can relive that moment complete with sights, sounds, vibrations, and even smells. Successive exposures result in a reduction of PTSD symptoms (Gerardi et al., 2008).

Virtual Reality Exposure

Desensitization is an *exposure therapy.* Similar to other such therapies, it involves exposing people to feared stimuli until their fears extinguish. In an important recent development, psychologists are now also using virtual reality to treat phobias. Virtual reality is a computer-generated, three-dimensional "world" that viewers enter by wearing a head-mounted video display. **Virtual reality exposure** presents computerized fear stimuli to clients in a realistic, yet carefully controlled fashion (Wiederhold & Wiederhold, 2005; Riva, 2009). It has already been used to treat fears of flying, driving, and public speaking as well as acrophobia (fear of heights), claustrophobia, and spider phobias (Arbona et al., 2004; Giuseppe, 2005; Meyerbröker & Emmelkamp, 2010; Müller et al., 2011) (Figure 13.3). Virtual reality exposure has also been used to create immersive distracting environments for helping patients reduce the experience of pain (Malloy & Milling, 2010).

Desensitization has been one of the most successful behavior therapies. A relatively new technique may provide yet another way to lower fears, anxieties, and psychological pain.

Eye Movement Desensitization

Traumatic events produce painful memories. Disturbing flashbacks often haunt victims of accidents, disasters, molestations, muggings, rapes, or emotional abuse. To help ease traumatic memories and post-traumatic stress, Dr. Francine Shapiro developed **eye movement desensitization and reprocessing (EMDR).**

In a typical EMDR session, the client is asked to visualize the images that most upset her or him. At the same time, a pencil (or other object) is moved rapidly from side to side in front of the person's eyes. Watching the moving object causes the person's eyes to dart swiftly back and forth. After about 30 seconds, clients describe any memories, feelings, and thoughts that emerged and discuss them with the therapist. These steps are repeated until troubling thoughts and emotions no longer surface (Shapiro, 2001; Shapiro & Forrest, 2004).

A number of studies suggest that EMDR lowers anxieties and takes the pain out of traumatic memories (Fleming, 2012; Seidler & Wagner, 2006). However, EMDR is highly

Virtual reality exposure Use of computer-generated images to present fear stimuli. The virtual environment responds to a viewer's head movements and other inputs.

Eye movement desensitization and reprocessing (EMDR) A technique for reducing fear or anxiety; based on holding upsetting thoughts in mind while rapidly moving the eyes from side to side.

THERAPIES **541**

controversial. Some studies, for example, have found that eye movements add nothing to the treatment. The apparent success of EMDR may simply be based on gradual exposure to upsetting stimuli, as in other forms of desensitization (Albright & Thyer, 2010). On the other hand, some researchers continue to find that EMDR is superior to traditional therapies (Greenwald, 2006; Solomon, Solomon, & Heide, 2009).

Is EMDR a breakthrough? Given the frequency of traumas in modern society, it shouldn't be long before we find out.

Operant Therapies—All the World Is a Skinner Box?

JOURNEY QUESTION 13.7 *What role do operant principles play in behavior therapy?*

Aversion therapy and desensitization are based on classical conditioning. Where does operant conditioning fit in? As you may recall, *operant conditioning* refers to learning based on the consequences of making a response. The operant principles most often used by behavior therapists to deal with human behavior are:

1. **Positive reinforcement.** Responses that are followed by reinforcement tend to occur more frequently. If children whine and get attention, they will whine more frequently. If you get *A*s in your psychology class, you may become a psychology major.
2. **Nonreinforcement and Extinction.** A response that is not followed by reinforcement will occur less frequently. If a response is not followed by reward after it has been repeated many times, it will extinguish entirely. After winning three times, you pull the handle on a slot machine 30 times more without a payoff. What do you do? You will likely stop.
3. **Punishment.** If a response is followed by discomfort or an undesirable effect, the response will be suppressed (but not necessarily extinguished).
4. **Shaping.** Shaping means reinforcing actions that are closer and closer approximations to a desired response. For example, to reward an intellectually disabled child for saying "ball," you might begin by reinforcing the child for saying anything that starts with a *b* sound.
5. **Stimulus control.** Responses tend to come under the control of the situation in which they occur. If you set your clock 10 minutes fast, it may be easier to leave the house on time in the morning. Your departure is under the stimulus control of the clock, even though you know it is fast.
6. **Time out.** A time-out procedure usually involves removing the individual from a situation in which reinforcement occurs. Time out is a variation of response cost: It prevents reward from following an undesirable response. For example, children who fight with each other can be sent to separate rooms and allowed out only when they are able to behave more calmly. (For a more thorough review of operant learning, return to Chapter 6.)

As simple as these principles may seem, they have been used very effectively to overcome difficulties in work, home, school, and industrial settings. Let's see how.

Nonreinforcement and Extinction

An extremely overweight mental patient had a persistent and disturbing habit: She stole food from other patients. No one could persuade her to stop stealing or to diet. For the sake of her health, a behavior therapist assigned her a special table in the ward dining room. If she approached any other table, she was immediately removed from the dining room. Any attempt to steal from others caused the patient to miss her own meal (Ayllon, 1963). Because her attempts to steal food went unrewarded, they rapidly disappeared.

What operant principles did the therapist in this example use? The therapist used *nonreward* to produce *extinction*. The most frequently occurring human behaviors lead to some form of reward. An undesirable response can be eliminated by *identifying* and *removing* the rewards that maintain it. But people don't always do things for food, money, or other obvious rewards. Most of the rewards maintaining human behavior are subtler. *Attention*, *approval*, and *concern* are common yet powerful reinforcers for humans (Figure 13.4).

Nonreward and extinction can eliminate many problem behaviors, especially in schools, hospitals, and institutions. Often, difficulties center on a limited number of particularly disturbing responses. *Time out* is a good way to remove such responses, usually by refusing to pay attention to a person who is misbehaving. For example, 14-year-old Terrel periodically appeared in the nude in the activity room of a training center for disturbed adolescents. This behavior always generated a great deal of attention from staff and other patients. As an experiment, the next time he appeared nude, counselors and other staff members greeted him normally and then ignored him. Attention from other patients rapidly subsided. Sheepishly, he returned to his room and dressed.

Reinforcement and Token Economies

Institutional settings, such as mental hospitals, halfway houses, schools for the intellectually disabled, programs for delinquents, and ordinary classrooms, also make use of reinforcement, in the form of *tokens* (symbolic rewards that can be exchanged for real rewards). Tokens may be printed slips of paper, check marks, points, or gold stars. Whatever form they take, tokens serve as rewards because they may be exchanged for candy, food, cigarettes, recreation, or privileges, such as private time with a therapist, outings, or watching television. They usually produce improvements in behavior (Maggin et al., 2011; Matson & Boisjoli, 2009).

By using tokens, positive responses can be *immediately rewarded*. For maximum impact, therapists select specific *target behaviors* (actions or other behaviors the therapist

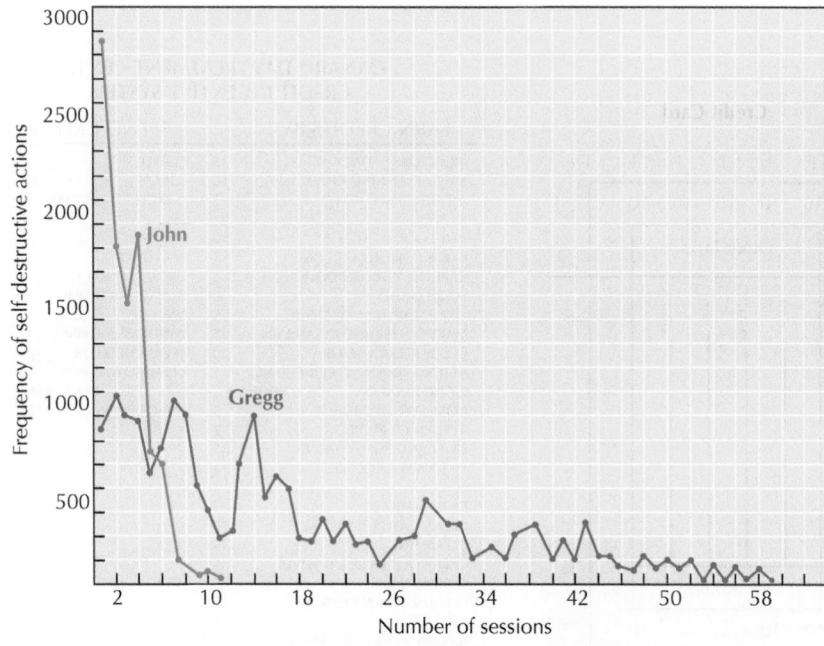

Figure 13.4 This graph shows extinction of self-destructive behavior in two autistic boys. Before extinction began, the boys received attention and concern from adults for injuring themselves. During extinction, the adults were taught to ignore the boys' self-damaging behavior. As you can see, the number of times that the boys tried to injure themselves declined rapidly. (Adapted from Lovaas & Simmons, "Manipulation of self-destruction in three retarded children." From *Journal of Applied Behavior Analysis*, 1969(2), 3. p. 147, Fig 1. Reprinted by permission of publisher.)

seeks to modify). Target behaviors are then reinforced with tokens. For example, a mute mental patient might first be given a token each time he or she says a word. Next, tokens may be given for speaking a complete sentence. Later, the patient could gradually be required to speak more often, then to answer questions, and eventually to carry on a short conversation in order to receive tokens. In this way, deeply withdrawn patients have been returned to the world of normal communication.

The full-scale use of tokens in an institutional setting produces a *token economy*. In a **token economy**, patients are rewarded with tokens for a wide range of socially desirable or productive activities (Spiegler & Guevremont, 2010). They must *pay* tokens for privileges and when they engage in problem behaviors (Figure 13.5). For example, tokens are given to patients who dress themselves, take required medication, arrive for meals on time, and so on. Constructive activities, such as gardening, cooking, or cleaning, may also earn tokens. Patients must *exchange* tokens for meals and private rooms, movies, passes, off-ward activities, and other privileges. They are *charged* tokens for disrobing in public, talking to themselves, fighting, crying, and similar target behaviors (Morisse et al., 1996; Spiegler & Guevremont, 2010).

Token economies can radically change a patient's overall adjustment and morale. Patients are given an incentive to change, and they are held responsible for their actions. The use of tokens may seem manipulative, but it actually empowers patients. Many "hopelessly" intellectually disabled, mentally ill, and delinquent people have been returned to productive lives by means of token economies (Field et al., 2004).

By the time they are ready to leave, patients may be earning tokens on a weekly basis for maintaining sane, responsible, and productive behavior (Miltenberger, 2012). Typically, the most effective token economies are those that gradually switch from tokens to *social rewards* such as praise, recognition, and approval. Such rewards are what patients will receive when they return to family, friends, and community.

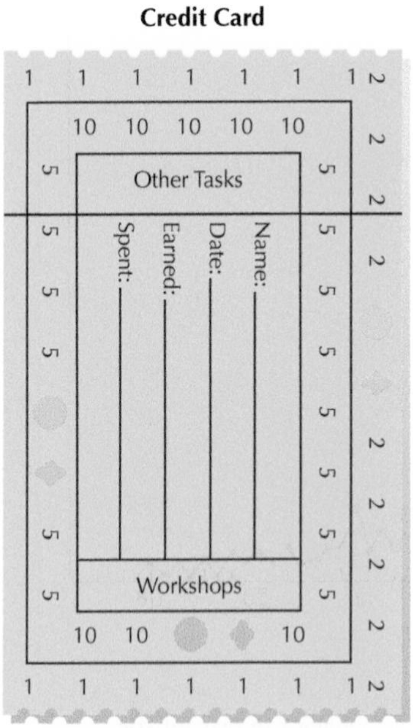

Credit Card

OXNARD DAY TREATMENT CENTER CREDIT INCENTIVE SYSTEM

EARN CREDITS BY		SPEND CREDITS FOR	
MONITOR DAILY	15	COFFEE	5
MENU PLANNING CHAIRMAN	50	LUNCH	10
PARTICIPATE	5	EXCEPT THURSDAY	15
BUY FOOD AT STORE	10	BUS TRIP	5
COOK FOR/PREPARE LUNCH	5	BOWLING	8
WIPE OFF KITCHEN TABLE	3	GROUP THERAPY	5
WASH DISHES	5-10	PRIVATE STAFF TIME	5
DRY AND PUT AWAY DISHES	5	DAY OFF	5-20
MAKE COFFEE AND CLEAN URN	15	WINDOW SHOPPING	5
CLEAN REFRIGERATOR	20	REVIEW WITH DR.	10
ATTEND PLANNING CONFERENCE	1	DOING OWN THING	1
OT PREPARATION	1-5	LATE 1 PER EVERY 10 MIN	
COMPLETE OT PROJECT	5	PRESCRIPTION FROM DR.	10
RETURN OT PROJECT	2		
DUST AND POLISH TABLES	5		
PUT AWAY GROCERIES	3		
CLEAN TABLE	5		
CLEAN 6 ASH TRAYS	2		
CLEAN SINK	5		
CARRY OUT CUPS & BOTTLES	5		
CLEAN CHAIRS	5		
CLEAN KITCHEN CUPBOARDS	5		
ASSIST STAFF	5		
ARRANGE MAGAZINES NEATLY	3		
BEING ON TIME	5		
MONITOR-ANN			

© Cengage Learning

Figure 13.5 Shown here is a token used in one token economy system. In this instance, the token is a card that records the number of credits earned by a patient. Also pictured is a list of credit values for various activities. Tokens may be exchanged for items or for privileges listed on the board. (After photographs by Robert P. Liberman.)

Token economy A therapeutic program in which desirable behaviors are reinforced with tokens that can be exchanged for goods, services, activities, and privileges.

RECITE

1. What two types of conditioning are used in behavior modification? _____ and _____

2. Shock, pain, and discomfort play what role in conditioning an aversion?

   a. conditioned stimulus
   b. unconditioned response
   c. unconditioned stimulus
   d. conditioned response

3. The three basic steps in systematic desensitization are: constructing a hierarchy, flooding the person with anxiety, and imagining relaxation. T or F?

4. Behavior modification programs aimed at extinction of an undesirable behavior typically make use of what operant principles?

   a. punishment and stimulus control
   b. punishment and shaping
   c. nonreinforcement and time out
   d. stimulus control and time out

5. Attention can be a powerful _____ for humans.

REFLECT

THINK CRITICALLY

6. A natural form of desensitization often takes place in hospitals. Can you guess what it is?

SELF-REFLECT

Have you ever become naturally desensitized to a stimulus or situation that at first made you anxious (for instance, heights, public speaking, or driving on freeways)? How would you explain your reduced fear?

See if you can give a personal example of how the following principles have affected your behavior: positive reinforcement, extinction, punishment, shaping, stimulus control, and time out.

ANSWERS

1. classical (or respondent), operant 2. c 3. F 4. c 5. reinforcer 6. Doctors and nurses learn to relax and remain calm at the sight of blood and other bodily fluids because of their frequent exposure to them.

Medical Therapies—Psychiatric Care

JOURNEY QUESTION 13.8 *How do psychiatrists treat psychological disorders?*

Psychotherapy may be applied to anything from a brief crisis to a full-scale psychosis. However, most psychotherapists *do not* treat patients with major depressive disorders, schizophrenia, or other severe conditions. Major mental disorders are more often treated medically, although combinations of medication and psychotherapy are also often helpful (Beck et al., 2009).

Three main types of **somatic** (body) **therapy** are *pharmacotherapy*, *electrical stimulation therapy*, and *psychosurgery*. Somatic therapy is often done in the context of psychiatric hospitalization. All the somatic approaches have a strong medical slant and are typically administered by psychiatrists, who are trained as medical doctors.

Drug Therapies

The atmosphere in psychiatric wards and mental hospitals changed radically in the mid-1950s with the widespread adoption of **pharmacotherapy** (FAR-meh-koe-THER-eh-pea), the use of drugs to treat psychopathology. Drugs may relieve the anxiety attacks and other discomforts of milder psychological disorders. More often, however, they are used to combat schizophrenia and major mood disorders (Julien, 2011).

What sort of drugs are used in pharmacotherapy? Three major types of drugs are used. All achieve their effects by influencing the activity of different brain neurotransmitters (Freberg, 2010). **Anxiolytics** (ANG-zee-eh LIT-iks), such as Valium, produce relaxation or reduce anxiety. **Antidepressants**, such as Prozac, are mood-elevating drugs that combat depression. **Antipsychotics** (also called **major tranquilizers**), such as Risperdal, have tranquilizing effects and reduce hallucinations and delusions. (See Table 13.1 for examples of each class of drugs.)

Are drugs a valid approach to treatment? Definitely. Drugs have shortened hospital stays, and they have greatly improved the chances that people will recover from major psychological disorders. Drug therapy has also made it possible for many people to return to the community, where they can be treated on an outpatient basis.

Somatic therapy Any bodily therapy, such as drug therapy, electroconvulsive therapy, or psychosurgery.

Pharmacotherapy The use of drugs to treat psychopathology.

Anxiolytics Drugs (such as Valium) that produce relaxation or reduce anxiety.

Antidepressants Mood-elevating drugs.

Antipsychotics (major tranquilizers) Drugs that, in addition to having tranquilizing effects, also tend to reduce hallucinations and delusional thinking.

Table 13.1 Commonly Prescribed Psychiatric Drugs

CLASS	EXAMPLES (TRADE NAMES)	EFFECTS	MAIN MODE OF ACTION
Anxiolytics (minor tranquilizers)	Ativan, Halcion, Librium, Restoril, Valium, Xanax	Reduce anxiety, tension, fear	Enhance effects of GABA
Antidepressants	Anafranil, Elavil, Nardil, Norpramin, Parnate, Paxil, Prozac, Tofranil, Zoloft	Counteract depression	Enhance effects of serotonin or dopamine
Antipsychotics (major tranquilizers)	Clozaril, Haldol, Mellaril, Navane, Risperdal, Thorazine	Reduce agitation, delusions, hallucinations, thought disorders	Reduce effects of dopamine

Source: Adapted from Freberg, 2010; Julien, 2011; and Kalat, 2013. © Cengage Learning

Courtesy Rodger Casier

The work of artist Rodger Casier illustrates the value of psychiatric care. Despite having a form of schizophrenia, Casier produces artwork that has received public acclaim and has been featured in professional journals.

Electroconvulsive therapy (ECT) A treatment for severe depression, consisting of an electric shock passed directly through the brain, which induces a convulsion.

Limitations of Drug Therapy

Regardless of their benefits, all drugs involve risks as well. For example, 15 percent of patients taking major tranquilizers for long periods develop a neurological disorder that causes rhythmic facial and mouth movements (Chakos et al., 1996). Similarly, although the drug *clozapine* (Clozaril) can relieve the symptoms of schizophrenia, 2 out of 100 patients taking the drug suffer from a potentially fatal blood disease (Ginsberg, 2006).

Is the risk worth it? Many experts think it is, because chronic schizophrenia robs people of almost everything that makes life worth living. It's possible, of course, that newer drugs will improve the risk/benefit ratio in the treatment of severe problems like schizophrenia. For example, the drug risperidone (Risperdal) appears to be as effective as Clozaril, without the same degree of lethal risk. But even the best new drugs are not cure-alls. They help some people and relieve some problems, but not all. It is noteworthy that for serious mental disorders, a combination of medication and psychotherapy almost always works better than drugs alone (Manber et al., 2008; Oestergaard & Møldrup, 2011). Nevertheless, when schizophrenia and major mood disorders are concerned, drugs will undoubtedly remain the primary mode of treatment (Leucht et al., 2011; Vasa, Carlino, & Pine, 2006).

Electrical Stimulation Therapy

In contrast to drug therapies, electrical stimulation therapies achieve their effects by altering the electrical activity of the brain. Electroconvulsive therapy is the first, and most dramatic, of these therapies. Widely used since the 1940s, it remains controversial to this day (Hirshbein & Sarvananda, 2008). Although ECT is mainly used to treat depression, it is still used to treat other disorders (Weiss, Allan, & Greenaway, 2012).

Electroshock

In **electroconvulsive therapy (ECT)** a 150-volt electrical current is passed through the brain for slightly less than a second. This rather drastic medical treatment for depression triggers a convulsion and causes the patient to lose consciousness for a short time. Muscle relaxants and sedative drugs are given before ECT to soften its impact. Treatments are given in a series of sessions spread over several weeks or months.

How does shock help? Actually, it is the seizure activity that is believed to be helpful. Proponents of ECT claim that shock-induced seizures alter or "reset" the biochemical and hormonal balance in the brain and body, bringing an end to severe depression and suicidal behavior (Medda et al., 2009) as well as improving long-term quality of life (McCall et al., 2006). Others have charged that ECT works only by confusing patients so they can't remember why they were depressed.

Not all professionals support the use of ECT. However, most experts seem to agree on the following: (1) At best, ECT produces only temporary improvement—it gets the patient out of a bad spot, but it must be combined with other treatments; (2) ECT can cause memory loss in some patients (Sienaert et al., 2010); (3) ECT should be used only after other treatments have failed; and (4) to lower the chance of a relapse, ECT should be followed by antidepressant drugs (McCall et al., 2011). All told, ECT is considered by many to be a valid treatment for selected cases of depression—especially when it rapidly ends wildly self-destructive or suicidal behavior (Medda et al., 2009; Pagnin et al., 2004). It's interesting to note that most ECT patients feel that the treatment helped them. Most, in fact, would have it done again (Bernstein et al., 1998; Smith et al., 2009).

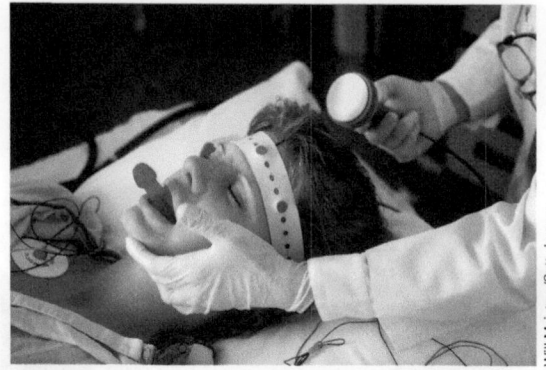

In electroconvulsive therapy, electrodes are attached to the head and a brief electrical current is passed through the brain. ECT is used in the treatment of severe depression.

Deep Brain Stimulation

Unlike ECT, **deep brain stimulation (DBS)** requires surgery to implant electrodes but allows for electrical stimulation of precisely targeted brain regions. (See Chapter 2 for more information about electrical stimulation of the brain.) In some studies, depressed patients who hadn't benefited from drug therapy and ECT improved when a specific brain region was stimulated (Kennedy et al., 2011; Sartorius et al., 2010). Stimulating pleasure centers in the brains of another group of patients also relieved depression (Schlaepfer et al., 2008). Also, unlike ECT, DBS can be used to treat disorders other than depression, such as obsessive-compulsive disorder (Haq et al., 2010).

Psychosurgery

Psychosurgery—any surgical alteration of the brain—is the most extreme medical treatment. The oldest and most radical psychosurgery is the lobotomy. In *prefrontal lobotomy*, the frontal lobes are surgically disconnected from other brain areas. This procedure was supposed to calm persons who didn't respond to any other type of treatment.

When the lobotomy was first introduced in the 1940s, there were enthusiastic claims for its success. But later studies suggested that some patients were calmed, some showed no change, and some became mental "vegetables." Lobotomies also produced a high rate of undesirable side effects, such as seizures, blunted emotions, major personality changes, and stupor. About the same time that such problems became apparent, the first antipsychotic drugs became available. Soon after, the lobotomy was abandoned (Mashour, Walker, & Martuza, 2005).

To what extent is psychosurgery used now? Psychosurgery is still considered valid by many neurosurgeons. However, most now use *deep lesioning*, in which small target areas are destroyed in the brain's interior. The appeal of deep lesioning is that it can have value as a remedy for some very specific disorders (Mashour, Walker, & Martuza, 2005). For instance, patients suffering from a severe type of obsessive-compulsive disorder may be helped by psychosurgery (Anderson & Booker, 2006; Dougherty et al., 2002).

It is worth remembering that psychosurgery cannot be reversed. Whereas a drug can be given or taken away and electrical stimulation can be turned off, you can't take back psychosurgery. Critics argue that psychosurgery should be banned altogether; others continue to report success with brain surgery. Nevertheless, it may have value as a remedy for some very specific disorders (Mashour, Walker, & Martuza, 2005; Sachdev & Chen, 2009).

Hospitalization

In 2008, about 3 million Americans received inpatient treatment for a mental health problem (National Institute of Mental Health, 2011a). **Mental hospitalization** involves placing a person in a protected setting where medical therapy is provided. Hospitalization by itself can be

Deep brain stimulation (DBS) Surgical procedure to implant electrodes in the brain, allowing for electrical stimulation of precisely targeted brain regions.

Psychosurgery Any surgical alteration of the brain designed to bring about desirable behavioral or emotional changes.

Mental hospitalization Placing a person in a protected, therapeutic environment staffed by mental health professionals.

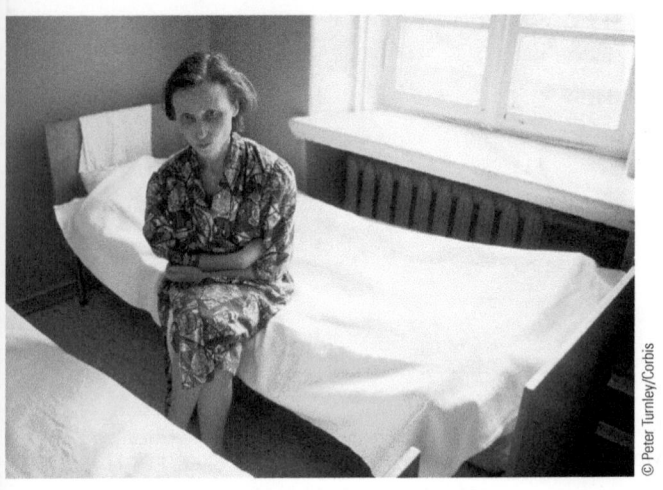

Depending on the quality of the institution, hospitalization may be a refuge or a brutalizing experience. Many state "asylums" or mental hospitals are antiquated and in need of drastic improvement.

a form of treatment. Staying in a hospital takes patients out of situations that may be sustaining their problems. For example, people with drug addictions may find it nearly impossible to resist the temptations for drug abuse in their daily lives. Hospitalization can help them make a clean break from their self-destructive behavior patterns (André et al., 2003).

At their best, hospitals are sanctuaries that provide diagnosis, support, refuge, and therapy. This is frequently true of psychiatric units in general hospitals and private psychiatric hospitals. At worst, confinement to an institution can be a brutal experience that leaves people less prepared to face the world than when they arrived. This is more often the case in large state mental hospitals. In most instances, hospitals are best used as a last resort, after other forms of treatment within the community have been exhausted.

Another trend in treatment is **partial hospitalization**. (Bales & Bateman, 2012). In this approach, some patients spend their days in the hospital but go home at night. Others attend therapy sessions during the evening. A major advantage of partial hospitalization is that patients can go home and practice what they've been learning. Overall, partial hospitalization can be just as effective as full hospitalization (Drymalski & Washburn, 2011; Kiser, Heston, & Paavola, 2006).

Deinstitutionalization

In the last 50 years the population in large mental hospitals has dropped by two thirds. This is largely a result of **deinstitutionalization**, or reduced use of full-time commitment to mental institutions. Long-term "institutionalization" can lead to dependency, isolation, and continued emotional disturbance (Novella, 2010). Deinstitutionalization was meant to remedy this problem.

How successful has deinstitutionalization been? In truth, its success has been limited (Talbott, 2004). Many states reduced mental hospital populations primarily as a way to save money. The upsetting result is that many chronic patients have been discharged to hostile communities without adequate care. Many former patients have joined the ranks of the homeless. Others are repeatedly jailed for minor crimes. Sadly, patients who trade hospitalization for unemployment, homelessness, and social isolation all too often end up rehospitalized or in jail (Markowitz, 2011).

Large mental hospitals may no longer be warehouses for society's unwanted, but many former patients are no better off in bleak nursing homes, single-room hotels, board-and-care homes, shelters, or jails. For every mentally ill American in a hospital, three are trapped in the criminal justice system (National Institute of Mental Health, 2010a). These figures suggest that jails are replacing mental hospitals as our society's "solution" for mental illness (Markowitz, 2011). Yet, ironically, high-quality care is available in almost every community. As much as anything, a simple lack of money prevents large numbers of people from getting the help they need (Torrey, 1996).

Halfway houses may be a better way to ease a patient's return to the community (Soyez & Broekaert, 2003). **Halfway houses** are short-term group-living facilities for people making the transition from an institution (mental hospital, prison, and so forth) to independent living. Typically, they offer supervision and support, without being as restricted and medically oriented as hospitals. They also keep people near their families. Most important, halfway houses can ease a person's return to "normal" life and reduce chances of being readmitted to a hospital (Davidson et al., 2010; Soyez & Broekaert, 2003).

Community Mental Health Programs

Community mental health centers, which offer a wide range of mental health services and psychiatric care, are a bright spot in the area of mental health care. Such centers try to help people avoid hospitalization, find answers to mental health problems, and improve mental health literacy (Jorm, 2012; Teed et al., 2007). Typically, they do this by providing short-term treatment, counseling, outpatient care, emergency services, and suicide prevention.

Partial hospitalization An approach in which patients receive treatment at a hospital during the day but return home at night.

Deinstitutionalization Reduced use of full-time commitment to mental institutions to treat mental disorders.

Halfway house A community-based facility for individuals making the transition from an institution (mental hospital, prison, and so forth) to independent living.

Community mental health center A facility offering a wide range of mental health services, such as prevention, counseling, consultation, and crisis intervention.

Mental health centers are also concerned with *prevention*. Consultation, education, and **crisis intervention** (skilled management of a psychological emergency) are used to prevent problems before they become serious. Also, some centers attempt to raise the general level of mental health in a community by combating unemployment, delinquency, and drug abuse (Tausig, Michello, & Subedi, 2004).

Have community mental health centers succeeded in meeting their goals? In practice, they have concentrated much more on providing clinical services than they have on preventing problems. This appears to be primarily the result of wavering government support (translation: money). Overall, community mental health centers have succeeded in making psychological services more accessible than ever before. Many of their programs rely on **paraprofessionals** (individuals who work in a near-professional capacity under the supervision of more highly trained staff). Some paraprofessionals are ex-addicts, ex-alcoholics, or ex-patients who have "been there." Many more are persons (paid or volunteer) who have skills in tutoring, crafts, or counseling or who are simply warm, understanding, and skilled at communication. Often, paraprofessionals are more approachable than doctors. This encourages people to seek mental health services that they might otherwise be reluctant to use (Everly, 2002; Farrand et al., 2009).

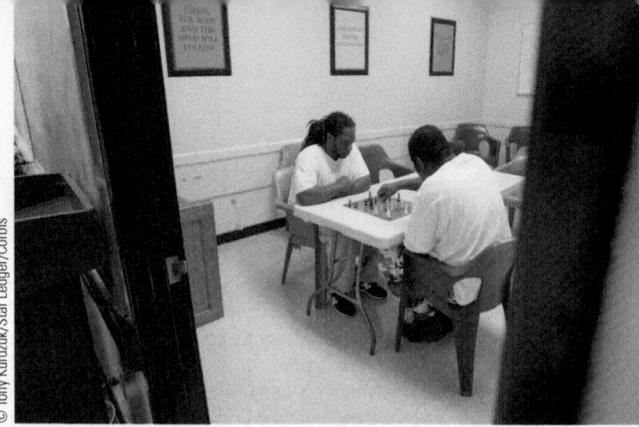

A well-run halfway house can be a humane and cost-effective way to ease former mental patients back into the community (Soyez & Broekaert, 2003).

study break Medical Therapies

RECITE

1. Pharmacotherapy doesn't really help mentally ill people get any better. T or F?
2. ECT is a modern form of pharmacotherapy. T or F?
3. Currently, the frontal lobotomy is the most widely used form of psychosurgery. T or F?
4. Deinstitutionalization is an advanced form of partial hospitalization. T or F?

REFLECT

THINK CRITICALLY

5. Residents of Berkeley, California, once voted on a referendum to ban the use of ECT within city limits. Do you think that the use of certain psychiatric treatments should be controlled by law?

SELF-REFLECT

Keeping in mind that all therapies, and especially medical therapies, have side effects (see, e.g., Casselle, 2009), when is it appropriate to use a medical therapy to treat someone with a mental illness? Why not use psychotherapy instead?

Why might you choose to combine a medical therapy and psychotherapy? Can you frame your reasons in terms of the stress-vulnerability model introduced in Chapter 12?

ANSWERS

1. F 2. F 3. F 4. F 5. The question of who can prescribe drugs, perform surgery, and administer ECT is controlled by law. However, psychiatrists strongly object to residents, city councils, or government agencies making *medical* decisions.

Therapies—Human to the Core

JOURNEY QUESTION 13.9 *Are various psychotherapies effective and what do they have in common?*

In this section, let's ask whether the psychotherapies work and what, if anything, they have in common. We have put this section *after* the section on medical therapies to stress that human relations are at the core of healing. Whether or not a patient under medical care is receiving a somatic treatment, that treatment is administered in a human context. In that sense, it doesn't matter if the healer is a psychotherapist, psychiatrist, social worker, hospital worker, or whatever. No matter what helping specialty you might be considering as a career, information you'll encounter in this section might prove invaluable.

Crisis intervention Skilled management of a psychological emergency.

Paraprofessional An individual who works in a near-professional capacity under the supervision of a more highly trained person.

Critical Thinking

Why is it risky to believe people who say their therapy was effective? An old joke among doctors is that a cold lasts a week without treatment and seven days with it. Perhaps the same is true of therapy. Someone who feels better after 6 months of therapy may have experienced a spontaneous remission—they just feel better because so much time has passed. Or perhaps the crisis that triggered the therapy is now nearly forgotten. Or maybe some sort of therapy placebo effect has occurred. Also, it's possible that the person has received help from other people, such as family, friends, or clergy.

To find out if therapy works, we could randomly place clients in an experimental group that receives therapy and a control group that does not. When this is done, the control group may show some improvement, even without receiving therapy (Lambert & Ogles, 2002; Schuck, Keijsers, & Rinck, 2011). Thus, we can conclude that the therapy is effective only if people in the experimental group improve more than those in the control group.

But isn't it unethical to withhold treatment from someone who really needs therapy? That's right. One way to deal with this is to use a *waiting-list* control group. In this case, people who are waiting to see a therapist are compared with those who receive therapy. Later, those on the waiting list will eventually also receive therapy.

If we combine the results of many experiments, it becomes clear that therapy *is* effective (Lipsey & Wilson, 1993; Shedler, 2010). In addition, studies have revealed that some therapies work best for specific problems (Bradley et al., 2005; Eddy et al., 2004). For example, behavioral, cognitive, and drug therapies are most helpful in treating obsessive-compulsive disorder.

OK. So how effective is psychotherapy? Judging the outcome of therapy is tricky. In a national survey, 9 out of 10 people who have sought mental health care say their lives improved as a result of the treatment (Consumer Reports, 2010; Kotkin, Daviet, & Gurin, 1996). Unfortunately, you can't just take people's word for it. (See "How Do We Know Therapy Actually Works?")

Psychologists are making steady progress in identifying "empirically supported" (or "evidence-based") therapies (Westen & Bradley, 2005). Rather than just relying on intuition, clinicians are seeking guidance from research experiments and guidelines developed through clinical practice (Carroll & Rounsaville, 2007; David & Montgomery, 2011). The end result is a better understanding of which therapies work best for specific types of problems. This trend is also helping to weed out fringe "therapies" that have little or no value.

Fortunately, there is direct evidence that therapy is beneficial. Hundreds of studies show a strong pattern of positive effects for psychotherapy, counseling, and other psychological treatments (Barlow, 2004; Moras, 2002; Shedler, 2010). Of course, results vary in individual cases. For some people, therapy is immensely helpful; for others, it is unsuccessful. Overall, it is effective for more people than not. Speaking more subjectively, a real success, in which a person's life is changed for the better, can be worth the frustration of several cases in which little progress is made.

Although it is common to think of therapy as a long, slow process, this is not normally the case (Shapiro et al., 2003). Research shows that about 50 percent of all clients feel better after between 13 and 18 weekly 1-hour therapy sessions (Howard et al., 1986). This means that the majority of clients improve after 6 months of therapy. Such rapid improvement is impressive in view of the fact that people often suffer for several years before seeking help. Unfortunately, because of high costs and limited insurance coverage, the average client receives only 5 therapy sessions, after which only 20 percent of all patients feel better (Hansen, Lambert, & Forman, 2002).

Core Features of Psychotherapy

What do psychotherapies have in common? We have sampled only a few of the many therapies in use today. For a summary of major differences among psychotherapies, see Table 13.2. To add to your understanding, let's briefly summarize what all techniques have in common.

Psychotherapies of various types share all or most of the following goals: restoring hope, courage, and optimism; gaining insight; resolving conflicts; improving one's sense of self; changing unacceptable patterns of behavior; finding purpose; mending interpersonal

Table 13.2 Comparison of Psychotherapies

	INSIGHT OR ACTION?	DIRECTIVE OR NONDIRECTIVE?	INDIVIDUAL OR GROUP?	THERAPY'S STRENGTH
Psychoanalysis	Insight	Directive	Individual	Searching honesty
Brief psychodynamic therapy	Insight	Directive	Individual	Productive use of conflict
Client-centered therapy	Insight	Nondirective	Both	Acceptance, empathy
Existential therapy	Insight	Both	Individual	Personal empowerment
Gestalt therapy	Insight	Directive	Both	Focus on immediate awareness
Behavior therapy	Action	Directive	Both	Observable changes in behavior
Cognitive therapy	Action	Directive	Individual	Constructive guidance
Rational-emotive behavior therapy	Action	Directive	Individual	Clarity of thinking and goals
Psychodrama	Insight	Directive	Group	Constructive reenactments
Family therapy	Both	Directive	Group	Shared responsibility for problems

Source: Adapted from Corsini & Wedding, 2011; and Prochaska & Norcross, 2010. © Cengage Learning

relations; and learning to approach problems rationally (Frank & Frank, 2004; Trull & Prinstein, 2013). To accomplish these goals, psychotherapies offer the following:

1. Perhaps more than any other single factor, effective therapy provides a **therapeutic alliance**, a *caring relationship* that unites the client and therapist as they work together to solve the client's problems. The strength of this alliance has a major impact on whether therapy succeeds (Meier et al., 2006; Muran & Barber, 2010). The basis for this relationship is emotional rapport, warmth, friendship, understanding, acceptance, and empathy.
2. Therapy offers a *protected setting* in which emotional *catharsis* (release) can take place. Therapy is a sanctuary in which the client is free to express fears, anxieties, and personal secrets without fearing rejection or loss of confidentiality.
3. All therapies to some extent offer an *explanation* or *rationale* for the client's suffering. Additionally, they propose a line of action that will end this suffering.
4. Therapy provides clients with a *new perspective* about themselves and their situations and a chance to practice *new behaviors* (Prochaska & Norcross, 2010). Insights gained during therapy can bring about lasting changes in clients' lives (Grande et al., 2003).

Basic Counseling Skills

A number of general helping skills can be distilled from the various approaches to therapy. These are points to keep in mind if you are ever called upon to comfort a person in distress, such as a troubled friend or relative (Kottler & Shepard, 2011; Sharf, 2012) (**Table 13.3**):

Table 13.3 Helping Behaviors

To help another person gain insight into a personal problem, it is valuable to keep the following comparison in mind:

BEHAVIORS THAT HELP	BEHAVIORS THAT HINDER
Active listening	Probing painful topics
Acceptance	Judging/moralizing
Reflecting feelings	Criticism
Open-ended questioning	Threats
Supportive statements	Rejection
Respect	Ridicule/sarcasm
Patience	Impatience
Genuineness	Placing blame
Paraphrasing	Opinionated statements

Source: Adapted from Kottler & Shepard, 2011. © Cengage Learning

Therapeutic alliance A caring relationship that unites a therapist and a client in working to solve the client's problems.

Be an Active Listener

People frequently talk "at" each other without really listening. A person with problems needs to be heard. Make a sincere effort to listen to and understand the person. Try to accept the person's message without judging it or leaping to conclusions. Let the person know you are listening, through eye contact, posture, your tone of voice, and your replies (Kottler & Shepard, 2011).

Reflect Thoughts and Feelings

One of the best things you can do when offering support to another person is to give feedback by simply restating what is said. This is also a good way to encourage a person to talk. If your friend seems to be at a loss for words, *restate* or *paraphrase* his or her last sentence. Here's an example:

Friend: I'm really down about school. I can't get interested in any of my classes. I flunked my Spanish test, and somebody stole my notebook for psychology.

You: You're really upset about school, aren't you?

Friend: Yeah, and my parents are hassling me about my grades again.

You: That sucks.

Friend: Yeah.

You: That must make you angry.

As simple as this sounds, it is very helpful to someone trying to sort out feelings. Try it. If nothing else, you'll develop a reputation as a fantastic conversationalist!

Don't Be Afraid of Silence

Counselors tend to wait longer before responding than do people in everyday conversations. Pauses of 5 seconds or more are not unusual, and interrupting is rare. Listening patiently lets the person feel unhurried and encourages her or him to speak freely.

Ask Open-Ended Questions

Because your goal is to encourage free expression, *open-ended questions* tend to be the most helpful. A *closed question* is one that can be answered yes or no. Open-ended questions call for an open-ended reply. Say, for example, that a friend tells you, "I feel like my boss has it in for me at work." A closed question would be, "Oh yeah? So, are you going to quit?" Open-ended questions such as "Do you want to talk about it?" or "How do you feel about it?" are more likely to be helpful.

Clarify Problems

People who have a clear idea of what is wrong in their lives are more likely to discover solutions. Try to understand the problem from the person's point of view. As you do, check your understanding often. For example, you might ask, "Are you saying that you feel depressed just at school? Or in general?" Remember, a problem well defined is often half solved.

Focus on Feelings

Feelings are neither right nor wrong. By focusing on feelings, you can encourage the outpouring of emotion that is the basis for catharsis. Passing judgment on what is said just makes people defensive. For example, a friend confides that he has failed a test. Perhaps you know that he studies very little. If you say, "Just study more and you will do better," he will probably become defensive or hostile. Much more can be accomplished by saying, "You must feel very frustrated" or simply, "How do you feel about it?"

Human Diversity

At the age of 23, the patient was clearly suffering from "ifufunyane," a form of bewitchment common in the Xhosa culture of South Africa. However, he was treated at a local hospital by psychiatrists, who said he had schizophrenia and gave him antipsychotic drugs. The drugs helped, but his family shunned his fancy medical treatment and took him to a traditional healer who gave him herbs for his ifufunyane. Unfortunately, he got worse and was readmitted to the hospital. This time, the psychiatrists included the patient's family in his treatment. Together, they agreed to treat him with a combination of antipsychotic drugs *and* traditional herbs. This time, the patient got much better—and his ifufunyane was alleviated, too (Niehaus et al., 2005).

As this example illustrates, **culturally skilled therapists** are trained to work with clients from various cultural backgrounds. To be culturally skilled, a counselor must be able to do all of the following (American Psychological Association, 2003b, 2008; Brammer, 2012; Fowers & Davidov, 2006):

- Adapt traditional theories and techniques to meet the needs of clients from non-European ethnic or racial groups.
- Be aware of his or her own cultural values and biases.
- Establish rapport with a person from a different cultural background.
- Be open to cultural differences without resorting to stereotypes.

- Treat members of racial or ethnic communities as individuals.
- Be aware of a client's ethnic identity and degree of acculturation to the majority society.
- Use existing helping resources within a cultural group to support efforts to resolve problems.

Cultural awareness has helped broaden our ideas about mental health and optimal development (Brammer, 2012). It is also worth remembering that cultural barriers apply to communication in all areas of life, not just therapy. Although such differences can be challenging, they are also frequently enriching (Uwe et al., 2006).

Avoid Giving Advice

Many people mistakenly think that they must solve problems for others. Remember that your goal is to provide understanding and support, not solutions. Of course, it is reasonable to give advice when you are asked for it, but make sure your advice is appropriate. For example, the student described earlier knows he needs to study. His problem is to understand why he doesn't *want* to study.

Accept the Person's Frame of Reference

Because we all live in different psychological worlds, there is no "correct" view of a life situation. Try to resist imposing your views on the problems of others. A person who feels that his or her viewpoint has been understood feels freer to examine it objectively and to question it. Understanding another person's perspective is especially important when cultural differences may create a barrier between a client and therapist (Jun, 2010). (See "Therapy and Culture—A Bad Case of 'Ifufunyane.'")

Maintain Confidentiality

Your efforts to help will be wasted if you fail to respect the privacy of someone who has confided in you. Put yourself in the person's place. Don't gossip.

These guidelines are not an invitation to play "junior therapist." Professional therapists are trained to approach serious problems with skills far exceeding those described here. However, the points made help define the qualities of a therapeutic relationship. They also emphasize that each of us can supply two of the greatest mental health resources available at any cost: friendship and honest communication.

The Future of Therapy—Back to the Future

JOURNEY QUESTION 13.10 *What will therapy be like in the future?*

Therapy has come a long way since the days of trepanning and demonology. Still, the search for ways to improve therapy remains an urgent challenge for those who devote their lives to

Culturally skilled therapist A therapist who has the awareness, knowledge, and skills necessary to treat clients from diverse cultural backgrounds.

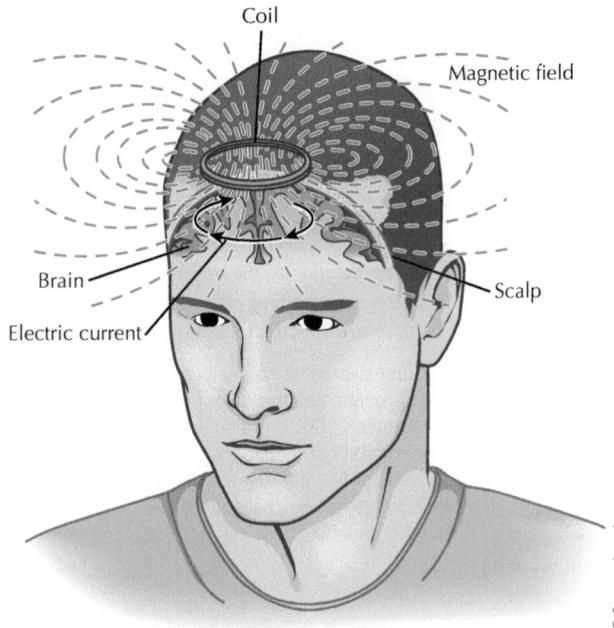

Figure 13.6 Transcranial magnetic stimulation (TMS) uses a small coil held near the surface of the scalp to create magnetic pulses that induce electrical activity in the underlying brain tissue. The result is a temporary blockage of normal brain activity. TMS can be used to study brain function and has already been applied as a medical therapy (Mantovani et al., 2010).

Labels on figure: Coil; Magnetic field; Brain; Scalp; Electric current

© Cengage Learning

helping others. Therapy in the future will likely include some things old and some things new (Norcross, Hedges, & Prochaska, 2002):

- More therapy provided by lower cost master's-level practitioners (counselors, social workers, and psychiatric nurses)
- Greater use of short-term therapy and solution-focused, problem-solving approaches
- More precisely targeted medical therapies with fewer side effects
- Greater reliance on group therapies and self-help groups run by paraprofessionals
- Increased use of Internet services and telephone counseling to distribute mental health services

As you might imagine, many of these predicted changes are based on pressures to reduce the cost of mental health services. Psychiatrists and clinical psychologists are expensive to train. There are too few to take on primary responsibility in all cases. Similarly, longer-term insight-oriented therapies, in particular psychoanalysis, are an expensive luxury.

New Medical Therapies

Neuroscience research continues to probe the functioning of the brain and its various parts in ever-greater detail (Freberg, 2010). As a result, more precisely targeted medical therapies with fewer side effects will continue to be discovered (Morgan & Ricke, 2008). For example, a new technique called **transcranial magnetic stimulation (TMS)** uses magnetic pulses to temporarily block activity in specific parts of the brain. Unlike surgical lesioning, TMS is noninvasive and reversible (Figure 13.6).

By applying TMS to parts of the frontal lobe, Paulo Boggio and his colleagues (2010) were able to change the way people made decisions while gambling. It is not a long stretch to imagine that this technique might become a powerful adjunct therapy together with cognitive therapy to treat compulsive gambling (Ladouceur, Lachance, & Fournier, 2009). Similarly, patients with obsessive-compulsive disorder have shown marked improvement when TMS disrupted brain areas involved in compulsive behavior (Mantovani et al., 2010).

Group Therapy

Because it is cost effective, **group therapy**—psychotherapy done with more than one person—will become more common in the future. This is a trend that began some 60 years ago when psychologists first worked with groups because there was a shortage of therapists. Many of the therapies we have discussed can be adapted for use in groups (Corey, 2012). Surprisingly, group therapy has turned out to be just as effective as individual therapy and has some special advantages (Burlingame, Fuhriman, & Mosier, 2003).

What are the advantages? In group therapy, a person can *act out* or directly experience problems. Doing so often produces insights that might not occur from merely talking about an issue. In addition, other group members with similar problems can offer support and useful input. Group therapy is especially good for helping people understand their personal relationships (McCluskey, 2002). For reasons such as these, a number of specialized groups have emerged. Because they range from Alcoholics Anonymous to Marriage Encounter, we will sample only a few examples.

Psychodrama

One of the first group therapies was developed by Jacob Moreno (1953), who called his technique *psychodrama*. In **psychodrama**, clients act out personal conflicts with others who play supporting roles (Blatner, 2006; McVea, Gow, & Lowe, 2011). Through role-playing, the client reenacts incidents that cause problems in real life. For example, Don, a disturbed teenager, might act out a typical family fight, with the therapist playing his father and with

Transcranial magnetic stimulation (TMS) Device that uses magnetic pulses to temporarily block activity in specific parts of the brain.

Group therapy Psychotherapy conducted in a group setting to make therapeutic use of group dynamics.

Psychodrama A therapy in which clients act out personal conflicts and feelings in the presence of others who play supporting roles.

other clients playing his mother, brothers, and sisters. Moreno believed that insights gained in this way transfer to real-life situations.

Therapists using psychodrama often find that role reversals are helpful. A **role reversal** involves taking the part of another person to learn how he or she feels. For instance, Don might role-play his father or mother, to better understand their feelings. A related method is the **mirror technique**, in which clients observe another person reenact their behavior. Thus, Don might briefly join the audience and watch as another group member plays his role. This would allow him to see himself as others do. Later, the group may summarize what happened and reflect on its meaning.

Family and Couples Therapy

Family relationships are the source of great pleasure and, all too often, of great pain. In **family therapy**, parents and children work as a group to resolve the problems of each family member. This is also called *couples therapy* when children are not involved (Scheinkman, 2008). Family and couples therapy tends to be time-limited and focused on specific problems, such as frequent fights or a depressed teenager. For some types of problems, family therapy may be superior to other approaches (Eisler et al., 2007; Trull & Prinstein, 2013).

Family therapists believe that a problem experienced by one family member is really the whole family's problem (Teyber & McClure, 2011). If the entire pattern of behavior in a family doesn't change, improvements in any single family member may not last. Family members, therefore, work together to improve communication, change destructive patterns, and see themselves and each other in new ways (Goldenberg & Goldenberg, 2004; Griffin, 2002).

Does the therapist work with the whole family at once? Family therapists treat the family as a unit, but they may not meet with the entire family at each session (Eisler et al., 2007). If a family crisis is at hand, the therapist may first try to identify the most resourceful family members who can help solve the immediate problem.

Group Awareness Training

Beginning in the 1960s and 1970s, the human potential movement led many people to seek personal growth experiences. Often, their interest was expressed by participation in sensitivity training or encounter groups. Participants in **sensitivity groups** take part in exercises that gently enlarge self-awareness and sensitivity to others. For example, in a "trust walk," participants expand their confidence in others by allowing themselves to be led around while blindfolded. **Encounter groups** are based on an honest expression of feelings, and intensely personal communication may take place. Typically, the emphasis is on tearing down defenses and false fronts.

There has also been much interest in various forms of large-group awareness training. **Large-group awareness training** refers to programs that claim to increase self-awareness and facilitate constructive personal change. The Garden Company, Lifespring, the Forum, the Hoffman Quadrinity Process, and similar commercial programs are examples. Like the smaller groups that preceded them, large-group training combines psychological exercises, confrontation, new viewpoints, and group dynamics to promote personal change.

Are sensitivity, encounter, and awareness groups really psychotherapies? These experiences tend to be positive, but they produce only moderate benefits (Faith, Wong, & Carpenter, 1995). Moreover, many of the claimed benefits may result simply from a kind of **therapy placebo effect**, in which improvement is based on a client's belief that therapy will help. Positive expectations, a break in daily routine, and an excuse to act differently can have quite an impact. Because of their low cost and versatility, however, groups undoubtedly will continue to grow in popularity as tools for solving problems and improving lives (Corey, 2012).

A group therapy session. Group members offer mutual support while sharing problems and insights.

Role reversal Taking the role of another person to learn how one's own behavior appears from the other person's perspective.

Mirror technique Observing another person reenact one's own behavior, like a character in a play; designed to help persons see themselves more clearly.

Family therapy Technique in which all family members participate, both individually and as a group, to change destructive relationships and communication patterns.

Sensitivity group A group experience consisting of exercises designed to increase self-awareness and sensitivity to others.

Encounter group A group experience that emphasizes intensely honest interchanges among participants regarding feelings and reactions to one another.

Large-group awareness training Any of a number of programs (many of them commercialized) that claim to increase self-awareness and facilitate constructive personal change.

Therapy placebo effect Improvement caused not by the actual process of therapy but by a client's expectation that therapy will help.

Popular TV psychologist Phillip McGraw was awarded a President's Citation from the American Psychological Association for his work in publicizing mental health issues (Meyers, 2006). Media psychologists have been urged to educate without actually doing therapy on the air. Some overstep this boundary, however. Do you think Dr. Phil sometimes goes too far?

Therapy at a Distance

Another cost-saving approach to psychotherapy is to use modern communications technologies (Ormay, 2006). Today, psychological services are available in the home through radio, television, telephone, and the Internet (Goss & Anthony, 2009). Not only is this generally less expensive, it also makes therapy available to people who, for a variety of reasons, cannot easily attend a traditional face-to-face session. Let's explore some advantages and disadvantages of getting help at a distance.

Mass Media Psychologists

By now you have probably heard a phone-in radio psychologist or watched one on television. On a typical program, participants describe problems arising from child abuse, loneliness, love affairs, phobias, sexual adjustment, or depression. The media psychologist then offers reassurance, advice, or suggestions for getting help. Such talk-radio and television programs may seem harmless, but they raise some important questions. For instance, is it reasonable to give advice without knowing anything about a person's background? Could the advice do harm? What good can a psychologist do in 3 minutes or even an hour?

In their own defense, mass media psychologists point out that listeners and viewers may learn solutions to their problems by hearing others talk. Many also stress that their work is educational, not therapeutic. Nevertheless, the question arises: When does advice become therapy? The American Psychological Association urges media psychologists to discuss problems only of a general nature, instead of actually counseling anyone.

Telephone and Internet Therapists

Of course, mass media psychologists must entertain as well as educate. Most distance therapy is conducted one-on-one via the telephone and the Internet. Regardless of how a therapist and client communicate, remember, perhaps the *key* feature of successful therapy is the establishment of an effective *therapeutic alliance*, which is a continuing relationship between two people. In this regard, different telephone and Internet therapies are more or less limited by a lack of interpersonal cues, such as facial expressions and body language. For example, brief e-mail messages are no way to make a diagnosis. And forget about facial expressions or body language—not even tone of voice reaches the e-mail therapist. Typing emotional icons (called *emoticons*) like little smiley faces (☺) or frowns (☹) is a poor substitute for real human interaction.

However, the Internet continues to provide new communication tools. Widely available and inexpensive technologies, such as Skype, make it easy to create two-way audio-video links that allow a client and therapist to see one another on computer monitors and to talk via speakerphones. Doing therapy this way still lacks the close personal contact of face-to-face interaction. However, it does remove many of the objections to doing therapy at a distance. It's very likely that distance services will continue to evolve (Riva & Wiederhold, 2006) and become a major source of mental health care in coming years (Schopp, Demiris, & Glueckauf, 2006).

It is worth noting that distance therapy does have some distinct advantages and disadvantages. For one thing, clients can more easily remain anonymous. (But beware that e-mail counseling may not be completely confidential and could be intercepted and misused.) Thus, a person who might hesitate to see a psychologist can seek help privately, on the phone or online. Of special concern is the fact that distance therapists may or may not be trained professionals (Bloom, 1998). And even if they are, questions exist about whether a psychologist licensed in one state can legally do therapy in another state via the telephone or the Internet.

In closing, under the right circumstances, distance therapies can be successful (Bauer et al., 2011; Brenes, Ingram, & Danhauer, 2011). For example, telephone counseling helps people quit smoking (Rabius, Wiatrek, & McAlister, 2012). Other studies have shown that depressed people benefit from Internet therapy (Titov, 2011). So, too, do people with social phobia and panic disorder (Carlbring et al., 2007; Klein, Richards, & Austin, 2006).

A Look Ahead

In the Psychology in Action section that follows, we will return briefly to behavioral approaches. There you will find a number of useful techniques that you may be able to apply to your own behavior. You'll also find a discussion of when to seek professional help and how to find it. Here's your authors' professional advice: This is information you won't want to skip.

 study break Contemporary Issues in Therapy

RECITE

1. Emotional rapport, warmth, understanding, acceptance, and empathy are the core of
   a. the therapeutic alliance
   b. large-group awareness training
   c. role reversals
   d. action therapy
2. Emotional _____ (release) in a protected setting is an element of most psychotherapies.
3. To aid a troubled friend, you should focus on facts rather than feelings, and you should critically evaluate what the person is saying to help him or her grasp reality. T or F?
4. Culturally skilled therapists always rely on their own cultural frame of reference. T or F?
5. Which therapy places great emphasis on role-playing?
   a. psychodrama
   b. awareness training
   c. family therapy
   d. encounter

REFLECT

THINK CRITICALLY

6. In your opinion, do psychologists have a duty to protect others who may be harmed by their clients? For example, if a patient has homicidal fantasies about his ex-wife, should she be informed?

SELF-REFLECT

What lies at the "heart" of psychotherapy? How would you describe it to a friend?

Which of the basic counseling skills do you already use? Which would improve your ability to help a person in distress?

Would you rather participate in individual therapy or group therapy?

ANSWERS

1. a 2. catharsis 3. F 4. F 5. a 6. According to the law, there is a duty to protect others when a therapist could, with little effort, prevent serious harm. However, this duty can conflict with a client's rights to confidentiality and with client–therapist trust. Therapists often must make difficult choices in such situations.

Psychology in Action

Self-Management and Seeking Professional Help

JOURNEY QUESTION 13.11 *How are behavioral principles applied to everyday problems and how could a person find professional help?*

As mentioned elsewhere in this book, you should seek professional help when a significant problem exists. For lesser difficulties you may want to try applying behavioral principles yourself (Martin & Pear, 2011; Watson & Tharp, 2007; see also Chapter 6).

Covert Punishment and Reward—Boosting Your "Willpower"

While behavior therapy is no cure-all, it does offer some simple tools that can help you modify your own behavior by making your less desirable behaviors less frequent while increasing the frequency of your more desired behaviors, Let's explore some of them.

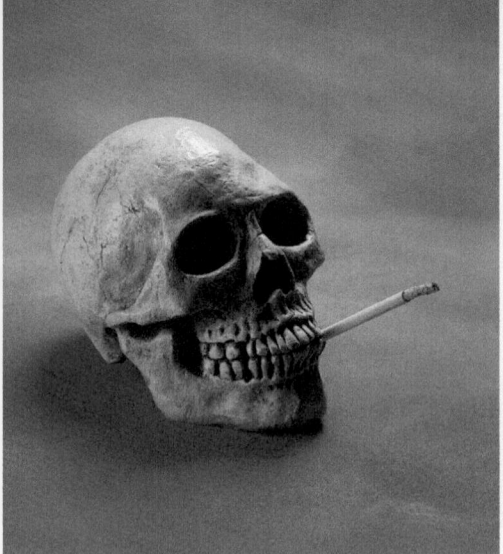
© Lawrence Manning/Corbis

Covert Sensitization

The use of intensive behavioral principles, such as electric shock, to condition an aversion seems remote from everyday problems. Even naturally aversive actions are difficult to apply to personal behavior. As mentioned earlier, for instance, rapid smoking is difficult for most smokers to carry out on their own. And what about a problem like overeating? Indeed, it would be difficult to eat enough to create a lasting aversion to overeating. (Although it's sometimes tempting to try.) In view of such limitations, psychologists have developed an alternative procedure that can be used to curb smoking, overeating, and other habits (Kearney, 2006; Watson & Tharp, 2007).

In **covert sensitization**, aversive imagery is used to reduce the occurrence of an undesired response. Here's how it's done: Obtain six cards and on each write a brief description of a scene related to the habit you wish to control. The scene should be so *disturbing* or *disgusting* that thinking about it would temporarily make you very uncomfortable about indulging in the habit. For smoking, the cards might read:

- "I am in a doctor's office. The doctor looks at some reports and tells me I have lung cancer. She says a lung will have to be removed and sets a date for the operation."
- "I am in bed under an oxygen tent. My chest feels caved in. There is a tube in my throat. I can barely breathe."
- "I wake up in the morning and smoke a cigarette. I begin coughing up blood."
- "My lover won't even kiss me because my breath smells bad."

The trick is to get yourself to imagine or picture vividly each of these disturbing scenes *several times* a day. Imagining the scenes can be accomplished by placing them under *stimulus control*. Simply choose something you do *frequently* each day (such as getting a cup of coffee or getting up from your chair). Next make a rule: Before you can get a cup of coffee or get up from your chair, or whatever you have selected as a cue, you must take out your cards and *vividly picture* yourself engaging in the action you wish to curb (eating or smoking, for example). Then *vividly picture* the scene described on the top card. Imagine the scene for 30 seconds.

After visualizing the top card, move it to the bottom so the cards are rotated. Make up new cards each week. The scenes can be made much more upsetting than the samples given here, which are toned down to keep you from being "grossed out."

Covert sensitization can also be used directly in situations that test your self-control. If you are trying to lose weight, for instance, you might be able to turn down a tempting dessert in this way: As you look at the dessert, visualize maggots crawling all over it. If you make this image as vivid and nauseating as possible, losing your appetite is almost a certainty. If you want to apply this technique to other situations, be aware that vomiting scenes are especially effective. Covert sensitization may sound as if you are "playing games with yourself," but it can be a great help if you want to cut down on a bad habit (Kearney, 2006). Try it!

Thought Stopping

As discussed earlier, behavior therapists accept that thoughts, like visible responses, can also cause trouble. Think of times when you have repeatedly "put yourself down" mentally or when you have been preoccupied by needless worries, fears, or other negative and upsetting thoughts. If you would like to gain control over such thoughts, thought stopping may help you do it.

In **thought stopping**, aversive stimuli are used to interrupt or prevent upsetting thoughts (Bakker, 2009). The simplest thought-stopping technique makes use of mild punishment to suppress upsetting mental images and internal "talk." Simply place a large, flat rubber band around your wrist. As you go through the day apply this rule: Each time you catch yourself thinking the upsetting image or thought, pull the rubber band away from your wrist and snap it. You need not make this terribly painful. Its value lies in drawing your attention to how often you form negative thoughts and in interrupting the flow of thoughts.

Covert sensitization Use of aversive imagery to reduce the occurrence of an undesired response.

Thought stopping Use of aversive stimuli to interrupt or prevent upsetting thoughts.

A second thought-stopping procedure requires only that you interrupt upsetting thoughts each time they occur. Begin by setting aside time each day during which you will deliberately think the unwanted thought. As you begin to form the thought, shout "Stop!" aloud, with conviction. (Obviously, you should choose a private spot for this part of the procedure!)

Repeat the thought-stopping procedure 10 to 20 times for the first 2 or 3 days. Then switch to shouting "Stop!" covertly (to yourself) rather than aloud. Thereafter, thought stopping can be carried out throughout the day, whenever upsetting thoughts occur. After several days of practice, you should be able to stop unwanted thoughts whenever they occur.

Covert Reinforcement

Earlier we discussed how punishing images can be used to decrease undesirable responses, such as smoking or overeating. Many people also find it helpful to covertly *reinforce* desired actions. **Covert reinforcement** is the use of positive imagery to reinforce desired behavior. For example, suppose your target behavior is, once again, not eating dessert. If this were the case, you could do the following (Kearney, 2006; Watson & Tharp, 2007):

> Imagine that you are standing at the dessert table with your friends. As dessert is passed, you politely refuse and feel good about staying on your diet.

These images would then be followed by imagining a pleasant, reinforcing scene:

> Imagine that you are your ideal weight. You look really slim in your favorite color and style. Someone you really like says to you, "Gee, you've lost weight. I've never seen you look so good."

For many people, of course, actual direct reinforcement (as described in the Psychology in Action section of Chapter 6) is the best way to alter behavior. Nevertheless, covert or "visualized" reinforcement can have similar effects. To make use of covert reinforcement, choose one or more target behaviors and rehearse them mentally. Then follow each rehearsal with a vivid, rewarding image.

Self-Directed Desensitization—Overcoming Common Fears

You have prepared for 2 weeks to give a speech in a large class. As your turn approaches, your hands begin to tremble. Your heart pounds and you find it difficult to breathe. You say to your body, "Relax!" What happens? Nothing! That's why the first step in desensitization is learning to relax voluntarily, by using the tension-release method described earlier in this chapter. As an alternative, you might want to try imagining a very safe, pleasant, and relaxing scene. Some people find such images as relaxing as the tension-release method (Rosenthal, 1993). Another helpful technique is to do some deep breathing. Typically, a person who is breathing deeply is relaxed. Shallow breathing involves little movement of the diaphragm. If you place your hand on your abdomen, it will move up and down if you are breathing deeply.

Once you have learned to relax, the next step is to identify the fear you would like to control and construct a fear hierarchy.

Procedure for Constructing a Fear Hierarchy

Make a list of situations (related to the fear) that make you anxious. Try to list at least 10 situations. Some should be very frightening and others only mildly frightening. Write a short description of each situation on a separate card. Place the cards in order from the least disturbing situation to the most disturbing. Here is a sample hierarchy for a student afraid of public speaking:

1. Being given an assignment to speak in class.
2. Thinking about the topic and the date the speech must be given.
3. Writing the speech; thinking about delivering the speech.
4. Watching other students speak in class the week before the speech date.
5. Rehearsing the speech alone; pretending to give it to the class.

Covert reinforcement Using positive imagery to reinforce desired behavior.

6. Delivering the speech to my roommate; pretending my roommate is the teacher.
7. Reviewing the speech on the day it is to be presented.
8. Entering the classroom; waiting and thinking about the speech.
9. Being called; standing up; facing the audience.
10. Delivering the speech.

Using the Hierarchy

When you have mastered the relaxation exercises and have the hierarchy constructed, set aside time each day to work on reducing your fear. Begin by performing the relaxation exercises. When you are completely relaxed, visualize the scene on the first card (the least frightening scene). If you can *vividly* picture and imagine yourself in the first situation twice *without a noticeable increase in muscle tension*, proceed to the next card. Also, as you progress, relax yourself between cards.

Each day, stop when you reach a card that you cannot visualize without becoming tense in three attempts. Each day, begin one or two cards before the one on which you stopped the previous day. Continue to work with the cards until you can visualize the last situation without experiencing tension (techniques are based on Wolpe, 1974).

By using this approach you should be able to reduce the fear or anxiety associated with things such as public speaking, entering darkened rooms, asking questions in large classes, heights, talking to members of the opposite sex, and taking tests (Watson & Tharp, 2007). Even if you are not always able to reduce a fear, you will have learned to place relaxation under voluntary control. This alone is valuable because controlling unnecessary tension can increase energy and efficiency.

Seeking Professional Help—When, Where, and How?

Chances are good that at some point you or someone in your family will benefit from mental health services of one kind or another. In one survey, 13.4 percent of all Americans received treatment for a mental health during the preceding year (National Institute of Mental Health, 2011a).

How would I know if I should seek professional help at some point in my life? Although there is no simple answer to this question, the following guidelines may be helpful:

1. If your level of psychological discomfort (unhappiness, anxiety, or depression, for example) is comparable to a level of physical discomfort that would cause you to see a doctor or dentist, you should consider seeing a psychologist or a psychiatrist.
2. Another signal to watch for is significant changes in behavior, such as the quality of your work (or schoolwork), your rate of absenteeism, your use of drugs (including alcohol), or your relationships with others.
3. Perhaps you have urged a friend or relative to seek professional help and were dismayed because he or she refused to do so. If *you* find friends or relatives making a similar suggestion, recognize that they may be seeing things more clearly than you are.
4. If you have persistent or disturbing suicidal thoughts or impulses, you should seek help immediately.

Locating a Therapist

If I wanted to talk to a therapist, how would I find one? Here are some suggestions that could help you get started:

1. **Colleges and universities.** If you are a student, don't overlook counseling services offered by a student health center or special student counseling facilities.
2. **Workplaces.** If you have a job, check with your employer. Some employers have employee assistance programs that offer confidential free or low-cost therapy for employees.
3. **Community or county mental health centers.** Most counties and many cities offer public mental health services. (These are listed in the phone book.) Public mental health

centers usually provide counseling and therapy services directly, and they can refer you to private therapists.

4. **Mental health associations.** Many cities have mental health associations organized by concerned citizens. Groups such as these usually keep listings of qualified therapists and other services and programs in the community.

5. **The Yellow Pages.** Psychologists are listed in the telephone book or on the Internet under "Psychologists," or in some cases under "Counseling Services." Psychiatrists are generally listed as a subheading under "Physicians." Counselors are usually found under the heading "Marriage and Family Counselors." These listings will usually put you in touch with individuals in private practice.

6. **Crisis hotlines.** The typical crisis hotline is a telephone service staffed by community volunteers. These people are trained to provide information concerning a wide range of mental health problems. They also have lists of organizations, services, and other resources in the community where you can go for help.

Table 13.4 summarizes all the sources for psychotherapy, counseling, and referrals we have discussed, as well as some additional possibilities.

Options *How would I know what kind of a therapist to see? How would I pick one?* The choice between a psychiatrist and a psychologist is somewhat arbitrary. Both are trained to do psychotherapy and can be equally effective as therapists (Seligman, 1995). Although a psychiatrist can administer somatic therapy and prescribe drugs, so can psychologists in New Mexico and Louisiana (Munsey, 2006). Besides, a psychologist can work in conjunction with a physician if such services are needed.

Fees for psychiatrists are usually higher, averaging about $160 to $200 an hour. Psychologists average about $100 an hour. Counselors and social workers typically charge about $80 per hour. Group therapy averages only about $40 an hour because the therapist's fee is divided among several people.

Be aware that most health insurance plans will pay for psychological services. If fees are a problem, keep in mind that many therapists charge on a sliding scale, or ability-to-pay basis, and that community mental health centers almost always charge on a sliding scale. In one way or another, help is almost always available for anyone who needs it.

Some communities and college campuses have counseling services staffed by sympathetic paraprofessionals or peer counselors. These services are free or very low cost. As mentioned earlier, paraprofessionals are people who work in a near-professional capacity under professional supervision. **Peer counselors** are nonprofessional persons who have

---

Table 13.4 Mental Health Resources

- Family doctors (for referrals to mental health professionals)
- Mental health specialists, such as psychiatrists, psychologists, social workers, and mental health counselors
- Religious leaders/counselors
- Health maintenance organizations (HMOs)
- Community mental health centers
- Hospital psychiatry departments and outpatient clinics
- University—or medical school—affiliated programs
- State hospital outpatient clinics
- Family service/social agencies
- Private clinics and facilities
- Employee assistance programs
- Local medical, psychiatric, or psychological societies

Source: National Institute of Mental Health, 2012b. © Cengage Learning

Peer counselor A nonprofessional person who has learned basic counseling skills.

learned basic counseling skills. There is a natural tendency, perhaps, to doubt the abilities of paraprofessionals. However, paraprofessional counselors are often as effective as professionals (Farrand et al., 2009).

Also, don't overlook **self-help groups**, which can add valuable support to professional treatment. Members of a self-help group typically share a particular type of problem, such as eating disorders or coping with an alcoholic parent. Self-help groups offer members mutual support and a chance to discuss problems. In many instances helping others also serves as therapy for those who give help (Burlingame & Davies, 2002). For some problems, self-help groups may be the best choice of all (Dadich, 2010; Galanter et al., 2005).

Qualifications   You can usually find out about a therapist's qualifications simply by asking. A reputable therapist will be glad to reveal his or her background. If you have any doubts, credentials may be checked and other helpful information can be obtained from local branches of any of the following organizations. You can also browse the websites listed here:

American Association for Marriage and Family Therapy (www.aamft.org)
American Family Therapy Academy (www.afta.org)
American Psychiatric Association (www.psych.org)
American Psychological Association (www.apa.org)
Association of Humanistic Psychology (www.ahpweb.org)
Canadian Psychiatric Association (www.cpa-apc.org)
Canadian Psychological Association (www.cpa.ca)
National Mental Health Association (www.nmha.org)

The question of how to pick a particular therapist remains. The best way is to start with a short consultation with a respected psychiatrist, psychologist, or counselor. This will allow the person you consult to evaluate your difficulty and recommend a type of therapy or a therapist who is likely to be helpful. As an alternative you might ask the person teaching this course for a referral.

Evaluating a Therapist   *How would I know whether or not to quit or ignore a therapist?* A balanced look at psychotherapies suggests that all techniques can be equally successful (Wampold et al., 1997). However, all *therapists* are not equally successful (Elliott & Williams, 2003). Ask yourself if you feel you are establishing a *therapeutic alliance* with your therapist. A therapist who is working *with* you is usually willing to use whatever method seems most helpful for a client. He or she is also marked by personal characteristics of warmth, integrity, sincerity, and empathy (Okiishi et al., 2003; Prochaska & Norcross, 2010). The *relationship* between a client and therapist is the therapist's most basic tool (Hubble, Duncan, & Miller, 1999; Prochaska & Norcross, 2010). This is why you must trust and easily relate to a therapist for therapy to be effective. Here are some danger signals to watch for in psychotherapy:

- Sexual advances by therapist
- Therapist makes repeated verbal threats or is physically aggressive
- Therapist is excessively blaming, belittling, hostile, or controlling
- Therapist makes excessive small talk; talks repeatedly about his/her own problems
- Therapist encourages prolonged dependence on him/her
- Therapist demands absolute trust or tells client not to discuss therapy with anyone else

Self-help group A group of people who share a particular type of problem and provide mutual support to one another.

An especially important part of the therapeutic alliance is agreement about the goals of therapy (Meier et al., 2006). It is, therefore, a good idea to think about what you would like to accomplish by entering therapy. Write down your goals and discuss them with your therapist during the first session. Your first meeting with a therapist should also answer all of the following questions (Somberg, Stone, & Claiborn, 1993):

- Will the information I reveal in therapy remain completely confidential?
- What risks do I face if I begin therapy?
- How long do you expect treatment to last?
- What form of treatment do you expect to use?
- Are there alternatives to therapy that might help me as much or more?

It's always tempting to avoid facing up to personal problems. With this in mind, you should give a therapist a fair chance and not give up too easily. But don't hesitate to change therapists or to terminate therapy if you lose confidence in the therapist or if you don't relate well to the therapist as a person.

 study break Self-Management and Seeking Professional Help

RECITE

1. Covert sensitization and thought stopping combine aversion therapy and cognitive therapy. T or F?
2. Like covert aversion conditioning, covert reinforcement of desired responses is also possible. T or F?
3. Exercises that bring about deep-muscle relaxation are an essential element in covert sensitization. T or F?
4. Persistent emotional discomfort is a clear sign that professional psychological counseling should be sought. T or F?
5. In many instances, a therapist's personal qualities have more of an effect on the outcome of therapy than does the type of therapy used. T or F?

REFLECT

THINK CRITICALLY

6. Would it be acceptable for a therapist to urge a client to break all ties with a troublesome family member?

SELF-REFLECT

How could you use covert sensitization, thought stopping, and covert reinforcement to change your behavior? Try to apply each technique to a specific example.

Just for practice, make a fear hierarchy for a situation you find frightening. Does vividly picturing items in the hierarchy make you tense or anxious? If so, can you intentionally relax using the tension-release method?

ANSWERS

1. T 2. T 3. F 4. T 5. T 6. Such decisions must be made by clients themselves. Therapists can help clients evaluate important decisions and feelings about significant persons in their lives. However, actively urging a client to sever a relationship borders on unethical behavior.

Chapter in Review

Summary

13.1 How did psychotherapy originate?

- 13.1.1 Early approaches to mental illness were dominated by superstition and moral condemnation.
- 13.1.2 Demonology attributed mental disturbance to demonic possession and prescribed exorcism as the cure.
- 13.1.3 In some instances, the actual cause of bizarre behavior may have been ergot poisoning.
- 13.1.4 More humane treatment began in 1793 with the work of Philippe Pinel in Paris.

13.2 Is Freudian psychoanalysis still used?

- 13.2.1 As the first true psychotherapy, Freud's psychoanalysis gave rise to modern psychodynamic therapies.
- 13.2.2 The psychoanalyst uses free association, dream analysis, and analysis of resistance and transference to reveal health-producing insights.
- 13.2.3 Psychoanalysts have become relatively rare because psychoanalysis is expensive and time intensive. Brief psychodynamic therapy (which relies on psychoanalytic theory but is brief and focused) is as effective as other major therapies. One example is interpersonal psychotherapy.
- 13.2.4 Some critics argue that traditional psychoanalysis receives credit for spontaneous remissions of symptoms. However, psychoanalysis is successful for many patients.

13.3 How do psychotherapies differ?

- 13.3.1 All psychotherapy aims to facilitate positive changes in personality, behavior, or adjustment.
- 13.3.2 Psychotherapies may be classified as insight, action, directive, nondirective, and combinations of these.
- 13.3.3 Therapies may be conducted either individually or in groups, and they may be time limited.

13.4 What are the major humanistic therapies?

- 13.4.1 Client-centered (or person-centered) therapy is nondirective, based on insights gained from conscious thoughts and feelings, and dedicated to creating an atmosphere of growth.
- 13.4.2 Unconditional positive regard, empathy, authenticity, and reflection are combined to give the client a chance to solve his or her own problems.
- 13.4.3 Existential therapies focus on the end result of the choices one makes in life. Clients are encouraged through confrontation and encounter to exercise free will and to take responsibility for their choices.
- 13.4.4 Gestalt therapy emphasizes immediate awareness of thoughts and feelings. Its goal is to rebuild thinking, feeling, and acting into connected wholes and to help clients break through emotional blockages.

13.5 How does cognitive therapy change thoughts and emotions?

- 13.5.1 Cognitive therapy emphasizes changing thought patterns that underlie emotional or behavioral problems. Changing the thought patterns can have a positive impact on emotions and behavior.
- 13.5.2 Aaron Beck's cognitive therapy focuses on changing several major distortions in thinking: selective perception, overgeneralization, and all-or-nothing thinking.
- 13.5.3 In a variation of cognitive therapy called rational-emotive behavior therapy (REBT), clients learn to recognize and challenge the irrational beliefs that are at the core of their maladaptive thinking patterns.

13.6 What is behavior therapy?

- 13.6.1 Behavior therapists use the learning principles of classical or operant conditioning to directly change human behavior.
- 13.6.2 In aversion therapy, classical conditioning is used to associate maladaptive behavior (such as smoking or drinking) with pain or other aversive events in order to inhibit undesirable responses.
- 13.6.3 In desensitization, gradual adaptation and reciprocal inhibition break the link between fear and particular situations.
- 13.6.4 Typical steps in desensitization are: Construct a fear hierarchy, learn to produce total relaxation. and perform items on the hierarchy (from least to most disturbing).
- 13.6.5 Desensitization may be carried out with real settings or it may be done by vividly imagining the fear hierarchy or by watching models perform the feared responses.
- 13.6.6 In some cases, virtual reality exposure can be used to present fear stimuli in a controlled manner.
- 13.6.7 A newer technique called eye movement desensitization and reprocessing (EMDR) shows promise as a treatment for traumatic memories and stress disorders. At present, however, EMDR is highly controversial.

13.7 What role do operant principles play in behavior therapy?

- 13.7.1 Operant principles, such as positive reinforcement, non-reinforcement, extinction, punishment, shaping, stimulus control, and time out, are used to extinguish undesirable responses and to promote constructive behavior.
- 13.7.2 Nonreward can extinguish troublesome behaviors. Often this is done by simply identifying and eliminating reinforcers, particularly attention and social approval.
- 13.7.3 To apply positive reinforcement and operant shaping, tokens are often used to reinforce selected target behaviors.
- 13.7.4 Full-scale use of tokens in an institutional setting produces a token economy. Toward the end of a token economy program, patients are shifted to social rewards such as recognition and approval.

13.8 How do psychiatrists treat psychological disorders?

- 13.8.1 Medical approaches to mental disorders, such as drugs, surgery, and hospitalization, are similar to medical treatments for physical ailments. All medical treatments for psychological disorders have pros and cons. Overall, however, their effectiveness is improving.

- 13.8.2 Three medical, or somatic, approaches to treatment are pharmacotherapy, electrical stimulation therapy (including electroconvulsive therapy [ECT]), and psychosurgery.

- 13.8.3 Community mental health centers seek to avoid or minimize mental hospitalization. They also seek to prevent mental health problems through education, consultation, and crisis intervention.

13.9 Are various psychotherapies effective and what do they have in common?

- 13.9.1 Effective psychotherapies are based on the therapeutic alliance, a protected setting, catharsis, insights, new perspectives, and a chance to practice new behaviors.

- 13.9.2 Psychotherapy is generally effective, although no single form of therapy is superior to others.

- 13.9.3 All of the following are helping skills that can be learned: active listening, acceptance, reflection, open-ended questioning, support, respect, patience, genuineness, and paraphrasing.

- 13.9.4 The culturally skilled counselor must be able to establish rapport with a person from a different cultural background and adapt traditional theories and techniques to meet the needs of clients from non-European ethnic groups.

13.10 What will therapy be like in the future?

- 13.10.1 New medical therapies, such as transcranial magnetic stimulation (TMS), will continue to be developed.

- 13.10.2 Therapy can be done with groups of people based on a simple extension of individual methods or based on techniques developed specifically for groups.

- 13.10.3 In psychodrama, individuals enact roles and incidents resembling their real-life problems. In family therapy, the family group is treated as a unit.

- 13.10.4 Sensitivity and encounter groups encourage positive personality change. Large-group awareness training attempts to do the same, but the benefits of such programs are questionable.

- 13.10.5 Media psychologists, telephone counselors, and Internet therapists may, on occasion, do some good. However, each has drawbacks, and the effectiveness of telephone counseling and Internet therapy has not been established.

- 13.10.6 Therapy by two-way audio-video link, such as Skype, shows more promise as a way to provide mental health services at a distance.

13.11 How are behavioral principles applied to everyday problems and how could a person find professional help?

- 13.11.1 Some personal problems can be successfully treated using self-management techniques, such as covert reinforcement, covert sensitization, thought stopping, and self-directed desensitization.

- 13.11.2 In covert sensitization, aversive images are used to discourage unwanted behavior. Thought stopping uses mild punishment to prevent upsetting thoughts. Covert reinforcement is a way to encourage desired responses by mental rehearsal.

- 13.11.3 Desensitization pairs relaxation with a hierarchy of upsetting images in order to lessen fears.

- 13.11.4 In most communities, a competent and reputable therapist can be located with public sources of information or through a referral.

- 13.11.5 Practical considerations such as cost and qualifications enter into choosing a therapist. However, the therapist's personal characteristics are of equal importance.

Interactive Learning

Log in to CengageBrain to access the resources your instructor requires. For this book, you can access:

CourseMate Go to CengageBrain.com to access Psychology CourseMate, where you will find an interactive eBook, glossaries, flashcards, quizzes, videos, Virtual Psychology Labs, and more.

Aplia If your professor has assigned Aplia:

1. Sign in to your account.
2. Complete the corresponding exercises as required by your professor.
3. When finished, click "Grade It Now" to see which areas you have mastered, which areas need more work, and detailed explanations of every answer.

Test Your Knowledge

Therapies

1. A scientific explanation of medieval "possessions" by "demons" is related to the effects of
   a. ergot poisoning
   b. trepanning
   c. exorcism
   d. unconscious transference

2. Which of the following is NOT a psychoanalytic concept?
   a. free association
   b. resistance
   c. transference
   d. storytelling

3. Spontaneous remission refers to the possibility that mental problems can get better due to the _____ .
   a. prescription of medication
   b. passage of time
   c. experience of therapy
   d. suddenness of life changes

4. An approach that is incompatible with insight therapy is
   a. individual therapy
   b. action therapy
   c. nondirective therapy
   d. group therapy

5. Carl Rogers did not believe in using _____ in therapy.
   a. empathy
   b. authenticity
   c. reflection
   d. confrontation

6. Filling in gaps in immediate self-awareness is one of the principal goals of
   a. REBT
   b. existential therapy
   c. person-centered therapy
   d. Gestalt therapy

7. A psychologist who is interested in overgeneralization and irrational beliefs is obviously a proponent of
   a. exposure therapy
   b. token economies
   c. systematic desensitization
   d. cognitive therapy

8. The *B* in the A-B-C of REBT stands for
   a. behavior
   b. belief
   c. being
   d. because

9. Classical conditioning principles are the basis for
   a. aversion therapy
   b. time out
   c. token economies
   d. EMDR

10. Reciprocal inhibition is an important principle in
    a. EMDR
    b. REBT
    c. desensitization
    d. the design of a token economy

11. Major tranquilizers are also known as
    a. anxiolytics
    b. antipsychotics
    c. antidepressants
    d. prefrontal sedatives

12. ECT is classified as a type of
    a. somatic therapy
    b. pharmacotherapy
    c. psychosurgery
    d. deep lesioning

13. Research shows that about ____ percent of people who have sought mental health treatment feel that the treatment helped.
    a. 90
    b. 50
    c. 80
    d. 100

14. When evaluating a therapy, one way to avoid being misled by a spontaneous remission of symptoms is to use a _____ control group.
    a. nondirective
    b. latent
    c. psychodynamic
    d. waiting-list

15. The therapeutic alliance involves
    a. warmth
    b. understanding
    c. acceptance
    d. all of the above

16. Culturally skilled therapists do all but one of the following; which does NOT apply?
    a. Be aware of the client's degree of acculturation.
    b. Use helping resources within the client's cultural group.
    c. Adapt standard techniques to match cultural stereotypes.
    d. Be aware of their own cultural values.

17. The mirror technique is frequently used in
    a. exposure therapy
    b. psychodrama
    c. family therapy
    d. EMDR

18. To date, the most acceptable type of distance therapy is
    a. mass media psychology
    b. commercial telephone counseling
    c. Internet therapy
    d. telehealth

19. Mild punishment is used in which self-management technique?
    a. thought stopping
    b. desensitization
    c. REBT
    d. time out

20. The tension-release method is an important part of
    a. covert reinforcement
    b. thought stopping
    c. desensitization
    d. peer counseling

References

Aamodt, M. G. (2010). *Industrial/ organizational psychology: An applied approach* (6th ed.). Belmont, CA: Cengage Learning/Wadsworth.

Abbott, K. R., & Sherratt, T. N. (2011). The evolution of superstition through optimal use of incomplete information. *Animal Behaviour, 82*(1), 85–92. doi:10.1016/j.anbehav.2011.04.002

Abe, N., Suzuki, M., Mori, E., et al. (2007). Deceiving others: Distinct neural responses of the prefrontal cortex and amygdala in simple fabrication and deception with social interactions. *Journal of Cognitive Neuroscience, 19*(2), 287–295. doi:10.1162/jocn.2007.19.2.287

Abraham, W. C. (2006). Memory maintenance: The changing nature of neural mechanisms. *Current Directions in Psychological Science, 15*(1), 5–8. doi:10.1111/j.0963-7214.2006.00396.x

Abrahamse, W., Steg, L., Vlek, C., et al. (2005). A review of intervention studies aimed at household energy conservation. *Journal of Environmental Psychology, 25*(3), 273–291. doi:10.1016/j.jenvp.2005.08.002

Adachi, P. J. C., & Willoughby, T. (2011a). The effect of violent video games on aggression: Is it more than just the violence? *Aggression & Violent Behavior, 16*(1), 55–62. doi:10.1016/j.avb.2010.12.002

Adachi, P. J. C., & Willoughby, T. (2011b). The effect of video game competition and violence on aggressive behavior: Which characteristic has the greatest influence? *Psychology of Violence, 1*(4), 259–274. doi:10.1037/a0024908

Adams, J. (2001). *Conceptual blockbusting* (4th ed.). New York: Basic Books.

Adamson, K. (2004). *Kate's journey: Triumph over adversity.* Redondo Beach, CA: Nosmada Press.

Adan, A., & Serra-Grabulosa, J. P. (2010). Effects of caffeine and glucose, alone and combined, on cognitive performance. *Human Psychopharmacology: Clinical & Experimental, 25*(4), 310–317. doi:10.1002/hup.1115

Addis, K. M., & Kahana, M. J. (2004). Decomposing serial learning: What is missing from the learning curve? *Psychonomic Bulletin & Review, 11*(1), 118–174. doi:10.3758/BF03206470

Adler, S. A., & Orprecio, J. (2006). The eyes have it: Visual pop-out in infants and adults. *Developmental Science, 9*, 189–206. doi:10.1111/j.1467-7687.2006.00479.x

Adolphs, R. (2008). Fear, faces, and the human amygdala. *Current Opinion in Neurobiology, 18*(2), 166–172. doi:10.1016/j.conb.2008.06.006

Adorno, T. W., Frenkel-Brunswik, E., Levinson, D. J., et al. (1950). *The authoritarian personality.* New York: Harper.

Adults and Children Together Against Violence. (2012). *About us.* Washington: Author. Retrieved April 30, 2012, from http://actagainstviolence.apa.org/about/what/index.html.

Advisory Council on the Misuse of Drugs. (2009). *MDMA ("ecstasy"): A review of its harms and classification under the Misuse of Drugs Act 1971.* London: Author. Retrieved February 18, 2012, from http://www.homeoffice.gov.uk/publications/drugs/acmd1/mdma-report?view=Binary

Afifi, T. O., Brownridge, D. A., Cox, B. J., et al. (2006). Physical punishment, childhood abuse, and psychiatric disorders. *Child Abuse & Neglect, 30*(10), 1093–1103. doi:10.1016/j.chiabu.2006.04.006

Agresti, J. D., & Smith, R. K. (2012). Gun control facts. *Just Facts.* Retrieved April 30, 2012, from http://justfacts.com/guncontrol.asp

Agrigoroaei, S., & Lachman, M. E. (2011). Cognitive functioning in midlife and old age: Combined effects of psychosocial and behavioral factors. *Journals of Gerontology, 66B*, 130–140. doi:10.1093/geronb/gbr017

Ahima. R. S., & Osei, S. Y. (2004). Leptin signaling. *Physiology & Behavior, 81*, 223–241. doi:10.1016/j.physbeh.2004.02.014

Ahluwalia, M. K., & Pellettiere, L. (2010). Sikh men post-9/11: Misidentification, discrimination, and coping. *Asian American Journal of Psychology, 1*(4), 303–314. doi:10.1037/a0022156

Ajzen, I. (2005). *Attitudes, personality and behaviour* (2nd ed.). New York: McGraw-Hill.

Åkerstedt, T. (2007). Altered sleep/wake patterns and mental performance. *Physiology & Behavior, 90*(2–3), 209–218. doi:10.1016/j.physbeh.2006.09.007

Albarracín, D., Johnson, B. T., & Zanna, M. P. (Eds.) (2005). *The handbook of attitudes.* Mahwah, NJ: Erlbaum.

Alberti, R., & Emmons, M. (2008). *Your perfect right* (9th ed.). San Luis Obispo, CA: Impact.

Alberto, P. A., & Troutman, A. C. (2009). *Applied behavior analysis for teachers* (8th ed.). Englewood Cliffs, NJ: Prentice Hall.

Albrecht, C. M., & Albrecht, D. E. (2011). Social status, adolescent behavior, and educational attainment. *Sociological Spectrum, 31*(1), 114–137. doi:10.1080/02732173.2011.525698

Albright, D. L., & Thyer, B. (2010). Does EMDR reduce post-traumatic stress disorder symptomatology in combat veterans? *Behavioral Interventions, 25*(1), 1–19.

Alcock, J. E. (2010). The parapsychologists lament. In S. Krippner & H. L. Friedman (Eds.), *Mysterious minds: The neurobiology of psychics, mediums, and other extraordinary people* (pp. 35–43). Santa Barbara, CA: Praeger.

Alcock, J. E., Burns, J., & Freeman, A. (2003). *Psi wars: Getting to grips with the paranormal.* Exeter, UK: Imprint Academic Press.

Aldhous, P. (2010, November 11). Is this evidence that we can see the future? *New Scientist.* Retrieved May 8, 2012, from http://www.newscientist.com/article/dn19712-is-this-evidence-that-we-can-see-the-future.html

Alegre, A. (2011). Parenting styles and children's emotional intelligence: What do we know? *The Family Journal, 19*(1), 56–62. doi:10.1177/1066480710387486

Alessandria, M., Vetrugno, R., Cortelli, P., et al. (2011). Normal body scheme and absent phantom limb experience in amputees while dreaming. *Consciousness & Cognition, 20*(4), 1831–1834. doi:10.1016/j.concog.2011.06.013

Ali, M. M., & Dwyer, D. S. (2010). Social network effects in alcohol consumption among adolescents. *Addictive Behaviors, 35*(4), 337–342. doi:10.1016/j.addbeh.2009.12.002

Allan, R. (2011). Type A behavior pattern. In R. Allan & J. Fisher (Eds.), *Heart and mind: The practice of cardiac psychology* (2nd ed., pp. 287–290). Washington, DC: American Psychological Association. doi:10.1037/13086-012

Allen, D., Carlson, D., & Ham, C. (2007). Well-being: New paradigms of wellness-inspiring positive health outcomes and renewing hope. *American Journal of Health Promotion, 21*(3), 1–9.

Allen, J. L., Lavallee, K. L., Herren, C., et al. (2010). DSM-IV criteria for childhood separation anxiety disorder: Informant, age, and sex differences. *Journal of Anxiety Disorders, 24*(8), 946–952. doi:10.1016/j.janxdis.2010.06.022

Allen, K., Blascovich, J., & Mendes, W. B. (2002). Cardiovascular reactivity in the presence of pets, friends, and spouses: The truth about cats and dogs. *Psychosomatic Medicine, 64*(5), 727–739.

Alleyne, M. D. (Ed.). (2011). *Anti-racism and multiculturalism: Studies in international communication.* Piscataway, NJ: Transaction Publishers.

Allport, G. W. (1958). *The nature of prejudice.* Garden City, NY: Anchor Books, Doubleday.

Allport, G. W. (1961). *Pattern and growth in personality.* New York: Holt, Rinehart, & Winston.

Altemeyer, B. (2004). Highly dominating, highly authoritarian personalities. *Journal of Social Psychology, 144*(4), 421–447. doi:10.3200/SOCP.144.4.421-448

Alter, A. L., Aronson, J., Darley, J. M., et al. (2010). Rising to the threat: Reducing stereotype threat by reframing the threat as a challenge. *Journal of Experimental Social Psychology, 46*, 166–171. doi:10.1016/j.jesp.2009.09.014

Altschuler, G. C. (2001). *Battling the cheats.* The New York Times: Education, Jan. 7, 15.

Alwin, D. F., Cohen, R. L., & Newcomb, T. M. (1991). *Political attitudes over the life span: The Bennington women after fifty years.* Madison, WI: University of Wisconsin Press.

Amabile, T., Hadley, C. N., & Kramer, S. J. (2002). Creativity under the gun. *Harvard Business Review, 80*(8), 52–61.

Amano, T. T., Duvarci, S. S., Popa, D. D., et al. (2011). The fear circuit revisited: Contributions of the basal amygdala nuclei to conditioned fear. *The Journal of Neuroscience: The Official Journal of the Society for Neuroscience, 31*(43), 15481–15489. doi:10.1523/JNEUROSCI.3410-11.2011

Ambady, N., & R. Rosenthal, R. (1993). Half a minute: Predicting teacher evaluations from thin slices of nonverbal behavior and physical attractiveness. *Journal of Personality & Social Psychology, 64*, 431–441. doi:10.1037/0022-3514.64.3.431

American Lung Association. (2012). *Secondhand smoke.* Retrieved February 8, 2012, from http://www.lungusa.org/stop-smoking/about-smoking/health-effects/secondhand-smoke.html.

American Psychiatric Association. (2000). *Diagnostic and statistical manual of mental disorders* (4th ed.). Washington, DC: Author.

American Psychiatric Association. (2012). *DSM-5: The future of psychiatric diagnosis.* Washington, DC: Author. Retrieved April 18, 2012, from http://www.dsm5.org/Pages/Default.aspx

American Psychological Association. (2003a). *Demographic shifts in psychology.* Washington, DC: Author. Retrieved May 9, 2012, from http://www.apa.org/workforce/snapshots/2003/demographic-shifts.aspx

American Psychological Association. (2003b). Guidelines on multicultural education, training, research, practice, and organizational change for psychologists. *American Psychologist, 58*(5), 377–402. doi:10.1037/0003-066X.58.5.377

American Psychological Association. (2007). *APA guidelines for the undergraduate psychology major*. Washington: Author. Retrieved April 30, 2012, from http://www.apa.org/ed/precollege/about/psymajor-guidelines.pdf

American Psychological Association. (2008). *Report of the Task Force on the Implementation of the Multicultural Guidelines*. Washington, DC: Author. Retrieved May 9, 2011, from http://www.apa.org/about/policy/multicultural-report.pdf

American Psychological Association. (2010). *Ethical principles of psychologists and code of conduct: 2010 amendments*. Washington, DC: Author. Retrieved May 9, 2012, from http://www.apa.org/ethics/code/index.aspx

Ancis, J. R., Chen, Y., & Schultz, D. (2004). Diagnostic challenges and the so-called culture-bound syndromes. In J. R. Ancis (Ed.), *Culturally responsive interventions: Innovative approaches to working with diverse populations* (pp. 213–222). New York: Brunner-Routledge.

Andersen, M. L., Poyares, D., Alves, R. S. C., et al. (2007). Sexsomnia: Abnormal sexual behavior during sleep. *Brain Research Reviews, 56*(2), 271–282. doi:10.1016/j.brainresrev.2007.06.005

Anderson, C. A. (1989). Temperature and aggression. *Psychological Bulletin, 106*, 74–96. doi:10.1037/0033-2909.106.1.74

Anderson, C. A. (2004). An update on the effects of violent video games. *Journal of Adolescence, 27*, 113–122. doi:10.1016/j.adolescence.2003.10.009

Anderson, C. A., & Bushman, B. J. (2002). Human aggression. *Annual Review of Psychology, 53*, 27–51. doi:10.1146/annurev.psych.53.100901.135231

Anderson, C. A., Anderson, K. B., & Deuser, W. E. (1996). Examining an affective aggression framework. *Personality & Social Psychology Bulletin, 22*(4), 366–376. doi:10.1177/0146167296224004

Anderson, C. A., Berkowitz, L. Donnerstein, E., et al. (2003). The influence of media violence on youth. *Psychological Science in the Public Interest, 4*, 81–100.doi:10.1111/j.1529-1006.2003.pspi_1433.x

Anderson, C.A., Gentile, D.A., & Buckley, K.E. (2007). *Violent video game effects on children and adolescents: Theory, research, and public policy*. New York: Oxford University Press.

Anderson, J. R. (2010a). *Cognitive psychology and its implications* (7th ed.). New York: Worth.

Anderson, K. J. (2010b). *Benign bigotry: The psychology of subtle prejudice*. New York: Cambridge University Press.

Anderson, M. C., & Green, C. (2001). Suppressing unwanted memories by executive control. *Nature, 410*(6826), 366–369. doi:10.1038/35066572

Anderson, M. C., Ochsner, K. N., Kuhl, B., et al., (2004). Neural systems underlying the suppression of unwanted memories. *Science, 303*, 232–235. doi:10.1126/science.1089504

Anderson, M. C., Reinholz, J., Kuhl, B. A., et al. (2011). Intentional suppression of unwanted memories grows more difficult as we age. *Psychology & Aging, 26*(2), 397–405. doi:10.1037/a0022505

Anderson, S. W., & Booker, M. B. (2006). Cognitive behavioral therapy versus psychosurgery for refractory obsessive-compulsive disorder. *The Journal of Neuropsychiatry & Clinical Neurosciences, 18*(1), 129. doi:10.1176/appi.neuropsych.18.1.129

André, C., Jaber-Filho, J. A., Carvalho, M., et al. (2003). Predictors of recovery following involuntary hospitalization of violent substance abuse patients. *The American Journal on Addictions, 12*(1), 84–89. doi:10.1080/10550490390143394

Andreasen, N. C., Nopoulos, P., Magnotta, V., et al. (2011). Progressive brain change in schizophrenia: A prospective longitudinal study of first-episode schizophrenia. *Biological Psychiatry, 70*(7), 672–679. doi:10.1016/j.biopsych.2011.05.017

Andresen, J. (2000). Meditation meets behavioural medicine: The story of experimental research on meditation. *Journal of Consciousness Studies, 7*(11–12), 17–73.

Anekonda, T. S. (2006). Resveratrol: A boon for treating Alzheimer's disease? *Brain Research Reviews, 52*(2), 316–326. doi:10.1016/j.brainresrev.2006.04.004

Annesi, J. J., & Marti, C. N. (2011). Path analysis of exercise treatment-induced changes in psychological factors leading to weight loss. *Psychology & Health, 26*(8), 1081–1098. doi:10.1080/08870446.2010.534167

Annett, M. (2002). *Handedness and brain asymmetry: The right shift theory*. Hove, UK: Psychology Press.

Annett, M., & Manning, M. (1990). Arithmetic and laterality. *Neuropsychologia, 28*(1), 61–69. doi:10.1016/0028-3932(90)90086-4

Antony, M. M., & Swinson, R. P. (2008). *The shyness and social anxiety workbook: Proven, step-by-step techniques for overcoming your fear* (2nd ed.). Oakland, CA: New Harbinger.

APA Center for Workforce Studies. (2010). *2009 APA member profiles*. Washington, DC: Author. Retrieved May 9, 2012, from http://www.apa.org/workforce/publications/09-member/table-03.pdf

Aradillas, E., Libon, D. J., & Schwartzman, R. J. (2011). Acute loss of spatial navigational skills in a case of a right posterior hippocampus stroke. *Journal of the Neurological Sciences, 308*(1–2), 144–146. doi:10.1016/j.jns.2011.06.026

Arbona, C. B., Osma, J., Garcia-Palacios, A., et al. (2004). Treatment of flying phobia using virtual reality: Data from a 1-year follow-up using a multiple baseline design. *Clinical Psychology & Psychotherapy, 11*(5), 311–323. doi:10.1002/cpp.404

Ariely, D., & Wertenbroch, K. (2002). Procrastination, deadlines, and performance: Self-control by precommitment. *Psychological Science, 13*(3), 219–224. doi:10.1111/1467-9280.00441

Arnett, J. J. (2004). *Emerging adulthood: The winding road from late teens through the twenties*. New York: Oxford University Press.

Arnett, J. J. (2010). Oh, grow up! Generational grumbling and the new life stage of emerging adulthood: Commentary on Trzesniewski & Donnellan (2010). *Perspectives on Psychological Science, 5*(1), 89–92. doi:10.1177/1745691609357016

Arnett, J. J. (2011). The cultural psychology of a new life stage. In L. A. Jensen (Ed.), *Emerging adulthood(s): The cultural psychology of a new life stage* (pp. 255–275). New York: Oxford University Press.

Arnett, J. J., & Galambos, N. L. (Eds.). (2003). *New directions for child and adolescent development: Exploring cultural conceptions of the transition to adulthood*. San Francisco: Jossey-Bass.

Arnsten, A., Mazure, C. M., & Sinha, R. (2012). This is your brain on meltdown. *Scientific American*, April, 48–53. doi:10.1038/scientificamerican0412-48

Aron, A., Fisher, H. E., Strong, G., et al. (2008). Falling in love. In S. Sprecher, A. Wenzel, & J. Harvey (Eds.), *Handbook of relationship initiation* (pp. 315–336). New York: Psychology Press.

Aronow, E., Altman Weiss, K., & Reznikoff, M. (2001). *A practical guide to the Thematic Apperception Test: The TAT in clinical practice*. New York: Brunner-Routledge.

Aronson, E. (2008). *The social animal* (10th ed.). New York: Worth.

Aronson, E., Wilson, T. D., & Akert, R. M. (2010). *Social psychology* (7th ed.). Englewood Cliffs, NJ: Prentice Hall.

Aronson, K. (2003) Alcohol: A recently identified risk factor for breast cancer. *Canadian Medical Association Journal, 168*(9), 1147–1148.

Arthur, W., & Doverspike, D. (2001). Predicting motor vehicle crash involvement from a personality measure and a driving knowledge test. *Journal of Prevention & Intervention in the Community, 22*(1), 35–42. doi:10.1300/J005v22n01_04

Artz, S. (2005). To die for: Violent adolescent girls' search for male attention. In D. J. Pepler, K. C. Madsen, et al. (Eds.), *The development and treatment of girlhood aggression* (pp. 137–160). Mahwah, NJ: Erlbaum.

Ary, D. V., Duncan, T. E., Biglan, A., et al. (1999). Development of adolescent problem behavior. *Journal of Abnormal Child Psychology, 27*(2), 141–150. doi:10.1023/A:1021963531607

Asch, S. E. (1956). Studies of independence and conformity: A minority of one against a unanimous majority. *Psychological Monographs, 70*(9, Whole No. 416). doi:10.1037/h0093718

Ash, D. W., & Holding, D. H. (1990). Backward versus forward chaining in the acquisition of a keyboard skill. *Human Factors, 32*(2), 139–146. doi:10.1177/001872089003200202

Ashby, F. G., & Maddox, W. T. (2005). Human category learning. *Annual Review of Psychology, 56*, 149–178. doi:10.1146/annurev.psych.56.091103.070217

Ashcraft, D. (2012). *Personality theories workbook* (5th ed.). Belmont, CA: Cengage Learning/Wadsworth.

Ashton, M. C. (2007). *Individual differences and personality*. San Diego: Elsevier.

Asmundson, G. J. G., & Taylor, S. (2005). *It's not all in your head*. London: Psychology Press.

Atkinson, R.C. & Shiffrin, R.M. (1968). Human memory: A proposed system and its control processes. In K. W. Spence & J. T. Spence (Eds.), *The psychology of learning and motivation* (Vol. 2, pp. 742–775). London: Academic Press. doi:10.1016/S0079-7421(08)60422-3

Au, S., & Stavinoha, P. L. (2008). *Stress-free potty training: A commonsense guide to finding the right approach for your child*. New York: AMACOM.

Aucoin, K. J., Frick, P. J., & Bodin, S. D. (2006). Corporal punishment and child adjustment. *Journal of Applied Developmental Psychology, 27*(6), 527–541.

Ausubel, D. P. (1978). In defense of advance organizers: A reply to the critics. *Review of Educational Research, 48*, 251–257. doi:10.2307/1170083

Avery, D. H., Eder, D. N., Bolte, M. A., et al. (2001). Dawn simulation and bright light in the treatment of SAD. *Biological Psychiatry, 50*(3), 205–216. doi:10.1016/S0006-3223(01)01200-8

Awadallah, N., Vaughan, A., Franco, K., et al. (2005). Munchausen by proxy: A case, chart series, and literature review of older victims. *Child Abuse & Neglect, 29*(8), 931–941. doi:10.1016/j.chiabu.2004.11.007

Axmacher, N., Do Lam, A. T. A., Kessler, H., et al. (2010). Natural memory beyond the storage model: Repression, trauma, and the construction of a personal past. *Frontiers in Human Neuroscience, 4*, 211. doi:10.3389/fnhum.2010.00211

Ayers, L., Beaton, S., & Hunt, H. (1999). The significance of transpersonal experiences, emotional conflict, and cognitive abilities in creativity. *Empirical Studies of the Arts, 17*(1), 73–82. doi:10.2190/4X8D-XTT4-FKKH-ECJ7

Ayllon, T. (1963). Intensive treatment of psychotic behavior by stimulus satiation and food reinforcement. *Behavior Research & Therapy, 1*, 53–61. doi:10.1016/0005-7967(63)90008-1

Baard, P. P., Deci, E. L., & Ryan, R. M. (2004). Intrinsic need satisfaction: A motivational basis of performance and well-being in two work settings. *Journal of Applied Social Psychology, 34*(10), 2045–2068. doi:10.1111/j.1559-1816.2004.tb02690.x

Babbie, E. R. (2013). *The practice of social research* (13th ed.). Belmont, CA: Cengage Learning/Wadsworth.

Baddeley, A. (2012). Working memory: Theories, models, and controversies. *Annual Review of Psychology, 63*, 1–29. doi:10.1146/annurev-psych-120710-100422

Baddeley, A., Eysenck, M. W., & Anderson, M. C. (2009). *Memory*. Hove, UK: Psychology Press.

Bahr, S. J., & Hoffmann, J. P. (2010). Parenting style, religiosity, peers, and adolescent heavy drinking. *Journal of Studies on Alcohol & Drugs, 71*(4), 539–543.

Bailey, C. H., & Kandel, E. R. (2004). Synaptic growth and the persistence of long-term memory: A molecular perspective. In M. S. Gazzaniga (Ed.), *The cognitive neurosciences* (3rd ed., pp. 647–663). Cambridge, MA: MIT Press.

Bailey, L. M., & McKeever, W. F. (2004). A large-scale study of handedness and pregnancy/birth risk events: Implications for genetic theories of handedness. *Laterality: Asymmetries of Body, Brain & Cognition, 9*(2), 175–188.

Baillargeon, R. (1991). Reasoning about the height and location of a hidden object in 4.5- and 6.5-month-old infants. *Cognition, 38*(1), 13–42. doi:10.1016/0010-0277(91)90021-U

Baillargeon, R. (2004). Infants' reasoning about hidden objects: Evidence for event-general and event-specific expectations. *Developmental Science, 7*(4), 391–424. doi:10.1111/j.1467-7687.2004.00357.x

Baillargeon, R., De Vos, J., & Graber, M. (1989). Location memory in 8-month-old infants in a nonsearch AB task. *Cognitive Development, 4*, 345–367. doi:10.1016/S0885-2014(89)90040-3

Bain, S. K., & Allin, J. D. (2005). Stanford-Binet Intelligence Scales, Fifth Edition. *Journal of Psychoeducational Assessment, 23*(1), 87–95. doi:10.1177/073428290502300108

Baird, A. D., Scheffer, I. E., & Wilson, S. J. (2011). Mirror neuron system involvement in empathy: A critical look at the evidence. *Social Neuroscience, 6*(4), 327–335. doi:10.1080/17470919.2010.547085

Baker, L., & McNulty, J. K. (2010). Shyness and marriage: Does shyness shape even established relationships? *Personality & Social Psychology Bulletin, 36*(5), 665–676. doi:10.1177/0146167210367489

Baker, T. B., Brandon, T. H., & Chassin, L. (2004). Motivational influences on cigarette smoking. *Annual Review of Psychology, 55*, 463–491. doi:10.1146/annurev.psych.55.090902.142054

Bakker, G. M. (2009). In defence of thought stopping. *Clinical Psychologist, 13*(2), 59–68. doi:10.1080/13284200902810452

Bales, D., & Bateman, A. W. (2012). Partial hospitalization settings. In A. W. Bateman & P. Fonagy (Eds.), *Handbook of mentalizing in mental health practice*, (pp. 197–226). Arlington, VA: American Psychiatric Publishing.

Balk, D. E., Lampe, S., Sharpe, B., et al. (1998). TAT results in a longitudinal study of bereaved college students. *Death Studies, 22*(1), 3–21. doi:10.1080/074811898201704

Balthazart, J. (2012). *Biology of homosexuality*. New York: Oxford University Press.

Bandura, A. (1971). *Social learning theory*. New York: General Learning Press.

Bandura, A. (2001). Social cognitive theory: An agentic perspective. *Annual Review of Psychology, 52*, 1–26. doi:10.1146/annurev.psych.52.1.1

Bandura, A., & Walters, R. (1959). *Adolescent aggression*. New York: Ronald.

Bandura, A., Blanchard, E. B., & Ritter, B. (1969). Relative efficacy of desensitization and modeling approaches for inducing behavioral, affective, and attitudinal changes. *Journal of Personality & Social Psychology, 13*(3), 173–199. doi:10.1037/h0028276

Bandura, A., Ross, D., & Ross, S. A. (1963). Vicarious reinforcement and imitative learning. *Journal of Abnormal & Social Psychology, 67*, 601–607. doi:10.1037/h0045550

Banich, M. T., & Compton, R. J. (2011). *Cognitive neuroscience* (3rd ed.). Belmont, CA: Cengage Learning/Wadsworth.

Banks, A., & Gartrell, N. K. (1995). Hormones and sexual orientation: A questionable link. *Journal of Homosexuality, 28*(3–4), 247–268. doi:10.1300/J082v28n03_04

Barabasz, A., & Watkins, J. G. (2005). *Hypnotherapeutic techniques* (2nd ed.). Washington, DC: Taylor & Francis.

Barber, N. (2010). Applying the concept of adaptation to societal differences in intelligence. *Cross-Cultural Research, 44*(2), 116–150. doi:10.1177/1069397109358041

Bardone-Cone, A. M., Joiner, Jr., T. E., Crosby, R. D., et al. (2008). Examining a psychosocial interactive model of binge eating and vomiting in women with bulimia nervosa and subthreshold bulimia nervosa. *Behaviour Research & Therapy, 46*(7), 887–894. doi:10.1016/j.brat.2008.04.003

Barelds, D. P. H., & Dijkstra, P. (2009). Positive illusions about a partner's physical attractiveness and relationship quality. *Personal Relationships, 16*(2), 263–283. doi:10.1111/j.1475-6811.2009.01222.x

Barkataki, I., Kumari, V., Das, M., et al. (2006). Volumetric structural brain abnormalities in men with schizophrenia or antisocial personality disorder. *Behavioural Brain Research, 169*(2), 239–247. doi:10.1016/j.bbr.2006.01.009

Barlow, D. H. (2000). Unraveling the mysteries of anxiety and its disorders from the perspective of emotion theory. *American Psychologist, 55*, 1247–1263. doi:10.1037/0003-066X.55.11.1247

Barlow, D. H. (2002). *Anxiety and its disorders* (2nd ed.). New York: Guilford.

Barlow, D. H. (2004). Psychological treatments. *American Psychologist, 59*(9), 869–878. doi:10.1037/0003-066X.59.9.869

Barnett, J., Behnke, S. H., Rosenthal, S., et al. (2007). In case of ethical dilemma, break glass: Commentary on ethical decision making in practice. *Professional Psychology: Research & Practice, 38*(1), 7–12. doi:10.1037/0735-7028.38.1.7

Barnier, A. J., McConkey, K. M., & Wright, J. (2004). Posthypnotic amnesia for autobiographical episodes: Influencing memory accessibility and quality. *International Journal of Clinical & Experimental Hypnosis, 52*(3), 260–279. doi:10.1080/0020714049052351

Baron, I. S. (2005). Test review: Wechsler intelligence scale for children (4th ed.). (WISC-IV). *Child Neuropsychology, 11*(5), 471–475. doi:10.1080/09297040590951587

Baron, R. A., Byrne, D., & Branscombe, N. R. (2012). *Mastering social psychology* (13th ed.). Boston: Pearson/Allyn & Bacon.

Baron-Cohen, S. (1985). Does the autistic child have a "theory of mind"? *Cognition, 21*, 37–46. doi:10.1016/0010-0277(85)90022-8

Barrett, D. (1993). The "committee of sleep": A study of dream incubation for problem solving. *Dreaming, 3*(2), 115–122.

Barron, F. (1958). The psychology of imagination. *Scientific American, 199*(3), 150–170. doi:10.1038/scientificamerican0958-150

Barrowcliff, A. L., & Haddock, G. (2006). The relationship between command hallucinations and factors of compliance: A critical review of the literature. *Journal of Forensic Psychiatry & Psychology, 17*(2), 266–298. doi:10.1080/14789940500485078

Barry, S. R., & Sacks, O. (2009). *Fixing my gaze*. New York: Basic Books.

Bar-Tal, D., & Labin, D. (2001). The effect of a major event on stereotyping: Terrorist attacks in Israel and Israeli adolescents' perceptions of Palestinians, Jordanians and Arabs. *European Journal of Social Psychology, 31*(3), 265–280. doi:10.1002/ejsp.43

Bartholow, B. D., & Anderson, C. A. (2002). Effects of violent video games on aggressive behavior. *Journal of Experimental Social Psychology, 38*(3), 283–290. doi:10.1006/jesp.2001.1502

Bartholow, B. D., Sestir, M. A., & Davis, E. B. (2005). Correlates and consequences of exposure to video game violence: Hostile personality, empathy, and aggressive behavior. *Personality & Social Psychology Bulletin, 31*(11), 1573–1586. doi:10.1177/0146167205277205

Bartram, B. (2006). An examination of perceptions of parental influence on attitudes to language learning. *Educational Research, 48*(2), 211–222. doi:10.1080/00131880600732298

Basadur, M., Runco, M. A., & Vega, L. A. (2000). Understanding how creative thinking skills, attitudes and behaviors work together. *Journal of Creative Behavior, 34*(2), 77–100. doi:10.1002/j.2162-6057.2000.tb01203.x

Basner, M., & Dinges, D. (2009). Dubious bargain: Trading sleep for Leno and Letterman. *Sleep, 32*(6), 747–752.

Bass, J., & Takahashi, J. S. (2010). Circadian integration of metabolism and energetics. *Science, 330*(6009), 1349–1354. doi:10.1126/science.1195027

Basson, R., Brotto, L. A., Laan, E., et al. (2005). Assessment and management of women's sexual dysfunctions: Problematic desire and arousal. *Journal of Sexual Medicine, 2*(3), 291–300. doi:10.1111/j.1743-6109.2005.20346.x

Bastian, B., & Haslam, N. (2006). Psychological essentialism and stereotype endorsement. *Journal of Experimental Social Psychology, 42*(2), 228–235. doi:10.1016/j.jesp.2005.03.003

Batelaan, N. M., de Graaf, R., Spijker, J., et al. (2010). The course of panic attacks in individuals with panic disorder and subthreshold panic disorder: A population-based study. *Journal of Affective Disorders, 121*(1–2), 30–38. doi:10.1016/j.jad.2009.05.003

Bateman, A. W., & Fonagy, P. (2012). Antisocial personality disorder. In A. W. Bateman & P. Fonagy (Eds.), *Handbook of mentalizing in mental health practice* (pp. 289–308). Arlington, VA: American Psychiatric Publishing.

Batson, C. D. (2006). "Not all self-interest after all": Economics of empathy-induced altruism. In D. De Cremer, M. Zeelenberg, et al. (Eds.), *Social psychology and economics* (pp. 281–299). Mahwah, NJ: Erlbaum.

Batson, C. D. (2010). Empathy-induced altruistic motivation. In M. Mikulincer & P. R. Shaver (Eds.), *Prosocial motives, emotions, and behavior: The better angels of our nature* (pp. 15–34). Washington, DC: American Psychological Association. doi:10.1037/12061-001

Batson, C. D., & Powell, A. A. (2003). Altruism and prosocial behavior. In T. Millon & M. J. Lerner (Eds.), *Handbook of psychology: Personality and social psychology* (Vol. 5, pp. 463–484). New York: Wiley.

Batterham, R. L., Cohen, M. A., Ellis, S. M., et al. (2003). Inhibition of food intake in obese subjects by peptide YY3-36. *New England Journal of Medicine, 349*(10), 941–948. doi:10.1056/NEJMoa030204

Bauer, J. J., McAdams, D. P., & Pals, J. L. (2008). Narrative identity and eudaimonic well-being. *Journal of Happiness Studies, 9*(1), 81–104. doi:10.1007/s10902-006-9021-6

Bauer, S., Wolf, M., Haug, S., et al. (2011). The effectiveness of Internet chat groups in relapse prevention after inpatient psychotherapy. *Psychotherapy Research, 21*(2), 219–226. doi:10.1080/10503307.2010.547530

Bauman, L. J., Karasz, A., & Hamilton, A. (2007). Understanding failure of condom use intention among adolescents: Completing an intensive preventive intervention. *Journal of Adolescent Research, 22*(3), 248–274. doi:10.1177/0743558407299696

Baumeister, R. F., & Bushman, B. (2011). *Social psychology and human nature* (2nd ed.). Belmont, CA: Cengage Learning/Wadsworth.

Baumeister, R. F., Campbell, J. D., Krueger, J. I., et al. (2003). Does high self-esteem cause better performance, interpersonal success, happiness, or healthier lifestyles? *Psychological Science in the Public Interest, 4*(1), 1–44. doi:10.1111/1529-1006.01431

Baumrind, D. (1991). The influence of parenting style on adolescent competence and substance use. *Journal of Early Adolescence, 11*(1), 56–95. doi:10.1177/0272431691111004

Baumrind, D. (2005). Patterns of parental authority and adolescent autonomy. In J. Smetana (Ed.), *New directions for child development: Changes in parental authority during adolescence* (pp. 61–69). San Francisco: Jossey-Bass.

Baumrind, D., Larzelere, R. E., & Cowan, P. A. (2002). Ordinary physical punishment: Is it harmful? *Psychological Bulletin, 128*(4), 580–589. doi:10.1037/0033-2909.128.4.580

Beans, D. R. (2009). *Integrative endocrinology*. New York: Routledge.

Bearman, P. S., Moody, J., & Stovel, K. (2004). Chains of affection: The structure of adolescent romantic and sexual networks. *American Journal of Sociology, 110*(1), 44–91. doi:10.1086/386272

Beck, A. T. (1991). Cognitive therapy. *American Psychologist, 46*(4), 368–375. doi:10.1037/0003-066X.46.4.368

Beck, A. T., Rector, N. A., Stolar, N., et al. (2009). *Schizophrenia: Cognitive theory, research, and therapy*. New York: Guilford.

Beck, B. L., Koons, S. R., & Milgrim, D. L. (2000). Correlates and consequences of behavioral procrastination. *Journal of Social Behavior & Personality, 15*(5), 3–13

Beck, H. P., Levinson, S., & Irons, G. (2009). Finding little Albert: A journey to John B. Watson's infant laboratory. *American Psychologist, 64*(7), 605–614. doi:10.1037/a0017234

Beeber, L. S., Chazan-Cohen, R., Squires, J., et al. (2007). The Early Promotion and Intervention Research Consortium (E-PIRC): Five approaches to improving infant/toddler mental health in Early Head Start. *Infant Mental Health Journal, 28*(2), 130–150. doi:10.1002/imhj.20126

Beeman, M. J., & Chiarello, C. (1998). Complementary right- and left-hemisphere language comprehension. *Current Directions in Psychological Science, 7*(1), 2–8. doi:10.1111/1467-8721.ep11521805

Beersma, D. G. M., & Gordijn, M. C. M. (2007). Circadian control of the sleep-wake cycle. *Physiology & Behavior, 90*(2–3), 190–195. doi:10.1016/j.physbeh.2006.09.010

Begley, S. (2006). *Train your mind, change your brain*. New York: Ballantine.

Behrend, D. A., Beike, D. R., & Lampinen, J. M. (2004). *The self and memory*. Hove, UK: Psychology Press.

Beirne-Smith, M., Patton, J., & Shannon, K. (2004). *Mental retardation: An introduction to intellectual disability* (7th ed.). Englewood Cliffs, NJ: Prentice Hall.

Bekinschtein, T. A., Shalom, D. E., Forcato, C., et al. (2009). Classical conditioning in the vegetative and minimally conscious state. *Nature Neuroscience 12*, 1343–1349. doi:10.1038/nn.2391

Belicki, K., Chambers, E., & Ogilvie, R. (1997). Sleep quality and nightmares. *Sleep Research, 26*, 637.

Bell, P. A., Greene, T., Fisher, J., et al. (2006). *Environmental psychology* (5th ed.). Mahwah, NJ: Erlbaum.

Bellezza, F. S., Six, L. S., & Phillips, D. S. (1992). A mnemonic for remembering long strings of digits. *Bulletin of the Psychonomic Society, 30*(4), 271–274.

Bem, S. L. (1974). The measurement of psychological androgyny. *Journal of Consulting & Clinical Psychology, 42*(2), 155–162. doi:10.1037/h0036215

Bem, S. L. (1975). Androgyny vs. the tight little lives of fluffy women and chesty men. *Psychology Today, 31*, 58–62.

Bem, S. L. (1981). Gender schema theory: A cognitive account of sex typing. *Psychological Review, 88*, 354–364. doi:10.1037/0033-295X.88.4.354

Ben Abdallah, N. M.-B., Slomianka, L., Vyssotski, A. L., et al. (2010). Early age-related changes in adult hippocampal neurogenesis in C57 mice. *Neurobiology of Aging, 31*(1), 151–161. doi:10.1016/j.neurobiolaging.2008.03.002

Benbow, C. P. (1986). Physiological correlates of extreme intellectual precocity. *Neuropsychologia, 24*(5), 719–725. doi:10.1016/0028-3932(86)90011-4

Benedetti, F. (2009). *Placebo effects: Understanding the mechanisms in health and disease*. New York: Oxford University Press.

Benitz, L. (2009). Becoming biliterate: A study of two-way bilingual immersion education. *Journal of Language, Identity, & Education, 8*(1), 54–57. doi:10.1080/15348450802620001

Benjafield, J. G. (2010). *A history of psychology* (4th ed.). New York: Oxford University Press.

Benjafield, J. G., Smilek, D., & Kingstone, A. (2010). *Cognition* (4th ed.). New York: Oxford University Press.

Benloucif, S., Bennett, E. L., & Rosenzweig, M. R. (1995). Norepinephrine and neural plasticity: The effects of xylamine on experience-induced changes in brain weight, memory, and behavior. *Neurobiology of Learning & Memory, 63*(1), 33–42. doi:10.1006/nlme.1995.1003

Bennett, P. (2011). *Abnormal and clinical psychology* (3rd ed.). New York: McGraw-Hill.

Bensafi, M., Zelano, C., Johnson, B., et al. (2004). Olfaction: From sniff to percept. In M. S. Gazzaniga (Ed.), *The cognitive neurosciences* (3rd ed., pp. 259–280). Cambridge, MA: MIT Press.

Ben-Shakhar, G., & Dolev, K. (1996). Psychophysiological detection through the guilty knowledge technique: Effect of mental countermeasures. *Journal of Applied Psychology, 81*(3), 273–281. doi:10.1037/0021-9010.81.3.273

Bensley, L., & Van Eenwyk, J. (2001). Video games and real-life aggression. *Journal of Adolescent Health, 29*(4), 244–257. doi:10.1016/S1054-139X(01)00239-7

Benson, H. (1977). Systematic hypertension and the relaxation response. *New England Journal of Medicine, 296*, 1152–1156.

Berman, S. L., Weems, C. F., & Stickle, T. R. (2006). Existential anxiety in adolescents: Prevalence, structure, association with psychological symptoms and identity development. *Journal of Youth & Adolescence, 35*(3), 303–310. doi:10.1007/s10964-006-9032-y

Bernard, R. S., Cohen, L. L., & Moffett, K. (2009). A token economy for exercise adherence in pediatric cystic fibrosis: A single-subject analysis. *Journal of Pediatric Psychology, 34*(4), 354–365. doi:10.1093/jpepsy/jsn101

Bernstein H. J., Beale M. D., Burns C., et al. (1998). Patient attitudes about ECT after treatment. *Psychiatric Annals, 28*(9), 524–527.

Bernstein, D. A., & Lucas, S. G. (2008). *Functional fixedness in problem solving*. In L.T. Benjamin (Ed.), *Favorite activities for the teaching of psychology* (pp. 143–144). Washington, DC: American Psychological Association.

Bernstein, D. M., & Loftus, E. F. (2009). How to tell if a particular memory is true or false. *Perspectives on Psychological Science, 4*(4), 370–374. doi:10.1111/j.1745-6924.2009.01140.x

Bernthal, M. J. (2003). How viewing professional wrestling may affect children. *The Sport Journal, 6*(3). Retrieved February 25, 2012, from http://www.thesportjournal.org/article/effect-professional-wrestling-viewership-children

Berntsen, D., & Thomsen, D. K. (2005). Personal memories for remote historical events: Accuracy and clarity of flashbulb memories related to World War II. *Journal of Experimental Psychology: General, 134*(2), 242–257. doi:10.1037/0096-3445.134.2.242

Berry, J. W., Phinney, J. S, Sam, D. L., et al. (2005). *Immigrant youth in cultural transition*. Mahwah, NJ: Erlbaum.

Berscheid, E. (2010). Love in the fourth dimension. *Annual Review of Psychology, 61*, 1–25. doi:10.1146/annurev.psych.093008.100318

Berscheid, E., & Regan, P. (2005). *The psychology of interpersonal relationships*. Englewood Cliffs, NJ: Prentice Hall.

Bersoff, D. M. (1999). Why good people sometimes do bad things: Motivated reasoning and unethical behavior. *Personality & Social Psychology Bulletin, 25*(1), 28–39. doi:10.1177/0146167299025001003

Beseler, C. L., Taylor, L. A., & Leeman, R. F. (2010). An item-response theory analysis of DSM-IV alcohol-use disorder criteria and "binge" drinking in undergraduates. *Journal of Studies on Alcohol & Drugs, 71*(3), 418–423.

Betancur, C., Velez, A., Cabanieu, G., et al. (1990). Association between left-handedness and allergy: A reappraisal. *Neuropsychologia, 28*(2), 223–227. doi:10.1016/0028-3932(90)90104-V

Beyers, W., & Seiffge-Krenke, I. (2010). Does identity precede intimacy? Testing Erikson's theory on romantic development in emerging adults of the 21st century. *Journal of Adolescent Research, 25*(3), 387–415. doi:10.1177/0743558410361370

Bhushan, B., & Khan, S. M. (2006). Laterality and accident proneness: A study of locomotive drivers. *Laterality: Asymmetries of Body, Brain & Cognition, 11*(5), 395–404. doi:10.1080/13576500500457458

Bialystok, E., & Barac, R. R. (2012). Emerging bilingualism: Dissociating advantages for metalinguistic awareness and executive control. *Cognition, 122*(1), 67–73. doi:10.1016/j.cognition.2011.08.003

Bialystok, E., & DePape, A.-M. (2009). Musical expertise, bilingualism, and executive functioning. *Journal of Experimental Psychology: Human Perception & Performance, 35*(2), 565–574. doi:10.1037/a0012735

Binder, J. L. (2004). *Key competencies in brief dynamic psychotherapy: Clinical practice beyond the manual*. New York: Guilford.

Binder, J., Zagefka, H., Brown, R., et al. (2009). Does contact reduce prejudice or does prejudice reduce contact? A longitudinal test of the contact hypothesis among majority and minority groups in three European countries. *Journal of Personality & Social Psychology, 96*(4), 843–856. doi:10.1037/a0013470

Binning, K. R., Sherman, D. K., Cohen, G. L., et al. (2010). Seeing the other side: Reducing political partisanship via self-affirmation in the 2008 presidential election. *Analyses of Social Issues & Public Policy, (1)*, 276–292. doi:10.1111/j.1530-2415.2010.01210.x

Birgegård, A., Norring, C., & Clinton, D. (2012). DSM-IV versus DSM-5: Implementation of proposed DSM-5 criteria in a large naturalistic database. *International Journal of Eating Disorders, 45*(3), 353–361. doi:10.1002/eat.20968

Biro, F. M., Galvez, M. P., Greenspan, L. C., et al. (2010). Pubertal assessment method and baseline characteristics in a mixed longitudinal study of girls. *Pediatrics, 126*(3), e583–e590. doi:10.1542/peds.2009-3079

Bisson, J. I., Ehlers, A., Matthews, R., et al. (2007). Psychological treatments for chronic post-traumatic stress disorder: Systematic review and meta-analysis. *British Journal of Psychiatry, 190*(2), 97–104. doi:10.1192/bjp.106.021402

Bitterman, M. E. (2006). Classical conditioning since Pavlov. *Review of General Psychology, 10*(4), 365–376. doi:10.1037/1089-2680.10.4.365

Bizer, G. Y., Hart, J., & Jekogian, A. M. (2012). Belief in a just world and social dominance orientation: Evidence for a mediational pathway predicting negative attitudes and discrimination against individuals with mental illness. *Personality & Individual Differences, 52*(3), 428–432. doi:10.1016/j.paid.2011.11.002

Bjorklund, D. F. (2012). *Children's thinking* (5th ed.). Belmont, CA: Cengage Learning/Wadsworth.

Bjorklund, D. F., & Hernández Blasi, C. (2012). *Child and adolescent development*. Belmont, CA: Cengage Learning/Wadsworth.

Bjornstrom, E. E. (2011). An examination of the relationship between neighborhood income inequality, social resources, and obesity in Los Angeles county. *American Journal of Health Promotion, 26*(2), 109–115. doi:10.4278/ajhp.100326-QUAN-93

Blackmore, S. (2000). First person: Into the unknown. *New Scientist, Nov 4,* 55.

Blackmore, S. (2004). *Consciousness: An introduction*. New York: Oxford University Press.

Blackwell, D. L., & Lichter, D. T. (2004). Homogamy among dating, cohabiting, and married couples. *Sociological Quarterly, 45*(4), 719–737. doi:10.1111/j.1533-8525.2004.tb02311.x

Blair, K. S., Richell, R. A., Mitchell, D. G. V., et al. (2006). They know the words, but not the music: Affective and semantic priming in individuals with psychopathy. *Biological Psychology, 73*(2), 114–123. doi:10.1016/j.biopsycho.2005.12.006

Blakemore, C., & Cooper, G. (1970). Development of the brain depends on the visual environment. *Nature, 228,* 477–478. doi:10.1038/228477a0

Blanchard, D. C., & Blanchard, R. J. (2003). What can animal aggression research tell us about human aggression? *Hormones & Behavior, 44*(3), 171–177. doi:10.1016/S0018-506X(03)00133-8

Blanchard, E. B., Kuhn, E., Rowell, D. L., et al. (2004). Studies of the vicarious traumatization of college students by the September llth attacks: Effects of proximity, exposure and connectedness. *Behaviour Research & Therapy, 42*(2), 191–205. doi:10.1016/S0005-7967(03)00118-9

Blatner, A. (2006). Current trends in psychodrama. *International Journal of Psychotherapy, 10*(3), 43–53.

Bloch, S. (2006). *Introduction to the psychotherapies* (4th ed.). New York: Oxford University Press.

Bloom, C. M., & Lamkin, D. M. (2006). The Olympian struggle to remember the cranial nerves: Mnemonics and student success. *Teaching of Psychology, 33*(2), 128–129. doi:1207/s15328023top3302_8

Bloom, J. W. (1998). The ethical practice of WebCounseling. *British Journal of Guidance & Counselling, 26*(1), 53–59. doi:10.1080/03069889800760061

Blunt, A., & Pychyl, T. A. (2005). Project systems of procrastinators: A personal project-analytic and action control perspective. *Personality & Individual Differences, 38*(8), 1771–1780. doi:10.1016/j.paid.2004.11.019

Bodner, E. (2009). On the origins of ageism among older and younger adults. *International Psychogeriatrics, 21*(6), 1003–1014. doi:10.1017/S104161020999055X

Boduroglu, A., Shah, P., & Nisbett, R. E. (2009). Cultural differences in allocation of attention in visual information processing. *Journal of Cross-Cultural Psychology, 40*(3), 349–360. doi:10.1177/0022022108331005

Boergers, J., Spirito, A., & Donaldson, D. (1998). Reasons for adolescent suicide attempts. *Journal of the American Academy of Child & Adolescent Psychiatry, 37*(12), 1287–1293. doi:10.1097/00004583-199812000-00012

Boggio, P. S., Campanhã, C., Valasek, C. A., et al. (2010). Modulation of decision-making in a gambling task in older adults with transcranial direct current stimulation. *European Journal of Neuroscience, 31*(3), 593–597. doi:10.1111/j.1460-9568.2009.07080.x

Bohbot, V., & Corkin, S. (2007). Posterior parahippocampal place learning in H.M. *Hippocampus, 17*(9), 863–872. doi:10.1002/hipo.20313

Bohlin, G., & Hagekull, B. (2009). Socio-emotional development: From infancy to young adulthood. *Scandinavian Journal of Psychology, 50*(6), 592–601. doi:10.1111/j.1467-9450.2009.00787.x

Bohner, G., & Dickel, N. (2010). Attitudes and attitude change. *Annual Review of Psychology, 62,* 391–417. doi:10.1146/annurev.psych.121208.131609

Boivin, D. B., Czeisler, C. A., & Waterhouse, J. W. (1997). Complex interaction of the sleep-wake cycle and circadian phase modulates mood in healthy subjects. *Archives of General Psychiatry, 54*(2), 145–152. doi:10.1001/archpsyc.1997.01830140055010

Boksa, P. (2009). On the neurobiology of hallucinations. *Journal of Psychiatry & Neuroscience, 34*(4), 260–262.

Bolbecker, A. R., Steinmetz, A. B., Mehta, C. S., et al. (2011). Exploration of cerebellar-dependent associative learning in schizophrenia: Effects of varying and shifting interstimulus interval on eyeblink conditioning. *Behavioral Neuroscience, 125*(5), 687–698. doi:10.1037/a0025150

Boldero, J. M., Moretti, M. M., Bell, R. C., et al. (2005). Self-discrepancies and negative affect: A primer on when to look for specificity and how to find it. *Australian Journal of Psychology, 57*(3), 139–147. doi:10.1080/00049530500048730

Bolt, D. M., Piper, M. E., Theobald, W. E., et al. (2012). Why two smoking cessation agents work better than one: Role of craving suppression. *Journal of Consulting & Clinical Psychology, 80*(1), 54–65. doi:10.1037/a0026366

Bonanno, G. A., Papa, A., Lalande, K., et al. (2004). The importance of being flexible. *Psychological Science, 15*(7), 482–487. doi:10.1111/j.0956-7976.2004.00705.x

Bond, R., & Smith, P. B. (1996). Culture and conformity: A meta-analysis of studies using Asch's (1952, 1956) line judgment task. *Psychological Bulletin, 119*(1), 111–137. doi:10.1037/0033-2909.119.1.111

Bongard, S., al'Absi, M., & Lovallo, W. R. (1998). Interactive effects of trait hostility and anger expression on cardiovascular reactivity in young men. *International Journal of Psychophysiology, 28*(2), 181–191. doi:10.1016/S0167-8760(97)00095-0

Bonham, V., Warshauer-Baker, E., & Collins, F. S. (2005). Race and ethnicity in the genome era: The complexity of the constructs. *American Psychologist, 60*(1), 9–15. doi:10.1037/0003-066X.60.1.9

Bonham, V., Warshauer-Baker, E., & Collins, F. S. (2005). Race and ethnicity in the genome era: The complexity of the constructs. *American Psychologist, 60*(1), 9–15.

Boniecki, K. A., & Britt, T. W. (2003). Prejudice and the peacekeeper. In T. W. Britt & A. B Adler (Eds.), *The psychology of the peacekeeper: Lessons from the field* (pp. 53–70). Westport, CT: Praeger.

Bonk, W. J., & Healy, A. F. (2010). Learning and memory for sequences of pictures, words, and spatial locations: An exploration of serial position effects. *American Journal of Psychology, 123*(2), 137–168.

Bood, S., Sundequist, U., Kjellgren, A., et al. (2006). Eliciting the relaxation response with the help of flotation-REST (Restricted Environmental Stimulation Technique) in patients with stress-related ailments. *International Journal of Stress Management, 13*(2), 154–175. doi:10.1037/1072-5245.13.2.154

Booker, J. M., & Hellekson, C. J. (1992). Prevalence of seasonal affective disorder in Alaska. *American Journal of Psychiatry, 149*(9), 1176–1182.

Bootzin, R. R., & Epstein, D. R. (2000). Stimulus control. In K. L. Lichstein & C. M. Morin. *Treatment of late life insomnia* (pp. 167–184). Thousand Oaks, CA: Sage.

Bora, E., Fornito, A., Radua, J., et al. (2011). Neuroanatomical abnormalities in schizophrenia: A multimodal voxelwise meta-analysis and meta-regression analysis. *Schizophrenia Research, 127*(1), 46–57. doi:10.1016/j.schres.2010.12.020

Borch-Jacobsen, M., & Shamdasani, S. (2011). *The Freud files: An inquiry into the history of psychoanalysis*. London: Cambridge University Press.

Bornstein, M. H., & Tamis-LeMonda, C. S. (2001). Mother-infant interaction. In A. Fogel & G. Bremmer (Eds.), *Blackwell handbook of infant development* (pp. 269–295). London: Blackwell.

Bornstein, R. F. (1996). Sex differences in dependent personality disorder prevalence rates. *Clinical Psychology: Science & Practice, 3*(1), 1–12. doi:10.1111/j.1468-2850.1996.tb00054.x

Bornstein, R. F. (2012). Rorschach score validation as a model for 21st-century personality assessment. *Journal of Personality Assessment, 94*(1), 26–38. doi:10.1080/00223891.2011.627961

Borod, J. C., Bloom, R. L., Brickman, A. M., et al. (2002). Emotional processing deficits in individuals with unilateral brain damage. *Applied Neuropsychology, 9*(1), 23–36.

Boroditsky, L. (2011). How language shapes thought. *Scientific American, February,* 62–65. doi:10.1038/scientificamerican0211-62

Boroditsky, L., & Gaby, A. (2010). Remembrances of times east: Absolute spatial representations of time in an Australian Aboriginal community. *Psychological Science, 21*(11), 1635–1639. doi:10.1177/0956797610386621

Boskey, E. (2011). Is oral sex safe sex? Retrieved May 9, 2012, from http://std.about.com/od/riskfactorsforstds/a/oralsexsafesex.htm

Botti, S., Orfali, K., & Iyengar, S. S. (2009). Tragic choices: Autonomy and emotional responses to medical decisions. *Journal of Consumer Research, 36*(3), 337–352. doi:10.1086/598969

Bouchard, Jr., T. J. (1983). Twins: Nature's twice-told tale. In *Yearbook of science and the future* (pp. 66–81). Chicago: Encyclopedia Britannica.

Bouchard, Jr., T. J. (2004). Genetic influence on human psychological traits: A survey. *Current Directions in Psychological Science, 13*(4), 148–151. doi:10.1111/j.0963-7214.2004.00295.x

Bouchard, Jr., T. J., Lykken, D. T., McGue, M., et al. (1990). Sources of human psychological differences: The Minnesota study of twins reared apart. *Science, 250,* 223–228. doi:10.1126/science.2218526

Bourgeois, J. A., Kahn, D., Philbrick, K. L., et al. (2009). *Casebook of psychosomatic medicine*. Washington, DC: American Psychiatric Publishing.

Bourne, E. J. (2010). *The anxiety & phobia workbook* (5th ed.). Oakland, CA: New Harbinger.

Bourne, V. J. (2008). Examining the relationship between degree of handedness and degree of cerebral lateralization for processing facial emotion. *Neuropsychology, 22*(3), 350–356. doi:10.1037/0894-4105.22.3.350

Bower, G. H. (1981). Mood and memory. *American Psychologist, 36,* 129–148.

Bower, G. H., & Springston, F. (1970). Pauses as recoding points in letter series. *Journal of Experimental Psychology, 83,* 421–430. doi:10.1037/h0028863

Boyle, S. H., Williams, R. B., Mark, D., et al. (2004). Hostility as a predictor of survival in patients with coronary artery disease. *Psychosomatic Medicine, 66*(5), 629–632. doi:10.1097/01.psy.0000138122.93942.4a

Boysen, G. A. (2011). The scientific status of childhood dissociative identity disorder: A review of published research. *Psychotherapy & Psychosomatics, 80*(6), 329–334. doi:10.1159/000323403

Bradbury, J. W., & Vehrencamp, S. L. (2011). *Principles of animal communication* (2nd ed.). Sunderland, MA: Sinauer.

Bradbury, T. N., & Karney, B. R. (2010). *Intimate relationships*. New York: Norton.

Bradley, R. T., McCraty, R., Atkinson, M., et al. (2010). Emotion self-regulation, psychophysiological coherence, and test anxiety: Results from an experiment using electrophysiological measures. *Applied Psychophysiology & Biofeedback, 35*(4), 261–283. doi:10.1007/s10484-010-9134-x

Bradley, R., Greene, J., Russ, E., et al. (2005). A multidimensional meta-analysis of psychotherapy for PTSD. *American Journal of Psychiatry, 162*(2), 214–227. doi:10.1176/appi.ajp.162.2.214

Bradshaw, C., Kahn, A. S., & Saville, B. K. (2010). To hook up or date: Which gender benefits? *Sex Roles, 62*(9–10), 661–669. doi:10.1007/s11199-010-9765-7

Bradshaw, S. D. (2006). Shyness and difficult relationships: Formation is just the beginning. In D. C. Kirkpatrick, D. S. Duck, et al. (Eds.), *Relating difficulty: The processes of constructing and managing difficult interaction* (pp. 15–42). Mahwah, NJ: Erlbaum.

Brainerd, C. J. (2003). Jean Piaget, learning research, and American education. In B. J. Zimmerman & D. H. Schunk (Eds.), *Educational psychology: A century of contributions* (pp. 251–287). Mahwah, NJ: Erlbaum.

Brakel, T. M., Dijkstra, A., Buunk, A. P., et al. (2011). Impact of social comparison on cancer survivors' quality of life: An experimental field study. *Health Psychology,* doi:10.1037/a0026572.

Bramerson, A., Johansson, L., Ek, L., et al. (2004). Prevalence of olfactory dysfunction: The Skovde population-based study. *Laryngoscope, 114*(4), 733–737. doi:10.1097/00005537-200404000-00026

Brammer, R. (2012). *Diversity in counseling* (2nd ed.). Belmont, CA: Cengage Learning/Wadsworth.

Brand, S., Gerber, M., Beck, J., et al. (2010). High exercise levels are related to favorable sleep patterns and psychological functioning in adolescents: A comparison of athletes and controls. *Journal of Adolescent Health, 46*(2), 133–141. doi:10.1016/j.jadohealth.2009.06.018

Brannon, L. (2011). *Gender: Psychological perspectives.* Boston: Pearson/Allyn & Bacon.

Brannon, L., & Feist, J. (2010). *Health psychology: An introduction to behavior and health* (7th ed.). Belmont, CA: Cengage Learning/Wadsworth.

Braun, K. A., Ellis, R., & Loftus, E. F. (2002). Make my memory: How advertising can change memories of the past. *Psychology & Marketing, 19,* 1–23. doi:10.1002/mar.1000

Braun-LaTour, K. A., & LaTour, M. S. (2004). Assessing the long-term impact of a consistent advertising campaign on consumer memory. *Journal of Advertising, 33*(2), 49–61.

Breedlove, S. M., Watson, N. V., & Rosenzweig, M. R. (2010). *Biological psychology: An introduction to behavioral and cognitive neuroscience* (6th ed.). Sunderland, MA: Sinauer Associates.

Brenes, G. A., Ingram, C. W., & Danhauer, S. C. (2011). Benefits and challenges of conducting psychotherapy by telephone. *Professional Psychology: Research & Practice, 42*(6), 543–549. doi:10.1037/a0026135

Bressan, P., & Pizzighello, S. (2008). The attentional cost of inattentional blindness. *Cognition, 106*(1), 370–383. doi:10.1016/j.cognition.2007.03.001

Bressi, C., Albonetti, S., & Razzoli, E. (1998). "Communication deviance" and schizophrenia. *New Trends in Experimental & Clinical Psychiatry, 14*(1), 33–39.

Bretherton, R., & Orner, R. J. (2004). Positive psychology and psychotherapy: An existential approach. In P. A. Linley & S. Joseph (Eds.), *Positive psychology in practice* (pp. 420–430). New York: Wiley.

Brewer, J. A., Mallik, S., Babuscio, T. A., et al. (2011). Mindfulness training for smoking cessation: Results from a randomized controlled trial. *Drug & Alcohol Dependence, 119*(1-2), 72–80. doi:10.1016/j.drugalcdep.2011.05.027

Brewer, N., & Wells, G. L. (2006). The confidence-accuracy relationship in eyewitness identification: Effects of lineup instructions, foil similarity, and target-absent base rates. *Journal of Experimental Psychology: Applied, 12*(1), 11–30. doi:10.1037/1076-898X.12.1.11

Brewer, N., & Williams, K. D. (Eds.). (2005). *Psychology and law: An empirical perspective.* New York: Guilford.

Briand, L. A., Flagel, S. B., Seeman, P., et al. (2008). Cocaine self-administration produces a persistent increase in dopamine D2-super(High) receptors. *European Neuropsychopharmacology, 18*(8), 551–556. doi:10.1016/j.euroneuro.2008.01.002

Bridges, K. M. B. (1932). Emotional development in early infancy. *Child Development, 3,* 324–334. doi:10.2307/1125359

Bridgett, D. J., Gartstein, M. A., Putnam, S. P., et al. (2009). Maternal and contextual influences and the effect of temperament development during infancy on parenting in toddlerhood. *Infant Behavior & Development, 32*(1), 103–116. doi:10.1016/j.infbeh.2008.10.007

Brinton, R. D., & Wang, J. M. (2006). Therapeutic potential of neurogenesis for prevention and recovery from Alzheimer's disease: Allopregnanolone as a proof of concept neurogenic agent. *Current Alzheimer Research, 3*(3), 185–190. doi:10.2174/156720506777632817

Britton, P. C., Duberstein, P. R., Conner, K. R., et al. (2008). Reasons for living, hopelessness, and suicide ideation among depressed adults 50 years or older. *American Journal of Geriatric Psychiatry, 16*(9), 736–741. doi:10.1097/JGP.0b013e31817b609a

Brodley, B. T. (2006). Nondirectivity in client-centered therapy. *Person-Centered & Experiential Psychotherapies, 5*(1), 36–52.

Brondolo, E., ver Halen, N. B., Libby. D., et al. (2011). Racism as a psychosocial stressor. In R. J. Contrada & A. Baum (Eds.), *The handbook of stress science: Biology, psychology, and health* (pp. 167–184). New York: Springer.

Brooks, M. (2009). Rise of the robogeeks. *New Scientist, 2697,* 34–36.

Brothen, T., & Wambach, C. (2001). Effective student use of computerized quizzes. *Teaching of Psychology, 28*(4), 292–294. doi:10.1207/S15328023TOP2804_10

Brower, A. M. (2002). Are college students alcoholics? *Journal of American College Health, 50*(5), 253–255. doi:10.1080/07448480209595716

Brown, A. S. (2012). *The tip of the tongue state.* New York: Psychology Press.

Brown, A. S., & Marsh, E. J. (2010). Digging into déjà vu: Recent research on possible mechanisms. In B. H. Ross (Ed.), *The psychology of learning and motivation: Advances in research and theory* (Vol. 53, pp. 33–62). San Diego: Elsevier. doi:10.1016/S0079-7421(10)53002-0

Brown, J. D. (2010). High self-esteem buffers negative feedback: Once more with feeling. *Cognition & Emotion, 24*(8), 1389–1404. doi:10.1080/02699930903504405

Brown, J. D., Cai, H., Oakes, M. A., et al. (2009). Cultural similarities in self-esteem functioning: East is east and west is west, but sometimes the twain do meet. *Journal of Cross-Cultural Psychology, 40*(1), 140–157. doi:10.1177/0022022108326280

Brown, L. M. (2005). *Girlfighting: Betrayal and rejection among girls.* New York: New York University Press.

Brown, M. J., Henriquez, E., & Groscup, J. (2008). The effects of eyeglasses and race on juror decisions involving a violent crime. *American Journal of Forensic Psychology, 26*(2), 25–43.

Brown, P. (1990). The name game. *Journal of Mind and Behavior, 11,* 385–406.

Brown, R., & Kulik, J. (1977). Flashbulb memories. *Cognition, 5,* 73–99. doi:10.1016/0010-0277(77)90018-X

Brown, R., & McNeill, D. (1966). The "tip of the tongue" phenomenon. *Journal of Verbal Learning & Verbal Behavior, 5,* 325–337. doi:10.1016/S0022-5371(66)80040-3

Brown, S. A., Tapert, S. F., Granholm, E., et al. (2000). Neurocognitive functioning of adolescents: Effects of protracted alcohol use. *Alcoholism: Clinical & Experimental Research, 24*(2), 164–171. doi:10.1111/j.1530-0277.2000.tb04586.x

Brown, S. D., Lent, R. W., Telander, K., et al. (2011). Social cognitive career theory, conscientiousness, and work performance: A meta-analytic path analysis. *Journal of Vocational Behavior, 79*(1), 81–90. doi:10.1016/j.jvb.2010.11.009

Brown, S. G., Roy, E., Rohr, L., et al. (2006). Using hand performance measures to predict handedness. *Laterality: Asymmetries of Body, Brain & Cognition, 11*(1), 1–14. doi:10.1080/13576500542000040

Brown, T. A., & Barlow, D. H. (2011). *Casebook in abnormal psychology* (4th. ed.). Belmont, CA: Cengage Learning/Wadsworth.

Browne, N., & Keeley, S. (2010). *Asking the right questions* (9th ed.). Englewood Cliffs, NJ: Prentice Hall.

Brownell, P. (2010). *Gestalt therapy: A guide to contemporary practice.* New York: Springer.

Bruner, J. (1973). *Going beyond the information given.* New York: Norton.

Bruner, J. (1983). *Child's talk.* New York: Norton.

Brunet, P. M., Mondloch, C. J., & Schmidt, L. A. (2010). Shy children are less sensitive to some cues to facial recognition. *Child Psychiatry & Human Development, 41*(1), 1–14. doi:10.1007/s10578-009-0150-0

Bryan, C. S., & Babelay, A. M. (2009). Building character: A model for reflective practice. *Academic Medicine, 84*(9), 1283–1288. doi:10.1097/ACM.0b013e3181b6a79c

Bryden, P. J., Bruyn, J., & Fletcher, P. (2005). Handedness and health: An examination of the association between different handedness classifications and health disorders. *Laterality: Asymmetries of Body, Brain & Cognition, 10*(5), 429–440. doi:10.1080/13576500442000193

Bucher, S. G. (2011). *344 questions: The creative person's do-it-yourself guide to insight, survival, and artistic fulfillment.* Berkeley, CA: New Riders Publishing.

Buck, J. A., & Warren, A. R. (2010). Expert testimony in recovered memory trials: Effects on mock jurors' opinions, deliberations and verdicts. *Applied Cognitive Psychology, 24*(4), 495–512. doi:10.1002/acp.1569

Buckle, P. (2011). 'The perfect is the enemy of the good'—Ergonomics research and practice. *Ergonomics, 54*(1), 1–11. doi:10.1080/00140139.2010.542251

Buckner, J. D., Ecker, A. H., & Cohen, A. S. (2010). Mental health problems and interest in marijuana treatment among marijuana-using college students. *Addictive Behaviors, 35*(9), 826–833. doi:10.1016/j.addbeh.2010.04.001

Buckworth, J., Lee, R. E., Regan, G., et al. (2007). Decomposing intrinsic and extrinsic motivation for exercise: Application to stages of motivational readiness. *Psychology of Sport & Exercise, 8*(4), 441–461. doi:10.1016/j.psychsport.2006.06.007

Buddie, A. M. (2004). Alternatives to twelve-step programs. *Journal of Forensic Psychology Practice, 4*(3), 61–70. doi:10.1300/J158v04n03_04

Budney, A. J., & Hughes, J. R. (2006). The cannabis withdrawal syndrome. *Current Opinion in Psychiatry, 19*(3), 233–238. doi:10.1097/01.yco.0000218592.00689.e5

Buehner, M. J., & May, J. (2003). Rethinking temporal contiguity and the judgement of causality: Effects of prior knowledge, experience, and reinforcement procedure. *Quarterly Journal of Experimental Psychology A: Human Experimental Psychology, 56*(5), 865–890. doi:10.1080/02724980244000675

Bukach, C. M., Cottle, J., Ubiwa, J., et al. (2012). Individuation experience predicts other-race effects in holistic processing for both Caucasian and Black participants. *Cognition*, doi:10.1016/j.cognition.2012.02.007.

Buller, D. J. (2005). *Adapting minds: Evolutionary psychology and the persistent quest for human nature.* Cambridge, MA: MIT Press.

Bunde, J., & Suls, J. (2006). A quantitative analysis of the relationship between the cook-medley hostility scale and traditional coronary artery disease risk factors. *Health Psychology, 25*(4), 493–500. doi:10.1037/0278-6133.25.4.493

Bundy, H., Stahl, D., & MacCabe, J. H. (2011). A systematic review and meta-analysis of the fertility of patients with schizophrenia and their unaffected relatives. *Acta Psychiatrica Scandinavica, 123*(2), 98–106. doi:10.1111/j.1600-0447.2010.01623.x

Bunn, G. C. (2007). Spectacular science: The lie detector's ambivalent powers. *History of Psychology, 10*(2), 156–178. doi:10.1037/1093-4510.10.2.156

Burchinal, M. R., Roberts, J. E., Riggins, R., et al. (2000). Relating quality of center-based child care to early cognitive and language development longitudinally. *Child Development, 71*(2), 339–357. doi:10.1111/1467-8624.00149

Burger, J. M. (2009). Replicating Milgram: Would people still obey today? *American Psychologist, 64*(1), 1–11. doi:10.1037/a0010932

Burger, J. M. (2011). *Personality* (8th ed.). Belmont, CA: Cengage Learning/Wadsworth.

Burger, J. M., & Lynn, A. L. (2005). Superstitious behavior among American and Japanese professional baseball players. *Basic & Applied Social Psychology, 27*(1), 71–76. doi:10.1207/s15324834basp2701_7

Burgess, C. A., & Kirsch, I. (1999). Expectancy information as a moderator of the effects of hypnosis on memory. *Contemporary Hypnosis, 16*(1), 22–31. doi:10.1002/ch.146

Burgess, M. C. R., & Weaver, G. E. (2003). Interest and attention in facial recognition. *Perceptual & Motor Skills, 96*(2), 467–480. doi:10.2466/PMS.96.2.467-480

Burka, J. B., & Yuen, L. M. (2008). *Procrastination: Why you do it, what to do about it.* Cambridge, MA: Perseus.

Burke, D., Hickie, I., Breakspear, M., et al. (2007). Possibilities for the prevention and treatment of cognitive impairment and dementia. *British Journal of Psychiatry, 190,* 371–372. doi:10.1192/bjp.bp.106.033407

Burlingame, G. M., & Davies, R. (2002). Self-help groups. In M. Hersen & W. H. Sledge (Eds.), *Encyclopedia of psychotherapy* (pp. 601–605). San Diego: Academic Press.

Burlingame, G. M., Fuhriman, A., & Mosier, J. (2003). The differential effectiveness of group psychotherapy: A meta-analytic perspective. *Group Dynamics: Theory, Research, & Practice, 7*(1), 3–12. doi:10.1037/1089-2699.7.1.3

Burlingame, G. M., McClendon, D. T., & Alonso, J. (2011). Cohesion in group therapy. *Psychotherapy, 48*(1), 34–42. doi:10.1037/a0022063

Burnett, R. C., Medin, D. L., Ross, N. O., et al. (2005). Ideal is typical.

Canadian Journal of Experimental Psychology, 59(1), 3–10. doi:10.1037/h0087453

Burns, G. W. (Ed). (2010). *Happiness, healing, enhancement: Your casebook collection for applying positive psychology in therapy.* New York: Wiley.

Burns, M. S., & Fahy, J. (2010). Brocas area: Rethinking classical concepts from a neuroscience perspective. *Topics in Stroke Rehabilitation, 17*(6), 401–410. doi:10.1310/tsr1706-401

Burt, S. A., McGue, M., Carter, L. A., et al. (2007). The different origins of stability and change in antisocial personality disorder symptoms. *Psychological Medicine, 37*(1), 27–38. doi:10.1017/S0033291706009020

Burton, C. M., & King, L. A. (2004). The health benefits of writing about intensely positive experiences. *Journal of Research in Personality, 38*(2), 150–163. doi:10.1016/S0092-6566(03)00058-8

Burtt, H. E. (1941). An experimental study of early childhood memory: Final report. *Journal of General Psychology, 58,* 435–439.

Bushnell, M. C., Villemure, C., & Duncan, G. H. (2004). Psychophysical and neurophysiological studies of pain modulation by attention. In D. D. Price & M. C. Bushnell (Eds.), *Psychological methods of pain control: Basic science and clinical perspectives* (pp. 99–116). Seattle: IASP Press.

Buss, A. H. (2012). *Pathways to individuality: Evolution and development of personality traits.* Washington, DC: American Psychological Association.

Buss, D. M. (2000). *The dangerous passion.* New York: Free Press.

Buss, D. M. (2007). The evolution of human mating. *Acta Psychologica Sinica, 39*(3), 502–512.

Buss, D. M. (2012). *Evolutionary psychology: The new science of the mind* (4th ed.). Boston: Pearson/Allyn & Bacon.

Butcher, J. N. (2011). *A beginner's guide to the MMPI-2* (3rd ed.). Washington, DC: American Psychological Association.

Butcher, J. N., Mineka, S., & Hooley, J. (2010). *Abnormal psychology* (14th ed.). Boston: Allyn & Bacon.

Butler, A. C., Chapman, J. E., Forman, E. M., et al. (2006). The empirical status of cognitive-behavioral therapy: A review of meta-analyses. *Clinical Psychology Review, 26*(1), 17–31. doi:10.1016/j.cpr.2005.07.003

Butler, J. C. (2000). Personality and emotional correlates of right-wing authoritarianism. *Social Behavior & Personality, 28*(1), 1–14. doi:10.2224/sbp.2000.28.1.1

Butler, M. G. (2001). *Overcoming social anxiety and shyness: A self-help guide using cognitive behavioral techniques.* New York: New York University Press.

Butler, R. (1954). Curiosity in monkeys. *Scientific American, 190*(18), 70–75. doi:10.1038/scientificamerican0254-70

Byrne, S., Barry, D., & Petry, N. M. (2012). Predictors of weight loss success: Exercise vs. dietary self-efficacy and treatment attendance.

Appetite, 58(2), 695–698. doi:10.1016/j.appet.2012.01.005

Cadinu, M., Maass, A., Rosabianca, A., et al. (2005). Why do women underperform under stereotype threat? Evidence for the role of negative thinking. *Psychological Science, 16*(7), 572–578. doi:10.1111/j.0956-7976.2005.01577.x

Caharel, S., Fiori, N., Bernard, C., et al. (2006). The effects of inversion and eye displacements of familiar and unknown faces on early and late-stage ERPs. *International Journal of Psychophysiology, 62*(1), 141–151. doi:10.1016/j.ijpsycho.2006.03.002

Cahill, L. (2006). Why sex matters for neuroscience. *Nature Reviews Neuroscience, 7*(6), 477–484. doi:10.1038/nrn1909

Cahn, B. R., & Polich, J. (2006). Meditation states and traits: EEG, ERP, and neuroimaging studies. *Psychological Bulletin, 132*(2), 180–211. doi:10.1037/0033-2909.132.2.180

Cain, S. (2012). *Quiet: The power of introverts in a world that can't stop talking.* New York: Crown Publishers/Random House.

Calabrese, F., Molteni, R., Racagni, G., et al. (2009). Neuronal plasticity: A link between stress and mood disorders. *Psychoneuroendocrinology, 34*(Suppl 1), S208–S216. doi:10.1016/j.psyneuen.2009.05.014

Calabria, B., Degenhardt, L., Briegleb, C., et al. (2010). Systematic review of prospective studies investigating "remission" from amphetamine, cannabis, cocaine, or opioid dependence. *Addictive Behaviors, 35*(8), 741–749. doi:10.1016/j.addbeh.2010.03.019

Callahan, C. M. (2006). Giftedness. In G. G. Bear & K. M. Minke (Eds.), *Children's needs III: Development, prevention, and intervention* (pp. 443–458). Washington, DC: National Association of School Psychologists.

Calzada, E. J., Fernandez, Y., & Cortes, D. E. (2010). Incorporating the cultural value of respeto into a framework of Latino parenting. *Cultural Diversity & Ethnic Minority Psychology, 16*(1), 77–86. doi:10.1037/a0016071

Cambron, M. J., Acitelli, L. K., & Pettit, J. W. (2009). Explaining gender differences in depression: An interpersonal contingent self-esteem perspective. *Sex Roles, 61*(11–12), 751–761. doi:10.1007/s11199-009-9616-6

Cameron, J. A., & Trope, Y. (2004). Stereotype-biased search and processing of information about group members. *Social Cognition, 22*(6), 650–672. doi:10.1521/soco.22.6.650.54818

Cameron, J., & Pierce, W. D. (2002). *Rewards and intrinsic motivation: Resolving the controversy.* Westport, CO: Bergin & Garvey.

Cammaroto, S., D'Aleo, G., Smorto, C., et al. (2008). Charles Bonnet syndrome. *Functional Neurology, 23*(3), 123–127.

Campbell, B. (2008). *Handbook of differentiated instruction using the multiple intelligences.* Boston: Pearson/Allyn and Bacon.

Canadian Psychological Association. (2012). *Careers in and related to psychology.* Ottawa, ON: Author. Retrieved April 30, 2012, from http://www.cpa.ca/students/career/careersinpsychology/

Canales, J. J. (2010). Comparative neuroscience of stimulant-induced memory dysfunction: Role for neurogenesis in the adult hippocampus. *Behavioural Pharmacology, 21*(5–6), 379–398. doi:10.1097/FBP.0b013e32833e16b6

Cannon, W. B. (1932). *The wisdom of the body.* New York: Norton.

Cannon, W. B. (1934). Hunger and thirst. In C. Murchinson (Ed.), *Handbook of general experimental psychology* (pp. 247–263). Worcester, MA: Clark University Press. doi:10.1037/11374-005

Cannon, W. B., & Washburn, A. L. (1912). An explanation of hunger. *American Journal of Physiology, 29,* 441–454.

Caplan, P. J. (1995). *They say you're crazy.* Reading, MA: Addison-Wesley.

Capron, C., & Duyme, M. (1992). Assessment of effects of socio-economic status on IQ in a full cross-fostering study. *Nature, 340,* 552–554. doi:10.1038/340552a0

Cardoso, S. H. (2000). Our ancient laughing brain. *Cerebrum, 2*(4), 15–30.

Carducci, B. J., & Fields, T. H. (2007). *The shyness workbook for teens.* Champaign, IL: Research Press.

Carlbring, P., Gunnarsdóttir, M., Hedensjö, L., et al. (2007). Treatment of social phobia: Randomized trial of internet-delivered cognitive-behavioural therapy with telephone support. *British Journal of Psychiatry, 190*(2), 123–128. doi:10.1192/bjp.bp.105.020107

Carlson, M., Marcus-Hewhall, A., & Miller, N. (1990). Effects of situational aggression cues: A quantitative review. *Journal of Personality & Social Psychology, 58*(4), 622–633. doi:10.1037/0022-3514.58.4.622

Carlson, N. R. (2010). *Physiology of behavior* (10th ed.). Boston: Allyn & Bacon.

Carnagey, N. L., & Anderson, C. A. (2004). Violent video game exposure and aggression: A literature review. *Minerva Psichiatrica, 45*(1), 1–18.

Carnagey, N. L., Anderson, C. A., & Bushman, B. J. (2007). The effect of video game violence on physiological desensitization to real-life violence. *Journal of Experimental Social Psychology, 43*(3), 489–496. doi:10.1016/j.jesp.2006.05.003

Carney, R. N., & Levin, J. R. (2001). Remembering the names of unfamiliar animals: Keywords as keys to their kingdom. *Applied Cognitive Psychology, 15*(2), 133–143. doi:10.1002/1099-0720(200103/04)15:2<133::AID-ACP687>3.0.CO;2-P

Carney, R. N., & Levin, J. R. (2003). Promoting higher-order learning benefits by building lower-order mnemonic connections. *Applied Cognitive Psychology, 17*(5), 563–575. doi:10.1002/acp.889

Carr, P. B., & Steele, C. M. (2010). Stereotype threat affects financial decision making. *Psychological Science, 21*(10), 1411–1416. doi:10.1177/0956797610384146

Carrico, A. R., & Riemer, M. (2011). Motivating energy conservation in the workplace: An evaluation of the use of group-level feedback and peer education. *Journal of Environmental Psychology, 31*(1), 1–13. doi:10.1016/j.jenvp.2010.11.004

Carroll, D. W. (2008). *Psychology of language* (5th ed.). Belmont, CA: Cengage Learning/Wadsworth.

Carroll, J. L. (2013). *Sexuality now: Embracing diversity* (4th ed.). Belmont, CA: Cengage Learning/Wadsworth.

Carroll, J. M., & Russell, J. A. (1996). Do facial expressions signal specific emotions? Judging emotion from the face in context. *Journal of Personality & Social Psychology, 70*(2), 205–218. doi:10.1037/0022-3514.70.2.205

Carroll, K. M., & Rounsaville, B. J. (2007). W(h)ither empirically supported therapies (ESTS)? Reply to commentaries. *Addiction, 102*(6), 867–869. doi:10.1111/j.1360-0443.2007.01897.x

Carroll, R. T. (2011). *The skeptic's dictionary: Superstition*. Retrieved May 7, 2012, from http://www.skepdic.com/superstition.html

Carskadon, M. A., Acebo, C., & Jenni, O. C. (2004). Regulation of adolescent sleep: Implications for behavior. *Annals of the New York Academy of Science, 1021*, 276–291. doi:10.1196/annals.1308.032

Cartwright, D. (2002). The narcissistic exoskeleton: The defensive organization of the rage-type murderer. *Bulletin of the Menninger Clinic, 66*(1), 1–18. doi:10.1521/bumc.66.1.1.23371

Cascio, W. F. & Aguinis, H. (2008). Industrial and organizational psychology 1963–2007: Changes, choices, and trends. *Journal of Applied Psychology, 93*, 1062–1081. doi:10.1037/0021-9010.93.5.1062

Casey, A. A., Elliott, M., Glanz, K., et al. (2008). Impact of the food environment and physical activity environment on behaviors and weight status in rural U.S. Communities. *Preventive Medicine, 47*(6), 600–604. doi:10.1016/j.ypmed.2008.10.001

Casey, P. (2001). Multiple personality disorder. *Primary Care Psychiatry, 7*(1), 7–11. doi:10.1185/135525701750167447

Casey-Campbell, M., & Martens, M. L. (2009). Sticking it all together: A critical assessment of the group cohesion–performance literature. *International Journal of Management Reviews, 11*(2), 223–246. doi:10.1111/j.1468-2370.2008.00239.x

Caspi, A., Roberts, B. W., & Shiner, R. L. (2005). Personality development: Stability and change. *Annual Review of Psychology, 56*, 453–484. doi:10.1146/annurev.psych.55.090902.141913

Caspi, A., Sugden, K., Moffitt, T. E., et al. (2003). Influence of life stress on depression: Moderation by a polymorphism in the 5-HTT gene.

Science, 301(5631), 386–389. doi:10.1126/science.1083968

Cassady, J. C. (2004). The influence of cognitive test anxiety across the learning-testing cycle. *Learning & Instruction, 14*(6), 569–592. doi:10.1016/j.learninstruc.2004.09.002

Casselle, G. (2009). What is it really like to have electroconvulsive therapy? *Journal of ECT, 25*(4), 289. doi:10.1097/YCT.0b013e3181a59f97

Castañeda, T. R., Tong, J., Datta, R., et al. (2010). Ghrelin in the regulation of body weight and metabolism. *Frontiers in Neuroendocrinology, 31*(1), 44–60. doi:10.1016/j.yfrne.2009.10.008

Castellano, J. A., & Frazier, A. D. (Eds.). (2011). *Special populations in gifted education: Understanding our most able students from diverse backgrounds*. Waco, TX: Prufrock Press.

Castro, J. R., & Rice, K. G. (2003). Perfectionism and ethnicity: Implications for depressive symptoms and self-reported academic achievement. *Cultural Diversity & Ethnic Minority Psychology, 9*(1), 64–78. doi:10.1037/1099-9809.9.1.64

Castro, J., Gila, A., Gual, P., et al. (2004). Perfectionism dimensions in children and adolescents with anorexia nervosa. *Journal of Adolescent Health, 35*(5), 392–398. doi:10.1016/j.jadohealth.2003.11.094

Castro-Schilo, L., & Kee, D. W. (2010). Gender differences in the relationship between emotional intelligence and right hemisphere lateralization for facial processing. *Brain & Cognition, 73*(1), 62–67. doi:10.1016/j.bandc.2010.03.003

Cattell, R. B. (1965). *The scientific analysis of personality*. Baltimore: Penguin.

Cattell, R. B. (1973). Personality pinned down. *Psychology Today, July*, 40–46.

Cavaco, S., Anderson, S. W., Allen, J. S., et al. (2004). The scope of preserved procedural memory in amnesia. *Brain: A Journal of Neurology, 127*(8), 1853–1867. doi:10.1093/brain/awh208

Cellard, C., Lefèbvre, A.-A., Maziade, M., et al. (2010). An examination of the relative contribution of saturation and selective attention to memory deficits in patients with recent-onset schizophrenia and their unaffected parents. *Journal of Abnormal Psychology, 119*(1), 60–70. doi:10.1037/a0018397

Centers for Disease Control and Prevention. (2003). *Deaths, percent of total deaths, and death rates for 15 leading causes of death in 5-year age groups, by race and sex: United States, 2000*. Atlanta: Author. Downloaded May 9, 2012, from http://www.cdc.gov/nchs/data/dvs/LCWK1_2000.pdf

Centers for Disease Control. (2011a). *HIV in the United States*. Atlanta: Author. Retrieved April 16, 2012, from http://www.cdc.gov/hiv/resources/Factsheets/PDF/us.pdf

Centers for Disease Control. (2011b). *Smoking cessation*. Atlanta, GA: Author. Downloaded February 8, 2012, from http://www.cdc.gov/

tobacco/data_statistics/fact_sheets/cessation/quitting/index.htm

Centers for Disease Control. (2012a). *Smokeless tobacco facts*. Atlanta, GA: Author. Downloaded February 8, 2012, from http://www.cdc.gov/tobacco/data_statistics/fact_sheets/smokeless/smokeless_facts/index.htm.

Centers for Disease Control. (2012b). *Sexually transmitted diseases (STDs)*. Atlanta: Author. Downloaded April 16, 2012, from http://www.cdc.gov/std/default.htm

Centofanti, A. T., & Reece, J. (2006). The cognitive interview and its effect on misleading postevent information. *Psychology, Crime & Law, 12*(6), 669–683. doi:10.1080/10683160600558394

Centre for Addiction and Mental Health. (2011). *Harm reduction: Its meaning and application for substance use issues position statement*. Toronto, Ontario: Author. Retrieved February 15, 2012, from http://www.camh.net/Public_policy/Public_policy_papers/harmreductionposition.html

Cervone, D., & Pervin, L. A. (2010). *Personality: Theory and research* (11th ed.). New York: Wiley.

Chabas, D., Taheri, S., Renier, C., et al. (2003). The genetics of narcolepsy. *Annual Review of Genomics & Human Genetics, 4*, 459–483. doi:10.1146/annurev.genom.4.070802.110432

Chaffee, J. (2012). *Thinking critically* (10th ed.). Belmont, CA: Cengage Learning/Wadsworth.

Chakos, M. H., Alvir, J. M. J., Woerner, M., et al. (1996). Incidence and correlates of tardive dyskinesia in first episode of schizophrenia. *Archives of General Psychiatry, 53*(4), 313–319. doi:10.1001/archpsyc.1996.01830040049009

Challacombe, F., Oldfield, V. B., & Salkovskis, P. M. (2011). *Break free from OCD: Overcoming obsessive compulsive disorder using CBT*. London: Vermillion.

Chalmers. D. J. (2010). *The character of consciousness*. New York: Oxford University Press.

Chambers, R. A., Taylor, J. R., & Potenza, M. N. (2003). Developmental neurocircuitry of motivation in adolescence: A critical period of addiction vulnerability. *American Journal of Psychiatry, 160*(6), 1041–1052. doi:10.1176/appi.ajp.160.6.1041

Chamorro-Premuzic, T., & Furnham, A. (2003). Personality predicts academic performance. *Journal of Research in Personality, 37*(4), 319–338. doi:10.1016/S0092-6566(02)00578-0

Chamorro-Premuzic, T., & Furnham, A. (2010). *The psychology of personnel selection*. New York: Cambridge University Press

Chan, G. C.-K., Hinds, T. R., Impey, S., et al. (1998). Hippocampal neurotoxicity of Δ-9-tetrahydrocannabinol. *Journal of Neuroscience, 18*(14), 5322–5332.

Chance, P. (2009). *Learning and behavior* (6th ed.). Belmont, CA: Cengage Learning/Wadsworth.

Chang, J.-H. (2009). Chronic pain: Cultural sensitivity to pain. In S. Eshun & R. A. R. Gurung (Eds.),

Culture and mental health: Sociocultural influences, theory, and practice (pp. 71–89). New York: Wiley-Blackwell. doi:10.1002/9781444305807.ch5

Chansler, P. A., Swamidass, P. M., & Cammann, C. (2003). Self-managing work teams: An empirical study of group cohesiveness in "natural work groups" at a Harley-Davidson Motor Company plant. *Small Group Research, 34*(1), 101–120. doi:10.1177/1046496402239579

Chao, R., & Tseng, V. (2002). Parenting of Asians. In M. H. Bornstein (Ed.), *Handbook of parenting* (Vol. 4): *Social conditions and applied parenting* (2nd ed., pp. 59–93). Mahwah, NJ: Erlbaum.

Chapman, R. A. (Ed.). (2006). *The clinical use of hypnosis in cognitive behavior therapy: A practitioner's casebook*. New York: Springer Publishing.

Charmaraman, L., & Grossman, J. M. (2010). Importance of race and ethnicity: An exploration of Asian, Black, Latino, and multiracial adolescent identity. *Cultural Diversity & Ethnic Minority Psychology, 16*(2), 144–151. doi:10.1037/a0018668

Charsky, D. (2010). From edutainment to serious games: A change in the use of game characteristics. *Games & Culture, 5*(2), 177–198. doi:10.1177/1555412009354727

Chasteen, A. L., Bhattacharyya, S., Horhota, M., et al. (2005). How feelings of stereotype threat influence older adults' memory performance. *Experimental Aging Research, 31*(3), 235–260. doi:10.1080/03610730590948177

Chaves, J. F. (2000). Hypnosis. In A. Kazdin (Ed.), *Encyclopedia of psychology* (Vol. 4, pp. 211–216). Washington, DC: American Psychological Association.

Cheal, M. L., Cooper, S., Jacobsen, T., et al. (2009). *APA membership: Past, present, and possible futures*. Paper presented to the American Psychological Association annual meeting, August 6–9, Toronto, Ontario.

Cheek, J., & Buss, A. H. (1979). *Scales of shyness, sociability and self-esteem and correlations among them*. Unpublished research, University of Texas. (Cited by Buss, 1980.)

Chein, J. M., & Fiez, J. A. (2010). Evaluating models of working memory through the effects of concurrent irrelevant information. *Journal of Experimental Psychology: General, 139*(1), 117–137. doi:10.1037/a0018200

Cheng, C., & Lin, Y. (2012). The effects of aging on lifetime of auditory sensory memory in humans. *Biological Psychology, 89*(2), 306–312. doi:10.1016/j.biopsycho.2011.11.003

Cheng, H., Cao, Y., & Olson, L. (1996). Spinal cord repair in adult paraplegic rats: Partial restoration of hind limb function. *Science, 273*(5274), 510. doi:10.1126/science.273.5274.510

Chess, S., & Thomas, A. (1986). *Know your child*. New York: Basic.

Chessick, R. D. (2010). Returning to Freud. *Journal of the American*

Academy of Psychoanalysis & Dynamic Psychiatry, 38(3), 413–440. doi:10.1521/jaap.2010.38.3.413

Cheyne, J. A. (2005). Sleep paralysis episode frequency and number, types, and structure of associated hallucinations. *Journal of Sleep Research, 14*(3), 319–324. doi:10. 1111/j.1365-2869.2005.00477.x

Cheyne, J. A., & Girard, T. A. (2009). The body unbound: Vestibular-motor hallucinations and out-of-body experiences. *Cortex, 45*(2), 201–215. doi:10.1016/j.cortex.2007.05.002

Cheyne, J. A., Rueffer, S. D., & Newby-Clark, I. R. (1999). Hypnagogic and hypnopompic hallucinations during sleep paralysis: Neurological and cultural construction of the nightmare. *Consciousness & Cognition, 8*, 319–337. doi:10.1006/ccog.1999.0404

Chipman, M., & Jin, Y. L. (2009). Drowsy drivers: The effect of light and circadian rhythm on crash occurrence. *Safety Science, 47*(10), 1364–1370. doi:10.1016/j. ssci.2009.03.005

Chisolm, T. H., Willott, J. F., & Lister, J. J. (2003). The aging auditory system: Anatomic and physiologic changes and implications for rehabilitation. *International Journal of Audiology, 42*(Suppl. 2), 2S3–2S10. doi:10.3109/14992020309074637

Choi, H., & Dancy, B. L. (2009). Korean American adolescents' and their parents' perceptions of acculturative stress. *Journal of Child & Adolescent Psychiatric Nursing, 22*(4), 203–210. doi:10.1111/j.1744-6171.2009.00200.x

Chomsky, N. (1975). *Reflections on language*. New York: Pantheon.

Chomsky, N. (1986). *Knowledge of language*. New York: Praeger.

Christakis, N. A., & Fowler, J. H. (2007). The spread of obesity in a large social network over 32 years. *New England Journal of Medicine, 357*(4), 370–379.

Christakis, N. A., & Fowler, J. H. (2008). The collective dynamics of smoking in a large social network. *New England Journal of Medicine, 358*(21), 2249–2258. doi:10.1056/NEJMsa0706154

Christakis, N. A., & Fowler, J. H. (2009). *Connected: The surprising power of our social networks and how they shape our lives*. New York: Little, Brown.

Christian, K. M., & Thompson, R. F. (2005). Long-term storage of an associative memory trace in the cerebellum. *Behavioral Neuroscience, 119*(2), 526–537. doi:10.1037/0735-7044.119.2.526

Christophersen, E. R., & Mortweet, S. L. (2003). *Parenting that works: Building skills that last a lifetime*. Washington, DC: American Psychological Association.

Chua, H. F., Boland, J. E., & Nisbett, R. E. (2005). Cultural variation in eye movements during scene perception. *Proceedings of the National Academy of Sciences, 102*(35), 12629–12633. doi:10.1073/pnas.0506162102

Cialdini, R. B. (2009). *Influence: Science and practice* (5th ed.). Boston: Allyn & Bacon.

Cialdini, R. B., & Griskevicius, V. (2010). Social influence. In R. F. Baumeister & E. J. Finkel (Eds.), *Advanced social psychology: The state of the science* (pp. 385–417). New York: Oxford University Press.

Cialdini, R. B., Reno, R. R., & Kallgren, C. A. (1990). A focus theory of normative conduct: Recycling the concept of norms to reduce littering in public places. *Journal of Personality & Social Psychology, 58*(6), 1015–1026. doi:10.1037/0022-3514.58.6.1015

Cipani, E., & Schock, K. (2007). *Functional behavioral assessment, diagnosis, and treatment: A complete system for education and mental health settings*. New York: Springer.

Cisler, J. M., & Koster, E. H. W. (2010). Mechanisms of attentional biases towards threat in anxiety disorders: An integrative review. *Clinical Psychology Review, 30*(2), 203–216. doi:10.1016/j.cpr.2009.11.003

Cisler, J. M., Olatunji, B. O., Feldner, M. T., et al. (2010). Emotion regulation and the anxiety disorders: An integrative review. *Journal of Psychopathology & Behavioral Assessment, 32*(1), 68–82. doi:10.1007/s10862-009-9161-1

Citrome, L. (2011). Neurochemical models of schizophrenia: Transcending dopamine. *Annals of Clinical Psychiatry, 23*(4), S10–S14.

Claessens, M. (2009). Mindfulness and existential therapy. *Existential Analysis, 20*(1), 109–119.

Clark, R., Anderson, N. B., Clark, V. R., et al. (1999). Racism as a stressor for African Americans. *American Psychologist, 54*(10), 805–816. doi:10.1037/0003-066X.54.10.805

Clayton, N. S., Russell, J., & Dickinson, A. (2009). Are animals stuck in time or are they chronesthetic creatures? *Topics in Cognitive Science, 1*(1), 59–71. doi:10.1111/j.1756-8765.2008.01004.x

Clayton, N. S., Yu, K. S., & Dickinson, A. (2001). Scrub jays (*Aphelocoma coerulescens*) form integrated memories of the multiple features of caching episodes. *Journal of Experimental Psychology: Animal Behavior Processes, 27*, 17–29. doi:10.1037/0097-7403.27.1.17

Cnattingius, S., Signorello, L. B., Ammerén, G., et al. (2000). Caffeine intake and the risk of first-trimester spontaneous abortion. *New England Journal of Medicine, 343*(25), 1839–1845.

Coates, D. D. (2012). "Cult commitment" from the perspective of former members: Direct rewards of membership versus dependency inducing practices. *Deviant Behavior, 33*(3), 168–184. doi:10.1080/01639625.2010.548302

Cobb, N. K., & Abrams, D. B. (2011). E-cigarette or drug-delivery device? Regulating novel nicotine products. *New England Journal of Medicine, 365*(3), 193–195. doi:10.1056/NEJMp1105249

Cohen, G. L., Garcia, J., Purdie-Vaughns, V., et al. (2009). Recursive processes in self-affirmation: Intervening to close the minority achievement gap. *Science, 324*(5925), 400–403. doi:10.1126/science.1170769

Cohen, S., Tyrrell, D. A., & Smith, A. P. (1993). Negative life events, perceived stress, negative affect, and susceptibility to the common cold. *Journal of Personality & Social Psychology, 64*(1), 131–140. doi:10.1037/0022-3514.64.1.131

Cohn, E., Bucolo, D., Pride, M., et al. (2009). Reducing white juror bias: The role of race salience and racial attitudes. *Journal of Applied Social Psychology, 39*(8), 1953–1973. doi:10.1111/j.1559-1816.2009.00511.x

Colangelo, J. J. (2007). Recovered memory debate revisited: Practice implications for mental health counselors. *Journal of Mental Health Counseling, 29*(2), 93–120.

Cole, T., Barrett, D. J. K., & Griffiths, M. D. (2011). Social facilitation in online and offline gambling: A pilot study. *International Journal of Mental Health & Addiction, 9*(3), 240–247. doi 10.1007/s11469-010-9281-6

Coles, C. D., & Black, M. M. (2006). Introduction to the special issue. *Journal of Pediatric Psychology Special Issue, 31*(1), 1–4. doi:10.1093/jpepsy/jsj036

Colin, A. K., & Moore, K., & West, A. N. (1996). Creativity, oversensitivity, and rate of habituation. *EDRA: Environmental Design Research Association, 20*(4), 423–427. doi:10.1016/0191-8869(95)00193-X

Collins, A. M., & Quillian, M. R. (1969). Retrieval time from semantic memory. *Journal of Verbal Learning & Verbal Behavior, 8*, 240–247. doi:10.1016/S0022-5371(69)80069-1

Collins, N. L., Cooper, M. L., Albino, A., et al. (2002). Psychosocial vulnerability from adolescence to adulthood: A prospective study of attachment style differences in relationship functioning and partner choice. *Journal of Personality, 70*(6), 965–1008. doi:10.1111/1467-6494.05029

Collins, W. A., & Gunnar, M. R. (1990). Social and personality development. *Annual Review of Psychology, 41*, 387–416. doi:10.1146/annurev.ps.41.020190.002131

Collop, N. A. (2005). Obstructive sleep apnea: treatment overview and controversies. In P. R. Carney, J. D. Geyer, & R. B. Berry (Eds.), *Clinical sleep disorders* (pp. 278–289). Philadelphia: Lippincott Williams & Wilkins.

Colvin, M. K., & Gazzaniga, M. S. (2007). *Split-brain cases*. Malden, MA: Blackwell Publishing.

Comer, R. J. (2013). *Abnormal psychology* (8th ed.). New York: Worth.

Compton, W. C. (2005). *An introduction to positive psychology*. Belmont, CA: Cengage Learning/Wadsworth.

Compton, W. C., & Hoffman, E. (2013). *Positive psychology: The science of happiness and flourishing* (2nd ed.). Belmont, CA: Cengage Learning/Wadsworth.

Confer, J. C., Easton, J. A., Fleischman, D. S., et al. (2010). Evolutionary psychology: Controversies, questions, prospects, and limitations. *American Psychologist, 65*(2), 110–126. doi:10.1037/a0018413

Conley, K. M., & Lehman, B. J. (2012). Test anxiety and cardiovascular responses to daily academic stressors. *Stress & Health, 28*(1), 41–50. doi:10.1002/smi.1399

Conlon, K. E., Ehrlinger, J., Eibach, R. P., et al. (2011). Eyes on the prize: The longitudinal benefits of goal focus on progress toward a weight loss goal. *Journal of Experimental Social Psychology, 47*, 853–855. doi:10.1016/j.jesp.2011.02.005

Conron, K. J., Mimiaga, M. J., & Landers, S. J. (2010). A population-based study of sexual orientation identity and gender differences in adult health. *American Journal of Public Health, 100*(10), 1953–1960. doi:10.2105/AJPH.2009.174169

Consumer Reports. (2012). *CRH survey: Antidepressants used by 78 percent of respondents with depression or anxiety*. Yonkers, NY: Author. Retrieved May 9, 2012, from http://pressroom.consumerreports.org/pressroom/2010/06/crh-survey-antidepressants-used-by-78-percent-of-respondents-with-depression-or-anxiety-.html

Conway, M. A., Cohen, G., & Stanhope, N. (1992). Very long-term memory for knowledge acquired at school and university. *Applied Cognitive Psychology, 6*(6), 467–482. doi:10.1002/acp.2350060603

Coolidge, F. L., & Wynn, T. (2009). *The rise of Homo Sapiens: The evolution of modern thinking*. New York: Wiley-Blackwell.

Cooper, J. (2007). *Cognitive dissonance: Fifty years of a classic theory*. Thousand Oaks, CA: Sage.

Cooper, J., Bennett, E. A., & Sukel, H. L. (1996). Complex scientific testimony: How do jurors make decisions? *Law & Human Behavior, 20*(4), 379–394. doi:10.1007/BF01498976

Cooper, M. J. (2005). Cognitive theory in anorexia nervosa and bulimia nervosa: Progress, development and future directions. *Clinical Psychology Review, 25*(4), 511–531. doi:10.1016/j.cpr.2005.01.003

Cooper, M., & McLeod, J. (2011). Person-centered therapy: A pluralistic perspective. *Person-Centered & Experiential Psychotherapies, 10*(3), 210–223. doi:10.1080/14779757.2011.599517

Cooper, R. P., Abraham, J., Berman, S., et al. (1997). The development of infants' preference for motherese. *Infant Behavior & Development, 20*(4), 477–488. doi:10.1016/S0163-6383(97)90037-0

Cooper, S. J. (2008). From Claude Bernard to Walter Cannon: Emergence of the concept of homeostasis. *Appetite, 51*(3), 419–427. doi:10.1016/j.appet.2008.06.005

Corballis, M. C. (2002). *From hand to mouth: The origins of language*. Princeton, NJ: Princeton University Press.

Corballis, M. C. (2010a). Handedness and cerebral asymmetry: An evolutionary perspective. In K. Hugdahl & R. Westerhausen (Eds.), *The two halves of the brain: Information processing in the cerebral hemispheres*. Cambridge, MA: MIT Press.

Corballis, M. C. (2010b). Visions of the split brain. *New Zealand Journal of Psychology, 39*(1), 5–7.

Corbin, W. R., & Fromme, K. (2002). Alcohol use and serial monogamy as risks for sexually transmitted diseases in young adults. *Health Psychology, 21*(3), 229–236. doi:10.1037/0278-6133.21.3.229

Corcoran, R. (2010). The allusive cognitive deficit in paranoia: The case for mental time travel or cognitive self-projection. *Psychological Medicine, 40*(8), 1233–1237. doi:10.1017/S003329170999211X

Coren, S. (1992). *The left-hander syndrome.* New York: Free Press.

Coren, S. (1996). *Sleep thieves.* New York: Free Press.

Corey, G. & Corey, M. S. (2010). *I never knew I had a choice: Explorations in personal growth* (9th ed.). Belmont, CA: Cengage Learning/Wadsworth.

Corey, G. & Corey, M. S. (2010). *I never knew I had a choice: Explorations in personal growth* (9th ed.). Belmont, CA: Cengage Learning/Wadsworth.

Corey, G. (2012). *Theory and practice of group counseling* (8th ed.). Belmont, CA: Cengage Learning/Wadsworth.

Corr, C. A., Nabe, C. M., & Corr, D. M. (2012). *Death and dying, life and living* (7th ed.). Belmont, CA: Cengage Learning/Wadsworth.

Correa-Chávez, M., Rogoff, B., & Arauz, R. M. (2005). Cultural patterns in attending to two events at once. *Child Development, 76*(3), 664–678. doi:10.1111/j.1467-8624.2005.00870.x

Corrigan, P. W., & Watson, A. C. (2005). Findings from the National Comorbidity Survey on the frequency of violent behavior in individuals with psychiatric disorders. *Psychiatry Research, 136*(2–3), 153–162. doi:10.1016/j.psychres.2005.06.005

Corsini, R. J., & Wedding, D. (2011). *Current psychotherapies* (9th ed.). Belmont, CA: Cengage Learning/Wadsworth.

Costa, Jr., P. T., & McCrae, R. R. (2006). Trait and factor theories. In J. C. Thomas, D. L. Segal, et al. (Eds.), *Comprehensive handbook of personality & psychopathology: Personality and everyday functioning* (Vol. 1, pp. 96–114). New York: Wiley.

Côté, J. E. (2006a). Emerging adulthood as an institutionalized moratorium: Risks and benefits to identity formation. In J. J. Arnett & J. L. Tanner (Eds.), *Emerging adults in America: Coming of age in the 21st century* (pp. 85–116). Washington, DC: American Psychological Association. doi:10.1037/11381-004

Côté, J. E. (2006b). Identity studies: How close are we to developing a social science of identity? An appraisal of the field. *Identity: An International Journal of Theory & Research, 6*, 3–25. doi:10.1207/s1532706xid0601_2

Court, J. H., & Court, P. C. (2001). Repression: R. I. P. *Australian Journal of Clinical & Experimental Hypnosis, 29*(1), 8–16.

Cowan, D. E., & Bromley, D. G. (2008). *Cults and new religions: A brief history.* Malden, MA: Blackwell.

Cowden, C. R. (2005). Worry and its relationship to shyness. *North American Journal of Psychology, 7*(1), 59–69.

Cowles, J. T. (1937). Food tokens as incentives for learning by chimpanzees. *Comparative Psychology,* Monograph, *14*(5, Whole No. 71).

Cox, R. H. (2011). *Sport psychology: Concepts and applications* (6th ed.). New York: McGraw-Hill.

Craig, E. (2012). Human existence (cún zài): What is it? What's in it for us as existential psychotherapists? *The Humanistic Psychologist, 40*(1), 1–22. doi:10.1080/08873267.2012.643680

Craig, L. (2006). Does father care mean fathers share? A comparison of how mothers and fathers in intact families spend time with children. *Gender & Society, 20*(2), 259–281. doi:10.1177/0891243205285212

Craik, F. I. M. (1970). The fate of primary items in free recall. *Journal of Verbal Learning & Verbal Behavior, 9*, 143–148. doi:10.1016/S0022-5371(70)80042-1

Crandall, C. S., Bahns, A. J., Warner, R., et al. (2011). Stereotypes as justifications of prejudice. *Personality & Social Psychology Bulletin, 37*(11), 1488–1498. doi:10.1177/0146167211411723

Crandall, C. S., Preisler, J. J., Aussprung, J. (1992). Measuring life event stress in the lives of college students: The Undergraduate Stress Questionnaire (USQ). *Journal of Behavioral Medicine, 15*(6), 627–662. doi:10.1007/BF00844860

Crane, L., Pring, L., Ryder, N., et al. (2010). Executive functions in savant artists with autism. *Research in Autism Spectrum Disorders, 5*(2), 790–797.

Crews, F. T., & Boettiger, C. A. (2009). Impulsivity, frontal lobes and risk for addiction. *Pharmacology, Biochemistry & Behavior, 93*(3), 237–247. doi:10.1016/j.pbb.2009.04.018

Crisp, A., Gowers, S., Joughin, N., et al. (2006). The enduring nature of anorexia nervosa. *European Eating Disorders Review, 14*(3), 147–152. doi:10.1002/erv.700

Crocker, J., & Park, L. E. (2004). The costly pursuit of self-esteem. *Psychological Bulletin, 130*(3), 392–414. doi:10.1037/0033-2909.130.3.392

Crooks, R., & Baur, K. (2011). *Our sexuality* (11th ed.). Belmont, CA: Cengage Learning/Wadsworth.

Cropley, A. (2006). In praise of convergent thinking. *Creativity Research Journal, 18*, 391–404. doi:10.1207/s15326934crj1803_13

Crown, C. L., Feldstein, S., Jasnow, M. D., et al. (2002). The cross-modal coordination of interpersonal timing. *Journal of Psycholinguistic Research, 31*(1), 1–23. doi:10.1023/A:1014301303616

Crowther, J. H., Sanftner, J., Bonifazi, D. Z., et al. (2001). The role of daily hassles in binge eating. *International Journal of Eating Disorders, 29*, 449–454. doi:10.1002/eat.1041

Cruse, D., Chennu, S., Chatelle, C., et al. (2011). Bedside detection of awareness in the vegetative state: A cohort study. *The Lancet, 378*(9809), 2088–2094. doi:10.1016/S0140-6736(11)61224-5

Csikszentmihalyi, M. (1997). *Creativity.* New York: HarperCollins.

Csikszentmihalyi, M., Abuhamdeh, S., Nakamura, J. (2005). Flow. In A. J. Elliot & C. S. Dweck, (Eds.), *Handbook of competence and motivation* (pp. 598–608). New York: Guilford.

Cuijpers, P., Geraedts, A. S., van Oppen, P., et al. (2011). Interpersonal psychotherapy for depression: A meta-analysis. *The American Journal of Psychiatry, 168*(6), 581–592. doi:10.1176/appi.ajp.2010.10101411

Culver, R., & Ianna, P. (1988). *Astrology: True or false?* Buffalo, NY: Prometheus Books.

Cummings, M. R. (2011) *Human heredity: Principles and issues* (9th ed.). Belmont CA: Cengage Learning/Wadsworth.

Curci, A., & Luminet, O. (2006). Follow-up of a crossnational comparison on flashbulb and event memory for the September 11th attacks. *Memory, 14*(3), 329–344. Doi:10.1080/09658210903081827

Curtis, D., Vine, A. E., McQuillin, A., et al. (2011). Case–case genome-wide association analysis shows markers differentially associated with schizophrenia and bipolar disorder and implicates calcium channel genes. *Psychiatric Genetics, 21*(1), 1–4. doi:10.1097/YPG.0b013e3283413382

Cytowic, R. E., & Eagleman, D. M. (2009). *Wednesday is indigo blue: Discovering the brain of synesthesia.* Cambridge, MA: MIT Press.

Czeisler, C. A., Duffy, J. F., Shanahan, T. L., et al. (1999). Stability, precision, and near-24-hour period of the human circadian pacemaker. *Science, 284*(5423), 2177–2181. doi:10.1126/science.284.5423.2177

Czeisler, C. A., Richardson, G. S., Zimmerman, J. C., et al. (1981). Entrainment of human circadian rhythms by light-dark cycles: A reassessment. *Photochemistry, Photobiology, 34*, 239–247. doi:10.1111/j.1751-1097.1981.tb08993.x

Dacre Pool, L., & Qualter, P. (2012). Improving emotional intelligence and emotional self-efficacy through a teaching intervention for university students. *Learning & Individual Differences,* doi:10.1016/j.lindif.2012.01.010.

Dadich, A. (2010). Expanding our understanding of self-help support groups for substance use issues. *Journal of Drug Education, 40*(2), 189–202.

Dai, D. Y. (2010). *The nature and nurture of giftedness: A new framework for understanding gifted education.* New York: Teachers College Press.

Damisch, L., Stoberock, B., & Mussweiler, T. (2010). Keep your fingers crossed! How superstition improves performance. *Psychological Science, 21*(7), 1014–1020. doi:10.1177/0956797610372631

Damman, M., Henkens, K., & Kalmijn, M. (2011). The impact of midlife educational, work, health, and family experiences on men's early retirement. *Journals of Gerontology, 66B*(5), 617–627. doi:10.1093/geronb/gbr092

Danaei, G., Ding, E. L., Mozaffarian, D., et al. (2009). The preventable causes of death in the United States: Comparative risk assessment of dietary, lifestyle, and metabolic risk factors. *PLoS Med, 6*(4), e1000058. doi:10.1371/journal.pmed.1000058.

Dane, S., & Erzurumluoglu, A. (2003). Sex and handedness differences in eye–hand visual reaction times in handball players. *International Journal of Neuroscience, 113*(7), 923–929. doi:10.1080/00207450390220367

Dang-Vu, T. T., McKinney, S. M., Buxton, O. M., et al. (2010). Spontaneous brain rhythms predict sleep stability in the face of noise. *Current Biology, 20*(15), R626–R627. doi:0.06/j.cub.200.06.032

Dani, J. A., & Balfour, D. J. K. (2011). Historical and current perspective on tobacco use and nicotine addiction. *Trends in Neurosciences, 34*(7), 383–392. doi:10.1016/j.tins.2011.05.001

Daniels, H. (2005). Vygotsky and educational psychology: Some preliminary remarks. *Educational & Child Psychology, 22*(1), 6–17.

Danziger, N., Prkachin, K. M., & Willer, J.-C. (2006). Is pain the price of empathy? The perception of others' pain in patients with congenital insensitivity to pain. *Brain: A Journal of Neurology, 129*(9), 2494–2507. doi:10.1093/brain/awl155

Darcy, A. M. (2011). Eating disorders in adolescent males: A critical examination of five common assumptions. *Adolescent Psychiatry, 1*(4), 307–312. doi:10.2174/2210677411101040307

Darley, J. M. (2000). Bystander phenomenon. In A. E. Kazdin (Ed.), *Encyclopedia of psychology* (Vol. 1, pp. 493–495). Washington, DC: American Psychological Association.

Darley, J. M., & Latané, B. (1968). Bystander intervention in emergencies: Diffusion of responsibility. *Journal of Personality & Social Psychology, 8*, 377–383. doi:10.1037/h0025589

Darling, C. A., Davidson, J. K., & Passarello, L. C. (1992). The mystique of first intercourse among college youth: The role of partners, contraceptive practices, and psychological reactions. *Journal of Youth & Adolescence, 21*(1), 97–117. doi:10.1007/BF01536984

Darou, W. S. (1992). Native Canadians and intelligence testing. *Canadian Journal of Counselling, 26*(2), 96–99.

Daruna, J. H. (2012). *Introduction to psychoneuroimmunology* (2nd ed.). San Diego: Academic Press.

Darwin, C. (1872). *The expression of emotion in man and animals.* Chicago: University of Chicago Press.

Davey, G. (2008). *Clinical psychology: Topics in applied psychology.* New York: Oxford University Press.

Davey, G. (Ed.) (2011). *Applied psychology.* New York: Wiley-Blackwell.

David, D., & Montgomery, G. H. (2011). The scientific status of psychotherapies: A new evaluative framework for evidence-based psychosocial interventions. *Clinical Psychology: Science & Practice, 18*(2), 89–99. doi:10.1111/j.1468-2850.2011.01239.x

David-Ferdon, C., & Hertz, M. F. (2009). *Electronic media and youth violence: a CDC issue brief for researchers.* Atlanta: Centers for Disease Control.

Retrieved May 9, 2012, from http://www.cdc.gov/violenceprevention/pdf/Electronic_Aggression_Researcher_Brief-a.pdf

Davidovitch, N., & Milgram, R. M. (2006). Creative thinking as a predictor of teacher effectiveness in higher education. *Creativity Research Journal, 18,* 385–390. doi:10.1207/s15326934crj1803_12

Davidson, J. E. (2003). Insights about insightful problem solving. In J. E. Davidson & R. J. Sternberg (Eds.), *The psychology of problem solving* (pp. 149–175). New York: Cambridge University Press. doi:10.1017/CBO9780511615771.006

Davidson, L., Shaw, J., Welborn, S., et al. (2010). "I don't know how to find my way in the world": Contributions of user-led research to transforming mental health practice. *Psychiatry: Interpersonal and Biological Processes, 73*(2), 101–113. doi:10.1521/psyc.2010.73.2.101

Davidson, R. J., Kabat-Zinn, J., Schumacher, J., et al. (2003). Alternations in brain and immune function produced by mindfulness meditation. *Psychosomatic Medicine, 65*(4), 564–570. doi:10.1097/01.PSY.0000077505.67574.E3

Davidson, T. L. (2000). Latent learning. In A. E. Kazdin (Ed.), *Encyclopedia of psychology* (Vol. 4, pp. 489–492). Washington, DC: American Psychological Association. doi:10.1037/10519-212

Davidson, W. B., Bromfield, J. M., & Beck, H. P. (2007). Beneficial academic orientations and self-actualization of college students. *Psychological Reports, 100*(2), 604–612. doi:10.2466/PR0.100.2.604-612

Davis, C., & Carter, J. C. (2009). Compulsive overeating as an addiction disorder: A review of theory and evidence. *Appetite, 53*(1), 1–8. doi:10.1016/j.appet.2009.05.018

Davis, D., & Follette, W. C. (2002). Rethinking the probative value of evidence. *Law & Human Behavior, 26*(2), 133–158. doi:10.1023/A:1014693024962

Davis, M. A. (2009). Understanding the relationship between mood and creativity: A meta-analysis. *Organizational Behavior & Human Decision Processes, 108*(1), 25–38. doi:10.1016/j.obhdp.2008.04.001

Davis, M. R., McMahon, M., & Greenwood, K. M. (2005). The efficacy of mnemonic components of the cognitive interview: Towards a shortened variant for time-critical investigations. *Applied Cognitive Psychology, 19*(1), 75–93. doi:10.1002/acp.1048

Davison, G. C., & Neale, J. M. (2006). *Abnormal psychology* (10th ed.). San Francisco: Jossey-Bass.

Day, D. O., & Moseley, R. L. (2010). Munchausen by proxy syndrome. *Journal of Forensic Psychology Practice, 10*(1), 13–36. doi:10.1080/15228930903172981

Dazzi, C., & Pedrabissi, L. (2009). Graphology and personality: An empirical study on validity of handwriting analysis. *Psychological Reports, 105,* 1255–1268. doi:10.2466/pr0.105.F.1255-1268

de Bono, E. (1992). *Serious creativity.* New York: HarperCollins.

de Jong, P. J., & Muris, P. (2002). Spider phobia. *Journal of Anxiety Disorders, 16*(1), 51–65. doi:10.1016/S0887-6185(01)00089-5

de Leon, C. F. M. (2005). Social engagement and successful aging. *European Journal of Ageing, 2*(1), 64–66.

de Rios, M. D., & Grob, C. S. (2005). Editors' introduction: Ayahuasca use in cross-cultural perspective. *Journal of Psychoactive Drugs, 37*(2), 119–121. doi:10.1080/02791072.2005.10399790

Dean, Jr., D., & Kuhn, D. (2007). Direct instruction vs. discovery: The long view. *Science Education, 91*(3), 384–397. doi:10.1002/sce.20194

Deardorff, J., Hayward, C., Wilson, K. A., et al. (2007). Puberty and gender interact to predict social anxiety symptoms in early adolescence. *Journal of Adolescent Health, 41*(1), 102–104. doi:10.1016/j.jadohealth.2007.02.013

DeCarolis, N. A., & Eisch, A. J. (2010). Hippocampal neurogenesis as a target for the treatment of mental illness: A critical evaluation. *Neuropharmacology, 58*(6), 884–893. doi:10.1016/j.neuropharm.2009.12.013

Decker, S. L., Brooks, J. H., & Allen, R. A. (2011). Stanford-Binet intelligence scales, fifth edition. In S. L. Decker, J. H. Brooks et al. (Eds.), *Handbook of pediatric neuropsychology* (pp. 389–395). New York: Springer.

Deckers, L. (2010). *Motivation: Biological, psychological, and environmental* (3rd ed.). Boston: Pearson/Allyn & Bacon.

Deckro, G. R., Ballinger, K. M., Hoyt, M., et al. (2002). The evaluation of a mind/body intervention to reduce psychological distress and perceived stress in college students. *Journal of American College Health, 50*(4), 281–287. doi:10.1080/07448480209603446

Deeb, S. S. (2004). Molecular genetics of color-vision deficiencies. *Visual Neuroscience, 21*(3), 191–196. doi:10.1017/S0952523804213244

Dein, S., & Littlewood, R. (2005). Apocalyptic suicide: From a pathological to an eschatological interpretation. *International Journal of Social Psychiatry, 51*(3), 198–210. doi:10.1177/0020764005056762

Delgado, B. M., & Ford, L. (1998). Parental perceptions of child development among low-income Mexican American families. *Journal of Child & Family Studies, 7*(4), 469–481. doi:10.1023/A:1022958026951

Dell, P. F. (2009). The long struggle to diagnose multiple personality disorder (MPD): MPD. In P. F. Dell & J. A. O'Neil (Eds.), *Dissociation and the dissociative disorders: DSM-V and beyond* (pp. 384–399). New York: Routledge.

Della Sala, S. (Ed.). (2010). *Forgetting.* Hove, UK: Psychology Press.

Demos, J. N. (2005). *Getting started with neurofeedback.* New York: Norton.

Denney, J. T., Rogers, R. G., Krueger, P. M., et al. (2009). Adult suicide mortality in the United States: Marital status, family size, socioeconomic status, and differences by sex. *Social Science Quarterly, 90*(5), 1167–1185. doi:10.1111/j.1540-6237.2009.00652.x.

Denollet, J., & Van Heck, G. L. (2001). Psychological risk factors in heart disease. *Journal of Psychosomatic Research, 51*(3), 465–468. doi:10.1016/S0022-3999(01)00230-6

DeSantis, A. D., & Hane, A. C. (2010). "Adderall is definitely not a drug": Justifications for the illegal use of ADHD stimulants. *Substance Use & Misuse, 45*(1–2), 31–46. doi:10.3109/10826080902858334

Deutsch, M. (1993). Educating for a peaceful world. *American Psychologist, 48*(5), 510–517. doi:10.1037/0003-066X.48.5.510

Deutschendorf, H. (2009). *The other kind of smart: Simple ways to boost your emotional intelligence for greater personal effectiveness and success.* New York: AMACOM.

Devine, D. J., Clayton, L. D., Dunford, B. B., et al. (2001). Jury decision making: Forty-five years of empirical research on deliberating groups. *Psychology, Public Policy, & Law, 7*(3), 622–727. doi:10.1037/1076-8971.7.3.622

Devlin, B., Daniels, M., & Roeder, K. (1997). The heritability of IQ. *Nature, 388*(6641), 468–471. doi:10.1038/41319

Devoto, A., Lucidi, F., Violani, C., et al. (1999). Effects of different sleep reductions on daytime sleepiness. *Sleep, 22*(3), 336–343.

DeWall, C. N., & Anderson, C. A. (2011). The general aggression model. In P. R. Shaver & M. Mikulincer (Eds.), *Human aggression and violence: Causes, manifestations, and consequences* (pp. 15–33). Washington, DC: American Psychological Association. doi:10.1037/12346-001

DeWall, C. N., Lambert, N. M., Slotter, E. B., et al. (2011). So far away from ones partner, yet so close to romantic alternatives: Avoidant attachment, interest in alternatives, and infidelity. *Journal of Personality & Social Psychology, 101*(6), 1302–1316. doi:10.1037/a0025497

Dewey J. (1910). *How we think.* Lexington, MA: D.C. Heath.

DeYoung, C. G., Flanders, J. L., & Peterson, J. B. (2008). Cognitive abilities involved in insight problem solving: An individual differences model. *Creativity Research Journal, 20*(3), 278–290. doi:10.1080/10400410802278719

Di Marzo, V., Goparaju, S. K., Wang, L., et al. (2001). Leptin-regulated endocannabinoids are involved in maintaining food intake. *Nature, 410*(6830), 822–825. doi:10.1038/35071088

Diano, S., Farr, S. A., Benoit, S. C., et al. (2006). Ghrelin controls hippocampal spine synapse density and memory performance. *Nature Neuroscience, 9,* 381–388. doi:10.1038/nn1656

Dickens, W. T., & Flynn, J. R. (2001). Heritability estimates versus large environmental effects: The IQ paradox resolved. *Psychological Review, 108,* 346–369. doi:10.1037/0033-295X.108.2.346

Dick-Niederhauser, A. & Silverman, W. K. (2006). Separation anxiety disorder. In J. E. Fisher & W. T. O'Donohue (Eds.), *Practitioner's guide to evidence-based psychotherapy* (pp. 627–633). New York: Springer. doi:10.1007/978-0-387-28370-8_62

Diener, E. (Ed.) (2009). *Assessing well-being: The collected works of Ed Diener.* New York: Springer.

Diener, E., & Chan, M. Y. (2011). Happy people live longer: Subjective well-being contributes to health and longevity. *Applied Psychology: Health & Well-Being, 3*(1), 1–43. doi:10.1111/j.1758-0854.2010.01045.x

Diener, E., Ng, W., Harter, J., et al. (2010). Wealth and happiness across the world: Material prosperity predicts life evaluation, whereas psychosocial prosperity predicts positive feeling. *Journal of Personality & Social Psychology, 99*(1), 52–61. doi:10.1037/a0018066

Diener, E., Scollon, C. N., & Lucas, R. E. (2009). In E. Diener (Ed.), *The evolving concept of subjective well-being: The multifaceted nature of happiness* (pp. 67–100). New York: Springer. doi:10.1007/978-90-481-2354-4_4

Diener, E., Tay, L., & Myers, D. G. (2011). The religion paradox: If religion makes people happy, why are so many dropping out? *Journal of Personality and Social Psychology, 101*(6), 1278–1290. doi:10.1037/a0024402

Dierdorff, E. C., & Wilson, M. A. (2003). A meta-analysis of job analysis reliability. *Journal of Applied Psychology, 88*(4), 635–646. doi:10.1037/0021-9010.88.4.635

Dieterich, S. E., Assel, M. A., Swank, P., et al. (2006). The impact of early maternal verbal scaffolding and child language abilities on later decoding and reading comprehension skills. *Journal of School Psychology, 43*(6), 481–494. doi:10.1016/j.jsp.2005.10.003

Dietrich, A., & Stoll, O. (2010). Effortless attention, hypofrontality, and perfectionism. In B. Bruya (Eds.), *Effortless attention: A new perspective in the cognitive science of attention and action* (pp. 159–178). Cambridge, MA: MIT Press.

Dikotter, F., Laamann, L., & Xun, Z. (2008). *Narcotic culture: A history of drugs in China.* Chicago: University of Chicago Press.

Dimberg, U., & Söderkvist, S. (2011). The voluntary facial action technique: A method to test the facial feedback hypothesis. *Journal of Nonverbal Behavior, 35*(1), 17–33. doi:10.1007/s10919-010-0098-6

Dimsdale, J. E. (2011). Medically unexplained symptoms: A treacherous foundation for somatoform disorders? *Psychiatric Clinics of North America, 34*(3), 511–513. doi:10.1016/j.psc.2011.05.003

Dinan, T. G. (2001). Stress, depression and cardiovascular disease. *Stress & Health: Journal of the International Society for the Investigation of Stress, 17*(2), 65–66. doi:10.1002/smi.895

Dingus, T. A., Klauer, S. G., Neale, V. L., et al. (2006). The 100-car naturalistic driving study: Phase II. Results of the 100-car field experiment. *National Highway Traffic Safety Administration Report No. DOT HS 810 593*. Retrieved May 9, 2012, from http://ntl.bts.gov/lib/jpodocs/repts_te/14302.htm

Dion, K. L. (2003). Prejudice, racism, and discrimination. In T. Millon & M. J. Lerner (Eds.), *Personality and social psychology. The comprehensive handbook of psychology* (Vol. 5, pp. 507–536). New York: Wiley.

Dirkzwager, A. J. E., Bramsen, I., & Van Der Ploeg, H. M. (2001). The longitudinal course of post-traumatic stress disorder symptoms among aging military veterans. *Journal of Nervous & Mental Disease, 189*(12), 846–853. doi:10.1097/00005053-200112000-00006

Distin, K. (2006). *Gifted children: A guide for parents and professionals*. London: Jessica Kingsley Publishers.

Dixon, M. J., Smilek, D., & Merikle, P. M. (2004). Not all synaesthetes are created equal: Projector versus associator synaesthetes. *Cognitive, Affective, & Behavioral Neuroscience, 4*(3), 335–343.

Dixon, M. J., Smilek, D., & Merikle, P. M. (2004). Not all synaesthetes are created equal: Projector versus associator synaesthetes. *Cognitive, Affective, & Behavioral Neuroscience, 4*(3), 335–343. doi:10.3758/CABN.4.3.335

Dixon, S. V., Graber, J. A., & Brooks-Gunn, J. (2008). The roles of respect for parental authority and parenting practices in parent-child conflict among African American, Latino, and European American families. *Journal of Family Psychology, 22*(1), 1–10. doi:10.1037/0893-3200.22.1.1

Dobricki, M., & Maercker, A. (2010). (Post-traumatic) embitterment disorder: Critical evaluation of its stressor criterion and a proposed revised classification. *Nordic Journal of Psychiatry, 64*(3), 147–152. doi:10.3109/08039480903398185

Dobson, K. S., Backs-Dermott, G. J., & Dozois, D. J. A. (2000). Cognitive and cognitive-behavioral therapies. In C. R. Snyder & R. E. Ingram (Eds.), *Handbook of psychological change: Psychotherapy processes and practices for the 21st century* (pp. 409–428). New York: Wiley.

Dodds, P. S., Muhamad, R., & Watts, D. J. (2003). An experimental study of search in global social networks. *Science, 301*(5634), 827–829. doi:10.1126/science.1081058

Dodson, E. R., & Zee, P. C. (2010). Therapeutics for circadian rhythm sleep disorders. *Sleep Medicine Clinics, 5*(4), 701–715. doi:10.1016/j.jsmc.2010.08.001

Doherty, M. J. (2009). *Theory of mind: How children understand others' thoughts and feelings*. New York: Psychology Press.

Doidge, N. (1997). Empirical evidence for the efficacy of psychoanalytic psychotherapies and psychoanalysis. *Psychoanalytic Inquiry, Suppl.*, 102–150. doi:10.1080/07351699709534161

Dollard, J., & Miller, N. E. (1950). *Personality and psychotherapy: An analysis in terms of learning, thinking and culture*. New York: McGraw-Hill.

Dombrowski, S. U., Sniehotta, F. F., Avenell, A., et al. (2007). Current issues and future directions in psychology and health: Towards a cumulative science of behaviour change: Do current conduct and reporting of behavioural interventions fall short of best practice? *Psychology & Health, 22*(8), 869–874. doi:10.1080/08870440701520973

Domellöf, E., Johansson, A., & Rönnqvist, L. (2011). Handedness in preterm born children: A systematic review and a meta-analysis. *Neuropsychologia, 49*(9), 2299–2310. doi:10.1016/j.neuropsychologia.2011.04.033

Domhoff, G. W. (2001). A new neurocognitive theory of dreams. *Dreaming, 11*, 13–33. doi:10.1023/A:1009464416649

Domhoff, G. W. (2003). *The scientific study of dreams: Neural networks, cognitive development, and content analysis*. Washington, DC: American Psychological Association.

Domhoff, G. W., & Schneider, A. (2008). Similarities and differences in dream content at the crosscultural, gender, and individual levels. *Consciousness & Cognition, 17*(4), 1257–1265. doi:10.1016/j.concog.2008.08.005

Domingo, R. A., & Goldstein-Alpern, N. (1999). "What dis?" and other toddler-initiated, expressive language-learning strategies. *Infant-Toddler Intervention, 9*(1), 39–60.

Domjan, M. (2010). *The principles of learning and behavior* (6th ed.). Belmont, CA: Cengage Learning/Wadsworth.

Donate-Bartfield, E., & Passman, R. H. (2004). Relations between children's attachments to their mothers and to security blankets. *Journal of Family Psychology, 18*(3), 453–458. doi:10.1037/0893-3200.18.3.453

Dooling, D. J., & Lachman, R. (1971). Effects of comprehension on retention of prose. *Journal of Experimental Psychology, 88*, 216–222. doi:10.1037/h0030904

Doran, S. M., Van Dongen, H. P., & Dinges, D. F. (2001). Sustained attention performance during sleep deprivation. *Archives of Italian Biology, 139*, 253–267.

Dorfman, J., Shames, J., & Kihlstrom, J. F. (1996). Intuition, incubation, and insight. In G. Underwood (Ed.), *Implicit cognition* (pp. 257–296). New York: Oxford University Press.

Dorman, M. F., & Wilson, B. S. (2004). The design and function of cochlear implants. *American Scientist, 92*(Sept/Oct), 436–445. doi:10.1511/2004.5.436

Dougherty, D. D., Baer, L., Cosgrove, G. R., et al. (2002). Prospective long-term follow-up of 44 patients who received cingulotomy for treatment-refractory obsessive-compulsive disorder. *American Journal of Psychiatry, 159*(2), 269–275. doi:10.1176/appi.ajp.159.2.269

Dovidio, J. F., & Gaertner, S. L. (1999). Reducing prejudice: Combating intergroup biases. *Current Directions in Psychological Science, 8*(4), 101–105. doi:10.1111/1467-8721.00024

Dovidio, J. F., & Penner, L. A. (2001). Helping and altruism. In M. Hewstone & M. Brewer (Eds.), *Handbook of social psychology* (pp. 162–195). London: Blackwell.

Dovidio, J. F., Gaertner, S. L., Kawakami, K., et al. (2002). Why can't we just get along? *Cultural Diversity & Ethnic Minority Psychology, 8*(2), 88–102. doi:10.1037/1099-9809.8.2.88

Dovidio, J. F., Glick, P., & Rudman, L. A. (Eds.). (2005). *On the nature of prejudice: Fifty years after Allport*. Malden, MA: Blackwell.

Dovidio, J. F., Piliavin, J. A., Schroeder, D. A., et al. (2006). *The social psychology of prosocial behavior*. Mahwah, NJ: Erlbaum.

Dow-Edwards, D. (2011). Translational issues for prenatal cocaine studies and the role of environment. *Neurotoxicology & Teratology, 33*(1), 9–16. doi:10.1016/j.ntt.2010.06.007

Dowling, K. W. (2005). The effect of lunar phases on domestic violence incident rates. *Forensic Examiner, 14*(4), 13–18.

Dozois, D. J. A., & Dobson, K. S. (2002). Depression. In M. M. Antony & D. H. Barlow (Eds.), *Handbook of assessment and treatment planning for psychological disorders* (pp. 259–299). New York: Guilford.

Dozois, D. J. A., & Dobson, K. S. (Eds.). (2004). *The prevention of anxiety and depression: Theory, research, and practice*. Washington, DC: American Psychological Association.

Drews, F. A., Yazdani, H., Godfrey, C. N., et al. (2009). Text messaging during simulated driving. *Human Factors, 51*(5), 762–770. doi:10.1177/0018720809353319

Drigotas, S. M., Rusbult, C. E., Wieselquist, J., et al. (1999). Close partner as sculptor of the ideal self: Behavioral affirmation and the Michelangelo phenomenon. *Journal of Personality & Social Psychology, 77*(2), 293–323. doi:10.1037/0022-3514.77.2.293

Drolet, G., Dumont, E. C., Gosselin, I., et al. (2001). Role of endogenous opioid system in the regulation of the stress response. *Progress in Neuro-Psychopharmacology & Biological Psychiatry, 25*(4), 729–741. doi:10.1016/S0278-5846(01)00161-0

Druckman, D., & Bjork, R. A. (1994). *Learning, remembering, believing: Enhancing human performance*. Washington, DC: National Academy Press.

Drummond, M., Douglas, J., & Olver, J. (2007). Anosmia after traumatic brain injury: A clinical update. *Brain Impairment, 8*(1), 31–40. doi:10.1375/brim.8.1.31

Dryden, W. (2011). *Understanding psychological health: The REBT perspective*. New York: Routledge/Taylor & Francis.

Drymalski, W. M., & Washburn, J. J. (2011). Sudden gains in the treatment of depression in a partial hospitalization program. *Journal of Consulting & Clinical Psychology, 79*(3), 364–368. doi:10.1037/a0022973

Duckitt, J., & Sibley, C. G. (2010). Personality, ideology, prejudice, and politics: A dual-process motivational model. *Journal of Personality, 78*(6), 1861–1893. doi:10.1111/j.1467-6494.2010.00672.x

Duckworth, A. L., Peterson, C., Matthews, M. D., et al. (2007). Grit: Perseverance and passion for long-term goals. *Journal of Personality & Social Psychology, 92*(6), 1087–1101. doi:10.1037/0022-3514.92.6.1087

Duffy, J. F., & Wright, Jr., K. P. (2005). Entrainment of the human circadian system by light. *Journal of Biological Rhythms, 20*(4), 326–338. doi:10.1177/0748730405277983

Duncan, J. (2005). Frontal lobe function and general intelligence: Why it matters. *Cortex, 41*(2), 215–217. doi:10.1016/S0010-9452(08)70896-7

Duncker, K. (1945). On problem solving. *Psychological Monographs, 58*(270).

Dunlop, S. M., & Romer, D. (2010). Adolescent and young adult crash risk: Sensation seeking, substance use propensity and substance use behaviors. *Journal of Adolescent Health, 46*(1), 90–92. doi:10.1016/j.jadohealth.2009.06.005

Durán, L. K., Roseth, C. J., Hoffman, P. (2010). An experimental study comparing English-only and Transitional Bilingual Education on Spanish-speaking preschoolers' early literacy development. *Early Childhood Research Quarterly, 25*(2), 207–217. doi:10.1016/j.ecresq.2009.10.002

Durand, V. M., & Barlow, D. H. (2013). *Essentials of abnormal psychology* (6th ed.). Belmont, CA: Cengage Learning/Wadsworth.

Dutta, T., & Mandal, M. K. (2005). The relationship of handedness and accidents: A meta-analytical review of findings. *Psychological Studies, 50*(4), 309–316.

Dutton, D. G., & Aron, A. P. (1974). Some evidence for heightened sexual attraction under conditions of high anxiety. *Journal of Personality & Social Psychology, 30*, 510–517. doi:10.1037/h0037031

Dvash, J., Gilam, G., Ben-Ze'ev, A., et al. (2010). The envious brain: The neural basis of social comparison. *Human Brain Mapping, 31*(11), 1741–1750. doi:10.1002/hbm.20972

Dyer, K. A. (2001). Dealing with death and dying in medical education and practice. *Journey of Hearts*. Retrieved May 9, 2012, from http://www.journeyofhearts.org/kirstimd/AMSA/outline.htm

Dyukova, G. M., Glozman, Z. M., Titova, E. Y., et al. (2010). Speech disorders in right-hemisphere stroke. *Neuroscience & Behavioral Physiology, 40*(6), 593–602. doi:10.1007/s11055-010-9301-9

Dywan, J., & Bowers, K. S. (1983). The use of hypnosis to enhance recall. *Science, 222*, 184–185. doi:10.1126/science.6623071

Dzokoto, V. A., & Adams, G. (2005). Understanding genital-shrinking epidemics in West Africa: Koro, juju, or mass psychogenic illness? *Culture, Medicine & Psychiatry, 29*(1), 53–78. doi:10.1007/s11013-005-4623-8

Eagly, A. H. (2009). The his and hers of prosocial behavior: An examination of the social psychology of gender. *American Psychologist, 64*(8), 644–658. doi:10.1037/0003-066X.64.8.644

Eardley, A. F., & Pring, L. (2007). Spatial processing, mental imagery, and creativity in individuals with and without sight. *European Journal of Cognitive Psychology, 19*(1), 37–58. doi:10.1080/09541440600591965

Eaton, D. K., Kann, L., Kinchen, S., et al. (2010). Youth risk behavior surveillance: United States, 2009. *MMWR Surveillance Summary, 59*(SS-5), 1–40. Retrieved May 9, 2012, from http://www.cdc.gov/mmwr/pdf/ss/ss5905.pdf

Ebben, M. R., & Spielman, A. J. (2009). Non-pharmacological treatments for insomnia. *Journal of Behavioral Medicine, 32*(3), 244–254. doi:10.1007/s10865-008-9198-8

Ebbinghaus, H. (1885). *Memory: A contribution to experimental psychology.* (H. A. Ruger & C. E. Bussenius, Trans.) New York: New York Teacher's College, Columbia University.

Eckerman, D. A. (1999). Scheduling reinforcement about once a day. *Behavioural Processes, 45*(1–3), 101–114. doi:10.1016/S0376-6357(99)00012-1

Eddy, K. T., Dutra, L., Bradley, R., et al. (2004). A multidimensional meta-analysis of psychotherapy and pharmacotherapy for obsessive-compulsive disorder. *Clinical Psychology Review, 24*(8), 1011–1030. doi:10.1016/j.cpr.2004.08.004

Edenfield, T. M., & Blumenthal, J. A. (2011). Exercise and stress reduction. In R. J. Contrada & A. Baum (Eds.), *The handbook of stress science: Biology, psychology, and health* (pp. 301–319). New York: Springer.

Eidelson, R. J., & Eidelson, J. I. (2003). Dangerous ideas. *American Psychologist, 58*(3), 182–192. doi:10.1037/0003-066X.58.3.182

Eifert, G. H., & Lejuez, C. W. (2000). Aversion therapy. In A. E. Kazdin (Ed.), *Encyclopedia of psychology* (Vol. 1, pp. 348–350). Washington, DC: American Psychological Association.

Eisenberg, N., Valiente, C., Fabes, R. A., et al. (2003). The relations of effortful control and ego control to children's resiliency and social functioning. *Developmental Psychology, 39*(4), 761–776. doi:10.1037/0003-066X.58.3.182

Eisendrath, S., Chartier, M., & McLane, M. (2011). Adapting mindfulness-based cognitive therapy for treatment-resistant depression. *Cognitive & Behavioral Practice, 18*(3), 362–370. doi:10.1016/j.cbpra.2010.05.004

Eisler, I., Simic, M., Russell, G. F. M., et al. (2007). A randomized controlled treatment trial of two forms of family therapy in adolescent anorexia nervosa: A five-year follow-up. *Journal of Child Psychology & Psychiatry, 48*(6), 552–560. doi:10.1111/j.1469-7610.2007.01726.x

Ekman, P. (1993). Facial expression and emotion. *American Psychologist, 48*(4), 384–392. doi:10.1037/0003-066X.48.4.384

Ekman, P., & Cordaro, D. (2011). What is meant by calling emotions basic. *Emotion Review, 3*(4), 364–370. doi:10.1177/1754073911410740

Ekman, P., Levenson, R. W., & Friesen, W. V. (1983). Autonomic nervous system activity distinguishes among emotions. *Science, 221*, 1208–1210. doi:10.1126/science.6612338

Ekonomou, A., Ballard, C. G., Pathmanaban, O. N., et al. (2011). Increased neural progenitors in vascular dementia. *Neurobiology of Aging, 32*, 2152–2161. doi:10.1016/j.neurobiolaging.2010.01.007

Elder, P. (2006). *Critical thinking: Learn the tools the best thinkers use.* Englewood Cliffs, NJ: Prentice-Hall.

Eldridge, M., Saltzman, E., & Lahav, A. (2010). Seeing what you hear: Visual feedback improves pitch recognition. *European Journal of Cognitive Psychology, 22*(7), 1078–1091. doi:10.1080/09541440903316136

Elkington, K. S., Hackler, D., McKinnon, K., et al. (2012). Perceived mental illness stigma among youth in psychiatric outpatient treatment. *Journal of Adolescent Research, 27*(2), 290–317. doi:10.1177/0743558411409931

Elli, K. A., & Nathan, P. J. (2001). The pharmacology of human working memory. *International Journal of Neuropsychopharmacology, 4*(3), 299–313. doi:10.1017/S1461145701002541

Ellickson, P. L., Martino, S. C., & Collins, R. L. (2004). Marijuana use from adolescence to young adulthood. *Health Psychology, 23*(3), 299–307. doi:10.1037/0278-6133.23.3.299

Elliott, M., & Williams, D. (2003). The client experience of counselling and psychotherapy. *Counselling Psychology Review, 18*(1), 34–38.

Elliott, R., & Farber, B. A. (2010). Carl Rogers: Idealistic pragmatist and psychotherapy research pioneer. In L. G. Castonguay, J. C. Muran, et al. (Eds.), *Bringing psychotherapy research to life: Understanding change through the work of leading clinical researchers* (pp. 17–27). Washington, DC: American Psychological Association.

Elliott, R., Sahakian, B. J., Matthews, K., et al. (1997). Effects of methylphenidate on spatial working memory and planning in healthy young adults. *Psychopharmacology, 131*, 196–206. doi:10.1007/s002130050284

Ellis, A. (1979). The practice of rational-emotive therapy. In A. Ellis & J. Whiteley (Eds.), *Theoretical and empirical foundations of rational-emotive therapy* (pp. 1–6). Monterey, CA: Brooks/Cole.

Ellis, A. (1995). Changing rational-emotive therapy (RET) to rational emotive behavior therapy (REBT). *Journal of Rational-Emotive & Cognitive Behavior Therapy, 13*(2), 85–89. doi:10.1007/BF02354453

Ellis, A., & Ellis, D. J. (2011). *Rational emotive behavior therapy.* Washington, DC: American Psychological Association.

Ellis, D. (2013). *Becoming a master student: Concise* (14th ed.). Belmont, CA: Cengage Learning/Wadsworth.

Ellison-Wright, I., & Bullmore, E. (2010). Anatomy of bipolar disorder and schizophrenia: A meta-analysis. *Schizophrenia Research, 117*(1), 1–12. doi:10.1016/j.schres.2009.12.022

Emerson, E. (2009). Relative child poverty, income inequality, wealth, and health. *Journal of the American Medical Association, 301*(4), 425–426. doi:10.1001/jama.2009.8

Emmorey, K., Grabowski, T., McCullough, S., et al. (2003). Neural systems underlying lexical retrieval for sign language. *Neuropsychologia, 41*(1), 85–95. doi:10.1016/S0028-3932(02)00089-1

Engelen, E., & Röttger-Rössler, B. (2012). Current disciplinary and interdisciplinary debates on empathy. *Emotion Review, 4*(1), 3–8. doi:10.1177/1754073911422287

Engle, D. E., & Arkowitz, H. (2006). *Ambivalence in psychotherapy: Facilitating readiness to change.* New York: Guilford.

Engler, B. (2009). *Personality theories* (5th ed.). Belmont, CA: Cengage Learning/Wadsworth.

Enns, M. W., Cox, B. J., & Clara, I. P. (2005). Perfectionism and neuroticism: A longitudinal study of specific vulnerability and diathesis-stress models. *Cognitive Therapy & Research, 29*(4), 463–478.

Enrici, I., Adenzato, M., Cappa, S., et al. (2011). Intention processing in communication: A common brain network for language and gestures. *Journal of Cognitive Neuroscience, 23*(9), 2415–2431. doi:10.1162/jocn.2010.21594

Epstein, S. (2003). Cognitive-experiential self-theory of personality. In T. Millon & M. J. Lerner (Eds.), *Comprehensive handbook of psychology: Personality and social psychology* (Vol 5, pp. 159–184). New York: Wiley.

Erez, D. L., Levy, J., Friger, M., et al. (2010). Assessment of cognitive and adaptive behaviour among individuals with congenital insensitivity to pain and anhidrosis. *Developmental Medicine & Child Neurology, 52*(6), 559–562. doi:10.1111/j.1469-8749.2009.03567.x

Erickson, C. D., & Al-Timimi, N. R. (2001). Providing mental health services to Arab Americans. *Cultural Diversity & Ethnic Minority Psychology, 7*(4), 308–327. doi:10.1037/1099-9809.7.4.308

Ericsson, K. A. (2000). How experts attain and maintain superior performance. *Journal of Aging & Physical Activity, 8*(4), 366–372.

Ericsson, K. A., & Charness, N. (1994). Expert performance. *American Psychologist, 49*(8), 725–747. doi:10.1037/0003-066X.49.8.725

Ericsson, K. A., & Chase, W. G. (1982). Exceptional memory. *American Scientist, 70*, 607–615.

Ericsson, K. A., Delaney, P. F., Weaver, G., et al. (2004). Uncovering the structure of a memorist's superior "basic" memory capacity. *Cognitive Psychology, 49*(3), 191–237. doi:10.1016/j.cogpsych.2004.02.001

Erikson, E. H. (1963). *Childhood and society.* New York: Norton.

Erlacher, D., & Schredl, M. (2004). Dreams reflecting waking sport activities: A comparison of sport and psychology students. *International Journal of Sport Psychology, 35*(4), 301–308.

Eschholz, S., Chiricos, T., & Gertz, M. (2003). Television and fear of crime: Program types, audience traits, and the mediating effect of perceived neighborhood racial composition. *Social Problems, 50*(3), 395–415. doi:10.1525/sp.2003.50.3.395

Essien, E. J., Monjok, E., Chen, H., et al. (2010). Correlates of HIV knowledge and sexual risk behaviors among female military personnel. *AIDS & Behavior, 14*(6), 1401–1414. doi:10.1007/s10461-010-9701-4

Ethier, K. A., Kershaw, T., Niccolai, L., et al. (2003). Adolescent women underestimate their susceptibility to sexually transmitted infections. *Sexually Transmitted Infections, 79*, 408–411. doi:10.1136/sti.79.5.408

Evans, G. W. (2006). Child development and the physical environment. *Annual Review of Psychology, 57*, 423–451. doi:10.1146/annurev.psych.57.102904.190057

Evardone, M., Alexander, G. M., & Morey, L. C. (2007). Hormones and borderline personality features. *Personality & Individual Differences, 44*(1), 278–287. doi:10.1016/j.paid.2007.08.007

Everly, G. S. (2002). Thoughts on peer (paraprofessional) support in the provision of mental health services. *International Journal of Emergency Mental Health, 4*(2), 89–92.

Ewen, R. B. (2009). *An introduction to theories of personality* (7th ed.). Hillsdale, NJ: Lawrence Erlbaum.

Eysenck, H. J. (1994). The outcome problem in psychotherapy: What have we learned? *Behaviour Research & Therapy, 32*(5), 477–495. doi:10.1016/0005-7967(94)90135-X

Eysenck, H. J. (Ed.). (1981). *A model for personality.* New York: Springer-Verlag.

Eysenck, M. W., Derakshan, N., Santos, R., et al. (2007). Anxiety and cognitive performance: Attentional control theory. *Emotion, 7*(2), 336–353. doi:10.1037/1528-3542.7.2.336

Fabrega, Jr., H. (2004). Culture and the origins of psychopathology. In U. P. Gielen, J. M., Fish, et al. (Eds.), *Handbook of culture, therapy, and healing* (pp. 15–35). Mahwah, NJ: Erlbaum.

Fahim, C., Stip, E., Mancini-Marïe, A., et al. (2005). Brain activity during emotionally negative pictures in schizophrenia with and without flat affect: An fMRI study. *Psychiatry Research: Neuroimaging, 140*(1), 1–15. doi:10.1016/j.pscychresns.2005.06.003

Fain, G. L. (2003). *Sensory transduction.* Sunderland, MA: Sinauer.

Faith, M. S., Wong, F. Y., & Carpenter, K. M. (1995). Group sensitivity training: Update, meta-analysis, and recommendations. *Journal of Counseling Psychology, 42*(3), 390–399. doi:10.1037/0022-0167.42.3.390

Falkowski, C. (2000). *Dangerous drugs.* Center City, MN: Hazelden Information Education.

Farah, M. J. (2004). *Visual agnosia* (2nd ed.). Cambridge, MA: MIT Press.

Farah, M. J. (2006). Prosopagnosia. In M. J. Farah & T. E. Feinberg (Eds.), *Patient-based approaches to cognitive neuroscience* (2nd ed., pp. 123–125). Cambridge, MA: MIT Press.

Farah, M. J., Haimm, C., Sankoorikal, G., et al. (2009). When we enhance cognition with Adderall, do we sacrifice creativity? A preliminary study. *Psychopharmacology, 202*(1–3), 541–547. doi:10.1007/s00213-008-1369-3

Faraut, B., Boudjeltia, K. Z., Dyzma, M., et al. (2011). Benefits of napping and an extended duration of recovery sleep on alertness and immune cells after acute sleep restriction. *Brain, Behavior, & Immunity, 25*(1), 16–24. doi:10.1016/j.bbi.2010.08.001

Farb, N. A. S., Segal, Z. V., Mayberg, H., et al. (2007). Attending to the present: Mindfulness meditation reveals distinct neural modes of self-reference. *Social Cognitive & Affective Neuroscience, 2*(4), 313–322. doi:10.1093/scan/nsm030

Farrand, P., Confue, P., Byng, R., et al. (2009). Guided self-help supported by paraprofessional mental health workers: An uncontrolled before-after cohort study. *Health & Social Care in the Community, 17*(1), 9–17. doi:10.1111/j.1365-2524.2008.00792.x

Farrell, M. J., Zamarripa, F., Shade, R., et al. (2008). Effect of aging on regional cerebral blood flow responses associated with osmotic thirst and its satiation by water drinking: A PET study. *Proceedings of the National Academy of Sciences, 105*(1), 382–387. doi:10.1073/pnas.0710572105

Farroni, T., Massaccesi, S., Pividori, D., et al. (2004). Gaze following in newborns. *Infancy, 5*(1), 39–60. doi:10.1207/s15327078in0501_2

Faurie, C., Bonenfant, S., Goldberg, M., et al. (2008). Socio-economic status and handedness in two large cohorts of French adults. *British Journal of Psychology, 99*(4), 533–554.

Fayek, A. (2010). *The crisis in psychoanalysis: In search of a lost doctrine.* Austin, TX: Bridgeway Books.

Federal Bureau of Investigation. (2011). *Crime in the United States, 2010.* Washington, DC: Author. Retrieved April 30, 2012, from http://www.fbi.gov/about-us/cjis/ucr/crime-in-the-u.s/2010/crime-in-the-u.s.-2010/violent-crime

Feingold, A. (1992). Gender differences in mate selection preferences. *Psychological Bulletin, 111*, 304–341.

Feldman, S. (2003). Enforcing social conformity: A theory of authoritarianism. *Political Psychology, 24*(1), 41–47. doi:10.1111/0162-895X.00316

Fellous, J.-M., & Ledoux, J. E. (2005). Toward basic principles for emotional processing: What the fearful brain tells the robot. In J.-M. Fellous & M. A. Arbib (Eds.), *Who needs emotions? The brain meets the robot* (pp. 79–115). New York: Oxford University Press.

Fenigstein, A. (2009). Private and public self-consciousness. In M. R. Leary &

R. H. Hoyle (Eds.), *Handbook of individual differences in social behavior* (pp. 495–511). New York: Guilford.

Fenn, K. M., Nusbaum, H. C., & Margoliash, D. (2003). Consolidation during sleep of perceptual learning of spoken language. *Nature, 425*(6958), 614–616. doi:10.1038/nature01951

Fenton, M. C., Keyes, K., Geier, T., et al. (2012). Psychiatric comorbidity and the persistence of drug use disorders in the United States. *Addiction, 107*(3), 599–609. doi:10.1111/j.1360-0443.2011.03638.x

Ferguson, C. J., & Dyck, D. (2012). Paradigm change in aggression research: The time has come to retire the General Aggression Model. *Aggression & Violent Behavior.* doi:10.1016/j.avb.2012.02.007.

Ferguson, C. J., & Garza, A. (2011). Call of (civic) Duty: Action games and civic behavior in a large sample of youth. *Computers in Human Behavior, 27*, 770–775. doi:10.1016/j.chb.2010.10.026

Ferguson, C. J., Miguel, C. N., & Hartley, R. D. (2009). A multivariate analysis of youth violence and aggression: The influence of family, peers, depression, and media violence. *Journal of Pediatrics, 155*(6), 904–908. doi:10.1016/j.jpeds.2009.06.021

Ferguson, K. (2011). *Stephen Hawking: Quest for a theory of everything.* New York: Palgrave MacMillan.

Fernald, A. (1989). Intonation and communicative intent in mothers' speech to infants: Is the melody the message? *Child Development, 60*(6), 1497–1510. doi:10.2307/1130938

Fernald, A., Perfors, A., & Marchman, V. A. (2006). Picking up speed in understanding: Speech processing efficiency and vocabulary growth across the 2nd year. *Developmental Psychology, 42*(1), 98–116. doi:10.1037/0012-1649.42.1.98

Féron, F., Perry, C., Cochrane, J., et al. (2005). Autologous olfactory ensheathing cell transplantation in human spinal cord injury. *Brain: A Journal of Neurology, 128*(12), 2951–2960. doi:10.1093/brain/awh657

Ferrari, J. R., & Scher, S. J. (2000). Toward an understanding of academic and nonacademic tasks procrastinated by students: The use of daily logs. *Psychology in the Schools, 37*(4), 359–366. doi:10.1002/1520-6807(200007)37:4<367::AID-PITS7>3.0.CO;2-Y

Festinger, L. (1957). *A theory of cognitive dissonance.* Stanford, CA: Stanford University Press.

Festinger, L., & Carlsmith, J. M. (1959). Cognitive consequences of forced compliance. *Journal of Abnormal & Social Psychology, 58*, 203–210. doi:10.1037/h0041593

Ficca, G., & Salzarulos, P. (2004). What in sleep is for memory. *Sleep Medicine, 5*, 225–230. doi:10.1016/j.sleep.2004.01.018

Ficca, G., Axelsson, J., Mollicone, D. J., et al. (2010). Naps, cognition and performance. *Sleep Medicine Reviews, 14*(4), 249–258. doi:10.1016/j.smrv.2009.09.005

Field, C. E., Nash, H. M., Handwerk, M. L., et al. (2004). A modification of the token economy for nonresponsive youth in family-style residential care. *Behavior Modification, 28*(3), 438–457. doi:10.1177/0145445503258995

Field, J. E., Kolbert, J. B., Cothers, L. M., et al. (2009). *Understanding girl bullying and what to do about it: Strategies to help heal the divide.* Thousand Oaks, CA: Corwin Press.

Fields, R. D. (2007). The shark's electric sense. *Scientific American, 297*(8), 74–81.

Fields, R. M., & Margolin, J. (2001). *Coping with trauma.* Washington, DC: American Psychological Association.

Filbey, F. M., Schacht, J. P., Myers, U. S., et al. (2009). Marijuana craving in the brain. *Proceedings of the National Academy of Sciences, 106*(31), 13016–13021. doi:10.1073/pnas.0903863106

Fine, C. (2010). *Delusions of gender.* New York: Norton.

Fink, M., & Taylor, M. A. (2003). *Catatonia: A clinician's guide to diagnosis and treatment.* London: Cambridge University Press.

Fink, M., Shorter, E., & Taylor, M. A. (2010). Catatonia is not schizophrenia: Kraepelin's error and the need to recognize catatonia as an independent syndrome in medical nomenclature. *Schizophrenia Bulletin, 36*(2), 314–320. doi:10.1093/schbul/sbp059

Fiore, D., Dimaggio, G., Nicoló, G., et al. (2008). Metacognitive interpersonal therapy in a case of obsessive-compulsive and avoidant personality disorders. *Journal of Clinical Psychology, 64*(2), 168–180. doi:10.1002/jclp.20450

Fireman, G., Kose, G., & Solomon, M. J. (2003). Self-observation and learning: The effect of watching oneself on problem solving performance. *Cognitive Development, 18*(3), 339–354. doi:10.1016/S0885-2014(03)00038-8

First, M. B., & Pincus, H. A. (2002). The DSM-IV text revision: Rationale and potential impact on clinical practice. *Psychiatric Services, 53*, 288–292. doi:10.1176/appi.ps.53.3.288

Fischer, A. H., Manstead, A. S. R., Rodriquez Mosquera, P. M., et al. (2004). Gender and culture differences in emotion. *Emotion, 4*(1), 87–94. doi:10.1037/1528-3542.4.1.87

Fischer, C., & Kächele, H. (2009). Comparative analysis of patients dreams in Freudian and Jungian treatment. *International Journal of Psychotherapy, 13*(3), 34–40.

Fischer, P., Kastenmüller, A., Greitemeyer, T. (2010). Media violence and the self: The impact of personalized gaming characters in aggressive video games on aggressive behavior. *Journal of Experimental Social Psychology, 46*(1), 192–195. doi:10.1016/j.jesp.2009.06.010

Fischer, P., Krueger, J. I., Greitemeyer, T., et al. (2011). The bystander-effect: A meta-analytic review on bystander intervention in dangerous and non-dangerous emergencies. *Psychological Bulletin, 137*(4), 517–537. doi:10.1037/a0023304

Fisher, R. P., & Geiselman, R. E. (1987). Enhancing eyewitness memory with the cognitive interview. In M. M. Gruneberg, P. E. Morris, et al. (Eds.), *Practical aspects of memory: Current research and issues* (pp. 34–39). Chinchester, U.K.: Wiley.

Fiske, S. T. (1993). Social cognition and social perception. *Annual Review of Psychology, 44*, 155–194. doi:10.1146/annurev.ps.44.020193.001103

Fiske, S. T., Cuddy, A. J. C., Glick, P., et al. (2002). A model of (often mixed) stereotype content: Competence and warmth respectively follow from perceived status and competition. *Journal of Personality & Social Psychology, 82*(6), 878–902. doi:10.1037/0022-3514.82.6.878

Flanagan, M. B., May, J. G., & Dobie, T. G. (2004). The role of vection, eye movements and postural instability in the etiology of motion sickness. *Journal of Vestibular Research: Equilibrium & Orientation, 14*(4), 335–346.

Flaskerud, J. H. (2009). What do we need to know about the culture-bound syndromes? *Issues in Mental Health Nursing, 30*(6), 406–407. doi:10.1080/01612840902812947

Flegal, K. M., Carroll, M. D., Ogden, C. L., et al. (2010). Prevalence and trends in obesity among US adults, 1999–2008. *Journal of the American Medical Association, 303*(3), 235–241. doi:10.1001/jama.2009.2014

Fleming, J. (2012). The effectiveness of eye movement desensitization and reprocessing in the treatment of traumatized children and youth. *Journal of EMDR Practice and Research, 6*(1), 16–26. doi:10.1891/1933-3196.6.1.16

Florida Medical Examiners Commission. (2010). *Drugs identified in deceased persons by Florida Medical Examiners: 2010 interim report.* Tallahassee, FL: Florida Medical Examiners Commission. Retrieved February 9, 2012, from http://www.fdle.state.fl.us/Content/getdoc/8a59bd00-c38d-4be1-ac06-715a273b552e/MEC-2010-Interim-Report.aspx

Floridi, L., Taddeo, M., & Turilli, M. (2009). Turing's imitation game: Still an impossible challenge for all machines and some judges: An evaluation of the 2008 Loebner contest. *Minds and Machines, 19*(1), 145–150. doi:10.1007/s11023-008-9130-6

Flowe, H. D., & Ebbese, E. B. (2007). The effect of lineup member similarity on recognition accuracy in simultaneous and sequential lineups. *Law & Human Behavior, 31*(1), 33–52. doi:10.1007/s10979-006-9045-9

Flowers, S. (2011). Mindfully shy. In B. Boyce (Ed.), *The mindfulness revolution: Leading psychologists, scientists, artists, and meditation teachers on the power of mindfulness in daily life* (pp. 166–176). Boston: Shambhala.

Flynn, B. S., Worden, J. K., Bunn, J. Y., et al. (2011). Evaluation of smoking prevention television messages based on the elaboration likelihood model. *Health Education Research, 26*(6), 976–987. doi:10.1007/s10979-006-9045-9

Flynn, J. R. (2007). *What is intelligence? Beyond the Flynn Effect*. New York: Cambridge.

Fochtmann, L. J. (1995). Intractable sneezing as a conversion symptom. *Psychosomatics, 36*(2), 103–112. doi:10.1016/S0033-3182(95)71679-6

Fogel, S. M., Nader, R., Cote, K. A., et al. (2007). Sleep spindles and learning potential. *Behavioral Neuroscience, 121*(1), 1–10. doi:10.1037/0735-7044.121.1.1

Foley, H. J., & Matlin, M. W. (2010). *Sensation and perception* (5th ed.). Boston: Pearson/Allyn and Bacon.

Folkman, S., & Moskowitz, J. T. (2004). Coping: Pitfalls and promise. *Annual Review of Psychology, 55*, 745–774. doi:10.1146/annurev.psych.55.090902.141456

Fontaine, K. R., Redden, D. T., Wang, C., et al. (2003). Years of life lost due to obesity. *Journal of the American Medical Association, 289*, 187–193. doi:10.1001/jama.289.2.187

Foo, P., Warren, W. H., Duchon, A., et al. (2005). Do humans integrate routes into a cognitive map? Map- versus landmark-based navigation of novel shortcuts. *Journal of Experimental Psychology: Learning, Memory, & Cognition, 31*(2), 195–215. doi:10.1037/0278-7393.31.2.195

Foot, M., & Koszycki, D. (2004). Gender differences in anxiety-related traits in patients with panic disorder. *Depression & Anxiety, 20*(3), 123–130. doi:10.1002/da.20031

Forgas, J. P., Cooper, J., & Crano, W. D. (Eds.) (2010). *The psychology of attitudes and attitude change*. New York: Psychology Press.

Forney, W. S., Forney, J. C., & Crutsinger, C. (2005). Developmental stages of age and moral reasoning as predictors of juvenile delinquents' behavioral intention to steal clothing. *Family & Consumer Sciences Research Journal, 34*(2), 110–126. doi:10.1177/1077727X05280666

Forsyth, D. R. (2010). *Group dynamics* (5th ed.). Belmont, CA: Cengage Learning/Wadsworth.

Forsyth, J. P., & Savsevitz, J. (2002). Behavior therapy: Historical perspective and overview. In M. Hersen & W. H. Sledge (Eds.), *Encyclopedia of psychotherapy* (Vol 1, pp. 259–275). San Diego: Academic Press.

Fortunato, L., Young, A. M., Boyd, C. J., et al. (2010). Hook-up sexual experiences and problem behaviors among adolescents. *Journal of Child & Adolescent Substance Abuse, 19*(3), 261–278. doi:10.1080/1067828X.2010.488965

Foster, C. A., Witcher, B. S., Campbell, W. K., et al. (1998). Arousal and attraction: Evidence for automatic and controlled processes. *Journal of Personality & Social Psychology, 74*(1), 86–101. doi:10.1037/0022-3514.74.1.86

Foster, S., & Ysseldyke, J. (1976). Expectancy and halo effects as a result of artificially induced teacher bias. *Contemporary Educational Psychology, 1*, 37–45. doi:10.1016/0361-476X(76)90005-9

Fougnie, D., & Marois, R. (2007). Executive working memory load induces inattentional blindness. *Psychonomic Bulletin & Review, 14*(1), 142–147. doi:10.3758/BF03194041

Fowers, B. J., & Davidov, B. J. (2006). The virtue of multiculturalism: Personal transformation, character, and openness to the other. *American Psychologist, 61*(6), 581–594. doi:10.1037/0003-066X.61.6.581

Fowler, J. H., & Christakis, N. A. (2010). Cooperative behavior cascades in human social networks. *Proceedings of the National Academy of Sciences, 107*(12), 5334–5338. doi:10.1073/pnas.0913149107

Frank, J. D., & Frank, J. (2004). Therapeutic components shared by all psychotherapies. In A. Freeman, M. J. Mahoney, et al. (Eds.), *Cognition and psychotherapy* (2nd ed., pp. 45–78). New York: Springer.

Franken, P., & Dijk, D.-J. (2009). Circadian clock genes and sleep homeostasis. *European Journal of Neuroscience, 29*(9), 1820–1829. doi:10.1111/j.1460-9568.2009.06723.x

Frankl, V. (1955). *The doctor and the soul*. New York: Knopf.

Franzoi, S. L., & Klaiber, J. R. (2007). Body use and reference group impact: With whom do we compare our bodies? *Sex Roles, 56*(3–4), 205–214. doi:10.1007/s11199-006-9162-4

Fraser, C. (2002). Fact and fiction: A clarification of phantom limb phenomena. *British Journal of Occupational Therapy, 65*(6), 256–260.

Freberg, L. A. (2010). *Discovering biological psychology* (2nd ed.). Belmont, CA: Cengage Learning/Wadsworth.

Frederickson, N., Petrides, K. V., & Simmonds, E. (2012). Trait emotional intelligence as a predictor of socioemotional outcomes in early adolescence. *Personality & Individual Differences, 52*(3), 323–328. doi:10.1016/j.paid.2011.10.034

Fredrickson, B. L. (2003). The value of positive emotions. *American Scientist, 91*, 330–335. doi:10.1511/2003.4.330

Fredrickson, B. L., & Branigan, C. (2005). Positive emotions broaden the scope of attention and thought-action repertoires. *Cognition & Emotion, 19*(3), 313–332. doi:10.1080/02699930441000238

Freedman, D. H. (2011). How to fix the obesity crisis. *Scientific American, February*, 40–47. doi:10.1038/scientificamerican0211-40

Freeman, D., & Garety, P. A. (2004). *Paranoia: The psychology of persecutory delusions*. New York: Routledge.

Freeman, J. H., & Steinmetz, A. B. (2011). Neural circuitry and plasticity mechanisms underlying delay eyeblink conditioning. *Learning & Memory, 18*, 666–677. doi:10.1101/lm.2023011

French, C. C., Fowler, M., McCarthy, K., et al. (1991). A test of the Barnum effect. *Skeptical Inquirer, 15*(4), 66–72.

French, S. E., Kim, T. E., & Pillado, O. (2006). Ethnic identity, social group membership, and youth violence. In N. G. Guerra & E. P. Smith (Eds.), *Preventing youth violence in a multicultural society* (pp. 47–73). Washington, DC: American Psychological Association.

Freud, S. (1900). *The interpretation of dreams*. London: Hogarth.

Freud, S. (1949). *An outline of psychoanalysis*. New York: Norton.

Freund, A. M., & Ritter, J. O. (2009). Midlife crisis: A debate. *Gerontology, 55*(5), 582–591. doi:10.1159/000227322

Fried, P. A., & Smith, A. M. (2001) A literature review of the consequences of prenatal marihuana exposure. *Neurotoxicology & Teratology, 23*(1), 1–11. doi:10.1016/S0892-0362(00)00119-7

Friedman, H. S. (2002). *Health psychology* (2nd ed.). Englewood Cliffs, NJ: Prentice-Hall.

Friedman, L. (2006). What is psychoanalysis? *Psychoanalytic Quarterly, 75*(3), 689–713.

Friedman, L. J. (2004). Erik Erikson on generativity: A biographer's perspective. In E. de St. Aubin, D. P. McAdams, et al. (Eds.), *The generative society: Caring for future generations* (pp. 257–264). Washington, DC: American Psychological Association. doi:10.1037/10622-016

Friedman, M., & Rosenman, R. H. (1983). *Type A behavior and your heart*. New York: Knopf.

Friese, M., Messner, C., & Schaffner, Y. (2012). Mindfulness meditation counteracts self-control depletion. *Consciousness & Cognition, 21*(2), 106–1022. doi:10.1016/j.concog.2012.01.008

Fritz, C. O., Morris, P. E., Acton, M., et al. (2007). Comparing and combining retrieval practice and the keyword mnemonic for foreign vocabulary learning. *Applied Cognitive Psychology, 21*(4), 499–526. doi:10.1002/acp.1287

Froufe, M., & Schwartz, C. (2001). Subliminal messages for increasing self-esteem: Placebo effect. *Spanish Journal of Psychology, 4*(1), 19–25.

Fry, R. (2012). *Improve your memory* (6th ed.). Belmont, CA: Cengage Learning/Wadsworth.

Frydman, M. (1999). Television, aggressiveness and violence. *International Journal of Adolescent Medicine & Health, 11*(3-4), 335–344. doi:10.1515/IJAMH.1999.11.3-4.335

Fu, J. H., Morris, M. W., Lee, S., et al. (2007). Epistemic motives and cultural conformity: Need for closure, culture, and context as determinants of conflict judgments. *Journal of Personality & Social Psychology, 92*(2), 191–207. doi:10.1037/0022-3514.92.2.191

Fuchs, C., & Obrist, M. (2010). HCI and society: Towards a typology of universal design principles. *International Journal of Human-Computer Interaction, 26*(6), 638–656. doi:10.1080/10447311003781334

Fukuda, K., & Ishihara, K. (2001). Age-related changes of sleeping pattern during adolescence. *Psychiatry & Clinical Neurosciences, 55*(3), 231–232. doi:10.1046/j.1440-1819.2001.00837.x

Funder, D. C. (2006). *The personality puzzle* (4th ed.). New York: Norton.

Funk, J. B. (2005). Children's exposure to violent video games and desensitization to violence. *Child & Adolescent Psychiatric Clinics of North America, 14*(3), 387–404. doi:10.1016/j.chc.2005.02.009

Furnham, A., Chamorro-Premuzic, T., & Callahan, I. (2003). Does graphology predict personality and intelligence? *Individual Differences Research, 1*(2), 78–94.

Gable, S. L., Reis, H. T., Impett, E. A., et al. (2004). What do you do when things go right? *Journal of Personality & Social Psychology, 87*(2), 228–245. doi:10.1037/0022-3514.87.2.228

Gadzella, B. M. (1995). Differences in processing information among psychology course grade groups. *Psychological Reports, 77*, 1312–1314. doi:10.2466/pr0.1995.77.3f.1312

Gaertner, S. L., Dovidio, J. F., Banker, B. S., et al. (2000). Reducing intergroup conflict: From superordinate goals to decategorization, recategorization, and mutual differentiation. *Group Dynamics, 4*(1), 98–114. doi:10.1037/1089-2699.4.1.98

Galambos, N. L., Barker, E. T., & Tilton-Weaver, L. C. (2003). Who gets caught at maturity gap? A study of pseudomature, immature and mature adolescents. *International Journal of Behavioral Development, 27*(3), 253–263. doi:10.1080/01650250244000326

Galankin, T., Shekunova, E., & Zvartau, E. (2010). Estradiol lowers intracranial self-stimulation thresholds and enhances cocaine facilitation of intracranial self-stimulation in rats. *Hormones & Behavior, 58*(5), 827–834. doi:10.1016/j.yhbeh.2010.08.006

Galanter, M., Hayden, F., Castañeda, R, et al. (2005). Group therapy, self-help groups, and network therapy. In R. J. Frances, S. I. Miller, et al. (Eds.), *Clinical textbook of addictive disorders* (3rd ed., pp. 502–527). New York: Guilford.

Galati, D., Scherer, K. R., & Ricci-Bitti, P. E. (1997). Voluntary facial expression of emotion: Comparing congenitally blind with normally sighted encoders. *Journal of Personality & Social Psychology, 73*(6), 1363–1379. doi:10.1037/0022-3514.73.6.1363

Galea, S., & Resnick, H. (2005). Post-traumatic stress disorder in the general population after mass terrorist incidents: Considerations about the nature of exposure. *CNS Spectrums, 10*(2), 107–115.

Galea, S., Ahern, J., Resnick, H., et al. (2002). Psychological sequelae of the September 11 terrorist attacks in New York City. *New England Journal of Medicine, 346*(13), 982–987. doi:10.1056/NEJMsa013404

Gallagher, S. (2004). Nailing the lie: An interview with Jonathan Cole. *Journal of Consciousness Studies, 11*(2), 3–21.

Galliher, R. V., Jones, M. D., & Dahl, A. (2011). Concurrent and longitudinal effects of ethnic identity and experiences of discrimination on psychosocial adjustment of Navajo adolescents. *Developmental Psychology, 47*(2), 509–526. doi:10.1037/a0021061

Gamache, G. (2004). *Essentials in human factors*. San Mateo, CA: Usernomics.

Ganis, G., Thompson, W. L., & Kosslyn, S. M. (2004). Brain areas underlying visual mental imagery and visual perception: An fMRI study. *Cognitive Brain Research, 20*(2), 226–241. doi:10.1016/j.cogbrainres.2004.02.012

Ganster, D. C., Fox, M. L., & Dwyer, D. J. (2001). Explaining employees' health care costs: A prospective examination of stressful job demands, personal control, and physiological reactivity. *Journal of Applied Psychology, 86*, 954–964. doi:10.1037/0021-9010.86.5.954

Garcia, E. E. (2008). Bilingual education in the United States. In J. Altarriba & R. R. Heredia (Eds.), *An introduction to bilingualism: Principles and processes* (pp. 321–343). Mahwah, NJ: Erlbaum.

Gardner, H. (2008). Birth and the spreading of a "meme." In J. Q. Chen, S. Moran, & H. Gardner (Eds.), *Multiple intelligences around the world* (pp. 3–16). San Francisco: Jossey-Bass.

Gardner, H. (2011). The theory of multiple intelligences. In M. A. Gernsbacher, R. W. Pew, L., et al. (Eds.), *Psychology and the real world: Essays illustrating fundamental contributions to society* (pp. 122–130). New York: Worth.

Garland, A. F., & Zigler, E. (1999). Emotional and behavioral problems among highly intellectually gifted youth. *Roeper Review, 22*(1), 41–44. doi:10.1080/02783199909553996

Garlow, S. J., Purselle, D. C., & Heninger, M. (2007). Cocaine and alcohol use preceding suicide in African American and white adolescents. *Journal of Psychiatric Research, 41*(6), 530–536. doi:10.1016/j.jpsychires.2005.08.008

Garnets, L. D., & Kimmel, D. (1991). Lesbian and gay male dimensions in the psychological study of human diversity. In J. D. Goodchilds (Ed.), *Psychological perspectives on human diversity in America* (pp. 137–189). Washington, DC: American Psychological Association. doi:10.1037/11105-004

Garrosa, E., Moreno-Jiménez, B., Liang, Y., et al. (2008). The relationship between socio-demographic variables, job stressors, burnout, and hardy personality in nurses: An exploratory study. *International Journal of Nursing Studies, 45*(3), 418–427. doi:10.1016/j.ijnurstu.2006.09.003

Gass, R. H., & Seiter, J. S. (2010). *Persuasion: Social influence and compliance gaining* (4th ed.). Boston: Allyn & Bacon.

Gastner, M. T., Shalizi, C. R., & Newman, M. E. J. (2005). Maps and cartograms of the 2004 US presidential election results. *Advances in Complex Systems, 8*(1), 117–123. doi:10.1142/S0219525905000397

Gates, A. I. (1917). Recitation as a factor in memorizing. *Archives of Psychology, 40*, 104.

Gathchel, R. J., & Oordt, M. S. (2003). Insomnia. In R. J. Gatchel & M. S. Oordt (Eds.), *Clinical health psychology and primary care: Practical advice and clinical guidance for successful collaboration* (pp. 135–148). Washington, DC: American Psychological Association. doi:10.1037/10592-008

Gauquelin, M. (1970). *Astrology and science*. London: Peter Davies.

Geary, N. (2004). Endocrine controls of eating: CCK, leptin, and ghrelin. *Physiology & Behavior, 81*(5), 719–733. doi:10.1016/j.physbeh.2004.04.013

Geddes, L. (2008). Could brain scans ever be safe evidence? *New Scientist, Oct 3*, 8–9.

Gegenfurtner, K. R., & Kiper, D. C. (2003). Color vision. *Annual Review of Neuroscience, 26*, 181–206. doi:10.1146/annurev.neuro.26.041002.131116

Geiselman, R. E., Fisher, R. P., MacKinnon, D. P., et al. (1986). Enhancement of eyewitness memory with the cognitive interview. *American Journal of Psychology, 99*, 385–401.

Genty, E., Breuer, T., Hobaiter, C., et al. (2009). Gestural communication of the gorilla (Gorilla gorilla): Repertoire, intentionality, and possible origins. *Animal Cognition, 12*(3), 527–546. doi:10.1007/s10071-009-0213-4

George, A. (2006). Living online: The end of privacy? *New Scientist, Sept 18*, 50–51.

Gerardi, M., Rothbaum, B. O., Ressler, K., et al., (2008). Virtual reality exposure therapy using a virtual Iraq: Case report. *Journal of Traumatic Stress, 21*(2), 209–213. doi:10.1002/jts.20331

Germain, A., Krakow, B., Faucher, B., et al. (2004). Increased mastery elements associated with imagery rehearsal treatment for nightmares in sexual assault survivors with PTSD. *Dreaming, 14*(4), 195–206. doi:10.1037/1053-0797.14.4.195

German, T. P., & Barrett, H. C. (2005). Functional fixedness in a technologically sparse culture. *Psychological Science, 16*(1), 1–5. doi:10.1111/j.0956-7976.2005.00771.x

German, T. P., & Defeyter, M. A. (2000). Immunity to functional fixedness in young children. *Psychonomic Bulletin & Review, 7*(4), 707–712. doi:10.3758/BF03213010

Gershman, S. J., & Niv, Y. (2010). Learning latent structure: Carving nature at its joints. *Current Opinion in Neurobiology, 20*(2), 251–256. doi:10.1016/j.conb.2010.02.008

Gershoff, E. T. (2002). Corporal punishment by parents and associated child behaviors and experiences: A meta-analytic and theoretical review. *Psychological Bulletin, 128*(4), 539–579. doi:10.1037/0033-2909.128.4.539

Gershoff, E. T., & Bitensky, S. H. (2007). The case against corporal punishment

of children: Converging evidence from social science research and international human rights law and implications for U.S. public policy. *Psychology, Public Policy, & Law, 13*(4), 231–272. doi:10.1037/1076-8971.13.4.231

Gerstein, E. R. (2002). Manatees, bioacoustics, and boats. *American Scientist, 90*(March–April), 154–163. doi:10.1511/2002.2.154

Geschwind, N. (1979). Specializations of the human brain. *Scientific American, 241*, 180–199. doi:10.1038/scientificamerican0979-180

Gever, J. (2009, May 19). APA: Major changes loom for bible of mental health. *MedPage Today*. Retrieved May 9, 2012, from http://www.medpagetoday.com/Meeting Coverage/APA/14270

Ghaemi, S. N. (2010). *The rise and fall of the biopsychosocial model: Reconciling art and science in psychiatry*. Baltimore, MD: Johns Hopkins University Press.

Giancola, P. R., Josephs, R. A., Parrott, D. J., et al. (2010). Alcohol myopia revisited: Clarifying aggression and other acts of disinhibition through a distorted lens. *Perspectives on Psychological Science, 5*(3), 265–278. doi:10.1177/1745691610369467

Giarratano, J. C., & Riley, G. (2004). *Expert systems, principles and programming* (4th ed.). Belmont, CA: Cengage Learning/Wadsworth.

Gibson, E. J., & Walk, R. D. (1960). The "visual cliff." *Scientific American, 202*(4), 67–71. doi:10.1038/scientificamerican0460-64

Gifford, E. V., & Shoenberger, D. (2009). Rapid smoking. In W. T. O'Donohue & J. E. Fisher (Eds.), *General principles and empirically supported techniques of cognitive behavior therapy* (pp. 513–519). New York: Wiley.

Gilchrist, A. L., Cowan, N., & Naveh-Benjamin, M. (2009). Investigating the childhood development of working memory using sentences: New evidence for the growth of chunk capacity. *Journal of Experimental Child Psychology, 104*(2), 252–265. doi:10.1016/j.jecp.2009.05.006

Gilhooly, K. J., Fioratou, E., Anthony, S. H. et al. (2007). Divergent thinking: Strategies and executive involvement in generating novel uses for familiar objects. *British Journal of Psychology, 98*, 611–625. doi:10.1111/j.2044-8295.2007.tb00467.x

Gillespie, C. F., & Nemeroff, C. B. (2007). Corticotropin-releasing factor and the psychobiology of early-life stress. *Current Directions in Psychological Science, 16*(2), 85–89. doi:10.1111/j.1467-8721.2007.00481.x

Gillespie-Lynch, K., Greenfield, P. M., Lyn, H., et al. (2011). The role of dialogue in the ontogeny and phylogeny of early symbol combinations: A cross-species comparison of bonobo, chimpanzee, and human learners. *First Language, 31*(4), 442–460. doi:10.1177/0142723711406882

Gino, F. & Flynn, F. J. (2011). Give them what they want: The benefits of explicitness in gift exchange. *Journal of Experimental Social Psychology, 47*, 915–922. doi:10.1016/j.jesp.2011.03.015

Ginsberg, D. L. (2006). Fatal agranulocytosis four years after clozapine discontinuation. *Primary Psychiatry, 13*(2), 32–33. doi:10.1176/appi.ajp.163.1.161

Giummarra, M. J., Gibson, S. J., Georgiou-Karistianis, N., et al. (2007). Central mechanisms in phantom limb perception: The past, present and future. *Brain Research Reviews, 54*(1), 219–232. doi:10.1016/j.brainresrev.2007.01.009

Giuseppe, R. (2005). Virtual reality in psychotherapy: Review. *CyberPsychology & Behavior, 8*(3), 220–230. doi:10.1089/cpb.2005.8.220

Gladwell, M. (2005). *Blink: The power of thinking without thinking*. New York: Little, Brown.

Glass, J., & Owen, J. (2010). Latino fathers: The relationship among machismo, acculturation, ethnic identity, and paternal involvement. *Psychology of Men & Masculinity, 11*(4), 251–261. doi:10.1037/a0021477

Glassgold, J. M., Beckstead, L., Drescher, J., et al. (2009). *Report of the American Psychological Association Task Force on appropriate therapeutic responses to sexual orientation*. Washington, DC: American Psychological Association. Retrieved April 9, 2012, from http://www.apa.org/pi/lgbt/resources/therapeutic-response.pdf

Gleason, J. B., & Ratner, N. B. (2009). *The development of language* (7th ed.). Boston: Allyn & Bacon.

Glenn, E. N. (Ed.). (2009). *Shades of difference: Why skin color matters*. Palo Alto, CA: Stanford University Press.

Glick, P. (2008). When neighbors blame neighbors: Scapegoating and the breakdown of ethnic relations. In V. M. Esses & R. A. Vernon (Eds.), *Explaining the breakdown of ethnic relations: Why neighbors kill: Social issues and interventions* (pp. 123–146). Malden, MA: Blackwell.

Global Footprint Network. (2011). *Footprint basics: Overview*. Oakland, CA: Author. Retrieved February 19, 2012, from http://www.footprintnetwork.org/en/index.php/GFN/page/footprint_basics_overview

Gloria-Bottini, F., Magrini, A., & Bottini, E. (2009). The effect of genetic and seasonal factors on birth weight. *Early Human Development, 85*(7), 439–441. doi:10.1016/j.earlhumdev.2009.02.004

Gobet, F. (2005). Chunking models of expertise: Implications for education. *Applied Cognitive Psychology, 19*(2), 183–204. doi:10.1002/acp.1110

Gobet, F., & Simon, H. A. (1996). Recall of random and distorted chess positions: Implications for the theory of expertise. *Memory & Cognition, 24*(4), 493–503. doi:10.3758/BF03200937

Göckeritz, S., Schultz, P. W., Rendón, T., et al. (2010). Descriptive normative beliefs and conservation behavior: The moderating roles of personal involvement and injunctive normative beliefs. *European Journal of Social Psychology, 40*(3), 514–523. doi:10.1002/ejsp.643

Godnig, E. C. (2003). Tunnel vision: Its causes & treatment strategies. *Journal of Behavioral Optometry, 14*(4), 95–99.

Gogate, L. J., Bahrick, L. E., & Watson, J. D. (2000). A study of multimodal motherese: The role of temporal synchrony between verbal labels and gestures. *Child Development, 71*(4), 878–894. doi:10.1111/1467-8624.00197

Goldberg, C. (2001). Of prophets, true believers, and terrorists. *The Dana Forum on Brain Science, 3*(3), 21–24.

Goldberg, R. (2010). *Drugs across the spectrum* (6th ed.). Belmont, CA: Cengage Learning/Wadsworth.

Golden, J. (2005). *Message in a bottle: The making of fetal alcohol syndrome.* Cambridge, MA: Harvard University Press.

Goldenberg, H., & Goldenberg, I. (2004). *Family therapy: An overview* (6th ed.). Pacific Grove, CA: Brooks/Cole.

Goldschmidt, L., Richardson, G. A., Willford, J. A., et al. (2011). School achievement in 14-year-old youths prenatally exposed to marijuana. *Neurotoxicology & Teratology.* doi:10.1016/j.ntt.2011.08.009

Goldstein, E. B. (2010). *Sensation and perception* (8th ed.). Belmont, CA: Cengage Learning/Wadsworth.

Goldstein, E. B. (2011). *Cognitive psychology: Connecting mind, research and everyday experience* (3rd ed.). Belmont, CA: Cengage Learning/ Wadsworth.

Goldstein, M. H., & Schwade, J. A. (2008). Social feedback to infants babbling facilitates rapid phonological learning. *Psychological Science, 19*(5), 515–523. doi:10.1111/j.1467-9280.2008.02117.x

Goldstein, M., Peters, L., Baillie, A., et al. (2011). The effectiveness of a day program for the treatment of adolescent anorexia nervosa. *International Journal of Eating Disorders, 44*(1), 29–38. doi:10.1002/eat.20789

Goldston, D. B., Molock, S. D., Whitbeck, L. B., et al. (2008). Cultural considerations in adolescent suicide prevention and psychosocial treatment. *American Psychologist, 63*(1), 14–31. doi:10.1037/0003-066X.63.1.14

Goman, C. K. (2008). *The nonverbal advantage: Secrets and science of body language at work.* San Francisco: Berrett-Koehler.

Gomez, R., & McLaren, S. (2007). The inter-relations of mother and father attachment, self-esteem and aggression during late adolescence. *Aggressive Behavior, 33*(2), 160–169. doi:10.1002/ab.20181

Gonzaga, G. C., Carter, S., & Buckwalter, J. G. (2010). Assortative mating, convergence, and satisfaction in married couples. *Personal Relationships, 17*(4), 634–644. doi:10.1111/j.1475-6811.2010.01309.x

Gonzalez, M., Durrant, J. E., Chabot, M., et al. (2008).What predicts injury from physical punishment? A test of the typologies of violence hypothesis. *Child Abuse & Neglect, 32*(8), 752–765. doi:10.1016/j.chiabu.2007.12.005

Gonzalez, V. M., Reynolds, B., & Skewes, M. C. (2011). Role of impulsivity in the relationship between depression and alcohol problems among emerging adult college drinkers. *Experimental & Clinical Psychopharmacology, 19*(4), 303–313. doi:10.1037/a0022720

González-Vallejo, C., Lassiter, G. D., Bellezza, F. S., et al. (2008). "Save angels perhaps": A critical examination of unconscious thought theory and the deliberation-without-attention effect. *Review of General Psychology, 12*(3), 282–296. doi:10.1037/a0013134

Goode, E. (1996). Gender and courtship entitlement: Responses to personal ads. *Sex Roles, 34*(3-4), 141–169. doi:10.1007/BF01544293

Goodman, G. S., Quas, J. A., Ogle, C. M. (2010). Child maltreatment and memory. *Annual Review of Psychology, 61*, 325–351. doi:10.1146/annurev.psych.093008.100403

Goodwin, R. D., Fergusson, D. M., & Horwood, L. J. (2005). Childhood abuse and familial violence and the risk of panic attacks and panic disorder in young adulthood. *Psychological Medicine, 35*(6), 881–890. doi:10.1017/S0033291704003265

Gopie, N., Craik, F. I. M., & Hasher, L. (2011). A double dissociation of implicit and explicit memory in younger and older adults. *Psychological Science, 22*(5), 634–640. doi:10.1177/0956797611403321

Gopnik, A. (2009). *The philosophical baby.* New York: Macmillan.

Gopnik, A., Meltzoff, A. N., & Kuhl, P. K. (2000). *The scientist in the crib: What early learning tells us about the mind.* New York: HarperCollins.

Gordon, A. K., & Kaplar, M. E. (2002). A new technique for demonstrating the actor-observer bias. *Teaching of Psychology, 29*(4), 301–303. doi:10.1207/S15328023TOP2904_10

Gordon, I., Zagoory-Sharon, O., Leckman, J. F., et al. (2010). Oxytocin and the development of parenting in humans. *Biological Psychiatry, 68*(4), 377–382. doi:10.1016/j.biopsych.2010.02.005

Gordon, K. A., Wong, D. D. E., Valero, J., J., et al. (2011). Use it or lose it? Lessons learned from the developing brains of children who are deaf and use cochlear implants to hear. *Brain Topography, 24*(3-4), 204–219. doi:10.1007/s10548-011-0181-2

Gorman, A. D., Abernethy, B., & Farrow, D. (2011). Investigating the anticipatory nature of pattern perception in sport. *Memory & Cognition, 39*(5), 894–901. doi:10.3758/s13421-010-0067-7

Goss, S., & Anthony, K. (2009). Developments in the use of technology in counselling and psychotherapy. *British Journal of Guidance & Counselling, 37*(3), 223–230. doi:10.1080/03069880902956967

Gourville, J. T., & Soman, D. (2005). Overchoice and assortment type: When and why variety backfires. *Marketing Science, 24*(3), 382–395. doi:10.1287/mksc.1040.0109

Grabe, M. (2006). *Integrating technology for meaningful learning.* Boston: Houghton Mifflin.

Grabill, K., Merlo, L., Duke, D., et al. (2008). Assessment of obsessive-compulsive disorder: A review. *Journal of Anxiety Disorders, 22*(1), 1–17. doi:10.1016/j.janxdis.2007.01.012

Grack, C., & Richman, C. L. (1996). Reducing general and specific heterosexism through cooperative contact. *Journal of Psychology & Human Sexuality, 8*(4), 59–68. doi:10.1300/J056v08n04_04

Grande, T., Rudolf, G., Oberbracht, C., et al. (2003). Progressive changes in patients' lives after psychotherapy. *Psychotherapy Research, 13*(1), 43–58. doi:10.1093/ptr/kpg006

Grandner, M. A., & Kripke, D. F. (2004). Self-reported sleep complaints with long and short sleep: A nationally representative sample. *Psychosomatic Medicine, 66*, 239–241. doi:10.1097/01.PSY.0000107881.53228.4D

Grangeon, M., Guillot, A., & Collet, C. (2011). Postural control during visual and kinesthetic motor imagery. *Applied Psychophysiology & Biofeedback, 36*(1), 47–56. doi:10.1007/s10484-011-9145-2

Granrud, C. E. (2006). Size constancy in infants: 4-month-olds' responses to physical versus retinal image size. *Journal of Experimental Psychology: Human Perception & Performance, 32*(6), 1398–1404. doi:10.1037/0096-1523.32.6.1398

Granrud, C. E. (2009). Development of size constancy in children: A test of the metacognitive theory. *Attention, Perception, & Psychophysics, 71*(3), 644–654. doi:10.3758/APP.71.3.644

Grant, B. (2010). Getting the point: Empathic understanding in nondirective client-centered therapy. *Person-Centered & Experiential Psychotherapies, 9*(3), 220–235.

Grant, B. F., Hasin, D. S., Stinson, F. S., et al. (2006). The epidemiology of DSM-IV panic disorder and agoraphobia in the United States: Results from the National Epidemiologic Survey on Alcohol and Related Conditions. *Journal of Clinical Psychiatry, 67*(3), 363–374. doi:10.4088/JCP.v67n0305

Grant, I., Gonzalez, R., Carey, C., et al. (2001). Long-term neurocognitive consequences of marijuana. In *National Institute on Drug Abuse Workshop on Clinical Consequences of Marijuana,* August 13, 2001, Rockville, MD.

Graves, J. L. (2001). *The emperor's new clothes.* Piscataway, NJ: Rutgers University Press.

Gravetter, F. J., & Wallnau, L. B. (2013). *Statistics for the behavioral sciences* (9th ed.). Belmont, CA: Cengage Learning/Wadsworth.

Gray, J. M., & Wilson, M. A. (2007). A detailed analysis of the reliability and validity of the sensation seeking scale in a UK sample. *Personality & Individual Differences, 42*(4), 641–651. doi:10.1016/j.paid.2006.08.019

Gredler, M. E. & Shields, C. C. (2008). *Vygotsky's legacy: A foundation for research and practice.* New York: Guilford.

Greenberg, D. L. (2004). President Bush's false "flashbulb" memory of 9/11/01. *Applied Cognitive Psychology, 18*(3), 363–370. doi:10.1002/acp.1016

Greene, D., & Lepper, M. R. (1974). How to turn play into work. *Psychology Today, 8*(4), 49.

Greene, E., & Heilbrun, K. (2011). *Wrightsman's psychology and the legal system* (7th ed.). Belmont, CA: Cengage Learning/Wadsworth.

Greenfield, P. M. (1997). You can't take it with you: Why abilities assessments don't cross cultures. *American Psychologist, 52*, 1115–1124. doi:10.1037/0003-066X.52.10.1115

Greenwald, R. (2006). Eye movement desensitization and reprocessing with traumatized youth. In N. B. Webb (Ed.), *Working with traumatized youth in child welfare: Social work practice with children and families* (pp. 246–264). New York: Guilford.

Greenwood, J. G., Greenwood, J. J. D., McCullagh, J. F., et al. (2006). A survey of sidedness in Northern Irish schoolchildren: The interaction of sex, age, and task. *Laterality: Asymmetries of Body, Brain & Cognition, 12*(1), 1–18. doi:10.1080/13576500600886630

Gregory, R. L. (1990). *Eye and brain: The psychology of seeing.* Princeton, NJ: Princeton University Press.

Gregory, R. L. (2000). Visual illusions. In A. Kazdin (Ed.), *Encyclopedia of psychology* (Vol 8, pp. 193–200). Washington, DC: American Psychological Association.

Gregory, R. L. (2003). Seeing after blindness. *Nature Neuroscience, 6*(9), 909–910.

Greitemeyer, T. (2010). Effects of reciprocity on attraction: The role of a partner's physical attractiveness. *Personal Relationships, 17*(2), 317–330. doi:10.1111/j.1475-6811.2010.01278.x

Grello, C. M., Welsh, D. P., & Harper, M. S. (2006). No strings attached: The nature of casual sex in college students. *Journal of Sex Research, 43*(3), 255–267. doi:10.1080/00224490609552324

Grenèche, J., Krieger, J., Bertrand, F., et al. (2011). Short-term memory performances during sustained wakefulness in patients with obstructive sleep apnea–hypopnea syndrome. *Brain & Cognition, 75*(1), 39–50. doi:10.1016/j.bandc.2010.10.003

Griffin, W. A. (2002). Family therapy. In M. Hersen & W. H. Sledge (Eds.), *Encyclopedia of psychotherapy* (pp. 787–791). San Diego: Academic Press.

Griffin-Fennell, F., & Williams, M. (2006). Examining the complexities of suicidal behavior in the African American community. *Journal of Black Psychology, 32*(3), 303–319. doi:10.1177/0095798406290469

Grigorenko, E. L. (2005). The inherent complexities of gene-environment interactions. *Journals of Gerontology*, *60B*(1), 53–64. doi:10.1093/geronb/60.Special_Issue_1.53

Grigorenko, E. L., & Sternberg, R. J. (2003). The nature-nurture issue. In A. Slater & G. Bremner (Eds.), *An introduction to developmental psychology* (pp. 64–91). Malden, MA: Blackwell.

Grilly, D. M., & Salamone, J. (2012). *Drugs, brain, and behavior* (6th ed.). Englewood Cliffs, NJ: Prentice Hall.

Grobstein, P., & Chow, K. L. (1975). Perceptive field development and individual experience. *Science*, *190*, 352–358.

Grodzinsky, Y., & Santi, A. (2008). The battle for Broca's region. *Trends in Cognitive Sciences*, *12*(12), 474–480. doi:10.1016/j.tics.2008.09.001

Gross, J. J. (2001). Emotion regulation in adulthood: Timing is everything. *Current Directions in Psychological Science*, *10*(6), 214–219. doi:10.1111/1467-8721.00152

Grubin, D., & Madsen, L. (2005). Lie detection and the polygraph: A historical review. *Journal of Forensic Psychiatry & Psychology*, *16*(2), 357–369. doi:10.1080/1478994041233 1337353

Guastello, D. D., & Guastello, S. J. (2003). Androgyny, gender role behavior, and emotional intelligence among college students and their parents. *Sex Roles*, *49*(11–12), 663–673. doi:10.1023/B:SERS.0000003136.67714.04

Guéguen, N. (2002). Status, apparel and touch: Their joint effects on compliance to a request. *North American Journal of Psychology*, *4*(2), 279–286.

Guéguen, N., & Pascual, A. (2003). Status and people's tolerance towards an ill-mannered person: A field study. *Journal of Mundane Behavior*, *4*(1), 29–36.

Guéguen, N., Jacob, C., & Meineri, S. (2011). Effects of the door-in-the-face technique on restaurant customers behavior. *International Journal of Hospitality Management*, *30*(3), 759–761. doi:10.1016/j.ijhm.2010.12.010

Guéguen, N., Marchand, M., Pascual, A., et al. (2008). Foot-in-the-door technique using a courtship request: A field experiment. *Psychological Reports*, *103*(2), 529–534. doi:10.2466/PR0.103.6.529-534

Guéguen, N., Martin, A., & Meineri, S. (2011). Similarity and social interaction: When similarity fosters implicit behavior toward a stranger. *The Journal of Social Psychology*, *151*(6), 671–673. doi:10.1080/00224545.2010.522627

Guéguen, N., Pascual, A., & Dagot, L. (2002). Low-ball and compliance to a request: An application in a field setting. *Psychological Reports*, *91*(1), 81–84. doi:10.2466/PR0.91.5.81-84

Guidetti, M., Conner, M., Prestwich, A., et al. (2012). The transmission of attitudes towards food: Twofold specificity of similarities with parents and friends. *British Journal of Health Psychology*, *17*(2), 346–361. doi:10.1111/j.2044-8287.2011.02041.x

Guillot, A. & Collet, C. (2008). Construction of the motor imagery integrative model in sport: A review

and theoretical investigation of motor imagery use. *International Review of Sport & Exercise Psychology*, *1*, 31–44. doi:10.1080/17509840701823139

Guillot, A., Collet, C., Nguyen, V. A., et al. (2009). Brain activity during visual versus kinesthetic imagery: An fMRI study. *Human Brain Mapping*, *30*(7), 2157–2172. doi:10.1002/hbm.20658

Gullette, D. L., & Lyons, M. A. (2005). Sexual sensation seeking, compulsivity, and HIV risk behaviors in college students. *Journal of Community Health Nursing*, *22*(1), 47–60. doi:10.1207/s15327655jchn2201_5

Gündogan, N. Ü., Durmazlar, N., Gümüs, K., et al. (2005). Projected color slides as a method for mass screening test for color vision deficiency (a preliminary study). *International Journal of Neuroscience*, *115*(8), 1105–1117.

Gurung, R. (2010). *Health psychology: A cultural approach* (2nd ed.). Belmont, CA: Cengage Learning/Wadsworth.

Güth, W., Levati, M. V., & von Wangenheim, G. (2010). Mutual interdependence versus repeated interaction: An experiment studying voluntary social exchange. *Rationality & Society*, *22*(2), 131–158.

Guthrie, R. V. (2004). *Even the rat was white: A historical view of psychology* (2nd ed.). Boston: Allyn & Bacon.

Haaken, J., & Reavey, P. (Eds.). (2010). *Memory matters: Contexts for understanding sexual abuse recollections*. New York: Routledge/Taylor & Francis.

Haas, B. W., Omura, K., Constable, R. T., et al. (2007). Is automatic emotion regulation associated with agreeableness? A perspective using a social neuroscience approach. *Psychological Science*, *18*(2), 130–132. doi:10.1111/j.1467-9280.2007.01861.x

Haber, R. N. (1970). How we remember what we see. *Scientific American*, *222*(5), 104–112. doi:10.1038/scientificamerican0570-104

Haber, R. N., & Haber, L. (2000). Eidetic imagery. In A. E. Kazdin (Ed.), *Encyclopedia of psychology* (Vol. 3, pp. 147–149). Washington, DC: American Psychological Association.

Hafer, C. L., & Bègue, L. (2005). Experimental research on just-world theory: problems, developments, and future challenges. *Psychological Bulletin*, *131*(1), 128–167. doi:10.1037/0033-2909.131.1.128

Haga, S. M., Kraft, P., Corby, E.-K. (2010). Emotion regulation: Antecedents and well-being outcomes of cognitive reappraisal and expressive suppression in crosscultural samples. *Journal of Happiness Studies*, *10*(3), 271–291. doi:10.1007/s10902-007-9080-3

Hagger, M., & Chatzisarantis, N. L.D. (2010). Causality orientations moderate the undermining effect of rewards on intrinsic motivation. *Journal of Experimental Social Psychology*, *46*(2), 485–489. doi:10.1016/j.jesp.2010.10.010

Haier, R. J., Jung, R. E., Yeo, R. A., et al. (2004). Structural brain variation and

general intelligence. *NeuroImage*, *23*, 425–433.

Haier, R. J., Siegel, B. V., Nuechterlein, K. H., et al. (1988). Cortical glucose metabolic rate correlates of abstract reasoning and attention studied with positron emission tomography. *Intelligence*, *12*, 199–217. doi:10.1016/0160-2896(88)90016-5

Haier, R. J., White, N. S., & Alkire, M. T. (2003). Individual differences in general intelligence correlate with brain function during nonreasoning tasks. *Intelligence*, *31*(5), 429–441. doi:10.1016/S0160-2896(03)00025-4

Hakun, J. G., Ruparel, K., Seelig, D., et al. (2009). Towards clinical trials of lie detection with fMRI. *Social Neuroscience*, *4*(6), 518–527. doi:10.1080/17470910802188370

Hales, D. (2013). *An invitation to health: Choosing to change* (15th ed.). Belmont, CA: Cengage Learning/Wadsworth.

Hall, J. (2006). *What is clinical psychology?* (4th ed.). New York: Oxford University Press.

Hall, N. C., Perry, R. P., Goetz, T., et al. (2007). Attributional retraining and elaborative learning: Improving academic development through writing-based interventions. *Learning & Individual Differences*, *17*(3), 280–290. doi:10.1016/j.lindif.2007.04.002

Hallahan, D. P., Kauffman, J. M., & Pullen, P. C. (2011). *Exceptional learners* (12th ed.). Englewood Cliffs, NJ: Merrill/Prentice Hall.

Halliday, G. (2010). Reflections on the meanings of dreams prompted by reading Stekel. *Dreaming*, *20*(4), 219–226. doi:10.1037/a0020880

Halpern, D. F. (2003). *Thought and knowledge: An introduction to critical thinking* (4th ed.). Mahwah, NJ: Erlbaum.

Halpern-Felsher, B. L., Cornell, J., Kropp, R. Y., et al. (2005). Oral versus vaginal sex among adolescents: Perceptions, attitudes, and behavior. *Pediatrics*, *115*, 845–851. doi:10.1542/peds.2004-2108

Hammond, D. C. (2008). Hypnosis as sole anesthesia for major surgeries: Historical & contemporary perspectives. *American Journal of Clinical Hypnosis*, *51*(2), 101–121. doi:10.1080/00029157.2008.10401653

Hancock, J. (2011). *Brilliant memory training: Stop worrying about your memory and start using it—to the full!* Upper Saddle River, NJ: FT Press.

Hancock, P. A., & Ganey, H. C. N. (2003). From the inverted-U to the extended-U: The evolution of a law of psychology. *Journal of Human Performance in Extreme Environments*, *7*(1), 5–14.

Handsfield, H. H. (2001). Resurgent sexually transmitted diseases among men who have sex with men. *Medscape Infectious Disease*, Medscape.com.

Hanley, S. J., & Abell, S. C. (2002). Maslow and relatedness: Creating an interpersonal model of self-actualization. *Journal of Humanistic Psychology*, *42*(4), 37–56. doi:10.1177/002216702237123

Hans, V. P., Kaye, D. H., Dann, B. M., et al. (2011). Science in the jury box: Jurors' comprehension of

mitochondrial DNA evidence. *Law & Human Behavior*, *35*(1), 60–71. doi:10.1007/s10979-010-9222-8

Hansen, C. J., Stevens, L. C., & Coast, J. R. (2001). Exercise duration and mood state: how much is enough to feel better? *Health Psychology*, *20*(4), 267–275. doi:10.1037/0278-6133.20.4.267

Hansen, N. B., Lambert, M. J., & Forman, E. M. (2002). The psychotherapy dose-response effect and its implications for treatment delivery services. *Clinical Psychology: Science & Practice*, *9*(3), 329–334. doi:10.1093/clipsy/9.3.329

Hanton, S., Mellalieu, S. D., & Hall, R. (2004). Self-confidence and anxiety interpretation: A qualitative investigation. *Psychology of Sport & Exercise*, *5*(4), 477–495. doi:10.1016/S1469-0292(03)00040-2

Hanyu, H., Sato, T., Hirao, K., et al. (2010). The progression of cognitive deterioration and regional cerebral blood flow patterns in Alzheimer's disease: A longitudinal SPECT study. *Journal of the Neurological Sciences*, *290*(1–2), 96–101. doi:10.1016/j.jns.2009.10.022

Haq, I. U., Foote, K. D., Goodman, W. G., et al. (2010). Smile and laughter induction and intraoperative predictors of response to deep brain stimulation for obsessive-compulsive disorder. *NeuroImage*, (Mar 10), [np].

Hardaway, C. A., & Gregory, K. B. (2005). Fatigue and sleep debt in an operational navy squadron. *International Journal of Aviation Psychology*, *15*(2), 157–171. doi:10.1207/s15327108ijap1502_3

Harden, K. P., Quinn, P. D., & Tucker-Drob, E. M. (2012). Genetically influenced change in sensation seeking drives the rise of delinquent behavior during adolescence. *Developmental Science*, *15*(1), 150–163. doi:10.1111/j.1467-7687.2011.01115.x

Harding, D. J., Fox, C., & Mehta, J. D. (2002). Studying rare events through qualitative case studies: Lessons from a study of rampage school shootings. *Sociological Methods & Research*, *31*(2), 174–217. doi:10.1177/0049124102031002003

Hardt, O., Einarsson, E. O., & Nader, K. (2010). A bridge over troubled water: Reconsolidation as a link between cognitive and neuroscientific memory research traditions. *Annual Review of Psychology*, *61*, 141–167. doi:10.1146/annurev.psych.093008.100455

Hare, R. D. (2006). Psychopathy: A clinical and forensic overview. *Psychiatric Clinics of North America*, *29*(3), 709–724. doi:10.1016/j.psc.2006.04.007

Harel, A., Gilaie-Dotan, S., Malach, R., et al. (2010). Top-down engagement modulates the neural expressions of visual expertise. *Cerebral Cortex*, *20*(10), 2304–2318. doi:10.1093/cercor/bhp316

Harker, L., & Keltner, D. (2001). Expressions of positive emotion in women's college yearbook pictures and their relationship to personality and life outcomes across adulthood. *Journal of Personality & Social*

Psychology, 80(1), 112–124. doi:10.1037/0022-3514.80.1.112

Harley, T. A. (2008). *The psychology of language: From data to theory* (3rd. ed.) Hove, UK: Psychology Press.

Harlow, H. F., & Harlow, M. K. (1962). Social deprivation in monkeys. *Scientific American, 207*, 136–146.

Harlow, J. M. (1868). Recovery from the passage of an iron bar through the head. *Publications of the Massachusetts Medical Society, 2*, 327–347.

Harm, D. L. (2002). Motion sickness neurophysiology, physiological correlates, and treatment. In K. M. Stanney (Ed.), *Handbook of virtual environments: Design, implementation, and applications* (pp. 637–661). Hillsdale, NJ: Erlbaum.

Harrigan, J. A. (2006). Proxemics, kinesics, and gaze. In J. A. Harrigan, R. Rosenthal, & R. Scherer (Eds.), *The new handbook of methods in nonverbal behavior research* (pp. 137–198). New York: Oxford University Press.

Harrington, R. (2013). *Stress, health and well-being: Thriving in the 21st century*. Belmont, CA: Cengage Learning/Wadsworth.

Harris, C. (2004). The evolution of jealousy. *American Scientist, 92*, 62–71.

Harris, J. C. (2010). *Intellectual disability: A guide for families and professionals*. New York: Oxford University Press.

Harris, L. R., & Jenkin, M. R. M. (Eds.) (2011). *Vision in 3D environments*. New York: Cambridge University Press.

Harrison, P. J., & Weinberger, D. R. (2005). Schizophrenia genes, gene expression, and neuropathology: On the matter of their convergence. *Molecular Psychiatry, 10*(1), 40–68. doi:10.1038/sj.mp.4001558

Hart, B., & Risley, T. R. (1999). *The social world of children learning to talk*. Baltimore, MD: Paul H. Brookes.

Hart, C. L., Ksir, C. J., & Ray, O. S. (2009). *Drugs, society, and human behavior* (13th ed.). New York: McGraw-Hill.

Hart, D., & Carlo, G. (2005). Moral development in adolescence. *Journal of Research on Adolescence, 15*(3), 223–233. doi:10.1111/j.1532-7795.2005.00094.x

Hartlep, K. L., & Forsyth, G. A. (2000). The effect of self-reference on learning and retention. *Teaching of Psychology, 27*(4), 269–271. doi:10.1207/S15328023TOP2704_05

Hartmann, E. (2008). The central image makes "big" dreams big: The central image as the emotional heart of the dream. *Dreaming, 18*(1), 44–57. doi:10.1037/1053-0797.18.1.44

Hartmann, E. (2010). The dream always makes new connections: The dream is a creation, not a replay. *Sleep Medicine Clinics, 5*(2), 241–248. doi:10.1016/j.jsmc.2010.01.009

Hartmann, P., Reuter, M., & Nyborg, H. (2006). The relationship between date of birth and individual differences in personality and general intelligence: A large scale study. *Personality & Individual Differences, 40*(7), 1349–1362. doi:10.1016/j.paid.2005.11.017

Hartung, C. M., Lefler, E. K., Tempel, A. B., et al. (2010). Halo effects in ratings of ADHD and ODD: Identification of susceptible symptoms. *Journal of Psychopathology & Behavioral Assessment, 32*(1), 128–137. doi:10.1007/s10862-009-9135-3

Hashibe, M., Straif, K., Tashkin, D. P., et al. (2005). Epidemiologic review of marijuana use and cancer risk. *Alcohol, 35*(3), 265–275. doi:10.1016/j.alcohol.2005.04.008

Hashimoto, I., Suzuki, A., Kimura, T., et al. (2004). Is there training-dependent reorganization of digit representations in area 3b of string players? *Clinical Neurophysiology, 115*(2), 435–447. doi:10.1016/S1388-2457(03)00340-7

Haycraft, E., & Blissett, J. (2010). Eating disorder symptoms and parenting styles. *Appetite, 54*(1), 221–224. doi:10.1016/j.appet.2009.11.009

Hayes, M. R., De Jonghe, B. C., & Kanoski, S. (2010). Role of the glucagon-like-peptide-1 receptor in the control of energy balance. *Physiology & Behavior, 100*(5), 503–510. doi:10.1016/j.physbeh.2010.02.029

Hayes, S. C., Strosahl, K. D., & Wilson, K. G. (2012). *Acceptance and commitment therapy: The process and practice of mindful change* (2nd ed.). New York: Guilford.

Hayne, H., & Rovee-Collier, C. (1995). The organization of reactivated memory in infancy. *Child Development, 66*(3), 893–906. doi:10.2307/1131957

Hayward, L. C., & Coles, M. E. (2009). Elucidating the relation of hoarding to obsessive compulsive disorder and impulse control disorders. *Journal of Psychopathology & Behavioral Assessment, 31*(3), 220–227. doi:10.1007/s10862-008-9106-0

Heath, R. G. (1963). Electrical self-stimulation of the brain in man. *American Journal of Psychiatry, 120*, 571–577.

Hebb, D.O. (1949). *The organization of behavior*. New York: Wiley & Sons.

Hebblethwaite, S., & Norris, J. (2011). Expressions of generativity through family leisure: Experiences of grandparents and adult grandchildren. *Family Relations, 60*(1), 121–133. doi:10.1111/j.1741-3729.2010.00637.x

Hecht, J. (2007). *The happiness myth: Why what we think is right is wrong*. New York: HarperCollins.

Hedden, T., Ketay, S., Aron, A., et al. (2008) Cultural influences on neural substrates of attentional control. *Psychological Science, 19*(1), 12–17. doi:10.1111/j.1467-9280.2008.02038.x

Hefferon, K., & Bonniwell, I. (2011). *Positive psychology: Theory, research and applications*. Buckingham: Open University Press.

Heiman, G. W. (2011). *Basic statistics for the behavioral sciences* (6th ed.). Belmont, CA: Cengage Learning/Wadsworth.

Heimann, M., & Meltzoff, A. N. (1996). Deferred imitation in 9- and 14-month-old infants: A longitudinal study of a Swedish sample. *British Journal of Developmental Psychology, 14*(Mar.), 55–64. doi:10.1111/j.2044-835X.1996.tb00693.x

Heinrichs, R. W. (2001). *In search of madness: Schizophrenia and neuroscience*. New York: Oxford University Press.

Heisel, M. J., Flett, G. L., & Hewitt, P. L. (2003). Social hopelessness and college student suicide ideation. *Archives of Suicide Research, 7*(3), 221–235. doi:10.1080/13811110301557

Helgeson, V. S. (2009). *The psychology of gender* (3rd ed.). Englewood Cliffs, NJ: Prentice Hall.

Hélie, S., & Sun, R. (2010). Incubation, insight, and creative problem solving: A unified theory and a connectionist model. *Psychological Review, 117*(3), 994–1024. doi:10.1037/a0019532

Helton, W. S. (2007). Skill in expert dogs. *Journal of Experimental Psychology: Applied, 13*(3), 171–178. doi:10.1037/1076-898X.13.3.171

Helton, W. S. (2009). Exceptional running skill in dogs requires extensive experience. *Journal of General Psychology, 136*(3), 323–332. doi:10.3200/GENP.136.3.323-336

Henderson, N. D. (1982). Human behavior genetics. *Annual Review of Psychology, 33*, 403–440. doi:10.1146/annurev.ps.33.020182.002155

Henderson, T. L., Roberto, K. A., & Kamo, Y. (2010). Older adults' responses to Hurricane Katrina: Daily hassles and coping strategies. *Journal of Applied Gerontology, 29*(1), 48–69. doi:10.1177/0733464809334287

Hennenlotter, A., Dresel, C., Castrop, F., et al. (2009). The link between facial feedback and neural activity within central circuitries of emotion: New insights from botulinum toxin-induced denervation of frown muscles. *Cerebral Cortex, 19*(3), 537–542. doi:10.1093/cercor/bhn104

Hennessey, B. A., & Amabile, T. M. (2010). Creativity. *Annual Review of Psychology, 61*, 569–598. doi:10.1146/annurev.psych.093008.100416

Henningsen, D. D., Henningsen, M. L. M., Eden, J., et al. (2006). Examining the symptoms of groupthink and retrospective sensemaking. *Small Group Research, 37*(1), 36–64. doi:10.1177/1046496405281772

Hennik-Kaminski, H., & Reichert, T. (2011). Using sexual appeals in advertising to sell cosmetic surgery: A content analysis from 1986 to 2007. *Sexuality & Culture, 15*(1), 41–55. doi:10.1007/s12119-010-9081-y

Henrich, J., Heine, S. J., & Norenzayan, A, (2010). The weirdest people in the world? *Behavioral & Brain Sciences, 33*, 61–135. doi:10.1017/S0140525X0999152X

Henry, P. K., Murnane, K. S., Votaw, J. R., et al. (2010). Acute brain metabolic effects of cocaine in rhesus monkeys with a history of cocaine use. *Brain Imaging & Behavior, 4*(3-4), 212–219. doi:10.1007/s11682-010-9100-5

Hepper, P. G., Wells, D. L., & Lynch, C. (2005). Prenatal thumb sucking is related to postnatal handedness. *Neuropsychologia, 43*(3), 313–315. doi:10.1016/j.neuropsychologia.2004.08.009

Hergenhahn, B. R. (2009). *An introduction to the history of psychology* (6th ed.). Belmont, CA: Cengage Learning/Wadsworth.

Hergenhahn, B. R., & Olson, M. (2009). *Introduction to the theories of learning* (8th ed.). Englewood Cliffs, NJ: Prentice Hall.

Heriot, S. A., & Pritchard, M. (2004). "Reciprocal inhibition as the main basis of psychotherapeutic effects" by Joseph Wolpe (1954). *Clinical Child Psychology & Psychiatry, 9*(2), 297–307. doi:10.1177/1359104504041928

Herman, J. L., & Tetrick, L. E. (2009). Problem-focused versus emotion-focused coping strategies and repatriation adjustment. *Human Resource Management, 48*(1), 69–88. doi:10.1002/hrm.20267

Hermanto, N., Moreno, S., & Bialystok, E. (2012). Linguistic and metalinguistic outcomes of intense immersion education: How bilingual? *International Journal of Bilingual Education and Bilingualism, 15*(2), 131–145. doi:10.1080/13670050.2011.652591

Hernstein, R., & Murray, C. (1994). *The bell curve*. New York: Free Press.

Herold, D. K. (2010). Mediating media studies: Stimulating critical awareness in a virtual environment. *Computers & Education, 54*(3), 791–798. doi:10.1016/j.compedu.2009.10.019

Herrmann, D. J., Yoder, C. Y., Gruneberg, M., et al. (2006). *Applied cognitive psychology: A textbook*. Mahwah, NJ: Erlbaum.

Hettich, P. I. (2005). *Connect college to career: Student guide to work and life transition*. Belmont, CA: Cengage Learning/Wadsworth.

Hiday, V. A., & Burns, P. (2010). Mental illness and the criminal justice system. In T. L. Scheid & T. N. Brown (Eds.), *A handbook for the study of mental health: Social contexts, theories, and systems* (2nd ed., pp. 478–498). New York: Cambridge University Press.

Higbee, K. L., Clawson, C., DeLano, L., et al. (1990). Using the link mnemonic to remember errands. *Psychological Record, 40*(3), 429–436.

Higgins, S. T., Heil, S. H., & Lussier, J. P. (2004). Clinical implications of reinforcement as a determinant of substance use disorders. *Annual Review of Psychology, 55*, 431–461. doi:10.1146/annurev.psych.55.090902.142033

Higham, P. A., & Gerrard, C. (2005). Not all errors are created equal: Metacognition and changing answers on multiple-choice tests. *Canadian Journal of Experimental Psychology, 59*(1), 28–34. doi:10.1037/h0087457

Hilgard, E. R. (1968). *The experience of hypnosis*. New York: Harcourt Brace Jovanovich.

Hilgard, E. R. (1977). *Divided consciousness* (pp. 32–51). New York: Wiley.

Hilgard, E. R. (1994) Neodissociation theory. In S. J. Lynn & J. W. Rhue (Eds.), *Dissociation: Clinical, theoretical and research perspectives* (pp. 32–51). New York: Guilford.

Hilsenroth, M. J. (2000). Rorschach test. In A. Kazdin (Ed.), *Encyclopedia of psychology* (Vol. 7, pp. 117–119). Washington, DC: American Psychological Association.

Hinrichs, K. T. (2007). Follower propensity to commit crimes of obedience: The role of leadership beliefs. *Journal of Leadership & Organizational Studies, 14*(1), 69-76. doi:10.1177/1071791907304225

Hintzman, D. L. (2005). Memory strength and recency judgments. *Psychonomic Bulletin & Review, 12*(5), 858-864. doi:10.3758/BF03196777

Hirshbein, L., & Sarvananda, S. (2008). History, power, and electricity: American popular magazine accounts of electroconvulsive therapy, 1940-2005. *Journal of the History of the Behavioral Sciences, 44*(1), 1-18. doi:10.1002/jhbs.20283

Hirstein, W. (2005). *Brain fiction: Self-deception and the riddle of confabulation.* Cambridge, MA: MIT Press.

Hobson, J. A. (2000). Dreams: Physiology. In A. Kazdin (Ed.), *Encyclopedia of psychology* (Vol 3, pp. 78-81). Washington, DC: American Psychological Association.

Hobson, J. A. (2001). *Consciousness.* New York: Freeman.

Hobson, J. A. (2005). Sleep is of the brain, by the brain and for the brain. *Nature, 437*(7063), 1254-1256. doi:10.1038/nature04283

Hobson, J. A., Pace-Schott, E. F., & Stickgold, R. (2000). Dream science 2000. *Behavioral & Brain Sciences, 23*(6), 1019-1035; 1083-1121. doi:10.1017/S0140525X00954025

Hodgins, H. S., & Adair, K. C. (2010). Attentional processes and meditation. *Consciousness & Cognition, 19*(4), 872-878. doi:10.1016/j.concog.2010.04.002

Hoerger, M., Chapman, B. P., Epstein, R. M., et al. (2012). Emotional intelligence: A theoretical framework for individual differences in affective forecasting. *Emotion, 12*(4), 716-725. doi:10.1037/a0026724

Hofer, B. K., & Yu, S. L. (2003). Teaching self-regulated learning through a "Learning to Learn" course. *Teaching of Psychology, 30*(1), 30-33. doi:10.1207/S15328023TOP3001_05

Hoff, E. (2006). How social contexts support and shape language development. *Developmental Review, 26*(1), 55-88. doi:10.1016/j.dr.2005.11.002

Hoff, E. (2009). *Language development* (4th ed.). Belmont, CA: Cengage Learning/Wadsworth.

Hoff, E., & Tian, C. (2005). Socioeconomic status and cultural influences on language. *Journal of Communication Disorders, 38*(4), 271-278. doi:10.1016/j.jcomdis.2005.02.003

Hoffart, A. (2005). Interpersonal therapy for social phobia: Theoretical model and review of the evidence. In M. E. Abelian (Ed.), *Focus on psychotherapy research* (pp. 121-137). Hauppauge, NY: Nova Science Publishers.

Hoffer, A., & Youngren, V. R. (2004). Is free association still at the core of psychoanalysis? *International Journal of Psychoanalysis, 85*(6), 1489-1492. doi:10.1516/QVFL-UVKB-WFEQ-XFVH

Hoffman, E. (2008). Abraham Maslow: A biographer's reflections. *Journal of Humanistic Psychology, 48*(4), 439-443. doi:10.1177/0022167808320534

Hofman, D. (2008). The frontal laterality of emotion: A historical overview. *Netherlands Journal of Psychology, 64*(3), 112-118. doi:10.1007/BF03076413

Hogan, E. H., Hornick, B. A., & Bouchoux, A. (2002). Focus on communications: Communicating the message: Clarifying the controversies about caffeine. *Nutrition Today, 37*, 28-35.

Hoge, C. W., Castro, C. A., Messer, S. C., et al. (2004). Combat duty in Iraq and Afghanistan, mental health problems, and barriers to care. *New England Journal of Medicine, 351*(1), 13-22. doi:10.1056/NEJMoa040603

Hohwy, J., & Rosenberg, R. (2005). Unusual experiences, reality testing and delusions of alien control. *Mind & Language, 20*(2), 141-162. doi:10.1111/j.0268-1064.2005.00280.x

Holden, C. (1980). Twins reunited. *Science, 80, Nov.*, 55-59.

Hollins, M. (2010). Somesthetic senses. *Annual Review of Psychology, 61*, 243-271. doi:10.1146/annurev.psych.093008.100419

Hollon, S. D., Stewart, M. O., & Strunk, D. (2006). Enduring effects for cognitive behavior therapy in the treatment of depression and anxiety. *Annual Review of Psychology, 57*, 285-315. doi:10.1146/annurev.psych.57.102904.190044

Holman, A., & Sillars, A. (2012). Talk about "hooking up": The influence of college student social networks on nonrelationship sex. *Health Communication, 27*(2), 205-216. doi:10.1080/10410236.2011.575540

Holman, E. A., Silver, R. C., Poulin, M., et al. (2008). Terrorism, acute stress, and cardiovascular health: A 3-year national study following the September 11th attacks. *Archives of General Psychiatry, 65*(1), 73-80. doi:10.1001/archgenpsychiatry.2007.6

Holmes, E. K., & Huston, A. C. (2010). Understanding positive father-child interaction: Children's, father's, and mother's contributions. *Fathering, 8*(2), 203-225. doi:10.3149/fth.1802.203

Holmes, J., & Adams, J. W. (2006). Working memory and children's mathematical skills: Implications for mathematical development and mathematics curricula. *Educational Psychology, 26*(3), 339-366. doi:10.1080/01443410500341056

Holmes, T. H., & Rahe, R. H. (1967). The social readjustment rating scale. *Journal of Psychosomatic Research, 11*(2), 213-218. doi:10.1016/0022-3999(67)90010-4

Holtzen, D. W. (2000). Handedness and professional tennis. *International Journal of Neuroscience, 105*(1-4), 101-119. doi:10.3109/00207450009003270

Hölzel, B. K., Lazar, S. W., Gard, T., et al. (2011). How does mindfulness meditation work? Proposing mechanisms of action from a conceptual and neural perspective. *Perspectives on Psychological Science, 6*, 537-559. doi:10.1177/1745691611419671

Holzinger, B., LaBerge, S., & Levitan, L. (2006). Psychophysiological correlates of lucid dreaming. *Dreaming, 16*(2), 88-95. doi:10.1037/1053-0797.16.2.88

Hooyman, N. & Kiyak, H. A. (2011). *Social gerontology: A multidisciplinary perspective* (9th ed.). Boston: Pearson/Allyn & Bacon.

Hopwood, C. J., Donnellan, M. B., Blonigen, D. M., et al. (2011). Genetic and environmental influences on personality trait stability and growth during the transition to adulthood: A three-wave longitudinal study. *Journal of Personality & Social Psychology, 100*(3), 545-556. doi:10.1037/a0022409

Horgan, J. (2005). The forgotten era of brain chips. *Scientific American, 293*(4), 66-73. doi:10.1038/scientificamerican1005-66

Horn, R. R., Williams, A. M., Scott, M. A., et al. (2005). Visual search and coordination changes in response to video and point-light demonstrations without KR. *Journal of Motor Behavior, 37*(4), 265-274.

Horne, R. S. C., Andrew, S., Mitchell, K., et al. (2001). Apnoea of prematurity and arousal from sleep. *Early Human Development, 61*(2), 119-133. doi:10.1016/S0378-3782(00)00129-8

Hortman, G. (2003). What do facial expressions convey? *Emotion, 3*(2), 150-166.

Horvath, L. S., Milich, R., Lynam, D., et al. (2004). Sensation seeking and substance use: A cross-lagged panel design. *Individual Differences Research, 2*(3), 175-183.

Hosch, H. M., & Cooper, D. S. (1982). Victimization as a determinant of eyewitness accuracy. *Journal of Applied Psychology, 67*, 649-652. doi:10.1037/0021-9010.67.5.649

Houghton, D. P. (2008). Invading and occupying Iraq: Some insights from political psychology. *Peace & Conflict: Journal of Peace Psychology, 14*(2), 169-192. doi:10.1080/10781910802017297

Howard, A., Pion, G. M., Gottfredson, G. D., et al. (1986). The changing face of American psychology: A report from the committee on employment and human resources. *American Psychologist, 41*, 1311-1327. doi:10.1037/0003-066X.41.12.1311

Howell, D. C. (2013). *Fundamental statistics for the behavioral sciences* (8th ed.). Belmont, CA: Cengage Learning/Wadsworth.

Howell, R. T., & Howell, C. J. (2008). The relation of economic status to subjective well-being in developing countries: A meta-analysis. *Psychological Bulletin, 134*(4), 536-560. doi:10.1037/0033-2909.134.4.536

Hsieh, P., Colas, J. T., & Kanwisher, N. (2011). Pop-out without awareness: Unseen feature singletons capture attention only when top-down attention is available. *Psychological Science, 22*(9), 1220-1226. doi:10.1177/0956797611419302

Huang, M.-H., & Rust, R. T. (2011). Sustainability and consumption. *Journal of the Academy of Marketing Science, 39*(1), 40-54. doi:10.1007/s11747-010-0193-6

Hubble, M.A., Duncan, B. L., & Miller, S. D. (Eds.) (1999). *The heart and soul of change: What works in therapy.* Washington, DC: American Psychological Association.

Hubel D. H., & Wiesel, W. N. (2005). *Brain & visual perception: The story of a 25-year collaboration.* New York: Oxford University Press.

Hübner, R., & Volberg, G. (2005). The integration of object levels and their content: A theory of global/local processing and related hemispheric differences. *Journal of Experimental Psychology: Human Perception & Performance, 31*(3), 520-541. doi:10.1037/0096-1523.31.3.520

Hughes, A. (2008). The use of urban legends to improve critical thinking. In L. T. Benjamin, Jr. (Ed.). *Favorite activities for the teaching of psychology.* Washington, DC: American Psychological Association.

Hughes, J. R., & Callas, P. W. (2011). Is delaying a quit attempt associated with less success? *Nicotine & Tobacco Research, 13*(12), 1228-1232. doi:10.1093/ntr/ntr207

Hughes, M., & Morrison, K., & Asada, K. J. K. (2005). What's love got to do with it? Exploring the impact of maintenance rules, love attitudes, and network support on friends with benefits relationships. *Western Journal of Communication, 69*(1), 49-66. doi:10.1080/10570310500034154

Hughes, M., Brymer, M., Chiu, W. T., et al. (2011). Posttraumatic stress among students after the shootings at Virginia Tech. *Psychological Trauma, 3*(4), 403-411. doi:10.1037/a0024565

Huijbregts, S. C., Séguin, J. R., Zelazo, P. D., et al. (2006). Interrelations between maternal smoking during pregnancy, birth weight and sociodemographic factors in the prediction of early cognitive abilities. *Infant & Child Development, 15*(6), 593-607. doi:10.1002/icd.480

Humes, K. R., Jones, N. A., & Ramirez, R. R. (2010). Overview of race and Hispanic origin: 2010. *U. S. Census Bureau News, 2010 Census Brief C2010BR-02.* Retrieved May 9, 2012, from http://www.census.gov/prod/cen2010/briefs/c2010br-02.pdf

Hunter, E. (1998). Adolescent attraction to cults. *Adolescence, 33*(131), 709-714.

Hunter, J. P., Katz, J., & Davis, K. D. (2003). The effect of tactile and visual sensory inputs on phantom limb awareness. *Brain, 126*(3), 579-589. doi:10.1093/brain/awg054

Huntsinger, C. S., & Jose, P. E. (2009). Parental involvement in children's schooling: Different meanings in different cultures. *Early Childhood Research Quarterly, 24*(4), 398-410. doi:10.1016/j.ecresq.2009.07.006

Huston, H. C., & Bentley, A. C. (2010). Human development in societal context. *Annual Review of Psychology, 61*, 411-437. doi:10.1146/annurev.psych.093008.100442

Hutchinson, S. R. (2004). Survey research. In K. deMarrais & S. D. Lapan (Eds.), *Foundations for research: Methods of inquiry in education and the social sciences: Inquiry and pedagogy across diverse contexts* (pp. 283–301). Mahwah, NJ: Erlbaum.

Hutchinson, S., Lee, L. H. L., Gaab, N., et al. (2003). Cerebellar volume of musicians. *Cerebral Cortex, 13*(9), 943–949. doi:10.1093/cercor/13.9.943

Hutchison, K. E., McGeary, J., Smolen, A., et al. (2002). The DRD4 VNTR polymorphism moderates craving after alcohol consumption. *Health Psychology, 21*(2), 139–146. doi:10.1037/0278-6133.21.2.139

Hyde, J. S., & DeLamater, J. D. (2011). *Understanding human sexuality* (11th ed.). New York: McGraw-Hill.

Hyde, J. S., & Else-Quest, N. (2013). *Half the human experience* (8th ed.). Cengage Learning/Wadsworth.

Hyman, R. (1996a). Evaluation of the military's twenty-year program on psychic spying. *Skeptical Inquirer, 20*(2), 21–23.

Hyman, R. (1996b). The evidence for psychic functioning: Claims vs. reality. *Skeptical Inquirer, 20*(2), 24–26.

Hyman, R. (2007). Talking with the dead, communicating with the future and other myths created by cold reading. In S. Della Sala (Ed.), *Tall tales about the mind & brain: Separating fact from fiction* (pp. 218–232). New York: Oxford University Press.

Hyman, S. E. (2011). Diagnosis of mental disorders in light of modern genetics. In D. A. Regier, W. E. Narrow, E. A. Kuhl, et al. (Eds.), *The conceptual evolution of DSM-5* (pp. 3–17). Arlington, VA: American Psychiatric Publishing.

Hysenbegasi, A., Hass, S. L., & Rowland, C. R. (2005). The impact of depression on the academic productivity of university students. *Journal of Mental Health Policy & Economics, 8*(3), 145–151.

Iacono, W. G. (2008). Effective policing: Understanding how polygraph tests work and are used. *Criminal Justice & Behavior, 35*(10), 1295–1308. doi:10.1177/0093854808321529

Iannetti, G. D., & Mouraux, A. (2010). From the neuromatrix to the pain matrix (and back). *Experimental Brain Research, 205*(1), 1–12. doi:10.1007/s00221-010-2340-1

Iannone, M., Bulotta, S., Paolino, D., et al. (2006). Electrocortical effects of MDMA are potentiated by acoustic stimulation in rats. *BMC Neuroscience,* February 16, 7–13. doi:10.1186/1471-2202-7-13

Ida, Y., & Mandal, M. K. (2003). Cultural differences in side bias: Evidence from Japan and India. *Laterality: Asymmetries of Body, Brain & Cognition, 8*(2), 121–133. doi:10.1080/713754478

Immordino-Yang, M. H. (2008). How we can learn from children with half a brain. *New Scientist, 2664*, 44–45.

Impett, E. A. Strachman, A., Finkel, E. J., et al. (2008). Maintaining sexual desire in intimate relationships: The importance of approach goals. *Journal of Personality & Social Psychology, 94*(5), 808–823. doi:10.1037/0022-3514.94.5.808

Impett, E. A., Gordon, A. M., Kogan, A., et al. (2010). Moving toward more perfect unions: Daily and long-term

consequences of approach and avoidance goals in romantic relationships. *Journal of Personality & Social Psychology, 99*(6), 948–963. doi:10.1037/a0020271

Ingham, A. G., Levinger, G., Graves, J., et al. (1974). The Ringelmann effect: Studies of group size and group performance. *Journal of Personality & Social Psychology, 10*, 371–384.

Innocence Project (2012). *Facts on post-conviction DNA exonerations.* Retrieved February 2, 2012, from http://www.innocenceproject.org/Content/Facts_on_PostConviction_DNA_Exonerations.php

Insel, T. R. (2010). Rethinking schizophrenia. *Nature, 468*(7321), 187–193. doi:10.1038/nature09552

Inzlicht, M., & Schmader, T. (Eds.) (2012). *Stereotype threat: Theory, process, and application.* New York: Oxford University Press.

Inzlicht, M., Gutsell, J. N., & Legault, L. (2012). Mimicry reduces racial prejudice. *Journal of Experimental Social Psychology, 48*(1), 361-365. doi:10.1016/j.jesp.2011.06.007

Iosif, A., & Ballon, B. (2005). Bad moon rising: The persistent belief in lunar connections to madness. *Canadian Medical Association Journal, 173*(12), 1498–1500. doi:10.1503/cmaj.051119

Isaacs, D. (2011). Corporal punishment of children: Changing the culture. *Journal of Paediatrics and Child Health, 47*(8), 491–492.doi:10.1111/j.1440-1754.2011.02143.x

Iversen, L. (2006). *Speed, ecstasy, Ritalin: The science of amphetamines.* New York: Oxford University Press.

Iyengar, S. S., & Lepper, M. R. (2000). When choice is demotivating: Can one desire too much of a good thing? *Journal of Personality & Social Psychology, 79*(6), 995–1006. doi:10.1037/0022-3514.79.6.995

Izard, C. E. (1990). Facial expressions and the regulation of emotions. *Journal of Personality & Social Psychology, 58*(3), 487–498. doi:10.1530/0022-3514.58.3.487

Izard, C. E. (2011). Forms and functions of emotions: Matters of emotion-cognition interactions. *Emotion Review, 3*(4), 371–378. doi:10.1177/1754073911410737

Izard, C. E., Fantauzzo, C. A., Castle, J. M., et al. (1995). The ontogeny and significance of infants' facial expressions in the first 9 months of life. *Developmental Psychology, 31*(6), 997–1013. doi:10.1037/0012-1649.31.6.997

Izard, C. E., Woodburn, E. M., & Finlon, K. J. (2010). Extending emotion science to the study of discrete emotions in infants. *Emotion Review, 2*(2), 134–136. doi:10.1177/1754073909355003

Jablonski, N.G., & Chaplin, G. (2000). The evolution of human skin coloration. *Journal of Human Evolution, 39*(1), 57–106. doi:10.1006/jhev.2000.0403

Jack, D. C., & Ali, A. (2010). *Silencing the self across cultures: Depression and gender in the social world.* New York: Oxford University Press.

Jackson, D., & Newberry, P. (2012). *Critical thinking: A user's manual.* Belmont, CA: Cengage Learning/Wadsworth.

Jackson, S. L. (2011). *Research methods: A modular approach* (2nd ed.). Belmont, CA: Cengage Learning/Wadsworth.

Jackson, T., Fritch, A., Nagasaka, T., et al. (2002). Towards explaining the association between shyness and loneliness: A path analysis with American college students. *Social Behavior & Personality, 30*(3), 263–270. doi:10.2224/sbp.2002.30.3.263

Jackson, T., Towson, S., & Narduzzi, K. (1997). Predictors of shyness: A test of variables associated with self-presentational models. *Social Behavior & Personality, 25*(2), 149–154. doi:10.2224/sbp.1997.25.2.149

Jacob, A., Prasad, S., Boggild, M., et al. (2004). Charles Bonnet syndrome: Elderly people and visual hallucinations. *British Medical Journal, 328*(7455), 1552–1554. doi:10.1136/bmj.328.7455.1552

Jacobs, J., Lega, B., & Anderson, C. (2012). Explaining how brain stimulation can evoke memories. *Journal of Cognitive Neuroscience, 24*(3), 553–563. doi:10.1162/jocn_a_00170

Jacobs, M. (2003). *Sigmund Freud.* Thousand Oaks, CA: Sage.

Jacobs, N., van Os, J., Derom, C., et al. (2008). Heritability of intelligence. *Twin Research & Human Genetics, 10*(Suppl), 11–14. doi:10.1375/twin.10.supp.11

Jacobs, S. R., & Dodd, D. K. (2003). Student burnout as a function of personality, social support, and workload. *Journal of College Student Development, 44*(3), 291–303. doi:10.1353/csd.2003.0028

Jacobson, S. W., Stanton, M. E., Dodge, N. C., et al. (2011). Impaired delay and trace eyeblink conditioning in school-age children with fetal alcohol syndrome. *Alcoholism: Clinical & Experimental Research, 35*(2), 250–264. doi:10.1111/j.1530-0277.2010.01341.x

Jacobs-Stewart, T. (2010). *Mindfulness and the 12 steps: Living recovery in the present moment.* Center City, MN: Hazelden Foundation.

Jaeggi, S. M., Buschkuehl, M., Jonides, J., et al. (2008). Improving fluid intelligence with training on working memory. *Proceedings of the National Academy of Sciences, 105*(19), 6829–6833. doi:10.1073/pnas.0801268105

Jaehnig, W., & Miller, M. L. (2007). Feedback types in programmed instruction: A systematic review. *Psychological Record, 57*(2), 219–232.

Jaffe, J., Beatrice, B., Feldstein, S., et al. (2001). Rhythms of dialogue in infancy. *Monographs of the Society for Research in Child Development, 66*(2), vi–131.

Jagaroo, V. (2009). *Neuroinformatics for neuropsychology.* New York: Springer.

Jahoda, G. (2007). Superstition and belief. *The Psychologist, 20*(10), 594–595.

Jamison, K. R. (2001). Suicide in the young: An essay. *Cerebrum, 3*(3), 39–42.

Janis, I. L. (1989). *Crucial decisions.* New York: Free Press.

Janis, I. L. (2007). Groupthink. In R. P. Vecchio (Ed.), *Leadership: Understanding the dynamics of power and influence in organizations* (2nd ed., pp. 163–176). Notre Dame, IN: University of Notre Dame Press.

Janssen, S. A., & Arntz, A. (2001). Real-life stress and opioid-mediated analgesia in novice parachute jumpers. *Journal of Psychophysiology, 15*(2), 106–113. doi:10.1027//0269-8803.15.2.106

Janus, S. S., & Janus, C. L. (1993). *The Janus report.* New York: Wiley.

Jarvin, L., & Sternberg, R. J. (2003). Alfred Binet's contributions to educational psychology. In B. J. Zimmerman & D. H. Schunk (Eds.), *Educational psychology: A century of contributions* (pp. 65–79). Mahwah, NJ: Erlbaum.

Jawahar, I. M., Stone, T. H., & Kisamore, J. L. (2007). Role conflict and burnout: The direct and moderating effects of political skill and perceived organizational support on burnout dimensions. *International Journal of Stress Management, 14*(2), 142–159. doi:10.1037/1072-5245.14.2.142

Jeffery, R. W., & Wing R. R. (2001). The effects of an enhanced exercise program on long-term weight loss. *Obesity Research, 9*(3), O193.

Jellinger, K. A. (2009). Review of *Interactive atlas of the human brain. European Journal of Neurology, 16*(3), e51. doi:10.1111/j.1468-1331.2008.02456.x

Jenkins, A. C., & Mitchell, J. P. (2011). Medial prefrontal cortex subserves diverse forms of self-reflection. *Social Neuroscience, 6*(3), 211–218. doi:10.1080/17470919.2010.507948

Jenkins, J. G., & Dallenbach, K. M. (1924). Oblivescence during sleep and waking. *American Journal of Psychology, 35*, 605–612.

Jerabek, I., & Standing, L. (1992). Imagined test situations produce contextual memory enhancement. *Perceptual & Motor Skills, 75*(2), 400.

Joffe, R. T. (2006). Is the thyroid still important in major depression? *Journal of Psychiatry & Neuroscience, 31*(6), 367–368.

Johnson, B. T., & Boynton, M. H. (2010). Putting attitudes in their place: Behavioral prediction in the face of competing variables. In J. P. Forgas, J., Cooper, & W. D. Crano (Eds.). *The psychology of attitudes and attitude change* (pp. 19–38). New York: Psychology Press.

Johnson, C. S., & Lammers, J. (2012). The powerful disregard social comparison information. *Journal of Experimental Social Psychology, 48*(1), 329–334. doi:10.1016/j.jesp.2011.10.010

Johnson, C. S., & Stapel, D. A. (2010). It depends on how you look at it: Being versus becoming mindsets determine responses to social comparisons. *British Journal of Social Psychology, 49*(4), 703–723. doi:10.1348/014466609X476827

Johnson, K. J., & Fredrickson, B. L. (2005). "We all look the same to me": Positive emotions eliminate the own-race bias in face recognition. *Psychological Science, 16*(11), 875–881. doi:10.1111/j.1467-9280.2005.01631.x

Johnson, S. (2005). *Everything bad is good for you: How today's popular culture is actually making us smarter.* New York: Riverhead.

Johnson, S. J., Batey, M., & Holdsworth, L. (2009). Personality and health: The mediating role of trait emotional intelligence and work locus of control. *Personality & Individual Differences, 47*(5), 470–475. doi:10.1016/j.paid.2009.04.025

Johnson, T. J. (2002). College students' self-reported reasons for why drinking games end. *Addictive Behaviors, 27*(1), 145–153. doi:10.1016/S0306-4603(00)00168-4

Johnson, W., Jung, R. E., Colom, R., et al. (2008).Cognitive abilities independent of IQ correlate with regional brain structure. *Intelligence, 36*(1), 18–28. doi:10.1016/j.intell.2007.01.005

Joinson, C., Heron, J., Von Gontard, A., et al. (2009). A prospective study of age at initiation of toilet training and subsequent daytime bladder control in school-age children. *Journal of Developmental & Behavioral Pediatrics, 30*(5), 385–393. doi:10.1097/DBP.0b013e3181ba0e77

Jones, K. L., & Streissguth, A. P. (2010). Fetal alcohol syndrome and fetal alcohol spectrum disorders: A brief history. *Journal of Psychiatry & Law, 38*(4), 373–382.

Jones, L., & Petruzzi, D. C. (1995). Test anxiety: A review of theory and current treatment. *Journal of College Student Psychotherapy, 10*(1), 3–15. doi:10.1300/J035v10n01_02

Jones, M. K., & Menzies, R. G. (1998). Danger ideation reduction therapy (DIRT) for obsessive-compulsive washers. *Behaviour Research & Therapy, 36*(10), 959–970. doi:10.1016/S0005-7967(98)00057-6

Jones, R. A. (2007). A discovery of meaning: The case of C. G. Jung's house dream. *Culture & Psychology, 13*(2), 203–230. doi:10.1177/1354067X07076596

Jones, R., Yates, W. R., & Zhou, M. (2002). Readmission rates for adjustment disorders: Comparison with other mood disorders. *Journal of Affective Disorders, 71*(1–3), 199–203. doi:10.1016/S0165-0327(01)00390-1

Jones, S. A. H., & Wilson, A. E. (2009). The horizon line, linear perspective, interposition, and background brightness as determinants of the magnitude of the pictorial moon illusion. *Attention, Perception, & Psychophysics, 71*(1), 131–142. doi:10.3758/APP.71.1.131

Jones, S. E., Mahmoud, S. Y., & Phillips, M. D. (2011). A practical clinical method to quantify language lateralization in fMRI using whole-brain analysis. *NeuroImage, 54,* 2937–2949. doi:10.1016/j.neuroimage.2010.10.052

Jones, S. R., & Fernyhough, C. (2007). A new look at the neural diathesis-stress model of schizophrenia: The primacy of social-evaluative and uncontrollable situations. *Schizophrenia Bulletin, 33*(5), 1171–1177. doi:10.1093/schbul/sbl058

Jones, S. S., & Hong, H.-W. (2001). Onset of voluntary communication: Smiling looks to mother. *Infancy, 2*(3), 353–370.

Jones, W. R., & Morgan, J. F. (2010). Eating disorders in men: A review of the literature. *Journal of Public Mental Health, 9*(2), 23–31. doi:10.5042/jpmh.2010.0326

Jonides, J., Lewis, R. L., Nee, D. E., et al. (2008). The mind and brain of short-term memory. *Annual Review of Psychology, 59,* 193–224. doi:10.1146/annurev.psych.59.103006.093615

Joo, E. Y., Tae, W. K., Lee, M. J., et al. (2010). Reduced brain gray matter concentration in patients with obstructive sleep apnea syndrome. *Sleep: Journal of Sleep & Sleep Disorders Research, 33*(2), 235–241.

Jordan, K. (2010). Vicarious trauma: Proposed factors that impact clinicians. *Journal of Family Psychotherapy, 21*(4), 225–237. doi:10.1080/08975353.2010.529003

Jorm, A. F. (2012). Mental health literacy: Empowering the community to take action for better mental health. *American Psychologist, 67*(3), 231–243. doi:10.1037/a0025957

Jouvet, M. (1999). *The paradox of sleep.* Boston: MIT Press.

Jowett, G. S. (2006). Brainwashing: The Korean POW controversy and the origins of a myth. In G. S. Jowett, & V. O'Donnell (Eds.), *Readings in propaganda and persuasion: New and classic essays* (pp. 201–211). Thousand Oaks, CA, Sage.

Juliano, L. M., & Griffiths, R. R. (2004). A critical review of caffeine withdrawal: Empirical validation of symptoms and signs, incidence, severity, and associated features. *Psychopharmacology, 176*(1), 1–29. doi:10.1007/s00213-004-2000-x

Julien, R. M. (2011). *A primer of drug action.* (12th ed.). New York: Worth.

Jun, H. (2010). *Social justice, multicultural counseling, and practice: Beyond a conventional approach.* Thousand Oaks, CA: Sage.

Jurd, R. R. (2011). TiNS special issue: Hippocampus and memory. *Trends in Neurosciences, 34*(10), 499–500. doi:10.1016/j.tins.2011.08.008

Jussim, L., & Harber, K. D. (2005). Teacher expectations and self-fulfilling prophecies: Knowns and unknowns, resolved and unresolved controversies. *Personality & Social Psychology Review, 9*(2), 131–155. doi:10.1207/s15327957pspr0902_3

Justman, S. (2011). From medicine to psychotherapy: The placebo effect. *History of the Human Sciences, 24*(1), 95–107. doi:10.1177/0952695110386655

Kagan, J. (2004). New insights into temperament. *Cerebrum, 6*(1), 51–66.

Kahneman, D. (2011). *Thinking, fast and slow.* New York: Farrar, Straus & Giroux.

Kahneman, D., & Tversky, A. (1972). Subjective probability: A judgment of representativeness. *Cognitive Psychology, 3,* 430–454. doi:10.1016/0010-0285(72)90016-3

Kahneman, D., Slovic, P., & Tversky, A. (1982). *Judgment under uncertainty: Heuristics and biases.* Cambridge, MA: Cambridge University Press.

Kail, R. V., & Cavanaugh, J. C. (2012). *Human development: A life-span view* (6th ed.). Belmont, CA: Cengage Learning/Wadsworth.

Kalat, J. W. (2013). *Biological psychology* (11th ed.). Belmont, CA: Cengage Learning/Wadsworth.

Kalat, J. W., & Shiota, M. N. (2012). *Emotion* (2nd ed.). Belmont, CA: Wadsworth.

Kallio, S., & Revonsuo, A. (2003). Hypnotic phenomena and altered states of consciousness: A multilevel framework of description and explanation. *Contemporary Hypnosis, 20*(3), 111–164. doi:10.1002/ch.273

Kalmijn, M. (2010). Educational inequality, homogamy, and status exchange in Black-White intermarriage: A comment on Rosenfield. *American Journal of Sociology, 115*(4), 1252–1263.

Kalyuga, S., & Hanham, J. (2011). Instructing in generalized knowledge structures to develop flexible problem solving skills. *Computers in Human Behavior, 27*(1), 63–68. doi:10.1016/j.chb.2010.05.024

Kalyuga, S., Renkl, A., & Paas, F. (2010). Facilitating flexible problem solving: A cognitive load perspective. *Educational Psychology Review, 22*(2), 175–186. doi:10.1007/s10648-010-9132-9

Kamimori, G. H., Johnson, D., Thorne, D., et al. (2005). Multiple caffeine doses maintain vigilance during early morning operations. *Aviation, Space, & Environmental Medicine, 76*(11), 1046–1050.

Kamin, L. J. (1981). *The intelligence controversy.* New York: Wiley.

Kampman, K. M. (2005). New medications for the treatment of cocaine dependence. *Psychiatry, 2*(12), 44–48.

Kapinos, K. A., & Yakusheva, O. (2011). Environmental influences on young adult weight gain: Evidence from a natural experiment. *Journal of Adolescent Health, 48*(1), 52–58. doi:10.1016/j.jadohealth.2010.05.021

Kaplan, A. (2008). Clarifying metacognition, self-regulation, and self-regulated learning: What's the purpose? *Educational Psychology Review, 20*(4), 477–484. doi:10.1007/s10648-008-9087-2

Kaplan, P. S. (1998). *The human odyssey.* Pacific Grove, CA: Brooks/Cole..

Kaplan, R. M., & Saccuzzo, D. P. (2013). *Psychological testing: Principles, applications, and issues* (8th ed.). Belmont, CA: Cengage Learning/Wadsworth.

Kapleau, P. (1966). *The three pillars of Zen.* New York: Harper & Row.

Kappe, R., & van der Flier, H. (2010). Using multiple and specific criteria to assess the predictive validity of the big five personality factors on academic performance. *Journal of Research in Personality, 44*(1), 142–145. doi:10.1016/j.jrp.2009.11.002

Kaptelinin, V., & Czerwinski, M. (Eds.). (2007). *Beyond the desktop metaphor: Design integrated digital work environments.* Cambridge, MA: MIT Press.

Karim, A. A., Hinterberger, T., Richter, J., et al. (2006). Neural internet: Web surfing with brain potentials for the completely paralyzed. *Neurorehabilitation & Neural Repair, 20*(4), 508–515. doi:10.1177/1545968306290661

Kark, R., & Eagly, A. H. (2010). Gender and leadership: Negotiating the labyrinth. In J. C. Chrisler & D. R. McCreary (Eds.), *Handbook of gender research in psychology: Gender research in social and applied psychology* (Vol 2, pp. 443–470). New York: Springer.

Karpicke, J. D., & Blunt, J. R. (2011). Retrieval practice produces more learning than elaborative studying with concept mapping. *Science, January,* doi:10.1126/science.1199327.

Kasser, T., & Ryan, R. M. (1993). A dark side of the American dream: Correlates of financial success as a central life aspiration. *Journal of Personality & Social Psychology, 65*(2), 410–422. doi:10.1037/0022-3514.65.2.410

Kasser, T., & Ryan, R. M. (1996). Further examining the American dream: Differential correlates of intrinsic and extrinsic goals. *Personality & Social Psychology Bulletin, 22*(3), 280–287. doi:10.1177/0146167296223006

Kassin, S. M. (2005). On the psychology of confessions: Does innocence put innocents at risk? *American Psychologist, 60*(3), 215–228. doi:10.1037/0003-066X.60.3.215

Kassin, S. M., Fein, S., & Markus, H. R. (2011). *Social psychology* (8th ed.). Boston: Houghton Mifflin.

Kataria, S. (2004). A clinical guide to pediatric sleep: Diagnosis and management of sleep problems. *Journal of Developmental & Behavioral Pediatrics, 25*(2), 132–133. doi:10.1097/00004703-200404000-00012

Katz, P. A. (2003). Racists or tolerant multiculturalists? *American Psychologist, 58*(11), 897–909.

Kaufman, A. S. (2000). Intelligence tests and school psychology: Predicting the future by studying the past. *Psychology in the Schools, 37*(1), 7–16.doi:10.1002/(SICI)1520-6807(200001)37:1<7::AID-PITS2>3.0.CO;2-H

Kaufman, J. C. (2009). *Creativity 101.* New York: Springer.

Kaufman, J. C., & Sternberg, R. J. (Eds.). (2010). *The Cambridge handbook of creativity.* New York: Cambridge University Press.

Kaufman, L., & Kaufman, J. H. (2000). Explaining the moon illusion. *Proceedings of the National Academy of Sciences, 97*(1), 500–505. doi:10.1073/pnas.97.1.500

Kawada, R., Yoshizumi, M., Hirao, K., et al. (2009). Brain volume and dysexecutive behavior in schizophrenia. *Progress in Neuro-Psychopharmacology & Biological Psychiatry, 33*(7), 1255–1260. doi:10.1016/j.pnpbp.2009.07.014

Kawai, K., Sugimoto, K., Nakashima, K., et al. (2000). Leptin as a modulator of sweet taste sensitivities in mice. *Proceedings of the National Academy of Sciences, 97*(20), 11044–11049. doi:10.1073/pnas.190066697

Kearney, A. J. (2006). A primer of covert sensitization. *Cognitive & Behavioral Practice, 13*(2), 167–175. doi:10.1016/j.cbpra.2006.02.002

Kearney, C. A., Sims, K. E., Pursell, C. R., et al. (2003). Separation anxiety disorder in young children: A longitudinal and family analysis. *Journal of Clinical Child & Adolescent Psychology, 32*(4), 593–598. doi:10.1207/S15374424JCCP3204_12

Kearney, C., & Trull, T. (2012). *Abnormal psychology and life: A dimensional approach.* Belmont, CA: Cengage Learning/Wadsworth.

Keating, C. (2010). Theoretical perspective on anorexia nervosa: The conflict of reward. *Neuroscience & Biobehavioral Reviews, 34*(1), 73–79. doi:10.1016/j.neubiorev.2009.07.004

Keefe, F. J., Abernethy, A. P., & Campbell, L. C. (2005). Psychological approaches to understanding and treating disease-related pain. *Annual Review of Psychology, 56*, 601–630. doi:10.1146/annurev.psych.56.091103.070302

Keegan, J., Parva, M., Finnegan, M., et al. (2010). Addiction in pregnancy. *Journal of Addictive Diseases, 29*(2), 175–191. doi:10.1080/10550881003684723

Keel, P. K., & Klump, K. L. (2003). Are eating disorders culture-bound syndromes? Implications for conceptualizing their etiology. *Psychological Bulletin, 129*(5), 747–769. doi:10.1037/0033-2909.129.5.747

Kegel, M., Dam, H., Ali, F., et al. (2009). The prevalence of seasonal affective disorder (SAD) in Greenland is related to latitude. *Nordic Journal of Psychiatry, 63*(4), 331–335. doi:10.1080/08039480902799040

Kell, C. A., Morillon, B., Kouneiher, F., et al. (2011). Lateralization of speech production starts in sensory cortices: A possible sensory origin of cerebral left dominance for speech. *Cerebral Cortex, 21*(4), 932–937. doi:10.1093/cercor/bhq167

Keller, E. F. (2010). Goodbye, nature vs nurture. *New Scientist*, Sept 20, 28–29.

Keller, M. C., & Young, R. K. (1996). Mate assortment in dating and married couples. *Personality & Individual Differences, 21*(2), 217–221.

Kelly, I. W. (1999). "Debunking the debunkers": A response to an astrologer's debunking of skeptics. *Skeptical Inquirer*, Nov.–Dec., 37–43.

Kelly, M. P., Strassberg, D. S., & Turner, C. M. (2006). Behavioral assessment of couples' communication in female orgasmic disorder. *Journal of Sex & Marital Therapy, 32*(2), 81–95. doi:10.1080/00926230500442243

Kendall-Tackett, K. (Ed.). (2010). *The psychoneuroimmunology of chronic disease: Exploring the links between inflammation, stress, and illness.* Washington, DC: American Psychological Association.

Kendler, K. S., & Schaffner, K. F. (2011). The dopamine hypothesis of schizophrenia: An historical and philosophical analysis. *Philosophy,* *Psychiatry, & Psychology, 18*(1), 41–63. doi:10.1353/ppp.2011.0005

Kendler, K. S., Thornton, L. M., & Prescott, C. A. (2001). Gender differences in the rates of exposure to stressful life events and sensitivity to their depressogenic effects. *American Journal of Psychiatry, 158*(4), 587–593. doi:10.1176/appi.ajp.158.4.587

Kennedy, S. H., Giacobbe, P., Rizvi, S. J., et al. (2011). Deep brain stimulation for treatment-resistant depression: Follow-up after 3 to 6 years. *The American Journal of Psychiatry, 168*(5), 502–510. doi:10.1176/appi.ajp.2010.10081187

Kenneth, M., Carpenter, K. M., & Hasin, D. S. (1998). Reasons for drinking alcohol. *Psychology of Addictive Behaviors, 12*(3), 168–184. doi:10.1037/0893-164X.12.3.168

Kenny, P. J., & Markou, A. (2006). Nicotine self-administration acutely activates brain reward systems and induces a long-lasting increase in reward sensitivity. *Neuropsychopharmacology, 31*(6), 1203–1211. doi:10.1038/sj.npp.1300905

Kenrick, D.T., Griskevicius, V., Neuberg, S.L., et al., (2010). Renovating the pyramid of needs: Contemporary extensions built upon ancient foundations. *Perspectives on Psychological Science, 5*, 292–314. doi:10.1177/1745691610369469

Kensinger, E. A. (2007). Negative emotion enhances memory accuracy: Behavioral and neuroimaging evidence. *Current Directions in Psychological Science, 16*(4), 213–218. doi:10.1111/j.1467-8721.2007.00506.x

Kernis, M. H., & Goldman, B. M. (2005). Authenticity, social motivation, and psychological adjustment. In J. P. Forgas, K. D. Williams, & S. M. Laham (Eds.), *Social motivation: Conscious and unconscious processes* (pp. 210–227). New York: Cambridge University Press.

Kernis, M. H., & Lakey, C. E. (2010). Fragile versus secure high self-esteem: Implications for defensiveness and insecurity. In R. M. Arkin, K. C. Oleson, & P. J. Carroll (Eds.), *Handbook of the uncertain self* (pp. 360–378). New York: Psychology Press.

Kerns, R. D., Sellinger, J., & Goodin, B. R. (2011). Psychological treatment of chronic pain. *Annual Review of Clinical Psychology, 7*, 411–434. doi:10.1146/annurev-clinpsy-090310-120430

Kessler, D. A. (2009). *The end of overeating: Taking control of the insatiable American appetite.* Emmaus, PA: Rodale Press.

Kessler, R. C. (2010). The prevalence of mental illness. In T. L. Scheid & T. N. Brown (Eds.), *A handbook for the study of mental health: Social contexts, theories, and systems* (2nd ed., pp. 46–63). New York: Cambridge University Press.

Kety, S. S. (1979, Sept.). Disorders of the human brain. *Scientific American, 241*, 202–214. doi:10.1038/scientificamerican0979-202

Keyes, C. L. M., & Haidt, J. (2003). Introduction: Human flourishing. In C. L. M. Keyes & J. Haidt (Eds.), *Flourishing* (pp. 3–12). Washington, DC: American Psychological Association.

Keysers, C., Xiao, D.-K., Földiák, P., et al. (2005). Out of sight but not out of mind: The neurophysiology of iconic memory in the superior temporal sulcus. *Cognitive Neuropsychology, 22*(3–4), 316–332. doi:10.1080/02643290442000103

Khan, O., Tselis, A., & Lisak, R. (2010). Getting to grips with myelin injury in progressive multiple sclerosis. *Brain: A Journal of Neurology, 133*(10), 2845–2851. doi:10.1093/brain/awq271

Kida, T. E. (2006). *Don't believe everything you think.* Buffalo, NY: Prometheus.

Kiecolt-Glaser, J. (2010). Stress, food, and inflammation: Psychoneuroimmunology and nutrition at the cutting edge. *Psychosomatic Medicine, 72*(4), 365–369. doi:10.1097/PSY.0b013e3181dbf489

Kiff, C. J., Lengua, L. J., & Bush, N. R. (2011). Temperament variation in sensitivity to parenting: Predicting changes in depression and anxiety. *Journal of Abnormal Child Psychology, 39*(8), 1199–1212. doi:10.1007/s10802-011-9539-x

Kim, E. H., & Gray, S. H. (2009). Challenges presenting in transference and countertransference in the psychodynamic psychotherapy of a military service member. *Journal of the American Academy of Psychoanalysis & Dynamic Psychiatry, 37*(3), 421–437. doi:10.1521/jaap.2009.37.3.421

Kim-Cohen, J., Moffitt, T. E., Caspi, A., et al. (2004). Genetic and environmental processes in young children's resilience and vulnerability to socioeconomic deprivation. *Child Development, 75*(3), 651–668. doi:10.1111/j.1467-8624.2004.00699.x

King, L. A., Richards, J. H., & Stemmerich, E. (1998). Daily goals, life goals, and worst fears: Means, ends, and subjective well-being. *Journal of Personality, 66*(5), 713–744. doi:10.1111/1467-6494.00030

King, N. J., Muris, P., & Ollendick, T. H. (2005). Childhood fears and phobias: Assessment and treatment. *Child & Adolescent Mental Health, 10*(2), 50–56. doi:10.1111/j.1475-3588.2005.00118.x

King, P. M. (2009). Principles of development and developmental change underlying theories of cognitive and moral development. *Journal of College Student Development, 50*(6), 597–620. doi:10.1353/csd.0.0104

Kingsley, C. H. & Lambert, K. G. (2006). The maternal brain. *Scientific American, 294*(1), 72–79.

Kinnunen, L. H., Moltz, H., Metz, J., et al. (2004). Differential brain activation in exclusively homosexual and heterosexual men produced by the selective serotonin reuptake inhibitor, fluoxetine. *Brain Research, 1024*(1-2), 251–254. doi:10.1016/j.brainres.2004.07.070

Kirby, D. B. (2008). The impact of abstinence and comprehensive sex and STD/HIV education programs on adolescent sexual behavior. *Sexuality Research & Social Policy, 5*(3), 18–27. doi:10.1525/srsp.2008.5.3.18

Kirchhoff, B. A. (2009). Individual differences in episodic memory: The role of self-initiated encoding strategies. *The Neuroscientist, 15*(2), 166–179. doi:10.1177/1073858408329507

Kirk, S. A., Gallagher, J. J., Coleman, M. R., et al. (2011). *Educating exceptional children* (13th ed.). Belmont, CA: Cengage Learning/Wadsworth.

Kirsch, I., (2005). The flexible observer and neodissociation theory. *Contemporary Hypnosis, 22*(3), 121–122. doi:10.1002/ch.2

Kirsch, I., & Lynn, S. J. (1995). The altered state of hypnosis. *American Psychologist, 50*(10), 846–858. doi:10.1037/0003-066X.50.10.846

Kirsh, S. J. (2010). *Children, adolescents, and media violence: A critical look at the research* (2nd ed.). Thousand Oaks, CA: Sage.

Kirveskari, E., Salmelin, R., & Hari, R. (2006). Neuromagnetic responses to vowels vs. tones reveal hemispheric lateralization. *Clinical Neurophysiology, 117*(3), 643–648. doi:10.1016/j.clinph.2005.11.001

Kiser, L. J., Heston, J. D., & Paavola, M. (2006). Day treatment centers/partial hospitalization settings. In T. A. Petti & C. Salguero (Eds.), *Community child & adolescent psychiatry: A manual of clinical practice and consultation* (pp. 189–203). Washington, DC: American Psychiatric Publishing.

Kisilevsky, B. S., Hains, S. M. J., Jacquet, A.-Y., et al. (2004). Maturation of fetal responses to music. *Developmental Science, 7*(5), 550–559. doi:10.1111/j.1467-7687.2004.00379.x

Kitayama, S., Markus, H. R., & Kurokawa, M. (2000). Culture, emotion, and well-being: Good feelings in Japan and the United States. *Cognition & Emotion, 14*, 93–124. doi:10.1080/026999300379003

Kjellgren, A., Buhrkall, H., & Norlander, T. (2011). Preventing sick-leave for sufferers of high stress-load and burnout syndrome: A pilot study combining psychotherapy and the flotation tank. *International Journal of Psychology & Psychological Therapy, 11*(2), 297–306.

Klahr, D., & Nigam, M. (2004). The equivalence of learning paths in early science instruction: Effects of direct instruction and discovery learning. *Psychological Science, 15*, 661–667. doi:10.1111/j.0956-7976.2004.00737.x

Klein, B., Richards, J. C., & Austin, D. W. (2006). Efficacy of internet therapy for panic disorder. *Journal of Behavior Therapy & Experimental Psychiatry, 37*(3), 213–238. doi:10.1016/j.jbtep.2005.07.001

Klein, D. W., & Kihlstrom, J. F. (1986). Elaboration, organization, and the self-reference effect in memory. *Journal of Experimental Psychology: General, 115*, 26–38. doi:10.1037/0096-3445.115.1.26

Klein, K., & Boals, A. (2001a). The relationship of life event stress and working memory capacity. *Applied Cognitive Psychology, 15*(5), 565–579. doi:10.1002/acp.727

Klein, K., & Boals, A. (2001b). Expressive writing can increase working memory capacity. *Journal of Experimental Psychology: General, 130*(3), 520–533. doi:10.1037/0096-3445.130.3.520

Klein, L. A., & Houlihan, D. (2010). Relationship satisfaction, sexual satisfaction, and sexual problems in sexsomnia. *International Journal of Sexual Health, 22*(2), 84–90. doi:10.1080/19317610903510489

Klohnen, E. C., & Luo, S. (2003). Interpersonal attraction and personality: What is attractive— self similarity, ideal similarity, complementarity or attachment security? *Journal of Personality & Social Psychology, 85*(4), 709–722. doi:10.1037/0022-3514.85.4.709

Klöppel, S., Mangin, J.-F., Vongerichten, A., et al. (2010). Nurture versus nature: Long-term impact of forced right-handedness on structure of pericentral cortex and basal ganglia. *Journal of Neuroscience, 30*(9), 3271–3275. doi:10.1523/JNEUROSCI.4394-09.2010

Knafo, D. (2009). Freud's memory erased. *Psychoanalytic Psychology, 26*(2), 171–190.

Kneer, J., Glock, S., & Rieger, D. (2012). Fast and not furious? Reduction of cognitive dissonance in smokers. *Social Psychology, 43*(2), 81–91. doi:10.1027/1864-9335/a000086

Knoll, J. L. IV., & Resnick, P. J. (2008). Insanity defense evaluations: Toward a model for evidence-based practice. *Brief Treatment & Crisis Intervention, 8*(1), 92–110. doi:10.1093/brief-treatment/mhm024

Knoops, K. T. B., de Groot, L. C., Kromhout, D., et al. (2004). Mediterranean diet, lifestyle factors, and 10-year mortality in elderly European men and women. *Journal of the American Medical Association, 292*(12), 1433–1439. doi:10.1001/jama.292.12.1433

Koch, I., Lawo, V., Fels, J., et al. (2011). Switching in the cocktail party: Exploring intentional control of auditory selective attention. *Journal of Experimental Psychology: Human Perception & Performance, 37*(4), 1140–1147. doi:10.1037/a0022189

Koch, W. H., & Pratarelli, M. E. (2004). Effects of intro/extraversion and sex on social internet use. *North American Journal of Psychology, 6*(3), 371–382.

Koda, S., & Sugawara, K. (2009). The influence of diet behavior and stress on binge-eating among female college students. *Japanese Journal of Psychology, 80*(2), 83–89.

Kohlberg, L. (1969). The cognitive-developmental approach to socialization. In A. Goslin (Ed.), *Handbook of socialization theory and research* (pp. 1–134). Chicago: Rand McNally.

Kohlberg, L. (1981). *Essays on moral development* (Vol. I): *The philosophy of moral development.* San Francisco: Harper.

Kohn, C. S., & Antonuccio, D. O. (2002). Treatment of kleptomania

using cognitive and behavioral strategies. *Clinical Case Studies, 1*(1), 25–38. doi:10.1177/1534650102001001003

Köke, A., Schouten, J. S., Lamerichs-Geelen, M. J. H., et al. (2004). Pain reducing effect of three types of transcutaneous electrical nerve stimulation in patients with chronic pain: A randomized crossover trial. *Pain, 108*(1–2), 36–42. doi:10.1016/j.pain.2003.11.013

Kolb, B., & Whishaw, I.Q. (2011). *Introduction to brain and behavior* (3rd ed.). New York: Freeman-Worth.

Kolb, B., Gibb, R., & Gorny, G. (2003). Experience-dependent changes in dendritic arbor and spine density in neocortex vary with age and sex. *Neurobiology of Learning & Memory, 79*(1), 1–10. doi:10.1016/S1074-7427(02)00021-7

Kolb, B., Mychasiuk, R., Williams, P., et al. (2011). Brain plasticity and recovery from early cortical injury. *Developmental Medicine & Child Neurology, 53*, 4–8. doi:10.1111/j.1469-8749.2011.04054.x

Komisaruk, B. R., Beyer-Flores, C., & Whipple, B. (2006). *The science of orgasm.* Baltimore, MD: Johns Hopkins University Press.

Kornhaber, M. L., & Gardner, H. (2006). Multiple intelligences: Developments in implementation and theory. In M. A. Constas & R. J. Sternberg (Eds.), *Translating theory and research into educational practice: Developments in content domains, large-scale reform, and intellectual capacity* (pp. 255–276). Mahwah, NJ: Erlbaum.

Kornilov, S. A., Tan, M., Elliott, J. G., et al. (2012). Gifted identification with aurora: Widening the spotlight. *Journal of Psychoeducational Assessment, 30*(1), 117–133. doi:10.1177/0734282911428199

Korol, C., Craig, K. D., & Firestone, P. (2003). Dissociative and somatoform disorders. In P. Firestone & W. L. Marshall (Eds.), *Abnormal psychology: Perspectives* (2nd ed., pp. 183–199). Toronto: Prentice Hall.

Kosslyn, S. M. (1983). *Ghosts in the mind's machine.* New York: Norton.

Kosslyn, S. M. (1985). Stalking the mental image. *Psychology Today, 19*(5), 22–28.

Kosslyn, S. M. (2005). Mental images and the brain. *Cognitive Neuropsychology, 22*(3–4), 333–347. doi:10.1080/02643290442000130

Kosslyn, S. M., Ball, T. M., & Reiser, B. J. (1978). Visual images preserve metric spatial information: Evidence from studies of image scanning. *Journal of Experimental Psychology: Human Perception & Performance, 4*, 47–60. doi:10.1037/0096-1523.4.1.47

Kosson, D. S., Suchy, Y., Mayer, A. R., et al. (2002). Facial affect recognition in criminal psychopaths. *Emotion, 2*(4), 398–411. doi:10.1037/1528-3542.2.4.398

Kotkin, M., Daviet, C., & Gurin, J. (1996). The Consumer Reports mental health survey. *American Psychologist, 51*(10), 1080–1082. doi:10.1037/0003-066X.51.10.1080

Kottler, J. A., & Chen, D. D. (2011). *Stress management and prevention:*

Applications to daily life (2nd ed.). New York: Routledge.

Kottler, J. A., & Shepard, D. S. (2011). *Introduction to counseling* (7th ed.). Belmont, CA: Cengage Learning/Wadsworth.

Kowert, P. A. (2002). *Groupthink or deadlock: When do leaders learn from their advisors? SUNY series on the presidency.* Albany, NY: State University of New York Press.

Krahé, B., & Möller, I. (2010). Longitudinal effects of media violence on aggression and empathy among German adolescents. *Journal of Applied Developmental Psychology, 31*(5), 401–409. doi:10.1016/j.appdev.2010.07.003

Krahé, B., Möller, I., Huesmann, L. R., et al. (2011). Desensitization to media violence: Links with habitual media violence exposure, aggressive cognitions, and aggressive behavior. *Journal of Personality & Social Psychology, 100*(4), 630–646. doi:10.1037/a0021711

Krakow, B., & Zadra, A. (2006). Clinical management of chronic nightmares: Imagery rehearsal therapy. *Behavioral Sleep Medicine, 4*(1), 45–70. doi:10.1207/s15402010bsm0401_4

Krall, E. A., Garvey, A. J., & Garcia, R. I. (2002). Smoking relapse after 2 years of abstinence: Findings from the VA Normative Aging Study. *Nicotine & Tobacco Research, 4*(1), 95–100. doi:10.1080/14622200110098428

Kramer, U., Despland, J.-N., Michel, L., et al. (2010). Change in defense mechanisms and coping over the course of short-term dynamic psychotherapy for adjustment disorder. *Journal of Clinical Psychology, 66*(12), 1232–1241. doi:10.1002/jclp.20719

Krantz, M. J., Sabel, A. L., Sagar, U., et al. (2012). Factors influencing QT prolongation in patients hospitalized with severe anorexia nervosa. *General Hospital Psychiatry, 34*(2), 173–177. doi:10.1016/j.genhosppsych.2011.08.003

Kteily, N. S., Sidanius, J., & Levin, S. (2011). Social dominance orientation: Cause or 'mere effect'?: Evidence for SDO as a causal predictor of prejudice and discrimination against ethnic and racial outgroups. *Journal of Experimental Social Psychology, 47*(1), 208–214. doi:10.1016/j.jesp.2010.09.009

Kübler-Ross, E. (1975). *Death: The final stage of growth.* Englewood Cliffs, NJ: Prentice-Hall.

Kuhl, P. K. (2004). Early language acquisition: Cracking the speech code. *Nature Reviews Neuroscience, 5*(11), 831–841. doi:10.1038/nrn1533

Kuiper, N. A., & McHale, N. (2009). Humor styles as mediators between self-evaluative standards and psychological well-being. *Journal of Psychology: Interdisciplinary & Applied, 143*(4), 359–376. doi:10.3200/JRLP.143.4.359-376

Kuther, T. L., & Morgan, R. D. (2010). *Careers in psychology: Opportunities in a changing world* (3rd ed.). Belmont, CA: Cengage Learning/Wadsworth.

LaBar, K. S. (2007). Beyond fear: Emotional memory mechanisms in the human brain. *Current Directions*

in Psychological Science, 16(4), 173–177. doi:10.1111/j.1467-8721.2007.00498.x

LaBerge, S. (2000). Lucid dreaming: Evidence and methodology. In F. E. Pace-Schott, M. Solms, et al. (Eds.), *Sleep and dreaming: Scientific advances and reconsiderations* (pp. 1–50). Cambridge, UK: Cambridge University Press.

Laborda, M. A., & Miller, R. R. (2011). S-R associations, their extinction, and recovery in an animal model of anxiety: A new associative account of phobias without recall of original trauma. *Behavior Therapy, 42*(2), 153–169. doi:10.1016/j.beth.2010.06.002

Labov, W. (1973). The boundaries of words and their meanings. In C. J. N. Bailey & R. W. Shuy (Eds.), *New ways of analyzing variation in English* (pp. 340–373). Washington, DC: Georgetown University Press.

LaBrie, R. A., & Shaffer, H. J. (2007). Gambling with adolescent health. *Journal of Adolescent Health, 40*(5), 387–389. doi:10.1016/j.jadohealth.2007.02.009

Lacayo, A. (1995). Neurologic and psychiatric complications of cocaine abuse. *Neuropsychiatry, Neuropsychology, & Behavioral Neurology, 8*(1), 53–60.

Lachman, M. E. (2004). Development in midlife. *Annual Review of Psychology, 55*, 305–331. doi:10.1146/annurev.psych.55.090902.141521

Lachman, M. E., Röcke, C., Rosnick, C., et al. (2008). Realism and illusion in Americans' temporal views of their life satisfaction: Age differences in reconstructing the past and anticipating the future. *Psychological Science, 19*(9), 889–897. doi:10.1111/j.1467-9280.2008.02173.x

Lackner, J. R., & DiZio, P. (2005). Vestibular, proprioceptive, and haptic contributions to spatial orientation. *Annual Review of Psychology, 56*, 115–147. doi:10.1146/annurev.psych.55.090902.142023

Ladouceur, R., Lachance, S., & Fournier, P.-M. (2009). Is control a viable goal in the treatment of pathological gambling? *Behaviour Research & Therapy, 47*(3), 189–197. doi:10.1016/j.brat.2008.11.004

Lagace, D. C. (2011). Does the endogenous neurogenic response alter behavioral recovery following stroke? *Behavioural Brain Research,* doi:10.1016/j.bbr.2011.08.045.

Lagos, P., Torterolo, P., Jantos, H., et al. (2009). Effects on sleep of melanin-concentrating hormone (MCH) microinjections into the dorsal raphe nucleus. *Brain Research, 1265*, 103–110. doi:10.1016/j.brainres.2009.02.010

Lam, R., & Mok, H. (2008). *Depression.* New York: Oxford.

Lamb, R. J., Kirby, K. C., Morral, A. R., et al. (2010). Shaping smoking cessation in hard-to-treat smokers. *Journal of Consulting & Clinical Psychology, 78*(1), 62–71. doi:10.1037/a0018323

Lamb, T. D. (2011). Evolution of the eye. *Scientific American, July,* 64–69.

Lambert, M. J., & Ogles, B. M. (2002). The efficacy and effectiveness of psychotherapy. In M. J. Lambert (Ed.), *Handbook of psychotherapy and behavior change* (5th ed., pp. 130–193). New York: Wiley.

Lammers, G. J., Bassetti, C., Billiard, M., et al. (2010). Sodium oxybate is an effective and safe treatment for narcolepsy. *Sleep Medicine, 11*(1), 105–106. doi:10.1016/j.sleep.2009.08.003

Lamont, K. T., Somers, S., Lacerda, L., et al. (2011). Is red wine a SAFE sip away from cardioprotection? Mechanisms involved in resveratrol-and melatonin-induced cardioprotection. *Journal of Pineal Research, 50,* 374–380. doi:10.1111/j.1600-079X.2010.00853.x

Lampinen, J. M., Neuschatz, J. S., & Cling, A. D. (2012). The psychology of eyewitness identification. Hove, UK: Psychology Press.

Lamprecht, R., Dracheva, S., Assoun, S., et al. (2009). Fear conditioning induces distinct patterns of gene expression in lateral amygdala. *Genes, Brain & Behavior, 8*(8), 735–743. doi:10.1111/j.1601-183X.2009.00515.x

Lamy, L., Fischer-Lokou, J., & Guéguen, N. (2012). Priming emotion concepts and helping behavior: How unlived emotions can influence action. *Social Behavior and Personality, 40*(1), 55–62. doi:10.2224/sbp.2012.40.1.55

Lan Yeung, V. W., & Kashima, Y. (2010). Communicating stereotype-relevant information: How readily can people individuate? *Asian Journal of Social Psychology, 13*(4), 209–220. doi:10.1111/j.1467-839X.2010.01313.x

Lanciano, T., Curci, A., & Semin, G. (2010). The emotional and reconstructive determinants of emotional memories: An experimental approach to flashbulb memory investigation. *Memory, 18*(5), 473–485. doi:10.1080/09658211003762076

Landa, Y., Silverstein, S. M., Schwartz, F., et al. (2006). Group cognitive behavioral therapy for delusions: Helping patients improve reality testing. *Journal of Contemporary Psychotherapy, 36*(1), 9–17. doi:10.1007/s10879-005-9001-x

Landau, J. D., & Leynes, P. A. (2006). Do explicit memory manipulations affect the memory blocking effect? *American Journal of Psychology, 119*(3), 463–479. doi:10.2307/20445353

Landau, M. J., Meier, B. P., & Keefer, L. A. (2010). A metaphor-enriched social cognition. *Psychological Bulletin, 136*(6), 1045–1067. doi:10.1037/a0020970

Lane, C. (2009). The slippery slope of bitterness disorder and other psychiatric diagnoses. *Psychology Today, June 3.* Retrieved May 9, 2012, from http://www.psychologytoday.com/blog/side-effects/200906/the-slippery-slope-bitterness-disorder-and-other-psychiatric-diagnoses

Langer, E. J. (2000). Mindful learning. *Current Directions in Psychological Science, 9*(6), 220–223. doi:10.1111/1467-8721.00099

Langleben, D. D. (2008). Detection of deception with fMRI: Are we there yet. *Legal & Criminological Psychology, 13*(1), 1–9. doi:10.1348/135532507X251641

Langleben, D. D., Dattilio, F. M., & Gutheil, T. G. (2006). True lies: Delusions and lie-detection technology. *Journal of Psychiatry & Law, 34*(3), 351–370. doi:10.1037/a0020970

Langleben, D. D., Loughead, J. W., Bilker, W. B., et al. (2005). Telling truth from lie in individual subjects with fast event-related fMRI. *Human Brain Mapping, 26*(4), 262–272. doi:10.1002/hbm.20191

Langone, M. D. (2002). Cults, conversion, science, and harm. *Cultic Studies Review, 1*(2), 178–186.

Larimer, M. E., Neighbors, C., LaBrie, J., et al. (2011). Descriptive drinking norms: For whom does reference group matter? *Journal of Studies on Alcohol & Drugs, 72*(5), 833–843.

Larsen, R. J., & Buss, D. M. (2010). *Personality psychology* (4th ed.). New York: McGraw-Hill.

Larsen, R. J., & Kasimatis, M. (1990). Individual differences in entrainment of mood to the weekly calendar. *Journal of Personality & Social Psychology, 58*(1), 164–171. doi:10.1037/0022-3514.58.1.164

Larsen, R.J., & Prizmic, Z. (2004) Affect regulation. In R. Baumeister & K. D. Voohs (Eds.), *Handbook of self-regulation: Research, theory, and applications* (pp. 40–61). New York: Guilford.

Larsson, B., Carlsson, J., Fichtel, Å., et al. (2005). Relaxation treatment of adolescent headache sufferers: Results from a school-based replication series. *Headache: The Journal of Head & Face Pain, 45*(6), 692–704. doi:10.1111/j.1526-4610.2005.05138.x

Larsson, J.-O., Larsson, H., & Lichtenstein, P. (2004). Genetic and environmental contributions to stability and change of ADHD symptoms between 8 and 13 years of age: A longitudinal twin study. *Journal of the American Academy of Child & Adolescent Psychiatry, 43*(10), 1267–1275. doi:10.1097/01.chi.0000135622.05219.bf

Latrofa, M., Vaes, J., Cadinu, M., et al. (2010). The cognitive representation of self-stereotyping. *Personality & Social Psychology Bulletin, 36*(7), 911–922. doi:10.1177/0146167210373907

Lattal, K. A., Reilly, M. P., & Kohn, J. P. (1998). Response persistence under ratio and interval reinforcement schedules. *Journal of the Experimental Analysis of Behavior, 70*(2), 165–183. doi:10.1901/jeab.1998.70-165

Laub, J. H., & Sampson, R. J. (2003). *Shared beginnings, divergent lives: Delinquent boys to age 70.* Cambridge, MA: Harvard University Press.

Laureys, S., & Boly. M. (2007). What is it like to be vegetative or minimally conscious? *Current Opinion in Neurology, 20,* 609–613.

Lawson, H. M., & Leck, K. (2006). Dynamics of Internet dating. *Social Science Computer Review, 24*(2), 189–208. doi:10.1177/0894439305283402

Lay, C., & Verkuyten, M. (1999). Ethnic identity and its relation to personal self-esteem. *Journal of Social Psychology, 139*(3), 288–299.

Lazar, S. W. (2005). Mindfulness research. In C. K. Germer, R. D. Siegel, et al. (Eds.), *Mindfulness and psychotherapy* (pp. 220–238). New York: Guilford.

Lazar, S. W., Bush, G., Gollub, R. L., et al. (2000). Functional brain mapping of the relaxation response and meditation. *Neuroreport, 11*(7), 1581–1585.

Lazarus, R. S. (1991a). Progress on a cognitive–motivational–relational theory of emotion. *American Psychologist, 46*(8), 819–834. doi:10.1037/0003-066X.46.8.819

Lazarus, R. S. (1991b). Cognition and motivation in emotion. *American Psychologist, 46*(4), 352–367. doi:10.1037/0003-066X.46.4.352

Le Pelley, M. E., Reimers, S. J., Calvini, G., et al. (2010). Stereotype formation: Biased by association. *Journal of Experimental Psychology: General, 139*(1), 138–161. doi:10.1037/a0018210

Le, T. N. (2011). Life satisfaction, openness value, self-transcendence, and wisdom. *Journal of Happiness Studies, 12*(2), 171–182. doi:10.1007/s10902-010-9182-1

Leal, M. C., Shin, Y. J., Laborde, M.-L., et al. (2003). Music perception in adult cochlear implant recipients. *Acta Oto-Laryngologica, 123*(7), 826–835. doi:10.1177/8755123312437050

Ledgerwood, A., & Trope, Y. (2010). Attitudes as global and local action guides. In J. P. Forgas, J., Cooper, & W. D. Crano (Eds.). *The psychology of attitudes and attitude change* (pp. 39–58). New York: Psychology Press.

LeDoux, J. E. (2000). Emotion circuits in the brain. *Annual Review of Neuroscience, 23,* 155–184. doi:10.1146/annurev.neuro.23.1.155

LeDoux, J. E., & Gorman, J. M. (2001). A call to action: Overcoming anxiety through active coping. *American Journal of Psychiatry. 158*(12), 1953–1955. doi:10.1176/appi.ajp.158.12.1953

Lee, M., Zimbardo, P. G., & Bertholf, M. (1977). Shy murderers. *Psychology Today, 11,* 69–70, 76, 148.

Lee, S. W., Clemenson, G. D., & Gage, F. H. (2011). New neurons in an aged brain. *Behavioural Brain Research,* doi:10.1016/j.bbr.2011.10.009.

Leenaars, A. A., Lester, D., & Wenckstern, S. (2005). Coping with suicide: The art and the research. In R. I. Yufit & D. Lester (Eds.), *Assessment, treatment, and prevention of suicidal behavior* (pp. 347–377). New York: Wiley.

Leeper, R. W. (1935). A study of a neglected portion of the field of learning: The development of sensory organization. *Pedagogical Seminary & Journal of Genetic Psychology, 46,* 41–75.

Lefcourt, H. M. (2003). Humor as a moderator of life stress in adults. In C. E. Schaefer (Ed.), *Play therapy with adults* (pp. 144–165). New York: Wiley.

Lefkowitz, E. S., & Zeldow, P. B. (2006). Masculinity and femininity predict optimal mental health: A belated test of the androgyny hypothesis. *Journal of Personality Assessment, 87*(1), 95–101. doi:10.1207/s15327752jpa8701_08

Lefrançois, G. R. (2012). *Theories of human learning: What the professors said* (6th ed.). Belmont, CA: Cengage Learning/Wadsworth.

Leiter, M. P., & Maslach, C. (2005). *Banishing burnout: Six strategies for improving your relationship with work.* San Francisco, CA: Jossey-Bass.

Leiter, M. P., Gascón, S., & Martínez-Jarreta, B. (2010). Making sense of work life: A structural model of burnout. *Journal of Applied Social Psychology, 40*(1), 57–75. doi:10.1111/j.1559-1816.2009.00563.x

Lejuez, C. W., Eifert, G. H., Zvolensky, M. J., et al. (2000). Preference between onset predictable and unpredictable administrations of 20% carbon-dioxide-enriched air: Implications for better understanding the etiology and treatment of panic disorder. *Journal of Experimental Psychology: Applied, 6*(4), 349–358. doi:10.1037/1076-898X.6.4.349

Lemma, A., Target, M., & Fonagy, P. (2011). The development of a brief psychodynamic intervention (dynamic interpersonal therapy) and its application to depression: A pilot study. *Psychiatry: Interpersonal & Biological Processes, 74*(1), 41–48. doi:10.1521/psyc.2011.74.1.41

Lemogne, C., Nabi, H., Zins, M., et al. (2010). Hostility may explain the association between depressive mood and mortality: Evidence from the French GAZEL cohort study. *Psychotherapy & Psychosomatics, 79*(3), 164–171. doi:10.1159/000286961

Lenton, A. P., & Bryan, A. (2005). An affair to remember: The role of sexual scripts in perceptions of sexual intent. *Personal Relationships, 12*(4), 483–498. doi:10.1111/j.1475-6811.2005.00127.x

Lenzenweger, M. F., & Gottesman, I. I. (1994). Schizophrenia. In V. S. Ramachandran (Ed.), *Encyclopedia of human behavior* (Vol 4, pp. 41–59). San Diego, CA: Academic.

León, I., & Hernández, J. A. (1998). Testing the role of attribution and appraisal in predicting own and other's emotions. *Cognition & Emotion, 12*(1), 27–43. doi:10.1080/026999398379763

Leor, J., Poole, W. K., & Kloner, R. A. (1996). Sudden cardiac death triggered by earthquake. *The New England Journal of Medicine, 334*(7), 413. doi:10.1056/NEJM199602033342514

Leotti, L. A., Iyengar, S. S., & Ochsner, K. N. (2010). Born to choose: The origins and value of the need for control. *Trends in Cognitive Sciences, 14*(10), 457–463. doi:10.1016/j.tics.2010.08.001

Lepage, J.-F., & Théret, H. (2007). The mirror neuron system: Grasping others' actions from birth? *Developmental Science, 10*(5), 513–523. doi:10.1111/j.1467-7687.2007.00631.x

Leppänen, J. M. (2011). Neural and developmental bases of the ability to recognize social signals of emotions. *Emotion Review, 3*(2), 179–188. doi:10.1177/1754073910387942

Lessow-Hurley, J. (2005). *Foundations of dual language instruction* (4th ed.). Boston: Allyn & Bacon.

Lester, D., & Yang, B. (2005). Regional and time-series studies of suicide in nations of the world. *Archives of Suicide Research, 9*(2), 123–133. doi:10.1080/13811110590903972

Lettvin, J. Y. (1961). Two remarks on the visual system of the frog. In W. Rosenblith (Ed.), *Sensory communication* (pp. 757–776). Cambridge, MA: MIT Press.

Leucht, S., Heres, S., Kissling, W., et al. (2011). Evidence-based pharmacotherapy of schizophrenia. *International Journal of Neuropsychopharmacology, 14*(2), 269–284. doi:10.1017/S1461145710001380

Leuner, B., & Gould, E. (2010). Structural plasticity and hippocampal function. *Annual Review of Psychology, 61*, 111–140. doi:10.1146/annurev.psych.093008.100359

LeUnes, A. (2008). *Sport psychology* (4th ed.). New York: Psychology Press.

Levant, R. F. (2001). Men and masculinity. In J. Worell (Ed.), *Encyclopedia of women and gender* (Vol. 2, pp. 717–727). San Diego: Academic Press.

Levant, R. F. (2003). Treating male alexithymia. In L. B. Silverstein, & T. J. Goodrich (Eds.), *Feminist family therapy: Empowerment in social context* (pp. 177–188). Washington, DC: American Psychological Association.

Levant, R. F., Good, G. E., Cook, S. W., et al. (2006). The Normative Male Alexithymia Scale: Measurement of a gender-linked syndrome. *Psychology of Men & Masculinity, 7*(4), 212–224. doi:10.1037/1524-9220.7.4.212

Levant, R. F., Hall, R. J., Williams, C. M., et al. (2009). Gender differences in alexithymia. *Psychology of Men & Masculinity, 10*(3), 190–203. doi:10.1037/a0015652

LeVay, S. (2011). *Gay, straight, and the reason why.* New York: Oxford University Press.

LeVay, S., & Baldwin, J. (2008). *Human sexuality* (3d ed.). Sunderland, MA: Sinauer Associates.

Levenson, E. A. (2012). Psychoanalysis and the rite of refusal. *Psychoanalytic Dialogues, 22*(1), 2–6. doi:10.1080/10481885.2012.646593

Levenston, G. K., Patrick, C. J., Bradley, M. M., et al. (2000). The psychopathic observer. *Journal of Abnormal Psychology, 109*, 373–385. doi:10.1037/0021-843X.109.3.373

Levesque, M. J., Steciuk, M., & Ledley, C. (2002). Self-disclosure patterns among well-acquainted individuals. *Social Behavior & Personality, 30*(6), 579–592. doi:10.2224/sbp.2002.30.6.579

Levett, L. M., Danielsen, E. M., Kovera, M. B., et al. (2005). The psychology of jury and juror decision making. In N. Brewer & K. D. Williams, (Eds.), *Psychology and law: An empirical perspective* (pp. 365–406). New York: Guilford

Levi, A. M. (1998). Are defendants guilty if they were chosen in a lineup? *Law & Human Behavior, 22*(4), 389–407. doi:10.1023/A:1025718909499

Levin, J. (2010). Gestalt therapy: Now and for tomorrow. *Gestalt Review, 14*(2), 147–170.

Levin, R., & Fireman, G. (2002). Nightmare prevalence, nightmare distress, and self-reported psychological disturbance. *Sleep: Journal of Sleep & Sleep Disorders Research, 25*(2), 205–212.

Levine, M., & Harrison, K. (2004). Media's role in the perpetuation and prevention of negative body image and disordered eating. In J. K. Thompson (Ed.), *Handbook of eating disorders and obesity* (pp. 695–717). New York: Wiley.

Levy, D. A. (2003). *Tools of critical thinking: Metathoughts for psychology.* Long Grove, IL: Waveland Press.

Levy, D. L., Coleman, M. J., Sung, H., et al. (2010). The genetic basis of thought disorder and language and communication disturbances in schizophrenia. *Journal of Neurolinguistics, 23*(3), 176–192. doi:10.1016/j.jneuroling.2009.08.003

Lew, A. R. (2011). Looking beyond the boundaries: Time to put landmarks back on the cognitive map? *Psychological Bulletin, 137*(3), 484–507. doi:10.1037/a0022315

Lewandowski, Jr., G. W., Aron, A., & Gee, J. (2007). Personality goes a long way: The malleability of opposite-sex physical attractiveness. *Personal Relationships, 14*(4), 571–585. doi:10.1111/j.1475-6811.2007.00172.x

Lewis, I., Watson, B., & White, K. M. (2009). Internet versus paper-and-pencil survey methods in psychological experiments: Equivalence testing of participant responses to health-related messages. *Australian Journal of Psychology, 61*(2), 107–116. doi:10.1080/00049530802105865

Lewis, M. (1995). Self-conscious emotions. *American Scientist, 83*(Jan–Feb), 68–78.

Leyendecker, B., Harwood, R. L., Comparini, L., et al. (2005). Socioeconomic status, ethnicity, and parenting. In T. Luster & L. Okagaki (Eds.), *Parenting: An ecological perspective* (2nd ed., pp. 319–341). Mahwah, NJ: Erlbaum.

Li, C., Ford, E. S., Zhao, G., et al. (2009). Associations of health risk factors and chronic illnesses with life dissatisfaction among U.S. adults: The Behavioral Risk Factor Surveillance System, 2006. *Preventive Medicine, 49*(2–3), 253–259. doi:10.1016/j.ypmed.2009.05.012

Lichtman, A. H., & Martin, B. R. (2006). Understanding the pharmacology and physiology of cannabis dependence In R. Roffman & R. S. Stephens (Eds.), *Cannabis dependence. Its nature, consequences and treatment* (pp. 37–57). New York: Cambridge University Press.

Lickliter, R., & Honeycutt, H. (2010). Rethinking epigenesis and evolution in light of developmental science. In M. S. Blumberg, J. H. Freeman, et al., (Eds.), *Oxford handbook of developmental behavioral neuroscience* (pp. 30–47). New York: Oxford University Press.

Liddell, S. K. (2003). *Grammar, gesture and meaning in American Sign Language.* Cambridge, MA: Cambridge University Press.

Liles, E. E., & Packman, J. (2009). Play therapy for children with fetal alcohol syndrome. *International Journal of Play Therapy, 18*(4), 192–206. doi:10.1037/a0015664

Lilienfeld, S. O., Ammirati, R., & Landfield, K. (2009). Giving debiasing away: Can psychological research on correcting cognitive errors promote human welfare? *Perspectives on Psychological Science, 4*(4), 390–398. doi:10.1111/j.1745-6924.2009.01144.x

Lilienfeld, S. O., Lynn, S. J., Ruscio, J., et al. (2010). *50 great myths of popular psychology: Shattering widespread misconceptions about human behavior.* London: Wiley-Blackwell.

Lilienfeld, S. O., Ruscio, J., & Lynn, S. J. (Eds.). (2008). *Navigating the mindfield: A user's guide to distinguishing science from pseudoscience in mental health.* Buffalo, NY: Prometheus Books.

Lin, F. R., Thorpe, R., Gordon-Salant, S., et al. (2011). Hearing loss prevalence and risk factors among older adults in the United States. *The Journals of Gerontology: Series A: Biological Sciences & Medical Sciences, 66A*(5), 582–590. doi:10.1093/gerona/glr002

Lin, T., & Peng, T. K. (2010). From organizational citizenship behaviour to team performance: The mediation of group cohesion and collective efficacy. *Management & Organization Review, 6*(1), 55–75. doi:10.1111/j.1740-8784.2009.00172.x

Lindemann, B. (2001). Receptors and transduction in taste. *Nature, 413*, 219–225. doi:10.1038/35093032

Linden, W. (2005). *Stress management: From basic science to better practice.* Thousand Oaks, CA: Sage.

Linderoth, B., & Foreman, R. D. (2006). Mechanisms of spinal cord stimulation in painful syndromes: Role of animal models. *Pain Medicine, 7*(Suppl. 1), S14–S26. doi:10.1111/j.1526-4637.2006.00119.x

Lindsey, B. J., Fabiano, P., & Stark, C. (2009). The prevalence and correlates of depression among college students. *College Student Journal, 43*(4, PtA), 999–1014.

Lipka, J., Miltner, W. H. R., & Straube, T. (2011). Vigilance for threat interacts with amygdala responses to subliminal threat cues in specific phobia. *Biological Psychiatry, 70*(5), 472–478. doi:10.1016/j.biopsych.2011.04.005

Lippke, S., Nigg, C. R., & Maddock, J. E. (2012). Health-promoting and health-risk behaviors: Theory-driven analyses of multiple health behavior change in three international samples. *International Journal of Behavioral Medicine, 19*(1), 1–13. doi:10.1007/s12529-010-9135-4

Lipsey, M. W., & Wilson, D. B. (1993). The efficacy of psychological, educational, and behavioral treatment: Confirmation from meta-analysis. *American Psychologist, 48*, 1181–1209. doi:10.1037/0003-066X.48.12.1181

Liu, Y., Gao, J., Liu, H., et al. (2000). The temporal response of the brain after eating revealed by functional MRI. *Nature, 405*, 1058–1062. doi:10.1038/35016590

Livingston, I, Doyle, J., & Mangan, D. (2010, April 25). Stabbed hero dies as more than 20 people stroll past him. *New York Post.* Retrieved May 9, 2012, from http://www.nypost.com/p/news/local/queens/passers_by_let_good_sam_die_5SGkf5XDP5oooudVuEd8fbI

Lodi-Smith, J., Geise, A. C., Roberts, B. W., et al. (2009). Narrating personality change. *Journal of Personality & Social Psychology, 96*(3), 679–689. doi:10.1037/a0014611

Loeber, R., & Hay, D. (1997). Key issues in the development of aggression and violence from childhood to early adulthood. *Annual Review of Psychology, 48*, 371–410. doi:10.1146/annurev.psych.48.1.371

Loehlin, J. C., McCrae, R. R., Costa, P. T., et al. (1998). Heritabilities of common and measure-specific components of the Big Five personality factors. *Journal of Research in Personality, 32*(4), 431–453. doi:10.1006/jrpe.1998.2225

Loftus, E. F. (2003). Make-believe memories. *American Psychologist, 58*(11), 867–873. doi:10.1037/0003-066X.58.11.867

Loftus, E. F., & Bernstein, D. M. (2005). Rich false memories: The royal road to success. In A. F. Healy (Ed.), *Experimental cognitive psychology and its applications* (pp. 101–113). Washington, DC: American Psychological Association.

Loftus, E. F., & Ketcham, K. (1994). *The myth of repressed memory: False memories and allegations of abuse* (pp. 101–113). New York: St. Martin's Press.

Loftus, E. F., & Palmer, J. C. (1974). Reconstruction of automobile destruction: An example of interaction between language and memory. *Journal of Verbal Learning & Verbal Behavior, 13*, 585–589. doi:10.1016/S0022-5371(74)80011-3

Lokuge, S., Frey, B. N., Foster, J. A., et al. (2011). Depression in women: Windows of vulnerability and new insights into the link between estrogen and serotonin. *Journal of Clinical Psychiatry, 72*(11), 1563–1569. doi:10.4088/JCP.11com07089

LoLordo, V. M. (2001). Learned helplessness and depression. In M. E. Carroll, & J. B. Overmier (Eds.), *Animal research and human health: Advancing human welfare through behavioral science* (pp. 63–77). Washington: American Psychological Association.

Long, C. R., Seburn, M., Averill, J. R., et al. (2003). Solitude experiences: Varieties, settings, and individual differences. *Personality & Social Psychology Bulletin, 29*(5), 578–583. doi:10.1177/0146167203029005003

Long, V. O. (1989). Relation of masculinity to self-esteem and self-acceptance in male professionals, college students, and clients. *Journal of Counseling Psychology, 36*(1), 84–87. doi:10.1037/0022-0167.36.1.84

López, S. R., & Guarnaccia, P. J. J. (2000). Cultural psychopathology. *Annual Review of Psychology, 51,* 571–598. doi:10.1146/annurev. psych.51.1.571

Lorenzo, G. L., Biesanz, J. C., & Human, L. J. (2010). What is beautiful is good and more accurately understood: Physical attractiveness and accuracy in first impressions of personality. *Psychological Science, 21*(12), 1777–1782. doi:10.1177/0956797610388048

Lounsbury, D. W., & Mitchell, S. G. (2009). Introduction to special issue on social ecological approaches to community health research and action. *American Journal of Community Psychology, 44*(3–4), 213–220. doi:10.1007/ s10464-009-9266-4

Lovaas, O., & Simmons, J. (1969). Manipulation of self-destruction in three retarded children. *Journal of Applied Behavior Analysis, 2,* 143–157. doi:10.1901/jaba.1969.2-143

Low, K. G., & Feissner, J. M. (1998). Seasonal affective disorder in college students: Prevalence and latitude. *Journal of American College Health, 47*(3), 135–137.

Lucas, R. E., & Diener, E. (2009). In E. Diener (Ed.), *Personality and subjective well-being* (pp. 75–102). New York: Springer.

Lucas, R. E., Clark, A. E., Georgellis, Y., et al. (2003). Reexamining adaptation and the set point model of happiness: Reactions to changes in marital status. *Journal of Personality & Social Psychology, 84*(3), 527–539. doi:10.1037/0022-3514.84.3.527

Lum, D. (2011). *Culturally competent practice: A framework for understanding* (4th ed.). Belmont, CA: Cengage Learning/Wadsworth.

Lum, J. A. G., & Bleses, D. (2012). Declarative and procedural memory in Danish speaking children with specific language impairment. *Journal of Communication Disorders, 45*(1), 46–58. doi:10.1016/j.jcomdis. 2011.09.001

Lumia, A. R., & McGinnis, M. Y. (2010). Impact of anabolic androgenic steroids on adolescent males. *Physiology & Behavior, 100*(3), 199–204. doi:10.1016/j. physbeh.2010.01.007

Lumley, M. A. (2004). Alexithymia, emotional disclosure, and health: A program of research. *Journal of Personality, 72*(6), 1271–1300. doi:10.1111/j.1467-6494.2004.00297.x

Lundh, L., Berg, B., Johansson, H., et al. (2002). Social anxiety is associated with a negatively distorted perception of one's own voice. *Cognitive Behaviour Therapy, 31*(1), 25–30. doi:10.1080/16506070252823634

Luppa, M., Heinrich, S., Angermeyer, M. C., et al. (2007). Cost-of-illness studies of depression A systematic review. *Journal of Affective Disorders, 98*(1–2), 29–43. doi:10.1016/j. jad.2006.07.017

Luria, A. R. (1968). *The mind of a mnemonist.* New York: Basic.

Lutter, M. (2007). Book review: Winning a lottery brings no happiness! *Journal of Happiness Studies, 8*(1), 155–160. doi:10.1007/s10902-006-9033-2

Luyten, P., & Blatt, S. J. (2011). Integrating theory-driven and empirically-derived models of personality development and psychopathology: A proposal for DSM-V. *Clinical Psychology Review, 31*(1), 52–68. doi:10.1016/j.cpr.2010. 09.003

Lykken, D. T. (1998). *A tremor in the blood: Uses and abuses of the lie detector.* New York: Plenum.

Lykken, D. T. (2001). Lie detection. In W. E. Craighead, & C. B. Nemeroff (Eds.), *The Corsini encyclopedia of psychology and behavioral science* (3rd ed., pp. 878–880). New York: Wiley.

Lyn, H., Franks, B., & Savage-Rumbaugh, E. S. (2008). Precursors of morality in the use of the symbols "good" and "bad" in two bonobos *(Pan paniscus)* and a chimpanzee *(Pan troglodytes). Language & Communication, 28*(3), 213–224. doi:10.1016/j. langcom.2008.01.006

Lynch, K. B., Geller, S. R., & Schmidt, M. G. (2004). Multi-year evaluation of the effectiveness of a resilience-based prevention program for young children. *Journal of Primary Prevention, 24*(3), 335–353. doi:10.1023/ B:JOPP.0000018052.12488.d1

Lynch, T. R., Robins, C. J., Morse, J. Q., et al. (2001). A mediational model relating affect intensity, emotion inhibition, and psychological distress. *Behavior Therapy, 32*(3), 519–536. doi:10.1016/S0005-7894(01)80034-4

Lynn, S. J., & Kirsch, I. (2006). Introduction: Definitions and early history. In S. J. Lynn & I. Kirsch (Eds.), *Essentials of clinical hypnosis: An evidence-based approach* (pp. 3–15). Washington, DC: American Psychological Association.

Lynn, S. J., & O'Hagen, S. (2009). The sociocognitive and conditioning and inhibition theories of hypnosis. *Contemporary Hypnosis, 26*(2), 121–125. doi:10.1002/ch.378

Lynne-Landsman, S. D., Graber, J. A., et al. (2011). Is sensation seeking a stable trait or does it change over time? *Journal of Youth & Adolescence, 40*(1), 48–58. doi: 10.1007/ s10964-010-9529-2

Lyons, R. (2011). The spread of evidence-poor medicine via flawed social-network analysis. *Statistics, Politics, & Policy, 2*(1). doi: 10.2202/ 2151-7509.1024.

Lyubomirsky, S., & Tucker, K. L. (1998). Implications of individual differences in subjective happiness for perceiving, interpreting, and thinking about life events. *Motivation & Emotion, 22*(2), 155–186. doi:10.1023/A: 1021396422190

Maas, J. (1999). *Power Sleep.* New York: HarperCollins.

MacDuffie, K., & Mashour, G. A. (2010). Dreams and the temporality of consciousness. *American Journal of Psychology, 123*(2), 189–197. doi:10.5406/amerjpsyc.123.2.0189

Macht, M., & Simons, G. (2011). Emotional eating. In I. Nykliĉek, A. Vingerhoets, & M. Zeelenberg (Eds.), *Emotion regulation and well-being* (pp. 281–295). New York: Springer.

MacIver, K., Lloyd, D. M., Kelly, S., et al. (2008). Phantom limb pain, cortical reorganization and the therapeutic effect of mental imagery. *Brain: A Journal of Neurology, 131*(8), 2181–2191. doi:10.1093/brain/ awn124

MacKay, D. G., & Hadley, C. (2009). Supra-normal age-linked retrograde amnesia: Lessons from an older amnesic (H.M.). *Hippocampus, 19*(5), 424–445. doi:10.1002/hipo.20531

Macklin, C. B., & McDaniel, M. A. (2005). The bizarreness effect: Dissociation between item and source memory. *Memory, 13*(7), 662–689. doi:10.1080/09658210444000304

Maddi, S. R. (2006). Hardiness: The courage to grow from stresses. *Journal of Positive Psychology, 1*(3), 160–168. doi:10.1080/17439760600619609

Maddi, S. R., Harvey, R. H., Khoshaba, D. M., et al. (2009). The personality construct of hardiness, IV: Expressed in positive cognitions and emotions concerning oneself and developmentally relevant activities. *Journal of Humanistic Psychology, 49*(3), 292–305. doi:10. 1177/0022167809331860

Maddock, J. E., Laforge, R. G., Rossi, J. S., et al. (2001). The College Alcohol Problems Scale. *Addictive Behaviors, 26,* 385–398. doi:10.1016/ S0306-4603(00)00116-7

Maddock, J., & Glanz, K. (2005). The relationship of proximal normative beliefs and global subjective norms to college students' alcohol consumption. *Addictive Behaviors, 30*(2), 315–323. doi:10.1016/j. addbeh.2004.05.021

Maddox, K. B. (2004). Perspectives on racial phenotypicality bias. *Personality & Social Psychology Review, 8*(4), 383–401. doi:10.1207/ s15327957pspr0804_4

Maggin, D. M., Chafouleas, S. M., Goddard, K. M., et al. (2011). A systematic evaluation of token economies as a classroom management tool for students with challenging behavior. *Journal of School Psychology, 49*(5), 529–554. doi:10.1016/j.jsp.2011.05.001

Maguire, E. A., Valentine, E. R., Wilding, J. M., et al. (2003). Routes to remembering: The brains behind superior memory. *Nature Neuroscience, 6*(1), 90–95. doi:10.1038/nn988

Mah, K., & Binik, Y. M. (2001). The nature of human orgasm: A critical review of major trends. *Clinical Psychology Review, 21*(6), 823–856. doi:10.1016/S0272-7358(00)00069-6

Mahler, H. I. M., Beckerley, S. E., & Vogel, M. T. (2010). Effects of media images on attitudes toward tanning. *Basic & Applied Social Psychology, 32*(2), 118–127. doi:10.1080/ 01973531003738296

Mahoney, A. E. J., & McEvoy, P. M. (2012). Changes in intolerance of uncertainty during cognitive behavior group therapy for social phobia. *Journal of Behavior Therapy & Experimental Psychiatry, 43*(2), 849–854. doi:10.1016/j.jbtep.2011.12.004

Maier, N. R. F. (1949). *Frustration.* New York: McGraw-Hill.

Mailis-Gagnon, A., & Israelson, D. (2005). *Beyond pain: Making the mind–body connection.* Ann Arbor: University of Michigan Press.

Maio, G. R., & Haddock, G. (2009). *The psychology of attitudes and attitude change.* Thousand Oaks, CA: Sage.

Maisel, E. (2011). The DSM-5 controversy. *Psychology Today, October 28.* Retrieved April 20, 2012, from http://www.psychologytoday. com/blog/rethinking-depression/ 201110/the-dsm-5-controversy

Maisto, S. A., Galizio, M., & Connors, G. J. (2011). *Drug use and abuse* (6th ed.). Belmont, CA: Cengage Learning/Wadsworth.

Malaspina, D., Reichenberg, A., Weiser, M., et al. (2005). Paternal age and intelligence: Implications for age-related genomic changes in male germ cells. *Psychiatric Genetics, 15*(2), 117–125. doi:10.1097/ 00041444-200506000-00008

Malhi, G. S., Tanious, M., Das, P., et al. (2012). The science and practice of lithium therapy. *Australian and New Zealand Journal of Psychiatry, 46*(3), 192–211. doi:10.1177/ 0004867412437346

Malloy, K. M., & Milling, L. S. (2010). The effectiveness of virtual reality distraction for pain reduction: A systematic review. *Clinical Psychology Review, 30*(8), 1011–1018. doi:10.1016/j.cpr.2010.07.001

Mamen, M. (2004). *Pampered child syndrome: How to recognize it, how to manage it and how to avoid it.* Carp, ON: Creative Bound.

Manber, R., Kraemer, H. C., Arnow, B. A., et al. (2008). Faster remission of chronic depression with combined psychotherapy and medication than with each therapy alone. *Journal of Consulting & Clinical Psychology, 76*(3), 459–467. doi:10.1037/0022-006X.76.3.459

Mandler, J. M., & McDonough, L. (1998). On developing a knowledge base in infancy. *Developmental Psychology, 34*(6), 1274–1288. doi:10.1037/0012-1649.34.6.1274

Mangan, M. A. (2004). A phenomenology of problematic sexual behavior occurring in sleep. *Archives of Sexual Behavior, 33*(3), 287–293. doi:10.1023/B:ASEB.0000026628. 95803.98

Mangels, J. A., Picton, T. W., & Craik, F. I. M. (2001). Attention and successful episodic encoding: An event-related potential study. *Brain Research, 11,* 77–95. doi:10.1016/ S0926-6410(00)00066-5

Manne, S. (2003). Coping and social support. In A. Nezu, C. Nezu, & P. Geller (Eds.), *Handbook of health psychology* (Vol. 9, pp. 51–74). New York: Wiley.

Manning, R., Levine, M., & Collins, A. (2007). The Kitty Genovese murder and the social psychology of helping: The parable of the 38 witnesses. *American Psychologist, 62*(6), 555–562. doi:10.1037/0003-066X.62.6.555

Manschreck, T. C. (1996). Delusional disorder: The recognition and management of paranoia. *Journal of Clinical Psychiatry, 57*(3, Suppl), 32–38.

Mansouri, A., & Adityanjee. (1995). Delusion of pregnancy in males: A case report and literature review. *Psychopathology, 28*(6), 307–311. doi:10.1159/000284942

Mantovani, A., Simpson, H. B., Fallon, B. A., et al. (2010). Randomized sham-controlled trial of repetitive transcranial magnetic stimulation in treatment-resistant obsessive-compulsive disorder. *International Journal of Neuropsychopharmacology, 13*(2), 217–227. doi:10.1017/S1461145709990435

Mantyla, T. (1986). Optimizing cue effectiveness: Recall of 600 incidentally learned words. *Journal of Experimental Psychology: Learning, Memory, & Cognition, 12*(1), 66–71. doi:10.1037/0278-7393.12.1.66

Maran, M. (2010). *My lie: A true story of false memory.* San Francisco: Jossey-Bass/Wiley.

Marcel, M. (2005). *Freud's traumatic memory: Reclaiming seduction theory and revisiting Oedipus.* Pittsburgh, PA: Duquesne University Press.

Margolin, G., & Gordis, E. B. (2000). The effects of family and community violence on children. *Annual Review of Psychology, 51*, 445–479. doi:10.1146/annurev.psych.51.1.445

Markoff, J. (2011). Computer wins on 'Jeopardy!': Trivial, it's not. *New York Times, February 16*, A1. Retrieved May 9, 2012, from http://www.nytimes.com/2011/02/17/science/17jeopardy-watson.html

Markowitz, F. E. (2011). Mental illness, crime, and violence: Risk, context, and social control. *Aggression & Violent Behavior, 16*, 36–44. doi:10.1016/j.avb.2010.10.003

Marks, D. F. (2000). *The psychology of the psychic.* Buffalo, NY: Prometheus.

Markus H. R., Ryff, C. D., Curhan, K., et al. (2004). In their own words: Well-being at midlife among high school and college educated adults. In O. G. Brim, C. D. Ryff, & R. C. Kessler (Eds.), *How healthy are we? A national study of well-being at midlife* (pp. 273–319). Chicago: University of Chicago Press.

Markus, H. R., Uchida, Y., Omoregie, H., et al. (2006). Going for the gold: Models of agency in Japanese and American contexts. *Psychological Science, 17*(2), 103–112. doi:10.1111/j.1467-9280.2006.01672.x

Markus, H., & Nurius, P. (1986). Possible selves. *American Psychologist, 41*, 954–969. doi:10.1037/0003-066X.41.9.954

Marshall, R. D., Bryant, R. A., Amsel, L., et al. (2007). The psychology of ongoing threat: Relative risk appraisal, the September 11 attacks, and terrorism-related fears. *American Psychologist, 62*(4), 304–316. doi:10.1037/0003-066X.62.4.304

Marsiglia, F. F., Kulis, S., Hecht, M. L., et al. (2004). Ethnicity and ethnic identity as predictors of drug norms and drug use among preadolescents in the US southwest. *Substance Use & Misuse, 39*(7), 1061–1094. doi:10.1081/JA-120038030

Martens, R., & Trachet, T. (1998). *Making sense of astrology.* Amherst, MA: Prometheus.

Martin, A. J., & Marsh, H. W. (2003). Fear of failure: Friend or foe? *Australian Psychologist, 38*(1), 31–38. doi:10.1080/0005006031000170699

Martin, E., & Weiss, K. J. (2010). Knowing moral and legal wrong in an insanity defense. *Journal of the American Academy of Psychiatry & the Law, 38*(2), 286–288.

Martin, G., & Pear, J. (2011). *Behavior modification: What it is and how to do it* (9th ed.). Upper Saddle River, NJ: Prentice-Hall.

Martin, L. R., Friedman, H. S., & Schwartz, J. E. (2007). Personality and mortality risk across the life span: The importance of conscientiousness as a biopsychosocial attribute. *Health Psychology, 26*(4), 428–436. doi:10.1037/0278-6133.26.4.428

Martin, W. L. B., & Freitas, M. B. (2002). Mean mortality among Brazilian left- and right-handers: Modification or selective elimination. *Laterality, 7*(1), 31–44. doi:10.1080/13576500143000104

Martinez-Gonzalez, M. A., Gual, P., Lahortiga, F., et al. (2003). Parental factors, mass media influences, and the onset of eating disorders in a prospective population-based cohort. *Pediatrics, 111*, 315–320. doi:10.1542/peds.111.2.315

Martynhak, B. J., Louzada, F. M., Pedrazzoli, M., et al. (2010). Does the chronotype classification need to be updated? Preliminary findings. *Chronobiology International, 27*(6), 1329–1334. doi:10.3109/07420528.2010.490314

Marx, B. P. (2009). Posttraumatic stress disorder and Operations Enduring Freedom and Iraqi Freedom: Progress in a time of controversy. *Clinical Psychology Review, 29*(8), 671–673. doi:10.1016/j.cpr.2009.02.004

Mashour, G. A., Walker, E. E., & Martuza, R. L. (2005). Psychosurgery: Past, present, and future. *Brain Research Reviews, 48*(3), 409–419. doi:10.1016/j.brainresrev.2004.09.002

Maslach, C., Schaufeli, W. B., & Leiter, M. P. (2001). Job burnout. *Annual Review of Psychology, 52*, 397–422. doi:10.1146/annurev.psych.52.1.397

Maslow, A. H. (1954). *Motivation and personality.* New York: Harper.

Maslow, A. H. (1967). Self-actualization and beyond. In J. F. T. Bugental (Ed.), *Challenges of humanistic psychology* (pp. 279–286). New York: McGraw-Hill.

Maslow, A. H. (1969). *The psychology of science.* Chicago: Henry Regnery.

Maslow, A. H. (1970). *Motivation and personality.* New York: Harper & Row.

Maslow, A. H. (1971). *The farther reaches of human nature.* New York: Viking.

Masquelier, G. (2006). *Gestalt therapy: Living creatively today.* Hove, UK: Psychology Press.

Masse, L. C. & Tremblay, R. E. (1997). Behavior of boys in kindergarten and the onset of substance use during adolescence. *Archives of General Psychiatry, 54*(1), 62–68. doi:10.1001/archpsyc.1997.01830130068014

Masters, J. L., & Holley, L. M. (2006). A glimpse of life at 67: The modified future-self worksheet. *Educational Gerontology, 32*(4), 261–269. doi:10.1080/03601270500494022

Masters, W. H., & Johnson, V. E. (1966). *Human sexual response.* Boston: Little, Brown.

Masters, W. H., & Johnson, V. E. (1970). *The pleasure bond: A new look at sexuality and commitment.* Boston: Little, Brown.

Masuda, T., Gonzalez, R., Kwan, L., et al. (2008). Culture and aesthetic preference: Comparing the attention to context of East Asians and Americans. *Personality & Social Psychology Bulletin, 34*(9), 1260–1275. doi:10.1177/0146167208320555

Mather, G. (2011). *Foundations of sensation and perception* (3rd ed.). Hove, UK: Psychology Press.

Mathy, F., & Feldman, J. (2012). What's magic about magic numbers? Chunking and data compression in short-term memory. *Cognition, 122*(3), 346–362. doi:10.1016/j.cognition.2011.11.003

Matossian, M. K. (1982). Ergot and the Salem witchcraft affair. *American Scientist, 70*, 355–357.

Matson, J. L., & Boisjoli, J. A. (2009). The token economy for children with intellectual disability and/or autism: A review. *Research in Developmental Disabilities, 30*(2), 240–248. doi:10.1016/j.ridd.2008.04.001

Matsumoto, D, & Juang, L. (2013). *Culture and psychology* (5th ed.). Belmont, CA: Cengage Learning/Wadsworth.

Mattanah, J. F., Lopez, F. G., & Govern, J. M. (2011). The contributions of parental attachment bonds to college student development and adjustment: A meta-analytic review. *Journal of Counseling Psychology, 58*, 565–596. doi:10.1037/a0024635

Matthew, C. T., & Sternberg, R. J. (2009). Developing experience-based (tacit) knowledge through reflection. *Learning & Individual Differences, 19*, 530–540. doi:10.1016/j.lindif.2009.07.001

Matthews, G., Deary, I. J., & Whiteman, M. C. (2009). *Personality traits* (3rd ed.). New York: Cambridge University Press.

Matthews, K. A., & Gallo, L. C. (2011). Psychological perspectives on pathways linking socioeconomic status and physical health. *Annual Review of Psychology, 62*, 501–530. doi:10.1146/annurev.psych.031809.130711

Matthews, P. H., & Matthews, M. S. (2004). Heritage language instruction and giftedness in language minority students: Pathways toward success. *Journal of Secondary Gifted Education, 15*(2), 50–55. doi:10.4219/jsge-2004-448

Mayer, J. D. (2005). A tale of two visions: Can a new view of personality help integrate psychology? *American Psychologist, 60*(4), 294–307. doi:10.1037/0003-066X.60.4.294

Mayer, J. D., Salovey, P., Caruso, D. R., et al. (2001). Emotional intelligence as standard intelligence. *Emotion, 1*(3), 232–242. doi:10.1037/1528-3542.1.3.232

Mayer, R. E. (1995). *Thinking, problem solving, and cognition.* New York: Freeman.

Mayer, R. E. (2004). Should there be a three-strikes rule against pure discovery learning? *American Psychologist, 59*(1), 14–19. doi:10.1037/0003-066X.59.1.14

Mayer, R. E. (2011). *Applying the science of learning.* Boston: Allyn & Bacon.

Mazzoni, G., Heap, M., & Scoboria, A. (2010). Hypnosis and memory: Theory, laboratory research, and applications. In S. J. Lynn, J. W. Rhue, et al. (Eds.), *Handbook of clinical hypnosis* (2nd ed., pp. 709–741). Washington, DC: American Psychological Association.

McAdams, D. P., & Pals, J. L. (2006). A new Big Five: Fundamental principles for an integrative science of personality. *American Psychologist, 61*(3), 204–217. doi:10.1037/0003-066X.61.3.204

McBurney, D. H., & White, T. L. (2010). *Research methods* (8th ed.). Belmont, CA: Cengage Learning/Wadsworth.

McCabe S. E., Knight, J.R., Teter, C.J., et al. (2005). Non-medical use of prescription stimulants among US college students: prevalence and correlates from a national survey. *Addiction, 100*, 96–106. doi:10.1111/j.1360-0443.2005.00944.x

McCabe, M. P., & Ricciardelli, L. A. (2004). Weight and shape concerns of boys and men. In Thompson, J. K. (Ed.), *Handbook of eating disorders and obesity* (pp. 606–634). New York: Wiley.

McCall, W. V., Prudic, J., Olfson, M., et al. (2006). Health-related quality of life following ECT in a large community sample. *Journal of Affective Disorders, 90*(2–3), 269–274. doi:10.1016/j.jad.2005.12.002

McCall, W. V., Rosenquist, P. B., Kimball, J., et al. (2011). Health-related quality of life in a clinical trial of ECT followed by continuation pharmacotherapy: Effects immediately after ECT and at 24 weeks. *The Journal of ECT, 27*(2), 97–102. doi:10.1097/YCT.0b013e318205c7d7

McCalley, L. T., de Vries, P. W., & Midden, C. J. H. (2011). Consumer response to product-integrated energy feedback: Behavior, goal level shifts, and energy conservation. *Environment and Behavior, 43*(4), 525–545. doi:10.1177/0013916510371053

McCarthy, B. W., & Fucito, L. M. (2005). Integrating medication, realistic expectations, and therapeutic interventions in the treatment of male sexual dysfunction. *Journal of Sex & Marital Therapy, 31*(4), 319–328. doi:10.1080/00926230590950226

McClelland, D. C. (1961). *The achieving society.* New York: Van Nostrand.

McClelland, D. C. (1975). *Power: The inner experience.* New York: Irvington.

McClelland, D. C. (1994). The knowledge-testing-educational complex strikes back. *American Psychologist, 49*(1), 66–69. doi:10.1037/0003-066X.49.1.66

McClelland, D. C., & Cheriff, A. D. (1997). The immunoenhancing effects of humor on secretory IgA and resistance to respiratory infections. *Psychology & Health*, *12*(3), 329–344. doi:10.1080/0887044970840671

McClelland, D. C., & Pilon, D. A. (1983). Sources of adult motives in patterns of parent behavior in early childhood. *Journal of Personality & Social Psychology*, *44*, 564–574. doi:10.1037/0022-3514.44.3.564

McClung, C. A. (2011). Circadian rhythms and mood regulation: Insights from pre-clinical models. *European Neuropsychopharmacology*, *21*, S683–S693. doi:10.1016/j.euroneuro.2011.07.008

McCluskey, U. (2002). The dynamics of attachment and systems-centered group psychotherapy. *Group Dynamics*, *6*(2), 131–142. doi:10.1037/1089-2699.6.2.131

McCormick, N. B. (2010). Sexual scripts: Social and therapeutic implications. *Sexual & Relationship Therapy*, *25*(1), 96–120. doi:10.1080/14681990903550167

McCrae, R. R., & Costa, P. T. (2001). A five-factor theory of personality. In L. A. Pervin & O. P. John (Eds.), *Handbook of personality* (pp. 139–153). New York: Guilford.

McDaniel, M. A., Maier, S. F., & Einstein, G. O. (2002). "Brain-specific" nutrients: A memory cure? *Psychological Science in the Public Interest*, *3*(1), 12–38. doi:10.1111/1529-1006.00007

McDermott, R., Johnson, D., Cowden, J., et al. (2007). Testosterone and aggression in a simulated crisis game. *Annals of the American Academy of Political & Social Science*, *614*(1), 15–33. doi:10.1177/0002716207305268

McGaugh, J. L., & Roozendaal, B. (2009). Drug enhancement of memory consolidation: Historical perspective and neurobiological implications. *Psychopharmacology*, *202*(1–3), 3–14. doi:10.1007/s00213-008-1285-6

McGrath, R. E., & Carroll, E. J. (2012). The current status of "projective" "tests". In H. Cooper (Ed.), *APA handbook of research methods in psychology: Foundations, planning, measures, and psychometrics* (Vol. 1, pp. 329–348). Washington, DC: American Psychological Association.

McGrath, R. E., & Moore, B. A. (Eds.). (2010). *Pharmacotherapy for psychologists: Prescribing and collaborative roles*. Washington, DC: American Psychological Association.

McGregor, I., McAdams, D. P., & Little, B. R. (2006). Personal projects, life stories, and happiness: On being true to traits. *Journal of Research in Personality*, *40*(5), 551–572. doi:10.1016/j.jrp.2005.05.002

McIntosh, W. D., Harlow, T. F., & Martin, L. L. (1995). Linkers and nonlinkers: Goal beliefs as a moderator of the effects of everyday hassles on rumination, depression, and physical complaints. *Journal of Applied Social Psychology*, *25*(14), 1231–1244. doi:10.1111/j.1559-1816.1995.tb02616.x

McKay, A. (2005). Sexuality and substance use: The impact of tobacco, alcohol, and selected recreational drugs on sexual function. *Canadian Journal of Human Sexuality*, *14*(1–2), 47–56.

McKay, E. (2008). *The human-dimensions of human-computer interaction: Balancing the HCI equation*. Amsterdam, Netherlands: IOS Press.

McKeever, L. (2006). Online plagiarism detection services: Saviour or scourge? *Assessment & Evaluation in Higher Education*, *31*(2), 155–165. doi:10.1080/02602930500262460

McKeever, W. F. (2000). A new family handedness sample with findings consistent with X-linked transmission. *British Journal of Psychology*, *91*(1), 21–39. doi:10.1348/000712600161655

McKenna, M. W., & Ossoff, E. P. (1998). Age differences in children's comprehension of a popular television program. *Child Study Journal*, *28*(1), 52–68.

McKim, W. A. (2007). *Drugs and behavior* (6th ed.). Englewood Cliffs, NJ: Prentice Hall.

McLay, R. N., & Spira, J. L. (2009). Use of a portable biofeedback device to improve insomnia in a combat zone, a case report. *Applied Psychophysiology & Biofeedback*, *34*(4), 319–321. doi:10.1007/s10484-009-9104-3

McLewin, L. A., & Muller, R. T. (2006). Childhood trauma, imaginary companions, and the development of pathological dissociation. *Aggression & Violent Behavior*, *11*(5), 531–545. doi:10.1016/j.avb.2006.02.001

McLoyd, V. C., & Smith, J. (2002). Physical discipline and behavior problems in African American, European American, and Hispanic children: Emotional support as a moderator. *Journal of Marriage & Family*, *64*(1), 40–53. doi:10.1111/j.1741-3737.2002.00040.x

McMahon, S., & Koltzenburg, M. (2005). *Wall & Melzacks textbook of pain* (5th ed.). London: Churchill Livingstone.

McManus, I. C., Moore, J., Freegard, M., et al. (2010). Science in the making: Right hand, left hand. III: Estimating historical rates of left-handedness. *Laterality: Asymmetries of Body, Brain & Cognition*, *15*(1–2), 186–208. doi:10.1080/13576500802565313

McNally, R. J., & Clancy, S. A. (2005). Sleep paralysis, sexual abuse, and space alien abduction. *Transcultural Psychiatry*, *42*(1), 113–122. doi:10.1177/1363461505050715

McNally, R. J., Clancy, S. A., & Barrett, H. M. (2004). Forgetting trauma? In D. Reisberg & P. Hertel (Eds.), *Memory & emotion* (pp. 129–154). New York: Oxford University Press.

McNamara, D. S., & Scott, J. L. (2001). Working memory capacity and strategy use. *Memory & Cognition*, *29*(1), 10–17. doi:10.3758/BF03195736

McNamara, P. (2011). *Spirit possession and exorcism: History, psychology, and neurobiology* (Vols. 1 & 2). Westport, CT: Praeger.

Mcquaid, N. E., Bibok, M. B., & Carpendale, J. I. M. (2009). Relation between maternal contingent responsiveness and infant social expectations. *Infancy*, *14*(3), 390–401. doi:10.1080/15250000902839955

McRobbie, H., & Hajek, P. (2007). Effects of rapid smoking on post-cessation urges to smoke. *Addiction*, *102*(3), 483–489. doi:10.1111/j.1360-0443.2006.01730.x

McVea, C. S., Gow, K., & Lowe, R. (2011). Corrective interpersonal experience in psychodrama group therapy: A comprehensive process analysis of significant therapeutic events. *Psychotherapy Research*, *21*(4), 416–429. doi:10.1080/10503307.2011.577823

Mecklinger, A. (2010). The control of long-term memory: Brain systems and cognitive processes. *Neuroscience & Biobehavioral Reviews*, *34*(7), 1055–1065. doi:10.1016/j.neubiorev.2009.11.020

Medda, P., Perugi, G., Zanello, S., et al. (2009). Response to ECT in bipolar I, bipolar II and unipolar depression. *Journal of Affective Disorders*, *118*(1–3), 55–59. doi:10.1016/j.jad.2009.01.014

Medhus, E. (2001). *Child rearing challenges*. Retrieved May 25, 2007, from http://www.drmedhus.com/childchallenges.htm

Meeks, T. W., & Jeste, D. V. (2009). Neurobiology of wisdom: A literature overview. *Archives of General Psychiatry*, *66*(4), 355–365. doi:10.1001/archgenpsychiatry.2009.8

Megreya, A. M., White, D., & Burton, A. M. (2011). The other-race effect does not rely on memory: Evidence from a matching task. *The Quarterly Journal of Experimental Psychology*, *64*(8), 1473–1483. doi:10.1080/17470218.2011.575228

Mehrabian, A. (2000). Beyond IQ: Broad-based measurement of individual success potential or 'emotional intelligence'. *Genetic, Social, & General Psychology Monographs*, *126*, 133–239.

Meier, P. S., Donmall, M. C., McElduff, P., et al. (2006). The role of the early therapeutic alliance in predicting drug treatment dropout. *Drug & Alcohol Dependence*, *83*(1), 57–64. doi:10.1016/j.drugalcdep.2005.10.010

Meijer, E. H., & Verschuere, B. (2010). The polygraph and the detection of deception. *Journal of Forensic Psychology Practice*, *10*(4), 325–338. doi:10.1080/15228932.2010.481237

Mejía, O. L., & McCarthy, C. J. (2010). Acculturative stress, depression, and anxiety in migrant farmwork college students of Mexican heritage. *International Journal of Stress Management*, *17*(1), 1–20. doi:10.1037/a0018119

Meltzoff, A. N. (2005). Imitation and other minds: The "Like Me" Hypothesis. In S. Hurley & N. Chater (Eds.), *Perspectives on imitation: From neuroscience to social science: Imitation, human development, and culture* (Vol. 2, pp. 55–77). Cambridge, MA: MIT Press.

Melzack, R. (1999). From the gate to the neuromatrix. *Pain*, Aug Suppl. 6, S121–S126. doi:10.1016/S0304-3959(99)00145-1

Melzack, R., & Katz, J. (2006). Pain in the 21st century: The neuromatrix and beyond. In G. Young, A. W. Kane, et al. (Eds.), *Psychological knowledge in court: PTSD, pain, and TBI* (pp. 129–148). New York: Springer.

Melzack, R., & Wall, P. D. (1996). *The challenge of pain*. Harmondsworth, UK: Penguin.

Memon, A., Meissner, C. A., & Fraser, J. (2010). The Cognitive Interview: A meta-analytic review and study space analysis of the past 25 years. *Psychology, Public Policy, & Law*, *16*(4), 340–372. doi:10.1037/a0020518

Mendolia, M. (2002). An index of self-regulation of emotion and the study of repression in social contexts that threaten or do not threaten self-concept. *Emotion*, *2*(3), 215–232. doi:10.1037/1528-3542.2.3.215

Meneses, G. D., & Beerlipalacio, A. (2005). Recycling behavior: A multidimensional approach. *Environment & Behavior*, *37*(6), 837–860. doi:10.1177/0013916505276742

Mercer, J. (2006). *Understanding attachment: Parenting, child care, and emotional development*. Westport, CT: Praeger.

Mercer, T., & McKeown, D. (2010). Interference in short-term auditory memory. *Quarterly Journal of Experimental Psychology*, *63*(7), 1256–1265. doi:10.1080/17470211003802467

Merens, W., Booij, L., Haffmans, P. M. J., et al. (2008). The effects of experimentally lowered serotonin function on emotional information processing and memory in remitted depressed patients. *Journal of Psychopharmacology*, *22*(6), 653–662. doi:10.1177/0269881107081531

Merhi, O., Faugloire, E., Flanagan, M., et al. (2007). Motion sickness, console video games, and head-mounted displays. *Human Factors*, *49*(5), 920–934. doi:10.1518/001872007X230262

Merlin, D. (2008). How culture and brain mechanisms interact in decision making. In C. Engel & W. Singer (Eds.), *Better than conscious? Decision making, the human mind, and implications for institutions* (pp. 191–205). Cambridge, MA: MIT Press.

Meyer, G. J., Finn, S. E., Eyde, L. D., et al. (2001). Psychological testing and psychological assessment: A review of evidence and issues. *American Psychologist*, *56*(2) 128–165. doi:10.1037/0003-066X.56.2.128

Meyerbröker, K., & Emmelkamp, P. M. G. (2010). Virtual reality exposure therapy in anxiety disorders: A systematic review of process-and-outcome studies. *Depression & Anxiety*, *27*(10), 933–944. doi:10.1002/da.20734

Meyers, L. (2006). Behind the scenes of the "Dr. Phil" show. *Monitor on Psychology*, *37*(9), 63.

Michaels, J. W., Blommel, J. M., Brocato, R. M., et al. (1982). Social facilitation and inhibition in a natural setting. *Replications in Social Psychology, 2,* 21–24.

Michalak, E. E., & Lam, R. W. (2002). Seasonal affective disorder: The latitude hypothesis revisited. *Canadian Journal of Psychiatry, 47*(8), 787–788. doi:10.1017/S1121189X00000300

Michaliszyn, D., Marchand, A., Bouchard, S., et al. (2010). A randomized, controlled clinical trial of in virtuo and in vivo exposure for spider phobia. *Cyberpsychology, Behavior, & Social Networking, 13*(6), 689–695. doi:10.1089/cyber.2009.0277

Michalko, M. (2001). *Cracking creativity.* Berkeley, CA: Ten Speed Press.

Michel, C., Caldara, R., & Rossion, B. (2006). Same-race faces are perceived more holistically than other-race faces. *Visual Cognition, 14*(1), 55–73. doi:10.1080/13506280500158761

Michel, G. F., & Tyler, A. N. (2005). Critical period: A history of the transition from questions of when, to what, to how. *Developmental Psychobiology, 46*(3), 156–162. doi:10.1002/dev.20058

Middaugh, S. J., & Pawlick, K. (2002). Biofeedback and behavioral treatment of persistent pain in the older adult: A review and a study. *Applied Psychophysiology & Biofeedback, 27*(3), 185–202. doi:10.1023/A:1016208128254

Mielke, H. W. (1999). Lead in the inner cities. *American Scientist, 87*(Jan.–Feb.), 62–73. doi:10.1511/1999.1.62

Mignot, E. (2001). A hundred years of narcolepsy research. *Archives of Italian Biology, 139,* 207–220.

Mikolajczak, M., Pinon, N., Lane, A., et al. (2010). Oxytocin not only increases trust when money is at stake, but also when confidential information is in the balance. *Biological Psychology, 85*(1), 182–184. doi:10.1016/j.biopsycho.2010.05.010

Mikulincer, M. & Shaver, P. R. (Eds.). (2010). *Prosocial motives, emotions, and behavior: The better angels of our nature.* Washington, DC: American Psychological Association.

Miles, L. K., Karpinska, K., Lumsden, J., et al. (2010). The meandering mind: Vection and mental time travel. *PLoS ONE, 5*(5): e10825. doi:10.1371/journal.pone.0010825

Milgram, S. (1963). Behavioral study of obedience. *Journal of Abnormal & Social Psychology, 67,* 371–378. doi:10.1037/h0040525

Milgram, S. (1965). Some conditions of obedience and disobedience to authority. *Human Relations, 18,* 57–76. doi:10.1177/001872676501800105

Milgram, S. (1967). The small-world problem. *Psychology Today, May,* 61–67.

Milgram, S., Bickman, L., & Berkowitz, L. (1969). Note on the drawing power of crowds of different size. *Journal of Personality & Social Psychology, 13,* 79–82. doi:10.1037/h0028070

Miller, D. T. (2006). *An invitation to social psychology.* Belmont, CA: Cengage Learning/Wadsworth.

Miller, E. K., & Cohen, J. D. (2001). An integrative theory of prefrontal cortex function. *Annual Review of*

Neuroscience, 24, 167–202. doi:10.1146/annurev.neuro.24.1.167

Miller, G. A. (1956). The magical number seven, plus or minus two: Some limits on our capacity for processing information. *Psychological Review, 63,* 81–97. doi:10.1037/0033-295X.101.2.343

Miller, G. E., Cohen, S., & Ritchey, A. K. (2002). Chronic psychological stress and the regulation of pro-inflammatory cytokines: A glucocorticoid-resistance model. *Health Psychology, 21*(6), 531–541. doi:10.1037/0278-6133.21.6.531

Miller, Jr., G. T., & Spoolman, S. (2011). *Environmental science* (13th ed.). Belmont, CA: Cengage Learning/Wadsworth.

Miller, J., & Garran, A. M. (2008). *Racism in the United States: Implications for the helping professions.* Belmont, CA: Cengage Learning/Wadsworth.

Miller, L. E., Grabell, A., Thomas, A., et al. (2012). The associations between community violence, television violence, intimate partner violence, parent–child aggression, and aggression in sibling relationships of a sample of preschoolers. *Psychology of Violence,* doi:10.1037/a0027254.

Miller, M. A., & Rahe, R. H. (1997). Life changes scaling for the 1990s. *Journal of Psychosomatic Research, 43*(3), 279–292. doi:10.1016/S0022-3999(97)00118-9

Miller, M., Hemenway, D., & Azraela, D. (2007). State-level homicide victimization rates in the US in relation to survey measures of household firearm ownership, 2001–2003. *Social Science & Medicine, 64*(3), 656–664. doi:10.1016/j.socscimed.2006.09.024

Miller, N. E. (1944). Experimental studies of conflict. In J. McV. Hunt (Ed.), *Personality and the behavior disorders* (Vol. 1, pp. 431–465). New York: Ronald Press.

Miller, N. E., & Bugelski. R. (1948). Minor studies of aggression: II. The influence of frustration imposed by the in-group on attitudes expressed toward out-groups. *Journal of Psychology, 25,* 437–442. doi:10.1080/00223980.1948.9917387

Miller, N., Pedersen, W. C., Earleywine, M., et al. (2003). A theoretical model of triggered displaced aggression. *Personality & Social Psychology Review, 7*(1), 75–97. doi:10.1207/S15327957PSPR0701_5

Miller, P. H. (2011). Piaget's theory: Past, present, and future. In U. Goswami (Ed.), *Piaget's theory: Past, present, and future* (pp. 649–672). Wiley-Blackwell.

Miller, R., Perlman, D., & Brehm, S. S. (2009). *Intimate relationships* (5th ed.). New York: McGraw-Hill.

Miller, W. R., & Munoz, R. F. (2005). *Controlling your drinking: Tools to make moderation work for you.* New York: Guilford.

Millman, R. B., & Ross, E. J. (2003). Steroid and nutritional supplement use in professional athletes. *American Journal on Addictions, 12*(Suppl 2), S48–S54. doi:10.1080/713830544

Milne, R., & Bull, R. (2002). Back to basics: A componential analysis of the original cognitive interview mnemonics with three age groups. *Applied Cognitive Psychology, 16*(7), 743–753. doi:10.1002/acp.825

Milner, B. (1965). Memory disturbance after bilateral hippocampal lesions. In P. Milner & S. Glickman (Eds.), *Cognitive processes and the brain* (pp. 97–111). Princeton, NJ: Van Nostrand.

Miltenberger, R. G. (2012). *Behavior modification: Principles and procedures* (5th ed.). Belmont, CA: Cengage Learning/Wadsworth.

Milton, J., & Wiseman, R. (1997). *Guidelines for extrasensory perception research.* Hertfordshire, UK: University of Hertfordshire Press.

Milton, J., & Wiseman, R. (1999). A meta-analysis of mass-media tests of extrasensory perception. *British Journal of Psychology, 90*(2), 235–240. doi:10.1348/000712699161378

Minda, J. P., & Smith, J. D. (2011). Prototype models of categorization: Basic formulation, predictions, and limitations. In E. M. Pothos & A. J. Wills (Eds.), *Formal approaches in categorization* (pp. 40–64). New York: Cambridge University Press.

Minton, H. L. (2000). Psychology and gender at the turn of the century. *American Psychologist, 55*(6), 613–615. doi:10.1037/0003-066X.55.6.613

Miotto, K., Darakjian, J., Basch, J., et al. (2001). Gamma-hydroxybutyric acid: Patterns of use, effects and withdrawal. *American Journal on Addictions, 10*(3), 232–241. doi:10.1080/105504901750532111

Mirsky, A. F., & Duncan, C. C. (2005). Pathophysiology of mental illness: A view from the fourth ventricle. *International Journal of Psycho-physiology, 58*(2–3), 162–178. doi:10.1016/j.ijpsycho.2005.06.004

Mirsky, A. F., Bieliauskas, L. M., Van Kammen, D. P., et al. (2000). A 39-year follow-up of the Genain quadruplets. *Schizophrenia Bulletin, 3,* 5–18.

Mischel, W. (2004). Toward an integrative science of the person. *Annual Review of Psychology, 55,* 1–22. doi:10.1146/annurev.psych.55.042902.130709

Mischel, W., & Shoda, Y. (2010). The situated person. In B. Mesquita, L. F. Barrett, & E. R. Smith (Eds.), *The mind in context* (pp. 149–173). New York: Guilford.

Mischel, W., Shoda, Y., & Smith, R. E. (2008). *Introduction to personality: Toward an integration* (8th ed.). Hoboken, NJ: Wiley.

Mistlberger, R. E. (2005). Circadian regulation of sleep in mammals: Role of the suprachiasmatic nucleus. *Brain Research Reviews, 49*(3), 429–454. doi:10.1016/j.brainresrev.2005.01.005

Mitchell, D. (1987). Firewalking cults: Nothing but hot air. *Laser, Feb.,* 7–8.

Mitchell, L. A., MacDonald, R. A. R., Knussen, C., et al. (2007). A survey investigation of the effects of music listening on chronic pain. *Psychology of Music, 35*(1), 37–57. doi:10.1177/0305735607068887

Mitchell, N. S., Dickinson, L. M., Allison Kempe, A., et al. (2010). Determining the effectiveness of Take Off Pounds Sensibly (TOPS), a nationally available nonprofit weight loss program. *Obesity, 19,* 568–573. doi:10.1038/oby.2010.202

Mitka, M. (2009). College binge drinking still on the rise. *Journal of the American Medical Association, 302*(8), 836–837. doi:10.1001/jama.2009.1154

Moerman, D. E. (2002). The meaning response and the ethics of avoiding placebos. *Evaluation & the Health Professions, 25*(4), 399–409. doi:10.1177/0163278702238053

Mogg, K., Bradley, B. P., Hyare, H., et al. (1998). Selective attention to food-related stimuli in hunger. *Behaviour Research & Therapy, 36*(2), 227–237. doi:10.1016/S0005-7967(97)00062-4

Moghaddam, B. (2002). Stress activation of glutamate neurotransmission in the prefrontal cortex. *Biological Psychiatry, 51*(10), 775–787. doi:10.1016/S0006-3223(01)01362-2

Moghaddam, F. M. (2007). *Multiculturalism and intergroup relations: Psychological implications for democracy in global context.* Washington, DC: American Psychological Association.

Mojtabai, R., Olfson, M., Sampson, N. A., et al. (2011). Barriers to mental health treatment: Results from the national comorbidity survey replication. *Psychological Medicine, 41*(8), 1751–1761. doi:10.1017/S0033291710002291

Mokdad, A. H., Marks, J. S., Stroup, D. F., et al. (2004). Actual causes of death in the United States, 2000. *Journal of the American Medical Association, 291,* 1238–1245. doi:10.1001/jama.291.10.1238

Molenberghs, P., Cunnington, R., & Mattingley, J. B. (2012). Brain regions with mirror properties: A meta-analysis of 125 human fMRI studies. *Neuroscience & Biobehavioral Reviews, 36*(1), 341–349. doi:10.1016/j.neubiorev.2011.07.004

Monahan, J., Steadman, H. J., Silver, E., et al. (2001). *Rethinking risk assessment: The MacArthur Study of Mental Disorder and Violence.* New York: Oxford University Press.

Montgomery, P., & Dennis, J. (2004). A systematic review of non-pharmacological therapies for sleep problems in later life. *Sleep Medicine Reviews, 8*(1), 47–62. doi:10.1016/S1087-0792(03)00026-1

Monti, M. M., Vanhaudenhuyse, A., Coleman, M. R., et al. (2010). Willful modulation of brain activity in disorders of consciousness. *New England Journal of Medicine, 362*(7), 579–589. doi:10.1056/NEJMoa0905370

Montoya, R. M., & Insko, C. A. (2008). Toward a more complete understanding of the reciprocity of liking effect. *European Journal of Social Psychology, 38,* 477–498. doi:10.1002/ejsp.431

Montreal Declaration on Intellectual Disabilities. (2004). Retrieved February 21, 2011, from http://www.mdri.org/mdri-web-2007/pdf/montrealdeclaration.pdf

Moore, S. A., & Zoellner, L. A. (2007). Overgeneral autobiographical memory and traumatic events: An evaluative review. *Psychological Bulletin, 133*(3), 419–437. doi:10.1037/0033-2909.133.3.419

Moore, T. O. (2001). Testosterone and male behavior: Empirical research with hamsters does not support the use of castration to deter human sexual aggression. *North American Journal of Psychology, 3*(3), 503–520.

Moran, F. (2010). *The paradoxical legacy of Sigmund Freud.* London: Karnac Books.

Moras, K. (2002). Research on psychotherapy. In M. Hersen & W. H. Sledge (Eds.), *Encyclopedia of psychotherapy* (Vol 2, pp. 525–545). San Diego: Academic Press.

Moreno, J. L. (1953). *Who shall survive?* New York: Beacon.

Moreno, M. M., Linster, C., Escanilla, O., et al. (2009). Olfactory perceptual learning requires adult neurogenesis. *Proceedings of the National Academy of Sciences, 106*(42), 17980–17985. doi:10.1073/pnas.0907063106

Moreno-Cabrera, J. (2011). Speech and gesture: An integrational approach. *Language Sciences, 33*(4), 615–622. doi:10.1016/j.langsci.2011.04.021

Morgan, J. E., & Ricker, J. H. (Eds.). (2008). *Textbook of clinical neuropsychology,* Washington, DC: Taylor & Francis.

Morgan, J. P. (Ed.). (2005). *Psychology of aggression.* Hauppauge, NY: Nova Science Publishers.

Morin, A. (2006). Levels of consciousness and self-awareness: A comparison and integration of various neurocognitive views. *Consciousness & Cognition, 15*(2), 358–371. doi:10.1016/j.concog.2005.09.006

Morisse, D., Batra, L., Hess, L., et al. (1996). A demonstration of a token economy for the real world. *Applied & Preventive Psychology, 5*(1), 41–46. doi:10.1016/S0962-1849(96)80025-4

Moritz, A. P., & Zamchech, N. (1946). Sudden and unexpected deaths of young soldiers. *American Medical Association Archives of Pathology, 42,* 459–494.

Morley, T. E., & Moran, G. (2011). The origins of cognitive vulnerability in early childhood: Mechanisms linking early attachment to later depression. *Clinical Psychology Review, 31*(7), 1071–1082. doi:10.1016/j.cpr.2011.06.006

Morrison, R. G., & Wallace, B. (2001). Imagery vividness, creativity and the visual arts. *Journal of Mental Imagery, 25*(3–4), 135–152.

Morrissey, A., & Brown, P. M. (2009). Mother and toddler activity in the zone of proximal development for pretend play as a predictor of higher child IQ. *Gifted Child Quarterly, 53*(2), 106–120. doi:10.1177/0016986208330563

Morsella, E., & Krauss, R. M. (2004). The role of gestures in spatial working memory and speech. *American Journal of Psychology, 117*(3), 411–424. doi:10.2307/4149008

Mosher, W. D., Chandra, C., & Jones, J. (2005). *Sexual behavior and selected health measures: Men and women 15–44 years of age, United States, 2002.* Atlanta: Centers for Disease Control. Retrieved May 9, 2012, from http://www.cdc.gov/nchs/data/ad/ad362.pdf

Mosley, M. (2011). Alien Hand Syndrome sees woman attacked by her own hand. *British Broadcasting Corporation Mobile News.* Retrieved January 3, 2012, from http://www.bbc.co.uk/news/uk-12225163

Mosley, P. E. (2009). Bigorexia: Bodybuilding and muscle dysmorphia. *European Eating Disorders Review, 17*(3), 191–198. doi:10.1002/erv.897

Most, S. B., Scholl, B. J., Clifford, E. R., et al. (2005). What you see is what you set: Sustained inattentional blindness and the capture of awareness. *Psychological Review, 112*(1), 217–242. doi:10.1037/0033-295X.112.1.217

Motivala, S. J., & Irwin, M. R. (2007). Sleep and immunity: Cytokine pathways linking sleep and health outcomes. *Current Directions in Psychological Science, 16*(1), 21–25. doi:10.1111/j.1467-8721.2007.00468.x

Müller, B. H., Kull, S., Wilhelm, F. H., et al. (2011). One-session computer-based exposure treatment for spider-fearful individuals: Efficacy of a minimal self-help intervention in a randomised controlled trial. *Journal of Behavior Therapy & Experimental Psychiatry, 42*(2), 179–184. doi:10.1016/j.jbtep.2010.12.001

Mundy, A. (2004). Divided we stand. *American Demographics, 26*(5), 26–31.

Munroe-Chandler, K., Hall, C., & Fishburne, G. (2008). Playing with confidence: The relationship between imagery use and self-confidence and self-efficacy in youth soccer players. *Journal of Sports Sciences, 26*(14), 1539–1546. doi:10.1080/02640410802315419

Munsey, C. (2006). RxP legislation made historic progress in Hawaii. *APA Monitor, June,* 42.

Muran, J. C., & Barber, J. P. (Eds.) (2010). *The therapeutic alliance: An evidence-based guide to practice.* New York: Guilford.

Murphy, B. C., & Dillon, C. (2011). *Interviewing in action in a multicultural world* (4th ed.). Belmont, CA: Cengage Learning/Wadsworth.

Murray, C. D., Pettifer, S., Howard, T., et al. (2007). The treatment of phantom limb pain using immersive virtual reality: Three case studies. *Disability & Rehabilitation, 29*(18), 1465–1469. doi:10.1080/09638280601107385

Murray, J. B. (2002). Phencyclidine (PCP): A dangerous drug, but useful in schizophrenia research. *Journal of Psychology, 136*(3), 319–327. doi:10.1080/00223980209604159

Murray, S., Holmes, J. G., & Griffin, D. W. (2003). Reflections on the self-fulfilling effects of positive illusions. *Psychological Inquiry, 14*(3-4), 2003, 289–295. doi:10.1080/1047840X.2003.9682895

Murrell, A. R., Christoff, K. A., & Henning, K. R. (2007). Characteristics of domestic violence offenders: Associations with childhood exposure to violence. *Journal of Family Violence, 22*(7), 523–532. doi:10.1007/s10896-007-9100-4

Music, G. (2011). *Nurturing natures: Attachment and children's emotional, sociocultural and brain development.* Hove, UK: Psychology Press.

Mussen, P. H., Conger, J. J., Kagan, J., et al. (1979). *Psychological development: A life span approach.* New York: Harper & Row.

Mustanski, B. S., Chivers, M. L., & Bailey, J. M. (2002). A critical review of recent biological research on human sexual orientation. *Annual Review of Sex Research, 13,* 89–140.

Myers, H. F., Lesser, I., Rodriguez, N., et al. (2002). Ethnic differences in clinical presentation of depression in adult women. *Cultural Diversity & Ethnic Minority Psychology, 8*(2), 138–156. doi:10.1037//1099-9809.8.2.138

Myers, L. (2007). The problem with DNA. *Monitor on Psychology, June,* 52–53.

Myrtek, M. (2007). Type A behavior and hostility as independent risk factors for coronary heart disease. In J. Jordan, B. Bardé, et al. (Eds.), *Contributions toward evidence-based psychocardiology: A systematic review of the literature* (pp. 159–183). Washington, DC: American Psychological Association.

Naitoh, P., Kelly, T. L., & Englund, C. E. (1989). *Health effects of sleep deprivation.* U.S. Naval Health Research Center Report, No. 89–46.

Najdowski, C. J. (2010). Jurors and social loafing: Factors that reduce participation during jury deliberations. *American Journal of Forensic Psychology, 28*(2), 39–64.

Nakamura, J., & Csikszentmihalyi, M. (2003). The motivational sources of creativity as viewed from the paradigm of positive psychology. In L. G. Aspinwall & U. M. Staudinger (Eds.), *A psychology of human strengths: Fundamental questions and future directions for a positive psychology* (pp. 257–269). Washington, DC: American Psychological Association.

Nakamura, Y., Goto, T. K., Tokumori, K., et al. (2011). Localization of brain activation by umami taste in humans. *Brain Research, 1406,* 18–29. doi:10.1016/j.brainres.2011.06.029

Nakayama, H. (2010). Development of infant crying behavior: A longitudinal case study. *Infant Behavior & Development, 33*(4), 463–471. doi:10.1016/j.infbeh.2010.05.002

National Academy of Sciences. (2003). *The polygraph and lie detection.* Washington, DC: The National Academies Press.

National Center for Chronic Disease Prevention and Health Promotion. (2011). *Tobacco use: Targeting the nation's leading killer.* Atlanta: Author. Retrieved April 16, 2012, from http://www.cdc.gov/nccdphp/publications/aag/osh.htm

National Institute of Child Health and Human Development. (2010a). *Link between child care and academic achievement and behavior persists into adolescence.* Washington, DC: Author. Retrieved May 9, 2012, from http://www.nichd.nih.gov/news/releases/051410-early-child-care.cfm

National Institute of Child Health and Human Development. (2010b). *Sudden infant death syndrome (SIDS).* Washington, DC: Author. Retrieved February 18, 2012, from http://www.nichd.nih.gov/health/topics/sudden_infant_death_syndrome.cfm

National Institute of Mental Health. (2010a). *Turning the corner, not the key, in treatment of serious mental illness.* Bethesda, MD: Author. Retrieved May 9, 2012, from http://www.nimh.nih.gov/about/director/2010/turning-the-corner-not-the-key-in-treatment-of-serious-mental-illness.shtml

National Institute of Mental Health. (2010c). *Suicide in the U.S.: Statistics and prevention.* Bethesda, MD: Author. Retrieved May 9, 2012, from http://www.nimh.nih.gov/health/publications/suicide-in-the-us-statistics-and-prevention/index.shtml

National Institute of Mental Health. (2011a). *Statistics.* Bethesda, MD: Author. Retrieved May 9, 2012, from http://www.nimh.nih.gov/statistics/index.shtml

National Institute of Mental Health. (2011b). *Warning signs of suicide.* Bethesda, MD: Author. Retrieved May 9, 2012, from http://www.nimh.nih.gov/health/topics/suicide-prevention/suicide-prevention-studies/warning-signs-of-suicide.shtml

National Institute of Mental Health. (2012a). *Depression.* Bethesda, MD: Author. Retrieved April 16, 2012, from http://www.nimh.nih.gov/health/publications/depression/complete-index.shtml#pub12

National Institute of Mental Health. (2012b). *How to find help.* Bethesda, MD: Author. Retrieved May 9, 2012, from http://www.nimh.nih.gov/health/topics/getting-help-locate-services/index.shtml

National Institute of Neurological Disorders and Stroke. (2007). *Brain basics: Understanding sleep.* NIH Publication No.06-3440-c. Bethesda, MD: Author. Retrieved February 18, 2012, from http://www.ninds.nih.gov/disorders/brain_basics/understanding_sleep.htm

National Institute on Alcohol Abuse and Alcoholism. (2008). *Tips for cutting down drinking.* Bethesda, MD: Author. Retrieved February 9, 2012, from http://pubs.niaaa.nih.gov/publications/Tips/tips.htm

National Institute on Drug Abuse. (2009). *Tobacco addiction.* Washington, DC: Author. Retrieved February 18, 2012, from https://www.drugabuse.gov/sites/default/files/tobaccorrs_v16_0.pdf

National Institute on Drug Abuse. (2010a). *NIDA InfoFacts: MDMA (Ecstasy).* Washington, DC: Author. Retrieved February 8, 2012, from http://www.drugabuse.gov/publications/infofacts/mdma-ecstasy

National Institute on Drug Abuse. (2010b). *Drugs, brains, and behavior: The science of addiction.* Washington, DC: Author. Retrieved February 18,

2012, from https://www.drugabuse.gov/sites/default/files/sciofaddiction.pdf

National Institutes of Health (2006). *Color vision deficiency*. Retrieved February 5, 2012, from http://ghr.nlm.nih.gov/condition/color-vision-deficiency

National Youth Violence Prevention Resource Center (2008). *Media violence facts and statistics*. Atlanta: Author. Downloaded May 2, 2010, from http://www.safeyouth.org/scripts/faq/mediaviolstats.asp

Nau, S. D., & Lichstein, K. L. (2005). Insomnia: Causes and treatments. In P. R. Carney, J. D. Geyer, et al. (Eds.), *Clinical sleep disorders* (pp. 157–190). Philadelphia, PA: Lippincott Williams & Wilkins.

Naveh-Benjamin, M., Guez, J., & Sorek, S. (2007). The effects of divided attention on encoding processes in memory: Mapping the locus of interference. *Canadian Journal of Experimental Psychology, 61*(1), 1–12.

Negriff, S., & Trickett, P. K. (2010). The relationship between pubertal timing and delinquent behavior in maltreated male and female adolescents. *Journal of Early Adolescence, 30*(4), 518–542. doi:10.1177/0272431609338180

Nehlig, A. (Ed.). (2004). *Coffee, tea, chocolate, and the brain*. Boca Raton, FL: CRC Press.

Neisser, U., Boodoo, G., Bouchard, T. J., et al. (1996). Intelligence: Knowns & unknowns. *American Psychologist, 51*, 77–101.

Neitz, J., & Neitz, M. (2011). The genetics of normal and defective color vision. *Vision Research, 51*(7), 633–651. doi:10.1016/j.visres.2010.12.002

Nelson, C. A. (1999). How important are the first 3 years of life? *Applied Developmental Science, 3*(4), 235–238. doi:10.1207/s1532480xads0304_8

Nelson, G., Van Andel, A. K., Curwood, S. E., et al. (2012). Exploring outcomes through narrative: The long-term impacts of better beginnings, better futures on the turning point stories of youth at ages 18–19. *American Journal of Community Psychology, 49*(1–2), 294–306. doi:10.1007/s10464-011-9466-6

Nelson, T. D. (2005). Ageism: Prejudice against our feared future self. *Journal of Social Issues, 61*(2), 207–221. doi:10.1111/j.1540-4560.2005.00402.x

Nelson, T. D. (2006). *The psychology of prejudice* (2nd ed.). Needham Heights, MA: Allyn & Bacon.

Nemeroff, C. B., Bremner, J. D., Foa, E. B., et al. (2006). Posttraumatic stress disorder: A state-of-the-science review. *Journal of Psychiatric Research, 40*(1), 1–21. doi:10.1016/j.jpsychires.2005.07.005

Neter, E., & Ben-Shakhar, G. (1989). The predictive validity of graphological inferences: A meta-analytic approach. *Personality & Individual Differences, 10*(7), 737–745. doi:10.1016/0191-8869(89)90120-7

Nettle, D. (2005). An evolutionary perspective on the extraversion continuum. *Evolution & Human Behavior, 26*, 363–373. doi:10.1016/j.evolhumbehav.2004.12.004

Nettle, D. (2006). The evolution of personality variation in humans and other animals. *American Psychologist, 61*(6), 622–631. doi:10.1037/0003-066X.61.6.622

Nettle, D. (2008). The personality factor: What makes you unique? *New Scientist*, Feb 9, 36–39.

Neubauer, A. C., & Fink, A. (2009). Intelligence and neural efficiency: Measures of brain activation versus measures of functional connectivity in the brain. *Intelligence, 37*(2), 223–229. doi:10.1016/j.intell.2008.10.008

Neufeind, J., Dritschel, B., Astell, A. J., et al. (2009). The effects of thought suppression on autobiographical memory recall. *Behaviour Research & Therapy, 47*(4), 275–284. doi:10.1016/j.brat.2008.12.010

Neufeld, R. W. J., Carter, J. R., Nicholson, I. R., et al. (2003). Schizophrenia. In P. Firestone & W. L. Marshall (Eds.), *Abnormal psychology: Perspectives* (2nd ed., pp. 343–370). Toronto: Prentice Hall.

Neukrug, E. S., & Fawcett, R. C. (2010). *Essentials of testing and assessment: A practical guide for counselors, social workers, and psychologists* (2nd ed.). Belmont, CA: Cengage Learning/Wadsworth.

Nguyen T. Q., Gwynn R. C., Kellerman S. E., et al. (2008). Population prevalence of reported and unreported HIV and related behaviors among the household adult population in New York City, 2004. *AIDS, 22*(2), 281–287. doi:10.1097/QAD.0b013e3282f2ef58

Nickell, J. (2001). John Edward: Hustling the bereaved. *Skeptical Inquirer*, Nov.–Dec., 19–22.

Nickerson, C., Diener, E., & Schwarz, N. (2011). Positive affect and college success. *Journal of Happiness Studies, 12*(4), 717–746. doi:10.1007/s10902-010-9224-8

Nickerson, R. S., & Adams, M. J. (1979). Long-term memory for a common object. *Cognitive Psychology, 11*, 287–307. doi:10.1016/0010-0285(79)90013-6

Niedzwienska, A. (2004). Metamemory knowledge and the accuracy of flashbulb memories. *Memory, 12*(5), 603–613. doi:10.1080/09658210344000134

Niehaus, D. J. H., Stein, D. J., Koen, L., et al. (2005). A case of "Ifufunyane": A Xhosa culture-bound syndrome. *Journal of Psychiatric Practice, 11*(6), 411–413. doi:10.1097/00131746-200511000-00009

Niehaus, J. L., Cruz-Bermúdez, N. D., & Kauer, J. A. (2009). Plasticity of addiction: A mesolimbic dopamine short-circuit? *American Journal on Addictions, 18*(4), 259–271. doi:10.1080/10550490902925946

Nielsen, M., & Dissanayake, C. (2004). Pretend play, mirror self-recognition and imitation: A longitudinal investigation through the second year. *Infant Behavior & Development, 27*(3), 342–365. doi:10.1016/j.infbeh.2003.12.006

Niemiec, C. P., Ryan, R. M., & Deci, E. L. (2009). The path taken: Consequences of attaining intrinsic and extrinsic aspirations in post-college life. *Journal of Research in Personality, 43*(3), 291–306. doi:10.1016/j.jrp.2008.09.001

Nisbett, R. E. (2005). Heredity, environment, and race differences in IQ: A commentary on Rushton and Jensen (2005). *Psychology, Public Policy, & Law, 11*(2), 302–310. doi:10.1037/1076-8971.11.2.302

Nisbett, R. E. (2009). *Intelligence and how to get it: Why schools and cultures count*. New York: Norton.

Nisbett, R. E., & Miyamoto, Y. (2005). The influence of culture: holistic versus analytic perception. *Trends in Cognitive Sciences, 9*(10), 467–473. doi:10.1016/j.tics.2005.08.004

Njeri, I. (1991, January 13). Beyond the melting pot. *Los Angeles Times*, E-1, E-8.

Noftle, E. E., & Fleeson, W. (2010). Age differences in big five behavior averages and variabilities across the adult life span: Moving beyond retrospective, global summary accounts of personality. *Psychology & Aging, 25*(1), 95–107. doi:10.1037/a0018199

Noice, H., & Noice, T. (1999). Long-term retention of theatrical roles. *Memory, 7*(3), 357–382.

Noland, J. S., Singer, L. T., Short, E. J., et al. (2005). Prenatal drug exposure and selective attention in preschoolers. *Neurotoxicology & Teratology, 27*(3), 429–438. doi:10.1016/j.ntt.2005.02.001

Nolen-Hoeksema, S. (2011). *Abnormal psychology* (5th ed.). New York: McGraw-Hill.

Norcross, J. C., Hedges, M., & Prochaska, J. O. (2002). The face of 2010: A Delphi poll on the future of psychotherapy. *Professional Psychology: Research & Practice, 33*(3), 316–322. doi:10.1037/0735-7028.33.3.316

Norem, J. K. (2002). *The positive power of negative thinking: Using defensive pessimism to harness anxiety and perform at your peak*. New York: Basic Books.

Norenzayan, A., & Nisbett, R. E. (2000). Culture and causal cognition. *Current Directions in Psychological Science, 9*, 132–135. doi:10.1111/1467-8721.00077

Norlander, T., Bergman, H., & Archer, T. (1998). Effects of flotation rest on creative problem solving and originality. *Journal of Environmental Psychology, 18*(4), 399–408. doi:10.1006/jevp.1998.0112

Norlander, T., Bergman, H., & Archer, T. (1999). Primary process in competitive archery performance: Effects of flotation REST. *Journal of Applied Sport Psychology, 11*(2), 194–209. doi:10.1080/10413209908404200

Norman, D. A. (1993). *Things that make us smart*. Menlo Park, CA: Addison-Wesley.

Norman, T. R. (2009). Melatonin: Hormone of the night. *Acta Neuropsychiatrica, 21*(5), 263–265. doi:10.1111/acn.2009.21.issue-510.1111/j.1601-5215.2009.00411.x

Northcutt, R. G. (2004). Taste buds: Development and evolution. *Brain, Behavior & Evolution, 64*(3), 198–206. doi:10.1159/000079747

Nosek, B. A., Greenwald, A. G., & Banaji, M. R. (2005). Understanding and using the implicit association test: II. Method variables and construct validity. *Personality & Social Psychology Bulletin, 31*(2), 166–180. doi:10.1177/0146167204271418

Novella, E. J. (2010). Mental health care in the aftermath of deinstitutionalization: A retrospective and prospective view. *Health Care Analysis, 18*(3), 222–238. doi:10.1007/s10728-009-0138-8

Nucci, L. P., & Gingo, M. (2011). The development of moral reasoning. In Goswami U. (Ed.), *The development of moral reasoning* (pp. 420–444). London: Wiley-Blackwell.

Nurnberger, J. I., & Zimmerman, J. (1970). Applied analysis of human behaviors: An alternative to conventional motivational inferences and unconscious determination in therapeutic programming. *Behavior Therapy, 1*, 59–69. doi:10.1016/S0005-7894(70)80057-0

O'Conner, T. G., Marvin, R. S., Rutter, M., et al. (2003). Child-parent attachment following early institutional deprivation. *Development & Psychopathology, 15*(1), 19–38. doi:10.1017/S0954579403000026

O'Connor, M. G., Sieggreen, M. A., Bachna, K., et al. (2000). Long-term retention of transient news events. *Journal of the International Neuropsychological Society, 6*(1), 44–51. doi:10.1017/S1355617700611050

O'Craven, K. M., & Kanwisher, N. (2000). Mental imagery of faces and places activates corresponding stimulus-specific brain regions. *Journal of Cognitive Neuroscience, 12*(6), 1013–1023. doi:10.1162/08989290051137549

O'Hare, A. E., Bremner, L., Nash, M., et al. (2009). A clinical assessment tool for advanced theory of mind performance in 5 to 12 year olds. *Journal of Autism & Developmental Disorders, 39*(6), 916–928. doi:10.1007/s10803-009-0699-2

O'Keeffe, C., & Wiseman, R. (2005). Testing alleged mediumship: Methods and results. *British Journal of Psychology, 96*(2), 165–179. doi:10.1348/000712605X36361

O'Leary, E. (2006). Person-centred gestalt therapy. In E. O'Leary & M. Murphy (Eds.), *New approaches to integration in psychotherapy* (pp. 25–37). New York: Routledge.

O'Neill, B. (2003). Don't believe everything you read online. *BBC News*. Retrieved April 21, 2009, from http://newswww.bbc.net.uk/1/hi/magazine/3151595.stm

O'Neill, P. (2005). The ethics of problem definition. *Canadian Psychology, 46*, 13–20. doi:10.1037/h0085819

O'Roark, A. M. (2001). Personality assessment, projective methods and a triptych perspective. *Journal of Projective Psychology & Mental Health, 8*(2), 116–126.

Oakley R. (2004). How the mind hurts and heals the body. *American Psychologist, 59*(1), 29–40. doi:10.1037/0003-066X.59.1.29

Oakley, D. A., & Halligan, P. W. (2010). Psychophysiological foundations of hypnosis and suggestion. In S. J. Lynn, J. W. Rhue, & I. Kirsch (Eds.). *Handbook of clinical hypnosis* (2nd ed., pp. 79–117). Washington, DC: American Psychological Association.

Oakley, D. A., Whitman, L. G., & Halligan, P. W. (2002). Hypnotic imagery as a treatment for phantom limb pain: Two case reports and a review. *Clinical Rehabilitation, 16*(4), 368–377. doi:10.1191/0269215502cr507oa

Oberauer, K., & Göthe, K. (2006). Dual-task effects in working memory: Interference between two processing tasks, between two memory demands, and between storage and processing. *European Journal of Cognitive Psychology, 18*(4), 493–519. doi:10.1080/09541440500423038

Oberle, E. (2009). The development of Theory of Mind reasoning in Micronesian children. *Journal of Cognition & Culture, 9*(1–2), 39–56. doi:10.1163/156853709X414629

Ochoa, J. G., & Pulido, M. (2005). Parasomnias. In P. R. Carney, J. D. Geyer, et al. (Eds.), *Clinical sleep disorders* (pp. 224–242). Philadelphia: Lippincott Williams & Wilkins.

Oestergaard, S., & Møldrup, C. (2011). Optimal duration of combined psychotherapy and pharmacotherapy for patients with moderate and severe depression: A meta-analysis. *Journal of Affective Disorders, 131*(1–3), 24–36. doi:10.1016/j.jad.2010.08.014

Ogden C. L., Carroll M. D., Curtin, L. R., et al. (2010). Prevalence of high body mass index in US children and adolescents, 2007–2008. *Journal of the American Medical Association, 303*(3), 242–249. doi:10.1001/jama.2009.2012

Ogden, C. L., & Carroll, M. D. (2010). *Prevalence of overweight, obesity, and extreme obesity among adults: United States, Trends 1960–1962 through 2007–2008.* Atlanta: Centers for Disease Control. Retrieved April 4, 2012, from http://www.cdc.gov/nchs/data/hestat/overweight/overweight_adult.pdf

Ogloff, J. R. P. (2006). Psychopathy/antisocial personality disorder conundrum. *Australian & New Zealand Journal of Psychiatry, 40*(6), 519–528. doi:10.1111/j.1440-1614.2006.01834.x

Ogrodniczuk, J. S., Piper, W. E., & Joyce, A. S. (2011). Effect of alexithymia on the process and outcome of psychotherapy: A programmatic review. *Psychiatry Research, 190*(1), 43–48. doi:10.1016/j.psychres.2010.04.026

Oishi, S., Kesebir, S., & Diener, E. (2011). Income inequality and happiness. *Psychological Science, 22*(9), 1095–1100. doi:10.1177/0956797611417262

Okiishi, J., Lambert, M. J., Nielsen, S. L., et al. (2003). Waiting for supershrink: An empirical analysis of therapist effects. *Clinical Psychology & Psychotherapy, 10*(6), 361–373. doi:10.1002/cpp.383

Olpin, M., & Hesson, M. (2010). *Stress management for life* (2nd ed.). Belmont, CA: Cengage Learning/Wadsworth.

Olson, J. M., & Zanna, M. P. (1993). Attitudes and attitude change. *Annual Review of Psychology, 44*, 117–154. doi:10.1146/annurev.ps.44.020193.001001

Olson, M. & Hergenhahn, B. R. (2009). *Introduction to the theories of learning* (8th ed.). Englewood Cliffs, NJ: Prentice Hall.

Olsson, A., Nearing, K, & Phelps, E. A. (2007). Learning fears by observing others: The neural systems of social fear transmission. *Social Cognitive & Affective Neuroscience, 2*(1), 3–11. doi:10.1093/scan/nsm005

Olsson, E. M. G., El Alaoui, S., Carlberg, B., et al. (2010). Internet-based biofeedback-assisted relaxation training in the treatment of hypertension: A pilot study. *Applied Psychophysiology & Biofeedback, 35*(2), 163–170. doi:10.1007/s10484-009-9126-x

Olszewski, P. K., Li, D., Grace, M. K., et al. (2003). Neural basis of orexigenic effects of ghrelin acting within lateral hypothalamus. *Peptides, 24*(4), 597–602. doi:10.1016/S0196-9781(03)00105-

Ong, A. D., Zautra, A. J., & Reid, M. C. (2010). Psychological resilience predicts decreases in pain catastrophizing through positive emotions. *Psychology & Aging, 25*(3), 516–523. doi:10.1037/a0019384

Onwuegbuzie, A. J. (2000). Academic procrastinators and perfectionistic tendencies among graduate students. *Journal of Social Behavior & Personality, 15*(5), 103–109.

Ooki, S. (2005). Genetic and environmental influences on the handedness and footedness in Japanese twin children. *Twin Research & Human Genetics, 8*(6), 649–656. doi:10.1375/twin.8.6.649

Opland, D. M., Leinninger, G. M., & Myers, M. G., Jr. (2010). Modulation of the mesolimbic dopamine system by leptin. *Brain Research, 1350*, 65–70. doi:10.1016/j.brainres.2010.04.028

Ord, T. J., Martins E. P., Thakur S., et al. (2005). Trends in animal behaviour research (1968–2002): Ethoinformatics and the mining of library databases. *Animal Behaviour, 69*(6), 1399–1413. doi:10.1016/j.anbehav.2004.08.020

Orenstein, P. (2011). *Cinderella ate my daughter.* New York: HarperCollins.

Orleans, C. T. (2000). Promoting the maintenance of health behavior change. *Health Psychology, 19*(Suppl. 1), 76–83. doi:10.1037/0278-6133.19.Suppl1.76

Orleans, C. T., Gruman, J., & Hollendonner, J. K. (1999). Rating our progress in population health promotion: Report card on six behaviors. *American Journal of Health Promotion, 14*(2), 75–82. doi:10.4278/0890-1171-14.2.75

Ormay, T. (2006). Cybertherapy: Psychotherapy on the Internet. *International Journal of Psychotherapy, 10*(2), 51–60.

Ormrod, J. E. (2011). *Educational psychology: Developing learners* (7th ed.). Boston: Allyn & Bacon.

Osgood, C. E. (1952). The nature and measurement of meaning. *Psychological Bulletin, 49*, 197–237. doi:10.1037/h0055737

Oskamp, S. (2002). Summarizing sustainability issues and research approaches. In P. Schmuck & W. P. Schultz (Eds.), *Psychology of sustainable development* (pp. 301–324). Dordrecht, Netherlands: Kluwer.

Oskamp, S., & Schultz, P. W. (2005). *Attitudes and opinions* (3rd ed.). Mahwah, NJ: Erlbaum.

Oster, H. (2005). The repertoire of infant facial expressions: An ontogenetic perspective. In J. Nadel & D. Muir (Eds.), *Emotional development: Recent research advances* (pp. 261–292). New York: Oxford University Press.

Oswald, D. L., & Chapleau, K. M. (2010). Selective self-stereotyping and women's self-esteem maintenance. *Personality & Individual Differences, 49*(8), 918–922. doi:10.1016/j.paid.2010.07.030

Otgaar, H., & Smeets, T. (2010). Adaptive memory: Survival processing increases both true and false memory in adults and children. *Journal of Experimental Psychology: Learning, Memory, & Cognition, 36*(4), 1010–1016. doi:10.1037/a0019402

Overmier, J. B., & LoLordo, V. M. (1998). Learned helplessness. In O'Donohue, W. T. (Ed.), *Learning and behavior therapy* (pp. 352–373). Boston, MA: Allyn & Bacon.

Owens, J., & Massey, D. S. (2011). Stereotype threat and college academic performance: A latent variables approach. *Social Science Research, 40*(1), 150–166. doi:10.1016/j.ssresearch.2010.09.010

Oyserman, D., Bybee, D., Terry, K., et al. (2004). Possible selves as roadmaps. *Journal of Research in Personality, 38*(2), 130–149. doi:10.1016/S0092-6566(03)00057-6

Page, K. (1999, May 16). The graduate. *Washington Post Magazine, 152*, 18–20.

Page, M. P. A., Madge, A., Cumming, N., et al. (2007). Speech errors and the phonological similarity effect in short-term memory: Evidence suggesting a common locus. *Journal of Memory & Language, 56*(1), 49–64.

Pagnin, D., de Queiroz, V., Pini, S., et al. (2004). Efficacy of ECT in depression: A meta-analytic review. *Journal of ECT, 20*(1), 13–20. doi:10.1097/00124509-200403000-00004

Palmer, S. E., & Beck, D. M. (2007). The repetition discrimination task: An objective method for studying perceptual grouping. *Perception & Psychophysics, 69*(1), 68–78. doi:10.3758/BF03194454

Pals, J. L. (2006). Narrative identity processing of difficult life experiences: Pathways of personality development and positive self-transformation in adulthood. *Journal of Personality, 74*(4), 1079–1110. doi:10.1111/j.1467-6494.2006.00403.x

Panksepp, J., & Pasqualini, M. S. (2005). The search for the fundamental brain/mind sources of affective experience. In J. Nadel & D. Muir (Eds.), *Emotional development: Recent research advances* (pp. 5–30). New York: Oxford University Press.

Panksepp, J., & Watt, D. (2011). What is basic about basic emotions? Lasting lessons from affective neuroscience. *Emotion Review, 3*(4), 387–396. doi:10.1177/1754073911410741

Papadatou-Pastou, M., Martin, M., Munafò, M. R., et al. (2008). Sex differences in left-handedness: A meta-analysis of 144 studies. *Psychological Bulletin, 134*(5), 677–699. doi:10.1037/a0012814

Papanicolaou, A. C. (Ed.) (2006). *The amnesias: A clinical textbook of memory disorders.* New York: Oxford University Press.

Paquette, D. (2004). Theorizing the father-child relationship: Mechanisms and developmental outcomes. *Human Development, 47*(4), 193–219. doi.org/10.1159/000078723

Paquette, V., Lévesque, J., Mensour, B., et al. (2003). "Change the mind and you change the brain": Effects of cognitive-behavioral therapy on the neural correlates of spider phobia. *NeuroImage, 18*, 401–409. doi:10.1016/S1053-8119(02)00030-7

Paradis, C. M., Solomon, L. Z., Florer, F., et al. (2004). Flashbulb memories of personal events of 9/11 and the day after for a sample of New York City residents. *Psychological Reports, 95*(1), 304–310. doi:10.2466/PR0.95.5.304-310

Park, G., Lubinski, D., Benbow, C. P. (2008). Ability differences among people who have commensurate degrees matter for scientific creativity. *Psychological Science, 19*(10), 957–961. doi:10.1111/j.1467-9280.2008.02182.x

Park, H. J., Li, R. X., Kim, J., et al. (2009). Neural correlates of winning and losing while watching soccer matches. *International Journal of Neuroscience, 119*(1), 76–87. doi:10.1080/00207450802480069

Park, H., & Lennon, S. J. (2008). Beyond physical attractiveness: Interpersonal attraction as a function of similarities in personal characteristics. *Clothing & Textiles Research Journal, 26*(4), 275–289. doi:10.1177/0887302X07309714

Park, N., Peterson, C., & Seligman, M. E. P. (2004). Strengths of character and well-being. *Journal of Social & Clinical Psychology, 23*(5), 603–619.

Parke, R. D. (2004). Development in the family. *Annual Review of Psychology, 55*, 365–399. doi:10.1146/annurev.psych.55.090902.141528

Parker, A., Ngu, H., & Cassaday, H. J. (2001). Odour and Proustian memory. *Applied Cognitive Psychology, 15*(2), 159–171. doi:10.1002/1099-0720(200103/04)15:2<159::AID-ACP694>3.0.CO;2-D

Parker, E. S., Cahill, L., & McGaugh, J. L. (2006). A case of unusual autobiographical remembering. *Neurocase, 12*(1), 35–49. doi:10.1080/13554790500473680

Parker, J. D. A. (2005). The relevance of emotional intelligence for clinical psychology. In R. Schulze & R. D. Roberts (Eds.), *Emotional intelligence: An international handbook* (pp. 271–287). Ashland, OH: Hogrefe & Huber.

Parker, P. D., & Salmela-Aro, K. (2011). Developmental processes in school burnout: A comparison of major developmental models. *Learning & Individual Differences, 21*, 244–248. doi:10.1016/j.lindif.2011.01.005

Parsons, K. M., Balcomb, K. C., III., Ford, J. K. B., et al. (2009). The social dynamics of southern resident killer whales and conservation implications for this endangered population. *Animal Behaviour, 77*(4), 963–971. doi:10.1016/j.anbehav.2009.01.018

Patall, E. A., Cooper, H., & Robinson, J. C. (2008). The effects of choice on intrinsic motivation and related outcomes: A meta-analysis of research findings. *Psychological Bulletin, 134*(2), 270–300. doi:10.1037/0033-2909.134.2.270

Paternoster, R., & Pogarsky, G. (2009). Rational choice, agency and thoughtfully reflective decision making: The short- and long-term consequences of making good choices. *Journal of Quantitative Criminology, 25*(2), 103–127. doi:10.1007/s10940-009-9065-y

Patterson, C. J. (2002). Lesbian and gay parenthood. In M. Bornstein (Ed.), *Handbook of Parenting* (Vol. 3): *Being and becoming a parent* (2nd ed., pp. 317–338). Mahwah, NJ: Erlbaum.

Paulhus, D. L. (1998). Interpersonal and intrapsychic adaptiveness of trait self-enhancement. *Journal of Personality & Social Psychology, 74*(5), 1197–1208. doi:10.1037/0022-3514.74.5.1197

Paulsson, T., & Parker, A. (2006). The effects of a two-week reflection-intention training program on lucid dream recall. *Dreaming, 16*(1), 22–35. doi:10.1037/1053-0797.16.1.22

Pavlov, I. P. (1927). *Conditioned reflexes.* Translated by G. V. Anrep. New York: Dover.

Payne, K. (2009). Winning the battle of ideas: Propaganda, ideology, and terror. *Studies in Conflict & Terrorism, 32*(2), 109–128. doi:10.1080/10576100802627738

Pedersen, A. F., Bovbjerg, D. H., & Zachariae, R. (2011). Stress and susceptibility to infectious disease. In R. J. Contrada & A. Baum (Eds.), *The handbook of stress science: Biology, psychology, and health* (pp. 425–445). New York: Springer.

Pedraza, C., García, F. B., & Navarro, J. F. (2009). Neurotoxic effects induced by gammahydroxybutyric acid (GHB) in male rats. *International Journal of Neuropsychopharmacology, 12*(9), 1165–1177. doi:10.1017/S1461145709000157

Peek, F., & Hanson, L. L. (2007). *The life and message of the real Rain Man: The journey of a mega-savant.* Port Chester, NY: Dude Publishing.

Penfield, W. (1957). Brain's record of past a continuous movie film. *Science News Letter,* April 27, 265.

Penfield, W. (1958). *The excitable cortex in conscious man.* Springfield, IL: Charles C Thomas.

Pennebaker, J. W. (2004). *Writing to heal: A guided journal for recovering from trauma and emotional upheaval.* Oakland, CA: New Harbinger Press.

Pennebaker, J. W., & Chung, C. K. (2007). Expressive writing, emotional upheavals, and health. In H. S.

Friedman & R. C. Silver (Eds.), *Foundations of health psychology* (pp. 263–284). New York: Oxford University Press.

Peplau, L. A. (2003). Human sexuality: How do men and women differ? *Current Directions in Psychological Science, 12*(2), 37–40. doi:10.1111/1467-8721.01221

Perin, C. T. (1943). A quantitative investigation of the delay of reinforcement gradient. *Journal of Experimental Psychology, 32*, 37–51. doi:10.1037/h0056738

Perloff, R. M. (2010). *The dynamics of persuasion: Communication and attitudes in the 21st century.* New York: Psychology Press.

Perls, F. (1969). *Gestalt therapy verbatim.* Lafayette, CA: Real People Press.

Perreault, S., & Bourhis, R. Y. (1999). Ethnocentrism, social identification, and discrimination. *Personality & Social Psychology Bulletin, 25*(1), 92–103. doi:10.1177/0146167299025001008

Perry, J. L., Joseph, J. E., Jiang, Y., et al. (2011). Prefrontal cortex and drug abuse vulnerability: Translation to prevention and treatment interventions. *Brain Research Reviews, 65*, 124–149. doi:10.1016/j.brainresrev.2010.09.001

Perry, R. P. (2003). Perceived (academic) control and causal thinking in achievement settings. *Canadian Psychology, 44*(4), 312–331. doi:10.1037/h0086956

Perry, R. P., Hladkyj, S., Pekrun, R. H., et al. (2001). Academic control and action control in the achievement of college students: A longitudinal field study. *Journal of Educational Psychology, 93*(4), 776–789.

Pesant, N., & Zadra, A. (2006). Dream content and psychological well-being: A longitudinal study of the continuity hypothesis. *Journal of Clinical Psychology, 62*(1), 111–121. doi:10.1002/jclp.20212

Pescatello, L. S. (2001). Exercising for health. *Western Journal of Medicine, 174*(2), 114–118.

Peters, W. A. (1971). *A class divided.* Garden City, NY: Doubleday.

Peterson, C., & Chang, E. C. (2003). Optimism and flourishing. In C. L. M. Keyes & J. Haidt (Eds.), *Flourishing* (pp. 55–79). Washington, DC: American Psychological Association.

Peterson, C., & Park, N. (2010). What happened to self-actualization? Commentary on Kenrick et al. (2010). *Perspectives on Psychological Science, 5*(3), 320–322. doi:10.1177/1745691610369471

Peterson, C., & Seligman, M. E. P. (2004). *Character strengths and virtues.* Washington, DC: American Psychological Association.

Peterson, C., & Vaidya, R. S. (2001). Explanatory style, expectations, and depressive symptoms. *Personality & Individual Differences, 31*(7), 1217–1223.

Peterson, D. R. (2001). Choosing the PsyD. In S. Walfish & A. K. Hess (Eds.), *Succeeding in graduate school: The career guide for psychology students* (pp. 53–60). Mahwah, NJ: Erlbaum.

Peterson, L. R., & Peterson, M. J. (1959). Short-term retention of individual verbal items. *Journal of Experimental Psychology, 58*, 193–198. doi:10.1037/h0049234

Peterson, P. C., & Husain, A. M. (2008). Pediatric narcolepsy. *Brain & Development, 30*(10), 609–623. doi:10.1016/j.braindev.2008.02.004

Petri, H. L., & Govern, J. M. (2013). *Motivation: Theory, research, and application* (6th ed.). Belmont, CA: Cengage Learning/Wadsworth.

Pett, M. A., & Johnson, M. J. M. (2005). Development and psychometric evaluation of the Revised University Student Hassles Scale. *Educational & Psychological Measurement, 65*(6), 984–1010. doi:10.1177/0013164405275661

Peverly, S. T., Brobst, K. E., Graham, M., et al. (2003). College adults are not good at self-regulation. *Journal of Educational Psychology, 95*(2), 335–346. doi:10.1037/0022-0663.95.2.335

Pezdek, K., Avila-Mora, E., & Sperry, K. (2010). Does trial presentation medium matter in jury simulation research? Evaluating the effectiveness of eyewitness expert testimony. *Applied Cognitive Psychology, 24*(5), 673–690. doi:10.1002/acp.1578

Phillips, D. A., & Lowenstein, A. E. (2011). Early care, education, and child development. *Annual Review of Psychology, 62*, 483–500. doi:10.1146/annurev.psych.031809.130707

Phillips, D. P., Liu, G. C., Kwok, K., et al. (2001). The Hound of the Baskervilles effect: Natural experiment on the influence of psychological stress on timing of death. *British Medical Journal, 323*(7327), 1443–1446. doi:10.1136/bmj.323.7327.1443

Phillips, K. W., Rothbard, N. P., & Dumas, T. L. (2009). To disclose or not to disclose? Status distance and self-disclosure in diverse environments. *Academy of Management Review, 34*(4), 710–732.

Piaget, J. (1951, original French, 1945). *The psychology of intelligence.* New York: Norton.

Piaget, J. (1952). *The origins of intelligence in children.* New York: International University Press.

Pickel, K. L., French, T. A., & Betts, J. M. (2003). A cross-modal weapon focus effect: The influence of a weapon's presence on memory for auditory information. *Memory, 11*(3), 277–292. doi:10.1080/09658210244000036

Piefke, M., Weiss, P., Markowitsch, H., et al. (2005). Gender differences in the functional neuroanatomy of emotional episodic autobiographical memory. *Human Brain Mapping, 24*, 313–324. doi:10.1002/hbm.20092

Piek, J. P. (2006). *Infant motor development.* Champaign, IL: Human Kinetics Publishers.

Pierrehumbert, B., Ramstein, T., Karmaniola, A., et al. (2002). Quality of child care in the preschool years. *International Journal of Behavioral Development, 26*(5), 385–396. doi:10.1080/01650250143000265

Pilgrim, D. (2011). The hegemony of cognitive-behaviour therapy in

modern mental health care. *Health Sociology Review, 20*(2), 120–132.

Piliavin, I. M., Rodin, J., & Piliavin, J. A. (1969). Good samaritanism: An underground phenomenon? *Journal of Personality & Social Psychology, 13*, 289–299. doi:10.1037/h0028433

Pineda, J. A. (Ed.). (2009). *Mirror neuron systems: The role of mirroring processes in social cognition.* New York: Humana Press.

Pinel, J. P. J., Assanand, S., & Lehman, D. R. (2000). Hunger, eating, and ill health. *American Psychologist, 55*(10), 1105–1116. doi:10.1037//0003-066X.55.10.1105

Pinel, P., & Dehaene, S. (2010). Beyond hemispheric dominance: Brain regions underlying the joint lateralization of language and arithmetic to the left hemisphere. *Journal of Cognitive Neuroscience, 22*(1), 48–66. doi:10.1162/jocn.2009.21184

Pinker, S. (2011). *The better angels of our nature: Why violence has declined.* New York: Viking.

Pinker, S., & Jackendoff, R. (2005). The faculty of language: What's special about it? *Cognition, 95*(2), 201–236. doi:10.1016/j.cognition.2004.08.004

Piper, Jr., A. (2008). Multiple personality disorder: Witchcraft survives in the twentieth century. In S. O. Lilienfeld, J. Ruscio, & S. J. Lynn (Eds.), *Navigating the mindfield: A user's guide to distinguishing science from pseudoscience in mental health* (pp. 249–268). Amherst, NY: Prometheus Books.

Pizam, A., Jeong, G.-H., Reichel, A., et al. (2004). The relationship between risk-taking, sensation-seeking, and the tourist behavior of young adults: A cross-cultural study. *Journal of Travel Research, 42*, 251–260. doi:10.1177/0047287503258837

Plassmann, H., O'Doherty, J., Shiv, B., et al. (2008). Marketing actions can modulate neural representations of experienced pleasantness. *Proceedings of the National Academy of Sciences, 105*(3), 1050–1054. doi:10.1073/pnas.0706929105

Plazzi, G., Vetrugno, R., Provini, F., et al. (2005). Sleepwalking and other ambulatory behaviours during sleep. *Neurological Sciences, 26*(Suppl3), s193–s198. doi:10.1007/s10072-005-0486-6

Pliner, P., & Mann, N. (2004). Influence of social norms and palatability on amount consumed and food choice. *Appetite, 42*(2), 227–237. doi:10.1016/j.appet.2003.12.001

Plous, S. (2003). *Understanding prejudice and discrimination.* New York: McGraw-Hill.

Plutchik, R. (2003). *Emotions and life.* Washington, DC: American Psychological Association.

Poland, J., & Caplan, P. J. (2004). The deep structure of bias in psychiatric diagnosis. In P. J. Caplan & L. Cosgrove (Eds.), *Bias in psychiatric diagnosis. A project of the association for women in psychology* (pp. 9–23). Lanham, MD: Jason Aronson.

Polemikos, N., & Papaeliou, C. (2000). Sidedness preference as an index of organization of laterality. *Perceptual & Motor Skills, 91*(3, Pt 2), 1083–1090. doi:10.2466/pms.2000.91.3f.1083

Polivy, J., & Herman, C. P. (2002). Causes of eating disorders. *Annual Review of Psychology, 53*, 187–213. doi:10.1146/annurev.psych.53.100901.135103

Pollner, M. (1998). The effects of interviewer gender in mental health interviews. *Journal of Nervous & Mental Disease, 186*(6), 369–373. doi:10.1097/00005053-199806000-00008

Polusny, M. A., Ries, B. J., Meis, L. A., et al. (2011). Effects of parents experiential avoidance and PTSD on adolescent disaster-related posttraumatic stress symptomatology. *Journal of Family Psychology, 25*(2), 220–229. doi:10.1037/a0022945

Pomaki, G., Supeli, A., & Verhoeven, C. (2007). Role conflict and health behaviors: Moderating effects on psychological distress and somatic complaints. *Psychology & Health, 22*(3), 317–335. doi:10.1080/14768320600774561

Popma, A., Vermeiren, R., Geluk, C., et al. (2007). Cortisol moderates the relationship between testosterone and aggression in delinquent male adolescents. *Biological Psychiatry, 61*(3), 405–411. doi:10.1016/j.biopsych.2006.06.006

Posada, G., Jacobs, A., Richmond, M. K., et al. (2002). Maternal caregiving and infant security in two cultures. *Developmental Psychology, 38*(1), 67–78. doi:10.1037/0012-1649.38.1.67

Post, J. M. (2011). Crimes of obedience: "groupthink" at Abu Ghraib. *International Journal of Group Psychotherapy, 61*(1), 49–66. doi:10.1521/ijgp.2011.61.1.48

Powell, D. H. (2004). Behavioral treatment of debilitating test anxiety among medical students. *Journal of Clinical Psychology, 60*(8), 853–865. doi:10.1002/jclp.20038

Powell, M. D. & Ladd, L. D. (2010). Bullying: A review of the literature and implications for family therapists. *American Journal of Family Therapy, 38*(3), 189–206. doi:10.1080/01926180902961662

Powell, R. A., & Honey, P. L. (2012). *Introduction to learning and behavior* (4th ed.). Belmont, CA: Cengage Learning/Wadsworth.

Power, M. (2010). *Emotion-focused cognitive therapy.* New York: Wiley/Blackwell.

Prat-Sala, M., & Redford, P. (2012). Writing essays: Does self-efficacy matter? The relationship between self-efficacy in reading and in writing and undergraduate students' performance in essay writing. *Educational Psychology, 32*(1), 9–20. doi:10.1080/01443410.2011.621411

Preckel, F., Holling, H., & Wiese, M. (2006). Relationship of intelligence and creativity in gifted and non-gifted students: An investigation of threshold theory. *Personality & Individual Differences, 40*(1), 159–170. doi:10.1016/j.paid.2005.06.022

Pressley, M. (1987). Are key-word method effects limited to slow presentation rates? An empirically

based reply to Hall and Fuson (1986). *Journal of Educational Psychology, 79*(3), 333–335. doi:10.1037/0022-0663.79.3.333

Price, D. D., Finniss, D. G., & Benedetti, F. (2008). A comprehensive review of the placebo effect: Recent advances and current thought. *Annual Review of Psychology, 59*, 565–590. doi:10.1146/annurev.psych.59.113006.095941

Price, J., & Davis, B. (2009). *The woman who can't forget: The extraordinary story of living with the most remarkable memory known to science—A memoir.* New York: Simon & Schuster.

Price, M., Mehta, N., Tone, E. B., et al. (2011). Does engagement with exposure yield better outcomes? components of presence as a predictor of treatment response for virtual reality exposure therapy for social phobia. *Journal of Anxiety Disorders, 25*(6), 763–770. doi:10.1016/j.janxdis.2011.03.004

Priluck, R., & Till, B. D. (2004). The role of contingency awareness, involvement, and need for cognition in attitude formation. *Journal of the Academy of Marketing Science, 32*(3), 329–344. doi:10.1177/0092070303257646

Prime, D. J., & Jolicoeur, P. (2010). Mental rotation requires visual short-term memory: Evidence from human electric cortical activity. *Journal of Cognitive Neuroscience, 22*(11), 2437–2446. doi:10.1162/jocn.2009.21357

Prochaska, J. O., & Norcross, J. C. (2010). *Systems of psychotherapy: A transtheoretical analysis* (7th ed.). Belmont, CA: Cengage Learning/Wadsworth.

Prokhorov, A. V., Kelder, S. H., Shegog, R., et al. (2010). Project aspire: An interactive, multimedia smoking prevention and cessation curriculum for culturally diverse high school students. *Substance Use & Misuse, 45*(6), 983–1006. doi:10.3109/10826080903038050

Provencher, M. D., Dugas, M. J., & Ladouceur, R. (2004). Efficacy of problem-solving training and cognitive exposure in the treatment of generalized anxiety disorder: A case replication series. *Cognitive & Behavioral Practice, 11*(4), 404–414. doi:10.1016/S1077-7229(04)80057-9

Puentes, J., Knox, D., & Zusman, M. E. (2008). Participants in "friends with benefits" relationships. *College Student Journal, 42*(1), 176–180.

Pychyl, T. A., Lee, J. M., Thibodeau, R., et al. (2000). Five days of emotion: An experience sampling study of undergraduate student procrastination. *Journal of Social Behavior & Personality, 15*(5), 239–254.

Quednow, B. B., Jessen, F., Kühn, K.-W., et al. (2006). Memory deficits in abstinent MDMA (ecstasy) users: Neuropsychological evidence of frontal dysfunction. *Journal of Psychopharmacology, 20*(3), 373–384. doi:10.1177/0269881106061200

Quinn, P. C., Bhatt, R. S., & Hayden, A. (2008). Young infants readily use proximity to organize visual pattern information. *Acta Psychologica,*

127(2), 289–298. doi:10.1016/j.actpsy.2007.06.002

Quinto-Pozos, D. (2008). Sign language contact and interference: ASL and LSM. *Language in Society, 37*(2), 161–189. doi:10.1017/S0047404508080251

Rabius, V., Wiatrek, D., & McAlister, A. L. (2012). African-American participation and success in telephone counseling for smoking cessation. *Nicotine & Tobacco Research, 14*(2), 240–242. doi:10.1093/ntr/ntr129

Rachman, S. (2004). *Anxiety* (2nd ed.). New York: Routledge.

Radvansky, G. A. (2011). *Human memory* (2nd ed.). Boston: Pearson/Allyn and Bacon.

Raid, G. H., & Tippin, S. M. (2009). Assessment of intellectual strengths and weaknesses with the Stanford-Binet Intelligence Scales—Fifth Edition (SB5). In J. A. Naglieri & S. Goldstein (Eds.), *Practitioner's guide to assessing intelligence and achievement* (pp. 127–152). New York: Wiley.

Ralston, A. (2004). *Between a rock and a hard place.* New York: Atria Books.

Ramachandran, V. S. (1995). 2-D or not 2-D—that is the question. In R. Gregory, J. Harris, P. Heard, & D. Rose (Eds.), *The artful eye* (pp. 249–267). Oxford: Oxford University Press.

Ramachandran, V. S. & Oberman, L. (2006). Broken mirrors: A theory of autism. *Scientific American, 295*(5), 62–69.

Ramsay, M. C., Reynolds, C. R., & Kamphaus, R. W. (2002). *Essentials of behavioral assessment.* New York: Wiley.

Rantanen, J., Metsäpelto, R. L., Feldt, T., et al. (2007). Long-term stability in the Big Five personality traits in adulthood. *Scandinavian Journal of Psychology, 48*(6), 511–518. doi:10.1111/j.1467-9450.2007.00609.x

Raposo, A., Han, S., & Dobbins, I. G. (2009). Ventrolateral prefrontal cortex and self-initiated semantic elaboration during memory retrieval. *Neuropsychologia, 47*(11), 2261–2271. doi:10.1016/j.neuropsychologia.2008.10.024

Rathus, R., Nevid, J., & Fichner-Rathus, L. (2010). *Human sexuality in a world of diversity* (7th ed.). Boston: Allyn & Bacon.

Rathus, S. A. (2011). *Childhood and adolescence: Voyages in development* (4th ed.). Belmont, CA: Cengage Learning/Wadsworth.

Rau, P. R. (2005). Drowsy driver detection and warning system for commercial vehicle drivers: Field operational test design, data analyses, and progress. *National Highway Traffic Safety Administration Paper Number 05-0192.* Retrieved February 18, 2012, from http://www-nrd.nhtsa.dot.gov/pdf/nrd-01/esv/esv19/05-0192-W.pdf

Rau, W., & Durand, A. (2000). The academic ethic and college grades: Does hard work help students to "make the grade"? *Sociology of Education, 73*(1), 19–38. doi:10.2307/2673197

Raun, K., von Voss, P., & Knudsen, L. B. (2007). Liraglutide, a once-daily human glucagon-like peptide-1 analog, minimizes food intake in severely obese minipigs. *Obesity,*

15(7), 1710–1716. doi:10.1038/oby.2007.204

Reason, J. (2000). The Freudian slip revisited. *The Psychologist, 13*(12), 610–611.

Reed, J. D., & Bruce, D. (1982). Longitudinal tracking of difficult memory retrievals. *Cognitive Psychology, 14*, 280–300. doi:10.1016/0010-0285(82)90011-1

Reed, S. K. (2013). *Cognition: Theory and applications* (9th ed.). Belmont, CA: Cengage Learning/Wadsworth.

Reevy, G. M., & Maslach, C. (2001). Use of social support: Gender and personality differences. *Sex Roles, 44*(7–8), 437–459. doi:10.1023/A:1011930128829

Regan, P. C., Levin, L., Sprecher, S., et al. (2000). Partner preferences: What characteristics do men and women desire in their short-term sexual and long-term romantic partners? *Journal of Psychology & Human Sexuality, 12*(3), 1–21. doi:10.1300/J056v12n03_01

Reid, M. R., Mackinnon, L. T., & Drummond, P. D. (2001). The effects of stress management on symptoms of upper respiratory tract infection, secretory immunoglobulin A, and mood in young adults. *Journal of Psychosomatic Research, 51*(6), 721–728. doi:10.1016/S0022-3999(01)00234-3

Reidy, D. A., & Riker, W. J. (Eds.). (2008). *Coercion and the state.* New York: Springer.

Reiff, S., Katkin, E. S., & Friedman, R. (1999). Classical conditioning of the human blood pressure response. *International Journal of Psychophysiology, 34*(2), 135–145. doi:10.1016/S0167-8760(99)00071-9

Reifman, A. S., Larrick, R. P., & Fein, S. (1991). Temper and temperature on the diamond: The heat-aggression relationship in major league baseball. *Personality & Social Psychology Bulletin, 17*(5), 580–585. doi:10.1177/0146167291175013

Reinberg, A., & Ashkenazi, I. (2008). Internal desynchronization of circadian rhythms and tolerance to shift work. *Chronobiology International, 25*(4), 625–643. doi:10.1080/07420520802256101

Reis, H. T., Maniaci, M. R., Caprariello, P. A., et al. (2011). Familiarity does indeed promote attraction in live interaction. *Journal of Personality & Social Psychology, Mar 7*, np.

Reis, S. M., & Renzulli, J. S. (2010). Is there still a need for gifted education? An examination of current research. *Learning & Individual Differences, 20*(4), 308–317. doi:10.1016/j.lindif.2009.10.012

Reisinger, D. (2008). Six degrees of separation is now three. *TechCrunch, Sept 3.* Retrieved May 9, 2012, from http://techcrunch.com/2008/09/03/six-degrees-of-separation-is-now-three

Reisner, A. D. (2006). A case of Munchausen syndrome by proxy with subsequent stalking behavior. *International Journal of Offender Therapy & Comparative Criminology, 50*(3), 245–254. doi:10.1177/0306624X05281880

Reiss, M., Tymnik, G., Koegler, P., et al. (1999). Laterality of hand, foot, eye, and ear in twins. *Laterality, 4*(3), 287–297. doi:10.1080/135765099396999

Reiss, S., & Havercamp, S. M. (2005). Motivation in developmental context: A new method for studying self-actualization. *Journal of Humanistic Psychology, 45*(1), 41–53. doi:10.1177/0022167804269133

Reivich, K., Gillham, J. E., Chaplin, T. M., et al. (2005). From helplessness to optimism: The role of resilience in treating and preventing depression in youth. In S. Goldstein & R. B. Brooks (Eds.), *Handbook of resilience in children* (pp. 223–237). New York: Kluwer Academic Publishers.

Reker, M., Ohrmann, P., Rauch, A. V., et al. (2010). Individual differences in alexithymia and brain response to masked emotion faces. *Cortex, 46*(5), 658–667. doi:10.1016/j.cortex.2009.05.008

Rentfrow, P. J. & Gosling, S. D. (2003). The do re mi's of everyday life: The structure and personality correlates of music preferences. *Journal of Personality & Social Psychology, 84*(6), 1236–1256. doi:10.1037/0022-3514.84.6.1236

Rentfrow, P. J., & Gosling, S. D. (2007). The content and validity of music-genre stereotypes among college students. *Psychology of Music, 35*(2), 306–326. doi:10.1177/0305735607070382

Rentfrow, P. J., Goldberg, L. R., & Levitin, D. J. (2011). The structure of musical preferences: A five-factor model. *Journal of Personality & Social Psychology, 100*(6), 1139–1157. doi:10.1037/a0022406

Rescorla, R. A. (1987). A Pavlovian analysis of goal-directed behavior. *American Psychologist, 42*, 119–129. doi:10.1037/0003-066X.42.2.119

Rescorla, R. A. (2004). Spontaneous recovery. *Learning & Memory, 11*(5), 501–509. doi:10.1101/lm.77504

Restak, R. M. (2001). *The secret life of the brain.* New York: Dana Press.

Revonsuo, A., Kallio, S., & Sikka, P. (2009). What is an altered state of consciousness? *Philosophical Psychology, 22*(2), 187–204. doi:10.1037/0951508090 2802850

Rhee, S. H., & Waldman, I. D. (2011). Genetic and environmental influences on aggression. In P. R. Shaver & M. Mikulincer (Eds.), *Human aggression and violence: Causes, manifestations, and consequences* (pp. 143–163). Washington, DC: American Psychological Association.

Rhine, J. B. (1953). *New world of the mind.* New York: Sloane.

Ribeiro, A. C., LeSauter, J., Dupré, C., et al. (2009). Relationship of arousal to circadian anticipatory behavior: Ventromedial hypothalamus: One node in a hunger arousal network. *European Journal of Neuroscience, 30*(9), 1730–1738. doi:10.1111/j.1460-9568.2009.06969.x

Rice, L., & Markey, P. M. (2009). The role of extraversion and neuroticism in influencing anxiety following computer-mediated interactions. *Personality & Individual Differences,* 46(1), 35–39. doi:10.1016/j.paid.2008.08.022

Richards, J. M., & Gross, J. J. (2000). Emotion regulation and memory: The cognitive costs of keeping one's cool. *Journal of Personality & Social Psychology, 79*(3), 410–424. doi:10.1037/0022-3514.79.3.410

Richmond, L. J. (2004). When spirituality goes awry: Students in cults. *Professional School Counseling, 7*(5), 367–375.

Ridenour, T. A., Maldonado-Molina M., Compton, W. M., et al. (2005). Factors associated with the transition from abuse to dependence among substance abusers: Implications for a measure of addictive liability. *Drug & Alcohol Dependence, 80*(1), 1–14.

Rideout, V., Foehr, U. G., & Roberts, D. F. (2010). *Generation M2: Media in the lives of 8–18 year-olds.* Menlo Park, CA: Kaiser Family Foundation. Retrieved May 9, 2012, from http://www.kff.org/entmedia/upload/8010.pdf

Riela, S., Rodriguez, G., Aron, A., et al. (2010). Experiences of falling in love: Investigating culture, ethnicity, gender, and speed. *Journal of Social & Personal Relationships, 27*(4), 473–493. doi:10.1177/0265407510363508

Rigakos, G. S., Davis, R. C., Ortiz, C., et al. (2009). Soft targets?: A national survey of the preparedness of large retail malls to prevent and respond to terrorist attack after 9/11. *Security Journal, 22*(4), 286–301. doi:10.1057/palgrave.sj.8350084

Riggio, H. R., & Garcia, A. L. (2009). The power of situations: Jonestown and the fundamental attribution error. *Teaching of Psychology, 36*(2), 108–112. doi:10.1080/00986280902739636

Riley, W., Jerome, A., Behar, A., et al. (2002). Feasibility of computerized scheduled gradual reduction for adolescent smoking cessation. *Substance Use & Misuse, 37*(2), 255–263.

Riquelme, H. (2002). Can people creative in imagery interpret ambiguous figures faster than people less creative in imagery? *Journal of Creative Behavior, 36*(2), 105–116. doi:10.1002/j.2162-6057.2002.tb01059.x

Ritchie, T. D., Sedikides, C., Wildschut, T., et al. (2011). Self-concept clarity mediates the relation between stress and subjective well-being. *Self & Identity, 10*(4), 493–508. doi:10.1080/15298868.2010.493066

Ritter, J. (1998). Uniforms changing the culture of the nation's classrooms. *USA Today,* Oct. 15, 1A, 2A.

Ritter, S. M., van Baaren, R. B., & Dijksterhuis, A. (2012). Creativity: The role of unconscious processes in idea generation and idea selection. *Thinking Skills & Creativity, 7*(1), 21–27. doi:10.1016/j.tsc.2011.12.002

Riva, G. (2009). Virtual reality: An experiential tool for clinical psychology. *British Journal of Guidance & Counseling, 37*(3), 337–345. doi:10.1080/03069880902957056

Riva, G., & Wiederhold, B. K. (2006). Emerging trends in cybertherapy: Introduction to the special issue. *Psychology Journal, 4*(2), 121–128.

Rizzolatti, G., & Craighero, L. (2004). The mirror-neuron system. *Annual Review of Neuroscience, 27*, 169–192. doi:10.1146/annurev.neuro.27.070203.144230

Rizzolatti, G., Fogassi, L., & Gallese V. (2006). Mirrors in the mind. *Scientific American, 295*(5), 54–61.

Roberts, B. W., & Mroczek, D. (2008). Personality trait change in adulthood. *Current Directions in Psychological Science, 17*(1), 31–35. doi:10.1111/j.1467-8721.2008.00543.x

Roberts, B. W., Kuncel, N. R., Shiner, R., et al. (2007). The power of personality: The comparative validity of personality traits, socioeconomic status, and cognitive ability for predicting important life outcomes. *Perspectives on Psychological Science, 2*(4),313–345. doi:10.1111/j.1745-6916.2007.00047.x

Roberts, R. E., Phinney, J. S., Masse, L. C., et al. (1999). The structure of ethnic identity of young adolescents from diverse ethnocultural groups. *Journal of Early Adolescence, 19*(3), 301–322. doi:10.1177/027243169901900300

Roberts, W. A. (2002). Are animals stuck in time? *Psychological Bulletin, 128*(3), 473–489.

Roberts, W. A. & Roberts, S. (2002). Two tests of the stuck-in-time hypothesis. *Journal of General Psychology, 129*(4), 415–429. doi:10.1080/00221300209602105

Robertson, L. C., & Sagiv, N, (2005). *Synesthesia: Perspectives from cognitive neuroscience.* New York: Oxford.

Robins, R. W., Gosling, S. D., & Craik, K. H. (1998). Psychological science at the crossroads. *American Scientist, 86*, 310–313. doi:10.1511/1998.4.310

Robinson, A. (2010). *Sudden genius? The gradual path to creative breakthroughs.* New York: Oxford University Press.

Robinson, D. N. (2008). *Consciousness and mental life.* New York: Columbia University Press.

Robinson, T. E., & Berridge, K. C. (2003). Addiction. *Annual Review of Psychology, 54*, 25–53. doi:10.1146/annurev.psych.54.101601.145237

Roca, M., Parr, A., Thompson, R., et al. (2010). Executive function and fluid intelligence after frontal lobe lesions. *Brain: A Journal of Neurology, 133*(1), 234–247. doi:10.1093/brain/awp269

Rock, A. (2004). *The mind at night: The new science of how and why we dream.* New York: Basic Books.

Rodd, Z. A., Bell, R. L., McQueen, V. K., et al. (2005). Chronic ethanol drinking by alcohol-preferring rats increases the sensitivity of the posterior ventral tegmental area to the reinforcing effects of ethanol. *Alcoholism: Clinical & Experimental Research, 29*(3), 358–366. doi:10.1097/01.ALC.0000156127.30983.9D

Roediger, H. L. III, & Amir, N., (2005). Implicit memory tasks: Retention without conscious recollection. In A. Wenzel & D. C. Rubin (Eds.), *Cognitive methods and their application to clinical research* (pp. 121–127). Washington, DC: American Psychological Association.

Roediger, H. L. III, & McDermott, K. B. (1995). Creating false memories: Remembering words not presented on lists. *Journal of Experimental Psychology: Learning, Memory, and Cognition, 21*(4), 803–814.

Roese, N. J., Pennington, G. L., Coleman, J., et al. (2006). Sex differences in regret: All for love or some for lust? *Personality & Social Psychology Bulletin, 32*(6), 770–780.

Roets, A., & Van Hiel, A. (2011). Allports prejudiced personality today: Need for closure as the motivated cognitive basis of prejudice. *Current Directions in Psychological Science, 20*(6), 349-354. doi:10.1177/0963721411424894

Roffman, J. L., Brohawn, D. G., Friedman, J, S., et al. (2011). MTHFR 677C>T effects on anterior cingulate structure and function during response monitoring in schizophrenia: A preliminary study. *Brain Imaging & Behavior, 5*(1), 65–75. doi:10.1007/s11682-010-9111-2

Rogers, C. R. (1959). A theory of therapy, personality, and interpersonal relationships, as developed in the client-centered framework. In S. Koch (Ed.), *Psychology: A study of a science* (Vol 3, pp. 184–256). New York: McGraw-Hill.

Rogers, C. R. (1961). *On becoming a person: A therapist's view of psychotherapy.* Boston: Houghton Mifflin.

Rogers, P., & Soule, J. (2009). Cross-cultural differences in the acceptance of Barnum profiles supposedly derived from Western versus Chinese astrology. *Journal of Cross-Cultural Psychology, 40*(3), 381–399. doi:10.1177/0022022109332843

Roizen, M. F., & Oz, M. C. (2006). *You on a diet: The owner's manual for waist management.* New York: Free Press.

Rollins, A. L., Bond, G. R., Lysaker, P. H., et al. (2010). Coping with positive and negative symptoms of schizophrenia. *American Journal of Psychiatric Rehabilitation, 13*(3), 208–223. doi:10.1080/15487768.2010.501297

Rolls, E. T. (2008). Top-down control of visual perception: Attention in natural vision. *Perception, 37*(3), 333–354. doi:10.1068/p5877

Roos, P. E., & Cohen, L. H. (1987). Sex roles and social support as moderators of life stress adjustment. *Journal of Personality & Social Psychology, 52*, 576–585. doi:10.1037/0022-3514.52.3.576

Rosa, N. M., & Gutchess, A. H. (2011). Source memory for action in young and older adults: Self vs. close or unknown others. *Psychology & Aging, 26*(3), 625–630. doi:10.1037/a0022827

Rosch, E. (1977). Classification of real-world objects: Origins and representations in cognition. In P. N. Johnson-Laird, & P. C. Wason (Eds.), *Thinking: Reading in cognitive science* (pp. 212–222). Cambridge, MA: Cambridge University Press.

Rosenhan, D. L. (1973). On being sane in insane places. *Science, 179*(4070), 250–258. doi:10.1126/science.179.4070.250

Rosenkranz, M.A., Jackson, D. C., Dalton, K. M., et al. (2003). Affective style and in vivo immune response: Neurobehavioral mechanisms. *Proceedings of the National Academy of Sciences, 100,* 11148–11152. doi:10.1073/pnas.1534743100

Rosenthal, M. (2013). *Human sexuality: From cells to society.* Belmont, CA: Cengage Learning/Wadsworth.

Rosenthal, R. (1973). The Pygmalion effect lives. *Psychology Today, Sept,* 56–63.

Rosenthal, R. (1994). Science and ethics in conducting, analyzing, and reporting psychological research. *Psychological Science, 5,* 127–134. doi:10.1111/j.1467-9280.1994.tb00644.x

Rosenthal, T. L. (1993). To soothe the savage breast. *Behavior Research & Therapy, 31*(5), 439–462. doi:10.1016/0005-7967(93)90126-F

Rosenthal, T. L., & Rosenthal, R. (1980). *The vicious cycle of stress reaction.* Copyright, Renate & Ted Rosenthal, Stress Management Clinic, Department of Psychiatry, University of Tennessee College of Medicine, Memphis, Tennessee.

Rosner, R. I. (2012). Aaron T. Beck's drawings and the psychoanalytic origin story of cognitive therapy. *History of Psychology, 15*(1), 1–18. doi:10.1037/a0023892

Rosnow, R. L. (2012). *Writing papers in psychology: A student guide to research papers, essays, proposals, posters, and handouts* (9th ed.). Belmont, CA: Cengage Learning/Wadsworth.

Ross, H. E., & Plug. C. (2002). *The mystery of the moon illusion.* Oxford: Oxford University Press.

Ross, M., Heine, S. J., Wilson, A. E., et al. (2005). Cross-cultural discrepancies in self-appraisals. *Personality & Social Psychology Bulletin, 31*(9), 1175–1188. doi:10.1177/0146167204274080

Ross, P. E. (2006). The expert mind. *Scientific American, 294*(7), 64–71.

Rossignol, S., & Frigon, A. (2011). Recovery of locomotion after spinal cord injury: Some facts and mechanisms. *Annual Review of Neuroscience, 34,* 413–440. doi:10.1146/annurev-neuro-061010-113746

Rothbart, M. K. (2007). Temperament, development, and personality. *Current Directions in Psychological Science, 16*(4), 207–212. doi:10.1111/j.1467-8721.2007.00505.x

Rotter, J. B. & Hochreich, D. J. (1975). *Personality.* Glenview, IL: Scott, Foresman.

Rozin, P., Kabnick, K., Pete, E., et al. (2003). The ecology of eating: Smaller portion sizes in France than in the United States help explain the French paradox. *Psychological Science, 14*(5), 450–454. doi:10.1111/1467-9280.02452

Rubenstein, C. (2002). What turns you on? *My Generation, July-Aug,* 55–58.

Rudd, M. D., Joiner, T. E., & Rajab, M. H. (2001). *Treating suicidal behavior.* New York: Guilford.

Rueckl, J. G., & Galantucci, B. (2005). The locus and time course of long-term morphological priming. *Language & Cognitive Processes, 20*(1), 115–138.

Rummens, J., Beiser, M., & Noh, S. (Eds.). (2003). *Immigration, ethnicity and health.* Toronto: University of Toronto Press.

Runco, M. A. (2004). Creativity. *Annual Review of Psychology, 55,* 657–687. doi:10.1146/annurev.psych.093008.100416

Runco, M. A. (2012). *Creativity: An interdisciplinary perspective.* New York: Routledge.

Runco, M. A., & Acar, S. (2012). Divergent thinking as an indicator of creative potential. *Creativity Research Journal, 24*(1), 66–75. doi:10.1080/10400419.2012.652929

Rushton, J. P., & Jensen, A. R. (2005). Thirty years of research on race differences in cognitive ability. *Psychology, Public Policy, & Law, 11,* 235–294. doi:10.1037/1076-8971.11.2.235

Russell, S., & Norvig, P. (2010). *Artificial intelligence: A modern approach* (3rd ed.). Englewood Cliffs, NJ: Prentice Hall.

Russo, M. B., Brooks, F. R., Fontenot, J., et al. (1998). Conversion disorder presenting as multiple sclerosis. *Military Medicine, 163*(10), 709–710.

Rutz, C., Bluff, L.A., Reed, N., et al. (2010). The ecological significance of tool use in New Caledonian crows. *Science, 329,* 1523–1526. doi:10.1126/science.1192053

Rutz, C., Bluff, L.A., Weir, A.A.S., et al. (2007). Video cameras on wild birds. *Science, 318,* 765. doi:10.1126/science.1146788

Ruva, C., McEvoy, C., & Bryant, J. B. (2007). Effects of pre-trial publicity and jury deliberation on juror bias and source memory errors. *Applied Cognitive Psychology, 21*(1), 45–67. doi:10.1002/acp.1254

Ryan, M. P. (2001). Conceptual models of lecture learning: Guiding metaphors and model-appropriate notetaking practices. *Reading Psychology, 22*(4), 289–312. doi:10.1080/02702710127638

Ryckman, R. M. (2013). *Theories of personality* (10th ed.). Belmont, CA: Cengage Learning/Wadsworth.

Ryff, C. D., & Singer, B. (2009). Understanding healthy aging: Key components and their integration. In V. L. Bengston, D. Gans, D., et al. (Eds.), *Handbook of theories of aging* (2nd ed., pp. 117–144). New York: Springer.

Ryff, C. D., Singer, B. H., & Palmersheim, K. A. (2004). Social inequalities in health and well-being: The role of relational and religious protective factors. In O. G. Brim, C. D. Ryff, et al. (Eds.), *How healthy are we? A national study of wellbeing at midlife* (pp. 90–123). Chicago: University of Chicago Press.

Saber, J. L., & Johnson, R. D. (2008). Don't throw out the baby with the bathwater: Verbal repetition, mnemonics, and active learning. *Journal of Marketing Education, 30*(3), 207–216. doi:10.1177/0273475308324630

Sachdev, P. S., & Chen, X. (2009). Neurosurgical treatment of mood disorders: Traditional psychosurgery and the advent of deep brain stimulation. *Current Opinion in Psychiatry, 22*(1), 25–31. doi:10.1097/YCO.0b013e32831c8475

Sack, R. L. (2010). Jet lag. *The New England Journal of Medicine, 362*(5), 440–447. doi:10.1056/NEJMcp0909838

Sackett, P. R., & Lievens, F. (2008). Personnel selection. *Annual Review of Psychology, 59,* 419–450. doi:10.1146/annurev.psych.59.103006.093716

Sacks, O. (2010). *The mind's eye.* New York: Knopf.

Saksida, L. M., & Wilkie, D. M. (1994). Time-of-day discrimination by pigeons. *Animal Learning & Behavior, 22,* 143–154. doi:10.3758/BF03199914

Salamone, J. D. (2007). Functions of mesolimbic dopamine: Changing concepts and shifting paradigms. *Psychopharmacology, 191*(3), 389. doi:10.1007/s00213-006-0623-9

Salimpoor, V. N., Benovoy, M. M., Larcher, K. K., et al. (2011). Anatomically distinct dopamine release during anticipation and experience of peak emotion to music. *Nature Neuroscience, 14*(2), 257–262. doi:10.1007/s00213-006-0623-9

Salisbury, A. G., & Burker, E. J. (2011). Assessment, treatment, and vocational implications of combat related PTSD in veterans. *Journal of Applied Rehabilitation Counseling, 42*(2), 42–49.

Sallinen, M., Holm, A., Hiltunen, J., et al. (2008). Recovery of cognitive performance from sleep debt: Do a short rest pause and a single recovery night help? *Chronobiology International, 25*(2–3), 279–296. doi:10.1080/07420520802210710

Salovey, P., & Mayer, J. (1997). *Emotional development and emotional intelligence.* New York: Basic.

Salthouse, T. A. (2004). What and when of cognitive aging. *Current Directions in Psychological Science, 13*(4), 140–144. doi:10.1111/j.0963-7214.2004.00293.x

Sam, D. L., & Berry, J. W. (2010). Acculturation: When individuals and groups of different cultural backgrounds meet. *Perspectives on Psychological Science, 5*(4), 472–481. doi:10.1177/1745691610373075

Sankofa, B. M., Hurley, E. A., Allen, B. A., et al. (2005). Cultural expression and black students' attitudes toward high achievers. *Journal of Psychology: Interdisciplinary & Applied, 139*(3), 247–259. doi:10.1037/1099-9809.14.4.336

Sansone, R. A., & Sansone, L. A. (2010). Road rage: What's driving it? *Psychiatry, 7*(7), 14–18.

Santelices, M. P., Guzmán G., M., Aracena, M., et al. (2011). Promoting secure attachment: Evaluation of the effectiveness of an early intervention pilot programme with mother–infant dyads in Santiago, Chile. *Child: Care, Health & Development, 37*(2), 203–210. doi:10.1111/j.1365-2214.2010.01161.x

Santrock, J. W. (2009). *Child development* (12th ed.). New York: McGraw-Hill.

Santrock, J. W. (2010). *A topical approach to lifespan development* (5th ed.). New York: McGraw-Hill.

Santrock, J. W., & Halonen, J. S. (2013). *Your guide to college success: Strategies for achieving your goals* (7th ed.). Belmont, CA: Cengage Learning/Wadsworth.

Sapolsky, R. (2005). Sick of poverty. *Scientific American, 293*(6), 92–99.

Sarason, I. G., & Sarason, B. R. (2005). *Abnormal psychology* (11th ed.). Mahwah, NJ: Prentice Hall.

Sartorius, A., Kiening, K. L., Kirsch, P., et al. (2010). Remission of major depression under deep brain stimulation of the lateral habenula in a therapy-refractory patient. *Biological Psychiatry, 67*(2), e9–e11. doi:10.1016/j.biopsych.2009.08.027

Sateia, M. J., & Nowell, P. D. (2004). Insomnia. *Lancet, 364*(9449), 1959–1973. doi:10.1016/S0140-6736(04)17480-1

Saunders, T., Driskell, J. E., Johnston, J. H., et al. (1996). The effect of stress inoculation training on anxiety and performance. *Journal of Occupational Health Psychology, 1*(2), 170–186. doi:10.1037/1076-8998.1.2.170

Sautter, J. M., Tippett, R. M., & Morgan, S. (2010). The social demography of Internet dating in the United States. *Social Science Quarterly, 91*(2), 554–575. doi:10.1111/j.1540-6237.2010.00707.x

Saxton, M. (2010). *Child language: Acquisition and development.* Thousand Oaks, CA: Sage.

Saxton, M., Houston-Price, C., & Dawson, N. (2005). The prompt hypothesis: Clarification requests as corrective input for grammatical errors. *Applied Psycholinguistics, 26*(3), 393–414. doi:10.1017/S0142716405050228

Saxvig, I. W., Lundervold, A. J., Gronli, J., et al. (2008). The effect of a REM sleep deprivation procedure on different aspects of memory function in humans. *Psychophysiology, 45*(2), 309–317. doi:10.1111/j.1469-8986.2007.00623.x

Schachter, S., & Wheeler, L. (1962). Epinephrine, chlorpromazine and amusement. *Journal of Abnormal and Social Psychology, 65,* 121–128.

Schacter, D. L. (1996). *Searching for memory: The brain, the mind, and the past.* New York: Basic Books.

Schacter, D. L., & Addis, D. R. (2008). The cognitive neuroscience of constructive memory: Remembering the past and imagining the future. In J. Driver, P. Haggard, et al. (Eds.), *Mental processes in the human brain* (pp. 27–47). New York: Oxford University Press.

Schafer, M., & Crichlow, S. (1996). Antecedents of groupthink: A quantitative study. *Journal of Conflict Resolution, 40*(3), 415–435. doi:10.1177/0022002796040003000

Schafer, M., & Crichlow, S. (2010). *Groupthink versus high-quality decision making in international relations.* New York: Columbia University Press.

Schaie, K. W. (1994). The course of adult intellectual development. *American Psychologist, 49*(4), 304–313. doi:10.1037/0003-066X.49.4.304

Schaie, K. W. (2005). *Developmental influences on adult intelligence: The*

Seattle longitudinal study. New York: Oxford University Press.

Scharinger, C., Rabl, U., Sitte, H. H., et al. (2010). Imaging genetics of mood disorders. *NeuroImage*, 3(3), 810–821. doi:10.1016/j.neuroimage.2010.02.019

Scheck, B., Neufeld, P., & Dwyer, J. (2000). *Actual innocence.* New York: Doubleday.

Scheinkman, M. (2008). The multi-level approach: A road map for couples therapy. *Family Process*, 47(2), 197–213.

Schenck, C. H., & Mahowald, M. W. (2005). Rapid eye movement and non-REM sleep parasomnias. *Primary Psychiatry*, 12(8), 67–74.

Schetter, C. D. (2011). Psychological science on pregnancy: Stress processes, biopsychosocial models, and emerging research issues. *Annual Review of Psychology*, 62, 531–558. doi:10.1146/annurev. psych.031809.130727

Schick, T., & Vaughn, L. (2011). *How to think about weird things: Critical thinking for a new age* (6th ed.). New York: McGraw-Hill.

Schiller, P. H., Slocum, W. M., Jao, B., et al. (2011). The integration of disparity, shading and motion parallax cues for depth perception in humans and monkeys. *Brain Research*, 1377, 67–77. doi:10.1016/ j.brainres.2011.01.003

Schilling, M. A. (2005). A "small-world" network model of cognitive insight. *Creativity Research Journal*, 17(2–3), 131–154. doi:10.1207/ s15326934crj1702&3_2

Schiraldi, G. R., & Brown, S. L. (2001). Primary prevention for mental health: Results of an exploratory cognitive-behavioral college course. *Journal of Primary Prevention*, 22(1), 55–67. doi:10.1023/A:1011040231249

Schlaepfer, T. E., Cohen, M. X., Frick, C., et al. (2008). Deep brain stimulation to reward circuitry alleviates anhedonia in refractory major depression. *Neuropsycho-pharmacology*, 33(2), 368–377. doi:10.1038/sj.npp.1301408

Schleicher, S. S., & Gilbert, L. A. (2005). Heterosexual dating discourses among college students: Is there still a double standard? *Journal of College Student Psychotherapy*, 19(3), 7–23. doi:10.1300/J035v19n03_03

Schlosberg, H. (1954). Three dimensions of emotion. *Psychological Review*, 61, 81–88. doi:10.1037/h0054570

Schlund, M. W. & Cataldo, M. F. (2010). Amygdala involvement in human avoidance, escape and approach behavior. *NeuroImage*, 53(2), 769–776. doi:10.1016/j.neuroimage.2010.06.058

Schmahmann, J. D. (2010). The role of the cerebellum in cognition and emotion: Personal reflections since 1982 on the dysmetria of thought hypothesis, and its historical evolution from theory to therapy. *Neuropsychology Review*, 20(3), 236–260. doi:10.1007/ s11065-010-9142-x

Schmalzl, L., Thomke, E., Ragnö, C., et al. (2011). "Pulling telescoped phantoms out of the stump": Manipulating the perceived position of phantom limbs using a full-body illusion. *Frontiers in Human*

Neuroscience, 5, doi:10.3389/ fnhum.2011.00121.

Schmelz, M. (2010). Itch and pain. *Neuroscience & Biobehavioral Reviews*, 34(2), 171–176. doi:10.1016/j. neubiorev.2008.12.004

Schmitt, D. P., & Allik, J. (2005). Simultaneous administration of the Rosenberg Self-Esteem Scale in 53 nations: Exploring the universal and culture-specific features of global self-esteem. *Journal of Personality & Social Psychology*, 89(4), 623–642. doi:10.1037/0022-3514.89.4.623

Schnakers, C. C., Perrin, F. F., Schabus, M. M., et al. (2009). Detecting consciousness in a total locked-in syndrome: An active event-related paradigm. *Neurocase*, 15(4), 271–277. doi:10.1080/13554790902724904

Schneider, K. J., Bugental, J. F. T., & Pierson, J. F. (2001). *The handbook of humanistic psychology.* Thousand Oaks, CA: Sage.

Schneider, K. J., Galvin, J., & Serlin, I. (2009). Rollo May on existential psychotherapy. *Journal of Humanistic Psychology*, 49(4), 419–434. doi:10.1177/0022167809340241

Schneiderman, N., Antoni, M. H., Saab, P. G., et al. (2001). Health psychology: Psychological and biobehavioral aspects of chronic disease management. *Annual Review of Psychology*, 52, 555–580. doi:10.1146/annurev.psych.52.1.555

Schoenberg, M. R., & Scott, J. G. (2008). *The black book of neuropsychology: A syndrome-based approach.* New York: Springer.

Schooler, C. (1998) Environmental complexity and the Flynn effect. In U. Neisser (Ed.), *The rising curve: Long-term gains in IQ and related measures* (pp. 67–79). Washington, DC: American Psychological Association.

Schopp, L. H., Demiris, G., & Glueckauf, R. L. (2006). Rural backwaters or front-runners? Rural telehealth in the vanguard of psychology practice. *Professional Psychology: Research & Practice*, 37(2), 165–173. doi:10.1037/0735-7028. 37.2.165

Schramm, D. G., Marshall, J. P., Harris, V. W., et al. (2012). Religiosity, homogamy, and marital adjustment: An examination of newlyweds in first marriages and remarriages. *Journal of Family Issues*, 33(2), 246–268. doi:10.1177/0192513X11420370

Schreiber, E. H., & Schreiber, D. E. (1999). Use of hypnosis with witnesses of vehicular homicide. *Contemporary Hypnosis*, 16(1), 40–44. doi:10.1002/ch.149

Schreiber, F. R. (1973). *Sybil.* Chicago: Regency.

Schroeder, J. E. (1995). Self-concept, social anxiety, and interpersonal perception skills. *Personality & Individual Differences*, 19(6), 955–958. doi:10.1016/S0191-8869(95)00108-5

Schroeder, S. (2008). Stranded in the periphery: The increasing marginalization of smokers. *New England Journal of Medicine*, 35(821), 2284. doi:10.1056/NEJMe0802708

Schuck, K., Keijsers, G. P. J., & Rinck, M. (2011). The effects of brief

cognitive-behaviour therapy for pathological skin picking: A randomized comparison to wait-list control. *Behaviour Research & Therapy*, 49(1), 11–17. doi:10.1016/j. brat.2010.09.005

Schuel, H., Chang, M. C., Burkman, L. J., et al. (1999). Cannabinoid receptors in sperm. In G. Nahas, K. M. Sutin, et al. (Eds.), *Marihuana and medicine* (pp. 335–345). Totowa, NJ: Humana Press.

Schultz, D. H., & Helmstetter, F. J. (2010). Classical conditioning of autonomic fear responses is independent of contingency awareness. *Journal of Experimental Psychology: Animal Behavior Processes*, 36(4), 495–500. doi:10.1037/a0020263

Schultz, D. P., & Schultz, S. E. (2012). *A history of modern psychology* (10th ed.). Belmont, CA: Cengage Learning/Wadsworth.

Schultz, D. P., & Schultz, S. E. (2013). *Theories of personality* (10th ed.). Belmont, CA: Cengage Learning/ Wadsworth.

Schultz, H. T. (2004). Good and bad movie therapy with good and bad outcomes. *The Amplifier: Official Newsletter of APA Division 46, Media Psychology*, Fall/Winter. Retrieved May 9, 2012, from http://www.apa.org/divisions/ div46/Amp%20Winter%2005/for%20 Website/ampwinter05.html#outcomes

Schuster, J., Hoertel, N., & Limosin, F. (2011). The man behind Philippe Pinel: Jean-Baptiste Pussin (1746–1811)— Psychiatry in pictures. *British Journal of Psychiatry*, 198(3), 198–241. doi:10.1192/bjp.198.3.241a

Schuster, M. A., Stein, B. D., Jaycox, L. H., et al. (2001). A national survey of stress reactions after the September 11, 2001, terrorist attacks. *New England Journal of Medicine*, 345(20), 1507–1512. doi:10.1056/NEJM200111153452024

Schwartz, S. J. (2008). Self and identity in early adolescence: Some reflections and an introduction to the special issue. *Journal of Early Adolescence*, 28(1), 5–15. doi:10.1177/0272431607308662

Schweckendiek, J., Klucken, T., Merz, C. J., et al. (2011). Weaving the (neuronal) web: Fear learning in spider phobia. *NeuroImage*, 54(1), 681–688. doi:10.1016/j.neuroimage. 2010.07.049

Schwenzer, M. (2008). Prosocial orientation may sensitize to aggression-related cues. *Social Behavior & Personality*, 36(8), 1009–1010. doi:10.2224/sbp.2008.36.8.1009

Schwitzgebel, E. (2011). *Perplexities of consciousness.* Cambridge, MA: MIT Press.

Sclafani, A., & Springer, D. (1976). Dietary obesity in adult rats: Similarities to hypothalamic and human obesity syndromes. *Psychology & Behavior*, 17, 461–471. doi:10.1016/0031-9384(76)90109-8

Scoboria, A., Mazzoni, G., Jarry, J. L., et al. (2012). Personalized and not general suggestion produces false autobiographical memories and suggestion-consistent behavior. *Acta Psychologica*, 139(1), 225–232. doi:10.1016/j.actpsy.2011.10.008

Scoboria, A., Mazzoni, G., Kirsch, I., et al. (2002). Immediate and persisting effects of misleading questions and hypnosis on memory reports. *Journal of Experimental Psychology: Applied*, 8(1), 26–32. doi:10.1037/1076-898X. 8.1.26

Scollon, C. N., & King, L. A. (2011). In R. Biswas-Diener R. (Ed.), *What people really want in life and why it matters: Contributions from research on folk theories of the good life* (pp. 1–14). New York: Springer.

Scollon, C. N., Koh, S., & Au, E. W. M. (2011). Cultural differences in the subjective experience of emotion: When and why they occur. *Social & Personality Psychology Compass*, 5(11), 853–864. doi:10.1111/j.1751-9004. 2011.00391.x

Scruggs, T. E. & Mastropieri, M. A. (2007). Science learning in special education: The case for constructed versus instructed learning. *Exceptionality*, 15(2), 57–74. doi:10.1080/09362830701294144

Scurfield, R. M. (2002). Commentary about the terrorist acts of September 11, 2001: Posttraumatic reactions and related social and policy issues. *Trauma Violence & Abuse*, 3(1), 3–14. doi:10.1177/15248380020031001

Sears, S., & Kraus, S. (2009). I think therefore I om: Cognitive distortions and coping style as mediators for the effects of mindfulness meditation on anxiety, positive and negative affect, and hope. *Journal of Clinical Psychology*, 65(6), 561–573. doi:10. 1002/jclp.20543

Seckel, A. (2000). *The art of optical illusions.* London: Carlton Books.

Segerdahl, P., Fields, W., & Savage-Rumbaugh, S. (2005). *Kanzi's primal language: The cultural initiation of primates into language.* New York: Palgrave MacMillan.

Segerstrom, S., & Miller, G. E. (2004). Psychological stress and the human immune system: A meta-analytic study of 30 years of inquiry. *Psychological Bulletin*, 130(4), 601–630. doi:10. 1037/0033-2909.130.4.601

Seidler, G. H., & Wagner, F. E. (2006). Comparing the efficacy of EMDR and trauma-focused cognitive-behavioral therapy in the treatment of PTSD: A meta-analytic study. *Psychological Medicine*, 36(11), 1515–1522. doi:10.1017/ S0033291706007963

Seitz, A., & Watanabe, T. (2005). A unified model for perceptual learning. *Trends in Cognitive Sciences*, 9(7), 329–334. doi:10.1016/j.tics.2005. 05.010

Sela, L., & Sobel, N. (2010). Human olfaction: A constant state of change-blindness. *Experimental Brain Research*, 205, 13–29. doi:10.1007/ s00221-010-2348-6

Seligman, M. E. P. (1972). For helplessness: Can we immunize the weak? In *Readings in Psychology Today* (2nd ed.). Del Mar, CA: CRM.

Seligman, M. E. P. (1989). *Helplessness.* New York: Freeman.

Seligman, M. E. P. (1995). The effectiveness of psychotherapy. *American Psychologist*, 50(12), 965–974.

Seligman, M. E. P. (2002). *Authentic happiness*. New York: Free Press.

Seligman, M. E. P. (2003). Positive psychology: Fundamental assumptions. *Source Psychologist*, *16*(3), 126–127.

Seligman, M. E. P., & Csikszentmihalyi, M. (2000). Positive psychology: An introduction. *American Psychologist*, *55*, 5–14. doi:10.1037/0003-066X.55.1.5

Selye, H. (1978). *The stress of life*. Oxford, England: McGraw-Hill.

Senécal, C., Julien, E., & Guay, F. (2003). Role conflict and academic procrastination: A self-determination perspective. *European Journal of Social Psychology*, *33*(1), 135–145. doi:10.1002/ejsp.144

Seybolt, D. C., & Wagner, M. K. (1997). Self-reinforcement, gender-role, and sex of participant in prediction of life satisfaction. *Psychological Reports*, *81*(2) 519–522. doi:10.2466/PR0.81.6.519-522

Seyle, D. C., & Newman, M. L. (2006). A house divided? The psychology of red and blue America. *American Psychologist*, *61*(6), 571–580. doi:10.1037/0003-066X.61.6.571

Shafer, C. S., & Hammitt, W. E. (1995). Congruency among experience dimensions, condition indicators, and coping behaviors in wilderness. *Leisure Sciences*, *17*, 263–279. doi:10.1080/01490409509513262

Shaffer, D. R. (2009). *Social and personality development* (6th ed.). Belmont, CA: Cengage Learning/Wadsworth.

Shaffer, D. R., & Kipp, K. (2010). *Developmental psychology: Childhood and adolescence* (8th ed.). Belmont, CA: Cengage Learning/Wadsworth.

Shafton, A. (1995). *Dream reader*. Albany, NY: SUNY Press.

Shanks, D. R. (2010). Learning: From association to cognition. *Annual Review of Psychology*, *61*, 273–301. doi:10.1146/annurev.psych.093008.100519

Shapiro, D. A., Barkham, M., Stiles, W. B., et al. (2003). Time is of the essence: A selective review of the fall and rise of brief therapy research. *Psychology & Psychotherapy: Theory, Research & Practice*, *76*(3), 211–235. doi:10.1348/147608303322362460

Shapiro, F. (2001). *Eye movement desensitization and reprocessing: Basic principles, protocols and procedures* (2nd ed.). New York: Guilford.

Shapiro, F., & Forrest, M. S. (2004). *EMDR: The breakthrough therapy for overcoming anxiety, stress, and trauma*. New York: Basic Books.

Shapiro, J. M. (2006). A "memory-jamming" theory of advertising. *Social Science Research Network*. Retrieved May 9, 2012, from http://papers.ssrn.com/sol3/papers.cfm?abstract_id=903474

Shapiro, S. L., & Walsh, R. (2006). The meeting of meditative disciplines and Western psychology: A mutually enriching dialogue. *American Psychologist*, *61*(3), 227–239. doi:10.1037/0003-066X.61.3.227

Sharf, R. S. (2012). *Theories of psychotherapy & counseling: Concepts and cases* (5th ed.). Belmont, CA: Cengage Learning/Wadsworth.

Shaver, P. R., & Mikulincer, M. (Eds.). (2011). *Human aggression and violence: Causes, manifestations, and consequences*. Washington, DC: American Psychological Association.

Shaw, E., & Delaporte, Y. (2011). New perspectives on the history of American sign language. *Sign Language Studies*, *11*(2), 158–204. doi:10.1353/sls.2010.0006

Shaywitz, B. A, Shaywitz, S. E., Pugh, K. R., et al. (1995). Sex differences in the functional organization of the brain for language. *Nature*, *373*, 607–609. doi:10.1038/373607a0

Shaywitz, S. E., & Gore, J. C. (1995). Sex differences in functional organization of the brain for language. *Nature*, *373*(6515), 607. doi:10.1038/373607a0

Shedler, J. (2010). The efficacy of psychodynamic psychotherapy. *American Psychologist*, *65*(2), 98–109. doi:10.1037/a0018378

Sheldon, K. M., Ryan, R. M., Rawsthorne, L. J., et al. (1997). Trait self and true self: Cross-role variation in the Big-Five personality traits and its relations with psychological authenticity and subjective well-being. *Journal of Personality & Social Psychology*, *73*(6), 1380–1393. doi:10.1037/0022-3514.73.6.1380

Shen, J., Botly, L. C. P., Chung, S. A., et al. (2006). Fatigue and shift work. *Journal of Sleep Research*, *15*(1), 1–5. doi:10.1111/j.1365-2869.2006.00493.x

Shepard, R. N. (1975). Form, formation, and transformation of internal representations. In R. L. Solso (Ed.), *Information processing and cognition: The Loyola Symposium* (pp. 87–122). Hillsdale, NJ: Erlbaum.

Shepherd, G. M. (2006). Smell images and the flavour system in the human brain. *Nature*, *444*(7117), 316–321. doi:10.1038/nature05405

Sherif, M., Harvey, O. J., White, B. J., et al. (1961). *Intergroup conflict and cooperation: The Robbers Cave experiment*. University of Oklahoma, Institute of Group Relations. Retrieved May 9, 2012 from http://psychclassics.yorku.ca/Sherif

Shermer, L. O., Rose, K. C., & Hoffman, A. (2011). Perceptions and credibility: Understanding the nuances of eyewitness testimony. *Journal of Contemporary Criminal Justice*, *27*(2), 183–203. doi:10.1177/1043986211405886

Shih, J. J., & Krusienski, D. J. (2012). Signals from intraventricular depth electrodes can control a brain-computer interface. *Journal of Neuroscience Methods*, *203*(2), 311–314. doi:10.1016/j.jneumeth.2011.10.012

Shillingsburg, M. A., Kelley, M. E., Roane, H. S., et al. (2009). Evaluation and training of yes-no responding across verbal operants. *Journal of Applied Behavior Analysis*, *42*(2), 209–223. doi:10.1901/jaba.2009.42-209

Shneerson, J. M. (2005). *Sleep medicine: A guide to sleep and its disorders* (2nd ed.). London: Blackwell.

Shneidman, E. S. (1987b). Psychological approaches to suicide. In G. R. VandenBos, and B. K. Bryant (Eds.), *Cataclysms, crises, and catastrophes: Psychology in action* (pp.147–184). Washington, DC: American Psychological Association.

Shorrock, S. T., & Isaac, A. (2010). Mental imagery in air traffic control. International *Journal of Aviation Psychology*, *20*(4), 309–324. doi:10.1080/10508414.2010.487008

Shrira, A., Palgi, Y., Ben-Ezra, M., et al. (2011). How subjective well-being and meaning in life interact in the hostile world? *The Journal of Positive Psychology*, *6*(4), 273–285. doi:10.1080/17439760.2011.577090

Shurkin, J. N. (1992). *Terman's kids*. Boston: Little, Brown.

Siefert, C. J. (2010). Screening for personality disorders in psychiatric settings: Four recently developed screening measures. In L. Baer & M. A. Blais (Eds), *Handbook of clinical rating scales and assessment in psychiatry and mental health* (pp.125–144). Totowa, NJ: Humana Press.

Siegel, D. J. (2007). *The mindful brain: Reflection and attunement in the cultivation of well-being*. New York: Norton.

Siegel, R. D. (2010). *The mindfulness solution: Everyday practices for everyday problems*. New York: Guilford.

Siegel, R. K. (2005). *Intoxication: The universal drive for mind-altering substances*. Rochester, VT: Park Street Press.

Siegler, R. S. (1989). Mechanisms of cognitive development. *Annual Review of Psychology*, *40*, 353–379. doi:10.1146/annurev.ps.40.020189.002033

Siegler, R. S. (2005). *Children's thinking* (4th ed.). Mahwah, NJ: Erlbaum.

Siegler, R. S., DeLoache, J. S., & Eisenberg, N. (2011). *How children develop* (3rd ed.). New York: Worth.

Sienaert, P., Vansteelandt, K., Demyttenaere, K., et al. (2010). Randomized comparison of ultra-brief bifrontal and unilateral electroconvulsive therapy for major depression: Cognitive side-effects. *Journal of Affective Disorders*, *122*(1–2), 60–67. doi:10.1016/j.jad.2009.06.011

Siever, L. J., & Koenigsberg, H. W. (2000). The frustrating no-man's-land of borderline personality disorder. *Cerebrum*, *2*(4), 85–99.

Sigelman, C. K., & Rider, E. A. (2012). *Life-span human development* (7th ed.). Belmont, CA: Cengage Learning/Wadsworth.

Silber, B. Y., & Schmitt, J. A. J. (2010). Effects of tryptophan loading on human cognition, mood, and sleep. *Neuroscience & Biobehavioral Reviews*, *34*(3), 387–407. doi:10.1016/j.neubiorev.2009.08.005

Silveri, M. C., Ciccarelli, N., & Cappa, A. (2011). Unilateral spatial neglect in degenerative brain pathology. *Neuropsychology*, *25*(5), 554–566. doi:10.1037/a0023957

Simeon, D., Guralnik, O., Knutelska, M., et al. (2002). Personality factors associated with dissociation: Temperament, defenses, and cognitive schemata. *American Journal of Psychiatry*, *159*, 489–491. doi:10.1176/appi.ajp.159.3.489

Simister, J., & Cooper, C. (2005). Thermal stress in the U.S.A.: Effects on violence and on employee behaviour. *Stress & Health*, *21*, 3–15. doi:10.1002/smi.1029

Simner, M. L., & Goffin, R. D. (2003). A position statement by the international graphonomics society on the use of graphology in personnel selection testing. *International Journal of Testing*, *3*(4), 353–364. doi:10.1207/S15327574IJT0304_4

Simons, D. A., & Wurtele, S. K. (2010). Relationships between parents' use of corporal punishment and their children's endorsement of spanking and hitting other children. *Child Abuse & Neglect*, *34*(9), 639–646. doi:10.1016/j.chiabu.2010.01.012

Simons, D. J., & Chabris, C. F. (1999). Gorillas in our midst: Sustained inattentional blindness for dynamic events. *Perception*, *28*, 1059–1074. doi:10.1068/p2952

Simons, D. J., & Levin, D. T. (1998). Failure to detect changes to people during a real-world interaction. *Psychonomic Bulletin & Review*, *5*(4), 644–649. doi:10.3758/BF03208840

Simon-Thomas, E. R., Role, K. O., & Knight, R. T. (2005). Behavioral and electrophysiological evidence of a right hemisphere bias for the influence of negative emotion on higher cognition. *Journal of Cognitive Neuroscience*, *17*(3), 518–529. doi:10.1162/0898929053279504

Simonton, D. K. (2009). Varieties of (scientific) creativity: A hierarchical model of domain-specific disposition, development, and achievement. *Perspectives on Psychological Science*, *4*(5), 441–452. doi:10.1111/j.1745-6924.2009.01152.x

Simpson, D. D., Joe, G. W., Fletcher, B. W., et al. (1999). A national evaluation of treatment outcomes for cocaine dependence. *Archives of General Psychiatry*, *57*(6), 507–514. doi:10.1001/archpsyc.59.6.538

Singer, J. D. (2005). Explaining foreign policy: U.S. decision-making and the Persian Gulf War. *Political Psychology*, *26*(5), 831–834.

Singer, M. T. (2003). *Cults in our midst: The continuing fight against their hidden menace*. San Francisco: Jossey-Bass.

Singer, M. T., & Addis, M. E. (1992). Cults, coercion, and contumely. *Cultic Studies Journal*, *9*(2), 163–189.

Singleton, J. L., & Newport, E. L. (2004). When learners surpass their models: The acquisition of American Sign Language from inconsistent input. *Cognitive Psychology*, *49*(4), 370–407. doi:10.1016/j.cogpsych.2004.05.001

Sinha, R., Garcia, M., Paliwal, P., et al. (2006). Stress-induced cocaine craving and hypothalamic-pituitary-adrenal responses are predictive of cocaine relapse outcomes. *Archives of General Psychiatry*, *63*(3), 324–331. doi:10.1001/archpsyc.63.3.324

Sipos, A., Rasmussen, F., Harrison, G., et al. (2004). Paternal age and schizophrenia: A population based cohort study. *British Medical Journal*,

329(7474), 1070. doi:10.1136/bmj.38243.672396.55

Sjöqvist, F., Garle, M., & Rane, A. (2008). Use of doping agents, particularly anabolic steroids, in sports and society. *Lancet*, 371(9627), 1872–1882. doi:10.1016/S0140-6736(08)60801-6

Skeels, H. M. (1966). Adult status of children with contrasting early life experiences. *Monograph of the Society for Research in Child Development*, 31(3), 1–56.

Skinner, B. F. (1938). *The behavior of organisms*. Englewood Cliffs, NJ: Prentice-Hall.

Skurnik, I., Yoon, C., Park, D. C., et al. (2005). How warnings about false claims become recommendations. *Journal of Consumer Research*, 31(4), 713–724. doi:10.1086/426605

Slocombe, K. E., Waller, B. M., & Liebal, K. (2011). The language void: The need for multimodality in primate communication research. *Animal Behaviour*, 81(5), 919–924. doi:10.1016/j.anbehav.2011.02.002

Sloman, A. (2008). The well-designed young mathematician. *Artificial Intelligence*, 172(18), 2015–2034. doi:10.1016/j.artint.2008.09.004

Slot, L. A. B., & Colpaert, F. C. (1999). Recall rendered dependent on an opiate state. *Behavioral Neuroscience*, 113(2), 337–344. doi:10.1037/0735-7044.113.2.337

Smedley, A., & Smedley, B. D. (2005). Race as biology is fiction, racism as a social problem is real. *American Psychologist*, 60(1), 16–26. doi:10.1037/0003-066X.60.1.16

Smith, A. P. (2005). Caffeine at work. *Human Psychopharmacology: Clinical & Experimental*, 20(6), 441–445. doi:10.1002/hup.705

Smith, A. P., Clark, R., & Gallagher, J. (1999). Breakfast cereal and caffeinated coffee: Effects on working memory, attention, mood and cardiovascular function. *Physiology & Behavior*, 67(1), 9–17. doi:10.1016/S0031-9384(99)00025-6

Smith, C. A., & Kirby, L. D. (2011). The role of appraisal and emotion in coping and adaptation. In R. J. Contrada & A. Baum (Eds.), *The handbook of stress science: Biology, psychology, and health* (pp. 195–208). New York: Springer.

Smith, C. S., Folkard, S., Tucker, P., et al. (2011). Work schedules, health, and safety. In J. C. Quick & L. E. Tetrick (Eds.), *Handbook of occupational health psychology* (2nd ed., pp. 185–204). Washington, DC: American Psychological Association.

Smith, J. D., Redford, J. S., & Haas, S. M. (2008). Prototype abstraction by monkeys (Macaca mulatta). *Journal of Experimental Psychology: General*, 137(2), 390–401. doi:10.1037/0096-3445.137.2.390

Smith, J. L., & Cahusac, P. M. B. (2001). Right-sided asymmetry in sensitivity to tickle. *Laterality*, 6(3), 233–238. doi:10.1080/13576500042000133

Smith, M. L., Cottrell, G. W., Gosselin, F., et al. (2005). Transmitting and decoding facial expressions. *Psychological Science*, 16(3), 184–189. doi:10.1111/j.0956-7976.2005.00801.x

Smith, M., Vogler, J., Zarrouf, F., et al. (2009). Electroconvulsive therapy: The struggles in the decision-making process and the aftermath of treatment. *Issues in Mental Health Nursing*, 30(9), 554–559. doi:10.1080/01612840902807947

Smith, T. W., & Traupman. E. K. (2011). Anger, hostility, and aggressiveness in coronary heart disease: Clinical applications of an interpersonal perspective. In R. Allan & J. Fisher (Eds.), *Heart and mind: The practice of cardiac psychology* (2nd ed., pp 187–198). Washington, DC: American Psychological Association.

Smith, T. W., Glazer, K., Ruiz, J. M., et al. (2004). Hostility, anger, aggressiveness, and coronary heart disease: An interpersonal perspective on personality, emotion, and health. *Journal of Personality*, 72(6), 1217–1270. doi:10.1111/j.1467-6494.2004.00296.x

Smith, T. W., Ruiz, J. M., & Uchino, B. N. (2004). Mental activation of supportive ties, hostility, and cardiovascular reactivity to laboratory stress in young men and women. *Health Psychology*, 23(5), 476–485. doi:10.1037/0278-6133.23.5.476

Smyth, J. D., Dillman, D. A., Christian, L. M., et al. (2010). Using the Internet to survey small towns and communities: Limitations and possibilities in the early 21st century. *American Behavioral Scientist*, 53(9), 1423–1448. doi:10.1177/0002764210361695

Smyth, J. M., & Pennebaker, J. W. (2008). Exploring the boundary conditions of expressive writing: In search of the right recipe. *British Journal of Health Psychology*, 13(1), 1–7. doi:10.1348/135910707X260117

Smyth, M. M., & Waller, A. (1998). Movement imagery in rock climbing. *Applied Cognitive Psychology*, 12(2), 145–157. doi:10.1002/(SICI)1099-0720(199804)12:2<145::AID-ACP505>3.0.CO;2-Z

Snow, C. P. (1961). Either-or. *Progressive*, Feb, 24.

Snowman, J., & McCown, R. (2011). *Psychology applied to teaching* (13th ed.). Belmont, CA: Cengage Learning/Wadsworth.

Snyder, A., Bahramali, H., Hawker, T., et al. (2006). Savant-like numerosity skills revealed in normal people by magnetic pulses. *Perception*, 35(6), 837–845. doi:10.1068/p5539

Snyder, C. R., Lopez, S. J., & Pedrotti, J. T. (2011). *Positive psychology: The scientific and practical explorations of human strengths* (2nd ed.). Thousand Oaks, CA: Sage.

Sobolewski, J. M., & Amato, P. R. (2005). Economic hardship in the family of origin and children's psychological well-being in adulthood. *Journal of Marriage & Family*, 67(1), 141–156. doi:10.1111/j.0022-2445.2005.00011.x

Soderstrom, M. (2007). Beyond babytalk: Re-evaluating the nature and content of speech input to preverbal infants. *Developmental Review*, 27(4), 501–532. doi:10.1016/j.dr.2007.06.002

Solomon, E. P., Solomon, R. M., & Heide, K. M. (2009). EMDR: An evidence-based treatment for victims of trauma. *Victims & Offenders*, 4(4), 391–397. doi:10.1080/15564880903227495

Solomon, J. L., Marshall, P., & Gardner, H. (2005). Crossing boundaries to generative wisdom: An analysis of professional work. In R. J. Sternberg & J. Jordan (Eds.), *A handbook of wisdom: Psychological perspectives* (pp. 272–296). New York: Cambridge University Press.

Solowij, N., Stephens, R. S., Roffman, R. A., et al. (2002). Cognitive functioning of long-term heavy cannabis users seeking treatment. *Journal of the American Medical Association*, 287, 1123–1131. doi:10-1001/pubs.JAMA-ISSN-0098-7484-287-9-joc11416

Soman, D. (2010). Option overload: How to deal with choice complexity. *Rotman Magazine*, Fall, 42–47.

Somberg, D. R., Stone, G., & Claiborn, C. D. (1993). Informed consent: Therapist's beliefs and practices. *Professional Psychology: Research & Practice*, 24(2), 153–159. doi:10.1037/0735-7028.24.2.153

Sommer, I. E. C. (2010). Sex differences in handedness, brain asymmetry, and language lateralization. In K. Hugdahl & R. Westerhausen (Eds.), *The two halves of the brain: Information processing in the cerebral hemispheres*. Cambridge, MA: MIT Press.

Sommers-Flanagan, J., & Sommers-Flanagan, R. (2008). *Clinical interviewing* (4th ed.). New York: Wiley.

Sorrell, J. M. (2009). Aging toward happiness. *Journal of Psychosocial Nursing & Mental Health Services*, 47(3), 23–26. doi:10.3928/02793695-20090301-14

Sousa, K., Orfale, A. G., Meireles, S. M., et al. (2009). Assessment of a biofeedback program to treat chronic low back pain. *Journal of Musculoskeletal Pain*, 17(4), 369–377. doi:10.3109/10582450903284828

Soussignan, R. (2002). Duchenne smile, emotional experience, and autonomic reactivity. *Emotion*, 2(1), 52–74. doi:10.1037/1528-3542.2.1.52

Soyez, V., & Broekaert, E. (2003). How do substance abusers and their significant others experience the re-entry phase of therapeutic community treatment: A qualitative study. *International Journal of Social Welfare*, 12(3), 211–220. doi:10.1111/1468-2397.00454

Spalding, K. L., Arner, E., Westermark, P. O., et al. (2008). Dynamics of fat cell turnover in humans. *Nature*, 453, 783–787. doi:10.1038/nature06902

Spano, R. (2005). Potential sources of observer bias in police observational data. *Social Science Research*, 34(3), 591–617. doi:10.1016/j.ssresearch.2004.05.003

Special, W. P., & Li-Barber, K. (2012). Self-disclosure and student satisfaction with facebook. *Computers in Human Behavior*, 28(2), 624–630. doi:10.1016/j.chb.2011.11.008

Spence, S. A., Kaylor-Hughes, C., Cooley, L., et al. (2009). Toward a cognitive neurobiological account of free association. *Neuropsychoanalysis*, 11(2), 151–163.

Spence, S., & David, A. (Eds.). (2004). *Voices in the brain: The cognitive neuropsychiatry of auditory verbal hallucinations*. London: Psychology Press.

Spencer-Thomas, S., & Jahn, D. R. (2012). Tracking a movement: U.S. milestones in suicide prevention. *Suicide & Life-Threatening Behavior*, 42(1), 78–85. doi:10.1111/j.1943-278X.2011.00072.x

Sperry, R. W. (1968). Hemisphere deconnection and unity in conscious awareness. *American Psychologist*, 23, 723–733. doi:10.1037/h0026839

Spiegler, M. D., & Guevremont, D. C. (2010). *Contemporary behavior therapy* (5th ed.). Belmont, CA: Cengage Learning/Wadsworth.

Spinella, M. (2005). Compulsive behavior in tobacco use. *Addictive Behaviors*, 30(1), 183–186. doi:10.1016/j.addbeh.2004.04.011

Spiro Wagner, P., & Spiro, C. S. (2005). *Divided minds: Twin sisters and their journey through schizophrenia*. New York, St. Martin's Press.

Sporer, S. L. (2001). Recognizing faces of other ethnic groups. *Psychology, Public Policy, & Law*, 7(1), 36–97. doi:10.1037/1076-8971.7.1.36

Springer, C. R., & Pear, J. J. (2008). Performance measures in courses using computer-aided personalized system of instruction. *Computers & Education*, 51(2), 829–835.

Springer, S. P., & Deutsch, G. (1998). *Left brain, right brain*. New York: Freeman.

Squire, L. R. (2004). Memory systems of the brain: A brief history and current perspective. *Neurobiology of Learning & Memory*, 82, 171–177. doi:10.1016/j.nlm.2004.06.005

Squire, L. R., & Wixted, J. T. (2011). The cognitive neuroscience of human memory since H.M. *Annual Review of Neuroscience*, 34(0147–006), 259–288. doi:10.1146/annurev-neuro-061010-113720

Sroufe, L. A., Egeland, B., Carlson, E., et al. (2005). Placing early attachment experiences in developmental context: The Minnesota Longitudinal Study. In K. E. Grossmann, K. Grossmann, & E. Waters, et al. (Eds.), *Attachment from infancy to adulthood: The major longitudinal studies* (pp. 48–70). New York: Guilford.

Stacks, A. M., & Oshio, T., Gerard, J., et al. (2009). The moderating effect of parental warmth on the association between spanking and child aggression: A longitudinal approach. *Infant & Child Development*, 18(2), 178–194. doi:10.1002/icd.596

Stall-Meadows, C., & Hebert, P. R. (2011). The sustainable consumer: An in situ study of residential lighting alternatives as influenced by infield education. *International Journal of Consumer Studies*, 35(2), 164–170. doi:10.1111/j.1470-6431.2010.00987.x

Stanovich, K. E. (2010). *How to think straight about psychology* (9th ed.). Boston: Allyn & Bacon.

Stapel, D. A., & Marx, D. M. (2007). Distinctiveness is key: How different types of self-other similarity moderate social comparison effects.

Personality & Social Psychology Bulletin, 33(3), 439–448. doi:10.1177/0146167206296105

Steele, C. M. (1997). A threat in the air: How stereotypes shape intellectual identity and performance. *American Psychologist*, 52(6), 613–629. doi:10.1037/0003-066X.52.6.613

Steele, C. M., & Aronson, J. (1995). Stereotype threat and the intellectual test performance of African Americans. *Journal of Personality & Social Psychology*, 69(5), 797–811. doi:10.1037/0022-3514.69.5.797

Steiger, A. (2007). Neurochemical regulation of sleep. *Journal of Psychiatric Research*, 41, 537–552. doi:10.1016/j.jpsychires.2006.04.007

Stein, L. M., & Memon, A. (2006). Testing the efficacy of the cognitive interview in a developing country. *Applied Cognitive Psychology*, 20(5), 597–605. doi:10.1002/acp.1211

Stein, M. B., & Stein, Dan J. (2008). Social anxiety disorder. *Lancet*, 371(9618), 1115–1125. doi:10.1016/S0140-6736(08)60488-2

Stein, M. D., & Friedmann, P. D. (2005). Disturbed sleep and its relationship to alcohol use. *Substance Abuse*, 26(1), 1–13. doi:10.1300/J465v26n01_01

Stein, M. I. (1974). *Stimulating creativity* (Vol. 1). New York: Academic.

Stein, M. T., & Ferber, R. (2001). Recent onset of sleepwalking in early adolescence. *Journal of Development, Behavior, & Pediatrics*, 22, S33–S35.

Steinberg, L (2001). Adolescent development. *Annual Review of Psychology*, 52, 83–110. doi:10.1146/annurev.psych.52.1.83

Steinmayr, R., & Spinath, B. (2009). The importance of motivation as a predictor of school achievement. *Learning & Individual Differences*, 19(1), 80–90. doi:10.1016/j.lindif.2008.05.004

Steketee, G., Frost, R. O., Tolin, D. F., et al. (2010). Waitlist-controlled trial of cognitive behavior therapy for hoarding disorder. *Depression & Anxiety*, 27(5), 476–484. doi:10.1002/da.20673

Stemler, S. E., & Sternberg, R. J. (2006). Using situational judgment tests to measure practical intelligence. In J. A. Weekley & R. E. Ployhart (Eds.), *Situational judgment tests: Theory, measurement, and application* (pp. 107–131). Mahwah, NJ: Erlbaum.

Stephens, K., Kiger, L., Karnes, F. A., et al. (1999). Use of nonverbal measures of intelligence in identification of culturally diverse gifted students in rural areas. *Perceptual & Motor Skills*, 88(3, Pt 1), 793–796. doi:10.2466/PMS.88.3.793-796

Stern, S. L., Dhanda, R., & Hazuda, H. P. (2001). Hopelessness predicts mortality in older Mexican and European Americans. *Psychosomatic Medicine*, 63(3), 344–351.

Sternberg, E. M. (2009). *Healing spaces: The science of place and well-being.* Cambridge, MA: Harvard University Press.

Sternberg, R. J. (1988). *The triangle of love.* New York: Basic.

Sternberg, R. J. (2004). Culture and intelligence. *American Psychologist*,

59(5), 325–338. doi:10.1037/0003-066X.59.5.325

Sternberg, R. J. (2007). Race and intelligence: Not a case of black and white. *New Scientist, Oct 27*, 16.

Sternberg, R. J. (2011). *Cognitive psychology* (6th ed.). Belmont, CA: Cengage Learning/Wadsworth.

Sternberg, R. J., & Grigorenko, E. L. (2005). Cultural explorations of the nature of intelligence. In A. F. Healy (Ed.), *Experimental cognitive psychology and its applications* (pp. 225–235). Washington, DC: American Psychological Association.

Sternberg, R. J., & Grigorenko, E. L. (2006). Cultural intelligence and successful intelligence. *Group & Organization Management*, 31(1), 27–39. doi:10.1177/1059601105275255

Sternberg, R. J., & Lubart, T. I. (1995). *Defying the crowd.* New York: The Free Press.

Sternberg, R. J., Grigorenko, E. L., & Kidd, K. K. (2005). Intelligence, race, and genetics. *American Psychologist*, 60(1), 46–59. doi:10.1037/0003-066X.60.1.46

Sternberg, R. J., Grigorenko, E. L., Kidd, K. K., et al. (2011). Intelligence, race, and genetics. In S. Krimsky & K. Sloan (Eds.), *Race and the genetic revolution: Science, myth, and culture* (pp. 195–237). New York: Columbia University Press.

Sterns, H. L., & Huyck, M. H. (2001). The role of work in midlife. In M. Lachman (Ed.), *The handbook of midlife development* (pp. 447–486). New York: Wiley.

Stetz, T., Button, S. B., & Porr, W. B. (2009). New tricks for an old dog: Visualizing job analysis results. *Public Personnel Management*, 38(1), 91–100.

Stewart, A. J., & Ostrove, J. M. (1998). Women's personality in middle age. *American Psychologist*, 53(11), 1185–1194. doi:10.1037/0003-066X.53.11.1185

Stewart-Williams, S. (2004). The placebo puzzle: Putting together the pieces. *Health Psychology*, 23(2), 198–206. doi:10.1037/0278-6133.23.2.198

Stickgold, R., & Walker, M. (2004). To sleep, perchance to gain creative insight? *Trends in Cognitive Sciences*, 8(5), 191–192. doi:10.1016/j.tics.2004.03.003

Stinson, F. S., Dawson, D. A., Chou, S. P., et al. (2007). The epidemiology of DSM-IV specific phobia in the USA: Result from the National Epidemiologic Survey on Alcohol and Related Conditions. *Psychological Medicine*, 37(7), 1047–1059. doi:10.1017/S0033291707000086

Stix, G. (2010). Alzheimer's: Forestalling the darkness. *Scientific American*, 302, 50–59. doi:10.1038/scientificamerican0610-50

Stix, G. (2011).The neuroscience of true grit. *Scientific American*, 304, 28–33. doi:10.1038/scientificamerican0111-29a

Stöber, J. (2004). Dimensions of test anxiety: Relations to ways of coping with pre-exam anxiety and uncertainty. *Anxiety, Stress & Coping*, 17(3), 213–226. doi:10.1080/1061580412331292615

Stoffregen, T. A., Faugloire, E., Yoshida, K., et al. (2008). Motion sickness and

postural sway in console video games. *Human Factors*, 50(2), 322–331. doi:10.1518/001872008X250755

Stokes, D. M. (2001, May-June). The shrinking filedrawer. *Skeptical Inquirer, May–June*, 22–25.

Stokes, D., & Lappin, M. (2010). Neurofeedback and biofeedback with 37 migraineurs: A clinical outcome study. *Behavioral & Brain Functions*, 6(Feb 2), ArtID 9; 10 pp. Retrieved May 9, 2012, from http://www.ncbi.nlm.nih.gov/pmc/articles/PMC2826281

Stone, J., Perry, Z. W., & Darley, J. M. (1997). "White men can't jump." *Basic & Applied Social Psychology*, 19(3), 291–306. doi:10.1207/15324839751036977

Stoppard, J. M., & McMullen, L. M. (Eds.). (2003). *Situating sadness: Women and depression in social context.* New York: New York University Press.

Strack, F., & Förster, J. (Eds.). (2009). *Social cognition: The basis of human interaction.* New York: Psychology Press.

Strack. F., Martin, L. L., & Stepper, S. (1988). Inhibiting and facilitating conditions of facial expressions: A non-obtrusive test of the facial feedback hypothesis. *Journal of Personality & Social Psychology*, 54, 768–777. doi:10.1037/0022-3514.54.5.768

Strange, J. R. (1965). *Abnormal psychology.* New York: McGraw-Hill.

Straub, R. (2012). *Health psychology* (3rd ed.). New York: Worth.

Strayer, D. L., Drews, F. A., & Crouch, D. J. (2006). A comparison of the cell phone driver and the drunk driver. *Human Factors*, 48(2), 381–391. doi:10.1518/001872006777724471

Strickler, E. M., & Verbalis, J. G. (1988). Hormones and behavior: The biology of thirst and sodium appetite. *American Scientist, May–June*, 261–267.

Stroebe, W., Papies, E. K., & Aarts, H. (2008). From homeostatic to hedonic theories of eating: Self-regulatory failure in food-rich environments. *Applied Psychology*, 57, 172–193. doi:10.1111/j.1464-0597.2008.00360.x

Strong, B., DeVault, C., & Cohen, T. C. (2011). *The marriage and family experience: Intimate relationships in a changing society* (11th ed.). Belmont, CA: Cengage Learning/Wadsworth.

Strongman, K. T. (2003). *The psychology of emotion: From everyday life to theory* (5th ed.). New York: Wiley.

Strote, J., Lee, J. E., & Wechsler, H. (2002). Increasing MDMA use among college students: Results of a national survey. *Journal of Adolescent Health*, 30(1), 64–72. doi:10.1016/S1054-139X(01)00315-9

Strubbe, M. J. (2005). What did Triplett really find? A contemporary analysis of the first experiment in social psychology. *American Journal of Psychology*, 118, 271–286.

Sturges, J. W., & Sturges, L. V. (1998). In vivo *systematic desensitization* in a single-session treatment of an 11-year old girl's elevator phobia. *Child & Family Behavior Therapy*, 20(4), 55–62. doi:10.1300/J019v20n04_04

Stuss, D. T., & Knight, R. T. (2002). *Principles of frontal lobe function.* New York: Oxford University Press.

Substance Abuse and Mental Health Services Administration. (2011). *Results from the 2010 National Survey on Drug Use and Health: Summary of national findings.* Rockville, MD: Author. Retrieved February 8, 2012, from http://oas.samhsa.gov/NSDUH/2k10NSDUH/2k10Results.pdf

Sue, D., Sue, D. W., Sue, D., et al. (2013). *Understanding abnormal behavior* (10th ed.). Belmont, CA: Cengage Learning/Wadsworth.

Suedfeld, P., & Borrie, R. A. (1999). Health and therapeutic applications of chamber and flotation restricted environmental stimulation therapy (REST). *Psychology & Health*, 14(3), 545–566. doi:10.1080/08870449908407346

Sugimoto, K., & Ninomiya, Y. (2005). Introductory remarks on umami research: Candidate receptors and signal transduction mechanisms on umami. *Chemical Senses*, 30(Suppl. 1), i21–i22. doi:10.1093/chemse/bjh093

Suinn, R. M. (1975). *Fundamentals of behavior pathology* (2nd ed.). New York: Wiley.

Suinn, R. M. (1999). Scaling the summit: Valuing ethnicity. *APA Monitor, March*, 2.

Suinn, R. M. (2001). The terrible twos: Anger and anxiety. *American Psychologist*, 56(1), 27–36. doi:10.1037/0003-066X.56.1.27

Suls, J. M., Luger, T., & Martin, R. (2010), The biopsychosocial model and the use of theory in health psychology. In J. M. Suls, K. W. Davidson, et al. (Eds.), *Handbook of health psychology and behavioral medicine* (pp. 15–27). New York: Guilford.

Sumerlin, J. R., & Bundrick, C. M. (1996). Brief index of self-actualization: A measure of Maslow's model. *Journal of Social Behavior & Personality*, 11(2), 253–271.

Sunnafrank, M., Ramirez, A., & Metts, S. (2004). At first sight: Persistent relational effects of get-acquainted conversations. *Journal of Social & Personal Relationships*, 21(3), 361–379. doi:10.1177/0265407504042837

Sutin, A. R., & Costa, Jr., P. T. (2010). Reciprocal influences of personality and job characteristics across middle adulthood. *Journal of Personality*, 78(1), 257–288. doi:10.1111/j.1467-6494.2009.00615.x

Suzuki, L., & Aronson, J. (2005). The cultural malleability of intelligence and its impact on the racial/ethnic hierarchy. *Psychology, Public Policy, & Law*, 11, 320–327. doi:10.1037/1076-8971.11.2.320

Svartdal, F. (2003). Extinction after partial reinforcement: Predicted vs. judged persistence. *Scandinavian Journal of Psychology*, 44(1), 55–64. doi:10.1111/1467-9450.00321

Sveticic, J., Milner, A., & De Leo, D. (2012). Contacts with mental health services before suicide: A comparison of indigenous with non-indigenous Australians. *General Hospital*

Psychiatry, 34(2), 185–191. doi:10.1016/j.genhosppsych.2011.10.009

Swann, Jr., W. B., Chang-Schneider, C., & Larsen McClarty, K. (2007). Do people's self-views matter? Self-concept and self-esteem in everyday life. American Psychologist, 62(2), 84–94. doi:10.1037/0003-066X.62.2.84

Swanson, S. A., Crow, S. J., Le Grange, D., et al. (2011). Prevalence and correlates of eating disorders in adolescents: Results from the national comorbidity survey replication adolescent supplement. Archives of General Psychiatry, 68(7), 714–723. doi:10.1001/archgenpsychiatry.2011.22

Swearer, S. M., Espelage, D. L. & Napolitano, S. A. (2009). Bullying prevention and intervention: Realistic strategies for schools. New York: Guilford.

Synhorst, L. L., Buckley, J. A., Reid, R., et al. (2005). Cross-informant agreement of the Behavioral and Emotional Rating Scale—2nd Edition (BERS-2) parent and youth rating scales. Child & Family Behavior Therapy, 27(3), 1–11. doi:10.1300/J019v27n03_01

Szabo, A. (2003). The acute effects of humor and exercise on mood and anxiety. Journal of Leisure Research, 35(2), 152–162.

Szaflarski, J. P., Rajagopal, A., Altaye, M., et al. (2011). Left-handedness and language lateralization in children. Brain Research. doi:10.1016/j.brainres.2011.11.026

Szollos, A. (2009). Toward a psychology of chronic time pressure: Conceptual and methodological review. Time & Society, 18(2–3), 332–350. doi:10.1177/0961463X09337847

Tackett, J. L., & Krueger, R. F. (2011). Dispositional influences on human aggression. In P. R. Shaver & M. Mikulincer (Eds.), Human aggression and violence: Causes, manifestations, and consequences (pp. 89–104). Washington, DC: American Psychological Association.

Talbot, N. L., & Gamble, S. A. (2008). IPT for women with trauma histories in community mental health care. Journal of Contemporary Psychotherapy, 38(1), 35–44. doi:10.1007/s10879-007-9066-9

Talbott, J. A. (2004). Deinstitutionalization: Avoiding the disasters of the past. Psychiatric Services, 55(10), 1112–1115. doi:10.1176/appi.ps.55.10.1112

Tal-Or, N., & Papirman, Y. (2007). The fundamental attribution error in attributing fictional figures' characteristics to the actors. Media Psychology, 9(2), 331–345. doi:10.1080/15213260701286049

Talley, P. F., Strupp, H. H., & Morey, L. C. (1990). Matchmaking in psychotherapy: Patient–therapist dimensions and their impact on outcome. Journal of Consulting & Clinical Psychology, 58(2), 182–188. doi:10.1037/0022-006X.58.2.182

Tam, H., Jarrold, C., Baddeley, A. D., et al. (2010). The development of memory maintenance: Children's use of phonological rehearsal and attentional refreshment in working memory tasks. Journal of Experimental Child Psychology, 107(3), 306–324. doi:10.1016/j.jecp.2010.05.006

Tamis-LeMonda, C. S., Bornstein, M. H., & Baumwell, L. (2001). Maternal responsiveness and children's achievement of language milestones. Child Development, 72, 748–767. doi:10.1111/1467-8624.00313

Tamis-LeMonda, C. S., Shannon, J. D., Cabrera, N. J., et al. (2004). Fathers and mothers at play with their 2- and 3-year-olds: Contributions to language and cognitive development. Child Development, 75(6), 1806–1820. doi:10.1111/j.1467-8624.2004.00818.x

Tang, C. Y., Eaves, E. L., Ng, J. C., et al. (2010). Brain networks for working memory and factors of intelligence assessed in males and females with fMRI and DTI. Intelligence, 38(3), 293–303. doi:10.1016/j.intell.2010.03.003

Tanner, D. C. (2007). Redefining Wernicke's area: Receptive language and discourse semantics. Journal of Allied Health, 36(2), 63–66.

Taraban, R., Rynearson, K., & Kerr, M. (2000). College students' academic performance and self-reports of comprehension strategy use. Reading Psychology, 21(4), 283–308. doi:10.1080/027027100750061930

Taris, T. W., Bakker, A. B., Schaufeli, W. B., et al. (2005). Job control and burnout across occupations. Psychological Reports, 97(3), 955–961. doi:10.2466/PR0.97.7.955-961

Tatum, J. L., & Foubert, J. D. (2009). Rape myth acceptance, hypermasculinity, and SAT scores as correlates of moral development: Understanding sexually aggressive attitudes in first-year college men. Journal of College Student Development, 50(2), 195–209. doi:10.1353/csd.0.0062

Taub, E. (2004). Harnessing brain plasticity through behavioral techniques to produce new treatments in neurorehabilitation. American Psychologist, 59(8), 692–704. doi:10.1037/0003-066X.59.8.692

Tauber, A. I. (2010). Freud, the reluctant philosopher. Princeton, NJ: Princeton University Press.

Tausig, M., Michello, J., & Subedi, S. (2004). A sociology of mental illness (2nd ed.). Englewood Cliffs, NJ: Prentice Hall.

Tavakoli, S., Lumley, M. A., Hijazi, A. M., et al. (2009). Effects of assertiveness training and expressive writing on acculturative stress in international students: A randomized trial. Journal of Counseling Psychology, 56(4), 590–596. doi:10.1037/a0016634

Tavris, C., & Aronson, E. (2007). Mistakes were made (but not by me): Why we justify foolish beliefs, bad decisions, and hurtful acts. New York: Harcourt.

Tay, L., & Diener, E. (2011). Needs and subjective well-being around the world. Journal of Personality & Social Psychology, 101(2), 354–365. doi:10.1037/a0023779

Taylor, C. A., Manganello, J. A., Lee, S. J., et al. (2010). Mothers' spanking of 3-year-old children and subsequent risk of children's aggressive behavior. Pediatrics, 125(5), e1057–e1065. doi:10.1542/peds.2009-2678

Taylor, D. J., & Roane, B. M. (2010). Treatment of insomnia in adults and children: A practice-friendly review of research. Journal of Clinical Psychology, 66(11), 1137–1147. doi:10.1002/jclp.20733

Taylor, G. J., & Taylor-Allan, H. L. (2007). Applying emotional intelligence in understanding and treating physical and psychological disorders: What we have learned from alexithymia. In R. Bar-On, M. J. G. Reuven, et al. (Eds.), Educating people to be emotionally intelligent (pp. 211–223). Westport, CT: Praeger.

Taylor, K. (2004). Brainwashing: The science of thought control. New York: Oxford University Press.

Taylor, S. E. (2011). The future of social-health psychology: Prospects and predictions. Social & Personality Psychology Compass, 5, 275–284. doi:10.1111/j.1751-9004.2011.00360.x

Taylor, S. E. (2012). Health psychology (8th ed.). New York: McGraw-Hill

Taylor, S. E., & Master, S. L. (2011). Social responses to stress: The tend-and-befriend model. In R. J. Contrada & A. Baum (Eds.), The handbook of stress science: Biology, psychology, and health (pp. 101–109). New York: Springer.

Taylor, S. E., Lerner, J. S., Sherman, D. K., et al. (2003). Are self-enhancing cognitions associated with healthy or unhealthy biological profiles? Journal of Personality & Social Psychology, 85(4), 605–615. doi:10.1037/0022-3514.85.4.605

Teed, E. L., Scileppi, J. A., Boeckmann, M., et al. (2007). The community mental health system: A navigational guide for providers. Boston: Allyn & Bacon.

Teglasi, H. (2010). Essentials of TAT and other storytelling assessments (2nd ed.). Hoboken, NJ: Wiley.

Tennesen, M. (2007). Gone today, hear tomorrow. New Scientist, March 10, 42–45.

Tennie, C., Greve, K., Gretscher, H., et al. (2010). Two-year-old children copy more reliably and more often than nonhuman great apes in multiple observational learning tasks. Primates, 51(4), 337–351. doi:10.1007/s10329-010-0208-4

Teo, A. R., & Gaw, A. C. (2010). Hikikomori, a Japanese culture-bound syndrome of social withdrawal? A proposal for DSM-5. Journal of Nervous & Mental Disease, 198(6), 444–449. doi:10.1097/NMD.0b013e3181e086b1

Terman, L. M., & Merrill, M. A. (1937/1960). Stanford-Binet Intelligence Scale. Boston: Houghton Mifflin.

Terman, L. M., & Oden, M. (1959). The gifted group in mid-life: Genetic studies of genius (Vol. 5). Stanford, CA: Stanford University Press.

Terry, C. (2006). History of treatment of people with mental illness. In J. R. Matthews, C. E. Walker, et al. (Eds.), Your practicum in psychology: A guide for maximizing knowledge and competence (pp. 81–103). Washington, DC: American Psychological Association.

Terry, D. J., & Hogg, M. A. (1996). Group norms and the attitude-behavior relationship. Personality & Social Psychology Bulletin, 22(8), 776–793. doi:10.1177/0146167296228002

Tewksbury, R., Higgins, G. E., & Mustaine, E. E. (2008). Binge drinking among college athletes and non-athletes. Deviant Behavior, 29(3), 275–293. doi:10.1080/01639620701588040

Teyber, E., & McClure, F. H. (2011). Interpersonal process in therapy: An integrative model (6th ed.). Belmont, CA: Cengage Learning/Wadsworth.

Thakral, P. P. (2011). The neural substrates associated with inattentional blindness. Consciousness & Cognition, 20(4), 1768–1775. doi:10.1016/j.concog.2011.03.013

Thase, M. E. (2006). Major depressive disorder. In F. Andrasik (Ed.), Comprehensive handbook of personality and psychopathology: Adult psychopathology (Vol 2, pp. 207–230). New York: Wiley.

The Nature Conservancy. (2012). Carbon footprint calculator. Arlington, VA: Author. Retrieved February 19, 2012, from http://www.nature.org/greenliving/carboncalculator

Thiessen, E. D., Hill, E. A., & Saffran, J. R. (2005). Infant-directed speech facilitates word segmentation. Infancy, 7(1), 53–71. doi:10.1207/s15327078in0701_5

Thomas, A. K., Bulevich, J. B., & Dubois, S. J. (2011). Context affects feeling-of-knowing accuracy in younger and older adults. Journal of Experimental Psychology: Learning, Memory, & Cognition, 37(1), 96–108. doi:10.1037/a0021612

Thomas, E. M. (2004). Aggressive behaviour outcomes for young children: Change in parenting environment predicts change in behaviour. Ottawa, ON: Statistics Canada. Retrieved February 25, 2012, from http://www.statcan.ca/cgi-bin/downpub/listpub.cgi?catno=89-599-MIE2004001

Thomas, M. (2009). Some needed changes in DSM-V: But what about children? Clinical Psychology: Science & Practice, 16(1), 50–53. doi:10.1111/j.1468-2850.2009.01142.x

Thompson, R. A., & Nelson, C. A. (2001). Developmental science and the media: Early brain development. American Psychologist, 56(1), 5–15. doi:10.1037/0003-066X.56.1.5

Thompson, R. F. (2005). In search of memory traces. Annual Review of Psychology, 56, 1–23. doi:10.1146/annurev.psych.56.091103.070239

Thornton, S. N. (2010). Thirst and hydration: Physiology and consequences of dysfunction. Physiology & Behavior, 100(1), 15–21. doi:10.1016/j.physbeh.2010.02.026

Thorpy, M. J. (2006). Cataplexy associated with narcolepsy: Epidemiology, pathophysiology and management. CNS Drugs, 20(1), 43–50.

Thrift, A. G. (2010). Design and methods of population surveys. *Neuroepidemiology, 34*(4), 267–269. doi:10.1159/000297758

Till, B. D., & Priluck, R. L. (2000). Stimulus generalization in classical conditioning: An initial investigation and extension. *Psychology & Marketing, 17*(1), 55–72. doi:10.1002/(SICI)1520-6793(200001)17:1<55::AID-MAR4>3.0.CO;2-C

Till, B. D., Stanley, S. M., & Priluck, R. (2008). Classical conditioning and celebrity endorsers: An examination of belongingness and resistance to extinction. *Psychology & Marketing, 25*(2), 179–196. doi:10.1002/mar.20205

Timmerman, C. K., & Kruepke, K. A. (2006). Computer-assisted instruction, media richness, and college student performance. *Communication Education, 55*(1), 73–104.

Tipples, J., Atkinson, A. P., & Young, A. W. (2002). The eyebrow frown: A salient social signal. *Emotion, 2*(3), 288–296. doi:10.1037/1528-3542.2.3.288

Tite, L. (2009). "The Obama Effect": Test-taking performance gap virtually eliminated during key moments of Obama's presidential run. *Research News@Vanderbilt.* Retrieved May 9, 2012, from http://news.vanderbilt.edu/2009/01/the-obama-effect-test-taking-performance-gap-story/

Titov, N. (2011). Internet-delivered psychotherapy for depression in adults. *Current Opinion in Psychiatry, 24*(1), 18–23. doi:10.1097/YCO.0b013e32833ed18f

Toates, F. (2011). *Biological psychology* (3rd ed.). Boston: Pearson/Allyn and Bacon.

Tober, G., & Strang, J. (Eds.) (2003). *Methadone matters: Evolving community methadone treatment of opiate addiction.* New York: Routledge/Taylor & Francis.

Tobler, N. S., Roona, M. R., Ocshorn, P., et al. (2000). School-based adolescent drug prevention programs: 1998 meta-analysis. *Journal of Primary Prevention, 20*, 275–337. doi:10.1023/A:1021314704811

Tolman, E. C., & Honzik, C. H. (1930). Degrees of hunger, reward and non-reward, and maze performance in rats. *University of California Publications in Psychology, 4*, 241–256.

Tolman, E. C., Ritchie, B. F., & Kalish, D. (1946). Studies in spatial learning: II. Place learning versus response learning. *Journal of Experimental Psychology, 36*, 221–229. doi:10.1037/h0060262

Tomasello, M. (2003). *Constructing a language: A usage-based theory of language acquisition.* Cambridge, MA: Harvard University Press.

Toneatto, T. (2002). Cognitive therapy for problem gambling. *Cognitive & Behavioral Practice, 9*(3), 191–199. doi:10.1016/S1077-7229(02)80049-9

Tononi, G., & Cirelli, C. (2003). Sleep and synaptic homeostasis: A hypothesis. *Brain Research Bulletin, 62*(2), 143–150. doi:10.1016/j.brainresbull.2003.09.004

Toro, C. T., & Deakin, J. F. W. (2007). Adult neurogenesis and schizophrenia: A window on abnormal early brain development? *Schizophrenia Research, 90*(1–3), 1–14. doi:10.1016/j.schres.2006.09.030

Torrey, E. F. (1996). *Out of the shadows.* New York: John Wiley & Sons.

Toyota, H., & Kikuchi, Y. (2005). Encoding richness of self-generated elaboration and spacing effects on incidental memory. *Perceptual & Motor Skills, 101*(2), 621–627.

Trainor, L. J., & Desjardins, R. N. (2002). Pitch characteristics of infant-directed speech affect infants' ability to discriminate vowels. *Psychonomic Bulletin & Review, 9*(2), 335–340. doi:10.3758/BF03196290

Travis, F., Arenander, A., & DuBois, D. (2004). Psychological and physiological characteristics of a proposed object-referral/self-referral continuum of self-awareness. *Consciousness & Cognition, 13*, 401–420. doi:10.1016/j.concog.2004.03.001

Traxler, M. J. (2011). *Introduction to psycholinguistics: Understanding language science.* New York: Wiley-Blackwell.

Treffert, D. A. (2010). *Islands of genius: The bountiful mind of the autistic, acquired, and sudden savant.* London: Jessica Kingsley Publishers.

Treffert, D. A., & Christensen, C. D. (2005). Inside the mind of a savant. *Scientific American, 293*(6), 108–113. doi:10.1038/scientificamerican1205-108

Tregear, S., Resto, J., Schoelles, K., et al. (2010). Continuous positive airway pressure reduces risk of motor vehicle crash among drivers with obstructive sleep apnea: Systematic review and meta-analysis. *Sleep: Journal of Sleep & Sleep Disorders Research, 33*(10), 1373–1380.

Trehub, S. E., Unyk, A. M., & Trainor, L. J. (1993a). Adults identify infant-directed music across cultures. *Infant Behavior & Development, 16*(2), 193–211. doi:10.1016/0163-6383(93)80017-3

Trehub, S. E., Unyk, A. M., & Trainor, L. J. (1993b). Maternal singing in cross-cultural perspective. *Infant Behavior & Development, 16*(3), 285–295. doi:10.1016/0163-6383(93)80036-8

Treves, T. A., & Korczyn, A. D. (2012). Modeling the dementia epidemic. *CNS Neuroscience & Therapeutics, 18*(2), 175–181. doi:10.1111/j.1755-5949.2011.00242.x

Triandis, H. C., & Suh, E. M. (2002). Cultural influences on personality. *Annual Review of Psychology, 53*, 133–160. doi:10.1146/annurev.psych.53.100901.135200

Trocmé, N., MacLaurin, B., Fallon, B., et al. (2001). Canadian incidence study of reported child abuse and neglect. Ottawa, ON: National Clearinghouse on Family Violence. Retrieved February 25, 2012, from http://www.phac-aspc.gc.ca/publicat/cissr-ecirc/.

Troll, L. E., & Skaff, M. M. (1997). Perceived continuity of self in very old age. *Psychology & Aging, 12*(1), 162–169. doi:10.1037/0882-7974.12.1.162

Trujillo, L. T., Kornguth, S., & Schnyer, D. M. (2009). An ERP examination of the different effects of sleep deprivation on exogenously cued and endogenously cued attention. *Sleep, 32*(10), 1285–1297.

Trull, T., & Prinstein, M. (2013). *Clinical psychology* (8th ed.). Belmont, CA: Cengage Learning/Wadsworth.

Tsai, G., & Coyle, J. T. (2002). Glutamatergic mechanisms in schizophrenia. *Annual Review of Pharmacology & Toxicology, 42*, 165–179. doi:10.1146/annurev.pharmtox.42.082701.160735

Tulving, E. (1989). Remembering and knowing the past. *American Scientist, 77*(4), 361–367.

Tulving, E. (2002). Episodic memory. *Annual Review of Psychology, 53*, 1–25. doi:10.1146/annurev.psych.53.100901.135114

Turenius, C. I., Htut, M. M., Prodon, D. A., et al. (2009). GABA(A) receptors in the lateral hypothalamus as mediators of satiety and body weight regulation. *Brain Research, 1262*, 16–24. doi:10.1016/j.brainres.2009.01.016

Turkheimer, E., Haley, A., Waldron, M., et al. (2003). Socioeconomic status modifies heritability of IQ in young children. *Psychological Science, 14*, 623–628. doi:10.1046/j.0956-7976.2003.psci_1475.x

Tversky, A., & Kahneman, D. (1981). The framing of decisions and the psychology of choice. *Science, 211*, 453–458. doi:10.1126/science.7455683

Tversky, A., & Kahneman, D. (1982). Judgments of and by representativeness. In D. Kahneman, P. Slovic, & A. Tversky (Eds.), *Judgment under uncertainty: Heuristics and biases* (pp. 84–98). Cambridge, MA: Cambridge University Press.

Twenge, J. M., & Campbell, W. K. (2001). Age and birth cohort differences in self-esteem: A cross-temporal meta-analysis. *Personality & Social Psychology Review, 5*(4), 321–344. doi:10.1207/S15327957PSPR0504_3

U.S. Census Bureau. (2011). *Poverty: Highlights.* New York: Author. Retrieved January 10, 2012, from http://www.census.gov/hhes/www/poverty/about/overview/index.html

U.S. Department of Energy. (2010). *Secretary Chu presents smart grid vision and announces $144 million in recovery act funding to transition to the smart grid.* Washington: Author. Retrieved May 9, 2012, from http://energy.gov/oe/articles/secretary-chu-presents-smart-grid-vision-and-announces-144-million-recovery-act-funding

U.S. Department of Energy Office of Science. (2011). *About the Human Genome Project.* Washington, DC: U.S. Department of Energy. Retrieved January 5, 2012, from http://www.ornl.gov/sci/techresources/Human_Genome/project/about.shtml

Underwood, B. J. (1957). Interference and forgetting. *Psychological Review, 64*, 49–60. doi:10.1037/h0044616

United Nations Programme on HIV/AIDS. (2010). *UNAIDS Report on the global AIDS epidemic 2010.* New York: Author. Retrieved April 16, 2012, from http://www.unaids.org/globalreport/Global_report.htm

Unsworth, G., & Ward, T. (2001). Video games and aggressive behaviour. *Australian Psychologist, 36*(3), 184–192. doi:10.1080/00050060108259654

Uwe P. Gielen, U. P., Fish, J. M., et al. (Eds.) (2006). *Handbook of culture, therapy, and healing.* Mahwah, NJ: Erlbaum.

Uziel, L. (2007). Individual differences in the social facilitation effect: A review and meta-analysis. *Journal of Research in Personality, 41*(3), 579–601. doi:10.1016/j.jrp.2006.06.008

Vaillant, G. E. (2002). *Aging well.* Boston: Little, Brown.

Vaillant, G. E. (2005). Alcoholics Anonymous: Cult or cure? *Australian & New Zealand Journal of Psychiatry, 39*(6), 431–436. doi:10.1111/j.1440-1614.2005.01600.x

Valadez, J. J. & Ferguson, C. J. (2012). Just a game after all: Violent video game exposure and time spent playing effects on hostile feelings, depression, and visuospatial cognition. *Computers in Human Behavior, 28*, 608–616. doi:10.1016/j.chb.2011.11.006

Valentine, S., Godkin, L., & Varca, P. E. (2010). Role conflict, mindfulness, and organizational ethics in an education-based healthcare institution. *Journal of Business Ethics, 94*(3), 455–469. doi:10.1007/s10551-009-0276-9

Valins, S. (1966). Cognitive effects of false heart-rate feedback. *Journal of Personality & Social Psychology, 4*, 400–408. doi:10.1037/h0023791

Valins, S. (1967). Emotionality and information concerning internal reactions. *Journal of Personality & Social Psychology, 6*, 458–463. doi:10.1037/h0024842

Valkenburg, P. M., Sumter, S. R., & Peter, J. (2011). Gender differences in online and offline self-disclosure in pre-adolescence and adolescence. *British Journal of Developmental Psychology, 29*(2), 253–269. doi:10.1348/2044-835X.002001

Vallerand, A. H., Saunders, M. M., & Anthony, M. (2007). Perceptions of control over pain by patients with cancer and their caregivers. *Pain Management Nursing, 8*(2), 55–63. doi:10.1016/j.pmn.2007.02.001

Vallerand, R. J., Paquet, Y., Philippe, F. L., et al. (2010). On the role of passion for work in burnout: A process model. *Journal of Personality, 78*(1), 289–312. doi:10.1111/j.1467-6494.2009.00616.x

Van Blerkom, D. L. (2012). *College study skills: Becoming a strategic learner* (7th ed.). Belmont, CA: Cengage Learning/Wadsworth.

van der Hart, O., Lierens, R., & Goodwin, J. (1996). Jeanne Fery: A sixteenth-century case of dissociative identity disorder. *Journal of Psychohistory, 24*(1), 18–35.

van der Kamp, J., & Cañal-Bruland, R. (2011). Kissing right? On the consistency of the head-turning bias in kissing. *Laterality: Asymmetries of Body, Brain & Cognition, 16*(3), 257–267. doi:10.1080/13576500903530778

van Dierendonck, D., & Te Nijenhuis, J. (2005). Flotation restricted environmental stimulation therapy (REST) as a stress-management tool: A meta-analysis. *Psychology & Health, 20*(3), 405–412. doi:10.1080/08870440412331337093

van Dierendonck, D., Díaz, D., Rodríguez-Carvajal, R., et al. (2008). Ryff's six-factor model of psychological well-being, a Spanish exploration. *Social Indicators Research, 87*(3), 473–479. doi:10.1007/s11205-007-9174-7

van Elst, L. T., Valerius, G., Büchert, M., et al. (2005). Increased prefrontal and hippocampal glutamate concentration in schizophrenia: Evidence from a magnetic resonance spectroscopy study. *Biological Psychiatry, 58*(9), 724–730. doi:10.1016/j.biopsych.2005.04.041

Van Lawick-Goodall, J. (1971). *In the shadow of man.* New York: Houghton Mifflin.

Van Rooij, J. J. F. (1994). Introversion-extraversion: Astrology versus psychology. *Personality & Individual Differences, 16*(6), 985–988. doi:10.1016/0191-8869(94)90243-7

Vandell, D. L. (2004). Early child care: The known and the unknown. *Merrill-Palmer Quarterly, 50*(3), 387–414. doi:10.1353/mpq.2004.0027

Vandewalle, G., Hébert, M., Beaulieu, C., et al. (2011). Abnormal hypothalamic response to light in seasonal affective disorder. *Biological Psychiatry, 70*(10), 954–961. doi:10.1016/j.biopsych.2011.06.022

Vanheule, S., Vandenbergen, J., Verhaeghe, P., et al. (2010). Interpersonal problems in alexithymia: A study in three primary care groups. *Psychology & Psychotherapy: Theory, Research & Practice, 83*(4), 351–362. doi:10.1348/147608309X481829

Vartanian, O., & Suedfeld, P. (2011). The effect of the flotation version of restricted environmental stimulation technique (REST) on jazz improvisation. *Music & Medicine, 3*(4), 234–238. doi:10.1177/1943862111407640

Vasa, R. A., Carlino, A. R., & Pine, D. S. (2006). Pharmacotherapy of depressed children and adolescents: Current issues and potential directions. *Biological Psychiatry, 59*(11), 1021–1028. doi:10.1016/j.biopsych.2005.10.010

Vasquez, E. A., Lickel, B., & Hennigan, K. (2010). Gangs, displaced, and group-based aggression. *Aggression & Violent Behavior, 15*(2), 130–140. doi:10.1016/j.avb.2009.08.001

Velakoulis, D., & Pantelis, C. (1996). What have we learned from functional imaging studies in schizophrenia? The role of frontal, striatal and temporal areas. *Australian & New Zealand Journal of Psychiatry, 30*(2), 195–209. doi:10.3109/00048679609076095

Venezia, M., Messinger, D. S., Thorp, D., et al. (2004). The development of anticipatory smiling. *Infancy, 6*(3), 397–406. doi:10.1207/s15327078in0603_5

Vernon-Feagans, L., Garrett-Peters, P., Willoughby, M., et al. (2011). Chaos, poverty, and parenting: Predictors of early language development. *Early Childhood Research Quarterly.* doi:10.1016/j.ecresq.2011.11.001

Videon, T. M. (2005). Parent-child relations and children's psychological well-being: Do dads matter? *Journal of Family Issues, 26*(1), 55–78. doi:10.1177/0192513X04270262

Viero, C., Shibuya, I., Kitamura, N., et al. (2010). Oxytocin: Crossing the bridge between basic science and pharmacotherapy. *CNS Neuroscience & Therapeutics, 16*(5), e138–e156. doi:10.1111/j.1755-5949.2010.00185.x

Visser, B. A., Bay, D., Cook, G. L., et al. (2010). Psychopathic and antisocial, but not emotionally intelligent. *Personality & Individual Differences, 48*(5), 644–648. doi:10.1016/j.paid.2010.01.003

Vlachou, S,. & Markou, A. (2011). Intracranial self-stimulation. In M. C. Olmstead (Ed.), *Animal models of drug addiction* (pp. 3–56). Totowa, NJ: Humana Press.

Vogel, E. K., Woodman, G. F., & Luck, S. J. (2006). The time course of consolidation in visual working memory. *Journal of Experimental Psychology: Human Perception & Performance, 32*(6), 1436–1451. doi:10.1037/a0016453

Vojdanoska, M., Cranney, J., & Newell, B. R. (2010). The testing effect: The role of feedback and collaboration in a tertiary classroom setting. *Applied Cognitive Psychology, 24*(8), 1183–1195. doi:10.1002/acp.1630

Volkow, N. D., Fowler, J. S., Wang, G.-J., et al. (2007). Dopamine in drug abuse and addiction: Results of imaging studies and treatment implications. *Archives of Neurology, 64*(11), 1575–1579. doi:10.1001/archneur.64.11.1575

Volkow, N. D., Gillespie, H., Mullani, N., et al. (1996). Brain glucose metabolism in chronic marijuana users at baseline and during marijuana intoxication. *Psychiatry Research: Neuroimaging, 67*(1), 29–38. doi:10.1016/0925-4927(96)02817-X

Volpicelli, J. R., Ulm, R. R., Altenor, A., et al. (1983). Learned mastery in the rat. *Learning & Motivation, 14*, 204–222. doi:10.1016/0023-9690(83)90006-1

Vuillermot, S., Weber, L, Feldon, J., et al. (2010). A longitudinal examination of the neurodevelopmental impact of prenatal immune activation in mice reveals primary defects in dopaminergic development relevant to schizophrenia. *Journal of Neuroscience, 30*(4), 1270–1287. doi:10.1523/JNEUROSCI.5408-09.2010

Vygotsky, L. S. (1962). *Thought and language.* Cambridge, MA: MIT Press.

Vygotsky, L. S. (1978). *Mind in society.* Cambridge, MA: Harvard University Press.

Wade, K. A., Green, S. L., & Nash, R. A. (2010). Can fabricated evidence induce false eyewitness testimony? *Applied Cognitive Psychology, 24*(7), 899–908. doi:10.1002/acp.1607

Wager, T. D., Rilling, J. K., Smith, E. E., et al. (2004). Placebo-induced changes in fMRI in the anticipation and experience of pain. *Science, 303*(Feb 20), 1162–1166. doi:10.1126/science.1093065

Wagstaff, G., Brunas-Wagstaff, J., Cole, J., et al. (2004). New directions in forensic hypnosis: Facilitating memory with a focused meditation technique. *Contemporary Hypnosis, 21*(1), 14–27. doi:10.1002/ch.284

Wainright, J. L., Russell, S. T., & Patterson, C. J. (2004). Psychosocial adjustment, school outcomes, and romantic relationships of adolescents with same-sex parents. *Child Development, 75*(6), 1886–1898. doi:10.1111/j.1467-8624.2004.00823.x

Wakefield, J. C. (1992). The concept of mental disorder. *American Psychologist, 47*(3), 373–388.

Walker, D. L., & Davis, M. (2008). Role of the extended amygdala in short-duration versus sustained fear: A tribute to Dr. Lennart Heimer. *Brain Structure & Function, 213*(1–2), 29–42. doi:10.1037/0003-066X.47.3.373

Walker, E., Kestler, L. Bollini, A., et al. (2004). Schizophrenia: Etiology and course. *Annual Review of Psychology, 55*, 401–430. doi:10.1146/annurev.psych.55.090902.141950

Walker, I., & Crogan, M. (1998). Academic performance, prejudice, and the Jigsaw classroom. *Journal of Community & Applied Social Psychology, 8*(6), 381–393. doi:10.1002/(SICI)1099-1298(199811/12)8:6<381::AID-CASP457>3.0.CO;2-6

Walker, M. P., & Stickgold, R. (2006). Sleep, memory, and plasticity. *Annual Review of Psychology, 57*, 139–166. doi:10.1146/annurev.psych.56.091703.070307

Walker, S. P., Wachs, T. D., Grantham-McGregor, S., et al. (2011). Inequality in early childhood: Risk and protective factors for early child development. *The Lancet, 378*(9799), 1325–1338. doi:10.1016/S0140-6736(11)60555-2

Wallach, M. A., & Kogan, N. (1965). *Modes of thinking in young children.* New York: Holt.

Walton, C. E., Bower, M. L., & Bower, T. G. (1992). Recognition of familiar faces by newborns. *Infant Behavior & Development, 15*(2), 265–269. doi:10.1016/0163-6383(92)80027-R

Wampold, B. E., Minami T., Tierney, S. C., et al. (2005). The placebo is powerful: Estimating placebo effects in medicine and psychotherapy from randomized clinical trials. *Journal of Clinical Psychology, 61*(7), 835–854. doi:10.1002/jclp.20129

Wampold, B. E., Mondin, G. W., Moody, M., et al. (1997). A meta-analysis of outcome studies comparing bona fide psycho-therapies. *Psychological Bulletin, 122*(3), 203–215. doi:10.1037/0033-2909.122.3.203

Wan, C. Y., Demaine, K., Zipse, L., et al. (2010). From music making to speaking: Engaging the mirror neuron system in autism. *Brain Research Bulletin, 82*(3–4), 161–168. doi:10.1016/j.brainresbull.2010.04.010

Wandersman, A., & Florin, P. (2003). Community interventions and effective prevention. *American Psychologist, 58*(6/7), 441–448. doi:10.1037/0003-066X

Wang, S. S., & Brownell, K. D. (2005). Public policy and obesity: The need to marry science with advocacy. *Psychiatric Clinics of North America, 28*(1), 235–252. doi:10.1016/j.psc.2004.09.001

Wang, S.-H., & Morris, R. G. M. (2010). Hippocampal-neocortical interactions in memory formation, consolidation, and reconsolidation. *Annual Review of Psychology, 61*, 49–79. doi:10.1146/annurev.psych.093008.100523

Ward, L., & Parr, J. M. (2010). Revisiting and reframing use: Implications for the integration of ICT. *Computers & Education, 54*(1), 113–122. doi:10.1016/j.compedu.2009.07.011

Wargo, E. (2008). The many lives of superstition. *APS Observer, 21*(9), 18–24.

Warren, D. J., & Normann, R. A. (2005). Functional reorganization of primary visual cortex induced by electrical stimulation in the cat. *Vision Research, 45*, 551–565. doi:10.1016/j.visres.2004.09.021

Washton, A. M., & Zweben, J. E. (2009). *Cocaine and methamphetamine addiction: Treatment, recovery, and relapse prevention.* New York: Norton.

Waterfield, R. (2002). *Hidden depths: The story of hypnosis.* London: Macmillan.

Watson, D. L. (2008). The fundamental attribution error. In L. T. Benjamin, Jr. (Ed.), *Favorite activities for the teaching of psychology* (pp. 248–251). Washington, DC: American Psychological Association.

Watson, D. L., & Tharp, R. G. (2007). *Self-directed behavior* (9th ed.). Belmont, CA: Cengage Learning/Wadsworth.

Watson, J. B. (1913/1994). Psychology as the behaviorist views it. *Psychological Review, 101*(2), 248–253. doi:10.1037/0033-295X.101.2.248

Watson, J. M., & Strayer, David L. (2010). Supertaskers: Profiles in extraordinary multitasking ability. *Psychonomic Bulletin & Review, 17*(4), 479–485. doi:10.3758/PBR.17.4.479

Watson, R. A., & Yeung, T. M. (2011). What is the potential of oligodendrocyte progenitor cells to successfully treat human spinal cord injury? *BMC Neurology, 11.* doi:10.1186/1471-2377-11-113

Waytz, A., Epley, N., & Cacioppo, J. T. (2010). Social cognition unbound: Insights into anthropomorphism and dehumanization. *Current Directions in*

Psychological Science, 19(1), 58–62. doi:10.1177/0963721409359302

Weaver, Y. (2009). Mid-life: A time of crisis or new possibilities? *Existential Analysis, 20*(1), 69–78.

Wechsler, D. (2008). *Wechsler Adult Intelligence Scale, Fourth Edition (WAIS-IV)*. San Antonio, TX: Pearson.

Wechsler, H., & Wuethrich, B. (2002). *Dying to drink*. Emmaus, PA: Rodale Books.

Wedding, D., & Corsini, R. J. (2011). *Case studies in psychotherapy* (6th ed.). Belmont, CA: Cengage Learning/Wadsworth.

Weekley, J. A. & Polyhart, R. E. (Eds.) (2006). *Situational judgment tests: Theory, measurement, and application*. Mahwah, NJ: Erlbaum.

Wegenek, A. R., & Buskist, W. (2010). *The insider's guide to the psychology major: Everything you need to know about the degree and profession*. Washington: American Psychological Association.

Wehr, T. A., Duncan, W. C., Sher, L., et al. (2001). A circadian signal of change of season in patients with seasonal affective disorder. *Archives of General Psychiatry, 58*(12), 1108–1114. doi:10.1001/archpsyc.58.12.1108

Weidenhammer, W., Linde, K., Streng, A., et al. (2007). Acupuncture for chronic low back pain in routine care: A multicenter observational study. *Clinical Journal of Pain, 23*(2), 128–135. doi:10.1097/01.ajp.0000210952.09127.df

Weinberg, R. A. (1989). Intelligence and IQ. *American Psychologist, 44*(2), 98–104. doi:10.1037/0003-066X.44.2.98

Weiner, B. A., & Carton, J. S. (2012). Avoidant coping: A mediator of maladaptive perfectionism and test anxiety. *Personality & Individual Differences, 52*(5), 632–636. doi:10.1016/j.paid.2011.12.009

Weingarten, K. (2010). Reasonable hope: Construct, clinical applications, and supports. *Family Process, 49*(1), 5–25. doi:10.1111/j.1545-5300.2010.01305.x

Weinstein, R. S., Gregory, A., & Strambler, M. J. (2004). Intractable self-fulfilling prophesies. *American Psychologist, 59*(6), 511–520. doi:10.1037/0003-066X.59.6.511

Weinstein, Y., & Shanks, D. R. (2010). Rapid induction of false memory for pictures. *Memory, 18*(5), 533–542. doi:10.1080/09658211.2010.483232

Weishaar, M. E. (2006). A cognitive-behavioral approach to suicide risk reduction in crisis intervention. In A. R. Roberts & K. R. Yeager, (Eds.), *Foundations of evidence-based social work practice* (pp. 181–193). New York: Oxford University Press.

Weiss, M., Allan, B., & Greenaway, M. (2012). Treatment of catatonia with electroconvulsive therapy in adolescents. *Journal of Child & Adolescent Psychopharmacology, 22*(1), 96–100. doi:10.1089/cap.2010.0052

Weisskirch, R. S. (2005). Ethnicity and perceptions relationship to ethnic identity development. *International Journal of Intercultural Relations,* *29*(3), 355–366. doi:10.1016/j.ijintrel.2005.053.008

Weissman, A. M., Jogerst, G. J., & Dawson, J. D. (2003). Community characteristics associated with child abuse in Iowa. *Child Abuse & Neglect, 27*(10), 1145–1159. doi:10.1016/j.chiabu.2003.09.002

Welch, R. D., & Houser, M. E. (2010). Extending the four-category model of adult attachment: An interpersonal model of friendship attachment. *Journal of Social & Personal Relationships, 27*(3), 351–366. doi:10.1177/0265407509349632

Wells, G. L. (2001). Police lineups: Data, theory, and policy. *Psychology, Public Policy, & Law, 7*(4), 791–801. doi:10.1037/1076-8971.7.4.791

Wells, G. L., & Olsen, E. A. (2003). Eyewitness testimony. *Annual Review of Psychology, 54*, 277–295. doi:10.1146/annurev.psych.54.101601.145028

Weltzin, T. E., Weisensel, N., Franczyk, D., et al. (2005). Eating disorders in men: Update. *Journal of Men's Health & Gender, 2*(2), 186–193. doi:10.1016/j.jmhg.2005.04.008

Wentland, J. J., & Reissing, E. D. (2011). Taking casual sex not too casually: Exploring definitions of casual sexual relationships. *Canadian Journal of Human Sexuality, 20*(3), 75–91.

Wernet, S. P., Follman, C., Magueja, C., et al. (2003). Building bridges and improving racial harmony: An evaluation of the Bridges Across Racial Polarization Program. In J. J. Stretch, E. M. Burkemper, et al., (Eds.), *Practicing social justice* (pp. 63–79). New York: Haworth Press.

Wertheimer, M. (1959). *Productive thinking*. New York: Harper & Row.

Werthmann, J., Roefs, A., Nederkoorn, C., et al. (2011). Can(not) take my eyes off it: Attention bias for food in overweight participants. *Health Psychology, 30*(5), 561–569. doi:10.1037/a0024291

Wesensten, N. J., Belenky, G., Kautz, M. A., et al. (2002). Maintaining alertness and performance during sleep deprivation: Modafinil versus caffeine. *Psychopharmacology, 159*(3), 238–247.

Wessel, I., & Wright, D. B. (Eds.). (2004). *Emotional memory failures*. Hove, UK: Psychology Press.

West, T. G. (1991). *In the mind's eye*. Buffalo, NY: Prometheus.

Westen, D., & Bradley, R. (2005). Empirically supported complexity: Rethinking evidence-based practice in psychotherapy. *Current Directions in Psychological Science, 14*(5), 266–271. doi:10.1111/j.0963-7214.2005.00378.x

Westera, W., Nadolski, R. J., Hummel, H. G. K., et al. (2008). Serious games for higher education: A framework for reducing design complexity. *Journal of Computer Assisted Learning, 24*(5), 420–432. doi:10.1111/j.1365-2729.2008.00279.x

Westrin, Å., & Lam, R. W. (2007a). Seasonal affective disorder: A clinical update. *Annals of Clinical Psychiatry, 19*(4), 239–246. doi:10.1080/10401230701653476

Westrin, Å., & Lam, R. W. (2007b). Long-term and preventative treatment for seasonal affective disorder. *CNS Drugs, 21*(11), 901–909. doi:10.2165/00023210-200721110-00003

Wethington, E. (2003). Turning points as opportunities for psychological growth. In C. L. M. Keyes & J. Haidt (Eds.), *Flourishing* (pp. 37–53). Washington, DC: American Psychological Association.

Wethington, E., Kessler, R. C., & Pixley, J. E. (2004). Turning points in adulthood. In O. G. Brim, C. D. Ryff, et al., (Eds.), *How healthy are we? A national study of well-being at midlife* (pp. 425–450). Chicago: University of Chicago Press.

Wexler, M. N. (1995). Expanding the groupthink explanation to the study of contemporary cults. *Cultic Studies Journal, 12*(1), 49–71.

Wheat, A. L., & Larkin, K. T. (2010). Biofeedback of heart rate variability and related physiology: A critical review. *Applied Psychophysiology & Biofeedback, 35*(3), 229–242. doi:10.1007/s10484-010-9133-y

White, J. (2006). *Intelligence, destiny and education: The ideological roots of intelligence testing*. New York: Brunner-Routledge.

White-Ajmani, M., & Bursik, K. (2011). What lies beneath: Dogmatism, intolerance, and political self-identification. *Individual Differences Research, 9*(3), 153–164.

Whitehouse, A. J. O., Maybery, M. T., & Durkin, K. (2006). The development of the picture-superiority effect. *British Journal of Developmental Psychology, 24*(4), 767–773. doi:10.1348/026151005X74153

Whitley, Jr., B. E. (1999). Right-wing authoritarianism, social dominance orientation, and prejudice. *Journal of Personality & Social Psychology, 77*(l), 126–134. doi:10.1037/0022-3514.77.1.126

Whitley, B. E., & Kite, M. E. (2010). *The psychology of prejudice and discrimination*, (2nd ed.). Belmont, CA: Cengage Learning/Wadsworth.

Whyte, J. (2000). Groupthink. In A. E. Kazdin, (Ed.), *Encyclopedia of psychology* (Vol. 4, pp. 35–38). Washington, DC: American Psychological Association.

Wickwire, E. M., Whelan, J. P., & Meyers, A. W. (2010). Outcome expectancies and gambling behavior among urban adolescents. *Psychology of Addictive Behaviors, 24*(1), 75–88. doi:10.1037/a0017505

Widner R. L., Otani, H., & Winkelman, S. E. (2005). Tip-of-the-tongue experiences are not merely strong feeling-of-knowing experiences. *Journal of General Psychology, 132*(4), 392–407. doi:10.3200/GENP.132.4.392-407

Wiederhold, B. K., & Wiederhold, M. D. (2005). Acrophobia. In B. K. Wiederhold & M. D. Wiederhold (Eds.), *Virtual reality therapy for anxiety disorders: Advances in evaluation and treatment* (pp. 157–164). Washington, DC: American Psychological Association.

Wiederman, M. W. (2001). Gender differences in sexuality: Perceptions, myths, and realities. *Family Journal-Counseling & Therapy for Couples & Families, 9*(4), 468–471. doi:10.1177/1066480701094019

Wigfield, A., & Eccles, J. (Eds.). (2002). *Development of achievement motivation*. San Diego: Academic Press.

Wilber, M. K., & Potenza, M. N. (2006). Adolescent gambling: Research and clinical implications. *Psychiatry, 3*(10), 40–46.

Wilder, D. A., Simon, A. F., & Faith, M. (1996). Enhancing the impact of counterstereotypic information. *Journal of Personality & Social Psychology, 71*(2), 276–287. doi:10.1037/0022-3514.71.2.276

Wilding, J., & Valentine, E. (1994). Memory champions. *British Journal of Psychology, 85*(2), 231–244. doi:10.1111/j.2044-8295.1994.tb02520.x

Wilkinson, D., & Abraham, C. (2004). Constructing an integrated model of the antecedents of adolescent smoking. *British Journal of Health Psychology, 9*(3), 315–333. doi:10.1348/1359107041557075

Wilkinson, D., Ko, P., Wiriadjaja, A., et al. (2009). Unilateral damage to the right cerebral hemisphere disrupts the apprehension of whole faces and their component parts. *Neuropsychologia, 47*(7), 1701–1711. doi:10.1016/j.neuropsychologia.2009.02.008

Wilkinson, M. (2006). The dreaming mindbrain: A Jungian perspective. *Journal of Analytical Psychology, 51*(1), 43–59. doi:10.1111/j.0021-8774.2006.00571.x

Wilkinson, R. G., & Pickett, K. E. (2006). Income inequality and population health: A review and explanation of the evidence. *Social Science & Medicine, 62*(7), 1768–1784. doi:10.1016/j.socscimed.2005.08.036

Wilkinson, R. G., & Pickett, K. E. (2007). The problems of relative deprivation: Why some societies do better than others. *Social Science & Medicine, 65*(9), 1965–1978. doi:10.1016/j.socscimed.2007.05.041

Wilkinson, R. G., & Pickett, K. E. (2009). Income inequality and social dysfunction. *Annual Review of Sociology, 35*, 493–511. doi:10.1146/annurev-soc-070308-115926

Willander, J., & Larsson, M. (2006). Smell your way back to childhood: Autobiographical odor memory. *Psychonomic Bulletin & Review, 13*(2), 240–244. doi:10.3758/BF03193837

Williams, D. G., & Morris, G. (1996). Crying, weeping or tearfulness in British and Israeli adults. *British Journal of Psychology, 87*(3), 479–505. doi:10.1111/j.2044-8295.1996.tb02603.x

Williams, G., Cai, X. J., Elliott, J. C., et al. (2004). Anabolic neuropeptides. *Physiology & Behavior. Special Reviews on Ingestive Science, 81*(2), 211–222. doi:10.1016/j.physbeh.2004.02.005

Williams, J. M. (2010). *Applied sport psychology: Personal growth to peak performance* (6th ed.). New York: McGraw-Hill.

Williams, R. B., Barefoot, J. C., & Schneiderman, N. (2003). Psychosocial risk factors for cardiovascular disease: More than one culprit at work. *Journal of the American Medical Association, 290*(16), 2190–2192. doi:10.1001/jama.290.16.2190

Williams, R. L., & Eggert, A. (2002). Note-taking predictors of test performance. *Teaching of Psychology, 29*(3), 234–237.

Williamson, D. A., Ravussin, E., Wong, M.-L., et al. (2005). Microanalysis of eating behavior of three leptin deficient adults treated with leptin therapy. *Appetite, 45*, 75–80. doi:10.1016/j.appet.2005.01.002

Wilson, S. L. (2003). Post-institutionalization: The effects of early deprivation on development of Romanian adoptees. *Child & Adolescent Social Work Journal, 20*(6), 473–483. doi:10.1023/B:CASW.0000003139.14144.06

Wilson, T. D. (2002). *Strangers to ourselves: Discovering the adaptive unconscious.* Cambridge Harvard University Press.

Wilson, T. D. (2009). Know thyself. *Perspectives on Psychological Science, 4*(4), 384–389. doi:10.1111/j.1745-6924.2009.01143.x

Wimpenny, J. H., Weir, A. A. S., Clayton, L., et al. (2009). Cognitive processes associated with sequential tool use in New Caledonian crows. *PLoS ONE, 4*(8): e6471. doi:10.1371/journal.pone.0006471. Retrieved May 9, 2012, from http://www.plosone.org/article/info%3Adoi%2F10.1371%2Fjournal.pone.0006471

Winfree, Jr., L. T., & Jiang, S. (2010). Youthful suicide and social support: Exploring the social dynamics of suicide-related behavior and attitudes within a national sample of US adolescents. *Youth Violence & Juvenile Justice, 8*(1), 19–37. doi:10.1177/1541204009338252

Winger, G., Woods, J. H., Galuska, C. M., et al. (2005). Behavioral perspectives on the neuroscience of drug addiction. *Journal of the Experimental Analysis of Behavior, 84*(3), 667–681. doi:10.1901/jeab.2005.101-04

Wingood, G.M., DiClemente, R.J., Bernhardt, J.M., et al. (2003). A prospective study of exposure to rap music videos and African American female adolescents' health. *American Journal of Public Health, 93*, 437–439. doi:10.2105/AJPH.93.3.437

Winkleby, M., Ahn, D., & Cubbin, C. (2006). Effect of cross-level interaction between individual and neighborhood socioeconomic status on adult mortality rates. *American Journal of Public Health, 96*(12), 2145–2153. doi:10.2105/AJPH.2004.060970

Winner, E. (2003). Creativity and talent. In M. H. Bornstein, L. Davidson, C. L. M. Keyes & K. Moore (Eds.), *Well-being: Positive development across the life course* (pp. 371–380). Mahwah, NJ: Erlbaum.

Winter, D. D. N., & Koger, S. M. (2010). *The psychology of environmental problems* (3rd ed.). New York: Psychology Press.

Wirth, M. M., Welsh, K. M., & Schultheiss, O. C. (2006). Salivary cortisol changes in humans after winning or losing a dominance contest depend on implicit power motivation. *Hormones & Behavior, 49*(3), 346–352. doi:10.1016/j.yhbeh.2005.08.013

Wise, R. A., & Safer, M. A. (2010). A comparison of what U.S. judges and students know and believe about eyewitness testimony. *Journal of Applied Social Psychology, 40*(6), 1400–1422. doi:10.1111/j.1559-1816.2010.00623.x

Wise, R. A., Gong, X., Safer, M. A., et al. (2010). A comparison of Chinese judges' and US judges knowledge and beliefs about eyewitness testimony. *Psychology, Crime & Law, 16*(8), 695–713. doi:10.1080/10683160903153893

Wiseman, R. (2009). *Owning up curriculum: Empowering adolescents to confront social cruelty, bullying, and injustice.* Champaign, IL: Research Press.

Wiseman, R., & Watt, C. (2006). Belief in psychic ability and the misattribution hypothesis: A qualitative review. *British Journal of Psychology, 97*(3), 323–338. doi:10.1348/000712605X72523

Witelson, S. F., Beresh, H., & Kigar, D. L. (2006). Intelligence and brain size in 100 postmortem brains: Sex, lateralization and age factors. *Brain: A Journal of Neurology, 129*(2), 386–398. doi:10.1093/brain/awh696

Witelson, S. F., Kigar, D. L., & Harvey, T. (1999). The exceptional brain of Albert Einstein. *Lancet, 353*, 2149–2153. doi:10.1016/S0140-6736(98)10327-6

Witherington, D. C., Campos, J. J., Anderson, D. I., et al. (2005). Avoidance of heights on the visual cliff in newly walking infants. *Infancy, 7*(3), 285–298. doi:10.1207/s15327078in0703_4

Witt, C. M., Schützler, L., Lüdtke, R., et al. (2011). Patient characteristics and variation in treatment outcomes: Which patients benefit most from acupuncture for chronic pain? *The Clinical Journal of Pain, 27*(6), 550–555. doi:10.1097/AJP.0b013e31820dfbf5

Wixted, J. T. (2004). The psychology and neuroscience of forgetting. *Annual Review of Psychology, 55*, 235–269. doi:10.1146/annurev.psych.55.090902.141555

Wixted, J. T. (2005). A theory about why we forget what we once knew. *Current Directions in Psychological Science, 14*(1), 6–9. doi:10.1111/j.0963-7214.2005.00324.x

Wohl, M. J. A., Pychyl, T. A., & Bennett, S. H. (2010). I forgive myself, now I can study: How self-forgiveness for procrastinating can reduce future procrastination. *Personality & Individual Differences, 48*(7), 803–808. doi:10.1016/j.paid.2010.01.029

Wolpe, J. (1974). *The practice of behavior therapy* (2nd ed.). New York: Pergamon.

Wolpin, M., Marston, A., Randolph, C., et al. (1992). Individual difference correlates of reported lucid dreaming frequency and control. *Journal of Mental Imagery, 16*(3–4), 231–236.

Wong, P. T. P. (2011). Positive psychology 2.0: Towards a balanced interactive model of the good life. *Canadian Psychology, 52*(2), 69–81. doi:10.1177/0022167811408729

Wong, W. (2012). *Essential study skills* (7th ed.). Belmont, CA: Cengage Learning/Wadsworth.

Wood, E., & Willoughby, T. (1995). Cognitive strategies for test-taking. In E. Wood, V. Woloshyn, et al. (Eds.), *Cognitive strategy instruction for middle and high schools* (pp. 5–17). Cambridge, MA: Brookline Books.

Wood, J. M., Nezworski, M. T., Lilienfeld, S. O., et al. (2003). The Rorschach Inkblot test, fortune tellers, and cold reading. *Skeptical Inquirer, 27*(4), 29–33.

Woodhill, B. M., & Samuels, C. A. (2004). Desirable and undesirable androgyny: A prescription for the twenty-first century. *Journal of Gender Studies, 13*(1), 15–28. doi:10.1080/0958923032000184943

Woodruff-Pak, D. S. (2001). Eyeblink classical conditioning differentiates normal aging from Alzheimer's disease. *Integrative Physiological & Behavioral Science, 36*(2), 87–108. doi:10.1007/BF02734044

Woods, A. M., Racine, S. E., & Klump, K. L. (2010). Examining the relationship between dietary restraint and binge eating: Differential effects of major and minor stressors. *Eating Behaviors, 11*(4), 276–280. doi:10.1016/j.eatbeh.2010.08.001

Woods, S. & West, M. (2010). *The psychology of work and organizations.* Belmont, CA: Cengage Learning/Wadsworth.

Woods, S. C., & Ramsay, D. S. (2011). Food intake, metabolism and homeostasis. *Physiology & Behavior, 104*(1), 4-7. doi:10.1016/j.physbeh.2011.04.026

Woods, S. C., Schwartz, M. W, Baskin, D. G., et al. (2000). Food intake and the regulation of body weight. *Annual Review of Psychology. 51*, 255–277. doi:10.1146/annurev.psych.51.1.255

Woollett, K., & Maguire, E. A. (2011). Acquiring "the knowledge" of London's layout drives structural brain changes. *Current Biology, 21*(24), 2109–2114. doi:10.1016/j.cub.2011.11.018

World Health Organization (2011). *WHO report on the global tobacco epidemic, 2011: Warning about the dangers of tobacco.* Geneva, Switzerland: Author. Retrieved February 8, 2012, from http://www.who.int/tobacco/global_report/2011/en/index.html

Woroch, B., & Gonsalves, B. D. (2010). Event-related potential correlates of item and source memory strength. *Brain Research, 1317*, 180–191. doi:10.1016/j.brainres.2009.12.074

Worthen, J. B., & Hunt, R. R. (2010). *Mnemonology: Mnemonics for the 21st century.* Hove, UK: Psychology Press.

Worthen, J. B., & Marshall, P. H. (1996). Intralist and extralist sources of distinctiveness and the bizarreness effect. *American Journal of Psychology, 109*(2), 239–263. doi:10.2307/1423275

Wraga, M. J., Boyle, H. K., & Flynn, C. M. (2010). Role of motor processes in extrinsically encoding mental transformations. *Brain & Cognition, 74*(3), 193–202. doi:10.1016/j.bandc.2010.07.005

Wraga, M., Shephard, J. M., Church, J. A., et al. (2005). Imagined rotations of self versus objects: An fMRI study. *Neuropsychologia, 43*(9), 1351–1361. doi:10.1016/j.neuropsychologia.2004.11.028

Wright, J. P., Dietrich, K. N., Ris, M. D., et al. (2008). Association of prenatal and childhood blood lead concentrations with criminal arrests in early adulthood. *Proceedings of the National Academy of Sciences, 5*(5), e101 doi:10.1371/journal.pmed.0050101

Wright, P. B., & Erdal, K. J. (2008). Sport superstition as a function of skill level and task difficulty. *Journal of Sport Behavior, 31*(2), 187–199.

Wrightsman, L. S., & Fulero, S. M. (2009). *Forensic psychology* (3rd ed.). Belmont, CA: Cengage Learning/Wadsworth.

Wyatt, J. W., Posey, A., Welker, W., et al. (1984). Natural levels of similarities between identical twins and between unrelated people. *The Skeptical Inquirer, 9*, 62–66.

Xu, T.-X., & Yao, W.-D. (2010). D1 and D2 dopamine receptors in separate circuits cooperate to drive associative long-term potentiation in the prefrontal cortex. *Proceedings of the National Academy of Sciences, 107*(37), 16366–16371. doi:10.1073/pnas.1004108107

Yahnke, B. H., Sheikh, A. A., & Beckman, H. T. (2003). Imagery and the treatment of phobic disorders. In A. A. Sheikh (Ed.), *Healing images: The role of imagination in health* (pp. 312–342). Amityville, NY: Baywood Publishing.

Yanchar, S. C., Slife, B. D., & Warne, R. (2008). Critical thinking as disciplinary practice. *Review of General Psychology, 12*(3), 265–281. doi:10.1037/1089-2680.12.3.265

Yang, Y., Tang, L., Tong, L., et al. (2009). Silkworms culture as a source of protein for humans in space. *Advances in Space Research, 43*(2), 1236–1242. doi:10.1016/j.asr.2008.12.009

Yapko, M. D. (2011). *Mindfulness and hypnosis: The power of suggestion to transform experience.* New York: Norton.

Yarmey, D. (2010). *Eyewitness testimony.* In J. M. Brown & E. A. Campbell (Eds.), *The Cambridge handbook of forensic psychology* (pp. 177–186). New York: Cambridge University Press.

Yedidia, M. J., & MacGregor, B. (2001). Confronting the prospect of dying. *Journal of Pain & Symptom Management, 22*(4), 807–819. doi:10.1016/S0885-3924(01)00325-6

Yeh, C. J. (2003). Age, acculturation, cultural adjustment, and mental health symptoms of Chinese, Korean, and Japanese immigrant youths. *Cultural Diversity & Ethnic Minority Psychology, 9*(1), 34–48. doi:10.1037/1099-9809.9.1.34

Yi, H., & Qian, X. (2009). A review on neurocognitive research in superior memory. *Psychological Science (China), 32*(3), 643–645.

Yiend, J. (2010). The effects of emotion on attention: A review of attentional processing of emotional information. *Cognition & Emotion, 24*(1), 3–47. doi:10.1080/02699930903205698

Yip, P. S. F., & Thorburn, J. (2004). Marital status and the risk of suicide: Experience from England and Wales, 1982–1996. *Psychological Reports, 94*(2), 401–407. doi:10.2466/PR0.94.2.401-407

Yokota, F., & Thompson, K. M. (2000). Violence in G-rated animated films. *Journal of the American Medical Association, 283*(20), 2716. doi:10.1001/jama.283.20.2716

Yonas, A., Elieff, C. A., & Arterberry, M. E. (2002). Emergence of sensitivity to pictorial depth cues: Charting development in individual infants. *Infant Behavior & Development, 25*(4), 495–514. doi:10.1016/S0163-6383(02)00147-9

Yontef, G. (2007). The power of the immediate moment in gestalt therapy. *Journal of Contemporary Psychotherapy, 37*(1), 17–23. doi:10.1007/s10879-006-9030-0

Yoonessi, A., & Baker, C. L. (2011). Contribution of motion parallax to segmentation and depth perception. *Journal of Vision, 11*(9). doi:10.1167/11.9.13

Yost, W. A. (2007) *Fundamentals of hearing: An introduction* (5th ed.). San Diego: Elsevier.

Young, R. (2005). Neurobiology of savant syndrome. In C. Stough (Ed.), *Neurobiology of exceptionality* (pp. 199–215). New York: Kluwer Academic Publishers.

Young, S. M., & Pinsky, D. (2006). Narcissism and celebrity. *Journal of Research in Personality, 40*(5), 463–471. doi:10.1016/j.jrp.2006.05.005

Yuille, J. C., & Daylen, J. (1998). The impact of traumatic events on eyewitness memory. In C. Thompson, D. Herrmann, et al. (Eds.), *Eyewitness memory: Theoretical and applied perspectives* (pp. 155–178). Mahwah, NJ: Erlbaum.

Zachariae, R. (2009). Psychoneuroimmunology: A bio-psycho-social approach to health and disease. *Scandinavian Journal of Psychology, 50*(6), 645–651. doi:10.1016/j.jrp.2006.05.005

Zaidi, Z. F. (2010). Gender differences in human brain: A review. *Open Anatomy Journal, 2*, 37–55. doi:10.2174/1877609401002010037

Zampetakis, L. A., & Moustakis, V. (2011). Managers' trait emotional intelligence and group outcomes: The case of group job satisfaction. *Small Group Research, 42*(1), 77–102. doi:10.1177/1046496410373627

Zarcadoolas, C., Pleasant, A., & Greer, D. S. (2006). *Advancing health literacy: A framework for understanding and action.* San Francisco: Jossey-Bass.

Zeidan, F., Johnson, S. K., Gordon, N. S., et al. (2010). Effects of brief and sham mindfulness meditation on mood and cardiovascular variables. *Journal of Alternative & Complementary Medicine, 16*(8), 867–873. doi:10.1089/acm.2009.0321

Zellner, D. A., Harner, D. E., & Adler, R. L. (1989). Effects of eating abnormalities and gender on perceptions of desirable body shape. *Journal of Abnormal Psychology, 98*(1), 93–96. doi:10.1037/0021-843X.98.1.93

Zemishlany, Z., Aizenberg, D., & Weizman, A. (2001). Subjective effects of MDMA ("Ecstasy") on human sexual function. *European Psychiatry, 16*(2), 127–130. doi:10.1016/S0924-9338(01)00550-8

Zentall, T. R. (2010). Coding of stimuli by animals: Retrospection, prospection, episodic memory and future planning. *Learning & Motivation, 41*(4), 225–240. doi:10.1016/j.lmot.2010.08.001

Zentall, T. R. (2011). Perspectives on observational learning in animals. *Journal of Comparative Psychology, 126*(2), 114–128. doi:10.1037/a0025381

Zentner, M., & Renaud, O. (2007). Origins of adolescents' ideal self: An intergenerational perspective. *Journal of Personality & Social Psychology, 92*(3), 557–574. doi:10.1037/0022-3514.92.3.557

Zhang R. L., Zhang Z. G., & Chopp, M. (2005). Neurogenesis in the adult ischemic brain: generation, migration, survival, and restorative therapy. *Neuroscientist, 11*(5), 408–416. doi:10.1177/1073858405278865

Zhang, B., Hao, Y. L., Jia, F. J., et al. (2010). Fatal familial insomnia: A middle-age-onset Chinese family kindred. *Sleep Medicine, 11*(5), 498–499. doi:10.1016/j.sleep.2009.11.005

Ziegler, M., Dietl, E., Danay, E., et al. (2011). Predicting training success with general mental ability, specific ability tests, and (un)structured interviews: A meta-analysis with unique samples. *International Journal of Selection & Assessment, 19*(2), 170–182. doi:10.1111/j.1468-2389.2011.00544.x

Zietsch, B. P., Miller, G. F., Bailey, J. M., et al. (2011). Female orgasm rates are largely independent of other traits: Implications for "female orgasmic disorder" and evolutionary theories of orgasm. *Journal of Sexual Medicine, 8*(8), 2305–2316. doi:10.1111/j.1743-6109.2011.02300.x

Zimbardo, P. (2007). *The Lucifer Effect: Understanding how good people turn evil.* New York: Random House.

Zimbardo, P. G., Haney, C., & Banks, W. C. (1973). A Pirandellian prison. *The New York Times Magazine*, April 8.

Zimbardo, P. G., Pilkonis, P. A., & Norwood, R. M. (1978). The social disease called shyness. In *Annual editions, personality and adjustment 78/79.* Guilford CT: Dushkin.

Zimmer, C. (2010). 100 trillion connections: New efforts probe and map the brain's detailed architecture. *Scientific American*, December, 58–63.

Ziv, I., Leiser, D., & Levine, J. (2011). Social cognition in schizophrenia: Cognitive and affective factors. *Cognitive Neuropsychiatry, 16*(1), 71–91. doi:10.1080/13546805.2010.492693

Zoccola, P. M., Green, M. C., Karoutsos, E., et al. (2011). The embarrassed bystander: Embarrassability and the inhibition of helping. *Personality & Individual Differences, 51*(8), 925–929. doi:10.1016/j.paid.2011.07.026

Zrenner, E., Bartz-Schmidt, K. U., Benav, H., et al. (2010). Subretinal electronic chips allow blind patients to read letters and combine them to words. *Proceedings of the Royal Society.* doi:10.1098/rspb.2010.1747 Retrieved May 9, 2012, from http://rspb.royalsocietypublishing.org/content/early/2010/11/01/rspb.2010.1747.full.pdf+html

Zucker, K. J. & Spitzer, R. L. (2005). Was the gender identity disorder of childhood diagnosis introduced into DSM-III as a backdoor maneuver to replace homosexuality? A historical note. *Journal of Sex & Marital Therapy, 31*(1), 31–42. doi:10.1080/00926230590475251

Zuckerman, M. (2002). Genetics of sensation seeking. In J. Benjamin, R. P. Ebstein, et al. (Eds.), *Molecular genetics and the human personality* (pp. 193–210). Washington, DC: American Psychiatric Publishing.

Name Index

Colin, K. A., 183
Collet, C., 316
Collins, A. M., 281, 282, 593
Collins, F. S., 602, 607
Collins, N. L., 106
Collins, R. L., 223
Collins, W. A., 105
Collop, N. A., 200
Colom, R., 73
Colvin, M. K., 75
Comer, R. J., 486
Comparini, L., 108, 109
Compton, R. J., 61, 78
Compton, W. C., 380, 531
Compton, W. M., 215
Confer, P., 591, 592
Confue, P., 549, 562
Conger, J. J., 111
Conley, K. M., 374
Conlon, K. E., 26, 27, 28
Conner, K. R., 520
Conner, M., 575
Connors, G. J., 210, 216, 222, 223
Constable, R. T., 392
Consumer Reports, 550
Conway, M. A., 289
Cook, G. L., 517
Cook, S. W., 387
Cooley, L., 529
Coolidge, F. L., 73
Cooper, C., 47
Cooper, D. S., 182
Cooper, G., 141, 146
Cooper, H., 378
Cooper, J., 575, 576, 577, 638
Cooper, M. J., 366
Cooper, M., 532
Cooper, M. L., 105
Cooper, R. P., 112
Cooper, S., 38
Cooper, S. J., 357
Corballis, M. C., 74, 88, 321
Corbin, W. R., 450
Corby, E.-K., 391
Corcoran, P. W., 500
Cordaro, D., 380
Coren, S., 88, 89, 90, 192
Corey, G., 421, 447, 554, 555
Corey, M. S., 421, 447
Corkin, S., 296
Cornell, J., 371
Corr, C. A., 130
Corr, D. M., 130
Correa-Chávez, M., 342
Corrigan, P. W., 500
Corsini, R. J., 49, 531, 551
Cortelli, P., 157
Cortes, D. E., 109
Cosgrove, G. R., 547
Costa, P. T., 406, 407, 408, 425
Côté, J. E., 122, 126
Cote, K. A., 194
Cothers, L. M., 423, 596
Cottle, J., 291
Cottrell, G. W., 385
Court, J. H., 294
Court, P. C., 294
Cowan, D. E., 587
Cowan, F., 427
Cowan, N., 278, 300

Cowan, P. A., 258
Cowden, C. R., 436
Cowden, J., 596
Cowles, J. T., 248
Cox, B. J., 257, 407, 467
Cox, R. H., 638
Coyle, J. T., 502
Craig, E., 533
Craig, K. D., 512
Craig, L., 108
Craighero, L., 79
Craik, F. M. I., 286, 287, 290
Craik, K. H., 34
Crandall, C. S., 476, 477, 600
Crane, L., 340
Cranney, A., 249
Crano, W. D., 575, 576
Crews, F. T., 78
Crichlow, S., 581
Crisp, A., 365
Crocker, J., 107
Crogan, M., 605
Crooks, R., 367, 371, 424
Cropley, A., 328
Crosby, R. D., 364, 366
Crouch, D. J., 42
Crow, S. J., 364
Crown, C. L., 112
Crowther, J. H., 471
Cruse, D., 83
Cruz-Bermúdez, N. D., 84, 211
Csikszentmihalyi, M., 35, 349, 373, 378
Cubbin, C., 455
Cuddy, A. J. C., 601
Cuijpers, P., 530
Culver, R., 24
Cumming, N., 275
Cummings, M. R., 97
Cunnington, R., 79
Curci, A., 296, 297
Curtis, D., 501, 506
Curwood, S. E., 418
Cytowic, R. E., 314
Czeisler, C. A., 192, 381
Czerwinski, M., 640

D
Dacre Pool, L., 393
Dagot, L., 583
Dahl, A., 122
Dai, D. Y., 339
D'Aleo, G., 161
Dalton, K. M., 453
Dam, H., 507
Damisch, L., 251, 333
Damman, M., 127
Danaei, G., 444, 445
Danay, E., 335
Dancy, B. L., 471
Dane, S., 90
Dang-Vu, T. T., 194
Danhauer, S. C., 556
Dani, J. A., 217
Daniels, H., 119
Daniels, M., 344
Danielsen, E. M., 638
Dann, B. M., 638
Danziger, N., 156
Darcy, A. M., 365

Darley, J. M., 20, 593, 601
Darling, C. A., 369
Darwin, C., 30, 385, 389
Das, M., 503
Das, P., 506
Datta, R., 360
Dattilio, F. M., 72
Davey, G., 18, 37, 534
David, A., 161
David, D., 550
David-Ferdon, C., 598
Davidov, B. J., 553, 606, 607, 608
Davidovitch, N., 328
Davidson, J., 325
Davidson, J. K., 369
Davidson, L., 548
Davidson, R. J., 208
Davidson, T. L., 260
Davidson, W. B., 414
Davies, R., 562
Daviet, C., 550
Davis, B., 273
Davis, C., 362
Davis, D., 331
Davis, E. B., 598
Davis, K. D., 157, 279
Davis, M. R., 281
Davis, R. C., 50
Davison, G. C., 501
Dawson, J. D., 458
Dawson, N., 111
Day, D. L., 485
Daylen, J., 182
Dazzi, C., 23
de Bono, E., 348
de Graaf, R., 509
de Groot, L. C., 446
de Jong, P. J., 240
De Jonghe, B. C., 360
De Leo, D., 519
de Leon, C. F. M., 129
de Queiroz, V., 547
de Rios, M. D., 191
De Vos, J., 118
de Vries, P. K., 250
Deakin, J. F. W., 503
Dean, D., Jr., 637
Deardorff, J., 121
Deary, I. J., 400, 404
DeCarolis, N. A., 503
Deci, E. L., 378
Decker, S. L., 335
Deckers, L., 356, 357, 375
Deckro, G. R., 208, 478
Deeb, S. S., 147
Defeyter, M. A., 325
Degenhardt, L., 210
Dehaene, S., 76
Dein, S., 586
DeLamater, J. D., 367
DeLano, L., 307
Delaporte, Y., 321
Delgado, B. M., 109
Delgado, J., 65
Dell, P. F., 512
Della Sala, S., 291, 292
DeLoache, J. S., 97
Demaine, K., 79
Dement, W., 201, 203
Demiris, G., 556

Demyttenaere, K., 547
Denney, J. T., 519, 520
Dennis, J., 199
Denollet, J., 473
DePape, A. M., 320
Derakshan, N., 374
DeSantis, A. D., 214
Desjardins, R. N., 112
Despland, J. -N., 462, 509
Deuser, W. E., 597
Deutsch, G., 74, 76, 90
Deutsch, M., 604
Deutschendorf, H., 389, 391, 393
DeVault, C., 371
Devine, D. J., 638
Devlin, B., 344
Devoto, A., 202
DeWall, C. N., 106, 596
DeYoung, C. G., 324
Dhanda, R., 465
Di Marzo, V., 360
Diano, S., 360
Diaz, D., 128
Dickel, N., 574
Dickinson, A., 253
Dickinson, L. M., 364
Dick-Niederhauser, A., 105
Dickens, W. T., 345
DiClemente, R. J., 263
Diener, E., 131, 132, 133, 376, 377, 448, 453, 455, 467, 479
Dierdorff, E. C., 634
Dieterich, S. E., 120
Dietl, E., 335
Dietrich, A., 639
Dietrich, K. N., 497
Dijk, D. -J., 357
Dijksterhuis, A., 328, 332
Dijkstra, A., 571
Dijkstra, P., 591
Dikotter, F., 218
Dillman, D. A., 49
Dillon, C., 429, 430
Dimaggio, G., 530
Dimberg, U., 390
Dimsdale, J. E., 512
Dinan, T. G., 473
Ding, E. L., 444, 445
Dinges, D. F., 192
Dingus, T. A., 46
Dion, K. L., 606
Dirkzwager, A. J. E., 512
Dissanayake, C., 119
Distin, K., 339
Dixon, M. J., 315
Dixon, S. V., 109
DiZio, P., 158
Do Lam, A. T. A., 463
Dobbins, I. G., 278
Dobie, T. G., 158
Dobricki, M., 491
Dobson, K. S., 506, 535
Dodd, D. K., 454, 455
Dodds, P. S., 559
Dodson, E. R., 358
Doherty, M. J., 118, 119
Doidge, N., 530
Dolev, K., 384
Dollard, J., 420, 421, 422
Dombrowski, S. U., 444

Holmes, T. H., 469
Hölzel, 208
Holzinger, B., 18, 227
Honey, P. L., 243, 247, 254
Hong, H. -W., 104
Honzik, C. H., 260
Hooley, J., 486
Hooyman, N., 129
Hopwood, C. J., 425
Horgan, J., 65
Horhota, M., 601
Horne, R. S. C., 201
Horney, K., 32
Hornick, B. K., 216
Hortman, G., 379
Horvath, L. S., 373
Horwood, L. J., 101
Hosch, H. M., 182
Houghton, D. P., 581
Houlihan, D., 200
Houser, M. E., 106
Houston-Price, C., 111
Howard, 550
Howell, C. J., 132
Howell, D. C., 620
Howell, R. T., 132
Hoyt, M., 208, 478
Hsieh, P., 141
Htut, M. M., 360
Huang, M.-H., 636
Hubble, M. A., 562
Hubel, D. H., 141
Hübner, R., 76
Huesmann, L. R., 264, 598
Hughes, A., 52
Hughes, J. R., 218, 223
Hughes, M., 371, 511
Huijbregts, S. C., 101
Human, L. J., 590
Humes, K. R., 36
Hummel, H. G. K., 250
Hunt, H., 330
Hunt, R. R., 305, 306
Hunter, E., 586
Hunter, J. P., 157
Hurley, E. A., 346
Husain, A. M., 201
Hutchinson, S. R., 49, 82
Hutchison, S. R., 221
Huyck, M. C., 128
Hyare, H., 174
Hyde, J. S., 34, 367, 413
Hyman, R., 179, 180, 501
Hysenbegasi, A., 467

I
Iacono, W. G., 384
Ianna, P., 24
Iannetti, G. D., 157
Iannone, M., 216
Ida, Y., 89
Immordino-Yang, M. H., 68
Impett, E. A., 371, 393, 479
Impey, S., 224
Ingham, A. G., 580
Ingram, C. W., 556
Insel, T. R., 501
Insko, C. A., 590
Inzlicht, M., 601, 606
Iosif, A., 54

Irons, G., 240
Irwin, M. R., 452
Isaac, A., 298
Ishihara, K., 192
Israelson, D., 157
Iversen, L., 214
Iyengar, S. S., 333
Izard, C. E., 104, 380, 390, 391, 393, 394

J
Jaber-Filho, J. A., 548
Jablonski, N. G., 607
Jack, D. C., 506
Jackendoff, 321
Jackson, D. C., 453
Jackson, S. L., 18, 21, 22, 26, 27, 46, 48
Jackson, T., 436
Jacob, A., 161
Jacob, C., 583
Jacobs, A., 105
Jacobs, J., 278
Jacobs, M., 31
Jacobs, N., 344
Jacobs, S. R., 454, 455
Jacobson, T., 237
Jacobs-Stewart, T., 222
Jaeggi, S. M., 346
Jaehnig, W., 249, 251
Jaffe, J., 112
Jagaroo, V., 72
Jahn, D. R., 522
Jahoda, G., 244
James, W., 30, 33, 387, 388, 390
Jamison, K. R., 520
Janessen, S. A., 66
Janis, I. L., 581
Jantos, H., 193
Janus, C. L., 368
Janus, S. S., 368
Jao, B., 168
Jarrold, C., 278
Jarvin, L., 334
Jasnow, M. D., 112
Jawahar, I. M., 570
Jaycox, L. H., 457
Jeffery, R. W., 364
Jekogian, A. M., 607
Jellinger, K. E., 72
Jenkins, A. C., 78
Jenkins, M. R. M., 167, 168
Jenni, O. C., 192
Jensen, A. R., 345
Jeong, G.-H., 373
Jerabek, I., 292
Jerome, A., 218, 267
Jessen, F., 216
Jeste, D. V., 346
Jia, F. J., 191
Jiang, S., 479
Jiang, Y., 78
Jin, J. L., 358
Joe, G. W., 215
Joffe, R. T., 86
Jogerst, G. J., 458
Johansson, A., 89
Johansson, H., 439
Johansson, L., 153
Johnson, B. T., 153, 222, 573, 575, 576

Johnson, C. S., 572
Johnson, D., 192, 596
Johnson, K. J., 174
Johnson, M. J. M., 470
Johnson, R. D., 305
Johnson, S., 345, 346
Johnson, S. J., 333, 392
Johnson, V. E., 368, 369
Johnson, W., 73
Joiner, T. E., Jr., 364, 366, 520
Joinson, C., 100
Jolicoeur, P., 275
Jones, J., 368
Jones, K. L., 101, 202, 340
Jones, L., 374
Jones, M. D., 122
Jones, M. K., 534
Jones, N. A., 36
Jones, R., 509
Jones, S. A. H., 172
Jones, S. E., 88
Jones, S. R., 502
Jones, S. S, 104
Jones, W. R., 365, 366
Jonides, J., 275, 278, 293, 346
Joo, E. Y., 200
Jordan, 241
Jorm, A. F., 548
Joseph, J. E., 78
Josephs, R. A., 220
Joughin, N., 365
Jouvet, M., 191, 196
Jowett, G. S., 586
Joyce, A. S., 387
Juang, L., 570, 571
Juliano, L. M., 216
Julien, E., 570
Julien, R. M., 211, 215, 217, 223, 545, 546
Jun, H., 553
Jung, C., 32, 401
Jung, R. E., 72, 80
Jurd, R. R., 84
Jussin, L., 45
Justman, S., 44

K
Kabnick, K., 363
Kächele, H., 529
Kagan, J., 102, 111, 342
Kahana, M. J., 286
Kahn, A. S., 371
Kahneman, D., 2, 314, 330, 331, 332, 333
Kail, R. V., 125
Kalat, J. W., 66, 82, 85, 96, 155, 211, 379, 385, 386, 425, 546
Kallgren, C. A., 571, 572
Kallio, S., 190, 204, 206
Kalish, D., 260
Kalmijn, M., 127, 589
Kalyuga, S., 325, 326, 327
Kamimori, G. H., 192
Kamin, L. J., 345
Kamo, Y., 469
Kamphaus, R. W., 430
Kampman, K. M., 215
Kandel, E., 298
Kann, L., 445, 447
Kanoski, S., 360

Kanwisher, N., 141, 316
Kapinos, K. A., 361
Kaplan, A., 8, 374
Kaplan, P. S., 106, 108
Kaplan, R. M., 334, 431, 433
Kaplar, M. E., 574
Kaptelinin, V., 640
Karasz, A., 450
Karim, A. A., 83
Karmaniola, A., 106
Karnes, F. A., 342
Karney, B. R., 589
Karoutsos, E., 593, 594
Kashima, Y., 606
Kasser, T., 375, 377
Kassin, S. M., 383, 579
Kastenmüller, A., 260
Kataria, S., 200
Katkin, E. S., 240
Katz, J., 156, 157, 599
Kauer, J. A., 84, 211
Kauffman, J. M., 338
Kaufman, A. S., 334
Kaufman, J. C., 328, 329, 349
Kaufman, J. H., 172
Kaufman, L., 172
Kawada, R., 503
Kawai, K., 361
Kawakamia, 599, 602
Kaye, D. H., 638
Kaylor-Hughes, C., 529
Kearney, A. J., 558, 559
Kearney, C. A., 105, 494, 495
Kee, D. W., 76
Keefe, F. J., 207
Keefer, L. A., 5724
Keegan, J., 101
Keel, P. K., 490
Keeley, S., 22
Kegel, M., 507
Keijsers, G. P. J., 550
Kelder, S. H., 447
Kell, C. A., 76
Keller, M. C., 590
Kellerman, S. E., 449
Kelley, M. E., 243
Kelly, I. W., 23
Kelly, M. P., 431
Kelly, S., 157
Kelly, T. L., 192
Keltner, D., 400
Kempe, A., 364
Kendall-Tackett, K., 452
Kendler, K. S., 65, 508
Kennedy, S. H., 547
Kenneth, M., 220
Kenny, P. J., 247
Kenrick, D. T., 378
Kensinger, E. A., 296, 297
Kernis, M. H., 402, 417
Kerns, R. D., 157
Kerr, M., 3
Kershaw, T., 449
Kesebir, S., 455
Kessler, D. A., 363, 364, 485
Kessler, H., 463
Kessler, R. C., 128, 491
Kestler, L., 500, 501, 502
Ketcham, K., 280
Kety, S. S., 496

Lewis, M., 119
Lewis, R. L., 275, 278, 293
Leyendecker, B., 108, 109
Leynes, P. A., 288, 292
Li, C., 445
Li, D., 360
Liang, Y., 454, 475
Li-Barber, K., 590
Libon, D. J., 84
Lichstein, K. L., 198, 199
Lichtenstein, P., 96
Lichter, D. T., 589
Lichtman, A. H., 223
Lickel, B., 458
Liddell, S. K., 321
Liebal, K., 321, 322
Lierens, R., 528
Lievens, F., 634
Lilienfeld, S. O., 18, 25, 52, 54, 179, 434
Liles, E. E., 101
Limosin, F., 528
Lin, F. R., 151
Lin, T., 571
Lin, Y., 274
Linde, K., 156
Lindemann, B., 154
Linden, W., 477
Linderoth, B., 156
Lindsey, B. J., 467
Linster, C., 175
Linton, D., 100
Lipka, J., 510
Lippke, S., 445
Lipsey, M. W., 550
Lisak, R., 65
Lister, J. J., 151
Little, B. R., 133, 418
Littlewood, R., 586
Liu, G. C., 383
Liu, H., 360
Liu, Y., 360
Livingston, I., 593
Lloyd, D. M., 157
Lodi-Smith, J., 418
Loehlin, J. C., 425
Loftus, E. F., 279, 280, 295
Lokuge, S., 506
LoLordo, A. M., 466, 506
Long, C. R., 571
Long, V. O., 424
Lopez, F. G., 105
Lopez, S. J., 35
López, S. R., 490
Lorenzo, G. L., 590
Loughead, J. W., 72
Lounsbury, D. W., 447
Lovaas, O., 543
Lovallo, W. R., 473
Low, K. G., 507
Lowe, R., 554
Lowenstein, A. E., 102, 106
Lubart, T. I., 330
Lubinski, D., 330
Lucas, R. E., 131, 132, 133
Lucas, S. G., 325
Lucidi, F., 202
Luck, S. J., 295
Lüdtke, R., 156
Luger, T., 444

Lum, D., 36
Lum, J. A. G., 283, 298
Lumia, A. R., 86
Lumley, M. A., 387, 391, 587
Lundervold, A. J., 191, 195
Lundh, L., 436
Luo, S., 592
Luppa, M., 445
Luria, A. R., 273
Lussier, J. P., 210
Lutter, M., 132
Luyten, P., 486
Lykken, D. T., 384, 425
Lyn, H., 322
Lynam, D., 373
Lynch, C., 89
Lynch, K. B., 108
Lynch, T. R., 391
Lynn, A. L., 244
Lynn, S. J., 25, 52, 205, 206
Lynne-Landsman, S. D., 373
Lyons, M. A., 373
Lyons, R., 448
Lyubomirsky, S., 475

M
Maas, J., 192
Maass, A., 601
MacCabe, J. H., 501
MacDuffie, K., 203
MacGregor, B, 130
Macht, M., 362
MacIver, K., 157
MacKay, D. G., 295
Mackinnon, L. T., 453
Macklin, C. B., 7
Maddi, S., 474, 475
Maddock, J. E., 221, 222, 445
Maddox, K. B., 601
Maddox, W. T., 317
Madge, A., 275
Madsen, L., 384
Maercker, A., 491
Maggin, D. M., 248, 543
Magnotta, V., 503
Magrini, A., 361
Magueja, C., 603
Maguire, E. A., 68, 300
Mah, K., 369
Mahler, H. I. M., 575
Mahmound, S. Y., 88
Mahoney A. E. J., 536
Mahowald, M.W., 199
Maier, N. R. F., 459
Maier, S. F., 300
Mailis-Gagnon, A., 157
Maio, G. R., 576
Maisel, E., 491
Maisto, S. A., 210, 216, 222, 223
Malach, R., 317
Malaspina, D., 501
Maldonado-Molina, M., 215
Malhi, G. S., 506
Mallik, S., 208
Malloy, K. M., 541
Mamen, M., 107
Manber, R., 546
Mancini-Marïe, A., 495
Mandal, M. K., 89
Mandler, J. M., 100

Mangan, D., 593
Mangan, M. A., 200
Manganello, J. A., 257
Mangels, J. A., 290
Mangin, J.-F., 89
Maniaci, M. R., 589, 590
Mann, N., 361
Manning, M., 90
Manning, R., 593
Manschreck, T. C., 497
Mansouri, A., 495
Manstead, A. S. R., 387
Mantovani, A., 554
Mantyla, T., 302
Maran, M., 295
Marcel, M., 413
Marchman, V. A., 111
Marchand, A., 240
Marchand, M., 582
Marcus-Newhall, A., 597
Margoliash, D., 191
Margolin, G., 598
Margolin, J., 457
Mark, D., 473
Markey, P. M., 404
Markoff, J., 341
Markou, A., 247
Markowitsch, H., 80
Markowitz, F. E., 500, 548
Marks, D. F., 179, 180
Marks, J. S., 445
Markus, H. R., 128, 386, 402, 417, 579
Marois, R., 166
Marsh, E. J., 286
Marsh, H. W., 467
Marshall, J. P, 589
Marshall, P. H., 305, 346, 457
Marston, A., 228
Marston, W., 384
Martens, M. L., 571
Martens, R., 24
Marti, C. N., 364
Martin, A. J., 467, 595
Martin, B. R., 223
Martin, E., 488
Martin, G., 557
Martin, L. L., 390, 468
Martin, L. R., 408
Martin, M., 89, 257
Martin, R., 444
Martin, W. L. B., 89
Martinez-Gonzalez, M. A., 366
Martinez-Jarreta, B., 453, 454, 455
Martino, S. C., 223
Martins, E. P, 37
Martuza, R. L., 547
Marvin, R. S., 105
Marx, B. P., 512
Marx, D. M., 572
Mashour, G. A., 203, 547
Maslach, C., 424, 454
Maslow, A., 32, 33, 183, 375, 376, 377, 414, 415, 416
Masquelier, 533
Massaccesi, S., 100
Masse, L. C., 122, 210
Massey, D. S., 601
Master, S. L., 479
Masters, W. H., 368, 369

Mastropieri, M. A., 637
Masuda, T., 175
Mather, G., 143, 144, 152, 166
Mathy, F., 278
Matlin, M. W., 146, 152
Matossian, M. K., 528
Matson, J. L., 543
Matsumoto, D., 570, 571
Mattanah, J. F, 102
Matthews, G., 400, 404
Matthews, K. L., 102, 214
Matthews, M. D., 376
Matthews, M. S., 320
Matthews, P. H., 320
Matthews, R., 457
Mattingley, J. B., 79
May, J. G., 158, 162
Mayberg, H., 207
Mayberry, M. T., 286
Mayer, A. R., 517
Mayer, J. D., 392, 393, 427
Mayer, R. E., 250, 261, 319
Mazure, C. M., 380, 456
Mazzoni, G., 280, 281
McAdams, D. P., 418, 427
McAlister, A. L., 556
McBurney, D. H., 44
McCabe, M. P., 365
McCabe, S. E., 214
McCall, W. V., 547
McCalley, L. T., 250
McCarley, R., 202
McCarthy, B. W., 371, 471
McCarthy, K., 25
McClelland, D. C., 346, 375, 422, 480
McClendon, D. T., 571
McClung, C. A., 381
McClure, F. H., 530, 536, 555
McCluskey, U., 554
McConkey, K. M., 206
McCormick, N. B., 370
McCown, R., 249, 260, 636
McCrae, R. R., 406, 407, 425
McCraty, A., 374
McCullagh, J. F., 88
McCullough, S., 321
McDaniel, M. A., 7, 300
McDermott, K. B., 280
McDermott, R., 596
McDonough, L., 100
McElduff, P., 551, 562
McEvoy, C., 280, 638
McEvoy, P. M., 536
McGaugh, J. L., 273, 279, 300
McGinnis, M.Y., 86
McGrath, R. E., 39, 433, 435
McGregor, L., 133, 418
McGue, M., 425, 517
McHale, N., 480
McIntosh, W. D., 468
McKay, A., 367
McKay, E., 640
McKeever, W. F., 89, 420
McKenna, M. W., 264, 598
McKeown, D., 275
McKim, W. A., 220
McKinney, S. M., 197
McKinnon, K., 492, 518
McLane, M., 535

Ruva, C., 280, 638
Ryan, M. P., 5
Ryan, R. M., 375, 378, 417
Ryckman, R. M., 401, 416
Ryder, N., 340
Ryff, C. D., 128, 133
Rynearson, K., 3

S
Saab, P. G., 453
Sabel, A. L., 364
Saber, J. L., 305
Saccuzzo, D. P., 334, 431, 433
Sachdev, P. S., 547
Sack, R. L., 358
Sackett, P. R., 634
Sacks, O., 80, 167
Saffran, J. R., 112
Sagan, C., 22, 635
Sagar, U., 364
Sagiv, N., 315
Sahakian, B. J., 214
Saksida, L. M., 253
Salamone, J. D., 65, 219
Salimpoor, V. N., 84
Salisbury, A. G., 512
Salkovskis, P. M., 511
Sallinen, M., 192
Salmela-Aro, K., 454
Salmelin, R., 88
Salovey, P., 392
Salthouse, T. A., 129
Saltzman, E., 249
Salzarulo, P., 194
Sam, D. L., 471
Sampson, N. A., 492
Sampson, R. J., 518
Samuels, C. A., 424
Sanftner, J., 471
Sankofa, B. M., 346
Sankoorikal, G., 214
Sansone, L. A., 458
Sansone, R. A., 458
Santelices, M. P., 105
Santi, A., 77
Santos, R., 374
Santrock, J. W., 5, 9, 13, 110,
    127–128, 301, 374, 420,
    467–468, 632
Sapolsky, R., 455
Sartorius, A., 547
Sateia, M. J., 198
Sato, T., 291, 497
Saunders, M. M., 157, 479
Sautter, J. M., 589
Savage-Rumbaugh, E., 322
Savage-Rumbaugh, S., 322
Saville, B. K., 371
Savsevitz, J., 538
Saxton, M., 110–111
Saxvig, I. W., 191, 195
Schabus, M. M., 83
Schacht, J. P., 223
Schachter, S., 388–390
Schacter, D. L., 279, 280
Schafer, M., 581
Schaffner, K. F., 65, 208
Schaie, W., 129
Schaufeli, W. B., 454
Scheck, B., 182

Scheffer, I. A., 79
Scheinkman, M., 555
Schenck, C. H., 199
Scher, S. J., 9
Scherer, K. R., 386
Schetter, C. D., 101
Schick, T., 24, 180
Schiller, P. H., 168
Schillling, M. A., 324
Schiraldi, G. R., 480
Schlaepfer, T. E., 547
Schleicher, S. S., 370
Schlosberg, H., 386
Schlund, M. W., 83, 256, 381
Schmader, T., 601
Schmahmann, J. D., 82
Schmalzl, L., 157
Schmidt, L. A., 435
Schmidt, M. G., 108
Schmitt, D. P., 402
Schmitt, J. A. J., 199
Schnakers, C. C., 83
Schneider, A., 203
Schneider, K. J., 32, 533
Schneiderman, N., 453, 474
Schnyer, D. M., 192
Schock, K., 430
Schoelles, K., 200
Schoenberg, M. R., 70
Scholl, B. J., 163
Schopp, L. H., 556
Schouten, J. S., 156
Schramm, D. G., 589
Schredl, M., 203
Schreiber, D. E., 281
Schreiber, E. H., 281
Schreiber, F. R., 512
Schroeder, D. A., 594
Schroeder, J. E., 436, 448
Schuck, K., 550
Schuel, H., 223
Schultheiss, O. C., 375
Schultz, D., 490
Schultz, D. H., 238
Schultz, D. P., 29, 30, 31, 235, 400,
    408, 421
Schultz, H. T., 39
Schultz, P. W., 576–577
Schultz, S. E., 29, 30, 31, 235, 400,
    408, 421
Schuster, J., 528
Schuster, M. A., 457
Schützler, L., 156
Schwade, J. A., 110
Schwartz, C., 191
Schwartz, F., 160
Schwartz, J. E., 408
Schwartz, M. W., 360
Schwartz, S. J., 122
Schwartzman, R. J., 84
Schwarz, N., 377
Schweckendiek, J., 240
Schwenzer, M., 597
Schwitzgebel, E., 190
Scileppi, J. A., 548
Sclafani, A., 363
Scoboria, A., 280, 281
Scollon, C. N., 131–133
Scott, J. G., 70
Scott, J. L., 307

Scruggs, T. E., 637
Sears, S., 207, 478
Seburn, M., 571
Sedikides, C., 401
Seelig, D., 72
Seeman, P., 66
Segal, Z. V., 207
Segerdahl, P., 322
Segerstrom, S., 452
Séguin, J. R., 101
Seidler, G. H., 541
Seiffge-Krenke, I., 126
Seiter, S. J., 577
Seitz, A., 175
Sela, L., 153
Seligman, M. E. P., 35, 383, 394, 416,
    465–467, 561
Sellinger, J., 157
Selye, H., 451–452
Semin, G., 296–297
Serlin, I., 533
Serra-Grabulosa, J. P., 216
Sestir, M. A., 598
Seybolt, D. C., 421
Seyle, C., 603
Shade, R., 356
Shafer, C. S., 571
Shaffer, D. R., 104, 118, 413,
    422–423
Shaffer, H. J., 537
Shafton, A., 196, 201
Shah, P., 175
Shalizi, C. R., 603
Shalom, D. E., 237
Shamdasani, S., 529–530
Shames, J., 349
Shanks, D. R., 234, 279, 295
Shannon, J. D., 108
Shannon, K., 340
Shapiro-Mendoza, C. K., 201
Shapiro, D. A., 550
Shapiro, F., 541
Shapiro, J., 280
Shapiro, S., 210
Sharf, R. S., 528, 531, 551
Sharpe, B., 434
Shaver, P. R., 458, 592, 596
Shaw, E., 321
Shaw, J., 548
Shaywitz, S. E., 80
Shedler, J., 530, 550
Shegog, R., 449
Sheikh, A. A., 540
Shekunova, E., 247
Sheldon, K. M., 417
Shen, J., 358
Shepard, D. S., 535–536, 551–552
Shepard, R. N., 315
Shephard, J. M., 315
Shepherd, G. M., 154
Sher, L., 507
Sherif, M., 604
Sherman, D. K., 257, 467, 603, 606
Sherratt, T. N., 244
Shields, C. C., 120
Shiffrin, R. M., 274
Shih, J. J., 83
Shillingsburg, M. A., 243
Shin, Y. J., 152
Shiner, R. L., 400, 425

Shiota, M. N., 379, 385–386
Shiv, B., 174
Shneerson, J. M., 197–199
Shneidman, E. S., 521
Shoda, Y., 420, 426
Shoenberger, D., 539
Shorrock, S. T., 298
Short, E. J., 224
Shorter, E., 499
Shrira, A., 133
Shurkin, J. N., 339
Sibler, B. Y., 199
Sibley, C. G., 600
Sidanius, J., 599
Siefert, C. J., 430
Siegel, B. V., 72, 80
Siegel, D. J., 2
Siegel, R. D., 182, 208
Siegel, R. K., 190–191
Siegler, R. S., 97, 117, 349
Sienaert, P., 547
Siever, L. J., 516
Sigelman, C. K., 100, 105
Signorello, L. B., 216
Sikka, P., 190
Sillars, A., 371
Silver, E., 500
Silveri, M. C., 74
Silverman, W. K., 105
Silverstein, S. M., 160
Simeon, D., 512
Simic, M., 555
Simister, J., 47
Simmonds, E., 392
Simmons, J., 543
Simner, M. L., 23
Simon-Thomas, E. R., 381
Simon, A. F., 599, 602
Simon, H. A., 327
Simons, D. J., 166, 257, 258, 291
Simons, G., 362
Simonton, D. K., 330, 448
Simpson, D. D., 215
Simpson, H. B., 554
Sims, K. E., 105
Singer, B., 128, 133
Singer, J. D., 581
Singer, L. T., 224
Singer, M. T., 587
Singleton, J. L., 321
Sinha, R., 215, 380, 456
Sjöqvist, F., 86
Skeels, H. M., 345
Skewes, M. C., 467
Skinner, B. F., 31, 242–245, 256
Skurnik, I., 279
Slife, B. D., 21, 26
Slocum, W. M., 168
Sloman, A., 344
Slomianka, L., 68
Slotter, E. B., 106
Smedley, A., 607
Smedley, B. D., 607
Smeets, T., 295
Smilek, D., 315
Smith, A. M., 224
Smith, A. P., 304, 469
Smith, C. A., 455, 456, 479
Smith, C. S., 358
Smith, E. E., 44

Subject Index/Glossary

A

Ablation (ab-LAY-shun), 70. Surgical removal of tissue.

Absolute threshold, 140. The minimum amount of physical energy necessary to produce a sensation.

Acceptance, 414

Accessibility (in memory), 292. Memories currently stored in memory that can be retrieved when necessary are both available and accessible.

Accommodation (in Piaget's theory), 114. The modification of existing mental patterns to fit new demands (that is, mental schemes are changed to accommodate new information or experiences).

Accommodation (in vision), 144. Changes in the shape of the lens of the eye.

Acculturative stress, 471. Stress caused by the many changes and adaptations required when a person moves to a foreign culture.

Achievement
  need for, 375
  self-confidence and, 376

Achondroplasia, 86

Acquisition, 237. The period in conditioning during which a response is strengthened.

Acromegaly, 85

Action potential, 63. The nerve impulse.

Activation-synthesis hypothesis, 202. An attempt to explain how dream content is affected by motor commands in the brain that occur during sleep but are not carried out.

Active listener, 5. A person who knows how to maintain attention, distractions, and actively gather information from lectures.

Active listening, 552

Actor-observer bias, 574. The tendency to attribute the behavior of others to internal causes while attributing one's own behavior to external causes (situations and circumstances).

Acupuncture, 156

Acute stress disorder, 512. A psychological disturbance lasting up to 1 month following stresses that would

produce anxiety in anyone who experienced them.

Adamson, Kate, 83

Adaptive behaviors, 379. Actions that aid attempts to survive and adapt to change conditions.

Adjustment disorder, 508–509. An emotional disturbance caused by ongoing stressors within the range of common experience.

Adler, Alfred, 32

Adolescence, 121. The culturally defined period between childhood and adulthood.
  characterization of, 120
  differences among, 121
  identity formation during, 121–122
  moral development in, 123–124, 127
  premature puberty in, 85
  puberty in, 121

Adrenal cortex, 86

Adrenal glands, 86. Endocrine glands that arouse the body, regulates salt balance, adjust the body to stress, and affect sexual functioning.

Adrenal medulla, 86

Adulthood. *See also* Emerging adulthood
  challenges of, 127–130
  happiness in, 130–131
  midlife crisis in, 128
  moral development in, 126–127
  personal factors, 132
  status criteria, 121

Advice giving, 553

Aerial perspective, 171

Affectional needs, 106. Emotional needs for love and affection.

Afterimages, 146–147

Age
  alcohol abuse, 220
  IQ and, 337
  regression, 207
  suicide rates, 519
  vision and, 144

Ageism, 129. Discrimination or prejudice based on a person's age.

Aggression, 458, 587. Any response made with the intent of causing harm, or achieving one's goals at the expense of another person.
  cause of, 587, 595–598
  manifestations of, 596
  prevention of, 598
  punishment and, 258

Agoraphobia (without panic) (ah-go-rah-FOBE-ee-ah), 509, 510. The fear that something

extremely embarrassing will happen if one leaves the house or enters unfamiliar situations.

Agreeableness, 406

Alarm reaction, 452. First stage of the GAS, during which bodily resources are mobilized to cope with a stressor.

Alcohol abuse
  age factors in, 220
  effects of, 220
  moderated drinking *vs.*, 221–222
  recognition of, 221
  treatment for, 222
  types of, 220–222

Alcohol myopia (my-OH-pea-ah), 220. Shortsighted thinking and perception that occurs during alcohol intoxication.

Alcoholics Anonymous (AA), 222

Alexithymia (a-LEX-ih-THIGH-me-ah), 386. A learned difficulty expressing emotions, more common in men.

Algorithm, 323. A learned set of rules that always lead to the correct solution of a problem.

All-or-nothing thinking, 318, 535. Classifying objects or events as absolutely right or wrong, good or bad, acceptable or unacceptable, and so forth.

Alpha waves, 193. Large, slow brainwaves associated with relaxation and falling asleep.

Altered state of consciousness (ASC), 190. A condition of awareness distinctly different in quality or pattern from waking consciousness.
  drug-induced, 210–215
  hypnosis as, 204–208

Alzheimer's disease (ALLS-hi-merz), 291, 496–497. An age-related disease characterized by memory loss, mental confusion, and, in its later stages, a nearly total loss of mental abilities.

Ambivalence, 461

Ambivalent attachment style, 106

American Psychological Association (APA)
  divisions of, 37
  ethical guidelines of, 28
  website, 11–12

American Sign Language (ASL), 321

Ames room, 160

Amnesia, 206

Amok, 490

Amphetamine psychosis, 214

Amphetamines, 214

Amygdala (ah-MIG-dah-luh), 83, 381. A part of the limbic system (within the brain) associated with fear responses.
  anatomy of, 381
  emotions and, 381

Anal stage, 409. The psychosexual state corresponding roughly to the period of toilet-training (ages 1 to 3).
  personality of, 412

Anal-expulsive personality, 412. A disorderly, destructive, cruel, or messy person.

Anal-retentive personality, 412. A person who is obstinate, stingy, or compulsive, and who generally has difficulty "letting go."

Anarchia, 494

Androgen, 367. Any of a number of male sex hormones, especially testosterone.

Androgyny (an-DROJ-ih-nee), 423–425. The presence of both "masculine" and "feminine" traits in a single person (as masculinity and femininity are defined within one's culture).

Anhedonia (an-he-DAWN-ee-ah), 215. An inability to feel pleasure.

Animal models, 37. In research, an animal whose behavior is used to derive principles that may apply to human behavior.
  surrogate mothers in, 104
  use of, 37–38

Animals
  language of, 320, 321–322
  time passage awareness of, 254

Anorexia nervosa (AN-uh-REK-see-yah ner-VOH-sah), 363–365. Active self-starvation or a sustained loss of appetite that has psychological origins.
  causes of, 365–366
  symptoms of, 365
  treatment of, 366

Antecedents, 234. Event that precede a response.

Anterograde amnesia, 295. Loss of the ability to form or retrieve memories for events that occur after an injury of trauma.

Anthropomorphic (AN-thro-po-MORE-fik) **error,** 47. The error of attributing human thoughts, feelings or motives to animals, especially as a way of explaining their behavior.

Antidepressants, 545. Mood-elevating drugs.

Antipsychotics (major tranquilizers), 545. Drugs that, in addition to having tranquilizing effects, also tend to reduced hallucinations and delusional thinking.
mode of action, 546

Antisocial behavior, 595. Any behavior that has a negative impact on other people.
causes of, 596–598
prevention of, 598
types of, 596

Antisocial personality (antisocial/ psychopathic personality), 518–519. A person who lacks a conscience; is emotionally shallow, impulsive, and selfish; and tends to manipulate others.

Anxiety, 462. Apprehension, dread, or uneasiness similar to fear but based on an unclear threat.
neurotic, 410–411
tests and, 374–375

Anxiety disorder, 489, 509–511. Disruptive feelings of fear, apprehension, or anxiety, or distortions in behavior that are anxiety related.
behavioral approach to, 514–515
causes of, 513–515
classification of, 509
cognitive approach to, 515
generalized, 509
humanistic-existential approach to, 514
obsessions in, 511
panic, 510
phobias, 510–511
psychodynamic approach to, 514

Anxiety reduction hypothesis, 515. Explains the self-defeating nature of avoidance responses as a result of reinforcing effects of relief from anxiety.

Anxiolytics (ANG-zee-eh LIT-iks), 545. Drugs (such as Valium) that produce relaxation or reduced anxiety.

Aphasia (ah-FAZE-yah), 77. A speech disturbance resulting from brain damage.

Apparent-distance hypothesis, 172. An explanation of the mood illusion stating that the horizon seems more distant than the night sky.

Applied psychology, 633. The use of psychological principles and research methods to solve practical problems.
educational, 636–637
environmental, 634–636
human factors, 639–640
industrial/organizational, 634
law, 637–638
sports, 638–639
Appreciation, 415

Approach-approach conflict, 460. Choosing between two positive, or desirable, alternatives.

Approach-avoidance conflict, 461. Being attracted to and repelled by the same goal or activity.
Arousal disorders, 371

Arousal theory, 373. Assumes that people prefer to maintain ideal, or comfortable levels of arousal.

Artificial intelligence (AI), 341. Refers to both the creation of computer programs capable of doing things that require intelligence when done by people, and to the resulting programs themselves.
Artificial hearing, 152
Asch experiment, 580–581

Assimilation, 114. In Piaget's theory, the application of existing mental patterns to new situations (that is, the new situation is assimilated to existing mental schemes).

Association areas (association cortex), 77. All areas of the cerebral cortex that are not primarily sensory or motor in function.
Association for Psychological Sciences (APS), 12–13

Associative learning, 234 The formation of simple associations between various stimuli and responses.

Astigmatism (ah-STIG-mah-tiz-em), 144. Defects in the cornea, lens or eye that cause some areas of vision to be out of focus.
Astrology
evidence against, 23–24
perceptions of, 24
personality profiles in, 24–25
popularity of, 24
Atkinson-Shiffrin model, 274

Attention deficit/hyperactivity disorder (ADHD), 214. A behavioral problem characterized by short attention span, restless movement, and impaired learning capacity.
Attention, value of, 183

Attitude, 574. A learned tendency to respond to people, objects, or institutions in a positive or negative way.
behavior and, 576
belief component of, 574–575
formation of, 575
persuasion and, 577
Attraction, interpersonal, 589–590

Attribution, 388, 573. The mental process of assigning causes to events. In emotion, the process of attributing arousal to a particular source.
making, 573–574
Auditory ossicles, 149

Authenticity, 533. In Carl Rogers' terms, the ability of a therapist

to be genuine and honest about his or her own feelings.

Authoritarian parents, 107. Parents who enforce rigid rules and demand strict obedience to authority.

Authoritarian (ah-thor-ih-TARE-ee-un) personality, 599. A personality pattern characterized by rigidity, inhibition, prejudice, and an excessive concern with power, authority, and obedience.

Authoritative parents, 107. Parents who supply firm and consistent guidance combined with love and affection.

Autonomic nervous system (ANS), 61, 382. The system of nerves carrying information to and from the internal organs and glands.
Autonomy, 415

Autonomy versus shame and doubt, 126. A conflict created when growing self-control (autonomy) is pitted against feelings of shame and doubt.

Availability (in memory), 292. Memories currently stored in memory are available.

Aversion therapy, 538. Suppressing an undesirable response by associating it with aversive (painful or uncomfortable) stimuli.
example of, 538–539
thought stopping in, 558–559

Avoidance learning, 257. Learning to make a response in order to postpone or prevent discomfort.
normal course of, 466

Avoidance-avoidance conflict, 460–461. Choosing between two negative, undesirable alternatives.
Avoidant attachment style, 106
Avoidant personality disorder, 516
Awareness levels, 411

Axons (AK-sahn), 62 Fibers that carries information away from the cell body of a neuron.
activity, measurement of, 62
interior of, 64
saltatory conduction of, 64–65

Axon terminals, 62. Bulb-shaped structures at the ends of axons that form synapses with the dendrites and somas of other neurons.

B
Barbiturates, 219

Barnum effect, 25, 52–53. The tendency to consider a personal description accurate if it is stated in very general terms.

Base rate, 331. The basic rate at which an event occurs over time, the basic probability of an event.

Basic emotions, 380–381. According to Robert Plutchik's theory, the most fundamental emotions are fear, surprise, sadness, disgust, anger, anticipation, joy, and acceptance.

Basic needs, 376. The first four levels of needs in Maslow's hierarchy, lower needs tend to be more potent than higher needs.

Basic suggestion effect, 205. The tendency of hypnotized persons to carry out suggested actions as if they were involuntary.

Behavior. *See also* Social behavior
adaptive, 379
biological perspective on, 34
disordered, 488
health-promoting, 446–447
helping, 551
hormonal link to, 86
ineffective, 476, 478–479
jury, 638
personality-based, 404
psychological perspective on, 34–35
self-managed, 265–268
situational effects of, 420
sociocultural perspective on, 36
targeted, 543–544
unconscious effects on, 31–32

Behavior modification, 538. The application of learning principles to change human behavior, especially maladaptive behavior.

Behavior therapy, 538. Any therapy designed to actively change behavior.
desensitization approach, 539–542
operant approach, 542–544

Behavioral assessment, 430–432. Recording the frequency of various behaviors.

Behavioral contract, 267. A formal agreement stating behaviors to be changed and consequence that apply.

Behavioral dieting, 364. Weight reduction based on changing exercise and eating habits, rather than temporary self-starvation.

Behavioral genetics, 425. The study of inherited behavioral traits and tendencies.

Behavioral medicine, 444. The study of behavioral factors in medicine, physical illness, and medical treatment.

Behavioral personality theory, 419. Any model of personality that emphasizes learning and observable behavior.

Behavioral risk factors, 444. Behaviors that increase the chances of disease, injury, or premature.
examples of, 444–445
STD-associated, 450

Behaviorism, 30. The school of psychology that emphasizes the study of overt, observable behavior.
  anxiety disorder approach of, 514–515
  key view of, 35
  learning and, 31
  personality theory of, 419–420
  radical, 30–31
  therapies of, 538–542
Beliefs
  attitude and, 574–575
  changing, 586–587
  false, 495–498
  just-world, 607
  in self, 421
  unproductive, 437
Bem Sex Role Inventory (BSRI), 423
Beta waves, 193. Small, fast brainwaves associated with being awake and alert.
Bias
  actor-observer, 574
  confirmation, 24–25
  participant, 44
  researcher, 44–45
  self-defeating, 436–437
Bilingualism, 320. A ability to speak two languages.
Binet, Alfred, 335
Binge drinking, 220–221. Consuming five or more drinks in a short time (four for women).
Binocular depth cues, 168–169
Biofeedback, 472–473. Information given to a person about his or her ongoing bodily activities, aids voluntary regulation of physical states.
Biological motives, 357. Innate motives based on biological needs.
Biological perspective, 34. The attempt to explain behavior in terms of underlying biological principles.
  aggression, 596
  emotions, 381–387
  intellectual disabilities, 339–340
  key view of, 34
  mood disorders, 506
  motivation, 357
  schizophrenic, 500–501
  sexual orientation, 370–371
Biological predisposition, 111. The presumed hereditary readiness of humans to learn certain skills, such as how to used language, or readiness to behavior in particular ways.
Biological rhythm, 191. Any repeating cycle of biological activity, such as sleep and waking cycles or changes in body temperatures.
Biopsychologists, 34

Biopsychosocial model, 444. Approach to which acknowledges that biological, psychological, and social factors interact to influence illness and health.
Bipolar disorders, 505. Emotional disorders involving both depression and mania or hypomania.
Bipolar I disorder, 505. A mood disorder in which a person has episodes of mania (excited, hyperactive, energetic, grandiose behavior) and also periods of deep depression.
Bipolar II disorder, 505. A mood disorder in which a person is mostly depressed (sad, despondent, guilt ridden) but has also had one or more episodes of mild mania (hypomania).
Birth injuries, 340
Blind spots, 144–145
Body language, 387
  emotional expression and, 387
Body reactions, 477–478
Body temperatures, 357
Borderline personality disorder, 516
Bottom-up processing, 160–161. Organizing perceptions by beginning with low-level features.
Brain. *See also specific regions*
  anatomy of, 73–74, 77–84
  chemicals, 65–66
  complexity of, 84
  emotions and, 381–382
  gender differences, 80
  hunger mechanisms in, 361–362
  image processing by, 314–316
  imaging techniques, 69–72
  injuries, 60
  long term memory and, 297–298
  plasticity of, 68–69
  psychoactive drugs and, 212
  schizophrenic, 498–499
  structures, 69–70
  surgical alteration of, 547
  vision gaps and, 144–146
Brainstem, 81. The lowest portions of the brain, including the cerebellum, medulla, pons, and reticular formation.
Brief psychodynamic therapy, 530. A modern therapy based on psychoanalytic theory but designed to produce insights more quickly.
Brightness constancy, 165. The apparent (or) relative brightness of objects remains the same as long as they are illuminated by the same amount of light.
Broca's (BRO-cahs) **area,** 77. A language area related to grammar and pronunciation.

Bulimia (bue-LIHM-ee-yah) **nervosa,** 364. Excessive eating (gorging) usually followed by self-induced vomiting and/or taking laxatives.
  causes of, 365–366
  symptoms of, 364
  treatment of, 366
Bullying, 596. The deliberate and repeated use of verbal or physical, direct or indirect aggression as a tactic for dealing with every-day situations.
Burnout, 454. A work-related condition of mental physical, and emotional exhaustion.
Bystander effect (bystander apathy), 593. Unwillingness of bystanders to offer help during emergencies or to become involved in others' problems.
  understanding of, 20
Bystander intervention
  arousal in, 594–595
  decision points in, 593–594

C
Caffeine, 216
Caffeinism, 216. Excessive consumption of caffeine leading to dependence and a variety of physical and psychological complaints.
Cannon-Bard theory, 388. States that activity in the thalamus causes emotional feelings and bodily arousal to occur simultaneously.
Cannon, Walter, 359–360
Cardinal trait, 404. A personality trait so basic that all of a person's activities relate to It.
Careers, 630, 633–640
Case study, 48. An in-depth focus on all aspects of a single person.
Catatonic schizophrenia, 499–500. Schizophrenia marked by stupor, rigidity, unresponsiveness, posturing, autism, and, sometimes agitated, purposeless behavior.
Causation, 48, 622. The act of causing some effect.
  correlation and, 622
Cause and effect, 43
Central nervous system (CNS), 60. The brain and spinal cord.
Central tendency, 615. The tendency for a majority of scores to fall in the midrange of possible values.
Central traits, 404. The core traits that characterize an individual personality.
Cerebellum (ser-ah-BEL-uhm), 82. A brain structure that controls posture, muscle tone, and coordination.
  damage to, 82

Cerebral (seh-REE-brel or ser-EH-brel) **cortex,** 73. The outer layer of the brain.
  hemispheres of, 74–75
  left-right functions, 75–76
  lobes of, 77–81
Cerebral hemispheres
  characterization of, 74
  handedness and, 88–89
  specialization of, 74–77
Character, 400. Personal characteristics that have been judged or evaluated; a person's desirable or undesirable qualities.
Checkers, 511
Children
  caring for, 126–127
  moral development of, 126
  obesity in, 362
  violent, 596
Chomsky, Noam, 111
Chromosomes, 96. Thread-like "colored bodies" in the nucleus of each cell that are made up of DNA.
Churchill, Winston, 500
Circadian (SUR-kay-dee-AN) **rhythms,** 357–358. Cyclical changes in body functions and arousal levels that vary on a schedule approximating a 24-hour day.
  effects of, 357–358
Clairvoyance, 178
Classical conditioning, 234. A form of learning in which reflex responses are associated with new stimuli.
  clinical applications for, 238
  in early learning, 240
  elements of, 236
  emotional response in, 240
  operant conditioning vs., 242
  Pavlov's experiment of, 235–236
  principles of, 237–239
  types of, 240–241
Cleaners, 511
Client-centered (or person-centered) therapy, 532–533. A nondirective therapy based on insights gained from conscious thoughts and feelings emphasizes accepting one's true self.
Clinical case study, 70. A detailed investigation of a single person, especially one suffering from injury or disease.
Clinical method, 48–49
Clinical psychologist, 38. A psychologist who specializes in the treatment of psychological and behavioral disturbances or who does research on such disturbances.
Closure, 162
Cocaine, 215
Cochlea
  definition of, 149
  implants of, 152
  side view of, 150

Coefficient of correlation, 47, 620–621. A statistical index ranging from −1.00 to +1.00 that indicates that and degree of correlation.

Coercion, 586. Being forced to change your beliefs or your behavior against your will.

Cognition (thinking), 314. The process of thinking or mentally processing information (images, concepts, words, rules, and symbols).
anxiety disorders and, 517
concept formation in, 317–318
creative, 328–330
images in, 314–316
language's role in, 318–322
problem solving and, 322–327
in social behavior, 572–576

Cognitive behavior therapy (CBT), 536. An approach combining cognitive and behavioral therapies to optimize treatment.

Cognitive development
overview of, 113–114
Piaget's theory of, 114–117
Vygotsky's sociocultural theory, 118–122

Cognitive dissonance theory, 577–578. An uncomfortable clash between self-image, thoughts, beliefs, attitudes or perceptions and one's behavior.

Cognitive interview, 281. Use of various cues and strategies to improve the memory of an eyewitness.

Cognitive learning, 234, 259–261. Higher-level learning involving thinking, knowing, understanding, and anticipation.

Cognitive map, 260. Internal images or other mental representations of an area (maze city campus, and so forth) that underlie an ability to choose alternative paths to the same goal.
function of, 259–260

Cognitive therapy, 534. A therapy directed at changing the maladaptive thoughts, beliefs, and feelings that underlie emotional and behavioral problems.
for depression, 534–535

College blues, 467–468

Color blindness, 147. A total inability to perceive, colors.

Color vision, 146–148

Color weakness, 147. An inability to distinguish some colors.

Commitment, 591. The deter-mination to stay in a long-term relationship with another person.

Common region, 163

Common sense, 18

Common traits, 402. Personality traits that are shared by most members of a particular culture.

Community health campaign, 447. A community wide education program that provides information about how to lessen risk factors and promote health.

Community mental health center, 548–549. A facility offering a wide range of mental health services, such as prevention, counseling, consultation, and crisis intervention.

Comorbidity (in mental disorders), 491. The simultaneous presence in a person of two or more mental disorders.

Companionate love, 591. Form of love characterized by intimacy and commitment but not passion.

Compensation, 463, 465. Counteracting a real or imagined weakness by emphasizing desirable traits or seeking to excel in the area of weakness or in other areas.

Compliance, 582–583. Bending to the requests of a person who has little or no authority or other form of social power.

Compression, 149

Computed tomographic scan (CT scan), 69, 503. A computer-enhanced X-ray image of the brain or body.

Computer-assisted instruction, 250

Concentrative meditation, 207. Mental exercise based on attending to a single object or thought.

Concept formation, 317. The process of classifying information into meaningful categories.

Concepts, 314. Generalized ideas representing a category of related objects or events.
types of, 317–318

Concrete operational stage, 116. Period of intellectual development during which children become able to use the concepts of time, space, volume, and number, but in ways that remain simplified and concrete, rather than abstract.

Condensation, 225. Combining several people objects, or events into a single dream image.

Conditioned emotional response (CER), 240. An emotional response that has been linked to a previously non-emotional stimulus by classical conditioning.

Conditioned response (CR), 236. A learned response elicited by a conditioned stimulus.

Conditioned stimulus (CS), 236. A stimulus that evokes a response because it has been repeatedly paired with an unconditioned stimulus.

Conditions of worth, 418. Internal standards used to judge the value of one's thoughts, actions, feelings, or experience.

Conductive hearing loss, 151. Poor transfer of sounds from the eardrum to the inner ear.

Cones, 144. Visual receptors for colors and daylight visual acuity.

Confidentiality, 553

Confirmation bias, 24–25. The tendency to remember or notice information that fits one's expectations.

Conflict, 459–462. A stressful condition that occurs when a person must choose between incompatible or contradictory alternatives.
forms of, 460–461
management of, 461–462

Conformity, 580–581. Bringing one's behavior into agreement or harmony with norms or with the behavior of others in a group.

Congenital problems, 101. Problems or defects that originate during prenatal development.,

Conjunctive concept, 317. A class of objects that have two or more features in common (for example, to qualify as an example of the concept an object must be both red and triangular).

Connotative meaning, 318. The subjective personal, or emotional meaning of a word or concept.

Conscience, 409, 410. The part of the superego that causes guilt when its standards are not met.

Conscientiousness, 407

Conscious, 409, 411. The region of the mind that includes all mental contents a person is aware of at any given moment.

Consciousness, 190. Mental awareness of sensations and perceptions of external events as well as self-awareness of internal events including thoughts, memories, and feelings about experiences and the self.
meditation and, 207–208
sleep and, 191–193
states of, 190–194

Consequences, 235. Effects that follow a response.

Conservation, 116. In Piaget's theory, mastery of the concept

that the weight, mass, and volume of matter remains unchanged (is conserved) even when the shape or appearance of objects changes.

Consolidation, 295–296. Process by which relatively permanent memories are formed in the brain.

Consummate love, 591. form of love characterized by intimacy, passion, and commitment.

Contact comfort, 104. A pleasant and reassuring feeling human and animal infants get from teaching or clinging to something soft and warm, usually their mothers.

Contiguity, 162

Contingency, 243

Continuation, 162

Continuous positive airway pressure (CPAP), 200

Continuous reinforcement, 251

Control, 20. Altering conditions that influence behavior.

Control group, 42. In a controlled experiment, the group of subjects exposed to all experimental conditions or variables except the independent variable.

Conventional moral reasoning, 124. Moral thinking based on a desire to please others or to follow accepted rules and values.

Convergence, 168–169

Convergent thinking, 328. Thinking directed toward discovery of a single established correct answer; conventional thinking.

Conversion disorder, 513. A bodily symptom that mimics a physical disability but is actually caused by anxiety or emotional distress.

Cookie guilt, 381

Coping
college blues, 467–468
with frustration, 459
with learned helplessness, 465–466
with stress, 456
with traumatic stress, 457

Coping statements, 479–480. Reassuring, self-enhancing statements that are used to stop self-critical thinking.
for test anxiety, 374–375

Correlation, 47, 620. The existence of a consistent, systematic relationship between two events, measures, or variables.

Correlational study, 47. A nonexperimental study designed to measure the degree of relationships (if any) between two or more events, measures or variables.

Digit-span test, 277
Dinklage, Peter, 86
Direct observation, 430–431. Assessing behavior through direct surveillance.
Discovery learning, 260. Learning based on insight and understanding.
Discrimination, 599. Treating members of various social groups differently in circumstances where their rights or treatment should be identical.
Discriminative stimuli, 254. Stimuli that precede rewarded and nonrewarded responses in operant conditioning.
examples of, 255
Disease-prone personality, 445. A personality type associated with poor health, marked persistent negative emotions, including anxiety, depression, and hostility.
Dishabituation, 183. A reversal of habituation.
Disjunctive concept, 317. A concern defined b the presence of at least one of several possible features (For example, to qualify an object must be either blue or circular.).
Disorganized schizophrenia, 499. Schizophrenia marked by incoherence, grossly disorganized behavior, bizarre thinking, and flat or grossly inappropriate emotions.
Displaced aggression, 458. Redirecting aggression to a target other than the actual source of one's frustration.
Displacement, 225. Directing emotions or actions toward safe or unimportant dream images.
Dissociative amnesia, 512. Loss of memory (partial or complete) for important information related to personal identity.
Dissociative disorder, 490. Temporary amnesia, multiple personality, or depersonalization.
Dissociative fugue, 512. Sudden travel away from home, plus confusion about one's personal identity.
Dissociative identity disorder, 512. The presence of two or more distinct personalities (multiple personality).
Dissociative state, 204–205
Disuse, 291. Theory that memory traces weaken when memories are not periodically used retrieved.
Divergent thinking, 328. Thinking that produces many ideas or alternatives; a major element in original or creative thought.

Diversity
broader view of, 36
in identity, 122
psychology's history and, 33–34
Dixon, Jeanne, 54
DNA (deoxyribonucleic acid) (dee-OX-see-RYE-bo-new-KLEE-ik), 96. A molecular structure that contains coded genetic information.
Dogmatism, 600. An unwarranted positiveness or certainty in matters of belief or opinion.
Dominant gene, 96. A gene whose influence will be expressed each time the gene is present.
Dominant hemisphere, 88. A term usually applied to the side of a person's brain that produces language.
Donahue, Phil, 519
Door-in-the-face effect, 582. The tendency for a person who has refused a major request to subsequently be more likely to comply with a minor request.
Double-blind experiment, 45. An arrangement in which both participants and experimenters are unaware of whether participants are in the experimental group or the control group, including who might have been administered a drug or placebo.
advantages of, 45
Down syndrome, 340
Drapetomania, 494
Dream processes, 225. Mental filters that hide the true meaning of dreams.
Dream symbols, 202. Images in dreams that serve as visible signs of hidden ideas, desires, impulses, emotions, relationships, and so forth.
Dreams
content of, 225–226
interpretation of, 226
REM sleep and, 201–202
remembering, 225
theories of, 202–203
using, 227–228
Drive, 356. The psychological expression of internal needs or valued goals. For example, hunger, thirst, or a drive for success.
Drug abuse. *See* Substance abuse
Drug interaction, 213. A combined effect of two drugs that exceeds the addition of one drug's effects to the other.
Drug tolerance, 211. A reduction in the body's response to a drug.
Drug-dependency insomnia, 198
Drugs therapy, 545–546
Dual process hypothesis of sleep, 194. Proposes that NREM sleep reduces the overall level of brain

activation, allowing unimportant memories to be forgotten while REM sleep sharpens memory for important events from the previous day.
Duerson, Dave, 59
Dwarfism, 85, 86
Dysosmia, 152
Dysthymic (dis-THY-mik) **disorder,** 505. Moderate depression that persists for 2 years or more.
Dysthymic disorders, 506–507

E
E-cigarettes, 218
Ear, anatomy of, 150, 152
Eating cues, 361, 364
Eating disorders
causes of, 365–368
men with, 365
symptoms of, 365
treatment of, 368
types of, 363–364
Echoic memory, 274. A brief continuation of sensory activity in the auditory system after a sound it heard.
Ecstasy. *See* MDMA (methylenedioxymethamphetamine)
Edison, Thomas, 347
Education
happiness and, 133
simulations for, 250
therapists, 38, 40
Educational psychology, 636–637. The field that seeks to understand how people learn and how teachers instruct.
Effector cells, 67
Efficient perceptions of reality, 414
Ego, 410. The executive part of personality that directs rational behavior.
function of, 410
Ego ideal, 410. The part of the superego representing ideal behavior, a source of pride when its standards are met.
function of, 410
Egocentric thought, 115. Thought that is self-centered and fails to consider the viewpoints of others.
Eidetic (eye-DET-ik) **imagery,** 299. The ability to retain a "projected" mental image long enough to use it as a source of information.
Elaborative processing, 278. Making memories more meaningful through processing that encodes links between new information and existing memories and knowledge, either at the lime of the original encoding or on subsequent retrievals.
application of, 301
Electra conflict, 409, 412. A girl's sexual attraction to her father and feelings of rivalry with her mother.

Electrical stimulation of the brain (ESB), 70. Direct electrical stimulation and activation of brain tissue.
Electroconvulsive shock (ECS), 295–296
Electroconvulsive therapy (ECT), 546–547. A treatment for severe depression, consisting of an electric shock passed directly through the brain, which induces a convulsion.
Electrode, 70. Any device (such as a wire, needle or metal plate) used to electrically stimulate or destroy nerve tissue or to record its activity.
Electroencephalograph (eh-LEK-tro-en-SEF-uh-lo-graf) **(EEG),** 71, 193. A device that detects, amplifies, and records electrical activity in the brain.
images from, 194
Electroencephalography, 71
Electronic aggression, 598
Emerging adulthood, 122, 123. A socially accepted period of extended adolescence now quite common in Western and Westernized societies.
Emotion, 379. A state characterized by physiological arousal, changes in facial expression, gestures, posture, and subjective feelings.
basic, 380–382
brain and, 381–382
contemporary model of, 390–391
death from, 382–383
development of, in infancy, 104
eating and, 362
expression of, 385–387
focus on, 552
in intuition, 333
lying and, 383–384
memory and, 296–297
in perceptions, 174–175
physiology of, 383–385
problem solving and, 326
reflective, 552
suppression of, 391
theories of, 387–391
Emotion-focused coping, 456. Managing or controlling one's emotional reaction to a stressful or threatening situation.
Emotional appraisal, 389. Evaluating the personal meaning of a stimulus or situation.
Emotional attachment, 104. An especially close emotional bond that infants form with their parents, caregivers, or others.
affectional needs and, 106–107
day care and, 106
effects of, 105
quality of, 105
styles of, 106

Emotional expression, 379. Outward signs that an emotion is occurring.

Emotional feelings, 379. The private, subjective experience of having an emotion.

Emotional intelligence, 392. The ability to perceive, use, understand, and manage emotions.
acquiring, 392–394
specific skills of, 393

Empathic arousal, 594. Emotional arousal that occurs when you feel some of another person's pain, fear, or anguish.

Empathy, 533. A capacity for taking another's point of view, the ability to feel what another is feeling.

Empathy-helping relationships, 595. Observation that we are most likely to help someone else when we feel emotions such as empathy and compassion.

Empirical evidence, 18
results of, 19

Encoding, 274. Converting information into a form in which it will be retained in memory.
strategies for, 301–302

Encoding failure, 289. Failure to store sufficient information to form a useful memory.
effects of, 289–291

Encounter group, 555. A group experience that emphasizes intensely honest interchanges among participants regarding feelings and reactions to one another.

Endocrine (EN-duh-krin) **system,** 84–86. Glands whose secretions pass directly into the bloodstream or lymph system.

Endogenous (en-DODGE-eh-nus) **depression,** 506. Depression that appears to be produced from within (perhaps by chemical imbalances in the brain), rather than as a reaction to life events.

Enrichment, 102. In development, deliberately making an environment more stimulating, nutritional, comforting, loving, and so forth.

Environment ("nurture"), 100. The sum of all external conditions affecting development, including especially the effects of learning.
deprivation and, 102
enrichment and, 102
expressions of, 102–103
in infancy, 101–103
IQ and, 347–349
personality and, 426–428

prenatal, 101
schizophrenia and, 500–501
sensitive periods, 101

Environmental psychology, 634–636. The formal study of how environments affect behavior.

Epinephrine (ep-eh-NEF-rin), 86. An adrenal hormone that tends to arouse the body, epinephrine is associated with fear (Also known as adrenaline),

Episodic (ep-ih-SOD-ik) **drive,** 358. A drive, like pain, that occurs in distinct episodes.

Episodic memory, 284. A subpart of declarative memory that records personal experiences that are liked with specific times and places.

Equal-status contact, 603
Erikson, Erik, 125
Erikson's psychosocial theory, 125–127

Erogenous (eh-ROJ-eh-nus) **zones,** 367, 409. Areas of the body that produced pleasure and/or provoke erratic desire.

Eros, 409. Freud's name for the "life instincts.
Erotomanic-type delusion, 497

Escape, 458. Reducing discomfort by leaving frustration situations or by psychologically withdrawing from them.

Escape learning, 256–257. Learning to make a response in order to end an aversive stimulus.

Essay tests, 11

Estrogen, 367. Any of a number of female sex hormones.

Estrus, 367. Changes in the sexual drives of animals that create a desire for mating, particularly used to refer to females in heat.

Ethics, 28, 553
Ethnicity
diversity in, 122
parenting styles, 108–109
suicide rates, 519

Ethnocentrism, 600. Placing one's own group or race at the center that is, tending to reject all other groups but one's own.

Evidence, collection of, 27

Evolutionary psychology, 34. Study of the evolutionary origins of human behavior patterns.
key view of, 36
mate selection of, 591–592

Excessive self-disclosure, 590

Excitement phase, 368. The first phase of sexual response, indicated by initial signs of sexual arousal.

Existential therapy, 533. An insight therapy that focuses on the elemental problems of existence, such as death, meaning, choice, and responsibility, and emphasizes making courageous life choices.

Expectancy, 238, 421. An anticipation concerning future events or relationships.

Experiential processing, 2, 314. Thought that is passive effortless, and automatic.

Experiment, 41. A formal trial undertaken to confirm or disconfirm a hypothesis about cause and effect.
conditioning, 235–237
on obedience, 580–581
on prejudice, 602–605

Experimental group, 42. In controlled experiment, the group of subjects exposed to the independent variable or experimental condition.

Experimental method, 46. Investigating causes of behavior through controlled experimentation.

Experimental subjects, 41. Humans (also referred to as participants) or animals whose behavior is investigated in an experiment.

Expert witnesses, 488

Explicit memory, 287. A memory that a person is aware of having; a memory that is consciously retrieved.

Expressive behaviors, 423–424. Behaviors that express or communicate emotion or personal feelings.

External frustration, 456–457

Extinction, 238. The weakening of a conditional response through removal or reinforcement.

Extracellular thirst, 366. Thirst caused by a reduction in the volume of fluids found between body cells.

Extraneous variables, 42. Conditions or factors excluded from influencing the outcome of an experiment.

Extrasensory perception (ESP), 52, 178–181. The purported ability to perceive events in ways that cannot be explained by known capacities of the sensory organs.
appraisal of, 178–180
fraud in, 179
implications of, 180–181
role of chance in, 179–180

Extreme marathons, 17

Extrinsic motivation, 378. Motivation based on obvious external rewards, obligations, or similar factors.

Extrovert, 401, 407. A person whose attention is directed outward; a bold, outgoing person.

Eye movement desensitization and reprocessing (EMDR), 541–542. A technique for reducing fear or anxiety; based on

holding upsetting thoughts in mind while rapidly moving the eyes from side to side.

Eyewitnesses, 280–281, 287, 291
Eyes
blind spots of, 144–145
structure of, 143–145

F

Facial agnosia (ag-KNOW-zyah), 80. An inability to perceive familiar faces.

Facial blends, 386
Facial expression
cultural differences in, 386
emotions displayed by, 386
gender differences in, 386–387
universality of, 385

Facial feedback hypothesis, 389–390. States that sensations from facial expressions help define what emotion a person favors.

False memory, 279. A memory that can seem accurate but it is not.
avoidance of, 280–282
example of, 280

False positive, 287
Familiarity, 589

Family therapy, 555. Technique in which all family members participated, both individually and as a group, to change destructive relationships and communication patterns.

Fantasy, 463. Fulfilling unmet desires in imagined achievements or activities.

Fathers, 108, 109
Faulty concepts, 318

Fear hierarchy, 539. A list of fears, arranged from least fearful to most fearful, for use in systematic desensitization.
construction of, 559–560

Fears
anxiety vs., 462
controlling, 240, 479–480
emotion and, 379, 380
evaluation, 436
learned, 240
learning, 240
neurology of, 83
social, 510–511, 601

Feedback, 248. Information returned to a person about the effects a response has had; also known as knowledge of results.
application of, 249–250
principle of, 249

Feeling of knowing, 285
Fellowship, with humanity, 415
Fetal alcohol syndrome (FAS), 101
Fetal damage, 340

Figure-ground organization, 161. Organizing a perception so that part of a stimulus appears to stand out as an object (figure) against a less prominent background (ground).

Firewalkers, 54

Five-factor model, 406–407. Proposes that there are five universal dimensions of personality.

Fixation (as a Freudian defense mechanism), 409, 412. A lasting conflict developed as a result of frustration or overindulgence.

Fixation (in problem solving), 325. The tendency to repeat wrong solutions or faulty responses, especially as a result of becoming blind to alternatives.

Fixed interval (FI) schedule, 253. A reinforcer is given only when a correct response is made after a set amount of time has passed since the last reinforced response. Responses made during the time interval are not reinforced.

Fixed ratio (FR) schedule, 252. A set number of correct responses must be made to get a reinforcer. For example, a reinforcer is given for every four correct reposes.

Flashbulb memory, 296–297. Memory created at times of high emotion that seems especially vivid.

Flat affect, 495

Flavors, 153–154

Flexibility, 328. In tests of creativity, the number of different types of solutions produced, indicates flexibility

Fluency, 328. In tests of creativity, fluency refers to the total number of solutions produced.

Fluid reasoning, 335

Flynn effect, 345, 346

Food intake, 199

Foot-in-the door effect, 582. The tendency for a person who has first complied with a small request to be more likely later to fulfill a larger request.

Forebrain, 83–84

Forgetting
card trick based on, 290
college students and, 291
cue-dependent, 292
curve of, 291
encoding failures and, 289–291
interference and, 293–294
retrieval failure and, 292–293
sleep and, 293
storage failures and, 291

Formal operational stage, 116. Period of intellectual development characterized by thinking that includes abstract, theoretical and hypothetical ideas.

Frame of reference, 553
defined, 32

Framing, 332–333. In thought, the terms in which a problem is stated or the way that it is structured.

Free association, 529. In psychoanalysis, the technique of having a client say anything that comes to mind, regardless of how embarrassing or unimportant it may seem.

Free will, 32, 414. The idea that human beings are capable of freely making choices or decisions.

Frequency distribution, 614. A table that divides an entire range of scores not a series of classes and then records the number of scores.

Frequency polygon, 614. A graph of a frequency distribution in which the number of scores falling in each class is represented by points on a line.

Frequency theory, 150. Holds that tones up to 4,000 hertz are converted to nerve impulses that match the frequency of each tone.

Freud, Anna, 32

Freud, Sigmund, 31–32, 408–411

Freudian slips, 32

Frontal lobes, 77. Areas of the cortex associated with movement, the sense of self, and higher mental functions.

Frustration, 456. A negative emotional state that occurs when one is prevented from reaching a goal.
factors affecting, 456–458
reactions to, 458–459
repeated, 457–458

Frustration-aggressive hypothesis, 597. States that frustration tends to lead to aggression.

Functional fixedness, 325. A rigidity in problem solving caused by an inability to see new uses for familiar objects.

Functional MRI (fMRI), 72. MRI technique that records brain activity.

Functional solution, 323. A detailed, practical, and workable solution.

Functionalism, 30. The school of psychology concerned with how behavior and mental abilities help people adapt to their environments.

Fundamental attribution error, 573. The tendency to attribute the behavior of others to internal causes (personality, likes, and so forth).

G

G-factor, 335. A general ability factor proposed to underlie intelligence, the core of general intellectual ability that involves reasoning, problem-solving ability, knowledge, and memory.

Gage, Phineas, 49

Galvanic skin response, 384

Gambler's fallacy, 537

Gardner, Howard, 343

GAS. *See* General adaptation syndrome (GAS)

Gate control theory, 156. Proposes that pain messages pass through neural "gates" in the spinal cord.

Gender differences
brain, 80
emotional expressions and, 386–387
life satisfaction and, 133
mood disorders, 506–507
puberty, 121
sexual arousal, 367–368
sexual response, 369
suicide rates, 519

Gender role, 422. The pattern of behaviors that are regarded as "male" or "female" by one's culture, sometimes also referred to as a sex role.
androgyny and, 423–424
consequences of, 422–423
personality and, 422–424

General adaptation syndrome (GAS), 451–452. A series of bodily reactions to prolonged stress, occurs in three stages: alarm, resistance, and exhaustion.

General solution, 323. A solution that correctly states the requirements for success but not in enough detail for further action.

Generalizations, 254

Generalized anxiety disorder, 509. A chronic state of tension and worry about work, relationships, ability, or impending disaster.

Generativity versus stagnation, 126. A conflict of middle adulthood in which self-interest is countered by an interest in guiding the next generation.

Genes, 96. Specific areas on the strand of DNA that carry hereditary information.
intellectual disabilities and, 340
sexual orientation and, 370–371

Genetic disorders, 101. Problems caused by defects in genes or by inherited characteristics.

Genital stage, 409. Period of full psychosexual development, marked by the attainment of mature adult sexuality
characterization of, 412

Gestalt psychology, 31. A school of psychology emphasizing the study of thinking, learning, and perception in whole units, not by analysis into parts.
history of, 31

Gestalt therapy, 533–534. An approach that focuses on immediate experience and awareness to help clients rebuild thinking, feeling, and acting into connected wholes; emphasizes the integration of fragmented experiences

GHB (gamma-hydroxybutyrate), 219

Ghost sickness, 490

Ghrelin, 360

Giftedness, 339. Either the possession of a high IQ or special talents or aptitudes.
identification of, 339
measurement of, 338–339

Gigantism, 85

Glove anesthesia, 513

Glucagon-like peptide I (GLP-1), 360

Goal, 356. The target or objective of motivated behavior.
happiness and, 133
setting of, 10
superordinate, 604

Grammar, 319. A set of rules for combining, language units into meaningful speech or writing.

Grandiose-type delusion, 493, 497

Graphical statistics, 614. Techniques for presenting numbers pictorially, often by plotting them on a graph.

Grasping reflex, 97

Group cohesiveness, 571. The degree of attraction among group member or their commitment to remaining in the group.

Group structure, 570–571. The network of roles, communication pathways, and power in a group.

Group therapy, 554–555. Psychotherapy conducted in a group setting to make therapeutic use of group dynamics.

Groupthink, 581. A compulsion by members of decision-making groups to maintain agreement, even at the costs of critical thinking.

Growth hormone, 85. A hormone, secreted by the pituitary gland, that promotes growth.

Growth needs, 376. In Maslow's hierarchy, the higher needs associated with self-actualization.

Guided discovery, 261

Guided imagery, 478. Intentional visual visualization of images that are calming, relaxing, or beneficial in other ways.

Guilty knowledge test, 384. Polygraph procedure involving testing people with knowledge only a guilty person could know.

Gustation, 152. The sense of taste.
Gut responses, 240

H

Habituation, 183. A decrease in perceptual response to a repeated stimulus.

Hair cells, 150. Receptor cells within the cochlea that transduce vibrations into nerve impulses.

Halfway house, 548. A community-based facility for individual making the transition from an institution (mental hospital, prison, and so forth) to independent living.

Hallucination, 160, 495. An imaginary sensation, such as seeing, hearing, or smelling things that don't exist in the real world.

Hallucinogen (hal-LU-sin-oh-jin), 222. A substance that alters or distorts sensory impressions.
  LSD, 222
  marijuana, 222–223
  PCP, 222
  types of, 222–223

Halo effect, 429. The tendency to generalize a favorable or unfavorable particular impression to unrelated details of personality.

Handedness, 87. A preference for the right of left hand in most activities.
  advantage left, 89–90
  advantage right, 89
  assessing, 87–88
  causes of, 88–89
Happiness, 131–132

Hardy personality, 474. A personality style associated with superior stress resistance.
  characteristics of, 474–475
  life events and, 475
Harm reduction strategy, 219

Hassle (microstressor), 469–471. Any distressing, day-to-day annoyance.
  impact of, 469–470
  study of, 470–471
Health
  behavior promoting, 446–447
  community, 447–448
  in middle-age, 127
  prevention programs and, 447
  psychosomatic disorders and, 471–472
  sexual, 448–450
  stress effects on, 451–453, 469–471
  subjective well-being and, 448

Health psychology, 444. Study of the ways in which cognitive and behavioral principles can be used to prevent illness and promote health.
Healthy solitude, 571
Hearing
  artificial, 152
  environmental damage to, 152

  loss of, 151–152
  processes of, 149–151
  stimulus for, 149
Hebb's rule, 68
Height in the picture plane, 170

Heredity ("nature"), 96. The transmission of physical and psychological characteristics from parents to offspring through genes.
  handedness and, 88–89
  IQ and, 344–348
  personality and, 424–425
  schizophrenia and, 501

Heuristic (hew-RIS-tik), 324. An strategy or technique that aids problem solving, especially by limiting the number of possible solutions to be tried.
  representativeness, 331

Hidden observer, 205. A detached part of the hypnotized person's awareness that silently observes events.

Hierarchy of human needs, 375–378. Abraham Maslow's ordering of needs, based on their presumed strength or potency.
  levels of, 377

Higher order conditioning, 237. Classical conditioning in which a conditioned stimulus is used to reinforce further learning that is, a CS is used as if it were a US.
  effects of, 238
Hikikomori, 490
Hindbrain, 81–82

Hippocampus (HIP-oh-CAMP-us), 84, 296. A brain structure, part of the limbic system, associated with emotion and the transfer of information from short term memory to long term memory.

Histogram, 614. A graph of a frequency distribution in which the number of scores falling in each class is represented by vertical bars.
Histrionic personality disorder, 516
HIV/AIDS, 449–450
Hoarders, 511

Homeostasis (HOE-me-oh-STAY-sis), 357. A steady state of body equilibrium.

Hormone, 85. A glandular secretion that affects bodily functions or behavior.
  behavioral effects of, 85
Horney, Karen, 32
Hospitalization. *See* Mental hospitalization
Huberty, James, 500
Hues, 143
Human development. *See also* Motor development
  growth sequence, 98
  height determination, 96–97
  levels of, 103

  milestones in, 125–127
  motor, 98–99

Human factors psychology (ergonomics), 639–640. A specialty concerned with making machines and work environments compatible with human physical capacities.
Human Genome Project, 96
Human nature, 414

Human–computer interaction (HCI), 640. The application of human factors to the design of computers and computer software.

Humanism, 32, 414–417. An approach to psychology that focuses on human experience, problems, potentials, and ideals.
  anxiety disorder approach of, 514
  development view of, 417–418
  history of, 32–33
  key feature of, 33
  key view of, 35
  therapies of, 532–534
Humanity, fellowship with, 415
Hunger
  eating and, 360–361
  external factors in, 361–362
  internal factors in, 359–361
  origins of, 359–360
  symptoms of, 359–361

Hyperopia (HI-per-OPE-ee-ah), 144. Difficulty focusing nearby objects (farsightedness).
Hypersomnia, 197

Hypnosis, 204. An altered state of consciousness characterized by narrow attention and increased suggestibility.
  demonstration of, 205
  effects of, 206–207
  reality of, 205–207
  theories of, 204–206

Hypnotic susceptibility, 206. One's capacity for becoming hypnotized.

Hypochondriac (HI-po-KON-dree-ak), 472. A person who complains about illnesses that appear to be imaginary.

Hypochondriasis (HI-pro-kon-DRY-uh-sis), 512–513. A preoccupation with fears of having a serious disease. Ordinary physical signs are interpreted as proof that the person has a disease, but no physical disorder can be found.
Hypopituitary, 85

Hypothalamus (HI-po-THAL-ah-mus), 83, 360. A small area of the brain that regulates emotional behaviors and motives.
  damage to, 360
  function of, 83–87

Hypothesis (hi-POTH-eh-sis), 26. A statement of the predicted outcome of an experiment or an

  educated guess about the relationship between variables.
  making of, 26–27

Hysteria, 432, 529. The presence of physical complaints for which no physical basis can be established.

I

Iconic (eye-KON-ick) **memory,** 274. A mental image or visual representation.

Id, 409. The primitive part of the personality that remains unconscious, supplies energy, and demands pleasure.
  function of, 409–410

Ideal self, 417. An idealized image of oneself (the person one would like to be).

Identification, 422. Feeling emotionally connected to a person and seeing oneself as like him or her.

Identification (in Freudian theory), 463. Taking on some of the characteristics of an admired person, usually as a way of compensating for perceived personal weaknesses or faults.
Identity
  diversity in, 122
  formation, 121–122, 126

Identity versus role confusion, 126. A conflict of adolescence, involving the need to establish a person identity.

Illogical thought, 328. Thought this is intuitive, haphazard or irrational.

Illusion, 160. A misleading or misconstrued perception.

Image, 314. Most often, a mental representation that has picture-like qualities, an icon.
  guided, 478
  kinesthetic, 316
  nature of, 315–316
  thinking and, 315
  use of, 316

Imitation, 422. An attempt to match one's own behavior to another person's behavior.
Immune system, 452–453

Implicit memory, 287. A memory that a person does not know exists; a memory that is retrieved unconsciously.
Impossible figure, 164

In-group, 571. A group with which a person identifies.

Inattentional blindness, 166. A failure to notice a stimulus because attention is focused elsewhere.

Incentive value, 356–357. The value of a goal above and beyond its ability to fill a need.

Incongruence, 416. A state that exists when there is a discrepancy between one's

experiences and self-image or between one's self-image and ideal self.
occurrence of, 417

Independent variable, 41. In an experiment, the condition being investigated as a possible cause of some change in behavior. The values that this variable takes are chosen by the experimenter.

Individual traits, 404. Personality traits that are shared by most members of a particular culture.

Individuating information, 606. Information that helps define a person as an individual, rather than as a member of a group or social category.

Inductive thought, 328. Thinking in which a general rule or principle is gathered from a series of specific examples, for instance, inferring the laws of gravity by observing many falling objects.

Industrial/organizational psychology, 634. A field that focuses on the psychology of work and on behavior within and organization.

Industry versus inferiority, 126. A conflict in middle childhood centered on lack of support for industrious behavior, which can result in feelings of inferiority.

Infants. *See also* Neonates
cognitive development, 113–120
depth perception of, 167–168
emotional development of, 104
eye movement of, 99–100
language development, 110–112
motor development of, 98–99
readiness of, 100
sensory development of, 99–100
sleep positions of, 201
social development, 104–106
stormy crying by, 105
traditional views of, 104
vision of, 99–100

Inferential statistics, 613. Mathematical tools used for decision making, for generalizing from small samples, and for drawing conclusions.
populations and, 623
samples in, 623
significant differences in, 623
use of, 622–623

Influence-type delusion, 495

Information
in operant conditioning, 243
rehearsing, 278
relearning, 287

Information bits, 277. meaningful units of information, such as numbers, letters, words, or phases.

Information chunks, 277. Information bits grouped into larger units.
learning to use, 299–300
processing of, 277–278

Informational view (of conditioning), 238. Perspective that explains learning in terms of information imparted by events in the environment.

Initiative versus guilt, 126. A conflict between learning to take initiative and overcoming feelings of guilt about doing so.

Insanity, 488. A legal term that refers to a mental inability to manage one's affairs or to be aware of the consequences of one's actions.

Insecure-ambivalent attachment, 105. An anxious emotional bond marked by both a desire to be with a parent or caregiver and some resistance to being reunited.

Insecure-avoidant attachment, 105. An anxious emotional bond marked by a tendency to avoid reunion with a parent or caregiver.

Insight, 324. A sudden mental reorganization of a problem that makes the solution obvious.
nature of, 325

Insomnia, 198. Difficulty in getting to sleep or staying asleep.
causes of, 198
remedies for, 199

Instrumental behaviors, 423. Behaviors directed toward the achievement of some goal; behaviors that are instrumental in producing some effect.

Integrity versus despair, 127. A conflict in old age between feelings of integrity and the despair of viewing previous life events with regret.

Intellectual disability (intellectual development disorder, formerly mental retardation), 339. The presence of a developmental disability involving a formal IQ score below 70 and a significant impairment of adaptive behavior.
causes of, 340
evaluation of, 339–340

Intellectualization, 463. Separating emotion from a threatening or anxiety provoking situation by talking or thinking about it in impersonal "intellectual" terms.

Intelligence, 335. An overall capacity to think rationally, act purposefully, and adapt to one's surroundings.
artificial, 341–342
culture and, 342–343
emotional, 392–394

measurement of, 335–338, 342
multiple, 343–344
overview of, 334
variations in, 338–340
wisdom reflected in, 346

Intelligence quotient (IQ), 336. An index of intelligence defined as a person's mental age divided by his or her chronological age and multiplied by 100.
deviation, 338
environment and, 344–345
gifted, 338–339
heredity and, 344–346
interpretation of, 337–340
multiple intelligences vs., 343–344
racial factors in, 345–346
success predictions of, 344–346

Interference, 293–294. The tendency for new memories to impair retrieval of older memories and the reverse.

Internet
surveys, 49–51
therapists, 556

Interpersonal attraction, 589–590. Social attraction to another person.

Interpersonal psychotherapy (IPT), 530. A brief dynamic psychotherapy designed to help people by improving their relationships with other people.

Intersubjective, 18

Interview (personality), 429. A face-to-face meeting held for the purpose of gaining information about an individual's personal history, personality traits, current psychological state, and so forth.

Intimacy, 591. Feelings of connectedness and affection for another person.

Intimacy versus isolation, 126. The challenge of overcoming a sense of isolation by establishing intimacy with others.

Intracellular thirst, 366. Thirst triggered when fluid is out of cells due to an increased concentration of salts and minerals outside the cell.

Intrauterine environment, 101

Intrinsic motivation, 378. Motivation that comes from within, rather than from external rewards; motivation based on personal enjoyment of a task or activity.

Introspection, 29. To look within, to examine one's own thoughts.

Introvert, 401. A person whose attention is focused inward; a shy, reserved, self-centered person.

Intuition, 331. Quick, impulsive thought that does not make use of formal logic or clear reasoning.
emotions in, 333
framing and, 332–333

representativeness, 331
underlying odds in, 331–332

Intuitive thought, 115. Thinking that makes little or no use of reasoning and logic.

Iodopsin, 146

Ions, 63

Ishihara test, 148

Isolation, 463. Separating contradictory thoughts or feelings into "logic-tight" mental compartments so that they do not come into conflict.

J

James-Lange theory, 387–388. States that emotional feelings follow physical arousal and come from awareness of such arousal.

James, William, 30

Jealous-type delusion, 497

Jet lag, 358

Jigsaw classroom, 604–605. A method of reducing prejudice, each student receives only part of the information needed to complete a project or prepare for a test.

Job analysis, 634

Johnson, Randi, 53

Jung, Carl, 32

Jury behavior, 638

Just-world beliefs, 607. Belief that people generally get what they deserve.

K

Kaczynski, Theodore, 501

Kanzi's hexagrams, 322

Kasparov, Garry, 341

Keyword method, 306. As an aid to memory, using a familiar word or image to link to items.

Kinesics (Kih-NEEZ-iks), 387. Study of the meaning of body movements, posture, hand gestures, and facial expression, commonly called body language.

Kinesthetic imagery, 316

Kinesthetic senses, 154. The senses of body movement and positioning.

Knowledge, 335

Knowledge of results (KR), 249. Informational feedback.

Koro, 490

Kudrow, Lisa, 39

L

Language, 314. Words or symbols, and rules for combining them that are used for thinking and communication.
animal, 321–322
development of, 110–112
gestural, 321
roots of, 111–112
structure of, 319–321
study of, 318–319
true, 320

Memory decay, 291. The fading or weakening of memories assumed to occur when memory traces become weaker.

Memory traces, 291. Physical changes in nerve cells or brain activity that take place when memories are stored.

Mental age, 336. The average mental ability displayed by people of a given age.

Mental disorder, 489. A significant impairment in psychological functioning. *See also* Psychotic disorders.
  anxiety-based, 508–513
  classifications of, 488–492
  comorbidity in, 491
  culturally based, 490
  dissociative, 490, 512
  DMS-IV-R categories of, 493
  labeling misuse, 492–494
  legal term for, 488
  medical therapies for, 545–549
  mood based, 504–507
  overview of, 489–490
  primitive treatment for, 528–530
  risks for, 491–492
  social stigma of, 492
  somatoform, 512–513
Mental health professionals, 39–40

Mental hospitalization, 547–548. Placing a person in a protected, therapeutic environment staffed by mental health professionals.

Mental images, 298. Mental pictures or visual depictions used in memory and thinking.
Mental processes, 114

Mental set, 347. The tendency to perceive a problem in a way that blinds us to possible solutions.

Mere presence, 579–580. The tendency for people to change their behavior just because of the presence of other people.

Meta-needs, 376–377. In Maslow's hierarchy, needs associated with impulses for self-actualization.
Metabolism, 85–86
Methadone, 219
Methamphetamine, 214
Microelectrode, 71

Microsleep, 192. A brief sift in brain-wave patterns to those of sleep.
Midlife crisis, 128
Milgram, Stanley, 583
Milgram's obedience studies, 584–585

Mindfulness, 208. A state of open, nonjudgmental awareness of current experience.

Mindfulness meditation, 207. Mental exercise based on widening attention to become aware of everything experienced at any given moment.

Minnesota Multiphasic Personality Inventory-2 (MMPI-2), 431–432. One of the best-known and most widely used objective personality questionnaires.

Mirror neuron, 77, 79. A neuron that becomes active when a motor action is carried out and when another organism is observed carrying out the same action.

Mirror technique, 555. Observing another person reenact one's own behavior, like character in a play, designed to help persons see themselves more clearly.
Misattribution, 389
Mistrust, cause of, 125
Mitchell, Edgar, 180

Mnemonic (nee-MON-ik), 8, 305. Any kind of memory system or aid.
  basic principles of, 305–307
  examples of, 306–307
  ideas in order, 307

Mock jury, 638. A group that realistically simulates a courtroom jury.

Mode, 615. A measure of central tendency found by identifying the most frequently occurring score in a group of scores.

Model (in learning), 262. A person who serves as an example.
  imitation of, 262–263
Monocular depth cues
  creation of, 169
  features of, 170–171

Mood, 380–381. A low-intensity, long-lasting emotional state.

Mood disorder, 489, 505. A major disturbance in mood or emotion, such as depression or mania.
  causes of, 506–507
  classification of, 505
  seasonal affective, 507
Moon illusion, 172

Moral anxiety, 409, 411. Apprehension felt when thoughts, impulses, or actions conflict with the superego's standards.

Moral development, 123. The development of values, beliefs, and thinking abilities that act as a guide regarding what is acceptable behavior.
  levels of, 123–124
  origins of, 123
Moro reflex, 97

Morphemes (MOR-feems), 319. The smallest meaningful units in a language, such as syllables or words.

Motherese (or parentese), 112. A pattern of speech used when talking to infants, marked by a higher-pitched voice, short, simple sentences; repetition, slower speech; and exaggerated voice inflections.

Mothers
  infant development and, 104–105
  influence of, 108
  language of, 112

Motivation, 356. Internal processes that initiate, sustain, direct, and terminate activities.
  emotional, 379–382
  extrinsic, 378
  hierarchy of, 375–378
  hunger as, 359–366
  intrinsic, 378
  model of, 356–357
Motives
  biological, 357
  creative, 378
  hunger as, 359–366
  learned, 357, 375
  sexual, 367–372
  stimulus, 357, 372–375
  thirst, 366
  types of, 357
Motor development, 98–99

Müller-Lyer (MEOO-ler-LIE-er) **illusion,** 177. Two equal-length lines tipped with inward or outward pointing Vs that appear to be of different lengths.

Multiculturalism, 606. Giving equal status, recognition, and acceptance to different ethnic and cultural groups.

Multiple approach-avoidance conflict, 461. Being simultaneously attracted to and repelled by each of several alternatives.

Multiple intelligences, 343–344. Howard Gardner's theory that there are several specialized types of intellectual ability.
Munchausen by proxy syndrome, 485
Musical personality, 405

Mutual interdependence, 604. A condition in which two or more persons must depend on one another to meet each

Myopia (my-OPE-ee-ah), 144. Difficulty focusing distant objects (nearsightedness).

N

Nanometers, 143
Narcissistic personality, 516
Narcissistic personality disorder, 516

Narcolepsy (NAR-koe-lep-see), 201. A sudden, irresistible sleep attack.
Narcotics, 218–219
Natural clinical tests, 49

Natural design, 640. Human factor's engineering that makes use of naturally understood perceptual signs.
Natural environment, 635–636

Natural selection, 30. Darwin's theory that evolution favors those plants and animals best suited to their living conditions.

Naturalistic observation, 46. Observing behavior as it unfolds in natural settings.
  correlation and causation in, 48
  limitations of, 46–47
Nearness, 162

Need, 356. An internal deficiency that may energize behavior.
  hierarchy of, 375–378
  incentives and, 356–357
  meta-, 376

Need for achievement (nAch), 375. The desire to excel or meet some internalized standard of excellence.

Need for power, 375. The desire to have social impact and control over others.

Need to affiliate, 589. The desire to associate with other people.

Negative after-potential, 64. A drop in electrical charge below the resting potential.
Negative afterimages, 147

Negative punishment (Response cost), 246. Removal of a positive reinforcers after a response is made.

Negative reinforcement, 245. Occurs when a response is followed by an end to discomfort or by the removal of an unpleasant event.

Negative relationship, 620. A mathematical relationship in which increases in one measure are matched by decreases in the other.

Negative self-statements, 479. Self-critical thoughts that increase anxiety and lower performance.
Neonates. *See also* Infants
  maturation in, 97–100
  temperament in, 102–103

Nerve, 61. A bundle of neuron axons.
  impulse of, 62, 63–65
Nervous systems, 60–61

Network model (of memory), 281. A mode of memory that views it as an organized system of linked information.

Neural networks, 66. Interlinked collections of neurons that process information in the brain.
  function of, 66–67
  inputs into, 67
Neurilemma, 68

Neurocognitive dream theory, 203. Proposal that dreams reflect everyday waking thoughts and emotions.

Neurogenesis (NOOR-oh-JEN-uh-sis), 68. The production of new brain cells.
  discovery of, 68–69

Neurological soft signs, 70. Subtle behavioral signs of nervous system dysfunction, including clumsiness, and awkward gait,